THE MEMOIRS OF RICHARD NIXON

Sidgwick & Jackson
London

Published simultaneously in Canada

First printing 1978
Printed in the United States of America

First published in Great Britain in 1978
by Sidgwick and Jackson Limited

Originally published in the United States
of America in 1978 by Grosset & Dunlap, Inc.

ISBN 0 283 98457 0

Printed in the United States of America

Some of the factual events in this book were treated
in greater detail in Six Crises *(Doubleday & Company, Inc.*
copyright © 1962 by Richard M. Nixon).

For
Pat, Tricia, and Julie

Contents

(Illustrations follow pages 212, 532, and 916.)

Sources and Acknowledgments

This is a memoir—a book of memories. Since memory is fallible and inevitably selective, I have tried whenever possible to check my recollections against the available records and to supplement them with contemporary sources. Some of these sources—memos, correspondence, public papers—are self-evident. A few of them need further elaboration.

Throughout my public career I have had the habit of making extensive handwritten notes about my ideas, conversations, activities, and speeches. These notes, most of them made on yellow legal pads, total more than 20,000 pages extending from my outlines for the debates in the 1946 campaign to the outlines of my resignation speech in 1974. They range from offhand observations to extremely detailed passages of dialogue.

Between 1954 and 1957, while I was Vice President, I made diary-type dictations covering 112 different meetings, conversations, or events. I cannot remember why I started or why I stopped making them, and they cover such a wide variety of subjects and personalities that there does not seem to have been any single purpose behind them. These diaries, which were dictated on Edison Voicewriter platters, were transcribed in 1961 when I wrote *Six Crises*, but I did not use them directly in that book and they are quoted here for the first time.

By historical necessity some of the events in the pre-presidential years that were treated in *Six Crises* are also dealt with in this book. The reader will find, however, that while the facts concerning the events have not changed, the passage of time has enabled me to analyze them with greater perspective, and the new context has made it necessary for me to treat them in a substantially different and more condensed manner than they were treated in that earlier account.

During the presidency, from November 1971 until April 1973 and again in June and July 1974, I kept an almost daily dictated diary. In this book these passages are introduced by the heading *Diary*. With the exception of a few that were subpoenaed by the Watergate Special Prosecutor, none of these diary cassettes was transcribed until the summer of 1976 in San Clemente. While I have excerpted the passages from them that appear in this book, no word has been changed without adding brackets to indicate the change. These dictated diaries do not have the orderliness of a written diary—often I would dictate on a subject one day and then expand on the same subject a day or two later. Because of this, in some cases, I have combined entries that deal with the same subjects but were dictated on different days. Diary entries dealing with Watergate, however, are always from the same dictating session on the same day.

For the Watergate period I have used some of the tape transcripts that are already public or that were used by the Special Prosecutor in different investigations and trials. In an effort to reconstruct as completely as possible what I knew and what I did in the crucial period immediately following the Watergate break-in, I asked Mrs. Marjorie Acker, a member of my staff since the vice presidential years, to type transcripts as well of the tapes of every conversation I had with H. R. Haldeman, John Ehrlichman, and Charles Colson for the month after my return to Washington following the break-in, June 20–July 20, 1972. I asked her to do the same for my conversations with Haldeman in May 1973, when we were discussing what we remembered of the events of June 23, 1972, when I authorized the meeting in which the CIA was asked to limit the FBI's investigation of Watergate.

There were many unintelligible passages on these new tapes. Even so, I believe that they have enabled me to give the most complete account of those days that has ever been given.

In this book I recount many conversations, some of them as direct quotes. Those dealing with Watergate are largely based on the language recorded on the White House tapes. Others are based on my handwritten notes or my dictated diaries. There are also extensive memoranda of conversations—"memcons"—covering most talks with foreign leaders, and I have been able to use these to confirm and supplement my notes and recollections. Conversations in which I did not take part are obviously dependent upon reports from the participants or on secondary sources. In a few cases, I have had to depend solely upon my memory of a conversation in re-creating it, but I have tried to limit this to exchanges in which the vividness of the words lodged them unforgettably in my mind.

This book could not have been written or published without the help of dozens of people, and I am deeply grateful to all of them.

The wonderful volunteer women who work every day taking care of the mail that comes into La Casa Pacifica spent many hours on the laborious but important proofreading of three drafts of the manuscript.

Cathy Price, Marnie Pavlick, Nora Kelly, Cindy Serrano-Mesa, and Meredith Johnson worked late hours and many weekends in order to type the manuscript and then proof galleys against original documents. Judy Johnson helped with a variety of typing and research tasks; Meredith Khachigian helped to proof the manuscript against the originals of my diary. When all the papers of my administration were impounded, Howard W. Smith, a private citizen, kindly sent us his complete set of the daily press office news releases and special briefing transcripts.

Robert Huberty and Mark Jacobsen, of the University of California, Irvine, did much of the detailed library research and newspaper checking.

In a work of this size the copy editors perform an enormous and vital task. I want to thank David C. Frost and Nancy Brooks of Grosset & Dunlap for their patience, diligence, and professional expertise. Others who assisted in various tasks were Jack Brennan, Bernard Shir-Cliff, Larry Gadd, Diana Price, and Robert and Cara Ackerman. The index was compiled by Robert Daugherty, and the photographs were assembled with the help of Ann Grier. I also appreciate the interest and encouragement I have received from my publishers: Harold Roth and Bob Markel of Grosset & Dunlap and Bill Sarnoff and Howard Kaminsky of Warner Books.

I am grateful to the dozens of former staff members and friends who took part in the events chronicled in this book and who gave hours of time to me and my staff as we worked to reconstruct those events fairly and accurately. I am also grateful to those who read different parts of the manuscript and gave valuable advice and assistance: General Brent Scowcroft, who concentrated on the sections dealing with international affairs and foreign policy; Ray Price, who gave editorial assistance and advice, particularly on the domestic policy sections of the presidency; and Herb Stein, who provided editorial assistance on the section dealing with the economy.

Rose Mary Woods was able to spend several months in San Clemente sharing her memories of the twenty-three years during which she served as my personal secretary and applying painstaking attention to detail in reading and checking the manuscript. Marje Acker also came out to help with these tasks. Loie Gaunt, who first joined my staff when I was in the Senate, has served tirelessly as a limitless source of information and help throughout the past three years.

Finally, there are the three people who have worked with me on this project from the beginning. My deep gratitude goes to Ken Khachigian and Diane Sawyer for their research and for pulling together much of the source material. And to Frank Gannon, my chief editorial assistant who organized the research and directed the project, my special appreciation.

RN

La Casa Pacifica
March 1978

Early Years
1913–1946

I was born in a house my father built. My birth on the night of January 9, 1913, coincided with a record-breaking cold snap in our town of Yorba Linda, California. Yorba Linda was a farming community of 200 people about thirty miles from Los Angeles, surrounded by avocado and citrus groves and barley, alfalfa, and bean fields.

For a child the setting was idyllic. In the spring the air was heavy with the rich scent of orange blossoms. And there was much to excite a child's imagination: glimpses of the Pacific Ocean to the west, the San Bernardino Mountains to the north, a "haunted house" in the nearby foothills to be viewed with awe and approached with caution—and a railroad line that ran about a mile from our house.

In the daytime I could see the smoke from the steam engines. Sometimes at night I was awakened by the whistle of a train, and then I dreamed of the far-off places I wanted to visit someday. My brothers and I played railroad games, taking the parts of engineers and conductors. I remember the thrill of talking to Everett Barnum, the Santa Fe Railroad engineer who lived in our town. All through grade school my ambition was to become a railroad engineer.

My first conscious memory is of running. I was three years old, and my mother was driving us in a horse-drawn buggy, holding my baby brother Don on her lap while a neighbor girl held me. The horse turned the corner leading to our house at high speed, and I tumbled onto the ground. I must have been in shock, but I managed to get up and run after the buggy while my mother tried to make the horse stop. The only aftereffect of this accident was that years later, when the vogue of parting hair on the left side came along, I still had to comb mine straight back to hide a scar caused by the fall.

Our life in Yorba Linda was hard but happy. My father worked at whatever jobs he could find. Thanks to a vegetable garden and some of our own fruit trees, we had plenty to eat despite our low income. We also had a cow that provided milk from which my mother made our butter and cheese.

I started first grade in Yorba Linda's schoolhouse when I was six. My mother had already taught me to read at home, and this head start enabled me to skip the second grade.

After homework and chores, I often sat by the fireplace or at the kitchen table immersed in a book or magazine. We took the Los Angeles *Times,* the *Saturday Evening Post,* and the *Ladies' Home Journal.* Aunt Olive, my mother's youngest sister, and her husband, Oscar Marshburn, lived in nearby Whittier and subscribed to the *National Geographic.* Nearly every time I visited them I borrowed a copy. It was my favorite magazine.

In 1922 my father sold our house and lemon grove in Yorba Linda, and we moved to Whittier. He did roustabout work in the oil fields, but although it paid well, this physical labor offered no challenge to a man of his ambition, intelligence, and lively imagination. Early on, my father could see that even though there were still very few automobiles and only one paved road in the area, the horseless carriage was an idea whose time was about to come. He borrowed $5,000 to buy some land on the main road connecting the growing towns of Whittier and La Habra. He cleared the lot, put in a tank and a pump, and opened the first service station in the eight-mile stretch between the two towns.

The enterprise was an almost instant success, and he soon opened a general store and market. He added a small counter for my mother's home-baked pies and cakes. One of her specialties was angel food cake. She insisted that it was at its best only when she beat fresh outdoor air into the batter before putting it into the oven. I remember her standing outside the kitchen door in the chilly predawn air, beating the batter with a big wooden spoon.

The grocery business expanded rapidly, and had it not been for the illnesses that struck our family, we would have been modestly well off by the standards of those times.

The Nixon Market was a "mom and pop" operation; the whole family worked in the store. In addition to waiting on the customers and keeping the accounts, inventory had to be taken, orders placed, and the shelves kept stocked. The store had to be cleaned and swept each night and sprayed for flies each day.

When I was older, I took over the fresh fruit and vegetable buying. Each morning I got up at four in order to be at the Seventh Street market in Los Angeles by five o'clock. I chose the best fruits and vegetables, bargained with the farmers and wholesalers for a good price, and then drove back to East Whittier to wash, sort, and arrange the produce in the store and be off to school by eight. It was not an easy life, but it was a good one, centered around a loving family and a small, tight-knit, Quaker community. For those who were willing to work hard, California in the 1920s seemed a place and time of almost unlimited opportunity.

The principle that opposites attract aptly describes my father and my mother. In the most important ways they were very much alike. Both were deeply religious. They were completely devoted to one another, and no sacrifice was too great for them to make for their children. But two more temperamentally different people could hardly be imagined.

My father, Francis Anthony Nixon, was known throughout his life as Frank. He was born on a farm in Ohio on December 3, 1878. His mother died of tuberculosis when he was eight, and her long illness left the family almost penniless. After her death the family moved to a small barren plot of land in eastern Ohio, where my father had to walk several miles each day to the nearest school. A newcomer, small in stature and dressed in ragged clothes, he was taunted by his schoolmates. He responded with a quick tongue and a ready pair of fists, and he soon became known as a natural fighter.

The family fortunes did not improve, and after he had finished the sixth grade he quit school and went to work. It was a necessary decision, but one he regretted all his life. Over the next few years he held many jobs, acquiring new skills with each. He drove an ox team hauling logs to a sawmill, worked as a carpenter, managed a potato farm, sheared sheep in Colorado, and installed early hand-crank telephones.

Throughout his life my father tried to better himself through work. He moved to Columbus, Ohio, and became a streetcar motorman. The insides of those early trolleys were heated by pot-bellied stoves, but the vestibules where the motormen stood were open. During the winter of 1906 his feet became frostbitten. Complaints to the company went unheeded, so he organized a protest by the motormen and conductors. They managed to get a bill passed in the state legislature requiring that the vestibules be enclosed and heated.

Nonetheless, the battle had left him frustrated and discouraged, and he decided to move to Southern California, where at least frostbite would not be a problem. In 1907 he got a job as a motorman on the Pacific Electric streetcar line that ran between Los Angeles and Whittier. In 1908 he met Hannah Milhous at a Valentine's Day party, and despite the reservations of her family because she had not finished college and because her suitor was not a Quaker, they were married four months later.

My father had an Irish quickness both to anger and to mirth. It was his temper that impressed me most as a small child. He had tempestuous arguments with my brothers Harold and Don, and their shouting could be heard all through the neighborhood. He was a strict and stern disciplinarian, and I tried to follow my mother's example of not crossing him when he was in a bad mood. Perhaps my own aversion to personal confrontations dates back to these early recollections.

He often argued vehemently on almost any subject with the customers he waited on in the store. His outbursts were not personal; they were just his way of putting life into a discussion. Unfortunately some of our customers did not appreciate this, and it was a standing family joke that my mother or one of us boys would rush to wait on some of our more sensitive customers before he could get to them.

Whatever talent I have as a debater must have been acquired from my father, from his love of argument and disputation. When I was on the debating team in college, he would often drive me to the debates and sit in the back of the room listening intently. On the way home he would dissect and analyze each of the arguments.

My father had a deep belief in the "little man" in America. He opposed the vested interests and the political machines that exercised so much control over American life at the beginning of the century. Because he thought that the Standard Oil trust was a blight on the American landscape, he chose to be supplied by the less well known Richfield Oil Company when he opened his service station in Whittier. As the Nixon Market grew, he became a vociferous opponent of chain stores. He feared that through their volume buying they would crush the independent operator and the family grocery store.

In those days before television and when radio was still in its infancy, conversation within the family and among friends was a major source of recreation. Lively discussions of political issues were always a feature of our family gatherings. My father started out as a hard-line Ohio Republican. In 1924, however, he became disenchanted with the stand-pat Republicanism of Harding and Coolidge. A populist strain entered his thinking, and that year he deserted his party to vote for the great

Wisconsin Progressive Senator Robert "Fighting Bob" La Follette. He even became an ardent supporter of the Townsend Plan, which proposed paying $200 a month to everyone over sixty who would spend the money and agree to retire, a program which was too liberal even for the New Deal. He supported Hoover in 1932 because Hoover was a "dry" and FDR a "wet" on prohibition. He never told me how he voted in 1936, but I always suspected that in the midst of the Depression he voted for Franklin D. Roosevelt rather than Alf Landon, whom he once described as a "stand-patter."

The dignity of labor was the keystone of my father's philosophy of life. He said that taking too seriously the biblical invitation to lean on the Lord encouraged laziness, and his favorite biblical passage was, "in the sweat of thy face shalt thou eat bread." During the long period when my brother Harold had tuberculosis—the years of the Great Depression—my father refused to let him go to the county tuberculosis hospital, one of the best in the country, on the ground that going there would be taking charity. would not take charity

My father's temper may have been exacerbated by a partial deafness that became almost total as he grew older. There were times I suspected him of provoking a commotion just so he could turn off his hearing aid and watch the drama unfold before him like a silent movie. But it is the love beneath his brusque and bristling exterior that I remember best. When he and my mother came to New York to see me off on the Herter Committee trip to Europe in 1947, Pat and I arranged a special treat for them. He particularly loved musical comedy, and I was able to get the best seats for the Broadway hit *Oklahoma!* We had to rush from the hotel to the theatre, and on the way he discovered that he had left his hearing aid in his room. He was determined that he would not spoil our evening, and I remember how intently he followed the play and how he laughed and applauded with the rest of the audience so that we would think he was having a good time, even though he could not hear a single word or a single note.

My father's interest in politics made him the most enthusiastic follower of my career from its beginnings. My success meant to him that everything he had worked for and believed in was true: that in America, with hard work and determination a man can achieve anything. During the years I was in Congress, I sent home copies of the daily *Congressional Record*. He read them cover to cover—something that no congressman or senator I knew ever took the time to do. When I was running for Vice President, he wrote a typically straightforward letter to one of the newspapers he had read years before, suggesting that it support me: "This boy is one of five that I raised and they are the finest, I think, in the United States. If you care to give him a lift I would say the *Ohio State Journal* is still doing some good."

Everyone who ever knew my mother was impressed with what a remarkable woman she was. She was born March 7, 1885, in southern Indiana into an Irish Quaker family of nine children. When she was twelve, her father decided to move to a new Quaker settlement in California. They loaded a railroad boxcar with many of their possessions, including horses and saddles, doors, and window frames, and arrived at Whittier in 1897, where my grandfather opened a tree nursery and planted an orange grove. After graduating from Whittier Academy, my mother went on to Whittier College. She loved history and literature, and she majored in languages, concentrating in Latin, Greek, and German. When she met and married my father, she had completed her second year of college. They had five sons and, with the exception of one named for my father, she named us after the early kings of England: Harold, born in 1909; Richard, born in 1913; Francis Donald, born in 1914; Arthur, born in 1918; and Edward, born in 1930.

My mother was always concerned and active in community affairs, but her most striking quality was a deep sense of privacy. Although she radiated warmth and love for her family, indeed, for all people, she was intensely private in her feelings and emotions. We never had a meal without saying grace, but except for special occasions when each of us boys would be called on to recite a verse from the Bible, these prayers were always silent. She even took literally the injunction from St. Matthew that praying should be done behind closed doors and went into a closet to say her prayers before going to bed at night.

Often when I had a difficult decision to make or a speech to prepare, or when I was under attack in the press, my mother would say, "I will be thinking of you." This was her quiet Quaker way of saying, "I will be praying for you"—and it meant infinitely more to me because of its understatement.

Many people who knew my mother in Whittier referred to her, even during her lifetime, as a Quaker saint. My cousin Jessamyn West recently wrote to me about my mother. She said, "I don't think of Hannah as a 'saint.' Saints, I feel, have a special pipeline to God which provides them a fortitude not given ordinary mortals. Hannah was not ordinary; but she did what she did and was what she was through a strength and lovingness which welled up out of her own good heart and because of her own indomitable character." The quality that made my mother so special, and that made people want to be close to her, was that although the inner serenity religion gave her shone through, she never wore her religion on her sleeve.

As a child I spent hours sitting at the piano in our living room picking out tunes. Shortly after I began school, I started taking piano lessons from my Uncle Griffith Milhous. He also taught me the fundamentals of the violin.

Probably because of Uncle Griffith's urgings, my parents decided to give my musical abilities a real test. My mother's sister Jane had studied piano at the Metropolitan School of Music in Indianapolis and was an accomplished performer and teacher. She lived with her own family in Lindsay, another Quaker enclave, in central California. It was decided that I should live with them for half a year and take lessons from her. Right after a family reunion at my grandmother's house in December 1924, I went home with Aunt Jane and Uncle Harold Beeson and my cousins Alden and Sheldon.

For six months I took daily piano lessons from Aunt Jane and violin lessons from a teacher in nearby Exeter, and walked a mile and a half each way to school with Alden and Sheldon. I enjoyed studying music, and I was able to memorize quite easily. Even today, more than fifty years later, I still remember some of the music I learned back in Lindsay.

Playing the piano is a way of expressing oneself that is perhaps even more fulfilling than writing or speaking. In fact, I have always had two great—and still unfulfilled—ambitions: to direct a symphony orchestra and to play an organ in a cathedral. I think that to create great music is one of the highest aspirations man can set for himself.

My parents came to bring me home in June 1925. Like any twelve-year-old I was happy to see them after what seemed like a very long time. As soon as he saw me alone, my youngest brother, Arthur, greeted me with a solemn kiss on the cheek. I later learned that he had asked my mother if it would be proper for him to kiss me since I had been away. Even at that early age he had acquired our family's reticence about open displays of affection.

A short time after we returned to Whittier, Arthur complained of a headache. The family doctor thought it was flu and ordered him to bed. Arthur's condition deteriorated quickly, and the doctor was unable to find the cause. He prescribed a series of tests, including a spinal tap. After that most painful of tests had been taken, I remember my father coming downstairs. It was the first time I had ever seen him cry. He said, "The doctors are afraid that the little darling is going to die."

Because Arthur required constant care and attention, Don and I were sent to stay with my Aunt Carrie Wildermuth in Fullerton. Just before we left, we went upstairs to see our brother. He had asked for one of his favorite dishes, tomato gravy on toast; we brought some up with us, and I remember how much he enjoyed it. Two days later he died.

The doctor said that it was tubercular encephalitis, but those words were too big, too cold, and too impersonal for us to grasp or understand. My father, who had been keeping the service station open on Sundays to accommodate the increasing weekend traffic on Whittier Boulevard, half believed that Arthur's death represented some kind of divine displeasure, and he never again opened the station or the market on a Sunday.

For weeks after Arthur's funeral there was not a day that I did not think about him and cry. For the first time I had learned what death was like and what it meant.

As a freshman in college I wrote a short essay about Arthur for an English composition course. I described the photograph of Arthur that my mother always kept in our living room, and I wrote, "Let me tell you, in a few words, something of my brother as I remember him."

> The first two or three years of my baby brother's life are rather indistinct in my memory for I was engrossed in the first years of my grammar school education. However, there were certain things concerned with my little brother's early development which did impress me. For example, I remember how his eyes changed from their original baby-blue to an almost black shade; how his hair, blond at first, became dark brown; how his mouth, toothless for five months, was filled with tiny, white teeth which, by the way, were exceedingly sharp when applied on soft fingers or toes which happened to get within their reach; how those little incoherent sounds of his finally developed into words and then into sentences; and how he learned to roll over, then to crawl, and finally to walk.
>
> Although I do not remember many incidents connected with my brother's early childhood, there were some which made a clear imprint on my mind. There was one time when he was asked to be a ring bearer at a wedding. I remember how my mother had to work with him for hours to get him to do it, because he disliked walking with the little flower girl. Another time, when he was about five years old, he showed the world that he was a man by getting some cigarettes out of our store and secretly smoking them back of the house. Unfortunately for him, one of our gossipy neighbors happened to see him, and she promptly informed my mother. I have disliked that neighbor from that time. . . .
>
> Again, I shall never forget how he disliked wearing "sticky" wool suits. As soon as he was able to read, he used to search the mail order catalogues for suits which weren't "sticky." . . .
>
> There is a growing tendency among college students to let their childhood beliefs be forgotten. Especially we find this true when we speak of the Divine Creator and his plans for us. I thought that I would also become that way,

but I find that it is almost impossible for me to do so. Two days before my brother's death, he called my mother into the room. He put his arms around her and said that he wanted to pray before he went to sleep. Then, with closed eyes, he repeated that age-old child's prayer which ends with those simple yet beautiful words:

"If I should die before I awake, I pray Thee, Lord, my soul to take."

There is a grave out now in the hills, but, like the picture, it contains only the bodily image of my brother.

And so when I am tired and worried, and am almost ready to quit trying to live as I should, I look up and see the picture of a little boy with sparkling eyes, and curly hair; I remember the childlike prayer; I pray that it may prove true for me as it did for my brother Arthur.

My oldest brother Harold's long bout with tuberculosis began several years before Arthur died, but it continued for more than ten years. It was especially hard for us to accept because he had always had such a robust enjoyment of life. He was tall and handsome with blue eyes and blond hair. At one point he grew a moustache that made him look quite rakish. In high school he had a stripped-down Model T Ford that he raced with his friends.

It was during Harold's long illness that my mother showed the depth of her character and faith. In those days, TB was almost always incurable, and the long, losing fight left its tragic mark on our whole family. First, Harold went to an expensive private sanatorium, and then he spent a few months in a cottage in the Antelope Valley in California, which is considerably drier than the Whittier area.

Finally, my mother decided to take him to live in Prescott, Arizona, which was supposed to be excellent for tubercular cures because of its dry climate and high elevation. She stayed with Harold in Prescott for almost three years. To make ends meet, she took care of three other bedridden patients. She cooked and cleaned, gave them bed baths and alcohol rubs, and did everything that a nurse does for a patient. Later, as she heard that one by one each had died, I could tell that she felt their deaths as deeply as if they had been her own sons'.

In addition to the wrenching physical and emotional strain of nursing, the very fact of separation from the rest of us was very hard on my mother. My father regularly made the fourteen-hour drive to Prescott with Don and me during Christmas and spring vacations, and we spent part of our summers there. During those two summers in Prescott, I worked at any odd job I could find. I was a janitor at a swimming pool, and once I helped pluck and dress frying chickens for a butcher shop. I also worked as a carnival barker at the Frontier Days festival that is still celebrated in Prescott every July.

Harold's illness continued to drag on. He became so thin it was almost painful to look at him. He was terribly unhappy and homesick in Prescott, so it was finally decided to let him come home, hoping that the familiar surroundings would compensate for the damper climate. He had a desperate will to live and refused to comply with the doctor's orders that he stay in bed. It was especially painful for us all because Harold was still so full of hope and had so much life in him. We kept hoping against hope that some mental lift might start him on the way back to physical recovery. When he said that he would like to go through the San Bernardino Mountains to see the desert, my father dropped everything to make plans for the trip. He rented one of the first house trailers on the market—a wooden structure built on a Reo truck chassis—and spent hours with Harold planning their route and their itinerary.

We saw them off one morning, expecting them to be gone for almost a month. They were back three days later. Harold had had another hemorrhage, and despite his insistence that they go on, my father knew that Harold would not be able to stand the rigors of living in the trailer. Harold told me that he was nevertheless glad they had taken even this short trip. I can still remember his voice when he described the beauty of the wild flowers in the foothills and the striking sight of snow in the mountains. I sensed that he knew this was the last time he would ever see them.

On March 6, 1933, Harold asked me to drive him downtown. He had seen an ad for a new kind of electric cake mixer he wanted to give our mother for her birthday the next day. He barely had the strength to walk with me into the hardware store. We had them wrap the mixer as a birthday present, and we hid it at home at the top of a closet.

The next morning he said that we should postpone giving our presents to mother until that night because he did not feel well and wanted to rest. About three hours later I was studying in the college library when I received a message to come home. When I got there, I saw a hearse parked in front of the house. My parents were crying uncontrollably as the undertaker carried out Harold's body. My mother said that right after I left for school Harold asked her to put her arms around him and hold him very close. He had never been particularly religious, but he looked at her and said, "This is the last time I will see you, until we meet in heaven." He died an hour later. That night I got the cake mixer out and gave it to my mother and told her that it was Harold's gift to her.

I loved my parents equally but in very different ways, just as they were very different people. My father was a scrappy, belligerent fighter with a quick, wide-ranging raw intellect. He left me a respect for learning and hard work, and the will to keep fighting no matter what the odds. My mother loved me completely and selflessly, and her special legacy was a quiet, inner peace, and the determination never to despair.

Three words describe my life in Whittier: family, church, and school.

The Milhous family was one of the oldest in the town, and counting sisters and cousins and aunts, it included scores of people. It was a matriarchy headed, first, by my great-grandmother Elizabeth Price Milhous. This remarkable woman, along with a forebear of hers, was the model for Eliza Cope Birdwell in Jessamyn West's charming novel *The Friendly Persuasion.* She died in 1923 at the age of ninety-six, when I was only ten, but I can remember her well.

My grandmother, Almira Burdg Milhous, lived to be ninety-four. At our traditional Christmas family reunions at her house she sat regally in her best red velvet dress as all the grandchildren brought their very modest presents to her. She praised them all equally, remarking that each was something she had particularly wanted. She seemed to take a special interest in me, and she wrote me verses on my birthday and on other special occasions. On my thirteenth birthday, in 1926, she gave me a framed picture of Lincoln with the words from Longfellow's "Psalm of Life" in her own handwriting beneath it: "Lives of great men oft remind us/We can make our lives sublime,/And departing, leave behind us/Footprints on the sands of time." I hung the picture above my bed at home, and to this day it is one of my fondest possessions. When I was in college my grandmother gave me a biography of Gandhi, which I read from cover to cover. Gandhi's concept of peaceful change and passive resistance appealed to her, and she had a deep Quaker opposition to any racial or religious prejudice.

Grandmother Milhous belonged to the generation of Quakers who used the plain speech. She would say, "Is thee going today?" or "Is this thine?" or "What are thy wishes?" I loved to listen when my mother and my aunts, none of whom used the plain speech in their own homes, would slip back into it while talking with her or with each other.

I grew up in a religious environment that was at once unusually strict and unusually tolerant. My mother and her family belonged to a branch of the Friends Church that had ministers, choirs, and virtually all the symbols of other Protestant denominations. The differences were the absence of water baptism and communion, and the heavy Quaker emphasis on silent prayer. My father had converted to Quakerism from his own rather robust Methodism at the time of his marriage, and he had the typical enthusiasm of a convert for his new religion. Our family went to church four times on Sunday—Sunday school, the regular morning service, Christian Endeavor in the late afternoon, and another service in the evening—and to Wednesday night services as well. During my high school and college years I also played the piano for various church services each week. My mother gave me a Bible when I graduated from eighth grade, and I never went to bed at night without reading a few verses.

Even the extensive religious activities of the Friends meetings in Yorba Linda and Whittier were not enough to satisfy my parents. They were both fascinated by the evangelists and revivalists of those times, and often we drove to Los Angeles to hear Aimee Semple McPherson at the Angelus Temple and Bob Shuler, her great competitor, at the Trinity Methodist Church.

While religion and prayer were very much a part of our family life, they were essentially personal and private. Perhaps because of this I never fell into the common practice of quoting the Bible in the speeches I made during my school years or later in my political life. When I was Vice President, President Eisenhower urged me to refer to God from time to time in my speeches, but I did not feel comfortable doing so.

I suffered my first political defeat in my junior year at Whittier High School, when I lost the election for president of the student body. I was appointed student body manager by the faculty, and it was my responsibility to handle the sale of tickets to football games and to persuade local businessmen to advertise in the school yearbook.

Our senior year, 1930, was the 2000th anniversary of the poet Vergil's birth, and the Latin teachers at school decided to put on a special dramatization of the *Aeneid* to commemorate the event. I was chosen to play Aeneas, and my girl friend, Ola Florence Welch, was his beloved Dido. It was my first experience in dramatics, and it is amazing that it was not my last.

The performance was sheer torture. First, the audience was bored stiff—Vergil obviously had not written the *Aeneid* for a high school assembly in Whittier, California. Second, the dramatically tender scene in which I embraced Dido evoked such catcalls, whistles, and uproarious laughter that we had to wait until they subsided before we could continue. Third, whoever rented the costumes had not taken into account the size of my feet—11D! I would guess that the silver boots I had to wear with my costume were no bigger than size 9. It took both Latin teachers and me several minutes to get them on and almost as long to get them off, and the hour on stage in them was agony beyond description and almost beyond endurance.

I had dreamed of going to college in the East. I finished third in my high school class, won the constitutional oratorical contests in my junior and senior years, and received the Harvard Club of California's award for outstanding all-around student. There was also a possibility of a tuition scholarship to Yale, but travel and living expenses would amount to even more than tuition, and by 1930 the Depression and the enormous expenses of Harold's illness had stripped our family finances to the bone. I had no choice but to live at home, and that meant that I would have to attend Whittier College. I was not disappointed, because the idea of college was so exciting that nothing could have dimmed it for me.

In college, as in high school, I continued to plug away at my studies. For the first time I met students who were able to get good grades without working very hard for them, but I needed the steady discipline of nightly study to keep up with all the courses and reading.

Each of my teachers made a great impression on me, but a few in particular touched my mind and changed my life.

Dr. Paul Smith was probably the greatest intellectual inspiration of my early years. I took his courses in British and American civilization, the American Constitution, and international relations and law. He was a brilliant lecturer, who always spoke without notes. His doctorate was from the University of Wisconsin, where he had studied under the great Progressive historian Glenn Frank. Dr. Smith's approach to history and politics was strongly influenced by the Progressive outlook, and it came as a revelation to me that history could be more than a chronicle of past events—that it could be a tool of analysis and criticism.

Albert Upton, who taught English and was the director of the drama club, was an iconoclast. Nothing was sacred to him, and he stimulated us by his outspoken unorthodoxy.

At the end of my junior year he told me that my education would not be complete until I read Tolstoy and the other great Russian novelists. That summer I read little else. My favorite was *Resurrection,* Tolstoy's last major novel. I was even more deeply affected by the philosophical works of his later years. His program for a peaceful revolution for the downtrodden Russian masses, his passionate opposition to war, and his emphasis on the spiritual elements in all aspects of life left a more lasting impression on me than his novels. At that time in my life I became a Tolstoyan.

Dr. J. Herschel Coffin influenced me in a different way. He taught a course called "The Philosophy of Christian Reconstruction," which I took in my senior year. This course was better known by its subtitle, "What Can I Believe?" It involved a weekly written self-analysis based on questions raised in class. We studied the theory of evolution, the literal authenticity of the Bible, and the nature of democracy, and at the beginning, middle, and end of the course, we had to write an essay answering the question, "What Can I Believe?"

On October 9, 1933, I described some of my impressions and problems at the beginning of the course. This composition gives a clearer picture of my beliefs, questions, and uncertainties as a college student than anything I could reconstruct today.

> Years of training in the home and church have had their effect on my thinking. . . . My parents, "fundamental Quakers," had ground into me, with the aid of the church, all the fundamental ideas in their strictest interpretation. The infallibility and literal correctness of the Bible, the miracles, even the whale story, all these I accepted as facts when I entered college four years ago. Even then I could not forget the admonition to not be misled by college professors who might be a little too liberal in their views! Many of those childhood ideas have been destroyed but there are some which I cannot bring myself to drop. To me, the greatness of the universe is too much for man to explain. I still believe that God is the creator, the first cause of all that exists. I still believe that He lives today, in some form, directing the destinies of the cosmos. How can I reconcile this idea with my scientific method? It is of course an unanswerable question. However, for the time being I shall accept the solution offered by Kant: that man can go only so far in his research and explanations; from that point on we must accept God. What is unknown to man, God knows.

I thought that Jesus was the Son of God, but not necessarily in the physical sense of the term: "He reached the highest conception of God and of value that the world has ever seen. He lived a life which radiated those values. He taught a philosophy which revealed those values to men. I even go so far as to say Jesus and God are one, because Jesus set the great example which is forever pulling men upward to the ideal life. His life was so perfect that he 'mingled' his soul with God's."

I wrote that the literal accuracy of the story of the resurrection was not as important as its profound symbolism: "The important fact is that Jesus lived and taught a life so perfect that he continued to live and grow after his death—in the hearts of men. It may be true that the resurrection story is a myth, but symbolically it teaches the great lesson that men who achieve the highest values in their lives may gain immortality. . . . Orthodox teachers have always insisted that the physical resurrection of Jesus is the most important cornerstone in the Christian religion. I believe that the modern world will find a real resurrection in the life and teachings of Jesus."

The populist elements of my father's politics, the Progressive influence of Paul Smith, the iconoclasm of Albert Upton, and the Christian humanism of Dr. Coffin gave my early thinking a very liberal, almost populist, tinge.

Thanks to my teachers I studied hard and received a first-rate education at Whittier. But academic pursuits were by no means the only—or the most important—part of my four years there. From the first week of school on, I was involved in extracurricular activities.

Whittier did not have any fraternities, but there was one social club, the Franklin Society, whose members had high social status on campus. One of the first students I met at college was Dean Triggs, who had just transferred to Whittier after two years at Colorado College, where he had belonged to a fraternity. He thought it undemocratic to have only one such club at Whittier, and he suggested that we start another. Albert Upton agreed to be our sponsor, and we decided to call ourselves the Orthogonian Society—the "Square Shooters."

While the Franklins were socially oriented, the Orthogonians recruited mostly athletes and men who were working their way through school. The Franklins posed for their yearbook pictures wearing tuxedos; we posed for our pictures wearing open-necked shirts. We were officially dedicated to what, with our collegiate exuberance, we called the Four B's: Beans, Brawn, Brain, and Bowels. Our motto was *Écrasons l'infâme*—"Stamp out evil"—and our symbol was a boar's head. Although only a freshman, I was elected the first president of the Orthogonians, and I wrote our constitution and our song.

College debating in those days was a serious pursuit and a highly developed art, and to me it provided not only experience with techniques of argument but also an intensive introduction to the substance of some issues I would deal with in later years.

Because of the way our college debates were organized, the team had to be prepared to argue either side of a question. This sort of exercise turned out to be a healthy antidote to certainty, and a good lesson in seeing the other person's point of view. Because of this debate training I became used to speaking without notes, a practice that was of great importance to me later in my political career. During my senior year I won the intercollegiate extemporaneous speaking contest of Southern California.

One of the topics we debated was free trade versus protectionism. Once I had thoroughly researched—and argued—both sides, I became a convinced free-trader and remain so to this day. Another topic was whether the Allied war debts should be canceled. Although once again I debated both sides, I became convinced that the economic recovery of Europe was more important than our insisting on payment of war debts. We also debated whether a free economy was more efficient than a managed economy. Though this was at the height of the early enthusiasm for the experiments of the New Deal, I surfaced from my immersion in both sides of that topic thoroughly persuaded of the superior merits of a free economy.

During the winter of my second year in college, the debate team made a 3,500-mile tour through the Pacific Northwest. My father let us take our family's eight-year-old, seven-passenger Packard for the trip. The leader of our debating team was Joe Sweeney, a red-headed Irishman with loads of self-assurance.

One of our stops was San Francisco. In those days shortly before the repeal of Prohibition, San Francisco was a wide-open town. We followed Sweeney down winding, colorful streets to a drugstore. He showed the man behind the counter a card one of the bellboys at the hotel had given him, and the man led us over to a wall covered with shelves of drugs. He pushed the wall and it opened like a door into a speakeasy. It was not a particularly boisterous place, although the smoky air and the casual attitude of the patrons made us feel that we had wandered into a veritable den of iniquity. I did not have the slightest idea what to drink, so Sweeney ordered a Tom Collins for me. Except for him, none of us had been in a speakeasy before, and I had never tasted alcohol, so it was a lark just to sit there watching the people, listening to their conversation, and admiring the barmaid who served our drinks.

I tried out for several plays in college, and I was usually given the character parts. I was the dithering Mr. Ingoldsby in Booth Tarkington's *The Trysting Place,* the Innkeeper in John Drinkwater's *Bird in Hand,* an old Scottish miner in a grim one-act play, *The Price of Coal,* and a rather flaky comic character in George M. Cohan's *The Tavern.* I also served as stage manager for the college productions of *The Mikado* and *The Pirates of Penzance.*

Student politics was necessarily low-keyed in a small school where everyone knew one another. My only major "campaign" was for president of the student body at the end of my third year. I was the candidate of the Orthogonian Society, and my opponent was Dick Thomson of the Franklin Society. We were good friends and did not feel much enthusiasm for running against each other.

I based my campaign on the controversial issue of allowing dancing on campus. I had no personal stake in it since I had not even known how to dance until Ola Florence forced me to learn a few steps at a party. My argument was strictly pragmatic: whether or not one approved of dancing—and most of the members of Whittier's board of trustees did not, as a matter of religious principle—most of the students were going to dance. Surely, I argued, it would be better to have dances on campus where they could be supervised, rather than off campus in some second-rate dance hall.

I won the election and then had to deliver on my promise. Herbert Harris, acting president of the college, helped me work out a compromise with the board of trustees whereby the board would rent the nearby Whittier Women's Club building, which had a fine ballroom. We held eight successful dances there during the year. The only problem now was that I had to attend. Ola Florence and several other coeds were very patient with me, but I fear that many new pairs of slippers were scuffed as a result of my attempts to lead my partners around the dance floor.

My happiest memories of those college days involve sports. In freshman year I played on the Poetlings basketball team, and we had a perfect record for the year: we lost every game. In fact, the only trophy I have to show for having played basketball is a porcelain dental bridge. In one game, jumping for a rebound, a forward from La Verne College hit me in the mouth with his elbow and broke my top front teeth in half.

Two factors have always motivated my great interest in sports. First, sports have provided necessary relief from the heavy burdens of work and study that I have assumed at every stage of my life. Second, I have a highly competitive instinct, and I find it stimulating to follow the great sports events in which one team's or one man's skill and discipline and brains are pitted against another's in the most exciting kind of combat imaginable.

Ever since I first played in high school, football has been my favorite sport. As a 150-pound seventeen-year-old freshman I hardly cut a formidable figure on the field, but I loved the game—the spirit, the teamwork, the friendship. There were only eleven eligible men on the freshman team, so despite my size and weight I got to play in every game and to wear a team numeral on my sweater. But for the rest of my college years, the only times I got to play were in the last few minutes of a game that was already safely won or hopelessly lost.

College football at Whittier gave me a chance to get to know the coach, Wallace "Chief" Newman. I think that I admired him more and learned more from him than from any man I have ever known aside from my father.

Newman was an American Indian, and tremendously proud of his heritage. Tall and ramrod-straight, with sharp features and copper skin, from his youngest days he was nicknamed Chief. He inspired in us the idea that if we worked hard enough and played hard enough, we could beat anybody. He had no tolerance for the view that how you play the game counts more than whether you win or lose. He believed in always playing cleanly, but he also believed that there is a great difference between winning and losing. He used to say, "Show me a good loser, and I'll show you a loser." He also said, "When you lose, get mad—but get mad at yourself, not at your opponent."

There is no way I can adequately describe Chief Newman's influence on me. He drilled into me a competitive spirit and the determination to come back after you have been knocked down or after you lose. He also gave me an acute understanding that what really matters is not a man's background, his color, his race, or his religion, but only his character.

One day during my last year at Whittier I saw a notice on the bulletin board announcing twenty-five $250 tuition scholarships to the new Duke University Law School in Durham, North Carolina. I applied, and only after I had won and accepted one did I learn that the students called this offer the "meat grinder," because of the twenty-five scholarships available for the first year, only twelve were renewed for the second.

When I arrived in Durham in September 1934, the photographs I had seen had not prepared me for the size and beauty of the Duke campus. For someone accustomed to California architecture and a small college like Whittier, Duke was like a medieval cathedral town. There were spires and towers and stained glass everywhere. Dozens of buildings were set in clusters amid acres of woods and gardens.

From the first day I knew that I was on a fast competitive track. Over half the members of my class were Phi Beta Kappas. Duke had adopted the Harvard case method, which involved memorizing the facts and points of law in hundreds of different cases and being able to stand up in class, recite them, and respond to sharp questioning. My memory was a great asset here, but I had never been faced with such an overwhelming mass of material. I sometimes despaired of pulling the memorized facts together into any meaningful knowledge of the law.

One night when I was studying in the library I poured out my fears and doubts to an upperclassman, Bill Adelson, who had noted the long hours I spent studying in the law library. He heard me out, sat back, looked me in the eye, and told me something I shall never forget: "You don't have to worry. You have what it takes to learn the law—an iron butt."

During my first two years at Duke I lived in a $5-a-month rented room; for my third year I joined three friends and moved into a small house in Duke Forest, about two miles from the campus. "Small house" is really an overstatement: it was a one-room clapboard shack without heat or inside plumbing, in which the four of us shared two large brass beds. As I look back, I am amazed that we lived so long and so contentedly in such primitive conditions, but at the time it seemed exciting and adventurous. We called the place Whippoorwill Manor, and we had a great time there.

There was a metal stove in the middle of the room, which we stuffed with paper at night; the first one up in the morning lighted it. While the paper burned, we pulled on our clothes by the fire's warmth. In order to save money, for breakfast I usually had a Milky Way candy bar. I left my razor behind some books in the law school library and shaved each morning in the men's room, enjoying the luxury of central heating and hot and cold running water. Each afternoon I played handball and then took a shower in the gym.

I was able to maintain the grades I needed to keep my scholarship, and I became a member of Duke's law review, a quarterly journal called *Law and Contemporary Problems.* My scholarship covered only tuition but I was able to supplement my income by working in the law library and doing research for Dean H. Claude Horack. I even found time for some political activity and was elected president of the Student Bar Association.

My three years at Duke provided an excellent legal background. Despite the fact that we had some intense discussions on the race issue, and while I could not agree with many of my Southern classmates on this subject, I learned in these years to understand and respect them for their patriotism, their pride, and their enormous interest in national issues. After my years at Duke I felt strongly that it was time to bring the South back into the Union.

As the last year at Duke Law School began, I had to think about what I would do after graduation. I expected to finish near the top of my class, but the job market was very bad. The recession of 1937 was about to wipe out what few gains had been made since the Depression began, and good jobs with good salaries were few. During the Christmas vacation of 1936 I decided to go to New York with my classmates Harlan Leathers and William Perdue and try my luck with some of the big law firms there. The only firm that showed any interest in me was Donovan, Leisure, Newton and Lombard. They wrote to me a month after the interview, but by that time I was no longer so keen on the idea of starting out in that cold and expensive city. At least we made use of our time in New York to see some plays—*Tobacco Road* was one—and to get the only seats we could afford in the upper reaches of the Metropolitan Opera House.

The Federal Bureau of Investigation recruited at Duke. I submitted an application and was called in for an interview. After that I never heard anything further from them. Many years later, when I was Vice President, I saw J. Edgar Hoover at a party at Alice Roosevelt Longworth's house and mentioned to him that I had once applied for a position as a special agent. He called me a few days later and said that he had looked up the file and found that my application had been approved. Just before the notification was to be mailed their appropriation request for the next year was cut; if it had come through, I might have had a career as a G-man for the FBI.

I decided to return home to Whittier and begin practicing law there. My family, including my eighty-eight-year-old grandmother, drove East for my graduation in June 1937. It was a proud day for them, made more so by the fact that on the day they arrived an announcement was made that I had finished third in my class and had been named a member of the prestigious national legal honor society, the Order of the Coif.

I arrived back in Whittier with good prospects but an uncertain future. First I had to pass the California bar. I would have just six weeks to study for the test for which most candidates allowed over two months; even worse, the three-day exam would include the extensive California code, which we had not studied at all at Duke.

Waiting for the results was an unnerving experience for me and my family. The scuttlebutt was that those who had passed received a simple notice in a regular envelope; those who failed received a large envelope containing all the papers necessary for applying to take the exam again. During the weeks of waiting for the results we eagerly checked the mailbox each day. Then one morning my mother returned from the mailbox in tears, holding the long-awaited envelope. It was a large one, obviously filled with papers. I did not want her to see my distress, so I went into the bathroom and shut the door before opening the envelope. Scuttlebutt notwithstanding, I had passed the exam: the letter was accompanied by voluminous instructions about making arrangements to be sworn in and other technical matters. I walked back to the kitchen and announced the good news.

I got a job in Whittier's oldest law firm, Wingert and Bewley. The first legal work I did involved the usual estate and divorce cases that fall to many young lawyers. I found the divorce cases unhappy and unsettling. At first I was surprised by some of the intimate matters people argued about, and equally surprised by the fact that they could calmly sit down and tell a stranger, even their lawyer, about them. I always tried to talk my clients into a reconciliation but seldom succeeded.

I enjoyed being a lawyer, and after a year the firm became Wingert, Bewley, and Nixon. Now for the first time I was no longer Frank and Hannah Nixon's son—I was Mr. Nixon, the new partner in Wingert and Bewley.

Young lawyers trying to get business for their firms are expected to join local clubs, so I began to participate extensively in community affairs. I joined the Kiwanis Club of La Habra and the 20–30 Club, a group for young business and professional men between those ages. By 1941 I had pretty well established myself in the community. I had been elected president of the 20–30 Club, and was president of the Whittier College Alumni Association, president of the Duke University Alumni of California, president of the Orange County Association of Cities, and the youngest member ever chosen for the Whittier College board of trustees. I was approached by several of the town's Republican leaders about running for the state assembly. I was flattered and interested by this suggestion, but the war intervened.

One day in 1938, Mrs. Lilly Baldwin, the director of the local amateur theatre group, telephoned me to ask if I would like to play the part of a prosecuting attorney in their upcoming production of Ayn Rand's courtroom drama, *The Night of January 16th*. I took the part and thoroughly enjoyed this experience in amateur dramatics.

Several months later I went to the casting tryouts for a production of George S. Kaufman and Alexander Woollcott's play, *The Dark Tower*. I thought I knew everyone in Whittier, but that night a beautiful and vivacious young woman with titian hair appeared whom I had never seen before. I found I could not take my eyes away from her. This new girl in town was Pat Ryan, and she had just begun teaching at Whittier High School. For me it was a case of love at first sight.

I got a friend to introduce us and then offered them both a ride home. On the way I asked Pat if she would like a date with me. She said, "I'm very busy." I said, "You shouldn't say that, because someday I am going to marry you!" We all laughed because it seemed so unlikely at that time. But I wonder whether it was a sixth sense that prompted me to make such an impetuous statement.

Pat's life deserves a volume of its own, and perhaps someday she will write that volume herself. It is an exceptional story, just as she is an exceptional woman with great independence, keen intelligence, and a warm sense of humor. She was born on March 16, 1912, in the little mining town of Ely, Nevada, and was christened Thelma Catherine Ryan. When she was a year old, her father decided to quit the mines and bring his family to a small ranch about twenty miles southwest of Los Angeles, near Artesia, California. There, the family of seven—her parents, a sister, and three brothers—lived in a house very much like the Nixons' in nearby Yorba Linda.

She decided to adopt the name her Irish father liked to call her, and became known to everyone as Pat. It is deeply irritating to be burdened with a name you dislike, and when our daughters were born Pat suggested that we give them only one name each, Patricia and Julie, so that they could change them or add to them when they were old enough to decide.

Her mother died of cancer when Pat was only thirteen, and Pat had to take her place, cooking and keeping house for her father and brothers. About the time she graduated from high school the long years in the mine took their toll and her father became ill with silicosis. Pat gave up her plans for college and nursed him until his death two years later. With her father gone and her brothers away at college, she was now completely on her own.

After her father died, Pat continued to live in the family house. She worked part-time as a teller in a bank and began attending classes at Fullerton Junior College. During the summer she heard that an elderly couple she knew was moving to New York and wanted someone to drive them across the country. Much to their surprise, this pretty, young girl asked for the job—and much to her surprise, she got it.

Pat was completely captivated by New York, and after only a few days she decided to stay there. She became a secretary and then took an X-ray technicians' course at Seton Hospital, which was run by the Sisters of Charity. She lived in the hospital annex and chauffeured the nuns around town when they went shopping.

Pat's goal had always been to continue her education, and after two years she returned to Los Angeles and registered at the University of Southern California. She supported herself by working forty hours a week as a research assistant to a professor. For a year she also worked as a salesperson in Bullock's Wilshire department store, and from time to time she was hired as an extra for crowd scenes in the movies. If you look closely, you can spot her in *Becky Sharp* and *Small Town Girl*. Offers of bigger parts and even a career in the movies could not distract her from her education, and she received a B.S. degree with honors from USC in 1937, the same year I graduated from Duke.

Pat's interest was marketing, and she expected to work for a department store. But jobs were hard to find, and when the opportunity arose to teach business courses at Whittier High School for $190 a month, she jumped at it. She was an immediate hit at the school, charming students and faculty alike. She was faculty adviser for the Student Pep Club and prepared programs for school assemblies and rallies. Because of her interest in dramatics, she decided to audition for the local theatre group. That was where she met the intense young man with the dark curly hair and the prominent nose who could not take his eyes away from her at the tryouts for *The Dark Tower*.

Pat and I began to see each other regularly. We went ice skating at the new indoor rink near Artesia, swimming at nearby beaches, and skiing in the mountains just outside Los Angeles. We were both movie fans and we often drove up to the large movie theatres in Hollywood. Fortunately Pat also liked football, so we went to as many Whittier and USC games as we could. She met my parents and they both liked her immediately. They were particularly impressed by her obvious strength of character and indomitable spirit.

In 1940 I sent Pat a May basket with an engagement ring set among the flowers. We were married on June 21, at a small family ceremony at the Mission Inn in Riverside, California. For our honeymoon we drove for two weeks through Mexico. We had very little money, so we had stocked up on canned foods in order to avoid the expense of restaurants. After we were on our way, we discovered that our friends had removed the labels from all the cans, and thus every meal became a game of chance. Several times we ended up having pork and beans for breakfast and grapefruit slices for dinner.

Back in Whittier I returned to my law office and Pat returned to teaching. Our life was happy and full of promise. As the 1940 elections approached, I strongly supported Wendell Willkie because, while I favored some of Roosevelt's domestic programs, particularly Social Security, I opposed his attempt to break the two-term tradition. I even made a couple of speeches for Willkie before small local groups in Whittier.

In 1941 Pat and I saved enough money to take a Caribbean cruise on the United Fruit Company's freight and passenger ship *Ulua.* Except for the fact that I was seasick for almost the entire trip, we enjoyed what turned out to be our last vacation for several years. My sharpest recollection of the trip is of the evening of June 22, 1941, when our elderly black steward told us that word had just come over the ship's radio that Hitler had invaded Russia. We both hoped this would lead to a Russian victory and Hitler's downfall. I despised Hitler, and despite my disenchantment with Stalin over the Hitler–Stalin pact, had no particular anti-Soviet or anticommunist feelings.

In December 1941, thanks to the recommendations of one of my professors from Duke, David Cavers, I was offered a job with the Office of Price Administration in Washington. The pay was only $3,200 a year, not nearly so much as Pat and I were making together with her teaching and my law practice. But it seemed a good opportunity to go to Washington and observe the working of the government firsthand. I also think that my mother was secretly relieved by this decision. Although it would take me far from Whittier again, she probably thought that if war came I would stay working in the government rather than compromise our Quaker principles by deciding to fight in the armed services.

One Sunday shortly before we were to leave for Washington, Pat and I decided to go to the movies in Hollywood. On the way we stopped for a visit at her sister Neva's house. When we arrived, Neva's husband,

Marc, said that he had just heard on the radio an unconfirmed report that the Japanese had bombed Pearl Harbor. I said I was sure that it was just one more of the frequent scare stories we all had been hearing, and we went on to the matinee. Shortly before the film was finished, the theatre manager interrupted with an announcement that all servicemen had been called to their units immediately. When we left the theatre, I saw the headline: *Japs Bomb Pearl Harbor.* The newsboy held up the paper as I walked over. He said, "We're at war, mister."

Early in January 1942 Pat and I drove across the country to a Washington that was now the capital of a nation at war. We found a small apartment nearby in Virginia, and I reported to the OPA office in one of the "temporary" buildings on Independence Avenue a few blocks from the Capitol.

I cannot say that my eight months at OPA were particularly happy ones, but at least they were instructive. I was an assistant attorney for the rationing coordination section, which dealt primarily with rationing rubber and automobile tires. One of the first lessons I learned was how government bureaucrats work. I went to Washington as a P-3 at $3,200 a year. I found that others with lesser academic records and not as much legal experience had come in as P-4s, a step higher, and some even as P-5s, at $4,600 a year. I made no complaints, but I did talk it over with some of the people I knew in personnel. One of my superiors, David Lloyd, who later became one of President Truman's top advisers, said, "Build a little staff. Request two or three people to assist you, and then we can raise you to a P-5." I said, "But I don't need a staff." "Then you won't get a promotion," he replied.

As a junior lawyer in the tire rationing division, I cannot say that I had much effect on OPA. But the experience had an enormous effect on the policies I later developed during my political career.

One impression that stayed with me was that while some career government workers were sincere, dedicated, and able people, others became obsessed with their own power and seemed to delight in kicking people around, particularly those in the private sector. It was hard enough to make rationing work even when we had the incentive of the war and the appeal to patriotism to back it up. I knew that once the war was over, rationing and price control would be almost impossible to enforce, and that the black marketeers, just like the bootleggers during the days of Prohibition, would be the only ones to profit from a continuation of the government-controlled system.

Many men in OPA were able to get draft deferments and spent the war in their offices. Despite my Quaker background and beliefs, I never considered doing this. When I heard that young lawyers were being recruited as officers for the Navy, I talked to Pat about it and applied for a commission. I was sent to the naval officer indoctrination school at Quonset Point, Rhode Island, in August 1942.

After two months at Quonset, where I learned to stand straight and keep my shoes shined, I listed "Ships and Stations" as my first choice for active duty. I expected to be assigned to a battle fleet in the South Pacific or the North Atlantic. I could hardly believe my eyes when I opened my orders and found that I was being sent to the Naval Air Station in Ottumwa, Iowa. When I reported for duty, I found that the station was still under construction. Its uncompleted runway stopped abruptly in the middle of a cornfield. My disappointment with this assignment was soon overcome by the warmth and friendliness of our new neighbors. Pat got a job in town as a bank teller and we settled in for an enjoyable taste of Midwest life.

Just when it began to seem that I might be landlocked in Iowa for the rest of the war, I saw a notice that applications for sea duty would be accepted from officers aged twenty-nine or younger. I was exactly twenty-nine, and I sent the application in immediately. Pat was worried about my safety, but she supported my decision to try to play a real part in the war effort.

I received orders to report to San Francisco for assignment overseas, and we went back to Whittier so that I could say goodbye to my family. It was a very painful visit. Although nothing was ever said, I knew that my mother and grandmother were deeply troubled by my decision. In World War I my Uncle Oscar had gone to France with the American Friends Service Committee and worked with the Red Cross as an orderly, tending wounded soldiers on both sides of the lines. I am sure that this was the kind of service they had hoped I would choose. It was a difficult decision for me to make, but I felt that I could not sit back while my country was being attacked. The problem with Quaker pacifism, it seemed to me, was that it could only work if one were fighting a civilized, compassionate enemy. In the face of Hitler and Tojo, pacifism not only failed to stop violence—it actually played into the hands of a barbarous foe and weakened home-front morale.

Family and friends came to see Pat and me off on the train to San Francisco. The Bewleys were there, along with my former secretary, Evlyn Dorn, and her husband, and some friends of Pat's and mine. My mother and father were there, along with Don and his wife, Clara Jane, and my youngest brother, Eddie, who was now twelve and looked like a carbon copy of me at that age. We all had breakfast at the Harvey House in Union Station. It was a painful meal, full of sad silences beneath the superficially cheerful conversation, and I was relieved when the train was finally announced. As Pat and I stood on the wooden block getting ready to board the train, I turned to take one last look. I think we all realized that we might never see each other again. My mother held her sorrow in, but my father began to sob. Pat and I watched them waving to us while the train pulled slowly out of the station until they disappeared in the distance.

Almost as soon as I left San Francisco I realized that I did not have a recent photograph of Pat to carry with me. I wrote to her and she went to a portrait studio and had one taken. I was happy when it arrived, but it made the separation even more painful for me.

I was assigned to the South Pacific Combat Air Transport Command at Nouméa on the island of New Caledonia. We were officially known as SCAT from our initials. Our unit was responsible for preparing manifests and flight plans for C-47 cargo and transport planes as they flew from island to island. The planes brought supplies in and flew the wounded out. We would unload the boxes and crates of supplies and then carefully carry aboard the stretchers of the critically wounded.

Like many assigned "down the line," I wanted to get where the action was, and I spent a lot of my time trying to get a battle-station assignment. Finally, in January 1944, I was assigned to Bougainville, which was a target for occasional Japanese bomber attacks. Shortly after I arrived, the Japanese staged an assault. When it was over, we counted thirty-five shell holes within a hundred feet of the air raid bunker six of us shared. Our tent had been completely destroyed.

Many fighter and bomber pilots came through Bougainville on their way to battle missions, and I felt that they deserved the best we could possibly give them. I used my SCAT resources to get small supplies of chopped meat and beer. Everyone in the unit had a nickname, and I was known as Nick Nixon. Whenever I received a fresh shipment, I opened "Nick's Hamburger Stand" and served a free hamburger and a bottle of Australian beer to flight crews who probably had not tasted anything to remind them of home in many weeks.

After serving on Bougainville, I requested and received an assignment as officer in charge of the SCAT detachment that was to support the invasion of Green Island. We landed in the bay in a PBY seaplane. The Japanese had already retreated, however, and the only danger came from a few straggling snipers and the ever-present giant centipedes.

The Seabees immediately went to work constructing an airstrip. A few days before it was completed, an Army B-29 bomber that had been seriously damaged flying over Rabaul had to use it for a crash landing even though some of the Seabees' equipment was still standing on it. It was dusk, almost dark, and we all cheered as the plane came in on its belly. Then we watched in horror as it crashed head-on into a bulldozer and exploded. The carnage was terrible. I can still see the wedding ring on the charred hand of one of the crewmen when I carried his body from the twisted wreckage.

My poker playing during this time has been somewhat exaggerated in terms of both my skill and my winnings. In Whittier any kind of gambling had been anathema to me as a Quaker. But the pressures of wartime, and the even more oppressive monotony, made it an irresistible diversion. I found playing poker instructive as well as entertaining and profitable. I learned that the people who have the cards are usually the ones who talk the least and the softest; those who are bluffing tend to talk loudly and give themselves away. One night in a stud poker game, with an ace in the hole, I drew a royal flush in diamonds. The odds against this are about 650,000 to 1, and I was naturally excited. But I played it with a true poker face, and won a substantial pot.

It was a lonely war for most of the men in the South Pacific, filled with seemingly interminable periods of waiting while the action unfolded thousands of miles away. We devoured the copies of *Life* magazine that filtered through to us, and, as much out of boredom as out of piety, I read and reread the old illustrated Bible that I had brought with me. Letters from home were the only thing we really had to look forward to, and I wrote to Pat every day during the fourteen months I was away. She has kept all those letters to this day.

When I was on Green Island I met Charles Lindbergh, who was flying combat missions testing new planes for the Air Force. The CO invited me to a small dinner in Lindbergh's honor, but I had to decline because a month before I had agreed to host a poker game. Today it seems incredible to me that I passed up an opportunity to have dinner with Charles Lindbergh because of a card game. But in the intense loneliness and boredom of the South Pacific our poker games were more than idle pastimes, and the etiquette surrounding them was taken very seriously. A quarter of a century later I was able to rectify this error when Charles and Anne Morrow Lindbergh accepted our invitation to attend a state dinner at the White House.

In July 1944 my overseas tour of duty was completed and I was ordered back to the States. I caught a cargo plane from Guadalcanal to Hawaii, and when we made a fueling stop at Wake Island in the middle of the night I got out to stretch my legs. For the first time I saw one of our war cemeteries. I shall never forget those white crosses, row after row after row of them, beginning at the edge of the runway and stretching out into the darkness on that tiny island so far away from home. I thought of all the men who were still out there fighting for these little bits of unfriendly and often barren ground, and I wondered, as I often had before, why Americans or the Japanese thought they were worth fighting and dying for. Of course, I knew that they were the essential stepping-stones for bringing the war home to Japan, and that we had to capture them just as the enemy had to defend them. But standing on Wake, waiting for the plane to be refueled, I was overcome with the ultimate futility of war and the terrible reality of the loss that lies behind it.

Congressman and Senator
1947–1952

As soon as I reached San Diego I phoned Pat, and she flew down from San Francisco, where, during my time overseas, she had been working as a price analyst for the OPA. I was at the airport gate waiting for her. She wore a bright red dress, and when she saw me standing there her eyes lighted up, and she ran to the barrier and threw her arms around me.

Although I was home now, I was still in the Navy. In January 1945 I received orders to go East to work on Navy contract terminations. During these last months of the war and the first months of peace we lived in Washington, Philadelphia, New York, and Baltimore.

Those were momentous times for Americans. In April Pat and I were in Bookbinders Restaurant in Philadelphia when our waiter came over and said he had just heard on the radio that FDR had died. Like everyone else, we were shocked and saddened by the news. A month later the war in Europe was over, and we saw the newsreels of Soviet and American troops shaking hands at the Elbe. In August Pat and I joined the throng in Times Square to celebrate V-J Day.

RUNNING FOR CONGRESS: 1946

Pat was expecting our first child, and now that the war was over we began to think seriously about what I should do in civilian life. The answer came in September in the form of a letter I received in Baltimore from Herman Perry. Manager of the Bank of America's Whittier branch, Perry was one of the community's Republican leaders. He had been a classmate of my mother's at Whittier College and was an old family friend. His letter was to the point:

> Dear Dick:
>
> I am writing you this short note to ask if you would like to be a candidate for Congress on the Republican ticket in 1946.
>
> Jerry Voorhis expects to run—registration is about 50–50. The Republicans are gaining.
>
> Please airmail me your reply if you are interested.
>
> Yours very truly,
> H. L. Perry
>
> P.S. Are you a registered voter in California?

Perry knew of my interest in politics from our discussions before the war about my running for the state assembly. But in 1941 I had been a newly married young lawyer just starting a career; in 1946 I would be a demobilized Navy lieutenant commander with a wife and child. It was clear that if I were to go after the congressional nomination seriously, it would require my full-time effort and attention. Pat and I would have to be able to support ourselves and finance the campaign at least until the primary in June. If I won the nomination, we could count on campaign funds from the party organization, although we would still have to pay all our personal expenses. With my pay, Pat's salary, and my poker winnings, we had managed to save $10,000 during the war. We had planned to use it to buy a house. Pat was dubious about spending our savings on what was at best a risky political campaign. But the more we thought about the possibility of returning to Washington as a congressional family, the more enthusiastic we became.

Two days later I called Perry and said that I was honored by his letter and excited by the prospect of running for Congress. When I told him that I could be in California to begin campaigning by the first of the year, he poured some cold water on my enthusiasm by saying that the nomination was not his to offer. He had written to me on behalf of a candidate search committee, known as the Committee of 100, established by the Twelfth District's Republican leaders to try to find someone who had a chance of beating Voorhis. He felt that if I were interested I would have a good chance, but the committee would probably interview several other candidates before deciding which one to endorse.

The next morning I wrote Perry a letter confirming my interest. I added: "I feel very strongly that Jerry Voorhis can be beaten, and I'd welcome the opportunity to take a crack at him. An aggressive, vigorous campaign on a platform of *practical* liberalism should be the antidote the people have been looking for to take the place of Voorhis's particular brand of New Deal idealism. My brief experience in Washington with the bureaucrats and my three and a half years in the Navy have given me a pretty good idea of what a mess things are in Washington."

I flew back to Whittier for the Committee of 100 dinner meeting at the William Penn Hotel on November 2, 1945. The group's search had produced six prospective candidates, and each of us was to make a speech describing the reasons for his candidacy. I wore my Navy uniform; I didn't own a civilian suit.

Since I drew the lot as last speaker on a long program, I decided that brevity would be as much appreciated as eloquence. In the first speech of my political career I described my view of the two conflicting opinions about the nature of the American system.

> One advocated by the New Deal is government control in regulating our lives. The other calls for individual freedom and all that initiative can produce.
>
> I hold with the latter viewpoint. I believe the returning veterans, and I have talked to many of them in the foxholes, will not be satisfied with a dole or a government handout. They want a respectable job in private industry where they will be recognized for what they produce, or they want the opportunity to start their own business.
>
> If the choice of this committee comes to me I will be prepared to put on an aggressive and vigorous campaign on a platform of practical liberalism and with your help I feel very strongly that the present incumbent can be defeated.

I returned to Baltimore to wait for the committee's decision. It was after two o'clock in the morning on November 29 when the phone rang in our apartment. Roy Day, a member of the committee, shouted into the phone, "Dick, the nomination's yours!" I had received sixty-three votes. My closest competitor, Sam Gist, a furniture store owner from Pomona, received twelve.

While I was waiting to be discharged from the Navy I began a crash course in politics and public affairs. Each night when I got home from work I pored over magazines, newspapers, and books about Congress and campaigns. I wrote to House Minority Leader Joe Martin, introducing myself as the prospective Republican nominee for the Twelfth District, and I visited him in his office in the Capitol. I talked with several Republican congressmen, seeking their evaluations of Voorhis. Through the Republican Campaign Committee I obtained his complete voting record, and I spent several days familiarizing myself with it. By the time of my discharge and return to California in January, I was confident that I knew Voorhis's record as well as he did himself. As it turned out, I knew it even better.

In the initial meetings with my campaign advisers, we agreed that the first thing I had to do was to become known throughout the district. While I was well known in the Whittier area, I was a stranger in all the other towns.

We began holding a series of "house meetings" in which Republican supporters would open up their houses to as many—or as few—of their friends and neighbors as were interested in coming to meet me. Over tea and coffee, I made brief remarks and then answered questions. These house meetings permitted me to meet hundreds of voters and helped me to enlist the women volunteers whose dedicated work is so important to any campaign. They also let me know what was really on the minds of the voters.

Pat was my best helper. Very soon after Tricia was born on February 21, she volunteered her time for typing press releases, mailing pamphlets, and keeping track of my schedule. She went to many of the house meetings with me and afterward gave thoughtful and sometimes quite persistent critiques of my performances.

Primary day was June 4. At that time California law permitted cross-filing, which meant that a candidate could enter the primaries of both parties. Thus the primary served as a trial heat for the later general election. Voorhis and I took advantage of this, and each of us was on the ballot as a candidate for both the Republican and Democratic nominations. When the votes were counted, each of us, as expected, had won the nomination of his own party. But in the combined vote totals, he had beaten me by about 7,500 votes. I knew I faced an uphill fight if I were to defeat him in November.

I was disappointed at not having done better, but I considered it significant and promising that this was Voorhis's weakest primary showing since 1936. The Twelfth District was basically conservative and Republican, and I was confident that we could recapture it if we could just maintain the intensity of the primary campaign right through the general election in November. "All we need," I wrote to Roy Day, now a key campaign adviser, "is a win complex and we'll take him in November."

The greatest advantage I had in 1946 was that the national trend that year was Republican. People were tired of the privations and shortages of four years of war, and in the burst of postwar prosperity they were beginning to bridle against the governmental regulations and interference that were written into so much of the New Deal legislation. In the

Twelfth District, as in many others across the country, returning veterans could not find homes at prices or rents they could afford; many could not find housing at all. The shortage of consumer goods was exacerbated by the many long strikes in 1946, and prices skyrocketed as a result. Some butcher shops in the district put signs in the window: "No meat today? Ask your congressman." My ads asked: "Are you satisfied with present conditions? Can you buy meat, a new car, a refrigerator, clothes you need? A vote for Nixon is a vote for change. Where are all those new houses you were promised? A vote for Nixon is a vote for change." The nationwide Republican campaign slogan in 1946 was, "HAD ENOUGH?" And the answer from the voters was clearly going to be a resounding "Yes!"

In anticipation of a Republican landslide, many Democrats tried to dissociate themselves from their party, and some even campaigned as critics of Truman and his policies. But Jerry Voorhis was far enough to the left of Truman that this was one problem I did not have to worry about.

Shortly before the campaign officially began in September, I received a request from a group called the Independent Voters of South Pasadena to participate in a debate with Voorhis. Most of my advisers were dubious about the idea, especially after they discovered that the Independent Voters group consisted predominantly of New Deal liberals. I felt, however, that as a challenger I could hardly turn down an invitation to debate my opponent.

As it turned out, the debate was not really a debate at all. It was more a joint public meeting in which each of us made an opening statement and then responded to questions from the floor. Voorhis spoke first in a rambling, discursive way about the nature of the executive–legislative relationship and the need for progressive legislation. He defended the record of the Truman administration. In my opening statement I made a hard attack on the bureaucratic red tape and bungling involved in the meat and housing shortages, and I called for strong action to prevent more of the strikes and labor disputes that had been hurting the economy so badly.

In the question period we were allotted three minutes for each answer. I tried to give brisk, concise responses, but Voorhis had trouble keeping within the time limit. There was one question, however, to which he had no trouble giving a short answer. He was asked whether he had once been a registered Socialist. He answered that he had, but only in the 1920s and during the early years of the Depression, when he felt that the two major parties weren't doing the job.

Then one of my supporters asked Voorhis to explain his "peculiar ideas about money"—a reference to his pet ideas on monetary reform, which had been known as his "funny money" program ever since he presented it in his book *Out of Debt, Out of Danger.* His colleagues in Congress had not been able to understand his program, and neither could the voters in Pasadena that night.

When it was my turn, one of Voorhis's supporters accused me of making false charges against Voorhis by claiming that he had been endorsed by the Political Action Committee of the Congress of Industrial Organizations. This question opened what became—at least after the fact—the most famous and controversial issue of the 1946 campaign.

The PAC had been established as a political arm of organized labor to support Franklin Roosevelt in the 1944 election. A sister organization, the National Citizens Political Action Committee (NCPAC), was set up to permit non-union participation. Until his death, labor leader Sidney Hillman served as chairman of both groups, and many other leaders of CIO-PAC also served on NCPAC. Both groups interviewed candidates and then made funds and campaign workers available to those whom they endorsed. It was estimated that in 1944 the two PAC organizations contributed over $650,000 to political campaigns. Although the leadership of both groups was non-Communist, the organizations were known to be infiltrated with Communists and fellow travelers who, because of their discipline, wielded an influence disproportionate to their numbers. Such influence was viewed as a problem because there was an emerging concern about Soviet postwar intentions and a corresponding apprehension about the communist movement in America.

Voorhis had been endorsed by CIO-PAC in 1944. In 1946, however, CIO-PAC decided to withhold its endorsement—ostensibly because he had not supported some measures in Congress considered important by the union leadership. In the spring of 1946, the Los Angeles County chapter of the NCPAC circulated a bulletin indicating that it was going to endorse Voorhis regardless of what CIO-PAC did. The May 31, 1946, issue of *Daily People's World,* the West Coast Communist newspaper, ran an article with the headline: *Candidates Endorsed by "Big Five."* The "Big Five" labor and progressive coalition was made up of CIO-PAC, NCPAC, the railroad brotherhoods, the Progressive AFL, and the Hollywood Independent Citizens Committee of the Arts, Sciences, and Professions. The *Daily People's World* article reported that the Big Five had interviewed the candidates and included the list of endorsements for the June 4 primary. The first name on the list was H. Jerry Voorhis. Following his name was this note: "No CIO endorsement." In answer, then, to my charge that he was endorsed by PAC, Voorhis had replied that he was not—that year—endorsed by *CIO*-PAC. To me that was an irrelevancy. The Los Angeles County chapter of NCPAC had a large number of Communists and fellow travelers, and, considering the close ties between the two PACs, I thought that the question of which PAC had endorsed him was a distinction without a difference.

When the question was raised in the South Pasadena debate, I pulled from my pocket a copy of the NCPAC bulletin announcing its endorsement recommendation and walked across the stage to show it to Voorhis. Reading aloud the names of the board members of each organization, many of which were the same, I demonstrated that there was little practical difference between a CIO-PAC endorsement and an NCPAC one.

Voorhis repeated his claim that CIO-PAC and NCPAC were separate organizations, but I could tell from the audience's reaction that I had made my point. A few days later Voorhis himself underscored it by sending a telegram to NCPAC headquarters in New York requesting that "whatever qualified endorsement the Citizens PAC may have given me be withdrawn." Had he repudiated the endorsement before he was backed onto the defensive and forced to act, the issue might never have developed. But since he had not, I thought then and still think that the endorsement was a legitimate issue to raise. Communist infiltration of labor and political organizations was a serious threat in those early postwar years, and a candidate's attitude toward endorsements by heavily infiltrated organizations was a barometer of his attitude toward that threat. Repudiation was also an essential weapon against infiltration.

After this debate, the PAC became a peripheral but heated issue in the campaign. While Voorhis equivocated, my campaign director, Harrison McCall, came up with the idea of passing out plastic thimbles saying: "Nixon for Congress—Put the Needle in the PAC."

This first "debate" was so successful that many of my supporters urged me to challenge Voorhis to other joint appearances. I had some reservations, because each one would require two or three days of concentrated preparation, and I did not want to take off any more time from campaigning. Murray Chotiner, the brilliant and no-nonsense public relations man who was running Bill Knowland's senatorial campaign and advising me part-time on mine, went straight to the point. "Dick," he said, "you're running behind, and when you're behind, you don't play it safe. You must run a high-risk campaign." He paused for a moment until I nodded my agreement, and then he said, "Good. I've already arranged for an announcement challenging Voorhis to more debates."

Voorhis accepted my challenge, and during the course of the campaign there were four more debates held in various towns in the district. They became very popular and drew overflow crowds. When the last one was held in San Gabriel the week before the election, more than a thousand people were crammed into the hall and loudspeakers had to be set up for the several hundred standing outside.

My research into Voorhis's record showed that of the more than a hundred bills he had introduced in Congress during the previous four years, only one had actually been passed into law. The effect of this bill was to transfer jurisdiction over rabbit breeders from the Department of the Interior to the Department of Agriculture. I began running a newspaper advertisement pointing out this rather insignificant legislative achievement. Voorhis replied with an ad under the headline: *Deception of the Voter Has No Place in American Politics.* He listed several of his congressional accomplishments, but they were either resolutions or speeches, not bills enacted into law.

At our fourth debate, at the Monrovia high school, Voorhis raised this issue and charged that my statements about his record were lies. I pointed out that none of the examples he cited was an actual bill that had been passed into law. To the delight of my supporters in the overflow audience of 1,200, I suggested that one had to be a rabbit to get effective representation in this congressional district.

Voorhis kept the issue alive, continuing to charge that I had lied about his record. In my opening remarks at our final debate I turned to him and said: "Congressman, I flatly challenge you to name one public bill of your authorship which passed both houses of Congress during the last four years." In his reply, he referred to a measure he wrote establishing National Employ the Physically Handicapped Week. My research into his record paid off again. In my rebuttal I produced a copy of the measure, handed it to Voorhis, and pointed out that this too was a resolution, not a bill.

Since no polls had been taken, I had no idea on Election Day how close the race might be. There were no voting machines, and the counting of the paper ballots lasted long into the following morning. But before we went to bed at about 4 A.M., it was clear that I had won. By the next afternoon the totals were complete. I had received 65,586 votes, and Voorhis received 49,994.

I was thirty-three years old, and the Twelfth District's new congressman.

In 1950, 1952, 1956, 1968, and 1972 I was again to experience the satisfaction of winning, and most of those campaigns were tough ones. But nothing could equal the excitement and jubilation of winning the first campaign. Pat and I were happier on November 6, 1946, than we were ever to be again in my political career.

By defeating a well-known figure like Voorhis, I briefly became a minor national celebrity. *Time* reported that I "turned a California grass-roots campaign (dubbed 'hopeless' by wheelhorse Republicans) into a triumph over high-powered, high-minded Democratic incumbent Jerry Voorhis" and added that I had "politely avoided personal attacks" on my opponent. *Newsweek* said, "In five Lincoln–Douglas debates, [Nixon] bested his opponent, New Dealer Jerry Voorhis, who admitted: 'This fellow has a silver tongue.' "

Despite later—and widespread—misconceptions, communism was not the central issue in the 1946 campaign. The PAC controversy provided emotional and rhetorical excitement, but it was not the issue that stirred or motivated most voters. The central issue in the 1946 campaign was the quality of life in postwar America. The loudest and longest applause given any line in any of the debates came when I said in the first one that "the time has come in this country when no labor leader or no management leader should have the power to deny the American people any of the necessities of life." Voorhis himself later wrote in his autobiography, *Confessions of a Congressman:* "The most important single factor in the campaign of 1946 was the difference in general attitude between the 'outs' and 'ins.' Anyone seeking to unseat an incumbent needed only to point out all the things that had gone wrong and all the troubles of the war period and its aftermath. Many of these things were intimate experiences in the everyday lives of the people." I took advantage of a nationwide phenomenon *Time* called "a cold but nonetheless angry voice raised against many things: price muddles, shortages, black markets, strikes, government bungling and confusion, too much government in too many things."

It was also true that although Voorhis was a hard-working and generally respected congressman, he was not really in tune with the voters of the district. I have no doubt that the Committee of 100 was right in its belief that any good Republican candidate would have had a chance of unseating Voorhis in 1946 despite his popularity and his incumbency.

Voorhis, the former Socialist, believed in large-scale government intervention, and I did not. He saw dark conspiracies among "reactionaries" and "monopolies," and I did not. He was generally an uncritical supporter of the labor unions, while I considered myself their critical friend. He advocated policies that I believed shackled and restricted American industry. His political views were 180 degrees away from mine. Most important, his votes in Congress on a wide range of issues did not represent the wishes of the voters in his district.

Since Voorhis was the front-runner and I a newcomer, I ran an especially vigorous campaign. I challenged his judgment and his voting record, a record that I appeared to know better than he did himself. If some of my rhetoric seems overstated now, it was nonetheless in keeping with the approach that seasoned Republican politicians were using that year. For example, when Henry Wallace campaigned for Democrats in California, Governor Earl Warren called him a spearhead of an attack "by leftist organizations that are attuned to the communist movement." Earlier in the year, Ohio Senator Robert Taft charged that Democratic congressional proposals "bordered on communism," while Joe Martin called for Republican victories in order to oust the Communists and fellow travelers from the federal government.

One of the most distorted charges subsequently made about the 1946 campaign involved my supporters. As I moved up the political ladder, my adversaries tried to picture me as the hand-picked stooge of oil magnates, rich bankers, real estate tycoons, and conservative millionaires. But a look at the list of my early supporters shows that they were typical representatives of the Southern California middle class: an auto dealer, a bank manager, a printing salesman, an insurance salesman, and a furniture dealer. What united them was no special vested interest but the fierce desire of average people to regain control of their own lives. Along with a majority of the voters in the Twelfth District, they had "had enough," and they decided to do something about it.

My first choice for a committee assignment was the prestigious Judiciary Committee. I was not surprised when I did not receive it, and I was pleased to be assigned to my second choice, the Education and Labor Committee. By one of those curious coincidences of history, another freshman assigned to that committee was a good-looking, good-humored young Democrat from Massachusetts named John Fitzgerald Kennedy. The newly elected members on the committee drew straws to determine their positions in the all-important seniority ranking. Kennedy drew the shortest straw among the Democrats, and I drew the shortest straw among the Republicans. As a result, he and I shared the dubious distinction of sitting at the opposite ends of the committee table, like a pair of unmatched bookends.

The Education and Labor Committee's work took up most of my time during 1947, my first year in Congress. We held months of hearings on legislation, which I supported, that passed into law as the Taft–Hartley Act in June 1947.

A public affairs group in McKeesport, Pennsylvania, asked the district's Democratic congressman, Frank Buchanan, to select the freshman from each party who seemed to have the brightest political future, and to invite them to debate the Taft–Hartley bill at a public meeting. Buchanan chose Kennedy and me, and on April 21, 1947, we had the first Kennedy–Nixon debate. McKeesport is near Pittsburgh, and for this meeting the normally Republican and conservative audience was augmented by a substantial number of anti-Taft–Hartley union men who introduced some acrimonious moments into the question period.

We took the *Capital Limited* back to Washington after the debate. We drew straws for the lower berth, and—this time—I won. We sat up late, talking far more about foreign policy than domestic issues. Kennedy and I were too different in background, outlook, and temperament to become close friends, but we were thrown together throughout our early careers, and we never had less than an amicable relationship. We were of the same generation—he was only four years younger than I; we were both Navy veterans; we both came to the House the same year; and we were both committed to devoting enormous energy to our work. Our exchanges in committee meetings and our discussions in the cloakrooms were never tinged with the personal acerbity that can make political differences uncomfortable. In those early years we saw ourselves as political opponents but not political rivals. We shared one quality which distinguished us from most of our fellow congressmen: neither of us was a backslapper, and we were both uncomfortable with boisterous displays of superficial camaraderie. He was shy, and that sometimes made him appear aloof. But it was shyness born of an instinct that guarded privacy and concealed emotions. I understood these qualities because I shared them.

Pat and I saw the inside of the White House for the first time on February 18, 1947, when we attended a reception the Trumans gave for the new members of the Eightieth Congress. On July 2 I was included in a group of four freshmen Republican congressmen for whom Representative Charles Kersten of Wisconsin had arranged a private meeting with the President. In the notes I made later that day, I described the Oval Office as a "big pleasant room," with "no gadgets" except for a pony express confidential pouch that Truman pointed out to us. Pictures of his family were on the table behind his desk, and also a model airplane that I assumed to be the presidential aircraft—an Air Force Constellation that Truman had named the *Sacred Cow*.

Truman made us all feel welcome and relaxed as we shook hands with him. We sat around the desk, and he spoke very earnestly about the necessity of rehabilitating Europe and emphasized his concern that peaceful German production should be encouraged. He said he was glad to see us even though we were Republicans, because he always considered it necessary for the two parties to cooperate in foreign affairs. He said, "Some of my best friends never agree with me politically."

He led us over to a big globe where he pointed to Manchuria and remarked on how rich it was in oil and mineral deposits. He said that the Soviets had devastated the whole region but that Manchuria would recover and become the next great productive area for the world. Then he turned the globe with the palm of his hand and pointed to the great mass of the Soviet Union. He said, "The Russians are like us, they look and act like us. They are fine people. They got along with our soldiers in Berlin very well. As far as I am concerned, they can have whatever they want just so they don't try to impose their system on others." He mentioned the accounts of Mrs. Roosevelt attending an international conference where the Soviet delegate was always obstructing action by saying that he had to clear the issue with the Kremlin. "That's just the way it was at Potsdam where I went with charitable feelings in view of their contributions in the war," Truman remarked. He said he could not understand what the Russians wanted as far as their policy toward Germany and toward Europe was concerned.

He told us that dropping the atomic bomb was an awful decision for him to make. Speaking of his job, he said, "It's the greatest show on earth, and it doesn't cost anything to the weekly newsman who covers the White House." I observed in my notes that Truman's strength was "his hominess, his democratic attitude, and his sincerity."

Twenty-two years later, when I was President, Pat and I flew to Independence to present Truman the piano he had played in the White House, for his presidential library. He was fighting a rough bout with flu, but his flair for pithy plain speaking was undiminished. I knew that he had long since changed his opinion of the Soviets. In 1969 he told me, "The Russians are liars—you can't trust them. At Potsdam they agreed to everything and broke their word. It's too bad the second world power is like this, but that's the way it is, and we must keep our strength."

Most freshmen received only one committee assignment, but Joe Martin, the new Republican Speaker, asked if I would be also willing to sit on the House Committee on Un-American Activities. Now that the Republicans controlled Congress, we would be held accountable for the committee's frequently irresponsible conduct. "We need a young lawyer on that committee to smarten it up," he said, and he added that he would consider my acceptance a personal favor. Put in this way, it was an offer I could not very well refuse. I accepted with considerable reluctance, however, because of the dubious reputation the committee had acquired under its former chairman, Martin Dies, a flamboyant and at times demagogic Texas Democrat.

My own attitude toward communism had recently changed from one of general disinterest to one of extreme concern. I do not recall being particularly disturbed when Roosevelt recognized the Soviet Union in 1934. During the Spanish Civil War the concerted press campaign against Franco—who was always described as a fascist rebel—led me to side with the Loyalists, whose communist orientation was seldom mentioned in the newspapers. At the time of the Hitler–Stalin pact I was strongly against Stalin, not because he was a Communist but because he was allied with Hitler, whom I despised; during the war I was pro-Russian, not because the Russians were Communists but because they were helping us fight Hitler. I was elated when both the United States and the Soviet Union supported the founding of the United Nations. As an admirer of Woodrow Wilson I felt that we had made a serious mistake in not joining the League of Nations, and I believed that the UN offered the world's best chance to build a lasting peace.

It was Churchill's Iron Curtain speech, delivered in Fulton, Missouri, in March 1946 that profoundly affected my attitude toward communism in general and the Soviet Union in particular. He said:

> From Stettin in the Baltic to Trieste in the Adriatic, an iron curtain has descended across the Continent. Behind that line lie all the capitals of the ancient states of Central and Eastern Europe. Warsaw, Berlin, Prague, Vienna, Budapest, Belgrade, Bucharest, and Sofia, all these famous cities and the populations around them lie in what I must call the Soviet sphere, and all are subject in one form or another, not only to Soviet influence, but to a very high, and, in many cases, increasing measure of control from Moscow.

I was jolted by these words, and at first I wondered if he had gone too far. But as the Communist subjugation of Eastern Europe became more and more apparent—with the takeover of Hungary in 1947 and Czechoslovakia in 1948—I realized that the defeat of Hitler and Japan had not produced a lasting peace, and freedom was now threatened by a new and even more dangerous enemy.

My maiden speech in the House on February 18, 1947, was the presentation of a contempt of Congress citation against Gerhart Eisler, who had been identified as the top Communist agent in America. When he refused to testify before the committee, he was held in contempt. I spoke for only ten minutes, describing the background of the case, and I concluded: "It is essential as members of this House that we defend vigilantly the fundamental rights of freedom of speech and freedom of the press. But we must bear in mind that the rights of free speech and free press do not carry with them the right to advocate the destruction of the very government which protects the freedom of an individual to express his views."

The only member who voted against the contempt citation was Vito Marcantonio of New York.

Eisler was finally indicted for passport fraud. Before he could be tried, however, he jumped bail and fled to East Germany, where he eventually became director of propaganda for the Communist regime.

At the end of 1947 I was appointed to a special legislative subcommittee of the Committee on Un-American Activities. We held some wide-ranging hearings into the nature of communist philosophy and practice, and on the basis of these I prepared a report outlining a new approach to the complicated problem of internal communist subversion. Most of the dedicated anticommunists felt that the best way to stop internal subversion was to outlaw the Communist Party. I believed that this approach would be inefficient and counterproductive. The practical effect of outlawing the party would only be to drive the hard core of true believers underground. I thought it made more sense to drive the Communist Party into the open so that we could know who its members were.

Another problem in this area was finding an objective way to define and identify Communist front organizations. Too many conservatives and other anticommunists applied broad and imprecise criteria, with the result that many extremely liberal and left-wing organizations were unfairly tarred with the communist brush. I felt that no matter how abhorrent the beliefs of any individuals or groups might be, as long as they did not receive financial support or orders from foreign governments, or engage in illegal activities, their right to their beliefs must be protected.

Working closely together, Karl Mundt of South Dakota and I prepared a bill that was introduced in the spring of 1948 and became known as the Mundt–Nixon bill. It was the first piece of legislation to emerge in ten years from the House Committee on Un-American Activities. It provided for the registration of all Communist Party members and required a statement of the source of all printed and broadcast material issued by organizations that were found to be Communist fronts. Under our bill, the identification of a group as a Communist front would be made by a Subversive Activities Control Board, which would investigate a group at the request of the Attorney General.

I was made floor manager for the debate on the bill; Vito Marcantonio was the floor leader for the Democrats. At the end of the first day's debate, I spoke briefly: "There is too much loose talk and confusion on the Communist issue. By passing this bill the Congress of the United States will go on record as to just what is subversive about communism in the United States. . . . It will once and for all spike many of the loose charges about organizations being Communist fronts because they happen to advocate some of the same policies which the Communists support."

The Mundt–Nixon bill passed the House on May 19, 1948, by a vote of 319 to 58. The Senate let it die in committee, and it was not until 1950 that some of its provisions were embodied in the McCarran Act. By then, of course, the nature of the question of internal communism had changed because of the Hiss case, and the harsher terms of the McCarran Act reflected that change.

It is important to remember that the perception of communism in American politics changed completely in the early postwar years. During the war, the Soviets were our allies against Hitler. The photographs of American and Russian soldiers shaking hands at the Elbe made a strong impression on many Americans, who looked forward to a new dawn of international peace and cooperation.

In the main, anticommunism in postwar America meant opposition to the kind of dictatorial state socialism that existed in Russia and that many Americans saw as a negation of everything America stood for. In the 1946 campaign, for example, when I talked about the "communist-dominated PAC," my remarks were generally understood in this context of dictatorial socialism versus free enterprise.

In the years 1946 to 1948 domestic communism was a peripheral issue. Until the Hiss case, it was generally not seen as a clear and present danger to our way of life. A poll in January 1948, for example, found that 40 percent of those questioned felt the American Communist Party posed no threat, while 45 percent believed that it posed a potential threat.

As the presidential election of 1948 approached, however, Truman must have begun to worry about the issue of internal security. Now that the Committee on Un-American Activities was in Republican hands, he may have decided that the best way to handle the issue was to cover up the evidence. On March 15, 1948, he ordered all federal departments and agencies to refuse future congressional requests or subpoenas for information regarding loyalty or security matters. This decision backfired because instead of defusing the issue it made it appear that Truman was trying to cover something up. Instead of admitting an error of judgment, Truman decided to tough it through. His course led him into the shoals of red herring that caused him so many problems, not only in the Hiss case but also two years later when McCarthy began his anticommunist career with the ostensible purpose of getting Truman to rescind this executive order.

It was the Hiss case that completely changed the public's perception of domestic communism. People were now alerted to a serious threat to our liberties. At the same time this new awareness unfortunately led to emotional excesses and demagogic imprecisions that clouded the issue more than they illuminated it.

THE HERTER COMMITTEE

On Monday, July 30, 1947, I was probably the most surprised man in Washington when I opened the morning newspaper and read that I had been chosen by Speaker Joe Martin to be one of the nineteen members of a select committee headed by Congressman Christian Herter of Massachusetts to go to Europe and prepare a report in connection with the foreign aid plan that the Secretary of State, General George C. Marshall, had unveiled at a Harvard commencement speech in June. I had not even spoken to Martin or anyone else about the committee because I had not thought there was any chance of being appointed to it.

The appointment was an unexpected honor and opportunity for me. My determination to work hard had paid off unexpectedly soon. I was also modest enough to recognize that geography and age had played a part in my selection. Martin wanted the committee to represent a cross section of the House, and I was the only Westerner and the youngest member appointed to it. I would now have an opportunity to work with some of the most senior and influential men in the House and a chance to show what I could do in the field of foreign affairs.

Most of my advisers in California were pleased with my appointment, but they wanted the committee's report to disown the bipartisan Truman–Vandenberg foreign policy that was being promoted in Washington to support the Marshall Plan. Just before we sailed for Europe, I received a long letter signed by half a dozen of my strongest supporters. It began, "We feel it appropriate to state our views at this time inasmuch as you are embarking on a trip on which you will be subjected first, to a skillful orientation program by the State Department and later, to no less skillfully prepared European propaganda. It is our hope and belief that, even in the midst of these powerful influences, you will be able to maintain the level-headed course you have followed in Congress." The conclusion was a straightforward partisan reminder that a presidential election was little more than a year away: "We believe there is only one fundamental cure for this whole situation—that is to rid ourselves of all the hangover philosophies of the New Deal by making a clean sweep in Washington and electing a Republican administration in 1948. This can be done provided the Republican members of Congress are wise enough to refuse to be drawn into support of a dangerously unworkable and profoundly inflationary foreign policy and, provided further, that the Democrats do not succeed in so dividing our party by bipartisan internationalism that there no longer is any way to tell who is a Republican."

The committee sailed from New York on the *Queen Mary* at the end of August. Despite all our briefings and studying, I do not think that any of us was really prepared for what we found in Europe. From the minute we stepped off the luxurious ship in Southampton it was clear that we had come to a continent tottering on the brink of starvation and chaos. In every country we visited the situation was the same: without American aid, millions would starve or die of diseases caused by malnutrition before the winter was over. The political facts were equally evident: without our food and aid, Europe would be plunged into anarchy, revolution, and, ultimately, communism.

Britain's Prime Minister, Clement Attlee, invited us to tea at 10 Downing Street, and we spent an hour with the Falstaffian Foreign Secretary, Ernest Bevin, whose recent speech advocating that all the gold at Fort Knox be divided up among the nations of the world tended to get the discussion off on the wrong foot.

If London was depressing, Berlin seemed hopeless. What once had been a great city was now block after block, mile after mile of charred desolation. It hardly seemed possible that three million people were still living amidst the rubble. As we stood in the vast ruined hall of what had been Hitler's Chancellery, small thin-faced German boys tried to sell us their fathers' war medals as souvenirs.

Despite the cautious reluctance of some of our embassy people, I insisted that we meet with the Communist Party leaders in each country we visited. We found that these men were usually more vigorous and impressive than their democratic counterparts. I was curious to see how their minds worked, and I also wanted to assess their relationship to the Soviet Union. I particularly remember our meeting with Giuseppe Di Vittorio, the Communist Secretary General of the Italian Labor Confederation. His office was decorated with red curtains and red walls, and he wore a small red flag in his lapel. I had seen most of the American labor leaders in action before the House Labor Committee, and Di Vittorio could have held his own with the best of them.

I asked him what kind of government policy he favored for Italian unions, and he replied that he would like to see labor be free from government control and have the right to strike.

"From your answer," I said, "I assume that you favor the kind of government we have in the United States, where labor is striking at this very moment, rather than the kind of government they have in Russia, where labor is dominated by the state and they haven't had a strike in the last twenty years."

After the translation, Di Vittorio gave me an icy look and said, "The gentleman and I are not speaking the same language. In a country like the United States the workers must strike to obtain their rights from the capitalist reactionaries and employers. In Russia there are no capitalist reactionaries and employers and therefore the right to strike need not exist."

I asked him if he had any criticisms to offer regarding American foreign policy. In the notes I made of the conversation, I wrote that "he proceeded to give our foreign policy a going over which would make Henry Wallace look like a piker." When he finished, I said, "We always welcome criticism of our policy, but may I ask whether you have ever criticized Russian policy so closely and in such detail?"

Di Vittorio gave me the same look as before and said, "Again the gentleman and I are not speaking the same language. The reason the foreign policy of the United States is necessarily imperialistic is that it is dominated by capitalists, reactionaries, and employers. In Russia there are no capitalists, reactionaries, and employers, and therefore it is impossible for the foreign policy of Russia to be imperialistic. Therefore it is not subject to criticism."

He was right: we were not speaking the same language. It struck me that Di Vittorio's expression of the party line was almost identical—right down to the phraseology—to that of the Communist leaders we had met in England and France. In my notes I concluded that "this indicates definitely then that the Communists throughout the world owe their loyalty not to the countries in which they live but to Russia."

If we saw the false face of an ostensibly patriotic communism in Britain, France, and Italy, we saw its true and brutal face in Greece and Trieste. In Greece we used an old cargo plane to fly up to the northern mountains to assess the military situation and the morale of the loyalist soldiers fighting against the Communist rebels. When we walked down the main street of a mountain town, the mayor introduced us to a girl whose left breast had been cut off by the Communists because she had refused to betray her brother, one of the loyalist leaders.

In Trieste, the large port on the Italian-Yugoslav border that was about to become a UN-mandated free city, I witnessed firsthand the violence that sometimes accompanied the communist threat.

We arrived the day before the UN mandate was to become effective. I was at the hotel, just beginning to unpack, when I heard loud singing. I looked out the window and saw a parade of about five hundred men and women. They were young, vigorous, and full of fight. Many were carrying red flags, and they were singing the stirring "Internationale" at the top of their lungs. The Communist Party headquarters was opposite the hotel, and as the parade passed by, each marcher raised his arm in a clenched-fist salute. I went down to see what was going on. Suddenly there was an explosion at the end of the block. The crowd cleared and I saw the body of a young man whose head had been blown off by a grenade thrown from a second-story window. For a frozen moment everyone stood looking at the blood gushing from his neck, but then rocks and bottles started flying. The police arrived and began chasing the Communist leaders.

A fleeing Communist, barreling through the crowd like a college fullback, hit an old woman and knocked her halfway across the street against the curb, where she lay motionless. This sort of thing continued all afternoon and evening. That day five people were killed and seventy-five were wounded by bombs and gunfire. I was sure that what was happening in Trieste would soon be re-enacted throughout Western Europe unless America helped to restore stability and prosperity.

A few weeks after we returned to Washington, the Herter Committee issued a number of reports based on the truckload of notes and papers we brought back with us. The common denominator of each report was a strong recommendation for economic aid for Europe. In the meantime I had taken a poll and found that 75 percent of my constituents in the Twelfth District were resolutely opposed to any foreign aid. This was the first time I had personally experienced the classic dilemma, so eloquently described by Edmund Burke, that is faced at one time or another by almost any elected official in a democracy: how much should his votes register his constituents' opinions, and how much should they represent his own views and convictions? After what I had seen and learned in Europe, I believed so strongly in the necessity of extending economic aid that I felt I had no choice but to vote my conscience and then try my hardest to convince my constituents.

I immediately prepared a series of columns for the local newspapers, and as soon as I could I went home and began an active round of speeches throughout the district describing what I had seen on the trip and why I felt that economic assistance was necessary if we were to save Europe from the twin specters of starvation and communism.

Fortunately, my appearances in the district were successful, and the whole experience ended up enhancing my popularity. On December 15, 1947, the House voted 313 to 82 in favor of the Marshall Plan. As everyone now knows, it was successful in every way: it saved Europe from starvation, it ensured Europe's economic recovery, and it preserved Europe from communism.

I learned a great deal from the Herter Committee trip. Above all, I now understood the reasons for the success of communism in Europe.

First, the Communist leaders were strong and vigorous: they knew what they wanted and were willing to work hard to get it. After this visit, I would never make the mistake of thinking, either because of the doubletalk party line jargon or because their manners are often crude, that Communist leaders are not very intelligent and very tough men.

Second, I saw how the leaders of postwar European communism understood the power of nationalism and were appropriating that power. While we were in Rome, for example, Communist posters for the upcoming municipal elections were plastered all over the city. These posters did not feature the hammer and sickle, or any other Communist symbol, nor did they depict the joys of some future workers' state. Instead, they were huge heroic pictures of the nineteenth-century patriot Garibaldi—who would have turned over in his grave had he known that his life's devotion to Italy and freedom was being manipulated by an international statist ideology ruled from Moscow.

Third, I saw how European communism was rolling in Soviet money. Unlike most of their democratic counterparts, the European Communist parties were well financed from Moscow.

Fourth, I saw that most of democratic Europe was either leaderless or, worse still, that many in the leadership classes had simply capitulated to communism. For the first time, I understood the vital importance of strong leadership to a people and a nation, and I saw the sad consequences when such leadership is lacking or when it fails. From just this brief exposure, I could see that the only thing the Communists would respect—and deal with seriously—was power at least equal to theirs and backed up by willingness to use it. I made a penciled note in Trieste that is as true today as it was thirty years ago: "One basic rule with Russians—never bluff unless you are prepared to carry through, because they will test you every time."

THE HISS CASE

Just before the House's summer recess in 1948, the Committee on Un-American Activities, chaired by J. Parnell Thomas of New Jersey, had heard testimony from Elizabeth Bentley, a courier for a Communist spy ring in Washington during the war. Looking for witnesses to corroborate her testimony, Robert Stripling, the committee's highly intelligent and dynamic young chief investigator, suggested that we subpoena a man who had been identified as a Communist functionary in the 1930s but who had left the party and was now a professionally well-respected and well-paid senior editor of *Time* magazine. That man was Whittaker Chambers.

When I first saw Chambers on the morning of August 3, just before he testified in public session, I could hardly believe this man was our witness. Whittaker Chambers was one of the most disheveled-looking persons I had ever seen. Everything about him seemed wrinkled and unpressed.

He began his testimony with the story of how, as a disaffected intellectual, he became a Communist in 1924. He told of his growing disillusion with Stalinism, and of his eventual break with the party in the late 1930s. Like many former Communists, Chambers had undergone a religious conversion. Now he feared and hated Communism with an almost mystical fervor. He said that he had been part of a Communist group whose primary aim was to infiltrate the government. Among the members of this group, he said, was Alger Hiss. He described their last meeting, in 1938, when Hiss had tearfully refused to join Chambers in leaving the Communist Party.

A ripple of surprise went through the room, because Hiss, who had not been mentioned in Miss Bentley's testimony, was a well-known and highly respected figure in New York and Washington. He had made a brilliant record at Harvard Law School and then served as a secretary to Supreme Court Justice Oliver Wendell Holmes. After a few years with private law firms in Boston and New York, Hiss had returned to Washington in 1933; like so many others he was drawn by the excitement and opportunities of the New Deal. He occupied a number of important government posts, ultimately becoming assistant to the Assistant Secretary of State and serving as one of President Roosevelt's advisers at the Yalta Conference with Stalin and Churchill. Hiss was acknowledged as one of the primary architects of the United Nations; he served as Secretary-General of the San Francisco Conference, at which the UN charter was drafted, and was then an adviser to the American delegation at the first General Assembly meeting in London. In 1947 he left the State Department to become president of the prestigious Carnegie Endowment for International Peace. John Foster Dulles, chairman of the Endowment's board of directors, was among those who had recommended and endorsed his selection.

Now here was Whittaker Chambers testifying that he had known Alger Hiss as a member of the Communist Party underground.

It may seem surprising in light of later events that Chambers's testimony that morning did not cause more of a stir. This was partly because his story was totally unexpected. Also, Chambers was such an unprepossessing figure that his story was not taken as seriously as it would have been had he been more forceful and impressive.

The next morning we received a telegram from Hiss asking to appear before us in order to deny Chambers's charge. We invited him to appear the next day.

As Alger Hiss stood to be sworn in on the morning of August 5, the difference between him and Chambers could not have been more striking. Hiss was tall, elegant, handsome, and perfectly poised as he categorically denied Chambers's charge. In a firm voice he said, "I am here at my own request to deny unqualifiedly various statements about me which were made before this committee by one Whittaker Chambers the day before yesterday." He lowered his voice for dramatic emphasis when he stated: "I am not and never have been a member of the Communist Party. I do not and never have adhered to the tenets of the Communist Party. I am not and never have been a member of any Communist front organization. I have never followed the Communist Party line, directly or indirectly."

He denied everything Chambers had said and added that he did not even know anyone named Chambers and, as far as he could remember, never had. When Mundt, as acting chairman, pointed out that Chambers had testified under oath when he said that he knew him, Hiss boldly rejoined, "I do know that he said that. I also know that I am testifying under those same laws to the contrary."

When Hiss finished his testimony people surged around him, to shake his hand and congratulate him on his performance, and to commiserate with him on the damage the committee had done him.

That same morning, President Truman held an informal press conference in the Oval Office. One of the reporters asked about our hearings. "Mr. President," he said, "do you think that the Capitol Hill spy scare is a 'red herring' to divert public attention from inflation?" After agreeing with the reporter's "red herring" characterization, Truman read a prepared statement that the hearings were doing "irreparable harm to certain people, seriously impairing the morale of federal employees, and undermining public confidence in the government."

While Truman's contemptuous dismissal of our hearings as a "red herring" had the effect of throwing his political weight against the investigation, he wielded still more effective powers. In his statement he reaffirmed his earlier order that all administrative agencies of the government refuse to turn over to a congressional committee information relating to the loyalty of any government employee.

Truman had honed his political skills in the rough and scandal-tainted Kansas City Democratic machine, and he never shied away from using any weapon available. Without question his goal throughout the Hiss case was to obstruct our efforts to uncover the facts.

The attack by the President, the impact of his executive directive, and Hiss's highly effective testimony combined to throw the committee into a panic by the time we met again in executive session that afternoon. The audience in the hearing room and the press seemed to have been completely convinced by Hiss, and we knew that we were in for a rough time for allowing Chambers to testify without having first verified his story. No one on the committee wanted to undergo such an assault from the President and the press right before the election. One of the members summed up the general opinion when he said, "We're ruined." I was the only member of the committee who argued in favor of holding our ground and pursuing the case further. Stripling, whose judgment was highly respected by all the members, strongly supported my position.

My reasoning was pragmatic. I felt that as far as the reputation of the committee was concerned, Chambers's testimony had already done its damage. Our critics would not be silenced just because we decided to drop the case, and I argued that we had more to gain than we had left to lose by seeing it through. I pointed out that the formulation of Chambers's charges and Hiss's response provided us with a unique angle to pursue. In most cases we were in the almost impossible position of having to prove whether or not an individual had actually been a Communist. This time, however, because of Hiss's categorical denials, we did not have to establish anything more complicated than whether the two men had known each other. I suggested that we examine Chambers again to see if he could substantiate his story. If he could, the committee would be vindicated; if he could not, we might then find out what bizarre or sinister motives had led him to lie about Hiss and thus at least be able to make a better defense for our mistake.

I already had some doubts about Hiss because for all the vehemence of his denials, he never actually said unequivocally that he did not know Chambers. There was always some qualifier. When Mundt described Chambers as a man "whom you say you have never seen," Hiss had interrupted and said, "As far as I know, I have never seen him."

The British sometimes say that someone is "too clever by half." That was my impression of Hiss: he was too suave, too smooth, and too self-confident to be an entirely trustworthy witness.

Stripling and I were finally able to convince the committee of the uncomfortable truth that we had indeed little left to lose, and it was decided that John McDowell, a thoughtful Republican from Pennsylvania, Eddie Hébert, a Louisiana Democrat who had been a newspaper reporter before entering politics, and I would take a crack at testing Chambers's story. We questioned him on August 7, a quiet Saturday morning, in a room in the deserted Federal Court House on Foley Square in lower Manhattan. I had made a long list of the kinds of things that a man would be likely to know and remember about a friend.

I began by giving him a chance to pull back, gently asking if we had correctly understood him to say that Hiss was a Communist.

"Could this have possibly been an intellectual study group?" I asked.

"It was in no wise an intellectual study group," Chambers firmly replied. "Its primary function was to infiltrate the government in the interest of the Communist Party."

Chambers had a wealth of detailed and intimate information about Hiss; virtually all of it turned out to be correct. He told us that in private Hiss called his wife Dilly or Pross and she called him Hilly; he told us about the cocker spaniel they had boarded in a kennel on Wisconsin Avenue in Washington when they took their summer holidays on the Eastern Shore in Maryland; he mentioned Hiss's simple tastes in food. He described Mrs. Hiss as a short, highly nervous woman who had a habit of blushing a fiery red when she became excited. He told us about the location and layout of the three houses and apartments Hiss had lived in during the years that he had known him, and described the several occasions on which he had stayed overnight in them.

Chambers told us that one of Hiss's hobbies was ornithology, and that he could still remember Hiss's excitement when he came home one morning after having seen a prothonotary warbler, a rare species.

After over two hours of exhaustive examination, I asked Chambers if he would be willing to take a lie detector test. Without hesitation, he said that he would. "You have that much confidence?" I asked. "I am telling the truth," he calmly replied.

If there turned out to be substance to Chambers's charges, Truman would be terribly embarrassed, and ordinarily this possibility alone might have spurred the Republicans on in an election year. But special factors in the Hiss case favored a cautious approach. Governor Thomas Dewey of New York was the Republican nominee for President. John Foster Dulles, one of those who had recommended Hiss for his job as president of the Carnegie Endowment, was Dewey's chief foreign policy adviser and was expected to be Secretary of State in a Dewey administration. The Hiss case, with its disturbing questions about "softness on communism," might become a two-edged sword that could hurt Dewey as much as Truman. I was aware that the Dewey campaign organization would undoubtedly be grateful if I decided to go along with the rest of the committee and let the case pass into a pre-election limbo.

On the basis of the testimony, I felt strongly that Hiss was lying. But before the case went any further, I wanted to follow up on a number of points that I did not think had been fully covered even in our marathon session. So I decided to visit Chambers at his farm in Westminster, Maryland, where I met Esther Chambers for the first time. She was a strikingly dark woman, who said very little but looked deeply sad and worried.

Once again, the richness and fullness of the detail of Chambers's memory were overwhelming. I told him point-blank that many people were charging that he had some hidden grudge or motive for what he was doing to Hiss. He was silent for a long time and then said: "Certainly I wouldn't have a motive which would involve destroying my own career." He said that privacy was almost an obsession with him and that appearing in public was one of the most painful things he had ever done in his life.

I happened to mention that I was a Quaker, and he said that Mrs. Hiss had been a Quaker when he knew her and that since then he had become a Quaker himself. He snapped his fingers and said, "That reminds me of something. Priscilla often used the plain speech in talking to Alger at home." From my own family, I knew how unlikely it would be for anyone but a close friend to know such an intimate detail. Of course, it was still possible that he could have learned it from someone, but the way he blurted it out convinced me that he was telling the truth.

Charles Kersten, an expert on Communist activities, urged that I discuss my findings with John Foster Dulles. On August 11, I called the Dewey campaign headquarters at the Roosevelt Hotel in New York and told Dulles that I thought he should look at Chambers's testimony before he made any kind of public statement on the case. That afternoon Kersten and I took the train up to New York to see him.

Kersten and I sat on a sofa in Dulles's suite while Foster and his brother, Allen, read through the transcripts of the three hearings. After they both had finished, Foster Dulles stood and paced back and forth across the room. "There's no question about it," he said. "It's almost impossible to believe, but Chambers knows Hiss." Allen Dulles agreed, and both felt that the case should be brought into the open by a public confrontation between the two men as soon as possible. Foster did not for a moment flinch from the potential embarrassment to himself as one of Hiss's sponsors for the presidency of the Carnegie Endowment. I told them I would keep them informed of any new developments.

After visiting Chambers's farm, I had called Bert Andrews, the Pulitzer Prize-winning head of the New York *Herald Tribune*'s Washington bureau. I knew that Andrews was an outspoken critic of the committee; he had recently written a book, *Washington Witch Hunt,* which was highly critical of the administration's loyalty program. I told Andrews that I believed Chambers was telling the truth, but that I wanted to put his story to every possible test. He agreed to go up with me and question Chambers thoroughly.

Andrews asked Chambers tough questions and bore down hard about the rumors that had begun to sweep Washington that he was an alcoholic and that he had a history of mental illness and institutional confinement. Chambers was unfazed and pointed out that rumors of this sort were typical of Communist smear campaigns.

By the time we got back to Washington, Andrews was more excited than I. He was convinced that Chambers was telling the truth, and he was now worried that Hiss would get off because of the careless methods and inefficient staff work that he felt had characterized committee hearings in the past. So was I.

Because of Truman's executive order we were not able to get any direct help from J. Edgar Hoover or the FBI. However, we had some informal contacts with a lower-level agent that proved helpful in our investigations.

When we called Hiss back before an executive session on August 16 he was in a very different temper than during our first encounter.

I told him that there were substantial areas of difference between his testimony and Chambers's, and that we wanted to give him an opportunity to explain these in executive session before we arranged a public confrontation. Hiss straightened his back and said, "I have been angered and hurt by the attitude you have been taking today that you have a conflict of testimony between two witnesses—one of whom is a confessed former Communist and the other is me—and that you simply have two witnesses saying contradictory things as between whom you find it most difficult to decide on credibility. I do not wish to make it easier for anyone who, for whatever motive I cannot understand, is apparently endeavoring to destroy me. I should not be asked to give details which somehow he may hear and then may be able to use as if he knew them before."

Then he introduced what was to become the main theme of his subsequent testimony: the idea that the *details* of the case were not important. He said, "The issue is not whether this man knew me and I don't remember him. The issue is whether he had a particular conversation that he has said he had with me, and which I have denied, and whether I am a member of the Communist Party or ever was, which he has said and which I have denied."

This was a crucial point. I had persuaded the committee to continue the hearings on precisely the ground that the details of the case *were* important because only the details could prove whether Hiss had lied when he said he did not know Chambers. His denial of even knowing Chambers was the primary factor that had discredited Chambers and the committee as well. If Hiss could now shift the hearings to the question of whether or not we could prove he was a Communist, we were finished.

I said that Chambers had been told that every answer he gave would be subject to the laws of perjury. Details concerning his alleged relationship with Hiss could be confirmed by third parties. That, I said, was the purpose of these questions.

Hiss asked if he could say something for the record. "Certainly," I replied.

With elaborate deliberation, he wrote something on the pad of paper in front of him. He said that he had written the name of a man he had known in the mid-1930s and who, he now remembered, had in fact done some of the things that Chambers claimed to have done. This man had spent several days in Hiss's house, sublet his apartment, borrowed money from him, and taken his car. But, Hiss said, he was reluctant to reveal the name directly because it might be leaked back to Chambers, who could then incorporate it into his perjurious tale.

The questioning resumed and once again Hiss quibbled about answering the questions Stripling and I asked him about the places he had lived on the grounds that his answers might get back to Chambers and be used against him. This coy reticence proved too much for the crusty Hébert. He said bluntly to Hiss, "Either you or Mr. Chambers is lying." Hiss coolly replied, "That is certainly true." Hébert came back, "And whichever one of you is lying is the greatest actor that America has ever produced."

The committee took a five-minute recess, and when the session resumed Hiss said he would reveal the name that he had earlier written on the pad.

He said, "The name of the man I brought in—and he may have no relation to this whole nightmare—is a man named George Crosley."

Thus George Crosley, the man who never was, the real red herring of the Hiss case, made his first appearance.

Hiss spent the better part of an hour and a quarter answering questions about George Crosley. Crosley was, he said, a free-loading free-lance journalist who had approached Hiss when he was counsel for the Senate's Nye Committee on Munitions and Armaments and asked for information for magazine articles he purported to be writing on the committee's activities. Hiss added that he frequently dealt with such requests from writers.

They had lunch a couple of times, he said, and Crosley asked for his help in finding a place to live because he wanted to bring his wife and baby down from New York for the rest of the summer while he wrote his articles. It happened that Hiss was about to move into a new house in Georgetown, with three months remaining in the lease of his old apartment. So he sublet the apartment to Crosley. When the Crosleys' furniture was late arriving from New York, Hiss said, he even let them stay in his new house for a few days. He added that in the end Crosley had welshed on the rent, and they had parted on less than friendly terms. Since 1935, Hiss said, he had never seen or heard from Crosley.

It was hard to believe that Hiss could have forgotten and then suddenly remembered someone like "Crosley," but we took the story at face value and questioned him about this mysterious journalist.

I asked him what Mrs. Crosley looked like, and he replied that she was "strikingly dark." I was the only member of the Committee who had ever seen Mrs. Chambers, and I knew that this described her perfectly. Now I felt sure that Hiss had known Chambers. Whether or not he had known him as George Crosley was the only question that remained to be answered. Next, I took him through a catalogue of Crosley's physical appearance, beginning with his height and weight. Then I asked, "How about his teeth?"

"Very bad teeth. That is one of the things I particularly want to see Chambers about. This man had very bad teeth, did not take care of his teeth."

"Did he have most of his teeth or just weren't well cared for?" Stripling asked.

"I don't think he had gapped teeth, but they were badly taken care of. They were stained and I would say obviously not attended to," Hiss replied.

Then, using Chambers's testimony as a guide, we took Hiss back over the ground of his life in the 1930s. We asked him the same questions that we had asked Chambers, and in almost every instance we got the same answers.

For most members of the committee, the exchange that clinched the case arose late in the day over the least likely subject. I asked Hiss if he had any hobbies, and he replied that he was interested in tennis and amateur ornithology. "Did you ever see a prothonotary warbler?" McDowell asked casually.

Hiss virtually lit up with excitement. "I have, right here on the Potomac."

"I saw one in Arlington," McDowell said.

"They come back and nest in those swamps," Hiss continued. "Beautiful yellow head, a gorgeous bird . . ."

There was a moment of telling silence as the significance of this exchange hit the committee.

We had promised Hiss a public confrontation with Chambers for August 25, which was still a week away. Now, however, there might be a third man in the mix—George Crosley—and with him a strange new twist had been added to the possibilities of mistaken identity. I felt that we had to have the meeting between Hiss and Chambers right away. If the whole thing were a mistake, it should be put right before any more damage was done. On the other hand, if Hiss had manufactured Crosley out of whole cloth to explain Chambers's damning testimony, I thought that it was equally important to flush him out before he had time to fill in more details of his deception.

I stayed very late at the office trying to decide the best thing to do. At 2 A.M. I phoned Stripling and said we could not wait a week and that I wanted a session arranged for that very afternoon. He said that he had reached the same conclusion and agreed to make the necessary arrangements.

The first Hiss–Chambers confrontation took place on August 17 at 5:35 P.M. in suite 1400 of the Commodore Hotel in New York.

The suite consisted of a living room and bedroom. The living room walls were decorated, ironically, with Audubon prints of birds. We put three chairs behind a table near the window for the committee members, and placed a single chair about eight feet away facing the table. There was a sofa against the wall, to the right of the chair.

When Hiss arrived, along with a friend from the Carnegie Endowment, he was pettish and irritable. When he was finally seated in the chair facing us, I told him that instead of waiting until August 25 we had decided that the cause of truth would be better served if he and Chambers could meet right away. We had therefore brought Chambers to this suite.

I asked that Chambers be brought in. The bedroom door behind Hiss opened, and Chambers walked through.

Hiss did not so much as look around while Chambers walked up behind him and then sat down on the sofa. He stared straight ahead at the window.

I began, "Mr. Chambers, will you please stand? And will you please stand, Mr. Hiss?"

The two men now stood and Hiss turned to face Chambers; they could not have been more than four or five feet apart.

"Mr. Hiss," I said, "the man standing here is Mr. Whittaker Chambers. I ask you now if you have ever known that man before?"

I do not think that I have ever seen one man look at another with more hatred in his eyes than did Alger Hiss when he looked at Whittaker Chambers. We opened the blinds so that there could later be no suggestion that bad light had hampered the identification.

Hiss now seemed genuinely uncertain and confused. He looked at me and said, "Will you ask him to say something?"

I asked Chambers to state his name and business. He said, "My name is Whittaker Chambers."

With this, Hiss took a step toward him, saying, "Would you mind opening your mouth wider?"

Chambers repeated his name, and Hiss became very impatient. "I said, would you open your mouth"—and he made a gesture with his fingers to show what he wanted him to do. Looking over at me, he said,

"You know what I am referring to, Mr. Nixon." What he meant was that he wanted to look at Chambers's teeth; Hiss's hand was not more than six inches from Chambers's mouth, and at that moment I wondered whether Chambers was tempted to bite his finger.

"May I ask whether his voice, when he testified before, was comparable to this?" Hiss asked. I looked around for something Chambers could read. The only reading matter in the room was a copy of *Newsweek*. As Chambers read from the magazine, Hiss studied his mouth intently, like a horse trader trying to guess the age of a potential purchase. Chambers paused, and Hiss said that the voice sounded a little different from the way he remembered Crosley's, and that the teeth were obviously much improved. Therefore, he said, without further checking he could not take an oath that Chambers was Crosley.

I asked Chambers whether he had had any major dental work done, and he mentioned some extractions and a plate made by his dentist, a Dr. Hitchcock. Hiss seemed satisfied with this information and said, "That testimony of Mr. Chambers, if it can be believed, would tend to substantiate my feeling that he represented himself to me in 1934 or 1935 or thereabouts as George Crosley, a free-lance writer of articles for magazines. I would like to find out from Dr. Hitchcock if what he has just said is true, because I am relying partly—one of my main recollections of Crosley was the poor condition of his teeth."

I said, "Mr. Hiss, do you feel that you would have to have the dentist tell you just what he did to the teeth before you could tell anything about this man?"

Hiss changed the subject and I began questioning Chambers.

"Mr. Chairman—" Hiss interrupted.

"Just a moment," I said, and returned to Chambers.

When Chambers said that he had stayed in Hiss's apartment for approximately three weeks, Hiss interrupted again and said, "Mr. Chairman, I don't need to ask Mr. Whittaker Chambers any more questions. I am now perfectly prepared to identify this man as George Crosley."

I have studied the testimony very closely, but I have never been sure why Hiss suddenly decided at this point to give up the charade. Just a few minutes earlier his "visual memory" had been so bad that he insisted on consulting dental charts before he could be sure of Chambers's identity. Now, he was so emphatic about his identification that when he was asked if he were absolutely certain, he said, "If he had lost both eyes and taken his nose off, I would be sure." He still, however, claimed that he had not known that Chambers/Crosley was a Communist.

Chambers was asked whether he could make a positive identification of Hiss as the Communist he had known and in whose house he had stayed. He answered, "Positive identification." Hiss suddenly shot up out of his chair and moved toward him, shaking his fist. His voice quavered with anger as he said, "May I say for the record at this point that I would like to invite Mr. Whittaker Chambers to make those same statements out of the presence of this committee, without their being privileged for suit for libel. I challenge you to do it, and I hope you will do it damned quickly."

Chambers had shown no fear at all when Hiss came toward him, but Hiss now was completely unnerved. I regretted that we had agreed to let him go early so he could keep a dinner appointment. I believe that if we had continued to press him we might have gotten even more contradictions out of him, if not an actual break. But as it was, we had quite enough.

The public confrontation between the two men came the following week on August 25, in the Caucus Room of the Old House Office Building. The room overflowed with people crowded in to witness the scene, and the heavy air was superheated by television lights.

Hiss used three basic tactics. At first he tried to confuse and belabor the details of the evidence. He once again brought up the importance of the dental work to explain his initial reluctance to identify Chambers as Crosley.

I said, "You have made much of the point of the bad teeth. You even asked the name of his dentist and wanted to consult with the dentist before you made the identification positive. My question may sound facetious, but I am just wondering: didn't you ever see Crosley with his mouth closed?"

He replied, "The striking thing in my recollection about Crosley was not when he had his mouth shut, but when he had his mouth open." With this answer the audience, which had started out on Hiss's side but had become restive because of his constant evasiveness, burst out laughing. Chairman Thomas called for order and said to Hiss, "If you've got any very humorous remarks in the way of answers, call me out later on and give them to me. I always like a good laugh, but let's not have any more laughing in here if we can possibly avoid it." Hiss was flailing about now, and he replied haughtily, "I understood the laughter to be at the question, not at the answer, Mr. Chairman. Maybe you or Mr. Nixon would like to withdraw to tell your jokes."

Equally ludicrous was Hiss's performance when he was shown a photostatic copy of a document bearing his signature and was asked to identify it. He hesitated and hedged, and said that he could not do so without seeing the original.

Mundt was completely exasperated by this reply and asked incredulously, "Could you be sure if you saw the original?"

"I could be surer," Hiss replied. Again there was laughter from the audience, and even his friends sitting in the front rows shook their heads uncomfortably.

His second tactic was to remind us of all the well-known and unquestionably patriotic people with whom he had worked and who thought highly of him. He named thirty-four, from John Foster Dulles and Harold Stassen to Cordell Hull and James Byrnes, and suggested that we consult them about his loyalty. This line of "innocence by association" did not get him anywhere with the committee, and did not seem to impress many people in the audience either.

His third tactic involved a renewed attempt to insist that the details of his and Chambers's conflicting stories made no difference because the only real issue was whether he had been a Communist. Once again I tried to expose the false logic behind this premise and to keep the hearings firmly on the ground of establishing whether he had committed perjury when he said he had not known Chambers.

"Mr. Hiss," I said, "you yourself have made an issue of the fact as to (1) whether you knew Chambers at all—that issue has now been resolved; and (2) how well you knew Chambers and whether you knew him as a Communist. That is the purpose of this questioning now."

The part of Hiss's testimony that seriously discredited him in the eyes of many was his story about his car. Chambers had testified that Hiss was such a dedicated Communist that when he bought a new Plymouth in 1936 he wanted to give his old car, a 1929 Ford roadster, to the Communist Party. It was strictly against party rules for a member of the underground to do anything that might publicly link him with the party, but Chambers said that Hiss had been so insistent that an exception was made, and an arrangement was worked out whereby the car was transferred through an intermediary.

Hiss's version was completely different. At one point in his testimony about George Crosley, he had said, "I sold him an automobile"; at another, "I gave him the use of the car"; at another, "I let him have it along with the rent." I pointed out these discrepancies to him, and said that it was hard to believe that he could not remember more precisely what he had done about the ownership of something as substantial as a car.

Thanks to some superb investigative work and a great stroke of luck, we accomplished the one thing Hiss had clearly never imagined possible: we found the papers he had signed transferring ownership of the car more than ten years before. The transaction turned out to have been highly unusual. Hiss had signed the car over to an automobile dealership for $25, and it had then immediately been signed over in the name of the dealership, for the same amount, to a man who turned out to have a record as a Communist organizer and who used a false address on the transfer papers. Nowhere did the name George Crosley appear; and we established that the transfer had not taken place in June 1935, when Hiss testified he had last seen Crosley, but almost a year later, in July 1936—exactly when Chambers had testified it happened.

The car transaction was incontrovertible evidence that Hiss had not been telling the truth and that he had known Chambers (or "Crosley") far better, far longer, and far later than he had testified. After his first appearance before the committee, Hiss had been besieged by well-wishers. At the end of this testimony, however, he and his attorney made their solitary way out of the hearing room. James Reston, who knew Hiss personally and was among those who had recommended him for his job at the Carnegie Endowment, reported in the New York *Times*, "Throughout these questions Mr. Hiss was calm, elaborately polite, but always he answered with a caution which angered members of the committee and, in the opinion even of his friends, hurt his case."

Chambers followed Hiss to the witness chair. When asked for his reaction to Hiss's testimony, he said simply, "Mr. Hiss is lying." His straightforward answers made Hiss's appear even more evasive and misleading.

I asked Chambers whether he might not have some kind of grudge against Hiss which would explain his apparent determination to tear him down and destroy him. To me, this exchange was the high point of the hearings, both as history and as drama.

I said, "Mr. Chambers, can you search your memory now to see what motive you can have for accusing Mr. Hiss of being a Communist at the present time?"

"What motive I can have?" he asked.

"Yes, do you, I mean, is there any grudge you have against Mr. Hiss over anything he has done to you?"

"The story has spread that in testifying against Mr. Hiss I am working out some old grudge, or motives of revenge or hatred," he said. "I do not hate Mr. Hiss. We were close friends, but we are caught in a tragedy of history. Mr. Hiss represents the concealed enemy against which we are all fighting, and I am fighting. I have testified against him with remorse and pity, but in a moment of history in which this nation now stands, so help me God, I could not do otherwise."

As soon as I had a chance to study all the testimony, I sent a four-page letter to John Foster Dulles summarizing my opinions and conclusions. I wrote: "Whether [Hiss] was guilty of technical perjury or whether it has been established definitely that he was a member of the Communist Party are issues which still may be open for debate, but there is no longer any doubt in my mind that for reasons only he can give, he was trying to keep the committee from learning the truth in regard to his relationship with Chambers."

This was the end of the committee's direct involvement in the Hiss case. The next step would depend on how Chambers reacted to Hiss's challenge to repeat his statements where they would not be protected by congressional immunity, so that Hiss could sue for libel. Two days after the public session on August 25, Chambers appeared on *Meet the Press*. The first question was about Hiss's challenge.

"Are you willing to repeat your charge that Alger Hiss was a Communist?" Chambers was asked.

"Alger Hiss was a Communist and may still be one," Chambers replied.

Hiss's friends assumed that he would sue Chambers immediately. Much to their consternation, he took no action for a month. Finally the Washington *Post*, one of his staunchest supporters, bluntly called his bluff in an impatient editorial declaring that Hiss himself had "created a situation in which he is obliged to put up or shut up."

Three weeks later, Hiss sued Chambers for libel. Legally Hiss's position seemed strong, because without corroborative evidence to back up his allegations Chambers could never prove them to any court's satisfaction. Hiss probably assumed that if Chambers had any such proof, it would have been produced during the committee hearings.

The case, which had already provided so many bizarre surprises, had not yet exhausted its supply.

Chambers was called by Hiss's lawyers for a pretrial deposition and in the course of routine questioning they asked him whether he had any documentary proof of his charges. He made no reply at the time, but he began agonizing over what he might have to do to defend his position.

Hiss's lawyers also questioned Mrs. Chambers. Chambers never told me specifically what had happened, but only that they had been very rough on her and had made her cry. He said that from that moment he realized that they were out to destroy him and that he must react accordingly. He told his lawyer that when the pretrial hearing resumed the next day, he had decided to introduce some documents he had recently retrieved from his wife's nephew in New York.

On November 17, Chambers turned over an envelope containing sixty-five pages of typewritten copies of State Department documents and four memos in Alger Hiss's handwriting. He explained to the stunned lawyers that when he decided to leave the party he had hidden these papers away as a sort of life insurance against any Communist attempts to blackmail or kill him.

The head of the Justice Department's Criminal Division was immediately summoned from Washington. He impounded the papers and obtained a court order enforcing secrecy on everyone concerned. Chambers returned to his farm assuming that it would only be a matter of a few days before the Justice Department brought the case to a grand jury and Hiss would be indicted. Two weeks passed, however, and nothing happened. On December 1, a small United Press story appeared in the Washington *Daily News* reporting that the Justice Department was considering dropping the case against Hiss. Another article stated that there were rumors that a perjury charge against Chambers was under consideration. It was hard to believe, but it appeared that the Justice Department was going to use the papers Chambers had produced not to prove that Hiss was a spy but as the basis for indicting Chambers for perjury because he had lied when he testified that he himself had never been involved in espionage.

These shattering new developments came at the worst possible time for me personally. Our second daughter, Julie, had been born on July 5, 1948. We had hoped to spend a few weeks with her and Tricia out of the sweltering heat of summertime Washington, but once again we were forced to cancel a planned vacation when the Hiss case had completely taken up the month of August. I promised Pat that we would take our first vacation in three years as soon as Congress recessed. We made reservations for a two-week Caribbean cruise at the beginning of December, and both of us looked forward to the trip.

On the day before we were to leave, I saw the article in the *Daily News*, and I was shocked that the Justice Department would be party to such a cynical maneuver. That afternoon Stripling and I drove to Chambers's farm.

I showed Chambers the newspaper report. He said, "This is what I have been afraid of."

He explained that he had turned over a considerable amount of documentary evidence, which had then been impounded by the Justice Department, and a court order prohibited him from disclosing the contents. "I will only say that they were a real bombshell," he told us.

We tried unsuccessfully to get some idea of what the papers contained. Finally I asked whether we were facing a situation in which the Justice Department alone would decide if any further action were to be taken.

"No, I wouldn't be that foolish," Chambers replied. "My attorney has photostatic copies, and also, I didn't turn over everything I had. I have another bombshell in case they try to suppress this one."

"You keep that second bombshell," I told him. "Don't give it to anybody except the committee."

When Stripling and I got back to Washington I was uncertain about what to do. I spent much of that night trying to decide whether to issue a subpoena for the rest of Chambers's material. I could not understand why Chambers would have withheld any important information from the committee hearings, and I could not help thinking that there might be some good reason the Justice Department was acting in this way.

After weighing all the factors, however, I decided that the case was too important to risk losing it now, so I asked Stripling to have subpoenas served on Chambers immediately for everything he had. "I mean *everything*," I said.

Our ship sailed from New York that afternoon. Pat and I relaxed in the lazy shipboard routine and enjoyed the company of the other members of Congress and their wives who were on board. We felt a sense of relief from the tremendous tension that had surrounded us in Washington. The next evening, however, I received a cable from Stripling:

> SECOND BOMBSHELL OBTAINED BY SUBPOENA 1 A.M. FRIDAY. CASE CLINCHED. INFORMATION AMAZING. HEAT IS ON FROM PRESS AND OTHER PLACES. IMMEDIATE ACTION APPEARS NECESSARY. CAN YOU POSSIBLY GET BACK?

The next morning, I received a cable from Andrews:

> DOCUMENTS INCREDIBLY HOT. LINK TO HISS SEEMS CERTAIN. LINK TO OTHERS INEVITABLE. RESULTS SHOULD RESTORE FAITH IN NEED FOR COMMITTEE IF NOT IN SOME MEMBERS. . . . NEW YORK JURY MEETS WEDNESDAY. . . . COULD YOU ARRIVE TUESDAY AND GET DAY'S JUMP ON GRAND JURY. IF NOT, HOLDING HEARING EARLY WEDNESDAY. MY LIBERAL FRIENDS DON'T LOVE ME NO MORE. NOR YOU. BUT FACTS ARE FACTS AND THESE FACTS ARE DYNAMITE. HISS'S WRITING IDENTIFIED ON THREE DOCUMENTS. NOT PROOF HE GAVE THEM TO CHAMBERS BUT HIGHLY SIGNIFICANT. STRIPLING SAYS CAN PROVE WHO GAVE THEM TO CHAMBERS. LOVE TO PAT. VACATION-WRECKER ANDREWS

I radioed Stripling to make arrangements for my return. The next morning I was picked up from the ship by a Coast Guard seaplane that took me to Miami, where I caught a flight to Washington. At the Miami airport reporters asked if I had any comment on the "pumpkin papers." I had no idea what they were talking about. When I reached Washington, Stripling filled me in on the latest turn of this extraordinary case.

I learned that Chambers had been in Washington on the day our subpoena was served on him, and he arranged to meet two of our investigators that night and drive back to his farm with them. They arrived very late. He led them into a frost-covered pumpkin patch. The flabbergasted investigators watched while he took the top off one of the pumpkins, reached inside, and pulled out three small metal microfilm cylinders. He explained that he had not wanted to leave anything in the house in case any other subpoenas or search warrants arrived in his absence. That morning, therefore, he had hollowed out a pumpkin and used it as a hiding place.

When the "pumpkin" microfilms were developed they yielded hundreds of pages of photostats. These represented a sampling of the classified documents Hiss gave to Chambers in the period just before Chambers left the party; they ran the gamut from inconsequential bureaucratic trivia to top-secret ambassadorial cables. Hiss's defense later claimed that the documents were unimportant and represented no threat to national security. That contention was shot down by expert testimony before the committee and at both trials. Some of the documents were relatively unimportant, but the State Department still felt in 1948, ten years after they had been taken from the government files, that publication of the complete "pumpkin papers" would be injurious to the national security. As important as the specific contents of the documents was the fact that many of even the substantively unimportant ones were coded, and anyone able to obtain copies of them could thus break our secret codes.

The "pumpkin papers" completely captured public attention. The uproar was tremendous, and even many of Hiss's erstwhile defenders had to admit that they had been wrong and the committee had been right.

Since the statute of limitations made prosecution for espionage impossible, the grand jury unanimously voted to indict Hiss on two counts of perjury. The first was for having lied when he testified that he had not unlawfully taken classified documents from the State Department and given them to Chambers; the second was for having lied when he testified that he had not seen Chambers after January 1, 1937.

There were two trials. The first ended with a hung jury divided 8 to 4 for conviction. At the second trial, the jury on January 21, 1950, unanimously found Hiss guilty. Shortly after the verdict had been announced, I received a telegram from Herbert Hoover. It read:

> THE CONVICTION OF ALGER HISS WAS DUE TO YOUR PATIENCE AND PERSISTENCE ALONE. AT LAST THE STREAM OF TREASON THAT HAS EXISTED IN OUR GOVERNMENT HAS BEEN EXPOSED IN A FASHION ALL MAY BELIEVE.

Hiss was sentenced to five years in prison. After serving forty-four months he was released on parole and sank into obscurity, working as a stationery and printing supplies salesman in New York.

To this day, Alger Hiss has emphatically insisted on his innocence and makes periodic attempts to clear himself. This tenacity, together with the passage of time and the vagaries of memory, has now and then been rewarded with favorable publicity and increasing acceptance. In 1975, for example, he was readmitted to the Massachusetts bar. Whenever the Hiss case is considered on the facts and the testimony, however, the verdict is the same: the evidence against him is still overwhelming.

It was very difficult for me to understand President Truman's conduct during our investigation of the Hiss case. I knew that he had defied his liberal advisers and supporters by proposing aid to the anticommunist governments in Greece and Turkey, and I considered him to be someone who understood the threat of communism and recognized the need to oppose its subversive spread.

Yet in the face of overwhelming evidence that Hiss was at best a perjurer and at worst a spy, Truman persisted in condemning our investigation as a "red herring" and, through his public statements and executive orders, doing everything in his power to obstruct it. Before the 1948 presidential election I could understand that he would do everything possible to contain the investigation in order to avoid political embarrassment. But I was surprised when, even after he had won the election, he continued this same stubborn course.

Bert Andrews, who had excellent sources in the White House, told me that when a Justice Department official showed Truman the typewritten documents that clearly seemed to implicate Hiss in espionage, Truman had furiously paced the floor in the Oval Office, saying over and over, "The son of a bitch—he betrayed his country!" At a press conference after Hiss was indicted, reporters asked Truman whether he still believed our investigation was a "red herring." Truman cut off one reporter abruptly and snapped: "I have made my position perfectly clear on that subject, and I have nothing further to say on it. My position hasn't changed. Period." When one of his aides later asked him about this, he replied, "Of course Hiss is guilty. But that damn committee isn't interested in that. All it cares about is politics, and as long as they try to make politics out of this communist issue, I am going to label their activities for what they are—a 'red herring.' "

Truman honestly believed that the investigation was politically motivated, and in return his motives were political. He finally approved a full Justice Department and FBI investigation, but for months he used the power and prestige of his office to obstruct the committee's work. But I did not think then, and I do not think now, that his actions were motivated by anything other than the political instincts of an intensely political man.

The Hiss case proved beyond any reasonable doubt the existence of Soviet-directed Communist subversion at the highest levels of American government. But many who had defended Hiss simply refused to accept the overwhelming evidence of his guilt. Some turned their anger and frustration toward me, as if I were somehow responsible for the fact that Hiss had taken them in. While there is no doubt that my reputation from the Hiss case launched me on the road to the vice presidency, it also turned me from a relatively popular young congressman, enjoying a good but limited press, into one of the most controversial figures in Washington, bitterly opposed by the most respected and influential liberal journalists and opinion leaders of the time.

I think that Foster Dulles expressed the real lesson of the Hiss case when he said, "The conviction of Alger Hiss is human tragedy. It is tragic that so great promise should have come to so inglorious an end. But the greater tragedy is that seemingly our national ideals no longer inspire the loyal devotions needed for their defense."

This, to me, went to the heart of the problem we faced then and in the years ahead: how could we instill in brilliant young Americans the same dedication to the philosophy of freedom that the Communists seemed to be able to instill in people like Hiss.

RUNNING FOR SENATOR: 1950

I attended the 1948 Republican National Convention in Philadelphia as an observer. I had great respect for the front-runners, Senator Robert Taft of Ohio and Governor Thomas Dewey of New York, but I believed that the Republicans needed a fresh face and a change in 1948, and I supported Harold Stassen of Minnesota—the one-time "boy wonder" of the Republican Party —for the presidential nomination. Dewey won the nomination on the third ballot, and he chose Earl Warren as his running mate.

Since I had won both the Democratic and Republican nominations for re-election to the House, I did a great deal of speaking for the national ticket across the country in the fall campaign. Although there was nothing specific I could put my finger on, I was not as optimistic about our chances as most Republicans were. The crowds I spoke to were large and friendly, but they did not convey the electricity that so often means the difference between victory and defeat. I was also bothered by Dewey's gingerly approach to Truman and by his refusal to rebut Truman's attacks on what he labeled the "do-nothing Eightieth Congress." Because of his temperament, overconfidence, and misjudgment, Dewey ran a lofty and detached campaign, while Truman behaved as if he really wanted the job. Truman won an eleventh-hour victory that stunned the forecasters. While I was deeply disappointed by Dewey's loss, I thought that our complacency had caught up with us.

Dewey's defeat and our loss of both houses of Congress turned me overnight into a junior member of the minority party, a "comer" with no place to go. For the first time I began to consider the possibility of trying to move up on my own instead of patiently waiting for seniority or party preferment in the House of Representatives.

The term of Sheridan Downey, California's Democratic senator, was to expire in 1950, and not long after the 1948 election I began to consider challenging Downey for his seat. At first glance the prospects were not promising. Downey was a popular and uncontroversial incumbent, and it was by no means clear that anyone could beat him.

Virtually all my political friends and advisers told me that running for the Senate would be tantamount to political suicide. But I recognized the worth of the nationwide publicity that the Hiss case had given me—publicity on a scale that most congressmen only dream of achieving. Running for the Downey seat was the only possibility for me to move up the political ladder at a time when my political stock was high. On August 11, 1949, I wrote to my friend and political adviser, Frank Jorgensen, summing up the situation as I saw it:

> I have built up quite a file of people who have written me pro and con on the Senate matter. Most of those who are against it, incidentally, are afraid of the risk of my losing the House seat. As I wrote you before, however, I have virtually reached the conclusion that although it is admittedly a long shot, it presents such an unusual opportunity that the risk is worth taking, provided, of course, that we do not have too determined an opposition in the primary. As I have told several of my friends here, unless the Republicans do make substantial gains in both the House and Senate in 1950, which necessarily would mean a Republican trend, I seriously doubt if we can ever work our way back into power. Actually, in my mind, I do not see any great gain in remaining a member of the House, even from a relatively good district, if it means that we would be simply a vocal but ineffective minority.
>
> On the other hand, if the trend is on, the chances for winning the Senate seat in California will be good. If the trend is not on, rewinning the House seat might prove to be a rather empty victory.

At the beginning of October Representative Helen Gahagan Douglas announced that she was going to run against Downey in the Democratic primary. Her entry brightened my prospects considerably. If Downey won the primary, he would be weakened by her attacks; if Mrs. Douglas won, she would be easier to beat than Downey.

During the fall I learned from Kyle Palmer, the astute political editor of the Los Angeles *Times,* that if I became a candidate for the Senate I would be endorsed by the *Times*. I received similar assurances about the San Francisco *Chronicle* and the Oakland *Tribune*. These endorsements were vital not only for the boost they would give my candidacy but because they would virtually assure that I would not face any opposition in the Republican primary.

On November 3, 1949—exactly one year before the election—I announced my candidacy for the Senate before a crowd of more than five hundred supporters in Pomona. I made a hard-hitting speech that foreshadowed the kind of campaign I planned to run. I said that the central issue of the campaign would be "simply the choice between freedom and state socialism." I charged that "the Democratic Party today, nationally and in our own state of California, has been captured and is completely controlled by a group of ruthless, cynical seekers-after-power who have committed that party to policies and principles which are completely foreign to those of its founders." I ended my speech with some lines that would be quoted frequently in later years: "There is only one way we can win," I said. "We must put on a fighting, rocking, socking campaign and carry that campaign directly into every county, city, town, precinct, and home in the state of California."

Thus began one of the most hectic and heated campaigns of my career. It had been hard enough to convince the voters in one traditionally Republican congressional district to elect me; now I had to campaign all through the second most populous state in the nation, seeking the support of millions of voters—most of them registered Democrats.

I decided to campaign all over California, and to get around I used a second-hand wood-paneled station wagon with "Nixon for Senator" signs nailed on each side. It was fitted with portable sound equipment, and as we came into a town we played a phonograph record of a popular song over the loudspeaker. That usually attracted at least half a dozen people at a busy street corner. Once a small crowd had gathered, I would speak for a few minutes and then answer questions.

At the beginning I often spoke to no more than a handful of bemused passersby. When the campaign began to gather steam, however, the crowds began to grow, and before long the presence of hecklers assured a large and lively audience at every stop. These hecklers were tightly organized bands sent out from local left-wing labor and political organizations. They tried to disrupt my speeches by a continuous counterpoint of critical questions and derisive observations. On one occasion in San Francisco, they even brought their own sound truck, and we engaged in an amplified debate. When a small band of them arrived outside a rally at Long Beach Municipal Auditorium, my driver turned up the loudspeaker and played a recording of one of the popular songs of the day,

"If I Knew You Were Coming I'd've Baked a Cake." My supporters roared their approval.

While I was beginning my campaign treks around the state, sparks were flying in the Democratic primary. Senator Downey had withdrawn from the race, citing health problems, and Mrs. Douglas was now opposed by Manchester Boddy, publisher of the Los Angeles *Daily News*. Boddy was well financed, and he campaigned with the genuine fervor of a lifelong Democrat who despised Mrs. Douglas's left-wing leanings. He referred to her and her followers as a "small subversive clique of red hots." His supporters attacked her voting record by comparing it with that of Vito Marcantonio, the only openly procommunist member of Congress.

Anyone could see that the Douglas and Marcantonio records were strikingly similar and the attacks coming from within her own party were as damaging as anything I could say. The subsequently controversial "pink sheet" that my campaign committee issued was, in fact, inspired by these earlier comparisons of the two voting records. Whatever interpretation was later placed on these facts, no one was ever able to challenge their accuracy. All we added was the mordant comment of the color of the paper.

The most serious damage to Mrs. Douglas was done by Senator Downey. On May 22, he publicly stated: "It is my opinion that Mrs. Douglas does not have the fundamental ability and qualifications for a United States Senator. . . . She has shown no inclination, in fact no ability, to dig in and do the hard and tedious work required to prepare legislation and push it through Congress." Referring to her voting record in the House, he said, "Mrs. Douglas gave comfort to the Soviet tyranny by voting against aid to both Greece and Turkey. She voted against the President in a crisis when he most needed her support and most fully deserved her confidence."

Mrs. Douglas ended up with less than 50 percent of the vote in the Democratic primary. Boddy got about 30 percent and, because crossover voting was still allowed, I received 20 percent. On the Republican side, I ran unopposed and received 740,000 votes—a record primary turnout. Thus the lines for the general election were clearly drawn. I had a completely unified Republican Party behind me, while the Democrats were divided and dispirited after a bitter primary.

Helen Gahagan had been a popular light opera and Broadway musical star during the 1920s. In 1931 she married Melvyn Douglas, one of Hollywood's most popular leading men. When the Democratic congressman from the Fourteenth District in Los Angeles retired in 1944, Helen

Douglas ran for his seat and won. She entered the House of Representatives in January 1945.

Mrs. Douglas was a handsome woman with a dramatic presence. She had many fans among the public and many admirers in the press and in the entertainment industry, but she was not, to put it mildly, the most popular member of the House of Representatives. Generally when two members of the House run against each other for another office their fellow congressmen maintain a friendly attitude and wish both of them well. But in our case, even many of the House Democrats let me know that they hoped I could defeat Helen Douglas.

One afternoon in 1950, I was working in my office when Dorothy Cox, my personal secretary, came in and said, "Congressman Kennedy is here and would like to talk to you."

Jack Kennedy was ushered in and I motioned him into a chair. He took an envelope from his breast pocket and handed it to me. "Dick, I know you're in for a pretty rough campaign," he said, "and my father wanted to help out."

We talked for a while about the campaign. As he rose to leave, he said, "I obviously can't endorse you, but it isn't going to break my heart if you can turn the Senate's loss into Hollywood's gain."

After he left I opened the envelope and found it contained a $1,000 contribution. Three days after I won in November, Kennedy told an informal gathering of professors and students at Harvard that he was personally very happy that I had defeated Mrs. Douglas.

The Douglas victory in the primary called for some rethinking of my strategy. My original plans had been geared to running against Downey, a popular moderate as well as an entrenched incumbent.

Now I found myself running against one of the most left-wing members of Congress—and a woman. I knew that I must not appear ungallant in my criticism of Mrs. Douglas. Consequently, I felt that the best strategy was to let her record do my work for me. She was out of step with the voters of California, and if I could prevent her formidable dramatic skills from clouding the issues, I was almost certain to win.

Throughout the campaign I kept her pinned to her extremist record. I pointed out that she had voted against Truman on military aid to Greece and Turkey, the key plank of the Truman Doctrine, which I had supported. She had also voted against bills requiring loyalty checks for federal employees and was one of only fourteen members of Congress who had voted against the security bill that allowed the heads of key national defense agencies, such as the Atomic Energy Commission, to discharge government workers found to be poor security risks. In a speech before the Conference on American-Soviet Cultural Cooperation, she had claimed that the obstacles to unity between the two countries were "deliberately created by sinister and dangerous forces in this country who have never given up their allegiance to the ideas of Hitler."

Mrs. Douglas had often appeared at meetings and addressed organizations that had been cited by the Attorney General's office during Truman's administration as "Communist and subversive." The Communist *Daily Worker* had selected Mrs. Douglas as "one of the heroes of the Eightieth Congress." Although I constantly questioned her wisdom and judgment in light of such a record, I never questioned her patriotism.

One of the most peculiar ineptitudes of the Douglas campaign was the attempt to charge that my voting record was actually more procommunist than hers. In her speeches she began saying that she was more anticommunist than I, and that I was the one who had voted with Marcantonio against key anticommunist issues. The decision to pursue this particular attack was clearly rooted more in desperation than in logic, because the charge that I was a communist sympathizer had no public credibility whatever. She made the further mistake of careless research on my voting record when she accused me of having voted five times with Marcantonio on key matters. In two of the five votes in question, I had not done so—although she had. In the third there was no vote of record. In the other two cases, she had seized on procedural technicalities to distort the record. She accused me of opposing aid to Korea when I had actually supported it, and of voting to cut a Korean aid program in half when in fact I had voted for a one-year bill rather than a two-year bill.

I made a statewide radio speech accusing her of glaring misstatements in a flyer that her campaign was circulating. I refuted each charge and repeated my challenge that she cite one instance in which I had misrepresented her record. Her side replied with a newspaper ad headed, *Thou Shalt Not Bear False Witness!*

Prominently placed in the ad was a desperate, ludicrous attack:

> NIXON–MARCANTONIO ISOLATIONISM
>
> Nixon's record of blind stupidity on foreign policy gave aid and comfort to the Communists. On every key vote Nixon stood with party liner Marcantonio against America in its fight to defeat Communism.

On October 12, four weeks before the election, a California poll was released showing that I had a 12 percent lead over Mrs. Douglas, with 34 percent still undecided. Panic must have swept the Douglas camp when this poll came out, because as the campaign entered its last weeks her attacks became more viciously personal. One of her campaign flyers printed on yellow paper read: "THE BIG LIE! Hitler invented it. Stalin perfected it. Nixon uses it. . . . YOU pick the Congressman the Kremlin loves!" She told one audience, "The temporary success of the Republican Party in 1946, with its backwash of young men in dark shirts, was short lived." She told an interviewer that she hated "Communist totalitarianism and Nazi totalitarianism and Mundt–Nixon totalitarianism." She called me a "peewee who is trying to scare people into voting for him" and customarily referred to me as a "pipsqueak."

In a campaign dispatch, the San Francisco *Chronicle* reported that "Nixon was dubbed 'tricky Dick' by Mrs. Douglas. She warned her listeners that if they want a depression again, elect Nixon. . . . She charged that Nixon had voted along with Congressman Vito Marcantonio on foreign affairs issues and the New Yorker always followed the Communist Party line. She said Nixon was attempting to 'steal' Democratic votes by 'harping' on her record." On October 23, she said that I was smearing her and denounced what she termed my "reaction at home and retreat abroad." She charged that I was "throwing up a smokescreen of smears, innuendos, and half-truths to try to confuse and mislead the voters." I responded immediately: "If it is a smear, it is by the record, and Mrs. Douglas made that record."

The New York *Times* captured the flavor of the campaign in a report from California that "Mrs. Douglas has been depicting her opponent as a red-baiting, reactionary enemy of labor and the common man. . . . Mr. Nixon has been assailing Mrs. Douglas as a flighty left-winger and an exponent of a regime that failed."

In addition to issues of foreign policy and internal security, the 1950 campaign involved several important California-related issues: offshore oil rights, water rights, and federal farm controls. On each, Mrs. Douglas held highly unpopular views. For example, on the question of rights to oil and mineral deposits in the tidelands just off the California coast, she alone of the twenty-three-member California congressional delegation voted to oppose state ownership and favor federal control.

Near the end of the campaign we scheduled a massive old-fashioned torchlight parade and rally in Los Angeles. I was introduced by movie actor Dick Powell. His wife, June Allyson, then pregnant, made a short and moving speech about the future of her unborn child.

I won the election by a margin of 680,000 votes, the largest plurality of any Senate winner that year. It was a good night for Republicans throughout the country as we picked up 30 House seats and 5 Senate seats.

Mrs. Douglas sent no personal message or even the traditional congratulations to me, although she did issue a brief statement: "It now seems certain that Richard Nixon has been elected and that California has two Republican senators." I did, however, receive a telegram from Senator Downey:

> PLEASE ACCEPT MY CONGRATULATIONS ON YOUR NOTABLE VICTORY AND MY BEST WISHES AND REGARDS.

The 1950 campaign became highly controversial because of the "rocking, socking" way in which I was said to have waged and won it. Mrs. Douglas and many of her friends and supporters claimed that I had impugned her loyalty and smeared her character, thus depriving the voters of the opportunity to make an honest choice.

Anyone who takes the trouble to go back through the newspapers and other sources of the period, however, will find that things happened as I have described them here.

Helen Gahagan Douglas waged a campaign that would not be equaled for stridency, ineptness, or self-righteousness until George McGovern's presidential campaign twenty-two years later. In the long run, however, even this probably made little difference. Helen Douglas lost the election because the voters of California in 1950 were not prepared to elect as their senator anyone with a left-wing voting record or anyone they perceived as being soft on or naive about communism. She may have been at some political disadvantage because she was a woman. But her fatal disadvantage lay in her record and in her views.

PRESIDENTIAL POLITICS: 1952

Although the 1952 presidential election was still two years away, Republicans in Congress and across the country were already beginning to gear up for it. We had come so close to winning with Dewey in 1948 that there was an almost desperate determination not to fail again. After twenty years out of power, Republicans could almost taste the victory we knew must be ours if only we could enter the election as a party united behind a strong candidate. As the new senator from the nation's second most populous state, I was caught up in this activity from my first days in the Senate.

Truman at this point was a tremendously unpopular President. After a humiliating defeat in the New Hampshire primary in March 1952, he decided not to run again. Even so, whoever the Democrats selected would still have to counter the weight of Truman's unpopularity and the public's disgust with the blatant corruption that even Adlai Stevenson, in reply to a question from the *Oregon Journal,* referred to as "the mess in Washington."

Truman stood in the eye of a hurricane of scandals that swirled around him while he did nothing. His military assistant presided over an influence-peddling scheme of such proportions that the free-lance agents trading in government contracts that grew up as a result came to be known, after their customary fee, as "5 percenters." Payoffs in the form of deep freezes went to Truman's Appointments Secretary, his naval aide, and his Treasury Secretary, among others.

A Senate investigation of the Reconstruction Finance Corporation revealed that its directors had been subject to manipulation for personal gain by top Democratic Party officials and by at least one member of the White House staff. But the tax scandals were the worst of all. A congressional inquiry produced a list of charges against officials in the then Bureau of Internal Revenue that included extortion, evading income tax, and preventing the audit of their own returns.

Of nine district tax collectors removed, one was a personal friend of Truman's, had figured in the RFC scandal, was sent to jail, and was later pardoned by President Johnson. Truman's Appointments Secretary was convicted of conspiracy in a tax case, sent to prison, and later pardoned by President Kennedy. The head of the Justice Department's Tax Division was convicted in the same case and was also pardoned by President Johnson.

In 1951 alone, 166 Internal Revenue officials were fired or forced to resign. It was no overstatement, then, when I kicked off my Western campaign in Pomona, to charge Truman with heading a "scandal-a-day" administration.

The two major Republican candidates were General Dwight Eisenhower and Senator Robert Taft of Ohio. Taft, the son of a President, had been in the Senate since 1939. He was known as "Mr. Republican" and would clearly be the choice of the party organizers and workers. He was generally described as a conservative, but his beliefs were far too complex—and he was far too intelligent and complicated a man—for any simple label. He was, to be sure, a strong anticommunist with an isolationist streak. Domestically, however, he was constantly trying to find creative solutions to America's social problems without having to resort to big government spending programs. Taft was universally respected in Congress, and perhaps his most ardent supporter was Bill Knowland, my senior colleague from California.

Eisenhower had been the Supreme Allied Commander in Europe during World War II. Immediately after the war he served as Army Chief of Staff. He was named president of Columbia University in 1948, but in 1950 he returned to the military as Supreme Commander of the North Atlantic Treaty Organization forces.

Throughout his military career, Eisenhower had been determinedly non-political, but after the war his heroic image made him a prize sought after by both political parties. According to Eisenhower, Truman had offered to back him for the Democratic presidential nomination in 1948. Eisenhower never told me why he refused Truman's offer. I feel there may have been several reasons. He probably felt the time wasn't right for him; he was reluctant to run as Truman's protégé, and—to the limited extent that he thought in partisan terms—he considered himself a Republican rather than a Democrat. Unlike Taft, Eisenhower could claim no grass roots base among the party faithful. But his engaging personality, his dazzling smile, and his great military successes had made "Ike" a genuine popular hero who could almost certainly win the election if he could first win the nomination.

By 1951 several small groups of influential Republicans were trying to persuade Eisenhower to run for the Republican nomination. Many of the more liberal elements of the party coalesced behind him. His leading supporter on Capitol Hill was Senator Henry Cabot Lodge of Massachusetts.

There were two other candidates, each of whom hoped that if the convention became deadlocked over Eisenhower and Taft it might turn to him: Harold Stassen and Earl Warren. Stassen's chances of nomination were remote at best. Warren, on the other hand, had been Dewey's running mate in 1948 and as a result of having won the California presidential primary as a favorite son, he would arrive at the convention in Chicago with a solid bloc of seventy delegates bound to stay with him until he decided to release them.

The first time I ever saw Dwight Eisenhower was on his triumphant return to the States after V-E Day in 1945. I was doing Navy contract termination work on Church Street in lower Manhattan, and the windows of my twentieth-floor office overlooked the route of his ticker-tape parade up Broadway. I could just make him out through the snowstorm of confetti, sitting in the back of his open car, waving and looking up at the cheering thousands like me who filled every window of the towering buildings. His arms were raised high over his head in the gesture that soon became his trademark.

I saw him closer up in 1948, when he briefed the members of the House of Representatives on the situation in Europe at a meeting held in the Library of Congress. In the summer of 1950, I saw him at even closer quarters at the Bohemian Grove, the site of the annual summer retreat of San Francisco's Bohemian Club, where each year members of this prestigious private men's club and their guests from all over the country gather amidst California's beautiful redwoods. Herbert Hoover used to invite some of the most distinguished of the 1,400 men at the

Grove to join him at his "Cave Man Camp" for lunch each day. On this occasion Eisenhower, then president of Columbia University, was the honored guest. Hoover sat at the head of the table as usual, with Eisenhower at his right. As the Republican nominee in an uphill Senate battle, I was about two places from the bottom.

Eisenhower was deferential to Hoover but not obsequious. He responded to Hoover's toast with a very gracious one of his own. I am sure he was aware that he was in enemy territory among this generally conservative group. Hoover and most of his friends favored Taft and hoped that Eisenhower would not become a candidate.

Later that day, Eisenhower spoke at the beautiful lakeside amphitheatre. It was not a polished speech, but he delivered it without notes and he had the good sense not to speak too long. The only line that drew significant applause was his comment that he did not see why anyone who refused to sign a loyalty oath should have the right to teach in a state university.

After Eisenhower's speech we went back to Cave Man Camp and sat around the campfire appraising it. Everyone liked Eisenhower, but the feeling was that he had a long way to go before he would have the experience, the depth, and the understanding to be President. But it struck me forcibly that Eisenhower's personality and personal mystique had deeply impressed the skeptical and critical Cave Man audience.

In May 1951 I went as a Senate observer to the World Health Organization conference in Geneva. Senator Frank Carlson of Kansas, one of Eisenhower's early supporters, arranged for me to meet Eisenhower at NATO headquarters in Paris. An aide ushered me into Eisenhower's office, and he rose from his desk to greet me. He was erect and vital and impeccably tailored, wearing his famous waist-length uniform jacket, popularly known as the "Eisenhower jacket." He motioned me to a large sofa against the wall, and his informality put me so completely at ease that we were able to talk very freely.

He spoke optimistically about the prospects for European recovery and development. Warming to the topic, he said, "What we need over here and what we need in the States is more optimism in order to combat the defeatist attitude that too many people seem to have."

He carefully steered away from American politics, but it was clear he had done his homework. He said that he had read about the Hiss case in *Seeds of Treason* by Ralph de Toledano and Victor Lasky. "The thing that most impressed me was that you not only got Hiss, but you got him fairly," he said. He also liked the emphasis I placed in some of my speeches on the need to take into account economic and ideological as well as military factors in fashioning foreign policy. "Being strong militarily just isn't enough in the kind of battle we are fighting now," he said. This impressed me because, then as now, it was unusual to hear a military man emphasize the importance of non-military strength.

It was not the substance of Eisenhower's conversation so much as his manner that most impressed me that afternoon. It was easy to see how he had been able to bring the leaders of the great wartime alliance together despite their many differences. I felt that in terms of experience and ability in handling foreign policy, Eisenhower was by far the best qualified of the potential presidential candidates. I felt that I was in the presence of a genuine statesman, and I came away convinced that he should be the next President. I also decided that if he ran for the nomination I would do everything I could to help him get it.

I did not know Bob Taft well, although I had met him several times while I was in the House of Representatives, particularly during the debates on the Taft–Hartley bill. He was highly respected in Washington, but even his strongest supporters acknowledged that he lacked some of the personality traits needed by a presidential candidate. He was an intelligent, high-minded patriot, but he was also very proud and very shy. This combination unfortunately made many people feel that he was arrogant. Taft was visibly uncomfortable with the personal "small change" of presidential politics—the handshaking and backslapping and endless importuning of local party leaders, and he was honest in a way that could be painfully blunt. I shall never forget seeing him on television during the New Hampshire primary. As he emerged from a building he began shaking hands. A little girl held out a pen and a piece of paper and asked for his autograph. Right on camera, he explained to her with devastating reasonableness that handshaking took less time than signing autographs, and since he had a very busy schedule he could not interrupt it to sign anything for her.

I think that next to Pat, Martha Taft was the most exceptional political wife I have ever known. She was as gracious and vivacious as her husband was shy and stiff. She had suffered a crippling stroke in 1950 and was confined to a wheelchair; Taft, who was completely devoted to her, took her everywhere with him, and at a dinner party it was a touching sight to see him cut her food and help feed it to her. People in Washington who knew these things about Taft admired him and made allowances because of them. But when it came to choosing a nominee the fact had to be faced that his abrasive personality would be a serious disadvantage in a presidential campaign.

I believed that the President elected in 1952 had first and foremost to be an expert in dealing with the serious international challenges facing America, and I had some serious reservations about Taft in this regard.

Before the elections in 1950 I had been invited to be the major speaker at the 36th Annual McKinley Day Dinner in Dayton, Ohio. My subject was the threat of communism at home and abroad. Taft had followed me with a short speech in which he said that, as he saw it, the greatest problem facing America at home or abroad was not communism but socialism. He urged therefore that we concentrate our efforts on fighting and defeating socialism. I did not like socialism any more than he did. What concerned me was his failure to recognize that many socialists were dedicated anticommunists. The major threat we faced was not socialism, but communist subversion supported by the international Communist movement, and Taft's failure to understand this distinction raised questions in my mind about his grasp of the whole international situation.

One day early in 1952, Taft came to see me. He was a man no more interested in small talk than I was, so he got right to the point. He said that we had many mutual friends in California and some of them had urged him to drop by and simply ask me for my support for his candidacy. "It wasn't something *I* felt I ought to do," he added with complete sincerity, "but I don't want to have any misunderstanding about my desire to have your support if you feel that my candidacy is consistent with your point of view."

I told him that I had enormous respect for his leadership in the Senate and had no doubt that in terms of domestic affairs he was the best qualified man to lead the country. It was with a great deal of sadness that I told him I personally felt that international affairs would be more important for the next President and that I had concluded Eisenhower was the best qualified in that area. Therefore I would be supporting his candidacy. I said I had already informed Knowland and Warren of my decision. I added that if Taft won the nomination he would have my wholehearted support and assured him that under no circumstances would I lend myself to a "stop Taft" movement at the convention.

He said that although he was naturally disappointed with my decision, he appreciated my frankness, and he was generous and respectful in his comments about Eisenhower. Bob Taft was a fine gentleman, and it was a great loss to the party, the Congress, and the nation when he died of cancer just a few months after Eisenhower was inaugurated.

On July 1, I flew to Chicago to take part in the platform hearings being held the week before the Republican National Convention.

I had first become aware that I might be considered as the nominee for Vice President a few months earlier when clues and signs began appearing in the press and the political rumor mills. However, I considered my chances almost impossibly remote. In retrospect, I see that the road to the ticket had begun on May 8, 1952, when, at Governor Dewey's invitation, I was the main speaker at the New York State Republican Party's annual fund-raising dinner at the Waldorf-Astoria. Because it was a presidential year, and because Dewey was both the former standard-bearer and one of the principal people behind Eisenhower, the dinner was a major occasion, and my speech would be broadcast on radio. I spent several hours making outlines, to be sure that I could say everything within the allotted half-hour radio time. I delivered it without notes in exactly twenty-nine minutes, and the audience gave me a standing ovation when it was over.

When I sat down next to Dewey after acknowledging the applause, he very deliberately snuffed out his cigarette, which he always held in a cigarette holder, grasped my hand, and earnestly said, "That was a terrific speech. Make me a promise: don't get fat, don't lose your zeal, and you can be President someday." I did not take him seriously, much less literally, because such compliments are commonplace in politics. But later that evening, during a small reception in his suite for some of his close friends, he asked me if I would object to his suggesting my name as a possible candidate for Vice President.

A few weeks later I was invited to meet with Eisenhower's inner circle of advisers in a suite at the Mayflower Hotel in Washington. The group included Herbert Brownell, the lawyer whom Eisenhower was later to name Attorney General, General Lucius Clay, and Harold Talbott, Dewey's chief fund-raiser. We had a wide-ranging discussion of foreign and domestic policy that lasted most of the afternoon. Nothing was said about the vice presidency, but it was clear that they were trying to get to know me better and to size me up.

Word of this meeting quickly made its way through the Washington grapevine, and rumors that I might be Eisenhower's running mate began to appear in the papers. One evening a few weeks before the convention, Pat and I had dinner with Alice Longworth, the witty, acerbic daughter of Teddy Roosevelt. I asked her if she thought I should take the nomination if Eisenhower offered it to me. I knew that Mrs. Longworth was an all-out Taft supporter. She did not like Eisenhower, and as far as I could tell she never did develop any liking for him.

In her typically outspoken way, she said, "Father used to tell me that being Vice President was the most boring job in the world. However," she added, "if Eisenhower gets the nomination, someone will have to go on that ticket who can reassure the party regulars and particularly the conservatives that he won't take everyone to hell in a handcart, and you are the best man to do it."

As we were leaving, Mrs. Longworth brought up the subject again and asked me whether I was giving it serious thought. I said that the prospect was too unlikely for me to take it very seriously. "I thought as much," she said disapprovingly. "You should be giving it a lot of thought, and you should talk to Pat about it so that just in case it does happen you aren't caught with your drawers down! If you ask me, and since you did I'll tell you again, if you're thinking of your own good and your own career you are probably better off to stay in the Senate and not go down in history as another nonentity who served as Vice President. Of course, Father's experience was different, and by some act of God you might become President too, but you shouldn't plan on it. For the good of the party, however, I think that you should take it if you have the chance."

Until this conversation, I had never taken the possibility of nomination seriously enough to consider that I might not want the job. The vice presidency had traditionally been a political dead end, and most Vice Presidents were old party wheelhorses or regional politicians added to balance the ticket. Theodore Roosevelt referred to the vice presidency as "taking the veil," and Harry Truman described the office as being about as useful as a fifth teat on a cow. Until Eisenhower completely changed the concept of the office, the Vice President was almost exclusively a ceremonial figure who went to the receptions and dedicated the dams the President didn't have time for. His only important functions were to cast occasional tie-breaking votes in the Senate and to be constantly ready to take over if the President died or were incapacitated. Today we think of the vice presidency as a stepping-stone to the presidency, but before 1952 it was more often a stepping-stone to political oblivion.

I did not have to know Eisenhower well to know that he would expect his Vice President to subordinate any personal ambitions to the President's programs and policies. It was one thing for me to believe that Eisenhower was the best man for the job; it was quite another to renounce my own political career just as it reached a national stage in the Senate. If I had had presidential ambitions—which I did not at that point—I probably would not have considered becoming Vice President.

When the Republican National Convention opened in Chicago on July 7, Bill Knowland, Minnesota Congressman Walter Judd, Colorado Governor Dan Thornton, and I were being touted as the most likely running mates for Eisenhower. Two days before the nominating session, Jack Knight, publisher and editor of the Chicago *Daily News*, went out on a political limb and predicted that Eisenhower and I would be the Republican nominees. A headline across the top of page one proclaimed: *GOP Ticket: Ike and Nixon, Predicts Knight.* I still considered this so unlikely that I sent someone out to buy a half a dozen copies of the paper. I said, "That will probably be the last time we'll see that headline, and I want to be able to show it to my grandchildren."

When I got back to the hotel around midnight, Pat was waiting up for me. For her, the worst part of politics was campaigning, and through two strenuous California campaigns in 1946 and 1950 she had been at my side every step of the way and took it all with good grace. Although campaigning did not come easily to her because of her deep-rooted sense of privacy, she did it superbly. But now that we actually had to consider the possibility of a long and grueling nationwide campaign, she was having second thoughts about what accepting the nomination could mean to us and to our young daughters.

About 4 A.M., after we had talked for hours, I suggested that we talk to Murray Chotiner. As a political professional, he might have a different perspective about the whole question.

When he arrived at our room I filled him in on our discussion and asked for his opinion. He answered in his usual blunt way. "There comes a point," he said, "when you have to go up or go out." He pointed out that even if I ran for Vice President and lost, I would still have my Senate seat. Or, if I became Vice President and did not like it, I could step down after the first term. "Think of it, Dick," he said, "any man who quits political life as Vice President as young as you are certainly hasn't lost a thing."

After Murray left, Pat and I talked about what he had said and we agreed that he was right. "I guess I can make it through another campaign," she said.

Eisenhower was nominated on the first ballot. The Taft forces were unhappy not just because they had been defeated but because of the strong-arm tactics they felt had been used on many delegates by Eisenhower's supporters under the direction of his floor manager, Governor Sherman Adams of New Hampshire.

When the convention adjourned for lunch, I decided to go back to my room at the Stock Yard Inn and sleep until the evening session when Eisenhower and his running mate would make their acceptance speeches. I had been up nearly all night talking to Pat and Murray, and the morning had been tiring because of the final frantic shiftings and maneuverings before the balloting. The room was not air-conditioned, and the temperature must have been 100 degrees when I opened the door. I stripped down to my shorts and lay on top of the covers, trying to think cool thoughts. Chotiner arrived a few minutes later, and he could scarcely contain his excitement. He told me that Eisenhower had approved a final list of acceptable running mates and then turned the actual selection over to his inner circle of advisers. One of them, Herb Brownell, had told Chotiner that I was on the list and asked where I could be reached if the need arose.

"It's still wishful thinking, Murray," I said.

I had just started to drift to sleep when the bedside phone rang. I could recognize Brownell's voice coming over the line, but it sounded very distant. I pressed the receiver against my ear and realized that he was talking to someone else.

"Yes, General," he was saying, "we have agreed unanimously, and it's Dick Nixon."

Then Brownell came on the line with me. He said simply, "We picked you."

For one of the few times I can remember, I was speechless.

"The general asked if you could come see him right away in his suite at the Blackstone Hotel," Brownell continued. "That is, assuming you want it!"

I felt hot, sleepy, and grubby, but there wasn't even time to shower or shave. I pulled my clothes on again and started down to the lobby. The ever-resourceful Chotiner somehow produced a limousine and a police motorcycle escort which sped us across town to Eisenhower's headquarters at the Blackstone.

Eisenhower beamed as he shook my hand and led me into the large sitting room of his suite. He introduced me to Mrs. Eisenhower, and the three of us chatted for a few minutes before she left us.

Almost immediately Eisenhower seemed to shift gears. He became very serious and formal. He said that he wanted his campaign to be a crusade for the things he believed in and the things he believed America stood for. "Will you join me in such a campaign?" he asked. I was a little taken aback by his formality, but I answered, "I would be proud and happy to."

"I'm glad you are going to be on the team, Dick," he said. "I think that we can win, and I know that we can do the right things for this country."

Suddenly he hit his forehead with the palm of his hand. "I just remembered," he said. "I haven't resigned from the Army yet!" He called in his secretary and dictated a letter to the Secretary of the Army. A few minutes later she brought the typed letter back to him.

While I watched as he read it over and signed it, I wondered what must be going through his mind. He had spent his entire adult life in the Army and had reached the pinnacle of fame and success. Now he was giving it up to plunge into politics. My guess is that if he could have known of the agonies he was to go through over the next eight years he would have had serious second thoughts.

As we talked, I was struck by Eisenhower's beguiling mixture of personal savvy and political naïveté. He began by telling me all the reasons he had not wanted to run for President, and how he had finally decided that it was his duty to run. Then, turning abruptly to his plans for his administration, he said, "Dick, I don't want a Vice President who will be a figurehead. I want a man who will be a member of the team. And I want him to be able to step into the presidency smoothly in case anything happens to me. Of course," he added with a grin, "we have to win the election first."

Eisenhower wanted his campaign to be waged as a crusade against the corruption of the Truman administration and against its foreign policy, which he felt had played into the Communists' hands in both Europe and Asia. It was clear that he envisaged taking an above-the-battle position, and that whatever hard partisan campaigning was required would be pretty much left to me. He said that as an upstanding young man and a good speaker I should be able not only to flail the Democrats on the corruption issue but also to personify the remedy for it. As for the communist threat, he said that the Hiss case was a text from which I could preach everywhere in the country.

Years later, in 1964, he told me my name had been first on the list he had submitted to his advisers for consideration. He added a bit sheepishly, "I must admit I thought at the time that you were two or three years older than you were."

I think there were several reasons that Eisenhower had put me on his list and that his advisers had chosen me. In 1952 Republican Party stalwarts viewed Eisenhower as the candidate of the Eastern liberal establishment. In order to hold the party together, he needed a moderate conservative from the Midwest or West who could serve as a bridge to the regular Republican Party organization, which had been sorely disappointed by Taft's defeat. Eisenhower also knew that to maintain his above-the-battle position he needed a running mate who was willing to engage in all-out combat, and who was good at it. In a sense, the hero needed a point-man.

There was undoubtedly a geographic element in his choice—the recognition of the postwar power and influence of the western United States and particularly of California. More than anyone else under serious consideration, I would also be able to appeal directly to the large number of younger voters and veterans.

I knew that some of Eisenhower's more liberal advisers had preferred Earl Warren to me, and that some of his more conservative advisers had preferred Bill Knowland, or even Bob Taft if he would accept. Perhaps my anticommunist credentials from the Hiss case were what most tilted the decision to me, because it was already clear that the communist challenge would be an important issue in the campaign.

Eisenhower finally looked at his watch. "We had both better begin getting ready for tonight," he said.

As we shook hands again at the door, two things were foremost in my mind. First, within a few hours I would be addressing the convention and millions of Americans on radio and television, and I had not yet prepared a single word or thought. Second, this possibility had seemed so remote that the only suit I had brought to Chicago was the wrinkled light gray one I was wearing. Pat too had been caught by surprise. She was lunching in a nearby restaurant when she heard a news bulletin that I was to be Eisenhower's running mate.

Chotiner and I went directly to the convention hall. We arrived shortly before the delegates were to begin the balloting for Vice President. I found Bill Knowland and asked him if he would do me the honor of placing my name in nomination. Knowland was not only a personal friend, but also the man whom Taft probably would have chosen as his running mate. Knowland said that he would be proud and happy to nominate me. I walked down the aisle to the Ohio delegation, and immediately spotted Senator John Bricker by his massive mane of white hair. When I asked if he would second my nomination, tears filled his eyes: "Dick," he said, "there isn't anybody in the world I would rather make a speech for, but after what they have said and done to Bob Taft over the last few months, I just cannot bring myself to do it. I would appreciate it if you would ask somebody else." I was taken aback by the depth of his feeling against the Eisenhower forces, and for the first time I realized how difficult and how important my role as a bridge between the party factions was going to be. I told Bricker that I appreciated his candor. I asked Governor Alfred Driscoll of New Jersey to deliver the main seconding speech in his place.

Since there was no opposition to my nomination, a motion was made that the rules be suspended and I be nominated by acclamation. At 6:33 P.M. I became the convention's nominee for Vice President. Joe Martin asked me to come up to the rostrum. Pat joined me on the convention floor and kissed me twice—the second time at the insistence of the photographers who had missed the first time.

It was to happen many times over the next two decades, but both Pat and I still remember that first time, and our surprise and elation at the thunderous sound of several thousand people shouting themselves hoarse and stamping their feet and clapping for us. I felt exhilarated—almost heady—as I looked out across the moving, shifting mass that filled the convention floor and galleries. Pat said later that for those few minutes it actually made her forget the long campaign that we would have to endure.

Joe Martin was beaming broadly. Pat kissed him, and his face flushed boyishly. I asked him whether he should not try to calm the people down, and he had to yell in my ear to make himself heard above the noise: "You know the old saying—gather in the hay while the sun is shining."

That night Eisenhower delivered his acceptance speech proclaiming his crusade. My acceptance speech followed his and closed both the evening and the convention. Standing before the delegates and the television cameras, still in my rumpled gray suit, I pledged myself to put on a "fighting campaign for the election of a fighting candidate," and also to work for a Republican-controlled House and Senate. In an attempt to begin healing wounds right away, I praised Joe Martin and Styles Bridges—both considered to be either pro-Taft or at best neutral toward Eisenhower—for their work at the convention and said how important it was that they be Speaker and Majority Leader in the next Congress.

The raucous audience suddenly grew still in anticipation of what it knew must be coming. "And then may I say this one word about a man that I consider to be a very great man. I am a relatively young man in politics. . . . But I do think I know something about the abilities of men in legislative life. And it seems to me that one of the greatest tragedies of the past two years, in the past four years, has been this: that one of the really great senators, one of the greatest legislative leaders in the history of America at the present time, instead of being chairman of the majority policy committee is chairman of the minority policy committee. And I say let's be sure that Senator Bob Taft is chairman of the majority policy committee after next January."

The frustration of the Taft supporters at having lost was added to the general sentiment for "Mr. Republican," and the convention went wild for him. In fact, it went too wild for the taste of some of Eisenhower's liberal advisers, who felt that Taft's ovation was more enthusiastic than Eisenhower's. Some of them even suggested that I had done this purposely in order to belittle Eisenhower and build myself up. This was my first, but by no means my last, run-in with this small but determined group.

The next evening I called on Taft at his hotel. He was obviously a terribly disappointed man, but not a beaten man. He took his defeat with good grace, and reassured me that he would work for Eisenhower's election. He told me that he was genuinely pleased that I was on the ticket.

My major job in the campaign, as I saw it, was to help heal the breach which had developed during the pre-convention period between the Taft and Eisenhower supporters. The problem was not the men at the top: Taft was a team player and he went all out in his support of the ticket. But many of Taft's partisans were bitter over their defeat and seemed likely to sit out the campaign. Most of the resentment was not aimed at Eisenhower personally, but at the men around him, and particularly the Eastern liberal faction that had managed his nomination, symbolized by Cabot Lodge, Sherman Adams, and Tom Dewey.

While they all knew that I had been for Eisenhower, they appreciated the fact that I had not been involved in any of the pre-convention attacks on Taft. Also, the Taft people tended to be organization minded, and they considered me to be a good organization man because both as congressman and senator I had spoken for party fund-raising and other affairs all over the country and thus was known personally to many of them. They knew that I would hit hard against communism and corruption, and they believed that it was essential to develop those issues if we were to pull in the candidates for the House and Senate who would assure us majorities in Congress.

That was why I was asked to keynote the Ohio State Republican Convention held in Columbus three weeks after the national convention. Two weeks later I made a similar speech on Republican Day at the Illinois State Fair. Illinois was a Taft state, and it was felt that through my speech I could stimulate the interest of the organization people on behalf of the ticket.

Right after the convention, Eisenhower went to Denver for a vacation, and I returned to Washington in a kind of daze. One of the many thousands of letters that poured in to my office was a handwritten one from a 1947 House classmate.

> Dear Dick:
>
> I was tremendously pleased that the convention selected you for V.P. I was always convinced that you would move ahead to the top —but I never thought it would come this quickly. You were an ideal selection and will bring to the ticket a great deal of strength.
>
> Please give my best to your wife and all kinds of good luck to you.
>
> Cordially,
> Jack Kennedy

Campaigns in those days still used whistle-stop trains, and that is how we began ours. Eisenhower's train, the *Look Ahead, Neighbor Special,* set out first for a tour of the Midwest. My own more prosaically named *Nixon Special* left on September 17 from Pomona, the town near Whittier where I had kicked off my campaigns for the House and Senate.

Nearly all the Nixons and Milhouses were on hand at the station that night. Even Earl Warren was carried away by the excitement. He introduced me graciously and concluded by saying, "I now present to you the next President of the United States." The laughter and applause which broke loose after his uncharacteristic slip of the tongue drowned out his embarrassed correction.

From the back platform of my train, I described the corruption in Truman's administration and lambasted "the mess in Washington."

Eisenhower would change all that, I said, and I promised to bring the message of Eisenhower's crusade to every corner of the country during the next two months.

THE FUND CRISIS

A few days before the Pomona kickoff, I had appeared in Washington on *Meet the Press.* After the broadcast, one of the reporters on the panel, the syndicated columnist Peter Edson, took me aside and said, "Senator, what is this 'fund' we hear about? There is a rumor to the effect that you have a supplementary salary of $20,000 a year, contributed by a hundred California businessmen. What about it?"

I told Edson that immediately after my election to the Senate I had met with several of my California supporters to discuss the best ways of being an effective senator. The biggest problem was the great distance between Washington and California. Everyone agreed that to be effective I should spend as much time as possible traveling around the state, making speeches and keeping in touch with the people in person and through the mail. But the statutory allowance provided for only one round trip between California and Washington per session, and since personal or strictly political material could not be sent free under the Senate frank, I would also have to pay for printing and postage of political mailings from my own funds. This could be expensive; for example, it had cost me over $2,000 a year just to send a Christmas card to each of the 20,000 people who had done volunteer work or made a contribution to my Senate campaign.

Murray Chotiner suggested that we think in terms of running a "permanent campaign" all through my six-year term, and Dana Smith, an attorney from Pasadena who had been finance chairman of my Senate campaign, suggested that we do some public fund-raising for it. He said that if we limited contributions to a relatively small amount and then had everything handled through a trustee, there could be no question about people trying to buy influence or about my gaining any personal profit.

In late 1950 Smith sent a letter to a few hundred campaign contributors outlining the purposes of this new fund. Several weeks later Smith sent out a second and more widely distributed mailing—this time an open letter to several thousand people on our campaign mailing lists. In the end, seventy-six had contributed an average of $240 each. No single contribution was more than $500, the limit Smith had set. The total amount we received for my fund was $18,235. Throughout the two years of its existence, all transactions were handled by Smith and paid by check. All expenditures were for mailing, travel, and other political activities. Not a cent was used for solely personal purposes.

I told Edson to call Smith for any information he needed for his story and gave him Smith's phone number in Pasadena.

Edson called Smith, who was happy to explain the fund to him. The same day, three other reporters also asked Smith about it, and he explained it to them. One of the three was Leo Katcher, a Hollywood movie writer who also covered the Los Angeles area for the New York *Post*.

On September 18, the day after our Pomona kickoff, the fund story exploded across the front page of the late morning edition of the New York *Post. Secret Nixon Fund!* the banner screamed; inside, another headline said: *Secret Rich Men's Trust Fund Keeps Nixon in Style Far Beyond His Salary.*

The story, written by Katcher, did not support the sensationalism of these headlines. In fact, the *Post*'s play of the story was so excessive that many editors dismissed it as a partisan ploy or relegated accounts of it to an inside page. The *Post*'s extreme liberal-left politics and Katcher's Hollywood gossip background lent weight to this interpretation. The editors of *Newsweek* decided that the story was a political stunt and that it would either be ignored or would backfire. Peter Edson's long and objective story on the fund appeared in many papers on the same day as Katcher's "exclusive," but its sober recounting of the facts sounded pale alongside the *Post*'s bombastic fantasy.

The Democrats, whose presidential nominee was Governor Adlai Stevenson of Illinois, tried to keep the *Post*'s version of the fund story going. They succeeded in making it a national issue when the Democratic National Chairman, Stephen Mitchell, demanded that I be thrown off the ticket or that we at least keep quiet about public morals. Other Democrats quickly chimed in that the whole Eisenhower crusade had been exposed as a phony.

About the only silence concerning the fund came from the Eisenhower train, where his staff had kept the story from him until early Friday morning so that he could devote his full attention to a major speech outlining his farm policy at Omaha on Thursday night. When they told him, he was surprised and upset. Concerned because his next scheduled speeches were on corruption, he told his staff, "Let's find out the facts before I shoot my mouth off."

After meeting with his principal advisers, Eisenhower released a statement:

> I have long admired and applauded Senator Nixon's American faith and determination to drive communist sympathizers from offices of public trust.
>
> There has recently been leveled against him a charge of unethical prac-

> tices. I believe Dick Nixon to be an honest man. I am confident that he will place all the facts before the American people fairly and squarely.
>
> I intend to talk with him at the earliest time we can reach each other by telephone.

Meanwhile, the *Nixon Special* moved up through the central California valley toward Oregon. Large crowds continued to turn out as hecklers transformed my speeches into sparring matches.

We delayed our departure from Chico, in northern California, to make telephone contact with the Eisenhower train in Nebraska. Senator Fred Seaton, who was acting as liaison between the Eisenhower and Nixon campaign trains, told me that he had a message that Eisenhower had penciled out that morning, recommending that I publish all documentary evidence I had to back up my position. He added that the general said he was ready to consult with me as soon as physically possible, explaining that our train schedules had apparently prevented a telephone conversation up to now. It was clear to me that Eisenhower was not committing himself.

By the beginning of the weekend, the whole nation was saturated with stories and rumors about the Nixon fund—and with speculation about Nixon's future. Late Friday night, after our train had pulled into a siding until morning, I ran into a reporter in the corridor, and he asked if I had any comment on the Washington *Post* and New York *Herald Tribune* editorials.

"What editorials?" I asked.

"Both the *Post* and *Herald Tribune* have editorials tomorrow morning saying that you ought to offer your resignation to General Eisenhower."

I felt as much of a jolt as if the train had suddenly started to move. I said I would not comment without having read the editorials and went back to my private car. I asked to see Murray Chotiner and Bill Rogers, who told me it was true. Since there was nothing that we could do about it, the staff had decided not to ruin my sleep by telling me. They showed me a copy of the *Herald Tribune* editorial. Although it avoided the question of whether I was actually guilty of anything, it concluded: "The proper course of Senator Nixon in the circumstances is to make a formal offer of withdrawal from the ticket. How this offer is acted on will be determined by an appraisal of all the facts in the light of General Eisenhower's unsurpassed fairness of mind."

For the first time I was struck by the enormity of the impending crisis. So far I had viewed it as a typical partisan attempt by the Democrats to derail my whistle-stopping attacks on the corruption issue. I had felt secure that I was on firm ground on the merits of the case and that I would therefore have nothing to worry about in the long run.

The demand for my resignation by the Washington *Post* was neither a surprise nor a particular concern. But the *Herald Tribune* was something altogether different. It was generally considered to be the most influential Republican paper in the East, if not in the country. Bert Andrews, who had worked so closely with me during the Hiss case, was traveling with Eisenhower as head of the *Trib*'s Washington bureau; I thought of the publishers and the editor as personal friends, and I knew that they were close to Eisenhower. If the *Herald Tribune* was calling for my resignation from the ticket, the fat was in the fire.

Chotiner was furious. "If those damned amateurs around Eisenhower just had the sense they were born with, they would recognize that this is a purely political attack and they wouldn't pop off like this," he said. He was assuming, as was I, that the *Herald Tribune* would not have published such an editorial unless people high in the councils of the Eisenhower campaign had indicated that it reflected their point of view.

It was essential that I get some firsthand information about where the people around Eisenhower—and, of course, Eisenhower himself—stood. We agreed that first thing in the morning, Rogers would call Dewey, and Chotiner would call Fred Seaton.

Perhaps the staff had been right in trying to protect my night's sleep, because by the time our discussion was over it was after 2 A.M. When I returned to our compartment, Pat woke up and I told her what had happened.

I was very tired and very discouraged by this time. "Maybe I am looking at this too much from my own standpoint," I said. "If the judgment of more objective people around Eisenhower is that my resignation would help him to win, maybe I ought to resign."

"You can't think of resigning," she said emphatically. With a typically incisive analysis she said flatly that if Eisenhower forced me off the ticket he would lose the election. She also argued strongly that unless I fought for my honor in the face of such an attack, I would mar not only my life but the lives of our family and particularly the girls.

The *Herald Tribune* editorial appeared on Saturday morning and had a predictable effect. Speculation began as to how much longer I could last on the ticket. One bright spot in a bleak day came when I learned that Bob Taft, when asked about the fund in an interview the day before, had replied bluntly: "I see no reason why a senator or representative should not accept gifts from members of his family or his friends or his constituents to help pay even personal expenses which are not paid by the government. The only possible criticism would arise if these donors asked for or received legislative or other favors. I know that no such motives inspired the expense payments in the case of Dick Nixon. Those who contributed to the fund probably agreed one hundred percent with his legislative position anyway." Karl Mundt had branded the *Post* story a "left-wing smear" and a "filthy" maneuver by a patently pro-Stevenson paper.

Before the day was over, Senator George Aiken of Vermont and former President Herbert Hoover had also come to my defense.

On Saturday afternoon the train arrived in Portland, Oregon. The crowd outside the hotel there was the ugliest we had met so far. They threw pennies into our car, and Pat was pushed and jostled as she walked alongside me. Our path was obstructed by people from the local Democratic organization with canes and dark glasses shaking tin cups labeled "Nickels for poor Nixon."

A message was waiting for me at the hotel switchboard: Sherman Adams, Eisenhower's campaign manager, had called me on an urgent matter. I told Chotiner to pass along the message that I would not talk with anyone except Eisenhower himself. Whatever happened, I was not going to be fobbed off on staff aides.

Jim Bassett, my press secretary, informed me that there had been an unofficial reaction from Eisenhower. During an off-the-record press conference on his train, the reporters traveling with Eisenhower had told him that the results of an informal poll taken among themselves had come out 40 to 2 in favor of dropping me from the ticket. Eisenhower told them, "I don't care if you fellows are 40 to 2. I am taking my time on this. Nothing's decided, contrary to your idea that this is a setup for a whitewash of Nixon." Then he added, "Of what avail is it for us to carry on this crusade against this business of what has been going on in Washington if we, ourselves, aren't clean as a hound's tooth?" Word of this inevitably leaked out, and the colorful phrase captured the public's imagination. Nixon would have to be clean as a hound's tooth.

Pat couldn't get over how unfair the whole thing was. "Not only isn't the fund illegal," she said, "but you know how you bent over backward to keep it public and to make sure that every cent was accounted for."

My mother was in Washington taking care of the girls when the crisis broke. On Saturday night, after reading the papers and listening to the radio news, she wrote out two telegrams. One I was not to hear about for several days. The other she sent to me:

> GIRLS ARE OKAY. THIS IS TO TELL YOU WE ARE THINKING OF YOU AND KNOW EVERYTHING WILL BE FINE. LOVE ALWAYS, MOTHER.

In our family, as I have said, the phrase "we are thinking of you" meant "we are praying for you." I was deeply touched by this message, but it also reminded me of all the people who were watching me and depending on me.

By Sunday morning there was still no direct word from Eisenhower. The tension had become so great that I could almost feel it in the air. The night before, Chotiner had suggested that since the Republican National Committee had allotted television time to the vice presidential candidate, I should ask for part of it to deliver a defense of the fund.

I spent the afternoon talking with my staff about the different possibilities for a television program. We were deep in this discussion when Tom Dewey called from New York. Dewey was never one to mince words. He said that he had been in touch with the Eisenhower train and confirmed what I already suspected: with only one or two exceptions, the circle around Eisenhower was a hanging jury as far as I was concerned. They wanted me to offer Eisenhower my resignation. Dewey was still one of my supporters, however, and he said that Eisenhower himself had not yet made a decision. "I think you ought to go on television," he said. "I don't think Eisenhower *should* make this decision. Make the American people do it. At the conclusion of the program, ask people to wire their verdict in to you. You will probably get over a million replies, and that will give you three or four days to think it over. At the end of that time, if it is 60 percent for you and 40 percent against you, say you are getting out as that is not enough of a majority. If it is 90 to 10, stay on. If you stay on, it isn't blamed on Ike, and if you get off, it isn't blamed on Ike. All the fellows here in New York agree with me."

I told him that was exactly what we had been discussing when he called. He urged me to start making plans right away, since the situation was too tense to wait much longer for a favorable resolution.

Later that night, I finally heard from Eisenhower. I took his telephone call without asking the others in the room to leave. They were all so intimately involved that I felt they had a right to be present at what might be the end of my vice presidential candidacy.

I could tell from Eisenhower's voice that although he was trying to buck me up, he was deeply troubled.

"You've been taking a lot of heat the last couple of days," he said. "I imagine it has been pretty rough."

"It hasn't been easy," I replied.

He said that it was very difficult for him to decide what was the best thing to do. "I have come to the conclusion," he said, "that you are the one who has to decide what to do. After all, you've got a big following in this country, and if the impression got around that you got off the ticket because I forced you off, it is going to be very bad. On the other hand, if I issue a statement now backing you up, in effect people will accuse me of condoning wrongdoing."

He paused as if waiting for me to fill the gap, but I let the line hang silent. After a moment he said that he had just been out to dinner with some of his friends. None of them knew what to do, but all of them agreed that I should have an opportunity to tell my side of the story to the country. "I don't want to be in the position of condemning an innocent man," he said. "I think you ought to go on a nationwide television program and tell them everything there is to tell, everything you can remember since the day you entered public life. Tell them about any money you have ever received."

"General," I asked, "do you think after the television program that an announcement could then be made one way or the other?"

He hesitated. "I am hoping that no announcement would be necessary at all," he replied, "but maybe after the program we could tell what ought to be done."

"General," I told him, "I just want you to know that I don't want you to give any consideration to my personal feelings. I know how difficult this problem is for you." I told him that if he thought my staying on the ticket would be harmful, I would get off it and take the heat. But I also told him that there comes a time to stop dawdling, and that once I had done the television program he ought to decide. "There comes a time in matters like this when you've either got to shit or get off the pot," I blurted out. "The great trouble here is the indecision," I added.

The language I used startled the men in the room with me, and I can only assume it had a similar effect on Eisenhower, who was certainly not used to being talked to in that manner. But he obviously remained unconvinced. He said, "We will have to wait three or four days after the television show to see what the effect of the program is."

There was nothing more to discuss. I would have to stake everything on a successful television speech. The conversation trailed off. His last words were, "Keep your chin up."

It seemed clear that Eisenhower would not have objected if I had told him that I was going to submit a resignation to him, which he could then choose to accept or not as the circumstances indicated. As I had told him, I was perfectly willing to do this, but the decision must be his. I felt that his indecision or his unwillingness to come out and ask for it relieved me of any obligation in that regard. It is one thing to offer to sign your own death warrant; it is another to be expected to draw it up yourself.

I told Pat about Eisenhower's call and asked her what she thought I should do. This whole episode had already scarred her deeply. The stress was so great that she had developed a painfully stiff neck and had to stay in bed. She was worried about how the girls would be affected by it, and she was constantly on the phone to my mother in Washington to make sure that things there were all right.

"We both know what you have to do, Dick," she said. "You have to fight it all the way to the end, no matter what happens."

That night I sat alone in my room and made my decision: I would stay and I would fight.

The Republican National Committee and the Senatorial and Congressional Campaign Committees agreed to put up $75,000 to buy a half hour of television time for me on Tuesday night, September 23. In those days, nationwide network broadcasts could originate only in New York, Chicago, and Los Angeles, so on Monday we flew from Portland back to Los Angeles. On the plane, I took some postcards from the pocket of the seat in front of me and began to put down some thoughts about what I might say.

I remembered the Truman scandal concerning a $9,000 mink coat given to a White House secretary, and I made a note that Pat had no mink—just a cloth coat. I thought of DNC Chairman Mitchell's snide comment that people who cannot afford to hold an office should not run for it, and I made a note to check out a quotation from Lincoln to the effect that God must have loved the common people because he made so many of them. I also thought about the stunning success FDR had in his speech during the 1944 campaign, when he had ridiculed his critics by saying they were even attacking his little dog Fala, and I knew it would infuriate my critics if I could turn this particular table on them. I made a note: "They will be charging that I have taken gifts. I must report that I did receive one gift after the nomination—a cocker spaniel dog, Checkers, and whatever they say, we are going to keep her."

During the flight Chotiner stopped by my seat for a brief chat and repeated something he had first observed three days earlier. He had shrewdly noted that all the Democrats except Stevenson were attacking me. "I smell a rat. I bet he has something to hide," Chotiner had said.

That evening, news arrived that proved Chotiner to be a prophet. Kent Chandler, a Chicago manufacturing executive, had sent a telegram to Stevenson charging that as governor of Illinois, Stevenson had promoted a "cash fund contributed by private individuals, which was paid to various of your official appointees to state jobs in order to supplement the salaries paid them by the state."

Within hours, Stevenson had issued a statement acknowledging the existence of such a fund saying: "The funds used for this purpose were left over from the 1948 campaign for governor, together with subsequent general contributions." His spokesman declined to elaborate, and Stevenson himself refused to meet with reporters.

Stevenson's statement did not address the subject of yet another revelation that day. A former Illinois state purchasing agent, William J. McKinney, revealed that he had made up a monthly list of business corporations and state suppliers who were solicited for expenses Stevenson felt could not be charged to the taxpayers. The amounts contributed reportedly ranged from $100 to $5,000. "They figured it would help them get business," McKinney said. Two men who had engaged in this solicitation admitted their roles while denying any impropriety.

Stevenson refused any further comment. Frustrated reporters signed a petition asking him for a news conference, but he said he doubted that it would be possible to hold one. At the end of the week, Stevenson finally released some information about his fund, showing that $18,744.96 had been turned over to him from his 1948 campaign. To this amount was added $2,900 in contributions from Chicago businessmen, for a total of $21,644.96. In fact, during the campaign the public never learned the real extent or disposition of these Stevenson funds; it was only revealed twenty-four years later, by Stevenson's official biographer, John Bartlow Martin, in *Adlai Stevenson of Illinois,* that Stevenson's disclosure had been less than candid. He had not stated that additional sums totaling almost $65,000 had been added to this fund in 1950, 1951, and 1952, bringing it to a total of $84,026.56. On September 26, 1952, long after the Stevenson-for-Governor Committee had been disbanded, and four days after the existence of the fund had been revealed, Stevenson wrote a personal check for more than $10,500 as reimbursement to the committee.

The final audit of this fund showed that $13,429.37 was expended for some rather broadly defined political purposes, including annual Christmas parties, gifts to newsmen, and an orchestra to play at a dance for Stevenson's sons. In one instance Stevenson used this political fund to make a small contribution to the Lake County Tuberculosis Association and then claimed the contribution as a personal deduction on his income tax returns.

The press treated Stevenson with kid gloves. His refusals to talk to reporters received only a mild reproach, and the obvious impropriety involved was all but ignored editorially. Johnson Kanady of the Chicago *Tribune* later wrote, "No newspaper was ever able to get details of the 1950 and 1951 Stevenson funds, and so far as I know no newspaperman with Stevenson, except me, tried very hard."

For me, one of the most depressing and infuriating aspects of the entire fund controversy was to see the blatant double standard that most of the press applied to reporting the Nixon fund and the Stevenson fund. But that would not become fully apparent until later, and in the meantime I had to concentrate all my efforts on trying to prepare my speech and master its delivery in the twenty-four hours before the broadcast.

The first part of the fund speech was the easiest to write. Paul Hoffman, chairman of Citizens for Eisenhower, had commissioned the firm of Price Waterhouse to make a complete audit of the fund and had retained the distinguished Los Angeles law firm of Gibson, Dunn, and Crutcher to prepare an opinion on its legality. I planned to present the summaries of these reports as part of my speech. Because the charges against me had become so bitter and so excessive, however, I knew that something more would be needed. I remembered Eisenhower's advice on the telephone: "Tell them everything you can remember," he had said. "Tell them about any money you have ever received."

I was proud of the way Pat and I had worked hard to earn what little we had. Knowing how closely the left and its sympathizers in the press would scrutinize everything about me after the Hiss case, I had been especially careful in my financial dealings. I knew that I could document and support everything I said. Up to that time, I doubt that any candidate had ever detailed his personal finances so thoroughly during an election campaign. Despite the repugnance I felt for such an invasion of our family's privacy, I could not help thinking about the dramatic impact such an unprecedented financial disclosure would have.

I told Pat what I was considering doing. It was too much for her. "Why do you have to tell people how little we have and how much we owe?" she asked.

"People in political life have to live in a fish bowl," I said, but I knew it was a weak explanation for the humiliation I was asking her to endure.

Now that I knew what I wanted to do with the speech, the writing became much easier. I worked all through the afternoon and evening in a suite in the Ambassador Hotel, scarcely bothering to touch the hamburgers that were ordered from room service.

By noon the next day the report from Gibson, Dunn, and Crutcher had arrived, confirming that there was nothing illegal about the fund. The accountants' report was taking longer than expected, however. Without it, the impact of whatever I said would be considerably lessened. It was essential that the crucial question of whether I had personally profited from the fund be independently and authoritatively answered.

Although I did not see any of the hundreds of telegrams that poured into the hotel on the afternoon before the speech, I was touched and heartened when I read many of them later that night.

Congressman Jerry Ford wired: "Over radio and newspapers I am in your corner 100 percent. Fight it to the finish just as you did the smears by the Communists when you were proving charges against Alger Hiss. All Michigan representatives feel as I do. I will personally welcome you in Grand Rapids or any other part of Michigan. Best personal regards."

The Minnesota lawyer and Republican Party leader, Warren Burger, and his wife, Vera, sent word that "your Minnesota friends have complete confidence in your personal and political integrity. We are looking forward to your speech tonight. Please call if there is anything we can do."

Whittaker Chambers sent an eloquent message: "Attack on you shows how deeply the enemy fears you as he always fears and seeks to destroy a combination of honesty and fighting courage. Be proud to be attacked for the attackers are the enemies of all of us. To few recent public figures does this nation owe so much as to you. God help us if we ever forget it."

An hour before we had to leave for the studio, a call came through from "Mr. Chapman" in New York. This was the codename that Tom Dewey had told us he would use for very sensitive calls. The long-distance line crackled as I heard Dewey's voice.

"Dick?"

"Yes."

"There has just been a meeting of all of Eisenhower's top advisers, and they have asked me to tell you that it is their opinion that at the conclusion of the broadcast tonight you should submit your resignation to Eisenhower. As you know, I have not shared this point of view, but it is my responsibility to pass this recommendation on to you."

I was stunned. "What does Eisenhower want me to do?" I asked in as even a voice as I could summon.

Dewey hedged, saying that he did not want to give the impression that he had spoken directly to Eisenhower or that the decision had been approved by Eisenhower himself. But in view of the close relationship between Eisenhower and those with whom Dewey had spoken, he felt that they would not have asked him to call me unless what he was suggesting represented Eisenhower's view as well.

"It's kind of late for them to pass on this kind of recommendation to me now," I said. "I've already prepared my remarks, and it would be very difficult for me to change them now."

Dewey said that he thought I should go ahead with my explanation of the fund as he had originally suggested. At the end, however, I should say that although I felt that I had done no wrong, I did not want my presence on the ticket to be in any way a liability to the Eisenhower crusade. Therefore, I should submit my resignation to Eisenhower and insist that he accept it.

"I've got another suggestion as to how you can follow this up and come out of all of it the hero rather than the goat," Dewey continued. "What you might do is announce not only that you are resigning from the ticket, but that you're resigning from the Senate as well. Then, in the special election which will have to be called for the Senate, you can run again and vindicate yourself by winning the biggest plurality in history."

The conversation was becoming unreal. Silence was the only possible response to this mind-boggling suggestion.

Dewey finally said, "Well, what shall I tell them you are going to do?"

I could barely control my temper. "Just tell them," I said, "that I haven't the slightest idea what I am going to do, and if they want to find out they'd better listen to the broadcast. And tell them I know something about politics too!" I slammed the receiver back into its cradle.

When I told Chotiner and Rogers about Dewey's suggestion, they were dumbfounded.

"You certainly aren't going to do it, are you?" Murray asked.

"I just don't know," I replied. "You two had better get out of here and give me a chance to think."

A few minutes later, it was time to go to the studio. As Pat and I emerged from our room, all activity came to a halt. Everyone came out into the corridor in a show of support, but not a word was spoken.

On the way, I went over my notes one final time. The figures from Price Waterhouse had arrived at the last minute, but I was worried about being able to memorize them and get them straight. One slip, or one mistake, and the credibility of the whole speech would be undermined.

Ted Rogers led us onto the stage of the empty 750-seat El Capitan theatre, which had been converted into a television studio by NBC. I had ordered that no one was to be there during the speech except for the director and technical crew. We arranged for the reporters to watch on a monitor in a separate room.

Ted showed me the set. It was a flimsy-looking, nondescript room with only a desk, a chair, and a bookcase set into the wall. I asked him to remove a small vase of flowers because I thought it looked out of place.

After a brief lighting and sound check we were ushered into a small room at the far side of the stage. Soon Ted was back, saying that there were only three minutes before we went on the air. I was suddenly overwhelmed by despair. My voice almost broke as I said, "I just don't think I can go through with this one." "Of course you can," Pat said matter-of-factly. She took my hand and we walked back onto the stage together.

"My fellow Americans," I began, "I come before you tonight as a candidate for the vice presidency and as a man whose honesty and integrity have been questioned."

As I continued to talk I began to feel that surge of confidence that comes when a good speech has been well prepared. I began to feel instinctively the rhythm of its words and the logic of its organization. I hardly had to look down at my notes at all. I felt warmed by the bright lights, and I opened up and spoke freely and emotionally. I talked as if only Pat were in the room and no one else were listening.

The speech was divided into four parts. I began by giving the facts about the fund and describing my personal finances. Then I went on the counterattack against Stevenson. The third section praised Eisenhower, and the fourth requested that my audience send letters and wires to the Republican National Committee in Washington to indicate whether they thought I should remain on or step down from the ticket.

I saw Ted Rogers come out of the director's booth and crouch down beside the camera in front of me. He held up the fingers of both hands and I knew that this was the signal that I had ten minutes left. I saw him when he held up one hand for five minutes, and then three fingers. By that time I was so wrapped up in what I was saying that I didn't see his signal for "ten seconds," "five seconds," or "cut." I was still talking when time ran out, standing in front of the desk with my arms stretched out toward the camera.

Suddenly I saw Ted Rogers stand up, and I realized that I had gone overtime. I couldn't believe it. I hadn't even given people the address of the Republican National Committee so that they would know where to send their telegrams. I felt almost dazed. I took a few steps forward and my shoulder grazed the side of the camera. I could hear Ted Rogers saying that they had waited until what sounded like the end of a sentence and faded the picture although I was still talking. Then Pat, Murray Chotiner, Pat Hillings, and Bill Rogers were standing in front of me. Pat embraced me, and I could only say, "I'm sorry I had to rush at the last; I didn't give the National Committee address. I should have timed it better." Everyone insisted that it had been a tremendous success, and I tried to smile and thank them for their support; but I felt drained and depressed.

While I was shaking hands with the cameramen, Ted Rogers ran in and said, "The telephone switchboard is lit up like a Christmas tree."

By the time we got back to the hotel and began to read some of the messages that were pouring in, I realized that, despite the problem with the ending, the speech had in fact been a great success. Apparently my emotional nerve endings had been rubbed so raw by the events of the previous few days that I was able to convey the intensity of my feelings to the audience.

Eisenhower was speaking in Cleveland that night. Along with Mamie and about thirty friends and staff members, he watched my speech on a television set in the manager's office above the hall where he was to speak. He sat on a chair directly in front of the set, with Mamie nearby.

I was told there was a brief silence in the small room in Cleveland when the television program was over. Mamie was sobbing and several others were holding back tears. Suddenly, the audience in the auditorium below, which had been listening to the speech on a radio hookup, began to chant, "We want Nixon! We want Nixon!" With the voice of the people literally ringing in his ears, Eisenhower turned to RNC Chairman Arthur Summerfield and said, "Well, Arthur, you certainly got your $75,000 worth tonight!"

After taking a few minutes alone to collect his thoughts, Eisenhower went down to the auditorium and told the cheering crowd, "I happen to be one of those people who, when I get into a fight, would rather have a courageous and honest man by my side than a whole boxcar of pussyfooters. I have seen brave men in tough situations. I have never seen anyone come through in better fashion than Senator Nixon did tonight." The crowd roared its approval.

But instead of declaring the case closed and affirming my place on the ticket, Eisenhower said that one speech was not enough to settle all the important questions that had been raised and that he would meet with me before reaching his final decision. He told the crowd that he was sending me a telegram asking me to fly to see him the next day in Wheeling, West Virginia, where he would be campaigning.

It turned out that Eisenhower's telegram, which got lost among the thousands of others that arrived that night, read:

> YOUR PRESENTATION WAS MAGNIFICENT. WHILE TECHNICALLY NO DECISION RESTS WITH ME, YOU AND I KNOW THE REALITIES OF THE SITUATION REQUIRE A PRONOUNCEMENT WHICH THE PUBLIC CONSIDERS DECISIVE. MY PERSONAL DECISION IS GOING TO BE BASED ON PERSONAL CONCLUSIONS. I WOULD MOST APPRECIATE IT IF YOU CAN FLY TO SEE ME AT ONCE. TOMORROW I WILL BE AT WHEELING, W. VA. WHATEVER PERSONAL AFFECTION AND ADMIRATION I HAD FOR YOU—AND THEY ARE VERY GREAT—ARE UNDIMINISHED.

All I heard that night was a wire service bulletin quoting Eisenhower as saying that one speech wasn't enough. I despaired when I heard this. "What more can he possibly want from me?" I angrily asked Chotiner. I had done everything I could, and if that were not enough I would do the only thing left and resign from the ticket. I would not humiliate myself further by going to Wheeling. I said that we would fly to my next scheduled campaign stop in Missoula, Montana, and wait there for Eisenhower to accept and announce my resignation.

I called Rose Mary Woods into my room, dictated the resignation, and told her to send it immediately. She typed it up, but instead of sending it she took it to Murray Chotiner, who read it and ripped it up. He said to Rose, "I don't blame him for being mad, and it would serve them right if he resigned now and Ike lost the election. But I think we ought to let things settle a little bit longer before we do anything this final."

A little later a call came through from Bert Andrews in Cleveland. He was enthusiastic in his praise for my speech, but when I filled him in on everything that had happened, his voice darkened and he spoke in flat, measured words. He even changed his form of address.

"Richard," he said, "you don't have to be concerned about what will happen when you meet Eisenhower. The broadcast decided that, and Eisenhower knows it as well as anyone else. But you must remember who he is. He is the general who led the Allied armies to victory in Europe. He is the immensely popular candidate who is going to win this election. He is going to be President, and he is the boss of this outfit. He will make this decision, and he will make the right decision. But he has the right to make it in his own way, and you must come to Wheeling to meet him and give him the opportunity to do exactly that."

I was impressed by Andrews's reasoning and chastened by his tone. In the aftermath of a tremendously emotional event I had failed to consider Eisenhower's point of view. For one thing, he hardly knew me. I should also have realized that it was perfectly logical for Eisenhower as a newcomer to politics to stand back and see what happened before he committed himself. I changed my mind and asked the staff to make arrangements for us to fly directly from Missoula to Wheeling.

We had landed at Wheeling, and I was just helping Pat on with her coat, when Chotiner rushed up to us.

It was one of the few times I ever heard awe in Murray Chotiner's voice. "The general is coming up the steps!" he said. No sooner were the words out than Eisenhower strode down the aisle behind him, hand outstretched, flashing his famous smile.

"General, you didn't need to come out to the airport," I said.

"Why not?" he grinned, "You're my boy!"

It was a cold night, with a heavy, dank smog covering Wheeling as we drove to the stadium for a rally. During the entire ride, Eisenhower never made any reference to the harrowing crisis we both had just been through. As I got to know him better, I discovered that this was characteristic, but I still recall the surreal quality of that twenty-minute drive during which he blithely talked about the comparative merits of whistle-stopping and rallies, as if nothing unusual had happened.

When we got to the stadium the roof of our convertible was put down and we sat together in the back, waving to the cheering crowds as the car drove around the track.

Eisenhower spoke first. He described me as "a man of courage and honor" who had been "subjected to a very unfair and vicious attack," and said that before I came to the podium he wanted to read to the audience two telegrams he had received. I had no idea what they were, so I listened as intently as everyone else in the crowd while he read:

> DEAR GENERAL: I AM TRUSTING THAT THE ABSOLUTE TRUTH MAY COME OUT CONCERNING THIS ATTACK ON RICHARD, AND WHEN IT DOES I AM SURE YOU WILL BE GUIDED RIGHT IN YOUR DECISION, TO PLACE IMPLICIT FAITH IN HIS INTEGRITY AND HONESTY. BEST WISHES FROM ONE WHO HAS KNOWN RICHARD LONGER THAN ANYONE ELSE. HIS MOTHER.

He then read a telegram from Arthur Summerfield informing him that all 107 of the 138 members of the Republican National Committee they had been able to reach had supported my staying on the ticket:

> THE COMMENT ACCOMPANYING THEIR UNANIMOUS RESPONSE WAS OVERWHELMINGLY ENTHUSIASTIC. . . . AS A MEMBER OF THE REPUBLICAN NATIONAL COMMITTEE IT GAVE ME GREAT SATISFACTION TO JOIN WITH MY COLLEAGUES IN THIS STIRRING TRIBUTE TO A TRULY GREAT AMERICAN WHO WALKED UNAFRAID THROUGH THE VALLEY OF DESPAIR AND EMERGED UNSCATHED AND UNBOWED. LET THERE BE NO DOUBT ABOUT IT—AMERICA HAS TAKEN DICK NIXON TO ITS HEART.

When I stood up to speak the ovation was overpowering. Everything I had to say was expressed in one sentence: "I want you to know that this is probably the greatest moment of my life."

After the speeches I saw Bill Knowland's familiar bulky form in the crowd of well-wishers, and when I reached him he grinned, grasped my hand, and said, "That was a great speech, Dick." All the pent-up emotion of the whole week burst out and tears filled my eyes. Knowland put his arm around me and I hid my face on his shoulder.

Afterward, Eisenhower invited Pat and me to see his private car on his campaign train. It turned out that he wanted a chance to talk to me alone because he had heard rumors of several other scandals involving my personal finances. In my response, I drew an analogy that would be familiar to him. "This is just like war, General," I said. "Our opponents are losing. They mounted a massive attack against me and have taken a bad beating. It will take them a little time to regroup, but when they start fighting back, they will be desperate, and they will throw everything at us, including the kitchen sink. There will be other charges, but none of them will stand up. What we must avoid at all costs is to allow any of their attacks to get off the ground. The minute they start one of these rumors, we have to knock it down just as quickly as we can." As a popular hero, Eisenhower had been treated extremely well by the press. I do not think he completely grasped what I was saying that night until he reached the White House and began to be treated as a politician.

In the car on the way to our hotel, Pat took my hand and held it without saying a word. I knew how fiercely proud she was that we had come through this painful crisis. But I also knew how much it had hurt her, how deeply it had wounded her sense of pride and privacy. I knew that from that time on, although she would do everything she could to help me and help my career, she would hate politics and dream of the day when I would leave it behind and we could have a happy and normal life for ourselves and our family.

I had begun the campaign feeling vigorous and enthusiastic. The fund crisis made me feel suddenly old and tired. It is said that you can live a year in a day. That is how I felt about this period: I lived several years during that single week.

I was deeply dispirited by much of the reaction to the fund. I was not surprised that the story was exploited by partisan Democrats. But I was disappointed and hurt that so many Republicans prejudged me without waiting for the facts, and I was bitterly disillusioned by the performance of the press. I regarded what had been done to me as character assassination, and the experience permanently and powerfully affected my attitude toward the press in particular and the news media in general.

While the fund was the most egregious press and partisan smear of the campaign, it was by no means the only one.

Less than a week before the election, the St. Louis *Post-Dispatch*, a staunchly pro-Stevenson newspaper, ran a front-page story charging that I had accompanied Dana Smith, the fund's trustee, to a Havana gambling club some six months earlier. The charge was a blatant lie. At the time the story put me in Havana, I was on a vacation thousands of miles away in Hawaii.

On October 28, just days before the election, the Democratic National Committee charged that my family and I owned real estate "conservatively valued at more than a quarter of a million dollars." In reaching this sum, they included the allegation that my brother Don owned a "swanky new drive-in restaurant" appraised at $175,000. In fact, Don was renting the property. What really infuriated me over this particular series of charges was the inclusion in the DNC calculations of a small farm in Pennsylvania and a modest house in Florida that my parents had bought for their retirement. These properties, which were not lavish by any standards, reflected the sum total of an entire life of hard work by my mother and father. I considered it despicable to attack my parents and suggest that they had unethically acquired expensive real estate.

Two days later, a Drew Pearson column appeared, characteristically teeming with innuendo and loose facts, which included information from my tax returns. Partisans in the Bureau of Internal Revenue had obviously leaked them to Pearson. Included in his laundry list of charges was one that Pat and I had falsely sworn to a joint property value of less than $10,000 in order to qualify for a $50 veterans' tax exemption on our California taxes. The charge was totally false. It turned out that a Mrs. Pat Nixon had filed for such an exemption on behalf of her husband, Richard—but they were a couple who coincidentally had the same names as ours. Pearson had not bothered to check with me before printing this lie five days *before* the election and he did not retract it until three weeks *after* it.

Also only after the election did information surface about a criminal scheme designed to malign my character and integrity. Someone forged a letter purporting to be from one oil company executive to another suggesting that I had been bought off for more than $52,000 a year to serve the oil industry in Washington. On the eve of the election, this patent forgery was delivered to the Democratic National Committee, which sent it to the New York *Post*. Even the *Post* decided not to risk printing such an obvious libel.

After the election, Drew Pearson continued trying to stir up interest in the story, so I called for a full investigation by the Senate Subcommittee on Privileges and Elections. The investigation proved conclusively that the letter was a forgery, and referred the matter to the Justice Department.

The fund smear had fallen short, and lies and forgery had also missed the target. But they all took their emotional toll on me and my family. It was not until long afterward that I found out that my proud and combative father had been reduced to bouts of weeping as each new smear surfaced.

The taste for politics soured, but my only recourse—and my instinct—was to fight back. I quickly came to feel a kinship with Teddy Roosevelt's description of the man in the arena "whose face is marred by dust and sweat and blood." Forgetful critics would later remember my counterattacks without recalling the lies and distortions that often bred them.

It would be many months before I could begin to put the agony of the fund crisis in perspective. I think that Eisenhower was impressed both by my toughness and by the political acumen I showed. He appreciated that from the start I had offered to resign if he wanted me to and that I had never consciously done anything to embarrass him.

I also learned some important lessons about politics and friendship. In politics, most people are your friends only as long as you can do something for them or something to them. In this respect I don't suppose that politics is much different from other walks of life—but the openly competitive nature of elections probably makes that fact stand out more starkly. Still, I shall never forget my surprise and disappointment about those who turned against me overnight when it looked as if I would have to leave the ticket.

THE 1952 ELECTION

After the fund crisis, the rest of the 1952 election campaign seemed tame. Voter studies and opinion polls showed that the demand for change and disgust with the corruption in the federal government were still among the most potent issues we had going for us. President Truman was extremely unpopular in 1952, as President Johnson was later in the dark days of Vietnam and as I was to become during Watergate. As with Johnson and me, some of Truman's unpopularity rubbed off on his party. Even Adlai Stevenson began putting distance between himself and the Truman administration.

By surviving the fund crisis, I forestalled the Democrats' attempt to short-circuit the corruption issue. In fact I emerged a far more effective and sought-after campaigner. My prominence after the fund speech revived public interest in the Hiss case and I reminded audiences across the country that Stevenson had given a deposition used in Hiss's first perjury trial that vouched for his reputation for veracity, integrity, and loyalty. This was *after* our committee hearings had proved that Hiss had lied about his relationship with Chambers.

I also criticized Secretary of State Dean Acheson, whose policies toward international Communism, I said, had lost us China, much of Eastern Europe, and had invited the Communists to begin the Korean war. I used a phrase that caught the public's attention—and the commentators' wrath—when I charged that Stevenson was a graduate of Acheson's "Cowardly College of Communist Containment."

Many years later, when I was President, Acheson and I became friends, and he was one of my most valued and trusted unofficial advisers. In this campaign, however, his clipped moustache, his British tweeds, and his haughty manner made him the perfect foil for my attacks on the snobbish kind of foreign service personality and mentality that had been taken in hook, line, and sinker by the Communists. Today I regret the intensity of those attacks. While I still believe that Acheson was wrong about Asia, he was right about Europe, where he helped make NATO a strong, durable bastion against Communist aggression.

In most elections, obviously, the opposing candidates are not overly fond of each other, but there is usually little or no personal antagonism. I felt instinctively negative toward Stevenson. I considered him to be far more veneer than substance, and I felt that beneath his glibness and mocking wit he was shallow, flippant, and indecisive. He reminded me of Oscar Wilde's definition of a cynic as a man who knows the price of everything and the value of nothing. Eisenhower shared my feelings. As late as 1957, when Dulles brought Stevenson into the State Department in an effort to assure the success of the NATO summit after the shock caused by *Sputnik*, Eisenhower was adamant against receiving him at the White House or having him attend the summit meetings in Paris. In fact, after Eisenhower's stroke the doctors ordered us to steer clear of discussion of Stevenson because it always caused the President's blood pressure to rise alarmingly.

Although he was not running himself, and although an embarrassed Stevenson tried to keep him in the background, President Truman was one of the main actors in the drama of the 1952 campaign. Harry Truman thrived on the cut and thrust of politics, and it was impossible for Stevenson to keep him out of the campaign. After Truman's unsuccessful attempt to interest Eisenhower in becoming his Democratic successor in the White House, the relations between the two men became strained and in the 1952 campaign, Truman attacked Eisenhower with a vengeance. Unlike most of the Democrats, who did not challenge Eisenhower's heroic status, Truman made typically dramatic—and typically irresponsible—charges about Eisenhower's expertise and even about his motives. Eisenhower was deeply offended by Truman's intimation that he had been politically involved in the Yalta and Potsdam agreements, which had effectively given Eastern Europe to the Communists. The charge was demonstrably untrue, but Eisenhower never got over his anger that Truman would even countenance, much less spread, such a deliberate slander.

As a result of this bitterness, Eisenhower would not have the traditional coffee at the White House with his predecessor before going to the Capitol for his inauguration. Instead, the two men met under the North Portico and, but for a bit of casual conversation, rode together in icy silence. Except for a chance meeting at the funeral of Chief Justice Fred Vinson in 1953, they did not meet again until 1961, after Eisenhower had left the White House.

Pat and I traveled 46,000 grueling miles during the 1952 campaign. I made 92 speeches, 143 whistle-stop appearances, visited 214 cities, and held several press conferences. Because of the fund episode, and because

I took the partisan lead that Eisenhower had avoided, I received much more attention than the usual vice presidential candidate—certainly far more than Stevenson's running mate, Senator John Sparkman of Alabama. In some areas I even outdrew Stevenson.

Everywhere I went I blasted the Democrats, linking Stevenson with Truman and Acheson and asking how the same people who had created the mess in Washington could be expected to clean it up. I called Acheson the "architect of striped-pants confusion." I told a Boston audience that if Stevenson were elected, "We can expect four more years of this same policy, because Mr. Stevenson received his education from Dean Acheson's wishy-washy State Department." I told another cheering audience that I would rather have a "khaki-clad President than one clothed in State Department pinks."

A week before the election, in a speech on October 27 at Texarkana, Arkansas, I said that Truman, Stevenson, and Acheson were "traitors to the high principles in which many of the nation's Democrats believe." In 1954 and in subsequent campaigns Truman charged that I had called him a traitor in this speech. Even when a tape recording was found and an exact transcript of my words was shown him, he refused to accept that what I had said was not as he had apparently remembered it.

Some of the rhetoric I used during this campaign was very rough. Perhaps I was unconsciously overreacting to the attacks made against me during and after the fund crisis; perhaps I was simply carried away by the partisan role Eisenhower had assigned me and the knowledge that someone had to fire up the party faithful and let them know a presidential campaign was being fought.

By the time the last Gallup poll appeared, a few days before the election, the trend was fairly clear:

Eisenhower–Nixon	47%
Stevenson–Sparkman	40%
Undecided	13%

Both Eisenhower and I campaigned right down to the wire, however, ending with a televised election eve rally at the Boston Garden. Later that night Pat and I flew to California.

I knew from my experiences in 1946 and 1950 that the longest day of a politician's life is Election Day, when millions are deciding his fate and he can do nothing whatever about it. After Pat and I voted early in the morning in East Whittier, I asked Bill Rogers if he would like to take a ride. We drove down to Laguna Beach, where we parked the car and walked several miles along the shore.

Some Marines from Camp Pendleton were throwing a football around on the beach, and we joined them for an impromptu game of touch football. One of the Marines had been staring at me for several minutes before he walked over to Rogers and said, "Say, isn't he some kind of a celebrity or something?" Rogers responded, "No, he is just Senator Nixon, running for Vice President." When I dropped a pass later in the game, one of the Marines jokingly remarked, "You'll make a better Vice President than a football player." Suddenly he caught himself and sheepishly added, "Sir."

We got back to the Ambassador Hotel in Los Angeles around four o'clock and I went straight to my room, got into my pajamas, and tried to take a nap. I told the staff that I did not want to hear any results until at least six, because anything before then would be too fragmentary and would just make everyone nervous. At six o'clock sharp there was a knock on my door, and about a dozen people burst into the room all talking at once. The polls had been closed only for an hour in the East, but already it looked like a landslide.

In the end, we won by over 6½ million votes: 55.1 percent to 44.4 percent. We picked up 22 seats in the House; and the final tally was 221 to 213 and 1 independent. In the Senate we picked up 1 seat, which gave us a bare majority of 1.

Vice President

1953–1960

January 20, 1953, the day of my first inauguration as Vice President, was mild and sunny. For the swearing-in ceremony my mother brought two Bibles that had been in the Milhous family for several generations.

That night we had a small family dinner at home before the inaugural balls. While the others were all talking about the great events of the day, my mother quietly took me aside and gave me a small piece of paper on which she had written a message for me. No one else saw her give it to me, and I did not read it until I was alone later that night. I put it in my wallet, and I have carried it with me ever since:

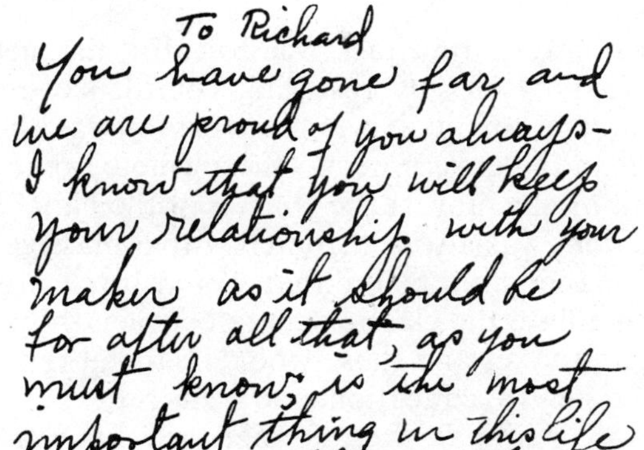
To Richard
You have gone far and
we are proud of you always—
I know that you will keep
your relationship with your
maker as it should be
for after all that, as you
must know, is the most
important thing in this life
With love Mother

Eisenhower's election ended twenty years of Democratic control of the White House. Winning control of the House and Senate made the victory doubly satisfying. But the tasks we faced were monumental.

The most immediate problems lay in the area of foreign policy. We were fighting an unpopular war in Korea, and Eisenhower had pledged in the election campaign to bring it to an honorable conclusion.

Although the U.S.S.R. was still far behind the United States in nuclear arms, it was moving dramatically forward. In Eastern Europe, the Soviet satellite nations formed a monolithic power bloc controlled from Moscow. The rigorously ideological Communist Chinese, still friendly with the Soviets and dependent upon them for economic and technological aid, were in an expansionist phase of their foreign policy.

Following World War II, the great free world alliance had been formalized by the establishment of NATO, and Europe had been rebuilt with American aid. But it was now becoming clear that both Britain and France had been so weakened by the war that it would not be long before their ability to help maintain security beyond their borders would be limited. The war had marked the beginning of the end —if not the end—of European colonialism. Symptomatic of this phenomenon was the crisis that would plague not only the Eisenhower administration but its successors as well: the deterioration of French control in Indochina. The tide of anticolonialism had not yet swept over Africa when Eisenhower took office. But eight years later, by the time he left, there were more than twenty new independent countries on that continent.

Other problem areas soon became apparent. The creation of the state of Israel in 1948 had planted seeds of hatred that would eventually explode into three full-scale wars. Nearby Iran, with its enormous oil reserves, was under the control of a left-leaning government that most observers feared would inevitably fall under Soviet domination. Latin America appeared secure on the surface, yet long years of dictatorships had laid the foundation for a period of instability and revolution.

At home Eisenhower's first task was to fulfill his pledge to clean up the "mess in Washington" by restoring confidence in the honesty of those serving in government. No less important was the job of rooting out security risks in the government—those who by reasons of disloyalty or poor judgment might subvert the policies of the United States.

The new President was also confronted with a massive problem in trying to develop an economic policy that would bring prosperity without war. He had to mediate the classic debate between those who urged him to cut spending and taxes and those who demanded that more money be spent for housing, health, education, and welfare.

Eisenhower was to find all these foreign and domestic issues less perplexing than his new duties as head of a divided political party. The division had been stark at the Chicago convention: the Eisenhower wing versus the so-called Old Guard Republicans led by Bob Taft.

Eisenhower had no taste for many of the rituals of politics. He recognized that he had the almost superhuman job of getting Republicans to think positively after having been the opposition for twenty years. In addition, while he had Republican majorities in both houses of Congress, those majorities were very thin, and in large measure they were based on Eisenhower's personal popularity rather than his party's strength. He recognized that it was his responsibility to broaden the base of the party so that it would be as strong as its leader, but he never felt at ease with most of the things he had to do to achieve that end.

INTERNATIONAL DIPLOMACY: 1953

Late in the spring of 1953, Eisenhower asked me to undertake a major trip to Asia and the Far East. He suggested that Pat come with me, and he urged that we visit as many countries as we possibly could.

From his wartime experiences, Eisenhower knew Europe and its leaders better than almost any other non-European in the world. But he did not know Asia or the Middle East well, and he was never one to overestimate his experience or knowledge. He also felt that Truman had seriously neglected both these important areas, and he tried to remedy this neglect during his own administration.

In the early 1950s most of the nations on our trip still knew very little about America or Americans. None of these nations had ever received an official visit from a President or Vice President. Their impressions of us were largely formed through bits and pieces of rumors and news, by contacts with individual Americans, and from exported Hollywood films about Chicago gangsters and cowboys and Indians. In those days the good will trip had not yet become a diplomatic cliché.

There were four specific purposes that my trip was meant to serve. It was intended to honor and reassure our friends and allies. It would also provide an opportunity for me to explain American policies in countries that had adopted a policy of neutrality. It would give me a firsthand look at the rapidly developing situation in Indochina. And it would give me an opportunity to assess Asian attitudes toward the emerging colossus of Communist China.

On October 5 Pat and I said goodbye to Tricia and Julie and boarded an Air Force four-engine Constellation at National Airport. It was a painful farewell, especially for Pat, who had never been away from the girls for more than two weeks; now we would be away from them for more than two months.

Our official party consisted of a chief of staff, Phil Watts; my administrative assistant, Chris Herter, Jr.; my secretary, Rose Woods; a Navy doctor; and a military aide to handle protocol matters. Only two Secret Service agents accompanied us on the trip. In comparison with what is provided for official trips today, this would be considered a pitifully small staff, but they more than made up in dedication what they lacked in numbers. There was relatively little press interest in the trip, and only one reporter from each of the three wire services came with us.

We had sent wires ahead to all our embassies indicating that I wanted strictly social events to be kept to a minimum. I let it be known that I was bringing only one dinner jacket and would not be packing a white tie or striped pants. Since we would not have more than four formal dinners in any one country, Pat took four formal gowns so that she could wear a different one on each occasion.

I also asked the State Department to arrange my schedule so that I could meet as many different kinds of people as possible—students, laborers, businessmen, intellectuals, politicians in and out of office, military men, farmers. I was told that this would be very unusual, very unorthodox, and very undiplomatic. I replied that unless these meetings were arranged for me I would have to arrange them on my own. There was the same kind of resistance when Pat requested her own itinerary. Wives of visiting officials from Washington customarily spent most of their days shopping or socializing. But Pat wanted to play an active part in the trip, visiting schools, hospitals, orphanages, clinics, museums, and marketplaces to meet the people and to let the people meet her. We deliberately ruled out shopping parties except on the few occasions when our embassy officials told us that our hosts would be offended if she did not purchase the local handicrafts.

Pat also asked to meet with representatives of women's organizations, and her visits gave great impetus to the new respect for women that was slowly beginning to develop in many of the countries we were visiting.

Phil Watts worked out a procedure whereby we were met at each stop by a senior foreign service officer from the embassy in the next country on our itinerary. During the flight the officer would update the briefings I had received before we left. This enabled me to conduct my meetings without using notes, a practice I had begun on the Herter Committee trip, when I found that using or making notes seems to inhibit spontaneous conversation. Some of the most useful conversations I have had during my visits with foreign leaders have been during automobile rides to and from airports, when only they and I and an interpreter were present.

Our first stops were in New Zealand and Australia, where we were warmly received. Of the many political leaders I met on this trip, by far the most impressive was Australia's Prime Minister Sir Robert Menzies. His extraordinary intelligence and profound understanding of issues, not only in the Pacific but throughout the world, made an indelible impression on me. Had he been born in Britain rather than in Australia, I am convinced that he would have been a great British Prime Minister in the tradition of Winston Churchill.

We plunged into Asia when we landed at Djakarta, Indonesia. We were greeted by President Sukarno, whose tastes were as rich as his people were poor. In no other country we visited was the conspicuous luxury of the ruler in such striking contrast to the poverty and misery of his people. Djakarta was a collection of sweltering huts and hovels. An open sewer ran through the heart of the city, but Sukarno's palace was painted a spotless white and set in the middle of hundreds of acres of exotic gardens. One night we ate off gold plate to the light of a thousand torches while musicians played on the shore of a lake covered with white lotus blossoms and candles floating on small rafts.

Sukarno was well educated and acutely aware that he exerted a magnetic hold over his people. He had led them to independence by ousting the hated Dutch rulers, and had given them a battle cry that stirred their pride and touched their hearts: *merdeka*—"freedom." But as a leader of almost unlimited power, Sukarno had become a mixture of political brilliance and corrosive vanity. He was very proud of his sexual prowess, which was the subject of countless rumors and stories—many of which he probably started himself. Be that as it may, his palaces were filled with some of the most exquisite women I have ever seen. My briefings had stressed this side of his character and his great susceptibility to flattery along these lines.

Sukarno was the main personification of a common problem in the newly created nation-states of Asia and Africa. He was a brilliant revolutionary leader but he was totally inept as a nation-builder once independence was achieved. Like Nasser in Egypt and Nkrumah in Ghana, he could be very successful in tearing down the old system, but he could not concentrate his attention on building a viable new one to replace it. These men could not lead their nations as effectively as they had led their revolutions, and their nations—and the world—are still paying the price for that failing.

Sukarno ruled with such an iron hand that the Communists had not been able to make much headway in Indonesia. But at our next stop, Malaya, we came face to face with the new kind of Communist warfare that was already threatening the stability of the entire region. Communist guerrilla forces were challenging the struggling Malayan government, which was just getting ready to make the break from British colonialism. The British were not making the mistake that the Americans made in the early days of the war in Korea and were to make later in

Vietnam, of trying to fight a guerrilla war with conventional tactics and traditional strategy. Instead, the British trained the natives and enlisted their wholehearted support in the fight against the insurgents.

In Kuala Lumpur I met with the High Commissioner, Field Marshal Sir Gerald Templer, a wiry, tough, emotional leader who had served under Eisenhower in North Africa. He told me, "What I am trying to do is convince all the native leaders and the native troops that this is *their* war, that they are fighting for *their* independence, and that once the guerrillas are defeated it will be *their* country and *their* decision to make as to whether they desire to remain within the British Commonwealth."

Both Templer and his wife worked closely with the local leaders and treated them with respect and dignity—something that had never occurred to the Dutch in Indonesia, that the French never learned in Vietnam, and that the Americans there learned only too late. We talked about the situation in Indochina and Templer shook his head sadly. "I hate to admit this because he's a real SOB, but what they need there is a Rhee." Events proved Templer right. Until strong leaders capable of providing stability appeared in Vietnam—first Diem and later Thieu—there was no solid opposition to Communist infiltration.

We spent six fascinating and frustrating days visiting Cambodia, Laos, and Vietnam, the three countries of French Indochina. Vietnam at that time was a nominal monarchy ruled by the emperor Bao Dai, whom the French had restored as a figurehead in 1949. He refused to lend his presence or even his support to the French military effort against the Communist Vietminh guerrilla forces unless France would make a guarantee of independence for Vietnam. This the French refused to do, and the result was a demoralizing standoff that benefited only the Communists.

Bao Dai rarely saw foreigners, but while I was in Saigon he invited me to visit him at his luxurious mountain resort in Dalat. He received me in a long room whose windows looked out at the jungle hills. Barefoot servants padded in noiselessly carrying silver trays laden with fresh fruit and cups of tea.

Bao Dai was opposed to any negotiations with the Communists. He said, "There is no point in trying to negotiate with them. At the least we would end up with a conference which would divide my country between us and them. And if Vietnam is divided, we will eventually lose it all."

From Saigon we flew to Vientiane, the capital of Laos, where I had a long meeting with Prince Souvanna Phouma, a young, Paris-educated member of the Laotian ruling family, who was then Prime Minister. Sixteen years later, when I was President, Souvanna Phouma was again

Prime Minister, and we worked closely together trying to prevent the Communists from taking over all of Indochina.

From Vientiane we flew to Hanoi. A brilliant sunset bathed the land below in gold as we flew above the muddy Red River snaking its way through the jungle toward the city. Driving to the residence of the French Commissioner General of Indochina, where we were to spend the night, I could see something of the city. Unlike Saigon, which was a sprawling cosmopolitan city teeming with the diversity of the many races that lived and traded there, Hanoi was like a prosperous provincial town in France. We drove down wide tree-shaded boulevards, and through ornate wrought-iron gates I caught glimpses of large villas set amidst lawns and gardens.

That night the Governor of North Vietnam, a French-educated Vietnamese, gave a dinner in our honor. In retrospect, my toast that night in Hanoi seems sad and ironic:

> The threat to this nation, although it has taken the form of a civil war, still derives its strength from an alien source. This source, to call it by its name, is totalitarian communism. . . .
>
> The struggle against the Vietminh in this country, therefore, is important far beyond the boundaries of Vietnam. On this battleground, stained with the blood of Vietnamese and Frenchmen and the peoples associated with France, are being defended the liberties and the continued national existence not only of Vietnamese, but also of Cambodians, Laotians, and of their neighbors to the west, to the south, and to the east. . . .
>
> We know that you are determined to resist aggression, even as we are determined to resist it. And we are resolved, as our past actions have proved, that you shall not fight unaided.

The next morning I boarded a French military transport plane. We were in the air before the sun was up, flying low over the dense jungle. We landed on a small airstrip, where several French commanding officers waited to greet us. As soon as the engines of our plane had stopped, I could hear what I had not heard for nine years: the thudding reverberation of artillery.

After I had met the French officers, one of them took me to the edge of the field and introduced me to their Vietnamese counterparts. I saw immediately a basic problem of the war. The French did nothing to hide the disdain they felt toward the Vietnamese. During the rest of my brief stay, without unnecessarily offending the French or embarrassing the Vietnamese, I made a point of trying to spend equal time with both groups.

I put on battle fatigues and a helmet and we drove to the front in a convoy of jeeps. There we watched an artillery barrage against a Vietminh division holding out in the jungle around Lai Cac, a hamlet about fifty miles from the Chinese border. I talked to both the French and the Vietnamese troops, and with the sound of the mortar fire raging around us, I told them that they were fighting on the very outpost of freedom and that the American people supported their cause and honored their heroism. I could see the inspiration this gave the Vietnamese soldiers, and I reflected that the French had forfeited their loyalty by not talking to them in this way.

When we returned to the airfield, I had lunch with the French officers in their mess. There, in the middle of the Vietnamese jungle, we had *bœuf bourguignon* washed down with an excellent Algerian red wine. When I thanked them for arranging such a fine meal in my honor, they replied that it was nothing special for them. I said that I would like to visit the Vietnamese soldiers' mess. This was an unpopular suggestion, but I persisted. Finally I was led to another cluster of tents, where the Vietnamese lived and ate. As we approached the mess tent, a sharp, unpleasant odor struck our noses. "What is that they're cooking?" I asked. One of the French officers crinkled his nose haughtily and said, "It's probably monkey." The Vietnamese soldiers were clearly moved by the fact that I had come to see them, and I repeated the things I had said to the officers in the French mess.

We were back in Hanoi by one o'clock. That afternoon Pat and I made a journey about twenty-five miles northwest of Hanoi to a large refugee camp at the town of Sontay. In every village along the way the provincial officials had turned out schoolchildren and Boy Scouts to cheer us. Banners with greetings in English and Vietnamese were stretched across the road.

Sontay was both heartrending and hopeful. Thousands of refugees, driven from their homes by the Communist guerrillas, lived in the crowded tents. Even during our short visit a steady stream of people carrying all they owned on their shoulders kept coming through the gate. These people seemed so at home with their sorrow that they conveyed a sense of dignity and even optimism which made me feel that, if the Communists could be defeated, the people of Vietnam could build a strong and successful nation. I never imagined that seventeen years later this war would still be going on, but fought by American troops instead of French, and that this very town Pat and I were visiting would serve as a prison camp for American prisoners of war.

That night, our last in Hanoi, the Commissioner General, Maurice Dejean, gave a formal dinner for us at his official residence. Except for the sprinkling of Vietnamese faces and the lush palms and orchids in the garden outside, the occasion might have been a mayoral banquet in Dijon or Toulouse, with starched linen napkins, sparkling crystal goblets, and silver candelabra.

Dejean was a polished and able diplomat, but his attitude displayed the same condescension that kept the French from dealing with the Vietnamese in a way that would have allowed a working partnership. In his toast, he referred to the toast delivered the night before by the Governor at the dinner he had given for us, remarking, "I could not stop myself on hearing it from feeling great pride in listening to a Vietnamese expressing himself with such clarity in a French so pure."

In my reply, I tried to stress the important part the Vietnamese would have to play if there were to be a victory against communism. Then I closed the toast on a personal note.

> Tomorrow morning we will leave this country. I do not know when we will return, but there is one final thought that I have, and I am sure Mrs. Nixon will have as we leave, and that is the thought of what a happy and great land this could be if only the aggressors in this land would stop their aggression. I realize that there has been talk of negotiation with the aggressors. We all want peace, but I think that we all realize too that the aggressors have not asked for peace, they have not asked to negotiate, and we all also realize that under no circumstances could negotiations take place which would in effect place people who want to be free and independent in perpetual bondage. Under the circumstances we leave with the confidence that this struggle which creates so much unhappiness and so much sorrow in this land will finally come to a victorious end.

In Cambodia we visited the haunting and majestic ruins at Angkor Wat, and I talked with King Sihanouk. I had met him earlier in the year when he was in Washington on an unofficial visit, and my first impressions were unfortunately confirmed. He was an intelligent man, but vain and flighty. He seemed prouder of his musical talents than of his political leadership, and he appeared to me totally unrealistic about the problems his country faced.

I left Vietnam, Laos, and Cambodia convinced that the French had failed primarily because they had not sufficiently trained, much less inspired, the Indochinese people to be able to defend themselves. They had failed to build a cause—or a cadre—that could resist the nationalist and anticolonialist appeals of the Communists.

The Vietnamese forces lived in deplorable conditions. They had no confidence in themselves, and they had no leader to inspire them. Most important, they did not have a battle cry, a *merdeka,* to make the difference between having to fight and wanting to fight.

But for this very reason, if the French were to pull out, Vietnam—and possibly Laos and Cambodia as well—would fall like husks before the fury of the communist hurricane. I decided, therefore, that the United

States would have to do everything possible to find a way to keep the French in Vietnam until the Communists had been defeated.

The Chinese Communists were training and supplying the Vietminh forces in Vietnam, but nowhere was their presence more ominously felt than on Formosa, where Generalissimo and Madame Chiang Kai-shek nurtured dreams and prepared plans for ousting the Communists from the mainland. I met with Chiang in his magnificent residence in Taipei. We talked for seven hours, Madame Chiang serving as our interpreter. When he talked about "China," Chiang made a sweeping gesture that made it clear that he did not mean just this small island to which his rule had been reduced, but the whole country beyond the horizon. I could not tell Chiang outright that his chances of reuniting China under his rule were virtually nonexistent, but I made it clear that American military power would not be committed to support any invasion he might launch. Although I felt his plans to return to the mainland were totally unrealistic, I was impressed by his high intelligence and his total dedication to the goal of freeing the Chinese people from Communist domination.

I arrived in Korea bearing a letter from Eisenhower to President Syngman Rhee. Rhee was unhappy with the Korean armistice that had been concluded in July. He refused to accept the division of his country, and he still cherished hopes of ruling a united nation.

Our ambassador in Seoul, Ellis Briggs, suspected that unless Rhee were made to understand our position, he might provoke an incident or even launch an attack against North Korea because of a mistaken belief that America would not leave him to fight alone. At the embassy I talked with Arthur Dean, our special negotiator in Korea, who knew that I was bringing a message for Rhee. Dean described him with great admiration. "I hope you aren't here to completely pull Rhee's teeth and take the fire out of him," he said. "He's a great leader, and a great friend in a part of the world where most of our friends are of the fair-weather variety."

Everywhere in Seoul I could see the legacy of wartime pain and privation. Small children in thin cotton pajamas shivered outside tarpaper huts that offered no protection from the freezing wind. It was obvious that South Korea—always a bleak, poor land—had paid a high price for its survival.

I met President Rhee the next day. He was a thin, small man wearing a dark blue suit and a dark blue tie. His firm handshake and spry walk belied his seventy-eight years. After some general conversation I said that I had some matters I would like to discuss with him personally. He nodded, and everyone else left the room.

Rhee studied me with a penetrating gaze while I told him that I was not only a representative of Eisenhower but someone who had a long and consistent record as a friend of Korea. I took Eisenhower's letter from my jacket and handed it to him. He held it gingerly with his fingers, almost as if he were weighing it.

With slow and deliberate movements he opened the envelope and unfolded the letter. In an even voice he read it aloud. In dignified but unmistakable language, Eisenhower made it clear that the United States would not tolerate any actions that might lead to a reopening of war and asked for specific reassurances from Rhee.

When he reached the end Rhee put the letter in his lap and stared down at it without saying anything. When he looked up his eyes were glistening with tears. "That is a very fine letter," he said.

Then he began to talk as if the letter did not exist. He described his attitude toward Japan; he talked about the future of Asia and the Pacific basin; he criticized the way we had administered the economic aid program. I tried to avoid pressing him too hard, but I finally brought him back to a discussion of the letter and of the assurances Eisenhower wanted. I said that I was speaking frankly to him because I thought it was of the highest urgency that he understand Eisenhower's position and make the commitment the President had requested in his letter.

"I too want to speak frankly to you," Rhee replied. "I am deeply appreciative of the aid my country has received from the United States and of my personal relationship with President Eisenhower. Because of this friendship I would not want to do anything that would not be in accord with the policies of the United States. On the other hand, I must think of Korea and, particularly, of the three million enslaved Koreans in the North. My obligation as a leader of the Korean people is to achieve unification of our country by peaceful means if possible but by force if necessary."

He paused. Then, as he continued, he ran his finger along the creases of the letter in his lap.

"I understand why the United States is anxious to maintain peace, and I am in basic agreement with that objective," he said. "But on the other hand a peace which leaves Korea divided would inevitably lead to a war which would destroy both Korea and the United States and I cannot agree to such a peace."

Suddenly he leaned toward me. "I pledge to you that before I take any unilateral action at any time I shall inform President Eisenhower first."

This was hardly the assurance Eisenhower had asked for, and I said firmly that it was essential for him to understand that under no circumstances should he take any action except by mutual agreement with Eisenhower. The meeting ended on this inconclusive note.

When I returned to the embassy I made extensive notes of our conversation. I had felt uncomfortable going as far as I did, but I knew that my mission would be a failure if because of any reticence or ineptness on my part, Rhee did not understand that the United States would not support any unilateral military attempt he might undertake to reunite his country.

My uncertainty increased the next day when Rhee told an interviewer, "I hope I will be able to convince President Eisenhower, through Vice President Nixon, that it is the right policy to finish this thing in Korea."

On the last night of our visit, Pat and I were the guests of honor at a show of Korean dancing and music. Midway through the performance there was a sharp crack, and the wooden platform at the back of the stage, on which a children's choir was standing, began to collapse. The audience gasped. When the children realized what was happening, they began screaming and crying.

Within a minute it was clear that no one had been hurt, and the audience's concern for the children's safety gave way to embarrassment that such a thing should have happened at a performance honoring foreign visitors. I knew that throughout the Far East, to lose face is the worst humiliation. It seemed as if Korea had lost face in this incident. The conductor threw up his hands and walked off the stage in embarrassment.

I suddenly thought of a way to rescue the evening from disaster. I jumped up from my seat and began to applaud. Pat saw what I was doing and immediately followed my lead. One by one, and then in larger groups, the audience joined us, and the applause grew louder and louder. The children, who had been frightened and then embarrassed by the accident, responded to the applause and began to smile. Finally the conductor returned, and the show went on.

When I paid a farewell call on Rhee the next day, he was very warm and friendly; I have no doubt he had been told about the incident with the choir. When we settled down alone again to talk, he took two pages of thin paper from his jacket. As he unfolded them, he said that he had typed them himself to ensure complete security. "The moment the Communists are certain that the United States controls Rhee," he said, "you will have lost one of your most effective bargaining points, and we will have lost all our hope. The fear that I may start some action is a constant check on the Communists. We are being very frank now, you and I, so you should know that the Communists think that America wants peace so badly that you will do anything to get it. At times, I am afraid that they are right. But they do not think that this is true as far as I am concerned, and I believe that you would be wrong to dispel their doubts in that respect. I shall send my reply to President Eisenhower's letter when you are in Tokyo tomorrow. I would like it to be delivered to President Eisenhower personally and then destroyed once he has seen it."

He handed me the notes he had been reading from and said, "You may want to use these in preparing your report of our meeting." At the end was an addition in his own handwriting: "Too much newspaper reports say Rhee has promised not to act independently. Such impression is not in line with our propaganda idea." As we shook hands at the door of his office, he said, "Any statements I have made about Korea acting independently were made to help America. In my heart I know that Korea cannot possibly act alone. We must act together with America. We realize that we will get everything as long as we travel together, and that we will lose everything if we do not."

I left Korea impressed by the courage and endurance of its people, and by the strength and intelligence of Syngman Rhee. I also gave much thought to Rhee's insight about the importance of being unpredictable in dealing with the Communists. The more I traveled and the more I learned in the years that followed, the more I appreciated how wise the old man had been.

Pat and I were Japan's first state guests since World War II. Everywhere we went in Japan we were cheered enthusiastically by hundreds of thousands who lined our motorcade routes. Those people were demonstrating a deep feeling I shared: that the war had been a tragedy and the time had come to re-establish the tradition of Japanese-American friendship that had previously existed for so many years.

In Tokyo I delivered a speech that made headlines around the world and stirred up a mild controversy at home. Before I left Washington, Foster Dulles and I had discussed what I should say about the touchy question of Japanese rearmament. Japanese disarmament had begun in 1946 and was formalized, at American insistence, by the Japanese Constitution in 1947. Privately we felt that some kind of Japanese armed defense force would soon be necessary to resist Communist domination of the Pacific. But in 1953 World War II was still a painfully recent memory, and we knew that the first mention of Japanese rearmament would raise storms of protest. Dulles thought that raising the subject first in Japan itself might help blunt the political impact in America, and I decided that an invitation to address a luncheon sponsored by the America-Japan Society and several other groups would provide the ideal forum. I said:

> Now if disarmament was right in 1946, why is it wrong in 1953? And if it was right in 1946 and wrong in 1953, why doesn't the United States admit for once that it made a mistake? And I'm going to do something that I think

> perhaps ought to be done more by people in public life. I'm going to admit right here that the United States did make a mistake in 1946.
>
> We made a mistake because we misjudged the intentions of the Soviet leaders. . . . We recognize that disarmament under present world conditions by the free nations would inevitably lead to war and, therefore, it is because we want peace and we believe in peace that we ourselves have rearmed since 1946, and that we believe that Japan and other free nations must assume their share of the responsibility of rearming.

The reaction in America to the speech was exactly what we had wanted: there was some speculation that I was launching a trial balloon, but many commentators simply assumed that I had gone too far on my own. Also as we had hoped, the speech had an enormously positive effect on the anticommunist leaders of Japan. What impressed all the Japanese, including the opposition parties, was that the United States admitted having made a mistake by imposing too harsh restrictions on their right to develop their ability to defend their country.

The highlight of my visit to the Philippines was my meeting with the President-elect, Ramón Magsaysay. We hit it off extremely well, and Pat remarked afterward that she had never seen two men of different cultural backgrounds who seemed to have so much in common. Magsaysay was dedicated to giving the Filipino people the kind of honest and efficient government very few of their postwar leaders had provided. He had the enthusiastic support of the young people, and he was a magnetic orator. His death in an airplane accident in 1957 was a tragedy for the Philippines and for all of free Asia.

The most exciting stop on the trip turned out to be Burma. This nation had recently received its independence from Britain, and its gentle, friendly people were having a difficult time combating persistent and skillful Communist infiltration.

On Thanksgiving Day we drove fifty miles into the jungle outside Rangoon to see the famous reclining Buddha in the town of Pegu. A luncheon was held for us at the city hall, and in honor of our American holiday the Burmese had managed to find a turkey that they served as the main course. We were scheduled to walk to the shrine, but during dessert the local police captain told our Secret Service agent that a walk would not be safe because the Communists had organized a demonstration. They had distributed anti-American signs, and a sound truck was whipping up the crowd. The police feared an unpleasant incident with hecklers and scuffling. There was even a real possibility of violence.

We had driven from Rangoon to Pegu with an armed escort because just a week earlier a guerrilla band had ambushed and killed some government officials traveling on the same road. Our Secret Service agent suggested that they bring our car around so that we could avoid the crowd by using the back door.

I said I thought we should go ahead with the walk to the shrine exactly as arranged. No crowd of Communist demonstrators should be allowed to alter the itinerary of the Vice President of the United States. Our local hosts were not keen on the walk, however, so Pat and I started alone out the door of the city hall and toward the temple. The crowd filled the street. I ordered the Secret Service agents and the Burmese security officials not to go in front but to stay behind us and to show no weapons. As we walked into the crowd, it backed away.

I went up to a man carrying a sign that said in English, "Go Back Warmonger." I gave him a friendly smile. "I notice these cards are addressed to Mr. Nixon," I said. "I am Nixon, and I am glad to know you. What's your name?" The man backed away in shocked surprise as I extended my hand to him. I then zeroed in on the man who seemed to be the leader, and said to him, "Your signs here are wrong. America doesn't want aggression. America wants peace. But what do you think about the countries who start aggressions, like the ones in Korea and Indochina?"

He shrugged uncomfortably, and replied in English. "That is different," he said.

"How different?" I asked.

"That is a struggle for national liberation," he replied.

I waited until I felt that the translation of this exchange had spread through the crowd and had a chance to sink in. Then I nodded my head as if he had explained everything perfectly. "Oh, I see, *they* are wars of national liberation," I said. I paused, then smiled and said, "Well, at least tell me how many children you have." Embarrassed, he began to sputter. The crowd laughed at his discomfiture, and one by one they put the signs down and began to move away. I was later told that by backing the leader down I had made him lose face with the people.

This experience bolstered my instinctive belief that the only way to deal with Communists is to stand up to them. Otherwise, they will exploit your politeness as weakness. They will try to make you afraid and then take advantage of your fears. Fear is the primary weapon of Communists.

The least friendly leader I met on this trip was Nehru. I had two private meetings with him in his office in New Delhi, one of them lasting for two hours. While I sat listening to Nehru's softly modulated British English, a uniformed waiter served us tangerine juice and cashews. "We need a generation of peace in order to consolidate our independence," he said. When I was President, I used his phrase "generation of peace" in many of my speeches as an expression of my own foreign policy goals.

Nehru spoke obsessively and interminably about India's relationship with Pakistan. He spent more time railing against India's neighbor than discussing either U.S.–Indian relations or other Asian problems. He strongly opposed the controversial proposal of U.S. aid to Pakistan, and I was convinced that his objection owed much to his personal thirst for influence, if not control, over South Asia, the Middle East, and Africa. Nehru was a great leader who had pulled together a disparate collection of races, states, and religions in a way that no other Indian leader could have done. But having led his nation to independence against great odds, he then forced it into official neutrality and made himself a spokesman for nations that wanted to remain similarly uncommitted. Had he devoted as much of his ability to solving India's internal economic and social ills as he did to playing his self-appointed role as spokesman for the underdeveloped nations of the Third World, Indian democracy might be more secure today.

Nehru's daughter, Indira Gandhi, was his official hostess during our visit. She was intelligent, poised, and gracious, and I felt her deep inner strength and determination. Her father clearly adored her, and in every way she was her father's daughter.

I met scores of presidents and princes and prime ministers during this trip, but for me the most memorable meeting was with the leader of the province of Madras, Rajagopalachari, a wizened contemporary of Gandhi. The afternoon I spent with Rajaji, as he was known, had such a dramatic effect on me that I used many of his thoughts in my speeches over the next several years, and to this day I can see in my mind's eye his small body, his large hawk nose, the fringe of wispy white hair around his ears, and his dark, piercing eyes as he sat on a straw mat, wearing just a *dhoti* and sandals.

Paul Hoffman, who had supervised the Marshall Plan before becoming president of the Ford Foundation, had told me he was one of the world's most gifted men. This was an understatement. After Rajaji's name in the three pages of notes I made about our conversation I wrote: "Infinitely wise."

We talked about the nature and appeal of communism. "Communism will never succeed in the long run," he said, "because it is based on a fundamental error. Self-interest is the motivating force for most human action. But by denying man the possibility of belief in God, the communists forfeit the possibility of any altruistic self-interest."

He was interested in learning what Eisenhower was like. "Is he religious?" he asked. "He is a very religious man," I replied, "but not so much in outward form as in inner spirit." Rajaji smiled. "That is typical of a military man," he said. "It's also typical for military men to be pacifists."

He spoke with great simplicity and emotion about the horror of the atomic bomb. "It was wrong to discover it," he said. "It was wrong to seek the secret of creation of matter. It isn't needed for civilian purposes. It is an evil thing, and it will destroy those who discovered it."

We discussed predestination, and I suggested that perhaps he was meant to lead India and South Asia along the paths of his ideas. He smiled sadly and said, "Oh, no, I am happy here. The world is unhappy, so why should I leave? I am seventy-four years old. In India, that is *very* old. My body is tired. Perhaps my brain is not, but younger men must be found to conduct the fight. Younger men like you," he said as he smiled again.

In Pakistan I met Ayub Khan, who was then commander of Pakistan's armed forces and had not yet assumed political power. I particularly enjoyed talking to him because, unlike most of his countrymen, he was not obsessed by the Pakistan–India problem. He did indicate his total contempt for the Hindus and his distrust of the Indians, but he was more anticommunist than anti-Indian. He was seriously concerned about the communist threat, both ideological and military, and about the danger that the Soviets would use India as a cat's-paw for establishing a major presence in South Asia. At that period in his career he was strongly pro-American and believed that Pakistan and the United States should be allies and friends.

Foster Dulles had not been able to visit Iran during his Middle East trip because of the unsettled conditions there at that time. A few months later a violent coup had taken place and the procommunist regime of Prime Minister Mohammed Mossadegh was overthrown by the military. A government supporting the Shah, Mohammed Riza Pahlevi, was installed under Prime Minister Fazollah Zahedi. Zahedi, whose son later served as ambassador to the United States while I was President, was intelligent and wise, with enormous strength of character. Without his leadership I am convinced Iran would not be an independent nation today.

The Shah was only thirty-four. He had just come through a harrowing experience—an attempt had been made to assassinate him. In our meetings he let Zahedi do most of the talking, but he listened intently and asked penetrating questions. I sensed an inner strength in him, and I felt that in the years ahead he would become a strong leader.

When our plane landed at National Airport on December 14, we drove to the White House, where Eisenhower invited us upstairs to have coffee with him and Mrs. Eisenhower.

The next day I received a two-page handwritten letter that, coming from one who meted out praise in very small and careful doses, I knew to be an extraordinarily warm and personal gesture.

> Dear Dick:
>
> Proud as I am of the record you—and Pat—established on your recent visit to a number of Asian countries, yet I must say I'm glad to have you home.
>
> We, by which I mean all the principal figures in the Administration, have missed your wise counsel, your energetic support and your exemplary dedication to the service of the country.
>
> On the purely personal side it was fine to see you both looking so well after the rigors of a trip that must have taxed the strength of even such young and vigorous people as yourselves. I look forward to some quiet opportunity when I can hear a real recital of your adventures and accomplishments.
>
> With warm personal regards,
>
> Sincerely,
> Dwight D. Eisenhower

The 1953 trip had a tremendously important effect on my thinking and on my career. It was an undisputed success in that it accomplished its stated objectives and more. But further, it established my foreign policy experience and expertise in what was to become the most critical and controversial part of the world.

The trip was highly educational for me. I learned much about the people of Asia through contact with hundreds of leaders and hundreds of thousands of ordinary citizens. I also saw three centuries of European colonialism on their deathbed, and I felt that I was able to diagnose the illness. I saw how the leaders and the masses of Asia longed for independence —whether or not they were ready for it, and whether or not they really understood it—because for them it meant dignity and respect. It meant being taken seriously and treated decently, and that was what they wanted.

I found that many people in these countries knew America only as an immensely powerful nation that both Communist propaganda and European snobbery had painted as crass and rapacious. I reassured them that we were not a colonial power, nor did we approve of the lingering colonialism of our European allies. Both Pat and I took every opportunity to let the people, as well as their leaders, know that America was genuinely interested in them, in their opinions, in their problems, and in their friendship. During years of oppression and repression the people had developed efficient underground communications networks, so that word of the little gestures we made quickly reverberated through a whole city or even a whole country.

This novel personal diplomacy made headlines everywhere we went and became, I think, one of the most significant contributions of the trip. In Singapore, for example, a front-page headline proclaimed: *Nixon Chats with Common Man,* and a news account of my arrival began by noting, "The American Vice President, Mr. Richard Nixon, yesterday found time to stretch his arm over a five-foot fence and offer his hand to an ordinary citizen of Malaya."

A columnist in Djakarta's mass-circulation *Abadi* wrote, "Maybe you readers would not believe that Vice President of the United States Richard Nixon yesterday helped fry sweet potatoes in a peasant's home between Bogor and Tjipanas. But that really happened yesterday. . . . Nixon even dropped in at a village coffee shop, and seated on a bamboo chair with Sukarno, had a chat with the proprietor."

Both Pat and I had a tremendous amount of personal contact with the people wherever we went. One day in the Philippines we shook hands with more than five thousand students at a 4-H exhibition. Later, as I walked through heavy crowds at a factory, my Filipino escort touched my arm and said, "That man back there, Mr. Vice President, said, 'He is not afraid to shake my hand even if my shirt is dirty!'" I shall never forget the look of quiet pride in my escort's face.

The New York *Times* surveyed its correspondents in each of the places we had visited and presented their observations in a front-page story on the day we returned home: "According to correspondents of the *Times* along his route, Mr. Nixon has shown that he has a knack for walking into delicate foreign political situations and saying the right things. In summary, the reports were that 'the common man of Asia liked this big, friendly, informal, democratic, serious young American, and got the impression that he likes them.'"

Today it may hardly seem a revelation that the peoples of Asia wanted to be treated with respect; but it was a lesson that the European nations did not learn sufficiently well or sufficiently soon in the years after World War II. In Hong Kong, the best run and most prosperous of the Asian cities I visited, I asked a local Chinese leader how the people would vote if offered independence. Without hesitation he said, "They would vote for independence by ten to one." I asked him why this was so, since the British presence had obviously materially benefited the people. He replied, "There is a saying that when the British establish a colony they build three things, in this order: a church, a racetrack, and a club to which Orientals cannot belong. That is an exaggeration but it is based upon a truth, and that is why we would always choose to be independent."

For better or worse, the colonial empires were disintegrating. The great question in the 1950s was who would fill the vacuum. Japan had the potential but was prohibited from doing so by the postwar treaties. None of the other countries in the region had the military and economic resources to defend itself unaided against Communist infiltration and subversion. It was clear to me that if the United States did not move, the Chinese or the Soviets, acting with or through the local Communist insurgent groups in each country, certainly would. The question, therefore, was not *whether* but *how*.

I learned much on this trip about the theory and practice of communism. In each country I saw how the Communists had carefully targeted their propaganda and aid where it did them the most good, and how they always presented themselves as being on the side of the people against the ruling classes—whether European or native. The Soviets were skillful with their propaganda and lavish with their money. But they, like us, were still interlopers in an Oriental world. The major new and unfathomable factor in Asia and the Pacific was Communist China. It was a giant looming beyond every Asian horizon—475 million people ruled by ruthless, disciplined ideologues. At a time when wishful thinkers in Washington and other Western capitals were saying that Communist China would not be a threat in Asia because it was so backward and underdeveloped, I was able to report firsthand that its influence was already spreading throughout the area.

With some countries, for example, the Chinese Communists had established student exchange programs, and large numbers of students were being sent to Red China for free college training. In Indonesia this amounted to as many as a thousand students a year, and I was shocked to find some of our embassies completely unconcerned about the impact this could have on the next generation of leaders.

I returned home convinced that, since the great battle in Asia was between communism and the free nations, we could not ignore the powerful Communist propaganda. I believed that the best way to undercut the appeal of the Communists was to confront them and show uncommitted observers that representatives of democratic nations were neither afraid of the Communists nor unable to debate them on any question. The most dramatic justification of this belief had come at the Pegu pagoda.

The trip also impressed upon me the tremendous spirit of enterprise and discipline in postwar Japan: it seemed as if everyone we saw—from farmers in the fields to factory hands on the assembly lines—was working feverishly. The country was still pretty much on its back in 1953, but after this trip there was no question in my mind that Japan would recover much more quickly than most Americans had predicted. When I got back to Washington I became a staunch advocate of close American-Japanese ties.

The 1953 trip had two lasting results. During those sixty-nine days I was able to meet not only those in power, but many of the younger up-and-coming generation whose careers developed over the next two decades as did my own. Each time I returned to these countries—as Vice President, as a private citizen, and then as President—I found that I was often dealing with people I had met on this first trip. The relationships that even these few early meetings had established and what I learned through these contacts were tremendously important to the development of my thinking about foreign affairs. It was as a result of this trip, too, that I knew that foreign policy was a field in which I had great interest and at least some ability.

One less significant but equally lasting result of this trip has been that neither Pat nor I has cared for champagne since. I would guess that during those two months we drank at least two cases of it. At every lunch and dinner and at almost every stop along the way, our hosts proudly produced bottles of fine French champagne and proposed toasts, which I then had to return. Before this, Pat and I had always enjoyed champagne as a way to celebrate a special occasion, but neither of us has willingly taken a glass of it since. When I was President, I would sip a little, as required when a toast was offered or returned, but I never actually finished a whole glass of the stuff.

JOE McCARTHY

One of the most serious problems we inherited from Truman was Joe McCarthy. As a Democratic friend put it to me, "Joe has been a snake in the grass for us. If you're not careful he'll become a viper in your bosom."

Both McCarthy and I had come to Washington in 1946. He was elected to the Senate as "the fighting Marine" after a brief career in local Wisconsin politics. I saw very little of him in those early years. He was a senator and I was a congressman, and we moved in different circles.

In February 1950, the month after Hiss was convicted of perjury, McCarthy gave a Lincoln Day speech to a Republican Women's Club in Wheeling, West Virginia. His subject was communist infiltration of government, and he ended by brandishing a paper that he said contained a list of individuals employed by the State Department who were known to the Secretary of State as members of the Communist Party. By the time he reached Salt Lake City the next day the number of names on the list had changed, but the charge remained the same.

Like everyone else in Washington, I read these stories with great interest. I also read them with great trepidation. Joe McCarthy had never been involved in fighting communists before, and I could not help wondering whether he understood the need for absolute accuracy and fairness in going after them. He called me shortly after he returned to Washington from Salt Lake City to ask whether, as a result of my work on the Hiss case, I had any files on communists in the State Department.

I told him that he was welcome to look through whatever files I had. But I urged that he be especially careful about facts. I noted that in his speeches he had talked about "card-carrying Communists." I told him he would be on firmer ground talking about the problems of security risks. He thanked me warmly for my advice and said I had made an important point. As the months went by, however, he continued to strike out indiscriminately.

I had a peculiar encounter with McCarthy in December 1950, at a small dinner-dance at the exclusive Sulgrave Club in Washington. Among the guests was Drew Pearson, who had been attacking McCarthy almost every day in his "Washington Merry-Go-Round" column. Although the two men were not seated near each other at the dinner table, it was clear that McCarthy was spoiling for a fight. Pearson seemed ready to give it to him.

There was dancing between the courses, and at one of the intermissions McCarthy went over to Pearson and said, "You know, I'm going to put you out of business with a speech in the Senate tomorrow. There isn't going to be anything left of you professionally or personally by the time I get finished with you." Pearson looked up impassively and said in a low voice, "Joe, have you paid your income taxes yet?" Pearson had been running articles about McCarthy's personal finances, and the remark infuriated him. He challenged Pearson to step outside, but some of the other guests intervened and got McCarthy to return to his seat.

As the party began to break up, I went downstairs to the cloakroom. There was Joe McCarthy with his big, thick hands around Pearson's neck. Pearson was struggling wildly to get some air. When McCarthy spotted me, he drew his arm back and slapped Pearson so hard that his head snapped back.

"That one was for you, Dick," he said.

I stepped between the two men and pushed them apart. "Let a good

Quaker stop this fight," I said. Pearson grabbed his overcoat and ran from the room. McCarthy said, "You shouldn't have stopped me, Dick," and went upstairs to bid his hostess good night.

Relations between McCarthy and Eisenhower had long been strained because of McCarthy's attacks on George Marshall.

After the election, I felt I should try to broker their feud. I began, therefore, to act as a go-between for McCarthy and the administration. I soon learned that the go-between is seldom popular with either side.

Most Republicans in the House and Senate were then still strongly pro-McCarthy and wanted Eisenhower to embrace him, while the predominantly liberal White House staff members opposed McCarthy and wanted Eisenhower to repudiate him. The President himself was torn. He disliked McCarthy personally, not only because of the attacks on Marshall but because of his coarse familiarity, which Eisenhower found distasteful. But he was reluctant to plunge into a bitter personal and partisan wrangle, aware that if he repudiated McCarthy or tried to discipline him, the Republican Party would split right down the middle in Congress and in the country. The unique personal good will that enabled Eisenhower to lead his party even while representing only its minority wing would have been severely damaged. So he hung back from provoking any confrontation.

Almost immediately, I found myself putting out brushfires started by McCarthy.

Two early nominations Eisenhower sent to the Senate were of James Bryant Conant, president of Harvard, as U.S. High Commissioner for Germany and of veteran diplomat Charles E. "Chip" Bohlen as ambassador to the Soviet Union. Conant had stirred up the ire of many anticommunists a few months earlier by flatly asserting that it was inconceivable that any member of the Harvard faculty was a Communist. McCarthy prepared to attack Conant's nomination on the Senate floor. Getting wind of his plan, I managed to talk him out of it. He agreed, instead, just to send a letter to Eisenhower expressing his opposition to the nomination. I was less successful, however, when the Bohlen nomination was debated several weeks later.

In the summer of 1953 McCarthy came across the tantalizing bit of information that William Bundy, one of Allen Dulles's brightest young men at the Central Intelligence Agency, had made a contribution to Alger Hiss's legal defense fund. McCarthy decided to investigate not only Bundy but the whole CIA. Allen Dulles asked me if I could do anything to help prevent a confrontation. He said that he had complete confidence in Bundy, and that his main interest was to keep the CIA out of the newspapers. I told McCarthy that I had seen Bundy's performance in several National Security Council meetings and he seemed to me a loyal American who was rendering vital service to the country.

"But what about his contribution to Hiss?" McCarthy persisted.

"Joe," I said, "you have to understand how those people up in Cambridge think. Bundy graduated from the Harvard Law School, and Hiss was one of its most famous graduates. I think he probably just got on the bandwagon without giving any thought to where the bandwagon was heading."

The next day I had lunch with McCarthy and the other Republicans on his subcommittee, Everett Dirksen, Karl Mundt, and Charles Potter. I enlisted their support, and McCarthy with obvious reluctance agreed to drop his investigation of Bundy and the CIA.

I tried to convince all parties—Eisenhower, the White House staff, the Cabinet, and many congressmen—that, while urging McCarthy to use restraint, we should consider each of his cases on its merits. I thought that until a break was unavoidable we should attack McCarthy only when his facts were wrong, and I hoped that in the meantime the anticommunist cause would not be irreparably damaged by his excesses. In August 1953, for example, he had discovered a Communist working in the Government Printing Office. He stretched the case far beyond its importance, but I argued against opposing him because there was at least some factual basis for his charges.

In his search for new areas of possible communist infiltration, McCarthy began investigations into the Army. The atom spy Julius Rosenberg had worked at an Army base, and McCarthy felt that where there had been one Communist there were likely to be more. At the end of December 1953, I invited him to Key Biscayne, where Bill Rogers, now Deputy Attorney General, and I double-teamed him about the dangers of pushing the Army investigation too hard.

I said that he should continue to go after communists in government. "It doesn't make any difference if they are in this administration or in previous ones," I told him. "If they are there, they should be out. But remember that this is your administration, and the people in it are just as dedicated as you are to cleaning out subversives." I suggested he talk with Robert Stevens, the Secretary of the Army. Rogers and I urged that he should think about moving into some new areas lest he become known as a "one-shot" senator.

McCarthy seemed to understand the good advice we were giving him, and before he left Florida he told some reporters that he planned to broaden his investigations to include questionable income tax settlements that had been made during the Truman administration. But no sooner had he returned to Washington than he was back in furious pursuit of communists and headlines.

In January 1954 McCarthy discovered Irving Peress, the Army dentist who was to lead to his downfall.

Peress had received a routine promotion even after he refused to answer a loyalty questionnaire. An Army investigation revealed that in fact Dr. Peress, by now a major, had not complied with its regulations and they decided to discharge him.

When McCarthy got wind of the incident and learned of Peress's membership in the far left-wing American Labor Party, he decided that he had hit pay dirt. He summoned Peress before a closed session of his subcommittee, where the dentist invoked the Fifth Amendment. A few days later Peress requested and received an honorable discharge from the Army. McCarthy hit the roof.

He subpoenaed General Ralph Zwicker, the commanding general, and three other officers. In a closed session Zwicker tried to explain how Peress had merely slipped through a loophole in Army red tape. As the commanding officer Zwicker accepted full responsibility, but he refused to name any individuals involved in processing Peress's case. McCarthy charged that Zwicker was shielding communists and said he was not fit to wear the uniform of an Army officer. He threatened to humiliate him in a public hearing the following week unless he changed his mind and decided to cooperate.

When Army Secretary Stevens learned of the incident, he ordered Zwicker not to appear at the public session, and announced that he would testify himself.

Once again I seemed to be the only person with enough credibility in both camps to suggest a compromise. Eisenhower was away on a golfing vacation, and I wanted to keep the situation from spilling over into a public brawl. However unconscionable McCarthy's treatment of Zwicker may have been, the fact remained that the Army was on very weak ground as far as the Peress case was concerned. The mistake may have been understandable, but it was a mistake.

Working closely with Jerry Persons, the White House congressional liaison officer, I arranged a meeting in my office in the Capitol. Stevens came with the Army's counsel, John Adams. Also present were Persons, Bill Rogers, Bill Knowland, Everett Dirksen, and Jack Martin, who had been Senator Taft's administrative assistant and was now on the White House staff.

Both Stevens and Adams seemed to have the naïve idea that they could go in and finesse the Peress case at the outset by admitting the Army's errors and then move on to the Zwicker incident and talk about how badly McCarthy had behaved. I said that they should certainly try to do that if they could, but I reminded them that it was McCarthy as chairman, not Stevens as witness, who would control the hearing.

We agreed that Dirksen should try to arrange a luncheon meeting with Stevens and McCarthy for the next day.

The luncheon was held in Dirksen's office, next door to mine in the Capitol. The meal consisted of fried chicken, peas, french fried potatoes, and hearts of lettuce. Within a few hours, the press had tagged it the "chicken luncheon," and that bland menu turned into one of the most controversial repasts of the 1950s.

From the beginning the meeting was stormy. In addition to McCarthy and Stevens, only the three Republican senators on McCarthy's subcommittee—Dirksen, Potter, and Mundt—were invited. As soon as the luncheon broke up Mundt filled me in on what had taken place. At first there had appeared to be no ground for compromise, but Mundt finally negotiated a written agreement that Army witnesses would appear and answer questions when called before McCarthy's subcommittee. There was an understanding, not mentioned in the agreement itself, that McCarthy would treat these witnesses respectfully.

Stevens telephoned me as soon as he got back to the Pentagon, and he seemed fairly happy with the way things had worked out. Within an hour, however, McCarthy casually told a reporter that Stevens could not have surrendered more "abjectly if he had gotten down on his knees."

Since the text of the Mundt agreement did not explicitly state that McCarthy would treat the witnesses respectfully, McCarthy's remark made the agreement appear to be a complete capitulation to him. Around 11:30 that night I got a call from Stevens. He was in a highly emotional state. He said that he had decided to issue a statement the following day and then resign. I told him to quit talking about resigning and suggested that in the morning we could talk about what kind of statement could be made.

At that point, Eisenhower returned to Washington. He immediately tried to get the luncheon participants to issue another statement that might resolve the situation. McCarthy proved adamant. The President then asked me to work with Stevens, Sherman Adams, and Jerry Persons in drafting a statement that Stevens could issue from the White House. We worked all afternoon in Persons's East Wing office while Eisenhower, probably to relieve the tremendous anger he felt, practiced chip shots on the South Lawn.

We took the draft to him in the Family Quarters, and he approved it. In the statement, Stevens said that he had received assurances from subcommittee members that there would be no more browbeating or humiliation of his officers and that he would "never accede to the abuse of Army personnel under any circumstances, including committee hearings."

A few days later, Eisenhower decided to issue his own statement on the Peress case. He mentioned his decision at a congressional leadership meeting on March 1, and I made a diary note about it:

> At the conclusion of the meeting, the President on his own initiative brought up the Stevens thing. He said that he was preparing to make the statement on it at his press conference and that one thing he wanted to say was that in fighting communism we could not destroy Americanism.
>
> Saltonstall [Senator Leverett Saltonstall of Massachusetts] said that he thought the Army had made a mistake in not admitting its error in the Peress case. The President reacted sharply and said that the Army had admitted it in a letter to McCarthy and in a public statement.
>
> Saltonstall came back by saying it had not admitted it clearly enough. Knowland very emphatically defended the Senators for the action they took at the luncheon with Stevens. He said that the Army's conduct in this case was inexcusable and that such a hearing on television would have been even worse than the situation with which we are confronted at this time. He tore sheets of paper off his note pad for emphasis. I don't know when I have seen him quite so stirred up on a matter as he was on this one.
>
> At the conclusion of the meeting the President said he was going to have a talk with me about this matter and attempt to get the thing in perspective.

By this time Eisenhower's reaction to the whole incident had become very emotional. As an Army man he was embarrassed by the Army's blunder and annoyed that it had been paraded through the newspapers. As party leader, he was worried about the way the issue was polarizing Republicans and giving the Democrats aid and comfort as the congressional elections approached. As President, he was offended by McCarthy's tactics, techniques, and personality. He wanted his statement to say that those who investigated communism were as great a danger as the communists themselves, and that the methods of investigators were the same as communist methods.

I believed that such a statement at that time would cause Eisenhower and the party more trouble than he or his White House staff and liberal friends who were urging it could imagine. A poll in January 1954 found that 50 percent of the people had a favorable opinion of McCarthy and only 29 percent had an unfavorable opinion.

I was again able to work out a compromise, and on March 3 Eisenhower opened his press conference by reading a long statement that adopted most of my suggestions and some of my language. It said: "In opposing communism, we are defeating ourselves if either by design or through carelessness we use methods that do not conform to the American sense of justice and fair play."

For almost three years the leaders of the Democratic Party had stood on the sidelines, watching the Republicans slug it out over McCarthy. As Lyndon Johnson, the Democratic Leader in the Senate, put it, "I will not commit my party to some high school debate on the subject 'Resolved, that communism is good for the United States,' with my party taking affirmative." But as both parties began to gear up for the 1954 elections, it became clear that the bitterly sensational Peress–Zwicker–Stevens affair had created a target of opportunity: McCarthy and McCarthyism could now safely be exploited by the Democrats.

On March 6, Adlai Stevenson, as titular head of the Democratic Party, fired the first shot of the off-year election campaign. In a televised speech he blasted Eisenhower's leadership and mocked what he portrayed as his weakness in refusing to confront and control McCarthy.

The immediate problem of who should reply to Stevenson was discussed at length during a Republican leadership meeting at the White House on March 8. Finally the President looked straight at me. "I am going to make a suggestion, even though he is present, that I think we probably ought to use Dick more than we have been," he said. "He can sometimes take positions which are more political than it would be expected that I take. The difficulty with the McCarthy problem is that anybody who takes it on runs the risk of being called a pink. Dick has had experience in the communist field, and therefore he would not be subject to criticism."

After the meeting, Eisenhower took me into his small private office next to the Oval Office. He said that he would recommend treating McCarthy and Stevenson with an easy backhand rather than making them the subject of the whole speech. One of the reasons he disliked McCarthy was that he felt McCarthy was drawing too much attention away from the administration's positive programs.

This was not a speech I looked forward to writing or delivering. No matter how it was done, it was bound to alienate large segments of the party and large segments of the public. What it really involved was what Eisenhower himself had purposely avoided for the past two years: determining the administration's policy on McCarthy. But now with the election coming up and the Democrats beginning to stir, it was clear that we could no longer afford the luxury of trying to deal piecemeal and behind the scenes with each new crisis McCarthy created.

The broadcast was set for Saturday night, March 13, so I would have only five days of preparation. I wrote dozens of outlines and drafts, and by Friday morning I felt that I had condensed them into a speech that was the best that could be done in the circumstances.

I had planned to spend Friday in seclusion going over my notes. I took a room at the Statler Hotel and left word that I was to be disturbed only in case of an emergency.

About 10 A.M., I was informed that I had an urgent call. It was Bill Knowland, furious because someone in the White House had leaked an unflattering item about him to a newspaper columnist. He said he could not put up with such internal sabotage any longer and was going to call a conference of the Senate Republicans to submit his resignation as Majority Leader. I tried to calm him down and convince him that he should wait until after my speech before doing anything.

I had just resumed work on the speech when a call came through from Tom Stephens, Eisenhower's Appointments Secretary, saying that the President had just asked if I could come over to talk to him before he went to Camp David for the weekend. I walked across Lafayette Square to the White House and was immediately ushered into the Oval Office. A few days later I recalled the conversation in my diary:

> He said that first, he didn't think I needed advice on a political speech, and that I had his complete confidence in my ability to handle it.
>
> He said, however, he felt that he knew what lifted people and he was convinced that it was necessary to get across to them that we had a progressive, dynamic program which benefited all the people.
>
> He did advise that I work a smile or two into the program. I told him that that was one of my difficulties and some people had suggested that was one thing I should try to do. He suggested I might work a smile in with regard to my comments on Stevenson. I told him that I planned to stick a few barbs into him, and then he suggested he was perfectly content that I do so but that he thought it was best to laugh at him rather than to hit him meanly.
>
> On Stevenson's attack on his defense program, he said, "What qualification does Stevenson have on this subject? Who is he?"
>
> He pointed out that Lincoln and Washington, our two greatest Presidents, were men who were subjected to considerable attack

> and who never indulged in personalities. He said, "Now be sure and don't put me on the same level, but it might be well subtly to work in that fact as you answer Stevenson."
>
> He suggested that I tell of Hiss and my part in that case. He said, "After all, there are great numbers of people who think that McCarthy got Hiss." He said, "I want you to know that I put you on the top of my list in Chicago because you had gotten Hiss and you had done it decently." He said that was also the reason he had selected me to do this broadcast.
>
> He said, "Try to get across to the people that we are working for a program for America, and that the little snapping at our heels isn't going to deter us." He suggested I might get in the fact he had commanded 5 million troops in Europe.

Stevenson's speech had been made before a cheering partisan audience at a Democratic fund-raising dinner; it had been one of his characteristically arch performances. I decided to try to convey the opposite impression, so I spoke in a calm and low-keyed manner in front of a plain backdrop. I purposely chose simple words and graphic examples. During my preparation for the speech, I tried always to bear in mind that my primary audience was the large middle ground of public opinion that believed that, regardless of McCarthy's tactics, there was no gentle way to deal with communists. I tried, therefore, to come up with some idea or some turn of phrase that would make my position memorable and unmistakable.

> Now, I can imagine some of you will say, "Why all this hullabaloo about being fair when you are dealing with a gang of traitors?" As a matter of fact, I have heard people say, "After all, we are dealing with a bunch of rats. What we ought to do is go out and shoot them."
>
> Well, I agree they are a bunch of rats. But just remember this. When you go out to shoot rats, you have to shoot straight, because when you shoot wildly, it not only means that the rats may get away more easily—but you make it easier on the rats. Also you might hit someone else who is trying to shoot rats, too. So, we have to be fair—for two very good reasons: one, because it is right; and two, because it is the most effective way of doing the job.

Eisenhower called me from Camp David with his congratulations. "As you know, Dick," he said, "I am not one who likes to use flattery, but I want you to know that I think you did a magnificent job and the very best that could have been done under the circumstances." I said that the speech would not satisfy either extreme of opinion; he replied he thought it would satisfy 85 percent of the people and that was what was important. "The people who are violently pro-McCarthy or anti-McCarthy will never be satisfied with anything except all-out war," he said. He seemed very pleased that I had smiled a couple of times during the speech and said that at one point he had turned to the others in the room with him and said, "There's that smile I told Dick to use."

At the meeting of legislative leaders the following Monday morning, Eisenhower was in the best spirits he had been in for a long time. My speech seemed to have buoyed him by giving voice to his own frustrations over McCarthy and by providing some focus for the administration's efforts.

The March 13 speech marked the beginning of a new phase of the McCarthy episode, a phase that turned out to be the beginning of the end. By the time the Army–McCarthy hearings began five weeks later, those who knew McCarthy said that he seemed to have fallen apart. In my diary for March 22, I recounted a conversation with Len Hall:

> Len seemed to feel that Joe was beginning to blow up and that he was in no condition whatever to attend a hearing and to participate in it.
>
> The same view was expressed by Karl Mundt when I talked to him on the phone. He had talked to Joe until two o'clock the night before and he said it was pretty grim with Jean [McCarthy's wife] almost in tears, and him having very little influence due to the fact that Joe said that he knew his political life was at stake and that he was not going to agree to anything that would make it difficult for him to defend himself.
>
> Len Hall said when he had been in to see Joe a couple of days before, when he came up to the apartment door Joe opened it and had a gun in his hand. Apparently he was carrying one all the time because of the threats that had been made against him.

Major shifts in public opinion now began to appear. A Gallup poll at the end of March showed that a solid 46 percent favored McCarthy and 36 percent disapproved of him. By August a dramatic reversal had occurred: while 36 percent still held firm in their approval, now 51 percent disapproved. As soon as the first cracks appeared in his public support, a startling erosion set in. Just a few months earlier the Republican National Committee had been calling McCarthy an asset to the party. Now there was an effort to write him off as soon as possible.

For almost two months, from April 22 to June 17, the grotesque melodrama of the Army–McCarthy hearings unfolded each day in the Senate Caucus Room. Eisenhower privately called the hearings "a damn shameful spectacle," and he urged that everything possible be done to get them over with as quickly as possible. But there was nothing we could do. The hearings became a national obsession. People stayed home from work to see the key confrontations. The posturing before the cameras on both sides repelled me, and after the first day I did not watch any of them. As I told a reporter, "I just prefer professional actors to amateurs."

On July 30, Vermont Republican Senator Ralph Flanders introduced Senate Resolution 301: "Resolved, That the conduct of the Senator from Wisconsin, Mr. McCarthy, is unbecoming a Member of the United States Senate, is contrary to senatorial traditions, and tends to bring the Senate into disrepute, and such conduct is hereby condemned." On August 2, by a vote of 75 to 12, the Senate adopted a resolution to appoint a select committee to consider the Flanders resolution. The committee was chaired by Senator Arthur V. Watkins, a stern Mormon from Utah. None of them, including the freshman senator from North Carolina, Sam Ervin, had taken a strong public stand on McCarthy.

After almost a month of hearings, the Watkins Committee unanimously recommended that McCarthy be censured on two counts: for contempt of the Senate because he had refused to appear before a subcommittee investigating his finances in 1952, and for his abuse of General Zwicker. The vote was postponed until after the November elections.

I was presiding over a tense Senate chamber when the final debate began on December 2. It was late afternoon by the time the vote was taken. A sudden hush fell over the Chamber as a lone figure came through the swinging doors at the back and walked slowly down the aisle. Joe McCarthy had arrived for the vote on his own censure. His arm was in a sling from an attack of bursitis that had kept him in the hospital for several days.

When the vote was taken, every Democrat voted against McCarthy; the Republicans split right down the middle, 22 for and 22 against. Among those voting against the resolution was Bill Knowland, the Minority Leader. The final vote was 67 to 22, and at 5:03 P.M. on December 2, Joseph R. McCarthy of Wisconsin became the third United States Senator ever to be censured by his colleagues. He sat quietly in his seat, staring at the bare desktop in front of him, surrounded by his supporters.

There was a brief procedural hassle when Styles Bridges of New Hampshire pointed out that as the word *censure* did not appear in the body of the resolution, it should be struck from the title. The parliamentarian advised me that Bridges was technically correct and that the resolution as formally passed was one of condemnation rather than censure.

But by this time the rhetoric did not matter. McCarthy had already left the chamber. For him it was all over.

Joseph McCarthy cast his shadow over four critical years of American politics. From the Wheeling speech in February 1950 to his condemnation in December 1954, intense controversy surrounded everything he said and did.

I remember a luncheon at the White House a few days after the chicken luncheon had brought the Stevens episode to fever pitch. As I noted in my diary at the time, everyone was very tense:

> At the luncheon, the President for some reason brought up the story of his old boxing instructor at West Point who he said used to hit him clear across the ring. He said that unless he got up smiling every time the boxing instructor would turn his back and walk out of the room.
>
> Apparently the purpose of the story was to see that everybody did not get too excited about the whole McCarthy incident and the attacks that he made.
>
> The President seems to have been convinced that people in the administration were actually afraid of McCarthy. Another purpose, I think, was the line he had been developing during the past week or so, that he wanted to see smiling faces around him.

My own feelings about Joe McCarthy were mixed. I never shared the disdain with which fashionable Washington treated him because of his lack of polished manners. In fact, I found him personally likable, if irresponsibly impulsive. At the end, I felt sorry for him as a man whose zeal and thirst for publicity were leading him and others to destruction. But it is despicable to make a racket of anticommunism or any other cause—to stir people up and then give them no positive leadership or direction. By the spring of 1954 J. Edgar Hoover was telling Eisenhower that McCarthy had reached a point where he was actually impeding the investigation of communists. As Eisenhower expressed it, "McCarthy is probably Malenkov's best helper in the United States."

I broke with McCarthy when he began to attack the administration openly. For some time he had picked up one of Senator Jenner's lines and been referring to the period before Eisenhower was elected as "twenty years of treason." In 1954, he began talking about "twenty-one years of treason," thus including the first year of Eisenhower's administration.

McCarthy was sincere, and I know from personal investigation that there was real substance to some of his charges. But he could not resist grossly exaggerating his facts. The communists and the compulsive anti-anticommunists, together with many who were as anticommunist as McCarthy himself, ended up discrediting everything the man had to say when McCarthy became the issue instead of communism.

CRISIS IN INDOCHINA: 1954

The names Vietnam and Indochina meant little to most Americans when, in March 1954, the first news stories appeared about the Communist siege of a remote French military outpost called Dien Bien Phu. Within a few weeks, however, we shared the daily agony and valor of its defenders, and we saw the threat of a Communist takeover in Vietnam bring America to the brink of war. After seven years of fighting and 50,000 men killed, there were serious questions in France about whether to continue the fight against Ho Chi Minh's Communist guerrillas.

A French withdrawal from Vietnam would have placed us in a very difficult position because American policy was predicated upon the vital importance of maintaining an independent Vietnam. Early in 1952 Truman's National Security Council had prepared a study of Southeast Asia that set forth what Eisenhower later referred to as the "falling domino" principle: that "the loss of any single country would probably lead to relatively swift submission to or an alignment with communism by the remaining countries of this group." The study described America's vital interests in the natural resources of this area—rubber and tin—and concluded that the French effort to defeat Ho Chi Minh's Communist Vietminh was "essential to the security of the free world, not only in the Far East but in the Middle East and Europe as well."

In February 1954, Eisenhower had sent two hundred Army mechanics as advisers to the French and Vietnamese forces. There was no serious opposition in Congress because the men would be in Vietnam only as technical advisers, and Eisenhower promised that they would not stay longer than June.

As the French and Vietminh settled in for a long siege, the press began to build up Dien Bien Phu as the first test since Korea of the free world's ability to resist Communist aggression. In Washington the Joint Chiefs of Staff, under their Chairman, Admiral Arthur Radford, devised a plan, known as Operation Vulture, for using three small tactical atomic bombs to destroy Vietminh positions and relieve the garrison. Both Eisenhower and Dulles, however, felt that nothing less than overt Chinese Communist aggression would be sufficient provocation for our going into Vietnam in any such a direct and unilateral way.

The Communist Chinese were the Vietminh's patrons and principal source of military supplies. At a congressional leadership meeting at the end of March, Eisenhower said that if the military situation at Dien Bien Phu became desperate he would consider the use of diversionary tactics, possibly a landing by Chiang Kai-shek's Nationalist forces on China's Hainan Island or a naval blockade of the Chinese mainland. Very simply, but dramatically, he said, "I am bringing this up at this time because at any time within the space of forty-eight hours, it might be necessary to move into the battle of Dien Bien Phu in order to keep it from going against us, and in that case I will be calling in the Democrats as well as our Republican leaders to inform them of the actions we're taking."

Reports of the situation in Dien Bien Phu were constantly changing, and our day-to-day attitude frequently reflected the shifting tides of the battle. I made a diary note of an NSC meeting on April 6:

> The President was in a very serious mood in this meeting. Dulles presented his plan about trying to get united action among the allies. I said that such a plan was all right as far as it goes but that, if it were limited to resisting overt aggression alone, it would not meet the real future danger in Asia. I said that we must adopt the principle of uniting together to resist subversive aggression of the Indochina and Chinese Civil War type. I pointed out that we had never yet found a formula to resist this kind of aggression on a united basis.
>
> The President said, "What about Korea?" I answered that Korea was a case of the Communists marching across a line even though it was technically in the same country and that, therefore, the united action principle applied because what was really involved was overt aggression.
>
> I also said that I didn't think the President should underestimate his ability to get the Congress and the country to follow his leadership. I suggested that more technicians could be sent to Indochina if the President asked for them. He asked Wilson to check on this immediately.
>
> From the conversation, however, it was quite apparent that the President had backed down considerably from the strong position he had taken on Indochina the latter part of the previous week. He seemed resigned to doing nothing at all unless we could get the allies and the country to go along with whatever was suggested and he did not seem inclined to put much pressure on to get them to come along.

The challenge we faced in 1954 was to convince the American people of the importance of Dien Bien Phu—that much more was at stake than the defense of some French troops besieged at a colonial outpost. No one, except possibly Admiral Radford, wanted American military intervention. We were all convinced, however, that unless the Communists knew that their so-called wars of liberation would be resisted by military means if necessary, they would not stop until they had taken over Southeast Asia, just as they had Eastern Europe.

Dulles spent several weeks trying to get the British and French to join us in concerted opposition to the Communists. The French government, however, was too much on the psychological defensive to be able to mount or sustain the kind of military and diplomatic offensive required.

Admiral Radford went to London to consult with Churchill, who said bluntly that if his people had not been willing to fight to save India for themselves, he did not think they would be willing to fight to save Indochina for the French. Churchill admitted that the rest of Indochina might fall if Vietnam were lost, but he did not foresee any threat to the rest of Southeast Asia, Japan, or Australia. Both Radford and I were astonished that Churchill, who had understood the communist problem so well as early as 1946, could have made this statement.

It was clear that we could not count on Britain or France for support in resisting communism in Indochina. If we decided to move, we would have to move on our own.

Early in April there was a respite from the crisis; it seemed that the French troops might be able to hold on at Dien Bien Phu. Eisenhower decided to go to Augusta for a few days, and Dulles, exhausted and disheartened by his unsuccessful attempts to promote allied unity, went to Canada. The news from Vietnam continued hopeful, and in order to extend his stay in Georgia, Eisenhower asked me to fill in for him at the American Society of Newspaper Editors' annual convention in Washington on April 16.

The ASNE convention is a prestigious and responsible forum, and I asked that all my remarks be off the record so that I could speak candidly. After delivering a prepared speech I agreed to take questions from the floor. I was asked whether I thought we would send American troops to Indochina if the French decided to withdraw and it was the only way to save Indochina from being taken over by the Communists. I said that I did not believe that "the presumption or the assumption which has been made by the questioner will occur, and I recognize that he has put it as a hypothetical question." Given those major reservations, however, I said that if sending American forces was the only way to avoid further Communist expansion in Asia, particularly in Indochina, "I believe that the executive branch of the government has to take the politically unpopular position of facing up to it and doing it, and I personally would support such a decision."

Two foreign reporters who were not at the meeting heard about my response and sent the story to their papers. By the next morning it was headline news all across America. It was widely interpreted as a trial balloon aimed at reversing the administration's policy, which, so far, had drawn the line at direct American military intervention in Vietnam.

I was concerned that Eisenhower might be upset over the incident, but he told me that if he had been confronted with a hypothetical question under similar circumstances he probably would have answered it the same way.

At a meeting with the Republican congressional leaders a week later, Eisenhower supported me when the matter was raised. I made a note of the meeting:

> Charlie Halleck, during the course of the discussion, said that the suggestion that American boys might be sent to Indochina "had really hurt," and that he hoped there would be no more talk of that type. The President, however, immediately stepped in and said he felt it was important that we not show a weakness at this critical time and that we not let the Russians think that we might not resist in the event that the Communists attempted to step up their present tactics in Indochina and elsewhere. He said that we had to think of whether it was best to take a strong stand now when we could or wait until later when we could not. He also pointed out that it was not well to tell the Russians everything as to what we would or would not do.

At the end of April the situation at Dien Bien Phu took another turn for the worse, and it did not look as if the French forces could hold on much longer. I made a diary note on April 29:

> The NSC meeting started at ten o'clock and did not end until one. The last hour and three-quarters was spent discussing Indochina.
>
> Radford reported on the military situation and on his conversations with the French and British. Bedell Smith read a message from Dulles which indicated considerable pessimism but that Dulles was going to stand firm for the American position.
>
> The President was extremely serious and seemed to be greatly concerned about what was the right course to take.
>
> After the reports were made, Harold Stassen said that he thought that decision should be to send ground troops if neces-

> sary to save Indochina, and to do it on a unilateral basis if that was the only way it could be done.
>
> The President himself said that he could not visualize a ground troop operation in Indochina that would be supported by the people of the United States and which would not in the long run put our defense too far out of balance. He also raised the point that we simply could not go in unilaterally because that was in violation of our whole principle of collective defense against communism in all places in the world.

After Stassen's proposal had been discussed, I said that in my judgment winning the war in Vietnam was not necessarily a question of committing a lot of ground troops to combat. Sending an Air Force contingent representing a unified alliance would have the double effect of letting the Communists know that we were going to resist further expansion in the area, and of bolstering the morale of the French and the Vietnamese troops. I suggested that we explore the possibilities of developing a Pacific coalition without the British, an alliance with Thailand, the Philippines, Indochina, Australia, New Zealand, and whatever other nations would join.

The next morning I met with Eisenhower and General Robert Cutler, his Special Assistant for National Security Affairs. Cutler reported that the NSC planning board had been discussing the possibility of telling our allies that if we went into Indochina, we might use the atom bomb. Eisenhower asked me what I thought about this idea; I said that whatever was decided about using the bomb, I did not think it was necessary to mention it to our allies before we got them to agree on united action. I emphasized, as I had at the NSC meeting, that it might not be necessary to have more than a few conventional air strikes by the united forces to let the Communists see that we were determined to resist. Eisenhower turned to Cutler and said, "First, I certainly do not think that the atom bomb can be used by the United States unilaterally, and second, I agree with Dick that we do not have to mention it to anybody before we get some agreement on united action."

On May 7, after a gallant but utterly hopeless defense of a territory that had been reduced to the size of a baseball field, the French garrison at Dien Bien Phu was overrun by the Vietminh. The almost universal reaction was relief that the crisis had ended without precipitating a major war. But while attempting to put the best face on it publicly, we knew that the defeat at Dien Bien Phu would probably lead to French withdrawal from Vietnam, and that America would either have to take over the burden of stopping Communist aggression in Indochina or abandon the entire region.

On May 20 the NSC discussed the possibility of keeping the two hundred American mechanics in Vietnam past June, but Eisenhower dismissed the idea. First, he said, the French were already going back on their word to keep up the fighting. Second, he said that such an extension would make our future relations with Congress very difficult, because he had given a solemn pledge that the mechanics would come out by June 15, and he intended to honor his pledge.

After the fall of Dien Bien Phu, the heart fell out of the French will to win, and the next several weeks of desultory battle were a holding action until a negotiated settlement could be reached at the Geneva Conference, which had opened eleven days before the fortress fell. Dulles was infuriated and dispirited by the plan to surrender half of Vietnam to the Communists. When the Indochina settlement was made on July 21, the United States did not sign it. I agreed with this decision. In fact, a month earlier, I had urged Dulles not to be part of any settlement that would result in the surrender of any part of Indochina to the Communists.

The press perceived Dulles, Radford, and me as the hawks in the Indochina crisis. To some extent Radford did believe that the early use of tactical nuclear weapons would convince the Communists that we meant business. Dulles and I both believed that if the Communists pushed too far we would have to do whatever was necessary to stop them. Eisenhower fully agreed, although I think that Dulles and I were probably prepared to stand up at an earlier point than he was. We all hoped that by being prepared to fight we would never actually have to do any fighting.

Years later, after Dulles was dead and America was deeply involved in a war in Vietnam under another President, Eisenhower was asked privately whether he and Dulles had agreed on the question of being ready to send troops into Vietnam. "All the way," Eisenhower said.

MEETING CHURCHILL

In June 1954, Prime Minister Winston Churchill and Foreign Secretary Anthony Eden visited the United States for meetings with Eisenhower and Dulles. I dictated an extensive diary note describing the visit, beginning with my first meeting with the great man:

> I met Churchill and Eden at the airport this morning. As he came down the steps of the airplane, he took each step alone by

himself although he was very hesitant in his steps when he arrived at the bottom. He shook hands and said that he was very happy to meet me for the first time. Later in the car he said that although this was the first time that he had met me that he had read of some of my statements and that he had admiration for them.

I was supposed to make a speech of introduction which I had spent an hour or so last night preparing even though it was only to be a minute and a half long. However, when Churchill saw the microphones he walked immediately over to them and took out a sheet of paper from which he read his own speech to the people who were at the airport.

We then got into the open car and rode into town. Churchill was rather slow to react to questions or statements but on the other hand after the conversation had gone on for a while his reactions picked up considerably.

He said that there was a period for four months in Roosevelt's last months that there was very little communication or understanding between him and the American government. This was in response to my remarks that I had just read the fourth volume of his memoirs. He said that Roosevelt was not himself at that time and that Truman did not know what was going on. In fact, he said that he was sure Truman had not been taken in on the great decisions that were being made. He felt Roosevelt made a great mistake in not developing his second in command when he knew that he himself was ill and could not be around much longer. I said that I often wondered what would have happened had the allies accepted his judgment with regard to the conduct of World War II, particularly in respect to the southern offensive rather than the Channel crossing. His only remark was, well it would have been very "handy to have Vienna."

The diary described the dinner the Eisenhowers gave that evening:

I think this was perhaps the most enjoyable occasion we have ever had at the White House. The crowd was relatively small—approximately 30—and the President, Churchill, et al. were in a relaxed, informal mood.

The President proposed a toast to General Marshall after he had proposed one to the Queen and Churchill had responded. He pointed out that both Churchill and Marshall had been his immediate superiors during the war and that he knew they would forgive him if he made a protocol exception and proposed a toast to Marshall. I looked at Marshall as the toast was being proposed and it was obvious that he was very deeply moved by this gesture.

After the guests who were not staying at the White House had gathered in one of the reception rooms downstairs we were all invited to come upstairs.

Eden was particularly impressed by the reports of our visit to Malaya—the occasion when we went out and met the troops he said made a great impression in Britain.

After we had finished dinner, we went in for cigars and after the President sat with Churchill for a little while he asked me to come over and sit by him and said, "This is one of the young men I have been telling you about and I want you to get acquainted with him." I asked Churchill about his writing his memoirs. He pointed out that he had started them in 1946 and that he did it all by dictation. I asked him if he used a machine and he said no; that the Americans had given him one of the best machines but he preferred a pretty girl to talk to rather than a machine.

We went down to the movie room and saw *The Student Prince*. The program was not over until about 12:30 A.M. During the program both Churchill and the President exchanged pleasantries which we could all hear and remarks about the movie. The movie significantly enough came out just the opposite to the way Edward VIII came out with Mrs. Simpson.

Pat sat at Churchill's right during the dinner and she said it was a very enjoyable evening from all standpoints. Mrs. Eisenhower watched over him as his food was being served and when he tried to cut a piece of the meat in half before putting it on his plate she told him the knives weren't sharp and that they had all been received as part of the White House set—this was part of the gold set that had been bought in Paris. Pat remarked how Mamie took things over just as if she were handling any youngster who happened to be visiting or any close friend.

Foster Dulles had his usual highball rather than the wines during dinner. Pat asked Churchill whether or not he would prefer that. He said no, that he usually had his first drink of whiskey at 8:30 in the morning and that in the evening he enjoyed a glass of champagne. I noted that Churchill was much sharper than he had been in the morning and he seemed to thrive on the fact that he was participating in these conferences. As a matter of fact, at the dinner he was just as quick as any person and he had—I learned later—not taken a nap in the afternoon but had played cards after the conference had been completed.

The last evening of Churchill's visit there was a stag dinner at the British Embassy. I attended as Eisenhower's representative and was therefore seated next to him at the table:

> I asked him how the three-day conference had affected him. He said that except for a few blackouts—and I assume he meant by that periods when he took a nap—that he had felt better during this conference than he had for some time. He said, "I always seem to get inspiration and renewed vitality by contact with this great novel land of yours which sticks up out of the Atlantic."
>
> During the course of the evening the conversation turned to General Lee and I asked his appraisal of Lee. He said that he thought he was one of the greatest men in American history and one of the greatest generals at any time. He said that somebody ought to "catch up in a tapestry or a painting the memorable scene of Lee riding back across the Potomac after he had turned down the command of the Union Armies in order to stay with the Southern side." He also said that one of the other great moments in the Civil War was at Appomattox when Lee pointed out to Grant that the officers owned their horses as personal property and asked that they be allowed to retain them. Grant said to have them take all of their horses—the enlisted men and the officers as well. "They will need them to plow their fields." Churchill said, "In the squalor of life and war, what a magnificent act."
>
> He reiterated his press club statement to the effect that we should have a policy of patience and vigilance. He said we could not deal with the Communists on the basis of weakness—that it had to be a policy of strength. He said he didn't like to call it a go-slow policy because that was not really a fair appraisal of the kind of policy he was advocating. He pointed out his record after World War I and also his Fulton, Missouri speech in properly appraising the communist threat and advocating means to meet it. He said, "I think that I have done as much against the Communists as McCarthy has done for them." He grinned and said, "Of course, that is a private statement. I never believe in interfering in the domestic politics of another country." He said that Bevan in England was just as much of a problem to him and to the British as was McCarthy to us. I asked him what it was that the British people didn't like about McCarthy and he said one

> thing they couldn't understand was why the Senate did not investigate all of the charges about his finances and other irregularities in getting elected and while he was Senator. I pointed out that very possibly Senators did not want to set the precedent of investigating a colleague for fear that it might someday react in a case against themselves.

I saw them off at the airport and Churchill was careful to see that I delivered some farewell remarks. I could tell that his declining health would soon cause him to give up the reins of leadership he had held for so long. While he was obviously not up to his best, he still was better than most leaders half his age. He had enormous experience, intelligence, and understanding of the forces that shape the world. My emotions were mixed as I said good-bye to him. I was honored to have met one of the world's greatest leaders, but I was saddened by the realization that he would soon be passing from the scene.

1954 ELECTIONS

It seemed as if the Eisenhower administration had hardly begun to settle in before it was time to fight the 1954 off-year election campaign. The Republicans' razor-thin majority of one in the Senate was the most obvious target for the Democrats, but they also had their sights set on regaining control of the House of Representatives.

It was clear that Eisenhower planned to remain above the battle. He said he did not want a heavy campaign schedule because he did not think it wise for the President to go on a barnstorming trip, and because at sixty-three he now needed more rest.

If Eisenhower had no taste for this campaign, I had little for it myself. In the eighteen months of his administration Eisenhower had maintained his personal popularity, but the party was as divided as it had been before he was elected. Indeed, the passing of Bob Taft and the ascent of Joe McCarthy had deepened the divisions within Republican ranks. The Democrats were making the most of our problems. Adlai Stevenson led the charge, telling his listeners that the Republican Party had "as many wings as a boardinghouse chicken" and that "caught between contradiction, apathy, and McCarthy, they act as confused as a blind dog in a meathouse." I led the counterattack, but my heart wasn't in the battle. Once again I realized how much the agony of the fund crisis had stripped the fun and excitement from campaigning for me.

Requests for campaign appearances on behalf of Republican congressmen and senators began flooding my office. They were worried about the effect Eisenhower's refusal to campaign would have on our chances. I decided that there was no choice for me but to lead the party in the election, so I threw myself into two full months of intensive campaigning. It was not a decision I made lightly, or enthusiastically.

As I made my first campaign trips into the country I was surprised to find how complacent the Republican organizers were. On September 19 I placed a conference call to Brownell, Summerfield, and Jerry Persons. I told them, "Don't give the President the idea that things are in good shape. They're not. If we don't get moving and get the issues working for us instead of killing us, we're going to lose fifty seats."

After a few weeks of campaigning around the country I decided I had to remove some of the simplistic ideas held by many of the political amateurs in the administration and even by some of the professionals at the Republican National Committee.

I wrote a memorandum to RNC Chairman Len Hall setting out some of my ideas. As far as the issues were concerned, I felt that we should be concentrating on the ones where we were strong and the Democrats were weak. "These are peace, communism, corruption, taxes," I wrote. "They are not unemployment and farm prices. If the voters on election day are thinking of unemployment and/or farm prices primarily, we will lose the election without any question. This is not because our position on these issues is not right and not because it is not salable if we had enough time to talk to each individual personally, but because these two issues are *defensive* from our standpoint while the others are *offensive* for our side and *defensive* for the other side."

I also addressed the McCarthy issue in terms of its impact on the party and the election:

> 1. Our handling of the issue has gained us no new support. Those people who were against us because they thought we tolerated McCarthy were against us anyway and will continue to vote on the other side because they consider the ADA [Americans for Democratic Action] gang as more anti-McCarthy than we are.
>
> 2. We have lost considerable support among Democrats whose reason for voting for us in '46, '50, and '52 was their distrust of the Truman administration on the handling of the domestic communist issue.
>
> 3. The greatest damage has been done in splitting the Republicans and causing apathy in our ranks.
>
> We can remedy to an extent the situations mentioned in 2 and 3 by emphasizing vigorously the Administration's anticommunist record and by attacking the other side for its past and present softness on the issue.

In discussing the communist issue during the campaign I emphasized as I had in 1950 and 1952 that the question as far as our opponents were concerned was not one of loyalty but of judgment. On a number of occasions I categorically dissociated the administration from McCarthy's reckless charge that the Democratic Party was the party of treason. I said, "There is only one party of treason in the United States—the Communist Party."

Eisenhower spent the first month of the campaign at the Denver White House. After a few hours of work in the morning he would golf in the afternoon. He followed my travels and activities closely, and at the end of September he wrote me a very warm letter: "Good reports have been reaching me from all parts of the country as a result of your intensive—and I am sure exhaustive—speaking tour. . . . Please don't think that I am not unaware that I have done little to lighten your load. On the contrary, I am, in point of fact, constantly suggesting other places for you to visit. You will have to consider these burdens I impose upon you the penalty for being such an excellent and persuasive speaker. One thing that is coming out of this is that you are constantly becoming better and more favorably known to the American public. This is all to the good."

As Election Day neared, the polls showed that the Democrats and Republicans were almost evenly matched. The campaign became increasingly bitter. As my campaigning seemed to be particularly effective, Stevenson and other Democrats, led by DNC Chairman Stephen Mitchell, zeroed in on me with a barrage of attacks. In a mocking reference to my successful good will tour in the Far East in 1953, Stevenson called my campaigning an "ill will tour." Mitchell, less elegant than Stevenson, called me a liar. The Washington *Post* and half a dozen other Democratic papers charged that I had taken over McCarthy's tactics—Stevenson characterized my campaigning as "McCarthyism in a white collar." I counterattacked hard, accusing Stevenson of trying to dismiss serious charges with quips and adding that he had derisively made a "typically snide and snobbish innuendo toward the millions of Americans who work in our shops and factories."

I continued to campaign right up to the wire. In the seven weeks between September 15 and November 2, I flew nearly 26,000 miles to visit 95 cities in 30 states, campaigning on behalf of 186 House, Senate, and gubernatorial candidates. During the last three weeks of the campaign I slept no more than five hours a night.

A few days before the election, Eisenhower made one of the typically gracious gestures that bound people so closely to him. At a time when I was exhausted and more than a little frustrated that very few of the Republican leaders seemed to be working as hard to win this election as I was, a letter arrived from the White House.

October 27, 1954

Dear Dick:

Whenever my burdens tend to feel unduly heavy, I admire all the more the tremendous job you have done since the opening of the present campaign. You have personally carried a back-breaking load of hard, tedious, day by day and state by state campaigning. And in doing so you have been undismayed by problems of time, distance, and physical effort.

I know we share the urgent hope that there may be returned to the Congress a Republican majority that will work with the Executive Branch in completing the program that we believe is in the best interests of all America. No man could have done more effective work than you to further that hope. Whatever the outcome next Tuesday, I can find no words to express my deep appreciation of the contribution you have made toward that goal.

Please tell Pat, too, that she has aroused my admiration as an able campaigner; there is no question but that she is the most charming of the lot.

With warm regard,

As ever,
D. E.

Pat and I stayed home election night, November 2. We sat together in front of the fireplace, and for a while I got up every few minutes to take calls from the campaign headquarters at the Republican National Committee. The news was mixed, and about what I expected. We lost 16 seats in the House and 2 seats in the Senate. This was substantially less than the usual off-year election loss for the party in power: during the previous fifty years, the average loss had been 40 in the House and 4 in the Senate. However, historical comparisons were small comfort. The Democrats regained control of the House and Senate; and Eisenhower, despite his enormous personal popularity, had to deal with a Democratic Congress for the last six years of his presidency.

At the first Cabinet meeting after the election, most members who were new to politics were downcast. I said that the important thing was to learn from this experience so that we would not repeat our mistakes. I pointed out that while we had fielded many outstanding candidates, we had also put forward some notably unexceptional ones. "There were just too many turkeys running on the Republican ticket," I told the Cabinet.

Then I took a little wind-up toy drummer from my pocket, released the catch, and put it on the Cabinet table. Everyone watched, puzzled, as the little fellow picked out a zigzag course across the polished surface and the sharp sound of his drum filled the room. "Gentlemen," I said, "we should take a lesson from this: this is no time to be depressed, and we have got to keep beating the drum about our achievements." Eisenhower beamed.

The 1954 election raised some disturbing questions for me. It was clear that Eisenhower was going to maintain his President-of-all-the-people posture and that, as long as we were a team, it would be my job to do the hard partisan campaigning. The prospect of having to go through it all again in another two years was depressing. It was also clear that I was going to continue to be the prime target for the Democrats' attacks. Eisenhower's popularity was too great and his above-the-battle strategy too successful to make attacking him worthwhile. But I was out front, a target of opportunity, and the more effective I was as a campaigner, the more determined many of the Democrats and their supporters in the media became to clobber me.

Although the fund crisis had thickened my skin, I still resented being portrayed as a demagogue or a liar or as the sewer-dwelling denizen of Herblock cartoons in the Washington *Post*. As the attacks became more personal, I sometimes wondered where party loyalty left off and masochism began. The girls were reaching an impressionable age, and neither Pat nor I wanted their father to become the perennial bad guy of American politics.

During the last week of the 1954 campaign, when I was so tired that I could hardly remember what it felt like to be rested, I decided that this would be my last campaign. I began to think more and more about what Murray Chotiner had said almost two and a half years earlier at the convention in Chicago: I should pretty much be able to write my own ticket after retiring from the vice presidency at age forty-four. By the time I made a nationally televised broadcast on election eve, I had decided not to run again in 1956 unless exceptional circumstances intervened to change my mind.

On Election Day, as we flew back to Washington, I took out my briefcase. A folder on top contained the several pages of handwritten notes I had made for the election-eve broadcast. Chotiner was in the seat next to me, and I handed them to him. "Here's my last campaign speech, Murray," I said to him. "You might like to keep it as a souvenir. It's the last one, because after this I am through with politics."

THE HEART ATTACK

September 24, 1955, was a hot Indian summer day in Washington. Around 5:30, I sat down to look over the *Evening Star*, and I noted a small item from Denver on the front page that the President was suffering from a slight case of indigestion. This was not unusual for him, and I turned to the sports pages without giving it a second thought. I was looking over the baseball scores when the phone rang.

"Dick, this is Jim Hagerty," the familiar voice said. "I have some bad news—the President has had a coronary."

"Are they sure?" I asked.

"We are absolutely sure," Hagerty replied. He had no further information, and we agreed that he would call me again as soon as he learned anything more. At the end of the conversation he said, "Dick, let me know where you can be reached at all times."

For several minutes I sat motionless, absorbing the full impact of the news. Not only was I concerned about Eisenhower's health; I was going to have to think about my own conduct in an unprecedented national crisis.

I called Bill Rogers, who was Acting Attorney General while Herb Brownell was in Spain, and asked him if he could come over. Rogers arrived just ahead of the reporters and cameramen who had rushed to our house as soon as Eisenhower's heart attack was announced in Denver. We agreed that we should not let them know I was there. I thought it was important that I not be seen or quoted until I had more information from Denver.

Rogers suggested that I spend the night at his home. He called his wife to pick us up and asked her to park on a side street behind my house. Fifteen minutes later Adele Rogers drove up in her Pontiac convertible, and Bill and I slipped out the side door. We walked quickly through my neighbor's backyard and piled into the car.

The Rogers house was well off the main road in Bethesda, Maryland. As soon as we arrived, I put in a call to Denver.

For the first time I learned that the attack had been officially diagnosed as a "mild" coronary thrombosis. Chances for recovery were good, but it was still too early to be sure of anything. After long discussions with Rogers and Jerry Persons and telephone conversations with various Cabinet members, it was decided that we would continue carrying on the nation's business as a united team until Eisenhower was able to return to his duties.

As I lay awake that night, I considered my future course. Assuming the best—that Eisenhower would be back on the job within a few weeks

—it would be foolish for me to do anything that the press could in any way interpret as being self-serving. Assuming the worst—that Eisenhower died or was completely incapacitated—there would be no question about my succession to the presidency; and if that happened it would be even more important that my conduct beforehand be above question. In the most likely situation—that Eisenhower would not be able to return for several weeks or months and a determination would have to be made about my taking over some of his responsibilities—it was equally important that nothing I did made it appear that I was seeking his power.

I knew that there would be many attempts to drive a wedge between Sherman Adams and me. Adams, the powerful Assistant to the President who was the White House Chief of Staff, was known as Eisenhower's most devoted and selfless staff member. The rumor had even spread around Washington that Adams's first words when he arrived back at the White House were: "It's quite a surprise to come back here and suddenly find yourself the President."

By Sunday morning I knew that I could not avoid the press any longer. But a press conference might appear self-serving, so I decided to let the reporters accompany Pat and me to church and then invite some of them home afterward for an informal chat.

We settled down in the living room, and I told them the little I knew about Eisenhower's condition. I described the team system he had created and said that I expected it to function smoothly until his return.

The reporters, of course, were after hard news, not talk about team spirit. They were looking for a statement about the political implications of Eisenhower's illness. There had already been speculation about whether Eisenhower would run again in 1956. A Gallup poll at the beginning of September had shown him preferred by 61 percent of the voters when matched up against Stevenson. Another Gallup poll taken at about the same time indicated that if Eisenhower did not run, I was the first choice among Republicans for the presidential nomination. I politely but firmly refused any questions about the political significance of Eisenhower's illness.

On Monday night Sherman Adams, Len Hall, Jerry Persons, Hall's press aide Lou Guylay, Rogers, and I met at Rogers's house to discuss the political aspects of the situation. Adams sat slightly apart from the rest of us. Whenever a question was addressed to him, he launched into a description of the fishing in Scotland. Finally it became clear that either he was determined not to engage in any substantive discussion until he could get to Denver and see Eisenhower's condition for himself, or else he was in something close to a state of shock.

I said that our main task was to prevent any scramble for the presidential nomination, at least until Eisenhower recovered and had had a chance to express his feelings about running again. Earlier that day Len Hall had flatly told reporters who had cornered him that the 1956 Republican ticket would be the same winning one as in 1952: Ike and Dick. Despite that necessary public show of optimism, I do not think any of us in that room believed that Eisenhower would run again, even if he recovered completely.

During the next two weeks I presided over various meetings in the White House, including the regular Cabinet and National Security Council meetings. I sat in the Vice President's chair, opposite the President's, and I was careful to act more as moderator than director. I signed several ceremonial documents "in behalf of the President," but I continued to work out of my office at the Capitol rather than in the White House. During those weeks I made it a point to visit Cabinet members in their own offices whenever a meeting was necessary, rather than asking them to come to my office. Despite all my precautions along these lines, and despite my determination to have as little to do with the press as I reasonably could, one or two members of the Cabinet seemed to feel that I was seeking publicity.

On October 8, exactly two weeks after Eisenhower's heart attack, I flew to Denver to see him. I was the first official visitor; after my visit the Cabinet members saw him according to rank. I was startled to see how pale and thin he was. But it was immediately clear that his mind was as sharp as ever, and he was able to talk about his heart attack with great detachment, although he had obviously been through an ordeal. "It hurt like hell, Dick," he told me. "I never let Mamie know how much it hurt."

Forty-eight days after his heart attack Eisenhower flew back to Washington. Thousands of cheering people lined the downtown streets in the autumn sunshine to cheer him as he returned to the White House. The country seemed to breathe a sigh of relief. There was no more need to worry—Ike was back.

RUNNING FOR RE-ELECTION: 1956

Since the 1954 campaign I had been considering leaving politics. I knew that Pat wanted to return to California. The only thing that made me hesitate was the unexpected situation created by Eisenhower's heart attack. Whereas before I had assumed that he would run again in 1956, now I was not at all sure. If he did not, I would be the next in line for the presidential nomination. A Gallup presidential preference poll after Eisenhower's heart attack, based on the assumption he would not be a candidate, showed me leading Earl Warren, 28 percent to 24 percent, followed by Dewey and Stassen with 10 percent each.

On December 26, 1955, Eisenhower called me into the Oval Office. He said that he had been giving a lot of thought to the coming election, and he wondered whether I ought to run for Vice President again or whether I might do better to accept a Cabinet post instead. He said that a Cabinet position such as Secretary of Defense would give me the kind of administrative experience, so important for a President, that the vice presidency did not offer. He pointed out that Herbert Hoover had been able to use his position as Secretary of Commerce to build a national reputation and a successful candidacy.

I was taken aback by this suggestion, although he seemed to be making it in a friendly and sincere spirit. He said that he was disappointed that other suitable candidates for the presidency had not emerged from the party during the last few years, and he referred to some of Gallup's trial heats in which Stevenson beat me by a fairly wide margin. He said it was too bad that my popularity had not grown more during the last three years.

For the first time I began to understand what was behind this conversation. Eisenhower's staff or his friends had evidently been sowing doubts in his mind, suggesting not only that I might lose if I ran on my own, but that I might be a drag on the ticket if I were his running mate again. It was hard not to feel that I was being set up, since more recent polls than the ones he was referring to showed me doing considerably better.

A few weeks later we had another conversation which covered the same ground. Eisenhower once again expressed his opinion that my own political future would be better served by taking a Cabinet post than by running again for Vice President. He seemed to be expecting a reply, and for a moment I felt as if the clock had been turned back to the fund crisis, when he had paused on the telephone so that I could offer him my resignation from the ticket. I had the same reaction now: as Vice President, I fully accepted that I was his to choose or his to dismiss. But I did not feel that my getting off the ticket would be the best thing for him or for the party, and I was not going to offer to do so.

As in 1952, my silence put the ball back into Eisenhower's court. Finally I said, "If you believe your own candidacy and your administration would be better served with me off the ticket, you tell me what you want me to do and I'll do it. I want to do what is best for you."

"No, I think we've got to do what's best for you," he replied.

Any doubts about Eisenhower's motives were removed when Foster Dulles independently initiated the same discussion and suggested that I might be named Secretary of Defense or succeed him as Secretary of State when he resigned. I was sure that Dulles had my best interests at heart.

From the point of view of historical experience, there was considerable merit in Eisenhower's and Dulles's suggestion. But neither of them took into account the derogatory way the media would have interpreted such a course or how it would have upset the many Republicans who still considered me Eisenhower's principal link with party orthodoxy.

Eisenhower had made a remarkable physical recovery, and within a short time after his return to Washington he resumed his regular schedule. But, as with many who have suffered heart attacks, his brush with death left him subject to debilitating bouts of depression. He would sit immobile for long periods of time, brooding silently about the future. Mamie Eisenhower was especially insistent that her husband not run for re-election. Her arguments ranged from the highly emotional to the coldly logical.

By the end of January, however, Eisenhower had in fact reached a tentative decision to run, which was strengthened by an excellent medical report on February 14. I think he decided to run again for several reasons. As in 1952 he felt it was his duty to his country. Also, he could not abide the idea that Adlai Stevenson might be his successor, and he was not confident of the election of any other Republican. I believe too that Eisenhower had a desire to finish what he had begun. He had strong feelings about what the Republican Party should be, and he knew that he had not been able to accomplish much in this area during his first term. He would need another four years to leave a lasting imprint on the party and on the nation.

Eisenhower declared his intention to run at a press conference on February 29. He invited a small group to join him in the Oval Office that night for the televised speech he was going to make announcing his decision. Jim Hagerty, Len Hall, Jerry Persons, Milton Eisenhower, and I sat on the sofas in front of the fireplace while Eisenhower sat at the desk facing the camera. When he had finished we all shook hands, and he invited us up to the Family Quarters for a drink. "I'll need some moral support with Mrs. Ike," he said with a sheepish grin.

As we sat in the living room at the end of the West Hall, Eisenhower was in a strangely subdued mood. He was glad that the decision had finally been made and announced, but he did not relish the campaigning that would now begin or even the prospect of four more years of the burdens of the presidency. "At least," he said, "I can say that I have done my duty."

Eisenhower had gone through a difficult period reaching his decision, and he had enjoyed the drama of announcing it. But I think the reaction of the reporters took him by surprise. He immediately had to respond to a barrage of political questions, and the first one had to do with me.

> Q: Mr. President, since your answer is affirmative, would you again want Vice President Nixon as your running mate?
>
> A: As a matter of fact, I wouldn't mention the vice presidency in spite of my tremendous admiration for Mr. Nixon, for this reason: I believe it is traditional that the Vice President is not nominated until after a presidential candidate is nominated; so I think that we will have to wait to see who the Republican convention nominates, and then it will be proper to give an expression on that point.

Responding to a follow-up question, he added: "I will say nothing more about it. I have said that my admiration and my respect for Vice President Nixon is unbounded. He has been for me a loyal and dedicated associate, and a successful one. I am very fond of him, but I am going to say no more about it."

I think that once the question was raised, Eisenhower had three basic reactions to having me as his running mate in 1956. First, his rule of thumb for making all political judgments was understandably never to do anything that would adversely affect his own chances of winning.

Second, while Eisenhower believed that he owed me the loyalty due a staunch and hard-working subordinate, and while he knew that I had supported him in situations that had clearly been against my own political interests, he did not feel that this loyalty required any special future commitment as far as the vice presidency was concerned.

Third, Eisenhower was used to the military system, in which men advanced by taking on the next toughest job and doing it well. He did not think in terms of grooming a successor or having a protégé—that was alien to the general-staff concept that everyone should serve the commanding general with equally unselfish fervor. When Eisenhower said that other candidates would be equally acceptable to him, he meant precisely that.

Further evidence of White House staff intrigue came when *Newsweek* reported Eisenhower's suggestion that I take a Cabinet position. I never could positively trace the source of the story, but it had come from a

White House insider. It was hard to believe that something so sensitive could leak without Eisenhower's approval. And if Eisenhower had approved the leak, perhaps I had been misreading him all along—perhaps he *was* determined to get me off the ticket and could not understand why I had not taken the hint.

The first question at Eisenhower's next news conference on March 7 concerned this *Newsweek* story.

> Q: Mr. President, there have been some published reports that some of your advisers are urging you to dump Vice President Nixon from the Republican ticket this year; and, secondly, that you yourself have suggested to Mr. Nixon that he consider standing aside this time and, perhaps, take a Cabinet post. Can you tell us whether there is anything to those reports?
>
> A: Well, now, as to the first one, I will promise you this much: if anyone ever has the effrontery to come in and urge me to dump somebody that I respect as I do Vice President Nixon, there will be more commotion around my office than you have noticed yet.
>
> Second, I have not presumed to tell the Vice President what he should do with his own future. . . .
>
> The only thing I have asked him to do is to chart out his own course, and tell me what he would like to do. I have never gone beyond that.

"Chart out his own course" immediately became a catchphrase for the columnists during the next several weeks. Everyone had his own interpretation of what Eisenhower meant, but it was generally taken to indicate varying degrees of indifference toward me, or even an attempt to put some distance between us.

By this time my disillusionment with the way Eisenhower was handling the matter and my lack of a burning desire to be Vice President began to affect my own attitude. After Eisenhower's press conference, I took a page of notepaper and drafted an announcement that I would not be a candidate in 1956. I mentioned it to Vic Johnston, the chief of staff of the Senatorial Campaign Committee, when he was in my office later that afternoon. Within a few hours, he was back with Len Hall and Jerry Persons. They said that if I announced I was withdrawing, the Republican Party would be split in two.

I said that it just is not possible in politics for a Vice President to "chart out his own course," and that if Eisenhower did not want me on the ticket I was damned if I was going to fight to stay on it. "It's up to him if he wants me," I said. "I can only assume that if he puts it this way, this must be his way of saying he'd prefer someone else."

Len Hall tried to calm me down. "That's not what he meant at all," he said. "Damn it, Dick, you and I have talked about this a hundred times if we've talked about it once. We all know that if this was anyone else it'd be different. But this is Ike, and you can't apply the kind of politically sophisticated standards to him that you do to anybody else."

I agreed to withhold any announcement for at least a few weeks. I later found out that about this same time Eisenhower himself had become unhappy with the way the story had developed and held several meetings in an effort to decide what he should do. Charlie Jones, president of Richfield Oil, told me about a small stag dinner at the White House during this period at which Eisenhower raised the question of the vice presidency. Some of the guests said that they thought he should make a change. They argued that if there was any possibility that I might lose Eisenhower any votes he should drop me like a hot potato. Jones was Eisenhower's contemporary and had been his friend for many years; he was one of the few who still called him Ike. After my critics had had their say, Jones looked across the table and said, "Ike, what in the hell does a man have to do to get your support? Dick Nixon has done everything you asked him to do. He has taken on the hard jobs that many of your other associates have run away from. For you not to support him now would be the most ungrateful thing that I can possibly think of."

On March 13, the first primary election of the 1956 campaign was held in New Hampshire.

That night Pat and I were having dinner with Alice Longworth. When we arrived at her big Victorian house on Massachusetts Avenue, she met us at the top of the stairs and said, "Have you been listening to the radio? There is a write-in for you in New Hampshire."

Mrs. Longworth could never resist anything political, and we were rushed through dinner. As we sipped coffee and listened to the radio in her drawing room filled with animal skins and photographs and other mementos of her father, I learned that my write-in vote was the big story of the New Hampshire primary.

Eisenhower could be well satisfied with the 56,464 voters who had gone out to mark the box next to his name on the ballot. But the big surprise was that almost 23,000 voters had written in my name on their ballots. I was elated, and I wondered what effect the news would have on the President.

When Eisenhower was asked about the New Hampshire results at his next press conference, he inched as near to an outright endorsement as he possibly could.

> Well, I will make this comment: apparently there are lots of people in New Hampshire that agree with what I have told you about Dick Nixon. . . .
>
> Anyone who attempts to drive a wedge of any kind between Dick Nixon

> and me has just as much chance as if he tried to drive it between my brother and me. . . .
>
> I want to say again what I said last week or a week before; I will say it in exactly the terms I mean: I am very happy that Dick Nixon is my friend. I am very happy to have him as an associate in government. I would be happy to be on any political ticket in which I was a candidate with him.
>
> Now, if those words aren't plain, then it is merely because people can't understand the plain unvarnished truth.
>
> I have nothing further to add.

Then, midway through a news conference on April 25, Eisenhower was asked, "Some time ago, Mr. President, you told us that you had asked Vice President Nixon to chart his own course and then report back to you. Has he done this?" Eisenhower replied, "Well, he hasn't reported back in the terms in which I used the expression that morning, no."

When I heard about this exchange, I knew the time had come to act. The more I thought about it, the more I was convinced that I could not get off the ticket without hurting Eisenhower more than helping him. I knew there would be no way to explain my leaving the ticket that would convince large numbers of party workers that I had not been dumped. These people were more my constituency than Eisenhower's and if they felt I had been treated badly they might decide to sit out the election.

Eisenhower had learned a great deal about politics since 1952, but he still did not like or understand those he called the "conservative party hacks" in Congress and in local Republican organizations throughout the country. He felt that they had no other place to go. But Eisenhower needed more than just their votes. He needed their wholehearted organizational support.

I disagreed with the premise that Eisenhower could pick up substantial votes from Democrats and independents by dropping me. Eisenhower now had a four-year record to run on and, particularly on economic, foreign policy, and internal security issues, that record was basically conservative. Stevenson would be the choice of liberals who preferred a softer line.

Early the next morning, April 26, I called the White House and said that I would like to see the President. That afternoon I sat across the desk from him in the Oval Office. "Mr. President," I said, "I would be honored to continue as Vice President under you. The only reason I waited this long to tell you was that I didn't want to do anything that would make you think I was trying to force my way onto the ticket if you didn't want me on it."

Eisenhower said that he was glad I felt that way and that he had wondered why I had taken so long to say so. He picked up the phone and asked for Jim Hagerty.

"Dick has just told me that he'll stay on the ticket," he told Hagerty. "Why don't you take him out right now and let him tell the reporters himself. And," he added, "you can tell them that I'm delighted by the news."

Eisenhower's imprimatur was enough to silence my potential opposition and bring his own White House staff in line—at least temporarily. Three weeks later, I received another unexpected boost when 32,878 voters wrote in my name on their ballots in the Oregon primary.

With the question of the ticket apparently settled, I expected smooth sailing until the convention. But a few weeks later Eisenhower was in the hospital being operated on for ileitis, and the whole question of his candidacy was superseded by concern about whether he would be able to complete his first term.

Jim Hagerty called me just before the operation began at about 2:30 A.M. on June 8. He told me that the President had just been put under anesthetic. "I know that this is really an unnecessary precaution," he said, "but I knew you would want to be ready in the unlikely case that any crisis arises in the next few hours, or, God forbid, that anything goes wrong with the operation."

Eisenhower recovered from the operation so quickly that there was never much doubt that he could complete his term. But the confidence that had grown up since his recovery from the heart attack was dealt a serious blow, and once again there was speculation about his running in November. Doubt rekindled presidential aspirations in some Republican breasts, and the fact that an eleventh-hour decision by Eisenhower not to run would make me the front-runner for the nomination resurrected the desire to "dump Nixon."

In the summer of 1956 Harold Stassen was at the height of his public stature as Eisenhower's "Secretary of Peace." As the President's Cabinet-level Adviser on Disarmament, Stassen was prominent and popular because of his conduct of the delicate Geneva disarmament talks with the Soviets.

Stassen had been among the first to call me in the days immediately following Eisenhower's heart attack the previous September pledging his support for the presidential nomination. But on July 20, 1956, he told Eisenhower that he had commissioned a private poll that showed I would lose more votes for Eisenhower than many other possible running mates, most particularly Governor Christian Herter of Massachusetts. Stassen thought Herter should be Eisenhower's running mate. Eisenhower later said that he found this proposal "astonishing"—not least because he knew that a week earlier Len Hall and Jim Hagerty had received a tentative agreement from Herter to place *my* name in nomination at the convention.

Eisenhower told Stassen that he was not going to dictate to the convention. Stassen asked if Eisenhower would mind if he tried to convince me to withdraw. "You are an American citizen, Harold," Eisenhower said, "and you are free to follow your own judgment in such matters."

Stassen thanked Eisenhower and left the White House. He called some of his supporters and told them that Eisenhower had said he supported an open convention. He then called Herter and told him that the President had been very interested in what he had to say and had authorized him to talk to Len Hall and me and to give us the benefit of his conclusions about the vice presidency. Stassen was clearly doing his best to edge all of us—Eisenhower, Herter, and me—to a confrontation. Three days later, on Monday, July 23, I received a letter from Stassen. In it he said: "I have concluded that I should do what I can to nominate Governor Chris Herter for Vice President at the coming convention. I sincerely hope that after careful reflection during the coming weeks you will conclude to join in supporting Chris Herter."

That afternoon Stassen called a press conference and announced his support for Herter's candidacy. Many supporters urged me to shrug off Stassen's effort as a clownish and transparent power play. But I knew that Stassen was a clever man and, except when blinded by ambition, a very able one. My concern was that if Stassen managed to raise doubts among the convention delegates in San Francisco about what Eisenhower really wanted, he might be able to create the kind of dangerously fluid situation in which the convention could be stampeded before the delegates realized what was happening. There were several potential vice presidential candidates eagerly waiting in the wings for just such a situation.

Eisenhower had left for an official visit to Panama immediately after his meeting with Stassen. He was furious when Stassen's press conference knocked his trip out of the headlines, and he authorized a curt statement: "The President pointed out to Mr. Stassen that, while he had every right as an individual to make any statement he so desired, it was also equally obvious that he could not make such a statement as a member of the President's official family." A few days later Sherman Adams informed Stassen that he would have to take a leave of absence from the White House staff if he intended to pursue his present course.

When Eisenhower arrived back in Washington things moved quickly. Herter called Sherman Adams to find out Eisenhower's real opinion of what had been happening. Adams told him that Eisenhower held him in very high esteem. If he wished to be a vice presidential candidate, that would be a matter of his own choosing, although Eisenhower had expected that in a second term he might be able to help in the international field and had already talked to Dulles about this possibility. That would not be possible, however, if Herter decided to run for Vice President. Herter said that he thought he would continue with his plans as they had stood prior to Stassen's press conference and arrange to place my name in nomination. He thought that would cut off any further attempts to make him Vice President.

Adams replied, "All right, let's consider it settled that way," and the Stassen bubble was burst less than twenty-four hours after it surfaced.

Herter telephoned Hall to tell him that he would nominate me, and Hall informed me of the news. Stassen was undeterred. He blithely told a press conference that the fact that Herter had been asked to nominate me was itself a confirmation of his very strong standing in the party. The next morning Herter held a press conference in Boston and formally endorsed me for the nomination.

On August 22, the day on which the convention was to select the vice presidential nominee, Stassen arrived at Eisenhower's suite at the St. Francis Hotel for an appointment with the President. He found himself confronted by Len Hall and Sherman Adams. Stassen produced a letter he planned to discuss with Eisenhower. It was an ultimatum addressed to Hall as Republican National Chairman, demanding that the nomination for Vice President be postponed until the next day.

Adams told Stassen that he could see Eisenhower only if he agreed beforehand to second my nomination and limit his conversation to informing the President of his agreement. Stassen finally seemed to get the message and agreed to accept these terms. Immediately after their meeting, Eisenhower held a televised news conference to announce: "Mr. Stassen called to see me a few minutes ago. . . . He said this morning that after several days here, he had become absolutely convinced that the majority of the delegates want Mr. Nixon. . . . He thought in order to get his own position clear before the convention and the American public, he was going to ask the convention chairman for permission this afternoon to second . . . the nomination of the Vice President, Mr. Nixon, for renomination."

While Eisenhower was making his announcement in San Francisco, I was four hundred miles away in Whittier. Early that morning I had learned that my father had suffered a ruptured abdominal artery and was not expected to live. He had rallied a little by the time we got to Whittier, and I was able to talk with him even though he was in great pain and in an oxygen tent. He said that he was feeling much better and insisted that I get back to San Francisco. Flashes of his old temper broke through the pain and medication as he said, "You get back there, Dick, and don't let that Stassen pull any more last-minute funny business on you."

That afternoon I watched the convention on TV in my parents' living room and saw Chris Herter place my name in nomination. Half an hour later the curtain finally came down on the "dump Nixon" movement when I was renominated by a vote of 1,323 to 1.

The following morning the doctor said my father was much better; he was certain the thrill that came with my renomination was a major factor in his improvement. When I suggested canceling my acceptance speech to stay with him, he practically blew his top. So Pat and I returned to San Francisco and that afternoon, with some valuable help from my old friend Father John Cronin, I finished my acceptance speech just minutes before we had to leave for the convention hall.

We returned to Washington after the convention, but a few days later I was called back to California because of my father's illness. The doctor told me that it was only his determination to see me defeat Stassen and be renominated that had kept him alive this long. Now his condition was rapidly worsening. He knew that the end was near, so he gave my mother instructions for his funeral and asked to be allowed to die at home rather than in the hospital. He died at 8:25 P.M. on September 4, 1956.

After the drama of the preliminaries, most of the 1956 campaign was relatively tame. Eisenhower invited several hundred party leaders to a picnic at his farm in Gettysburg to kick off the campaign. Stevenson had already opened his with a stinging attack on the Eisenhower administration as a "ruthless" government "with a false front." Eisenhower, always thin-skinned about criticism and especially resentful of Stevenson, was furious and wanted to hit back. He phoned me on the morning of the picnic, and my note of our conversation shows the way he worked when he wanted something political done:

> The President called me this morning and he said, "Look, you are going to speak up there at Gettysburg today."
>
> He said, "Of course, everybody is now noting that you are talking the new high level. However, I think today you ought to take notice of some of these attacks that have been made on the administration and on me." He said, "I think that when Stevenson calls this administration racketeers and rascals, when they say we are heartless in dealing with the problems of the people and

> the problems of the farmers, when they say we have no peace and no prosperity, I want them to be called on it. I would like for you to do so and if you have to praise me that will be okay. I, of course, will be a little embarrassed by that but I know you have to do it to answer. I suggest something along the lines: Do you want to go back to war in order to have prosperity under the Democrats? After all, there were 9 million unemployed in 1939 before World War II, and also a great number before the Korean war.
>
> I told him I agreed that Stevenson was swinging very wildly. He said, "Of course, it isn't necessary to attack him personally but we should point out that he is wrong."
>
> I then talked to Brownell and he said, "I don't think we could win with a so-called high level campaign. It has to be fair but you have to take the opposition on. It has to be hard-hitting."

There was warm sunshine that afternoon as Eisenhower played host at his farm. Everyone gathered in a big tent set up on the lawn for the speeches. I followed Eisenhower's instructions and sank some solid barbs into Stevenson and the Democrats. Then he got up and began his speech by praising me. He said: "There is no man in the history of America who has had such a careful preparation as has Vice President Nixon for carrying out the duties of the presidency, if that duty should ever fall upon him."

Eisenhower came out to National Airport on the morning of September 18 to see Pat and me off on our first campaign swing. He said that this campaign should be based on the administration's record, and that there was no need to indulge in "the exaggerations of partisan political talk." In 1948 Harry Truman had campaigned to cries of "Give 'em hell." Eisenhower's parting admonition in 1956 was, "Give 'em heaven."

I followed this advice for the first two days of the campaign. The press corps was stupefied, and the Republican audiences disappointed, when I delivered serious, low-key speeches without any of the tough campaign rhetoric both groups looked forward to hearing from me. As Stevenson's attacks on Eisenhower and me grew increasingly shrill and irresponsible, I knew that it was only a matter of time before I would have to go on the offensive against him.

We arrived in Eugene, Oregon, for a big rally, and I gave my "give 'em heaven" speech. Once again I could tell that the audience felt let down. It was midnight before I went to bed, but I couldn't get to sleep. Around 5:30 in the morning I got out of bed and went into the living room of our suite to work on some hard-hitting additions to my basic speech. Suddenly I felt as if a great weight had been lifted from me. I had not realized how frustrating it had been to suppress the normal partisan instincts and campaign with one arm tied behind my back while Stevenson bombarded us with malicious ridicule and wild charges. I went over to the grand piano in one corner of the suite and began playing Brahms's Rhapsody in G. I had just launched into Sinding's "Rustle of Spring" when Pat came in and said, "What on earth are you doing? Dick, you'll wake up the whole hotel—it isn't even 7:30 yet."

My new speech delighted audiences, and for the first time the campaign began to catch fire.

The underlying issue of the campaign was still Eisenhower's health and the fact that if anything happened to him I would become President. From the start I came under intense and bitter fire. Describing the Democratic National Convention in Chicago in August, *Newsweek* stated:

> From the opening crack of the gavel in Chicago until the last lusty cheer echoed and died, Nixon was the target. Speakers pronounced his name with a sneer, as though it were an obscene epithet. He was attacked as "the vice-hatchet man," "the White House pet midget," a traveler of "the low road." . . . In attacking Nixon, the Democrats, in effect, were asking: "Do you want a man like this in the White House? Remember, he'll be President if you re-elect Mr. Eisenhower and Ike dies."

Stevenson had told the delegates: "The American people have the solemn obligation to consider with the utmost care who will be their President if the elected President is prevented by a higher will from serving his full term."

He pointed out that seven of our Presidents had come into office "as a result of such an indirect selection." He pulled out all stops in a speech in Flint, Michigan, on October 17:

> There is no man who can safely say he knows where the Vice President stands. This is a man of many masks. Who can say they have seen his real face? . . .
>
> In these critical days, America cannot afford the risk of having a President or a Vice President who treats a tragic war as an occasion for political demagoguery, and who spreads ill will instead of good will abroad.

He described the vice presidency as "this nation's life insurance policy," and he concluded that the election of the Eisenhower–Nixon ticket would mean that the nation would "go for four years uninsured."

On October 4, I made a nationwide television broadcast answering questions piped in live from newsmen in eight cities. This experiment proved so successful that I used the televised question-and-answer format in every election campaign until 1972.

Even though television was beginning to come into its own as a campaign tool —by 1956, 73 percent of American homes had a television set —we still mounted an old-fashioned down-to-the-wire effort that was as physically punishing as all the others had been. Pat and I made three cross-country campaign sweeps in a chartered plane. Because I was carrying the main load of campaigning for the administration, and because I myself was an issue in the campaign, I was accompanied by the largest press contingent ever assigned to a vice presidential candidate. I held at least one and sometimes two press conferences every working day. The New York *Times* reported that I was "adroitly . . . running a campaign that has to be seen to be believed."

From the start of the campaign, the polls had fairly consistently shown Eisenhower and me ahead. In the final days and even hours of the campaign, three foreign crises erupted that effectively finished off what few hopes of winning Stevenson might have had. The American people rally around the President in times of international crisis, and this was no exception. On October 19 a brief revolt broke out in Communist Poland, and on October 23 the Hungarian rebellion began in Budapest and quickly spread through the country before Soviet troops rolled in to crush it. I called Nikita Khrushchev the "Butcher of Budapest"—a sobriquet that stuck and was repeated around the world. Then, on October 29, Israel invaded Egypt after several months of dispute over access to the Suez Canal. On November 5, the day before our election, British and French paratroops landed in Egypt to support the Israeli invasion and to protect their own rights there.

Eisenhower and Dulles put heavy public pressure on Britain, France, and Israel to withdraw their forces from Suez. In retrospect I believe that our actions were a serious mistake. Nasser became even more rash and aggressive than before, and the seeds of another Mideast war were planted. The most tragic result was that Britain and France were so humiliated and discouraged by the Suez crisis that they lost the will to play a major role on the world scene. From this time forward the United States would by necessity be forced to "go it alone" in the foreign policy leadership of the free world. I have often felt that if the Suez crisis had not arisen during the heat of a presidential election campaign a different decision would have been made.

Stevenson made a desperate election-eve speech, going even further than he had before, bluntly reminding the voters that, because of Eisenhower's health, his election would probably mean voting me into the White House:

> Distasteful as this matter is, I must say bluntly that every piece of scientific evidence we have, every lesson of history and experience, indicates that a Republican victory tomorrow would mean that Richard M. Nixon probably would be President of this country within the next four years. . . .
>
> Distasteful as it is, this is the truth, the central truth, about the most fateful decision that American people have to make tomorrow.
>
> I have confidence in that decision.

Many considered this a crude and tasteless appeal, and it probably lost Stevenson more support than it gained. When the votes were counted the next night, the Eisenhower–Nixon ticket won 57 percent of the vote, carrying forty-one of the forty-eight states.

On election night Pat and I joined the Eisenhowers at a victory celebration at the Sheraton-Park Hotel. I had rarely seen Eisenhower in higher spirits; he was genuinely elated at what looked like a real landslide from the moment the first fragmentary returns started coming in. By the time the returns from the Midwest were tallied, however, it was clear that Eisenhower's personal victory was not going to spill over into the state or congressional races. Despite one of the biggest landslides in presidential history, Eisenhower was the first President in 108 years who could not carry at least one house of Congress for his party.

Eisenhower simply could not understand how this could happen, just as I found it difficult to understand when it happened to me in 1972. He became more and more subdued as we sat there slowly sipping highballs and watching television for the latest returns. "You know why this is happening, Dick?" he said. "It's all those damned mossbacks and hardshell conservatives we've got in the party. I think that what we need is a new party."

This was not the first time that Eisenhower had blamed the conservatives for the party's problems. In many cases he was justified in being exasperated and annoyed by the splits within the party; in others, he lacked the tolerance for diversity that someone more schooled in politics would have had. Eisenhower's thoughts turned to the crowd waiting for us in the ballroom below and he said, "You know, I think I will talk to them about Modern Republicanism." "Modern Republicanism" was a popular phrase at that time, particularly in the press, for the kind of liberalism that commentators described as the antithesis of Taftite conservatism.

I thought it would be a mistake for Eisenhower to talk about as controversial a party issue as Modern Republicanism on an occasion like this and risk offending the party regulars downstairs and across the country. But I also knew that Eisenhower would say whatever he wanted.

Stevenson conceded at about 1:30 A.M., and Eisenhower went downstairs and said that his victory was a victory for Modern Republicanism. As I had feared, many party regulars took these words either as a boast that he had won the victory by himself, or as a threat that those within the party who did not share his views would gradually be replaced by those who did. There was just enough truth in both interpretations to start the second term off on a slightly sour note in some Republican circles.

A few days before the end of the year I received a letter from the White House.

> Dear Dick:
>
> As both 1956 and our first administration draw to a close, I want to tell you, in a personal letter, what I have so often expressed publicly. In these last four years you have brought to the office of the Vice President a real stature that formerly it had not known; you have proved yourself an able and popular "Ambassador" to our friends in many other parts of the world; and you have worked tirelessly and effectively to interpret to the people of America—and to forward—the policies of the administration. For all of this I am personally indebted to you, and gratified that you have so capably filled all of my expectations.
>
> Also—somewhat to my chagrin—I find that while I have thanked what seem to be thousands of people from Maine to California for their help in the political campaign, I have never expressed my appreciation to you for carrying the brunt of the state-by-state effort. I know you were rewarded as, of course, I could not fail to be, by the verdict of the voters. But I do want to express to you, and to your loyal and overworked staff, my tremendous gratitude for all that you did to bring about the final result.
>
> With affectionate regard to Pat and the children, and, as always, my best to yourself,
>
> As ever,
> Dwight Eisenhower

OPERATION MERCY

The Hungarian uprising of 1956 captured the sympathy of the American people. In November and December 1956, after crushing the last flickers of rebellion, the Soviets reimposed their brutal and oppressive control over the Hungarian people. Many tried to escape across the border into Austria, and, to the great embarrassment of the determinedly neutral Austrian government, the number of refugees soon reached several thousand a day.

The Soviets and their Hungarian puppets accused the United States of having provoked the uprising by assuring the Hungarian rebels that we would aid them if they revolted against their government. Much to our dismay and embarrassment some of the freedom fighters seemed to agree. They blamed us for first encouraging them to revolt and then sitting back while the Soviets cut them down.

On December 13, Eisenhower called me back to Washington from a brief pre-Christmas holiday Pat and I were taking in New York and asked me to meet with Dulles to discuss some ideas they had about this problem. Eisenhower had offered asylum to 21,500 of the more than 100,000 refugees who had already escaped to Austria, and more were pouring over the borders each day. This had not been a particularly popular decision. There was considerable opposition in Congress to letting in any refugees at a time of domestic unemployment, and public opinion was not yet strongly committed to the humanitarian aspects of the situation. Because Eisenhower had acted under temporary provisions of the existing law, he wanted more permanent legislation to handle the refugee question. He also hoped more would be permitted to enter the United States.

Dulles said that Eisenhower wanted me to lead an emergency mission to Austria that would focus national attention on the plight of the refugees. Then, when I returned, I could prepare a report that could be used to buttress the case for new legislation. My mission would be called Operation Mercy.

Partly from fear that an embarrassing diplomatic incident might develop and partly because of their characteristic desire for orderliness, the Austrians pretty much sanitized my scheduled visit to the refugee camp at the frontier town of Andau. I met a few refugees, but most of the people I talked to were Austrian or Red Cross officials.

That night the Austrian government gave a dinner in my honor. When we returned to the American Embassy, I told our ambassador, Llewellyn "Tommy" Thompson, that I wanted to go to the border and get a real look at what was happening there. Thompson arranged for a car, and, together with Bill Rogers, Congressman Bob Wilson of California, and Bob King, my administrative assistant, I went back to Andau.

In the bleak refugee center at the border we saw the real agony and the heroism of the Hungarian freedom fighters.

Some of those who had just escaped that night were university students who spoke English, and they told us about the suffering that was still going on in Budapest and throughout Hungary.

"Do you feel that the Voice of America and Radio Free Europe played a part in encouraging the revolution?" I asked. Looks of surprise came over their faces as my deliberately undiplomatic question was translated. One of them blurted out the answer—"Yes."

I was later told that that simple exchange broke the ice and convinced the refugees that I wasn't going to try to sweep their situation under the carpet.

One of the refugee leaders told me that many people escaped through the deep forests that covered the border for some miles to the north. Once across, the refugees would wait in the barn of some friendly farmer until they could be brought to the refugee center. He asked me if I would like to go along while they picked up that night's "crop," as he called it. I said that I would; he smiled and said, "Well, sir, you will have to travel the way we do."

I climbed into the back of a large hay wagon coupled to a tractor. We left the lights of the refugee center behind, following the winding road that ran between the forest on one side and the farms on the other. At one farm, we picked up a young man who said he had hidden for three days before he had finally made a dash across the border about five hours before.

It was after six o'clock in the morning by the time we got back to the center, and I could only say some hasty farewells before the long drive back to Vienna. After a quick shower and change at the ambassador's residence, I was only a few minutes late for a nine o'clock meeting.

I returned to Washington on Christmas Eve, and by working through the holiday I was able to submit my report to Eisenhower on New Year's Day.

I urged that the McCarran–Walter Act regulating immigration be amended so that we could make a flexible response to this situation. I said that it would not be wise or realistic to tie ourselves down to either a fixed number of refugees or a fixed percentage of the total number. "I believe that the countries which accept these refugees will find that rather than having assumed a liability, they have acquired a valuable national asset," I wrote. I was disappointed by the hardhearted attitude many Americans seemed to have toward the Hungarian refugees. I felt the same way when there was similar resistance to the Cuban refugees in 1959 and to the Vietnamese refugees in 1975.

When I reflect on the Hungarian uprising of 1956, and the Czechoslovakian rebellion of 1968, I still feel an utter hopelessness about what we can do to help the people in the Communist countries of Central and Eastern Europe. The combined realities of their geographic position and the difficulty of arranging the kind of joint military operation with our European allies that would be required to be effective mean that we simply cannot and will not use our armed forces in the event that they engage in open rebellion against their Communist dictators. Consequently, it is irresponsible to urge them to armed rebellion, raising their hopes and encouraging them to risk their lives without any prospect of assistance from us. But I do not feel that it is an acceptable alternative to slam down the Iron Curtain and accept the idea that they are destined to live forever under Communist rule.

Peaceful change is the only practicable answer. Admittedly it is not a very satisfactory one because such change could take a generation, maybe even a century. In the meantime we must seize every opportunity that may arise to increase contact and communication with the people of these countries so that they will know we share their hopes for a better and freer life.

THE PRESIDENT'S STROKE

On November 25, 1957, I received a terse phone call from Sherman Adams, asking me to come to the White House right away.

As soon as the door closed behind us he said, "The President has suffered a stroke."

We were silent for a moment. "How serious is his condition?" I asked.

"We'll know more in the morning," he replied. "Right now he's more confused and disoriented than anything else. It will take a few days before the doctors can assess the damage. This is a terribly, terribly difficult thing to handle," Adams said. "You may be President in twenty-four hours."

In fact, the stroke had been relatively mild. Eisenhower's ability to read, write, and reason had suffered no damage, and the only aftereffect was an occasional hesitancy in finding the right word, an impairment about which he was painfully self-conscious but that was scarcely noticeable to others. He made a point in public of appearing to be in complete control, but those of us who saw him in private caught occasional glimpses of the serious psychological effect the stroke had on him. He was depressed by the fear that he could no longer bring to the presidency the physical or mental qualities it required, and this was a serious blow to his morale. "This is the end," he said when he first heard the diagnosis. "Mamie and I are farmers from now on."

He was deeply disturbed by some of the press coverage of his condition during his recovery, especially references to occasional misspoken words. He did have some difficulty in speaking at times but by iron discipline and will power he overcame it. Some editorial writers and columnists even suggested he should resign or delegate interim powers to me—much as they recoiled at the idea of my succeeding him in office.

One day when he seemed particularly depressed by these attacks, I told him that he should consider the source and ignore them. The most important point, I reminded him, was that there was nothing the matter with his brain. "The trouble with most politicians is that their mouths move faster than their brains. With you it is the other way around."

This broke the tension, and he laughed more heartily than I had heard him laugh for weeks.

I had always felt that Eisenhower could cut down considerably on his workload without neglecting his essential duties. I told him there was no reason that individual Cabinet officers should not make more decisions on their own, particularly domestic ones. Eisenhower agreed, but he was sensitive about taking any step that might be interpreted as an admission that he could no longer handle the full job. Within a few months he was again attending every meeting and allowing the discussions to ramble on as if it were his duty to be bored for his country as well as to lead it.

An important result of his stroke was the procedure that Eisenhower established in case of any future debilitating illness during his term. When Congress took no action to fill the constitutional void with regard to presidential disability, Bill Rogers, Foster Dulles, and I worked with Eisenhower to develop a plan that would suffice at least for the balance of his administration. Eisenhower personally drafted and sent to me a letter setting forth the procedures to be followed. The entire determination of fitness was to be made by the President and Vice President. If during some future illness Eisenhower concluded that he could no longer perform his duties, he would tell me and I would then become acting President with full authority until he decided he was able to resume his duties. If he were incapable of making or expressing a decision, I was to act on my own authority after appropriate consultation and serve as acting President until such time as he decided he was sufficiently recovered to resume. This plan was no substitute for a permanent constitutional solution, but it was a workable arrangement, which, fortunately, never had to be put to the test. Kennedy wrote a similar letter to Lyndon Johnson before his inauguration.

This issue was formally settled by the adoption in 1967 of the Twenty-fifth Amendment to the Constitution.

SOUTH AMERICA: 1958

In the spring of 1958 I could already see the November elections shaping up as a disaster. Secretary of Labor Jim Mitchell and I were desperately—and unsuccessfully—trying to talk our colleagues in the Cabinet into a job-stimulating tax cut that would get the economy moving again and possibly help Republican chances. Therefore I was not enthusiastic when Assistant Secretary of State Roy Rubottom, Jr., asked me in early March if I would consider heading our official delegation to the inauguration of the new President of Argentina, Arturo Frondizi. The dictator Juan Perón had been overthrown in 1955, and Frondizi was the winner of Argentina's first free elections in twenty years.

I said that I could not take on another foreign trip at that time, but in the next few days both Dulles and Eisenhower made it clear that they felt it was important for me to go, and I had little choice but to agree. Rubottom immediately began lobbying for one or two extra stops, and by the end of the week, the itinerary included every country in South America except Brazil, where I had represented Eisenhower at the inauguration of President Kubitschek in 1956, and Chile, whose President was to have been in Washington on a state visit at the time I would have been in Chile.

The CIA had warned that although the Communist Party had been officially suppressed in most South American countries, I might have to face occasional demonstrators; but I expected the trip to be so uneventful that I advised several reporters not to bother coming with us.

In Montevideo, Uruguay, our first stop, the crowds were warm and friendly; only a few hecklers displayed signs as we drove past the University of the Republic. Later in the visit I arranged an unscheduled stop at the University. I walked through the campus, shaking hands and answering questions. When several communist students tried to interrupt me, they were shouted down by the rest, and I left amid cheers.

Ambassador Robert Woodward told me that this brief stop had been a tremendous success. He said that South Americans above all have contempt for fear or timidity and admire courage and the dramatic gesture.

We received warm receptions from the people in Argentina, Paraguay, and Bolivia. By the time we reached Peru, it was clear that the communists would have to resort to more extreme tactics if they were to succeed in spoiling the trip.

They did. When we got back to our Lima hotel after lunch with President Manuel Prado, there was a large crowd in front, obviously less than friendly and more than curious. The whistles and catcalls were loud and menacing. It was clear that the demonstrations were entering a more dangerous phase.

The next day's schedule included a visit to the old and distinguished San Marcos University. The communists had openly boasted that they would prevent me from going there, and both the rector of the university and the chief of police had let it be known that they hoped we would cancel the visit. Most of our embassy officials felt that I should cancel rather than risk an incident that might have a serious effect on our relations with Peru.

I said that I would call it off only if the rector or the chief of police issued a statement requesting me to do so. An embassy staff member made some phone calls and returned to inform us that the rector was afraid the communist students might blame him for depriving them of the incident they were hoping to provoke, and the chief of police did not want to run the risk of being charged with inability to maintain order. We consulted with several Peruvian government leaders. Each wanted the visit canceled, but none would take the responsibility for canceling it.

My administrative assistant, Bill Key, proposed an alternate solution. He suggested that, instead of going to San Marcos, I visit Lima's Catholic University, where the students were much more responsible and disciplined, and where the rector had said he would welcome a visit.

I asked Ambassador Ted Achilles what he thought I should do. He took a long time before he answered me. Finally he said, "I believe from a personal standpoint you should make a decision not to go. But from the standpoint of the United States, I will have to say that your failing to go may lead to some very detrimental publicity reactions throughout the hemisphere."

I slept very little that night. The crowd outside the hotel had grown large and ugly, and around midnight it started chanting anti-American and anti-Nixon slogans.

In the morning, the first thing everyone wanted to know was what I had decided. I said I had not yet made a final decision.

I asked Pat to stay behind at the hotel when I left for my first activity that morning, a wreath-laying ceremony at the statue of José de San Martín, the liberator of Peru. The custom is to place the wreath and then stand at attention for about thirty seconds in silence. That morning, however, I must have stood there for at least two minutes. I knew that as soon as I returned to the car I would have to give the order that would take us either to San Marcos or to Catholic University.

After laying the wreath, I turned and walked over to one of my three Secret Service agents, Jack Sherwood, and said, "San Marcos." Then I walked quickly to my car.

For two blocks before we reached the gates of San Marcos, we could hear the thousands of demonstrators chanting, "*Fuera Nixon! Fuera Nixon!*"—"Go Home Nixon!" Sometimes the chant became "*Muera Nixon! Muera Nixon!*"—"Death to Nixon!" I did not want a provocative retinue of embassy officials or policemen to accompany me onto the campus. Only my interpreter, Colonel Vernon Walters, and Jack Sherwood were with me as I walked toward the solid wall of screaming demonstrators that blocked the gate. I shouted, "I want to talk to you. Why are you afraid of the truth?" Walters shouted the translation.

I shouted a few more sentences, hoping to get them to listen. Suddenly a rock hit Sherwood in the face, breaking a tooth. A shower of rocks rained down on us. I realized that we had no choice but to leave. As we drove away, I stood up in the convertible and shouted, "You are cowards, you are afraid of the truth!" Sherwood held my legs as the car swerved into the street.

We drove directly to Catholic University, and as I entered the auditorium everyone rose in a tremendous ovation. After about thirty minutes, as I was answering a question, Sherwood came over and whispered, "We'd better get out of here; the gang from San Marcos is on its way."

We left just in time. When we got near our hotel, however, we could see that a great part of the San Marcos mob had preceded us. I assumed that the ringleaders were expecting us at the front entrance, so I had the driver let us out a short distance away. We walked as quickly as we could, and we were only about fifty feet from the entrance when the crowd realized who we were, and a shrill, savage cry went up. But surprise was on our side, and, in wedge formation, we were able to cover the rest of the distance in just a few moments.

I was about to go through the door of the hotel when one of the demonstrators blocked my way. I thought he was going to speak to me or shout at me; instead, he spit in my face. When I got upstairs, Pat rushed over and embraced me. She had been watching the mob from our hotel room, and she said, "It wasn't just hate those people had in their eyes. It was a sort of frenzy that frightened me."

For the rest of the day, wherever I went I was hailed as a hero by the citizens of Lima. The incident at San Marcos had shocked and shamed patriotic Peruvians, and cheering crowds tried to erase the memory of the jeering students. Late in the afternoon I held a press conference.

I told the reporters that the greatest danger a non-Communist nation faced was from the handful of activists and infiltrators who could impose their will on the whole society. I said that the story of the San Marcos incident was the story of how some 200 trained agitators had led a demonstration of 2,000 students, bringing disgrace to the whole of Peru.

On the flight from Lima to Quito, Ecuador, we tried to call Tricia and Julie on the plane's radio telephone in order to reassure them that we were all right, but it was impossible to make a connection. We received a message from Eisenhower: "Dear Dick. Your courage, patience, and calmness in the demonstration directed against you by radical agitators have brought you a new respect and admiration in our country." And Clare Boothe Luce sent a one-word wire: "Bully."

In Bogotá, Colombia, we received a disturbing message from the chief of the Secret Service in Washington: "The Central Intelligence Agency advises the Secret Service in Washington that information has been received relating to rumors of a plot to assassinate the Vice President in Venezuela." I cabled ahead to have our ambassador tell the Venezuelan government that if it wanted to cancel my visit I would understand. Right up until our arrival, however, the Venezuelan officials reported that everything was completely under control.

We landed at Maiquetía Airport, just outside Caracas, on the morning of May 13. We could hear yelling and whistling even before the plane's engines had cut off. Pat and I stood at attention at the top of the ramp while the honor guard fired a nineteen-gun salute and a band played the Venezuelan and American national anthems. The landing strip had been cleared except for the official welcoming party. The large crowd of demonstrators stood behind the fences at the edge of the runways and on the observation deck on the roof of the terminal building. A red carpet ran from the foot of the stairs to the terminal building where the motorcade was assembled to take us the twelve miles into Caracas.

As we started to descend the stairs, Walters whispered in my ear, "They aren't friendly." That much was clear from the whistles and catcalls that had kept up a raucous counterpoint to both anthems. As I shook hands, the welcoming party seemed determined to ignore the screams of the crowd. The Venezuelan chief of security assured me, "Oh, they are just kids. They are harmless."

I took Pat's arm and started walking along the red carpet toward the terminal. The others fell in quickly behind us. We had almost reached the terminal door when the band leader suddenly began playing the Venezuelan anthem again. We stopped and stood at attention. For a second it seemed as if it had begun to rain, and then I realized that the crowd on the observation deck just above our heads was showering us with spit. It fell on our faces and our hair. I saw Pat's bright red suit grow dark with tobacco-brown splotches. After we passed through the terminal and walked out in front, we were surrounded by the demonstrators. While we waited for Sherwood and our other agents to clear the way to the car they continued to pelt us. Pat leaned over the barricade toward a young girl who had just spit at her. The girl's face was contorted with hate. When Pat put her hand on the girl's shoulder and smiled at her, it was as if something snapped inside the girl, and she turned her head away and broke into sobs.

Finally our agents were able to clear a path. I got into the first car, along with the Foreign Minister. Pat and the Foreign Minister's wife were in the second car. The embarrassed Foreign Minister kept offering me his handkerchief to wipe some of the spit off my clothes. Finally I snapped at him, "Don't bother. I am going to burn these clothes as soon as I can get out of them."

He tried to explain what had happened. "The Venezuelan people have been without freedom so long that they tend now to express themselves more vigorously perhaps than they should," he said. "In our new government we do not want to do anything which would be interpreted as a suppression of freedom."

"If your new government doesn't have the guts and good sense to control a mob like the one at the airport, there soon will be no freedom for anyone in Venezuela," I replied.

As we entered Caracas, a barrage of rocks flew toward us, and a mob ran out from the side streets and alleys. Our driver pushed the accelerator to the floor and we got through.

About four blocks from the Panteón Nacional a solid wall of vehicles was strung across the street from the sidewalk to the traffic island in the center. A steady flow of cars in the opposite direction made it impossible to drive over the island. We pulled to a stop. For a moment everything seemed suspended. Then Sherwood said, "Here they come." Hundreds of people suddenly appeared from the streets and alleys, running toward our car. Our Venezuelan motorcycle escort evaporated. Our only protection was our augmented detail of twelve courageous Secret Service agents who did a superhuman job in trying to fend off the mob.

We realized that we were completely alone as the first rock hit the car window, lodging itself in the glass and spraying us with tiny slivers. One sliver hit the Foreign Minister in the eye, and he started to bleed heavily. He tried to stop the blood, moaning over and over, "This is terrible. This is terrible."

I saw a thug with an iron pipe work his way up to the car. He was looking right at me as he began trying to break the window. Once again the glass held, but flying slivers hit Walters in the mouth. Both Sherwood and I caught some in the face. Suddenly the car began to move, and the idea that we had somehow broken free gave me a surge of relief. Then I realized that the crowd was rocking the car back and forth—slower and higher each time. I remembered that it was a common tactic for mobs to turn a car over and then set it on fire.

I believe that at that moment, for the first time, each of us in the car realized we might actually be killed. My first thought was of Pat. I looked through the rear window and was relieved to see that the mob was concentrating on us and ignoring her car.

Suddenly Sherwood pulled out his revolver and said, "Let's get some of these sons of bitches." I told him to hold his fire. Once a gun went off the crowd would go berserk and that would be the end of us.

Finally the press truck in front of us managed to break out of the jam and swerve over the traffic island and into the lane of traffic coming from the opposite direction. Like a blocker leading a running back, the truck cleared a path for us. Our driver gunned the engine and shot around the truck, picking up speed. I was greatly relieved to see Pat's car right behind us.

We had been trapped for only twelve minutes, but it seemed like a lifetime. Our police motorcycle escort suddenly appeared again and started signaling our driver to follow. The Foreign Minister began talking about getting back on schedule, and it dawned on me that the escort was leading us to the Panteón for the wreath-laying ceremony. As we reached the next intersection I called out to the driver to turn quickly, and as he did the motorcycles rode on. The Foreign Minister looked panic-stricken. He cried, "We cannot leave our protection. We've got to follow the police escort!" I looked at him and said, "If that's the kind of protection we are going to get, we are better off going it alone."

I told the driver that the important thing was not to go anyplace where we would be expected. There would certainly be another mob waiting at the Panteón and also at the government guesthouse where we were scheduled to stay. By some miracle Pat's car and the truck carrying the reporters and photographers were following right behind. I asked the driver to pull over, and I walked back to make sure that she was all right. Several reporters ran up. I gave them a brief rundown of the situation and told them that I had decided to go directly to the embassy.

It was an immense relief to drive through the embassy gate and see the American flag flying from the roof. Pat and I showered and changed. By the time I came back downstairs, word had arrived that a bloodthirsty mob of several thousand had been waiting for us at the Panteón plaza, and later investigation revealed a cache of Molotov cocktails ready to be thrown at us during the ceremony. I also learned that the members of the ruling military junta were on their way to the embassy to make an official apology. One of the ambassador's aides wanted to have our battered limousine taken around to the back of the building so that it would not embarrass them. I said, "Leave it where it is. It's time that they see some graphic evidence of what communism really is."

I held a press conference late in the afternoon and made the same point that I had made in Lima: that the men and women who had led the riots could not claim to be loyal to their country because their first loyalty was to the international Communist conspiracy. I said that it would be very dangerous to ascribe the riots to the fact that after ten years of repressive dictatorship the people did not know how to exercise restraint in enjoying their new freedom. Those mobs were communists led by Communists, and they had no devotion to freedom at all.

That night Pat and I had dinner alone in our room at the embassy. Around nine o'clock there was a knock on the door and Rubottom and the ambassador asked if they could have a word with me. I didn't see how I could take another meeting at this point and started to tell them so when Rubottom said that a new crisis had arisen because of a news report that had just been received from Washington. Eisenhower had dispatched two companies of airborne infantry and two companies of Marines to the Caribbean to be "in a position to cooperate with the Venezuelan government if assistance is requested." The Venezuelan radio was apparently reporting this precautionary measure as a full-scale invasion.

I could hardly believe my ears. Why hadn't the White House consulted us before doing such a thing? Only later did we find out that communications between Caracas and Washington had been cut for a critical period immediately after the riot that afternoon. The last message the State Department had received before the cutoff was a flash report that the local security system had completely broken down, that anti-American mobs were on the loose, and that I was under attack. Eisenhower had acted on the basis of this message. We immediately tried to rectify the situation by issuing a statement that the Venezuelan authorities had the situation well in hand and that we saw no need for outside assistance.

The next morning I felt that we should leave Venezuela as soon as possible. The junta members were pleading that I attend the luncheon they had planned in my honor that afternoon, and they guaranteed that they would deliver me safely to the airport immediately afterward. I accepted their invitation, even though I still had trepidations about their ability to maintain security.

From the moment they arrived at the embassy to escort me to the luncheon, however, I realized that my fears had been unnecessary. It looked as if they had come to declare war rather than take me to lunch. The courtyard was filled with tanks and jeeps and armored cars. There were twelve truckloads of troops flanking our limousines. The security extended even to the food; they had replaced the caterer lest our food be tampered with.

After the luncheon, we were escorted to our cars. The limousine in which I was riding with the Provisional President was an arsenal on wheels. The floor was piled with submachine guns, revolvers, rifles, tear gas canisters, and ammunition clips; there was hardly room for our feet.

I saw that the junta had decided to make a symbolic point by taking me along the same route I had traveled the day before. This time, however, the streets were almost empty and heavily patrolled by armed soldiers. The few civilians I saw were holding handkerchiefs to their faces. At first I thought this was a protest sign, but when I saw the police wearing gas masks I realized that the whole area had been tear-gassed.

The airport was like a ghost town; the terminal was empty and eerily silent. After shaking hands with our hosts, Pat and I went up the steps to our plane. At the top we turned and waved briefly to the small group standing below.

A large crowd came out to greet us when we landed at National Airport in Washington. Eisenhower was there, along with the Cabinet, the leaders of Congress, and the diplomatic corps. Tricia and Julie were waiting for us at the bottom of the stairs, and they could hardly contain their tears of joy.

For several weeks after our return from South America, neither Pat nor I could appear anywhere in public without people standing up to applaud. For the first time I pulled even with Kennedy in the Gallup presidential trial heat polls. The positive reaction to the Caracas incident was naturally satisfying. But I never forgot how lucky we were to get out alive from what I had thought was going to be the most boring trip we had ever taken.

THE RESIGNATION OF SHERMAN ADAMS

Congress was in an ugly mood in the summer of 1958. The Republicans were fighting each other more than they were fighting the Democrats, and the Democrats were frantically digging up every possible issue they could throw at us in the fall elections. I paid little attention in June when charges were brought against Sherman Adams by the Subcommittee on Legislative Oversight of the House Interstate and Foreign Commerce Committee. It appeared that some of Adams's hotel bills had been paid by a New England industrialist named Bernard Goldfine. The Democrats charged that Adams had done favors for Goldfine and claimed they had uncovered a case of influence-peddling in the White House. Goldfine denied the charges, and on June 11 Jim Hagerty, speaking on behalf of the President, characterized the allegations as "completely false."

Stories of Adams's immense influence with Eisenhower and his cold and abrupt personal demeanor were a standard feature of many Washington dinner parties and gossip columns. For the Democrats he was a natural target as the President's Chief of Staff. Two days after Hagerty's flat denial, Adlai Stevenson accused Adams of "hypocrisy." Such criticism was to be expected from the Democrats. But many of Adams's most vocal and unrelenting critics turned out to be Republicans.

The day after Stevenson made his attack, Barry Goldwater, who was running for re-election to the Senate, called Adams a political liability. Unfortunately for Adams, he was not able to depend on compensating support from liberal Republicans. He had been so successful and so evenhanded in his role as Eisenhower's "no man" that he had few friends when he came under serious attack.

The next day, June 15, a story appeared in the New York *Post* that excited public opinion more than the accusations about hotel bills: the *Post* reported that Goldfine had given Adams a vicuña coat. Most people did not have the slightest idea what a vicuña coat was, but it sounded expensive.

With Eisenhower's approval, Adams testified before the subcommittee. He admitted to a lack of prudence in his dealings with Goldfine, and he made a favorable impression as an honest man who would not intentionally use his public influence for private profit. Eisenhower stood by him staunchly. At a press conference the next day, he replied to a question about Adams by saying: "I need him."

But Eisenhower's personal popularity was not as high as it had been, and he was increasingly plagued by his lame-duck status. His defense of Adams had surprisingly little influence on Republican leaders. Bill Knowland, the Minority Leader in the Senate, called for Adams's resignation, and Republican state chairmen around the country clamored for Adams's head.

Meanwhile the story grew more troublesome. It turned out that Goldfine had paid bills for and given presents to several senators and governors; the hotel bills for Adams and his family amounted to over $3,000; and the subcommittee found that Goldfine had deducted some of the money spent on Adams as business expenses.

A temporary respite occurred when it was discovered that Goldfine's hotel room had been bugged by a House committee investigator who had been found listening in an adjoining room, along with Jack Anderson, then an assistant to columnist Drew Pearson. The investigator was forced to resign.

Then the controversy resumed when, on July 10, it was revealed that Goldfine had paid not only Adams's hotel bills but also those of Senator Fred Payne, a Republican coming up for re-election in Maine.

On July 14, in the midst of this political turmoil, the Middle East erupted. King Faisal and other members of the royal family of Iraq were murdered during a successful military takeover. Fearing that Syria would follow suit and cross the frontier into Lebanon, Lebanese President Camille Chamoun asked for American help. On July 15, Eisenhower ordered the Marines into Lebanon. He asked me to come to his office that morning. He was pacing the floor, and for the first time he conveyed to me his frustration with the Adams situation. He said, "Here on a day that I am making a decision that could involve the United States in war, I have to be worried about this damned Goldfine–Adams business." He said nothing to indicate any lack of support for Adams, but I could tell that his patience was wearing thin. He asked me to keep him advised of anything I thought he should know about the situation.

Just before Congress adjourned in late August, Eisenhower and I talked about the Adams case. "Some people have been telling me that the issue has quieted down considerably in the past few weeks," he said.

I felt I had to be completely frank with him about the political implications. I said that the Democrats would inevitably make the Adams case a major campaign issue and Republican candidates would eventually have to take sides. I told him that most of our candidates would probably come out against Adams.

He thought for a moment, then said, "Well, Sherm could use that as a good reason for his resigning—that he did not want his presence in the administration to be an embarrassment to the Republican Party or to me." He then suggested, "Why don't you have a talk with Sherm after Congress adjourns? See how he feels about this, and let him know what he's going to be up against once the campaign begins."

When Congress adjourned on August 24, I kept a long-standing promise to Pat and the girls and took them by train to The Greenbrier in West Virginia. Every vacation we had planned since coming to Congress in 1947 had been cut short, but this time I really thought it would be different.

On the morning we arrived, however, Eisenhower called from the White House: "I wonder if you could talk to Sherm now that the Congress is out." He had heard that the Adams issue might be brought up at the Republican National Committee meeting in Chicago in a few days and had asked the RNC Chairman, Meade Alcorn, to try to avoid a public discussion of Adams. "I was really hoping," Eisenhower said, "that we could get the matter resolved before then."

I had a brief meeting with Eisenhower the next day, August 26. He asked me to talk bluntly to Adams about the political realities of the situation we faced. He did not authorize me to say that he wanted him to resign, but it was clear that he wanted the result of our conversation to be Adams's resignation.

I gave Adams my straightforward appraisal of the present situation from a political standpoint. I told him that most of the candidates and party leaders across the country believed that he should resign.

"Who will take my place? I've never heard anyone suggested," Adams said bluntly.

I replied that only Eisenhower could answer that question, and I had not discussed it with him. He pressed me further to try to determine whether I was expressing my own views, reporting on the views of others, or actually reflecting the President's position.

Before I left, Adams pinned me down with a direct question: "What do you think is the President's view?" I replied, "He hasn't told me to tell you this, Sherm, so I am only expressing my personal view. But I believe that the President thinks you are a liability and that you should resign."

Adams rather abruptly terminated the conversation by saying, "Well, I will have to talk to the boss myself." From the way he talked about "seeing the boss," it seemed clear that he was not going to take my hints and that he intended to hang on as long as he could.

Sherman Adams had earned the reputation of keeping icy cold no matter how hot the situation. In this case, however, I could see that the strain was beginning to tell. While I was in his office he took a bottle of pills from his desk, poured a couple of the tablets into his hand, and swallowed them with a glass of water. I felt deeply sorry for him.

I went to the Oval Office to report to Eisenhower on our meeting. I told him that I had just talked to Adams as he had asked, but that Adams was clearly not going to budge without first talking directly to him personally.

Adams saw Eisenhower that same afternoon. I was called over to the Oval Office a while later and found the President hitting 5-irons on the South Lawn. He made no mention of Adams, but said, "I'm going to play some golf this afternoon, Dick, and I wonder if you would like to join me."

We drove out to Burning Tree. Ann Whitman, Eisenhower's personal secretary, had warned me that he was in a "sour mood," and it showed up in his golf game. He told me it was the worst round he had had in months.

On the ride home he finally opened up: "Sherm won't take any of the responsibility. He leaves it all to me. Still, I can't fire a man who is sincere just for political reasons. He must resign in a way I can't refuse." He added, "I think Sherm must have misunderstood what you said. You had better write me an aide-mémoire on your conversation."

When I mentioned that Adams had raised the question of his replacement, Eisenhower's face flushed, and he said curtly and coldly, "That's my problem, not his." He looked out the car window for a minute and then said, "He has a heart condition. He might use that as a reason for resigning." Then he told me to ask Meade Alcorn to report the facts to Adams. He said, "I want Alcorn to really lay it on the line with him." He did not make a personal judgment on Adams except to say, "It's incredible, because with all these things that have been coming out one by one in the press, Sherm sees no wrong whatever in anything that he has done."

Later that evening I went back to The Greenbrier to rejoin Pat and the girls. Eisenhower went to his summer White House in Newport, and Adams went to his vacation home in New Brunswick.

Meade Alcorn was able to forestall any public action by the Republican state chairmen and campaign officials when they met in Chicago. He did, however, take a confidential poll, and found the overwhelming majority in favor either of Eisenhower's firing Adams or of Adams's voluntarily submitting his resignation. On September 4, Eisenhower phoned Alcorn from Newport and said that he had received some disturbing messages from party leaders and contributors concerning "the matter we discussed the other day." They had apparently told him that an association between a man like Goldfine and the chief assistant to the President was a reflection upon the White House that Eisenhower should not allow to continue.

Eisenhower was upset. He told Alcorn to work with me to settle the matter as quickly as possible. "I want to solve this as soon as we can after the Maine election so that it isn't hanging around during the campaign," he said. "This is the way I feel. It doesn't seem as if Sherm is going to do anything about it, and I am going to leave this entirely in your hands."

Adams was called back from his vacation in Canada on September 15. At eleven that morning Alcorn came to my office at the Capitol so that we could plan our strategy. The halls were swarming with reporters who sensed a crisis brewing, so I suggested to Alcorn that he meet with Adams alone. If the two of us left my office and went to the White House together, the reporters would follow us and it might become impossible to accomplish our objective of giving Adams a dignified opportunity to resign.

Alcorn met with Adams at two o'clock that afternoon in Adams's White House office. After the meeting Alcorn called to report that it had been a long and difficult session; Adams had hung on, stubborn to the last. Finally, Alcorn convinced him that we were acting at the direct request of the President.

On September 22, Sherman Adams flew to Newport and met with Eisenhower. He officially informed him that he had decided to resign, and Eisenhower said that he would accept the resignation but only with the deepest regret. Adams flew back to Washington, and that night announced his resignation in a nationally televised speech.

I called Adams's resignation a tragic loss to the country. I am convinced that he was personally an honest man who would not in any circumstances have allowed any decision he made to be influenced by his friends or by any gifts he received. Adams had come to Washington as a man of modest means, and as far as I knew he left with less than he had when he arrived. But he had not heeded one of the oldest political maxims: it is not necessary to prove guilt of the men around the President—the appearance of guilt is enough to destroy their usefulness.

Sherman Adams was cold, blunt, abrasive, at times even rude. But I never doubted that he always did what he believed "the boss" wanted and expected him to do, and he kept the complicated wheels of the executive office turning during more than one major crisis.

Why hadn't Eisenhower himself talked to Adams, his closest associate and the top man on his staff? Why did he use Alcorn and me for this painful task? General Walter Bedell Smith, Eisenhower's chief of staff in World War II, provided an important insight into Eisenhower's personality and his technique of leadership one night when he was reminiscing about his years with Eisenhower. He was very tired, and he uncharacteristically began showing his emotions. Tears began to stream down his cheeks, and he blurted out his pent-up feelings. "I was just Ike's prat boy," he said. "Ike always had to have a prat boy, someone who'd do the dirty work for him. He always had to have someone else who could do the firing, or the reprimanding, or give any orders which he knew people would find unpleasant to carry out. Ike always has to be the nice guy. That's the way it is in the White House, and the way it will always be in any kind of an organization that Ike runs."

Over the years a story spread that Adams and I were deadly enemies, the two major rivals for power in the Eisenhower White House. The fact is that we were neither friends nor enemies. We worked together in harness for the President. I was probably not Adams's first choice for Vice President, and certainly Adams was jealously protective of his prerogatives during the time of the President's major illnesses. But Adams was not against me; he was for Eisenhower.

What was it that Eisenhower saw in Sherman Adams that made him choose him in the first place?

I once asked Eisenhower if there was a single quality he valued above all in selecting a man for a top position on his staff. He thought for a long time—so long that I wondered if he had forgotten my question. Then he looked at me and said, "Selflessness. Selflessness is the most important attribute a member of any organization can have. He must always consider that his first responsibility is to do his job well, regardless of whether it serves his own self-interest or not."

Adams had this quality. He had no political ambitions; he did not seek any other position; unlike many White House aides, he was not trying to advance his own career. All he was interested in was serving "the boss" as best he could. And ironically, it was this interest that made Adams so many enemies. In making the President look good, Adams made himself look bad. But it was also this quality of selflessness that made him—except for his tragic misjudgments in his relationship with Goldfine—such an outstanding and successful chief of the White House staff.

1958 ELECTIONS

Off-year elections for the House, Senate, and state houses are often even more bitter and divisive than presidential elections. This was particularly true in 1958. As the year began, the economy was turning downward. Heated intraparty battles were taking place in a number of key states, including California. In this summer of discontent for the Republican Party, Eisenhower's popularity sank below 50 percent for the only time in his eight years in the White House

Eisenhower, always reluctant to involve himself in partisan politicking, would be able to do even less than in 1954 because of his health. And once again most of the Cabinet members were planning to sit out the campaign.

In the aftermath of Caracas, my popularity was now at its highest point. If I wanted to run for the presidency in 1960, it would be risky to put myself again in the position of Eisenhower's political point-man. Tom Dewey was almost passionately insistent that I not become involved: "I know that Ike won't do it, and I know that all those old party wheelhorses will tell you stories that will pluck your heartstrings, but you're toying with your chance to be President. Don't do it, Dick. You've already done enough, and 1960 is what counts now."

But I was deluged by appeals from across the country to appear on behalf of Republican candidates. In the end, I took on the task because it had to be done, and because there wasn't anyone else to do it.

In the campaign I traveled all over the country, doing what little I could. Some of the candidates were personal friends and good men who deserved to be elected or re-elected to Congress. But the more I traveled the more I appreciated the truth of Richard Rovere's observation in *The New Yorker* that I was "climbing into harness with a bunch of wheelhorses scarcely capable of drawing their own weight." In the last weeks of the campaign I labored under a feeling of total hopelessness.

The defeat was massive, and November 4, 1958, was one of the most depressing election nights I have ever known. The statistics still make me wince. In the Senate, the Democratic majority increased by 13 seats, bringing the proportion up to 62 to 34. They increased their majority by 47 seats in the House, thus outnumbering the Republicans by a whopping 282 to 153. Republicans won only 8 of 21 gubernatorial contests, and the Democrats now controlled 34 of the 48 state houses. The defeats in crucial states, among them California and Ohio, meant that the party would have to face the formidable task of rebuilding its state organizations if I was to have any hopes of carrying them in 1960. The reasons for the defeat were fairly easy to analyze, but the disappointment was still great. I knew that this defeat would make the campaign coming up in less than two years the most difficult of my career.

The next morning I heard that one television commentator had told his viewers that the big winner of 1958 was Nelson Rockefeller—who had been elected governor of New York by a wide margin—and the big loser was Richard Nixon. It seemed that the worst fears of my friends and advisers had been realized. My campaigning had had little visible effect, had gained me little thanks or credit, and had tarred me with the brush of partisan defeat at a time when my potential rivals for the nomination, Rockefeller and Barry Goldwater, were basking in the glory of victory. Perhaps Dewey had been right: I should have sat it out.

After the depressing ordeal of the 1958 disaster, I welcomed the opportunity to represent Eisenhower at the dedication of the American Chapel in St. Paul's Cathedral in London.

My major speech on this trip was to the English-Speaking Union at London's historic Guildhall on November 27.

I said that a new kind of battle was being fought, especially in the countries of Asia, the Middle East, Africa, and Latin America, where the leaders of those countries were struggling to satisfy their peoples' desire for the physical well-being and material comfort advanced nations enjoy. They would prefer to attain these objectives and retain their freedom—but if they believed that was impossible, they would choose progress even without liberty. "No people in the world today," I said, "should be forced to choose between bread and freedom."

I closed by saying that we should speak less of the threat of communism and more of the promise of freedom; that we should adopt as our primary objective not the defeat of communism but the victory of plenty over want, of health over disease, and of freedom over tyranny.

The trip gave me an opportunity to meet with and obtain the views of Britain's major political leaders on foreign policy issues. I was particularly impressed by the high intelligence and common sense that Prime

Minister Harold Macmillan displayed in a long discussion we had on what policy we should follow in dealing with the Soviet Union.

While we were in London I met with Winston Churchill at his house in Hyde Park Gate. I was surprised by how old and feeble he had become. As we talked about world affairs, however, he became more animated and by the end of our conversation there were flashes of the old brilliance.

After almost an hour, I said that I would not impose upon him any longer. He insisted on seeing me to the door. I was sad to see that he could not move without the assistance of his aide, who supported him as he walked. As the door swung open, we could see the lights from the movie cameras and all the reporters and photographers standing on the step. With sudden surprising strength, Churchill pushed his aide aside and almost seemed to puff himself up as he stood beside me. The cameras rolled and the flashbulbs popped, and the picture of the scene shows the proud, strong, upright Churchill of people's memory rather than the sad reality of time and age that I had just seen in private in his sitting room.

CASTRO: 1959

On January 1, 1959, Fidel Castro led his rebel army in triumph through the streets of Havana. He had defeated and ousted the repressive Batista regime, and he promised justice and freedom for the people of Cuba.

Castro had received a generally favorable press in the United States as the leader of a successful revolution against a right-wing dictator. Within the Eisenhower administration, however, opinions about him were mixed. Most of the State Department's Latin American experts advocated immediate recognition of Castro's government. But Allen Dulles and others in the CIA and NSC felt that we should delay such action until we had a better fix on Castro: was he an unwitting front man for the Communists, or perhaps even a Communist himself?

Eisenhower had not yet made a decision on this issue when Castro accepted an invitation to speak in Washington at a meeting of the American Society of Newspaper Editors on April 17, 1959. The President refused to see him, but Herter urged that I meet with Castro informally as I might be able to gain for the administration additional information about his background and insight into his views. On Sunday, April 19, we met alone in the Vice President's formal office in the Capitol, and for three hours we discussed his political views, his attitude toward the United States, and other international issues.

After that meeting I dictated a long memorandum for Eisenhower,

Herter, and Foster and Allen Dulles summarizing our conversation and describing my impressions. In it I noted Castro's reaction to my urging that he declare himself in favor of elections at the earliest possible time:

> He went into considerable detail as he had in public with regard to the reasons for not holding elections, emphasizing particularly that "the people did not want elections because the elections in the past had produced bad government."
>
> He used the same argument that he was simply reflecting the will of the people in justifying the executions of war criminals and his overruling the acquittal of Batista's aviators. In fact he seemed to be obsessed with the idea that it was his responsibility to carry out the will of the people whatever it might appear to be at a particular time. . . .
>
> It was this almost slavish subservience to prevailing majority opinion—the voice of the mob—rather than his naïve attitude toward communism and his obvious lack of understanding of even the most elementary economic principles which concerned me most in evaluating what kind of a leader he might eventually turn out to be. That is the reason why I spent as much time as I could trying to emphasize that he had the great gift of leadership, but that it was the responsibility of a leader not always to follow public opinion but to help to direct it in the proper channels—not to give the people what they think they want at a time of emotional stress but to make them want what they ought to have. I pointed out that it might be very possible that the people of Cuba were completely disillusioned as far as elections and representative government were concerned but that this placed an even greater responsibility on him to see that elections were held at the very earliest date, and thereby to restore the faith of the people in democratic processes. Otherwise, the inevitable result would be the same dictatorship against which he and his followers had fought so gallantly. I used the same argument with regard to freedom of the press, the right to a fair trial before an impartial court, judge, and jury, and on other issues which came up during the course of the conversation. In every instance he justified his departure from democratic principles on the ground that he was following the will of the people. I, in my turn, tried to impress upon him the fact that while we believe in majority rule that even a majority can be tyrannous and that there are certain individual rights which a majority should never have the power to destroy. . . .
>
> Whatever we may think of him he is going to be a great factor in the development of Cuba and very possibly in Latin American affairs generally. He seems to be sincere. He is either incredibly naïve about communism or under Communist discipline—my guess is the former, and as I have already implied his ideas as to how to run a government or an economy are less developed than those of almost any world figure I have met in fifty countries.
>
> But because he has the power to lead to which I have referred, we have no choice but at least to try to orient him in the right direction.

Castro's actions when he returned to Cuba convinced me that he was indeed a Communist, and I sided strongly with Allen Dulles in presenting this view in NSC and other meetings. In early 1960 Eisenhower became convinced we were right and that steps should be taken to support the anti-Castro forces inside and outside Cuba. I was present at the meeting in which Eisenhower authorized the CIA to organize and train Cuban exiles for the eventual purpose of freeing their homeland from the Communists.

The irony, and the tragedy, of Castro's coming to power was that the Cuban people were rid of a right-wing dictator only at the cost of accepting a left-wing dictator who turned out to be far worse. From the U.S. point of view, Batista at least was friendly; Castro turned out to be an implacable and dangerous enemy.

KHRUSHCHEV AND THE "KITCHEN DEBATE"

Early in 1959 Eisenhower approved a recommendation by the United States Information Agency for me to represent the United States at the opening of the American National Exhibition in Moscow in July.

It may be difficult for those who do not remember the late 1950s to understand the nature of the relations between the Communist nations and the free world then. Russia was still shrouded in much of the sinister mystery of the Stalin era. The Iron Curtain was pulled tight across Europe, and Soviet missiles were feared in Bonn, Paris, London—and in Washington.

Nikita Khrushchev, a crude bear of a man who had risen from the ranks, was the leader of the Communist Party. Khrushchev's rough manners, bad grammar, and heavy drinking caused many Western journalists and diplomats to underestimate him. But despite his rough edges, he had a keen mind and a ruthless grasp of power politics.

Bluntly ignoring Western invitations for disarmament and détente, Khrushchev openly continued to stockpile missiles, build submarines, and test nuclear weapons. The bellicose way in which Khrushchev flaunted his new leadership in rocketry made many believe that he would have no qualms about using it to unleash a nuclear war.

Few foreigners had been invited to meet Khrushchev, and those who did were often deeply disturbed by him. At times he was almost seductively charming; at other times he was boorish and obtuse. Some visitors came away swearing that he was the devil incarnate; others came away swearing that he was just a drunk. All thought he was a bully.

For this trip to the Soviet Union, I undertook the most intense preparation I had ever made for a trip or meeting. I read everything I could find about the Soviet Union and its peoples. Pat and I spent several evenings learning Russian words and phrases. I received briefings from the State Department and the CIA and familiarized myself with the backgrounds of the Soviet leaders I would be likely to meet. By the time I left for Moscow on July 22, I was prepared to discuss any of the more than a hundred topics or problems of Soviet-American relations that Khrushchev was likely to bring up.

I asked the few Westerners who had met and talked to Khrushchev what he was like and what I could expect from him. Many said that of prime importance was to leave absolutely no doubt in his mind about the sincerity of our dedication to peace. Khrushchev would be scrutinizing my conduct for any hints of belligerence, they warned, so, as Walter Lippmann put it, I should bend over backward not to rock the boat. Others, equally expert, felt that Khrushchev would fasten on any sign of weakness or appeasement on my part and exploit it to his advantage.

I wanted to get the advice of Foster Dulles, who was then in Walter Reed Hospital with terminal cancer. When I arrived he was sitting in a wheelchair, a red plaid bathrobe covering his shrunken frame. His voice was weak, and between sentences he would suck on an ice cube to dull the burning in his throat.

"What above everything else should I try to get across to Khrushchev?" I asked him.

As usual he took time to consider his answer, and he expressed his thoughts with customary firmness and logic.

"Khrushchev does not need to be convinced of our good intentions," he said. "He knows we are not aggressors and do not threaten the security of the Soviet Union. He understands us. But what he needs to know is that we also understand him. In saying that he is for peaceful competition, he really means competition between his system and ours only in our world, not in his. He must be made to understand that he cannot have it both ways. Point the record out to him, that we have concrete proof of the Kremlin's activities around the world. He should be told that until he puts a stop to such activities, his call for reducing of tensions and for peaceful coexistence will have a completely false and hollow ring."

We chatted a little longer. Then Dulles looked out the window. "It's too fine a day for you to be in here," he said. "You should be out golfing." Those were his last words to me. He died four days later, on May 24, 1959.

Foster Dulles and I were friends. Although there were considerable differences in our ages and backgrounds, we shared a fascination with the world and the same basic outlook on America's role in it. Dulles was by no means politically inexperienced or naïve, but as Secretary of State he was frequently traveling and always busy, so he used me as his political eyes and ears to keep him abreast of what was going on in Washington, especially in Congress. Many nights I would have cocktails or dinner with him, and then we would sit for hours talking our way around the world. It was an incomparable opportunity for me to learn from one of the great diplomats of our time.

Most people who did not know Dulles thought him severe, dour, almost ascetic. The press generally presented him as a cold fish, devoid of human emotions, who talked with abstract righteousness about "massive retaliation" and about going to the "brink of war." Dulles was, indeed, a brilliant, disciplined, and deeply religious man who saw many dimensions of principle and logic in every issue he encountered. But he was also a man who thought that the life of each individual on earth was important and precious because it was the gift of God.

Dulles appreciated the considerable leeway Eisenhower gave him in the conduct of foreign affairs, and he was constantly aware of the responsibilities and obligations involved. "I never want to be a burden on the President," he would say to me when a controversy was brewing. "As a friend, I want you to tell me whenever you believe that I have become a burden, either politically or otherwise." He recognized the fundamental truth a public man must never forget—that he loses his usefulness when he, rather than his policy, becomes the issue. In this respect Foster Dulles was perhaps the most conscientious public man I have ever known.

At a time when the political and intellectual climate in the West appeared to be moving slowly but steadily toward advocacy of shortsighted and opportunistic arrangements with the Soviets, Dulles was made to seem and sound like a throwback to cold war rigidity. But he saw his work as a high calling, and a few months before his death he said, "Communism is stubborn for the wrong; let us be steadfast for the right. A capacity to change is indispensable. Equally indispensable is the capacity to hold fast to that which is good."

World leaders and heads of government came to Dulles's funeral, as well as the foreign secretaries and foreign ministers who were his opposite numbers. Few came because they loved him; most had often disagreed with him. But they all respected him for his integrity and for his profound dedication to the principles of peace, freedom, and justice that motivated every decision he made.

Shortly before I left for Moscow, Congress passed the Captive Nations resolution, as it had every year since 1950. Eisenhower issued the proclamation provided for in the resolution urging Americans to "study the plight of the Soviet-dominated nations and to recommit themselves to the support of the just aspirations of those captive nations." While the fact that Eisenhower issued the proclamation just a week before I left for Moscow was coincidental, I knew that Khrushchev might interpret it as an intentionally belligerent action.

We left Friendship Airport in an Air Force jet on July 22. The reception awaiting us in Moscow was cool and controlled. Deputy Premier Frol Kozlov gave a long welcoming speech while the American and Soviet flags hung limp in the warm afternoon air. But there were no bands, no anthems, and no crowds.

Llewellyn "Tommy" Thompson, whom I had first met in Austria in 1956, was now our ambassador in Moscow. We talked for a long time in the secure room on the second floor of Spaso House, the ambassador's official residence; in every country our embassy has a room that is constantly guarded and swept for listening devices. Thompson told me that the Soviet leaders were furious about the Captive Nations resolution, and the airport reception was probably only the first sign of their disapproval. He said that they were particularly sensitive to such criticism because their relations with some of the satellite countries were strained.

Because of the time change I could scarcely sleep that night, and around 5:30 I woke my Secret Service agent, Jack Sherwood, and told him I wanted to go to the famous Danilovsky market, where farmers bring their vegetables and meat. It would be a good way to get a sense of the city and its people before starting my official schedule. Sherwood and I were joined by a Russian security policeman who served as driver and interpreter.

As I walked through the crowded aisles between the stalls, word of my arrival spread quickly. Soon a crowd had gathered.

For almost an hour I mingled with the crowd, answering questions, caught up in the friendly and spontaneous exchange. As I was about to leave, several people asked if I had any tickets to the American Exhibition. I said I had none but would be delighted to buy some for my new friends there in the market so they could be my guests. I had Sherwood hand the spokesman for the group a hundred-ruble note, enough for a hundred tickets. The spokesman handed it back, explaining that the problem was not the cost of the tickets but the fact that the government made them available only to selected persons. We all laughed about the problem, and I shook hands and left. The next day the three largest Soviet newspapers, *Pravda, Izvestia,* and *Trud,* headlined the incident, accusing me of having tried to "bribe" and "degrade" Soviet citizens by offering them money.

Later that morning, I went to the Kremlin for my first meeting with Khrushchev. He was standing at the far corner of his large office, examining a small model of the Soviet rocket that had recently been fired into outer space. We shook hands for the photographers. He was shorter than I expected, but otherwise he looked exactly like his photographs—the girth, the brash smile, the prominent mole on his cheek.

While the reporters and photographers were present Khruchshev chatted amiably about the fine Moscow weather. He praised my London Guildhall speech and said that he too welcomed the kind of peaceful competition I had described in it. Then he waved the photographers out and gestured toward a long conference table with chairs on both sides.

Abruptly the atmosphere changed, and Khrushchev launched into a tirade against the Captive Nations resolution. He called it a stupid and frightening decision and he asked whether war would be the next step. "Heretofore, the Soviet government thought Congress could never adopt a decision to start a war," he said. "But now it appears that, although Senator McCarthy is dead, his spirit still lives. For this reason the Soviet Union has to keep its powder dry."

I tried to explain how the resolution had come about and suggested we go on to other subjects. But he was not to be deterred. Blustering, he tried to twist it into a justification for Soviet arms. Finally I said, "At the White House we have a procedure for breaking off long discussions that seem to get nowhere. President Eisenhower says, 'We have beaten this horse to death; let's change to another.' Perhaps that is what you and I should do now."

Khrushchev's face remained impassive while the translator interpreted my words. "I agree with the President's saying that we should not beat one horse too much," he said, "but I still cannot understand why your Congress would adopt such a resolution on the eve of such an important state visit. It reminds me of a saying among our Russian peasants, that 'people should not go to the toilet where they eat.' " By this time his face was flushed with anger, and he said, "This resolution stinks. It stinks like fresh horse shit, and nothing smells worse than that!"

Khrushchev watched me closely while the translation was made. I decided to call his bluff, and in his own terms. I remembered from some of the briefing materials that Khrushchev had in his youth worked as a herder of pigs. I also remembered from my childhood that horse manure was commonly used as fertilizer—but that a neighbor had once used a load of pig manure, and the stench was overpowering.

Looking straight into Khrushchev's eyes but speaking in a conversational tone, I replied, "I am afraid that the Chairman is mistaken. There is something that smells worse than horse shit—and that is pig shit."

For a split second after the translator had finished, Khrushchev's face hovered on the borderline of rage. Then he suddenly burst into a broad smile. "You are right there," he said, "so perhaps you are right that we should talk about something else now. However, I must warn you that you will hear about this resolution during your visit here." On this subject if on few others, Khrushchev kept his word.

We drove from the Kremlin to take a look at the American Exhibition before it opened officially that evening. One of the first displays we came to was a model television studio, and a young engineer asked if we would like to try out a new color television taping system by recording greetings that could be played back during the Exhibition. Khrushchev seemed suspicious, but when he saw a group of Soviet workmen near the display the actor in him took over. Before I knew what he was doing he had scrambled onto the platform and was talking for the cameras and playing to the gallery.

"How long has America existed?" he asked me. "Three hundred years?"

"One hundred and eighty years," I replied.

Khrushchev was unfazed. "Well, then, we will say America has been in existence for one hundred and eighty years, and this is the level she has reached," he said, taking in the whole Exhibition hall with a broad wave of his arm. "We have existed not quite forty-two years, and in another seven years we will be on the same level as America." The audience was obviously enjoying his boasting, and he continued. "When we catch up with you, in passing you by, we will wave to you," he said, looking over his shoulder and waving goodbye to an imaginary America.

Pointing to a burly Russian worker standing in the front of the crowd, he asked, "Does this man look like a slave laborer? With men of such spirit, how can we lose?"

I pointed to an American worker and said, "With men like that *we* are strong! But these men, Soviet and American, work together well for peace, even as they have worked together in building this Exhibition. This is the way it should be." I added, "If this competition in which you plan to outstrip us is to do the best for both of our peoples and for peoples everywhere, there must be a free exchange of ideas. You must not be afraid of ideas. After all, you don't know everything."

Khrushchev, furious, jumped in. "If *I* don't know everything, *you* don't know anything about communism," he shouted, "except fear of it!"

Walking through the Exhibition, we soon arrived at its most controversial attraction. This was a full-size model of a middle-class American home, priced at $14,000 and full of conveniences that dazzled the Russians. The Soviet press called it the "Taj Mahal" and insisted that it did not represent the way that an average American family really lived. I told Khrushchev that this was the kind of home that might be owned by an American steelworker, but either he did not believe me or he was unwilling to admit that it was true. We stopped in the model kitchen, and our exchange there turned into a debate that reverberated around the world.

Unlike our encounter in the model television studio, our "kitchen debate" was not televised, but it was widely reported—with a dramatic photograph showing me prodding my finger in Khrushchev's chest for emphasis. He was defensive, declaring that Russian houses, too, would have the modern equipment displayed in the American exhibit; and he was aggressive, arguing that it was better to have just one model of washing machine than many. When I asked if it wasn't better to be arguing about the relative merits of washing machines than about the relative strengths of rockets, he shouted, "Your generals say we must compete in rockets. Your generals say they are so powerful they can destroy us. We can also show you something so that you will know the Russian spirit. We are strong, we can beat you."

I replied, "No one should ever use his strength to put another in the position where he in effect has an ultimatum. For us to argue who is the stronger misses the point. If war comes we both lose."

Khrushchev tried to turn the tables, accusing me of issuing an ultimatum. "We, too, are giants," he declared. "You want to threaten—we will answer threats with threats."

I told him we would never engage in threats. "You wanted indirectly to threaten me," he shouted. "But we have the means to threaten too."

Finally he was ready to move to less belligerent ground. He said, "We want peace and friendship with all nations, especially with America." I responded, "We want peace, too."

Standing next to Khrushchev during this heated exchange was one of his chief aides, a young party official named Leonid Brezhnev.

We returned to the Kremlin, where Pat and Mrs. Khrushchev joined us for a lavish luncheon. We toasted each other with champagne and, following our host's lead, threw our glasses into the fireplace. Then we were served caviar on silver dishes.

The following night we gave a dinner for Khrushchev at the American Embassy. Midway through the evening he began describing the beauties of the Russian countryside. Suddenly he said that we should not wait to see them, and he insisted that Pat and I spend the night in his dacha outside Moscow: he would join us there the next day for the scheduled meetings. Half an hour later we were in a limousine speeding down deserted roads. Soon we were in the forest, where the air was cooler and the darkness seemed deep and still. Khrushchev's dacha, which had been a Czarist summer home, was almost as large as the White House. It was surrounded by acres of grounds and gardens, and on one side the forest dropped down to the banks of the Moskva River.

Khrushchev and his wife arrived late the next morning. With the gusto of a social director he immediately took everything in hand. "First, let's have pictures taken in front of the house," he said, "and then we can take a ride on the Moskva River so that you can see how the slaves live."

"Oh, yes, the captives," I said, determined not to let him provoke me on that again.

Boats were waiting at the dock, and we followed the winding Moskva upriver for almost an hour. Several times groups of bathers swam out from the shore and surrounded the boat, cheering Khrushchev and clamoring to shake our hands. The first time this happened I was amused by Khrushchev's asking the swimmers, "Do you feel like captive people?" But I soon realized it was a setup. "You never miss a chance to make propaganda, do you?" I asked him. "No, no," he insisted, "I don't make propaganda. I tell the truth."

We had lunch on the lawn under a canopy of magnificent birch trees; the scene could have been out of Chekhov. When we sat down, Khrushchev made some playful verbal jabs. When Anastas Mikoyan started to speak in English to Pat, Khrushchev accused him of trying to be a Romeo when he was too old for the part. Then he told him, "Now look here, you crafty Armenian, Mrs. Nixon belongs to me. You stay on your side of the table." With his finger he drew an imaginary line down the middle of the starched white tablecloth between Pat and Mikoyan. "This is an iron curtain," he said. "And don't you step over it!"

One of the first courses was a Siberian delicacy, raw whitefish sliced very thin and spiced with salt, pepper, and garlic. Khrushchev took a generous portion and smiled approvingly when he saw me do the same. "It was Stalin's favorite dish," he remarked as he took a large mouthful. "He said it put steel in his backbone."

When the plates had been cleared, I expected that Khrushchev and I would excuse ourselves and settle down for serious talk. But he made no move to go. Instead, as we all sat there he began boasting about the power and accuracy of Soviet rockets and missiles. He cast a chill over the table by casually admitting that accidents can happen. A couple of months earlier, for example, he had been worried when a Soviet ICBM malfunctioned and overshot its course by 1,250 miles. At first he had been afraid that it might land in Alaska, but fortunately it fell into the ocean.

I asked him why the Soviets bothered to continue building bombers if they were so far advanced in missile production. Khrushchev answered, "We have almost stopped production of bombers, because missiles are much more accurate and not subject to human failure and human emotions. Humans are frequently incapable of dropping bombs on their assigned targets because of emotional revulsion. That is something you don't have to worry about in missiles."

When I asked him about submarines, Khrushchev said, "We are building as many submarines as we can." Mikoyan shot him a quick glance and said, "The Chairman means we are building as many submarines as we need for our defense."

I asked about the development of solid fuels for powering missiles; Khrushchev replied, "Well, that is a technical subject which I am not capable of discussing."

By this time the atmosphere had become fairly tense. Pat smiled at Khrushchev and said, "I'm surprised that there is a subject that you're not prepared to discuss, Mr. Chairman. I thought that with your one-man government you had to know everything and have everything firmly in your own hands."

Mikoyan came suavely to his leader's rescue. "Even Chairman Khrushchev does not have enough hands for all he has to do, so that is why we are here to help him," he said.

Finally I said quietly that it was largely because of belligerent talk from the Soviet leaders that the world was as fearful of war as it was. "I hope you don't think that you can hold a meeting of Communists from fifty-one countries in Moscow without our knowing what they are up to and what kind of directives they are getting. Just recently in Poland, you openly declared that the Soviet Union supports communist revolutions everywhere."

"We are against terror against individuals," he replied, "but if we go to the support of a communist uprising taking place in another country, that is a different question. If the bourgeoisie doesn't surrender power peacefully, then it is true that force may be necessary."

"In other words, you consider that workers in capitalist states are 'captives' whose liberation is justified?" I asked.

Khrushchev blustered and said that it wasn't interference if the Soviets were supporting a genuine internal uprising.

I asked him about the fact that the Soviet newspapers and radio had openly endorsed the terrorism against Pat and me in Venezuela. The Soviet press had expressed complete sympathy with the mob that had tried to kill us there.

Khrushchev paused for a moment and then leaned across the table toward me. In a low voice, thick with emotion, he said, "We have a saying that 'you are my guest, but truth is my mother,' so I will answer your very serious question. You were the target of the righteous indignation of the people there. Their acts were not directed against you personally, but against American policy—against the failure of your American policy."

"I accept your right to have your own opinion and to have sympathy for these violent acts," I said. "But I want to point out that when great military power like that of the Soviet Union is coupled with such revolutionary opinions and sympathies, there is a grave danger of matters getting out of control. This is why such strong men like Eisenhower and you should meet. But such meetings would have to take place on a basis of give and take. You are one of the most effective spokesmen for your own views that I have ever seen, Mr. Chairman. But you have only one theme. You say that the United States is always wrong, and the Soviet Union is never wrong. Peace cannot be made that way."

This fired him anew and he began another long harangue which lasted almost an hour. As he finally wound down, I said, "My question is whether there is any room for negotiation in your position. Suppose I were the President of the United States sitting here across the table from you instead of the Vice President. Is your position so fixed that you would not even listen to the President?"

Perhaps he was tired by his long monologue. He was obviously not interested in pursuing the question further, because he answered me with a vague reference to Berlin and soon rose to indicate that the luncheon was at an end.

It had been 3:30 when we sat down; it was almost nine o'clock when we finally rose from the table. Everyone seemed a little dazed. We had been talking for over five hours.

Khrushchev's intention had been to bully us—to overwhelm us with Soviet military strength and his willingness to use it. Like most tyrants, he considered the trapped audience and the interminable monologue important weapons in his personal arsenal. But I had deprived him of their use that afternoon. Tommy Thompson confirmed what I had already guessed: the ordinary instincts of most of the Americans who met Khrushchev were to be pleasant and agreeable with him, and he took this courtesy as a sign of weakness. After that long luncheon at the dacha I knew that my intuition had been right. Khrushchev would respect only those who stood up to him, who resisted him, and who believed as strongly in their own cause as he believed in his.

At the end of my trip I made an unprecedented radio and television address to the Soviet people. Tommy Thompson and Professor William Y. Elliott of Harvard, who had come at my request as a member of my party, helped me prepare my remarks. Thompson suggested that I mention the incident at the market. He said that the Soviet press had made so much of it that it would be on many of my listeners' minds. In my speech I simply described what had happened, but this was the first time anyone could remember that *Pravda* had been criticized publicly, and the incident stirred debate among the Russian people long after I was gone.

Looking to the future, I said that "to me the concept of coexistence is completely inadequate and negative." I went on to explain: "Coexistence

The Nixon family in Yorba Linda in 1916. From left: Harold, Frank, Donald, Hannah, Richard.

The Nixon brothers in Yorba Linda in 1922. From left: Donald, seven, in the tire; Richard, nine; Harold, thirteen, already sick with tuberculosis, wearing a bathrobe; and Arthur, four.

Fullerton High School orchestra, sophomore year, 1928.

RN in East Whittier in 1927.

The last photograph of Harold, who died in 1933, and RN.

UNITED PRESS INTERNATIONAL

Number 23 on the Whittier College football team, October 1933.

RN in front of "Nick's Hamburger Stand" on Bougainville in the South Pacific in 1944.

ARLEN BLAKE

The photograph of Pat that RN carried with him during the war.

Tricia and her parents in the yard of their house in Whittier in 1946.

KEYSTONE PHOTO SERVICE

AMERICA NEEDS
NEW LEADERSHIP NOW!
ELECT
RICHARD M.
NIXON
YOUR CONGRESSMAN
World War II Navy Combat Veteran
A vote for NIXON is a vote for new, progressive and EFFECTIVE leadership— for a change!

The first political campaign: opposing Jerry Voorhis for the House of Representatives from California's Twelfth District.

RN and John F. Kennedy (back row at right) in a radio interview with other freshman members of the Eightieth Congress in January 1947.

RENI NEWSPHOTO SERVICE

The Hiss case: examining the "pumpkin papers" microfilm with Robert Stripling.

Campaigning for the U.S. Senate in California's San Joaquin Valley in 1950.

RAY GEERS STUDIO

Photo from 1950 Senate election campaign poster.

Rose Mary Woods became RN's secretary in 1951.

UNITED PRESS INTERNATIONAL

Receiving the nomination for Vice President at the 1952 Republican National Convention in Chicago.

Letter from John F. Kennedy after receiving the Republican vice presidential nomination. Text of the letter appears on page 91.

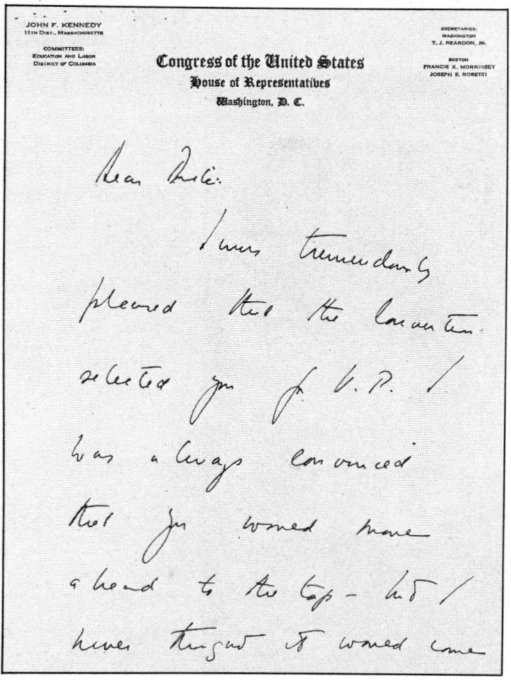

JOHN F. KENNEDY
11TH DIST., MASSACHUSETTS

COMMITTEES:
EDUCATION AND LABOR
DISTRICT OF COLUMBIA

Congress of the United States
House of Representatives
Washington, D. C.

SECRETARIES:
WASHINGTON
T. J. REARDON, JR.
BOSTON
FRANCIS X. MORRISSEY
JOSEPH E. ROSETTI

Dear Dick:

I was tremendously pleased that the Convention selected you for V.P. I was always convinced that you would move ahead to the top - but I never thought it would come

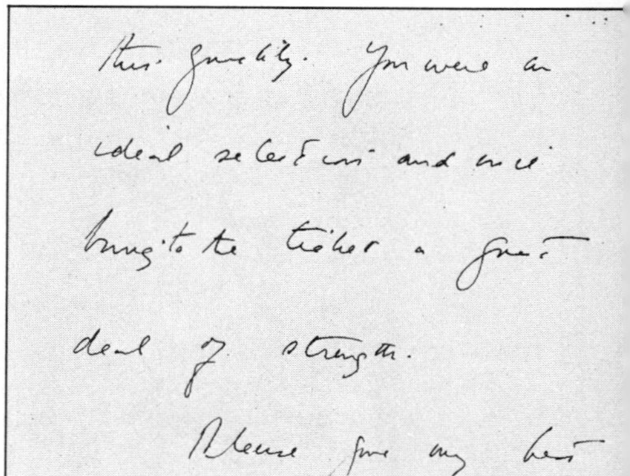

this quickly. You were an ideal selection and will bring to the ticket a great deal of strength.

Please give my best to your wife and all kinds of good luck to you.

Cordially
Jack Kennedy

The Fund Speech: September 23, 1952.

RN discloses, Stevenson refuses. The front page of *The New York Times* after RN and Eisenhower met in Wheeling, West Virginia, following the Fund Speech.

EISENHOWER CALLS NIXON VINDICATED; COMMITTEE VOTES TO RETAIN NOMINEE; STEVENSON BARS DATA ON ILLINOIS FUND

GIFT PLAN BACKED

Governor Says Program Lessened Sacrifice of Low-Paid Key Aides

RECIPIENTS' NAMES SECRET

Nominee Undecided on Listing the Identities of Donors, He Tells Baltimore Backers

Text of the Stevenson speech in Baltimore, Page 23.

By W. H. LAWRENCE
Special to THE NEW YORK TIMES.

SPRINGFIELD, Ill., Sept. 24—Gov. Adlai E. Stevenson of Illinois declared today that he had no intention of making public any details of the fund from which he gave secret extra compensation to some appointive Illinois state officials.

The Democratic Presidential nominee asserted he did not believe any useful purpose would be served by publicizing the names of the officials helped or the amounts they received. He also said that he did not know whether he would make public a list of the contributors who made possible these gifts "around Christmas time

Associated Press Wirephoto

THEY "STAND TOGETHER": Gen. Dwight D. Eisenhower and his running mate, Senator Richard M. Nixon, left, respond to cheers of crowd that greeted them after they met last night in Senator Nixon's plane at airport in Wheeling, W. Va.

CANDIDATES MEET

Airport Greeting Warm—General Calls Senator a 'Man of Honor'

TICKET HARMONY ASSURED

Californian Now 'Stands Higher Than Ever,' Eisenhower Says of His Explanation

Texts of Eisenhower and Nixon speeches in Wheeling, Page 21.

By JAMES RESTON
Special to THE NEW YORK TIMES.

WHEELING, W. Va., Sept. 24—Gen. Dwight D. Eisenhower said tonight that his Vice Presidential running mate, Senator Richard M. Nixon of California, had been "completely vindicated" of charges in connection with a privately raised expense fund.

Speaking before a cheering and enthusiastic crowd here, the Republican Presidential nominee announced that the 107 members of the Republican National Committee who could be reached had all voted for retaining Mr. Nixon on the ticket. There are 138 members on the full committee.

General Eisenhower declared he believed Senator Nixon "had been

Inauguration Day 1953. From left: Presidents Truman, Eisenhower, and Hoover.

SINGAPORE *Standard*

THIS wire fence was no barrier as the U.S. Vice-President, Mr. Richard M. Nixon reached over it to shake hands with peons, clerks and people of all walks of life, as they crowded round to meet him while he was leaving the V.I.P. room at Kallang airport yesterday. — Standard photo.

NIXON CHATS WITH COMMON MAN

Standard Staff Reporter

WITHIN 15 minutes of his arrival in Singapore yesterday Mr. Richard Nixon, America's youngest Vice-President and President Eisenhower's personal ambassador, got down to meeting the ordinary people of Singapore's varied communities.

The Vice-President turned away from the pomp and ceremony of an official reception at Kallang Airport to shake hands with 20 or more of the hundreds of ordinary Singapore working men and boys who had stood for several hours under a broiling sun to see America's second most important man.

To the chagrin of hundreds of security men and high police officers who guarded the disembarkation apron, Mr. Nixon leaned over a wire fence and shook hands with a tiny Malay boy.

Broad grins of approval spread over the faces of the crowd and they surged forward to shake the hand of one of America's most popular politicians.

1953 trip: front page of the Singapore *Standard,* October 25, 1953.

1953 trip: with Generalissimo and Madame Chiang Kai-shek in Taipei.

UNITED PRESS INTERNATIONAL

1953 trip: with President Syngman Rhee in Seoul.

1953 trip: while I was in meetings, Pat insisted on having her own schedule of activities. Here she visits the Shwedagon Pagoda in Burma. Her guide (left) is U Thant, later secretary-general of the United Nations.

1953 trip: with Prime Minister Nehru and his daughter Indira Gandhi.

Letter from President Eisenhower following the 1953 trip. Text of the letter appears on page 134.

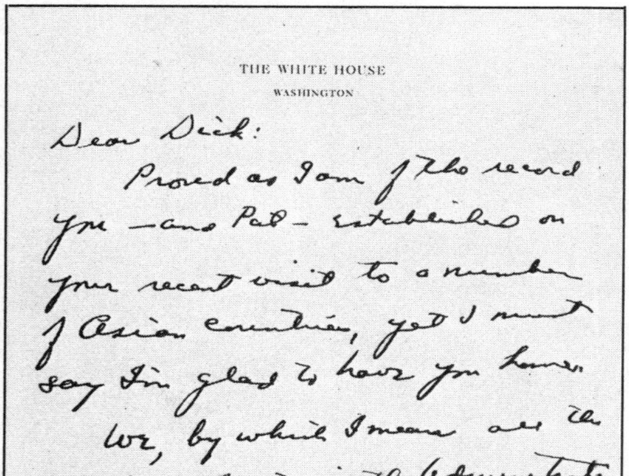

THE WHITE HOUSE
WASHINGTON

Dear Dick:

Proud as I am of the record you—and Pat—established on your recent visit to a number of Asian countries, yet I must say I'm glad to have you home.

We, by which I mean all the principal figures in the Administration, have missed your wise counsel, your energetic support and your exemplary dedication to the service of the country.

On the purely personal side it

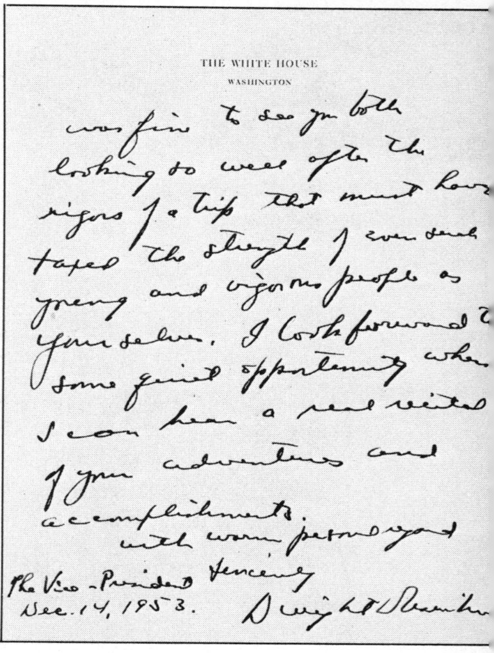

THE WHITE HOUSE
WASHINGTON

was fine to see you both looking so well after the rigors of a trip that must have taxed the strength of even such young and vigorous people as yourselves. I look forward to some quiet opportunity when I can hear a real recital of your adventures and accomplishments.

With warm personal regard
Sincerely
Dwight D. Eisenhower

The Vice-President
Dec. 14, 1953.

Inauguration Day 1957. President Eisenhower stands with two of his grandchildren, Anne and David Eisenhower; RN with Tricia and Julie. This was the first meeting between David and Julie, who were to be married twelve years later.

RN's first and only White House news conference as Vice President, in November 1957, following President Eisenhower's stroke.

WIDE WORLD PHOTOS

GEORGE SILK/*Life Magazine* © 1952 TIME INC.

Frank Nixon in Whittier in 1952.

WAYNE MILLER/*Life Magazine* © 1952 TIME INC.

RN with Hannah Nixon in 1952.

Caracas: RN's limousine after the mob attack on May 13, 1958.

UNITED PRESS INTERNATIONAL

With Queen Elizabeth II in London, November 1958.

Sir Winston Churchill pushed aside his aide to stand alone before the cameras at his door in Hyde Park Gate, London, November 1958.

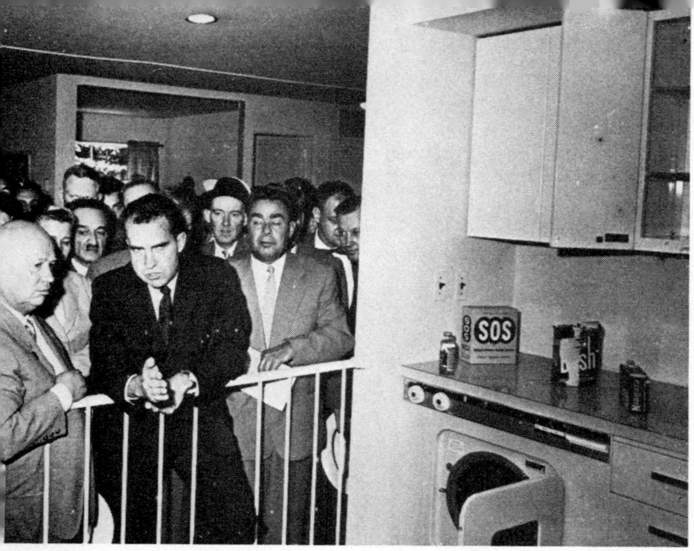

WIDE WORLD PHOTOS

Making a point with Khrushchev in the "kitchen debate" at the American Exhibition in Moscow in 1959. Leonid Brezhnev is at right.

UNITED PRESS INTERNAT

With Fidel Castro in RN's office at the U.S. Capitol, April 19, 1959.

With President Eisenhower at Washington's Griffith Stadium for the first baseball game of the season on April 18, 1960.

UNITED PRESS INTERNATIONAL

implies that the world must be divided into two hostile camps with a wall of hate and fear between. What we need today is not two worlds but one world where different peoples choose the economic and political systems which they want, but where there is free communication among all the peoples living on this earth."

I tried to make clear what lay at the heart of our differences with the Soviet leadership: not which system was better, but whether one nation should seek to impose its system on other nations. Recalling Khrushchev's famous prediction that our grandchildren would live under communism, I said: "Let me say that we do not object to his saying this will happen. We only object if he tries to bring it about. . . . We prefer our system. But the very essence of our belief is that we do not and will not try to impose our system on anybody else. We believe that you and all other peoples on this earth should have the right to choose the kind of economic or political system which best fits your particular problems without any foreign intervention."

After leaving the Soviet Union, we made a brief visit to one of the captive nations—Poland.

The Polish government was extremely sensitive to the fact that Khrushchev had received a noticeably cool reception when he had recently visited Warsaw, and therefore no public announcement had been made of the time of our arrival or the route our motorcade would take. But the people knew, thanks to Radio Free Europe and the underground network that survives even in tightly controlled Communist societies.

It was a Sunday, and many people did not have to be at work. As we left the airport we soon were greeted, first by small clusters, and then by huge throngs of people, waving, clapping, shouting, cheering, many with tears streaming down their faces. Hundreds threw bouquets of flowers into my car, into Pat's car, even into the press buses that followed behind. The government security forces were totally unprepared. Time and again the motorcade was stopped by the surging crowds pressing forward, shouting "*Niech żyje Ameryka*"—"long live America"—and "*Niech żyje Eisenhower*," "*Niech żyje Nixon.*" A quarter of a million people turned out that Sunday. Despite the presence of Soviet troops, and the fact that they share a common border with the Soviet Union, on that Sunday the people of Poland demonstrated dramatically not only their friendship for the United States but also their detestation of their Communist rulers and Soviet neighbors.

When we landed in Washington on August 5, we were welcomed by a large and enthusiastic crowd. The Soviet trip had an enormous impact in America. The film clip of my first encounter with Khrushchev at the Exhibition had been shown on U.S. television, and the coverage of our other meetings had presented me as the man who stood up to Khrushchev.

There was a disadvantage to this reputation, however. Some press observers suggested that if I became President I might not be able to get along with Khrushchev, and Khrushchev subsequently did everything he could to lend credence to this theory.

1960 CAMPAIGN

Of the five presidential campaigns in which I was a direct participant, none affected me more personally than the campaign of 1960. It was a campaign of unusual intensity. Jack Kennedy and I were both in the peak years of our political energy, and we were contesting great issues in a watershed period of American life and history.

Our differences were distinct. He preached the orthodox Democratic gospel of government activism, making sweeping promises and issuing rhetorical challenges to leap ahead into an era of new leadership and social welfare. I carried the banner of constructive postwar Republicanism, bred of conservative beliefs that a healthy private sector and individual initiative set the best pace for prosperity and progress. But beyond these differences, the way the Kennedys played politics and the way the media let them get away with it left me angry and frustrated.

Kennedy and I entered the 1960 race fairly evenly matched in terms of our personal campaigning strengths and weaknesses. My most formidable asset was that, since Caracas and my confrontation with Khrushchev, I was probably the best known political figure in the country after Eisenhower. The polls showed that people thought of me as the more experienced candidate, and I intended to stress my experience in the campaign. Perhaps most important of all, I was physically, mentally, and emotionally ready for this campaign, and I was enthusiastically looking forward to it. I knew it would be an uphill battle, but I felt I could win.

On the other side of the ledger, my most serious liability was the weakness of my Republican Party base. In 1960 there were 50 million Americans of voting age who considered themselves Democrats and only 33 million who considered themselves Republicans. In the disastrous 1958 elections, Republican candidates had won only 43 percent of the total votes cast. The Republican Party was at its lowest ebb since 1936, and 1960 boded to be a bad year for anyone who ran with an (R) after his name on the ballot.

I considered Kennedy's biggest assets to be his wealth and the appeal of his personal style. Some Republican strategists thought that these would weigh against him, but I felt that in the new decade of the sixties, after eight years of Eisenhower's rather grandfatherly manner, people might be ready for an entirely new style of presidential leadership. He would also be able to count on strong party unity. Unlike Republicans, Democrats are usually able to swallow their differences and unite behind their party's nominee.

Kennedy had two principal political liabilities. In my judgment one was only apparent—his Catholicism; the other was real—his lack of experience. The religion issue would cut several ways and would probably end up as an advantage for Kennedy. The pockets of fundamentalist anti-Catholic prejudice that still existed were concentrated in states that I stood to win anyway. But many Catholics would vote for Kennedy because he was Catholic, and some non-Catholics would vote for him just to prove they were not bigoted. The experience issue, however, was one on which Kennedy was vulnerable. He had been an active senator for nearly eight years and had established a reputation for the caliber of his mind and the quality of his staff, but he had not carved out any particular areas of expertise.

Just as I was sure that Kennedy would be the Democratic nominee, I was almost as sure that Lyndon Johnson would be his running mate. Both men were superb campaigners and politicians, and a Kennedy–Johnson ticket would be ideally balanced in age, experience, region, and religion. It might be an uneasy and joyless marriage of convenience, but it was a ticket that would unite the party by assuring Southern conservative support even though the ticket was headed by a Northern liberal.

The obvious Republican equivalent of the Kennedy–Johnson ticket would have been a Nixon–Rockefeller ticket. I made the gesture of offering him the position when we met in New York on July 22. As I expected, he declined. I was not altogether sorry, because Rockefeller's independent temperament would have made him a much more difficult running mate for me to deal with than Johnson would be for Kennedy. But his refusal left me without the option of the kind of finely balanced ticket the Democrats had achieved.

Kennedy made a strong impression and received a great deal of favorable publicity during the Democratic National Convention, which was held in Los Angeles in mid-July. Before the Republicans convened in Chicago on July 25, my pollster, Claude Robinson, placed the Kennedy–Johnson ticket 55 percent to 45 percent ahead of any ticket the Republicans might field.

Just after 11 P.M. on Wednesday, July 27, the state of Arizona moved to make unanimous my nomination as Republican candidate for President of the United States. I immediately called a meeting of thirty-two Republican Party leaders to confer on the selection of the vice presidential nominee.

Before the convention there had been six names on my list of possible running mates: Ambassador to the United Nations Henry Cabot Lodge of Massachusetts; Senator Thruston Morton of Kentucky; Congressman Walter Judd of Minnesota; Congressman Gerald Ford of Michigan; Secretary of the Interior Fred Seaton of Nebraska; and Secretary of Labor Jim Mitchell of New Jersey.

By the time I met with the leaders in my suite at the Blackstone Hotel, I had narrowed the list to three: Judd, Morton, and Lodge. Both Judd and Morton urged that I select a man with a national reputation who would appeal to wider political constituencies than I might otherwise attract. Morton wanted the position badly, but he magnanimously recommended that I choose Lodge. Eisenhower had also urged me to select him.

Lodge had the greatest support among the assembled party leaders, and overall, I thought he was the right choice. While I was concerned that his domestic views were more liberal than mine, I had no doubt that if the need ever arose he would be able to take over and serve as President with great distinction. At 2:30 A.M. I telephoned him and asked him to be my running mate. He accepted and immediately made plans to come to Chicago.

My next task was the final preparation of my acceptance speech. I wanted to use the speech to break the stolid and unimaginative stereotype of Eisenhower and his administration that had been presented by Kennedy and the Democrats at their convention. I wanted to challenge people with the rather daring idea that a Republican campaign could be exciting and even inspiring. I asked Rockefeller to introduce me to the convention. He understood that the unity of the party would depend largely on his words, and he came through effectively—as did Goldwater, when he spoke.

I declared my intention to wage a campaign unprecedented in scope: "I announce to you tonight—and I pledge to you—that I personally will carry this campaign into every one of the fifty states of this nation between now and November 8." In an election between evenly matched contenders, every vote—and thus every state—would be important.

I believed the key issue of the campaign would be experience, and in my acceptance speech I brought home that message.

I asked all Americans to join in meeting what I believed was to be the exciting challenge we faced in the years ahead:

> We shall build a better America . . . in which we shall see the realization of the dreams of millions of people not only in America but throughout the world—for a fuller, freer, richer life than men have ever known in the history of mankind.
>
> What we must do is wage the battles for peace and freedom with the

> same . . . dedication with which we wage battles in war. . . . The only answer to a strategy of victory for the Communist world is a strategy of victory for the free world. Let the victory we seek . . . be the victory of freedom over tyranny, of plenty over hunger, of health over disease, in every country of the world.

The publicity surrounding the Republican convention and my acceptance speech succeeded as I had hoped they would. Gallup reported a decisive switch from the pre-convention results: now Nixon–Lodge led Kennedy–Johnson, 53 percent to 47 percent. But I knew that the immediate impact of the convention and the speech would soon wear off, and the projections about the election itself were that we would be neck and neck until the finish.

An entirely new factor entered American political campaigning in 1960 with the first televised debates between the two presidential candidates.

An incumbent seldom agrees willingly to debate his challenger, and I knew that the debates would benefit Kennedy more than me by giving his views national exposure, which he needed more than I did. Further, he would have the tactical advantage of being on the offensive. As a member of Eisenhower's administration, I would have to defend the administration's record while trying to move the discussion to my own plans and programs. But there was no way I could refuse to debate without having Kennedy and the media turn my refusal into a central campaign issue. The question we faced was not whether to debate, but how to arrange the debates so as to give Kennedy the least possible advantage.

We agreed to a series of four appearances. The second and third were to be, in effect, joint press conferences. The first and fourth would more nearly resemble a debate format: each candidate would make opening and closing statements, and a panel of reporters would ask questions. One of these two programs would be devoted exclusively to domestic issues, the other exclusively to foreign policy. Determining our preferred order of these two broadcasts turned out to be one of my most important decisions of the campaign—and one of my biggest mistakes.

Since there was no precedent for this kind of televised debate, we could only guess which program would have the larger audience. Foreign affairs was my strong suit, and I wanted the larger audience for that debate. I thought more people would watch the first one, and that interest would diminish as the novelty of the confrontation wore off. Most of my advisers believed that interest would build as the campaign progressed, and that the last program, nearest Election Day, would be the most important one. I yielded to their judgment and agreed that in the negotiations to set up the debates I would agree to scheduling the domestic policy debate first and the foreign policy debate last.

I began my fifty-state campaign with two trips into the South in mid-August. The first was to North Carolina, my home for three years when I had been at Duke. We received a warm welcome, and the successful visit was marred only by a seemingly small incident: I bumped my knee getting into a car in Greensboro. The immediate pain soon passed, and I thought no more about it. But twelve days later the knee became intensely painful, and tests showed it was badly infected. I required massive doses of penicillin and other antibiotics—and two weeks in bed at Walter Reed Hospital.

All the plans I had made for seizing the initiative by extensive early campaigning were now useless. It was painful when my knee was injected with antibiotics, but it was even more painful to know that each day I was falling behind Kennedy and losing precious time in the campaign.

I was finally able to leave the hospital on Friday, September 9. After only a weekend at home I began an intensive two-week tour covering 15,000 miles and twenty-five states. The first day of that tour was representative of the entire schedule. We took an early morning flight from Baltimore to appear at a rally in Indianapolis, from Indianapolis we flew to Dallas for a motorcade and rally, and from Dallas to San Francisco for a rally at the airport and one downtown in Union Square. I got to bed at 2 A.M. Eastern time.

This pace was bound to tell. Within three days I was running a fever of over 103 degrees, but I continued to keep my schedule. I can now see that I should have accepted the advice of my campaign manager, Bob Finch, my chief scheduler, Jim Bassett, and other members of my staff who urged that my hospital stay was a compelling and legitimate reason to abandon the pledge I had made to carry my campaign to all fifty states of the Union. But having made the pledge, I was stubborn and determined to carry it through. I felt that I had to move decisively to catch up with Kennedy. While I was in the hospital he had regained the lead in the Gallup poll by a slender 51 percent to 49 percent. So instead of lightening my campaign load, I intensified it to make up for lost time.

In the first week after leaving the hospital, I covered fourteen states. In the second week, I covered eleven states. After less than a day at home in Washington, I took a night flight to Chicago, where a crowd of 5,000 was waiting at the airport. After making a short speech and shaking some hands, we moved on to the street rallies that had been planned in each of the five election wards we were to drive through. It was after 1 A.M. before I got to bed. The first debate with Kennedy was set for that evening, September 26.

In the morning I was scheduled to make a speech to the annual convention of the carpenters' union, so I had only the afternoon for an uninterrupted review of my notes for the debate. When I arrived at the studio I was mentally alert but I was physically worn out, and I looked it. Between illness and schedule, I was ten pounds underweight. My collar was now a full size too large, and it hung loosely around my neck.

Kennedy arrived a few minutes later, looking tanned, rested, and fit. My television adviser, Ted Rogers, recommended that I use television makeup, but unwisely I refused, permitting only a little "beard stick" on my perpetual five o'clock shadow.

During the debate Kennedy was continually on the offensive, attacking Eisenhower's policies and calling them ineffective. His solution was a more active and interventionist federal government. I did not disagree with many of the goals he outlined, but I sharply attacked the means he advocated to achieve them.

While most of the questions dealt with substantive issues, it was a question of no real substance that hurt me. One of the reporters referred to a response Eisenhower had made a month earlier at the end of a press conference when asked what major ideas I had contributed as Vice President: "If you give me a week, I might think of one." Eisenhower had meant, "Ask me at next week's conference"—but he immediately knew that it had come out wrong, and he called me that afternoon to express his regret. The Democrats leaped on Eisenhower's slip to undercut my emphasis on experience and to imply that Eisenhower was less than enthusiastic about my candidacy.

Most of the editorial writers who based their opinions on substance rather than image, even in the pro-Kennedy Washington *Post* and St. Louis *Post-Dispatch,* called the debate a draw, but postdebate polls of the television audience gave the edge to Kennedy. Ralph McGill of the Atlanta *Constitution*, who supported Kennedy, observed that those listening to the debate on radio reported that I had had the better of it. This was small comfort, since the television audience had been five to six times larger than the radio audience.

It is a devastating commentary on the nature of television as a political medium that what hurt me the most in the first debate was not the substance of the encounter between Kennedy and me, but the disadvantageous contrast in our physical appearances. After the program ended, callers, including my mother, wanted to know if anything was wrong, because I did not look well.

The second debate was scheduled for October 7, eleven days later, in Washington. I knew I had to counter the visual impression of the first debate. A four-a-day regimen of rich milkshakes helped me put on weight, and this time I agreed to use makeup.

I immediately took the offensive, hitting at Kennedy's vulnerabilities.

In May he had made a rash statement after the Soviets had shot down one of our U-2 spy planes, suggesting that Eisenhower should apologize to Khrushchev. I argued that an American President should never apologize for action taken to defend America's security. I also hammered hard on Kennedy's shortsighted unwillingness to defend the offshore islands of Quemoy and Matsu, occupied by Chiang Kai-shek's forces.

After the second debate, the consensus was that I had had the better of it. The New York *Times* reported that I "clearly made a comeback, came out ahead." A New York *Herald Tribune* editorial stated that I had "clearly won the second round." But 20 million fewer people had watched this debate than had watched the first one.

In the third debate, on October 13, I appeared in a studio in Los Angeles while Kennedy spoke from New York. I continued on the offensive throughout. Once again I hit hard on the Quemoy–Matsu issue, stating that Kennedy's willingness to surrender the islands to the Communists under threat of war was no different from submitting to blackmail. Shortly after the third debate I learned that one of Kennedy's top foreign policy advisers had telephoned Secretary of State Herter to say that Kennedy did not want to give the Communists the impression that America would not stand united against aggression and was therefore prepared to revise his position in order not to appear to oppose the administration on this issue. I saw this as Kennedy's way of trying to slide away from an unpopular position, and my immediate inclination was not to let him get away with it. But the Quemoy–Matsu situation was so tense, and the importance of America's role in discouraging Communist aggression was so great, that I decided not to press the point if Kennedy modified his stand. I pointed out how his changed attitude reflected his lack of experience, and then let the issue drop.

The fourth and final debate took place in New York on October 21. This was the foreign policy debate, which we had hoped would have the largest audience. Instead, the number of viewers stubbornly remained 20 million fewer than for the first.

The day before, afternoon newspaper headlines had proclaimed: *Kennedy Advocates U.S. Intervention in Cuba; Calls for Aid to Rebel Forces in Cuba.* I knew that Kennedy had received a CIA briefing on the administration's Cuban policy and assumed that he knew, as I did, that a plan to aid the Cuban exiles was already under way on a top-secret basis. His statement jeopardized the project, which could succeed only if it were supported and implemented secretly.

I knew that this matter would be raised in our debate. In order to protect the secrecy of the planning and the safety of the thousands of men and women involved in the operation, I had no choice but to take a completely opposite stand and attack Kennedy's advocacy of open intervention in Cuba. This was the most uncomfortable and ironic duty I have had to perform in any political campaign. I shocked and disappointed many of my own supporters and received support from all the wrong places for what I considered to be all the wrong reasons. I was praised in the Washington *Post* for my restraint. Within a few days Kennedy modified his position; but only a fraction of the debate audience ever was aware of that. In that debate, Kennedy conveyed the image—to 60 million people—that he was tougher on Castro and communism than I was.

Those who claim that the "great debates" were the decisive turning point in the 1960 campaign overstate the case. To ascribe defeat or victory to a single factor in such a close contest is at best guesswork and oversimplification.

The public opinion polls seem to indicate that the debates had little significant effect on the outcome of the election. Before the first debate, Gallup had shown Kennedy ahead, 51 percent to 49 percent. Seven weeks later, after all debates and intensive nationwide campaigning, Gallup showed Kennedy with 50.5 and me with 49.5. On Election Day the polls were virtually even: 49.7 percent for Kennedy, 49.6 percent for me.

As for television debates in general, I doubt that they can ever serve a responsible role in defining the issues of a presidential campaign. Because of the nature of the medium, there will inevitably be a greater premium on showmanship than on statesmanship.

After the last debate, with just over two weeks left before the election, I intensified my efforts even more. The polls showed me slightly behind, but I could sense a momentum beginning to develop, and I felt that with a final push we could go over the top.

I continued the killing pace of the rally speeches and in the last week added several fifteen-minute television talks on the major issues. I tried to draw even more sharply my major differences with Kennedy over domestic issues, primarily the economy. The government spending programs he was proposing would raise the federal budget some $15 billion and set off rounds of higher prices. I wanted to reach as many voters as I could in these last days, and television would have been the ideal way. But television time costs money, and our campaign had run short. We could afford only one telethon, which we scheduled for the day before the election.

From the earliest days of the campaign I had planned to keep Eisenhower in reserve as a political weapon that would be the more powerful for having been sparingly used. We felt that his appearances in the last two weeks of the campaign might tip the balance to me in some close areas in key states. Eisenhower fully agreed with my strategy at the outset. But as Kennedy began to attack the record of his administration—especially on the phony issue of the alleged "missile gap," which insulted Eisenhower's intelligence as well as his competence—he began to bridle under his self-imposed restraint.

I was to have lunch with Eisenhower at the White House on October 31 to discuss a specially expanded campaign schedule, which he had suggested undertaking. The night before the luncheon Pat received a phone call from Mamie Eisenhower. She was distraught and said that Eisenhower was not up to the strain campaigning might put on his heart. But he was so determined to get out and answer the attacks on his record that she could not dissuade him. She begged Pat to have me make him change his mind without letting him know that she had intervened. "Ike must never know I called you," she said.

The next morning I received an urgent call from the White House physician, Major General Howard Snyder. He told me he could not approve a heavy campaign schedule for the President. Eisenhower's dander was up because of Kennedy's attacks, but the strain of intense campaigning might be too much for his limited cardiac reserves. "I know what he *wants* to do, and he usually won't take my advice," Snyder said. "Please, either talk him out of it or just don't let him do it—for the sake of his health."

I had rarely seen Eisenhower more animated than he was when I arrived at the White House that afternoon. An expanded itinerary had been worked out that included several additional stops in the crucial areas of downstate Illinois, upstate New York, and Michigan, where the race was believed to be particularly close. He was confused—to put it mildly—when I opened the discussion with half a dozen rather lame reasons for his not carrying out the expanded itinerary. At first he was hurt and then he was angry. But I stood my ground and insisted that he should limit himself to the original schedule and to the election eve telecast with Lodge and me. He finally acquiesced. His pride prevented him from saying anything, but I knew that he was puzzled and frustrated by my conduct.

Those who traveled with Eisenhower for his few appearances during that final week said that they had never seen him show such partisan fervor, not even in his own campaigns. In retrospect, it seems possible that if he had been able to carry out his expanded campaign schedule, he might have had a decisive impact on the outcome of the election. For example, his appearance in southern Illinois, which would have had extensive coverage in eastern Missouri as well, might have tipped the balance in those states that Kennedy won by razor-thin margins.

Under the circumstances, however, I could make no other decision than to discourage him and limit his participation. It was not until years later that Mrs. Eisenhower told him the real reason for my sudden change of mind regarding his campaigning.

After one last frenetic week, it was over. Since the convention in August I had traveled over 65,000 miles and visited all fifty states. I had made 180 scheduled speeches and delivered scores of impromptu talks and informal press conferences. There was nothing more I could have done. I did not let up once, nor did my staff. The campaign had an intensity of spirit that was at once exhausting and uplifting.

We flew to California to vote and wait for the results, which would begin coming in around six o'clock, after the polls closed in the East. To make the long afternoon pass more quickly, Pat took Tricia and Julie to Beverly Hills to have their hair done. I eased the tension of the wait by driving south on the Pacific Coast Highway with Don Hughes, Jack Sherwood, and a Los Angeles police driver. Hughes remarked that he had never been to Tijuana, so we continued all the way to Mexico. We were back in Los Angeles by the time the first results were coming in.

Any election night is an emotional roller coaster ride, but election night in 1960 was the most tantalizing and frustrating I have ever experienced. The Texas results went back and forth; Ohio leaned my way; but Pennsylvania was going to Kennedy. The Daley machine was holding back the Chicago results until the downstate Republican counties had reported and it was known how many votes the Democrats would need to carry the state. The overall trend seemed to favor Kennedy, but at midnight I was fast closing the gap of 1.7 million votes that had opened up between us early in the evening. It was problematical whether I could overtake him, but the race was still not over. Even so, most of the press had already predicted a substantial Kennedy victory, and there was tremendous pressure from reporters and commentators for me to concede. I decided to make a brief statement acknowledging the apparent trend of the returns thus far.

Pat, fierce with pride, adamantly opposed making any statement and said that she would not join me. A few minutes later, as I tried to jot down notes on what to say, she came into my room and said, "I think we should go down together." I do not know which quality I loved more—the fight or the warmth. It is at such moments, when you see the effect it has on your family, that the ache of losing is the greatest.

At 12:15 A.M. we went downstairs to the ballroom of the Ambassador Hotel. I said, "If the present trend continues, Senator Kennedy will be the next President of the United States." Our loyal supporters in the ballroom were yelling, "Don't give up!" and "You're still going to win!" Pat could barely manage to keep back the tears. I wanted only to get away to the solitude of our suite.

Julie shook me awake at six the next morning. Kennedy's lead had narrowed to 500,000 votes, and there were stories of massive vote frauds in Chicago and Texas. Everett Dirksen urged me to request a recount and demanded that I not concede. He warned that once I had conceded, voting records would be destroyed or otherwise disappear, and a recount would be impossible. After his call I sat alone for a few minutes reviewing the situation.

We had made a serious mistake in not having taken precautions against such a situation, and it was too late now. A presidential recount would require up to half a year, during which time the legitimacy of Kennedy's election would be in question. The effect could be devastating to America's foreign relations. I could not subject the country to such a situation. And what if I demanded a recount and it turned out that despite the vote fraud Kennedy had still won? Charges of "sore loser" would follow me through history and remove any possibility of a further political career. After considering these and many other factors, I made my decision and sent Kennedy a telegram conceding the election.

I had planned to sleep on the long flight back to Washington, but I found I could not. Instead, I thought about how close we had come and what we should have done differently.

The 1960 election was the closest presidential contest since Harrison–Cleveland in 1888. Kennedy received 34,221,000 votes and I received 34,108,000: a difference of only 113,000. The shift of one-half vote per precinct could have changed the outcome.

We found Washington astir with talk of election fraud. Many Republican leaders were still urging me to contest the results and demand recounts. Eisenhower himself urged that course, offering to help raise the money needed for recounts in Illinois and Texas.

There is no doubt that there was substantial vote fraud in the 1960 election. Texas and Illinois produced the most damaging, as well as the most flagrant, examples. In one county in Texas, for example, where only 4,895 voters were registered, 6,138 votes were counted. In Chicago a voting machine recorded 121 votes after only 43 people had voted; I lost this precinct, 408–79. The Washington journalist and editor Benjamin Bradlee, a close friend of Kennedy's, has written in his book, *Conversations with Kennedy,* that Kennedy called Mayor Daley on election night to find out how things were shaping up in Chicago. "Mr. President," Daley reportedly said, "with a little bit of luck and the help of a few close friends, you're going to carry Illinois."

Several years after Kennedy's death, New York *Times* columnist Tom Wicker wrote in the foreword of Neal Peirce's *The People's President:* "Nobody knows to this day, or ever will, whom the American people really elected President in 1960. Under the prevailing system,

John F. Kennedy was inaugurated, but it is not at all clear that this was really the will of the people or, if so, by what means and margin that will was expressed."

As experienced as I was in politics by 1960, I encountered several new and unexpected factors, each of which had a strong influence on the outcome of the election.

First, there was the substantial and influential power that the emergence of television as the primary news medium gave the reporters, commentators, and producers. It was largely they who decided what the public would hear and see of the campaign.

Another new political phenomenon was the way so many reporters in 1960 became caught up in the excitement of Kennedy's campaign and infected with his personal sense of mission. This bred an unusual mutuality of interests that replaced the more traditional skepticism of the press toward politicians. Theodore H. White described this in his book *The Making of the President 1960*:

> By the last weeks of the campaign, those forty or fifty national correspondents who had followed Kennedy since the beginning of his electoral exertions into the November days had become more than a press corps—they had become his friends and, some of them, his most devoted admirers. When the bus or the plane rolled or flew through the night, they sang songs of their own composition about Mr. Nixon and the Republicans in chorus with the Kennedy staff and felt that they, too, were marching like soldiers of the Lord to the New Frontier.

Writing to me after the election, Willard Edwards, the Chicago *Tribune*'s veteran political analyst, put it more bluntly. He referred to the "staggering extent of . . . slanted reporting" as "one of the most, if not the most, shameful chapters of the American press in history."

The other unique aspect of this campaign was the Kennedy organization and technique. I had been through some pretty rough campaigns in the past, but compared to the others, going into the 1960 campaign was like moving from the minor to the major leagues. I had an efficient, totally dedicated, well-financed, and highly motivated organization. But we were faced by an organization that had equal dedication and unlimited money that was led by the most ruthless group of political operators ever mobilized for a presidential campaign.

Kennedy's organization approached campaign dirty tricks with a roguish relish and carried them off with an insouciance that captivated many politicians and overcame the critical faculties of many reporters. I should have anticipated what was coming as I observed some of what went on in Kennedy's brilliant but coldly mechanical destruction of Hubert Humphrey in the primaries. In his autobiography, *The Education of a Public Man,* published sixteen years later, Humphrey wrote that the Kennedy organization was undeniably impressive and successful. "But underneath the beautiful exterior," he added, "there was an element of ruthlessness and toughness that I had trouble either accepting or forgetting."

Finally, I was not prepared for the blatant and highly successful way the Kennedys repeatedly made religion an issue in the campaign even as they professed that it should not be one. Led by Robert Kennedy, they managed to turn the election partially into a referendum on tolerance versus bigotry. From this point on I had the wisdom and wariness of someone who had been burned by the power of the Kennedys and their money and by the license they were given by the media. I vowed that I would never again enter an election at a disadvantage by being vulnerable to them—or anyone—on the level of political tactics.

During the 1972 campaign, in the diary I was keeping at the time, I reflected on what might have happened if I had won the presidency in 1960:

> If we had known then as much about how to campaign, etc., as we know now we would have probably won in 1960. Whether that would have been a good thing or a bad thing I am not sure. I am speaking now not personally but so far as the country was concerned. It might have been that we would have continued the establishment types in office too long and would not have done the job we should have done as far as the country was concerned. On the other hand, had we won in 1960 we would have handled the Cuban Bay of Pigs crisis much differently, and would probably have faced down the Russians and saved Cuba from Castro, with all the implications that might have had for the future. I think also that we would have handled Vietnam quite differently, and would have used our power effectively very early in the war if we had found it necessary to use it at all. In any event, history was certainly kind to us by arranging for the Cuban missile confrontation to come in 1962, which sealed the fate as far as the gubernatorial election was concerned. Had we won the gubernatorial election, as I have often pointed out, I would have inevitably been nominated in 1964 and would have lost. Of course, you could write the script a different way—had we won [in 1962] Kennedy might not have been going to Texas and Oswald might never have shot him and under the circumstances we might have had a re-run of the '60 campaign with a better

chance to win than was the case after the Kennedy assassination and the martyr halo which Johnson was able to clutch to his brow as against Goldwater.

Within a few days after the election I was already thinking about what we would do next after my fourteen years in public life came to an end on January 20, 1961.

Pat and I went directly from the inaugural ceremony to the F Street Club, where Admiral and Mrs. Lewis Strauss were the hosts at a farewell luncheon for President and Mrs. Eisenhower.

When I said goodbye to Eisenhower, he held my hand for a long time as he shook it. For a moment I thought he was going to become emotional, but he said simply, "I want you and Pat to come up and visit us in Gettysburg very soon." I said that we would.

That night Pat and I had a quiet dinner at home with Tricia and Julie. They were very subdued. Both said that if I had not been cheated in Chicago and a couple of other places, we would be having this dinner at the White House. Despite the way I felt I told them that this was no time for bitterness and that one benefit of losing the election was that I would be home for dinner more often. When school was out we could do some traveling together.

My Secret Service protection had ended at noon, but I had my official car and chauffeur until midnight. John Wardlaw had been my driver for almost eight years, and I asked him if he would mind coming back after dinner for one last ride through the city.

The streets were snarled with traffic, made worse by the snow and ice. Hundreds of cars and rented limousines were lined up outside the hotels, waiting to pick up men in tails and women in long gowns on their way to the inaugural balls. No one noticed us as we drove past the White House and headed through the streets toward Capitol Hill.

I asked John to park in the space reserved for the Vice President's car, and I got out and walked up the broad stone stairs. A surprised guard let me in, and I walked past the entrance to the Senate Chamber and down the long corridor to the Rotunda, the dome of the Capitol rising above it. The only sound was the echo of my heels on the bare stone floor.

I opened a door and went onto the balcony that looks out across the west grounds of the Capitol. I had stood there many times before. It is one of the most magnificent vistas in the world, and it never seemed more beautiful than at this moment. The mall was covered with fresh snow. The Washington Monument stood out stark and clear against the luminous gray sky, and in the distance I could see the Lincoln Memorial. I stood looking at the scene for at least five minutes. I thought about the great experiences of the past fourteen years. Now all that was over, and I would be leaving Washington, which had been my home since I arrived as a young congressman in 1947.

As I turned to go inside, I suddenly stopped short, struck by the thought that this was not the end—that someday I would be back here. I walked as fast as I could back to the car.

Private Citizen
1961–1967

The day after Kennedy's inauguration, Pat and I flew to Eleuthera in the Bahamas to spend a few days with friends, trying to relax while we discussed our plans for the immediate future.

During my fourteen years of public service, we had lived a comfortable but simple life. After we paid the costs of moving from Washington to Los Angeles, our sole asset other than personal effects was a $48,000 equity in our house in Washington. I felt that I owed it to Pat to take a job that would pay well enough to support a reasonably comfortable life and send our daughters to good colleges, and also give me time with them to make up for the long hours and days I had had to spend away from home during the vice presidency. I also wanted a job that would allow me to stay at least a little involved in politics.

Pat and I wanted to move back to California, so I decided to accept an offer from the Los Angeles law firm of Adams, Duque, and Hazeltine. In 1946, when I was running against Voorhis, Earl Adams had offered me a job with the firm in the event I lost the election. As I told him jokingly, it had taken me only fourteen years to get the right qualification. We did not want to take Tricia and Julie out of school in the middle of the year, so we decided that Pat would stay with them in Washington and I would live in Los Angeles until June.

It was not an easy time. Relatives and friends wanted me to stay with them, but I preferred to be alone, so I rented a small bachelor apartment on Wilshire Boulevard not far from the office. I learned to fix my own meals. Fortunately, I have never been fussy about food and I actually learned to enjoy heating a TV dinner and eating it alone while reading a book or magazine.

I had thought that I could move right into the work of the law firm, just as I had done with every other challenging new job. For several weeks, however, I found it difficult to concentrate and almost impossible to work up much enthusiasm. I realized I was experiencing the letdown of defeat.

In 1968 I had a different and completely unexpected experience: the fatigue and letdown of victory. But then there was the challenge of setting up a new administration. In 1961 I found that virtually everything I did seemed unexciting and unimportant by comparison with national office. When you win, you are driven by the challenges you have to meet; when you lose, you must drive yourself to do whatever is required.

The last thing I wanted to do was talk to people about the election. But many of those who called or wrote had supported me so loyally over the years that I felt an obligation to see them or at least to talk to them by phone. Requests for public appearances and speeches continued to pour in. But aside from the fact that I was simply "talked out" from the campaign, I believed that the new administration should have the traditional honeymoon of freedom from partisan criticism.

As time went on I began to adjust to my new life and even to enjoy it. In the spring Pat and the girls came out, and we spent Easter vacation by the ocean in Santa Monica. The girls loved the beach and the warm weather, and their enthusiasm about California began to rub off on me.

THE BAY OF PIGS

I became increasingly interested in taking up my role as titular leader of the Republican Party. I was disturbed by some of Kennedy's early foreign policy actions. During his first weeks in office he was confronted with a crisis involving Communist aggression in Laos. After an initial show of strength in one of his first press conferences, he pulled back and ended up accepting a supposedly neutral government that everyone knew would be heavily influenced by the Communists. I decided that it was time for the administration's honeymoon to end, and I agreed to give a speech before the Executives Club of Chicago on May 5, 1961.

Because my speech was to deal with foreign policy, I asked the White House to allow Allen Dulles to give me a CIA briefing. My request was approved, and we arranged to meet at my house in Washington at six o'clock on April 19.

Two days earlier, while I was still in California, I heard the news that anti-Castro rebel forces had landed in Cuba at a spot unhappily known as the Bay of Pigs. During the next few days the news reports were frustratingly sketchy and incomplete, but it was clear that the invaders had met with considerable resistance and had not been able to achieve much initial success.

While I was waiting for Dulles on April 19, I picked up the afternoon Washington *Star,* and read more pessimistic—but still inconclusive—reports about the invasion. Dulles sent word that he would be late, and when he finally arrived shortly after 7:30, he looked nervous and shaken.

I asked him if he would like a drink, and Dulles replied, "I certainly would—I really need one. This is the worst day of my life!"

"What's wrong?" I asked.

He shook his head. "Everything is lost," he said dejectedly. "The Cuban invasion is a total failure."

Dulles explained that after his election Kennedy had given his go-ahead to the invasion plans formulated under Eisenhower, and the CIA had continued to train the Cuban exiles. However, some of Kennedy's advisers urged him to call off the action on the ground that if our support became known, America's prestige in the world would be badly damaged. They held out the specter of World War III if the Soviet Union decided to intervene, and they painted grim pictures of the repercussions if the invasion failed.

The invasion had been planned for February, but Kennedy postponed it while internal debate raged within the administration. Finally on April 15 Kennedy decided to go ahead. There was sad admiration in Dulles's voice when he said, "It took great courage for the President to overrule some of his advisers and order the invasion to proceed." But the nervous aides made a final attempt to dissuade Kennedy, and he tried to keep both sides happy by making last-minute compromises. He canceled two of the three air strikes that were intended to knock out Castro's air force and to provide air cover for the invasion forces. The Free Cuban forces landing in the Bay of Pigs found themselves sitting ducks for Castro's Soviet-made bombers. By holding back the air support, Kennedy had doomed the operation.

At first the White House and Adlai Stevenson, our ambassador to the United Nations, completely denied any American involvement in the invasion. Then Kennedy had to deny the denials. Our international prestige suffered a double blow—first for having mounted an unsuccessful invasion and then for trying to deny it.

Dulles stared at the floor. "I should have told him that we must not fail," he said. "And I came very close to doing so, but I didn't. It was the greatest mistake of my life."

I spent the morning of April 20 on Capitol Hill conferring with the Republican leaders. We agreed that the situation was too serious for partisanship. We all had to stand behind the President until the crisis was over. When I got home early that afternoon, I found a note from

Tricia next to the telephone in the hall: "JFK called. I knew it! It wouldn't be long before he would get into trouble and have to call on you for help." I dialed the familiar White House number. The operator immediately put my call through to the President. Sounding tense and tired, he wasted no time on small talk. He said, "Dick, could you drop by to see me?"

Kennedy was standing at his desk in the Oval Office talking to Lyndon Johnson. We greeted each other with solemn handshakes. The atmosphere was tense.

After Johnson left the room, Kennedy motioned me to one of the small sofas near the fireplace; he sat in his rocking chair. "I had a meeting with the members of the Cuban Revolutionary Council," he said. "Several of those who were there had lost their sons, brothers, or other close relatives or friends in this action. Talking to them and seeing the tragic expressions on their faces was the worst experience of my life."

I asked about the Cubans' morale. He said, "Last night they were really mad at us. But today they have calmed down a lot and, believe it or not, they are ready to go out and fight again if we will give them the word and the support."

With that he jumped up from his chair and began pacing back and forth in front of his desk. His anger and frustration poured out in a profane barrage. Over and over he cursed everyone who had advised him: the CIA, the Chairman of the Joint Chiefs of Staff, members of his White House staff. "I was assured by every son of a bitch I checked with—all the military experts and the CIA—that the plan would succeed," he said.

Everything had been going so well for him; a few days earlier he stood high in the polls, and his press was overwhelmingly favorable. Now he was in deep trouble, and he felt that he was the innocent victim of bad advice from men whom he had trusted. He paced up and down with his fists clenched tightly.

After he had blown off some steam, he returned to his rocking chair. For a moment the room was silent. It suddenly struck me how alone he must feel—how wronged yet how responsible.

He looked over at me and said, "What would you do now in Cuba?" Without any hesitation I replied, "I would find a proper legal cover and I would go in. There are several justifications that could be used, like protecting American citizens living in Cuba and defending our base at Guantánamo. I believe that the most important thing at this point is that we do whatever is necessary to get Castro and communism out of Cuba."

He seemed to think about what I said, and then he shook his head. "Both Walter Lippmann and Chip Bohlen have reported that Khrushchev is in a very cocky mood at this time. This means that there is a good chance that, if we move on Cuba, Khrushchev will move on Berlin. I just don't think we can take the risk, in the event their appraisal is correct."

I explained that I looked at Cuba in the larger context of Communist ambitions around the world. Khrushchev would probe and prod in several places at the same time, and as soon as we showed any weakness, he would create a crisis to take advantage of us. I said that we should take some action in both Cuba and Laos, including if necessary a commitment of American air power.

"I just don't think we ought to get involved in Laos," Kennedy said, "particularly where we might find ourselves fighting millions of Chinese troops in the jungles." This was a complete reversal of what he had said on television in March about the vital importance of defending Laos. "In any event," he continued, "I don't see how we can make any move in Laos, which is thousands of miles away, if we don't make a move in Cuba, which is only ninety miles away."

I was surprised and disappointed that he did not make the logical connection between his own statements: that the Communist threat was indivisible, and unless it was resisted everywhere there was really no point in resisting it anywhere. But I knew that this was no time to try to convince him of that; this was a crisis—he wanted and needed my support.

I said, "I will publicly support you to the hilt if you make such a decision in regard to either Laos or Cuba, and I will urge all other Republicans to do likewise. I realize that some political observers say you might risk political defeat in 1964 if either the Cuban or Far East crisis involves an American armed forces commitment. I want you to know that I am one who will never make that a political issue if such action becomes necessary."

For a moment he seemed lost in thought, weighing what I had said. Then he gave a slight shrug of his shoulders and said, "The way things are going and with all the problems we have, if I do the right kind of job, I don't know whether I am going to be here four years from now."

We had been talking for almost an hour, and I felt that I had at least lightened his burden by listening to him and by assuring him that I would not turn this crisis into a partisan exercise.

"It really is true that foreign affairs is the only important issue for a President to handle, isn't it?" he said. "I mean, who gives a shit if the minimum wage is $1.15 or $1.25, in comparison to something like this?"

We walked out to the covered porch alongside the Oval Office. The spring flowers in the Rose Garden were in full bloom. A White House car was waiting for me in the driveway.

As he walked to the car with me, he said that Pat Brown was concerned because a poll showed him running behind me for governor of California. Although supporters had suggested I run, I didn't have the slightest intention of doing so, and I was very surprised that Kennedy and Brown were discussing that possibility.

We shook hands, and he turned and walked back up the path to his office. His hands were thrust in his jacket pockets, but his head was bowed and his usually jaunty walk seemed slow. At that moment I felt empathy for a man who had to face up to a bitter tragedy that was not entirely his fault but was nonetheless his inescapable responsibility.

I flew to Chicago on May 5 to make the Executives Club address.

I began by stressing that as far as I was concerned, criticism of the new administration should be responsible and constructive, and focus only on issues of substance. Still, I was concerned about the way Kennedy had handled the Bay of Pigs, and I wanted to make my concerns known. I said, "Those who talk constantly of our prestige would seem to believe that we are in a popularity contest with other countries to see who was most liked and admired. What we must remember is that we are in a fight for our lives."

My greatest concern was that Kennedy, having been burned in Cuba, would be reluctant to stand up to the Communists in the other places like Laos, Vietnam, or Berlin. I said that "the worst thing that could flow from our failure in Cuba is not the temporary drop in prestige which seems to obsess too many observers but that this failure may discourage American policymakers from taking decisive steps in the future because there is a risk of failure."

There was a long round of applause when I said that we should learn at least one lesson from the Cuban invasion: "Whenever American prestige is to be committed on a major scale we must be willing to commit enough power to obtain our objective even if all of our intelligence estimates prove wrong. Putting it bluntly, we should not start things in the world unless we are prepared to finish them."

After this speech I found that I was back in the national limelight as leader of the "loyal opposition." Any concerns I might have had that time would hang heavy in private life were soon dispelled. With the demands of the law firm, my personal and political correspondence, unavoidable travel, routine office work, preparation of the columns I was writing for the Times-Mirror syndicate, and planning for a book I had agreed to write, this was one of the busiest periods of my life. As usual, the ones who suffered most, and most silently, were my family. One of my reasons for moving to California was to have more time with Pat and the girls, but I think I saw them even less that year than I had when we were in Washington.

By December 1961, I was more tired than I had been at the end of the 1960 campaign. I was almost ten pounds underweight from strain and fatigue, and I became short-tempered at home and at the office.

It was ironic that while I was writing a book about handling crises, I had let myself get so run-down that I was not in good shape for making a decision which created a major new crisis for me and my family.

RUNNING FOR GOVERNOR: 1962

The pressures to run for governor began almost from the day I arrived back in California.

Friends, old supporters, and business and party leaders from all over the state approached me by letter, phone, or in person, urging me to run. I replied that I wasn't interested in running for anything so soon after the 1960 presidential election, and urged that they look elsewhere for a candidate.

But the pressure continued and by the beginning of the summer I began for the first time to consider seriously the possibility of running. My intuition was unchanged—I still thought it would be a case of running for the wrong office at the wrong time.

I had a long talk with Eisenhower at the El Dorado Country Club near Palm Springs. He thought that I should run for governor in 1962 and then run for the presidency again in 1964. He said, "It has been my experience that when a man is asked by a majority of the leaders of his party to take on an assignment, he must do so or risk losing their support in the future. If you don't run and the Republican candidate loses, you will be blamed for it, and you will be through as a national political leader."

A few weeks later I wrote a long letter to Eisenhower outlining the pros and cons of running. In this letter I expressed the deepest underlying reason for my apparent indecisiveness and lack of enthusiasm:

> Another argument which is made against my running is that from the time I started the campaign in January through the period I served in office, I would have to devote my attention almost exclusively to the problems of California. It is true that Rockefeller has been able to comment at times on national and international issues but my own belief is that our problems here are so complex and also we are, frankly, physically so far away from the centers of national and international news media that I simply do not believe it would be possible for me to continue to speak at all constructively on national and international issues if I decided to run for governor.

The polls were then indicating that I could defeat Brown fairly easily; one had me beating him 5 to 3. I am not sure that Eisenhower's advice would have been the same had he thought there was a considerable risk of my losing.

Rose Woods had come to California to be my secretary at the law firm. She called me at home on the afternoon of July 11 to tell me that Whittaker Chambers had died. The news hit me hard. I knew that Chambers had not been well, but he had survived so much in his life that I suppose I had come to think of him as indestructible. Now he was dead.

That night I reread the last letter he had written to me, shortly after I had returned to California in February 1961:

> It seems possible that we may not meet again—I mean at all. So forgive me if I say here a few things which, otherwise, I should not presume to say.
>
> You have decades ahead of you. Almost from the first day we met (think, it is already 12 years ago) I sensed in you some quality, deep-going, difficult to identify in the world's glib way, but good, and meaningful for you and multitudes of others. I do not believe for a moment that because you have been cruelly checked in the employment of what is best in you, what is most yourself, that that check is final. It cannot be. . . .
>
> You have years in which to serve. Service is your life. You must serve. You must, therefore, have a base from which to serve.
>
> Some tell me that there are reasons why you should not presently run for governor of California. Others tell me that you would almost certainly carry the state. I simply do not know the facts. But if it is at all feasible, I, for what it is worth, strongly urge you to consider this.

Friends whose political judgment I respected were sharply divided as to what I should do. Eisenhower, Tom Dewey, and J. Edgar Hoover urged me to run for governor so that I could have a new political base. Herbert Hoover and General Douglas MacArthur advised me to run for Congress so that I would have a forum from which I could address national and international issues. MacArthur put it in his characteristically oracular way: "California is a great state but it is too parochial. You should be in Washington, not Sacramento."

Early in August I had a long talk with Bob Finch. We discussed some of the political forces that would be arrayed against me if I ran.

First, there would be the all-out opposition of the Kennedy administration. They would do everything they could to stop me from getting a new political lease on life by winning the governorship. Nor could I count on the support of the many California Republicans who favored Rockefeller or Goldwater for President in 1964. The two men would be opposing each other as the convention neared, but they would join in opposing me now.

Joe Shell, the Republican leader in the state assembly, had already begun to campaign for the gubernatorial nomination, and had picked up considerable conservative support and money. Finally, there was Pat Brown himself. Although generally considered something of a bumbler, he was in the enviable political position of being a man whom no one particularly disliked.

By the end of the conversation I was more convinced than ever that my first intuition was right: I should not run for governor in 1962. The word found its way back to Washington, and within a couple of days I received a call from Len Hall and Cliff Folger urgently requesting to talk with me before I announced my decision. The next afternoon they were on a plane for California.

Hall said, "Either you run or you're finished in national politics. In 1962 you'll have Rockefeller running in New York, another strong candidate for governor in Pennsylvania, another in Michigan. Who will remember Dick Nixon? You can only win in '64 if you run and win for governor now." They both stressed how much Eisenhower was counting on me to run and win.

My own political judgment at that point told me that Kennedy would be almost unbeatable in 1964. If I ran for governor I felt I would have to pledge to spend the full term in Sacramento. That would leave someone else to square off in 1964 against Kennedy, his money, and his tactics.

The real problem was that I had no great desire to be governor of California. Equally compelling was my knowledge of how strongly Pat felt against my running. She thought that we owed it to ourselves as well as to Tricia and Julie to spend more time with them during their adolescent years.

My inclination was against making the race. But Eisenhower's advice and the pressures brought to bear by Hall and Folger, by Whittaker Chambers's letter, and by the importunings of many close friends began to tip the balance in favor of a decision to run.

I dreaded bringing up the subject with Pat and Tricia and Julie, so I left it until the last possible moment. I had asked Bob Finch to arrange a press conference on September 27, when I would announce my decision. On September 25, as we all sat around the table after dinner, I described some of the factors and the conflicting advice I had been receiving and weighing. I said that I was now thinking of running, but I wanted to know their feelings before I made up my mind.

Pat, as I expected, took a strong stand against it. Many women would give everything they have to be a celebrity, but Pat has always been one of those rare individuals whose ego does not depend on public attention. Her deepest feelings have always been private, and she shares them only with her family and loved ones. She had been by my side through all the invective and controversy of the congressional campaigns; she had endured nobly and silently the agony of the fund crisis; and during the vice presidency she had constantly balanced the requirements of national office with the importance of maintaining a normal and loving home for Tricia and Julie. But there had been so many campaigns and dinners and trips that after the 1960 defeat she had looked forward to building a new and private life in California for ourselves and the girls. She said, "If you run this time, I'm not going to be out campaigning with you as I have in the past." Tricia and Julie at fifteen and thirteen were still too young to exert a major influence on my decision, but I wanted to hear their views. When Julie saw that Pat and I had such a strong difference of opinion, she said that she would approve whatever I decided. Tricia was the only one who took a positive line: "I am not sure whether you should run," she said, "but I kind of have the feeling that you should just to show them you aren't finished because of the election that was stolen from us in 1960!"

We talked about it for almost an hour. Finally I went upstairs to my study. I sat at my desk and started to make some notes for the press conference, announcing that I had decided not to run for governor.

Half an hour later Pat came in. She sat down on the sofa, outside the pool of light cast by my desk lamp. Her face was in the shadows, but I could tell from her voice that she was fighting not to show her tremendous disappointment. "I have thought about it some more," she said, "and I am more convinced than ever that if you run it will be a terrible mistake. But if you weigh everything and still decide to run, I will support your decision. I'll be there campaigning with you just as I always have."

"I'm making notes to announce that I won't be running," I said, pointing to the yellow pad before me on the desk.

"No," she said firmly, "you must do whatever you think is right. If you think this is right for you, then you must do it."

We sat for some time in silence. Then she came over to me, put her hand on my shoulder, kissed me, and left the room. After she had gone, I tore off the top sheet of paper and threw it into the wastebasket. On a fresh page I began making notes for an announcement that I had decided to run.

On September 27 I held a press conference at the Statler Hilton Hotel in Los Angeles.

I said I had two decisions to announce. The first was that I would not be a candidate for President of the United States in 1964. The second was that I would be a candidate for governor of California in 1962.

This wasn't enough for many of the reporters, who demanded more. One of them referred to General William Tecumseh Sherman's famous statement, "If nominated I will not run and if elected I will not serve." I told him, "I think General Sherman's statement meant that he wasn't a candidate. Calvin Coolidge's statement was that he did not choose to run. The Nixon statement is that I shall not be a candidate in 1964."

Pat Brown greeted my announcement by immediately stating that despite my claim to the contrary, I would be a candidate for President in 1964: "He sees the governorship of this state only as a stepping-stone for his own presidential ambitions."

Instead of beginning to plan strategy and plot the campaign, I now had to spend the next three months writing and editing the final draft of my book, *Six Crises*. I had undertaken to write it a few months after Kennedy's inauguration, when the prospect of running for anything in 1962 had seemed unthinkable. Now I was up against a publisher's deadline at the very time that I had to make vital decisions about the campaign.

As I traveled through the state before the June primary, I met with a lot of heckling—but it was different from the heckling in 1950. Then I had been heckled by the far left; now I was being heckled by the far right. Members of the ultra right-wing John Birch Society had infiltrated a considerable number of Republican organizations. One of the costliest and most difficult decisions I made was to disavow support for or from any Republican candidate who was a member of the John Birch Society and who would not repudiate the extremist statements of the society's founder, Robert Welch, namely that President Eisenhower was "a dedicated, conscious agent of the Communist conspiracy," and that Foster Dulles was "a Communist agent."

Congressmen John Rousselot and Edgar Hiestand were two of my closest personal and political friends. But both were members of the John Birch Society. Whether or not they personally believed any or all of Welch's accusations, neither would repudiate them. Thus I lost not only their support but the support of their friends in two heavily Republican districts. Politically it was a no-win proposition, but as a matter of conscience I had no choice. I could not accept support from an extremist group whose leader had defamed Eisenhower and Dulles.

The primary was held on June 5. Although I won easily, Shell got over a third of the vote. I took that as a portent of the kind of Republican defections I might have to expect in November.

Fortunately my campaign organization was excellent and already was functioning smoothly; some of those who participated gained valuable experience that served us well six years later in my campaign for the presidency. Bob Haldeman was campaign manager; Maurice Stans was finance chairman. Herb Klein was my major press adviser, and a young man named Ron Ziegler worked on his staff.

Immediately after the primary, pressure began for a candidates' debate. Brown was now running ahead in the polls, so I felt that a debate would be in my interest. Brown tried to avoid a debate for just that reason, and the closest we got was a joint appearance before a group of newspaper editors and publishers in San Francisco on October 1. The Los Angeles *Times* ran a front-page account of the session under the headline: *Brown and Nixon in Violent Clash.*

After Brown and I made brief opening statements, one of the first to ask a question was Tom Braden, publisher of the Oceanside *Blade Tribune.* Braden was a liberal columnist whom Pat Brown had appointed to the State Board of Education.

"I wanted to ask you whether you as Vice President, or as a candidate for governor, think it proper for a candidate for governor, morally and ethically, to permit his family to receive a secret loan from a major defense contractor in the United States?" he said.

The chairman of the meeting jumped in immediately. "Mr. Nixon, you don't need to answer that question if you don't want to. I would rule it out on the basis that it is outside the issues of this campaign."

"As a matter of fact, Dr. Robinson, I insist on answering it," I replied. "I welcome the opportunity of answering it. Six years ago, my brother was in deep financial trouble. He borrowed $205,000 from the Hughes Tool Company. My mother put up as security for that loan practically everything she had—a piece of property, which, to her, was fabulously wealthy, and which now is producing an income of $10,000 a year to the creditor.

"My brother went bankrupt six years ago. My mother turned over the property to the Hughes Tool Company. Two years ago in the presidential election, President Kennedy refused to make a political issue out of my brother's difficulties and out of my mother's problems, just as I refused to make a political issue out of any of the charges made against the members of his family.

"I had no part or interest in my brother's business. I had no part whatever in the negotiation of this loan. I was never asked to do anything by the Hughes Tool Company and never did anything for them. And yet, despite President Kennedy's refusing to use this as an issue, Mr. Brown, privately, in talking to some of the newsmen here in this audience, and his hatchetmen have been constantly saying that I must have gotten some of the money—that I did something wrong.

"Now it is time to have this out. I was in government for fourteen years as a congressman, as a senator, as Vice President. I went to Washington with a car and a house and a mortgage. I came back with a car and a house and a bigger mortgage.

"I have made mistakes, but I am an honest man. And if the Governor of this state has any evidence pointing up that I did anything wrong in this case, that I did anything for the Hughes Tool Company, that I asked them for this loan, then instead of doing it privately, doing it slyly, the way he has—and he cannot deny it, because newsmen in this audience have told me that he has said, 'We are going to make a big issue out of the Hughes Tool Company loan'—now, he has a chance.

"All the people of California are listening on television. The people of this audience are listening. Governor Brown has a chance to stand up as a man and charge me with misconduct. Do it, sir!"

Brown was taken completely off guard by the way I had turned the issue around, and he made an unsuccessful attempt to deny that he and his staff had been raising it in the campaign. In fact, they continued to raise it throughout the campaign. The media loved the story and played it up big—both because it made such tantalizing copy and because it was so damaging to me.

I felt that I came out considerably ahead of Brown in this meeting; apparently he agreed, because he refused to participate in other joint appearances when I challenged him to do so.

Aside from the Hughes loan and my repudiation of the John Birch Society, my biggest problem in the campaign was the question of my actual interest in being governor of California. Despite my constant disclaimers of any plans to run for presidency in 1964, I was simply not able to convince many people. A poll taken during the campaign showed the extent of the difficulty: 36 percent thought I was interested in serving as governor, 64 percent thought I was interested in running for President.

Looking back, I recognize that there was a measure of truth in what the polls showed the public perceived. I thought that Kennedy would be unbeatable, so my disclaimers of any interest in running for President were absolutely honest. But I was really not all that eager to be governor of California.

Despite my efforts to campaign on the issues, every press conference brought questions about the personal attacks being made against me—I must have answered the question about the Hughes loan at least a hundred times. Reporters never tired of asking if I had repudiated the John Birch Society, or of having me reiterate my refusal to support Rousselot and Hiestand. There was no morning, afternoon, or evening that I did not deny that I was planning to use the governorship as a stepping-stone to a presidential candidacy in 1964. Most reporters showed little interest in the many detailed proposals I made on the cost of state government, crime, education, or the necessity for creating a better business climate in California.

On the evening of October 22 President Kennedy reported in a dramatic television address that the Soviets had moved medium-range nuclear missiles into Cuba. He announced a U.S. naval blockade of Cuba and demanded that the Soviets dismantle and remove the missiles immediately. The world waited tensely for Khrushchev's response to this direct challenge. For almost two days, America seemed to be tottering on the brink of nuclear war. As always in time of international crisis, the nation rallied behind the President. I strongly supported Kennedy's actions in a statement I made in Oakland and a statewide television address in San Diego.

The Cuban missile crisis completely dominated the news for the last days of the 1962 campaign. Now I knew how Stevenson must have felt when Suez and the Hungarian rebellion flared up in the last days before the election in 1956. I knew that any chance I might have had of narrowing Brown's lead in the polls was now gone.

We had to play the dreary drama through to its conclusion on election night. I left for the hotel early in the afternoon, telling my family that I would call as soon as I had an idea how it was going.

It was all over before midnight even though the numerical vote was still close. I knew the state well enough to know that votes in districts not yet reported would not be enough to carry me over. I went to bed around three o'clock, and when I got up four hours later, the worst was confirmed. I had lost to Brown by 297,000 out of nearly 6 million votes cast.

Herb Klein went downstairs to read my concession statement. I watched on the television in my room as the reporters harassed him, demanding that I come down and make a personal appearance. They were so persistent that Klein finally came up to my room and asked if I would consider meeting them. The anger and frustration, the disappointment and fatigue struggling inside me burst out. I said, "Screw them. I'm not going to do it. I don't have to, and I'm not going to. You read them my concession message to Brown, Herb, and if they want to know where I am you can tell them that I've gone home to be with my family."

Klein went back downstairs. Just as I was leaving, I looked at the television for a moment and heard the insulting tone of the reporters still asking, "Where's Nixon?"—as if I had some obligation to appear before them.

I said, "I'm going down there," and started toward the elevator. I walked into the press room and went up to the platform where Herb was talking at the microphone. I had not had time to shave. I felt terrible, and I looked worse.

I began, "Good morning, gentlemen. Now that Mr. Klein has made his statement, and now that all the members of the press are so delighted that I have lost, I'd like to make a statement of my own."

I could see many of the reporters exchanging glances. This didn't sound like the abject performance they had been hoping for.

I thanked my staff and the many volunteer workers in my campaign, and I assessed the Republican victories in New York, Pennsylvania, Ohio, and Michigan. I congratulated Brown on his victory.

Then I returned to my main theme: "At the outset I said a couple of things with regard to the press that I noticed some of you looked a little irritated about. And my philosophy with regard to the press has never really gotten through. And I want it to get through.

"This cannot be said for any other American political figure today, I guess. Never in my sixteen years of campaigning have I complained to a publisher, to an editor, about the coverage of a reporter. I believe a reporter has got a right to write it as he feels it. I believe if a reporter believes that one man ought to win rather than the other, whether it's on television or radio or the like, he ought to say so. I will say to the reporters sometimes that I think, well, look, I wish you'd give my opponent the same going over that you give me.

"And as I leave the press, all I can say is this: for sixteen years, ever since the Hiss case, you've had a lot of—a lot of fun—that you've had an opportunity to attack me, and I think I've given as good as I've taken."

I continued, "I leave you gentlemen now and you will now write it. You will interpret it. That's your right. But as I leave you I want you to know—just think how much you're going to be missing.

"You won't have Nixon to kick around anymore, because, gentlemen, this is my last press conference, and it will be one in which I have welcomed the opportunity to test wits with you. I have always respected you. I have sometimes disagreed with you. But unlike some people, I've never canceled a subscription to a paper, and also I never will.

"I believe in reading what my opponents say, and I hope that what I have said today will at least make television, radio, and the press first recognize the great responsibility they have to report all the news and, second, recognize that they have a right and a responsibility, if they're against a candidate, to give him the shaft, but also recognize if they give him the shaft, put one lonely reporter on the campaign who will report what the candidate says now and then.

"Thank you, gentlemen, and good day."

The people in the room were stunned into silence. I know that Herb was shocked and disappointed. I turned to him and said, "Herb, I did that for you. These guys deserved it, and I'm glad I did it."

To the great majority of my supporters and virtually all of the press, my so-called last press conference was a personal and political disaster. Maury Stans told me that he thought it would cost me $100,000 a year in new legal clients. My critics and opponents exulted in what they interpreted as the ultimate, self-inflicted blow. Columnist Mary McGrory called it "Richard Nixon's Last Hurrah" and reported: "Nixon carried on for fifteen minutes in a finale of intemperance and incoherence perhaps unmatched in American political annals. He pulled the havoc down around his ears, while his staff looked on aghast."

The reaction was not all negative. I received thousands of letters and wires from friends and supporters across the country who said they were glad that someone finally had the guts to tell the press off.

I have never regretted what I said at the "last press conference." I believe that it gave the media a warning that I would not sit back and take whatever biased coverage was dished out to me. In that respect, I think that the episode was partially responsible for the much fairer treatment I received from the press during the next few years. From that point of view alone, it was worth it.

On the Sunday night following the election, Howard K. Smith appeared on ABC television with a half-hour special program called "The Political Obituary of Richard Nixon." His four guests were intended to represent a cross section of my friends and foes over the years: Murray Chotiner and Jerry Ford spoke as longtime friends, lamenting that my defeat and my press conference seemed to mark the end of my political career. Jerry Voorhis talked bitterly about the 1946 campaign. The fourth participant was Alger Hiss. Smith matter-of-factly asked him how he felt about my conduct during the Hiss–Chambers case. In an arrogantly tolerant tone of voice, Hiss said, "He was less interested in developing the facts objectively than in seeking ways of making a preconceived plan appear plausible. I regard his actions as motivated by ambition, by personal self-serving."

The immediate uproar that followed this remark helped to turn me from the sore loser of the "last press conference" into something of an injured party. The ABC switchboard lit up with hundreds of calls even before the program was finished. Eighty thousand letters and telegrams protesting Hiss's appearance poured in over the next several days. President Eisenhower called Jim Hagerty, then an executive at ABC, to tell him that he was astonished at the incredibly bad taste of putting Hiss on the air to comment on my defeat.

If ABC was prepared to write my political obituary, those within the Kennedy administration were not inclined to leave anything to chance. They did everything possible to drive a final nail into the coffin. Three months after I lost the governor's race, my income tax returns were subjected to an exhaustive audit. Years later, in 1973, the IRS supervisor in charge wrote to Rose Woods to explain that although he had informed his Washington superiors of "no change" in the original audit, they sent the case back to him three separate times—persistently citing articles in newspapers and magazines as reasons for assessing me further taxes. Each time, this auditor courageously resisted, acidly noting: "We don't work cases by what the news media and magazines say; we base our findings on facts."

It was hard for me to believe that such tactics would persist even after I had been defeated for a second time and marked by political observers everywhere as a man without a political future.

Department of Justice files leaked to the New York *Times* in 1972 showed that within months of his brother's inauguration, Attorney General Robert Kennedy used the Justice Department to try to develop evidence that would justify bringing criminal charges against my mother and brother over the matter of the Hughes loan. The probe, according to this report, cleared members of my family of any wrongdoing. The political motivation behind this use of a federal agency was manifest. I especially resented the attempt to get at me through my family. These instances of abuse of the Internal Revenue Service and the Justice Department for political purposes were typical of the partisan vindictiveness that pervaded the Kennedy administration.

NEW YORK LAWYER: 1963

Shortly after the election I took a vacation in Florida with Bebe Rebozo, whom I had first met there in 1951. We had become close friends over the years. After a few days in Miami, we flew to Nassau, and as soon as school let out Pat and the girls joined us there for the Thanksgiving holidays.

During this trip I had a long talk with my old friend Elmer Bobst, chairman of the board of the Warner-Lambert Pharmaceutical Company. He strongly urged me to leave California and move to New York. He pointed out that now that I had lost the election nothing tied me to California; that business opportunities would be much greater in New York; and that I would find life there much more interesting and stimulating.

The more I thought about the move, the more evenly balanced the arguments seemed. I was reluctant to uproot Pat and the girls again, but since the election California held much less charm for them, and I found they were quite excited by the prospect of living in New York.

A move to New York would of course have a major impact on my political status. Despite my defeat by Brown, I could still play an important, if not uncontested, leadership role in the Republican Party in California. But leaving my political base and moving to a state in which all political power was firmly held by Nelson Rockefeller, my principal rival, would be an announcement that I was ruling myself out as an active political figure for the foreseeable future.

A move to New York would mean giving up any thought of becoming a candidate for President in 1964, and running for any office in New York was out of the question. I think this factor influenced Pat as much as any other. She felt strongly that now was the time for me to get out of the political arena once and for all. Having in effect overruled the family when I ran for governor in 1962, I thought that now it was their turn. We would move to New York as soon as I could find the right job and make the necessary arrangements.

A few months later I joined the Wall Street law firm of Mudge, Stern, Baldwin, and Todd, which became Nixon, Mudge, Rose, Guthrie, and Alexander. We bought a ten-room cooperative apartment that was, coincidentally, in the same building in which Nelson Rockefeller lived.

Before beginning my new job, I was determined to keep a longstanding promise to Pat and the girls. On June 12 we set out on a six-week vacation in Europe and the Middle East with our friends Jack and Helene Drown and their daughter, Maureen.

From our welcome abroad, no one would have guessed that I had lost two elections in the past three years and that my prospects for any political comeback seemed extremely remote. Everywhere we went we were received as if I were still Vice President.

Our schedule was full: in addition to the rigorous sightseeing involved in traveling with three teenaged girls, I had a number of meetings and talks with foreign leaders. Generalissimo Francisco Franco received me at his summer residence in Barcelona. I had never met him before, and I expected to find the rigid and unpleasant dictator pictured in the press. Instead, I found a subtle, pragmatic leader whose primary interest was maintaining the internal stability necessary to Spain's progress.

President de Gaulle invited Pat and me to have lunch with him in Paris. The luncheon—a simple meal, elegantly prepared and served—was held outdoors on a patio behind the Elysée Palace. After lunch de Gaulle rose and proposed a warm and typically eloquent toast. He said that he knew I had suffered some difficult defeats, but he predicted that at some time in the future I would be serving my nation in a very high capacity.

Perhaps the most indelible memory I have of this trip is my first sight of the Berlin Wall. We were taken on a tour of the drab city of East Berlin, but the oppressive number of Communist police who unsubtly accompanied us meant we had hardly any chance to talk to the people. That night I decided to go back. We walked through Checkpoint Charlie and stood waiting for a taxi. A man dressed in work clothes came up and whispered in my ear, "We are glad you came to East Berlin. Don't let us down. The Americans are our only hope." Then he quickly walked away.

We found a taxi and went to a restaurant where an excellent Hungarian orchestra played gypsy music. I was recognized, and after dinner I went up to the bandstand and banged out the "Missouri Waltz" on the piano.

While we were in Cairo, President Nasser arranged a special trip for us to the site of the Aswan dam. When we arrived around midnight, the temperature was still over 100 degrees. Huge Soviet cranes and bulldozers were working around the clock. When our Egyptian hosts showed us the plans for the dam, they proudly proclaimed that there were very few Russians working on the project. I could tell from the appearance of the drivers, however, that a substantial number of them were Russian.

Nasser invited Pat and me to his surprisingly modest house in Cairo. He was a man of superior intelligence and great charisma. Despite the bombast of his public utterances, I was impressed by his dignity and quiet manner in private. He was eager to have my assessment of the current attitudes and intentions of the Soviet leaders. He ventured some criticisms of President Kennedy's policy toward Israel, but I gave him no encouragement, and he quickly caught the hint and changed the subject. Several times he expressed his warm feeling for Eisenhower.

I emphasized as politely as I could that I thought his first priority should be the welfare and progress of his own people. This was a course that Nasser could not bring himself to follow. Like Sukarno and Nkrumah, Nasser had devoted the best of his energies to revolution. Now he was more interested in a grandiose crusade for Arab unity than he was in the vital but less glamorous tasks of managing and improving Egypt's economic, political, and social structure. His attitude toward Israel served his political purpose, beyond his blind intolerance of the Jews; if Israel had not existed, Nasser would have had to invent something to take its place. Arab unity needed a common cause, and the destruction of Israel filled the bill.

We were awed by the Pyramids and by the Valley of the Kings at Luxor, but equally impressive to me was what I learned about modern Egypt and its ruler. I could see that, despite its terrible poverty, the country was moving ahead and would eventually exert enormous influence throughout the Middle East. I could also see that, despite Israel's superior technology and training, the Egyptians and the Arabs would in the end submerge the Israelis and defeat them by sheer weight of numbers unless some accommodation were reached. Closer relations between the United States and Israel's Middle Eastern enemies were going to be of the utmost importance, not only to Israel itself but also to the prevention of a confrontation between the great powers in the Middle East.

President Kennedy was in Rome on a state visit while we were there. One afternoon the phone rang in our hotel room and the operator informed me that the President was calling. Sounding happy and relaxed, he said that he had heard we were in Rome and just wanted to say hello. We exchanged brief pleasantries. This was to be the last time I talked to him; five months later he was dead.

For Pat, Tricia, Julie, and me, this trip was one of the happiest times of our lives. What made it so special was that it gave us a chance to be together as a family. We walked through castles and cathedrals in Spain; we explored the ruins of the Parthenon in Athens and of the Forum in Rome; we rode in gondolas in Venice and went to the top of the Eiffel Tower in Paris; we sailed down the Rhine and listened to Big Ben chime the hours at London's Houses of Parliament.

Nevertheless, it was a thrill to see the Statue of Liberty below us as our plane came in to New York. Vacation time was over, and I immediately devoted my full energies to my new responsibilities as a Wall Street lawyer.

From the first day at my new job I was sure that I had made the right decision in moving to New York. New business came to Nixon, Mudge, and the firm expanded as we had hoped it would.

The chance to see old friends in the New York area and to make new ones gave our family the stimulation and the revitalized outlook on life that we needed after the California campaign. One night less than two weeks after we had moved into our new apartment, Pat looked across the dinner table and said to me, "I hope we never move again."

By the summer of 1963, although I was barely settled into my New York law practice, I was already getting calls and letters from friends and party leaders across the country urging me to run again for the presidency in 1964. Goldwater, they said, would drive off almost everyone except the party's most conservative fringe; and Rockefeller would split the party down the middle. I could sympathize with their concerns, but my instinct was to stay completely out of it.

I strongly felt that I should not seek the nomination in 1964. Despite Kennedy's recent slippage in the polls, his lackluster domestic record, and his crisis-prone foreign policy, I felt that he was almost certainly going to be re-elected. With party unity and a favorable press added to the advantages of being an incumbent, Kennedy would be virtually unbeatable. I could not idly consider the thought of subjecting Pat, the girls, or myself to the tension and disappointment of another losing campaign against Kennedy. I was also well aware that after my defeats in 1960 and 1962, another defeat in 1964 might so brand me with a loser image that I could never recover.

I also had to consider the motives of those who were urging me to run. Many of them were opposed to Goldwater's candidacy for reasons I did not share. I liked Goldwater personally. He was direct and sincere and deeply patriotic. He had a tendency to be impulsive and to shoot from the hip, but I knew that he was also well intentioned and open to advice. Even though Goldwater was farther to the right of my centrist position than Rockefeller was to the left of it, I felt that Goldwater's deviation from midstream at least put him deeper into Republican territory, while Rockefeller's made him practically a liberal Democrat on many issues.

I received a call from our upstairs neighbor on the morning of September 3, inviting me for cocktails that afternoon. When I arrived Rockefeller greeted me warmly, and after an exchange of small talk, we quickly settled down to a serious discussion.

"I'm going to go for the nomination," he said. "I am not going to back out this time. If I did, I would appear to be unstable. In my opinion, Kennedy will be a one-termer. He has messed up on all issues—Vietnam, the international monetary situation, the Atlantic alliance, civil rights."

He continued, "I have nothing to lose. I would worry if Barry won, because he's just too shallow. He only went to college for one year. He doesn't have a good staff, and he has a very superficial approach to problems. I will take on the task of stopping Barry. If I don't he's going to get it by default."

He turned to his other rivals. "Romney wants to run," he said, "but the regular Republicans don't like his independent attitude toward the party. His greatest weakness is that he knows too little of the world and is too sure of what he doesn't know. Bill Scranton wants to run, but only if he's drafted, and there just isn't a draft around with Bill Scranton's name on it."

He paused, then leaned closer to me. "Dick, you can't run actively. You *could,* but it would be a big mistake, and you don't make that kind of mistake. What we both have to recognize is that you and I are the only ones qualified on both foreign and national issues to serve as President. Despite some differences, we have generally agreed on basic policies."

I kept silent and tried to look noncommittal. Finally he said, "What I want to suggest is that, if you will support me now, if there is a deadlock at the convention, I will support you."

I thanked him for his candor but said that I planned not to participate personally in the campaign, except to support whoever was nominated. I did not respond to his suggestion that we make a deal.

As Thanksgiving approached, I held firm to my plan that unless something completely unexpected happened, I would not become a candidate in 1964; I would not endorse anyone before the convention; and I would try to remain on good terms with all the potential candidates so that I could play the role of party unifier regardless of who won.

I flew to Dallas on November 20 to attend a board meeting of the Pepsi-Cola Company, one of our firm's clients. Several local reporters asked for an interview, and the next day I met with them briefly at my hotel. I had read that demonstrations were planned against Kennedy and Johnson, who were to visit Dallas the next day. I told the reporters that, however strongly people felt about particular issues or personalities, the President and Vice President deserved to be treated with respect wherever they appeared.

Early on the morning of November 22 on the way to the Dallas airport I saw the flags displayed along the motorcade route for the presidential visit. Arriving in New York, I hailed a cab home. We drove through Queens toward the 59th Street Bridge, and as we stopped at a traffic light, a man rushed over from the curb and started talking to the driver. I heard him say, "Do you have a radio in your cab? I just heard that Kennedy was shot." We had no radio, and as we continued into Manhattan a hundred thoughts rushed through my mind. The man could have been crazy or a macabre prankster. He could have been mistaken about what he had heard; or perhaps a gunman might have shot at Kennedy but missed or only wounded him. I refused to believe that he could have been killed.

As the cab drew up in front of my building, the doorman ran out. Tears were streaming down his cheeks. "Oh, Mr. Nixon, have you heard, sir?" he asked. "It's just terrible. They've killed President Kennedy."

Later in the day I called Edgar Hoover in Washington. He came right on the line and without wasting words I asked, "What happened? Was it one of the right-wing nuts?"

"No," he replied, "it was a Communist." Months later Hoover told me that Oswald's wife had disclosed that Oswald had been planning to kill me when I visited Dallas and that only with great difficulty had she managed to keep him in the house to prevent him from doing so.

I never felt the "there but for the grace of God go I" reaction to Kennedy's death that many people seemed to imagine I would. After eight years as Vice President I had become fatalistic about the danger of assassination. I knew that given the number of people who, for whatever reasons, want to kill a President, it takes a combination of luck and the law of averages to keep him alive. I did not think of Kennedy and myself as interchangeable: I did not think that if I had won in 1960 it would have been I rather than he riding through Dealey Plaza in Dallas at that time, on that day.

Since the 1960 election there had been no love lost between Kennedy and me; I had been critical of his performance as President. But I admired his ambition and his competitiveness, and I could feel the terrible impact this tragedy would have on his closely knit family. I remembered how I had felt when first Arthur and then Harold had died, and I wished that there was something that I could do to ease the Kennedys' grief.

That night I sat up late in my library. Long after the fire had gone out I wrote a letter to Jacqueline Kennedy.

Richard M. Nixon
810 Fifth Avenue
New York, N.Y. 10021

November 23

Dear Jackie,

In this tragic hour Pat and I want you to know that our thoughts and prayers are with you.

While the hand of fate made Jack and me political opponents I always cherished the fact that we were personal friends from the time we came to the Congress together in 1947. That friendship evidenced itself in many ways including the invitation we received to attend your wedding.

Nothing I could say now could add to the splendid tributes which have come from throughout the world to him.

But I want you to know that the nation will also be forever grateful for your service as First Lady. You brought to the White House charm, beauty and elegance as the official hostess for America, and the mystique of the young in heart which was uniquely yours made an indelible impression on the American consciousness.

If in the days ahead we could be helpful in any way we shall be honored to be at your command.

Sincerely,
Dick Nixon

A few weeks later I received her reply:

Dear Mr Vice President -

I do thank you for your most thoughtful letter -

You two young men - colleagues in Congress - adversaries in 1960 - and now look what has happened - Whoever thought such a hideous thing could happen in this country -

I know how you must feel - so long on the path - so closely missing the greatest prize - and now for you, all the question comes up again - and you must commit all you and your family's hopes and efforts again - Just one thing I would say to you - if it does not work out as you have hoped for so long - please be consoled by what you already have - your life and your family -

We never value life enough when we have it - and I would not have had Jack live his life any other way - though I know his death could have been prevented, and I will never cease to torture myself with that -

But if you do not win - please think of all that you have - With my appreciation - and my regards to your family - I hope your daughters love Chapin School as much as I did - Sincerely

Jacqueline Kennedy

The three most significant political developments in the period after Kennedy's death were the enormous strength that Goldwater began to pick up among party workers and organizers across the country, the consummate skill with which Lyndon Johnson conducted himself during his first weeks and months in the White House, and the emergence of Henry Cabot Lodge as a serious contender for the Republican presidential nomination. Johnson was able to consolidate the nation's grief over Kennedy's death, and by the first weeks of 1964 it was widely believed by objective observers in both parties that no one could beat him in November. The March 10 New Hampshire presidential primary surprised most political professionals when, as the result of a well-organized write-in campaign, Lodge came in first.

One advantage of my New York law practice was that it allowed me to travel extensively abroad to see some of the firm's international clients. In this way I was also able to visit old friends from my vice presidential days and make new ones. As a private citizen, I was able to meet with opposition leaders as well as government officials, and my business and legal contacts gave me a much more rounded view of local issues and attitudes than I had gained as an official visitor.

I took the first of these trips immediately after the New Hampshire primary, visiting Lebanon, Pakistan, Malaysia, Thailand, Vietnam, the Philippines, Hong Kong, Taiwan, and Japan. Everywhere I went I heard about America's declining prestige, and I heard expressions of dismay that the world's strongest nation was showing so little positive leadership. Perhaps most disturbing of all, I saw for myself how dangerously different the reality of the situation in Vietnam was from the version of it being presented to the American people at home.

The Asian leaders I talked with looked at Laos, where we had suffered an unqualified disaster because of Kennedy's naïve willingness to accept a "neutralist" coalition regime that was known to be a convenient cover for the Communist Pathet Lao guerrillas. They looked at Cuba, where our indecisiveness during the Bay of Pigs had given the Communists their greatest propaganda victory in many years. And now they were looking at Vietnam, where after years of encouraging and building up the anticommunist Saigon government, we seemed reluctant to support the measures needed to defeat the Communists. To our Asian friends and allies it looked as if a combination of political expediency, public apathy, distorted reporting in the media, and partisan politics was undermining America's will to fight against communism in Asia.

In Pakistan I saw my old friend, President Ayub Khan. He spoke sadly about what he believed had been American collusion in the murder of President Ngo Dinh Diem in Vietnam on November 1, 1963, three weeks before Kennedy's assassination. "I cannot say—perhaps you should never have supported Diem in the first place. But you did support him for a long time, and everyone in Asia knew it. Whether they approved or disapproved, they knew it. And then, suddenly, you didn't support him anymore—and Diem was dead." He shook his head and continued, "Diem's murder meant three things to many Asian leaders: that it is dangerous to be a friend of the United States; that it pays to be neutral; and that sometimes it helps to be an enemy! Trust is like a thin thread, and when it is broken it is very hard to put together again."

In Bangkok, Prime Minister Thanom Kittikachorn warned against any relaxation of the war against the Vietcong. If Vietnam were to fall, he said, Communist influence would have a green light in Southeast Asia. Pote Sarasin, the distinguished scholar-diplomat who had been Thailand's ambassador in Washington when I was Vice President, said that Johnson's eagerness to begin talks with the Vietcong would only encourage them to hold out for better terms. "What America should do," he said, "is convince the Vietcong that they cannot win their struggle either in South Vietnam or in Washington. Then you should present them with a final offer that they can accept or reject. If they reject it, then you should prosecute the war relentlessly."

I arrived at Saigon's Tan Son Nhut Airport on a hot rainy afternoon. Sandbags were piled up around the hangars, and armed soldiers patrolled the runways.

The Vietnamese military leaders I met fully understood the nature of their enemy. One told me, "It is the same as when they were the Vietminh. They will stop at nothing, and they will settle for nothing short of winning everything. We cannot compromise with them, and we cannot negotiate with them. This has to be a fight to the finish. With your help and support, we are ready to fight them and beat them."

Both the Americans and the Vietnamese military leaders were distressed that Washington was holding them back from launching air raids into North Vietnam as well as ground raids into Laos to cut off the pipeline of Vietcong arms and supplies known as the Ho Chi Minh trail. Many American officers I talked to thought they were being restrained because of the election year at home, and some of them blamed the highly distorted reports in the American media.

During a long conversation over dinner with Cabot Lodge, who was then U.S. ambassador to South Vietnam, I described my concerns. He listened attentively and took a long time before he replied. "I know that a lot of people are impatient with the way things are going here," he said, "and I know that the military men don't like being held back. But there's a bigger and broader problem that can't be settled by fighting over it. The problem in South Vietnam is less military than economic. The Vietcong draw their strength from hungry peasants, and if we want to wean them from communism we shouldn't shoot at them—we should distribute food to them."

Lodge argued against pursuing the Vietcong forces into Laos or Cambodia. Even more surprising to me, he said American troops should avoid fighting the Vietcong except to retaliate when Americans were killed. I could hardly believe that I was hearing this from one as versed as Cabot Lodge in the tactics and techniques of international communism. I wondered whether he felt it was his duty to defend the administration's policy regardless of his own feelings, or whether he had actually been converted by the academic theorists around Johnson who thought that the problem of communism in Southeast Asia could be solved by economic development.

What I saw and heard on this trip convinced me that Johnson's Vietnam policy would not succeed.

In our discussions in Saigon, Lodge was eager to have my reading of the political situation at home. He thought that Johnson was highly vulnerable and could be beaten. Reversing Goldwater's "Southern strategy," he argued that a moderate Republican concentrating on the Northern cities could do very well. It was clear that he was thinking of himself as that Republican. Several years later, in fact, he told me that if he had won the Oregon primary in May he had planned to resign and return home to campaign for the nomination.

In Taiwan I was the houseguest of Chiang Kai-shek, who was predictably critical of our Vietnam policy. He said that we could never win without invading North Vietnam, and he laughed at the Strategic Hamlet Program then being pursued. "It is the familiar fallacy that economic development will defeat the Communists," he said. He leaned closer to me and almost whispered, "But only bullets will really defeat them!"

I met with Japanese Prime Minister Ikeda in Tokyo; like the other leaders I had seen he was concerned by America's apparent crisis of confidence over its policy in Vietnam. Minister of State Sato and former Prime Minister Kishi felt that the key to victory in Vietnam lay with China and Russia, and they suggested that American policy on Vietnam be formulated in terms of the great-power interests involved there.

When I returned home from this trip on April 15 I found that Vietnam was not nearly of as much interest in Washington as the race developing among Lodge, Goldwater, and Rockefeller, and by the battle of wills shaping up over whether Johnson would allow Bobby Kennedy a place on the ticket as his running mate. Asia seemed far away, and attention was focused on the Oregon primary, in which many expected Lodge to repeat his New Hampshire victory.

During April and May the polls continued to show Rockefeller doing well with voters; but in the area that counted—getting convention delegates—Goldwater was on the way to winning the nomination by a landslide. Some of my supporters still refused to give up, and they mounted a write-in effort for me in the Nebraska primary on May 12. The 42,800 votes I received there represented an astonishingly strong showing, but I had no illusions that this would slow the Goldwater bandwagon, let alone stop it. Rockefeller won a surprise victory in the Oregon primary, thus eliminating Lodge. But Goldwater's victory in the all-important California primary on June 2 eliminated Rockefeller. Last-ditch efforts to launch campaigns for Governor William Scranton of Pennsylvania and Governor George Romney of Michigan proved too little and too late. Goldwater had the nomination locked up long before the convention began in San Francisco.

THE GOLDWATER CAMPAIGN: 1964

Goldwater was nominated on the first ballot. I had asked that as the former standard-bearer I be given the honor of presenting the nominee to the convention before his acceptance speech; I looked upon this as the first and best chance to begin the ministry of party unity that I expected to preach right through Election Day in November. I singled out Scranton, Romney, Lodge, and Rockefeller by name as men of whom the Republican Party could be proud as we entered the campaign of 1964—just as in my acceptance speech in 1952 I had named Bridges, Martin, and Taft for the same reasons of party unity. I said, "Before this convention we were Goldwater Republicans, Rockefeller Republicans, Scranton Republicans, Lodge Republicans, but now that this convention has met and made its decision, we are Republicans, period, working for Barry Goldwater for President of the United States. And to those few, if there are some, who say that they are going to sit it out or take a walk, or even go on a boat ride, I have an answer: in the words of Barry Goldwater in 1960, 'Let's grow up, Republicans, let's go to work'—and we shall win in November."

I tried to stress Goldwater's Republicanism and to place him in the historical tradition of other Republican nominees. In an attempt to build drama around his first appearance before the convention as its nominee, and to go over the heads of the reporters and ask the American people to listen and judge for themselves, I concluded: "I ask you tonight, look at this man. Listen to him for the next thirty minutes. Forget the too harsh criticisms of his critics and forget even perhaps the too complimentary compliments of his friends. Remember, this is the moment of truth. Judge him as he is. Make this decision yours, not as someone else tells you to make it."

I had worked hard to find the right turn of phrase to close the speech, and I had finally found one that satisfied me: "He is the man who earned and proudly carries the title of Mr. Conservative. He is the man who, by the action of this convention, is now Mr. Republican. And he is the man who, after the greatest campaign in history, will be Mr. President—Barry Goldwater."

The speech seemed to have the desired effect of pleasing the different party factions. As Goldwater strode to the rostrum he was greeted by a long ovation. Here was the best opportunity he would have to heal the party's wounds and unite it behind him for the campaign ahead.

To my dismay, Goldwater proceeded to deliver a strident, divisive speech. He said, "Anyone who joins us in all sincerity we welcome. Though those who don't care for our cause, we don't expect to enter our ranks in any case." Half of those in the crammed Cow Palace cheered wildly. The other half sat in stunned silence: they had just been read out of the Goldwater campaign and out of the party. And he was not yet finished. He said, "Extremism in the defense of liberty is no vice! . . . Moderation in the pursuit of justice is no virtue!" This was the statement that, more than any other, enabled Johnson and the Democrats to put the skids under his campaign.

Goldwater had won the nomination, but if he had ever had any chance to win the presidency, he lost it that night with that speech.

I felt almost physically sick as I sat there on the platform. Not only did Goldwater fail to close the rifts in the party and heal its wounds; he opened new wounds and then rubbed salt in them. It was terribly sad to see a man throw away his chance for something he wanted and had worked very hard to get. But my major concern was for the thousands of Republican candidates across the country who would now be doomed to spend their campaigns trying to explain away the man at the top of the ticket.

From Goldwater's point of view, his speech was an unforgivable folly. It should have been his aim to unify the party while moving it to the right. Losing to Johnson, who was running as Kennedy's successor, need not have been ruinous. If Goldwater could have minimized congressional and state losses in 1964 and then picked up a few seats by campaigning in 1966, he would have been in a very strong position to reclaim the nomination in 1968, when the odds would favor a Republican.

Unless someone got to Goldwater and toned him down, the Republican nomination in 1968 might not be worth anything to anyone.

I knew Goldwater's speech had greatly disturbed Eisenhower. I waited until he had been back in Gettysburg for a few days before I called him to suggest two ideas.

"General," I said, "you are the only person Barry will listen to, and you are the only person who can do something that will at least give Republican candidates a fighting chance."

"Well," he asked hesitantly, "what do you think I could do?" I suggested that he meet with Goldwater. "I know you have your doubts," I said, "but I know that Barry can be very reasonable. I am sure that he would respond to any advice you gave him about the campaign."

Eisenhower agreed to a meeting on the condition I be present. He also agreed to my second suggestion, that a Republican "summit conference" of party leaders be held a few days after our meeting with Goldwater. With Goldwater's cooperation we could turn this summit meeting into a highly publicized display of party unity. It would give Goldwater a chance to start his campaign anew, on a basis of moderation and unity.

To set the stage, I suggested to Goldwater that we take steps to quiet the controversy still raging over his acceptance speech. I offered to write a letter asking for clarification, and then to make public both my letter and his reply. He agreed, and in his letter he substantially modified his controversial "extremism" statement. He wrote: "If I were to paraphrase the two sentences in question in the context in which I uttered them I would do it by saying that wholehearted devotion to liberty is unassailable and that halfhearted devotion to justice is indefensible."

When I read this I breathed a sigh of relief. At least he had not used the codeword *extremism.* Rockefeller had hung the extremist tag around Goldwater's neck in the primaries, and Goldwater's acceptance speech had turned it into a noose. I hoped this letter would loosen it a bit, but my hopes were soon dashed. The master political operator of our time, Lyndon B. Johnson, knew that he had a devastatingly good issue, and with invaluable assistance from Goldwater's numerous gaffes in the campaign, he tied the extremist tag so tight on Goldwater that it choked the political life out of him.

Goldwater came to Gettysburg on August 6. Eisenhower did not want us at his farm so we crowded into his small office in town. He began the meeting with some straight talk. In fact I had seldom, if ever, heard Eisenhower lay it on the line the way he did on this occasion. He told Goldwater that he ought to stop shooting from the hip. He suggested that Goldwater give a speech discussing the charges of extremism that had been made against him and admit that he may have encouraged them by the language of his acceptance speech.

Goldwater responded just as candidly. He said that it was not in his nature to be cautious. He could understand that Eisenhower was particularly sensitive about those of his comments that were taken to be critical of the Eisenhower administration, but he had not meant anything personal by them. On the whole, however, Goldwater took a conciliatory line. This, and the impending publication of our exchange of letters, seemed to bode well for the success of the upcoming summit meeting.

The summit meeting of party leaders, candidates, governors, and aides met at the rambling old Hotel Hershey in Hershey, Pennsylvania, on August 12.

The main session was held behind closed doors. Goldwater made a speech in which he considerably modified some of his most extreme positions. Then Goldwater, Rockefeller, Romney, Scranton, Eisenhower, and I engaged in a rambling and falsely optimistic discussion of how the campaign should be run. Of course, the real purpose of the exercise was to make effective use of the press conference to be held at the end. This was to be Goldwater's chance to emerge as the leader and spokesman of a united party.

The press conference was crammed with reporters and TV cameras. Eisenhower, Scranton, and I sat flanking Goldwater and his running mate, New York Congressman Bill Miller, as the flashbulbs popped and the cameras whirred. To my amazement and disappointment, after all our planning Goldwater did not grasp the opportunity the meeting had given him. Instead he stated that he did not consider his speech earlier in the day to have been conciliatory, and he would not agree that he had made any concessions on issues of substance. The rest of the press conference was a typical Goldwater performance. He himself brought up his controversial statement that he would consider giving military commanders in the field control over the use of tactical nuclear weapons and, under intense questioning, refused to back away from it. When one reporter asked about his policy toward Germany, I saw Eisenhower wince when Goldwater replied, "I think that Germany originated the modern concept of peace through strength."

Eisenhower was infuriated by Goldwater's performance. I learned later that on the drive back to Gettysburg he said, "You know, before we had this meeting I thought that Goldwater was just stubborn. Now I am convinced that he is just plain dumb."

While the "Spirit of Hershey" may have fooled some of the press and the public, the politicians weren't taken in for a minute. A sense of doom enveloped the Goldwater campaign, and very few national leaders wanted any part of it. Nelson Rockefeller and most of his major supporters sat it out. George Romney concentrated on his own gubernatorial campaign in Michigan. Scranton was a good soldier and tried to help, but his efforts had little effect even with his own supporters; and Eisenhower played hardly any role.

My office in New York was swamped with speaking invitations from candidates all over the country. Many were old friends and supporters; others were promising new candidates who had the ill fortune to be running their first races in a year of dismal presidential prospects. I decided to devote five solid weeks to campaigning.

It was frustrating for me to see as inept a candidate as Goldwater running for President. It was especially heartbreaking because Republican voters seemed to be interested in the campaign that year; everywhere I went I found the audiences big and enthusiastic. But time after time the senatorial or congressional candidate on whose behalf I was to speak begged me to avoid associating his candidacy with Goldwater. It was a difficult tightrope to walk, but I usually found some way to praise the local candidates independently of expressing, as I did in every speech I gave, my personal support for Goldwater. I made over 150 appearances in thirty-six states. But it was a hopeless task. From the time the campaign began I knew that we were going to lose heavily.

Election Day was November 3. By eight o'clock in New York all three networks were projecting a Johnson landslide. The next morning I got up early to check the final reports on the campaigns for House and Senate. It was a Republican disaster: we had lost 37 seats in the House, 2 in the Senate, and over 500 in state legislatures. Most of the new young candidates Eisenhower and I had tried to encourage failed in their first bids for public office.

One Republican winner was not on the ballot. The week before the end of the campaign, Ronald Reagan made a nationwide television broadcast on Goldwater's behalf. Reagan's views were as conservative as Goldwater's, but he had what Goldwater lacked: the ability to present his views in a reasonable and eloquent manner. The broadcast started a ground swell of support that swept Reagan into the California governor's office in 1966 and into the race for the presidential nomination in 1968.

Goldwater took his defeat with grace, and Johnson resisted what must have been a great temptation to crow over his landslide. It was Nelson Rockefeller who tried to turn the disaster to his own advantage. The day after the election, he issued a statement aimed at reading Goldwater and his followers—and, by indirection, those like me who had supported Goldwater—out of the party. I had intended to make no comment on the results until after a "cooling-off" period, but Rockefeller's attack changed my mind.

On November 5, I held a press conference. I complimented Goldwater, saying that he had fought courageously against great odds. I said that those who had divided the party in the past could not now expect to unite it in the future. At the end, I pulled out all stops and said that Rockefeller was a spoilsport and a divider, and that there now was so much antipathy to him among Republicans throughout the country that he could no longer be regarded as a party leader anywhere outside New York.

As I expected, this press conference stirred up a furor. But I had said what needed to be said in order to avert an irreconcilable split between conservatives and liberals within the party. At first timidly and then in larger numbers, other party leaders joined me in calling for a cooling-off period and for renouncing recriminations over 1964, so that the party could be united for a comeback in 1966.

REVIEWING THE SITUATION: 1965

While I did not have any illusions about the extreme state of disarray in which the 1964 defeat left the Republican Party, I did not completely share the widespread pessimism about the future. Within just a few months after the election I could see developing in the Democratic Party the political climate that would bring Lyndon Johnson down from his pinnacle of popularity and force him to decide not to run for re-election in 1968. Soon Johnson would have to deal with the fact that the left wing of his own party was as extreme and self-righteous as the Republican right wing. Johnson's magic seemed to be wearing thin even at the height of his power. The Eastern media had been contemptuous of his Texas ways when he was Vice President, and now that he was no longer Kennedy's legatee but had been elected on his own, a newly critical tone began to appear in some of his coverage.

I saw no reason that the Republican Party could not make a comeback in 1966—if only we could keep it from falling apart in the meantime.

I felt that two things would be necessary to keep the party together: we would have to be on constant guard against attempts by leaders of the left or the right to take over the party; and we would have to convince the party rank and file that there were better times ahead. I knew from experience that this would be hard, boring, and sometimes thankless work. But this was the job that I increasingly saw as my own. It was pragmatism more than altruism that led me to take it on, because I believed that whoever did would gain a significant advantage in the race for the 1968 presidential nomination. This enabled me to reconcile the paradox of having to help my Republican competitors—Rockefeller, Romney, and Reagan. I felt that if the base of the party were not expanded, the 1968 nomination would be worthless. If the party were expanded by the victories of others, I thought I had a good chance of benefiting from its greater strength.

I did not reveal to my family or anyone else that this was what I had in mind. I knew that Pat and the girls would again be disappointed. But I had finally come to the realization that there was no other life for me but politics and public service. Even when my legal work was at its most interesting I never found it truly fulfilling. I told some friends at this time that if all I had was my legal work, I would be mentally dead in two years and physically dead in four. I knew that they thought I was exaggerating; but I was telling the truth about the way I thought and felt.

On January 9, 1965, after a small family party to celebrate my fifty-second birthday, I sat in my study to look back on the past year and look ahead into the future.

I reflected on the fact that Winston Churchill had been in his mid-fifties when he lost his position of leadership in the House of Commons in 1929, and most of his contemporaries had then written him off as a political leader. But Churchill refused to write himself off. I took heart from the example of his refusal to give up just because people thought he was finished. I wrote down some "New Year's Resolutions for 1965":

—Set great goals.
—Daily rest.
—Brief vacations.
—Knowledge of all weaknesses.
—Better use of time.
—Begin writing book.
—Golf or some other kind of daily exercise.
—Articles or speeches on provocative new international and national issues.

I put down my yellow pad, turned out the light, and stared into the fire. For the first time in seven years, I started not only to think seriously about running for the presidency again but to think about where I should begin.

It was still much too early to make any final decision, much less any announcement, about running for President again. Besides, I was convinced that any attempt at presidential politics before the party had had a chance to rebuild itself for 1966 would be self-defeating. The party's best interests and my own dovetailed on this point: until the organization had been restored to the point that the nomination would be worth something to whoever won it, I would be foolish to make any commitment. But if I was interested in running, it would be equally foolish not to begin laying plans and harnessing some of the good will I had built up in the 1964 campaign. Barry Goldwater was a vocal adherent of this view. At the Republican National Committee meeting in Chicago on January 22 he introduced me as the man "who worked harder than any one person for the ticket." He turned to me and said, "Dick, I will never forget it. I know that you did it in the interests of the Republican Party and not for any selfish reasons. But if there ever comes a time I can turn those into selfish reasons, I am going to do all I can to see that it comes about."

I began making lists of the odds for and against my nomination in 1968. There was no denying that the odds against were formidable. After 1960 and 1962, I had what every politician dreads most, a loser image. In fact, after the "last press conference," I had a *sore* loser image.

Almost equally serious was my lack of political funds. For the first time in my life I was making a solid six-figure income from the law firm and from my book royalties and writing fees. But we had an expensive apartment, and one daughter in private school and the other in college. After all the frugal years in Washington, I felt that Pat and the girls deserved the best, and I would not have them stint in order to bankroll another candidacy.

Another serious problem was the lack of a political base. By leaving California I had become in political terms a man without a country. It was almost unprecedented for a major candidate to build a serious presidential campaign without having the party machinery in his home state working for him. New York, however, was Rockefeller turf, and the New York Republican organization would actually be working against me. Rockefeller had made this clear from the beginning, and I was effectively frozen out of any major role in New York Republican politics.

Although the odds against me were heavy, there were also some points in my favor. One was my position as front-runner for the presidential nomination in polls of Republican voters. In the summer of 1966, for example, the Gallup poll gave me a lead of almost 2 to 1 over my nearest competitor, Henry Cabot Lodge. My many years of labor in the Republican vineyards were being rewarded by the support of the party organization in most of the country.

Another advantage was that, like me or not, the press seemed to consider me the most consistently newsworthy of the potential presidential candidates. Even though I did not hold an office, I could count on overflow attendance any time I called a press conference, and wherever I traveled local television usually covered my speeches and appearances.

In my judgment, however, the most important thing in my favor was less tangible and more substantive than polls or press coverage. I was confident that because of my background and experience, particularly in the field of foreign policy, I had the best grasp of the issues and trends that would determine the campaign and the election. Whether this was in fact true, I believed it was true, and the confidence that belief gave me was itself a tremendous advantage.

Since the best way to prepare for 1968 was to do well in 1966, I decided to begin some rudimentary planning for the coming year's election campaign. In the middle of 1965, Maurice Stans, Al Cole, and Peter Flanigan began raising money for my travels on behalf of the party and its candidates in the 1966 elections.

The issues that were to dominate the political dialogue of the latter part of the 1960s were already taking shape by the middle of the decade. In May 1964 President Johnson had told the graduating class of the University of Michigan that "in your time we have the opportunity to move not only toward the rich society and the powerful society, but upward to the Great Society." Johnson observed quite correctly that "the solution to these problems does not rest on a massive program in Washington," but the fatal flaw of his Great Society was precisely its inclination to establish massive federal programs. The price tag was astronomical. In five years, Johnson's spending for the poor doubled, from $12.5 billion to $24.6 billion. Federal funds for health and education jumped by over $18 billion.

As I read the legislative messages that poured out of the White House during the first few months of 1965, I could see that Johnson had fallen into the trap that snares so many believers in big government: he was promising far more than ever could be achieved. Even allowing for a healthy dose of oratorical overstatement, the Great Society promised so much to so many that, instead of inspiring people to work hard to attain its goals, it made people impatient and angry when the goals were not immediately achieved without effort on their part.

I knew that Johnson would soon be bitterly disappointed by the ingratitude of those he tried to help. His Great Society programs spawned a new constituency of government dependents who would always demand more than he could give. Johnson was a man who needed praise, but he would get precious little of it from them.

I also anticipated the breakdown of performance of the Great Society programs themselves. The Great Society was created by liberal academics and bureaucrats steeped in the myths of the New Deal. When its theoretical high-mindedness ran up against the self-interested tough-mindedness of the people it was intended to serve, there was certain to be conflict.

The philosophical distinction between the Republican and Democratic parties was never clearer than in the middle 1960s. It was therefore the perfect time for Republicans to lead an active opposition. I fully recognized, however, that one of our biggest problems lay in our public image as a "negative" party. Goldwater's rhetoric had much to answer for in this regard. Republicans had always been tagged as reactionary, but after his campaign we were portrayed as reckless and racist.

Republicans needed to leapfrog the Democrats on the Great Society issues and get ahead of them. The Democrats were the majority party, but it seemed to me that the great strength of the Republicans lay in our ability to lead effectively on the local level, much as the great strength of the Democrats rested on their ability to mobilize the resources of Washington.

In a number of speeches during 1965, I urged my audiences to be Lincoln Republicans: liberal in their concern for people and conservative in their respect for the rule of law. I deliberately used the terms *liberal* and *conservative,* which in 1964 had been the sorrow of the party, to show how they had been abused and distorted almost beyond recognition. I said, "If being a liberal means federalizing everything, then I'm no liberal. If being a conservative means turning back the clock, denying problems that exist, then I'm no conservative."

I stressed that the Republican Party must have no room for racism. I made it clear that contrary to what some conservatives might have thought, George Wallace did not belong in the Republican Party. I was equally critical of the black activists and the extremists in the civil rights movement. When the Watts district of Los Angeles was swept by black rioters, arsonists, and looters in the summer of 1965, I refused to accept that such outbursts were the inevitable result of any systematic racism of American society. In my judgment, the real culprits in the race riots of the 1960s were neither society nor the police, but the extremists of both races who encouraged the idea that people need obey only the laws with which they agree.

Another widespread concern during this period was the general tone of American society and the growth of permissiveness. Psychologists, preachers, and parents worried as traditional standards of social and sexual behavior were flouted or abandoned. I felt that to a large degree these excesses reflected the malaise of affluence. In some cases, however, they represented a real change in American culture, and I felt that rather than just bemoaning them Republicans should try to understand them.

Increasingly in the forefront in 1965 was the war in Vietnam. I had become deeply concerned about the contrast between the actual situation I found when I visited Vietnam in 1964 and what the Johnson administration was telling the American people. I concluded that Johnson hoped to achieve a quick negotiated settlement before antiwar dissent within the Democratic Party and media criticism began undercutting his Great Society legislation.

Johnson had not leveled with the American people and told them why we were fighting in Vietnam or how deeply American troops were actually involved. To some extent he was trapped by his own words in the campaign. He had said: "We are not about to send American boys 9,000 or 10,000 miles away from home to do what Asian boys ought to be doing for themselves." He was expanding the war, and it would be difficult to explain why he considered it necessary without arousing the ire of the antiwar forces and the skepticism of the average citizen.

The price of Johnson's dissembling was high, and I was to inherit that debt: the "credibility gap." The government lost the confidence of the people, which I believe it could have kept had Johnson taken the risk and fully explained the war and patiently educated the people about it.

This was Johnson's strategic mistake—and it was a serious one. It was compounded by a no less serious tactical mistake.

By limiting the military effort to retaliation and small-scale operations, he forfeited the military initiative to the Communists. Johnson seemed to believe that restraint on his part—partly an effort to placate the left wing of his party—would be interpreted by the Communists as proof of his sincerity in seeking a negotiated settlement. He did not see how they could refuse to come to the conference table when faced with anyone as reasonable as he was determined to be.

Successful negotiation requires the creation of conditions that make it advantageous for the other party to do what you want. For a favorable outcome in Vietnam, it would have been necessary for the United States to employ its great economic and military power to demonstrate convincingly to the Communists that aggression would not pay and that it would be more desirable for them to negotiate a settlement. The Johnson administration pursued a policy of only the most gradual escalation of the air and ground war. What this policy actually accomplished was to convince the Communists that the United States lacked the will to win in Vietnam and could be worn down with propaganda directed against both our domestic front and our allies around the world.

As I saw it, Johnson should have told the American people about our role in Vietnam frankly and without any rosy predictions. The country should have been informed how difficult and costly the struggle would be. He also should have portrayed the stakes more convincingly. The United States was not just fighting to maintain an independent South Vietnam, but also to defeat the indirect aggression of China and the Soviet Union under the guise of a "war of national liberation." General Vo Nguyen Giap, the North Vietnamese military commander, had stated that the war against South Vietnam was a model for the Communist movement around the world: if such a style of aggression could succeed there, it could work elsewhere.

After the Munich Conference in 1937, Winston Churchill warned the House of Commons that "the idea that safety can be purchased by throwing a small state to the wolves is a fatal delusion." What had been true of the betrayal of Czechoslovakia to Hitler in 1938 was no less true of the betrayal of South Vietnam to the Communists advocated by many in 1965. The fall of free Vietnam to outside aggression would have sent shock waves throughout Asia. As I put it in many of my speeches, "If America gives up on Vietnam, Asia will give up on America."

To me the choice lay not, as many doves thought, between *this war* and *no war*—but between *this war* and a *bigger war later* when the Communists would be stronger and more confident.

In my speeches in 1965 I sought to justify and explain the American commitment in Southeast Asia. I pointed out that we were not like the French colonialists, who had been fighting to stay in Vietnam. We were fighting to get out once aggression had been defeated.

On January 26, 1965, in a speech to the Sales Executives Club of New York I stated bluntly that we were losing the war in Vietnam. I urged that we take the war to North Vietnam by naval and air bombing of the Communists' supply routes in South Vietnam and by destroying the Vietcong staging areas in North Vietnam and Laos. "It is dangerous and foolhardy to try to gloss over the truth as to what the war in Vietnam really involves," I said. "The war in Vietnam is not about Vietnam but about Southeast Asia." I warned that we must not delude ourselves with schemes for coalition governments or neutralization. "Neutrality where the Communists are concerned means three things: we get out; they stay in; they take over." Any negotiated settlement would inevitably lead only to further Communist demands. "We finally get back to the very difficult decision we have to make," I said. "We must realize that there is no easy way out. We either get out, surrender on the installment plan through neutralization, or we find a way to win."

Unlike some of the extremist "hawks," I did not think that we should use nuclear weapons in Vietnam. Nor did I think that we should rely on a strategy of committing increasing numbers of American troops to land battles. I said that we should instead "quarantine" the war in Vietnam by using our air and sea power to close off the outside interference from Laos and North Vietnam that made it possible for the Vietcong to practice their guerrilla terrorism. "If that were accomplished," I said, "the South Vietnamese would have a fair chance to defeat the Vietcong in battle."

I was aware that this policy would risk involving Red China, so I added: "There are risks, yes. But the risks of waiting are much greater. This becomes apparent when we look ahead and realize that if South Vietnam is lost, and Southeast Asia is lost, and the Pacific becomes a Red Sea, we could be confronted with a world war where the odds against us would be far greater."

At the end of the speech I acknowledged that "the course of action I advocate is one that is not popular in America and would probably not get a vote of confidence in Congress or by a Gallup or Harris poll." But I felt that what I had proposed was the right way, in fact the only way, to deal with the problem of Vietnam.

Two weeks later, on February 6, the Vietcong began a new stage in the escalation of the war by shelling the Army barracks at our air base near Pleiku; Johnson responded with a statement that since Hanoi had embarked upon a more aggressive course of action, "We have no choice now but to clear the decks and make absolutely clear our continued determination to back South Vietnam in its fight to maintain its independence." He ordered retaliatory air raids in North Vietnam.

I spent another four days in Saigon in September 1965. I found the situation a bit improved from eighteen months before, particularly in terms of the morale among the South Vietnamese. But American and Vietnamese military officials still seemed frustrated. They felt they were being held back because Washington thought this would encourage negotiations, while the enemy was making advances. When I appeared on *Meet the Press* after my return from Vietnam, for example, I said: "I don't know what President Johnson presently thinks with regard to negotiations, but certainly I think continued talk on his part . . . suggesting that we only want peace, that we want to negotiate, has the effect of prolonging the war rather than bringing it to a close. I think President Johnson has got to make it clear to the world and to the people of South Vietnam that our objective is a free and independent South Vietnam with no reward and no appeasement of aggressors." I repeated my call for more air and sea power against North Vietnam.

During 1965 the volume of political mail, phone calls, and speaking requests coming into my office took a quantum leap. Rose was working twelve and fourteen hours a day. Pat came down to pitch in. By the end of the year it was clear that I would have to begin building a personal staff —not just for the 1966 campaign but with an eye to being ready for 1968. In January 1966, Pat Buchanan, a young editorial writer for the St. Louis *Globe-Democrat,* joined my staff as a researcher and speech-writer.

1966 ELECTIONS

As the 1966 elections neared, I began carefully assessing the opportunities they presented and the risks they entailed for me. The risks were obvious. If the party went down to defeat or even failed to make a reasonable comeback, my adversaries in the press and my political competitors in the party would say that Nixon, the perennial loser, had once again dragged the party down to defeat, and that we needed new faces to win in 1968. However, Republicans had good reason to be optimistic about the 1966 elections, and if I had a hand in a sweeping party victory, it would not go unnoticed in the party ranks.

Between the end of the 1964 debacle and the beginning of the 1966 campaign, I had logged 127,000 miles visiting forty states to speak before more than 400 groups. I helped to raise more than $4 million in contributions to the party.

Early in 1966 I began to concentrate specifically on the fall campaign. My speaking schedule intensified. Tom Evans and Len Garment, both lawyers with our firm, were often in my office talking more politics than law. John P. Sears, a twenty-five-year-old associate in the firm, volunteered afterhours work. The fund-raising efforts of Cole, Stans, and Flanigan were stepped up and formalized in three committees, the major one of which was called Congress '66. RNC Chairman Ray Bliss refused our request for committee funds to rent a plane on the ground that this would be showing favoritism for me over other potential presidential candidates. So we raised the money on our own. It was a political miracle that we were able to do it all by ourselves.

On March 12 I attended the Gridiron Dinner of the press in Washington. Johnson had sent his regrets, and Hubert Humphrey was sitting in for him. Later in the evening, however, after many of the speeches and skits were completed, Johnson burst into the room, followed by the presidential entourage.

As he was being escorted from the dais after the toasts he greeted me and said that he would like me to stop by to have coffee with him the next morning.

As I got off the elevator on the second floor of the White House, a butler greeted me and escorted me to Johnson's room. He was sitting in bed in his pajamas. "Hello, Dick," he said. His voice was extremely hoarse, and he looked tired, almost to the point of exhaustion.

We discussed the situation in Vietnam. I told him my views regarding the need to take stronger actions to bring the North Vietnamese to the conference table. I said that I had defended the administration's policy in all the foreign countries I visited. He nodded. "I am receiving the benefit from the support I gave you and Ike in the foreign policy field in the eight years you were here," he said.

He then turned to my recommendations regarding a harder line in Vietnam. "China's the problem there," he said. "We can bomb the hell out of Hanoi and the rest of that damned country, but they've got China right behind them, and that's a different story."

I had not been in the room long when the door opened and Mrs. Johnson walked in, wearing a dressing gown. She greeted me warmly, got into bed beside her husband, and joined us for the remainder of our conversation.

He shifted gears and in muted tones began talking like a man arriving at the end of his term, rather than a President in full control of events. "When I leave this office, Bobby, Hubert, or you will have the problem of China on your hands," he said. I urged a diplomatic communication with China as soon as possible. "Mr. President," I said, "time is on their side. Now is the time to confront them on the diplomatic front." Johnson did not respond, but I sensed he agreed with me.

I said that since it was an election year, I would be out campaigning and making speeches for Republican candidates just as he had done for Democrats in 1954 and 1958 when the Republicans were in office. "I know you will understand and not take any criticism I make on issues as being directed personally at you," I said.

"I know, Dick," he replied. "We politicians are just like lawyers who get together for a drink after fighting each other like hell in the courtroom."

Johnson got up and walked to his dressing room closet, where he chose a pair of presidential cufflinks from his jewelry box and gave them to me. We shook hands and I said goodbye.

The 1966 campaign was one that I thoroughly enjoyed. With very few exceptions I was able to give my enthusiastic endorsement to the Republican candidates. I personally picked the districts and states in which I felt I could be effective, and I was pretty much on my own because the other big guns on the national scene were tied up with their own campaigns. The polls indicated that the Democrats were going to take a fairly substantial beating, and I could feel a tremendous confidence and enthusiasm in the crowds I met and spoke to. But rumors began to circulate that Johnson was planning a last-minute grandstand play that would restore public confidence right before the election. I knew him well enough to know that such a move would be entirely in character for him, so I assumed a position of watchful waiting.

At the end of September Johnson made a surprise announcement that he was going to meet with President Nguyen Van Thieu of South Vietnam and other Vietnamese and allied leaders in Manila in late October, just two weeks before the election. In the newspaper column I was writing at this time I bluntly noted the widespread skepticism that greeted this announcement. I wrote, "From diplomats in Tokyo to members of the President's own party in Washington, the question is being posed: Is this a quest for peace or a quest for votes?"

At the conclusion of their Manila meetings on October 25, Johnson, Thieu, and the leaders of Australia, Korea, New Zealand, the Philippines, and Thailand issued a joint communiqué. It offered an American and allied troop withdrawal from South Vietnam within six months, contingent upon a North Vietnamese withdrawal of forces, cessation of their support of Vietcong infiltration, and a general lessening of the levels of violence in the war.

I was on a campaign trip when we received a copy of the Manila Communiqué, and I stayed up a good part of the night analyzing it. I called in Rose Woods and Pat Buchanan and dictated several pages of notes. I asked them to travel ahead to the next stop so that Buchanan could begin incorporating my thoughts into a working draft.

By the time I got back to New York, I had a long, point-by-point analysis of what Johnson had agreed to at Manila, which I issued to the press on November 3, five days before the election. It began by pointing out that the apparently promising offer of mutual U.S. and North Vietnamese troop withdrawals was far more illusory than real.

I stated that "the effect of this mutual withdrawal would be to leave the fate of South Vietnam to the Vietcong and the South Vietnamese Army. . . . The South Vietnamese Army could not prevail for any length of time over the Communist guerrillas without American advisers, air support, and logistical backing. Communist victory would most certainly be the result of 'mutual withdrawal' if the North Vietnamese continued their own logistical support of the Communist guerrillas. . . ." The situation in 1966, when the South Vietnamese were totally untrained and unprepared to defend themselves, was very different from that in 1969, when in my presidency we were able to propose a mutual withdrawal with the assurance that our Vietnamization policies would prepare the South Vietnamese to defend themselves. I said that if I understood the Manila Communiqué correctly, it offered to tie American withdrawals to the level of fighting indulged in by the Vietcong. "If this inference is accurate," I continued, "then we have offered to surrender a decisive military advantage at the Manila Conference."

My statement was printed in full in the New York *Times* and was widely reviewed and discussed. It was treated as major news, particularly because up to that time I had consistently supported our goals in Vietnam, even while I raised questions about the tactics being used to achieve them.

If the Manila meeting had been intended to help the Democrats in the election, it backfired completely. The press was almost insultingly cynical about Johnson's motives. The doves attacked the Manila Communiqué as bellicose, and the hawks attacked it as amounting to surrender on the installment plan.

My criticism of the Manila Communiqué apparently hit a particularly raw nerve in the White House. Johnson's press conference on November 4 opened with some questions that revealed the cynical attitude of the press toward him. Johnson was tired and testy, and when a reporter asked him for a comment on my statement, something inside him seemed to break.

"I do not want to get into a debate on a foreign policy meeting in Manila with a chronic campaigner like Mr. Nixon," he replied. "It is his problem to find fault with his country and with his government during a period of October every two years. If you will look back over his record, you will find that to be true. He never did really recognize and realize what was going on when he had an official position in the government. You remember what President Eisenhower said, that if you would give him a week or so he would figure out what he was doing.

"Since then he has made a temporary stand in California, and you saw what action the people took out there. Then he crossed the country to New York. Then he went back to San Francisco, hoping that he would be in the wings, available if Goldwater stumbled. But Goldwater didn't stumble. Now he is out talking about a conference that obviously he is not well prepared on or informed about."

Reporters stole glances at one another to make sure that they were hearing correctly. Lady Bird Johnson was seated behind her husband. She was trying to smile, but shaking her head slightly.

Johnson began defending the terms of the Manila Communiqué against the charges in my statement. He said that the Communists should have no doubts about our determination to leave Vietnam as soon as the conditions of mutual withdrawal, suspension of infiltration, and a decrease in fighting were met. "They know that," he said, "and we ought not try to confuse it here and we ought not try to get it mixed up in a political campaign here. Attempts to do that will cause people to lose votes instead of gaining them. And we ought not have men killed because we try to fuzz up something. When the aggression, infiltration, and violence cease, not a nation there wants to keep occupying troops in South Vietnam. Mr. Nixon doesn't serve his country well by trying to leave that kind of impression in the hope that he can pick up a precinct or two, or a ward or two."

While Johnson was holding this press conference in Washington, I was at La Guardia Airport in New York, about to board a plane for a campaign appearance in Waterville, Maine. As soon as we were strapped into our seats, Pat Buchanan leaned over and said, "You remember that you asked me to listen to Johnson's press conference just in case he said something about your statement on the Manila Communiqué? Well, I listened, and you're not going to believe what he did."

When Buchanan told me what had happened I realized for the first time how worried Johnson was beneath his booming exterior. He had spoken in desperation, not in malice. I knew that if I handled myself well, this could turn into both a Republican and a personal windfall. When I returned to the airport after my speech at Waterville, a reporter asked me what I thought and how I felt about being personally attacked by the President of the United States. I said, "Now President Johnson and I can disagree about that, but let's disagree as gentlemen. Let's disagree as men who are trying to find the right way. Let me say that the best way is not a one-man way, not just LBJ's way but the two-party way. We need a bipartisan program for Vietnam in which both participate, rather than just a one-party program in which he says, 'I know best and all of the rest of you, if you ever take me on, then I'll hit you personally.' That's all I'm asking him to do. Let's be gentlemen about this and have our discussions in a reasonable way."

With just a few days left before the election, I suddenly found myself the center of national attention. Editorialists and columnists who had had little use for me in the past defended my integrity against Johnson's intemperate attack. Eisenhower called me from Gettysburg and said, "Dick, I could kick myself every time some jackass brings up that goddamn 'give me a week' business. Johnson has gone too far on this, and there will be a very strong backlash in your favor. I just wanted you to know that I'm issuing a statement down here." Eisenhower's statement, which was widely reported, said that I was "one of the best informed, most capable, and most industrious Vice Presidents in the history of the United States."

The Republican Congressional Campaign Committee offered me a half-hour of the network television time that had been allotted to it by NBC.

I opened the broadcast by getting right to the point. I said:

> As you have no doubt gathered from that introduction, I was subjected last week to one of the most savage personal assaults ever leveled by the President of the United States against one of his political opponents. . . .
>
> I shall answer it not for myself but because of a great principle that is at stake. It is the principle of the right to disagree, the right to dissent. That means the right to disagree with any government official, even the President of the United States.

I used most of the speech to make the case for a Republican Congress, but at the end I returned to Johnson's attack. I said:

> I understand that the President of the United States may be listening to this program tonight. I want to direct these comments to him personally. Mr. President: For fourteen years I had the privilege of serving with you in Washington. I respected you then, I respect you now. I respect you for the

great office you hold—an office that we both sought and that you won. I respect you for the great energies you devote to that office, and my respect has not changed because of the personal attack you made on me. You see, I think I understand how a man can be very, very tired and how his temper then can be very short. And if a Vice President or a former Vice President can be bone weary and tired, how much more tired would a President be after a journey like yours?"

I closed the broadcast by offering Johnson my continued support in his search for peace and freedom abroad and progress at home.

The speech was a success, it renewed my credentials as a national spokesman and a fighting campaigner. It also served to identify me with the Republican victory that now seemed almost certain in the election two days hence.

I enjoyed listening to the 1966 election returns. By the end of the night, Republicans had won a net of 47 House seats, 3 Senate seats, 8 governorships and 540 seats in state legislatures. My predictions—that we would win 40 House seats, 3 Senate seats, 6 governorships and 700 state legislature seats—which had seemed so unrealistically optimistic when I made them six months earlier were vindicated with a vengeance.

The election was personally satisfying to me in that the Republicans made gains in the South, defeating Democratic backlash candidates in Arkansas, where Winthrop Rockefeller won, and in Maryland, where Spiro Agnew defeated a Democrat who was running on a subtly racist line. I had specifically predicted that Rockefeller and Agnew would win.

After the last returns were in and our victory was confirmed, I rounded up a small party to go to El Morocco for a victory supper of spaghetti and red wine. There was a lot for me to celebrate. The first major hurdle had been met, faced, and surmounted in style. There were more hurdles ahead, but this was an auspicious start. It was gratifying to know that I had played a major part in this Republican victory—a prerequisite for my own comeback.

"A HOLIDAY FROM POLITICS"

I fully realized that my efforts in the campaign had been only one of many factors in the Republican triumph. We had been the recipients of a massive anti-Johnson windfall. But no matter what the reasons, I had indisputably played a central part, and for the first time in ten years I was identified with a smashing victory.

The campaign of 1966 had another important effect: it softened the remaining jagged memories of the "last press conference." For one of the few times in my political career, Johnson's attack made me the wounded party. He had not, in fact, been far off. I *was* something of a chronic campaigner, always out on the stump raising partisan hell. But my years in the "wilderness" and the simple process of growing older had probably rounded off some of the hard edges of the younger Nixon. I emerged from the campaign of 1966 as a seasoned senior Republican statesman who could still deliver some effective political licks.

On the day after the election I issued a statement of my belief that the results represented a repudiation of Johnson's policies. I also underscored the message for Hanoi and Peking that the new House of Representatives would be much stronger than its predecessor in supporting a U.S. policy of "no reward for aggression."

Throughout the campaign many of my friends, advisers, and supporters had urged me to gear up my own organization to be ready to go public with my presidential candidacy as soon as the election—and, we hoped, the great Republican victory—had taken place. Such advice made perfect sense in traditional terms, but I had already decided to try a highly unconventional idea: instead of plunging into the arena, I was going to bide my political time. When I had appeared on *Issues and Answers* two days before the election, I announced: "I am going to take a holiday from politics for at least six months with no political speeches scheduled whatever. What the future holds I don't know."

I wanted to run for President in 1968, but I wanted to leave open, until the last possible moment, the option of deciding *not* to run.

Our family spent a relaxed holiday in Key Biscayne. We went sailing with Bebe Rebozo on his boat, the *Coco Lobo,* and spent hours on the beach reading, swimming, and talking about everything except politics. I knew that Pat and the girls were secretly hoping that the moratorium on politics would go on and on.

Shortly after we got back to New York, Peter Flanigan and Maury Stans came to see me. It was the day before Thanksgiving. They said that the time had come to make a move if I had any intention of being a candidate in 1968. Romney was off and running, and Reagan's supporters were talking about renewing the Goldwater conservative movement. There was even talk of another Goldwater candidacy. Nelson Rockefeller was in the wings, ready to pick up the ball if others stumbled. Each hopeful was trying to get party leaders and workers committed to him, and unless I could give my personal supporters some reason to hold out, I might one day find that they had been snatched up by my rivals. Flanigan and Stans wanted to organize a Nixon for President Club and begin some preliminary low-key organizing and fund-raising. I told them that I considered the ability to remain officially undecided for as long as possible to be one of my greatest advantages. Not only would this allow me more independence, but the speculation about my intentions guaranteed far more media attention than I would have if I announced. Therefore, I would publicly neither approve nor disapprove their activity. But I assured them that I agreed completely with their analysis of the need to begin organizing.

A few months later, about the time I was emerging from a meeting with Willy Brandt in Bonn, the formation of the first Nixon for President Committee was announced in Washington.

On January 7 and 8, 1967, I held planning meetings at the Waldorf Towers. I said: "I'm not going to be coy with my oldest friends and closest advisers. I want you to proceed with plans for winning the Republican presidential nomination next year."

I made it clear that my six-month moratorium, while admittedly a risk, was carefully calculated. George Romney could be out front taking the heat from the press and the pundits while I continued my quiet planning and foreign travel. "But make no mistake," I said, "while I am lying back I want you to work your tails off getting the job done. We will have to work harder and better than the other candidates to win."

I decided to begin building a personal political staff so that I could be ready to plunge into the battle as soon as my moratorium ended. I enlisted Raymond K. Price, Jr., a former chief editorial writer for the New York *Herald Tribune,* to be my principal idea man and speechwriter; he would also work on a book I was considering along the lines of Wendell Willkie's *One World.* In addition to Price, Dwight Chapin, a young advertising executive, joined the staff to serve as a personal aide.

On January 1, 1967, my law firm had merged with the firm of Caldwell, Trimble, and Mitchell, which specialized in municipal bonds. I struck up an immediate friendship with the husky, outwardly gruff senior partner, John Mitchell. Although he had never been involved in a campaign, I felt from our conversations that he had an instinctive talent for politics. As a result of his extensive work with state and local governments in providing legal advice on bond issues, he had an exceptionally wide network of political contacts. Within a few months I was beginning to turn increasingly to him for advice and counsel on political matters.

I decided to use the time during my moratorium on active politics to make a series of foreign study trips. I wanted to bring my impressions up to date and to renew my contacts and refine my ideas about current conditions in the world. By undertaking these trips I was building on my political strong suit, my knowledge of foreign affairs. I also believed this was the best possible way to ensure that I would be able to frame foreign policy issues in a way that would be both effective and responsible, and, if I became President, to ensure that I could get a head start on what to me were the most important decisions a President faces.

I scheduled four trips: to Europe and the Soviet Union in March, to Asia in April, to Latin America in May, and to Africa and the Middle East in June. By this time Robert Ellsworth, an exceptionally able former congressman from Kansas then practicing law in Washington, had arranged to spend approximately half his time helping with my campaign-that-was-not-yet-a-campaign. Ellsworth had a special interest in foreign and defense matters, and he helped make arrangements for the trips through the State Department and the embassies of the countries I would visit. He accompanied me on the first trip and on part of another; Ray Price was on the second; my friend Bebe was on the third to Latin America; and Pat Buchanan on the fourth.

In these 1967 worldwide trips I met the leaders, met the people, and saw at first hand the problems, opportunities, and dangers confronting the United States. The result was to reinforce some views I already strongly held and to modify others.

The trip to Europe and the Soviet Union was to begin on March 5. As usual I requested a CIA briefing before departure; and for the first time since I had left office it was refused. Since such briefings are a privilege—not a right—for a private citizen, no official explanation was given. Unofficially I was told that Johnson was still furious over the Manila Communiqué incident and that he had expressly forbidden the CIA to give me any help or guidance.

This was a very disturbing trip for me. I had not made a systematic tour of the NATO nations since 1963, and I was shocked by the extent to which our relations with them had deteriorated. The Europeans were deeply offended by our failures to consult with them, or even to inform them of decisions we made that touched on their defenses and their destinies. Everywhere I heard the same story: under Kennedy and Johnson, we had shown in a variety of ways how little we valued our allies and how little we appreciated the importance of NATO.

I saw Konrad Adenauer, for the last time. As I entered his room, he embraced me with almost embarrassing warmth. Standing back, his hands still on my shoulders, he said, "Thank God you are here. Your visit is like manna from heaven." This great architect of postwar Europe was depressed about Europe's future. "I am worried, my friend," he said. He predicted that when de Gaulle left the scene, the Communist

Party in France, and then in Italy, would gain strength. He completely discounted the Soviet Union's alleged interest in hastening peace in Vietnam, and the popular speculation that the Soviets would turn toward the West out of fear of China. "Make no mistake about it," he said, "they want the world. The whole world. Most of all they want Europe, and to get Europe they know they must destroy Germany. We need you to keep us strong and free. But you also need us." Adenauer urged—as had de Gaulle four years before—that we tilt our policy toward Communist China to counterbalance the growing Soviet threat.

I was surprised to find a similar concern about Soviet strategy expressed by almost everyone I talked with on this trip. In Rome President Saragat and Foreign Minister Fanfani agreed that the Soviets were determined to keep the war going in Vietnam. Like Adenauer, however, they felt that the primary threat from communism was in Europe rather than in Asia. Fanfani said, "NATO is what really counts, but too many people in your country take it for granted and think that Vietnam is the most important thing because that is where you are fighting the Communists. America is like the man confronted with a small fire in his barn when his house is falling apart for want of repairs."

My old friend Manlio Brosio, the Italian diplomat who was then Secretary General of NATO after having served in Washington for six years and in Moscow for five, emotionally and emphatically expressed his doubts about Soviet intentions. "I know the Russians," he said. "They are great liars, clever cheaters, and magnificent actors. They cannot be trusted. They consider it their duty to cheat and lie." A Belgian I talked with pithily expressed his own skeptical view of détente: "It is like the Virgin Birth. I accept it, but I don't believe it."

I had been refused a visa to visit Poland on this trip and was therefore surprised to receive one from Romania. Even so, I assumed that I would get one of the cold-shoulder receptions that Communist governments are particularly good at. But from the moment Ellsworth and I stepped off the plane in Bucharest, it was clear that this was going to be a remarkable visit. Everywhere we were greeted with outbursts of friendship from the people.

I called on the Romanian Communist Party's Secretary General, Nicolae Ceauşescu, at the Central Committee Building. We had a long talk, ranging over the spectrum of East-West relations. I doubted that any true détente with the Soviets could be achieved until some kind of rapprochement could be reached with Communist China. If its 800 million people remained isolated, within twenty years China could pose a grave threat to world peace. I said that I thought the United States could do little to establish effective communications with China until the Vietnam war was ended. After that, however, I thought we could take steps to normalize relations with Peking. Ceauşescu was guarded in his reaction, but I could tell that he was interested to hear me talking in this way, and that he agreed with what I said.

On my trip to Asia in April I wanted to evaluate the situation in Vietnam and the importance of the conflict to Vietnam's neighbors. I also particularly wanted to learn how Asian leaders were viewing China and its future relationship with the rest of Asia and the world.

Many Americans were primarily Europeanists in their approach to foreign affairs, dismissing Asia as relatively unimportant. But the United States is a Pacific power, and rapid changes were taking place in Asia—where more than half the human race lived—that might well determine the world's future. Japan would soon be the world's third-ranking industrial power, behind the United States and the Soviet Union. Some of the most rapid rates of economic progress anywhere were being achieved by the nations of non-Communist Asia. And mainland China potentially posed the greatest threat to peace during the final third of the twentieth century.

I met with Prime Minister Sato, former Prime Minister Kishi, and a number of other Japanese political officials. The Japanese leaders felt strongly that the United States must remain in Asia, and that it was vital that we continue to help defend South Vietnam. They were keenly aware that, because of memories of World War II, there were limits to the leadership Japan could exercise. Nonetheless, they acknowledged the need for regional cooperation to contain the Communist challenge.

I visited Chiang Kai-shek at a lake resort on Taiwan. Chiang still dreamed of returning to the mainland, and once again he urged that America support such an effort. He argued that the Chinese on the mainland were disenchanted with their leaders and ready to rally to another force. A Nationalist invasion of the mainland, he said, would end the threat of a Red Chinese atomic bomb, end Chinese support of the Vietnam war, and end the chance of a Sino-Soviet rapprochement.

Chiang was a friend and unquestionably one of the giants of the twentieth century. I wondered whether he might be right, but my pragmatic analysis told me that he was wrong. His burning desire to return to the mainland was understandable and admirable. But it was totally unrealistic in view of the massive power the Communists had developed.

In Vietnam, despite the military's optimistic prediction, I became further convinced that continuation of the administration's policy of fighting a defensive war of attrition would inevitably lead to defeat. It was small comfort to learn the enemy was losing more men than we were. It had become America's war, and the South Vietnamese were not being adequately trained and equipped to defend themselves. The Communists were willing to continue fighting regardless of losses. They had a total commitment to victory. We had, at most, a partial commitment to avoid defeat. If this situation continued, in the end they would win.

Every leader I talked to in Asia expressed support for a strong American position in Vietnam. But I also found on this trip a growing concern about Communist China. Some who had adamantly opposed any change of American policy toward China had come around to the view that some new and direct relationship between the two nations was essential if there were to be any chance at all after the Vietnam war was over to build a lasting peace in Asia in which free nations would have a chance to survive.

In Latin America in May I found that Kennedy's Alliance for Progress had raised expectations too high. The leaders I met with expressed their disappointment and urged that the United States develop a new approach to attract the private investment from both the United States and Europe that the Latin American economies desperately needed in order to make any meaningful progress.

In Africa in June the leaders emphasized their desire to have more aid from the United States rather than depend on their former colonial masters. But I was discouraged by the fact that, with a few exceptions, the new black African nations simply did not have the trained leadership to achieve their goals in any forseeable future.

I visited Israel just after that country's victory in the June war. In a long conversation with General Yitzhak Rabin I pointed out that Israel had a stake in the outcome of the war in Vietnam. He was obviously interested in my analysis that if the United States were defeated or humiliated in Vietnam, the American people could well turn isolationist and be unwilling to come to the aid of other small nations, like Israel, who depended on us for survival.

I was impressed by the courage and toughness of the Israeli leaders and people. But I was disturbed by the fact that their swift and overwhelming victory over the Arabs had created a feeling of overconfidence about their ability to win any war in the future, and an attitude of total intransigence on negotiating any peace agreement that would involve return of any of the territories they had occupied. Their victory had been too great. It left a residue of hatred among their neighbors that I felt could only result in another war, particularly if the Russians were to step up military aid to their defeated Arab clients.

I summarized my conclusions from these trips first in a speech at the Bohemian Grove and then in an article for the quarterly *Foreign Affairs*.

If I were to choose the speech that gave me the most pleasure and satisfaction in my political career, it would be my Lakeside Speech at the Bohemian Grove in July 1967. Because this speech traditionally was off the record it received no publicity at the time. But in many important ways it marked the first milestone on my road to the presidency.

The setting is possibly the most dramatic and beautiful I have ever seen. A natural amphitheatre has been built up around a platform on the shore of a small lake. Redwoods tower above the scene, and the weather in July is usually warm and clear. Herbert Hoover had always delivered the Lakeside Speech, but he had died in 1964, and I was asked if I would deliver the 1967 speech in his honor. It was an emotional assignment for me and also an unparalleled opportunity to reach some of the most important and influential men, not just from California but from across the country.

In the speech I pointed out that we live in a new world—"never in human history have more changes taken place in the world in one generation"—and that this is a world of new leaders, of new people, of new ideas.

I led the audience on a tour of the world, tracing the changes and examining the conflicts, finding both danger and opportunity as the United States entered the final third of the twentieth century. I urged the need for strong alliances and continued aid to the developing nations; but I also urged that we should provide our aid more selectively, rewarding our friends and discouraging our enemies and encouraging private rather than government enterprise.

Turning to the Soviet Union, I noted that even as the Soviet leaders talked peace they continued to stir up trouble, to encourage aggression, and to build missiles. I urged that we encourage trade with the Soviet Union and Eastern Europe, and that "diplomatically we should have discussions with the Soviet leaders at all levels to reduce the possibility of miscalculation and to explore the areas where bilateral agreements would reduce tensions." But we should insist on reciprocity: "I believe in building bridges but we should build only our end of the bridge." And in negotiations we must always remember "that our goal is different from theirs. We seek peace as an end in itself. They seek victory, with peace being at this time a means toward that end."

Looking ahead, I said:

> As we enter this last third of the twentieth century the hopes of the world rest with America. Whether peace and freedom survive in the world depends on American leadership.
>
> Never has a nation had more advantages to lead. Our economic superiority is enormous; our military superiority can be whatever we choose to make

> it. Most important, it happens that we are on the right side—the side of freedom and peace and progress against the forces of totalitarianism, reaction, and war.
>
> There is only one area where there is any question—that is whether America has the national character and moral stamina to see us through this long and difficult struggle.

To me, that would be the central question at issue in 1968.

The subject of my October 1967 *Foreign Affairs* article was "Asia After Vietnam." In it I stressed the importance of Asia to the United States and the world, and concluded with a section on U.S. policy toward China:

> Some counsel conceding to China a "sphere of influence" embracing much of the Asian mainland and extending even to the island nations beyond; others urge that we eliminate the threat by pre-emptive war. Clearly, neither of these courses would be acceptable to the United States or to its Asian allies. Others argue that we should seek an anti-Chinese alliance with European powers, even including the Soviet Union. Quite apart from the obvious problems involved in Soviet participation, such a course would inevitably carry connotations of Europe vs. Asia, white vs. non-white, which could have catastrophic repercussions throughout the rest of the non-white world in general and Asia in particular. . . . Only as the nations of non-Communist Asia become so strong—economically, politically, and militarily—that they no longer furnish tempting targets for Chinese aggression, will the leaders in Peking be persuaded to turn their energies inward rather than outward. And that will be the time when the dialogue with mainland China can begin.
>
> For the short run, then, this means a policy of firm restraint, of no reward, of a creative counterpressure designed to persuade Peking that its interests can be served only by accepting the basic rules of international civility. For the long run, it means pulling China back into the world community—but as a great and progressing nation, not as the epicenter of world revolution.

Soon after I got back to New York on June 24 I began checking to find out how the political situation had developed during my absence. Things were moving so fast that even the few months I was away had produced an almost completely different political landscape.

I found that sentiment was beginning to turn very decisively in my favor. But everyone was still asking the big question: after two defeats, could I shake my "loser image"? It appeared more and more that the presidential primaries offered the only way to show that I could win.

Ronald Reagan was one of the potential presidential candidates who denied any interest in the nomination. I had seen him at the Bohemian

Grove in July where Senator George Murphy, he, and I had a candid discussion of the political situation as we sat outdoors on a bench under one of the giant redwoods. I told him about my tentative plans to enter the primaries. I assured him that it was my intention to do everything possible to unite the party and to campaign only against Johnson and his administration, and not against any fellow Republicans.

Reagan said that he had been surprised, flattered, and somewhat concerned about all the presidential speculation surrounding him. He did not want to be a favorite son, he said, but he would probably have to allow it in order to assure party unity in California. He said that he would not be a candidate in the primaries.

On July 17, I flew to Gettysburg to see Eisenhower. I looked forward, as usual, to discussing politics and world affairs with him, but now we had another subject of mutual interest. Julie and his grandson David had been seeing a great deal of each other while at college. Actually, though it was not known to the respective families, they had already decided to marry.

We ate lunch alone on the screened-in porch overlooking the farm. We had chicken with noodles and a salad garnished with pickled watermelon rind, which he proudly said he had helped to make. "The rind wasn't thick enough," he said as he helped himself to more.

Eisenhower had been quite animated at lunch, but afterward he looked tired and had to grope for words. He was particularly fatigued after we took a short walk to the barn, but he was firm in the advice he gave me. He advised me against making Vietnam a political issue because many Republicans supported Johnson's goals, although questioning the means he was using to achieve them. He agreed with my long-held view that Johnson's greatest error in prosecuting the war was not having used more power at the outset. He said he knew from his own military experience that gradual escalation did not work. He said, "If an enemy battalion is defending a hill, you give me two battalions and I'll take the hill—but at a terrible cost in casualties. Give me a division and I'll take it without a fight."

Eisenhower asked if Goldwater was still writing a newspaper column. "Barry is the least qualified man I know to write on foreign policy," he said. "He has charm and he is very likable, but he is just not smart." He felt that Scranton was the best qualified of any of the men who had not held national office.

He also talked about Johnson. "Lyndon is too poll-conscious and too sensitive about press criticism," he said. "I told him that directly. I said, 'You are the President, don't worry about jackasses like Fulbright and Morse.' " He added, "The difficulty with Johnson is that he is only interested in what people will approve, and that makes it difficult to get people to believe him."

That fall of 1967 I visited most of the Republican governors and party leaders in their home states. They all wanted to know my plans, but I said only that I was considering entering the primaries and would be grateful for any advice they had. While this position did not commit me or call for any commitments from them, it reinforced their determination to see how I would do in the primaries before deciding whom to support.

In fact, it looked as if many Republicans were using my possible candidacy as an excuse for remaining uncommitted to anyone else. Many Southern leaders, particularly, were holding back on these grounds. In their hearts they would have preferred Reagan, but they had been burned by Goldwater and had learned a lesson of political pragmatism. If they thought I was the man who could win, they would support me.

I was in my law office in New York on Saturday, September 30, 1967, when Rose came in to tell me that my brother Don was on the telephone. I was in a conference, so I asked Rose to tell him I would return the call. She began to cry and said, "No, you should talk to him. Your mother just died."

My mother had suffered a stroke two years before, and we had reluctantly put her in a nursing home in Whittier. Whenever I was in the Los Angeles area I drove out to see her. She never gave any signs of awareness and could speak only in monosyllables, but I felt sure that in the deep recesses of her mind she recognized me.

She had always hated the idea of being in a rest home, but she needed constant attention from nurses and doctors that would have been impossible to provide either at Don's house or in our New York apartment. There were times when I regretted that we did not do whatever was necessary to keep her in one of our homes. There was no doubt, however, that it was better for her to be where she could receive proper care. I also knew that she would have wanted it that way, because she never wanted to be a burden to her family.

Perhaps because I was prepared intellectually for the idea of her death, it took some time before the emotional impact of it hit me. By the time I got home about an hour later, Pat had told the girls. They were in tears; they loved their grandmother very much, although it would not have been possible for them to love her as much as she loved them. Her love was all-encompassing and totally unselfish—never expecting or wanting anything in return. I did not cry when I heard the news, nor when I talked with Pat and the girls in the apartment, nor on the plane to California for the funeral. My principal thought was a feeling of deep regret that I had not done as much for her as I might have if I had not been so busy with my own career and concerns.

My mother had been a great admirer of Billy Graham, even before he became famous. She had attended one of his first crusades in Southern California and spoken to him afterward, and he never forgot her in the years that followed. As soon as he heard of her death, he called me from his home in North Carolina and said that he wanted to come to the funeral. The service was held in the same Friends Church in East Whittier where as a child I had played the piano for Sunday School and sung in the choir. It was in this church that my father's funeral service had been held eleven years earlier.

The church was full, and many of my mother's Whittier friends and acquaintances had to stand outside because of the great number of reporters, whose presence I deeply resented, who filled the back and side aisles. At the end of the service the family were the first to leave the church and walk by the open casket. My mother was not pretty, but she was beautiful, and she looked as beautiful in death as she had in life.

The local minister and Billy were standing at the door as we left. I shook hands with the minister and then, as I shook hands with Billy, our eyes met. I could no longer control my pent-up emotions. I broke into tears. He threw his arms around me and said, "Let it all out."

We walked out into the sunlight and rode from the church to Rose Hills Memorial Park. My mother was buried in the family plot, alongside my father, my brothers Arthur and Harold, her mother and father, and her sister Elizabeth, who died of cancer. Only one reporter had the bad manners to stick a microphone in my face and ask how I felt. I just walked past him. I did not want to stay around the places that reminded me so painfully of my mother, so Pat and I went directly to the airport from the cemetery and were soon on our way back to New York.

While Pat slept, I closed my eyes and thought back on my mother's life. She had worked so hard and given so much of herself to others. I remembered the last time we had talked before she had her stroke. She had just had an operation, and although she was in terrible pain she never once complained about it.

I knew that her chances of recovery were very small. Words were utterly inadequate, so all I could say was, "Mother, don't give up."

She pulled herself up in the bed, and with sudden strength in her voice she said, "Richard, don't *you* give up. Don't let anybody tell you you are through."

Only later did I find out that just before her operation she had read a column in the Los Angeles *Times* speculating that I was through as far as any chances of regaining national office were concerned.

"Richard, don't you give up. Don't let anybody tell you you are through." What a typical sentiment, I thought as the plane flew eastward into nightfall. What a marvelous legacy.

The Republican front-runner during the preprimary period was George Romney. I knew that Romney had a head start, but I also suspected that his lack of experience might make him politically accident-prone. Reports from his campaign organization confirmed this suspicion. His statement that he had been successfully "brainwashed" by his official hosts during his study tour of Vietnam was his worst, but by no means his only, gaffe during this period.

From my point of view, the most interesting question about Romney was whether Nelson Rockefeller was using him as a stalking horse for his own candidacy.

I saw Eisenhower again on October 17. By now the political situation was beginning to develop very quickly, and he was outspoken in analyzing the various political personalities who might play a role in 1968.

I told him of my high regard for Jerry Ford. He agreed but was afraid that Ford was not exciting enough. "We need someone who can charge up the troops," he said. He called Mel Laird "the smartest of the lot, but he is too devious." In December 1968, after I had selected Laird as Secretary of Defense, Eisenhower expressed the same doubts. After the two men had a meeting in January, however, Eisenhower told me he thought I had made a good choice. Flashing his famous grin, he said, "Of course Laird is devious, but for anyone who has to run the Pentagon and get along with Congress, that is a valuable asset."

We discussed Rockefeller's intentions and his chances. Eisenhower said, "His major liability is that his becoming a candidate would resurrect all the hard feelings of 1964 at a time when it is imperative to get the party together."

As usual we talked about the situation in Vietnam. I said that I thought we should quarantine North Vietnam by mining its harbors. Eisenhower said that he thought we would need a declaration of war in order to justify such action under international law. He took a hard line, however, regarding the proposals to stop the bombing of North Vietnam. He said, "Who wants to stop it? The Communists want to stop it because it is hurting them. Therefore, we should continue it."

He thought that Johnson's hesitations at crucial occasions had been damaging. He thought he had made a serious mistake in restricting the bombing of North Vietnam, and that Johnson had been about a year and a half too late at every stage: in committing U.S. troops, in initiating the bombing, and in building up public support for the war.

I asked him what he thought of the idea of switching to a volunteer army when the war ended. He strongly opposed it and said that he had written a thesis on the topic at the War College. He had investigated all the options and concluded that universal military training was a good idea. "Besides," he added, "it would be good for the hippie generation."

He looked up suddenly. "Look at that beautiful bluejay," he said. We watched the bird for a few moments. Eisenhower's brow furrowed as he tried to pick up his train of thought, and it was painful for me to watch him struggling to remember. Finally he sighed and said, "If only the time would come when men would sit down and rationally settle their differences in peace."

By the end of 1967 I knew that I had to make a final decision about running. The Nixon for President organization was ready to shift into high gear as soon as I gave the signal. Johnson's personal and political insecurity had become obvious; his party was ready to split apart under pressure from Eugene McCarthy and Bobby Kennedy on the left and from George Wallace on the right. The chances for a Republican to be elected President in 1968 looked better all the time. My chances of being that Republican had also improved over the year. I was the first choice of Republicans for the nomination in almost every Gallup poll taken in 1967; most of the party's organizational leaders either wanted to support me or, at least, felt that I had earned a shot at the nomination by the hard labor I had done for the party during the dark times after Goldwater's defeat. However, many of my strongest supporters were still not sure that I could throw off my "loser image" and lead the party to victory. As I had foreseen, everything was going to depend on the primaries.

In October 1967 the Gallup poll's presidential trial heat had shown me running ahead of Johnson for the first time, 49 percent to 45 percent. Even though he regained the lead in November, this showing did much to improve my chances.

In all the conversations that I had in the latter part of 1967, seeking advice about what to do, I did not reveal to anyone my inner doubts about becoming a candidate. Late on the night of December 22, 1967, I committed some of them to paper.

It had been a long day—lunch with my law partners, an afternoon meeting with key campaign advisers, and in the evening our annual Christmas party at our apartment, at which I played Christmas carols on the piano and Tom Dewey led the singing in his rich baritone. After the party, Pat and I went to the kitchen to thank Manolo and Fina Sanchez for the splendid job they had done in serving over a hundred guests.

We realized again, as we had so many times before, how fortunate we were to have had the loyal and efficient services of this remarkable Spanish couple who had come to us as refugees from Cuba in 1961. Then I retreated to the quiet of my library. Manolo had laid a fire, and the room had a comforting, familiar warmth.

I sat in my easy chair and took a fresh yellow pad. I wrote: "I have decided personally against becoming a candidate." Then I summarized my thoughts:

—Unlike some of the political newcomers, I did not want the presidency in order to *be* someone.

—Losing again could be an emotional disaster for the family. The memories of 1960 and 1962 were still painful.

—Perhaps I had lost the spirit and zeal essential to survive the ordeal of a long presidential campaign—particularly one that begins on the tortuous primary route. I wrote, "Combat is the essence of politics." Yet I really did not relish the combat and had to force myself to develop the fighting spirit necessary to inspire others.

—I was tired of having to ask for support from political and business leaders and even from old friends.

—There would be no draft at the convention. People were still hesitating about their support, and I continued to hear the message that the party needed a winner.

—I was bored by the charade of trying to romance the media. They were being relatively courteous at this period, but I knew the majority opposed my views and would strongly oppose my candidacy.

—"Personally, I have had it. I want nothing else." Even as I wrote the words I was surprised by my ambivalence regarding the presidency. As if to restore some balance I noted that neither was the practice of law what I wanted for the rest of my life.

—A good candidate must have five qualities: brains, heart, judgment, guts, and experience. I felt that I measured up to four of them. But I was not sure whether I still had the heart—whether I had not reached the time in life when I lacked the zeal to continue a political career.

—Many of my friends did not want my place in history to be determined by the defeats of 1960 and 1962. They argued that defeat should not be my epitaph. That argument never had much appeal to me because I had a fatalistic, almost deterministic, view of history—that history makes the man more than the man makes history.

Finally, I startled myself again by writing at the bottom of the page a thought that I had never expected to have: "I don't give a damn."

I put down my pen and just sat looking into the fire and thinking. I had somehow always known that if everything worked out right, I could have another presidential candidacy. The road had been tiring and at times unbearably lonely. Had I come all this way to avoid the clash? I *did* want to run. Every instinct said yes. But now, on the brink of that decision, I was surprised to find myself procrastinating.

On Christmas Day, I had a long discussion with Pat, Tricia, and Julie. Pat said that she was completely happy with our life in New York, but whatever I decided, she was resigned to helping out. Tricia and Julie were now grown up, and I gave great weight to their opinions. Julie was a sophomore at Smith College. She had never really accepted the loss in 1960. She said, "You have to do it for the country." Tricia, a senior at Finch College, spoke in more personal terms. "If you don't run, Daddy, you really will have nothing to live for."

With the New Hampshire primary less than three months away, I could not prolong the final decision much longer. It was clear that in the busy holiday atmosphere at home, I would not be able to do any concentrated thinking. I decided therefore to go to Florida for a few days to relax and think in solitude.

As I left on December 28, Pat took my arm and kissed me. "Whatever you do, we'll be proud of you," she said. "You know we love you."

Bebe Rebozo met me at the airport, and we went directly to a villa at the Key Biscayne Hotel. I had telephoned Billy Graham and asked if he could come down and join us. For the next three days I walked on the beach and thought about the most important decision of my life. On the first night we sat up late talking about theology and politics and sports. Billy read aloud the first and second chapters of Romans. The next afternoon I invited him to join me for a walk along the beach. He had been very sick with pneumonia and was still recuperating, so we decided not to tax his strength by walking too far. I told him that I was genuinely torn on the question of whether to run. One part of me wanted to more than anything else, but another part of me rebelled at the thought of all it would entail. It was far from certain that I could win the nomination; even if I did, that would be only the prelude to an even more arduous campaign. Ten months of campaigning would mean great stress and strain on me and on my family, especially Pat.

We had become so involved in our conversation that we walked more than a mile—all the way to the old Spanish lighthouse at the tip of Key Biscayne. By the time we got back, Billy was weak and exhausted. He went upstairs to rest while Rebozo and I watched the Green Bay Packers defeat the Dallas Cowboys 21–17 in subfreezing weather in Green Bay. That night, New Year's Eve, we had dinner at the Jamaica Inn, where I had reserved my favorite table beside a small waterfall.

As Billy was getting ready to leave the next day, I went to his room and sat looking out at the ocean while he finished packing. "Well, what is your conclusion?" I asked. "What should I do?" Billy closed his suitcase and turned toward me. "Dick, I think you should run," he said. "If you don't you will always wonder whether you should have run and whether you could have won or not. You are the best prepared man in the United States to be President." He talked about the problems facing America and how much greater and more serious they were now than in 1960. He said that I had been denied the chance to provide leadership in 1960, but now, providentially, I had another chance. "I think it is your destiny to be President," he said.

I stayed in Florida for another week. One morning when I went to the hotel from my villa to pick up my mail, I found a letter from David Eisenhower.

> Dear Mr. Nixon,
>
> During my past visit, Julie told me of the difficult decisions you were facing and of the strong possibility that you might not run for President. I hoped that an appropriate moment would arise to say something about it to you in person, but the subject seemed so delicate that the words and the moment eluded me. . . .
>
> The most discouraging aspect of politics, when I rationally consider my ambitions in life, is its thanklessness. My Grandad is now regarded as a simple country bumpkin and a sweet old General. The liberal element, since it does control educational and journalistic media to a vast degree, has distorted his personal and public image possibly forever. Yet I feel his efforts were, for himself and many others, the source of genuine satisfaction since he served his country to the best of his ability and touched the lives of millions.
>
> Everything I say must be a tremendous understatement since I have never endured a political campaign or political life in its most taxing form. Politics is a sacrifice, in terms of one's family, privacy, and countless other aspects of a man's life. This I have seen. It is rare when someone possesses such wisdom and insight that he should be called upon to sacrifice himself and to serve. But I sincerely feel that you have it and that America needs the guidance you could render. I also feel that America will come to realize this in due time, if it doesn't already. . . .
>
> Only you can determine whether to run is worth the effort and the hardships or not. I simply hoped to tell you a little of how I felt on the matter. . . .
>
> Sincerely,
> David

By January 9, my fifty-fifth birthday, I was back in New York. My mind was made up, but I decided to wait until Julie could come home from school for a weekend so that I could tell the whole family at the same time.

On January 15, we were all together for dinner. I asked Rose Woods to join us—she had been through so much with us that she was virtually a part of the family. I felt she should be present at this moment. I waited until dinner was over, and then I asked Manolo and Fina to join us.

I said that, as they probably guessed, I had reached a decision. I knew that Pat was not in favor of my running, and that was the one factor that finally weighed most heavily in my mind against it. But I had increasingly come to understand that politics was not just an alternative occupation for me. It was my life. Although it would be a long, hard road, I felt that this time I could win. Finally, I said, "I have decided to go. I have decided to run again."

There was a brief pause. Then Pat said, "I know what you are asking us to do, and what you are asking of yourself. Now that the decision is made, I will go along with it."

Tricia picked up her water glass and proposed a toast. She said, "Whatever happens, we will win either way!" Fina, standing next to Manolo, said, "You are the man to lead the country! This was determined before you were born! "

1968 Campaign and Election

I began my second campaign for the presidency with a press conference on the afternoon of February 2, 1968, in the Holiday Inn at Manchester, New Hampshire. I came to the microphones and announced, "Gentlemen, this is *not* my last press conference."

Anticipating the central question, I said at the outset that I had considered the "he can't win" problem and had decided to enter all the primaries to prove that I *could* win. As a challenge to Nelson Rockefeller —who was, I was convinced, behind George Romney's candidacy—I said that the next Republican nominee must be selected not in smoke-filled rooms but in the "fires of the primaries."

I had some reasons for confidence about the chances for success of my primary strategy. The most recent nationwide Gallup poll of Republicans gave me a commanding 40 percent lead over Romney, and I led Rockefeller by a comfortable 14 percent. Given these generally reassuring figures, I had three major concerns about the New Hampshire primary. First, there was always the danger of an upset; no candidate can be confident of an election when 32 percent of the voters are undecided. I had to show that I could be a winner, but I could not let the proud and independent voters of New Hampshire think me arrogant or start regarding Romney as an underdog. Second, there was always the danger of making a mistake. I knew that the media would analyze and examine everything I did and said, and I would have to be extraordinarily careful of the image and tone my campaign projected. Third, there was the danger of allowing the primary campaign to split the Republican ranks so deeply that whoever won would inherit a dispirited and disunited party. Johnson's popularity ratings were low because of North Korea's seizure of the intelligence ship *Pueblo* in January, the Tet offensive in Vietnam in February, and the bitter disunity being stirred up among the Democrats by Minnesota Senator Eugene McCarthy's antiwar candidacy. Even considering these factors, it would still be very difficult for any Republican to challenge Lyndon Johnson, a resourceful politician armed with the powers of incumbency.

The Vietnam war was the dominant issue in New Hampshire, as it was throughout the campaign. I wanted the war to end, but in a manner that would save the South Vietnamese people from military defeat and subjection to the domination of the North Vietnamese Communist regime.

I felt that there were a number of unexplored avenues to probe in finding a way to end the war. I believed that we could use our armed strength more effectively to convince the North Vietnamese that a military victory was not possible. We also needed to step up our programs for training and equipping the South Vietnamese so that they could develop the capability of defending themselves. Most important, I believed that we were not making adequate use of our vast diplomatic resources and powers. The heart of the problem lay more in Peking and Moscow than in Hanoi.

As a candidate it would have been foolhardy, and as a prospective President, improper, for me to outline specific plans in detail. I did not have the full range of information or the intelligence resources available to Johnson. And even if I had been able to formulate specific "plans," it would have been absurd to make them public. In the field of diplomacy, premature disclosure can often doom even the best-laid plans.

To some extent, then, I was asking the voters to take on faith my ability to end the war. A regular part of my campaign speech was the pledge: "New leadership will end the war and win the peace in the Pacific."

I never said that I had a "plan," much less a "secret plan," to end the war; I was deliberately straightforward about the difficulty of finding a solution. As I told the AP on March 14, 1968, there was "no magic formula, no gimmick. If I had a gimmick I would tell Lyndon Johnson."

Although Romney campaigned vigorously and spent large sums of money—much of which was rumored to have come from Rockefeller—the polls continued to move against him.

I was in the middle of a campaign swing through a number of small towns when Pat Buchanan came up after a speech and said that he had to talk to me alone. He guided me to a nearby men's room and said that he had just heard from a reporter that Romney was going to hold a press conference and pull out of the race. I was utterly astonished, and I asked my staff to watch Romney's press conference and fill me in. Their report was in the broad grins they wore when they walked into my room after the broadcast. Personally I was disappointed by Romney's withdrawal. Even though I had knocked him out of the ring, now I would win without having actually defeated an opponent in the election—and the test of the election was, after all, the reason I had decided to enter the primaries in the first place.

Despite Romney's withdrawal, we continued publicly to forecast my vote at only 45 percent to 50 percent of the total. While I hoped and expected to win more, I believed it was better to understate the prospects than to overstate them.

On the night of March 12, Pat and I went to a victory celebration at national Nixon headquarters in New York. I was pleasantly surprised when I polled 78 percent of the vote. Even without Romney in the race, my win was hailed as significant, and it dwarfed the handful of write-in votes that had been solicited by some of Rockefeller's unofficial supporters.

The New Hampshire results changed the political picture for both parties. On the Democratic side, Johnson won with 49.5 percent of the vote, but Senator Eugene McCarthy's unorthodox antiwar candidacy received a phenomenal 42.4 percent. The media attention and analysis concentrated so heavily on McCarthy that many people got the impression he had actually won—and, for all practical purposes, he had. Four days after McCarthy had shown that Johnson might be defeated, Senator Robert Kennedy of New York announced his candidacy for the nomination. Many of the conscientious antiwar liberals felt that Kennedy was cynically moving in to usurp the fruits of McCarthy's labors. Liberal New York *Post* columnist Murray Kempton charged that Kennedy had merely waited until Johnson was "bloodied in New Hampshire," and that Kennedy was a coward for coming "down the hills to shoot the wounded."

On the Republican side, Romney's withdrawal and my victory put pressure on Rockefeller, and on March 21 he called a press conference. I fully expected him to declare his candidacy. Instead he announced, "I have decided today to reiterate unequivocally that I am not a candidate campaigning directly or indirectly for the presidency of the United States." He said he would "do nothing in the future by word or deed to encourage" a presidential draft and that he had signed an affidavit taking his name out of the Oregon primary. For emphasis he added, "The terms of the affidavit are precise. They plainly declare that I am not, and will not be, a candidate for the presidency."

Rockefeller talked about the need for party unity, and admitted, "Quite frankly, I find it clear at this time that a considerable majority of the party's leaders want the candidacy of former Vice President Richard Nixon, and it appears equally clear that they are keenly concerned and anxious to avoid any such divisive challenge within the party as marked the 1964 campaign."

Governor Spiro T. Agnew of Maryland was watching the broadcast in his office in Annapolis with a group of friends and reporters. Agnew was a sponsor of the National Draft Rockefeller Committee, which had been formed in Annapolis just three days before, and he fully expected Rockefeller to announce his candidacy. Agnew told the reporters that he was "tremendously surprised and greatly disappointed" by Rockefeller's decision.

The next week I met with Agnew for two hours, and I was impressed by his intelligence and poise. After that meeting he told reporters that he still liked Rockefeller and was not yet ready to announce his support for me. But in speaking of me, he said, "I have high regard for him. He's the front-runner."

I had scheduled a nationwide radio speech for Sunday evening, March 31, to outline my views on the Vietnam war. I intended to propose that America vigorously try to convince the Soviet Union to reduce its military support for North Vietnam. I also planned to deliver a sharp critique of the Johnson policy of gradualism on the military front.

On Saturday afternoon, as I was putting the final touches on my speech before the taping, I received word that Johnson had asked the television networks for time the next night. I had no alternative but to postpone my speech.

I spent most of Sunday campaigning in Milwaukee. Because I would be airborne during Johnson's speech, I asked Pat Buchanan to listen to it and to meet me at La Guardia Airport with a report when I landed.

When Buchanan gave me his report, I was stunned. Johnson had described his latest attempts at de-escalating the war and stressed his personal dedication to obtaining peace. Then he made one of the most unexpected announcements in American political history. He said that he did not believe that he should devote even an hour of his day to any personal partisan causes. "Accordingly," he continued, "I shall not seek, and I will not accept, the nomination of my party for another term as your President."

When reporters clamored for my statement, I flippantly said that this was "the year of the dropouts": Romney, Rockefeller, and now Johnson. While the dropout label might have been apt for the first two, I was justifiably criticized for thus characterizing Johnson's action.

The upshot of these events was that the next primary, held in Wisconsin on April 2, was rendered almost meaningless. I won 79.4 percent of the Republican vote, and McCarthy swamped noncandidate Johnson, 56 percent to 34 percent.

Two days after the Wisconsin primary Martin Luther King, Jr., was assassinated in Memphis, Tennessee. The uproar set off by Johnson's announcement had not yet subsided, and now the nation was about to go through brief but intense agony as shock turned to disillusion, disillusion to despair, and despair to hatred and violence. Within an hour after King's death, looting and vandalism broke out in Washington, within six blocks of the White House. That same evening scattered and sporadic fighting and looting occurred in New York's Harlem and Bedford-Stuyvesant. Soon disorders were breaking out across the nation. The next day, the rioting and vandalism became arson and death. Seven were killed and over 350 arrested in Chicago as rioters pillaged a long stretch of downtown stores. The National Guard was called out there, as well as in Detroit, Boston, and elsewhere.

On Sunday, April 7, I flew to Atlanta to pay my respects to the King family. I went to their home and met his four children, still dazed over their father's murder. I saw Mrs. King in her room, where she was resting; I was moved by her poise and serenity. She thanked me for coming, and we talked about my first meeting with her husband, on the occasion of the independence of Ghana in 1957. I told her how impressed I had been by his insistence that the realization of his dream of equal opportunity for all should be accomplished by peaceful rather than violent means. Two days later I returned to Atlanta for the funeral.

The idealism of Martin Luther King, Jr., expressed in his words and actions, was his unique contribution to the civil rights cause. He worked to resist the extremists in the movement, those who wished to resort to violence to reach their goals. Perhaps their pressure sometimes caused him to be more extreme in his public views than he otherwise would have been. Yet one could reason with him. Like his colleagues, he did not enjoy hearing that patience would be required to achieve his goals; but as a practical man, he realized that this was the case. His death left black America without a nationally recognized leader who combined responsibility with charisma. Others were reasonably effective, but none could match his mystique and his ability to inspire people—white as well as black—and to move them.

I canceled all political activity for two weeks after Dr. King's death. Then I flew to Washington for an April 19 appearance before the American Society of Newspaper Editors. My speech and the lively question-

and-answer session that followed went over well, and a few days later I received a letter from Eisenhower.

> Dear Dick:
>
> My morning's paper carried excerpts from your speech before the Nation's Editors. I think it was superb. Moreover, I applaud your Q. and A. format—it gives you opportunity for spontaneity, humor, and hard-hitting observations.
>
> Casual word-of-mouth reports coming to me about your campaign's progress are far brighter than a few weeks ago. At first all the self-appointed experts were still saying, "Dick is well prepared for the presidency, but he cannot be elected." Now, by and large—and my reports come not only from locals but from visitors throughout the country—the refrain has changed to "Of course, Nixon is well prepared for the presidency, now we must see if we can elect him." This is real progress and if the trend continues it will not be long before doubt has become conviction. . . .
>
> Devotedly,
> Ike E

The cheer I received from Eisenhower's letter was particularly welcome—and timely; within a week Nelson Rockefeller was back in the race against me.

On April 30 Rockefeller convened a press conference in Albany and announced a complete turnaround. He explained that the "dramatic and unprecedented events of the past weeks have revealed in most serious terms the gravity of the crisis that we face as a people," and declared his candidacy.

Rockefeller made his announcement on the day of the Massachusetts primary. Governor John Volpe, one of my early supporters, had insisted on running as a favorite son candidate. Thanks to write-in votes, Rockefeller managed to squeeze out a half percentage-point victory over Volpe. The victory was embarrassing to Volpe, irritating to me, and a great boost to Rockefeller. All thirty-four Massachusetts delegates went to him, and his campaign got a good send-off.

Rockefeller entered the race too late to have his name on the ballot in any of the remaining primaries. I was certain that his late entry was calculated to spare himself the risk of losing.

With Rockefeller back in the race, I began listening for the faint hoofbeats of another aspiring candidate. Ronald Reagan could not win a two-man contest with me at the convention; but with Rockefeller to chip away at me from the left, Reagan would very likely begin seeing visions of a greater role than favorite son of the California delegation.

Therefore, I was not surprised that Reagan had assented to his name's being placed on the ballot by Nebraska state officials for its May 14 primary. He disavowed any personal encouragement of the effort, but his supporters mounted a substantial effort on his behalf, including several statewide prime-time showings of a very effective half-hour television documentary. Rockefeller's supporters launched a write-in campaign and bought 247 television spots and 564 newspaper ads. Despite their efforts, I topped Reagan 70 percent to 22 percent, while Rockefeller limped in at only 5 percent. This was the most competitive Republican primary so far, and I was gratified by the results.

The key primary was now Oregon, the last one I would enter; the June 4 contest in California was Reagan's—I had decided not to risk dividing the party by challenging his favorite son status. For the time being at least, Rockefeller and Reagan shared a common strategy: to slow me down, brake my momentum, and buy time for a final attack at the convention in Miami Beach. I was worried about Oregon because Reagan's people were spending heavily in an attempt to make a last-minute sweep. They eventually spent several hundred thousand dollars in the state, and Rockefeller's forces, seeking write-in votes, did the same.

I doubled my efforts in Oregon, and, unlike Reagan and Rockefeller, I went to the state to campaign. Reagan could not go because he was professing not to be a candidate, and Rockefeller apparently felt he could not afford to because a defeat would look even worse if he had campaigned there.

So Reagan showed his documentary and Rockefeller ran hundreds of ads, but my strategy paid off. I received more than 73 percent of the vote in this final primary test, with Reagan trailing at 23 percent and Rockefeller at 4 percent.

That night in my suite in the Benson Hotel in Portland I had some of the same sense of satisfaction that I had had on election night 1966. It was far from over, but things were falling into place.

In June 1967 Bob Haldeman gave me a memorandum on the use of media in a modern presidential campaign. He stressed that creative thought had to be given to developing ways to use television. "The time has come," he wrote, "for political campaigning—its techniques and strategies—to move out of the dark ages and into the brave new world of the omnipresent eye." Haldeman correctly argued that a candidate could make hundreds of speeches during a campaign and still only meet directly with a few hundred thousand potential new supporters. Such a frenetic pace, in the meantime, causes a candidate to "become punchy, mauled by his admirers, jeered and deflated by his opponent's supporters (and paid troublemakers), misled by the super-stimulation of one frenzied rally after another. He has no time to think, to study his opponent's strategy and statements, to develop his own strategy and statements. No wonder the almost inevitable campaign dialogue borders so near the idiot level."

The most important recommendation in the Haldeman memo was to develop new ways to use television.

A group of my advisers spent an afternoon in New York, watching old television news clips from over the years that showed me in a wide variety of formal and informal situations. The goal was to match the candidate with the medium, to determine exactly what manner of presentation would be the most effective. They analyzed each performance and decided that the more spontaneous the situation, the better I came across. This insight led to the decision that I would use the question-and-answer technique extensively, not only in press conferences and public question sessions with student audiences but also in my paid political programming.

In the campaign this evolved into the "man in the arena" concept, in which I stood alone, with no podium, in the center of a stage surrounded by an audience in bleacherlike tiers. In this setting I was asked questions by a panel of private citizens, sometimes joined by local reporters.

In 1968 the South was to be one of the most important regions in terms of winning both the nomination and the election. In 1964 Governor George Wallace of Alabama had mounted an essentially racist campaign in three Democratic Party primaries, and his strong showing embarrassed party leaders. In 1968 Wallace decided to expand his appeal along more generally conservative lines and make his bid via a third party. He was working to get his name on the general election ballot in as many states as possible.

On the Republican side, it was Ronald Reagan who set the hearts of many Southern Republicans aflutter. He spoke their conservative language articulately and with great passion, and there was always a possibility that Southern delegates could be lured at the last minute by his ideological siren song. Until I had the nomination, therefore, I had to pay careful attention to the dangers of a sudden resurgence on the right. Equally dangerous would be a serious intraparty split that would deliver the Reaganites into Wallace's camp.

On May 31, I flew to Atlanta for one of the most important conferences of the pre-convention period. The Southern Republican state chairmen were meeting, and I spent several hours over two days with these officials individually and in various groups. There was no pretense about the purpose of my visit: I was doing serious courting and hard counting.

I had invited Senator Strom Thurmond to Atlanta, and he sat in on one of the meetings. Thurmond was a former governor of South Carolina and Dixiecrat candidate for President in 1948 on the States' Rights ticket. In 1964 he had switched from the Democratic to the Republican Party and supported Barry Goldwater. Now he was among the strongest Republican leaders in the South, and his support was essential to me.

I had been consulting privately with Thurmond for several months, and I was convinced that he would join my campaign if he were satisfied on the two issues of paramount concern to him. The more important of these was national defense. As a member of the Senate Armed Services Committee he believed that America should be unquestionably first in the world in military power; I agreed with him completely. The second issue was parochial: Thurmond wanted tariffs against textile imports to protect South Carolina's position in the industry. I reluctantly went along with him on this issue because of political realities, but I told him that we should try first to get Japan and other countries to agree voluntarily to reduce their exports to the United States before we took the tariff route. On civil rights, Thurmond knew my position was very different from his. I was for the Civil Rights Act of 1964; he was against it. Although he disagreed with me, he respected my sincerity and candor. He knew that I would enforce the law, but that I would not make the South the whipping boy.

I emerged from this meeting with Thurmond's pledge of support, which would become a valuable element in my ability to thwart any moves by Reagan on my right.

I watched the California primary returns on television in our New York apartment with Pat, Tricia, Julie, and David Eisenhower. Because of the time difference, I stayed up only long enough to get a sense of the trend. It was clear that Bobby Kennedy was gaining back the initiative he had lost to McCarthy in Oregon. I believed that Hubert Humphrey had waited too long before declaring his candidacy, and I saw no way a Kennedy juggernaut could be stopped once it had acquired the momentum of a California victory. As I went to bed, I said, "It sure looks like we'll be going against Bobby." David and Julie said they would stay up watching and give me a report in the morning.

It was not long before I dimly heard David's voice calling my name over and over. "Mr. Nixon. Excuse me, sir. Mr. Nixon." I finally opened my eyes and saw David standing in my room. "What is it?" I asked. "They shot Kennedy," he said. "He's still alive, but he's unconscious. He was shot right after his victory speech."

With millions of other Americans I thought, how could such ghastly tragedy be revisited on the Kennedy family? Who had done it, and why? When would this madness come to an end?

The next day I was working in my study when Pat came in, tears in her eyes. She said, "Dick, that poor boy just died. It's on the radio."

Bobby Kennedy and I were political antagonists, representing wholly different constituencies and philosophies. There was nothing similar about our beliefs or styles. But we shared, as all politicians do, membership in an unchartered club of those who devote their energies and themselves to public life and public service. I was, as I had always been, fatalistic about danger. But I was saddened and appalled by such tragic human waste.

Pat and I attended the funeral mass at St. Patrick's Cathedral in New York, and we were deeply moved by the eloquent eulogy delivered by his brother, Teddy.

All the candidates observed a moratorium on campaigning in the weeks following the funeral. President Johnson ordered round-the-clock Secret Service protection for all presidential candidates and their families.

I renewed my campaigning at the end of June, and except for occasional periods of rest there was no stopping until Election Day, November 5.

As the convention neared, I kept my lead despite formidable efforts by the Rockefeller and Reagan forces to dislodge and attract delegates. Because Rockefeller had declined to fight me in the primaries, he had only one card left to play: the "loser" issue. He would try to demonstrate that he had a better chance to win in November than I did.

To this end he launched a ludicrous "battle of the polls." In a formal telegram sent to me and made public on July 9, Rockefeller proposed, first, that I meet him in a debate, and second, that I join him in commissioning a poll to test our relative strengths in areas of large electoral votes. The results of these polls would be given to the delegates at the convention, who could use them to decide upon their nominee. I had never heard of such a ridiculous way to determine a party's nominee. This was clearly a last-ditch effort, born of desperation.

Although I rejected the offer of a joint poll, Rockefeller went ahead on his own. He hired a polling firm—and then spent millions of dollars on a massive national advertising campaign in an obvious attempt to affect public opinion at the time his polls were being made. Just before the convention, Rockefeller began releasing the results of the polls, which showed him ahead of me in the key electoral states.

My strategy was to wait it out. My own polls showed me doing as well as, or even better than, Rockefeller in the same key states. I was sorely tempted to fire back, but I didn't. I felt certain of defeating Rockefeller, and I didn't want to let him draw me into internecine warfare that could only hurt my chances in the fall.

While Rockefeller continued his charade of the polls, I maintained a heavy schedule aimed at solidifying the delegate support I already had and at collecting additional delegates to ensure a first-ballot victory. To this end, I felt it was essential to obtain Eisenhower's endorsement.

Eisenhower was reluctant to become involved in a pre-convention fight. I knew that he would prefer to bestow his endorsement after the convention, when it would have a symbolic unifying effect on the party. But I knew that he wanted me to get the nomination, and I asked Bryce Harlow, one of his former top aides now supporting me, to write to Eisenhower urging him to endorse me before the convention.

I visited Eisenhower at Walter Reed Hospital in Washington on July 15. His smile had not dimmed, but the deep wrinkles in his face showed that age and illness had taken their toll. After some small talk, he brought up the question of the endorsement. Our importunings had apparently been effective; without any hesitation or qualifications he said, "Dick, I don't want there to be any more question about this. You're my choice, period." He agreed to release his endorsement on July 18. His statement was strong and straightforward, and it meant a great deal to me:

> The issues are so great, the times so confusing, that I have decided to break personal precedent and speak out to endorse a presidential candidate prior to the national convention. . . .
>
> I support Richard M. Nixon as my party's nominee for the presidency of the United States. I do so not only because of my appreciation of the distinguished services he performed for this nation during my own administration but even more because of my admiration of his personal qualities: his intellect, acuity, decisiveness, warmth, and above all, his integrity. I feel that the security, prosperity, and solvency of the United States and the cause of world peace will best be served by placing Dick Nixon in the White House in January 1969.

After the announcement was released, he sent me a copy with a handwritten note across the top: "Dear Dick—This was something I truly enjoyed doing—DE."

On July 26 I went to Washington for the intelligence briefing President Johnson had offered to all presidential candidates. He had briefed George Wallace earlier that day, and when I got to the White House, Johnson, Secretary of State Dean Rusk, and Walt Rostow, the President's National Security Adviser, were waiting for me.

The central issue of the briefing was Vietnam. On the question of whether we should unilaterally stop the bombing in North Vietnam, Johnson spoke feelingly of the men who were serving in South Vietnam and the letters he had to write to the next of kin of those who had died.

"Do I tell that boy that we'll stop bombing and let 30 percent more trucks filled with ammunition and guns come south so that they will have a better chance to kill him?" he asked.

Rusk, one of the ablest and most honorable men ever to serve as Secretary of State, made the point that the rest of Asia would be in a "panic" if the United States were to withdraw from Vietnam without an honorable peace settlement. He said that he held this view completely apart from the domino theory, which he considered simplistic. He believed that American withdrawal from Vietnam would leave the Chinese Communists as the only major power on the Asian mainland, thus creating the panic.

The critical part of the briefing concerned the bombing halt. Johnson returned to this point several times. He said he had, in fact, made an offer involving a halt, which both the Soviets and the North Vietnamese were seriously considering. He said bitterly that, as far as we were concerned, previous halts had produced nothing. He was also firm that he would insist on a quid pro quo: "We must get something from them if we halt the bombing," he said. He assured me that no halt was planned at that moment. He was prepared to wait as long as the North Vietnamese and their Soviet sponsors took to come to reasonable terms. I said that I would continue to support our goals in Vietnam even though I would be critical of some of the tactics that had been used. I also pledged not to undercut our negotiating position just in case the Communists came around and agreed to the conditions Johnson would insist upon in return for a bombing halt.

When the briefing was over and the others had left, Johnson seemed almost to deflate before my eyes. He looked old and terribly tired. His voice sounded hollow as he detailed at considerable length his decision not to run again. He gave many reasons and explained the many clues that he said he had been dropping since August 1967. At no point, however, did he mention Eugene McCarthy or Bobby Kennedy, or the pressures their candidacies were causing.

By the time he walked me to the door, he was his old self again, fully in command. He praised J. Edgar Hoover; he told me of his gratitude for Eisenhower's support; he complimented me on my family; he said that he had just received a letter from David Eisenhower supporting his position on Vietnam.

As we shook hands he said, "You know, Dick, all the talk about me being obsessed with power is just hogwash. I never cared about having any goddamn power. The only thing that appeals to me about being President is the opportunity it provides to do some good for the country. That's all."

While Johnson was telling me about his use of power, I was thinking of ways to keep power out of the hands of Nelson Rockefeller. He was far from giving up. He continued his frantic polling up to the eve of the convention, and he arrived in Miami Beach with armloads of statistics to distribute to the delegates. His efforts seemed to have minimal effect.

While Rockefeller was working openly, Reagan continued to be coy about his candidacy. But there was no doubt about his intentions. Before the convention Reagan had been flying Southern delegates to California to meet with him, making ideological appeals that were difficult for them to resist. Three weeks before the convention he had set off on a tour of the South with Clifton White, his chief delegate-hunter, in tow.

When Reagan arrived at the convention, he immediately began "dropping in" at delegation meetings, charming the delegates with his personality and speaking ability. Finally, on Monday, August 5, he moved into the open. Bill Knowland emerged from a California delegation caucus to announce it had passed a resolution recognizing that "Governor Reagan in fact is a leading and bona fide candidate for President."

It was not long before a new catchword began making the rounds in Miami Beach: *erosion.* Both Rockefeller and Reagan had an interest in convincing delegates that I had not yet sewn up the nomination, and they joined forces to attempt to show that my strength was eroding and that I was losing delegates.

Lieutenants of both candidates buttonholed delegates arriving in Miami, begging them to believe that I had not yet locked up the nomination. While this frantic activity was going on in Miami, I spent the last few days before the convention at Montauk Point on the eastern tip of Long Island working on my acceptance speech.

On the day Reagan's candidacy was announced, Pat and I flew to Miami Beach. We were welcomed by large and enthusiastic crowds. As soon as we reached the penthouse suite of the Hilton Plaza Hotel, I called John Mitchell.

"John, what's the count?" I asked. He chuckled and answered with characteristic coolness and confidence, "I told you that you didn't need to worry, Dick. We've got everything under control." When I put the same question to Dick Kleindienst, who with Mitchell had responsibility for our delegate operation, he was equally confident. Still, the marriage of convenience between Rockefeller and Reagan was now operating at full force. Rockefeller worked on the Northern and Midwestern states while Reagan tried to breach my Southern flank.

But the months of arduous labor were paying off. Strom Thurmond and Senator John Tower of Texas went to work, visiting or telephoning each delegation personally. Tirelessly they shored the Southern dike against Reagan's rising waters. Tower called it "the thin gray line which never broke."

Holding the South was not our only problem; there were other trouble spots. Governor James Rhodes of Ohio, for example, insisted on remaining a favorite son, thus tying up all the Ohio votes, most of which would have gone to me, on the crucial first ballot. George Romney also refused to cede his favorite son status, although the majority of his delegates supported me.

But by Wednesday night, August 7, I was satisfied that I had the votes to win. After checking and double-checking I saw no way that Reagan or Rockefeller could pull it off. Their talk of "erosion" was pure political gamesmanship, and nothing short of a miracle could bring either of them a victory even on a later ballot.

Some observers claimed that I was smug and complacent about winning the nomination. Any idea that the convention was a boring coronation ceremony ignored the months of backbreaking work that had laid the foundation for my success. What truly galled the critics and commentators who did not favor my candidacy was that they could not honestly maintain that the party bosses had arranged my victory. As the only candidate who ran the primary gauntlet from beginning to end, it could hardly be argued that I was not the choice of the people of my party.

As the nominations began, I invited a small group of friends and staff to join my family in our suite. Pat, Tricia and her guest Ed Cox, and Julie and David were there, as well as Rose Woods, Bob Haldeman, Pat Buchanan, Dwight Chapin, Ray Price, and Len Garment. John Mitchell was in constant touch from his communications trailer command post outside the convention hall. Rogers Morton was my floor manager, helping put out fires and giving last-minute pep talks to wavering delegates. Dick Kleindienst roamed the convention floor, keeping a close watch on his charges until the last vote was counted.

Ted Agnew placed my name in nomination. Mitchell had asked him if he would like to have the assignment and had suggested that, if he did a good job, he would be among those considered for the second spot on the ticket. To that extent, at least, Agnew's speech was an audition.

The balloting began. First, Alabama. We had been able to hold the line against the Reagan inroads, and I won 14 votes to his 12. Wally Hickel delivered all but 1 of Alaska's 12 votes, and Barry Goldwater kept all Arizona's votes in the Nixon column. The first problem state on the roll call was Florida. When I got 32 out of the state's 34 votes, the initial danger point had passed.

In Illinois, despite Chuck Percy's last-minute switch to Rockefeller, I won 50 of the 58 delegates.

There were no surprises in any of the states from Massachusetts through Nevada. The second critical point was coming: New Jersey.

Just before the balloting reached that state, John Mitchell called me from his command post trailer. "Dick," he said, "I think you're going to have a pleasant surprise in New Jersey. But Cliff Case may never let you cross the Hudson River again." To counter liberal Senator Clifford Case's recalcitrance, Mitchell had enlisted the help of Frank "Hap" Farley, a Republican stalwart from Atlantic City, and broken open the New Jersey delegation. Case's ego was involved, since he had decided at the last minute to run as a favorite son. But his candidacy was patently a front for Rockefeller, and we had to try to persuade the Nixon supporters in the delegation to assert their independence. Outflanked and defeated, Case did not give up easily or gracefully. The internal fight was bitter, and he finally demanded that the delegation be polled. Each member was thus called upon to declare his choice publicly. The strategy failed; as each name was read, and as each delegate called out, "Nixon," the television screen showed Case sulking in his chair, humiliated and hurt. As I watched him on the screen, I thought of the work we had done together in the House and how my campaigning for him in 1954 had helped to win him his Senate seat by a bare 3,000 votes. Those bonds were loosened that night, and our relationship would never again be the same. I had 18 of New Jersey's 40 delegates.

When the roll call reached New York, I managed to pick up four votes on Rockefeller's home ground. I was a little surprised when Jim Rhodes refused to yield his favorite son status and held the Ohio delegation. Pennsylvania Governor Ray Shafer, like Chuck Percy, had gone over to Rockefeller at the last minute. By breaking his neutrality he made his delegation fair game, however, and we raided it with considerable success: I got 22 of the state's 64 votes.

There were no surprises left. Wisconsin put me over the top. I was pleased that the deciding vote came from a primary state.

The final count gave me 692 votes, 25 more than needed. Ronald Reagan, in a unifying gesture in keeping with his posture of being a strong party man, moved that the nomination be made unanimous by acclamation.

We had come halfway up the mountain. I knew from the experiences of 1960 and 1962 that the next half would be by far the more difficult to climb.

Rockefeller called a few minutes later to congratulate me. When I told him that I understood his disappointment, he laughed and said, "Ronnie didn't come through for us as well as we expected." He complimented me on my successful strategy and pledged his total support for the final drive in November.

Now I had to make my decision on a running mate. Two weeks earlier

John Mitchell and I had tentatively—and very privately—concluded that the nod should go to Agnew. But like most important decisions, this one would not be final until it was announced. I still wanted to test it, to weigh alternatives, to hear other views. It was a tentative choice, and still reversible.

In talking with Agnew I had been impressed by him as a man who seemed to have a great deal of inner strength. Though he had no foreign policy experience, his instincts in this area appeared to parallel mine. He had a good record as a moderate, progressive, effective governor. He took a forward-looking stance on civil rights, but he had firmly opposed those who resorted to violence in promoting their cause. As a former county executive of Baltimore County, he had a keen interest in local as well as state government. He expressed deep concern about the plight of the nation's urban areas. He appeared to have presence, poise, and dignity, which would contribute greatly to his effectiveness both as a candidate and, if we should win, as Vice President.

From a strictly political standpoint, Agnew fit perfectly with the strategy we had devised for the November election. With George Wallace in the race, I could not hope to sweep the South. It was absolutely necessary, therefore, to win the entire rimland of the South—the border states—as well as the major states of the Midwest and West. Agnew fit the bill geographically, and as a political moderate he fit it philosophically.

In my two meetings with him before the convention I never raised the possibility that he might be considered for the vice presidential spot. When I asked him what he might want to do if we won in November, he said he would not be interested in a Cabinet position but would like to be considered for a federal court appointment if an opening occurred.

In the series of meetings I held that night after the nomination, lasting into the early morning hours, I purposely gave no clue to my tentative choice—or even that I had one. The names most mentioned by those attending were the familiar ones: Romney, Reagan, John Lindsay, Percy, Mark Hatfield, John Tower, George Bush, John Volpe, Rockefeller—with only an occasional mention of Agnew, sometimes along with Governors John Love of Colorado and Daniel Evans of Washington.

The meetings produced no strong consensus for any candidate, but they did gradually tend to eliminate all except Agnew. Before finally deciding, I asked each of two close friends and long-time associates: would he himself be my running mate?

The first was Bob Finch. Bob was probably my closest friend in politics, and after winning the lieutenant governorship of California in 1966 he had become a rising star in the party. I was sure of his answer, but I told him, "You have many of Lindsay's best attributes. You have youth and freshness, and you would have great appeal to the party and to independent voters." He was deeply moved by my suggestion, but he strongly rejected it, arguing that the leap from lieutenant governor to Vice President would be perceived as too great. Besides, he was my former aide and a long-time personal friend, and there would be charges of cronyism. Also, he and Reagan had already developed a rivalry in California, and Reagan's supporters would be extremely irritated if he were chosen.

Next, I took Rogers Morton aside. I had immense respect for Morton, and we saw eye to eye on nearly all issues. As a congressman from Maryland, he knew Agnew well. I asked him for a totally honest, candid appraisal of him. Morton stretched his giant frame and paused for a moment to collect his thoughts. Agnew, he said, was potentially a very good candidate, though he had a tendency to be "lazy." He hastened to add that he did not mean this in a derogatory way, but only as a warning that if Agnew were placed on the ticket, he would have to be given a heavy schedule. I then surprised Morton by saying, "Rog, maybe you would be the better choice for me."

Morton smiled for a moment and then became completely serious. He said that as a member of the House he lacked the credentials for the job—or at least credibility as a candidate. "If you want to know the truth," he said, "If it's between me and Ted Agnew, Ted would be the stronger candidate."

That pretty well clinched it for me. Had Morton said that he wanted it, even at that late moment I might well have picked him. Politically he had the same border-state advantages as Agnew. I knew him far better than I knew Agnew, and I considered him one of the best campaigners, one of the ablest individuals, and one of the most astute politicians in the party.

Finally, after a last review with Mitchell, I decided: it would be Agnew. I asked Morton to telephone him.

About an hour later I went downstairs to tell the waiting press corps. Absolute shock and surprise greeted my announcement. Soon after I announced my choice, Agnew met with the press and acquitted himself well under a barrage of subtly hostile rapid-fire questions. Admitting that his name was not exactly a household word, he assured everybody that he would work to change that situation.

I turned immediately to putting the final touches on my acceptance speech. No other campaign speech would be as important, because none would have a larger or more attentive audience.

As I was getting ready to leave for the convention hall, a minor revolt developed over my selection of Agnew. Some of the party's liberal elements, led by New York Congressman Charles Goodell and Rhode Island Governor John Chafee, sought to enlist John Lindsay to carry their banner in a floor challenge to Agnew. When Lindsay declined—in fact, with Brownell acting as intermediary, Lindsay agreed to place Agnew's name in nomination—the dissidents got George Romney to lead the challenge.

My first reaction was that the politicking was a harmless way to let the delegates blow off steam. But as I thought more about this challenge, it began to make me angry. Nothing was more important this year than Republican unity. We could not afford a replay of 1964. I asked Mitchell for suggestions. He was unconcerned: "Ah, screw 'em, Dick. It'll blow over." Mitchell was a superb manager, but he lacked the political experience to foresee the effect of an apparently unimportant episode like this. I told him, "John, we've got to look past the exigencies of the moment. I'm not going to stand for this kind of revolt. If the sore losers get away with something like this now, they'll do the same damn thing during my presidency. It's a test of my leadership, and I'm going to stand firm. I don't want Agnew's first national exposure to be humiliation."

I told him that I expected him to impose whatever discipline he could on the delegates because I wanted to lose as few votes as possible on this challenge.

The revolt was cut short when Agnew received 1,128 votes to Romney's 186. A few days after the convention Romney wrote to me: "I assume you received my note of August 9 and the attached press release on the vice presidency insurrection. As someone said afterwards, it was like a good big burp! It relieved the tension and united your support."

As Pat and I approached the podium in the convention hall, the roar was deafening. Except for winning the election, very few things are more satisfying to a political candidate than the moment of accepting a presidential nomination.

In 1960 I had had to defend Eisenhower's record: now in 1968 I was the challenger against an incumbent administration, and I felt that a tougher approach was called for. I described the problems America faced exactly as I saw them:

> America is in trouble today not because her people have failed but because her leaders have failed.
>
> When the strongest nation in the world can be tied down for four years in a war in Vietnam with no end in sight;
>
> When the richest nation in the world can't manage its own economy;
>
> When the nation with the greatest tradition of the rule of law is plagued by unprecedented lawlessness;

When a nation that has been known for a century for equality of opportunity is torn by unprecedented racial violence;

And when the President of the United States cannot travel abroad or to any major city at home without fear of a hostile demonstration—then it's time for new leadership for the United States of America.

My fellow Americans, tonight I accept the challenge and the commitment to provide that new leadership for America.

I had written the conclusion of the speech as a personal testimony to the political and social opportunity we have in the United States. It was intentionally dramatic, and it was completely true.

Tonight, I see the face of a child.

He lives in a great city. He is black, or he is white. He is Mexican, Italian, Polish. None of that matters. What matters, he's an American child.

That child in that great city is more important than any politician's promise. He is America. He is a poet. He is a scientist, he is a great teacher, he is a proud craftsman. He is everything we ever hoped to be and everything we dare to dream to be.

He sleeps the sleep of a child and he dreams the dreams of a child.

And yet when he awakens, he awakens to a living nightmare of poverty, neglect, and despair.

He fails in school.

He ends up on welfare.

For him the American system is one that feeds his stomach and starves his soul. It breaks his heart. And in the end it may take his life on some distant battlefield.

To millions of children in this rich land, this is their prospect of the future.

But this is only part of what I see in America.

I see another child tonight.

He hears a train go by at night and he dreams of far away places where he'd like to go.

It seems like an impossible dream.

But he is helped on his journey through life.

A father who had to go to work before he finished the sixth grade, sacrificed everything he had so that his sons could go to college.

A gentle, Quaker mother, with a passionate concern for peace, quietly wept when he went to war but she understood why he had to go.

A great teacher, a remarkable football coach, an inspirational minister encouraged him on his way.

A courageous wife and loyal children stood by him in victory and also defeat.

And in his chosen profession of politics, first there were scores, then hundreds, then thousands, and finally millions who worked for his success.

And tonight he stands before you—nominated for President of the United States of America.

On the whole the convention came off very well. It looked good on television, and the first post-convention Gallup poll showed me leading Humphrey 45 percent to 29 percent—a 16 percent margin.

Immediately after the convention, our entourage flew to California. On the way, Agnew and I stopped in Texas to meet with President Johnson, Secretary of State Rusk, Deputy Defense Secretary Cyrus Vance, and CIA Director Richard Helms. They gave us a full-scale intelligence briefing, ordered by Johnson for each of the nominees.

Johnson and Rusk came out to meet the presidential helicopter that flew us to the LBJ Ranch. It was a very hot day, and we soon had our coats off. Johnson was expansive and cordial, and I could see that he was already enjoying his role as a noncandidate in this election year.

After our meeting we had a delicious lunch of steak and fresh corn on the cob, followed by Lady Bird's homemade toll-house cookies. Johnson drove me from the ranch house to the helicopter pad. On the way he went by the little house where he was born and showed me the plot of land where his parents were buried. After seeing Johnson at his ranch, I understood what Billy Graham had meant when he said that Johnson "loved the land" and always wanted to go back to it.

As I started to board the helicopter, Johnson's dog darted past my legs into the cabin. There was a great deal of laughter, and I practically had to pick the animal up and carry him down the steps. Johnson shouted in mock anger, "Dick, here you've got my helicopter, you're after my job, and now you're gonna take my dog."

There were going to be seven key states in the 1968 presidential campaign: New York, California, Illinois, Ohio, Pennsylvania, Texas, and Michigan. Of these I had won only California and Ohio in 1960. This time I had to win at least three in order to have a chance of winning the election.

The Deep South had to be virtually conceded to George Wallace. I could not match him there without compromising on the civil rights issue, which I would not do. But I would not concede the Carolinas, Florida, Virginia, or any of the states on the rim of the South. These states became the foundation of my strategy; added to the states that I expected to win in the Midwest, the Great Plains, the Rocky Mountains, and the Far West, they would put me over the top and into the White House.

Because of the Wallace candidacy I expected the race to be very close. My polls showed that Wallace's vote was overwhelmingly Democratic but that when his name was not included in the poll sampling, his votes came to me on more than a two-to-one basis, especially in the South. Therefore it was essential that I keep the Wallace vote as low as possible. A major theme that we used very effectively in key states such as Florida, North Carolina, South Carolina, Tennessee, Kentucky, and Virginia was that Wallace couldn't win. Our message to would-be Wallace voters was: "Don't waste your vote."

While the Democrats gathered in Chicago for their convention, I went to Key Biscayne to rest and think. With Bobby Kennedy gone, I knew that Humphrey would get the nomination. Eugene McCarthy nonetheless continued his quixotic candidacy. Although the outcome of such a contest was a foregone conclusion, most of the media sympathized with McCarthy and the coverage given his challenge would have national impact, regardless of its actual influence on the convention's choice.

Thousands of young people had converged on Chicago for the Democratic convention. Many were sincere protesters against the Vietnam war, but some were little more than semiprofessional agitators and educated hoodlums. A series of clashes with the Chicago police finally erupted into a pitched battle on the night of Humphrey's nomination.

Like millions of other Americans watching television that night, I did not want to believe my eyes. It seemed as if the Democrats' convention was confirming every indictment of their leadership that I had made in my campaign speeches. Television magnified the agony of Chicago into a national debacle. I knew, of course, that the impact of Humphrey's nomination would now be seriously undermined. He would have to spend his entire campaign trying to patch up the divisions in his party. Even before the confrontation with the police, McCarthy and his zealous followers had been embittered by the convention because their efforts to pass a peace plank in the platform were defeated.

Humphrey chose Senator Edmund S. Muskie of Maine as his running mate. A former governor who had shown great political skill in getting re-elected in a traditionally Republican state, Muskie was a strong addition to the ticket.

My first scheduled stop in the 1968 presidential campaign was a motorcade through downtown Chicago on September 4. In some respects this was a risk because the city was still tense and reeling from the Democratic convention and from the criticism being leveled against Mayor Richard Daley and the Chicago police force. The risk paid off. As our motorcade passed through Chicago's Loop at noontime, an estimated half million people turned out in genuine good cheer, with frequent outbursts of enthusiastic support. The contrast with the bitter confrontation that Humphrey was now tied to could not have been greater.

I knew that Humphrey would not remain in his slump forever. His was the majority party, and as Tom Wicker of the New York *Times* put it, "No Republican, as has often been said, unites the Democrats the way

Nixon does." Humphrey would soon begin to recover his early losses. The only questions were when and by how much?

The first Gallup poll after the Democratic convention showed that I still had a substantial lead:

Nixon	43%
Humphrey	31%
Wallace	19%
Undecided	7%

But the problem with being the front-runner is that you are the target for everyone behind you.

Though painted as an underdog, Humphrey was not alone in his battle. In addition to his designated partisans, he had in his corner the giant combine of American organized labor. Although intellectuals, upper-middle-class liberals, and young people had temporarily deserted Humphrey, the union bosses never wavered. Under George Meany's orders, labor unions across the country provided Humphrey with millions of dollars, tens of thousands of marching feet, sophisticated direct mail and data processing, and other costly facilities. Although the union leadership was solidly behind Humphrey, the rank and file was far from united. Hundreds of thousands of blue-collar Democrats had voted for George Wallace in the primaries, and Humphrey would not necessarily inherit their support.

The anti-Nixon and anti-Wallace union propaganda eventually began paying off for Humphrey, but he needed more. The stigma of Chicago was not so easily erased. Lyndon Johnson stayed home in the White House, and Humphrey became a handy target for everyone on the left who hated the Johnson administration and the Vietnam war. During Humphrey's first weeks of campaign appearances, he was subjected to persistent heckling; the chant "Dump the Hump" dogged his steps. At one point he was driven almost to tears in front of the television cameras when he could not finish a speech before a derisive audience.

In an attempt to separate himself from Johnson on the war issue, Humphrey delivered a nationally televised speech from Salt Lake City on September 30. He said that his first priority as President would be to end the war and obtain an honorable peace. Although he continued to oppose a unilateral withdrawal of forces, he said that he would stop the bombing of North Vietnam "as an acceptable risk for peace because I believe it could lead to success in the negotiations and thereby shorten the war."

Humphrey's speech was shrewd. While it scarcely differed from Johnson's position, he made it sound like a major new departure. As antiwar columnist Joseph Kraft put it, the speech "has to be judged more by the music than the words. . . . The important thing is that the Humphrey campaign may finally be getting off the ground." The New York *Times* also concluded that Humphrey's proposal "may be a frail straw for doves to clutch at, but it is more hopeful than anything the administration or the Republican candidate has so far offered." By this point the doves *were* clutching at straws; they were beginning to realize that, however disappointed they were with Humphrey, and however disillusioned by Chicago, unless something were done to knock down my commanding lead in the polls, I was going to be elected President on November 5.

Liberal support and money started pouring back into Humphrey's campaign. Humphrey's problems with hecklers considerably abated; they began instead to focus their efforts on disrupting my campaign. These were not the hecklers of the American and British campaign tradition who press candidates with barbed questions and comments. These were anarchistic mobs. As soon as the speeches began they would start shouting, chanting simplistic and often obscene slogans, less to be heard themselves than to prevent the speaker from being heard. It was not an exercise in debate but a descent into hate.

Waving fists, carrying signs, shouting filth and obscenities, demonstrators made life miserable for me as well as for Pat, Tricia, and Julie when they made campaign appearances on my behalf.

These episodes were the saddest aspect of the 1968 campaign. They were symbolic of the things that were wrong with America that year. To this day I cannot understand the twisted logic that escalates the right of free speech into a license for hysteria and mob violence.

Encouraged by the reaction to his Salt Lake City speech, Humphrey began issuing challenges to me to debate him. I was determined not to be lured into a confrontation, since Humphrey was still far behind me in the polls, and would therefore be the beneficiary of any debate. Besides, as Humphrey knew, there was no way that he and I could have a debate without including George Wallace. Wallace's candidacy was depriving me of a substantial number of votes, and anything I did to elevate Wallace would be self-destructive. It was not fear but self-interest that determined my decision on the debates. Naturally my unwillingness to debate gave Humphrey a major campaign issue. On October 15, he told an audience that I was "Richard the Silent" and "Richard the Chicken-Hearted."

Polls taken after the election indicated that if George Wallace had not run for President in 1968, I might have received the same overwhelming mandate then that Eisenhower had received in 1952. But Wallace was a spoiler. He would siphon off the protest votes of people who were fed up with the policies of the Great Society. I had to try my best to hold down the Wallace vote, but I had to do it in a responsible manner. Humphrey and his advisers saw that Wallace could be used as a blockade against me. As Tom Wicker put it, "As for Wallace, without his heavy-breathing presence in the race Humphrey might as well go home to Waverly and raise turkeys."

If Humphrey could not get enough electoral votes to become President, he could still end up in the White House by making sure that I didn't get enough either. Under the Constitution, if no candidate received a majority of electoral votes, the election would be decided in the House of Representatives. Since the Democrats controlled the House, it was almost certain that Humphrey would make a deal with Wallace and thus emerge as the thirty-seventh President. Toward the end of the campaign I challenged Humphrey to agree that the winner of the popular vote should get the support of the loser, but he avoided the issue and refused to agree.

Having failed to make measurable inroads on my lead, Humphrey—and the media—began concentrating on Agnew. Because of his total lack of previous experience in national campaigning, it did not take long to catch him in a slip and magnify it into a cause célèbre. He naïvely used inflammatory codewords when he referred to Humphrey as "soft on crime" and "soft on communism," and he jokingly called reporter Gene Oishi "the fat Jap."

No one felt worse than Agnew about such embarrassing misjudgments, and I admired him for the way he stood up to the vicious onslaught of national political exposure—the cruel cartoons, the slashing attacks, the stinging commentaries. I tried to reassure him, telling him that these efforts were mainly a way of using him to get at me.

In contrast to their treatment of Agnew, the news media gave Muskie such encomiums as James Reston's "The most refreshing figure in the American campaign is Ed Muskie of Maine." A headline proclaimed in the Washington *Post*: *"Abe Lincoln Quality" Seen as Muskie Campaign Surges*. Muskie emerged from the campaign the favorite of the media—clearly presidential timber for 1972. This infatuation with Muskie could not have pleased Humphrey, but he had to acknowledge and use it. By the end of September he was telling audiences, "If you have any doubts about the top of the ticket, please settle it on the basis of No. 2."

During the two weeks before Election Day I was campaigning eighteen and twenty hours a day. At each appearance I tried to have some new ammunition to fire at Humphrey. In Cincinnati I quoted a statement he had made two years earlier, when riots were convulsing the country: that if he were living in a slum, he could "lead a mighty good revolt" himself. I said that this kind of talk was "adult delinquency" and "not worthy of a Vice President."

At Springfield, Ohio, I hit another key issue, loss of respect for America. "We must gain respect for America in the world. A burned American library, a desecrated flag, a ship captured by international outlaws on the high seas—these are the events which in effect squeeze the trigger which fires the rifle which kills young Americans." One reporter wrote, "There was speculation that the 'old Nixon' had broken through—the slashing campaigner of earlier campaigns who eventually hurt his reputation by his tough attacks." But I felt it was essential to take the battle to Humphrey after his weeks of much harsher rhetorical assaults.

I was especially intent on getting across my stark differences with Humphrey on the issues of crime and justice. His statement about leading a "revolt" was the kind of rationalization many liberals produced to justify the riotous disorders of the 1960s. I charged that Humphrey had exaggerated and overemphasized poverty as a cause of crime and that contrary to what the administration believed and preached, the war on poverty was not a war on crime, and it was no substitute for a war on crime.

Though inflation was on the rise in 1968 and the economic storm signals were clear, the actual detrimental effects of Johnson's guns-and-butter policy were not apparent until after I entered the White House. Consequently, Humphrey was able to campaign on a platform of prosperity while making the classic Democratic charge that every Republican since Herbert Hoover had a compulsion to make people unemployed.

For his part, Humphrey attacked me with characteristic gusto. He charged that I was "joining forces with the most reactionary elements in American society." Variously, he characterized me as someone likely to "weasel" and as one who "has sacrificed national interest for political demagogy."

On October 28 Humphrey claimed that I was about to unleash a "vicious final week of campaigning." He warned: "Batten down the hatches for the most desperate and cynical display of political irresponsibility ever seen in America." In the very same speech without missing a beat, Humphrey expressed *his* sense of political responsibility by charging that I was "urging a mad escalation of the nuclear arms race [and] advocating an increasing militarization of American life and American foreign policy."

In fact, despite what Humphrey and other Democratic spokesmen were saying, both my rhetoric and actions were restrained in the 1968 campaign. Because of my lead, there was no need for overkill. And because national unity was so fragile that year, I didn't want to enter the White House after a bitterly divisive campaign.

After the Democratic convention, I led Humphrey 43 percent to 31 percent, and a few weeks later 46 percent to 31 percent. During the last few weeks of the campaign, however, the gap narrowed dramatically, and the election turned out to be a cliff-hanger. The trend was reversed as traditional Democrats returned to the party of their fathers, and as the effects of George Wallace's spoiler candidacy were felt. Additionally, toward the end of the campaign the antiwar liberals decided to bury the hatchet and vote for Humphrey. Less than two weeks before Election Day, Eugene McCarthy finally endorsed Humphrey.

More than anything else, Humphrey had Lyndon Johnson to thank for the eleventh-hour masterstroke that almost won him the election.

On October 31 I was to address a nationally televised rally at Madison Square Garden in New York. I set aside a couple of quiet hours in the afternoon, and I was sitting in my study at home making notes for the speech later that evening when the telephone rang. It was a White House operator: the President was placing a conference call to Humphrey, Wallace, and me. A moment later Lyndon Johnson was on the line.

He got right to the point. There had been a breakthrough in Paris, he said, and after wide consultations among his advisers, he had decided to call a total bombing halt over North Vietnam. He would make the announcement on television in two hours. As Johnson went on, I thought to myself that whatever this meant to North Vietnam, he had just dropped a pretty good bomb in the middle of my campaign.

Johnson said, rather defensively, "I'm *not* concerned with an election. *You* all *are* concerned with an election. *I* don't think this concerns an election. I think all of you want the same thing. So I thought if I laid it on the line that way, and presented it to you, you would at least have a complete, full understanding of all the facts."

Johnson explained that he had not been able to persuade Saigon to agree to the provisions of the bombing halt, so that South Vietnam would not be joining in the announcement.

When Johnson finished and we had asked some perfunctory questions, George Wallace said, "I'm praying for you."

Humphrey said, "We'll back you up, Mr. President."

I thanked Johnson for making the call and seconded Humphrey's pledge of support.

The telephone call over, I could feel my anger and frustration welling up. Johnson was making the one move that I thought could determine the outcome of the election. Had I done all this work and come all this way only to be undermined by the powers of an incumbent who had decided against seeking re-election?

I remembered how categorical Johnson had been at our briefing earlier that summer. Then he had been contemptuous of those who wanted a bombing halt, and his arms had sliced the air as he insisted that he was not going to let one ammunition truck pass freely into South Vietnam carrying the weapons to kill American boys.

In fact, the bombing halt came as no real surprise to me. I had known for several weeks that plans were being made for such an action; the announcement was the other shoe that I had been waiting for Johnson to drop. What I found difficult to accept was the timing. Announcing the halt so close to the election was utterly callous if politically calculated, and utterly naïve if sincere.

I had learned of the plan through a highly unusual channel. It began on September 12, when Haldeman brought me a report from John Mitchell that Rockefeller's foreign policy adviser, Henry Kissinger, was available to assist us with advice. In 1967 Kissinger had served Johnson as a secret emissary, passing Johnson's offers for a bombing halt to the North Vietnamese via French intermediaries. At one point Johnson even recommended a direct meeting, but the North Vietnamese were recalcitrant, and the "Kissinger channel" came to an end in October 1967. Kissinger, however, retained the respect of Johnson and his national security advisers, and he continued to have entrée into the administration's foreign policy inner circles.

I knew that Rockefeller had been offering Kissinger's assistance and urging that I make use of it ever since the convention. I told Haldeman that Mitchell should continue as liaison with Kissinger and that we should honor his desire to keep his role completely confidential.

Two weeks after his first meeting with Mitchell, Kissinger called again. He said that he had just returned from Paris, where he had picked up word that something big was afoot regarding Vietnam. He advised that if I had to say anything about Vietnam during the following week, I should avoid any new ideas or proposals. Kissinger was completely circumspect in the advice he gave us during the campaign. If he *was* privy to the details of negotiations, he did not reveal them to us. He considered it proper and responsible, however, to warn me against making any statements that might be undercut by negotiations I was not aware of.

I asked Haldeman to have Bryce Harlow call the Republican Senate Minority Leader, Everett Dirksen. "Have Ev tell Lyndon that I have a message from Paris," I suggested. "Leave the hint that I know what's going on, and tell Ev to nail Lyndon hard to find out what's happening."

I also told Haldeman to have Agnew ask Dean Rusk whether there was anything to "rumors" we had heard.

That same day I sent a memo to my key staff thinkers and writers ordering them to put the Vietnam monkey on Humphrey's back, *not* Johnson's. I wanted to make it clear that I thought it was Humphrey rather than the President who was playing politics with the war.

A few days later Haldeman sent me a memorandum with more information from Kissinger via Mitchell.

> Our source feels that there is a better than even chance that Johnson will order a bombing halt at approximately mid-October. This will be tied in with a big flurry of diplomatic activity in Paris which will have no meaning but will be made to look important.

After covering other diplomatic matters, the memo continued:

> Our source does not believe that it is practical to oppose a bombing halt but does feel thought should be given to the fact that it may happen—that we may want to anticipate it—and that we certainly will want to be ready at the time it does happen. . . .
>
> Our source is *extremely* concerned about the moves Johnson may take and expects that he will take some action before the election.

That same day I learned that Dean Rusk had reassured Agnew that there were no new developments and that the administration would not "cut our legs off" with an announcement in October. If there were any change, he said, Johnson would call me right away. Rusk did say, however, that although there was nothing currently planned, the situation was "fast-changing."

On October 9, the North Vietnamese in Paris publicly called on Johnson to stop the bombing while he still had the power to do so. Johnson, of course, knew what the public did not know: secret negotiations for a bombing halt were already taking place.

Three days later we received another secret report from Kissinger saying that there was a strong possibility that the administration would move before October 23. Kissinger strongly recommended that I avoid making any statements about Humphrey's hurting the prospects of peace. Rather cryptically, Kissinger reported that there was "more to this than meets the eye." I thought that this report from Kissinger was uncomfortably vague. Why was he trying to get me to avoid making statements about Vietnam and why was he so insistent about laying off Humphrey? One factor that had most convinced me of Kissinger's credibility was the length to which he went to protect his secrecy. But what if Johnson's people knew that he was passing information to me and were feeding him phony stories? In such a tense political and diplomatic atmosphere, I was no longer sure of anything.

Over the next few days rumors became rampant that something big was about to happen in Paris. Reporters demanded to know what was happening, and in response to their questions, the White House press office released a statement that there were no breakthroughs in Paris and no change in the situation.

I was campaigning in Missouri on October 16 when word arrived from the White House that Johnson wanted to clarify matters with a conference call to all three candidates. When the call came, I was in Kansas City's Union Station, about to address a large rally in the main waiting room. I took his call in a tiny room behind the platform. The "room" was like a telephone booth with a glass door. Throughout our conversation people wandered by, staring quizzically at me jammed into this closet.

We had a bad connection, so that I had to strain to make out Johnson's words. He told us to read his Press Secretary's statement. There was no breakthrough in Paris. The rumors were wrong. He urged us not to say anything. He said that there had in fact been some movement by Hanoi, but that anything might jeopardize it. I asked for some assurance that he was still insisting on reciprocity from the Communists for any concessions on our part, and Johnson replied that he was maintaining that three points had to be met: (1) Prompt and serious talks must follow any bombing halt; (2) Hanoi must not violate the Demilitarized Zone; and (3) the Vietcong or the North Vietnamese would not carry out large-scale rocket or artillery attacks against South Vietnam's major cities. If these conditions were fulfilled, of course, I would support whatever arrangements Johnson could work out.

When I saw Johnson that night at the annual Al Smith Dinner in New York, he gave me further assurances that he would not accept any arrangement without reciprocity, and again requested that I be careful about what I had to say on Vietnam. After the dinner I instructed Haldeman to pass the word that, in view of Johnson's request, I would not be making any major speeches criticizing the conduct of the war.

Speaking in Rochester the next day, I said, "If a bombing pause can be agreed to in Vietnam . . . one which will not endanger American lives, and one which will increase the chances for bringing a peaceful and honorable solution to the war, then we are for it." I added, "We do not want to play politics with peace." But, of course, that was inevitably what was happening.

Vietnam was becoming the hottest national issue no matter how much the candidates soft-pedaled it. If there was nothing I could do about Johnson's motivations in this matter, I was determined to make absolutely sure that, if he did stop the bombing, it would at least be done according to the minimum safeguards that I insisted be met.

I was asked the next day about the rumors during a regionally broadcast question-and-answer session televised live from Boston. For the first time, while reiterating my position I suggested that something might be taking place. "There seems to be some movement," I said. "We can't be sure. I have been thoroughly briefed on this, but I won't disclose those briefings." It was a weak answer, but I didn't know what more I could say.

On October 22, Bryce Harlow received information from a source whose credibility was beyond question. It was from someone in Johnson's innermost circle, and, as events turned out, it was entirely accurate. I read Harlow's memorandum several times, and with each reading I became angrier and more frustrated:

> The President is driving exceedingly hard for a deal with North Vietnam. Expectation is that he is becoming almost pathologically eager for an excuse to order a bombing halt and will accept almost any arrangement. . . .
>
> Clark Clifford, [Joseph] Califano, and Llewellyn Thompson are the main participants in this effort. [George] Ball is in also, though somewhat on the fringe.
>
> Careful plans are being made to help HHH exploit whatever happens. White House staff liaison with HHH is close. Plan is for LBJ to make a nationwide TV announcement as quickly as possible after agreement; the object is to get this done as long before November 5 as they can. . . .
>
> White Housers still think they can pull the election out for HHH with this ploy; that's what is being attempted.

I fired off a battery of orders: have Mitchell check with Kissinger; have Dirksen and Tower blast the moves by the White House; have Dirksen call Johnson and let him know we were on to his plans. I even considered having Harlow fly to Vietnam to talk to General Andrew Goodpaster to get a firsthand military view of the situation there. But I was simply venting my frustration; no matter what I did, Johnson continued to hold the whip hand.

The initial results of my orders raised some doubts about Harlow's secret source. Kissinger had not heard anything about Johnson's plan, and when Ev Dirksen confronted Johnson with the rumor, he denied it with a vehemence that convinced even his skeptical old friend. He said that there was nothing new to report from Paris, and he chided Dirksen for being taken in by such obvious rumors at this stage of his life.

The next day, October 24, Harlow reported from his source that an agreement had been reached with the North Vietnamese the day before, and that it would be announced shortly. I found this hard to believe, but Harlow emphasized that considering his source, there could be no doubt about the accuracy of the report. If it were true, it meant that the settlement had already been reached when Johnson had told Dirksen that no settlement was even being contemplated.

In retrospect I cannot fault Johnson for his secrecy, but I was angry at his lack of candor with me. I felt that he should at least have dropped the pretense that he would keep me fully informed. I would not have used this information if our sources had been opposed to Johnson's policies and were trying to undermine them by talking to us. But they felt that Johnson was using the war to help Humphrey, and that was politics, not policy.

I immediately decided that the only way to prevent Johnson from totally undercutting my candidacy at the eleventh hour was for me to make public the fact that a bombing halt was imminent. In addition I wanted to plant the impression—which I believed to be true—that his motives and his timing were not dictated by diplomacy alone.

I knew that Johnson wanted nothing more than to be able to set peace in motion before he left the presidency. If he waited until after the election, the Communists might decide to hold out in order to deal with the new administration. The next ten days might be Johnson's last chance to redeem his record, and I could not begrudge him the effort. Vietnam had consumed him politically and personally, and negotiating a peace would help him regain much of what he had lost to that conflict.

I was also convinced, however, that Johnson had additional motives. I knew him well enough to know that everything he did was weighed a second time on a strictly political scale. Moreover, Harlow's source had made it clear that, contrary to popular impression, the political liaison between Humphrey and the White House was very active. Adept and dedicated partisans such as Clark Clifford and George Ball would see to it that any political benefits to be gained for Humphrey would not be overlooked. I knew that I would be walking a fine line between political necessity and personal responsibility, but I believed that the actions of Johnson and many of those around him were sufficiently political to permit my taking at least some action.

On October 26, therefore, I issued a statement concerning the peace talks:

> In the last thirty-six hours I have been advised of a flurry of meetings in the White House and elsewhere on Vietnam. I am told that top officials in the administration have been driving very hard for an agreement on a bombing halt, accompanied possibly by a cease-fire, in the immediate future. I have since learned these reports are true.
>
> I am . . . told that this spurt of activity is a cynical, last-minute attempt by President Johnson to salvage the candidacy of Mr. Humphrey. This I do not believe.

> At no time in the campaign have I found the President anything but impartial and candid in his dealings with the major presidential contenders about Vietnam. . . .
>
> In every conversation I have had with him he has made it clear that he will not play politics with this war.

While I believed that Johnson would not go out of his way to help Humphrey unless he were forced to meet a clear-cut partisan challenge, the last thing I wanted to do was to give the President an excuse to get angry with me in public. I hoped to avoid Johnson's going all out for Humphrey with every resource at the command of the White House.

There was nothing more I could do. Even though I knew what was coming—had known about it for weeks—the timing and impact were completely in Johnson's hands.

At the Madison Square Garden rally on October 31 I responded to the bombing halt announcement in what I considered the only responsible way: "I will say that as a presidential candidate, and my vice presidential candidate joins me in this, that neither he nor I will say anything that might destroy the chance to have peace." One reporter wrote, "President Johnson gave Richard M. Nixon a trick and Vice President Humphrey a treat for Halloween when he announced a complete halt to the bombing of North Vietnam last night." The bombing halt unquestionably resulted in a last-minute surge of support for Humphrey. The militant liberals came back to the fold. Even those McCarthy zealots who had pledged never to support Humphrey now had an excuse to vote for him. The bombing halt also undercut one of my most effective campaign issues—the inability of the Democratic leadership to win a permanent peace. Studies made after the election showed that public opinion had been particularly volatile during this period, and the hope that the halt might lead to a peace settlement resulted in massive voter shifts to Humphrey.

The Democrats' euphoria was dampened on November 2, when President Thieu announced that his government would not participate in the negotiations Johnson was proposing.

Thieu's reaction was totally predictable. He watched American politics no less carefully than did the leaders in Hanoi. Given his disapproval of any bombing halt, and the fact that Humphrey was now talking like a dove, it was scarcely in Thieu's interest to acquiesce in a bad bargain. By holding back his support, Thieu fostered the impression that Johnson's plan had been too quickly conceived and too shakily executed.

On the heels of Thieu's recalcitrance, I asked Bob Finch to put the word out to newsmen that the prospects for peace were not as advanced as Johnson's announcement might have made them seem. Providing background in his capacity as an "aide to Richard Nixon," Finch explained, "We had the impression that all the diplomatic ducks were in position." Then for the record he said, "I think this will boomerang. It was hastily contrived."

Johnson saw the news story with Finch's comments. He was furious, and he made his displeasure known. Bryce Harlow urged me to call Johnson to calm him down—and I did so Sunday morning, November 3.

"Who's this guy Fink?" Johnson asked. "Why is he taking out after me?"

I said, "Mr. President, that's Finch, not Fink."

He ignored my correction and continued to refer to Finch as "Fink."

I pointed out that my public statements on the issue were responsible, but that I had to respond to developments as I saw them. He calmed down, and the rest of our conversation was relatively cordial.

On the day of Thieu's announcement, I told a Texas rally: "In view of the early reports that we've had this morning, the prospects for peace are not as bright as they looked only a few days ago." It was Saturday, November 2, less than three days before the election. Bombing halt or no, the campaign had to continue. I decided to treat Johnson's announcement as a potentially beneficial diplomatic move botched by lack of planning rather than as a straight political ploy. I told my staff to get our spokesmen asking why we didn't have the agreement worked out with our allies.

I knew the gap was closing. With the help of hundreds of thousands of dollars in last-minute campaign contributions and loans, Humphrey appeared to be outspending us in television commercials in the week before the election.

I scheduled a four-hour telethon—two hours for the eastern United States and two for the West—the day before the election. Bud Wilkinson acted as moderator, reading the questions to me as they were phoned in from across the country. Some of my advisers had thought such a costly and tiring effort was not needed, but I overruled them. I remembered 1960 and felt I should do everything possible that might make the difference in a close election. It was my best campaign decision. Had we not had that last telethon, I believe Humphrey would have squeaked through with a close win on Election Day.

I felt we could not afford to do anything that would augment the advantage that Humphrey was getting from sympathetic treatment in the national media. Whatever the reason—sympathy for his temporary underdog status; preference for his liberal views; or simply his likability—Humphrey benefited from favorable press coverage.

Though I had sensed this instinctively during the campaign, I had no idea that the favoritism toward Humphrey was so strong until Edith Efron's carefully researched book, *The News Twisters,* was released in

1971. In it she documented the number of words spoken "for" and "against" me by reporters on the three networks. She found that the ratios were 11 to 1, 67 to 1, and 65 to 1—all "against." She did the same thing for Humphrey and found that only one of the three networks showed a larger ratio of "against" than "for," and that was by a much smaller margin of 6 to 1. She concluded:

> If Richard Nixon is President of the United States today, it is in spite of ABC-TV, CBS-TV, and NBC-TV. Together they broadcast the quantitative equivalent of a New York *Times* lead editorial against him every day—for five days a week for the seven weeks of his campaign period. And every editorial technique was employed on three networks to render the pro-Nixon side less "forceful" than the anti-Nixon side. Indeed, to speak of "forceful" pro-Nixon opinion is impossible. It does not exist.

Pat and I voted by absentee ballot in 1968; for once we did not have to get up early to be photographed voting. We got to the airport in Los Angeles before ten o'clock that morning to board our campaign plane, the *Tricia*. The cabin was decorated with campaign posters and balloons. As I passed by a poster with our campaign slogan, "Nixon's the One," I said aloud to no one in particular, "I hope it's right."

As the plane taxied toward the runway, I sank into the chair in my private compartment. I was tired but I felt confident. I knew that the wide gap of the early campaign had closed and that all the polls showed the race was too close to call. But somehow I believed that this year would be different from 1960.

Although I felt instinctively confident this time, I took the precaution of preparing my family for the worst. I asked Pat, Tricia, Julie, and David to come to my private office compartment. I told them how proud I was of their tireless campaigning. I said that it would be almost impossible for me to lose this election by popular vote. But it *could* happen, and I wanted them to be prepared just in case. What I really wanted them to be ready for was an electoral stalemate. "If that happens," I told them, "there won't be any winner or loser tonight. The election would be thrown into the House of Representatives, and I can't even guess how we would handle that situation."

I was sure that each of them wondered whether I knew something or had seen some poll that had led me to prepare them for losing. In fact, that afternoon a reporter had asked me for a comment on a Harris poll showing Humphrey winning by three points, approximately two million votes. I felt that Harris might have weighted his sample in the metropolitan areas and that Gallup, whose last poll showed me still leading by two points, was more accurate. "Even though it will be extremely close, we can win," I said. "In fact, I think we probably will. If we don't win, we'll simply go on to other projects which, from a personal viewpoint, may give us more satisfaction. And we won't have the spotlight of the world on us and on every movement that we make."

The *Tricia* touched down at Newark Airport just after six o'clock, and an hour later we were settled into our suite on the thirty-fifth floor of the Waldorf Towers in New York, where we would await the returns. Before I left Pat and the girls in their room, I said jokingly that at least this time we would not have to endure a twenty-four-hour ordeal as we had in 1960. I felt that by midnight or one o'clock Eastern time, when there were sufficient California returns to indicate a trend, we would know for sure.

While the polls were closing in the East and Midwest, I treated myself to a long hot soak in the huge bathtub. I took my time shaving and dressing, and then I called Haldeman to find out what was happening.

The first meaningful results were in by 8:45 P.M. They ran roughly 41 percent to 36 percent in my favor. For the next half hour my percentage remained the same, and Humphrey's moved up to 38 percent.

Then returns began pouring in. At 9:15 I had a 5 percent lead in New Jersey and a slight lead in Pennsylvania, but I was behind by 2 percent in Texas. Humphrey was walking away with Massachusetts, which was no surprise, but I had fallen hopelessly behind in Connecticut, a state I had hopes of winning. I kept reminding everyone that it was still too early to see any shape in the numbers or percentages.

When I checked the national returns again at 9:30, Humphrey had moved up another point while I remained at 41 percent. In Maryland I held a 12-point lead. In Pennsylvania, with the cities still out, I was leading by 5 points. With 10 percent of the Texas vote in, I trailed Humphrey by 8 points. I asked Haldeman to check our contacts in New Jersey. He reported: "It's tight, but we'll win it."

Just after 10 P.M. Humphrey pulled even with me in the national returns. I was shaken by the early returns from Illinois, which gave me 35 percent to Humphrey's 56 percent and Wallace's 8 percent. Since I knew that Mayor Daley would, as usual, hold back dozens of Cook County precincts, these figures were doubly disturbing. The news from Ohio was not encouraging either. With 27 percent of the vote in, I trailed Humphrey by three points.

The network commentators had begun playing with the numbers and speculating about a possible Humphrey upset.

At 10:15, however, my lead was holding in New Jersey and Pennsylvania, and I was reported ahead by 6 points in South Carolina. Ohio had improved: with 30 percent of the votes in, I had gained on Humphrey and trailed him there by only 1 point. The momentum there was in my direction, and since the late votes would be from the rural areas and small towns, I was fairly confident of Ohio.

At 10:25 I started playing with some possibilities on my notepad. If I won California, Ohio, Illinois, Missouri, and Maryland, and added them to my other states, I would have 288 electoral votes—18 more than I needed. Losing Missouri and Maryland, however, would leave me 4 votes shy of winning. These figures did not include the crucial toss-ups in Texas, New Jersey, Pennsylvania, New Mexico, South Carolina, Hawaii, or Washington. My estimate was conservative; but no matter how the numbers were arranged, it was close.

I thought back to what I had told Pat, the girls, and David earlier in the evening. I had been wrong—once again it was going to be an all-night vigil. I was glad that they were staying in a different room. I had decided to put them in a separate suite and not to meet with them until after I was relatively sure of the outcome. I knew how worried they would be until the winner had been decided, and I did not want to make them feel that they had to keep up a cheerful front for my sake.

At 10:30 the national results were still the same—Humphrey and I were running neck and neck, while Wallace had 18 percent. I was behind in Missouri, Pennsylvania, Delaware, and Ohio and ahead in New Jersey and Maryland, all with 41 percent or less of their votes in.

At 11 P.M. word arrived that something had gone wrong with the voting tabulation in Dallas and the votes could not be counted until the next day. That was alarming news. I feared that Texas Democrats were fully as capable of stealing votes in 1968 as they had been in 1960, and I told Haldeman to find out what the hell was happening and what we could do about it.

At 11:30 I asked Murray Chotiner to come in. He had been following the results as closely as I had, and we had arrived at the same figures. So far I had 231 solid electoral votes. But there were disturbing intimations that the momentum was with Humphrey. By midnight he had moved ahead in the popular vote. A half hour later, NBC showed him leading by about 600,000.

In 1968, as in 1960, the election was apparently going to be determined by the same key states: Illinois, California, Ohio, Missouri, and Texas. All were close. I was counting on Ohio and California. I had high hopes for Texas, but I knew that Johnson and Governor John Connally had fired up the recalcitrant state Democratic organization to get behind Humphrey, and that made Texas a question mark. Missouri was also going to be a seesaw. Mitchell was confident that Missouri would come through and I had learned to trust his confidence.

As Ohio and California moved more solidly into my column, the balance seemed to hang on Illinois, where I now had a substantial lead of almost 100,000 votes. But a number of Cook County precincts were still unreported.

In those early hours of November 6, confident that I had won Illinois and thus the election, I became irritated with Daley's stubbornness in not releasing the count in Cook County. I called Bryce Harlow and told him to get Larry O'Brien, Humphrey's campaign manager, on the phone. "Bryce, lay it on the line. Don't fool around. Tell O'Brien to tell Hubert to quit playing games. We've won Illinois, so let's get this thing over with." Harlow reached O'Brien's suite, but either he was not there or would not take the call.

Just before 3 A.M., for the first time in that long night, I allowed myself the luxury of self-assurance.

I had won the presidency.

I called in Bob Finch, Murray Chotiner, John Mitchell, and Bob Haldeman. We reviewed the totals. I told them that I was sure of all the big ones, including California, Illinois, Ohio, and Missouri.

"Any objections?" I asked.

There were no objections.

I placed calls to Ted Agnew and Nelson Rockefeller. They agreed that victory was just a matter of time. Then I called in my senior staff. We sat and talked for almost two hours while we waited for the reported results to confirm our predictions. Several times I asked Mitchell or Haldeman to call our people in the key states to break loose better information than the TV commentators seemed able to supply. They always came back with the same message: Don't worry—things are going well—we're almost there. *Almost*. I had been *almost* there in 1960. Finally, around five o'clock, Mitchell and Haldeman persuaded me to try to nap. It was clear that the outcome would not be definite until the morning, and at this point I had been up for almost twenty-two hours. I couldn't get to sleep, and after half an hour I got up again.

Just before 8 A.M. Haldeman brought in word that both NBC and ABC had declared me the winner in California and Ohio. But there was still no movement in Illinois, and that was what I needed to confirm victory. One more state. At 8:30 the door burst open and Dwight Chapin rushed in. "ABC just declared you the winner!" he shouted. "They've projected Illinois. You got it. You've won."

We hurried into the sitting room where the television set was on, and we watched as ABC continued to survey the electoral vote count. After we had watched for a few moments, I put a hand on John Mitchell's shoulder and said, "Well, John, we had better get down to Florida and get this thing planned out." Before Mitchell could respond, tears welled up in his eyes. He said very quietly, "Mr. President, I think I'd better go up to be with Martha." This was a doubly moving moment for us both. It was the first time that anyone addressed me by the title I had just won. It was also the first time that Mitchell had directly referred to his wife's problems, which I knew had been an immense emotional strain on him. Martha had been in a rest home during the last weeks of the campaign, and I fully understood his desire to be with her now.

I went down the hall to the suite where Pat and the girls were waiting. They were so physically and emotionally exhausted that there wasn't the elation one would normally expect. We all kissed and embraced. Julie went to her room and then called me in. She opened her briefcase and pulled out a piece of crewelwork she had done during campaign flights around the country. It was the Great Seal of the United States, with the inscription "To RN—JN" stitched at the bottom. "Daddy, I never had any doubt you would win," she said as she hugged me. "I just wanted something to be ready right away to prove it."

I sat alone with Pat, and she told me that it had been a terribly difficult night for her. The speculation by the commentators about Illinois had driven her to tears. Waves of nausea had swept over her as she feared that we would have to experience a repeat of the outrageous frauds of 1960. When I told her it was all over, she asked emotionally, "But Dick, are we sure of Illinois? Are we completely sure?" I answered, very firmly, "Absolutely. The votes are in, and there is no way that it can be turned around at this point." Then I held her, and she burst into tears of relief and joy.

I returned to my room and took an hour's nap. I got up at ten o'clock and shaved and dressed. There was still no word from Humphrey, and I could not do anything until he conceded. At 10:35 Haldeman came in with the news that NBC had finally projected my victory. A few minutes later CBS did the same.

At about 11:30 Hubert Humphrey called. His voice, usually so cheerful and confident, was full of fatigue and disappointment. But he was as gracious in defeat as he had been tenacious in combat. When I saw his wife Muriel and the other members of his family standing with him when he appeared on television a little while later, I felt sorrier for them than for him. After all, politics was *his* chosen profession. But I knew from experience how bitter and crushing defeat is for the people one loves.

As soon as Humphrey had finished his concession, Pat, Tricia, Julie, David, and I went down to the ballroom of the Waldorf-Astoria, where hundreds of supporters had remained, keeping the all-night vigil with us. The applause was thunderous. Although I had often thought about what I would say if this occasion came, what I finally said was spontaneous.

I told about receiving Humphrey's phone call, and of how I had told him I knew what it was like to lose a close one. The audience erupted in cheers when I said: "Having lost a close one eight years ago and having won a close one this year, I can say this—winning's a lot more fun."

I philosophized a moment about defeat: "A great philosophy is never one without defeat. It is always one without fear. What is important is that a man or a woman engage in battle, be in the arena."

I referred to an incident during our whistle-stop trip through Ohio:

> I saw many signs in this campaign. Some of them were not friendly and some were very friendly. But the one that touched me the most was the one that I saw in Deshler, Ohio, at the end of a long day of whistle-stopping. A little town, I suppose five times the population was there in the dusk, almost impossible to see—but a teenager held up a sign, "Bring Us Together."
>
> And that will be the great objective of this administration at the outset, to bring the American people together.

When we arrived back at our Fifth Avenue apartment, early in the afternoon, Manolo and Fina were not there, so I suggested to Pat that we all go out for lunch. Then I realized that we could no longer just casually "go out for lunch." She and the girls went into the kitchen and fixed bacon and eggs, and we all sat in my library for this postelection feast.

When Manolo and Fina came back a little later, they reminded me of the reason for their absence. Never imagining that the election would spill over into the following day, they had arranged to take their oaths of citizenship that afternoon. Manolo said, "Mr. President, next time *we* will be able to vote for you. We are now United States citizens."

When the others had left the library, I went to the record player and selected one of my favorites, the musical score from *Victory at Sea* by Richard Rodgers. I put it on and turned the volume up high. My thoughts meshed with the music. The battle had been long and arduous. We had suffered reverses and won victories. The struggle had been hard fought. But now we had won the final victory. The music captured the moment for me better than anything I could say or think or write.

PRESIDENT-ELECT

On November 6 we flew aboard an Air Force jet to Key Biscayne for a postelection rest. On the way we stopped in Washington so that I could visit Eisenhower at Walter Reed Hospital. Few moments in my life have been more satisfying than entering his room as the President-elect. When he saw me, his face brightened and he said, "Congratulations, Mr. President!"

I think Eisenhower had wanted me to win the election as much as I did. He urged me to describe for him every detail of the long election night and morning, and he beamed with pleasure all the while.

Our flight south was happy. Election night had been too draining for celebration, and this was the first time we were really able to relax and savor the joy of having finally reached the top of the mountain after a long and arduous journey.

I drove from Key Biscayne to Opa-Locka Airport to meet with Humphrey and Muskie and their families, who were on their way to a vacation in the Virgin Islands. I asked Humphrey if he would consider becoming ambassador to the United Nations. He asked for time to think about the offer. At the end of the meeting, Humphrey told reporters that the election was over and the national interest must prevail over partisan interest. "He's going to be our President," Humphrey said, "and I'm going to be one of his fellow citizens."

Thus, on the sunny tarmac in Florida, a familiar and moving moment in American political tradition took place: a symbolic message of nonpartisan reassurance was sent to our countrymen and to a watching world.

After a five-day rest in Key Biscayne we returned to New York to begin putting together an administration. Once again we stopped in Washington, this time for luncheon at the White House with President and Mrs. Johnson.

After a gracious meal Lady Bird and Pat began a room-by-room inspection of the entire mansion while Johnson had scheduled a series of briefings for me. On our way to the West Wing we stopped in his bedroom. The room was dominated by a canopied four-poster bed. There were a large closet and dressing room, in addition to a white-tiled bathroom. "I wanted you to know about this," Johnson said as he showed me how to open a small safe concealed in the wall.

When we entered the Cabinet Room, the briefers were already waiting for us: Secretary of State Dean Rusk, Secretary of Defense Clark Clifford, Chairman of the Joint Chiefs of Staff General Earle Wheeler, Director of Central Intelligence Richard Helms, and National Security Adviser Walt Rostow.

The main subject was Vietnam. The travail of the long war was etched on the faces around me. These were all able and intelligent men. They had wanted desperately to end the war before leaving office, but they had not succeeded. They seemed very nearly worn out. They had no new approaches to recommend to me. I sensed that, despite the disappointment of defeat, they were relieved to be able to turn this morass over to someone else.

They all emphasized that the United States must see the war through to a successful conclusion—with negotiations if possible, but with continued fighting if necessary. They agreed that an American bug-out, or a negotiated settlement that could be interpreted as a defeat, would have a devastatingly detrimental effect on our allies and friends in Asia and around the world. Clark Clifford, who during my administration became one of the most outspoken critics of the war, was an ardent supporter of Johnson's policies that afternoon.

When Johnson and I returned to the Oval Office after the briefing, he talked with a sense of urgency. "There may be times when we disagree, and, if such time comes, I will let you know privately," he said. "But you can be sure that I won't criticize you publicly. Eisenhower did the same for me. I know what an enormous burden you will be carrying." He said that he wanted to do everything he could to help me succeed. "The problems at home and abroad are probably greater than any President has ever confronted since the time of Lincoln," he said. Johnson and I had been adversaries for many years, but on that day our political and personal differences melted away. As we stood together in the Oval Office, he welcomed me into a club of very exclusive membership, and he made a promise to adhere to the cardinal rule of that membership: stand behind those who succeed you.

My first staff appointment was Rose Mary Woods as my personal secretary. Rose had been part of my political life since 1951. She combined professional skill with unexcelled personal charm. And she had total dedication. Her faith about my future had never wavered, even when my own sometimes did.

I asked Bob Haldeman to be my Chief of Staff. His role, as we envisaged it, would be administrative rather than substantive. He would examine the paperwork to ensure that opposing views were included and then bring the material to me for my decision; he would be a funnel rather than a filter. His intelligence and his capacity for detaching his personal prejudices from the examination of issues made him the ideal man for the job. He would also be the gatekeeper of the Oval Office. This would place him in the unenviable position of having to say no to a lot of people who felt they needed to see me personally and often, but I knew that his strong ego would be able to handle the jealousy and unpopularity such a role inevitably engenders.

I had strong opinions, many of them derived from my experiences and observations during the Eisenhower years, about the way a President should work. In my view, then and now, the key to a successful presidency is in the decision-making process. I felt that the matters brought before a President for decisions should be only those that cannot or should not be made at a lower level on the White House staff, or by the Cabinet member responsible for them. This was a lesson I had learned directly from Eisenhower, whose staff had too often cluttered his schedule with unimportant events and bothered him with minor problems that drained his time and energy. I knew that I could absorb far more material by reading it than by talking about it, and I have invariably found that staff members will present problems more concisely and incisively in writing than they will in meetings.

I had attended hundreds of Cabinet meetings as Vice President, and I felt that most of them were unnecessary and boring. On the few issues that cut across all departments, such as the economy, group discussions would sometimes be informative. But the day had long since passed when it was useful to take an hour and a half to have the Secretary of Defense and the Secretary of State discuss the Secretary of Transportation's new highway proposal. Therefore I wanted to keep the Cabinet meetings in my administration to a minimum. I felt that the better each Cabinet member performed his job, the less time I should have to spend discussing it with him except for major questions of politics or policy. If we were going to run government with a clear eye for efficiency and a tough approach to wastefulness, we would have to have good managers who could immerse themselves in detail and learn the job. I was willing to trade flamboyance for competence. I had also seen the hazards of appointing Cabinet members who were too strong-willed to act as part of a team. I wanted people who would fight to the finish in private for what they thought was right but would support my decision once it was made.

I was fully conscious that I had won the presidency with a narrow plurality of the popular vote. I knew that some of my choices for Cabinet posts would have to serve, even if only symbolically, to unite the country, and "bring us together." I wanted to have some Democrats in the Cabinet or in Cabinet-level posts, but Humphrey turned down the UN ambassadorship, and Senator Henry Jackson of Washington turned down an offer to be Secretary of Defense.

For the UN post we approached President Kennedy's brother-in-law Sargent Shriver, whom Johnson had appointed ambassador to France. Shriver expressed great interest and sent me a message stating the conditions for his acceptance. Among other things he required a pledge that the federal poverty programs would not be cut. It was intolerable to have a prospective ambassadorial appointee making demands relating to domestic policy, so I told Bill Rogers to inform Shriver that I had decided against him and to let him know why. Rogers reported that Shriver realized that he had overstepped himself and had tried to backpedal, claiming that he had not meant his message to set forth conditions but to make suggestions. I told Rogers to say that my decision remained unchanged.

In addition to some Democrats, I had hoped to bring some black leaders into my Cabinet. I offered the UN post to Ed Brooke, but he felt he could make a greater contribution by staying in the Senate. I urged the

Executive Director of the Urban League, Whitney Young, to be Secretary of Housing and Urban Development, but he declined, saying that he felt he could do more for his cause working outside the government. What he meant, of course, was that serving in a Republican Cabinet would be the political kiss of death for anyone who wanted a role of real leadership in the black community.

In this respect I was reaping the harvest of the Goldwater campaign. In 1960 I had received 32 percent of the black vote; in 1964 Goldwater received only 6 percent. I was able to increase the Republican share of the black vote to 12 percent in 1968, but the false impression that Goldwater was a racist was still too prevalent for an easy relationship to exist between the black community and a Republican administration. I regretted this fact, but I knew that there was nothing I could say that would change it. I would have to show by my actions in office that I was indeed President of all the American people.

The Cabinet gradually began to take shape. As a group, its members were less conservative than Eisenhower's Cabinet, and in fact somewhat to the left of my own centrist positions. But each man knew his subject and each brought both competence and imagination to his job.

Bill Rogers, a strong administrator, would have the formidable job of managing the recalcitrant bureaucracy of the State Department. He was a resourceful negotiator, and as a personal friend I knew that I could trust him to work with me on the most sensitive assignments in domestic as well as foreign policy. During his service as Attorney General in the Eisenhower years he had demonstrated that he could get along with Congress. I felt that the almost institutionalized enmity between Senator Fulbright's Foreign Relations Committee and the White House had become damaging to the national interest, and I thought Rogers could thaw that freeze.

For the Defense Department I chose Melvin Laird of Wisconsin, a veteran of seventeen years in the House of Representatives and an expert on defense appropriations. Mel Laird was respected by his congressional colleagues as a strong man and a shrewd politician.

Even as John Mitchell was helping me develop a list of candidates for Attorney General, I decided that I would try to persuade him to accept the position himself. I wanted someone who shared my concern about permissiveness in the courts and even in many law enforcement agencies. Mitchell was tough, intelligent, and fair. Moreover, I counted him my most trusted friend and adviser and I wanted to have his advice available, not just on legal matters but on the whole range of presidential decision-making.

David Kennedy, head of the Continental Illinois National Bank and Trust Company in Chicago, brought to the Treasury Department his experience and expertise in international finance. He also met my requirement that my Secretary of the Treasury not be part of the New York–Boston banking establishment that had dominated the department for too long. Winton "Red" Blount for Postmaster General, Walter Hickel for Interior, Clifford Hardin for Agriculture, Maurice Stans for Commerce, George Shultz for Labor, Bob Finch for Health, Education, and Welfare, George Romney for Housing and Urban Development, and John Volpe for Transportation rounded out the Cabinet.

I had invited Ted Agnew and his wife, Judy, to Key Biscayne right after the election to begin making plans for his role in the administration. I told Agnew that I wanted him to assume policy-making responsibilities, and I suggested that he have an office in the West Wing of the White House, the first time in history that a Vice President would do so. I asked him to draw on his experience as a state official by taking the major responsibility for federal-state relations. I urged him to start immediately to use his role as President of the Senate to get to know Congress and its members, to work with them, and to serve as their primary liaison with the White House.

When Eisenhower selected Foster Dulles as his Secretary of State, he wanted him to be his chief foreign policy adviser, a role Dulles was uniquely qualified to fill. From the outset of my administration, however, I planned to direct foreign policy from the White House. Therefore I regarded my choice of a National Security Adviser as crucial. Considering the importance I placed on the post, I made my choice in an uncharacteristically impulsive way.

I knew that Henry Kissinger had served for many years as a foreign policy adviser to Nelson Rockefeller. I had also heard that in the period before the 1968 Republican convention, while Rockefeller and I were rivals for the nomination, Kissinger had privately made a number of disparaging comments about my competence in the field. But I expected this from a Rockefeller associate, and I chalked it up to politics. During the last days of the campaign, when Kissinger was providing us with information about the bombing halt, I became more aware of both his knowledge and his influence.

John Mitchell arranged for Kissinger and me to meet on November 25 in my transition office in the Hotel Pierre in New York. Since neither of us was interested in small talk, I proceeded to outline for him some of the plans I had for my administration's foreign policy. I had read his book *Nuclear Weapons and Foreign Policy* when it first appeared in 1957, and I knew that we were very much alike in our general outlook in that we shared a belief in the importance of isolating and influencing the factors affecting worldwide balances of power. We also agreed that whatever else a foreign policy might be, it must be strong to be credible

—and it must be credible to be successful. I was not hopeful about the prospects of settling the Vietnam war through the Paris talks and felt that we needed to rethink our whole diplomatic and military policy on Vietnam. Kissinger agreed, although he was less pessimistic about the negotiations than I was. I said that I was determined to avoid the trap Johnson had fallen into, of devoting virtually all my foreign policy time and energy to Vietnam, which was really a short-term problem. I felt that failing to deal with the longer-term problems could be devastating to America's security and survival, and in this regard I talked about restoring the vitality of the NATO alliance, and about the Middle East, the Soviet Union, and Japan. Finally I mentioned my concern about the need to re-evaluate our policy toward Communist China, and I urged him to read the *Foreign Affairs* article in which I had first raised this idea as a possibility and a necessity.

Kissinger said he was delighted that I was thinking in such terms. He said that if I intended to operate on such a wide-ranging basis, I was going to need the best possible system for getting advice. Kennedy had replaced NSC strategic planning with tactical crisis management; and Johnson, largely because of his concern with leaks, had reduced NSC decision-making to informal weekly luncheon sessions with only a few advisers. Kissinger recommended that I structure a national security apparatus within the White House that, in addition to coordinating foreign and defense policy, could also develop policy options for me to consider before making decisions.

I had a strong intuition about Henry Kissinger, and I decided on the spot that he should be my National Security Adviser. I did not make a specific offer to him then, but I made it clear that I was interested in having him serve in my administration. I guessed that he would want to think about our conversation, and also that he would feel an obligation to discuss it with Rockefeller.

I met with Kissinger again two days later and asked him if he would like to head the NSC. He replied that he would be honored to accept. He immediately began assembling a staff and analyzing the policy choices that I would have to address as soon as I took office. From the beginning he worked with the intensity and stamina that were to characterize his performance over the years.

The combination was unlikely—the grocer's son from Whittier and the refugee from Hitler's Germany, the politician and the academic. But our differences helped make the partnership work.

Daniel Patrick Moynihan had one of the most innovative minds for domestic policy in the country. Like Kissinger a Harvard professor, he had served as Assistant Secretary of Labor in the Kennedy and Johnson administrations. I had read several of his articles before the 1968 campaign, and I found his thinking refreshing and stimulating. Unlike so many liberal academics, Moynihan was free of professional jargon and ideological cant. He had helped design the Great Society poverty programs, but he was not afraid to acknowledge that many of them had failed, and he was ready to apply the lessons learned from that failure to devising new programs that might work.

I met with Moynihan to explore his views and to sound him out about coming to the White House. Although he quickly made known his opposition to the Vietnam war, he was clearly interested by the opportunity. Our shared conviction that the current welfare system had to be totally reformed helped to cement the rapport I immediately felt with him. I told Moynihan about my intention to establish an Urban Affairs Council, describing it as the domestic policy equivalent of the National Security Council in foreign affairs. "That's a capital idea!" he exclaimed. Then I asked him if he would like to head it. He accepted immediately. Even when I thought Pat Moynihan was wrong about a particular issue or problem, I found his intellect scintillating and challenging. As I said after he had left the administration and returned to Harvard, "I disagreed with a lot of what he said—but he certainly did light up the place!"

I created a new Cabinet-level position, Counsellor to the President, for my old friend and adviser Arthur Burns. I thought that his conservatism would be a useful and creative counterweight to Moynihan's liberalism.

I could remember as if it were only yesterday sitting in Eisenhower's suite in the Blackstone Hotel in 1952 and wondering whether he knew what he was getting himself in for as I watched him sign his letter of resignation from the Army. He had not been in politics very long and was bound to be surprised by many of the things that happened. But I had been involved in presidential politics for almost two decades, and I was determined to be as prepared as anyone ever had been for the power and position I was about to assume. Therefore, despite the demands of daily events during this transition period, I set aside time to think about the condition of the nation and the world I would be inheriting from Johnson and about how I wanted my presidency to change and improve things.

Like Eisenhower, I was about to assume four different hats: as head of state I would have to deal with foreign affairs; as head of government I would have to provide domestic leadership and legislative programs; as Commander in Chief I would have the ultimate authority and responsibility for America's armed forces; and as leader of the Republican Party

I would have to do something to breathe new life into the national, state, and local party organizations.

As I looked at America's foreign policy during the 1960s, I felt that it had been held hostage, first under Kennedy to the cold war and then under Johnson to the Vietnam war. Our tendency to become preoccupied with only one or two problems at a time had led to a deterioration of policy on all fronts. I did not feel that there should be any single foreign policy priority. There were many priorities, moving in tandem, each affecting the others. To the extent that I would have to start somewhere, I felt that I had to put Europe at the top of the list. Only when we had secured our Western alliance would we be on sufficiently solid footing to begin talks with the Communists. NATO was in disarray, largely because of the failure of the United States to consult adequately with our European allies.

In the Far East, Japan, now the second most productive nation in the free world, was beginning to have doubts about the credibility of America's defense commitments. Our control of the island of Okinawa was a constant irritant in our relations.

In the Middle East the truce that followed the June war of 1967 was continually interrupted by intermittent fighting. The United States seemed to be unable to do anything more than arm Israel against the next Arab onslaught. Egypt and Syria, Israel's two major potential enemies, were receiving Soviet arms, and this turned the already explosive area into an international powder keg, that, when it exploded, might lead not only to another war between Israel and its neighbors, but also to a direct confrontation between the United States and the Soviet Union.

From Communist China there was only ominous silence. Except for sterile and sporadic talks between the American and Chinese ambassadors in Warsaw, a gulf of twenty years of noncommunication separated the world's most populous nation from the world's most powerful nation.

As I looked at America's position in the world and examined our relations with other nations, I could see that the central factor in 1968 on the eve of my presidency was the same as it had been in 1947 when I first went to Europe with the Herter Committee: America now, as then, was the main defender of the free world against the encroachment and aggression of the Communist world.

For twenty-five years, I had watched the changing face of communism. I had seen prewar communism, luring workers and intellectuals with its siren call of equality and justice, reveal itself as an aggressive imperialistic ideology during the postwar period of the Marshall Plan. Despite the most nobly ringing rhetoric, the pattern was tragically the same: as soon as the Communists came to power, they destroyed all opposition. I had watched the Soviets' phenomenal recovery from the devastation of war and their costly but successful struggle to achieve for communism the selling point of potential prosperity. At home I had seen the face of underground subversive communism when it surfaced in the Hiss case, reminding people not only that it existed, but that its purpose was deadly serious.

In the late 1940s and during the 1950s I had seen communism spread to China and other parts of Asia, and to Africa and South America, under the camouflage of parties of socialist revolution, or under the guise of wars of national liberation. And, finally, during the 1960s I had watched as Peking and Moscow became rivals for the role of leadership in the Communist world.

Never once in my career have I doubted that the Communists mean it when they say that their goal is to bring the world under Communist control. Nor have I ever forgotten Whittaker Chambers's chilling comment that when he left communism, he had the feeling he was leaving the winning side. But unlike some anticommunists who think we should refuse to recognize or deal with the Communists lest in doing so we imply or extend an ideological respectability to their philosophy and their system, I have always believed that we can and must communicate and, when possible, negotiate with Communist nations. They are too powerful to ignore. We must always remember that they will never act out of altruism, but only out of self-interest. Once this is understood, it is more sensible—and also safer—to communicate with the Communists than it is to live in icy cold-war isolation or confrontation. In fact, in January 1969 I felt that the relationship between the United States and the Soviet Union would probably be the single most important factor in determining whether the world would live at peace during and after my administration.

I felt that we had allowed ourselves to get in a disadvantageous position vis-à-vis the Soviets. They had a major presence in the Arab states of the Middle East, while we had none; they had Castro in Cuba; since the mid-1960s they had supplanted the Chinese as the principal military suppliers of North Vietnam; and except for Tito's Yugoslavia they still totally controlled Eastern Europe and threatened the stability and security of Western Europe.

There were, however, a few things in our favor. The most important and interesting was the Soviet split with China. There was also some evidence of growing, albeit limited, independence in some of the satellite nations. There were indications that the Soviet leaders were becoming interested in reaching an agreement on strategic arms limitation. They also appeared to be ready to hold serious talks on the anomalous situation in Berlin, which, almost a quarter century after the war had ended, was still a divided city and a constant source of tension, not just between the Soviets and the United States, but also between the Soviets and Western Europe. We sensed that they were looking for a face-saving formula that would lessen the risk of confrontation in the Mideast. And we had some solid evidence that they were anxious for an expansion of trade.

It was often said that the key to a Vietnam settlement lay in Moscow and Peking rather than in Hanoi. Without continuous and massive aid from either or both of the Communist giants, the leaders of North Vietnam would not have been able to carry on the war for more than a few months. Thanks to the Sino-Soviet split, however, the North Vietnamese had been extremely successful in playing off the Soviets and the Chinese against each other by turning support for their war effort into a touchstone of Communist orthodoxy and a requisite for keeping North Vietnam from settling into the opposing camp in the struggle for domination within the Communist world. This situation became a strain, particularly for the Soviets. Aside from wanting to keep Hanoi from going over to Peking, Moscow had little stake in the outcome of the North Vietnamese cause, especially as it increasingly worked against Moscow's own major interests vis-à-vis the United States. While I understood that the Soviets were not entirely free agents where their support for North Vietnam was concerned, I nonetheless planned to bring maximum pressure to bear on them in this area.

I was sure that Brezhnev and Kosygin had been no more anxious for me to win in 1968 than Khrushchev had been in 1960. The prospect of having to deal with a Republican administration—and a Nixon administration at that—undoubtedly caused anxiety in Moscow. In fact, I suspected that the Soviets might have counseled the North Vietnamese to offer to begin the Paris talks in the hope that the bombing halt would tip the balance to Humphrey in the election—and if that was their strategy, it had almost worked.

After the election Johnson proposed that as President and President-elect he and I attend a summit meeting with the Soviets in the period before my inauguration. I understood his desire to make one last dramatic demonstration of his dedication to peace, but I saw no solid basis for concluding that the Soviet leaders were prepared to negotiate seriously on any critical issue. Nor did I want to be boxed in by any decisions that were made before I took office.

The most that might come from such a last-minute summit would be a "spirit," like the "Spirit of Glassboro" that followed Johnson's meeting with Kosygin in New Jersey in 1967 or the "Spirit of Camp David" that followed Eisenhower's meeting with Khrushchev in 1959. It was my feeling that such "spirits" were almost entirely spurious and that they actually worked heavily to the Soviets' advantage. Since public opinion played no role whatever in the Communist system, such summit "spirit" was a one-way street in their direction, because the optimistic attitudes that characterized American public opinion after a summit made it harder for us to assume a tough line in our postsummit dealings with the Soviets.

During the transition period Kissinger and I developed a new policy for dealing with the Soviets. Since U.S.–Soviet interests as the world's two competing nuclear superpowers were so widespread and overlapping, it was unrealistic to separate or compartmentalize areas of concern. Therefore we decided to link progress in such areas of Soviet concern as strategic arms limitation and increased trade with progress in areas that were important to us—Vietnam, the Mideast, and Berlin. This concept became known as linkage.

Lest there be any doubt of my seriousness in pursuing this policy, I purposely announced it at my first press conference when asked a question about starting SALT talks. I said, "What I want to do is to see to it that we have strategic arms talks in a way and at a time that will promote, if possible, progress on outstanding political problems at the same time—for example, on the problem of the Mideast and on other outstanding problems in which the United States and the Soviet Union acting together can serve the cause of peace."

Linkage was something uncomfortably new and different for the Soviets, and I was not surprised when they bridled at the restraints it imposed on our relationship. It would take almost two years of patient and hard-nosed determination on our part before they would accept that linkage with what we wanted from them was the price they would have to pay for getting any of the things they wanted from us.

We made our first contacts with the Soviets during the transition period. In mid-December Kissinger met with a Soviet UN diplomat who was, as we knew, actually an intelligence officer. I wanted it made clear that I was not taken in by any of the optimistic rhetoric that had characterized so much of recent Soviet–American relations. Kissinger therefore stated that while the tendency during the last few years had been to emphasize how much our two nations supposedly had in common, the Nixon administration felt that there were real and substantial differences between us and that an effort to lessen the tension created by these differences should be the central focus of our relationship. Kissinger also said that I did not want a pre-inauguration summit meeting and that if they held one with Johnson I would have to state publicly that I would not be bound by it. Nothing more was heard about this summit project.

We received a prompt reply from Moscow. Our UN contact reported that the Soviet leadership was "not pessimistic" because of the election of a Republican President. He said that the Soviet leadership had expressed an interest in knowing if I desired to "open channels of communication." It was with this in mind that I said in my inaugural address, "After a period of confrontation, we are entering an era of negotiation. Let all nations know that during this administration our lines of communication will be open."

VIETNAM

The most pressing foreign problem I would have to deal with as soon as I became President was the war in Vietnam. During the transition Kissinger began a review of all possible policies toward Vietnam, distilling them into specific options that ran the gamut from massive military escalation to immediate unilateral withdrawal. A strong case could be made for each option.

For example, it could be argued that military victory was still possible if I would remove the restrictions Johnson had placed on our commanders in the field and allow them to use our massive power to defeat the enemy. The most serious of these constraints was the bombing halt; because of it the Communists had been able to regroup their forces and amass supplies for a new offensive. Those who favored the escalation option argued that just the threat of an invasion of North Vietnam would tie down North Vietnamese troops along the DMZ; that mining Haiphong Harbor would cripple the enemy's supply lines; and that free pursuit of the Communist forces into Laos and Cambodia would blunt their ability to continue making hit-and-run attacks against our forces in South Vietnam. Renewed bombing would reinforce these other moves. That, in essence, was the escalation option. It was an option we ruled out very early.

The opinion polls showed a significant percentage of the public favored a military victory in Vietnam. But most people thought of a "military victory" in terms of gearing up to administer a knockout blow that would both end the war and win it. The problem was that there were only two such knockout blows available to me. One would have been to bomb the elaborate systems of irrigation dikes in North Vietnam. The resulting floods would have killed hundreds of thousands of civilians. The other possible knockout blow would have involved the use of tactical nuclear weapons. Short of one of these methods, escalation would probably have required up to six months of highly intensified fighting and significantly increased casualties before the Communists would finally be forced to give up and accept a peace settlement. The domestic and international uproar that would have accompanied the use of either of these knockout blows would have got my administration off to the worst possible start. And as far as escalating the conventional fighting was concerned, there was no way that I could hold the country together for that period of time in view of the numbers of casualties we would be sustaining. Resorting to the escalation option would also delay or even destroy any chance we might have to develop a new relationship with the Soviet Union and Communist China.

At the other end of the spectrum from escalation was the case for ending the war simply by announcing a quick and orderly withdrawal of all American forces. If that were done, the argument went, the Communists would probably respond by returning our POWs after the last American had departed.

There were some undeniably compelling political arguments to recommend this particular course. As one of my friends in Congress put it, "You didn't get us into this war, so even if you end it with a bad peace, by doing it quickly you can put the blame on Kennedy and Johnson and the Democrats. Just go on TV and remind people that it was Kennedy who sent the 16,000 Americans in there, and that it was Johnson who escalated it to 540,000. Then announce that you're bringing them all home, and you'll be a hero."

As I saw it, however, this option had long since been foreclosed. A precipitate withdrawal would abandon 17 million South Vietnamese, many of whom had worked for us and supported us, to Communist atrocities and domination. When the Communists had taken over North Vietnam in 1954, 50,000 people had been murdered, and hundreds of thousands more died in labor camps. In 1968, during their brief control of Hué, they had shot or clubbed to death or buried alive more than 3,000 civilians whose only crime was to have supported the Saigon government. We simply could not sacrifice an ally in such a way. If we suddenly reneged on our earlier pledges of support, because they had become difficult or costly to carry out, or because they had become unpopular at home, we would not be worthy of the trust of other nations and we certainly would not receive it.

As far as I was concerned, almost everything involving a Vietnam settlement was negotiable except two things: I would not agree to anything that did not include the return of all our POWs and an accounting for our missing in action; and I would not agree to any terms that required or amounted to our overthrow of President Thieu.

I was aware that many Americans considered Thieu a petty and corrupt dictator unworthy of our support. I was not personally attached to Thieu, but I looked at the situation in practical terms. As I saw it, the alternative to Thieu was not someone more enlightened or tolerant or democratic but someone weaker who would not be able to hold together the contentious factions in South Vietnam. The South Vietnamese needed a strong and stable government to carry on the fight against the efforts of the Vietcong terrorists, who were supported by the North Vietnamese Army in their efforts to impose a Communist dictatorship on the 17 million people of South Vietnam. My determination to honor our commitment to Thieu was a commitment to stability, and that is exactly why the Communists were so insistent upon securing his downfall as part of a settlement. For three and a half years, until the fall of 1972, the North Vietnamese insisted upon our willingness to overthrow or sacrifice Thieu as a sine qua non for a settlement. Once they dropped this demand serious negotiations began.

I began my presidency with three fundamental premises regarding Vietnam. First, I would have to prepare public opinion for the fact that total military victory was no longer possible. Second, I would have to act on what my conscience, my experience, and my analysis told me was true about the need to keep our commitment. To abandon South Vietnam to the Communists now would cost us inestimably in our search for a stable, structured, and lasting peace. Third, I would have to end the war as quickly as was honorably possible.

Since I had ruled out a quick military victory, the only possible course was to try for a fair negotiated settlement that would preserve the independence of South Vietnam. Ideally the war could be over in a matter of months if the North Vietnamese truly wanted peace. Realistically, however, I was prepared to take most of my first year in office to arrive at a negotiated agreement.

In mid-December I told Kissinger that I wanted to send a message to North Vietnam. We decided to use Jean Sainteny as an intermediary. Sainteny was a French businessman who had spent many years in Indochina and who still knew personally many of the leaders in both North and South Vietnam, including Ho Chi Minh. I had first met Sainteny in the South of France in 1965, and Kissinger knew him as well.

My first message, which Sainteny gave to the North Vietnamese in Paris, set forth in conciliatory terms our proposals for a negotiated settlement. Eleven days later we received a reply charging that Saigon was holding up the opening of the Paris peace talks and that we supported the "absurd demands" of the South Vietnamese leaders. "If the U.S. wishes," their note concluded, "it may communicate its general ideas, and its specific ideas for making more precise points than are already known, for our serious examination." When he handed this reply to Sainteny, Mai Van Bo, Hanoi's representative in Paris, commented, "At the beginning, I believe that the question is to know if the U.S. wants peace, if it really wishes to withdraw its troops from South Vietnam, or if it only talks of this to make it possible to do nothing."

I waited only two days to reply, sending word through Sainteny that "the Nixon administration is willing to negotiate seriously and in good faith." The North Vietnamese reply to this message still took a hard line, but I was neither surprised nor discouraged; I had never expected to end the long war quickly or easily. In my inaugural address I reiterated my desire to reach a peaceful settlement if possible, but I left no doubts about my determination to see through to an honorable conclusion the commitment we had undertaken. I said: "To all those who would be tempted by weakness, let us leave no doubt that we will be as strong as we need to be for as long as we need to be."

The Vietnam war was complicated by factors that had never occurred before in America's conduct of a war. Many of the most prominent liberals of both parties in Congress, having supported our involvement in Vietnam under Kennedy and Johnson, were now trying to back off from their commitment. Senators and congressmen, Cabinet members and columnists who had formerly supported the war were now swelling the ranks of the antiwar forces. In 1969 I still had a congressional majority on war-related votes and questions, but it was a bare one at best, and I could not be sure how long it would hold. Another unusual aspect of this war was that the American news media had come to dominate domestic opinion about its purpose and conduct and also about the nature of the enemy. The North Vietnamese were a particularly ruthless and cruel enemy, but the American media concentrated primarily on the failings and frailties of the South Vietnamese or of our own forces. In each night's TV news and in each morning's paper the war was reported battle by battle, but little or no sense of the underlying purpose of the fighting was conveyed. Eventually this contributed to the impression that we were fighting in military and moral quicksand, rather than toward an important and worthwhile objective.

More than ever before, television showed the terrible human suffering and sacrifice of war. Whatever the intention behind such relentless and literal reporting of the war, the result was a serious demoralization of the home front, raising the question whether America would ever again be able to fight an enemy abroad with unity and strength of purpose at home. As *Newsweek* columnist Kenneth Crawford wrote, this was the first war in our history when the media was more friendly to our enemies than to our allies. I felt that by the time I had become President the way the Vietnam war had been conducted and reported had worn down America's spirit and sense of confidence.

As I prepared to enter the presidency, I regarded the antiwar protesters and demonstrators with alternating feelings of appreciation for their concerns, anger at their excesses, and, primarily, frustration at their apparent unwillingness to credit me even with a genuine desire for peace. But whatever my estimation of the demonstrators' motives—and whatever their estimate of mine—I considered that the practical effect of their activity was to give encouragement to the enemy and thus prolong the war. They wanted to end the war in Vietnam. So did I. But they wanted to end it immediately, and in order to do so they were prepared to abandon South Vietnam. That was something I would not permit.

The final returns of the 1968 presidential election showed that I had defeated Humphrey by only 500,000 votes—43.3 percent to 42.6 percent. But George Wallace had received 13.5 percent, nearly 10 million votes. My votes and Wallace's totaled 56.8 percent, and together they represented a clear mandate: after almost four decades in which the federal government had insatiably drawn power to itself, the American voters wanted a change of direction away from Washington paternalism. As I considered the situation that could confront me when I assumed responsibility as head of government, the major question as I saw it was: given an opposition Congress and an essentially liberal bureaucracy, how far would I be able to go toward carrying out this mandate?

I was the first newly elected President since Zachary Taylor 120 years earlier to take office with both houses of Congress controlled by the opposition party. If I were to get legislation passed, I would need a coalition of bipartisan support.

Throughout my presidency my strongest and most dependable support in foreign affairs came from conservatives in both parties. I came to depend particularly on a group of Southern Democrats including Sonny Montgomery of Mississippi, George Mahon of Texas, William Colmer of Mississippi, and Joe Waggonner, Eddie Hébert, and Otto Passman of Louisiana in the House, and Dick Russell of Georgia, John Stennis of Mississippi, and John McClellan of Arkansas in the Senate.

Unfortunately, there was no similar coalition I could tap for support on domestic policy. In that area I knew that the different interests of different groups would coincide on some issues and diverge on others. Liberals would seldom think that I had gone far enough, and conservatives would often think I had gone too far. On every issue I would have to gather enough borderline members of each persuasion to pass my legislation. To get my programs through Congress I would have to devise complex political strategies. To prevent things I opposed from being enacted I would have to be prepared to bear the political and public relations consequences of vetoing large amounts of legislation.

I won the 1968 election as a Washington insider, but with an outsider's prejudices. The behind-the-scenes power structure in Washington is often called the "iron triangle": a three-sided set of relationships composed of congressional lobbyists, congressional committee and subcommittee members and their staffs, and the bureaucrats in the various federal departments and agencies. These people tend to work with each other year after year regardless of changes in administrations; they form personal and professional associations and generally act in concert.

I felt that one of the reasons I had been elected was my promise to break the hammerlock Washington holds over the money and decisions that affect American lives. I wanted to break open the iron triangle and start turning money and power back to the states and cities, and I wanted to throw the red tape out the window. But Washington is a city run primarily by Democrats and liberals, dominated by like-minded newspapers and other media, convinced of its superiority to other cities and other points of view; from the beginning I knew my chances of succeeding with the kinds of domestic reforms I had in mind were slim.

I urged the new Cabinet members to move quickly to replace holdover bureaucrats with people who believed in what we were trying to do. I warned that if they did not act quickly, they would become captives of the bureaucracy they were trying to change. "In effect, we want to reverse the whole trend of government over the last eight years. We may only have four years in which to do it, so we can't waste a minute," I said. I urged them to resist the Washington habit of recruiting their staffs solely from Eastern schools and companies and instead to branch out and get new blood from the South, the West, and the Midwest. "We can't depend on people who believe in another philosophy of government to give us their undivided loyalty or their best work," I concluded. "For some reason this is something that the supposedly idealistic Democrats have always been better at recognizing than the supposedly hard-nosed Republicans. If we don't get rid of those people, they will either sabotage us from within, or they'll just sit back on their well-paid asses and wait for the next election to bring back their old bosses."

As I saw it, America in the 1960s had undergone a misguided crash program aimed at using the power of the presidency and the federal government to right past wrongs by trying to legislate social progress. This was the idea behind Kennedy's New Frontier and Johnson's Great Society. The problems were real and the intention worthy, but the method was foredoomed. By the end of the decade its costs had become almost prohibitively high in terms of the way it had undermined fundamental relationships within our federal system, created confusion about our national values, and corroded American belief in ourselves as a people and as a nation.

The 1960s had been a decade of great restlessness and change. Prodded by the emotional power of Kennedy's liberal rhetoric, new sensitivities—some sincere, some merely fashionable—developed regarding the black, the poor, and the young in our society.

This was the period of what social critic Henry Fairlie has called "the politics of expectation," when the President held out the promise of solutions by means of federal programs to the problems of poverty and racial discrimination, thereby raising the expectations of millions of people—and, of course, securing the support of millions of voters. From 1960 to 1969 the cost of welfare benefits for families with dependent children nearly tripled. More than a quarter of a trillion federal dollars was spent between 1964 and 1969 in an attempt to eradicate poverty and inequality. But instead of solving problems, these programs themselves became part of the problem, by raising hopes they proved unable to fulfill.

Billions of dollars were poured into new federally sponsored programs and agencies to help the poor, but the poor frequently did not see much of this money because it went to pay the salaries of the social workers and the overhead of the vast new poverty bureaucracy, much of it composed of middle-class whites, that administered the programs and agencies. Housing and education services were tied up in red tape and foundered on the fundamentally mistaken notion that the poor can be talked or taught out of their poverty.

In 1961 John Kennedy had challenged people to "ask not what your country can do for you—ask what you can do for your country." By the end of the decade, however, many people were asking why the federal government had not done all the things it had promised and undertaken to do for them.

Perhaps most demoralizing of all, the working poor watched while the nonworking poor made as much money—and in some cases even more money—by collecting welfare payments and other unemployment benefits. This began a bitter cycle of frustration, anger, and hostility.

I wanted to be an activist President in domestic policy, but I wanted to be certain that the things we did had a chance of working. "Don't promise more than we can do," I told the Cabinet. "But do more than we can promise."

I had watched the sixties from outside the arena of leadership, but I had strong feelings about what I had seen happen. I saw the mass demonstrations grow remote from the wellsprings of sensitivity and feeling that had originally prompted them, and become a cultural fad. And the new sensitivity to social inequities that was awakened at the beginning of the decade had, by the middle of the sixties, spawned an intolerance for the rights and opinions of those who disagreed with the vocal minority. I had no patience with the mindless rioters and professional malcontents, and I was appalled by the response of most of the nation's political and academic leaders to them. The political leadership seemed unable to make the distinction between a wrong that needed to be set right and the use of such a wrong as a justification for violating the privileges of democracy. The young demonstrators held firmly to their beliefs, while the adults seemed stricken with ambivalence about their own guilt and doubts about their own values. By proving themselves vulnerable to mob rule, the political and academic leaders encouraged its spread. Contemptuous of most of their professors, encouraged by others on the faculty and in the political arena, and spotlighted by the rapt gaze of television cameras, the demonstrators and their demonstrations continued and grew, and so did the often rationalized or romanticized violence connected with them.

I was ready to take a stand on these social and cultural issues; I was anxious to defend the "square" virtues. In some cases—such as opposing the legalization of marijuana and the provision of federal funds for abortions, and in identifying myself with unabashed patriotism—I knew I would be standing against the prevailing social winds, and that would cause tension. But I thought that at least someone in high office would be standing up for what he believed.

Since the advent of television as our primary means of communication and source of information modern Presidents must have specialized talents at once more superficial and more complicated than those of their predecessors. They must try to master the art of manipulating the media not only to win in politics but in order to further the programs and causes they believe in; at the same time they must avoid at all costs the charge of trying to manipulate the media. In the modern presidency, concern for image must rank with concern for substance—there is no guarantee that good programs will automatically triumph. "Elections are not won or lost by programs," I once reminded Haldeman in a memo. "They are won or lost by how these programs are presented to the country and how the political and public relations considerations are handled." I do not like this situation; I can remember a time in American politics when it was not the case. But today it is a fact of life, and anyone who seeks a position of influence in politics must cope with it; anyone who seeks a position of leadership must master it.

I knew that as President my relations with the media would be at best an uneasy truce. Some of the problems were simply institutional. The media see themselves as adversaries of government, and consider it their obligation to be skeptical. The government knows that there is no such thing as a perfect program, and searches for ways to mitigate criticism sufficiently well and long enough to get something accomplished. Often the tension between the two results from nothing more than this. But in my case the problems were more than just institutional. The majority of New York and Washington newspaper and television reporters, news executives, columnists, and opinion-makers are liberals. I am not, and for many years we had looked at each other across an ideological chasm that Vietnam only deepened further. After the press treatment I received during the Hiss case and the fund episode, and after the flagrant media favoritism for Kennedy in 1960, I considered the influential majority of the news media to be part of my political opposition. Whatever the reasons—institutional, ideological, or simply those based on personality—my relationship with them was somehow different even from that of other political figures whom they disliked or with whom they disagreed. I knew that I must expect no generosity, even for mistakes; I knew that my conduct and that of my family would be held up to the most severe scrutiny; and I felt that if anything ever went seriously wrong, the media would jump in and give me a fight for my political life.

I was prepared to have to do combat with the media in order to get my views and my programs to the people, and despite all the power and public visibility I would enjoy as President, I did not believe that this combat would be between equals. The media are far more powerful than the President in creating public awareness and shaping public opinion, for the simple reason that the media always have the last word.

I also felt that it would be important to establish a more direct relationship with the media outside New York and Washington. I did not want all the views and opinions reaching me filtered through the *Times*, the *Post*, and the three television networks. Therefore I asked for a daily summary of the main ideas and opinions expressed across the country in news reports, editorials, columns, and articles from fifty newspapers, thirty magazines, and the two major wire services.

Within the White House I created the post of Director of Communications for the executive branch. Herb Klein, who had served as my press spokesman in 1960 and 1962, headed this new office. One of his tasks was to stay in touch with the media in the rest of the country, bring their reports to me, and get my ideas out to them. I named Ron Ziegler, my twenty-nine-year-old campaign press assistant, as Press Secretary.

As I assembled my Cabinet and senior staff during this transition period, I thought that one of our most important tasks would be to place our stamp on the federal bureaucracy as quickly and as firmly as we possibly could. Ever since Andrew Jackson and the era of "To the victor belong the spoils," the Democrats had understood and excelled at acting on this premise. I could remember my concern when Eisenhower, upon entering office after twenty years of uninterrupted Democratic power, failed to press his Cabinet members and other appointees to Republicanize their agencies and departments. After the eight Kennedy–Johnson years the need was hardly less great, and at every meeting during the transition and the first months of my administration I urged, exhorted, and finally pleaded with my Cabinet and other appointed officials to replace holdover Democrats with Republicans who would be loyal to the administration and support my programs.

Week after week I watched and listened while even the Cabinet members who had been in politics long enough to know better justified retaining Democrats in important positions in their departments for reasons of "morale" or in order to avoid controversy or unfavorable publicity. Looking back, I think that Eisenhower, because of his many years of experience with the Army, understood that the combination of human nature and the inertia of institutions will generally override even the most determined attempts to change them. Once the opportunity had passed, it was too late to correct this failure during my first term. I could only console myself with the determination that, if I were re-elected in 1972, I would not make the same mistake of leaving the initiative to individual Cabinet members.

I knew that I was assuming the role of Commander in Chief at what was perhaps the most troubled time in the history of our armed forces. Never before had our fighting men been subjected to such criticism—and never to such obloquy—during wartime. Among the most serious effects of the antiwar movement in America was its effect on the morale and discipline of our armed forces both at home and on the battlefield, and the problem became worse as the expanded monthly draft calls began bringing in more young men who had been infected by antiwar attitudes. As I looked ahead to the end of the Vietnam war, I saw that we could end the recruitment of our armed forces through universal conscription and create an all-volunteer force. In 1969 I introduced this plan, and by 1973 the civilian draft had been completely eliminated.

I addressed the problems of the military in a speech I gave a few months later at the Air Force Academy commencement exercises in June 1969. I said, "It is open season on the armed forces. . . . The military profession is derided in some of the so-called best circles of America. Patriotism is considered by some to be a backward fetish of the uneducated and unsophisticated." While it was undeniably important to keep the power of the military firmly under civilian control and to check wastefulness in military programs, I also considered it important to let our armed forces know that their Commander in Chief stood behind them. I told the cadets in Colorado Springs, "The American defense establishment should never be a sacred cow, but on the other hand, the American military should never be anybody's scapegoat."

By 1968 I had been dedicated to the Republican Party and its electoral fortunes for twenty-two years. Unfortunately the party had not emerged much strengthened from the 1968 election despite our victory at the top of the ticket. Perhaps the problems were too deep-seated for any easy solution. The fact was that the Democrats had controlled both houses of Congress for all but two of the past thirty years. From the outset of my administration, I decided that I would use the power of incumbency to help the Republican Party and to enhance its electoral prospects. I took it as a serious responsibility as leader of the party to inject some much-needed old-time partisan fire and spirit into Republican veins. Although off-year elections almost always go against the party in the White House, I hoped that we could at least hold our own in 1970. By 1972 I hoped to have restored vitality to the Republican organization and to have identified and encouraged a new generation of winning Republican candidates.

In the meantime I would also have to keep an eye on my own political position. The victory over Humphrey had been far too close for comfort. If it had not been for the debacle of the Chicago convention and the burden of Johnson's unpopularity, Humphrey might have won. There was no reason to expect that the Democrats would be so obliging as to provide me with similar advantages in 1972. If they were able to unite around Teddy Kennedy or Muskie or even Humphrey again, they would be very hard to beat. Therefore I decided that we must begin immediately keeping track of everything the leading Democrats did. Information would be our first line of defense.

I met with President Johnson again on December 12. I sat on one of the sofas in front of the fireplace in the Oval Office while he sat in the king-size rocking chair that he had brought in to replace Kennedy's smaller one. He began by stressing the need for maintaining secrecy on all matters involving national security. This comment was prompted by my recent announcement that I planned to revive the moribund National Security Council. Johnson was dubious about this decision, and as he warmed to his subject he sat on the edge of his rocker and leaned forward until his face was just inches from mine.

Jabbing his finger at my chest, his voice raised, he said, "Let me tell you, Dick, I would have been a damn fool to have discussed major decisions with the full Cabinet present, because I knew that if I said something in the morning, you could sure as hell bet it would appear in the afternoon papers. It's the same thing with the National Security Council. Everybody there's got their damned deputies and note-takers with them sitting along the wall. I will warn you now, the leaks can kill you. I don't even let Hubert sit in on some of those meetings for fear his staff might let something out. And even with all the precautions I take, things still leak."

Johnson shifted his massive frame to one side of the chair and rocked toward me again. "If it hadn't been for Edgar Hoover," he said, "I couldn't have carried out my responsibilities as Commander in Chief. Period. Dick, you will come to depend on Edgar. He is a pillar of strength in a city of weak men. You will rely on him time and time again to maintain security. He's the only one you can put your complete trust in."

I told Johnson that I knew one of his greatest disappointments was that he had not been able to end the war before leaving office. I assured him that we would do everything possible to bring the war to an early and honorable conclusion, and that when the goal was accomplished I would see to it that he received the credit due him. I told him he could be proud of having stood up to his critics, particularly those in his own party.

Johnson mentioned, as he had at our meeting during the summer, the letter of support that David Eisenhower had written to him. He said, "That was a time when I wasn't receiving a whole lot of letters like that from college students." He looked over his shoulder at the Rose Garden. His eyes moistened and his voice softened. "I am mighty proud of my family and particularly proud of my two sons-in-law, who are fighting in Vietnam," he said. "You can be equally proud of your family."

My daughter Julie first met David Eisenhower at his grandfather's second inauguration in 1957, when they were both eight years old. They did not see each other at all during the early 1960s; it was a geographical coincidence that brought them together again. In 1966 David began his freshman year at Amherst College and Julie began her freshman year at Smith College, only a few miles away. One day he called her on an impulse and asked if he could come over to see her. They met, they fell in love, and just before the start of their sophomore year they told Pat and me that they planned to marry.

On the night their engagement was announced I wrote a note for Julie and left it on her bed table.

The wedding was set for December 22. I told Julie that she should give serious consideration to waiting until after the inauguration and being married in the White House. That was a unique privilege, and I wanted to be sure that she did not renounce it lightly. But both she and David felt that they wanted their wedding ceremony to be as personal and non-political as it possibly could.

RICHARD M. NIXON

November 22, 1967

Dear Julie —

I suppose no father believes any boy is good enough for his daugter.

But I believe both David and you are lucky to have found each other —

Fina often says — "Miss Julie always brings life into the home"

In the many years ahead you will have ups and downs but I know you will always "bring life into your home" wherever it is —

Love

Daddy

Dr. Norman Vincent Peale's Marble Collegiate Church in New York had played such an important and happy part in our family's life since we moved to New York that Julie felt very deeply about being married there and about having all reporters and cameramen excluded from the ceremony.

Just as the preparations had reached their height on the evening of the rehearsal and the wedding party dinner, I came down with the flu and had to be given medication to lower my fever. I was determined, however, not to miss any of the events and not to let Julie or David know that I was not feeling well.

The church was beautifully decorated for Christmas with fresh pine boughs and red bows draped over the balconies and a large wreath behind the altar. Red and white poinsettias banked the entire front of the church and surrounded the small white prie-dieu on which David and Julie knelt during the ceremony.

The most memorable moment for me was when I gave Julie away at the altar. She suddenly turned and kissed me. This impulsive, spontaneous gesture brought tears to the eyes of many in the church—including mine.

It was not until I had joined Pat in our pew that the reality of what was happening hit me. Until now I had always thought of our family as a complete unit. Now it would be larger, but it would also be different. I could not help thinking back to one of my first conversations with Paul Douglas, the senator from Illinois, shortly after I had entered the Senate in 1950. One day we had lunch together and he asked me about my family. I told him about Tricia and Julie, and suddenly he became very pensive. He said, "I've got a little girl that all of a sudden became a teenager without my realizing it. It wasn't long ago she was just a tiny girl. Now she's a young lady, and I was so caught up in my work that I missed the years in between. Don't let that happen to you."

Pat and I had always been careful to set aside time each day to spend with the girls. But there were all the times when we were away campaigning or on official trips or when we would suddenly be called on to fill in for the Eisenhowers and would not be able to have dinner at home.

Our family time together in California before I embarked on the governor's race had been far too brief. I knew that Pat and the girls thought that the move to New York would finally put an end to politics. But here we were, almost six years later, and I was the President-elect. I felt tremendous joy and pride watching my daughter get married but I couldn't help wondering if it would not have been possible to have spent even a little more time with her, and regretting that I had not tried harder to do so.

Mamie Eisenhower had been hospitalized a week earlier with a respiratory infection, so she as well as General Eisenhower saw the wedding from Walter Reed Hospital on a closed-circuit television hookup. Eisenhower had been unhappy about the length of David's hair, and he told me that he had offered him a hundred dollars if he would have it cut short. David usually respected his grandfather's wishes, but he got only a light trim. I could not help noticing at the ceremony that despite Eisenhower's concern, David's hair was considerably shorter than any of his college friends' in the wedding party, and I thought that at least in comparative terms he might have put in a claim for the reward, but he never did—and Eisenhower never paid.

The reception after the ceremony was held at the Plaza Hotel. David and Julie chose "Edelweiss" from *The Sound of Music* as their first dance. I do not think I have ever felt lighter on my feet than when I tapped David's shoulder and cut in for my dance with the bride. In my toast I mentioned the joyous things that had happened that day: the Apollo VIII astronauts had gone into the first manned moon orbit; the North Koreans had released the crew of the *Pueblo*; and the wedding.

When they were ready to leave for their honeymoon in Florida, Julie threw her bridal bouquet—into Tricia's waiting hands. During the wedding Julie had worn the same thin blue garter that Mamie Doud had worn on July 1, 1916, when she married Lieutenant Dwight Eisenhower. Julie had therefore given David a different garter to throw to the waiting groomsmen.

That night Pat and I sat in front of the fire in our apartment and talked about the day and how beautiful Julie had looked and about how perfect the ceremony had been. But I know that we were both thinking about time: about how fast it goes, and about how little of it there is to do the important things with the people who really matter to you.

As I anticipated becoming President, I found that I was awed by the prospect but not fearful of it. I felt prepared. I had the advantage of experience and of the detachment that comes from being out of office. The "wilderness years" had been years of education and growth.

I had no illusions about either the difficulty of the challenge or about my ability to meet it. I felt I knew what would *not* work. On the other hand, I was less sure what *would* work. I did not have all the answers. But I did have definite ideas about the changes I felt were needed.

As 1968 came to a close, I was a happy man. At Key Biscayne a wreath hung on the front door and a beautifully trimmed Christmas tree stood in the living room. David and Julie came over from their honeymoon retreat in Palm Beach to join Pat and Tricia and me for Christmas dinner. Far out in space Apollo VIII orbited the moon while astronaut

Frank Borman read the story of the Creation from the Book of Genesis. Those were days rich with happiness and full of anticipation and hope.

On Sunday morning, January 19, 1969, Pat and I attended Norman Vincent Peale's morning service at Marble Collegiate Church, and in the afternoon we boarded the plane Johnson had sent to bring us to Washington.

I spent my last evening as a private citizen putting the final touches on my inaugural address. At about eight o'clock Eisenhower called me from Walter Reed.

"Hi, Dick!" he said. "I want to wish you the best on what I am sure will be a great day tomorrow." He paused for a moment. "I have only one regret. This is the last time that I can call you Dick. From now on it will always be Mr. President."

THE PRESIDENCY
1969–1972

On inauguration day, January 20, 1969, I woke at 7:45 A.M. and had breakfast with Pat in our suite. Then we attended a prayer service in the State Department Auditorium before driving to the White House. As our car slowly turned into the driveway, we could see the Johnsons waiting for us on the porch under the North Portico.

We went in for the traditional coffee and rolls in the Red Room. "I think maybe you should deliver my address today, Hubert," I said to Humphrey in an attempt to keep the mood light.

"That's what I had planned to do, Dick," he replied with a smile.

I remembered from 1961 how painful this ceremony could be for a man who had lost a close election, and I was touched by Humphrey's graceful show of good humor.

During the short ride to the Capitol, Johnson waved to the crowds lining the route and carried on a lively conversation all the way. That night I dictated a note about what he said:

> Riding down to the Capitol, Johnson spoke with very strong feeling with regard to Muskie and Agnew.
>
> He said that at a dinner the night before, a group of people were talking about how much Muskie had contributed to the campaign. He, Johnson, had replied that all the press had slobbered over Muskie, but when it came down to votes Muskie had

delivered Maine with four votes, whereas Agnew could take credit or at least a great deal of the credit on South Carolina, North Carolina, Virginia, Tennessee, and Kentucky. Obviously, he liked Agnew and had very little use for Muskie.

For the swearing in, Pat held the same two Milhous family Bibles that she had held in 1953 and 1957. I had requested that they be opened to Isaiah 2:4: "They shall beat their swords into plowshares, and their spears into pruning hooks: nation shall not lift up sword against nation, neither shall they learn war any more."

After Chief Justice Earl Warren administered the oath, I delivered my inaugural address.

My major theme was peace. I said: "The greatest honor history can bestow is the title of peacemaker. This honor now beckons America. . . . If we succeed, generations to come will say of us now living that we mastered our moment, that we helped make the world safe for mankind. This is our summons to greatness."

When we were ready to begin the inaugural parade from the Capitol back to the White House, I saw that the Secret Service had put the top on the presidential limousine. The agent in charge explained that there were several hundred demonstrators along the route and there had already been some skirmishes with the police and the other spectators.

For the first few blocks the cheering crowds were friendly. Around 12th Street I could see protest signs waving above a double line of police struggling to keep the crowd back. Suddenly a barrage of sticks, stones, beer cans, and what looked like firecrackers began sailing through the air toward us. Some of them hit the side of the car and fell into the street. I could hear the protesters' shrill chant: "Ho, Ho, Ho Chi Minh, the NLF is going to win." A Vietcong flag was lifted, and there was a brief scuffle as some in the crowd tried to tear it down. Seconds later we rounded the corner onto 15th Street, and the atmosphere changed completely. A loud cheer rose from the crowds on the sidewalks in front of the Washington Hotel and the Treasury Building. I was angered that a group of protesters carrying a Vietcong flag had made us captives inside the car. I told the driver to open the sun roof and to let the other agents know that Pat and I were going to stand up so the people could see us.

That night we attended each of the four inaugural balls. It was about 1:30 A.M. when we returned to the White House. Tricia and Julie found the refrigerator stocked with butter brickle ice cream and Dr Pepper, left by the Johnson girls.

I sat down at the grand piano in the center hall of the Family Quarters and played "Rustle of Spring" and a song I had composed for Pat before we were married.

When we had all gathered on the sofas in the West Hall Pat said with a happy sigh, "It's good to be home." Everyone looked up. The White House was now our home.

The White House is both a national museum and a home. The great historical rooms are primarily on the ground and first floors—the East Room, the Green, Blue, and Red Rooms, and the State Dining Room. The private rooms on the second and third floors are known as the Residence or the Family Quarters. Their personality changes with every administration.

In decorating our Family Quarters Pat chose yellows, blues, and golds—sunny, California colors. Tricia, who lived with us until her marriage in 1971, took Lynda Bird Johnson's room, which looked out over Pennsylvania Avenue and Lafayette Park. The bright and airy third-floor Solarium, which had been a schoolroom for the Kennedy children and then a no-adults-admitted teenage party room for Luci and Lynda Johnson, became our family room.

Yet even in the Family Quarters, history surrounds you. When I asked for a regular bed rather than the large canopied four-poster used by Johnson, the bed that was brought out of storage for me turned out to have been first Truman's and then Eisenhower's. I could not help thinking that here was a case in which politics had literally bred strange bedfellows.

From John Adams to Theodore Roosevelt the President and his staff worked in the White House itself. But TR's family of six children and their menagerie of cats, dogs, raccoons, snakes, a pony, and a bear proved too much and he requested the addition of a West Wing.

The West Wing is actually a small three-story office building. On the ground floor are the Oval Office, the Cabinet Room, and another meeting room, which we called the Roosevelt Room. During World War II an East Wing was added to provide additional offices for the President's staff and the staff of the First Lady.

Even after Pat had warmed the Oval Office with a rich blue and gold rug and vibrant gold sofas and curtains, it was still undeniably formal. I decided, therefore, to have a second and more comfortable office in the old Executive Office Building, which is next to the White House, separated from it by a narrow closed-off street. Reporters usually referred to the EOB office as my "small hideaway office," but it was almost as large as the Oval Office. Pat filled the shelves with my favorite books and decorated it with some of the mementos I had collected over the years. There were many family photographs, but the one that meant the most to me was a picture of Pat, Tricia, Julie, and me, taken on the day we moved back to California after I lost the 1960 presidential election. Julie once wrote to me, "I like to think that the reason you kept it on your desk was that it symbolized the happiness that we felt as a family in the midst of a difficult defeat and a difficult new start for you in private life after serving so many years as congressman, senator, and Vice President." I preferred working and thinking surrounded by these personal things rather than by the formal atmosphere of the Oval Office.

From the first days, I also used the Lincoln Sitting Room on the second floor of the White House for the work I did at night after dinner. It is a small room that was used as an office by Lincoln's secretaries, John Hay and John Nicolay. Pat added a few special touches to the decoration, including my favorite old brown velvet easy chair and footstool that I had brought from my study in our New York apartment.

For the Oval Office I requested the antique desk that I had used in my ceremonial office in the Capitol when I was Vice President. For the EOB office we brought in the desk and chair Eisenhower had used in the Oval Office. It had been in storage since Kennedy decided to replace it with a desk Franklin D. Roosevelt had used during his presidency.

Above the mantel in the Oval Office, Johnson had a portrait of FDR holding the Atlantic Charter. I replaced it with a Gilbert Stuart portrait of George Washington. Following White House tradition, I personally selected portraits of three predecessors for the Cabinet Room. I chose Eisenhower, Woodrow Wilson, and Theodore Roosevelt.

Lyndon Johnson had been captivated by gadgets and electronic equipment and he felt a constant need to know what was being said about him in the press and on television. Standing against the wall of the Oval Office to the left of his desk was a large specially constructed cabinet with insulated sides and a thick glass top, housing two constantly clattering wire service news tickers. Next to it, a long low cabinet concealed three large-screen color TV sets arranged side by side. Using a special remote control device, Johnson could watch the three networks simultaneously while switching back and forth among them for the sound. There was a similar three-set console in the small office adjacent to the Oval Office, and still another in the President's bedroom. I told Haldeman that I would like a single set put in the small office, and that all the others were to be removed, along with the wire service machines.

I discovered a mass of wires and cables underneath Johnson's bed. I was told that some were for his telephones, some were remote control wires for the TV sets, and some were for tape recording equipment connected to the phones. I asked that they all be removed.

One other piece of Johnsonian paraphernalia was the shower in the President's private bathroom in the Residence. It consisted of half a dozen different jets and showerheads, controlled by a complicated panel of knobs. My first few attempts at using it nearly flung me out of the stall, so I asked that it be replaced with a regular overhead fixture.

I slept only about four hours my first night in the White House, and was up at 6:45 A.M. While I was shaving, I remembered the hidden safe that Johnson had shown me during our visit in November. When I opened it, the safe looked empty. Then I saw a thin folder on the top shelf. It contained the daily Vietnam Situation Report from the intelligence services for the previous day, Johnson's last day in office.

I quickly read through it. The last page contained the latest casualty figures. During the week ending January 18, 185 Americans had been killed and 1,237 wounded. From January 1, 1968 to January 18, 1969, 14,958 men had been killed and 95,798 had been wounded. I closed the folder and put it back in the safe and left it there until the war was over, a constant reminder of its tragic cost.

On February 17 Soviet Ambassador Anatoly Dobrynin came to the White House to pay his first official call.

I told him that I wanted to have completely open communications with him and with the leaders of his government.

"Both you and I, Mr. Ambassador, recognize the very fundamental differences that exist between us," I said. "We may or may not be able to settle them. I hope that we will. But you and I must at least make sure that no differences arise between us because of lack of communication."

Kissinger had suggested that we develop a private channel between Dobrynin and him. I agreed that Dobrynin might be more forthcoming in strictly private and unpublicized meetings and we arranged for him to arrive unseen through a seldom-used East Wing door so that no one need know they had met. Within a short time they were meeting weekly, often over lunch.

When Dobrynin said that his government wanted to begin talks in the area of arms limitation, I expressed my feeling that progress in one area must logically be linked to progress in other areas.

"History makes it clear that wars result not so much from arms, or even from arms races, as they do from underlying political differences and political problems," I said. "So I think it is incumbent on us, when we begin strategic arms talks, to do what we can in a parallel way to defuse critical political situations like the Middle East and Vietnam and Berlin, where there is a danger that arms might be put to use."

Before Dobrynin left, he handed me an official seven-page note from Moscow which indicated that the Soviets were prepared to move forward on a whole range of topics, including the Middle East, Central Europe, Vietnam, and arms control.

This note seemed to augur well for our policy of linkage. The major question, of course, was whether the Soviets would follow up on their words with action.

EUROPE AND de GAULLE

On February 23 I left Washington for an eight-day working visit to Europe. I wanted this trip, my first abroad as President, to establish the principle that we would consult with our allies before negotiating with our potential adversaries. I also wanted to show the world that the new American President was not completely obsessed with Vietnam, and to dramatize for Americans at home that, despite opposition to the war, their President could still be received abroad with respect and even enthusiasm.

Most important, I felt that President de Gaulle's cooperation would be vital to ending the Vietnam war and to my plans for beginning a new relationship with Communist China. France had diplomatic relations with Hanoi and Peking, and Paris would be the best place to open secret channels of communication between us and them. But de Gaulle had become seriously alienated from America during the last several years. In 1966 he had NATO headquarters removed from France. Whether we would be able to use Paris as a site for our diplomatic overtures would depend on my ability to overcome the estrangement that had grown up between us and to establish a relationship of trust and confidence with de Gaulle.

The first stop was Brussels, where I set the tone for the trip when I told the North Atlantic Council, "I have come for work, not for ceremony; to inquire, not to insist; to consult, not to convince; to listen and learn, and to begin what I hope will be a continuing interchange of ideas and insight."

In London I had a luncheon with Queen Elizabeth, and a long informal conversation with nineteen prominent British citizens. I had a private talk with Prime Minister Wilson in a comfortable room at 10 Downing Street. A warm fire cast a glow over the room and after a few minutes Wilson leaned back in his chair and put his feet up on the table. He was wearing carpet slippers. Our conversation ranged from America's position in Vietnam to Britain's role in Europe. Wilson had met the Soviet leaders when he visited Moscow, and he offered his impressions of their different personalities. He said that if Brezhnev had been born in Britain he probably would have ended up Secretary General of the Trades Union Council, and if Kosygin had been an Englishman he would likely have become Chairman of Imperial Chemical Industries.

A potentially awkward situation arose when Wilson gave a small dinner party for me at 10 Downing Street. In 1962 the British magazine *New Statesman* had described my defeat by Pat Brown as "a victory for decency in public life." John Freeman, who had then been the magazine's editor, had recently been appointed British ambassador in Washington. That evening at Downing Street would be the first time that he and I would be in the same room in an intimate social setting.

I decided to relieve the tension by addressing it directly. In my toast after dinner I said that American journalists had written far worse things about me than had appeared in Freeman's magazine. It was now a part of the past and best forgotten. "After all," I said, "he's the new diplomat, and I'm the new statesman."

The men thumped the table and called, "Hear, hear." When I sat down, Wilson slid his menu to me. On the back of it he had written: "That was one of the kindest and most generous acts I have known in a quarter of a century in politics. Just proves my point. You can't guarantee being born a lord. It is possible—you've shown it—to be born a gentleman."

We had feared antiwar demonstrations, and a few took place during this trip, but none could mar the overwhelmingly friendly reaction of the large crowds that greeted us everywhere we went in London, Paris, Bonn, Brussels, Berlin, and Rome. Whenever possible, I took impromptu walks or plunged into the crowds to shake hands and meet people.

The high point of this trip personally and substantively was my series of meetings with de Gaulle. When *Air Force One* taxied to the terminal at Orly Airport, I could see him standing coatless at the foot of the ramp. I had been told that the temperature was just above freezing, but I immediately took off my overcoat. As we shook hands, de Gaulle greeted me in English—a virtually unprecedented personal gesture for him.

When we met privately that afternoon at the Elysée Palace, the first topic of discussion was the Soviet Union.

He said that the central fact of life for postwar Europe was the Soviet threat, but he believed that the Soviets themselves had become preoccupied with China. He said, "They are thinking in terms of a possible clash

That was one of the kindest and most generous acts I have known in a quarter of a century in politics.

Just proves my point.

You can't guarantee being born a lord. It is possible — you've shown it — to be born a gentleman.

H.

DINNER

in honour of

The President of the

United States of America

The Rt. Hon.
The Prime Minister

10 Downing Street,
25th February, 1969

with China, and they know they can't fight the West at the same time. Thus I believe that they may end up opting for a policy of rapprochement with the West." He thought that the Russians' traditional fear of German armies would give added impetus to whatever inclination they already had toward détente.

"As far as the West is concerned," he continued, "what choice do we have? Unless you are prepared to go to war or to break down the Berlin Wall, then there is no alternative policy that is acceptable. To work toward détente is a matter of good sense: if you are not ready to make war, make peace."

"If the Russians made a move," I asked, "do you think they believe that the United States would react with strategic weapons? And do the Europeans have confidence that we would move in answer to a Soviet attack, or the threat of an attack, by massive conventional ground forces?"

"I can only answer for the French," he replied. "We believe that the Russians know that the United States could not allow them to conquer Europe. But we also believe that if the Russians marched, you would not use nuclear weapons right away, since it would imply a total effort to kill everyone on the other side. If both the Russians and the United States were to use tactical nuclear weapons, Europe would be destroyed. Western Europe and the United Kingdom would be destroyed by Soviet tactical weapons, and East Germany, Poland, Czechoslovakia, and Hungary would be destroyed by American tactical weapons. Meanwhile, the United States and the Soviet Union would not be harmed."

That night there was a state dinner at the Elysée. I talked with Madame de Gaulle, a woman of great strength and character. Her main concerns were her husband and her family. She observed, "The presidency is temporary—but the family is permanent."

The next day de Gaulle and I met in the Grand Trianon Palace at Versailles. "Louis XIV ruled Europe from this room," he said as we stood at one of the huge windows looking out over acres of formal gardens.

We talked about the tragic effect World War II had had on the great nations of Europe. He compressed volumes of history into a single sentence when he said, "In the Second World War, all the nations of Europe lost. Two were defeated."

I turned our conversation to China. As we talked, I could see that his thinking paralleled my own. "I have no illusions about their ideology," he said, "but I do not feel that we should leave them isolated in their rage. The West should try to get to know China, to have contacts, and to penetrate it."

"In looking down the road," I said, "as I pursue my talks with the Soviets, I too might want to keep an anchor to windward with respect to China. In ten years, when China has made significant nuclear progress, we will have no choice. It is vital that we have more communications with them than we have today."

"It would be better for you to recognize China before you are obliged to do so by the growth of China," he agreed.

We returned to Paris from Versailles late in the afternoon, and that night I was host for a return dinner in de Gaulle's honor. He confirmed his acceptance of my invitation to visit the United States, and we agreed that a working visit similar to this one would be the most useful. We settled on January or February 1970 as the best time.

In his toast that night de Gaulle said, "As I am learning to know you better—and by this visit you have given me that opportunity which I consider historic—I appreciate more the statesman and the man that you are."

I felt that the new entente cordiale between the Presidents of France and the United States expressed by his words would alone have made the European trip worthwhile.

We discussed Vietnam at our meeting on my last day in France. America had become deeply involved in Vietnam despite de Gaulle's warnings and without seeking his advice, so I opened the session by asking, "Mr. President, what would you do regarding Vietnam?"

He paused for a long time before he spoke. "What is it you expect me to do, Mr. President?" he asked. "Do you want me to tell you what I would do if I were in your place? But I am not in your place!"

He said that he believed the only way to end the war was by conducting negotiations on political and military issues simultaneously and by establishing a calendar for the departure of our troops. "I do not believe that you should depart with undue haste."

He leaned forward and placed his large hands flat on the table and said, "I recognize that France had some part in this as she did not give the Vietnamese freedom early enough and thus enabled the Communists to pose as the champions of national independence, first against us and then against you. But you Americans can make this kind of settlement because your power and wealth are so great that you can do it with dignity."

When he suggested that direct conversations with the North Vietnamese would be the best way to make progress, I indicated great interest in attempting this. De Gaulle said nothing more and our meetings drew to a close, but I felt confident that the message would be passed to the North Vietnamese Embassy.

Our last stop was at the Vatican, where I met with Pope Paul VI. We discussed the whole range of world issues and problems, but he was particularly interested to learn about my plans concerning Vietnam. He talked about the importance of resisting the spread of communism in

Southeast Asia. He recalled how the Communists had murdered Christians and suppressed religion after they took over North Vietnam in 1954, and with emotion in his voice he agreed that America should continue to hold the line against the Communists in South Vietnam.

I felt that the European trip had accomplished all the goals we set for it. It showed the NATO leaders that a new and interested administration which respected their views had come to power in Washington. It served warning on the Soviets that they could no longer take for granted —nor take advantage of—Western disunity. And the TV and press coverage had a positive impact at home, instilling, however briefly, some much needed pride into our sagging national morale.

EISENHOWER

President Eisenhower's rapidly failing health cast a sad shadow over the early days of my presidency. He had been in Walter Reed Hospital since April 1968, and there was little hope that he would ever leave it.

When I visited him before my trip, he had asked me to extend his regards to some of his old friends, particularly de Gaulle. "I don't think we handled him right, now that I look back on it," he had said. "Roosevelt and Churchill were too inconsiderate of him. They treated his pride as if it were just vanity, and they never saw that a few gestures of recognition might have made him less antagonistic toward us."

When I went to see him after I returned from Europe, I was so shocked at the deterioration of his condition that later I made a note, "Looked like a corpse—waxen face." As soon as he saw me, however, he brightened, raised his hand, and called out, "Hi!"

Even though it was visibly painful for him to talk, he insisted on having a conversation. "You know, the doctors say I'm getting better," he said. Always the optimist, perhaps he believed it.

I told him that the leaders of Europe had sent their regards to him, and I said, "You were absolutely right about de Gaulle." I told him that the Pope had said he was praying for him and hoping that a miracle might occur and bring about his complete recovery.

Shortly after noon on Friday, March 28, I had walked back from an NSC meeting to the Oval Office with Haldeman, Kissinger, and Mel Laird. While we were talking, Dr. Walter Tkach, the White House physician, entered the room. Standing near the door he said, "Mr. President, President Eisenhower just died." I knew that he had been sinking fast, but the news hit me so hard that I could not speak. A wave of sadness swept over me, and I could not hold back tears.

Mamie met us at the door of the presidential suite when we arrived at

Walter Reed. I embraced her and told her how we all shared her loss. Julie and David had been there when he died. David was pale and shaken, and I could see that Julie had been crying.

When I got back to the White House, I decided to go to Camp David to write the eulogy I would deliver in the Capitol Rotunda on Sunday.

I talked with Mamie briefly on the telephone about plans for the funeral service, and then she said, "Maybe you would like to know the last thing Ike said to me before he died. You know how weak he was, but he was wide awake. He knew I was sitting there, and he said, 'I have always loved my wife. I have always loved my children. I have always loved my grandchildren. And I have always loved my country.' " I wrote down the words because I knew that I would want to use them in the eulogy.

Perhaps the best description I can give of Dwight Eisenhower is that he had a warm smile and icy blue eyes. It was not a case of being outwardly warm and inwardly cold. Rather, beneath his captivating personal appearance was a lot of finely tempered hard steel. He had exceptional warmth; but there was always a reserve, even an aloofness, that balanced it. Masses of people all over the world thought they knew him, but the people closest to him, his friends and colleagues who loved or admired him, understood that even they did not really know him well.

While most people probably remember him for his engaging, outgoing personality, I remember him for his decisive leadership. He was at his best in times of crisis and when he had to deal with great issues. It has become popular to think of the 1950s in nostalgic terms as a time of domestic apathy and international stability. But in fact, Eisenhower became President just as America and the world had reached a turning point in history, when the proliferation of nuclear weapons and the rise of Soviet militancy had forever changed the nature of international relations.

One of the questions Eisenhower had to address was whether we would utilize our nuclear advantage and fight a total war or confine ourselves to applying only limited military strength. I made a diary dictation describing Eisenhower's decisive approach to this question at an NSC meeting on March 25, 1954:

> At the NSC meeting this morning there was a discussion of what the strategy of the United States should be in the event of a major war with the Soviet Union. The Joint Chiefs of Staff had a division on this point. The President took over in as emphatic a manner as I have ever seen him use. He stated that he felt this was a problem for the Commander in Chief primarily. He said that the only policy we could follow once war was started against

> us was to win victory. That under no circumstances could we hold back punches because of some feeling that total victory might bring greater problems than if victory were obtained through limited war. He said, in effect, that there was no possibility of a limited-war concept in view of the type of enemy we had and the type of weapons with which we have to reckon. He said we are talking about sizes of bombs and potential destructive power in fantastic amounts and that the casualties would reach 7 million one day, 8 million another possibly. He said in other words they would be in "Amos and Andy" figures.
>
> He softened it to an extent by suggesting that the Joint Chiefs talk to him about it privately at any time to attempt to convince him, if they wanted, that his view was wrong. At the present time, he was convinced that this is the only sound position to take.
>
> The only qualification he made was that we might consider not using our strongest weapon if we felt from a military standpoint the reaction would be so great as to make that use unadvisable. For example, he told of how the allies had discovered thousands of tons of much more deadly gas than anybody had believed existed when they overran the German positions in World War II. The Germans had not used it because they realized they were more vulnerable to gas in their constricted positions than were the Allies.
>
> He also objected to a paragraph which said that we should insist on countries in effect being free and democratic after the war. He pointed out that in the next war every country would come out a dictatorship inevitably and would have to remain a dictatorship for some time. He, of course, said they would try in the United States to return to a free economy as soon as possible but that it would be more difficult in the future than it had been in the past wars.

While he had an engaging, outgoing personality, he also had a very definite sense of dignity. He was not the kind of man who appreciated undue familiarity. I remember the chilling looks he gave to those who tugged at his sleeve or slapped him on the back. In this respect he could not have been more different from Lyndon Johnson, who seemed unable to carry on a conversation without nudging or poking or even shaking the other person. General Jerry Persons, who had been with Eisenhower during the war years and then served as his Director of Congressional Relations before succeeding Adams as chief of the White House staff in 1958, told me of an occasion in 1959 when Eisenhower called him in shortly before Johnson was due to arrive for a meeting. "I want you to stand between Lyndon and me," Eisenhower told him. "My bursitis is kicking up, and I don't want him to grab me by the arm."

What seemed most characteristic of Eisenhower was his determined optimism. He was constantly waging a battle for high spirits on his staff. Hardly a meeting went by without some exhortation to cheerfulness. "Long faces don't win hard battles," he once told the Cabinet. "Why can't our people have a grin on their face instead of always a frown?" he asked during a meeting with legislative leaders. Yet though he enjoyed a good joke, he saw little humor in the weighty problems of his office, and he did not particularly like it when others introduced humor into serious discussions.

One afternoon early in his administration, a legislative leadership meeting debated whether to prepare the public for the horrors of nuclear war. Eisenhower strongly felt that something had to be done to develop civil defense and national preparedness. At one point, Senator Eugene Millikin, a conservative Republican from Colorado, recalled what a Colorado governor once said when confronted with some excessively dire predictions regarding his policies: "Well, if things are so bad maybe what we ought to do is paint our asses white and run with the antelope." Everyone laughed, but Eisenhower's laughter was not very enthusiastic. As we returned to the discussion, he said, rather shortly, "Well, maybe we won't even have time to paint our asses white if they begin to drop the bombs and we are not prepared for it."

Eisenhower often said that he himself never read newspaper editorial columns or looked at the political cartoons; in fact he was extremely sensitive about them, as evidenced in a diary note I made in June 1954, when Eisenhower gave vigorous expression to his views about press criticism:

> At the legislative leaders meeting on Monday morning, June 21, Jerry Persons brought up an article which had been written by Drew Pearson to the effect that the President was not going to support Bridges and several other senators.
>
> The President blew his top and said that he wished that everybody in his whole organization would quit reading the columnists and quit reporting such incidents to him.

Eisenhower was not used to being criticized, and he found criticism hard to take. He never forgave Truman for his widely quoted quips about his lack of political experience during the 1952 campaign. "Why, this fellow don't know any more about politics than a pig knows about Sunday," Truman once said.

At one point during the administration we were planning a big bipartisan rally to build support for the mutual security program. I suggested that Truman, who supported the program, be invited to appear on the platform. A cold, hard look came over Eisenhower's face, and he said that he would not appear on the same platform with Truman no matter what was at stake.

As a political leader, Eisenhower knew that he was much stronger than his party. He felt that by doing a good job he could pull his party up; and he did not want his party to drag him down. The serious erosion of Republican strength during the years of his presidency was in some measure the result of this hands-off, arm's-length attitude. Yet he knew better than most politicians how to move people, how to rally the nation to his support, and how to inspire their faith and win their trust—and these are the essence of politics.

Contrary to the generally held view that Eisenhower was a staid standpatter, he actually welcomed and encouraged new and even unorthodox ideas.

Early in 1954 I made a diary note of a conversation I had with Persons in which I was especially struck by his description of Eisenhower's style:

> He said that the difficulty with some of the people around the President is that every word that the President spoke they took as gospel. Jerry said that those who worked with him before knew that they should not do this and that the President many times would take a very forward position and finally settle upon one which was not so far out front.
>
> "Yep," he said, "Ike sure likes to hit those fungoes out there and see what happens to them!"

To many, Dwight Eisenhower seemed a rather kindly and benign grandfather, but his own view of himself and his conception of the presidency were quite different. He saw himself in very active terms as the man responsible for doing the right thing for America.

The last time I saw Eisenhower was two days before his death. His doctor greeted me outside the entrance to the presidential suite. "How's he doing?" I asked.

"I'm afraid there's not much hope, Mr. President," he replied.

I talked with Eisenhower for about fifteen minutes before the doctor came in to indicate that I should leave. Eisenhower obviously did not want me to go. But I could see that he was tiring fast, so I shook hands with him and walked quickly to the door.

It struck me that this was probably the last time I would see him alive.

I turned impulsively and tried to keep the emotion out of my voice as I said: "General, I just want you to know how all the free people of Europe and millions of others in the world will forever be in your debt for the leadership you provided in war and peace. You can always take great pride in the fact that no man in our history has done more to make America and the world a better and safer place in which to live."

His eyes were closed as I spoke, but after a brief moment he opened them and lifted his head from the pillow. With an unusual formality he said, "Mr. President, you do me great honor in what you have just said."

Then he slowly raised his hand to his forehead in a final salute.

OPERATION BREAKFAST

We had wondered whether a new President and a serious new peace overture would produce a breakthrough that would end the Vietnam war. The North Vietnamese gave us the answer in February when they launched a small-scale but savage offensive into South Vietnam. It was a deliberate test, clearly designed to take the measure of me and my administration at the outset.

My immediate instinct was to retaliate. Kissinger and I agreed that if we let the Communists manipulate us at this early stage, we might never be able to negotiate with them from a position of equality, much less one of strength. Johnson had made this mistake and had never been able to recover the initiative.

This view was shared by General Creighton Abrams, the U.S. Commander in Vietnam, and by Ambassador Ellsworth Bunker in Saigon. When the Communists stepped up their offensive, both Abrams and Bunker recommended B-52 bombing runs against their supply lines in the Cambodian sanctuaries.

Bill Rogers and Mel Laird opposed this recommendation. They feared the fury of Congress and the media if I expanded the war into Cambodia. But Kissinger argued, "What do we care if the New York *Times* clobbers us now if it helps us end the war sooner?" I agreed with him, but I decided to postpone a final decision about the bombing until I returned from the European trip, because a leak of plans to bomb Cambodia might have triggered serious antiwar demonstrations abroad. I directed that a cable be sent to Bunker through regular channels saying that all discussions of bombing should be suspended. I simultaneously sent a top secret "back-channel" message—a routing outside the official system—to General Abrams telling him to ignore the message to Bunker and to continue planning the B-52 strikes on a contingency basis even though I would have to withhold approval until after my trip.

While I was in Europe, the Communist offensive intensified. At a press conference two days after my return I was asked what our reaction would be. "We have not moved in a precipitate fashion," I said, "but the fact that we have shown patience and forbearance should not be considered as a sign of weakness. . . . An appropriate response to these attacks will be made if they continue."

Ten days later, on the morning of my next press conference, the North Vietnamese mounted a new attack across the DMZ. In reply to a question about whether my patience was growing thin with this kind of provocation, I said, "You may recall that on March 4, when I received a similar question, at an earlier stage in the attacks, I issued what was interpreted widely as a warning. It will be my policy as President to issue a warning only once, and I will not repeat it now. Anything in the future that is done will be done."

On Sunday, March 16, I met for two hours with Rogers, Laird, Kissinger, and General Earle Wheeler, the Chairman of the Joint Chiefs, to review the military and diplomatic situation in Vietnam.

I asked for the latest casualty figures. Because of the Communist offensive, they were high. Three hundred fifty-one Americans had died during the past week, 453 the week before, and 336 the week before that.

Our intelligence reports indicated that over 40,000 Communist troops had secretly been amassed in a zone ten to fifteen miles wide just inside the Cambodian border. Cambodia was a neutral country. We respected that neutrality, but the Communists were blatantly violating it by launching raids across the Cambodian border into South Vietnam and then retreating to the safety of their jungle sanctuaries.

"Gentlemen," I said, "we have reached the point where a decision is required: to bomb or not to bomb."

I assured everyone that I understood the problems and recognized the risks involved in bombing the sanctuaries, no matter how justified such action might be.

"But we have to look at what we're up against," I continued. "The state of play in Paris is completely sterile. I am convinced that the only way to move the negotiations off dead center is to do something on the military front. That is something they will understand."

I said that short of resuming the bombing of North Vietnam, this was the only military action we could take that might succeed in saving American lives and getting the peace negotiations moving.

I concluded, "I have decided to order the bombing to begin as soon as possible. Tomorrow, if the weather is good enough."

The weather was good, and on March 17, B-52 bombers struck the Communist sanctuaries inside the Cambodian border. The Pentagon gave the secret bombing the codename Menu, and the various target areas were designated by different mealtimes. The attack on the first area was called Operation Breakfast. It was the first turning point in my administration's conduct of the Vietnam war.

Maximum precautions were taken to keep the bombing secret, for several reasons. We knew that Prince Sihanouk, the head of the Cambodian government, strongly objected to the presence of the North Vietnamese army in his country. As early as 1968, he had asked the United States to retaliate against the North Vietnamese, either with "hot pursuit" on the ground or by bombing the sanctuaries. We also knew that because of Cambodia's neutral status, Sihanouk could not afford to endorse our actions officially. Therefore, as long as we bombed secretly, we knew that Sihanouk would be silent; if the bombing became known publicly, however, he would be forced to protest it publicly.

We also anticipated that as long as the bombing remained secret, the North Vietnamese would find it difficult to protest since they were officially denying that they had any troops in Cambodia.

Another reason for secrecy was the problem of domestic antiwar protest. My administration was only two months old, and I wanted to provoke as little public outcry as possible at the outset.

In order to preserve the secrecy of the bombing, we informed only Richard Russell and John Stennis, the Chairman and the ranking member of the Senate Armed Services Committee. Although Russell was beginning to have doubts about the war in general, both men thought that the bombing was the right decision, and both said that they would back me up in the event that it became public.

Soon after Operation Breakfast began, there was a steady decline in American casualties in South Vietnam.

EC-121

Less than a month after the secret bombing of the Communist sanctuaries in Cambodia began, we were suddenly confronted with a major crisis from a completely unexpected quarter of the Communist world.

Just before seven in the morning on April 15, my bedside phone began ringing. It was Kissinger. He informed me of reliable but as yet unconfirmed reports that North Korean jets had shot down one of our Navy reconnaissance planes with thirty-one men aboard.

As soon as I got to the Oval Office, I read the fragmentary intelligence reports. The North Koreans had shot down a four-engine propeller-driven EC-121 Navy aircraft which was on a regular reconnaissance mission off the North Korean coast. Such flights had been made for almost twenty years under standing orders that the aircraft not approach closer than forty nautical miles to the coast of North Korea, well outside the international territorial limit.

It was remotely possible that the men aboard the EC-121 had been taken captive in North Korea as the *Pueblo* crew had been fifteen months earlier. All during the day we assumed the worst—that the men were dead—but hoped for the best.

I reacted in the same way and with the same instincts that I had felt when the North Vietnamese offensive began: we were being tested, and therefore force must be met with force.

At ten the next morning, Washington time, I met with the NSC in the Cabinet Room to consider how we would respond to our first international crisis.

Both Rogers and Laird urged restraint. They reasoned that this might be a completely isolated incident, and thought we should stay our hand until we were completely sure what had happened and why. Ted Agnew disagreed. With obvious frustration he asked, "Why do we always take the other guy's position?"

Nothing was decided that morning, but two serious options emerged. Option One involved retaliation by sending a military strike against a North Korean airfield. Option Two involved continuing the EC-121 reconnaissance flights but sending combat escorts with them to ward off any future incidents.

Neither option was ideal. The North Koreans were well armed, and if we chose Option One we would have to be prepared to suffer further losses and to confront the possibility of reopening the fighting in Korea. And Option Two, while it would clearly establish the principle of our right to fly reconnaissance missions in international airspace, was admittedly a very weak protest against what appeared to be the murder of thirty-one men and a deliberate affront to American honor. Americans would rightly wonder about the value of our costly overseas commitments if we could not adequately protect our men and our honor in a situation that was as clear-cut as this one.

In midafternoon we received word that two bodies had been recovered from the water, along with some of the debris of the plane, ninety miles from the coast. There could be no more hope that there had been any survivors nor could there be any doubt that the incident was a calculated and cold-blooded challenge.

Intelligence reports indicated that shooting down the EC-121 was an isolated provocation like the seizure of the *Pueblo*. One of them pointed out that April 14 was the birthday of North Korea's leader, Kim Il-sung, and it was even possible that this was his macabre birthday present to himself. The case against retaliation was strongly supported in an urgent cable from Ambassador William Porter in Seoul, warning that any major military action we took would end up playing into the hands of North Korea's extremist leadership.

On the other hand, Kissinger and I continued to feel that retaliation was important. As he put it, a strong reaction from the United States would be a signal that for the first time in years the United States was sure of itself. It would shore up the morale of our allies and give pause to our enemies. We discussed the possibility that the North Koreans would respond with an attack on South Korea. Kissinger said that he did not believe that would happen, but, if it did, we had to be prepared to take whatever steps were necessary to bring the North Koreans to their knees.

I said that plans should be initiated for Option One. And since Option Two, the immediate resumption of the intelligence flights with fighter escorts, did not preclude the subsequent use of Option One, I decided to go ahead and announce its implementation at a press conference the next morning.

At the press conference, on April 18, I announced: "I have today ordered that these flights be continued. They will be protected. This is not a threat; it is simply a statement of fact."

In the meantime, we began to discuss a third possibility: Option Two backed up with a second round of bombing of the North Vietnamese sanctuaries in Cambodia. This would avoid the risks of a direct retaliation against North Korea, and still would be an effective way to impress the Communist leaders of both North Korea and North Vietnam with our resolve to support our allies and resist aggression.

Before we reached the go stage of the Option One bombing plan, I decided to call it off and adopt this combination of Option Two and a renewal of the secret Menu bombing in Cambodia. This second round, aimed at the next target area, would be called Operation Lunch.

Kissinger still felt that our credibility vis-à-vis the Communist world was at stake in our response to this deliberate challenge. The Soviets, the North Vietnamese, and the Chinese would all be watching. "If we strike back, even though it's risky," he said, "they will say, 'This guy is becoming irrational—we'd better settle with him.' But if we back down, they'll say, 'This guy is the same as his predecessor, and if we wait he'll come to the same end.' "

I still agreed that we had to act boldly; I was just not convinced that this was the time to do it. It was a calculated risk that the North Koreans would not escalate the situation any further if we retaliated with a single strike against one of their airfields. But what if they did and we suddenly found ourselves at war in Korea? As long as we were involved in Vietnam, we simply did not have the resources or public support for another war in another place.

I also had to consider the fact that except for Agnew and Mitchell, most of my top national security advisers, particularly Rogers and

Laird, were strongly opposed to Option One. Kissinger agreed that we could ill afford a Cabinet insurrection at such an early date in the administration. He also agreed that congressional and public opinion were not ready for the shock of a strong retaliation against the Communists in North Korea.

Making my decision in favor of Option Two turned out to be easier than getting it carried out. Despite my April 18 directive—and the public announcement of it—we were faced with a series of postponements, excuses, and delays from the Pentagon, and it was nearly three weeks before my order was implemented. Even worse, we discovered that without informing the White House, the Pentagon had also canceled reconnaissance flights in the Mediterranean. Thus from April 14 to May 8, the United States had not conducted its scheduled aerial reconnaissance in the Mediterranean and the North Pacific—two of the most sensitive areas of the globe.

I was surprised and angered by this situation. The North Koreans would undoubtedly think that they had succeeded in making us back off the reconnaissance flights. Thanks to this incident I learned early in my administration that a President must keep a constant check not just on the way his orders are being followed, but on whether they are being followed at all.

Before long, other issues absorbed us and the EC-121 incident was largely forgotten. Yet I remained troubled by the response we had made —or, as I saw it, that we had failed to make. I told Kissinger, "They got away with it this time, but they'll never get away with it again."

On April 28, de Gaulle resigned as President of France. He had staked his political future on the outcome of a plebiscite involving Senate and regional reforms.

In addition to the public statement wishing de Gaulle well, I wrote him a personal letter. I said, "The message I sent to you through official channels could not convey adequately my deep sense of personal loss when you announced your retirement," and that "I believe history will record that your resignation was a great loss to France and to the cause of freedom and decency in the world."

I extended an open invitation to him and Madame de Gaulle to visit the United States, and at the end I wrote, "Putting it in blunt terms—in this age of mediocre leaders in most of the world—America's spirit needs your presence."

When this letter was personally delivered to him at Colombey, de Gaulle read it and said, "He is a true comrade." Then he sat down at his desk and wrote a reply to be sent back the same day:

> Dear Mr. President:
>
> Your gracious official message and your very warm personal letter touched me deeply. Not only because you occupy the high office of President of the United States, but also because they are from you, Richard Nixon, and I have for you—with good reason—esteem, confidence, and friendship as great and as sincere as it is possible to have.
>
> Perhaps one day I will have the occasion and the honor to see you again; in the meantime, I send you from the bottom of my heart all my best wishes for the successful accomplishment of your immense national and international task.
>
> Would you please give Mrs. Nixon my most respectful regards, to which my wife adds her warm wishes. For you, my dear Mr. President, the assurance of my feeling of faithful and devoted friendship.
>
> Charles de Gaulle

De Gaulle died a year and a half later. I went to Paris for the funeral service in Notre Dame Cathedral, and afterward paid my respects to Georges Pompidou, once de Gaulle's deputy, and now his successor.

Pompidou was rightly known as a rather unemotional man, and he had had his differences with de Gaulle over the years. But after waiting a moment for him to begin the conversation, I looked over and saw that he was choked up and could not speak.

Remembering how I felt after Eisenhower's death, I waited silently until he had composed himself. The two of us had lived and worked for so many of our public years in the shadows of two giants, Eisenhower and de Gaulle. Now both were dead.

Pompidou sighed, and looking at me, said, *"Enfin seuls."* He too must have been thinking about this bond we had shared; now we were alone.

LEAKS AND WIRETAPS

Leaks about the Vietnam war had plagued Lyndon Johnson during the last years of his presidency. At first he was frustrated, then angered, and, finally, nearly obsessed by the need to stop them. He tried to circumvent leaks by working with fewer and fewer people, until he was making national security policy in private Tuesday afternoon luncheon meetings with a tight circle of trusted advisers. I have already described how, when he heard that I had decided to reactivate the NSC system, he told me about his experiences with leaks and predicted that it would be a decision I would regret.

I soon learned that his concerns were fully justified. The leaks began almost with the start of my administration, and before long I experienced firsthand the anger, worry, and frustration that Johnson had described. In the first five months of my presidency, at least twenty-one major stories based on leaks from materials in the NSC files appeared in New York and Washington newspapers. A CIA report listed forty-five newspaper articles in 1969 that contained serious breaches of secrecy.

Within a matter of days after the NSC held its first meeting on the Middle East on February 1, the details of the discussion that had taken place were leaked to the press. Eisenhower, whom I had personally briefed on this meeting, considered any leak of classified foreign policy information whether in war or peace, treasonable. When he saw the news story he telephoned Kissinger and warned him in no uncertain terms. "Tighten your shop," he said. "Get rid of people if you have to, but don't let this go on."

On April 4 the New York *Times* carried a story about Soviet missile deployment based on highly classified information gathered in secret intelligence surveys.

On April 1 an NSC directive was issued that called for a comprehensive new study of alternative policies for Vietnam, including, for the sake of completeness, the radical option of unilateral withdrawal. On April 6, five days after the study was submitted, the New York *Times* reported that the United States was considering a unilateral withdrawal. This came as a shock to our allies and undoubtedly gave encouragement to our enemies.

On April 22 the *Times* ran a story based on our planning sessions for the coming disarmament talks with the Soviets. Two days later the *Times* had a detailed report of our deliberations on whether to post an intelligence ship off North Korea. The next day the *Times* reported a leak from "reliable sources" on our negotiations for arms sales to King Hussein.

I talked with Edgar Hoover and John Mitchell about this problem. Hoover's three suggestions were to conduct background checks on those suspected as possible sources of leaked information, to have them tailed, or to place wiretaps on their telephones. Tapping, he said was the only really effective means of uncovering leakers. He told me that tapping had been authorized by every President starting with FDR.

It was decided that when leaks occurred Kissinger would supply Hoover with the names of individuals who had had access to the leaked materials and whom he had any cause to suspect. I authorized Hoover to take the necessary steps—including wiretapping—to investigate the leaks and find the leakers.

On May 1 the New York *Times* ran a leak from an administration study of the U.S. strategic force posture, including options for improvement ranging from antiballistic missiles to offensive systems and the cost estimates for each. On May 6 the same reporter had an inside story of our deliberations during the EC-121 crisis.

I was in Key Biscayne on May 9, when the early edition of the New York *Times* carried on its front page a disclosure we had been fearing for months. The secret bombing was no longer secret. The headline read: *Raids in Cambodia by U.S. Unprotested.* The story was filed from Washington, and the reporter attributed his information to Nixon administration sources.

The Cambodian bombing policy had worked well. It had saved American lives, the enemy was suffering, and the pressure to negotiate was building. The *Times* leak threatened everything.

Kissinger was enraged, and I was as well. He immediately speculated that the leak must have come from State or Defense. We knew that State Department bureaucrats routinely leaked. But in this particular case, Rogers was the only person at State who had been told about the bombing, and I was certain that he would never leak secret information.

Nor were we naïve about the Pentagon's proclivity for leaking whatever would make the Pentagon look good or advance its positions. But this leak would embarrass Mel Laird and was likely to cause him some uncomfortable moments at coming Capitol Hill hearings.

As I had when several of the earlier leaks had appeared, I suggested that Kissinger take a hard and objective look at his own staff: if there were any leakers in the NSC, better to find out now. Kissinger agreed and during the day he talked by phone with Hoover.

According to Hoover's memo of the conversations, Kissinger expressed our shared feeling that the leaks were more than just damaging; they were potentially dangerous to national security. Kissinger sent Hoover the names of four individuals who had access to the leaked materials. The FBI immediately installed four wiretaps.

I wanted maximum secrecy on this wiretap project and I also instructed that the taps be taken off as soon as possible. I knew that a leak about the wiretaps would be a blow to the morale of the White House staff, and provide a potent issue for the domestic antiwar groups and a propaganda weapon for the North Vietnamese. In fact the average number of warrantless wiretaps per year during my presidency was less than in any administration since Franklin D. Roosevelt's. But I felt that what previous Presidents had done in this regard would matter little if the press and the antiwar activists found out about what Nixon was doing.

Meanwhile, the leaks continued. On May 20 the Washington *Post* carried a leak of my plans to meet with President Thieu. On May 22 the New York *Times* reported sensitive details of an administration debate over whether to test a new missile warhead before the SALT talks began. On June 3 the *Times* published an article based on an NSC memo, issued only a week earlier, outlining our fallback position for the negotiations with the Japanese on Okinawa. Its premature revelation seriously undermined our bargaining position; even before the negotiations began, the Japanese side knew how far we were willing to compromise.

That same day the Washington *Star* published a story about the administration's decision to begin troop withdrawals from Vietnam. This leak undercut Thieu, whom we had assured that we would make the announcement jointly lest the Communists interpret it as a sign that we had begun to abandon South Vietnam.

From 1969 to early 1971, seventeen individuals were wiretapped by the FBI in an effort to find the source of national security leaks. The group included four newsmen and thirteen White House, State, and Defense Department aides. I was only asked to approve the program itself and not each individual tap. Today, nine years later, I cannot reconstruct the particular events that precipitated each of them.

There was an eighteenth national security tap, one on syndicated columnist Joseph Kraft. I remember being disturbed that Kraft, who had very good sources in the White House and NSC staffs and at the State and Defense Departments, was in direct contact with the North Vietnamese. I know that I told Ehrlichman on at least one occasion that Kraft's contacts with the North Vietnamese were all that we were interested in.

I cannot recall specifically, however, what made me decide to act. I authorized a tap on Kraft's home phone in Washington, but the FBI was reluctant to place a tap at that location. Consequently I authorized a plan to install a tap without using the FBI, but we abandoned this effort when the FBI arranged for a tap on Kraft during one of his trips to Paris to see the North Vietnamese.

Unfortunately none of these wiretaps turned up any proof linking anyone in the government to a specific national security leak.

For at least twenty-five years, every President and Attorney General authorized wiretaps to obtain intelligence in both foreign and domestic security matters. It was not until 1972—over a year after the last of our national security taps had been removed—that the Supreme Court ruled that national security taps on American citizens must be authorized by a court-ordered warrant if the subject had no "significant connection with a foreign power, its agents or agencies."

In the early years of my administration I saw the government's ability to function effectively in international affairs being undermined by leaks which I felt were a violation of law as well as of the code of honorable behavior. Particularly where leaks involving Vietnam were concerned, as long as Americans were fighting and dying there I had no patience with the argument that the people who leaked information did so because they opposed the war on moral grounds. So even though I disliked wiretapping and felt that it was at best a technique of only limited usefulness, it seemed to be our only chance to find out who was behind the leaks, and to stop them.

When our efforts to discover the source of the leaks failed, we began conducting our foreign policy planning in smaller groups. It is an ironic consequence of leaking that instead of producing more open government, it invariably forces the government to operate in more confined and secret ways. So it was that the widely reported impression of a Nixon administration "paranoia" about secrecy developed. Secrecy unquestionably exacts a high price in the form of a less free and creative interchange of ideas within the government. But I can say unequivocally that without secrecy there would have been no opening to China, no SALT agreement with the Soviet Union, and no peace agreement ending the Vietnam war.

VIETNAM: PUBLIC OFFERS AND SECRET OVERTURES

During the first months of the administration, despite the Communist offensive in February and despite the stalemate at the Paris talks, I remained convinced that the combined effect of the military pressure from the secret bombing and the public pressure from my repeated invitations to negotiate would force the Communists to respond. In March I confidently told the Cabinet that I expected the war to be over in a year. We had taken the initiative in Paris and proposed the restoration of the DMZ as a boundary between North and South Vietnam and advanced the possibility of a simultaneous withdrawal of American and North Vietnamese troops from the South. For his part, President Thieu offered to begin talks with the North Vietnamese on the question of a political settlement, and to permit free elections.

But the North Vietnamese yielded nothing. They insisted that political and military issues were inseparable, that American troops must be withdrawn unilaterally, and that Thieu must be deposed as a precondition to serious talks.

In mid-April we increased the diplomatic pressure. Kissinger showed Dobrynin a page of three points that I had initialed. In diplomatic usage, this was a sign that I considered them to be extremely important. Their message was unmistakable:

> 1. The President wishes to reiterate his conviction that a just peace is achievable.
>
> 2. The President is willing to explore avenues other than the existing negotiating framework. For example, it might be desirable for American and North Vietnamese negotiators to meet separately from the Paris framework to discuss general principles of a settlement If the special US and DRV negotiators can achieve an agreement in principle, the final technical negotiations can shift back to Paris.
>
> 3. The USG is convinced that all parties are at a crossroads and that extraordinary measures are called for to reverse the tide of war.

Kissinger told Dobrynin that U.S.–Soviet relations were involved because, while we might talk about progress in other areas, a settlement in Vietnam was the key to everything.

Dobrynin said that we had to understand the limitations of Soviet influence on Hanoi, and he added that the Soviet Union would never threaten to cut off supplies to their allies in North Vietnam. He promised, however, that our proposals would be forwarded to Hanoi within twenty-four hours.

After weeks passed with no response, we decided to take the initiative once again. In a televised speech on May 14 I offered our first comprehensive peace plan for Vietnam. I proposed that the major part of all foreign troops—both U.S. and North Vietnamese—withdraw from South Vietnam within one year after an agreement had been signed. An international body would monitor the withdrawals and supervise free elections in South Vietnam. I warned the enemy not to confuse our flexibility with weakness. I said, "Reports from Hanoi indicate that the enemy has given up hope for a military victory in South Vietnam, but is counting on a collapse of will in the United States. There could be no greater error in judgment."

There was no serious response from the North Vietnamese, either in Hanoi or Paris, to my May 14 proposals. I had never thought that peace in Vietnam would come easily; for the first time I had to consider the possibility that it might not come at all. Nonetheless, I decided to continue on the course we had planned, in the hope that the enemy would decide to take up our proposals and join us in the search for a settlement.

Early in the administration we had decided that withdrawing a number of American combat troops from Vietnam would demonstrate to Hanoi that we were serious in seeking a diplomatic settlement; it might also calm domestic public opinion by graphically demonstrating that we were beginning to wind down the war.

Mel Laird had long felt that the United States could "Vietnamize" the war—that we could train, equip, and inspire the South Vietnamese to fill the gaps left by departing American forces. In March Laird returned from a visit to South Vietnam with an optimistic report about the potential of the South Vietnamese to be trained to defend themselves. It was largely on the basis of Laird's enthusiastic advocacy that we undertook the policy of Vietnamization. This decision was another turning point in my administration's Vietnam strategy.

President Thieu was among those who objected to the proposed plan for American withdrawals from South Vietnam. I privately assured him through Ambassador Bunker that our support for him was steadfast. In order to dramatize this pledge, I proposed that we meet on Midway Island in the Pacific. Thieu readily accepted, and we met there on June 8.

After our meeting we both made brief statements to reporters. I announced that, as a consequence of Thieu's recommendation and the assessment of our own commander in the field, I had decided to order the immediate redeployment from Vietnam of approximately 25,000 men. This involved some diplomatic exaggeration, because both Thieu and Abrams had privately raised objections to the withdrawals.

I said that in the months ahead I would consider further troop withdrawals, based on three criteria: the progress in training and equipping the South Vietnamese armed forces; the progress of the Paris talks; and the level of enemy activity.

Although Thieu was somewhat mollified by the Midway meeting, he was still deeply troubled. He knew that the first American withdrawals would begin an irreversible process, the conclusion of which would be the departure of all Americans from Vietnam.

To make sure the message of Midway was not lost on Hanoi, I spelled it out when we arrived back at the White House. I told the people gathered on the South Lawn to welcome us that the combination of my May 14 peace plan and the Midway troop withdrawal left the door to peace wide open. "And now we invite the leaders of North Vietnam to walk with us through that door," I said.

At the end of June it looked as if we might be getting a response of sorts from Hanoi. There seemed to be a lull in the fighting, and our intelligence indicated that some North Vietnamese units were being withdrawn from South Vietnam. Le Duc Tho, the Politburo member who was the Special Adviser to the North Vietnamese delegation at the Paris talks, suddenly returned to Hanoi, and there was speculation that he had been called back to receive new negotiating instructions.

This military lull continued through early July. Although the evidence was still entirely circumstantial, and although the dangers of appearing overeager were as great as ever, I decided to try once again to cut through whatever genuine doubts or misunderstandings might still be holding Hanoi back. I decided to "go for broke" in the sense that I would attempt to end the war one way or the other—either by negotiated agreement or by an increased use of force.

One reason for making this decision at this time was my feeling that unless I could build some momentum behind our peace efforts over the next several weeks, they might be doomed to failure by the calendar. Once the summer was over and Congress and the colleges returned from vacation in September, a massive new antiwar tide would sweep the country during the fall and winter. Then, with the approaching dry season in Vietnam, there was almost sure to be a renewed Communist offensive during the Tet holiday period in February. By early spring the pressures of the November 1970 elections would make congressional demands for more troop withdrawals impossible to stop and difficult to ignore.

After half a year of sending peaceful signals to the Communists, I was ready to use whatever military pressure was necessary to prevent them from taking over South Vietnam by force. During several long sessions, Kissinger and I developed an elaborate orchestration of diplomatic, military, and publicity pressures we would bring to bear on Hanoi.

I decided to set November 1, 1969—the first anniversary of Johnson's bombing halt—as the deadline for what would in effect be an ultimatum to North Vietnam.

Since November 1 was only three and a half months away, there was no time to waste. On July 15 I wrote a personal letter to Ho Chi Minh. Once again Jean Sainteny acted as our courier. I met with him at the White House so that he would be able to talk at firsthand about my strong desire for peace. But I also told him to say that, unless some serious breakthrough had been achieved by the November 1 deadline, I would regretfully find myself obliged to have recourse "to measures of great consequence and force."

My letter to Ho Chi Minh was sent to Sainteny by secret courier and on July 16 he delivered it to Xuan Thuy, head of the regular North Vietnamese delegation in Paris, for transmittal to Hanoi. In it I tried to convey both the sincerity and the urgency of our desire for a settlement:

> I realize that it is difficult to communicate meaningfully across the gulf of four years of war. But precisely because of this gulf, I wanted to take this opportunity to reaffirm in all solemnity my desire to work for a just peace. . . .
>
> As I have said repeatedly, there is nothing to be gained by waiting. . . .
>
> You will find us forthcoming and open-minded in a common effort to bring the blessings of peace to the brave people of Vietnam. Let history record that at this critical juncture, both sides turned their face toward peace rather than toward conflict and war.

With this letter I felt that I had gone as far as I could until the North Vietnamese indicated that they too were interested in an agreement. Now we would have to wait to see how Ho Chi Minh responded. As far as I was concerned, my letter put the choice between war and peace in his hands.

In a few days word was flashed to us that the North Vietnamese were proposing a secret meeting between Kissinger and Xuan Thuy.

On July 23, I flew to the South Pacific for the splashdown of Apollo XI. This was to be the first leg of an around-the-world trip that included stops in Guam, the Philippines, Indonesia, Thailand, South Vietnam, India, Pakistan, Romania, and Britain. In honor of Apollo's accomplishment, we gave the trip the codename Moonglow.

The trip provided the perfect camouflage for Kissinger's first secret meeting with the North Vietnamese. It was arranged that Kissinger would go to Paris, ostensibly to brief French officials on the results of my meetings. While there he would meet secretly with Thuy.

The first stop after the Apollo splashdown was on the island of Guam. Shortly after we arrived I conducted an informal press conference with the reporters covering the trip. It was there that I enunciated what at first was called the Guam Doctrine and has since become known as the Nixon Doctrine.

I stated that the United States is a Pacific power and should remain so. But I felt that once the Vietnam war was settled, we would need a new Asian policy to ensure that there were no more Vietnams in the future. I began with the proposition that we would keep all our existing treaty commitments, but that we would not make any more commitments unless they were required by our own vital interests.

In the past our policy had been to furnish the arms, men, and matériel to help other nations defend themselves against aggression. That was what we had done in Korea, and that was how we had started out in Vietnam. But from now on, I said, we would furnish only the matériel and the military and economic assistance to those nations willing to accept the responsibility of supplying the manpower to defend themselves. I made only one exception: in case a major nuclear power engaged in aggression against one of our allies or friends, I said that we would respond with nuclear weapons.

The Nixon Doctrine announced on Guam was misinterpreted by some as signaling a new policy that would lead to total American withdrawal from Asia and from other parts of the world as well. In one of our regular breakfast meetings after I returned from the trip Senate Majority Leader Mike Mansfield articulated this misunderstanding. I emphasized to him, as I had to our friends in the Asian countries, that the Nixon Doctrine was not a formula for getting America *out* of Asia, but one that provided the only sound basis for America's staying *in* and continuing to play a responsible role in helping the non-Communist nations and neutrals as well as our Asian allies to defend their independence.

When we landed in Bucharest, Romania, on August 2, I became the first American President to make a state visit to a Communist satellite country.

President Nicolae Ceauşescu is a strong, independent leader who had cultivated good relations with the Chinese in spite of the fact that he had to walk a very fine line lest the Soviets decide to intervene in Romania as they had in Hungary in 1956 and in Czechoslovakia in 1968. So far he had walked that line with consummate skill.

I had been briefed to expect a courteous reception, but the size and spontaneous enthusiasm of the crowds exceeded all our expectations. At one point Ceauşescu and I were literally swept up by the dancing in the streets.

Romania had good diplomatic relations with the North Vietnamese, and I knew that anything I said would be repeated to them, so I used one of my meetings with Ceauşescu to reinforce my message to Hanoi. I said, "We cannot indefinitely continue to have two hundred deaths a week in Vietnam and no progress in Paris. On November 1 this year—one year after the halt of the bombing, and after the withdrawal of some of our troops and several reasonable offers for peaceful negotiations—if there is no progress, we must re-evaluate our policy."

I told him that in order to get peace we might have to open another channel of communications between the two sides. Ceauşescu said he would do everything he could to be helpful in furthering negotiations.

The story of Kissinger's secret meetings with the North Vietnamese, which began on August 4, 1969, and extended over the next three years, is an extraordinary one, full of classic cloak-and-dagger episodes, with Kissinger riding slouched down in the back seats of speeding Citroëns, eluding inquisitive reporters, and putting curious embassy officials off the scent.

The first conversation took place in Jean Sainteny's Paris apartment in the fashionable Rue de Rivoli, where Kissinger met with Xuan Thuy and Mai Van Bo.

Kissinger opened by saying that he wanted to convey a message from me personally. He reminded them that November 1 would be the first anniversary of the bombing halt. During this time the United States had made what we considered significant moves: we had ended troop reinforcements, we had observed a partial bombing halt and then a total bombing halt, and we had already withdrawn 25,000 combat troops and offered to accept the result of free elections. As far as we could see, there had been no significant response. Now, in order to expedite negotiations, I was ready to open another channel of contact with them. "But at the same time," Kissinger added, "I have been asked to tell you in all solemnity, that if by November 1 no major progress has been made toward a solution, we will be compelled—with great reluctance—to take measures of the greatest consequences." He pointed out that in their propaganda and in the Paris discussions, the North Vietnamese were attempting to make this "Mr. Nixon's war." "We do not believe that this is in your interest," he said, "because if it is Mr. Nixon's war, then he cannot afford not to win it."

Xuan Thuy replied with a relatively restrained restatement of Hanoi's most extreme position: he called for the complete withdrawal of all American forces and observance of the National Liberation Front's ten points, which in effect provided for total Communist domination over South Vietnam. He insisted on maintaining the patent fiction that there were no North Vietnamese troops in South Vietnam. He also continued to demand that we overthrow President Thieu before any agreement could be reached.

Finally Kissinger decided that he had said all he could to representatives who were not actually empowered to negotiate. Exercising his tremendous skill, he brought the conversation around to a mellower tone, saying, "We would prefer to have the Vietnamese as friends rather than as enemies. I believe that we must make an effort to find a solution between now and November 1."

The three men shook hands and departed separately to avoid attracting any attention.

Having put the Nixon Doctrine on record and having begun to put pressure on Hanoi, I decided it was time to assume the offensive in the public forum of the Paris peace talks. The diplomats and reporters who had become accustomed to Cabot Lodge's usually complacent demeanor were surprised when he rose from his chair on August 7, looked directly at the Communist delegates, and said, "We have done all that we can do by ourselves to bring a negotiated peace in Vietnam. Now it is time for you to respond." The press called it his toughest talk since taking over in January as chief U.S. negotiator.

Ho Chi Minh's reply to my July letter arrived dated August 25. In it, he referred to "the war of aggression of the United States against our people" and said that he was "deeply touched at the rising toll of death of young Americans who have fallen in Vietnam by reason of the policy of American governing circles."

In response to my statement that we would be willing to discuss any proposal or program that might lead to a negotiated settlement, he said that the ten-point program of the NLF had "earned the sympathy and support of the peoples of the world." He concluded:

> In your letter you have expressed the desire to act for a just peace. For this the United States must cease the war of aggression and withdraw their troops from South Vietnam, respect the right of the population of the South and of the Vietnamese nation to dispose of themselves, without foreign influence.

Considering the tone of my letter to him, and even taking into account the stridency of communist jargon, there was no doubt that Ho's reply was a cold rebuff.

After receiving this unpromising reply, I knew that I had to prepare myself for the tremendous criticism and pressure that would come with stepping up the war.

On September 3, Ho Chi Minh died. There were rumors of a struggle over the succession for several days before Premier Pham Van Dong emerged as the Hanoi Politburo's leading figure. Veteran Vietnam-watchers were at a loss to predict what effect this would have on the war.

In the middle of September I announced the withdrawal of another 35,000 troops by December 15. In my statement I pointed out that the withdrawal of 60,000 troops was a significant step and that "the time for meaningful negotiations has therefore arrived." This announcement was intended to let the new leaders of North Vietnam know that I was not assuming that they were bound by Ho's reply to my letter.

Two days later, in a speech at the opening of the UN General Assembly, I said that "the time has come for peace. And in the name of peace, I urge all of you here—representing 126 nations—to use your best diplomatic efforts to persuade Hanoi to move seriously into the negotiations which could end this war."

On September 20 Kissinger received a letter from Sainteny, who had been in Hanoi for Ho Chi Minh's funeral and, while he was there, had had a long conversation with Pham Van Dong. The new Premier was notably unvituperative in his references to the United States. When Sainteny stressed that he knew how eager I was for peace from his own conversation with me, Dong said, "I see that they have convinced you. But we, we are not able to take them at their words: only acts will convince us."

Since this conversation had taken place before my mid-September troop withdrawal, I felt that I had supplied the deed to prove our words. Once again the choice lay with Hanoi.

In the weeks remaining before November 1, I wanted to orchestrate the maximum possible pressure on Hanoi. I was confident that we could bring sufficient pressure to bear on the diplomatic front. But the only chance for my ultimatum to succeed was to convince the Communists that I could depend on solid support at home if they decided to call my bluff. However, the chances I would actually have that support were becoming increasingly slim.

There had been serious riots and disorders on more than a score of college campuses during the winter and spring of 1969, the causes of which covered a wide spectrum of frustrations of which Vietnam was by no means the predominant one. Students at Berkeley demanded an autonomous College for Ethnic Studies. Black students seized the administration building at Duke and demanded a nongraded black education program and money for a black student union. One hundred black students, armed with rifles and shotguns, held the student union at Cornell University and demanded that disciplinary reprimands to three black students be revoked. The faculty first refused and then capitulated on the issue. The University of Pennsylvania administration decided to avoid a confrontation with student war protesters by taking down American flags and putting them in storage.

I was disgusted—and I said so—by the capitulation of professors and administrators to students using force. I praised those who held firm—like San Francisco State College's Dr. S. I. Hayakawa, who ripped out the wires of a public address system set up by radicals in violation of campus regulations, and Rev. Theodore Hesburgh of Notre Dame, who announced he would give protesters who substituted "force for rational persuasion" fifteen minutes, and then suspend them from the university; five minutes after that, if they continued the disturbance, they would be expelled.

During the first months of my presidency Vietnam was not the primary issue in campus demonstrations largely because Johnson's bombing halt had suspended the most actively controversial aspect of the war, and my announced plans to establish an all-volunteer Army and our reform of the draft, which made it less threateningly disruptive, also helped in this regard.

I knew that this situation was bound to change. As the fall term began on college campuses, and as Congress returned from its summer recess, newspapers and television began reflecting signs of a new level of intensity in the antiwar movement. There was talk of holding a "Moratorium," a nationwide day of protest, on October 15, right in the period most crucial to the success of my November 1 ultimatum.

In a press conference on September 26, in answer to a question about the Moratorium and other public protests against the war, I said, "Now, I understand that there has been and continues to be opposition to the war in Vietnam on the campuses, and also in the nation. As far as this kind of activity is concerned, we expect it. However, under no circumstances will I be affected whatever by it."

I was fully aware of the furore that this statement would cause. But having initiated a policy of pressure on North Vietnam that now involved not only our government but foreign governments as well, I felt that I had no choice but to carry it through. Faced with the prospect of demonstrations at home that I could not prevent, my only alternative was to try to make it clear to the enemy that the protests would have no effect on my decisions. Otherwise my ultimatum would appear empty.

We continued to keep up the diplomatic pressure on the Soviets. On September 27, Kissinger told Dobrynin that the apparent failure of all our requests for Soviet help toward ending the war made it very difficult for us to carry on more than basic diplomatic relations between our two countries.

I telephoned Kissinger in the middle of this discussion, and we talked for a few minutes. When they resumed their conversation, Kissinger said, "The President just told me in that call that as far as Vietnam is concerned, the train has just left the station and is now headed down the track."

Dobrynin tried to ease the atmosphere with a diplomatic turn of phrase. "I hope it's an airplane rather than a train," he said, "because an airplane can still change its course in flight."

Kissinger replied, "The President chooses his words very carefully, and I am sure he meant what he said. He said, 'train.' "

As another part of our efforts to apply pressure on Hanoi, I ordered a survey of non-Communist nations shipping to North Vietnam. We found that Cyprus, Malta, Singapore, and Somalia were among the countries with registered ships going to Hanoi. When the first two governments refused to cooperate with us, I ordered their foreign aid programs cut off. Singapore and Somalia agreed to cut down the shipping under their flags.

I met with the Republican congressional leadership and told them that the next sixty days would be of the utmost importance for the ending of the war. "We are going to need unity more than we have ever needed it before," I said. "I can't tell you everything that will be going on, because if there is to be any chance of success, it will have to be done in secret. All I can tell you is this: I am doing my damnedest to end the war. I am approaching the whole question with only two operating principles: I won't make it hard for the North Vietnamese if they genuinely want a settlement; but I will not be the first President of the United States to lose a war."

Later the same day I moved the pressure on Hanoi up a notch when I met with nine Republican senators and planted a story that I knew would leak. I did not have to wait long. In eight days Rowland Evans and Robert Novak ran a column saying that I was considering blockading Haiphong and invading North Vietnam. I wanted this rumor to attract some attention in Hanoi. Although I never knew for sure that it did, I do know that it attracted the attention of Mel Laird. He and Bill Rogers immediately urged that before taking any drastic action I consider the very low American casualty rates over the last few months and the improved performance of the South Vietnamese as a result of our stepped-up Vietnamization program.

VIETNAM MORATORIUM

The antiwar forces on the campuses, in Congress, and in the media had coalesced around the Vietnam Moratorium scheduled for October 15 in Washington. The plan was to hold similar demonstrations in different cities on the fifteenth of each month until the war was over.

By the first week of October, the pent-up fury reached full force. There were antiwar speeches, teach-ins, and rallies. The controversy over my Supreme Court nomination of Judge Clement Haynsworth, the debate over welfare reform, the defeat of a Republican incumbent by an antiwar Democrat in a special election in Massachusetts, the vocal impatience of some civil rights leaders with the pace of our integration policy—all prominently in the news—created the impression of an administration reeling under siege. These factors were lumped together in the media and labeled a crisis of leadership. The headline in *Newsweek* was *Mr. Nixon in Trouble,* and *Time* devoted its National Affairs section to describing *Nixon's Worst Week*: "It did not take an alarmist of Chicken Little proportions to discern that bits of sky were falling on the Nixon administration."

Pronouncements of no-confidence and predictions of political paralysis were widespread. On October 7 David Broder wrote in the Washington *Post* that "it is becoming more obvious with every passing day that the men and the movement that broke Lyndon Johnson's authority in 1968 are out to break Richard Nixon in 1969. The likelihood is great that they will succeed again." A few days later Dean Acheson warned against "the attempt being made from so many sources to destroy Nixon." In an exclusive interview in the New York *Times* he said, "I think we're going to have a major constitutional crisis if we make a habit of destroying Presidents."

My deliberate refusal to acknowledge these dire predictions itself became an element of the supposed crisis. *Time* reported, "Nixon seemed unconcerned and aloof from it all," and the magazine's Washington bureau chief, Hugh Sidey, found my attitude "perhaps as alarming as the events themselves in the most trying time Nixon has yet had in office."

My real concern was that these highly publicized efforts aimed at forcing me to end the war were seriously undermining my behind-the-scenes attempts to do just that. Weeks later, in a meeting with Cabot Lodge, the North Vietnamese ambassador recited statements made by leading Senate doves. The New York *Times* reported that Le Duc Tho, "with a wide grin," told an American visitor about Senator Fulbright's accusation that I was trying to prolong the war with Vietnamization. Although publicly I continued to ignore the raging antiwar controversy, I had to face the fact that it had probably destroyed the credibility of my ultimatum to Hanoi.

On October 13 Ron Ziegler announced that I would make a major address to the nation concerning Vietnam on Monday, November 3.

This announcement was generally interpreted as either an attempt to undercut the October 15 Moratorium, then only two days away, or as a sign that the Moratorium had already been successful in forcing me to reconsider my Vietnam policy. In fact, I hoped that the announcement of a major speech for two days after the November 1 deadline would give Hanoi second thoughts about fishing in our troubled domestic waters.

On October 14, I knew for sure that my ultimatum had failed when

Kissinger informed me that Radio Hanoi had just broadcast a letter from Premier Pham Van Dong to the American people. In it Dong declared:

> This fall large sectors of the U.S. people, encouraged and supported by many peace- and justice-loving American personages, are launching a broad and powerful offensive throughout the United States to demand that the Nixon administration put an end to the Vietnam aggressive war and immediately bring all American troops home. . . .
>
> We are firmly confident that with the solidarity and bravery of the peoples of our two countries and with the approval and support of peace-loving people in the world, the struggle of the Vietnamese people and U.S. progressive people against U.S. aggression will certainly be crowned with total victory.
>
> May your fall offensive succeed splendidly.

To indicate the seriousness with which I viewed this blatant intervention in our domestic affairs, I asked Agnew to hold a press conference at the White House. He called Dong's letter an "incredible message" and read excerpts of it for the cameras. He said, "The leaders and sponsors of tomorrow's Moratorium, public officials, and others leading these demonstrations should openly repudiate the support of the totalitarian government which has on its hands the blood of 40,000 Americans."

I considered the question period that followed Agnew's remarks a disgraceful performance on the part of the White House press corps. As if it were our fault that Dong had written this letter, one reporter asked, "Mr. Vice President, let us take the bull by the horns. Isn't seizing upon this letter a last-minute attempt to dampen down the Moratorium by the administration?"

The media generally either played down the Dong letter or indicated that the administration had unreasonably fastened upon it as an excuse for the repression of legitimate dissent.

I had to decide what to do about the ultimatum. I knew that unless I had some indisputably good reason for not carrying out my threat of using increased force when the ultimatum expired on November 1, the Communists would become contemptuous of us and even more difficult to deal with. I knew, however, that after all the protests and the Moratorium, American public opinion would be seriously divided by any military escalation of the war.

A quarter of a million people came to Washington for the October 15 Moratorium. Despite widespread rumors that some of the more radical left-wing organizations would provoke violent confrontations with police, the demonstrations were generally peaceful.

Opinion within the administration was divided over how to respond. Kissinger urged that I do nothing at all and let the protest run its course, lest I upset our foreign policy strategy. John Ehrlichman, however, was upset by our apparent indifference to the sincere fervor of many of the protesters and urged that I declare a National Day of Prayer on October 15 as a show of tacit support for the underlying goal of peace.

The Washington *Post* praised the protesters and said that the Moratorium was "a deeply meaningful statement" of the anguish they felt about the war. Elsewhere, however, reservations were expressed. The Washington *Star,* for example, said, "What counts is whether the demonstration, regardless of intention, does in fact give encouragement to Hanoi and thereby presumably prolongs the war." As if in answer to that point, the Vietcong Radio said that the Communists had gained "strong encouragement" from the Moratorium.

The Vietnam Moratorium raised, for the first but by no means the last time in my administration, a basic and important question about the nature of leadership in a democracy: should the President or Congress or any responsible elected official let public demonstrations influence his decisions?

I had strong opinions about this question, and I decided to address it head on. I asked that one letter be selected from all those we had received criticizing my press conference statement that I would not be affected by the protests and that a reply be prepared to it.

The letter the staff chose was from a student at Georgetown University. In it, he stated, "It has been my impression that it is not unwise for the President of the United States to take note of the will of the people; after all, these people elected you, you are their President, and your office bears certain obligations. Might I respectfully suggest that the President reconsider his pre-judgment."

I replied, "If a President—any President—allowed his course to be set by those who demonstrate, he would betray the trust of all the rest. Whatever the issue, to allow government policy to be made in the streets would destroy the democratic process. It would give the decision, not to the majority, and not to those with the strongest arguments, but to those with the loudest voices. . . . It would allow every group to test its strength not at the ballot box but through confrontation in the streets."

On the night of October 15 I thought about the irony of this protest for peace. It had, I believed, destroyed whatever small possibility may still have existed of ending the war in 1969. But there was nothing I could do about that now. I would have to adjust my plans accordingly and carry on as best I could. At the top of the page of preliminary notes I was making for my November 3 speech, I wrote: "Don't get rattled—don't waver—don't react."

THE SILENT MAJORITY

After the Moratorium attention immediately began to focus on my speech. Most doves in the media and Congress assumed that I had been so impressed—or so frightened—by the Moratorium that I had decided to announce major new troop withdrawals in order to blunt the impact of the next Moratorium scheduled for November 15. An AP wire story on October 20 stated that I might offer a cease-fire in the speech, and some papers reported this in front-page headlines. Flora Lewis, writing in the Boston *Globe,* stated categorically that I would announce the withdrawal of 300,000 men during 1970 and that I had ordered the Pentagon to work out the necessary schedules. Dan Rather, on a special CBS news report on the Moratorium, claimed that I was considering stepped-up troop withdrawals, fewer B-52 raids, a reduction in fighting, and perhaps even a cease-fire before the end of the year. In the Senate, Hugh Scott called for a unilateral cease-fire. Since he was Minority Leader, his statement was widely interpreted as a White House trial balloon. Hubert Humphrey predicted that I would announce a major program for the "systematical and accelerated withdrawal of U.S. forces" from Vietnam.

How far off the mark these predictions and expectations were can be seen in notes I made for the November 3 speech in the early morning hours of October 22:

> They can't defeat us militarily in Vietnam.
> They can't break South Vietnam.
> Include a paragraph on *why* we are there.
> They cannot break us.

As the November 1 deadline approached, three factors strongly influenced my thinking about the ultimatum. The first was that American casualty figures in Vietnam had been reaching new lows. I knew that these reductions might be a ploy on the part of the Communists to make escalating the fighting that much more difficult for me.

The second factor was the possibility that the death of Ho Chi Minh might have created new opportunities for reaching a settlement that deserved a chance to develop.

The third factor was a conversation I had on October 17 with Sir Robert Thompson, the British expert on guerrilla warfare.

"What do you think of the 'option to the right'?" I asked. "What would you think if we decided to escalate?"

Thompson was clearly not in favor of escalation because it would risk a major American and worldwide furore and still not address the central problem of whether the South Vietnamese were sufficiently confident and prepared to defend themselves against a renewed Communist offensive at some time in the future. His estimate was that, continuing the current U.S. policy and assuming South Vietnamese confidence that we would not pull out, victory could be won within two years. He thought that our only chance for a negotiated settlement in the meantime would be if it were clear to Hanoi that we were there for the duration. I asked if he would go to Vietnam and make a personal study of the situation there for me and report as soon as possible.

When I asked Thompson whether he thought it was important for us to see it through in Vietnam, he said, "Absolutely. In my opinion the future of Western civilization is at stake in the way you handle yourselves in Vietnam."

In view of these three factors, and recognizing that the Moratorium had undercut the credibility of the ultimatum, I began to think more in terms of stepping up Vietnamization while continuing the fighting at its present level rather than of trying to increase it. In many respects Vietnamization would be far more damaging to the Communists than an escalation that, as Thompson had pointed out, would not solve the basic problem of South Vietnamese preparedness, and that would stir up serious domestic problems in America.

It was important that the Communists not mistake as weakness the lack of dramatic action on my part in carrying out the ultimatum. We would be able to demonstrate our continuing resolve to the North Vietnamese on the battlefield, but I thought that the Soviets would need a special reminder. Therefore when Ambassador Dobrynin came to the White House for a private meeting on the afternoon of October 20, I decided to use the encounter to make our position absolutely clear to the Soviet leadership.

Kissinger accompanied Dobrynin to the Oval Office, and after greetings were exchanged the ambassador said that he had received an aide-mémoire from his government, with instructions to read it to me.

"Go ahead, Mr. Ambassador," I said.

"I am instructed to frankly inform the President that Moscow is not satisfied with the present state of relations between the U.S.S.R. and the U.S.," he began. "Moscow feels that the President should be frankly told that the method of solving the Vietnam question through the use of military force is not only without perspective, but also extremely dangerous. . . . If someone in the United States is tempted to make profit from Soviet–Chinese relations at the Soviet Union's expense, and there are some signs of that, then we would like to frankly warn in advance that such line of conduct, if pursued, can lead to a very grave miscalculation and is in no way consistent with the goal of better relations between the U.S. and the U.S.S.R."

Dobrynin seemed a little uncomfortable with my silence when he had finished reading from the paper. After a moment I leaned back in my chair and opened the center drawer of my desk. I took out a yellow pad and slid it across toward him.

"You'd better take some notes," I said.

He took the pad and put it on his lap.

"You have been candid, Mr. Ambassador, and I will be equally so. I, too, am disappointed in U.S.–Soviet relations. As of today, I have been in this office for nine months. The babies should have been born by now. Instead, there have been several miscarriages."

Taking some of the major issues—the Middle East, trade, European security, Berlin—I analyzed point by point the problems with each. Most arose from Soviet intransigence or jockeying for position.

Turning to China, I said, "Anything we have done or are doing with respect to China is in no sense designed to embarrass the Soviet Union. On the contrary, China and the United States cannot tolerate having a situation develop in which we are enemies, any more than we want to be permanent enemies of the Soviet Union. Therefore, we expect to make moves in trade and exchanges of persons and eventually in diplomacy. I want to repeat that this is not directed against the Soviet Union. Within ten years, China will be a nuclear power, capable of terrorizing many other countries. The time is running out when the Soviet Union and the United States can build a different kind of world."

Having put in the hook this far, I pulled it hard. "The only beneficiary of U.S.–Soviet disagreement over Vietnam is China," I said, "and therefore this is the last opportunity to settle these disputes."

Before Dobrynin could interrupt, I moved on to Vietnam. "Prior to the bombing halt, which, as you are aware, will be one year old on November 1, Ambassador Bohlen and Ambassador Thompson and Ambassador Harriman pointed out to President Johnson that the Soviet Union could not do anything as long as we were bombing a fellow socialist country. They said that the Soviet Union would be very active with its help if we stopped. The bombing halt was then agreed to, but the Soviet Union has done nothing to help."

At this Dobrynin raised his hand as if to be called on, but I waved it down. "Of course, we now have an oblong table at the talks in Paris, and I know the Soviet Union contributed something to that, but we do not consider that a great achievement. All the conciliatory moves for the past year have been made by us."

I said that I had concluded that perhaps the Soviet Union did not want to end the war in Vietnam. "You may think that you can break me," I said. "You may believe that the American domestic situation is unmanageable. Or you may think that the war in Vietnam costs the Soviet Union only a small amount of money while it costs us a great many lives. I do not propose to argue with this kind of assessment. On the other hand, Mr. Ambassador, I want you to understand that the Soviet Union is going to be stuck with me for the next three years and three months, and during all that time I will keep in mind what is being done right now, today. If the Soviet Union will not help us get peace, then we will have to pursue our own methods for bringing the war to an end. We cannot allow a talk-fight strategy to continue without taking action.

"Let us be frank, Mr. Ambassador," I continued. "All you have done is repeat the same tired old slogans that the North Vietnamese used six months ago. You know very well they can lead nowhere. It is time to get discussions started, because, I can assure you, the humiliation of a defeat is absolutely unacceptable to my country. I recognize that the Soviet leaders are tough and courageous. But so are we."

I stopped only a moment and then went on. "I hope that you will not mind this serious talk," I said. "If the Soviet Union found it possible to do something in Vietnam, and the Vietnam war ended, then we might do something dramatic to improve our relations, indeed, something more dramatic than could now be imagined. But until then, I have to say that real progress will be very difficult."

Dobrynin waited to see if I would go on. This time I did not.

"Does this mean that there can be no progress?" he asked.

"Progress is possible," I replied, "but it would have to be confined essentially to what is attainable in diplomatic channels. The war can drag on, in which case we will find our own way to bring it to an end. There is no sense in just repeating the proposals of the last six months."

I wanted no reply to this, so I brought the meeting to a close by saying, "The whole world wants us to get together. I, too, want nothing so much as to have my administration remembered as a watershed in American and Soviet relations. But let me repeat that we will not hold still for being diddled to death in Vietnam."

With that I rose, shook his hand, and escorted him to the door.

Kissinger came back in after he had seen Dobrynin to his car. "I wager that no one has ever talked to him that way in his entire career!" he said. "It was extraordinary! No President has ever laid it on the line to them like that."

"We shouldn't have any illusions that it will do any good or make any difference," I said, "but it is good to let them know that we're not as big fools as the requirements of diplomacy may sometimes make us seem."

I received much conflicting advice concerning what I should say on November 3. Rogers and Laird urged me to concentrate on the hopes for peace, Rogers emphasizing the Paris talks and Laird stressing the prospects of Vietnamization. The majority of the White House staff, the

Cabinet members, and the congressional leaders I consulted advocated that I use the speech to establish beyond any doubt my sincere desire for peace.

Kissinger was advocating a very hard line. He felt that if we backed off, the Communists would become totally convinced that they could control our foreign policy through public opinion. And Dean Acheson sent word that any announcement of withdrawal schedules would put us at a disadvantage in negotiations.

Speculation about the speech reached fever pitch as the date approached. I welcomed this because I knew that the more it was talked about, the bigger the audience would be.

I kept my own counsel, and very few people knew the way my thinking was really going or the surprise I was planning for the antiwar agitators who thought that their street marches could force me to make foreign policy the way they wanted.

I went to Camp David for a long weekend on October 24 and worked twelve to fourteen hours a day writing and rewriting different sections of the speech. Haldeman cleared most of my schedule during the following week so that I could continue the work uninterrupted.

By Friday the speech had gone through twelve drafts, and I was ready to take it to Camp David for a final review. Senate Majority Leader Mike Mansfield had written down his thoughts in a memorandum, and he asked that I read it before I made any final decisions about what I would say.

I read Mansfield's memorandum later that night. He began by stating: "The continuance of the war in Vietnam, in my judgment, endangers the future of this nation." He said that it was more than just the loss of lives or the waste of money and resources that concerned him. "Most serious," he wrote, "are the deep divisions within our society to which this conflict of dubious origin and purpose is contributing."

He said that he would give articulate public support to "any or all of the following decisions if in your responsibility you decide that they are necessary, as well they may be, to a rapid termination of the war in Vietnam." He then listed actions that amounted to a unilateral cease-fire and withdrawal. "I know that a settlement arrived at in this fashion is not pleasant to contemplate," he wrote, "especially in view of the dug-in diplomatic and military positions which, unfortunately, were assumed over the past few years." The memo was signed, "With the greatest respect."

I realized that with this memorandum Mansfield was offering what would be the last chance for me to end "Johnson's and Kennedy's war." I interpreted his references to it as a "conflict of dubious origin" and to the military positions "unfortunately" assumed over the past few years as signals that he would even allow me to claim that I was making the best possible end of a bad war my Democratic predecessors had begun. I knew that the opponents of the war would irrevocably become my opponents if my speech took a hard line. But I could not escape the fact that I felt it would be wrong to end the Vietnam war on any terms I believed to be less than honorable.

I worked through the night. About 4 A.M. I wrote a paragraph calling for the support of "the great silent majority of Americans." I went to bed, but after two hours of restless sleep I was wide awake, so I got up and began work again. By 8 A.M. the speech was finished. I called Haldeman, and when he answered, I said, "The baby's just been born!"

The message of my November 3 speech was that we were going to keep our commitment in Vietnam. We were going to continue fighting until the Communists agreed to negotiate a fair and honorable peace or until the South Vietnamese were able to defend themselves on their own—whichever came first. At the same time we would continue our disengagement based on the principles of the Nixon Doctrine: the pace of withdrawal would be linked to the progress of Vietnamization, the level of enemy activity, and developments on the negotiating front. I emphasized that our policy would not be affected by demonstrations in the streets.

At least in part because of the very different expectations that had been built up around this speech, my strongly expressed determination to stand and fight came as a surprise to many people and therefore had a greatly increased impact. I called on the American people for their support:

> I have chosen a plan for peace. I believe it will succeed.
>
> If it does succeed, what the critics say now won't matter. If it does not succeed, anything I say then won't matter. . . .
>
> And so tonight—to you, the great silent majority of my fellow Americans—I ask for your support.
>
> I pledged in my campaign for the presidency to end the war in a way that we could win the peace. I have initiated a plan of action which will enable me to keep that pledge.
>
> The more support I can have from the American people, the sooner that pledge can be redeemed; for the more divided we are at home, the less likely the enemy is to negotiate at Paris.
>
> Let us be united for peace. Let us also be united against defeat. Because let us understand: North Vietnam cannot defeat or humiliate the United States. Only Americans can do that.

Very few speeches actually influence the course of history. The November 3 speech was one of them. Its impact came as a surprise to me; it was one thing to make a rhetorical appeal to the Silent Majority—it was another actually to hear from them.

After the speech I had dinner by myself in the Lincoln Sitting Room. I did not listen to the TV commentators, but the rest of the family did, and they were livid with anger. They said that the comment and analyses broadcast by the network news correspondents criticized both my words and my motives. Instead of presenting impartial summaries of what I had said and cross sections of political and public reaction, most of the reporters talked about the speech they thought I should have given. Tricia came in and said, "They talked as if they had been listening to a different speech than the one you made."

But there were signs that the critics and the commentators were unrepresentative of public opinion. The White House switchboard had been lighted up from the minute I left the air. The calls continued for hours, and soon the first waves of telegrams began to arrive. After I took calls from Cabinet officers, staff, and others—including Dean Acheson—I began to realize that the reaction to the speech was exceeding my most optimistic hopes.

I was too keyed up to sleep very well that night. The various reports of the public response to the speech excited me; the reports of the television coverage rankled me. Later I made a note: "Before November 3 a majority of the press expected RN to cave, and those who did not expected him to have a violent reaction to the demonstrations. He surprised them by doing neither. The RN policy is to talk softly and to carry a big stick. That was the theme of November 3."

By morning the public reaction was confirmed. The White House mail room reported the biggest response ever to any presidential speech. More than 50,000 telegrams and 30,000 letters had poured in, and the percentage of critical messages among them was low. A Gallup telephone poll taken immediately after the speech showed 77 percent approval.

There was no mistaking that the Silent Majority speech had hit a responsive chord in the country. In fact, for the first time, the Silent Majority had made itself heard.

The outpouring of popular support had a direct impact on congressional opinion. By November 12, 300 members of the House of Representatives—119 Democrats and 181 Republicans—had cosponsored a resolution of support for my Vietnam policies. Fifty-eight senators—21 Democrats and 37 Republicans—had signed letters expressing similar sentiments.

The November 3 speech was both a milestone and a turning point for my administration. Now, for a time at least, the enemy could no longer count on dissent in America to give them the victory they could not win on the battlefield. I had the public support I needed to continue a policy of waging war in Vietnam and negotiating for peace in Paris until we could bring the war to an honorable and successful conclusion.

During the weeks after November 3 my Gallup overall-approval rating soared to 68 percent, the highest it had been since I took office. Congressional reaction was so positive that I took the unprecedented step of personally appearing before both the House and Senate and addressing them separately to thank them for their support.

At the same time I was under no illusions that this wave of Silent Majority support could be maintained for very long. My speech had not proposed any new initiatives; its purpose had been to gain support for the course we were already following. I knew that under the constant pounding from the media and our critics in Congress, people would soon be demanding that new actions be taken to produce progress and end the war.

One result of the unexpected success of the November 3 speech was the decision to take on the TV network news organizations for their biased and distorted "instant analysis" and coverage. Unless the practice were challenged, it would make it impossible for a President to appeal directly to the people, something I considered to be of the essence of democracy.

A few days after the speech, Pat Buchanan sent me a memorandum urging a direct attack on the network commentators and a few days later he submitted a speech draft that did so in very direct and articulate language. Ted Agnew's hard-hitting speeches had attracted a great deal of attention during the fall, and I decided that he was the right man to deliver this one. I toned down some of Buchanan's rhetoric and gave it to Agnew. We further moderated some sections that Agnew thought sounded strident, and then he edited it himself so that the final version would be his words. He decided to deliver the speech in Des Moines, Iowa, on November 13.

When the advance text arrived at the networks, there was pandemonium; all three decided to carry the speech live. For thirty minutes, Agnew tore into the unaccountable power in the hands of the "unelected elite" of network newsmen. He said, "A small group of men, numbering perhaps no more than a dozen anchormen, commentators, and executive producers, settle upon the film and commentary that is to reach the public. They decide what 40 to 50 million Americans will learn of the day's events in the nation and in the world." Referring to my November 3 speech, he said that my words had been unfairly subjected to "instant analysis and querulous criticism."

The national impact of Agnew's Des Moines speech was second only to that of my November 3 speech. Within a few hours telegrams began arriving at the White House; the switchboards were tied up all night by people calling to express their relief that someone had finally spoken up, and within a few days thousands of letters began pouring in from all over the country.

The networks purposely ignored the widespread public support Agnew's words received and tried to label the speech as an attempt at government "repression." The president of CBS, Frank Stanton, called it "an unprecedented attempt by the Vice President of the United States to intimidate a news medium which depends for its existence upon government licenses." The president of NBC, Julian Goodman, said that Agnew's "attack on television news is an appeal to prejudice." George McGovern reflected left-wing and liberal congressional reaction when he said, "I feel that the speech was perhaps the most frightening single statement ever to come from a high government official in my public career."

Some voices were raised on Agnew's side. Jerry Ford said that if the media distorted the news, they should be called to account: "I don't know why they should have a halo over their heads," he said. George Christian, President Johnson's last Press Secretary, said that LBJ had been concerned about the very questions Agnew raised, but he had been afraid to make a speech about them because he knew it would be interpreted as an attack on freedom of the press.

Even some of our severest critics admitted that Agnew's complaints were not unfounded. Writing in the *Saturday Review*, for example, British journalist Henry Brandon stated, "The Vice President made a few telling points. Instant commentary based on a hasty reading of a speech without much time for contemplation is hazardous and can lead to rash conclusions or unfair criticism."

After the tremendous success of my November 3 speech, an element of desperation entered into the planning of the November Vietnam Moratorium, known as the New Mobe. We received alarming reports that several militant groups involved in the New Mobe now felt that only a violent confrontation could adequately dramatize their concerns. Because of the radical background of some of the New Mobe organizers, many congressmen who had supported the October Moratorium managed to be unavailable for comment before the New Mobe began and out of town while it was going on.

On November 15 the New Mobe arrived. In San Francisco, while some of the crowd of 125,000 yelled "Peace!" Black Panther leader David Hilliard insisted, "We will kill Richard Nixon. We will kill any [one] that stands in the way of our freedom."

In Washington, 250,000 demonstrators surged into the city, causing the Washington *Post* to rhapsodize: "To dig beneath the rhetoric is to discover something extraordinary, and quite beautiful. Those who were here . . . are here in support of what is best about this country." At the

Washington Monument, Dick Gregory brought the crowd to its feet when he said, "The President says nothing you kids do will have any effect on him. Well, I suggest he make one long distance call to the LBJ Ranch." And later in the day came scattered episodes of violence. A group of protesters battled with police as they made their way through the streets knocking out windows. At the Justice Department protesters shouting "Smash the state!" stormed the building, tore down the American flag, burned it, and raised the Vietcong flag in its place.

I had never imagined that at the end of my first year as President I would be contemplating two more years of fighting in Vietnam. But the unexpected success of the November 3 speech had bought me more time, and, bolstered by Sir Robert Thompson's optimistic estimate that within two years we would be able to achieve a victory—either in the sense of an acceptable negotiated settlement or of having prepared the South Vietnamese to carry the burden of the fighting on their own—I was prepared to continue the war despite the serious strains that would be involved on the home front. Two years would bring us to the end of 1971 and the beginning of the 1972 campaign, and if I could hold the domestic front together until then, winning an honorable peace would redeem the interim difficulties.

As 1970 began, I envisioned a year of limited and even diminishing battlefield activity. I also envisioned the continuation of Kissinger's activity in the secret channel. I was rather less optimistic than Kissinger regarding the prospect of a breakthrough in the secret negotiations but I agreed that we must continue to pursue them as long as there was even a possibility they would be successful. Kissinger and I agreed that at the very least they would provide an indisputable record of our desire for peace and our efforts to achieve it.

I was disappointed but not surprised by the apparent ineffectiveness of our attempts in 1969 to get the Soviets to apply pressure on North Vietnam. But I understood the pressures placed on Moscow by the rivalry with Peking for ascendancy in the Communist world, and I felt that the important thing was to keep the Soviets aware that while we might recognize their inability to decrease their support of Hanoi or to apply pressure on the North Vietnamese to negotiate a settlement, we would not tolerate any major increase in aid or belligerent encouragement. Not surprisingly, the greatest incentive for Soviet cooperation in Vietnam was our new relationship with the Chinese, but that would not become a major factor until the middle of 1971.

I do not know whether or how I would have acted differently if at the end of 1969 I had known that within less than four months I would be forced to order an attack on the Communist sanctuaries in Cambodia, or that the next two years would once again bring America to the brink of internal disruption over Vietnam. At the same time I would have to walk a constantly higher tightrope trying to support our allies and our fighting men while not pushing the increasingly powerful antiwar forces in Congress into passing legislation that would cut off funds for the war or require our withdrawal.

All this lay ahead. As I sat in my study in San Clemente on New Year's Day thinking about these problems, I actually allowed myself a feeling of cautious optimism that we had weathered the worst blows from Vietnam and had only to hold firm until time began to work in our favor. I suppose that in some respects the Vietnam story is one of mutual miscalculation. But if I underestimated the willingness of the North Vietnamese to hang on and resist a negotiated settlement on any other than their own terms, they also underestimated my willingness to hold on despite the domestic and international pressures that would be ranged against me.

1969: PRESIDENT AND CONGRESS

I was determined to be an activist President in domestic affairs. I had a definite agenda in mind, and I was prepared to use the first year of the presidency to knock heads together in order to get things done. "The country recognizes the need for change," I told the first meeting of my new Urban Affairs Council, "and we don't want the record written that we were too cautious."

But it didn't take long to discover that enthusiasm and determination could not overcome the reality that I was still the first President in 120 years to begin his term with both houses of Congress controlled by the opposition party. I sent over forty domestic proposals to Congress that first year, including the first major tax reform package since Eisenhower's first term, a proposal to reorganize foreign aid, a message on electoral reform, the first presidential message in our history dealing with the explosive problems of population growth, and some twenty proposals dealing with crime and drug and pornography control. Only two of these proposals were passed: draft reform and our tax bill. Legislation that would take the Post Office Department out of politics and turn it into a non-partisan corporation soon followed. We won some tactical legislative victories over the Democratic opposition, but it soon became clear that my attempts to get Congress to approve creative and comprehensive proposals were going to be resisted.

Three major congressional battles that first year illustrated the kind of problems I would face in my dealings with Congress throughout my first term. There was the cliff-hanging one-vote margin of victory on my request for an anti-ballistic missile (ABM) system, underscoring the uncomfortably narrow bipartisan coalition I had to depend on when it came to foreign policy and defense issues. Then there were the battles over the Supreme Court vacancies: with the Haynsworth nomination at the end of 1969 and the Carswell nomination at the beginning of 1970, Congress, in an unprecedented partisan display, refused to confirm two successive presidential Supreme Court nominees. Finally, our bold attempt to reform the federal welfare system—the Family Assistance Plan—illustrated the problem of the Senate's tendency to fracture into special interest groups. As George Shultz later summed it up. "He who walks in the middle of the road gets hit from both sides."

It was clear to me by 1969 that there could never be absolute parity between the U.S. and the U.S.S.R. in the area of nuclear and conventional armaments. For one thing, the Soviets are a land power and we are a sea power. For another, while our nuclear weapons were better, theirs were bigger. Furthermore, absolute superiority in every area of armaments would have been meaningless, because there is a point in arms development at which each nation has the capacity to destroy the other. Beyond that point the most important consideration is not continued escalation of the number of arms but maintenance of the strategic equilibrium while making it clear to the adversary that a nuclear attack, even if successful, would be suicidal.

Consequently, at the beginning of the administration I began to talk in terms of *sufficiency* rather than *superiority* to describe my goals for our nuclear arsenal. Putting an end to the arms race meant working out trade-offs with the Soviets, and I wanted us to have the most bargaining chips from the outset in order to get the best deal. I said that Congress must not send me to the negotiating table as the head of the second strongest nation in the world.

This is where the ABM came in. The Soviets had indicated that they were willing to reach agreement on defensive arms limitation. Most of the liberals in Congress, the media, and the academic community tended to take them at face value in this regard and feared that a congressional vote for an ABM system would destabilize the existing arms balance and compel the Soviets to increase their own construction programs, thus losing a precious opportunity and moving the arms race up another notch.

I thought they were wrong. I thought the Soviets' primary interest in opening arms negotiations at that point was that without an ABM we would be in a disadvantageous negotiating position. Our intelligence reports indicated that in 1969 the Soviets spent the equivalent of $25 billion on nuclear weapons. They deployed more than a hundred intercontinental ballistic missiles (ICBMs) while we deployed none; they added several nuclear missile-firing submarines to their Navy while we added none; and they deployed forty new ABMs around Moscow. We knew that even as the debate in Congress over an American ABM was raging, the Soviets had initiated work on more ICBMs and ABMs, as well as major new radar systems in conjunction with their deployment; they were also building additional submarine missiles. I felt that tactically we needed the ABM as a bargaining chip for negotiations with the Soviets: they already had an ABM system, so if we went into negotiations without one we might have to give up something else, perhaps something more vital. In that sense, we had to have it in order to be able to agree to forgo it. I tried to persuade Congress that what the ABM vote represented was really a philosophical turning point in America's strategic credibility.

I knew that the vote on ABM would reverberate around the world as a measure of America's resolve. The minute the Europeans or the Japanese decided that we could not be depended upon to keep our commitments and stand up to the Soviets, the American position in Europe and the Far East would be severely damaged. But as I saw it, the ABM vote involved the much deeper question of whether Americans still believed that we stood for something in the world and that we must be willing to bear the burden of resisting aggression against our allies and friends. I believed that the majority of Americans felt this way; but as long as there was any doubt about it among our enemies, the temptations to test us would be that much stronger. The ABM vote would be the first significant congressional vote on defense measures in my administration, and I wanted the signal to go out that we had not lost our national sense of purpose and resolve—because I did not think we had.

Unfortunately, Vietnam soured the debate. It had convinced the liberals that America suffered from too belligerent a posture and made them determined to curb our military spending. As Stewart Alsop wrote in his column, "There are, of course, perfectly rational arguments against the ABM. But a great deal of the opposition to ABM is essentially emotional—it is the liberals' way of getting back at the generals for Vietnam." The liberals hated the war and they thought our best solution was just to get out. I hated the war too, but I thought we had to end it in a way that would keep our commitment to South Vietnam. I thought the liberals had deluded themselves: America would not make the world safer by acting dishonorably.

One good argument against the ABM was that many people—Eisenhower, incidentally, among them—doubted the efficacy of defensive weapons systems and preferred to put our money into building our offensive capability. There were also technical objections involving the cost of the system measured against the increased levels of defense it would actually produce. These arguments lost me support among some responsible conservatives and moderates whose votes I might otherwise have had, and made the tension even greater as we headed into the final vote.

The ABM vote actually involved a request for additional appropriations to carry on a building program that had begun under President Johnson. The system of extensive ABM coverage he had proposed in 1967 was called Sentinel. The reduced version I decided to propose in 1969 was called Safeguard.

Once I had made the decision, we faced the biggest congressional battle of the first term. We would be fairly sure of carrying the House; but in the Senate, where the powerful liberal forces were headed by Teddy Kennedy, it was clearly going to be very close. Democratic Senator Henry Jackson, a strong proponent of national defense, led the fight for us. He said that it was just like war, and we were going to have to fight it like war if we wanted to win.

We blanketed Capitol Hill with White House staff members. This was our first major attempt to use the delicate technique of persuasion without pressure, and we were constantly having to adjust our strategy as the daily reports indicated that we were not pushing hard enough with one congressman or that we were coming on too strong with another. I started out with a heavy schedule of calls and meetings with congressmen, but after the initial contacts had been made and the arguments presented I concluded that I was squandering presidential prestige that might be needed later. Some legislators tried to use the ABM vote as a bargaining chip of their own. In one case a powerful committee chairman hinted that I could have his support in exchange for approving a major federal installation in his district.

I felt we were fighting with one hand tied behind our back because we could not publicly explain the bargaining chip rationale for the ABM, nor could we reveal the intelligence reports of Soviet arms. Kissinger and I used these arguments in congressional briefings and meetings, but the liberal forces were well organized and were largely able to control the public debate.

The Senate would cast the first vote on ABM, and from the outset it was clear that the vote would be close. One of the key figures was the independent Republican senator, Margaret Chase Smith. Both sides sought to win her support; Mike Mansfield said he'd never seen so many men publicly woo one woman. Seemingly unrelated issues and events were weighed for the import they might have for the ABM vote. Thus, one of the arguments raised against retaliation when the North Koreans shot down our EC-121 in April was that the resulting furore would strengthen the anti-ABM forces. And when Teddy Kennedy's car went off a bridge at Chappaquiddick in July, the effectiveness of his leadership against the ABM was significantly reduced. As the time of the vote neared, I told Bryce Harlow, "Make sure that all our guys are there all the time. Don't let anyone get sick. Don't even let anyone go to the bathroom until it's all over."

When the vote was taken on August 6 it was in the form of three separate amendments to the bill that, if they had been adopted, would have halted construction of the ABM. All three were defeated. On the first and most important amendment—which would have prohibited all spending for Safeguard deployment, the Senate divided 50–50. Under Senate rules a tie vote would have defeated the amendment anyway, but Agnew cast his tie-breaking vote and the final tally read 51–50.

Even though the margin of victory was razor thin, the vote established that America was still prepared to maintain its military strength. I am absolutely convinced that had we lost the ABM battle in the Senate, we would not have been able to negotiate the first nuclear arms control agreement in Moscow in 1972. But the one-vote margin was undeniably a nerve-racking one, and it confirmed my resolve to pour every possible resource of money and manpower into the congressional elections of 1970 in order to shore up our position in Congress and make our margin more secure.

The Supreme Court is always keenly aware of political and social trends. During the 1950s and 1960s, under the leadership of Chief Justice Earl Warren, the Court had become unprecedentedly politically active. Like many legal and political moderate conservatives, I felt that some Supreme Court Justices were too often using their interpretation of the law to remake American society according to their own social, political, and ideological precepts.

By the time of the 1968 political campaign Warren was seventy-seven years old. It was unlikely that he would be able to lead the Court through the next four—or possibly eight—years of what might become the Nixon administration. On June 13, 1968, he sent his resignation to Lyndon Johnson "effective at your pleasure."

On June 26, Johnson nominated Abe Fortas to be Chief Justice. Fortas had been an Associate Justice since Johnson appointed him to the Court in 1965. Shortly after his nomination as Chief Justice was announced, it came to light that while on the Court, Fortas, a close friend of Johnson's, had performed a number of personal and political chores for him. This was a clear violation of the principle of separation of powers. It was also discovered that Fortas had accepted a $15,000 fee for a lecture series at American University. One of Fortas's former law partners had raised the money from influential business and financial leaders—men who might have interests in cases coming before the Supreme Court.

On October 2 Fortas asked Johnson to withdraw his nomination. By then it was then too close to the election for Johnson to make another nomination without seeming blatantly political. Thus whoever won the election would have the opportunity of selecting a Chief Justice at the beginning of his presidency.

Shortly after I was elected, I asked Bill Rogers to approach Chief Justice Warren and work out an understanding with regard to the timing of his resignation. Warren agreed to stay on until the end of the Court's session in June, and I asked John Mitchell to begin looking for a candidate to replace him. I was the thirty-seventh President, but the man I nominated would be only the fifteenth Chief Justice in our history. It was not a selection to be made lightly or hastily.

My first choice was former Attorney General Herb Brownell. There was only one drawback: he had been Eisenhower's Attorney General in 1957 at the time of the Little Rock school crisis, and I knew that many Southerners were still deeply embittered by his role in the use of federal troops to enforce integration. After getting negative reactions from key Southern senators, Mitchell told Brownell that his confirmation fight would be messy. Brownell said that such a controversy would not be in the interests of the nation or of the new administration, and he asked to be removed from consideration.

I asked Mitchell to sound out Tom Dewey, but as I expected, he ruled himself out because of his age. He was already sixty-six, and he felt strongly that any Chief Justice should serve for at least ten years.

I also considered Associate Justice Potter Stewart, an articulate dissenter from many of the Warren Court's activist decisions. On April 30, however, he came to the White House and said he wanted me to know that, in terms of the morale of the other Justices, he did not believe it was in the best interests of the Court to have one of the Associate Justices elevated to Chief Justice.

As the search continued, I developed five criteria for the selection process. The next Chief Justice must have a top-flight legal mind; he must be young enough to serve at least ten years; he should, if possible, have experience both as a practicing lawyer and as an appeals court judge; he must generally share my view that the Court should interpret the Constitution rather than amend it by judicial fiat; and he must have a special quality of leadership that would enable him to resolve differences among his colleagues so that, as often as possible, the Court would speak decisively on major cases with one voice or at least with a strong voice for the majority opinion.

I reviewed the list of appeals court judges Mitchell prepared for me and began looking particularly into the record of Judge Warren E. Burger of the District of Columbia Court of Appeals. I had been impressed by excerpts from one of Burger's speeches on the role of law and order in society that I read in 1967 in *U.S. News & World Report*. I had used several ideas from it in my speeches during the 1968 campaign. Mitchell gave me some of Burger's opinions to read, and I was impressed by their forcefulness and clarity. I knew Warren Burger to be philosophically a moderate conservative and personally an impressive man. On May 21 I nominated him as Chief Justice of the United States. He was confirmed readily and sworn in on June 23.

As I was nearing my decision on a new Chief Justice, I unexpectedly had the opportunity to fill another seat on the Supreme Court when Abe Fortas suddenly submitted his resignation.

Life magazine had recently disclosed further improprieties involving Fortas's finances and potential conflicts of interest, and I had told Mitchell that as a courtesy and on a completely confidential basis, we should keep Chief Justice Warren informed about the new charges emerging from the Justice Department's ongoing investigation. Warren was grateful because he felt that the new information represented a serious threat to the reputation of the Court; he was convinced that Fortas had no choice but to step down.

It was a difficult time for Fortas. I felt that the press had to some extent singled him out for criticism as a belated way of getting at Johnson, and I called him the day he announced his resignation and expressed my sympathy. Still, there was no question that he had been astonishingly indiscreet, and that it was important for the Court that he resign.

Once again I asked John Mitchell to direct the search for a Supreme Court Justice. We selected Judge Clement F. Haynsworth of South Carolina and announced his nomination on August 18, 1969. Haynsworth came from a distinguished legal family, was fifty-six years old, and had served with great distinction for twelve years on the Fourth Circuit Court of Appeals.

Harsh criticism began as soon as I announced the nomination. Civil rights organizations immediately called Haynsworth a racist; one group said he was a "laundered segregationist." George Meany claimed that his record was antilabor. The press picked up these themes and played daily variations on them. Soon the pack mentality took hold in Washington. Organized interest groups went to work, and letter and phone campaigns began putting pressure on the Senate.

Senator Birch Bayh of Indiana became the leader of the anti-Haynsworth forces. During Haynsworth's confirmation hearings, Bayh charged him with conflict of interest, claiming that he should have disqualified himself in several cases involving litigants who were customers of a company in which he owned stock. These disclosures had been investigated several years earlier by then Attorney General Robert Kennedy and by Judge Simon Sobeloff of the Fourth Circuit, who both found no conflict of interest. John Frank, the leading legal authority on disqualification of judges, testified at the time that not only did Haynsworth have no obligation to disqualify himself, he had an affirmative responsibility to rule on the cases in question. But the truth never caught up with Bayh's charges as he and other liberal Democrats on the Senate Judiciary Committee worked with a cooperative press corps to discredit Haynsworth.

Bayh and his supporters ended up maintaining that it was no longer sufficient that a nominee had not engaged in any impropriety; now there must be no "appearance" of impropriety. Thus opponents of a nominee could raise an "appearance" of impropriety by false charges and thereby defeat him. It was a vicious circle: the nominee would not be condemned for what he had done but for what he had been accused of having done by his detractors.

Few senators were candid enough to admit on the record the real grounds for their opposition to Haynsworth, but one anonymously told a reporter, "Conflict of interest is so much jazz; we are against him for what he believes."

In the middle of the furore, a delegation of Republican senators led by the Minority Whip, Robert Griffin of Michigan, came to the White House to ask me to withdraw the Haynsworth nomination. They explained the pressure they were under and the political leverage that was being brought to bear on them by labor and the press.

I refused. In fact, I went further and said that I would not withdraw Haynsworth's name even if he himself asked me to. There was a basic constitutional principle involved, the right of a President to choose his nominees for the Supreme Court. There was also a human element. To withdraw Haynsworth's name while he was under such bitter partisan fire might destroy his reputation, driving him from the bench and from public service. I made it clear that I planned to see the nomination through to the end.

On November 21 the Senate had rejected the Haynsworth nomination, 55 to 45, with seventeen Republicans joining the liberal Democrats in opposition.

On December 4 Haynsworth came to the White House, and we talked for an hour in the Oval Office. He seemed confused and dazed by what had happened. He is a quiet, refined, and extraordinarily kind man. When he said that the ordeal had been harder on his wife than on him, I thought about how Pat had felt during the fund crisis, and I hoped that the private hell they must have endured would not leave them scarred for life as ours had done. That night I wrote a note: "Haynsworth was the victim of forces he probably did not understand."

On January 19, 1970, two months after the Haynsworth vote, I nominated Judge G. Harrold Carswell of the Fifth Circuit Court of Appeals in Florida. I had told Mitchell to make sure that our second nominee was absolutely above personal or professional reproach; the fact that Carswell owned no stocks or securities seemed to put him beyond even the "appearance" of impropriety that had contributed to Haynsworth's defeat.

It did not take long for the liberal opposition to Carswell to start. As if on cue, the ritual charges of "racist" were made in the media and in Congress. Any conservative Southern judge would have to expect this kind of attack, and I was not surprised by it. Unfortunately, we had missed one statement from Carswell's distant past. In 1948, as a Democratic candidate for the Georgia legislature, he had said, "Segregation of the races is proper and the only practical and correct way of life in our states. I have always so believed and I shall always so act." Carswell had renounced his twenty-two-year-old views, but the damage was irreparable. I was distressed that we had overlooked this unfortunate statement, but I did not believe that youthful indiscretions that had been recanted and redeemed should be held against an individual in later years.

Carswell had looked highly qualified on paper; the exceptionally rigorous scrutiny to which he was subjected, with various senators and their staffs determined to dig out anything bad they could find and then present it in the worst possible light, revealed that he was not as highly qualified as we had thought. I still believe that Carswell would have passed muster by the standards of other times. But the post-Haynsworth partisan fallout was too intense. The word *mediocre* was increasingly used to describe him and his career. His defenders were placed in the position of having to prove a negative—that he was not mediocre.

When the vote was taken on April 8, the Carswell nomination was rejected, 51 to 45. It was cold and reasoned anger that impelled me to make a statement the next day commenting on the Senate's action. If the Northern liberals had tasted victory in defeating my second nominee, I was determined that they would at least pay a political price for it in the South. I said:

> I have reluctantly concluded that it is not possible to get confirmation for a Judge on the Supreme Court of any man who believes in the strict construction of the Constitution, as I do, if he happens to come from the South. . . .

> When you strip away all the hypocrisy, the real reason for their rejection was their legal philosophy, a philosophy that I share, of strict construction of the Constitution, and also the accident of their birth, the fact that they were born in the South. . . .
>
> And I have concluded, therefore, that the next nominee must come from outside the South, since this Senate, as it is presently constituted, will not approve a man from the South who shares my views of strict construction of the Constitution.

Looking back I have no quarrel with some of those senators who voted against Carswell because of their belief that he lacked the superior intellectual and judicial qualities to be a Supreme Court Justice. But I still believe that many of the senators who voted against him used the issue of his competence as camouflage for their real reason, which was their disapproval of his constitutional philosophy.

On April 14, 1970, I nominated Federal Circuit Court of Appeals Judge Harry A. Blackmun. An Eisenhower appointee who had practiced law for twenty years prior to ten and a half years of distinguished service on the federal bench, Blackmun was a Northerner, from Minnesota. He was unanimously confirmed by the Senate on May 12.

Within a week in September 1971, Supreme Court Justices Hugo Black and John Harlan both submitted letters of retirement to me for reasons of health.

After my experience with the Carswell and Haynsworth appointments, I did not intend to make the same mistakes again. I was still determined, however, that those appointed be strict constructionists, and I still wanted to find a qualified Southerner. This time I also wanted to find a qualified woman. Above all, I wanted to be sure that my nominees would be confirmed.

Now I decided that while John Mitchell would once again play the leading role in recommending possible candidates, I would try to elicit some independent evaluations.

Our search for a woman nominee was serious and intense, and accompanied, I might add, by Pat's cogent and determined lobbying on every available occasion. But we found that in general the women judges and lawyers qualified to be nominated for the Supreme Court were too liberal to meet the strict constructionist criterion I had established.

On October 19, 1971, I asked Mitchell to extend to Lewis Powell, a Virginia attorney and a former president of the American Bar Association, an offer to fill one of the vacancies. Powell was reluctant because he was sixty-four years old, but that night I telephoned him and urged him to take it. The next afternoon he called Mitchell and accepted the nomination.

My friend and White House Special Counsel Dick Moore suggested that I consider Assistant Attorney General William Rehnquist for the other vacancy. Rehnquist had been first in his class at Stanford Law School and then served as a clerk to Supreme Court Justice Robert Jackson. Apart from his unquestioned legal qualifications and his moderately conservative philosophy, Rehnquist's most attractive attribute was his age: he was only forty-seven and could probably serve on the Court for twenty-five years. Mitchell shared Moore's high opinion of Rehnquist and enthusiastically endorsed him.

When I announced Powell and Rehnquist as my nominees on national television on October 21, there were the predictable charges that I was packing the Court with ultraconservatives, and the Senate dragged its feet in order to give the critics time to try to knock down the new nominees. But they were so obviously highly qualified that only the most partisan opposition could be raised. Both men were confirmed, Powell on December 6 and Rehnquist on December 10, by overwhelming votes.

I consider my four appointments to the Supreme Court to have been among the most constructive and far-reaching actions of my presidency. Some critics have characterized my appointments as an effort to create a "Nixon Court." It is true that the men I appointed shared my conservative judicial philosophy and significantly affected the balances of power that had developed in the Warren Court. But as individuals they were each dedicated and able constitutional lawyers who often disagreed on major cases. When I appointed them, I told each that I would never try to influence his judgment and that his only loyalty should be to the law and not to me. Their decisions in cases that affected me politically or personally reflected the fact that they accepted my admonition.

From the first days of my administration I wanted to get rid of the costly failures of the Great Society—and I wanted to do it immediately. I wanted the people who had elected me to see that I was going to follow through on my campaign promises. The worst offender was the welfare system, and welfare reform was my highest domestic priority.

It was Pat Moynihan who made an uncharacteristic plea for caution. In several long sessions in the Oval Office he paced back and forth in front of my desk, waving his arms to punctuate his argument. "All the Great Society activist constituencies are lying out there in wait," he said, "poised to get you if you try to come after them: the professional welfarists, the urban planners, the day-carers, the social workers, the public housers. Frankly, I'm terrified at the thought of cutting back too fast. Just take Model Cities. The urban ghettos will go up in flames if you cut it out."

Moynihan wanted to take a year to consolidate our domestic situation before proposing any domestic legislation. But a year was simply too long, so I pushed the Cabinet and staff to develop a program of creative and innovative social legislation as soon as possible.

The current welfare system was a mess. It was inefficient and inconsistent. Payment for equivalent families could range from as high as $263 a month in one state to $39 a month in another. In most states higher payments were made to fatherless families; not surprisingly, families split up in order to collect more money. From 1961 to 1967, 93 percent of the families added to the welfare rolls had absent fathers. There was a rise in illegitimacy; by 1969 over 69 percent of welfare births in New York City were out of wedlock. There were loopholes that meant an individual could earn more on welfare than working for the minimum wage and that a woman earning over $12,000 a year might still be eligible for welfare benefits. There were also flagrant problems of fraud, along with the graft that plagues any big system with a multitude of different regulations and large amounts of money.

Seething beneath the surface of the welfare problem was a disturbing undercurrent of racial friction. Moynihan summarized this in a memo to me on May 17, 1969: "In the present time the service-dispensing groups in the society—teachers, welfare workers, urban planners, nutrition experts, etc., etc.—are preoccupied with the black problem and almost at times seem to resent hearing there are whites who are in difficulty or marginally so." Moynihan pointed out that the current services strategy for welfare tended not only to exclude working-class whites—and 60 percent of low income workers were white—but to create a group of middle-class whites and blacks who were in what he called the "resentment business":

> They earn very good livings making the black poor feel put upon, when they are, which is often the case, and also when they are not. . . .
>
> On average, I would suppose for example, that the white women who teach Head Start children earn about three times as much per hour as the black men who fathered the children. And for all this the results are really rather marginal so far as the children are concerned. In the meantime the black poor *seem* to be favored over the white near poor, the loud mouths get louder and temperatures rise.

The result of this situation was that, as one magazine writer described it, we were on the brink of "The Revolt of the White Lower Middle Classes."

After several months of study and discussion of every aspect of the problem, we devised the Family Assistance Plan, which I announced in a televised address on domestic legislation on August 8, 1969.

The Great Society programs had poured billions of dollars into supplying a formidable range of social services for the poor; if you could prove that your income was below a certain level you could qualify for any number of free or subsidized goods and services. I felt that this kind of approach encouraged a feeling of dependence and discouraged the kind of self-reliance that is needed to get people on their feet. I thought that people should have the responsibility for spending carefully and taking care of themselves. I abhorred snoopy, patronizing surveillance by social workers which made children and adults on welfare feel stigmatized and separate. The basic premise of the Family Assistance Plan was simple: what the poor need to help them rise out of poverty is money.

The answer we came up with was also simple, but revolutionary: we decided to provide federal financial aid not just to the unemployed poor, but to the working poor. Payments would go not just to families with fatherless children but to families in which the fathers lived at home. By providing a federal income floor we would ease the financial burden on the states; by setting nationwide standards and establishing automated payment procedures we hoped to cut down on red tape, and before long to eliminate social services, social workers and the stigma of welfare.

But there was something else that was revolutionary about FAP. It was not a simple guaranteed income. The plan required that everyone who accepted benefits must either accept work or training for work if suitable jobs were available within a reasonable distance. The bottom line was—no work, no welfare. The only exceptions would be the aged, the infirm, and mothers of pre-school children.

FAP was a risk. I knew that. We would be making thirteen million more people eligible for federal help than were currently eligible in an effort to reward work and not punish the poor for holding jobs. We would be incurring a first-year cost increase of $4 billion on the speculation that once people were not penalized for work—once they were certain they could earn more in jobs than solely on welfare—they would prefer to work. We hoped that the stability that the increased money would provide would be an incentive to get better and better paying jobs, ultimately taking people off the welfare rolls. It was a speculation that no one was certain would work. For these reasons FAP had a rocky passage through my own staff and Cabinet, where Moynihan, Finch, Ehrlichman and Secretary of Labor George Shultz defended it against the criticisms of the opposing conservative faction led by Arthur Burns, Ted Agnew, and Budget Director Robert Mayo.

I knew that we were taking a chance with FAP. But I also knew that the current system was a disaster that deteriorated faster every year. And FAP was the only plan with any chance of changing that.

In many respects I was in a very peculiar situation: less than eight months after my inauguration as the first Republican President in eight years, I was proposing a piece of almost revolutionary domestic legislation that required me to seek a legislative alliance with Democrats and liberals; my own conservative friends and allies were bound to oppose it. I thought the biggest danger would be the attack from the right. I was in for a surprise.

Predictably, conservatives denounced the plan as a "megadole" and a leftist scheme. But then, after a brief round of praise from columnists, editorialists, and academics, the liberals turned on the plan and practically pummeled it to death. They complained that the dollar amounts were not enough and the work requirements were repressive. In fact, FAP would have immediately lifted 60 percent of the people then living in poverty to incomes above that level. This was a real war on poverty, but the liberals could not accept it. Liberal senators immediately began to introduce extravagant bills of their own that had no hope of passage. As Moynihan observed, it was as if they could not tolerate the notion that a conservative Republican President had done what his liberal Democratic predecessors had not been bold enough to do.

The interest groups reacted no more admirably. The National Welfare Rights Organization, purportedly representing the interests of welfare recipients, formed an alliance with the social workers who were threatened with extinction, and denounced the plan. NWRO called it an "act of political repression" and accused the administration of conspiring to starve children. The plan was even called "racist," despite the fact that immediately upon passage it would have provided roughly 40 percent more money to blacks living in fourteen Southern states—and in 1969 slightly more than half the black population lived in the South. NWRO held noisy hearings at which welfare recipients testified, "We only want the kind of jobs that will pay $10,000 or $20,000" and "You'd better give me something better than I'm getting on welfare." NWRO proposed its own plan, which was introduced in the Senate by George McGovern, to guarantee a $6,500 income to every family of four. Such a plan would have put about half of America on welfare.

We fought hard. On April 16, 1970, thanks in large part to the leadership of Jerry Ford with help from Wilbur Mills, FAP passed the House.

But the Senate Finance Committee, with Southern conservatives in key positions and no coordinated endorsement from the liberals, kept the plan on ice. On July 1, 1970, Moynihan wrote to me: "I fear the chances are now less than even that Family Assistance will be passed this year, and if not this year, not this decade." He said that no Republican was resisting efforts to kill the measure and that "increasingly the Democrats see an opportunity to deny you this epic victory and at the same time blame you for the defeat."

During the fall I put pressure on the Senate Finance Committee, but my efforts failed. On November 20 the committee voted the measure down, 10–6. In 1971 the House again passed the bill and again the Senate Finance Committee bottled it up. Ultimately only the sections of FAP providing guaranteed incomes for the aged and disabled passed the full Congress.

By 1971 the momentum for FAP had passed and I knew it. I still believed in the validity of the idea, but I no longer believed in the political timing. In 1969 the American people had been ready for change; in 1971 they were thinking of other things—of Vietnam and the economy. By 1971 there was also the prospect of the 1972 election; I did not want to be in a losing fight with the conservatives over FAP in an election year. Therefore, in the summer of 1972 when I was given a choice either to endorse a more costly version of the bill proposed by Senator Ribicoff or to stay with our original FAP even though it would surely fail, I decided on the latter. FAP finally died in the Senate Finance Committee in 1972—an idea ahead of its time.

APOLLO XI

For me the most exciting event of the first year of my presidency came in July 1969 when an American became the first man to walk on the moon. The moon landing was the culmination of a program begun a dozen years earlier after the Soviets launched Sputnik, the first man-made orbiting satellite. American public opinion was jolted at the thought of the Soviets in control of outer space, but Eisenhower and most of his advisers were not so disturbed. Sherman Adams, for example, told a predominantly Republican audience that the so-called satellite race was just "an outer space basketball game." I believed that this flippant remark was wrong in substance and disastrous in terms of public opinion. The next night I told an audience in San Francisco, "We could make no greater mistake than to brush off this event as a scientific stunt of more significance to the man in the moon than to men on earth."

In Cabinet and NSC meetings during this time I strongly advocated a sharp increase in our missile and space programs. Eisenhower finally came around to this view and approved a proposal for manned space vehicles. While he justified this decision on military grounds, I felt that something far more basic was involved. I believe that when a great nation drops out of the race to explore the unknown, that nation ceases to be great.

The manned space program was already well under way when President Kennedy captured the national imagination in 1961 by setting the goal of a moon landing by the end of the decade. President Johnson was an enthusiastic supporter of NASA, and under his administration the Apollo program made great strides.

I decided that when the Apollo XI astronauts actually landed on the moon, the occasion should be well and widely marked. Working with NASA officials, we made plans for a televised phone conversation from the White House to the moon. In addition to planting an American flag on the lunar surface, the astronauts would leave behind a plaque bearing our signatures and a message that read:

HERE MEN FROM THE PLANET EARTH
FIRST SET FOOT UPON THE MOON
JULY, 1969 A.D.
WE CAME IN PEACE FOR ALL MANKIND

On Sunday night, July 20, Apollo VIII astronaut Frank Borman, Bob Haldeman, and I stood around the TV set in the private office and watched Neil Armstrong step onto the moon. Then I went into the Oval Office next door where TV cameras had been set up for my split-screen phone call to the moon.

Armstrong's voice came through loud and clear. I said, "Because of what you have done the heavens have become a part of man's world. And as you talk to us from the Sea of Tranquillity, it inspires us to redouble our efforts to bring peace and tranquillity to earth."

After a journey of almost half a million miles to the moon and back, Apollo XI landed less than two miles from the prearranged target about a thousand miles southwest of Hawaii in the Pacific Ocean. I was there to welcome the astronauts home. Because the mission's command module was named *Columbia,* I had asked the Navy band to play "Columbia, the Gem of the Ocean" as the astronauts stepped from the helicopter onto the aircraft carrier *Hornet*'s deck.

When I talked with them through the window of their quarantine chamber, it was hard to contain my enthusiasm or my awe at the thought that the three men on the other side of that glass had just returned from the moon. I said impulsively, "This is the greatest week in the history of the world since the Creation." When I talked to Billy Graham a few days later, he said, "Mr. President, I know exactly how you felt, and I understand exactly what you meant, but, even so, I think you may have been a little excessive."

The Apollo program ended on December 19, 1972, with the splashdown of Apollo XVII. By then, the public had become blasé about the ever-present hazards of space as well as the excitement of its challenge. The program had also begun to fall victim to the introverted attitude that threatened so much new technology in the 1970s. This contributed to the congressional refusal to support my proposal to continue our supersonic jet transport program, which I considered essential if America were to retain its lead in the field of commercial aviation. The argument went, as long as one person on earth is poor, not a dollar should be spent on space. In my opinion, however, exploration of space is one of the last of the great challenges to the American spirit. Space is perhaps the last frontier truly commensurate with America's capacity for wonder.

LYNDON JOHNSON: DECEMBER 1969

On Thursday, December 11, 1969, Lyndon Johnson was in Washington, and I invited him to the White House for breakfast. I met him in the Red Room and we went right into the first-floor family dining room, where I had arranged the table so that he could look into the fire. Without his asking, a bottle of liquid saccharin had been placed by his plate and the waiter brought him very light coffee.

He was extremely agitated about charges that while he was President he had used his influence to get his friends special deals for land acquisition and federal loans for their geriatrics center in Texas. Several times during breakfast he returned to this subject. But he also had some fascinating afterthoughts on the Vietnam bombing halt and on his dealings with the Soviets.

Late that night I dictated some recollections of our meeting; this was one of the handful of detailed dictations I made before I began keeping an almost daily dictated diary in November 1971.

Lyndon Johnson was such an intensely physical man that it is probably impossible for words to convey what being with him was like. I think this dictation gives at least some sense of the range of impressions and emotions a conversation with him might generate:

> He seemed to have gotten considerably heavier, and I noted that when he got excited he breathed very hard and on the [geriatrics center] point even seemed to have tears in his eyes.
>
> He reviewed in detail his attitude on Vietnam negotiations and his relations with the Russians. He again told me, as he had in California, that his major mistake as President was in "trust-

ing the Russians" too much. He said that he thought that Eisenhower got along well with the Russians for the first six or seven years of his term due to the fact that "they feared Ike" because of what Dulles had threatened to do in Korea [use the A-Bomb]. He thought the reason Ike had difficulties in the last year was because some of the fear had been dissipated. He thought the same thing had happened to Kennedy when he tried to placate the Russians up until the time of the Cuban missile crisis. He thought that he had gone through the same experience during his years in office.

He recounted that Kosygin at Glassboro had indicated that the Russians would be willing to help out on Vietnam and had set out a proposition which Johnson said he would like to consider. Johnson suggested that they meet again in New York. When they met Johnson had studied the Kosygin proposition with Rusk and McNamara and made a counterproposal which Kosygin said was "different from his but in the ball park." Johnson confidently expected that something would happen. Two weeks went by without result. Rusk called Dobrynin in and was stonewalled on the matter. Two weeks later Thompson [U.S. ambassador in Moscow] called on Gromyko and got a cold shoulder. Nothing at all came from this initiative.

He said at the time of the bombing halt Harriman told him "at least twelve times" that they had assurances from the North Vietnamese that if the bombing were halted, the "understanding" with regard to shelling cities would be carried out. He felt that the Russians had given a similar assurance along these lines.

He said that all the bombing pauses were a mistake and he had accomplished nothing. Each one of them was undertaken only because of some assurance that he received, either through Russian or other sources, that there would be a positive reaction from the other side. He said that he did not want to call a bombing halt late in the campaign unless he was absolutely convinced he had a "deal." He knew he would be charged with having done it for political reasons.

He spoke with considerable bitterness about *Look*'s article on his brother. He told the story of one of his big financial supporters, who also had a brother who got into lots of trouble; [the man's] mother insisted on his doing something for the brother and he finally gave him a job driving a truckload of dynamite across the state. "He stopped at a roadside stand, had a couple of beers, propositioned the waitress to marry him, and went off down the road, and then a tree moved in front of him."

He spoke warmly of Agnew and said that he had a high opinion of him when he had been governor of Maryland. Agnew apparently had given him strong support on his foreign policy.

He felt that newspapermen are just naturally vicious and are not happy unless they are attacking somebody. He felt that he was free from such attacks during his first year in office only because Goldwater was his opponent and that as soon as Goldwater was out of the way it was inevitable that they would take him on. "The press just isn't happy unless they are attacking who happens to be President" was his conclusion.

He gave me at least a twenty-minute monologue on the geriatric center, referring very movingly to his having determined to build such a center due to the fact that the mayor of his home town had spent the last years of his life in a rest home which was just like a "hawg pen" and that his mother also spent some time in such a place.

He told the story about his going on the ticket [in 1960] and said he did so because Sam Rayburn insisted that he had to stop Nixon since Nixon had "called him a traitor." Johnson recalled that while I was Vice President, I had called him up to the rostrum in the Senate one day and shown him the speech which they were referring to. Johnson had shown it to Rayburn later, and Rayburn simply brushed it aside and said that I had said it another time. In any event Rayburn believed that was the case until he died.

As we were leaving he spoke very warmly of the courtesies we had extended him and to his girls and to Lady Bird.

THE FIRST YEAR

By the end of 1969, after almost a year in the White House, I felt that the administration was operating as an effective team.

Bob Haldeman had proved that, contrary to accepted belief, it is possible to make the White House run efficiently, to get the most out of people, and to prepare for decisions with sufficient information in sufficient time. Haldeman should get the credit for this, because he was made to pay the price for it. From the outset there were conflicts between the Cabinet and the White House staff, as there are in every presidency. Stories spread about Haldeman's alleged rudeness to Cabinet members and party leaders. Most of the stories were apocryphal, although I am sure that some were not. Haldeman was a quick, cogent thinker with limited tolerance for those whose decisiveness and dedication did not match his own. He had great expectations, and he drove the White House staff to meet them.

There were conflicts of viewpoint and clashes of personality in the Nixon administration, but no human organization ever has been or ever will be free of them. The most important of these conflicts—because of its potential effect on policy—involved Bill Rogers, Henry Kissinger, and Mel Laird. When three such distinctive personalities and temperaments were added to the already volatile institutional mix of the State Department, the NSC, and the Pentagon, it was inevitable that there would be fireworks. To Rogers's credit, it must be said that in many cases his primary concern was simply to be kept informed of what was going on. He had to testify before several congressional committees, and the secrecy with which our decisions customarily—and usually necessarily—were surrounded often placed him in an embarrassing position. I once jokingly remarked that Laird did not have this problem because he would answer questions and state his views whether he was informed or not.

Rogers and Laird occasionally carried on sensitive dealings and negotiations without coordinating them with the White House. In some cases this was inadvertent, when they lacked information about our secret diplomacy; sometimes it was done to preclude Kissinger's or my own disapproval; and sometimes, I think, it was done just to show themselves, their departments, and the press that they were capable of independent action. In some cases the results were harmless or even positive, but in a few cases the outcome threatened to undercut our policy and credibility with foreign countries.

Eventually the relationship between Kissinger and Rogers took on a fairly combative aspect. Kissinger bridled at my assignment in 1969 and 1970 of all Middle Eastern problems to Rogers. He felt that Rogers was overly influenced by the pro-Arab elements of the State Department, and that he did not have the necessary skill or subtlety or a sense of broad foreign policy strategy. Kissinger also worried when foreign policy power seemed to become dispersed, and he was concerned by Rogers's direct access to the Oval Office. Rogers felt that Kissinger was Machiavellian, deceitful, egotistical, arrogant, and insulting. Kissinger felt that Rogers was vain, uninformed, unable to keep a secret, and hopelessly dominated by the State Department bureaucracy. The problems became increasingly serious as the years passed. Kissinger suggested repeatedly that he might have to resign unless Rogers was restrained or replaced.

Since I valued both men for their different views and qualities, I tried to keep out of the personal fireworks that usually accompanied anything in which they were both involved. In this regard, Haldeman rendered valiant service since he ended up as a sort of DMZ between the two, and between them and me. Finally, even Haldeman had difficulties mediating the strongly held views of these proud and powerful men, and by the end of 1969 I was beginning to include John Mitchell in many foreign policy decisions so that he could provide a stabilizing personal influence.

The clashes between my liberal and conservative domestic advisers were perhaps more cerebral but no less dramatic or deeply felt. During the summer and fall I had gradually moved John Ehrlichman into the position of coordinating all domestic programs and issues. He had a strong creative streak and a refreshingly acerbic sense of humor, and I considered him to be the ideal choice to bring to domestic policy the same intellectually wide-ranging but organizationally disciplined approach that Kissinger had brought so successfully to foreign policy.

On the personal side, the biggest surprise of the first year for Pat and me was that we had not been prepared for the paradoxical combination of loss of privacy and sense of isolation that we experienced in the White House. When I was Vice President we had had many official obligations, but at the end of the day we went home to our family in a residential area of Washington where we did our shopping in the local markets, and had a large circle of friends with whom we could unwind and relax. But the President and First Lady soon discover that everything they do or say is potentially news. They are surrounded by Secret Service agents, staff members, communications teams, medics and doctors, transportation aides, and scores of reporters and photographers whose only job is to try to get a word with them or a picture of them. Any moments of real privacy suddenly seem especially precious, and increasingly Pat and I liked to spend time at Camp David, in Key Biscayne, and at our home in San Clemente, California.

At the same time I discovered how isolated from the reality of American life a President can feel in the White House. For all its cosmopolitan self-confidence, Washington is a parochial city preoccupied by politics and gossip—which at times in Washington are the same thing. Like other Presidents before and after me, I felt a need to get out of the White House and out of Washington in order to keep some sense of perspective.

Looking back over 1969, I saw it as a beginning—a solid beginning. We had held our own. The new year would begin a new decade, and I looked forward to the opportunity to leave the turbulent 1960s behind and begin a new era of creative and peaceful progress for America and the world.

1970

From a political standpoint, my approach to the question of civil rights for black Americans was similar to my approach to the question of Israel. In each case, I was in the unique position of being politically unbeholden to the major pressure group involved, and this meant that I was more readily trusted by opposing or competing groups; this, in turn, meant that I had more flexibility and freedom to do solely what I thought was the right thing.

During the 1960s, particularly under President Johnson, there had been great strides in making the laws ensure the guaranteed rights of every American. With the passage of the Civil Rights Act of 1964 and the Voting Rights Act of 1965, almost every legislative roadblock to equality of opportunity for education, jobs, and voting had been removed. But passing legislation in Washington was one thing; enforcing it throughout the country was another. Expectations had been raised too high, and some black extremists now advocated and engaged in violent action in their efforts to pressure the federal government to hasten the rate of real progress.

Two weeks after the 1964 Civil Rights Act was passed, the first new outbreaks of racial violence occurred. The Harlem riots of 1964 were followed by the 1965 Watts riot, in which arson, looting, sniping, even killing suddenly became the preferred tools of many of the new activists of both races. George Wallace used the inevitable white backlash to build a formidable third party candidacy in 1968.

When I came into office in 1969, the black extremists were still riding high. Despite the laws, the money spent on the problem, and the significant progress that had in fact been made, black Americans appeared to be more dissatisfied with their lot at the end of the 1960s than they were at the beginning, and tensions between black and white had never been higher. I felt that as a Republican and a moderate conservative I had a better chance of achieving an accommodation between the races than a Democrat or a liberal who was publicly committed to one particular constituency. In formulating my policies I tried to strike a moderate balance. Inevitably I dissatisfied the people on both extremes. As I told members of my staff at one of our early meetings, "I could deliver the Sermon on the Mount and the NAACP would criticize the rhetoric. And the diehard segregationists would criticize it on the grounds that I was being motivated solely by public pressure rather than by conscience. So let's just tackle the problems instead of talking about them. We will be judged by what we do rather than what we say on this issue."

Finally, I knew that we had to attack the problem on a number of fronts. I felt that while education would be the most difficult and the most important, there were also questions of jobs, of welfare reform, of encouraging minority business enterprise, and of housing.

A few weeks after the inauguration, Pat Moynihan brought Rev. Ralph Abernathy, president of the Southern Christian Leadership Conference, and several of his associates to the White House. I had first met Abernathy in 1957 when he was Martin Luther King's chief lieutenant. While he may have been a good lieutenant, I could see that he had not developed into a good general; he lacked the vision and the wisdom that King had had in such a remarkable degree. Most of the Cabinet and key members of the White House staff assembled in the Roosevelt Room to meet with Abernathy, but the long session was a shambles because he was either unprepared or unwilling, or both, to have a serious discussion. Instead he postured and made speeches. He began by reading a list of demands and spent the rest of the time restating them in more colorful ways. Nonetheless he seemed pleased that we had made this effort and at the end he thanked me profusely for taking the time to meet with them. When he left the Cabinet Room he walked into the briefing room and told reporters that he had just sat through "the most disappointing, the most fruitless of all the meetings we had had up to this time."

Moynihan was embarrassed and outraged. He came into the Oval Office and paced the floor and said, "After the way you and the rest of us listened and indicated our sincere desire to find solutions to the problems, he goes into the press room and pisses on the President of the United States. It was unconscionable and I promise you it will never happen again."

Moynihan had been surprised by Abernathy's conduct, but I wasn't. I said, "The problem as I see it, is that they don't think that I care. We must demonstrate to them that we *do* care by our actions and not just by our words."

It was ironic that Moynihan, who was among the strongest advocates of civil rights programs in my administration, provided the very words over which we were subsequently accused of being reactionaries in a memo he wrote to me early in 1970. In it he set forth a number of positive initiatives he felt we should undertake. In a section clearly referring to the desirability of cooling inflated rhetoric, he wrote:

> The time may have come when the issue of race could benefit from a period of "benign neglect." The subject has been too much talked about. The forum has been too much taken over by hysterics, paranoids, and boodlers on all sides. We may need a period in which Negro progress continues and racial rhetoric fades.

The phrase *benign neglect* was seized upon out of context to characterize the administration's attitude toward blacks and other minorities. It was a term that caught on and was played back to us every time we tried to do something constructive in the civil rights area. Moynihan was deeply distressed by this incident and offered to resign. Of course, I refused his offer.

A good job is as basic and important a civil right as a good education, and many blacks and members of other minorities were being prevented from getting good jobs because of the policies of the major labor unions which excluded them from membership or discriminated against them in hiring and promotion. Therefore the first problem we addressed was unemployment. I asked Secretary of Labor George Shultz to see what could be done. He proposed a plan which would require all contractors working on federally funded construction projects to pledge a good faith effort toward the goal of hiring a representative number of minority workers.

Shultz pointed out that of the 1.3 million construction workers in the United States, only 106,000 were black, and 80 percent of those were in the lowest paid category of laborers; of the 130,000 building apprentices in the country, only 5,000 were black.

As Vice President I had been chairman of Eisenhower's Committee on Government Contracts, which made substantial progress in using persuasion and publicity to encourage companies with government contracts to hire more minority workers. I felt that the plan Shultz devised, which would require such action by law, was both necessary and right. We would not fix quotas, but would require federal contractors to show "affirmative action" to meet the goals of increasing minority employment. For example, in Philadelphia the goal would be to increase it from 4 percent to 26 percent between 1969 and 1973. Other cities would have other goals.

Congressional conservatives joined organized labor in vehemently opposing this plan. They considered it heretical for a Republican President to propose such a thing—and heresy is rarely politically popular. Right up to his death in September 1969, Everett Dirksen urged me to abandon it. In a meeting in the Cabinet Room with the legislative leaders he said, in his characteristically colorful way, "As your leader in the Senate of the United States, it is my bounden duty to tell you that this thing is about as popular as a crab in a whorehouse. You will split your own party if you insist on pursuing it. And, Mr. President, I do not think that I myself will be able to support you on this ill-conceived scheme."

By the end of October 1969, a contract was awarded that put the plan into effect for six construction unions working on a federally funded hospital in Philadelphia. What became known as the Philadelphia Plan was soon extended to building trades unions in New York, Pittsburgh, Seattle, Los Angeles, St. Louis, San Francisco, Boston, Chicago, and Detroit.

George Meany hit the roof, charging that the administration was making the unions a whipping boy and trying to score "brownie points" with civil rights groups. Union lobbyists applied tremendous political power and pressure to members of Congress, and damaging amendments were adopted by the Senate. We carried the battle to the floor of both houses. Eventually, due in large part to the leadership of Jerry Ford and Hugh Scott, our efforts paid off. Both the Senate and House rejected the amendments, which would have gutted the Philadelphia Plan.

Getting the plan written into law turned out to be easier than implementing the law. There were some initial successes, but I was disappointed that we received only lukewarm support from most of the national black leaders, who tended either to minimize the results we had achieved, or to complain that we had not gone far enough. Once again I had to wonder whether the black leadership was not more interested in dramatic tokenism than in the hard fight for actual progress.

An important area where we were able to make a considerable impact was in the field of minority business enterprise. During the 1968 campaign I had delivered a radio address entitled "Bridges to Human Dignity" in which I urged new efforts to bring members of minority groups into the economic mainstream. Unless they were to be a permanent inferior economic class apart from other Americans, we had to find ways to give qualified blacks and other minorities a stake in the American private enterprise system. During the transition period I delegated this responsibility to Secretary of Commerce Maurice Stans and told him that I considered it to be of the highest priority. The statistics demonstrate that while we did not attain all the goals we set for ourselves, we made substantial progress in this area.

When I entered office in 1969, minority enterprises were getting only $8 million of business through government contracts. By 1972 they were getting $242 million. In the same period the total of all government grants, loans, and guarantees directed toward helping minority business enterprises had jumped from $200 million to $472 million. Of the 100 largest black-owned businesses in 1975, more than two-thirds had been formed since 1968. Most important, all of this activity was reflected at the cash register, where receipts of black-owned businesses jumped from $4.5 billion in 1968 to $7.2 billion in 1972.

The most explosive of the civil rights issues during my presidency were the questions of school desegregation and busing. Fifteen years had passed since the Supreme Court handed down its landmark decision that laws requiring segregated schools were unconstitutional in *Brown* v. *Board of Education.* After the *Brown* decision, segregation by law—de jure segregation—was illegal as well as wrong; where it could be proved to exist, the law could be used to stop it. It was more difficult to deal with the problem of unequal education for black and white students because of segregation which existed, not as a result of conscious discrimination by law, but as the natural outgrowth of economic and social patterns within individual communities and neighborhoods—de facto segregation.

Despite a great deal of rhetoric and a few highly publicized symbolic confrontations during the Kennedy and Johnson administrations, very little progress was made in ending the dual school system in the South. When I came into office in January 1969, 68 percent of black children in the South were still going to all-black schools and 78.8 percent were going to schools that were 80 percent or more black.

The question in 1969 was whether the courts should try to correct the remnants of de jure segregation, which existed primarily in the South, by forcibly mixing the races in the schools. The principal tool by which this was to be accomplished was busing, whereby schoolchildren would be put on buses and driven to different schools within the district until the racial balance in each school reflected the racial balance in the community as a whole. One alternative to busing was for Congress to provide money to upgrade inferior education wherever it existed and thereby remedy the problem without disrupting the neighborhood school.

I wanted to eliminate the last vestiges of segregation by law, and I wanted to do it in a way that treated all parts of the nation equally. I was determined that the South would not continue to be a scapegoat for Northern liberals. I was not willing, however, to impose wholesale busing, because I believe strongly in the neighborhood school. Even more important, I do not believe that schoolchildren should be torn from their home environments and, solely because of their race, be forced to go to distant schools where they might not be welcome or even safe. Compulsory segregation was wrong; but compulsory racial balancing was also wrong.

I believed that with the right approach we could persuade people in the South and elsewhere not just to obey the law because it was the law, but gradually to bring them to an understanding and acceptance of the wisdom and humanity that lay behind it. In the meantime, I felt that as long as the law was not being deliberately disobeyed, the federal government should be an instrument of persuasion rather than an engine of coercion; the President should be the conciliator rather than the divider.

I felt that, to the greatest extent possible, plans for desegregation should be made by school boards, local communities, and the courts in each area or region, rather than by bureaucrats in HEW in Washington.

Many school districts decided not to forestall the inevitable and simply complied with the desegregation deadlines which had been laid down by the Supreme Court in 1968. Some districts decided to resist any change and submitted proposals for delays that were patently obstructionist. We rejected a number of these proposals and cut off federal funds. Others, however, tried to find solutions in responsible and responsive ways, and we planned to grant these districts limited and supervised delays.

But on October 29, 1969, just as the school year was getting under way, the Supreme Court handed down a unanimous decision that required every school district to terminate segregated school systems *at once*. I felt that the Court had set a deadline that was unrealistic and would be impossible to meet, but I had no choice other than to enforce the ruling.

At my next press conference I was asked about my policy on school desegregation. I replied that it was "to carry out what the Supreme Court has laid down. I believe in carrying out the law even though I may have disagreed as I did in this instance with the decree."

I felt obliged to uphold the law; but I did not feel obliged to do any more than the minimum the law required, while hoping that the Court would eventually see how its well-intentioned ruling was both legally and socially counterproductive. One thing I was determined to ensure was that the many young liberal lawyers in HEW and in the Justice Department's Civil Rights Division would not treat this decision as a carte blanche for them to run wild through the South enforcing compliance with extreme or punitive requirements they had formulated in Washington.

The Court's February deadline for immediate desegregation passed without incident. Some of the remaining segregated schools complied; some closed down; others ignored it and waited to see what would happen. Even before that, George Wallace had urged the South to defy the federal government and talked about running for President in 1972. A national Gallup poll found that more than half of those responding felt that school integration was going too fast.

I appointed a Cabinet Committee on Education to consider the problem at the highest level. I told them, "First of all I want everyone, but especially the Negro leaders, to know that our motto around here is 'I care.' The President cares about the situation and he plans to do something about it. The important thing, however, is to keep things in their proper perspective. Once we have made it clear that the law is being upheld and no segregation is legal anywhere in the country, I think we should take into account the possibility that local communities, black and white, might want to keep a certain degree of separation. That's why I want to put our federal money into the best possible education in each school. We've got to stop using the classrooms and the kids as the cutting edges for social and economic problems that will have to be solved elsewhere. Our goal should be education, not litigation."

A week later, Senator Richard Russell of Georgia came to the White House to transmit the views of four Southern governors that HEW bureaucrats were going around the South stirring up trouble and inciting suits. "I don't know what I'd do in your place, Mr. President," my ailing friend said. "I only know you've got a problem that won't go away and will get worse unless you do something about it. The people of Georgia are more worked up over this problem than anything I've seen in all of my years in politics."

I decided that the time had come to issue a major policy statement from the White House. On March 24 I released an 8,000-word statement covering every aspect of the civil rights issue. I reaffirmed my support for desegregation and my opposition to busing; I also indicated that the primary reliance should be on cooperation with local authorities and on voluntary compliance with the law rather than on federal involvement and enforcement. I said that my first priority would be maintaining and improving the quality of public education, and I announced that I would request $1.5 billion over two years for helping school districts desegregate. Reaction to this statement split between those who wanted to coerce the South to comply with the Court's ruling and those who were willing to take a chance on persuasion.

I was convinced that involvement on the part of local leaders and officials was the first prerequisite for a successful policy of persuasion. At the suggestion of my Cabinet Committee, seven of the Southern states which were still in various degrees of noncompliance with the Court's ruling formed State Advisory Committees on school desegregation. On June 24 I met with the Mississippi State Advisory Committee in the White House; there were fifteen members, nine whites and six blacks.

One of the black members said to me, "The day before yesterday I was in jail for going to the wrong beach. Today, Mr. President, I am meeting you. If that's possible anything can happen."

Over the next few weeks I met with all of the other state committees, and with each of them I stressed the same points. First, I condemned the hypocrisy in much of the North about the segregation problem. I affirmed my belief that the South should be treated with understanding and patience, but I also stressed the need to solve the problem through peaceful compliance. Second, I emphasized my commitment to the principle of local leadership to solve local problems. I got across subtly but unmistakably the point that if they did not act to solve the problem I would be forced to act to carry out my responsibility to enforce the law of the land.

Most of the whites who attended these meetings believed that the Court's decision was wrong; and some of the blacks entered the meetings with a skeptical view because they thought that only strong federal intervention would bring about compliance with the law. The meetings showed that it was possible for both sides to meet and talk about their concerns.

I knew that I was walking a fine line between the instant integrationists and the segregation-forever extremists, but I felt that the risk would be well worth it if we could solve the problem without getting the federal government involved.

At the end of July, I received a long memorandum from Harry Dent, my Southern political liaison man. He wrote that there was "a dangerous, growing concern in the Southern and conservative political communities—a concern that the administration is heading left in an effort to quiet those who have been against the administration." He said there was a feeling that " 'the squeaky wheel gets the grease' " and that at a recent meeting most of the Southern Republican chairmen had expressed the feeling that "We've been good guys too long and have gotten nothing but rhetoric while the bad guys have been in the streets getting all the attention and action."

On August 6, the same day that the Georgia State Advisory Committee came to the White House, I met with the leading conservative senators and Southern Republicans, including Ed Gurney of Florida, Barry Goldwater, Strom Thurmond, and John Tower. They complained bitterly that the administration had turned sharply to the left on the civil rights issue. Demands were made that I fire Jerris Leonard, Assistant Attorney General for the Civil Rights Division, and others who had been working to implement my policies. I listened to them and told them I was actually restraining bureaucrats from HEW and the Justice Department who wanted to move more aggressively, and in my opinion irresponsibly, on the South. At the same time I emphasized that I had a responsibility to carry out the law of the land and that I was determined to meet that responsibility.

On August 14 I flew to New Orleans to join the Louisiana State Advisory Committee, which was holding its first meeting. Before I arrived the members had become hopelessly deadlocked. After talking to each one individually, I was able to convince them of the need for progress and they agreed to make another try.

As the beginning of the new school year approached, tension began to mount. Would my faith in the power of persuasion be justified? Or would federal troops have to be called out to enforce integration?

At the end of August I personally asked Billy Graham to record some TV appeals in support of voluntary compliance. He made a videotape that was shown in all the Southern states, and I am convinced it had a very positive and powerful influence.

To my great relief, the policy worked. Schools in the South and all across the country opened in the fall of 1970 without violence and in compliance with the Supreme Court's order. The dramatic success of our Southern school desegregation program is eloquently told by the statistics. By 1974 only 8 percent of black children in the South were attending all-black schools, down from 68 percent in the fall of 1968.

My personal philosophy regarding the problem of busing and civil rights issues generally was set forth in detail in a memorandum I wrote to John Ehrlichman on January 28, 1972:

> I begin with the proposition that freedom of choice in housing, education, and jobs must be the right of every American. My support for family assistance, even though I have serious doubts as to whether it will work, is primarily based on the conclusion that only by such a program does freedom of choice have any chance to become a reality for millions of families who live below the poverty line. By freedom of choice of course I mean in the deepest philosophical sense and not in the narrow obstructionist sense that the term was used in fighting the school cases in the South in 1966–67 and 68. Legally segregated education, legally segregated housing, legal obstructions to equal employment must be totally removed.
>
> On the other hand I am convinced that while legal segregation is totally wrong, forced integration of housing or education is just as wrong.
>
> I realize that this position will lead us to a situation in which blacks will continue to live for the most part in black neighborhoods and where there will be predominantly black schools and predominantly white schools in the metropolitan areas. While I cannot go as far as Scammon in contending that those who insist on forced integrated education are really practicing white supremacy there is unfortunately a grain of truth in it. . . .
>
> In any event I believe there may be some doubt as to the validity of the

> Brown philosophy that integrating education will pull up the blacks and not pull down the whites. But while there may be some doubt as to whether segregated education is inferior there is no doubt whatever on another point —that education requiring excessive transportation for students is definitely inferior. I come down hard and unequivocally against busing for the purpose of racial balance. . . .
>
> Having made all these points I come down hard on another point which I think is absolutely overriding. This country is not ready at this time for either forcibly integrated housing or forcibly integrated education. . . .
>
> We simply have to face the hard fact the law cannot go beyond what the people are willing to support. This is true insofar as Prohibition is concerned. It is far more true with regard to education and even more true with regard to housing where economic considerations enter the picture. . . .
>
> We cannot sweep this issue under the rug. It is going to explode all over the landscape during this next year. . . . My feelings on race as you know are if anything ultraliberal. But I cannot duck the responsibility for coming down on the side which is right. . . . Even if I should become convinced—and I don't think it would be possible to convince me—that forced integration of education and housing was in the best interests of blacks and not too detrimental to whites I could not possibly support it in good conscience. What I am saying through this memorandum, is that as a matter of conscience I have reached a conclusion motivated not by politics but by my considered evaluation of all the issues involved, that I must speak to these two controversial issues now firmly without equivocation and if necessary through the advocacy of a constitutional amendment.

Although I considered the idea of a constitutional amendment at that time, I now believe that it would have exacerbated the already volatile issues of integrated education and housing with which we were confronted.

Personally I had always felt that the real issue in school desegregation was that of quality education. In my opinion, the *Brown* decision was based on the principle that the dual school system in the South was wrong not because segregation was wrong per se, but because in practice it produced Negro schools that were educationally inferior. To my mind, subsequent Court decisions have muddied the waters by assuming, incorrectly, that the issue involved race rather than education. I simply do not believe that education is the great leveler of social barriers that it was thought to be by the framers of the Great Society programs. I feel that home environment has more to do with success in life than has any amount of integrated education; busing black children from poor families to richer white schools will have little effect on how they learn.

During the years I was President I placed primary emphasis on better education in neighborhood schools. In a message to Congress on March 16, 1972, I proposed directing over $2.5 billion mainly toward improving the education of children from poor families. I hoped by doing this that we could retrieve a lost generation of children who had been doomed to inferior education in the central cities.

Controversy continued to rage over the interpretation of the Supreme Court's decisions on busing. Some lower courts ordered or approved busing plans that went much further than the Supreme Court had intended, and in 1972 Chief Justice Burger issued a memorandum for the guidance of courts across the country, making it clear that the high Court did not *require* busing for the purpose of achieving racial balance.

Just before I resigned in 1974, the Supreme Court further endorsed my position by holding that unless school districts were gerrymandered for the purpose, or with the intent, of segregating blacks from whites, the law did not require busing to ensure racial balance. In his opinion, Chief Justice Burger wrote that "no single tradition in public education is more deeply rooted than local control."

As far as my administration's overall record on civil rights is concerned, I believe we can point with justifiable pride to what was accomplished in the area of peacefully desegregating schools in the South. As Pat Moynihan put it in a memo shortly after the school year began in 1970, "There has been more change in the structure of American public school education in the past month than in the past 100 years."

CAMBODIA AND KENT STATE

As 1970 began, our intelligence indicated that Communist infiltration from North into South Vietnam was increasing substantially. The North Vietnamese had also begun moving large numbers of troops and equipment into Cambodia and Laos.

In view of this enemy activity I felt that we had to think about initiatives we could undertake to show the enemy that we were still serious about our commitment in Vietnam.

On February 21 Kissinger had his second secret meeting in Paris with the North Vietnamese. The situation had changed dramatically since the first meeting in August, largely because my November 3 speech had strengthened my position at home. A Gallup poll at the end of January found that 65 percent of the nation approved of my handling of Vietnam. Even more disturbing for the North Vietnamese must have been the knowledge that we were now talking to their two major military patrons: the Soviets had recently proposed four-power discussions on the Berlin question in Bonn, and the Chinese Communists had agreed to resume the ambassadorial talks with us in Warsaw.

This time Le Duc Tho joined Xuan Thuy in participating in the talks with Kissinger. Tho was a member of the Hanoi Politburo, which meant that the talks now had at least reached the decision-making level.

Trying to capitalize on the reaction to my speech, Kissinger emphatically warned them not to underestimate the strong support I had for my Vietnam policy. "I know that here in Paris you see many Americans who are extremely sympathetic to your position. But in the last election the big bloc of votes was not on the left but on the right. President Nixon can appeal to people whom President Johnson could not reach," he told them. Le Duc Tho countered suavely that it was his impression that since August the antiwar movement in the United States had surged higher than ever. He said that he had seen many statements by the Senate Foreign Relations Committee, by the Democratic Party, and by Clark Clifford demanding the total withdrawal of American forces and the change of the Thieu government. Tho bluntly told Kissinger, "The present administration of Thieu–Ky–Khiem is opposed by the people and the press of the U.S., as by the great majority of the people of South Vietnam."

Kissinger had felt from the start that Tho's bombast concealed genuine North Vietnamese doubts and worries. This appraisal seemed to be borne out later in the meeting when the North Vietnamese became more conciliatory. In fact, it appeared that they were ready to begin serious negotiations in the private channel. They suggested another meeting for March 16.

When Kissinger returned to Washington he reported that "this has been an important meeting, certainly the most important since the beginning of your administration and even since the beginning of the talks in 1968."

At the end of Kissinger's memo proposing our strategy for the next secret meeting, I wrote a short note about the way I thought he should deal with the North Vietnamese at their next session. "Don't haggle so much over 'what did they mean by this or that,' " I wrote. "They thrive on this kind of discussion. Come directly to the hard decisions on the two major issues and say 'we will leave details to subordinates'—otherwise you will spend two days on details and make no progress on substance. We need a breakthrough on principle—and substance. Tell them we want to go immediately to the core of the problem."

When they met again on March 16, Kissinger told the North Vietnamese that if a settlement could be reached, we would have all our troops out of Vietnam within sixteen months. They appeared interested but remained noncommittal. Kissinger's conclusion was that "two more meetings should tell the story."

A few days later an unexpected event completely altered the situation. On March 18, while the Cambodian head of state Prince Sihanouk was visiting Moscow, he was overthrown by a bloodless military coup that brought to power General Lon Nol, a strong anti-Communist.

Lon Nol's coup came as a complete surprise. The CIA had received no indication that the opposition to Sihanouk had gone so far. "What the hell do those clowns do out there in Langley?" I asked Bill Rogers impatiently.

My immediate inclination was to do everything possible to help Lon Nol, but Rogers and Laird strongly recommended that we hold back. They pointed out that Moscow, Peking, and Hanoi would be in great turmoil and suspect us of having financed and staged the coup. If we provided economic and military aid now, they argued, we would confirm such suspicions and possibly even supply the North Vietnamese with a pretext for abandoning their official facade of noninvolvement and thereby unleash a full-scale invasion of Cambodia. Helms also urged restraint. He reported that the Lon Nol government was unlikely to survive. It would put us in a very bad light, he said, to rush aid to a government that might be overthrown even before our aid arrived.

I decided to withhold any aid for at least a week, during which time Lon Nol, whose troops fought surprisingly well against the highly trained Communist Khmer Rouge and North Vietnamese, proceeded on his own to cut off a major source of Communist supplies by closing the Cambodian port of Sihanoukville.

Against this background Kissinger prepared for another meeting with the North Vietnamese in Paris. Before he left, he sent me a memo requesting approval for the strategy he wanted to follow. He felt that the time had come for our side to be very firm and find out whether the Communists really meant to negotiate. I approved this strategy and even strengthened it. "Put a time limit on it," I wrote on his memo.

The meeting lasted almost five hours. The North Vietnamese were not forthcoming. Kissinger felt that they had been confused by the events in Cambodia, which they charged us with having engineered. Following my instructions, he proposed that a time limit be set for reaching an agreement in the secret talks. When they would not agree to this, he suggested that the channel be closed down until one side or the other had something new to discuss.

The whole situation over Cambodia and Vietnam was becoming so tense that I felt I had to make a very painful personal decision. Although I knew how much Pat and Julie were counting on it, I canceled our plans to attend David's graduation from Amherst and Julie's graduation from Smith later in the spring. Pat had never known the joy of having a parent attend any of her graduations, and I knew that she had been looking forward to Julie's. Julie was also terribly disappointed. She tried to hold back her tears, and she pointed out that only a few small radical groups were involved, and that everyone she knew—including students who opposed the war and my administration—felt that I should be able to attend the ceremony.

Ted Agnew felt particularly strongly about this. "Don't let them intimidate you, Mr. President," he said, barely restraining his indignation. "You may be President, but you're her father, and a father should be able to attend his daughter's graduation." The Secret Service, however, had received reports of several protest demonstrations that were already being planned against me, and the possibility of an ugly incident that would mar the graduation, not just for us but for all the other students and parents, was too great to risk.

Despite the impasse in the secret talks and the worsening military situation in Cambodia, I decided to go ahead with the troop withdrawal scheduled for April 20. I discussed the issue at length with Kissinger, and we agreed that the time had come to drop a bombshell on the gathering spring storm of antiwar protest.

Vietnamization had progressed to the point that, for the first time, we felt we could project our troop withdrawals over the next year. We decided, therefore, that instead of announcing a smaller number over a shorter period, I would announce the withdrawal of 150,000 men over the next year.

The withdrawal figure came as a dramatic surprise when I revealed it in a speech on April 20. The only Communist reaction was an escalation of the fighting.

By the end of April, the Communists had a quarter of Cambodia under control and were closing in on Phnom Penh. It was clear that Lon Nol needed help to survive. If the Communists succeeded in overthrowing him, South Vietnam would be threatened from the west as well as the north. This situation would jeopardize our troop withdrawal program and would also virtually assure a Communist invasion of South Vietnam as soon as the last American had left.

Support for Lon Nol was to be discussed at an NSC meeting on April 22. I woke up early that morning and dictated a memorandum to Kissinger:

> Assuming that I feel the way today at our meeting as I feel this morning (it is 5 A.M., April 22), I think we need a bold move in Cambodia to show that we stand with Lon Nol.
>
> I do not believe he is going to survive. There is, however, some chance that he might, and in any event we must do something symbolic to help him survive.
>
> We have really dropped the ball on this one due to the fact that we were taken in with the line that by helping him we would destroy his "neutrality"

and give the North Vietnamese an excuse to come in. Over and over again we fail to learn that the Communists never need an excuse to come in.

They didn't need one in Hungary in 1956 when the same argument was made by the career State people and when Dulles bought it because he was tired and it was during the campaign.

They didn't need one in Czechoslovakia when the same argument was made by the State people. And they didn't need one in Laos where we lost a precious day by failing to make the strike that might have blunted the whole offensive before it got started, and in Cambodia, where we have taken a completely hands-off attitude by protesting to the Senate that we have only a delegation of seven State Department jerks in the embassy, and would not provide any aid of any kind because we were fearful that if we did so it would give them a "provocation" to come in.

They are romping in there, and the only government in Cambodia in the last twenty-five years that had the guts to take a pro-Western and pro-American stand is ready to fall . . .

I will talk to you about this after the NSC meeting.

The Communist sanctuaries in Cambodia were in two main areas. The Parrot's Beak is a sliver of land that pushes into South Vietnam and reaches within thirty-three miles of Saigon. A particularly strong ARVN [South Vietnamese Army] force was stationed on the border in this area. Our intelligence reports indicated that the heaviest Communist concentration was in another border area, the Fishhook, a thin, curving piece of Cambodian territory jutting right into the heart of South Vietnam, about fifty miles northwest of Saigon. This was the primary area of operation for what intelligence referred to as COSVN—the Central Office of South Vietnam. COSVN was the Communists' floating command post of military headquarters, supplies, food, and medical facilities. The Fishhook was thus the nerve center of the Communist forces in the sanctuaries, and it would be strongly defended. The initial intelligence estimates projected that the heavy fortifications and the concentration of Communist troops in the area might result in very high casualties in the first week of the operation.

I began to consider letting the ARVN go into the Parrot's Beak and sending a mixed force of American and South Vietnamese troops into the Fishhook. Giving the South Vietnamese an operation of their own would be a major boost to their morale as well as provide a practical demonstration of the success of Vietnamization. It would also be a good diversionary cover for the more important and more difficult Fishhook operation.

I never had any illusions about the shattering effect a decision to go into Cambodia would have on public opinion at home. I knew that opinions among my major foreign policy advisers were deeply divided over the issue of widening the war, and I recognized that it could mean personal and political catastrophe for me and my administration.

On Sunday night, April 26, I reached my decision. We would go for broke. The ARVN would go into the Parrot's Beak and a joint ARVN–U.S. force would go into the Fishhook.

On Monday morning I met with Rogers, Laird, and Kissinger. It was a tense meeting, because even though Rogers and Laird had by now given up hope of dissuading me from taking some action in Cambodia, they still thought they could convince me not to involve American troops. Rogers said, "It will cost us great casualties with very little gain. And I just don't believe it will be a crippling blow to the enemy." Laird said, "I'm not really opposed to going after the COSVN, but I'm not happy with the way this is being implemented." He was more upset, it seemed, with an apparent snub of the Pentagon in our decision-making process. He also suggested that General Abrams might not approve of the COSVN operation, but backed away when Kissinger contradicted him. Nevertheless, immediately after our meeting I sent a back-channel cable to Abrams, ordering him to send me the "unvarnished truth" about the way he felt.

A joint response from Abrams and U.S. Ambassador Ellsworth Bunker indicated full support on their part. Speaking specifically of the attack on the Fishhook, they wrote: "We both agree that attack on this area should have maximum unsettling effect on the enemy, who has considered until now his sanctuaries immune to ground attack." Abrams added his personal views in a separate paragraph: "It is my independent view that these attacks into the enemy's sanctuaries in Cambodia are the military move to make at this time in support of our mission in South Vietnam both in terms of security of our own forces and for advancement of the Vietnamization program."

That night I sat alone going over the decision one last time. It was still not too late to call the operation off: the Parrot's Beak action would not begin until the next morning, and the Fishhook not until two days after that. I took a pad and began to make a list of the pluses and minuses of both operations. The risk and danger involved were undeniably great; there was no assurance of success on the battlefield and there was the certainty of an uproar at home. But there was also no question that the continued existence of the Cambodian sanctuaries would threaten the safety of the remaining American troops in South Vietnam and almost guarantee a Communist invasion as soon as we had pulled out.

Early the next morning I showed Kissinger my notes. He blinked his eyes as he took a piece of paper from the folder he was carrying and handed it to me. It was a list almost identical to mine. "I did the same thing, Mr. President," he said, "and it looks like we're both able to make a good case both ways on it."

I said that as far as I was concerned, the simple fact of showing the Communists that we intended to protect ourselves and our allies put all the weight on one side. "Now that we have made the decision there must be no recriminations among us," I said. "Not even if the whole thing goes wrong. In fact, *especially* if the whole thing goes wrong."

South Vietnam's announcement of the Parrot's Beak operation came over the wires on Wednesday, April 29. Within minutes the leading Senate doves were in front of the TV cameras, demanding that I disavow Thieu's offensive and not send any American troops into Cambodia. All during the day I continued to work on the speech I would deliver the next night announcing the operation. I asked Rose to call Julie for me. "I don't want to get her upset, but it's possible that the campuses are really going to blow up after this speech," I said, "so could you just say I asked if she and David could come down from school to be with us."

That night I found it difficult to get to sleep. After tossing fitfully for an hour or so, I got up and sat in the Lincoln Sitting Room until 5:30. At nine o'clock I walked over to my EOB office to go over the first pages of the typed speech. That afternoon I had Haldeman and Kissinger come over so I could read the announcement to them. I asked Kissinger to brief George Meany, because I knew that labor support would be vital. A little later he reported that Meany supported my decision wholeheartedly. Kissinger had less success with his own NSC staff. Three of his top assistants decided to resign in protest over my decision.

Shortly before delivering the speech from the Oval Office, I went to the White House Theatre to brief the bipartisan congressional leadership. I said I understood that many of them would oppose the decision I had made. I knew how they felt about it, and I respected their feelings. "I just want you to know that whether you think it's right or wrong, the reason I have decided to do this is that I have decided it's the best way to end the war and save the lives of our soldiers," I told them.

I looked around the room. The faces were intent and strained. Some of the strongest doves were there: Fulbright, Mansfield, Aiken, Kennedy. The sincerity of my words must have reached them, even though they remained opposed to the decision I had made. As I left the room, everyone stood and applauded.

I began the speech by describing how the Communists had responded to my recently announced troop withdrawal by stepping up their attacks throughout Indochina. "To protect our men who are in Vietnam and to guarantee the continued success of our withdrawal and Vietnamization programs," I said, "I have concluded that the time has come for action."

I used a map to explain the geographic and strategic importance of the Cambodian sanctuaries and to describe the South Vietnamese operation in the Parrot's Beak. Then I announced that a joint U.S.–Vietnamese force would go into the Fishhook.

I stressed that this was not an invasion of Cambodia. The sanctuaries were completely occupied and controlled by North Vietnamese forces. We would withdraw once they had been driven out and once their military supplies were destroyed. The purpose, I said, was not to expand the war into Cambodia, but to end the war in Vietnam by making peace possible.

Setting my decision in its widest context, I continued, "If, when the chips are down, the world's most powerful nation, the United States of America, acts like a pitiful, helpless giant, the forces of totalitarianism and anarchy will threaten free nations and free institutions throughout the world."

For an hour after the speech I sat with my family in the Solarium while they discussed the speech and tried to gauge the reactions to it. Then I went to the Lincoln Sitting Room and began returning calls that had come in after the speech.

Just after 10:30 I was informed that Chief Justice Warren Burger was at the gate with a letter for me. I instructed the Secret Service agent on duty to have him shown up immediately.

"I didn't want to disturb you, Mr. President," Burger said, "but I wanted you to know that I think your speech tonight had a sense of history and destiny about it."

I said that the critics had already begun denouncing the speech and the decision, but he said that he was sure it would be supported by the people. "I think anyone who really listened to what you said will appreciate the guts it took to make the decision," he added. He also pointed out that anyone who thought about it would realize that, as a shrewd politician, I would obviously not do anything that might damage Republican chances in the November elections unless I felt that it was absolutely necessary for national security.

"Speaking in the greatest confidence, Mr. Chief Justice," I said, using his formal title as I always did when addressing him, "I am realist enough to know that if this operation doesn't succeed—or if anything else happens that forces my public support below a point where I feel I can't be re-elected—I would like you to be ready to be in the running for the nomination in 1972."

When I finally went to my bedroom around three o'clock, I found a note from Julie.

Dear Daddy,

I was very proud of you tonight. You explained the situation in Vietnam perfectly—I am sure the American people will realize why you made your decision. I especially want to tell you how effective—and heartfelt—your final message to the people of South and North Vietnam, the Soviet Union, and the United States was. I feel that the strongest message which resulted from your speech was: We cannot abandon 17 million people to a living death, and we cannot jeopardize the chances for future world peace by an unqualified pull-out of Vietnam.

I know you are right and, again, I am so proud.

Love,
Julie

Reactions to the speech were along predictable lines. Senator Muskie said, "This speech confirms a judgment that I've been reluctant to reach: the President has decided to seek a military method of ending this war rather than a negotiated method." Senator Walter Mondale of Minnesota said, "This is not only a tragic escalation, which will broaden the war and increase American casualties, but is outright admission of the failure of Vietnamization."

The New Republic began a front-cover editorial with the sentence: "Richard Nixon is going down in history, all right, but not soon enough," and said my speech was "insensitive," "phony," "a fraud," "indifferent," and "dangerous." The New York *Times* said I was "out of touch" with the nation.

In Britain, *The Economist* took a different point of view: "It is not the Americans who have brought the war to Cambodia, but the Communists. For years, North Vietnam has violated the neutrality of this country—with barely a chirp of protest from the rest of the world. . . . To condemn the United States for 'invading' neutral Cambodia is about as rational as to condemn Britain for 'invading' formally neutral Holland in 1944."

Despite very little sleep, I was up early on the morning after the speech. I went to the Pentagon for a firsthand briefing on the Cambodian operation from the Joint Chiefs and their top advisers. As I walked through the halls to the briefing room, I was mobbed by people cheering and trying to shake my hand. "God bless you!" "Right on!" "We should have done this years ago!" they shouted.

The atmosphere in the briefing room was generally positive if somewhat more restrained. A huge map of the battle area almost covered one wall. Different colored pins indicated the positions and movements of the various forces. As the briefers described the initial success of the operation, I found myself studying the map more and more intently. I noted that in addition to the Parrot's Beak and the Fishhook, four other areas were marked as occupied by Communist forces.

Suddenly I asked, "Between the ARVN and ourselves, would we be able to mount offensives in all of those other areas? Could we take out *all* the sanctuaries?"

The reply to my question emphasized the very negative reaction any such action would receive in the media and Congress.

"Let me be the judge as far as the political reactions are concerned," I said. "The fact is that we have already taken the political heat for this particular operation. If we can substantially reduce the threat to our forces by wiping out the rest of the sanctuaries, now is the time to do it."

Everyone seemed to be waiting for someone else to speak. Usually I like to mull things over, but I made a very uncharacteristic on-the-spot decision. I said, "I want to take out all of those sanctuaries. Make whatever plans are necessary, and then just do it. Knock them all out so that they can't be used against us again. Ever."

As I left the Pentagon after the briefing, once again employees rushed into the halls. By the time I reached the lobby, I was surrounded by a friendly, cheering crowd. One woman was particularly emotional as she thanked me on behalf of her husband, who was serving in Vietnam. As I thought of these men and women with loved ones fighting in Vietnam, I could not help thinking about those students who took advantage of their draft deferments and their privileged status in our society to bomb campuses, set fires, and tyrannize their institutions.

"I have seen them," I said about our soldiers in Vietnam. "They're the greatest. You see these bums, you know, blowing up the campuses. Listen, the boys that are on the college campuses today are the luckiest people in the world, going to the greatest universities, and here they are burning up the books, storming around about this issue. . . . Then out there, we have kids who are just doing their duty. And I have seen them. They stand tall, and they are proud."

That afternoon, while the tempest of reaction over Cambodia continued to build, I decided to get my family away from the White House for at least a few hours of relaxation after the great tension we had all experienced. It was a warm, clear day, so I suggested that we sail down the Potomac to Mount Vernon on the *Sequoia*.

It is the custom for all naval vessels passing Mount Vernon to honor George Washington, who is buried there. When we neared the spot, I had everyone move onto the deck and face the shore. Pat was next to me, then David, Julie, and Bebe Rebozo. As we passed by the first President's tomb, over the *Sequoia*'s loudspeaker came "The Star-Spangled Banner." We all stood at attention until the last note died away.

By the time the *Sequoia* had returned to Washington, the indignant reaction to my "bums" statement that morning at the Pentagon had almost overwhelmed the response to the Cambodia speech itself.

All through the spring of 1970 the country had faced wave after wave of violent campus unrest. As with the disturbances at the beginning of 1969, the issues were largely campus-oriented, dealing with disciplinary regulations, campus administration, and minority admissions.

What distinguished many of the 1970 campus disturbances from all earlier ones was the increase in bombings and violence connected with them. Radical groups openly encouraged the bombing of institutions of which they disapproved.

In the academic year 1969–70 there were 1,800 demonstrations, 7,500 arrests, 462 injuries—two-thirds of them were to police—and 247 arsons and 8 deaths.

April 1970 had been a particularly violent month. For the second time, a bank near the University of California at Santa Barbara was set on fire. A fire was set at the University of Kansas that destroyed buildings worth $2 million. At Ohio State University protesters demanding the admission of more black students and the abolition of ROTC on campus engaged in a six-hour battle with police. There were 600 arrests and 20 wounded. Governor James Rhodes finally had to call in 1,200 national guardsmen and impose a curfew to quiet the campus.

It was criminal and barbarous to burn banks as a protest against capitalism or to burn ROTC buildings as a protest against militarism. But to me the most shocking incidents were those that I considered to be directed at the very quality of intellectual life that should characterize a university community. In March, an arsonist caused $320,000 damage to the University of California library at Berkeley. At the end of April as part of a demonstration in support of Black Panthers charged with murder in New Haven, $2,500 worth of books were set on fire in the basement of the Yale Law School.

The most shameful incident occurred at Stanford University. On April 24 an anti-ROTC group set a fire at the university's center for behavioral studies. One of the offices that was completely gutted belonged to a visiting Indian anthropologist, Professor M. N. Srinivas. His personal notes, files, and manuscripts went up in flames.

When Pat Moynihan told me about this tragedy, I wrote to Professor Srinivas:

> As did countless other Americans, I responded with disbelief at the news

> that your study at the Center for Advanced Studies in the Behavioral Sciences had been firebombed, and that much of the work of a lifetime had been destroyed.
>
> It can be small consolation for you to know that the overwhelming proportion of the American people, and of the American academic community, utterly reject the tactics of the person or persons who did this. To say that they are deranged, does not excuse them. To say, what is more probably the case, that they are simply evil, does not make them go away.
>
> I hope that the great insights of social anthropology that you have brought to your studies might serve in this moment to help you understand this tragedy. Please at all events know that you are an honored and welcome guest, whose work is appreciated and valued in this nation as indeed throughout the world.

I do not think that anyone who heard my comments at the Pentagon or who heard the tape recording of it, had any doubt that when I talked about "bums" burning up the books and blowing up the campuses, I was referring to the arsonists at Berkeley and Yale and the Stanford firebombers and others like them. The Washington *Post* headline the next morning accurately reflected my meaning: *Nixon Denounces Campus "Bums" Who Burn Books, Set Off Bombs.*

But the front-page headline in the New York *Times* conveyed a slightly different meaning: *Nixon Puts "Bums" Label on Some College Radicals;* and the inside continuation of the story was headlined: *Nixon Denounces "Bums" on Campus.*

Within a few days, it was the widespread impression that I had referred to all student protesters as "bums."

The media coverage and interpretation of the "bums" statement added fuel to the fires of dissent that were already getting out of control on many campuses. The National Student Association called for my impeachment, and editors of eleven Eastern colleges, including most of the Ivy League schools, ran a common editorial in their campus newspapers calling for a nationwide academic strike.

At the University of Maryland, just outside Washington, fifty people were injured when students ransacked the ROTC building and skirmished with police. In Kent, Ohio, a crowd of hundreds of demonstrators watched as two young men threw lighted flares into the Army ROTC building on the campus of Kent State University, and burned it to the ground. Governor Rhodes called in the National Guard. He said that 99 percent of the Kent State students wanted the school to remain open, and that the rest were "worse than the brownshirts."

On Monday, May 4, I asked Haldeman to come to the EOB office to go over trip schedules with me. He looked agitated. "Something just came over the wires about a demonstration at Kent State," he said. "The National Guard opened fire, and some students were shot."

I was stunned. "Are they dead?" I asked.

"I'm afraid so. No one knows why it happened."

It appeared that an uneasy confrontation had begun brewing around noon. Finally, a large crowd of students began throwing rocks and chunks of concrete at the guardsmen, forcing them up a small hill. At the top the soldiers turned, and someone started shooting.

In the newspaper the next day I saw the pictures of the four young people who had been killed. Two had been bystanders; the other two had been protesting a decision they felt was wrong. Now all four were dead, and a call was going out for nationwide demonstrations and student strikes. Would this tragedy become the cause of scores of others? I could not get the photographs out of my mind. I could not help thinking about the families, suddenly receiving the news that their children were dead because they had been shot in a campus demonstration. I wrote personal letters to each of the parents, even though I knew that words could not help.

Those few days after Kent State were among the darkest of my presidency. I felt utterly dejected when I read that the father of one of the dead girls had told a reporter, "My child was not a bum."

Kent State also took a heavy toll on Henry Kissinger's morale. Members of his staff had resigned because of Cambodia, and former Harvard colleagues whom he had considered among his most loyal friends wrote bitter letters to him demanding that he make his professed moral position credible by resigning.

On a day several of these letters arrived, he came into my office and sat staring disconsolately out the window. Finally he said, "I still think you made the right decision as far as foreign policy considerations were involved. But in view of what has happened I fear I may have failed to advise you adequately of the domestic dangers."

I told him that I had been fully aware of both the military and the political risks. I had made the decision myself, and I assumed full responsibility for it. Finally I said, "Henry, remember Lot's wife. Never turn back. Don't waste time rehashing things we can't do anything about."

I was shocked and disappointed when an apparently intentional leak to the press revealed that Bill Rogers and Mel Laird had been opposed to my Cambodian decision. The operation was still in a critical stage, and I called Rogers and told him that I felt the Cabinet should get behind a decision once it had been made by the President.

Walter Hickel, the Secretary of the Interior, chose a more public way to express his conviction that I should listen to the students and spend more time with the Cabinet. In what he later explained as a mishap, a copy of a letter he had written to me raising these points was already going out over the AP wire before it had been delivered to the White House. Several other Cabinet and administration members also took public positions of less than full support.

In the midst of all the furore, it meant a great deal to me when one of the two living Americans who could really know what I was going through wrote to me.

I received a note from Johnson City: "Dear Mr. President," it read, "I hope you have a chance to read this. My best always. LBJ." Attached to it was a recent column by one of Johnson's former assistants, John P. Roche, entitled "The President Makes the Decisions." It began: "What distinguishes the Republican regime from that of Lyndon Johnson is that Mr. Nixon announced an 'open administration,' with the consequence that everyone above the rank of GS-15 feels free to comment on the wisdom of the President's actions." After noting examples of Cabinet members dissociating themselves from my Cambodian decision, Roche concluded by making the point that "Nixon was elected to make a choice and he made it. One can attack it on the merits if he so chooses, that is, say it was mistaken. Or one can support his actions (as I do). But under the Constitution no one has the right to impeach his decision because he did not consult Senator Fulbright, Secretary Finch, Pat Moynihan or the International Security Affairs section of the Pentagon."

Kent State triggered a nationwide wave of campus protests. The daily news reports conveyed a sense of turmoil bordering on insurrection. Hundreds of college campuses went through a paroxysm of rage, riot, and arson. By the end of the first week after the killings, 450 colleges and universities were closed by student or faculty protest strikes. Before the month was over, the National Guard had been called out twenty-four times at twenty-one campuses in sixteen states.

A national day of protest was hastily called to take place in Washington on Saturday, May 9. I felt that we should do everything possible to make sure that this event was nonviolent and that we did not appear insensitive to it. Ehrlichman urged that we make whatever gestures of communication were possible. Kissinger, however, took a particularly hard line on the demonstrators. He was appalled at the violence they provoked and at the ignorance of the real issues they displayed. He felt strongly that I should not appear more flexible until after the Cambodian operation was successfully completed. As he put it, we had to make it clear that our foreign policy was not made by street protests.

I decided to try to defuse the tension by holding a press conference.

The risks were high, and my staff was deeply divided about the wisdom of having one at this time. Most of the reporters and commentators were bound to be bitterly critical, and it was highly possible that an acrimonious session would only make things worse. Nonetheless I decided to go ahead, and the conference was announced for prime time on Friday evening, May 8.

I could feel the emotions seething beneath the hot TV lights as I entered the East Room at ten o'clock Friday night. Almost all the questions were about the Cambodian operation and Kent State.

The first question was whether I had been surprised by the intensity of the protests and whether they would affect my policy in any way. I replied that I had not been surprised by the intensity of the protests. I knew that those who protested did so because they felt that my decision would expand the war, our involvement in it, and our casualties. "I made the decision, however, for the very reasons that they are protesting," I said. "I am concerned because I know how deeply they feel. But I know that what I have done will accomplish the goals that they want. It will shorten this war. It will reduce American casualties. It will allow us to go forward with our withdrawal program. The 150,000 Americans that I announced for withdrawal in the next year will come home on schedule. It will, in my opinion, serve the cause of a just peace in Vietnam."

One reporter asked what I thought the students were trying to say in the demonstration that was about to take place in Washington. I wanted my answer to this question to be compassionate but not weak. I said, "They are trying to say that they want peace. They are trying to say that they want to stop the killing. They are trying to say that they want to end the draft. They are trying to say that we ought to get out of Vietnam. I agree with everything that they are trying to accomplish. I believe, however, that the decisions that I have made, and particularly this last terribly difficult decision of going into the Cambodian sanctuaries which were completely occupied by the enemy—I believe that that decision will serve that purpose, because you can be sure that everything that I stand for is what they want."

Immediately after the press conference I began returning some of the dozens of phone calls that had come in and placing calls to others. I was agitated and uneasy as the events of the last few weeks raced through my mind.

I slept for a few hours and then went to the Lincoln Sitting Room. I put on a record of Rachmaninoff's Second Piano Concerto and sat listening to the music. Manolo heard that I was up and came in to see if I would like some tea or coffee. Looking out the windows I could see small groups of young people beginning to gather on the Ellipse between the White House and the Washington Monument. I mentioned that I considered the Lincoln Memorial at night to be the most beautiful sight in Washington, and Manolo said that he had never seen it. Impulsively I said, "Let's go look at it now."

This event was spontaneous on my part and I purposely did not take any staff members along or alert any reporters to accompany me. Thus it was especially frustrating when the newspapers reported that I had been unable to communicate with the young people I met, and that I had shown my insensitivity to their concerns by talking about inconsequential subjects like sports and surfing. Some of this mistaken impression apparently came from the students themselves. One of them told a reporter, "He wasn't really concerned with why we were here." Another said that I had been tired and dull and rambled aimlessly from subject to subject.

In a meeting a few days later John Ehrlichman referred to the problems that I had created by talking about sports to students who had traveled hundreds of miles to protest my war policies. I was tired and tense, and I snapped at him about the problems a President has when even his own staff believes the false stories that are spread about him.

That night I dictated a long memorandum describing what had actually taken place, and I sent it to Haldeman with another memo analyzing my frustrations about this incident:

> The attached is a memorandum of what actually took place at the Lincoln Memorial.
>
> After you read it, I think you will share my complete frustration with regard to coverage of my activities. I can understand why John Ehrlichman got the idea from the news reports that I was tired and all I talked about was surfing and nonsensical things. . . .
>
> As I evaluated the situation, this was the one time this group of students—most of whom perhaps were middle class or lower middle class—most of whom were about as poor as I was when I was in college and who had driven all this long distance to Washington—this was the only time they had ever talked to a President of the United States. They will see me many times discuss these heated, angry subjects that they would hear about later at the Monument, and that they hear in their classrooms. Perhaps the major contribution I could make to them was to try to lift them a bit out of the miserable intellectual wasteland in which they now wander aimlessly around.
>
> I do not write this memorandum to you critically of our staff, because I think it is the best staff any President has had by far in terms of loyalty, willingness to work, etc.
>
> The only problem is that we seem to lack on the staff any one individual who really understands or appreciates what I am trying to get across in terms of what a President should mean to the people. Not news; not gimmicks like rushing out to that Negro junior college with a covey of newsreels following. All of this seems to be big stuff and I realize makes big news—perhaps it is.

But on the other hand, I really wonder in the long run if this is all the legacy we want to leave.

If it is, then perhaps we should do our job as easily as we can, as expeditiously as we can, and get out and leave the responsibilities of the government to the true materialists—the socialists, the totalitarians who talk idealism but rule ruthlessly without any regard to the individual considerations—the respect for personality that I tried to emphasize in my dialogue with the students.

I dictated this long diary-like memorandum describing the visit to the Lincoln Memorial because I wanted to make a record of what was for me a memorable event, and because I wanted to knock down the idea that I would have engaged in the kind of inane conversations the news reports had indicated.

Manolo and I got out of the car at approximately 4:40 and walked up the steps to the Lincoln statue. . . .

By this time a few small groups of students had begun to congregate in the rotunda of the Memorial. I walked over to a group of them . . . and shook hands. They were not unfriendly. As a matter of fact, they seemed somewhat overawed, and, of course, quite surprised.

When I first started to speak to the group there were approximately eight in it. I asked each of them where they were from and found that over half were from upper New York State. At this point, all of them were men. There were no women. To get the conversation going I asked them how old they were, what they were studying, the usual questions. . . .

Two or three of them volunteered that they had not been able to hear the press conference because they had been driving all night in order to get here. I said I was sorry they had missed it because I had tried to explain in the press conference that my goals in Vietnam were the same as theirs—to stop the killing and end the war—to bring peace. Our goal was not to get into Cambodia by what we were doing, but to get out of Vietnam.

They did not respond, so I took it from there by saying that I realized that most of them would not agree with my position, but I hoped that they would not allow their disagreement on this issue to lead them to fail to give us a hearing on some other issues where we might agree. And also particularly I hoped that their hatred of the war, which I could well understand, would not turn into a bitter hatred of our whole system, our country, and everything that it stood for.

I said, I know that probably most of you think I'm an SOB, but I want you to know that I understand just how you feel. I recall that when I was just a little older than you, right out of law school and ready to get married, how excited I was when Chamberlain came home from Munich and made his famous statement about peace in our time. I had heard it on the radio. I had so little in those days that the prospect of going into the service was almost unbearable and I felt that the United States staying out of any kind of conflict was worth paying any price whatever. I pointed out, too, the fact that I came from a Quaker background. I was as close to being a pacifist as anybody could be in those times. As a result I thought at that time, that Chamberlain was the greatest man alive, and when I read Churchill's all-out criticism of Chamberlain I thought Churchill was a madman.

In retrospect, I now realize I was wrong. I think now that Chamberlain was a good man, but that Churchill was a wiser man and that we in the world are better off than we would be because Churchill had not only the wisdom but the courage to carry out the policies that he believed were right even though there was a time when both in England and all over the world he was extremely unpopular because of his "anti-peace" stand.

I then tried to move the conversation into areas where I could draw them out. I said that since some of them had come to Washington for the first time I hoped that while they were young that they would never miss an opportunity to travel. One of them said that he didn't know whether he could afford it, and I said I didn't think I could afford it either when I was young but my wife and I borrowed the money for a trip we took to Mexico and then one to Central America. The fact is, you must travel when you are young. If you wait until you can afford it you will be too old to enjoy it. When you're young, you can enjoy it. . . .

At that time a girl joined the group and since I had been discussing California I asked if anybody there was from California. She spoke up and said she was from Los Altos and I said that was one of my favorite towns in Northern California and I hoped it was as beautiful as I remembered it. She did not respond.

In trying to draw her out, I told the rest of the group that when they went to California that they would see there what massive strides we could take to deal with the problem of the environment which I knew they were all interested in. I said that right below where I live in California there was the greatest surfing beach in the world, that it was completely denied to the public due to the fact that it was Marine Corps property, and that I had taken steps to release some of this property for a public beach so that the terribly overcrowded beaches further north could be unburdened, and so that the people could have a chance to enjoy the natural beauty which was there. I said that one of the thrusts of our whole "quality of life" environmental program was to take our government property and put it to better uses and not simply to continue to use it for military or other purposes because it had been used for that way from time immemorial.

Most of them seemed to nod in agreement when I made this point.

I then spoke of how I hoped that they would have the opportunity to know not only the United States but the whole world. I said most people will tell you to go to Europe. I said Europe was fine, but it's really an older version of America. It is worth seeing, but the place that I felt they would particularly enjoy visiting would be Asia.

I told them my great hopes that during my administration, and certainly during their lifetime, that the great mainland of China would be opened up so that we could know the 700 million people who live in China who are one of the most remarkable people on earth. Most of them seemed to nod in agreement when I made this point. . . .

I then moved on to the Soviet Union. Then one of them asked me what Moscow was like, and I said "gray." It's very important if you go to Russia, of course, to see Moscow because of the historical and governmental operations that are there, but if you really want to know Russia, its exciting variety and history, you must go to Leningrad. I said that in Russia Leningrad was really a more interesting place to visit. The people were really more outgoing there since they were not so much under control and domination of the central government.

I also said that in terms of beautiful cities, they would find Prague and Warsaw of much more architectural beauty than Moscow. I made this point because I was speaking directly to one of the students who said he was a student of architecture. In fact, there were two who said they were studying architecture and I thought that they would be interested. But the most important point I made about Russia was that they should go to places like Novosibirsk, a raw, new city in the heart of Siberia, and Samarkand in Asian Russia where the people were Asians rather than Russians.

One of them asked whether it would be possible to get a visa to such cities, and I said I was sure they could and if any of them took a trip to Russia and wanted to contact my office I would help out. This seemed to get a little chuckle from them.

I then moved back to the problem and my thrust then that what really mattered in the world was people rather than cities and air and water and all other things that were material. I said, for example, of all the countries I have visited in Latin America, Haiti is probably the poorest . . . but that the Haitians, as I recalled from 1955, while they were poor, had a dignity and a grace which was very moving, and that I always had wanted to return, not because there was anything in Haiti worth seeing in terms of cities or good food, etc., but because the people had such character.

I then made this same point again with regard to the people I had seen in Asia and India and returned again to the United States, where I again emphasized the importance of their not becoming alienated from the people of this country, its great variety.

I expressed distress that on the college campuses the blacks and whites, while they now go to school together, have less contact with each other than they had when they weren't. . . . This seemed to get through, although none of them had much to say and none of them responded specifically.

By this time the group around me had begun to get considerably larger. I would say that the original group of approximately eight to ten had now become perhaps thirty and some of those who seemed to be more leader types and older began to take part in the conversation.

One spoke up and said, "I hope you realize that we are willing to die for what we believe in."

I said, I certainly realize that. Do you realize that many of us when we were your age were also willing to die for what we believed in and were willing to do so today? The point is that we were trying to build a world in which you will not have to die for what you believe in, in which you are able to live for it.

I put in one brief comment with regard to the point I had made in the press conference, that while we had great differences with the Russians we had to find a way to limit nuclear arms and I had hoped that we could make some progress in that direction. They seemed to have very little interest in that subject. Perhaps it was because we moved through so fast and perhaps because they were overawed by the whole incident.

Then another spoke up and said, "We are not interested in

what Prague looks like. We are interested in what kind of life we build in the United States."

I said the whole purpose of my discussing Prague and other places was not to discuss the city but the people. For the next twenty-five years the world is going to get much smaller. We are going to be living in all parts of the world and it is vitally important that you know and appreciate and understand people every place, wherever they are, and particularly understand the people in your own country.

I said, I know that the great emphasis that is currently being put on the environment—the necessity to have clean air, clean water, clean streets—that, as you know, we have a very bold program going further than any has ever gone before to deal with some of these subjects. But I want to leave just one thought with you. Cleaning up the air and the water and the streets is not going to solve the deepest problems that concern us all. Those are material problems. They must be solved. They are terribly important. . . . But you must remember that something that is completely clean can also be completely sterile and without spirit.

What we all must think about is why we are here—what are those elements of the spirit which really matter. And, here again, I returned to my theme of thinking about people rather than about places and about things. I said candidly and honestly that I didn't have the answer, but I knew that young people today were searching, as I was searching forty years ago, for an answer to this problem. I just wanted to be sure that all of them realized that ending the war, and cleaning up the streets and the air and the water, was not going to solve spiritual hunger which all of us have and which, of course, has been the great mystery of life from the beginning of time. . . .

By this time the dawn was upon us, the first rays of the sun began to show, and they began to climb up over the Washington Monument and I said I had to go, and shook hands with those nearest to me, and walked down the steps.

A bearded fellow from Detroit was taking a picture as I began to get in the car. I asked him if he wouldn't like to get in the picture. He stepped over with me and I said, Look, I'll have the President's doctor take the picture, and Tkach took the picture. He seemed to be quite delighted—it was, in fact, the broadest smile that I saw on the entire visit. As I left him I said . . . that I knew he had come a long way for this event and I knew, too, that he and his colleagues were terribly frustrated and angry about our policy and opposed to it. I said, I just hope your opposition doesn't turn into a blind hatred of the country, but remember this is a great country, with all of its faults. I said, If you have any doubt about it, go down to the passport office. You won't see many people lining up to get out of the country. Abroad, you will see a number lining up to get in.

He smiled and took it all in good humor. We shook hands, and I got into the car and drove away.

I knew that those days in April and May were as hard for my staff as they were for me. Haldeman, Ehrlichman, and Kissinger, in particular, had borne the brunt of the Cambodian crisis. I wanted to do something to show how much I appreciated their strength and support. While we were in Key Biscayne over the weekend of May 15, I asked Bebe if his girl friend, Jane Lucke, would mind doing a little sewing for me.

On the plane back to Washington I asked Haldeman, Ehrlichman, and Kissinger to come to my cabin. When they arrived, I thanked them for all that they had done. "In fact," I said, "you deserve something like the Purple Heart for all the wounds you have sustained in the line of duty over the past few weeks."

They all laughed and said that they had only done their jobs.

"No," I continued, "you have done more than your jobs, and I have devised a new award—a Blue Heart, for those who are true blue."

I gave them each a small heart made from blue cloth. "This will be our secret," I said, "but I wanted you to know how much I appreciate what you have done."

Public opinion seemed to rally during the weeks after Kent State, when the military success of the Cambodian operation became increasingly apparent.

On May 20 the New York Building and Construction Trades Council sponsored a parade to City Hall in support of the President. There had already been scattered incidents of scuffling between the hardhats and various groups of antiwar demonstrators, especially after Mayor John Lindsay had ordered the flag on City Hall to be flown at half-staff as part of a "Day of Reflection" about the Kent State tragedy. The hardhats decided to show their support for our war aims, and more than 100,000 people came out to march with them.

I invited the leaders of the construction workers' unions to come to the White House. A photograph was taken of their hard hats on the Cabinet table. I gave a short briefing about the background of the Cambodian operation, and as I shook hands with them, one man said, "Mr. President, if someone would have had the courage to go into Cambodia sooner, they might have captured the bullet that took my son's life."

In the middle of May, *Newsweek* published a remarkable Gallup poll. It showed that 65 percent approved of my handling of the presidency; 30 percent of these described themselves as "very satisfied." Fifty percent approved of my decision to send troops into Cambodia; 39 percent disapproved; and 11 percent had no opinion. In response to the question, "Who do you think was primarily responsible for the deaths of four students at Kent State?" 58 percent blamed "demonstrating students" while only 11 percent blamed the National Guard.

On May 30, one month after the Cambodian operation began, I made a televised report to the nation on the progress to date. After conferring with General Abrams, I could state that this had been the most successful operation of the Vietnam war. We had already captured almost as much in enemy arms, equipment, ammunition, and food during the past month in Cambodia alone as we had captured in all of Vietnam during all of 1969.

On June 30, exactly on schedule and exactly as I had promised, we announced the departure of the last American troops from Cambodia. The operation had been a complete success. We had captured enough individual weapons to equip seventy-four full strength North Vietnamese infantry battalions; enough rice to feed all the Communist combat battalions estimated to be in South Vietnam for about four months; 143,000 rockets, mortars, and recoilless rifle rounds—equivalent to the amount used in about 14 months of fighting; 199,552 antiaircraft rounds, 5,482 mines, 62,022 grenades, and 83,000 pounds of explosives; 435 vehicles were captured and 11,688 bunkers and other military structures were destroyed.

Most important, the Cambodian operation had destroyed the Communists' capability of launching a spring offensive against our forces in South Vietnam. Our casualties had dropped from 93 a week in the six months before the operation to 51 per week in the six months after; and the performance of the ARVN had demonstrated that Vietnamization was working. The 150,000-man troop withdrawal I had announced on April 20 could go forward on schedule. And, finally, the pressure against Lon Nol had been reduced, and he was now expected to be able to survive. That would mean that Sihanoukville, the major port of entry for Soviet and Chinese heavy weapons into the Cambodian sanctuaries, would remain closed.

On the day of the previously announced departure from Cambodia the Senate passed the Cooper–Church amendment, the first restrictive vote ever cast on a President in wartime. In essence it demanded that I remove all American troops from Cambodia by July 1. The symbolism of the timing was as serious as the action itself was meaningless, since all Americans had already left Cambodia.

Kissinger's first secret meeting with the North Vietnamese since the Cambodian operation took place on September 7. Instead of the propaganda and vituperation he had expected, he found the friendliest atmosphere of any of the sessions so far. Summing up the meeting for me, he wrote, "Not only did they change their tone, but they also indicated a readiness to move on substance. They in effect dropped their demand for a six-month 'unconditional' withdrawal schedule, made no mention of the ten points, and indicated that they would reconsider their political proposals. They are very anxious to continue this channel, coming back repeatedly with proposals to meet again when I insisted that this channel required major progress."

I was somewhat skeptical about his optimism, because beneath the friendly atmosphere and the new elements of accommodation, the North Vietnamese still insisted that a settlement could be reached only if we deposed President Thieu. On Kissinger's memo, next to the reference to Thieu, I wrote, "This is probably the breaking point unless we can find a formula"—and it was hard to see how even Kissinger's negotiating skill could find a middle ground on that particular issue.

A follow-up meeting was scheduled for September 27. On Kissinger's memo describing the approach he planned, I wrote: "I would only suggest that I would try to get sooner at the heart of the question. Do they mean business—or is this just another rehash?"

The meeting of September 27 dashed all hopes of a breakthrough. The North Vietnamese were argumentative and repetitive. They made it clear that their tactic would be to isolate Thieu as the man who stood in the way of peace. Kissinger broke off the meeting without setting a date for another one.

Since it seemed unlikely that the secret talks were going to produce any solid progress, I decided to present publicly a significant new peace plan.

Because of the success of the Cambodian operation, I felt that now, for the first time, we could consider agreeing to a cease-fire in place in South Vietnam without first requiring that the North Vietnamese agree to withdraw their forces. As long as the Communist troops in South Vietnam could not depend on the Cambodian sanctuaries for supplies, ammunition, and reinforcements, I felt that the ARVN forces, which had been greatly improved and strengthened by more than a year of Vietnamization, would soon be able to defend themselves and their country.

In addition to a cease-fire in place throughout Indochina, the other key points of my new plan were an all-Indochina peace conference to be followed by a negotiated timetable for the withdrawal of all U.S. troops, a political settlement which reflected "the existing relationship of political forces in South Vietnam," and immediate release of all prisoners on both sides.

I presented this plan on television on October 7. Five days later I announced that 40,000 more troops would be withdrawn by Christmas. These two moves went so far toward removing the obstacles to a settlement that they effectively silenced the domestic antiwar movement by placing the burden squarely on the North Vietnamese to begin serious negotiations. But Hanoi stayed silent, and the secret channel in Paris remained closed.

THE HUSTON PLAN

By 1970 the evolutionary cycle of violent dissent spawned an ugly offshoot: the urban underground of political terrorists urging murder and bombing.

The most prominent of these groups were the Black Panthers and the Weathermen. The Black Panthers was founded in 1966 by Bobby Seale and Huey Newton while they were working for the Office of Economic Opportunity. Newton said they would exert power not through political channels but through a capacity for destruction. Eldridge Cleaver, the Panther "Minister of Communication," urged that the masses be spurred toward "revolutionary temptation to kidnap American ambassadors, hijack American airplanes, blow up American pipelines and buildings and to shoot anyone who uses guns and other weapons in the bloodstained service of imperialism against the people."

The Black Panthers had bases in urban areas all around the country. Because their organization was small and highly disciplined, it was extremely difficult to obtain advance information about their plans or the places they intended to strike. In 1969 and 1970 two members pleaded guilty to the murder of a suspected informant.

In 1969 police said they found a cache of Panther weapons that included a submachine gun, thirteen rifles, a handmade grenade, and thirty firebombs. Five policemen were wounded in a Chicago gun battle in July; in November, again in Chicago, two policemen were killed and six wounded, and one Black Panther was killed in another shoot-out. In December, Los Angeles police and Panthers engaged in a four-hour gun battle. In 1969 alone, 348 Panthers were arrested for serious crimes, including murder, armed robbery, rape, and burglary. "Off the Pig" was the Black Panther slogan.

The Weathermen were a terrorist offshoot of the Students for a Democratic Society. At their National Council meeting in 1969, the Weathermen decided to begin a new campaign of underground warfare, police murder, and bombing. "Revolutionary violence is the only way," they stated subsequently in their first public communiqué. With as many as a thousand estimated members, the Weather Underground separated into secret floating commando-type units. As with the Black Panthers, there was no way of knowing where or how they were going to strike.

Terrorists caused no fewer than 174 major bombings and bombing attempts on campus in the school year 1969–70. Cities were now targets as well. On March 6 a large townhouse in Greenwich Village exploded. Three bodies were found in the wreckage, along with fifty-seven sticks of dynamite, plumbing pipes stuffed with dynamite and roofing nails, and fragmentation bombs. It was a Weatherman bomb factory. There was evidence of Weatherman involvement in the planting of two bombs that same day in police facilities in Detroit. On March 12 explosions in three midtown Manhattan buildings caused the evacuation of some 15,000 people. A terrorist group calling itself Revolutionary Force 9 took the credit. In one twenty-four-hour period, there were more than 400 bomb scares in New York City. On March 30 police found dynamite in a Weatherman bomb factory in Chicago.

Fear was increasingly generated throughout the country. It was accompanied by demands for effective government action. A New York *Times* editorial stated, "The actual and threatened bombings of the past few days must not be glossed over as the action of idealistic if misguided revolutionaries; they are the criminal acts of potential murderers. . . . The mad criminals who threaten and bomb must be recognized for what they are and prosecuted with the full force not only of the law but of the community they would rule and ruin."

J. Edgar Hoover informed me that FBI agents had begun to pick up rumors of a calculated nationwide terrorist offensive by radical student groups using arson, bombing, and kidnaping of university and government officials. Violence was increasing in the high schools. Plane hijackings were up from 17 in 1968 to 33 in 1969.

From January 1969 through April 1970 there were, by conservative count, over 40,000 bombings, attempted bombings, and bomb threats—an average of over eighty a day. Over $21 million in property was destroyed. Forty-three people were killed. Of these 40,000 incidents, 64 percent were by bombers whose identity and motive were unknown.

On March 25 I sent Congress a message asking for urgent legislation to mete out the death penalty in cases where bombs caused the death of others. But weeks passed, and nothing had been done.

On May 25 the New York *Times* published excerpts from a "Declaration of War" issued by the Weathermen: "Within the next 14 days," it said, "we will attack a symbol or institution of Amerikan injustice." Two weeks and one day later a dynamite time bomb exploded in New York police headquarters. A handwritten communication signed "Weatherman" was sent to the Associated Press claiming that they had planted the bomb because "the pigs in this country are our enemies."

The Black Panthers were closely affiliated with North Korean groups and with radical Arab terrorists. We knew that Weathermen identified with North Vietnam, Cuba, and North Korea. I was eager to learn whether the foreign support went beyond ideological sympathy. I was sure that it did; the patterns were too clear. But the intelligence community never had a conclusive answer. Not until 1977 would the New York *Times* report that the FBI had developed evidence of direct support for the Weathermen from both Cuba and North Vietnam. Cuban and North Vietnamese agents counseled them, and the Cuban intelligence agency guided and paid for their escape from the FBI. Cuban military officers instructed them in "practical weaponry."

Now that this season of mindless terror has fortunately passed, it is difficult—perhaps impossible—to convey a sense of the pressures that were influencing my actions and reactions during this period, but it was this epidemic of unprecedented domestic terrorism that prompted our efforts to discover the best means by which to deal with this new phenomenon of highly organized and highly skilled revolutionaries dedicated to the violent destruction of our democratic system.

I turned for assistance in this effort to the various intelligence agencies. Working together, they developed a program to counter revolutionary violence. Three years later this program would be publicly revealed and labeled the Huston Plan. It was attacked as an authorization of Gestapo tactics bent on violating personal liberties. In the light of more recent revelations, we now know that this program did not involve the use of any measures not previously employed by federal law enforcement and intelligence agencies.

J. Edgar Hoover had become director of the Bureau of Investigation in 1924 and over the next forty years was hailed as a national hero. In the mid-sixties, however, he sensed that the temper of the times was turning against him. A new liberalism was fashionable, in which there appeared to be more concern for the rights of the accused than for the protection of the innocent. Now that his career was nearing its end he was determined not to give anyone ammunition in his last years to damage him or his organization. He had always been rigidly territorial when it came to the functions and prerogatives of the FBI. He totally distrusted the other intelligence agencies—especially the CIA—and, whenever possible, resisted attempts to work in concert with them. He was sensibly reluctant to go out on a limb for anyone, lest he find himself suddenly alone.

For more than twenty years, FBI agents had, when necessary, gathered foreign intelligence and evidence of foreign subversion and intelligence about domestic violence by secret break-ins. Between 1942 and 1968, apart from the foreign targets, domestic groups suspected of subversive or violent illegal activities were the targets of over 200 of these break-ins, which were known as "black bag" jobs.

In 1966, threatened with a congressional investigation and liberals in control of the Justice Department, Hoover summarily canceled all FBI black bag jobs and secret mail-opening operations. He also drastically decreased the use of room bugs since they, too, required surreptitious entry, and in 1967 he also cut back the recruitment of student and campus informants.

Just as Hoover cut back on these practices, domestic violence began increasing at an alarming rate. The Johnson administration reacted with great concern. Top administration officials put pressure on the FBI to obtain information about the potential rioters and their activities and even developed extraordinary additional programs of their own.

For example, whereas his predecessor restricted the role of the FBI in racial demonstrations exclusively to investigating "subversive involvement," in 1967 the new Attorney General, Ramsey Clark, ordered the FBI to "use the maximum resources, investigative and intelligence, to collect and report all facts bearing upon the question as to whether there has been or is a scheme or conspiracy by any group of whatever size, effectiveness, or affiliation to plan, promote, or aggravate riot activity." Clark's Assistant Attorney General for the Civil Rights Division, John Doar, went even further: he expressed concern that the FBI was not taking a "broad spectrum approach" to intelligence collection and evaluation, and was instead focusing too narrowly on "traditional subversive groups" and on persons suspected of specific statutory violations.

Clark and Doar set up a central unit for coordinating riot intelligence from informants in the Great Society poverty, community relations, and legal services programs. By 1968 they had over 3,000 people reporting on their neighbors.

In the late 1960s, under pressure from the White House and from Ramsey Clark at the Justice Department, the small domestic intelligence division at the Pentagon, which had been created in 1963, was dramatically expanded. By 1968, 1,500 Army intelligence agents were monitoring various civilian groups, ranging from the Poor People's March and the Mobilization Committee to protests by welfare mothers and classes in black studies. Later, in 1971, Mel Laird, with my approval, abolished the military intelligence program. By that time it had amassed files on more than 100,000 people.

In 1970 the already uneasy relationship between the CIA and FBI was exacerbated when the CIA refused to give Hoover the name of an FBI agent who had assisted them on a case without first having sought Hoover's permission. Hoover retaliated by cutting off all liaison between the FBI and the CIA. I received reports that Hoover's action, coupled with the general lack of coordination among the various intelligence agencies, had left us with an insufficient intelligence capability at a time when terrorist violence was at fever pitch. Weeks later, reportedly irritated further by criticism within the intelligence community, he proceeded to cut off all liaison with all other intelligence agencies, retaining communication only with the White House.

On June 5, 1970, I called a meeting with Hoover, Helms of the CIA, Lieutenant General D. V. Bennett of the Defense Intelligence Agency, and Vice Admiral Noel Gayler, Director of the National Security Agency. Haldeman, Ehrlichman, Bob Finch, and Tom Huston were also present. Huston was a young lawyer and former Defense Intelligence Agency aide whose assignments on the White House staff included the problem of violence from radicals. He was seriously concerned about the inadequacies of the U.S. intelligence apparatus, both in the face of domestic violence and in comparison to the intelligence capabilities of Communist-bloc countries.

I told the group that I wanted to know what the problems were in intelligence-gathering and what had to be done to solve them. I wanted their report submitted to me jointly, and I asked Hoover to act as chairman for this purpose.

The committee formed a study group to evaluate the situation and draw up alternatives. A report was drafted that was approved by the heads of the CIA, DIA, and NSA. Then it went to Hoover, who added, as footnotes to the body of the document, his personal objections to several of the sections.

The report was completed on June 25, 1970. It was officially called "Special Report Interagency Committee on Intelligence (Ad Hoc)."

The report opened with a brief analysis of the problems confronting us, ranging from the Black Panthers and the Weathermen to Communist infiltrators. It differentiated radical terrorist groups from those that merely indulged in incendiary rhetoric. It gave a summary of the available intelligence techniques, the current restrictions on them, and the advantages and disadvantages of lifting those restrictions.

There was only one technique which Hoover had no objection to seeing expanded—the National Security Agency's coverage of overseas telephone and telegraph communications. He had strong objections to the four central possibilities discussed: resumption of covert mail-opening, resumption of black bag jobs, increased electronic surveillance, and an increase in campus—therefore young—informants.

In a separate memo recommending the two most controversial methods, covert mail-opening and surreptitious entry, Huston indicated that the former would be primarily targeted at foreign intelligence and cases of suspected espionage, and the latter would be resumed against foreign targets when they might provide information that could break a code, and possibly against other "urgent and high priority internal security targets," namely, "the Weathermen and Black Panthers."

The final technique discussed in the plan was military intelligence. Hoover objected to an increase in military undercover agents. The group also requested budget increases for each agency—which Hoover approved—and recommended the creation of an intelligence coordinating committee which would ensure that coordination existed between the disparate intelligence-gathering activities of the government. Hoover objected to this.

When I learned of Hoover's dissent from the committee's otherwise unanimous approval of the report, I felt that it was primarily a case of his inability to overcome his natural resistance to cooperating with the CIA or the other intelligence agencies. Beyond that, I thought he was afraid that if he agreed to cooperate, and was on record as having done so, the other agencies might use this to undercut him through leaks.

On July 14, following Huston's recommendations, I turned down an increase in military intelligence activities and approved relaxation of restrictions on the other techniques. I felt they were necessary and justified by the violence we faced. I was satisfied that none of the special techniques would be used indiscriminately, and that none of them represented any threat to legitimate dissent. The express domestic targets—the Black Panthers and the Weathermen—had announced their intentions to kidnap and assassinate and were already building an arsenal of weapons to carry out their threat.

On July 23 Huston sent a memo to the heads of the intelligence agencies notifying them of my decision.

When Hoover learned about this, he appealed to John Mitchell. He said he thought the possibility of public exposure was too great to justify the risks. Mitchell conveyed Hoover's arguments to me, adding that he agreed with Hoover. I knew that if Hoover had decided not to cooperate, it would matter little what I had decided or approved. Even if I issued a direct order to him, while he would undoubtedly carry it out, he would soon see to it that I had cause to reverse myself. There was even the remote possibility that he would resign in protest.

On July 28, five days later, before the plan could be implemented, I withdrew my approval.

The irony of the controversy over the Huston Plan did not become apparent until a 1975 investigation revealed that the investigative techniques it would have involved had not only been carried out long before I approved the plan but continued to be carried out after I had rescinded my approval of it.

It is clear that when a nation confronts dire situations someone is going to act. People will not stand by and let criminals destroy life and property. If the President does not decide how to meet the emergency, someone at a lower level will. I would rather it be the President exercising his judgment than the FBI agent in the field. As Senator Frank Church said in hearings on intelligence agency activities, the Huston Plan "was limited to techniques far more restrictive than the far-reaching methods that were employed by the FBI during the years that we have reviewed."

The bombing and violence continued unabated, and more than once I wondered whether the Huston Plan, if it had been in operation, might have detected and prevented the death and destruction. In August a policeman was killed and six others were wounded in a series of gun battles with the Black Panthers and another black militant group in Philadelphia. That same month, a bomb planted in a research center at the University of Wisconsin took the life of a graduate student working there; four other people were injured. On October 8 there were several bomb explosions—reportedly the work of the Weathermen—at the University of Washington and in two northern California towns. Five buildings were hit by dynamite blasts in Rochester, New York, on October 12; a research center in Irvine, California, was demolished by a bomb on October 18. On March 1, 1971, the U.S. Capitol was bombed by the Weather Underground.

I believe today as I believed then that in view of the crisis of terrorism and violence visited upon countless innocent people, the recommendations made to me by the interagency intelligence group in its 1970 report were justified and responsible. Critics who later contended that the recommendations were repressive and unlawful had the luxury of a calmer environment. They did not face the exigencies of a critical period in which the President, whose paramount responsibility is to ensure the safety of all citizens, was forced to consider measures that would undoubtedly be unacceptable in more tranquil times.

In the 1960s an FBI official report claimed that the results of just one surreptitious entry helped bring about the "near disintegration" of the Ku Klux Klan. Was the FBI right or wrong in taking that action? Did the threat of murder and violence by Klan members warrant an infringement on its members' liberties?

My decision to approve the recommendations of the Huston Plan, like the decisions of President Roosevelt to incarcerate thousands of Japanese-Americans and of President Lincoln to suspend the constitutional guarantee of habeas corpus, will always be debated. In the 1970s did the threatened and actual bombings of the Weathermen, and the brutal assaults of the Black Panthers, justify an intrusion on their liberties? When the issue juxtaposes the lives of innocent citizens against the possible curtailment of personal liberties we all cherish, the answers are never easy.

Sometimes the letter of one law will conflict with the spirit of another, and that is when the President must choose. He cannot throw up his hands in dismay, because inaction may be as devastating as wrong action. The question is: What is the law, and how is it to be applied with respect to the President in fulfilling the duties of his office? Precedents over the years have sanctioned some degree of latitude in the use by Presidents of emergency measures to meet emergency situations. I believe such latitude is necessary, and at times vital, to defend the nation and to protect innocent people whose lives are threatened by criminal forces. Jefferson was talking about this problem in 1810 when he noted:

> A strict observance of the written laws is doubtless one of the high duties of a good citizen, but it is not the highest. The laws of necessity, of self-preservation, of saving our country when in danger, are of a higher obligation. . . . To lose our country by a scrupulous adherence to written law, would be to lose the law itself, with life, liberty, property and all those who are enjoying them with us; thus absurdly sacrificing the end to the means.

I think it would be disastrous if, in an excess of prohibitory zeal, we were to tie the President's hands now and in the future, limiting him to the mechanical functions of executing the precise letter of the law, because laws cannot foresee every circumstance. We have to place faith in his judgment; we have to weigh the potential for abuse of power if we allow him reasonable latitude to act, against the potential harm that may result if we too narrowly restrict that latitude.

WAR IN JORDAN

America's Middle Eastern policy under Presidents Kennedy and Johnson was aimed primarily at supplying the arms and money to enable Israel to defend itself against its potential enemies.

This policy seemed to be successful. In 1967 the numerically inferior Israeli forces were able to defeat and humiliate the Soviet-armed Egyptians and Syrians in less than a week of fighting. As a result of this Six-Day War, the Israelis expanded their territory by occupying several areas along the banks of the Suez Canal, on the Sinai Peninsula, on the west bank of the Jordan River, in Jerusalem, and in the Golan Heights along the Israeli-Syrian border. The victory was overwhelming—so overwhelming that it was inevitable that further wars would be fought by Israel's neighbors for repossession of these conquered and occupied territories.

After the war high-level visits between Moscow and Cairo, Damascus, and Baghdad produced a massive new infusion of Soviet money, men, and matériel. The Soviets wanted to maintain their presence in the Middle East, not because of ideological support for the cause of Arab unity but because it was through Egypt and the other Arab countries that the Soviets could gain access to what the Russians had always wanted—land, oil, power, and the warm waters of the Mediterranean. As I commented to Bill Rogers, "The difference between our goal and the Soviet goal in the Middle East is very simple but fundamental. *We* want peace. *They* want the Middle East."

The potential for a confrontation between the United States and the U.S.S.R. loomed large. If the Soviets were committed to Arab victories, and we were committed to Israeli victories, it did not require much imagination to see how we both might be drawn in even against our wills—and almost certainly against our national interests.

At the beginning of my administration, I assigned the Middle East exclusively to Bill Rogers and his Assistant Secretary of State for Near Eastern and South Asian Affairs, Joseph Sisco. I did this partly because I felt that Kissinger's Jewish background would put him at a disadvantage during the delicate initial negotiations for the reopening of diplomatic relations with the Arab states. Primarily, however, I felt that the Middle East required full time and expert attention. As I told Kissinger, "You and I will have more than enough on our plate with Vietnam, SALT, the Soviets, Japan, and Europe."

It was clearly in America's interests to halt the Soviet domination of the Arab Mideast. To do so would require broadening American relations with the Arab countries. Within the first few months of my administration I began taking the first steps in this direction.

At the beginning of April 1969, King Hussein of Jordan made a state visit to the United States. In our last meeting before he left I told him that I was deeply troubled because the absence of diplomatic relations with some of the governments in the Middle East precluded our playing a constructive role in the region. Although he made no reply at the time,

I knew that Hussein would carry this message back to the other Arab leaders.

The next day, I met with Mahmoud Fawzi, who had come to Washington as a personal emissary of President Nasser of Egypt. I told him that we regretted the United States did not have formal relations with Egypt. I said that I did not believe there would ever be a settlement that would fully satisfy either side, but I was confident that a mutually acceptable compromise could be achieved if the United States could establish a new relationship with Egypt and the Arab nations. "Of course, this will require trust between the parties, and I know that trust has to be deserved and earned," I said.

The key to peace in the Middle East lay as much in Moscow as it did in Cairo or Damascus. Therefore when our new ambassador to the Soviet Union, Jacob Beam, presented his credentials in April 1969, I had him deliver a personal letter from me to Premier Kosygin. In it I said that it was essential that both our countries exert a calming influence in the Middle East, and that no outside power seek any advantage in the area at the expense of any other.

On September 25, 1969, Golda Meir came to Washington for a state visit. In Israeli terms she was a "hawk," and a hard-liner opposed to surrendering even an inch of the occupied territory Israel had won in the 1967 war. Mrs. Meir conveyed simultaneously the qualities of extreme toughness and extreme warmth; when the survival of her country was involved, the toughness was predominant. She requested twenty-five Phantom jets and eighty Skyhawk fighters and complained about the delays in delivery of planes that had already been approved. She also asked for low-interest loans of $200 million a year for periods up to five years. I reassured her that our commitments would be met.

At the state dinner in her honor she expressed concern regarding our moves toward détente with the Soviets. I told her that we had no illusions about their motives. I said, "Our Golden Rule as far as international diplomacy is concerned is: 'Do unto others as they do unto you.' "

"Plus ten percent," Kissinger quickly added.

Mrs. Meir smiled. "As long as you approach things that way, we have no fears," she said.

In December 1969, Bill Rogers gave a speech in which he outlined what became known as the "Rogers Plan" for peace in the Middle East. This plan was based on the principle of the return of the occupied Arab territories in exchange for Arab assurances of Israel's territorial integrity. In strictly practical terms, the provision for return of occupied territories meant that the Rogers Plan had absolutely no chance of being accepted by Israel.

Rogers and the State Department argued that the plan offered the best hope for peace, since the return of the occupied territories would at least remove for the Arabs the hated reminder of their humiliating defeat. Kissinger countered that the plan encouraged the extremist elements among the Arabs, gratuitously offended the Israelis, and earned the contempt of the Soviets, who saw it as playing naïvely into their hands. As Kissinger predicted, the Rogers Plan drew fierce criticism from the Israelis and made Rogers, as Kissinger frequently reminded me, "the most unpopular man in Israel."

I knew that the Rogers Plan could never be implemented, but I believed that it was important to let the Arab world know that the United States did not automatically dismiss its case regarding the occupied territories or rule out a compromise settlement of the conflicting claims. With the Rogers Plan on the record, I thought it would be easier for the Arab leaders to propose reopening relations with the United States without coming under attack from the hawks and pro-Soviet elements in their own countries.

On January 31, 1970, I received what Kissinger termed the first Soviet threat of my administration. Significantly, it involved the Middle East. It came in the form of a letter from Premier Kosygin that stated: "We would like to tell you in all frankness that if Israel continues its adventurism, to bomb the territory of U.A.R. and of other Arab states, the Soviet Union will be forced to see to it that the Arab states have means at their disposal, with the help of which a due rebuff to the arrogant aggressor could be made."

My reply was carefully low-keyed: I urged a more positive Soviet response to the Rogers Plan and proposed discussions on limiting arms supplies to the Middle East.

In the meantime a different kind of diplomatic problem had arisen closer to home. Many members of the American Jewish community and its political friends had decided to boycott the state visit of President Georges Pompidou of France as a protest against his recent sale to Libya of more than a hundred Mirage jet fighters.

Shortly before Pompidou's arrival, I received word that neither Governor Rockefeller nor Mayor Lindsay would officially greet him in New York nor attend the dinner in his honor at the Waldorf-Astoria Hotel on the last night of his visit. I fully understood the importance of the Jewish vote in New York, but, as I said to Haldeman, "It's completely hypocritical to treat Pompidou this way when they slobbered all over Kosygin when he was there—and *he's* the direct cause of the whole damn problem." I told Kissinger, "I consider this unconscionable conduct towards an official guest of the United States of America, and I will not tolerate it. Nor will I lead people to believe that it has any effect whatsoever on me."

After four days in Washington, the Pompidous visited Cape Kennedy and San Francisco before flying to Chicago. There, obscenity-screaming demonstrators broke through police lines and jostled the Pompidou party. Madame Pompidou was shaken by the incident, and Bus Mosbacher, our Chief of Protocol, informed me that she was going to fly home to Paris the next morning.

I told Mosbacher, "I don't care what you have to do, but I don't want her to leave."

I decided to fly to New York and attend the Waldorf-Astoria dinner that Rockefeller and Lindsay were boycotting. My appearance at the dinner came as a dramatic surprise, and nothing I said in our many talks over the years on substantive matters did as much to win Pompidou's friendship and cooperation as this gesture.

At the beginning of March I decided to postpone our delivery of Phantom jets to Israel. I had heard that the Soviets were coming under renewed pressures from their Arab clients to surpass the new American deliveries to Israel, and I hoped that since Israel was already in a strong military position, I could slow down the arms race without tipping the fragile military balance in the region. I also believed that American influence in the Middle East increasingly depended on our renewing diplomatic relationships with Egypt and Syria, and this decision would help promote that goal.

On March 12 I received a personal letter from Mrs. Meir. She said, "It is true that our pilots are very good, but they can be good only when they have planes. Lately some rumors have reached me that your decision may be negative or at best postponed. I absolutely refuse to believe it. If, God forbid, this were true, then we would feel really forsaken."

Israel had survived only because its people were ready to fight and die for it. I could understand their reluctance to accept our assurances instead of our jet fighters at a time when they faced a possible attack.

As I had told Pompidou, "If you put yourself in the position of Dayan, Rabin, Eban, or Mrs. Meir, who are intelligent and tough people, you must admire them: there they sit, a very few people, surrounded by enemies, and the fact is, they aren't prepared to take advice even from the President of the United States." I tried to reassure Mrs. Meir that if it ever came to the test of a crisis—as it did in September 1970 and again in October 1973—then we would be found fully and firmly on Israel's side. In the meantime, I realized that my new policy would cause much pain and many problems. I also realized that it would be misunderstood and denounced by many on both sides. What I was trying to do, however, was to construct a completely new set of power relationships in the Middle East—not only between Israel and the Arabs, but also among the United States, Western Europe, and the Soviet Union.

One of the main problems I faced in this regard was the unyielding and shortsighted pro-Israeli attitude prevalent in large and influential segments of the American Jewish community, Congress, the media, and in intellectual and cultural circles. In the quarter century since the end of World War II this attitude had become so deeply ingrained that many saw the corollary of not being pro-Israeli as being anti-Israeli, or even anti-Semitic. I tried unsuccessfully to convince them that this was not the case.

There was a wave of criticism in the media and in Congress when my decision to postpone the Phantom deliveries was announced. Israeli Ambassador Rabin knew the decision was coming and complained to Kissinger that we were failing to meet our responsibilities. I was annoyed that a number of the senators who were urging that we send more military aid to save Israel were opposing our efforts to save South Vietnam from Communist domination. I dictated a memorandum to Kissinger describing my feelings and pointing out the danger for Israel of relying on the prominent liberal and dove senators of both parties to come through in the event a crisis arose in which Israel was attacked by the Arabs or was even threatened directly by Soviet power:

> What they must realize is that these people are very weak reeds. They will give Israel a lot of lip service, but they are peace at any price people. When the chips are down they will cut and run, not only as they are presently cutting and running in Vietnam, but also when any conflict in the Mideast stares them straight in the face.
>
> On the other hand, their real friends (to their great surprise) are people like Goldwater, Buckley, RN et al., who are considered to be hawks on Vietnam but who, in the broader aspects, are basically not cut-and-run people whether it is in Vietnam, the Mideast, Korea, or any place else in the world. . . .
>
> They must recognize that our interests are basically pro-freedom and not just pro-Israel because of the Jewish vote. We are *for* Israel because Israel in our view is the only state in the Mideast which is *pro*-freedom and an effective opponent to Soviet expansion. We will oppose a cut-and-run policy either in Vietnam or Cuba or the Mideast or NATO or anyplace else in the world. This is the kind of friend that Israel needs and will continue to need, particularly when the going gets very tough in the next five years. . . .
>
> What all this adds up to is that Mrs. Meir, Rabin, et al., must trust RN completely. He does not want to see Israel go down the drain and makes an absolute commitment that he will see to it that Israel always has "an edge." On the other hand, he must carry with him not just the Jewish constituency in New York and Pennsylvania and California and possibly Illinois which voted 95 percent against him, but he must carry with him the 60 percent of the American people who are in what is called the silent majority, and who

> must be depended upon in the event that we have to take a strong stand against Soviet expansionism in the Mideast. Only when the Israeli leaders realize this fact are they going to have any kind of security which will be reliable. . . .
>
> We are going to stand up in Vietnam and in NATO and in the Mideast, but it is a question of all or none. This is it cold turkey, and it is time that our friends in Israel understood this.
>
> We are going to be in power for at least the next three years and this is going to be the policy of this country. Unless they understand it and act as if they understood it beginning now, they are down the tubes.

Throughout the spring there were sporadic but bitter outbreaks of fighting between Israel and Egypt and Syria. At the beginning of June 1970, Rogers sent me a memorandum proposing a U.S. peace initiative, and on June 25 he announced that we would encourage the parties "to stop shooting and start talking."

On August 7, an uneasy cease-fire was declared. It was a major accomplishment for Rogers and Sisco. Even though the cease-fire was violated by Egypt almost before the ink was dry, it established the United States as the honest broker accepted by both sides.

On August 17 Kissinger and I met with Ambassador Rabin. He said emotionally that Mrs. Meir and the Israeli government were unsettled because the United States did not seem to accept the evidence that serious Egyptian cease-fire violations were taking place. He said that Soviet surface-to-air missiles had been moved into the forward area along the Suez Canal, changing the entire balance of power in the area. Unless something were done, it would be just a matter of time before the Egyptians attacked. The Israelis therefore wanted to send air strikes against these missile complexes. The attrition of their aircraft would be very high, however, unless we gave them the special electronic jamming equipment and missiles they were requesting.

"Israel must understand that I have no illusions about Soviet motives," I said. "Perhaps I even understand them better than Israel itself. We have launched our cease-fire initiative with no preconceived notions as to Soviet good will. On the other hand, it was important that the initiative be made so that it is on the record."

I pointed out that American public opinion would be very important if another war began in the Middle East. This was why I had wanted America to be the prime mover of the cease-fire proposal, and why I wanted Israel to be scrupulously careful in observing it. "If our peace initiative fails, everyone should be able to recognize who is at fault," I said. "And I hope that it will not be Israel."

I said that I would approach the Soviets through special channels concerning their involvement in the current crisis. "I completely agree with you," I said, "that the Soviets are the main cause of Middle East tensions, and that if they were removed from the situation Israel would be able to handle matters without difficulty."

A month later our policy of building a new balance of power in the Middle East was put to the test of war.

At the beginning of September, the extremist Palestinian guerrillas became increasingly active. One group of them hijacked four commercial airliners and blew them up after holding the hundreds of passengers, most of them Americans, hostage for several days. It seemed likely that a serious showdown was going to be unavoidable, so I decided to revoke my earlier order and to send more military aid and more Phantom jets to Israel.

On September 15 a full-blown crisis erupted in Jordan. The Palestinian extremist leaders, backed by Syrian arms and aid, had stirred up the Palestinian refugees living in Jordan and threatened to provoke a civil war against Hussein's regime. When Kissinger reported this news to me, he said, "It looks like the Soviets are pushing the Syrians and the Syrians are pushing the Palestinians. The Palestinians don't need much pushing."

The situation was confused, and until we had reliable information or intelligence about what was really going on, I felt it was important to keep as cool as possible. I was scheduled to leave on a two-day trip to Kansas City and Chicago, and I decided to keep to the schedule.

However, one thing was clear. We could not allow Hussein to be overthrown by a Soviet-inspired insurrection. If it succeeded, the entire Middle East might erupt in war: the Israelis would almost certainly take pre-emptive measures against a Syrian-dominated radical government in Jordan; the Egyptians were tied to Syria by military alliances; and Soviet prestige was on the line with both the Syrians and the Egyptians. Since the United States could not stand idly by and watch Israel being driven into the sea, the possibility of a direct U.S.–Soviet confrontation was uncomfortably high. It was like a ghastly game of dominoes, with a nuclear war waiting at the end.

The next morning the phone rang at 8:00 in my Chicago hotel suite. It was Kissinger, calling with the news that civil war had broken out in Jordan. Palestinian rebel forces were fighting Hussein's troops, and Syrian tanks were poised and ready on the border. That afternoon, I talked to a group of reporters and editors and told them that we might have to intervene if Syrian tanks or troops or any of the Arab League Iraqi troops already encamped in Jordan moved against Hussein. When the afternoon newspapers appeared, headlines announced: *Nixon Warns Reds: Keep Out*.

The next day, September 18, we received a note from the Kremlin stating that the Soviets had no intention of intervening in Jordan, urging us not to intervene, and suggesting that we discourage others—in other words, Israel—from doing so.

I had one of my regular breakfast meetings with Mike Mansfield that morning. Mansfield strongly opposed any American military involvement in the Mideast, and I was able to tell him that, based on the Soviet note, I was optimistic that we could work things out without a confrontation. He raised his hands over his head and slowly brought them down to the table as he closed his eyes and said: "Praise Allah!"

At eleven o'clock that same morning I had an appointment with Golda Meir, who was in the United States on an unofficial visit.

When Mrs. Meir was ushered into the Oval Office, I could see from her fixed smile that she was in a very stern mood. I opened by saying that I was not naïve about Soviet intentions and that I was aware of the difficulties that cease-fire violations had caused Israel.

"In my view, Mr. President," she replied, "the American response to our reports about cease-fire cheating was slow, and your initial acquiescence encouraged additional violations." She asked Rabin to explain, and on the rug he spread out three large Israeli intelligence maps pinpointing the specific violations.

Mrs. Meir said that Israel's problems were not caused primarily by the Arabs. They were the direct result of the Soviet presence and Soviet military equipment. The Egyptians did not even know how to operate the surface-to-air missiles the Soviets had given them, and Soviet personnel had had to be interspersed at all levels within the Egyptian military. She said that Israeli pilots had already met Soviet pilots in air-to-air combat over the Suez Canal.

Mrs. Meir continued. "Now, in my opinion, I think you should go to the Soviets directly and demand an adjustment of the situation if the negotiations are to continue."

I assured Mrs. Meir that we had already sent several strong notes to the Soviets through diplomatic channels. I said that I wanted her to understand the major principles underlying American policy in the Mideast. We were under no illusions concerning the Soviet intent and involvement in the region, and we recognized that something had to be done about Egyptian cease-fire violations. We did not intend to permit the military balance in the Middle East to be disturbed, and we were prepared to work with her in developing a military aid program that would be appropriate for the strategy the Israelis adopted.

Mrs. Meir said that Israel would not move precipitately into Jordan; she agreed that it was preferable to have Hussein solve the problem himself.

Reports from Jordan indicated hard fighting throughout the country, with Hussein's troops holding their own or better. Then, on September 18 word was flashed to the White House Situation Room that Syrian tanks had crossed the border into northern Jordan. The next day we learned that the invasion force had numbered at least a hundred tanks. We moved quickly and decisively on the diplomatic front. Kissinger drafted a very stern note and delivered it to the Soviets; Rogers issued a strong public statement calling on Syria to halt its invasion. By early evening it appeared that about half the Syrian tanks had returned to Syria.

"They're testing us," I said to Kissinger, "and the test may not be over yet."

On the night of September 21 at around ten o'clock another message was received in the Situation Room: about three hundred Syrian tanks had crossed the Jordanian border. They had broken through the Jordanian defenses and were rumbling almost unopposed along the roads toward Amman. By the next morning, however, most of these tanks had also been pulled back. The testing was continuing, moving a few notches higher each time. We would have to decide what to do very soon, or it might be too late to do anything.

We decided to pursue a very hard but very quiet line. I authorized Kissinger to call Ambassador Rabin and suggest that he inform his government that we would be fully in support of Israeli air strikes on Syrian forces in Jordan if this became necessary to avoid a Jordanian defeat. I decided to put 20,000 American troops on alert and moved additional naval forces into the Mediterranean.

In the end Jordan under Hussein's courageous leadership saved itself. By the morning of September 22, the Syrian tanks were once again heading back toward the border. Rabin called early in the afternoon to confirm that the tanks had left Jordan and that the rebel forces were in disarray. He ascribed Hussein's victory to the tough American position, the Israeli threat, and the superb fighting by Hussein's troops.

CRISIS IN CUBA

On Friday, September 18, while I was waiting for Golda Meir to arrive for her meeting in the Oval Office, I received an urgent memo from Kissinger. It was headed "TOP SECRET/SENSITIVE/EYES ONLY." Its first sentence stated: "Analysis of reconnaissance flight photography over Cuba has this morning confirmed the construction of a probable submarine deployment base in Cienfuegos Bay." If the intelligence was correct, it meant that the Soviets were building a nuclear submarine base on Cuba.

So far the details were very sketchy. On August 4 Yuli Vorontsov, the Minister Counselor of the Soviet Embassy and Chargé in Dobrynin's absence, had delivered a note to Kissinger expressing concern over alleged anti-Castro activity by Cuban revolutionary groups in the United States. The note stressed that the Soviets were adhering to the understanding President Kennedy had agreed to in 1962, which included a provision that the Soviets would not put nuclear weapons on Cuban territory in return for our assurance that we would not undertake or support military action to overthrow Castro.

Regular U-2 reconnaissance flights over Cuba in August showed nothing unusual. In September, however, the photographs revealed that construction had begun on the shores of Alcatraz Island, a tiny dot of land off Cuba's southern coast in the middle of Cienfuegos Bay. A submarine tender was anchored to four buoys in the deep-water basin, and submarine nets were strung across the harbor. A large complex of barracks, administrative buildings, and recreation facilities was almost completed on Alcatraz Island.

When a U-2 had discovered Soviet missile sites in Cuba in October 1962, President Kennedy revealed their presence in a nationwide television speech and had Adlai Stevenson display the enlarged photographs at the UN General Assembly. These actions placed Khrushchev in an almost impossible situation in terms of his international prestige. He was able, however, to use the universal fear of war to put pressure on Kennedy, thus making himself appear responsible for resolving the crisis and reaching a peaceful settlement. So instead of dealing with Khrushchev from the position of immense nuclear superiority that we still held in 1962, Kennedy ended up by agreeing to refrain from any anti-Castro activities in return for Khrushchev's removal of the Soviet missiles from Cuba.

In view of what had happened in the 1962 crisis, I decided that I would not force a public confrontation unless I had no other choice, and I would not deal with the Soviets from anything less than a position of unyielding strength.

I wrote a note to Kissinger: "I want a report on a crash basis on: (1) What CIA can do to support *any* kind of action which will irritate Castro; (2) What actions we can take which we have not yet taken to boycott nations dealing with Castro; (3) Most important, what actions we can take, covert or overt, to put missiles in Turkey—or a sub base in the Black Sea—anything which will give us some trading stock."

During the next few days further U-2 flights confirmed our worst fears. The construction was proceeding at a rapid pace, and unless we acted quickly and decisively, we would wake up one morning to find a fully functioning nuclear-equipped Soviet submarine base ninety miles from our shores.

Not all my advisers agreed on the need for immediate action. Bill Rogers was particularly forceful in an NSC meeting on September 23, urging that we keep the situation completely quiet until after the November elections. I did not feel, however, that the crisis would keep that long, and I directed the NSC to work on a contingency plan.

On September 24 Dobrynin requested an appointment with me to deliver the Kremlin's reply concerning proposals we had made recently regarding a possible summit meeting. I was surprised by the boldness of this request. The Soviets apparently thought we were still unaware of what they were doing in Cuba, and were clearly planning to take us by surprise with a fait accompli, just as they had in 1962. Kissinger and I agreed that he should meet with Dobrynin and see what the Soviets were up to.

The next morning, the New York *Times* ran a story by its distinguished foreign correspondent C. L. Sulzberger that "initial information" suggested that a naval installation for nuclear submarines was being built in Cienfuegos. Because the information was vague and unconfirmed and because Sulzberger's column appeared on the paper's editorial pages, there was a chance that the story might not be picked up for several days. When Kissinger and Dobrynin met in the Map Room that morning, neither mentioned the column nor the alleged base. Dobrynin, in fact, reported that the Soviet leaders were interested in holding a summit, and he even proposed dates. Kissinger suggested that he return to the White House later that afternoon for a reply.

However, at a press briefing across the river in the Pentagon, a Deputy Assistant Secretary inadvertently revealed that there was evidence that a Soviet submarine facility was possibly being constructed in Cuba. Confronted with this leak, Kissinger had to meet with reporters. He tried to finesse the situation as much as possible, but the story was in the news that evening.

Kissinger told me that when Dobrynin came back to the White House at 5:30 that afternoon his face was ashen. To Dobrynin's surprise and then to his discomfort, Kissinger studiously ignored the afternoon's events and began by stating calmly that he had my answer concerning the proposed summit. In principle, he said, I would agree to a meeting in Moscow in either June or September 1971. Finally he said that he wanted to talk about the press statements that had come out of the Pentagon and his own press conference earlier that afternoon. He had implied to the reporters that we did not yet know whether there actually was a submarine base in Cuba. He told Dobrynin that he had done this deliberately in order to give the Soviets an opportunity to withdraw without a public confrontation.

"I want you to know, however, that we have no illusions about this matter," Kissinger added. "We know there is a base in Cuba, and we will view it with the utmost gravity if construction continues and the base remains."

Dobrynin tried to minimize the problem, but Kissinger persisted. We were giving the Soviets an opportunity to pull out because we did not want a public confrontation. But we would not shrink from other measures, including public ones, if we were forced into them.

Dobrynin asked whether we considered that the 1962 understandings on Cuba had been violated. Kissinger replied that we did. Cuba was a place of extreme sensitivity for us, and we considered that the installation of the submarine base had been carried out with maximum deception. Dobrynin said that he would immediately inform the Kremlin of what Kissinger had said.

I gave orders that absolutely no further news leaks about the submarine base were to occur until we received the Soviet reply. The entire success of our strategy of keeping the crisis low key depended on keeping a tight lid on the story. I knew from the 1962 experience that a serious war scare would sweep the country if the real story of Cienfuegos hit the headlines.

We were able to keep the secret so well that during the next few days several prominent political leaders and journalists dismissed Cienfuegos as a trumped-up crisis. Senator Fulbright, the Chairman of the Senate Foreign Relations Committee, charged the administration with "hoodwinking the American people" and said that stories of nuclear submarine bases in Cuba were aimed at getting Congress to approve generous appropriations for the Pentagon. I did nothing to discourage such mistaken opinions; in fact, I did everything possible to carry on business as usual. The most recent U-2 flights indicated a slowing of activity at Cienfuegos, so on September 27 I left for a week-long trip to Europe.

On October 6, our first morning back in Washington, Dobrynin called to arrange an appointment with Kissinger. He handed Kissinger a note in which the Soviet government reaffirmed the 1962 understanding about Cuba and stated that it was not doing anything in Cuba that would contradict that understanding. When Kissinger showed me the note, I was tremendously relieved. Our strategy had worked. The Soviets had decided to take advantage of the maneuverability a low profile afforded. They were backing away from the crisis by denying that it had ever existed.

We could not, however, accept Dobrynin's vague declaration as the definitive settlement of such a serious incident. A few days later Kissinger handed him a note from me that welcomed the Soviet reply but specifically outlined our interpretation of the 1962 understanding. I wrote, "The U.S. government understands that the U.S.S.R. will not establish, utilize, or permit the establishment of any facility in Cuba that can be employed to support or repair Soviet naval ships capable of carrying offensive weapons, i.e. submarines or surface ships armed with nuclear-capable, surface-to-surface missiles." To nail down the details so that there would be no further "misunderstandings," I listed five specific actions that we would consider violations of the 1962 agreement.

Dobrynin objected to the bluntness of some of the language, but he hinted that the question would soon be put to rest. A few days later TASS, the Soviet government news agency, issued a statement that no submarine base existed, thus putting the Soviets officially on record.

The crisis was over. After some face-saving delays, the Soviets abandoned Cienfuegos. Through strong but quiet diplomacy we had averted what would have been known as the Cuban Nuclear Submarine Crisis of 1970 and which, like its predecessor, might have taken us to the brink of nuclear confrontation with the Soviet Union.

The events at Cienfuegos Bay convinced me that I had chosen the right course in dealing with another Communist threat in Latin America —this one in Chile.

In Chile's presidential elections of September 4, 1970, a pro-Castro Marxist, Salvador Allende, came in first with a 36.3 percent plurality. Under Chilean law Allende's slim plurality was insufficient for election, and the Chilean Congress would choose the new President on October 24. The CIA estimated that Cuba had pumped about $350,000 into the Allende campaign. Allende's own intentions, stated in a campaign speech, were clear: "Cuba in the Caribbean and a Socialist Chile in the Southern Cone will make the revolution in Latin America."

Allende had run for President three times before and been defeated each time. In the Chilean elections of 1962 and 1964 Presidents Kennedy and Johnson had authorized CIA expenditures of almost $4 million to avert a Communist takeover in Chile. Knowing this, and knowing that nearly two-thirds of Chile's voters had rejected Allende, I directed the CIA to provide support for Allende's opponents in order to prevent his election by the Chilean Congress.

We live in a far from ideal world. As long as the Communists supply external funds to support political parties, factions, or individuals in other countries, I believe that the United States can and should do the same and do it secretly so that it can be effective. Under Communist standards of morality, governments are meant to be subverted and elections influenced. To me it would have been the height of immorality to allow the Soviets, the Cubans, and other Communist nations to interfere with impunity in free elections while America stayed its hand. It is a peculiar double standard that would require us alone to stand abjectly aside as democracies are undermined by countries less constrained by conscience. In Chile we sought to help non-Communist parties have at least the same resources as the lavishly financed pro-Allende forces.

In mid-October I was informed that our efforts were probably not going to be successful; therefore I instructed the CIA to abandon the operation. Allende was inaugurated President of Chile on November 3.

I was extremely troubled by this. I believed, as had my two predecessors, that a Communist regime in Cuba exporting violence, terrorism, and revolution throughout Latin America was dangerous enough. An Italian businessman who called on me before the Chilean election had cautioned, "If Allende should win, and with Castro in Cuba, you will have in Latin America a red sandwich. And, eventually, it will all be red." Such fears were realized when, soon after Allende came to power, Cuban intelligence agents began operating from a base in Chile, exporting revolution to Bolivia, Argentina, Brazil, and Uruguay.

After three years of inefficient administration, during which the Chilean economy suffered from a series of crippling strikes, Allende was overthrown by the Chilean military in September 1973, and according to conflicting reports, was either killed or committed suicide during the coup.

America was being tested in the fall of 1970—by war in Vietnam; by the threat of war in the Middle East; by the introduction of threatening nuclear capabilities in Cuba. In Chile the test was just as real, although much subtler.

Communist leaders believe in Lenin's precept: Probe with bayonets. If you encounter mush, proceed; if you encounter steel, withdraw. I had feared that in our handling of the EC-121 incident in 1969 the Communists may have thought they had encountered mush. While our effort to prevent Allende from coming to power failed, at least in 1970 in Jordan and in Cuba, their probing had encountered our unmistakable steel.

1970 ELECTIONS

Shortly before the 1970 congressional campaign began, Pat Buchanan sent me an eleven-page memorandum analyzing *The Real Majority,* a new book which claimed that the elections in 1970 and 1972 would be decided by what the authors, Richard Scammon, Kennedy's Director of the Census Bureau, and Ben Wattenberg, a former Johnson speechwriter, called the "Social Issue."

In what became a highly publicized formulation, Scammon and Wattenberg described the average American voter in the next election as a forty-seven-year-old housewife from the outskirts of Dayton, Ohio, whose husband was a machinist. "To know that the lady in Dayton is afraid to walk the streets alone at night," they wrote, "to know that she has a mixed view about blacks and civil rights because before moving to the suburbs she lived in a neighborhood that became all black, to know that her brother-in-law is a policeman, to know that she does not have the money to move if her new neighborhood deteriorates, to know that she is deeply distressed that her son is going to a community junior college where LSD was found on the campus—to know all this is the beginning of contemporary political wisdom."

The purpose of *The Real Majority* was to persuade Democrats to stop playing so heavily to the fashionable but unrepresentative constituencies of the young, the poor, the racial minorities, and the students. Once the Democrats got on the right side of the Social Issue, the book argued, they could win the election by taking the offensive on the economy, which was the Republicans' weak point.

If this analysis was right, and I agreed with Buchanan that it was, then the Republican counterstrategy was clear: we should preempt the Social Issue in order to get the Democrats on the defensive. We should aim our strategy primarily at disaffected Democrats, at blue-collar workers, and at working-class white ethnics. We should set out to capture the vote of the forty-seven-year-old Dayton housewife.

I had decided not to do any active campaigning in 1970. I felt confident that I would not be needed because in Ted Agnew we had the perfect spokesman to reach the silent majority on the Social Issue. Our strategy worked brilliantly at first. The Social Issue had liberals on the run everywhere, with Agnew in hot rhetorical pursuit. He stirred up predictable emotions—Hubert Humphrey called him the "brass knuckles of the administration"—but in fact his salvos were remarkably restrained for campaign rhetoric and hit right on target.

When the campaign began to heat up around the middle of September, I was deeply involved in preparations for my second European trip, which lasted from September 27 to October 5. When I left, it seemed as if we actually had a chance to pull off an upset victory and pick up some seats. When I returned, I discovered that we were in serious trouble in almost every major race.

The problem was that we had peaked too early on the Social Issue. Democrats know how to read too, and they had obviously taken the lessons of *The Real Majority* to heart. Adlai Stevenson III, running for the Senate in Illinois, responded to attacks on his ultraliberal record with a highly emotional invocation of his war record. *Newsweek* dryly called it "the most improbable speech" in his political career and noted that the Illinois Senate race "was offering final proof that this is the year when even the proudest liberals feel they had better pay major attention to the flag and to all the traditional values, yearnings, and fears of Richard Nixon's silent majority." Running for the Senate in California, Ted Kennedy's liberal protégé John Tunney used TV commercials that showed him riding around in a police car.

As the campaign progressed and the Democrats successfully blunted the Social Issue, they unleashed a full-scale attack on us about the economy, which was undeniably having problems. They hammered at the fact that unemployment had climbed to 5.5 percent and insisted it was going to go higher still.

We commissioned a quick private poll that indicated that as things stood we were going to lose thirty House seats and possibly all but one of the key Senate seats. I decided to reverse my earlier decision and announced that I would campaign personally for our candidates in a number of key races. During the three weeks before the election I devoted seven full days to campaigning for candidates in twenty-two states.

Almost everywhere I went during the campaign there were bands of demonstrators. As I was entering a hall in New Jersey, a young man reached out and as he shook my hand shouted a few obscenities at me. I motioned the Secret Service back, and I stood looking at him while he screamed, "You're guilty of murder every day you fight this war." I said to him, very quietly, so that he had to lean a little bit forward to hear me, "Have you been to Vietnam?" He seemed surprised, and hesitated before he said, "No." I looked at him again for a moment before I said, "Our men are fighting there so you won't have to fight there or anyplace else in your lifetime." By this time he had released his grip on my arm, and I walked directly into the hall.

I would not have wanted Pat or the girls to see some of the things the demonstrators did or hear some of the things they shouted, and I was concerned about the vast majority of individuals and families who had come out in high spirits for a presidential rally and suddenly found themselves in the midst of an ugly confrontation.

While I was talking to a crowd of about 5,000 supporters at California's San Jose Municipal Auditorium, a crowd of about 2,000 demonstrators beat on the doors all around the building. As I walked the few steps to my car after the speech, I could see protesters gathered on the other side of the police barricades just a hundred feet away. They were chanting their favorite slogans, including "One, two, three, four—we don't want your fucking war," and I could not resist showing them how little respect I had for their juvenile and mindless ranting.

I stood on the hood of the car and gave them the V-sign that had become my political trademark. It had a predictable effect, and a chorus of jeers and boos began. Then I saw something coming toward me. When it hit the roof of the car, I realized that it was a rock. Suddenly rocks and eggs and vegetables were flying everywhere. Within seconds I was inside the car and Secret Service agents were following emergency evacuation procedures. Unfortunately one of the cars in the motorcade behind us stalled, and its windows and windows in the press bus were broken by rocks. Several people, including Secret Service agents, were hit by rocks and flying glass.

The local police chief may have exaggerated when he said it was an act of God that I got out safely. But the dents in the presidential limousine and the broken glass from the bus were real enough, and the possibility of a more serious incident having developed was very disturbing. The organizer of the demonstration proudly claimed credit for the mêlée, saying that the Peace and Freedom Party and other antiwar groups had staged the demonstration to call attention to their claim that I was a "war criminal" who was not welcome in California. He said, "After dropping that many bombs on the Vietnamese people how can anyone associated with the government claim to be upset about people throwing some eggs and rocks at Nixon? What's so precious about Nixon that he can't take a few eggs when he can dish out so many bombs?"

We flew to San Clemente from San Jose, and that night I sat in my study for over an hour, thinking about what had happened and about how I should respond. As far as I knew this was the first time in our history that a mob had physically attacked the President of the United States. I did not care what these demonstrators or their leaders thought about me personally, but if they did not respect the office of the presidency, I thought that people should be made to recognize that fact and take sides on it.

Two days later, at a rally at Sky Harbor Airport in Phoenix, I discussed the San Jose incident.

I wanted to cut through the fashionable notion that all our troubles were the result of the supposedly immoral war in Vietnam. It was time to brand this alibi for violence as the pure nonsense it was. "Those who carry a 'peace' sign in one hand and throw a bomb or a brick with the other are the super hypocrites of our time," I said. "Violence in America today is not caused by the war; it is not caused by repression. There is no romantic ideal involved. Let's recognize these people for what they are. They are not romantic revolutionaries. They are the same thugs and hoodlums that have always plagued the good people."

The speech was interrupted many times by loud cheers from the noontime audience. One of the loudest came when I said, "And now could I add a personal note? The terrorists, the far left, would like nothing better than to make the President of the United States a prisoner in the White House. Well, let me just set them straight. As long as I am President, no band of violent thugs is going to keep me from going out and speaking with the American people wherever they want to hear me and wherever I want to go. This is a free country, and I fully intend to share that freedom with my fellow Americans. This President is not going to be cooped up in the White House."

I told Haldeman that I wanted to have the film of this speech rebroadcast as my election night address to the nation.

What happened next was one of those mistakes that it is hard to believe could actually have been made. The film we had of the Phoenix speech turned out to be a poor quality black-and-white videotape. The picture was grainy, and the sound, bouncing from the walls of the huge airport hangar, was shrill and occasionally slightly garbled. Everyone who worked on it remarked that it was terrible; some of the TV technicians wondered whether it was even of minimum broadcast quality. But election eve was two days away, there was no time for lengthy debates, and no one wanted to assume the responsibility for saying that we should not use it. The editing was completed just in time for the tape to be rushed to the studios for broadcast.

The result was a disaster. The quality was so bad that many TV stations received calls from outraged Republicans who were convinced that the program must have been sabotaged by the Democrats. Even worse, it was followed immediately by Senator Muskie's election eve broadcast on behalf of the Democratic candidates. In contrast to the harsh tone of my Phoenix speech, Muskie sounded calm and measured as he spoke from the homey setting of his summer house in Cape Elizabeth, Maine. What should have been a comparison based on substance thus became a comparison based on tone, and there was no doubt that Muskie emerged the winner. As John Mitchell put it, the Phoenix speech made me sound as if I were running for District Attorney of Phoenix, rather than the President of the United States addressing the American people at the end of an important national campaign.

In a postelection memo I dictated to Haldeman dissecting our performance in the 1970 election, I talked about the ill-fated Phoenix broadcast:

> There is a good lesson out of this. . . . It is that in this age of television, technical quality is probably more important than the content of what is said. We learned this from the first debate with Kennedy, and now we have had to relearn it in fortunately a less decisive forum in our handling of this particular matter. The important thing is for us not to brush it off as something that "wasn't all that bad" but to recognize that it was a mistake and to be sure that kind of mistake is not made again.

Election Day was November 3. We lost nine House seats and gained two in the Senate. In fact this was an excellent showing because in past election years in which unemployment was on the rise the average loss of seats by the party controlling the White House was forty-six. In that respect we had defied overwhelming historical trends. It was also particularly gratifying to me that some extreme liberals were among those senators retired by the voters. The greatest disappointment was the drubbing we took in the gubernatorial contests, where we lost eleven state houses and ended up with only twenty-one Republican governors in the fifty states.

The most important result of the 1970 election was that the shaky coalition of support we had to rely on in the Senate was now replaced by a slim but more dependable majority on foreign policy and national defense issues.

Despite this fact and despite the fact that our losses in the House were substantially smaller than the off-year defeats of previous administrations, the postelection media analysis, led by the TV networks and the news magazines, treated the election as a significant political failure for me and a serious setback to my chances for being re-elected. *Newsweek*'s cover featured Senator Muskie and the story inside reported that the Democrats now dared to dream that I might be "retired" in 1972.

Although our first efforts to consolidate a constituency based on the Social Issue had met with only mixed success, I still felt that the basic strategy was right.

In the lengthy post-mortem I dictated for Haldeman, I turned my sights toward 1972. I said that we should start now to weed out lackluster Republican House, Senate, and gubernatorial candidates, help them get other jobs, and replace them with candidates who could win.

At least two major candidates had been defeated in 1970 because of their involvement in political scandals, and I urged that we take precautions against this particular hazard. The personal ethics and conduct of our candidates had to be above suspicion or reproach. I wrote: "We cannot afford to have anybody on our ticket in 1972 who will pose this problem to us. We must be absolutely ruthless in bringing such matters to the attention of candidates and getting them cleaned up, or getting the candidate off the ticket if he has such a problem and cannot clean it up."

I said that I thought it was imperative that we get politics out of the White House either by introducing dynamic campaign management into the Republican National Committee or by setting up a special presidential re-election committee. I wrote, "I want to be in the position where I can honestly say the White House does not have its hand in the political maneuvering that is going to begin the moment the new Congress comes in session."

Agnew, I said, should "de-escalate the rhetoric without de-escalating the substance of his message." He should be shown fighting for something, rather than just railing against everything.

I wrote that I hoped we could get some enthusiasm into the RNC, and I urged that people be "upbeat and act as if they were having some fun in carrying out assignments." This extended to my own schedule, where

I wanted more spontaneity and less gimmickry. Somehow we weren't getting across to people all the activities at the White House—the social evenings, the worship services, the special parties. I added, "This must be done, incidentally, without trying to make the President a laughing boy, and without having Martha Mitchell appear to be the only one who seems to enjoy being in Washington!"

Finally I wrote that I was going to take the advice of nearly all those around me and firmly and flatly keep out of my re-election campaign until as late as possible in 1972.

In fact my determination to keep politics out of the White House was short-lived. I should have known that the attempt would be futile. As each day brought the election closer, and as the competition heightened, the need for action and information became irresistible. Democratic Presidents since FDR had excelled—and reveled—in flexing the formidable political muscle that goes with being the party in the White House. I planned to take no less advantage of it myself. So I ended up keeping the pressure on the people around me to get organized, to get tough, and to get information about what the other side was doing. Sometimes I ordered a tail on a front-running Democrat; sometimes I urged that department and agency files be checked for any indications of suspicious or illegal activities involving prominent Democrats. I told my staff that we should come up with the kind of imaginative dirty tricks that our Democratic opponents used against us and others so effectively in previous campaigns.

John Mitchell was going to be my campaign manager, but he would have his hands full organizing and running the Committee to Re-elect the President. Increasingly I turned to Chuck Colson to act as my political point-man. Colson had joined the administration in late 1969 in the role of White House liaison with special interest groups. He worked on policy matters with energy and devotion. He spent hours with labor groups, veterans' organizations, ethnic minorities, and religious groups. He was positive, persuasive, smart, and aggressively partisan. His instinct for the political jugular and his ability to get things done made him a lightning rod for my own frustrations at the timidity of most Republicans in responding to attacks from the Democrats and the media. When I complained to Colson I felt confident that something would be done, and I was rarely disappointed.

I was confident that I could win re-election in a contest on the issues in 1972. That only reinforced my determination not to let the other side be politically tougher than we were.

1971

The first months of 1971 were the lowest point of my first term as President. The problems we confronted were so overwhelming and so apparently impervious to anything we could do to change them that it seemed possible that I might not even be nominated for re-election in 1972. Early in January it was announced that unemployment had reached 6 percent—the highest point since 1961. In February we became involved in the Laotian operation, which turned out to be a military success but a public relations disaster. In May 200,000 antiwar demonstrators converged on Washington and, led by hard-core agitators who had been openly encouraged by the North Vietnamese, mounted a violent but unsuccessful attempt to close down the government for a day. In June the publication of the Pentagon Papers assaulted the principle of government control over classified documents. The economy was in bad shape and did not look like it was going to get better very soon. On the foreign exchange markets the dollar hit its lowest point since 1949. As the opinion polls registered my losses, they marked Muskie's gains. The Soviets had set back détente by their adventurism in Cuba and the Middle East, and the likelihood of a breakthrough in SALT or the other outstanding issues between us seemed remote. Similarly our tentative approaches to Communist China appeared to have fallen on deaf ears. Without these levers to bring pressure to bear on Hanoi it looked as if the war could drag on indefinitely, although the increasing strength and confidence of the antiwar forces in Congress might mean a sudden termination vote or cutoff of funds at almost any time.

Having hit the lowest of low points in 1971, we suddenly rebounded with a series of stunning successes, among them the announcement of the China trip, a breakthrough in the SALT negotiations, an extremely popular and apparently effective economic program including a freeze of wages and prices, and the scheduling of a Soviet summit. These and other things gave us a momentum that carried right into the presidential election year of 1972.

The year 1971 proved the political maxim that one should never despair until the votes have been cast and counted. Something can always turn up, often from an unexpected source or quarter, that utterly transforms one's situation and one's prospects.

LAM SON

Before our successful Cambodian operation in 1970, it was estimated that 85 percent of the heavy arms used by the Communists in South Vietnam had come by sea through the port of Sihanoukville. Once we closed that route, everything had to come overland through Laos down the Ho Chi Minh trail. By mid-December 1970, Laos was clogged with men and supplies, the bulk of which would be moved into Cambodia for a 1971 spring offensive.

On January 18, 1971, in a meeting with Laird, Rogers, Helms, Kissinger, Colonel Alexander Haig, Kissinger's deputy, and Admiral Thomas H. Moorer, Chairman of the Joint Chiefs of Staff, I authorized a major military operation to cut the Ho Chi Minh trail by attacking enemy forces in Laos. Because of the problem of American domestic opinion and because the South Vietnamese wanted to prove how successful Vietnamization had been, we decided that the operation would be an ARVN exercise; the United States would supply only air cover and artillery support. The principal American contribution would be ferrying troops and supplies by helicopter, gunship support, and B-52 raids. Even the operation's codename was Vietnamese: Lam Son 719.

On February 8, a 5,000-man ARVN force crossed the border into Laos. The Communists put up stronger resistance than had been anticipated, and the American military command in Saigon failed to respond to this unexpectedly intense level of combat with the necessary increase in air cover for the invading forces. The resulting ARVN casualties were heavy, but they continued to fight courageously.

The South Vietnamese forces quickly recovered from these initial setbacks, and most of the military purposes of Lam Son were achieved within the first few weeks as the Communists were deprived of the capacity to launch an offensive against our forces in South Vietnam in 1971.

In view of the operation's substantial success and because of signs that the Communists were trying to prepare a major counteroffensive, the ARVN commanders decided to withdraw early. On March 18 they began what was to have been a strategic retreat. Our air support was inadequate, however, and under severe enemy pounding some of the ARVN soldiers panicked. It took only a few televised films of ARVN soldiers clinging to the skids of our evacuation helicopters to reinforce the widespread misconception of the ARVN forces as incompetent and cowardly.

The net result was a military success but a psychological defeat, both in South Vietnam, where morale was shaken by media reports of the retreat, and in America, where suspicions about the possibility of escalation had been aroused and where news pictures undercut confidence in the success of Vietnamization and the prospect of ending the war.

Sir Robert Thompson wrote to Kissinger from Vietnam shortly after Lam Son ended. He praised its military success and stated that the major factor in the war was now the question of South Vietnamese psychology and confidence. Thanks to Lam Son there was no Communist offensive in 1971 despite the largest influx of matériel in the history of the war. American and South Vietnamese casualties were reduced, and Vietnamization continued at a steady pace.

I still agree with Kissinger's assessment of Lam Son at the end of March 1971 when he said, "If I had known before it started that it was going to come out exactly the way it did, I would still have gone ahead with it."

On March 29, 1971, just days after the withdrawal of ARVN troops from Laos, First Lieutenant William Calley, Jr., was found guilty by an Army court-martial of the premeditated murder of twenty-two South Vietnamese civilians. The public furore over Lam Son had just begun to settle down, and now we were faced with still another Vietnam-related controversy. This one had been simmering since the fall of 1969, when the murders were first revealed.

It was in March 1968, ten months before I became President, that Calley led his platoon into My Lai, a small hamlet about 100 miles northeast of Saigon. The village had been a Vietcong stronghold, and our forces had suffered many casualties trying to clear it out. Calley had his men round up the villagers and then ordered that they be shot; many were left sprawled lifeless in a drainage ditch.

Calley's crime was inexcusable. But I felt that many of the commentators and congressmen who professed outrage about My Lai were not really as interested in the moral questions raised by the Calley case as they were interested in using it to make political attacks against the Vietnam war. For one thing, they had been noticeably uncritical of North Vietnamese atrocities. In fact, the calculated and continual role that terror, murder, and massacre played in the Vietcong strategy was one of the most underreported aspects of the entire Vietnam war. Much to the discredit of the media and the antiwar activists, this side of the story was only rarely included in descriptions of Vietcong policy and practices.

On March 31 the court-martial sentenced Calley to life in prison at hard labor. Public reaction to this announcement was emotional and sharply divided. More than 5,000 telegrams arrived at the White House, running 100 to 1 in favor of clemency.

John Connally and Jerry Ford recommended in strong terms that I use my powers as Commander in Chief to reduce Calley's prison time. Connally said that justice had been served by the sentence, and that now the reality of maintaining public support for the armed services and for the war had to be given primary consideration. I talked to Carl Albert and other congressional leaders. All of them agreed that emotions in Congress were running high in favor of presidential intervention.

I called Admiral Moorer on April 1 and ordered that, pending Calley's appeal, he should be released from the stockade and confined instead to his quarters on the base. When this was announced to the House of Representatives, there was a spontaneous round of applause on the floor. Reaction was particularly strong and positive in the South. George Wallace, after a visit with Calley, said that I had done the right thing. Governor Jimmy Carter of Georgia said that I had made a wise decision. Two days later I had Ehrlichman announce that I would personally review the Calley case before any final sentence was carried out.

By April 1974, Calley's sentence had been reduced to ten years, with eligibility for parole as early as the end of that year. I reviewed the case as I had said I would but decided not to intervene. Three months after I resigned, the Secretary of the Army decided to parole Calley.

I think most Americans understood that the My Lai massacre was not representative of our people, of the war we were fighting, or of our men who were fighting it; but from the time it first became public the whole tragic episode was used by the media and the antiwar forces to chip away at our efforts to build public support for our Vietnam objectives and policies.

THE WHITE HOUSE TAPES

From the very beginning I had decided that my administration would be the best chronicled in history. I wanted a record of every major meeting I held, ranging from verbatim transcripts of important national security sessions to "color reports" of ceremonial events. Unfortunately the system proved cumbersome, because it was not always convenient or appropriate to have someone in the room taking notes. In many cases it inhibited conversation. We also found that the quality of prose varied as much as the quality of perception, and too many of the reports ended up more hagiography than history. Finally, during the period that Lam Son was being planned and discussed, I decided to reinstall a tape recording system.

The existence of the tapes was never meant to be made public—at least not during my presidency. I thought that afterward I could consult the tapes in preparing whatever books or memoirs I might write. Such an objective record might also be useful to the extent that any President feels vulnerable to revisionist histories—whether from within or without his administration—and particularly so when the issues are as controversial and the personalities as volatile as they were in my first term.

The first President known to make tapes of his conversations was Franklin Roosevelt, who reportedly had a microphone placed in a lamp in the Oval Office. There is evidence that Eisenhower taped some of his conversations. President Kennedy taped some of his office conversations and phone calls, and more than 180 such recordings are now in the Kennedy Library kept under restrictions imposed by the Kennedy family.

Lyndon Johnson had a taping system for his office phone, his bedroom phone, the phone at Camp David, the phone at his ranch in Johnson City, and the phone at his office in Austin. In addition to the phone equipment, he had room microphones placed in the Cabinet Room and in the private office next to the Oval Office. At one point there was also a recording device that could pick up conversations in the room outside the Oval Office where Johnson's visitors would wait before being ushered in to see him. The Johnson system was operated manually, which permitted him to decide which conversations to record. In the Cabinet Room buttons were attached to the underside of the table in front of his chair, and I have been told that in the private office the system was activated by buttons concealed behind the television console in the Oval Office.

Johnson frequently had the tapes transcribed as soon as the conversation had ended. According to the White House grapevine, Johnson taped the conversation when he met privately with Bobby Kennedy to inform him that he would not be the 1964 vice presidential nominee. Immediately after their meeting Johnson asked to have the tape transcribed. When the typist played the tape, however, she found that the entire conversation was inaudible. A tape technician concluded that Kennedy must have carried a small scrambling device with him as a precaution.

Johnson thought that my decision to remove his taping system was a mistake; he felt his tapes were invaluable in writing his memoirs.

Although I was not comfortable with the idea of taping people without their knowledge, I was at least confident that the secrecy of the system would protect their privacy. I thought that recording only selected conversations would completely undercut the purpose of having the taping system; if our tapes were going to be an objective record of my presidency, they could not have such an obviously self-serving bias. I did not want to have to calculate whom or what or when I would tape. Therefore, a system was installed that was voice-activated; talking would trigger the tape machines. Beginning in February recording devices were placed in the Oval Office, the Cabinet Room, and the EOB office. I rejected the suggestion that recording equipment be placed on phones in the Family Quarters and in Key Biscayne and San Clemente; I wanted to record only the official business of the presidency. Recorders were installed on phones in the Oval and EOB offices, the Lincoln Sitting Room, and on the office phone at Camp David.

Initially, I was conscious of the taping, but before long I accepted it as part of the surroundings.

I never listened to a tape until June 4, 1973, when I had to do so because of the Watergate investigation. None of the tapes was transcribed until September 1973, when I was faced with the subpoenas of the Ervin Committee and the Special Prosecutor.

THE KENNEDY PORTRAITS

In February 1971, Pat invited Jacqueline Kennedy Onassis and her children to have dinner with our family and see the official portraits of President Kennedy and herself before the public unveiling ceremony. It was a particularly moving occasion for us because none of them had been inside the White House since the agonizing days immediately after President Kennedy's assassination.

Pat gave explicit orders that the visit be kept secret until it was over so that no reporters or cameramen would intrude on their privacy. We welcomed them in the Diplomatic Reception Room and then took them to see the portraits, which had been painted by a New York artist Jackie had personally chosen.

John Kennedy, Jr., who was ten, and his sister, Caroline, who was thirteen, were very enthusiastic about each of the portraits. Jackie, however, did not make any comments about them. I thought that this might be because she was embroiled in a controversy with the artist who had sold a reproduction of the painting and sketches of her to a national magazine. Pat later told me that when she invited Rose Kennedy to see the portraits, Mrs. Kennedy had stood silently in front of her son's bowed figure for a long time. Finally she said, "I never saw Jack look like that."

Later I made some notes about our dinner:

We had drinks in the West Hall before going in to dinner. The butler, Allen, had been in the White House while the Kennedys were here, and he greeted Jackie warmly. I noticed that he put ice in her white wine at dinner, and she explained that it had been her custom to have this when she was here.

The children were served milk at Jackie's request, and John, Jr., said, "Milk is so bad in foreign countries. It's icky!"

Jackie was very bright and talkative. As we went into the second-floor Dining Room, which she had had converted from Margaret Truman's bedroom, we talked about how Alice Longworth had her appendix out in it. She said that Jack and she practically suffocated when the room was being renovated because of the paint smell. In fact, they had moved to the other end of the floor until the painting was completed.

I recalled that one of the problems of campaigning was that in many hotels, and particularly in the smaller cities, the rooms were often freshly painted before we arrived. It is difficult enough to sleep on the road, but the smell of paint makes it impossible.

She recalled that once when Jack was in the Senate, she had "peeked into your office just across the hall." She also recalled the picture that was taken in Chicago when the three of us arrived on the same plane early in 1960. I reminded her that she had been reading Allen Drury's *Advise and Consent* on the plane. "I never finished it," was her response.

We talked in very general terms about all the changes that had taken place in the years since she had been in the White House. Of course I was determined to keep the conversation away from anything that would distress her or make the visit sad. At one point she looked at me and said, "I always live in a dream world."

TRICIA'S WEDDING

Tricia first met Ed Cox at a high school dance in 1963. A year later, when she was a freshman at Finch College and he was a freshman at Princeton, he was her escort at the International Debutante Ball, an annual charity event held in New York. They began to date but found themselves at times falling into disagreements about politics. Ed was a Republican, but in the Eastern liberal tradition; during the summer of 1968 he worked for Ralph Nader.

One day late in 1969 Tricia told me that they were becoming serious about each other, but she was concerned about their continuing political differences. Since both of them were extremely strong-willed and articulate, these discussions were often heated. I said that the important thing was the way they felt about each other; if they were truly in love, I said, that was all that mattered and political problems would work themselves out. As time went on, their political differences virtually evaporated as their affection for each other grew steadily stronger.

One November weekend in 1970, Ed Cox came into my study at Camp David and said rather formally, "Mr. President, as I'm sure you know, I am very much in love with Tricia. I would like your permission to ask her to marry me."

I had known Ed for several years, and I told him that what was important was what Tricia wanted and that I was sure she would say yes.

We announced their engagement on Pat's birthday, March 16, after a dinner in honor of Prime Minister John Lynch of Ireland. We asked Tricia if she would like to have a White House wedding. It was entirely up to her and Ed, but we felt it would be something they would remember all their lives. Pat suggested that, since they had chosen June 12, we could have it outdoors in the Rose Garden.

The night before the wedding I wrote a short note to Tricia and slipped it under her door after she had gone to bed.

The day of the wedding dawned cloudy. Intermittent light drizzle was predicted until around four—just when the ceremony was scheduled to begin. I called Tricia and asked her how she felt about taking the risk and counting on the weather clearing as forecast.

"I would prefer to have it in the Rose Garden as we planned," she said.

"Then that's the way we'll do it," I replied.

When I left for the Residence around three, the rain had tapered off slightly, but the sky was still a threatening, sullen gray.

Tricia has described the scene in the Family Quarters when she emerged from her room, dressed in her wedding gown and veil, to join Pat and Julie, who were waiting for her in the West Hall.

> Mama and Julie looked so beautiful that suddenly I felt the event would be beautiful too. They exclaimed over the wedding gown and the fact that the diamond pendant necklace Edward had given me was the perfect length for the V-neck gown. Daddy appeared from the elevator, and said that everyone looked lovely. He went into his room and reappeared shortly in morning coat and striped pants which suited him well because he has the height to do it justice.

By 4:15 the young military officers who serve as White House social aides had gathered the 400 guests into the long ground-floor corridor and were waiting to learn whether to usher them outside into the Rose Garden or upstairs into the East Room. I called for the latest Air Force

June 12, 1971
12:10 AM

THE WHITE HOUSE

WASHINGTON

Dear Tricia –

Well Today is the day you begin a long and exciting journey –

I want you to know how proud I have been of you through the years – some of them – pretty difficult for you I'm sure.

The years ahead will be happy ones because you will make them so.

Your strength of
character will see you
through whatever comes—
You have made
the right choice and
I am sure Eddie + you
will look back on
this time and be able
to say—
"The day indeed was
splendid"—
Love
Daddy

weather report. Now a clearing front that would last for about fifteen minutes was expected to move into the area at about 4:30. I told Haldeman to pass the word along: we would begin at 4:30.

The rain stopped, the plastic covers were removed from the chairs, and the guests were ushered to their places. At 4:30 Julie and the bridesmaids began the procession down the long curving white staircase into the garden. Tricia described the scene:

> Along the green carpeted path Daddy and I smiled at each other as if to say, "No rain yet!" The Army Strings sounded glorious as we approached the garden entrance. Lucy Winchester smiled from ear to ear like the Cheshire Cat as we walked through the entrance. Julie was ahead of us in her ephemeral-looking palest of mint gown, walking in a stately manner into the most breathtaking sight I had ever seen in the United States.
>
> The Rose Garden was a crown of natural beauty, with the gazebo the most spectacular jewel of the crown. Flowers which were exquisite in their own right were intertwined with one another, and out of this composition emerged a creation of beauty that surpassed the beauty of the individual flowers. For once, mankind had improved on nature.
>
> When Julie had almost reached the steps leading to the platform where the minister stood waiting, Lucy whispered, "Go," to us. I released my train which Lucy quickly bent to arrange. Then I turned to Daddy and said, "All right."
>
> We proceeded slowly down the aisle. I recall smiling generally but seeing no specific face. The crowd was one blur until we reached the first row and I saw Mama and gave her a special smile. Eddie and I exchanged little happy smiles as Daddy and I ascended the steps.

The marriage ceremony, which Tricia and Ed had written themselves, was beautiful. When it was over and the groom had kissed the bride, instead of walking immediately up the aisle they went over first to Pat and me and then to the Coxes, to embrace us and to thank us for this day.

There was dancing at the reception in the East Room afterward. Ed and Tricia had chosen "Lara's Theme" from *Dr. Zhivago* for the first waltz. When the band began playing "Thank Heaven for Little Girls," I broke in to dance with Tricia while Ed danced with Pat. This was the first time I danced in the White House. After dancing with Tricia, I cut in and danced with Pat. She is an excellent dancer, and the guests broke into delighted applause as she steered me around the floor. Then I danced with Julie. I knew that she missed David, who was now in the Navy and had been assigned to sea duty in the Mediterranean. I whispered in her ear that I would never forget how beautiful she was on her wedding day two and a half years before.

I saw Lynda Bird Johnson, standing alone, and I asked her to dance and told her how impressed I had been by her beauty and grace when I saw her on television when she and Chuck Robb had been married in the White House in 1967.

After the newlyweds had left for a honeymoon at Camp David, Pat, Julie, Bebe Rebozo, and I sat in the Residence watching the TV specials.

It had been a wonderful day. Even the weather had turned out to be a friend. It was a day that all of us will always remember, because all of us were beautifully, and simply, happy.

THE PENTAGON PAPERS

On Sunday morning, June 13, I picked up the New York *Times*. In the top left-hand corner there was a picture of me standing with Tricia in the Rose Garden. *Tricia Nixon Takes Vows* was the headline. Next to the picture was another headline: *Vietnam Archive: Pentagon Study Traces 3 Decades of Growing U.S. Involvement.*

The story described a 7,000-page study of American involvement in Southeast Asia from World War II through 1968, which had been commissioned by Robert McNamara, Johnson's Secretary of Defense. It contained verbatim documents from the Defense Department, the State Department, the CIA, the White House, and the Joint Chiefs of Staff. The *Times* announced that it planned to publish not only portions of the study but many of the original documents as well. The newspaper did not say that all these materials were still officially classified "Secret" and "Top Secret." In fact, this was the most massive leak of classified documents in American history.

The McNamara study had been officially titled "The History of U.S. Decision-Making Process on Vietnam." Before long, however, the media had created a more dramatic label: "The Pentagon Papers."

The documents had been illegally turned over to the *Times,* and I believed that the paper acted irresponsibly in publishing them. The *Times* admitted having been in possession of them for more than three months before publishing them, but had never once sought comment from anyone in the government, or inquired whether publication of any of the classified material might threaten national security or endanger the lives of our men in Vietnam.

The defense and intelligence agencies raced to obtain copies of the study in order to assess the impact of its disclosure. The National Security Agency was immediately worried that some of the more recent documents could provide code-breaking clues. They feared that information about signal and electronic intelligence capabilities would be spotted by the trained eyes of enemy experts. The State Department was alarmed because the study would expose Southeast Asia Treaty Organization contingency war plans that were still in effect. The CIA was worried that past or current informants would be exposed; they said that the study would contain specific references to the names and activities of CIA agents still active in Southeast Asia. In fact, one secret contact dried up almost immediately. A tremor shook the international community because the study contained material relating to the role of other governments as diplomatic go-betweens; several of them made official protests. Dean Rusk issued a statement that the documents would be valuable to the North Vietnamese and the Soviets.

On consideration, we had only two choices: we could do nothing, or we could move for an injunction that would prevent the New York *Times* from continuing publication. Policy argued for moving against the *Times*; politics argued against it.

The McNamara study was primarily a critique of the way Kennedy and Johnson had led the nation into war in Vietnam. It recounted Kennedy's decision to support the coup that ousted President Diem in 1963 and resulted in Diem's death, causing General Maxwell Taylor to comment that one of our worst mistakes was our connivance in the Diem overthrow—"nothing but chaos came as a result." News reports said the document proved that Johnson had told the American people that he was not going to escalate the war, while privately planning an escalation from 17,000 to 185,000 American men. After the release of the papers James Reston wrote of the "deceptive and stealthy American involvement in the war under Presidents Kennedy and Johnson."

Nevertheless, publication of the Pentagon Papers was certain to hurt the whole Vietnam effort. Critics of the war would use them to attack my goals and my policies.

But to me, there was an even more fundamental reason for taking action to prevent publication. An important principle was at stake in this case: it is the role of the government, not the New York *Times*, to judge the impact of a top secret document. Mel Laird felt that over 95 percent of the material could be declassified, but we were all still worried about whatever percent—even if it were only 1 percent—that should not be. If we did not move against the *Times* it would be a signal to every disgruntled bureaucrat in the government that he could leak anything he pleased while the government simply stood by.

The *Times*'s decision to publish the documents was clearly the product of the paper's antiwar policy rather than a consistent attachment to principle. In the early 1960s Otto Otepka, a State Department employee, had shown classified documents relating to lax security procedures in the department to senators who were investigating the problem. Otepka believed that his action was justified because it was the only way to correct what he considered a dangerous situation. The *Times* had no sympathy for Otepka's action and expressed its editorial indignation:

> Orderly procedures are essential if the vital division of power between legislative and executive branches is not to be undermined. The use of "underground" methods to obtain classified documents from lower-level officials is a dangerous departure from such orderly procedures.

The Washington *Post* had also been outraged:

> If any underling in the State Department were free at his own discretion to disclose confidential cables or if any agent of the Federal Bureau of Investigation could leak the contents of secret files whenever he felt like it, the Executive Branch of the Government would have no security at all.

When the *Times*'s publisher, Arthur Sulzberger, was asked about the government's concern that publication of the Pentagon Papers undermined the faith of foreign governments in our ability to deal in confidence, he was reported to have said, "Oh, that's a lot of baloney. I mean, really."

On Tuesday, June 15, the Justice Department moved to enjoin the *Times* from publication until the government could review the documents and verify that they caused no national security problems. In the meantime, the Washington *Post*, the Boston *Globe*, and the St. Louis *Post-Dispatch* had obtained copies and started publication on their own.

In court the *Times*'s counsel argued at one point that even if publication of the Pentagon Papers contributed to the delay of the return of our POWs, protection of the First Amendment made that a risk we should be willing to take. I was outraged. I did not consider that rights conveyed by the First Amendment for the publication of these documents superior to the right of an American soldier to stay alive in wartime.

At the outset I had hoped that former Presidents Truman and Johnson would join me in taking a strong public stand against such leaks of classified material. As far as I know, however, Truman made no comment. And after talking to Johnson, Bryce Harlow reported that Johnson felt that whatever he said now would be turned against him by the Washington *Post* and the New York *Times*. Those papers, he said, were merely trying to "re-execute" him. Harlow said Johnson had talked in bitter outbursts, accusing the "professors" who wrote the study of misconstruing contingency plans as actual presidential decisions. The authors of the study had all been involved in the actions they were "bitching" about now, Johnson had said, adding that he had never made a decision of any consequence on escalation or the use of troops without the full concurrence of McNamara and others in his administration.

On June 30, the Supreme Court ruled on our effort to prevent publication: the government lost, 6 to 3. One of the majority opinions agreed that the disclosures might have a serious impact on the national interest but said this was still no basis for sanctioning entire restraint on the press. Chief Justice Burger, in his dissent, criticized the undue haste of the Court's deliberation and the *Times*'s failure to consult the government: "To me it is hardly believable that a newspaper long regarded as a great institution in American lives would fail to perform one of the basic and simple duties of every citizen with respect to the discovery or possession of stolen property or secret government documents. . . . This duty rests on taxi drivers, justices, and the New York *Times*."

The Pentagon Papers leak came at a particularly sensitive time. We were just three and a half weeks away from Kissinger's secret trip to China, and the SALT talks were under way. Sir Robert Thompson had written in April saying that the major factor now influencing the course of the war was psychological: our military policy was working on the battlefield, but division in America was causing the North Vietnamese to stall in Paris. There had been violent demonstrations in Washington in May. On May 31, at the secret Paris talks, Kissinger offered our most far-reaching proposal yet. On June 13 the Pentagon Papers were published, and on June 22 the Senate voted its first resolution establishing a pull-out timetable for Vietnam. Before long, the North Vietnamese would slam the door on our new proposal and begin building up for a new military offense.

We had lost our court battle against the newspaper that published the documents, but I was determined that we would at least win our public case against the man I believed had stolen them, Daniel Ellsberg. A former Pentagon aide, Ellsberg had come under suspicion soon after the first installments from the study appeared. Whatever others may have thought, I considered what Ellsberg had done to be despicable and contemptible—he had revealed government foreign policy secrets during wartime. He was lionized in much of the media. CBS devoted a large segment of the network news to a respectful interview with him even while he was still a fugitive from the FBI.

On June 28, a Los Angeles grand jury indicted him on one count of theft of government property and one count of unauthorized possession of documents and writings related to national defense.

"I think I've done a good job as a citizen," Ellsberg told the throng of admirers outside the courthouse.

Kissinger, Haldeman, Ehrlichman, and I had met on the afternoon of June 17 to assess the situation. Kissinger had known Ellsberg at Harvard and said he was bright but emotionally unstable.

In various interviews Ellsberg had said he was convinced that I intended to escalate the war rather than pull troops out of Vietnam. He said that increased public opposition would be necessary to force unilateral withdrawal. I felt that there was serious reason to be concerned about what he might do next. During his years at the Defense Department, he had had access to some of the most sensitive information in the entire government. And the Rand Corporation, where he had worked before he gave the Pentagon Papers to the *Times*, had 173,000 classified documents in its possession. I wondered how many of these Ellsberg might have and what else he might give to the newspapers.

Ellsberg was not our only worry. From the first there had been rumors and reports of a conspiracy. The earliest report, later discounted, centered on a friend of Ellsberg, a former Defense Department employee who was then a Fellow at the Brookings Institution. I remembered him from the early days of the administration when I had asked Haldeman to get me a copy of the Pentagon file on the events leading up to Johnson's announcement of the bombing halt at the end of the 1968 campaign. I wanted to know what had actually happened; I also wanted the information as potential leverage against those in Johnson's administration who were now trying to undercut my war policy. I was told that a copy of the bombing halt material and other secret documents had been taken from the Pentagon to Brookings by the same man. I wanted the documents back, but I was told that one copy of the bombing halt report had already "disappeared"; I was sure that if word got out that we wanted it, the copy at Brookings might disappear as well.

In the aftershock of the Pentagon Papers leak and all the uncertainty and renewed criticism of the war it produced, my interest in the bombing halt file was rekindled. When I was told that it was still at Brookings, I was furious and frustrated. In the midst of a war and with our secrets being spilled through printing presses all over the world, top-secret government reports were out of reach in the hands of a private think tank largely staffed with antiwar Democrats. It seemed absurd. I could not accept that we had lost so much control over the workings of the government we had been elected to run—I saw absolutely no reason for that report to be at Brookings, and I said I wanted it back right now—even if it meant having to get it surreptitiously. My determination only increased when I learned of a 1969 Brookings circular announcing a new study of Vietnam, due in 1971, to be based in part on "executive branch documents." The director of the study was Dr. Daniel Ellsberg.

We learned that an aide to Elliot Richardson at the State Department had given Ellsberg access to the current Vietnam documents in 1970. Even after the information in them was leaked, presumably by Ellsberg,

Richardson had refused to remove the aide. It was also well known that a number of people on Kissinger's staff had friends and contacts at Brookings, and I wondered if any of them had provided Ellsberg and his friends with documents and materials.

In early July, John Mitchell reported that the Justice Department had continuing indications that Ellsberg had acted as part of a conspiracy; we received a report that the Soviet Embassy in Washington had received a set of the Pentagon Papers before they had been published in the New York *Times*; I was told that some of the documents provided to the newspapers were not even part of the McNamara study. Once again we were facing the question: what more did Ellsberg have, and what else did he plan to do?

In the meantime Ellsberg was successfully using the press, television talk shows, and antiwar rallies to promote the concept of unlawful dissent. Kissinger said that we were in a "revolutionary" situation.

Even as our concern about Ellsberg and his possible collaborators was growing, we learned that J. Edgar Hoover was dragging his feet and treating the case on merely a medium-priority basis; he had assigned no special task forces and no extra manpower to it. He evidently felt that the media would automatically make Ellsberg look like a martyr, and the FBI like the "heavy," if it pursued the case vigorously. Mitchell had been told that Hoover was sensitive about his personal friendship with Ellsberg's father-in-law. Finally, other agencies, principally the Defense Department, were conducting simultaneous investigations, and Hoover strongly resisted sharing his territory with anyone.

I did not care about any reasons or excuses. I wanted someone to light a fire under the FBI in its investigation of Ellsberg, and to keep the departments and agencies active in pursuit of leakers. If a conspiracy existed, I wanted to know, and I wanted the full resources of the government brought to bear in order to find out. If the FBI was not going to pursue the case, then we would have to do it ourselves. Ellsberg was having great success in the media with his efforts to justify unlawful dissent, and while I cared nothing for him personally, I felt that his views had to be discredited. I urged that we find out everything we could about his background, his motives, and his co-conspirators, if they existed.

I was also determined not to sit back while the Democratic architects of our Vietnam involvement tried to make me pay for the war politically. I wanted a good political operative who could sift through the Pentagon Papers as well as State and Defense Department files and get us all the facts on the Bay of Pigs, the Diem assassination, and Johnson's 1968 bombing halt. We were heading into an election year, in which the Vietnam war was almost certainly going to be the biggest issue. I wanted ammunition against the antiwar critics, many of whom were the same men who, under Kennedy and Johnson, had led us into the Vietnam morass in the first place. Finally, I wanted a revision of the classification system that would ensure that only legitimate foreign policy secrets were classified, but that those that were classified stayed secret.

On July 17, 1971, Ehrlichman assigned Egil "Bud" Krogh, a young lawyer on the Domestic Council staff, to head the leak project. David Young, a lawyer who was formerly a Kissinger aide, Howard Hunt, a former CIA agent, and G. Gordon Liddy, a former FBI man, worked with him. A year and a half later I learned for the first time that because their job was plugging leaks, Young had jokingly put up a sign establishing himself as a "Plumber."

On July 23, the morning before we were scheduled to present our formal position at the SALT talks in Helsinki, the New York *Times* carried a front-page leak of our fallback negotiating position. I tried to motivate Krogh in the strongest terms, and I told him, "We're not going to allow it. We just aren't going to allow it." The Plumbers pushed the departments to investigate with interviews and polygraph tests. An August 13 New York *Times* report was based on a CIA report we had received at the White House only a few days earlier. The information in the story was traceable to a highly secret CIA intelligence source. By fall the CIA reported that we were in the midst of the worst outbreak of leaks since 1953. I urged everyone to keep the pressure on.

On Labor Day weekend, 1971, Krogh's group organized a break-in at the office of Ellsberg's psychiatrist in an attempt to get information from his files on his motivation, his further intentions, and any possible co-conspirators.

I do not believe I was told about the break-in at the time, but it is clear that it was at least in part an outgrowth of my sense of urgency about discrediting what Ellsberg had done and finding out what he might do next. Given the temper of those tense and bitter times and the peril I perceived, I cannot say that had I been informed of it beforehand, I would have automatically considered it unprecedented, unwarranted, or unthinkable. Ehrlichman says that he did not know of it in advance, but that he told me about it after the fact in 1972. I do not recall this, and the tapes of the June–July 1972 period indicate that I was not conscious of it then, but I cannot rule it out.

Today the break-in at Ellsberg's psychiatrist's office seems wrong and excessive. But I do not accept that it was as wrong or excessive as what Daniel Ellsberg did, and I still believe that it is a tragedy of circumstances that Bud Krogh and John Ehrlichman went to jail and Daniel Ellsberg went free.

In hindsight I can see that, once I realized the Vietnam war could not be ended quickly or easily and that I was going to be up against an anti-war movement that was able to dominate the media with its attitudes and values, I was sometimes drawn into the very frame of mind I so despised in the leaders of that movement. They increasingly came to justify almost anything in the name of forcing an immediate end to a war they considered unjustified and immoral. I was similarly driven to preserve the government's ability to conduct foreign policy and to conduct it in the way that I felt would best bring peace. I believed that national security was involved. I still believe it today, and in the same circumstances, I would act now as I did then. History will make the final judgment on the actions, reactions, and excesses of both sides; it is a judgment I do not fear.

By late September the Plumbers unit began to disband. Before long, too, the natural cycle of concern over the Pentagon Papers ran its course and our thoughts turned to other matters.

It is an interesting sidelight of the Pentagon Papers episode that our efforts to document the role of the Kennedy administration in the Diem assassination and the Bay of Pigs did not prove easy. The CIA protects itself, even from Presidents. Helms refused to give Ehrlichman the agency's internal reports dealing with either subject. At one point he told Ehrlichman on the phone that even he did not have a copy of one of the key Bay of Pigs reports. He also expressed concern about all the people, and specifically Howard Hunt, who he said would like to run around in the agency's "soiled linen."

Helms finally brought me several of the items after I had requested them from him personally. I promised him I would not use them to hurt him, his predecessor, or the CIA. "I have one President at a time," he responded. "I only work for you." When Ehrlichman read the materials Helms had delivered, however, he found that several of the reports, including the one on the Bay of Pigs, were still incomplete.

The CIA was closed like a safe, and we could find no one who would give us the combination to open it.

1971: ECONOMIC CONTROLS

I have always believed that America's economy operates best with the least possible government interference. Yet in August 1971 I proposed a series of economic controls and reforms that left even long-time wage and price control advocates breathless.

The economy that Eisenhower had bequeathed to Kennedy in January 1961 was remarkably stable, with a rate of inflation of about 1.5 percent. By 1968, largely because of the effects of the Vietnam war, inflation had soared to 4.7 percent. But the war was not the only cause of inflation. Johnson had tried to satisfy everyone; he had encouraged the American people to believe that even in time of war they could have butter as well as guns. The fact was that the expansion of the Great Society was financed by deficit spending.

The major theme of my economic policy in 1969 and 1970 was the rejection of government "jawboning" of business and labor as a way of restraining inflation. It had become clear during the Johnson administration that voluntary "guideposts" for wage and price increases were ineffective. I also strongly opposed mandatory government controls on wages and prices because I felt that controls would constitute interference in the free market and, once begun, would end up building a bureaucracy that would have dictatorial power to regulate business and labor.

By the end of 1969 there were hopeful signs that inflation was abating. But in the early spring of 1970 we ran into difficulty. Unemployment, fueled in part by the reduction in the armed services resulting from our troop withdrawals, rose to 5 percent; the inflation rate had still not declined and a sharp decline in the stock market further intensified apprehension about the economy.

Over my objections Congress sent me sweeping legislation that empowered the President to control prices, wages, and salaries. Since my strong opposition to controls was well known, I viewed the bill as a political ploy on the part of the Democratic Congress aimed at putting the ball publicly in my court. To a certain extent the ploy worked. Although I would not accept a complete move to a mandatory system of wage and price controls, I feared that if I refused to take some action I might exacerbate the general lack of confidence that was itself beginning to harm the economy and hamper its chances of recovery.

Therefore, in June 1970, I made a televised address on the economy that contained the basic steps I was proposing to try to slow the rate of inflation. I announced plans to appoint a National Commission on Productivity, with members to be chosen from business, labor, the general public, and the government. The job of the commission would be to achieve a balance between costs and productivity that would lead to more stable prices. I instructed the Council of Economic Advisers to issue periodic "inflation alerts" that would spotlight the significant areas of wage and price increases and to analyze their impact on price levels. This move was intended to test the idea that publicity about past or prospective price and wage increases would deter business and labor from inflationary behavior. I established an interagency Regulations and Purchasing Review Board to determine whether federal actions were driving up prices and costs and to bring about corrective actions if that were the case.

None of these steps had any significant effect on the economy in 1970. So I tried again. The budget I submitted in January of 1971 was set to be balanced at full employment and run a deficit to help take up the slack when unemployment was high. Along with this new "full employment" budget policy, there would have to be a rate of monetary expansion sufficient to move the economy up on the desired path.

When I briefed the Republican congressional leaders on this budget, which in effect endorsed the concept of deficit spending in periods of high unemployment, Congressman Les Arends of Illinois shook his head sadly and said, "Mr. President, I'll support you as I always do, but I'm going to have to burn up a lot of old speeches denouncing deficit spending."

I answered, "I'm in the same boat."

The economy remained sluggish in the early months of 1971. There were signs of improvement ahead, but patience had worn thin, and we ran out of time. Demands for action poured down on the White House from all sides. Media criticism of our policies became intense. Republicans as well as Democrats reflected the pressure they were receiving from their constituents and vociferously called for new policies to deal more positively with unemployment and inflation. Most of the critics and many of the economists hammered away on one theme: the need to have some program of mandatory government control of prices and wages.

On June 26, 1971, I met with my economic advisers at Camp David. We discussed the problems and our options for dealing with them at great length. After weighing all the factors, I decided to remain on the present course with one exception. For several months I had been concerned about conflicting views on the economy that filtered out of different parts of the administration and helped to create a sense of disarray and confusion in the country. My solution to the problem of too many voices was to designate a single voice: an economic spokesman who would be the authoritative source for my administration's economic policy. I selected John Connally for this role.

As Treasury Secretary, Connally was the senior Cabinet officer with economic responsibility. More important, he was an articulate speaker who could convey his determination to carry out presidential decisions vigorously.

On June 29 Connally briefed the White House press corps on the decisions we had reached at Camp David. He handed down what became known as the "four noes" when he announced that there would be no wage and price review board, no mandatory wage and price controls, no tax cut, and no increase in government spending.

In response to reporters' questioning, Connally forcefully insisted that the economy was expanding and that better days lay ahead. But even

Connally's skills could not redeem the troubled economic, psychological, and political situation that had been building up over several years.

In the briefing I held for congressional leaders after my July 15 China announcement, I found that for every one who expressed support of that dramatic foreign initiative, at least twice as many used the opportunity to express concern about our domestic economic policies and to urge new actions to deal with the problems of unemployment and inflation. After this meeting Connally and I concluded that the time had come to act.

"If we don't propose a responsible new program, Congress will have an irresponsible one on your desk within a month," he said. I knew that he was right, and I authorized him to obtain privately the views of our senior economic advisers and then to prepare a report for me that included action options for me to consider.

Connally's report was ready on August 6. By nature he always favored the "big play," so I had expected that he would recommend something bold. But even I was not prepared for the actions he proposed. He urged, in effect, total war on all economic fronts, including across-the-board wage and price controls. "I am not sure this program will work. But I *am* sure that anything less will not work," he said. He also advised me to let the issue "sit and simmer" for a while, even if it meant letting matters worsen a bit. If that happened then the actions I took would look all the better.

However, an unexpected development forced us to accelerate dramatically our economic timetable. In the second week of August the British ambassador appeared at the Treasury Department to ask that $3 billion be converted into gold. Whether we honored or denied this request, the consequences of our action would be fraught with danger: if we gave the British the gold they wanted, then other countries might rush to get theirs. If we refused, then that would be an admission of our concern that we could not meet every potential demand for conversion into gold. Connally deferred giving his answer, but we knew that we would very soon have to confront a major crisis concerning the international economic position of the United States.

Acting on Connally's recommendations, I called a high-level meeting at Camp David for August 13. Fifteen economic experts, White House staff members, and a speechwriter assembled there, some arriving by secret routes lest news of the meeting itself trigger a wave of international speculation.

These were the men who understood the intricate complexities of economics: John Connally, Arthur Burns, George Shultz, Paul McCracken, and Herbert Stein from my Council on Economic Advisers; Peter Peterson, head of the Council of International Economic Policy; and Paul

Volcker, Treasury Undersecretary for Monetary Affairs. From my personal staff there were Haldeman, Ehrlichman, and Bill Safire.

I began by laying down the ground rules that I would insist upon being followed over the next few days until I officially announced my decision: "In the past, leaks have compromised our positions on various issues. Between now and Monday, no one here is to say anything."

I then turned the meeting over to Connally, who succinctly described the actions that the experts had been working on: closing the "gold window" and allowing the dollar to float; imposing a 10 percent import tax that would be mainly a bargaining chip to discourage foreign countries from depressing their currencies in order to promote their exports; reinstating the investment tax credit to stimulate the business community; providing new income tax relief; and repealing the excise tax on automobiles to encourage higher sales.

He left for last the action that would be perceived by the American people as the most dramatic and significant: a ninety-day freeze on wages and prices. No large or permanent bureaucracies would be created; these controls would be monitored for the duration by a Pay Board, a Price Board, and a Cost of Living Council.

Herbert Stein, who subsequently became Chairman of my Council of Economic Advisers, later wrote of those Camp David sessions:

> The tense psychological condition in the country, the remoteness and beauty of the Camp David setting, the orderly and disciplined conduct of the business there, and the surprising and sweeping character of the decisions taken make the August 13–15 meeting one of the most dramatic events in the history of economic policy.

While there was relatively strong, though skeptical, support among those present for the freeze and the other domestic actions, there was substantial disagreement on closing the gold window—in other words suspending the convertibility of the dollar into gold.

The strongest opposition came from Arthur Burns, Chairman of the Federal Reserve Board. He wanted us to wait. Even if all the arguments were right, he said, he still felt that there was no rush. He warned that I would take the blame if the dollar were devalued. "*Pravda* would write that this was a sign of the collapse of capitalism," he said. On the economic side he worried that the negative results would be unpredictable: the stock market could go down; the risk to world trade would be greater if the trade basis changed; and there might be retaliation by other countries.

I always gave great weight to Burns's opinions because of my respect for his superior intellect and because he always followed the practice he once described to me of "telling the President what he *needs* to hear, not just what he *wants* to hear." This was to be one of the few cases in which I did not follow his recommendations. I decided to close the gold window and let the dollar float. As events unfolded, this decision turned out to be the best thing that came out of the whole economic program I announced on August 15, 1971.

I decided to announce these decisions on Sunday night so that the new policy would be known before the stock markets opened on Monday morning.

As I worked with Bill Safire on my speech that weekend I wondered how the headlines would read: would it be *Nixon Acts Boldly*? Or would it be *Nixon Changes Mind*? Having talked until only recently about the evils of wage and price controls, I knew I had opened myself to the charge that I had either betrayed my own principles or concealed my real intentions. Philosophically, however, I was still against wage-price controls, even though I was convinced that the objective reality of the economic situation forced me to impose them.

The public reaction to my television speech was overwhelmingly favorable. On the networks, 90 percent of the Monday newscasts were devoted to it, and most of the focus was on the brilliant briefing that John Connally had given during the day. From Wall Street the news came in numbers: 33 million shares were traded on the New York Stock Exchange on Monday, and the Dow Jones average gained 32.93 points.

Over the next months the New Economic Policy began to take hold. The inflation rate in 1971, before the freeze, was 3.8 percent. It fell to 1.9 percent during the freeze, and then, after a bulge when the freeze ended, it ran around 3.0 percent for the rest of 1972. The unemployment rate, which had been 6.1 percent when the new policy was initiated, fell to 5.1 percent at the end of 1972.

A Harris poll taken six weeks after the announcement showed that, by 53 percent to 23 percent, Americans believed my economic policies were working.

Over the next two and a half years the economy went through three additional phases of wage and price controls before all controls were finally lifted in the spring of 1974.

Phase II, which began in November 1971, was our answer to getting out of the controls before they broke down or became permanent. In this phase the controls, although still mandatory and widespread, were much less comprehensive.

The switch into Phase III in January 1973, as we expected, caused some outcry as repressed prices began moving up. In June 1973, this time over the objection of many of my advisers, I reimposed a temporary, limited freeze to settle public anxiety, which by then was compounded by Watergate, and to dampen a rise in prices taking place simply because a freeze was anticipated. If this freeze only further complicated a bad situation, at least it produced a side benefit that was wryly summarized by George Shultz: "At least we have now convinced everyone else of the rightness of our original position that wage-price controls are not the answer," he said.

When mandatory wage and price controls came to a complete end in 1974, the aftermath was far from pleasant. Energy shortages and high food costs contributed to an increase in inflation and to recession, and the pressures that built up after the period of controls led into the destructive double-digit inflation that plagued the early months of the Ford administration. Three years after controls had completely ended, both unemployment and inflation hovered around 7 percent, and there was even nostalgia for the "good old days" in 1971 when we had only 4 percent inflation and 6 percent unemployment.

What did America reap from its brief fling with economic controls? The August 15, 1971, decision to impose them was politically necessary and immensely popular in the short run. But in the long run I believe that it was wrong. The piper must always be paid, and there was an unquestionably high price for tampering with the orthodox economic mechanisms.

In concentrating on the most urgent economic problem of my administration—the inflation–unemployment problem—I have tended to highlight the area in which we felt it necessary to depart dramatically from the free market and then painfully work our way back to it. But there were also a number of economic steps during my administration that better reflected my economic philosophy and that may be more important in the longer run.

For example, in 1969 we reduced income taxes and relieved more than six million low-income people from the burden of paying any income taxes at all. By 1973 we had freed agriculture of almost all production controls for the first time in thirty-five years. We abolished numerous controls on international capital movements that had been imposed in the 1960s, and we took the lead in establishing a worldwide system of free exchange rates. We pushed legislation through Congress authorizing negotiations for reduction of barriers to international trade, and the first of these negotiations was held in Tokyo in September 1973. We also began moves to reduce or eliminate regulations in the fields of transportation and finance that were burdensome on industry and expensive to consumers.

Some people think of the free market as a matter of concern only to businessmen. But when I came into office, one of the severest and most unfair restraints on the free market was the military draft, which is a way of compelling service from everyone rather than hiring service from those who supply it voluntarily. Thus the elimination of the draft and the introduction of a volunteer Army in January 1973 were also major steps to meaningful economic freedom.

Conservatives are always at a disadvantage when speaking about economics because their belief that some pain may be necessary now to save the patient later is conventionally interpreted by liberal politicians and commentators as "heartlessness" or "callous indifference to human suffering."

It is unfortunate that the *politics* of economics has come to dictate action more than the *economics* of economics. Not surprisingly, when prudence clashes with political reality, the latter sometimes triumphs. Like all oversimplifications, this one sounds too cynical; but I can personally attest to how even someone with strong economic ideas can be affected by the sting of criticism and the clamor of those who want a different policy.

Government enterprise is the most inefficient and costly way of producing jobs. Through the private enterprise system, with all its faults, the United States in its 200 years has waged the most successful war on poverty in the history of civilized man. Private enterprise is an instrument that produces change and encourages progress; government enterprise almost invariably discourages change and inhibits progress.

It is significant to note that our major Communist competitor, the Soviet Union, has found it necessary to turn to *our* way to increase production. At a time when the Communists are by necessity providing increased incentives for more efficient producers, the United States seems to be slowly but surely turning *their* way by discouraging incentives.

America today is at a watershed as far as our economic and political system is concerned. Federal, state, and local taxes now take 40 percent of our net national product. If this percentage continues to rise, we will soon reach a point at which people will be working more for the government than for themselves. If that day ever comes, then we will no longer have the private enterprise system that has made America the freest and most prosperous nation in the world. We can only hope that statesmen of both parties will see the danger of this situation and not allow it to come to pass.

SALT BREAKTHROUGH AND BERLIN SETTLEMENT

There were dire predictions that the announcement that I would be going to China, which I made on July 15, 1971, would seriously damage U.S.–Soviet relations. Exactly the opposite occurred. On October 12 a joint announcement issued in Washington and Moscow confirmed that I would visit the Soviet Union three months after returning from China.

A U.S.–Soviet summit was at last possible because of two achievements: progress in the Strategic Arms Limitation Talks before the China overture was revealed, and progress on a Berlin settlement after the China announcement had been made.

The SALT talks, which had begun at the end of 1969, had quickly bogged down because the two sides differed on the proper scope of an agreement. Stated in its simplest form, the Soviets wanted to conclude an agreement dealing only with the limitation of defensive ABM systems. We, however, wanted to conclude a comprehensive agreement covering not only defensive systems like the ABMs but also offensive weapons like Intercontinental Ballistic Missiles (ICBMs) and Multiple Independently-targetable Re-entry Vehicles (MIRVs).

On January 9, 1971, I sent a personal message to Brezhnev stressing the necessity of linking offensive and defensive weapons if an agreement were to be reached.

Two weeks later Kissinger met with Dobrynin, who had just returned from lengthy consultations with Brezhnev in Moscow. At this meeting Dobrynin suggested late summer for a summit meeting and indicated that a SALT agreement might be worked out along the compromise lines we had suggested: an ABM-only formula coupled with a freeze on offensive weapons while further talks took place.

On March 12, however, Dobrynin delivered a reply to our proposed SALT agreement that seemed to return to earlier hard-line insistence on ABM-only terms. After having made what appeared to be considerable progress in our relations, it looked as if we were in for another period of testing by the Soviets.

Perhaps this sudden about-face was one final test they felt they had to make, or perhaps Brezhnev was just covering his own flanks on the eve of a Party Congress. Whatever the reason, on March 26 Dobrynin received a new set of instructions from Moscow, and they embodied the breakthrough we had been waiting for: the Soviets would agree to continued talks and a freeze on offensive weapons after reaching an ABM agreement.

The SALT talks in Vienna, under the leadership of our chief negotiator, Gerard Smith, and the secret exchanges of messages through Kissinger and Dobrynin immediately became more intense and serious. The major problem, as I saw it, was going to be the American negotiating position. Congressional doves were treating the Soviet ABM-only proposal as a way to chalk up a belated victory over the administration on the ABM issue and urged that I accept immediately.

I felt that it would be disastrous to go into the final SALT negotiations in this position. I believed that the only effective way to achieve nuclear arms limitation was to confront the Soviets with an unacceptable alternative in the form of increased American armaments and the determination to use them.

On April 20 I met for an hour and a half in the Cabinet Room with a group of Senate Republicans. I said, "If SALT is to have a chance, we cannot give away in the Senate things we might want to negotiate with the Soviets. They will say, 'Why should we continue to negotiate SALT when the United States is going to take these actions unilaterally?' The Soviets have strong reasons to have an agreement, but we know for a fact that they will only deal from strength and that they only respect those who have strength; otherwise they have historically moved into the power vacuums."

On May 12 Dobrynin delivered to Kissinger the latest Soviet proposals regarding SALT. They had dropped the last remaining objectionable provision. Now we had our breakthrough. I appeared before the television cameras in the White House briefing room at noon on May 20.

"As you know," I began, "the Soviet-American talks on limiting nuclear arms have been deadlocked for over a year. As a result of negotiations involving the highest level of both governments, I am announcing today a significant development in breaking the deadlock." I read the statement, which was being released at the same moment in Moscow. Its wording was purposely vague: it said only that we had agreed to concentrate on an ABM agreement and that they had agreed on "certain measures" with respect to the limitation of offensive weapons.

The Berlin talks reached a successful conclusion in late August. After sixteen months of negotiation in which we were represented by our Ambassador to West Germany, Kenneth Rush, the United States, in cooperation with the United Kingdom and France, reached an agreement with the Soviets on Berlin that dissipated some of the tension accumulated over twenty-six years of the city's divided existence. The agreement contained provisions that would prevent harassment of travelers and visitors from West Berlin to East Berlin and East Germany, make available to West Berliners passports to the Communist-controlled section, and ensure West Berlin's representation abroad by the Bonn government. Before 1971 it was common to consider Berlin and the Middle East as the greatest stumbling blocks in U.S.–U.S.S.R. relations. By removing at least one of these obstacles we were able to clear the way for a summit meeting.

The announcement of the Soviet Summit for May 1972 came as a complete surprise. The Detroit *Free Press* titled its editorial *Another Rabbit from Hat of the Ever-Amazing Nixon.* The *Wall Street Journal* said that the scheduling of two summits "reflects the most optimistic view of world politics that any President has held for a good many years."

Not all the reactions were positive. George Meany, who had been able to restrain his enthusiasm for the China announcement, now suggested that I might also want to visit Allende in Chile and Castro in Cuba. "If he's going to visit the louses of the world," Meany asked, "why doesn't he visit them all?"

The important thing was that our patient preparation of linkage had paid off handsomely. We would have a Chinese trip and a Soviet Summit as well.

INDO-PAKISTAN WAR

On the morning of November 4 I met in the Oval Office with the Prime Minister of India, Indira Gandhi. Her visit to Washington came at a critical time. Eight months earlier there had been a rebellion in East Pakistan against the government of President Yahya Khan. Indian officials reported that nearly 10 million refugees fled from East Pakistan into India. We knew that Yahya Khan eventually would have to yield to East Pakistan's demands for independence, and we urged him to take a more moderate and conciliatory line. We could not have known the extent to which India would seize this opportunity not just to destroy Pakistan's control of East Pakistan but to weaken West Pakistan as well.

Mrs. Gandhi complimented me highly on the way I was winding down the war in Vietnam and on the boldness of the China initiative. We talked about the uneasy situation in Pakistan, and I stressed how important it was that India not take any actions that would exacerbate it.

She earnestly assured me that India was not motivated in any way by anti-Pakistan attitudes. "India has never wished the destruction of Pakistan or its permanent crippling," she said. "Above all, India seeks the restoration of stability. We want to eliminate chaos at all costs."

I later learned that, even as we spoke, Mrs. Gandhi knew that her generals and advisers were planning to intervene in East Pakistan and were considering contingency plans for attacking West Pakistan as well.

Even though India was officially neutral and continued to receive foreign aid from us, Mrs. Gandhi had gradually become aligned with the Soviets and received substantial economic and military aid from Moscow. President Ayub Khan and his successor, Yahya Khan, had responded by developing Pakistan's relations with the People's Republic of China. With Moscow tied to New Delhi and Peking tied to Islamabad, the potential for the subcontinent's becoming a dangerous area of confrontation between the Communist giants was great.

In our conversation that morning I was disturbed by the fact that although Mrs. Gandhi professed her devotion to peace, she would not make any concrete offers for de-escalating the tension. Yahya Khan had agreed to move his troops away from the border if India would do the same, but she would not make a similar commitment.

I said, "Absolutely nothing could be served by the disintegration of Pakistan. For India to initiate hostilities would be almost impossible to understand." I said that in some respects the situation was similar to that in the Middle East: just as American and Soviet interests were involved there, so Chinese, Soviet, and American interests were at stake in South Asia and the Indian subcontinent. "It would be impossible to calculate precisely the steps which other great powers might take if India were to initiate hostilities," I said.

A month later, primed with Soviet weapons, the Indian Army attacked East Pakistan. Fighting also erupted along the border with West Pakistan, but it was impossible to tell whether the Indian objective there was to pin down Pakistani forces or whether the action was the prelude to a full-scale attack. Battle plans of such dimension are not formulated in less than a month, and I could not help thinking that Mrs. Gandhi had purposely deceived me in our meeting. I was also concerned that the Soviets had ignored several clear signals from us that we would react very unfavorably if they supported India in an invasion of Pakistan. I felt that one of the primary Soviet motives was to show the world that, despite the much heralded Sino-American rapprochement, the U.S.S.R. was still the premier Communist power. In fact, the Soviets moved troops to the Chinese border in an unsubtle attempt to tie up Chinese forces and prevent them from going to the aid of Pakistan.

I felt it was important to discourage both Indian aggression and Soviet adventurism, and I agreed with Kissinger's recommendation that we should demonstrate our displeasure with India and our support for Pakistan.

To coordinate our planning, Kissinger convened a meeting of the Washington Special Action Group (WSAG), composed of representatives from State, Defense, CIA, and the NSC. He found that the State Department felt that independence for East Pakistan was inevitable and desirable, and that India had limited aims in East Pakistan and no designs on West Pakistan. The risk of Soviet or Chinese intervention, according to this reasoning, was small. The State Department, therefore, argued that we should keep calm, sit back, and let the inevitable happen.

I completely disagreed with this bland assessment. I wanted to let the Soviets know that we would strongly oppose the dismemberment of Pakistan by a Soviet ally using Soviet arms. Kissinger, therefore, summoned Soviet Chargé Vorontsov to the White House and told him that this crisis had once again brought our relations to a watershed because we considered that promoting a war in the Indian subcontinent was inconsistent with improved relations between us.

Kissinger said that we wanted a cease-fire and the withdrawal of all Indian troops from Pakistan. Once the fighting had stopped, the parties could begin to negotiate a political settlement of the problem. We recognized that political autonomy for East Pakistan would be the probable outcome of a political solution, and we were willing to work in that direction. The main point was that the fighting should stop and the danger of a great power confrontation should be removed.

The next day I wrote a letter to Brezhnev that left no doubts about my feelings:

> The objective fact now is that Indian military forces are being used in an effort to impose political demands and to dismember the sovereign state of Pakistan. It is also a fact that your government has aligned itself with this Indian policy. . . .
>
> I am convinced that the spirit in which we agreed that the time had come for us to meet in Moscow next May requires from both of us the utmost restraint and the most urgent action to end the conflict and restore territorial integrity in the subcontinent.

At eleven that night, Vorontsov delivered a note replying to the points Kissinger had made the day before. It accused the United States of not having been active enough in maintaining peace, and it proposed an immediate cease-fire coupled with a demand that Pakistan immediately recognize the independence of East Pakistan. The Soviets clearly intended to play a hard line. What we had to do, therefore, was remain absolutely steadfast behind Pakistan. If we failed to help Pakistan, then Iran or any other country within the reach of Soviet influence might begin to question the dependability of American support. As Kissinger put it, "We don't really have any choice. We can't allow a friend of ours and China's to get screwed in a conflict with a friend of Russia's."

On December 9 Vorontsov arrived with a long letter from Brezhnev. In an attempt to put the shoe on the other foot, he said that the crux of the problem lay in finding ways to exert influence on Yahya Khan to give up East Pakistan. Kissinger felt that the cordial tone of the letter at least indicated some responsive movement on the Soviet side, but I expressed my doubts.

In the meantime, the crisis had taken a disturbing turn. Through intelligence sources we learned that at a meeting of the Indian Cabinet

Mrs. Gandhi had led a discussion of plans to expand the war on the western front and to invade West Pakistan. Kissinger called in the Indian Ambassador, virtually told him that we knew his government's plans, and demanded that the Ambassador urge New Delhi to reconsider any precipitate action.

The Soviet Minister of Agriculture happened to be visiting Washington at this time. I knew he was a close friend of Brezhnev's, so I asked him to carry back a personal message to Brezhnev from me, conveying my seriousness in saying that it was incumbent upon the two of us as the leaders of the two nuclear superpowers not to allow our larger interests to become embroiled in the actions of our smaller friends.

Later that afternoon I authorized Admiral Moorer to dispatch a task force of eight ships, including the nuclear aircraft carrier *Enterprise,* from Vietnam to the Bay of Bengal.

The military situation in East Pakistan was hopeless. The numerically superior Indians had been joined by fierce Bengali rebels, and Yahya Khan's forces were in total retreat. The almost unbelievable cruelty of the fighting on both sides had turned the situation into a nightmare. Millions of people were left homeless before the fighting ended.

Finally, Yahya Khan recognized that he should follow the course of action we had been recommending: that he could no longer defend East Pakistan and that he should concentrate his forces in the defense of West Pakistan, in which event I indicated he would have my complete support. On December 9 Pakistan accepted the UN General Assembly's call for a cease-fire. India rejected it, however, and tension was still rising along the border in West Pakistan, as I wrote another letter to Brezhnev, calling on him to join me in ending the crisis before we ourselves were dragged into it. I began by stating that, in our view, his proposal for the political independence of East Pakistan had been met by Pakistan's own action. Then I wrote:

> This must now be followed by an immediate cease-fire in the West. If this does not take place, we would have to conclude that there is in progress an act of aggression directed at the whole of Pakistan, a friendly country toward which we have obligations.
>
> I therefore propose an immediate joint appeal for a complete cease-fire.
>
> Meanwhile, I urge you in the strongest terms to restrain India with which, by virtue of your treaty, you have great influence and for whose actions you must share responsibility.

On December 11 we waited all day for a reply from Brezhnev. This delay was intolerable, since the possibility of an Indian attack on West

Pakistan increased with each passing hour. On December 12, shortly before I was to fly to the Azores for a Franco-American Summit with President Pompidou on the international monetary crisis, a brief reply arrived from Moscow, stating simply that the government of India had no intention of taking any military action against West Pakistan.

I immediately sent back a message that the Indian assurances lacked any concreteness. In view of the urgency of the situation and the need for concerted action, I proposed that we continue consultations through the secret Kissinger-Dobrynin channel. I added that I could not emphasize too strongly that time was of the essence to avoid consequences that neither of us wanted.

Despite the urgent tone of my message, the hot-line wires were cold until 5 A.M. the next day, when a three-sentence message arrived that the Soviets were conducting a "clarification" of the circumstances in India and would inform us of the results without delay.

In Washington on December 14 Vorontsov handed Haig another message from the Kremlin. Once again it offered only vague assurances that India had no intention of taking any military action against Pakistan. Since this reply offered no improvement over the earlier message I agreed with Kissinger that Haig should call Vorontsov and tell him so.

On the flight from the Azores back to Washington, Kissinger talked to the three pool reporters flying aboard *Air Force One*. One of them asked if there were any danger that the crisis might deteriorate to the point that it would affect my plans to go to the summit. "Not yet," Kissinger replied, "but we will have to wait and see what happens in the next few days." The reporters immediately realized that they had just been given a big story. "Should we infer from that statement that if the Russians don't begin to exercise a restraining influence very soon, the plans for the President's trip might be changed?" one asked.

Kissinger replied, "We are definitely looking to the Soviets to become a restraining influence in the next few days, and if they continue to deliberately encourage military actions, we might have to take a new look at the President's plans."

As soon as the plane landed, the reporters rushed to share their notes with their colleagues and file their stories. The early evening news programs flashed the report around the country and around the world.

Kissinger summoned Vorontsov to the White House and told him that I had been concerned that the Soviet leaders were not doing everything possible to arrive at a settlement. In view of their continued delays, I had begun to believe that they were dealing only in words, with the intention of letting events on the ground dictate the ultimate outcome.

"It is not President Nixon's style to threaten," Kissinger said. "He has long sought a genuine change in U.S.–Soviet relations. Despite his desire, however, your government has proceeded to equip India with great amounts of sophisticated armaments. If the Soviet government were to support or to pressure other foreign leaders to dismember or to divide an ally of the United States, how can they expect progress in our mutual relationships?"

The next day, Kissinger called Vorontsov back and showed him the text of a letter I had written to Kosygin urging that our countries take prompt and responsible steps to ensure that the military conflict not spread and that assurances be given against territorial acquisition by either side.

Vorontsov complained that the Indians were proving very resistant to Soviet pressure. Kissinger replied, "There is no longer any excuse. The President has made any number of personal appeals, all of which have been rejected, and it is now time to move."

Vorontsov said that the Soviets were prepared unconditionally to guarantee that there would be no Indian attack on West Pakistan or on Kashmir. But to do this publicly would mean that they were, in effect, speaking for a friendly country. In other words, the Soviets would urge the Indians to accept a cease-fire as long as they did not have to do so publicly. Without the prospect of Soviet support and aid, the Indians were almost certain to agree to a settlement.

The next day Yahya Khan's forces in East Pakistan surrendered unconditionally. On December 17 the explosive situation on the western front was also resolved when Pakistan accepted the Indian offer of a cease-fire there. By using diplomatic signals and behind-the-scenes pressures we had been able to save West Pakistan from the imminent threat of Indian aggression and domination. We had also once again avoided a major confrontation with the Soviet Union.

The Indo-Pakistan war involved stakes much higher than the future of Pakistan—and that was high enough. It involved the principle of whether big nations supported by the Soviet Union would be permitted to dismember their smaller neighbors. Once that principle was allowed, the world would have become more unstable and unsafe.

The Chinese played a very cautious role in this period. They had troops poised on the Indian border, but they would not take the risk of coming to the aid of Pakistan by attacking India, because they understandably feared that the Soviets might use this action as an excuse for attacking China. They consequently did nothing, but the presence of their forces probably had a deterrent effect on India.

Three days after the cease-fire was arranged, we sent the Chinese a brief description of its major points. We concluded, "It is the U.S. view that recent events in South Asia involve sobering conclusions. The governments of the People's Republic of China and the United States should not again find themselves in a position where hostile global aims can be furthered through the use of proxy countries."

As a result of the Indo-Pakistan crisis, my respect and regard for Mrs. Gandhi diminished. A few months later, in March 1972, after having seen a film biography of Mahatma Gandhi—who was no relation to her—during a weekend at Key Biscayne, I dictated a brief reflection in the diary I had begun keeping in November 1971.

Diary

As I saw Gandhi's assassination and heard his words on violence, I realized how hypocritical the present Indian leaders are, with Indira Gandhi talking about India's victory wings being clipped when Shastri went to Tashkent, and her duplicitous attitude toward us when she actually had made up her mind to attack Pakistan at the time she saw me in Washington and assured me she would not. Those who resort to force, without making excuses, are bad enough—but those who resort to force while preaching to others about their use of force deserve no sympathy whatever.

One of the most serious incidents of the Indo-Pakistan crisis occurred on our domestic front. On December 14, while we were still uncertain whether India would attack West Pakistan, syndicated columnist Jack Anderson published verbatim excerpts of the minutes of the WSAG meetings of December 2, 4, and 6. The minutes revealed Kissinger's statements to the group relaying my strong pressure to "tilt" toward Pakistan, which differed from the posture that had been adopted by some State Department sources as well as from the more neutral public position we embraced in order to exercise greater leverage on all parties. From a diplomatic point of view, the leak was embarrassing; from the point of view of national security, it was intolerable.

The leak came as a shock because WSAG meetings had been attended by only the highest-ranking members of the military intelligence organizations and the State Department. We learned that Rear Admiral Robert O. Welander believed that one of the leaked documents had to have come from his office, which handled liaison between the Joint Chiefs of Staff and the National Security Council. Bud Krogh and David Young were assigned to investigate.

Suspicion centered on a young Navy yeoman assigned to Welander's office. In the course of questioning, Young learned that for some time the yeoman had been making copies of secret NSC documents. He had regularly rifled burn bags for carbons or Xerox copies, and in some cases he actually took documents for copying out of Kissinger's and Haig's briefcases. On one occasion he copied a memo of Kissinger's conversation with Chou En-lai during the first secret mission to Peking. He passed these documents to his superiors in the Pentagon.

We were not able to establish beyond doubt that the yeoman was Anderson's source. However, circumstantial evidence was strong. They were personally acquainted and had met on several occasions. Whether or not he had disclosed classified information to Anderson, the fact remained that he had jeopardized the relationship of the JCS to the White House.

I was disturbed—although not perhaps really surprised—that the JCS was spying on the White House. But I was, frankly, very reluctant to pursue this aspect of the case because I knew that if it were explored, like so many other sensitive matters it would wind up being leaked to the media where it would be completely distorted, and we would end up doing damage to the military at a time when it was already under heavy attack.

The yeoman himself presented a similar problem. I felt the circumstantial evidence that he had provided information to Anderson was convincing, and I knew that such actions could not be tolerated.

> *Diary*
>
> What concerns me about this story is the Ellsberg complex that drove the yeoman to put out the information. His spying on the White House for the Joint Chiefs is something that I would not particularly be surprised at, although I don't think it's a healthy practice. But his proceeding to put out top secret information to a newspaper columnist, because he disagreed with the policy on India, is the kind of practice that must, at all costs, be stopped.

I felt, however, that it would be too dangerous to prosecute the yeoman. He had traveled with Kissinger and others on a number of secret missions and had had access to other top-secret information, which, if disclosed, could have jeopardized our negotiations with China and with North Vietnam. In this respect he was a potential time bomb that might be triggered by prosecution. We had him transferred to a remote post in Oregon and kept him under surveillance, including wiretaps for a time, to make sure that he was not dispensing any more secret information. It worked: there were no further leaks from him.

With vice presidential running mate Henry Cabot Lodge at the 1960 Republican National Convention.

Democratic vice presidential candidate Lyndon Johnson and Senate Minority Leader Everett Dirksen visit RN when an infected knee forced him into the hospital during the 1960 campaign.

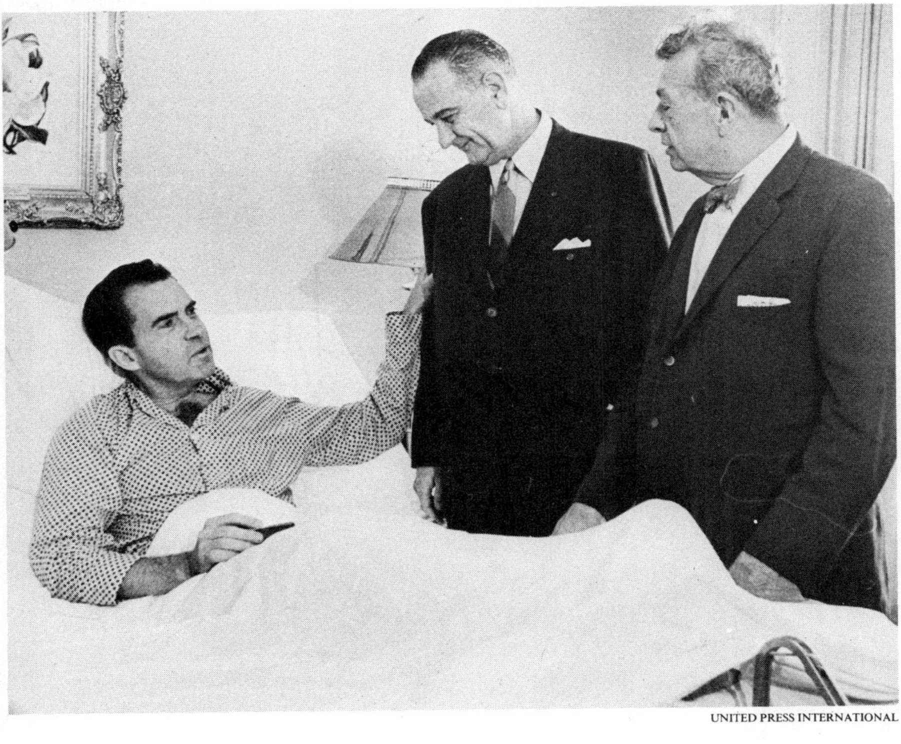

UNITED PRESS INTERNATIONAL

UNITED PRESS INTERNATIONAL

The Nixon–Kennedy debates: the first was on September 26, 1960, in Chicago.

HANK WALKER/*Life Magazine* © 1960 TIME INC.

Election Night 1960: conceding that if the trend continues, John F. Kennedy will be elected President.

One of the Nixon family's favorite photographs, taken on their arrival in California in 1961. Checkers is in the foreground.

The "last press conference" following the 1962 election for governor of California. Herb Klein is standing in the background.

RALPH CRANE/*Life Magazine* © 1962 TIME INC.

With Checkers in Central Park after the move to New York in 1963.

UNITED PRESS INTERNATIONAL

A grainy wire service photo from South Vietnam during the Asian trip in September 1965.

Relaxing in Key Biscayne before the 1968 campaign.

The Nixons and the Agnews at the Republican National Convention at Miami Beach, August 1968.

DIRCK HALSTEAD/UNITED PRESS INTERNATIONAL

Campaigning in 1968 in Philadelphia.

A candid photo taken by Dwight Chapin in RN's hotel suite after his election as President on November 6, 1968. The TV screen shows the Illinois returns that clinched the victory. John Mitchell looks on as RN holds Julie's victory gift—the Great Seal of the United States in crewelwork.

DWIGHT CHAF

UNITED PRESS INTERNATIONAL

Meeting with Vice President Hubert Humphrey two days after the 1968 election, at the airport at Opa-Locka, Florida.

Escorting Julie on December 22, 1968, the day of her wedding to David Eisenhower.

RICHARD WINBURN

WHITE HOUSE PH

Inauguration Day, January 20, 1969. Chief Justice Earl Warren administers the oath. Pat holds two Milhous family Bibles.

The last photo of RN and General Eisenhower.

WHITE HOUSE PHOTO

With President Charles de Gaulle in Paris in February 1969. Behind RN are (left) National Security Adviser Henry Kissinger and Secretary of State William Rogers.

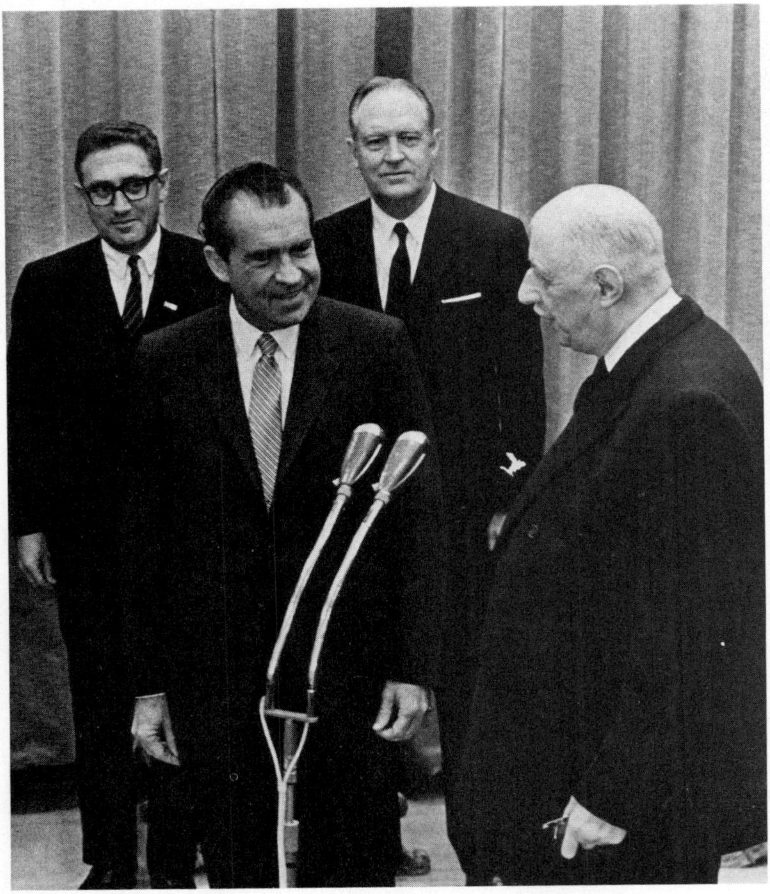

WHITE HOUSE PHOTO

WHITE HOUSE PHOTO

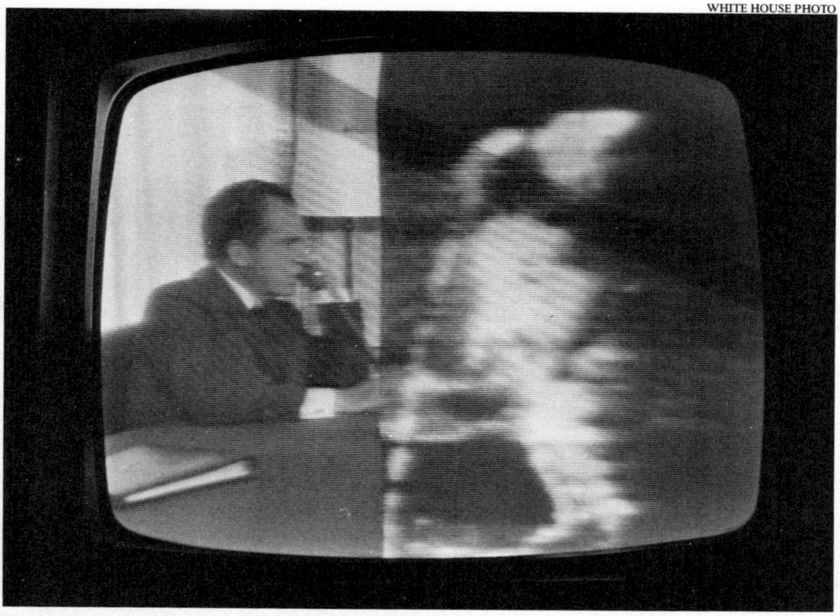

The telephone conversation between the earth and the moon: talking to the Apollo XI astronauts from the Oval Office in July 1969.

RN with former President Johnson and John McCormack in May 1970, at a White House luncheon honoring McCormack when he retired as Speaker of the House of Representatives.

WHITE HOUSE PHOTO

©1970 FRED J.MAROON

In the Oval Office in 1970 with staff aides John Ehrlichman, Henry Kissinger, and Bob Haldeman (seated).

In the Lincoln Sitting Room with Henry Kissinger.

WHITE HOUSE PHOTO

RN at the picture window of Aspen Lodge at Camp David.

WHITE HOUSE PHOTO

Visiting with U.S. troops in Vietnam in July 1969.

WHITE HOUSE PHOTO

Hats of construction union leaders on the table in the Roosevelt room at the White House after the Cambodian operation in May 1970.

"Working the fence" at the airport at Bangor, Maine, in 1971.

WHITE HOUSE PHOTO

WHITE HOUSE PHOTO

RN with Michael Newton, poster child for Better Hearing and Speech Month Campaign, 1971.

Pat practicing her personal diplomacy at an orphanage in Ivory Coast during her African trip in January 1972.

WHITE HOUSE PHOTO

WHITE HOUSE PHOTO

One of the Nixon family's favorite photographs of the White House years, taken in the Blue Room during the Christmas holidays in 1971.

WHITE HOUSE PHOTO

Escorting Tricia in the Rose Garden on June 12, 1971, the day of her wedding to Edward Cox.

WHITE HOUSE PHOTO

Dancing at Tricia's wedding reception in the East Room.

SIX GREAT GOALS

Although Vietnam and other foreign problems dominated most of 1971, this was the year in which I challenged Congress to pass domestic legislation that would result in what I called a "New American Revolution." Undeterred by Congress's lack of interest in diffusing power and returning it to the people, I once again urged action on proposals—some of which I had first sent up in 1969—that would begin changing the whole size and shape of the federal government. In my State of the Union address on January 22, 1971, I used blunt language to describe the need for the programs I was proposing. "Let's face it," I said. "Most Americans today are simply fed up with government at all levels."

In a speech that I consider the most comprehensive and constructive statement on my domestic policy that I made as President, I listed six great goals for the American nation and the American people: welfare reform; full prosperity in peacetime; restoring and enhancing the natural environment; improving health care and making it available more fairly to more people; strengthening and renewing state and local government; and a complete reform of the federal government.

The response from Congress continued to be disappointing and frustrating. Welfare reform, government reorganization, the comprehensive health care programs, and dozens of other programs and pieces of legislation continued to be casualties of congressional inaction.

PAT

Most people would probably say that it takes stamina, strength, or determination to succeed in political life. Pat once said that what political life most requires is "heart"—and she is right. That is true of politics at its best and public life at its finest.

"Heart" is a combination of personal communication and human understanding that is based on a liking for people because you respect them rather than because you need their votes or their support. It is a quality that Pat possesses in abundance. It was her gift to the White House and to the country from the moment she became First Lady.

She stepped into the demanding new role without breaking stride. She set up staff offices in the East Wing and took a personal interest in every aspect of the operation of the White House. She was as concerned about having fresh flowers in the public rooms for the daily tours as she was in being completely briefed on every state visitor.

Each of us loved the White House and looked for ways to share its history and beauty with others, but it was Pat who made it happen.

She had loudspeakers set up near the fence on the South Grounds so that while they were waiting people standing in line for the tour could hear about the history of the rooms they were about to see. She arranged special tours for the blind that allowed them for the first time to touch the historic objects in the different rooms. Pat also recorded an introduction for the first "talking history" of the White House so that those who could not see it would nevertheless have a sense of sharing and belonging when they were there.

The girls reflected their mother's sense of caring and generosity. Tricia, who lived with us until her marriage, tutored young children from one of the city's elementary schools, and she thought of imaginative ways to bring young people into the White House—meeting with 1,000 Boy Scouts on the South Lawn, having a Halloween party for 350 children from less privileged areas of Washington. In the spring of 1970 she was the hostess for 2,000 children who blanketed the lawn for a concert by the D.C. Youth Orchestra. All this was in addition to her regular schedule of receptions, teas, and speaking engagements.

During our first summer in the White House, Julie volunteered as a guide at the Visitors Office, taking delighted tourists on special trips through the gardens and up to the historical rooms on the second floor. In the afternoons, she gave special tours for the handicapped. Even when she was studying for a master's degree and later while an editor for the *Saturday Evening Post,* she maintained a heavy schedule of speeches and visits throughout the country.

Pat arranged for private contributions so that the outside of the White House could be illuminated at night for the city's residents as well as for tourists. Inside, she transformed the House with her unerring sense of color and design, and her extraordinary energy. Working with White House Curator Clement Conger, and Edward V. Jones of Albany, Georgia, an authority on Federal period art, architecture, and furniture, she raised the money to bring more than 500 carefully selected pieces of early American furniture and art to the public rooms of the White House. With Carlisle Humelsine, the head of the Colonial Williamsburg Foundation, she was instrumental in the refurbishment of the West Wing of the White House.

The girls and I took great pride in the fact that after Pat was finished with her work, the many artists, historians, architects, and decorators who came to visit said that the White House had never looked more beautiful.

I can take credit for only one innovation in our White House redecorating program. One night as we were arriving home from some social function, I noticed that the flags were flying over many of the federal buildings but not over the White House. My military assistant, Don Hughes, informed me that the flag could be flown at night only if it were lighted. I asked him to have a floodlight installed on the roof and, from that time on, the flag flew over the White House day and night.

There is a deep common bond among all those who have shared in life at the White House. Pat and I particularly wanted to make the families of all former Presidents and Vice Presidents, regardless of their party or their politics, feel welcome.

Pat suggested that we compile a register of all living direct descendants of former Presidents, and over the years we invited many of them to White House functions. In this way we met Calvin Coolidge's son, some of Grover Cleveland's grandchildren, Roosevelts from Oyster Bay and Hyde Park, and dozens of Adamses.

We made sure that approval was given for the Johnson family to have additional Secret Service protection when they traveled abroad. I periodically called Johnson and Humphrey to ask their advice, and sometimes just to chat and let them know I understood the burdens they had borne.

Pat's idea of having a visitor to the White House was to visit with them. She has always disliked making formal speeches, and instead of dropping by a reception just long enough to say a few words for the benefit of the reporters and television cameras, she preferred spending her time mixing personally with the guests and talking to them. One afternoon it would be 450 dieticians, then 670 wives of financial leaders from foreign countries, or the 1,200 members of the White House Conference on Food, Nutrition, and Health, or the 350 American Farm Bureau Women.

It frustrated me that her backbreaking schedule received so little attention from the press. But all that mattered to her was that she had made people feel welcome.

Each morning Pat would go over some of the more than 1,000 letters she received every week and sign replies to them. She believed that if people took the time to write to her that they deserved a personal reply. In the afternoon, after her regular schedule of receptions and teas, she might take retarded children for a cruise on the *Sequoia,* or plan a special event such as the Thanksgiving dinner to which she invited hundreds of older citizens—not VIPs, but people who might never have a chance to see the White House otherwise. Then, in the evenings, she would often have some function at the White House or be scheduled to make an appearance somewhere in the city.

She left us all breathless. By our second year in the White House we had set a record of 50,000 guests.

There is a modern notion that every First Lady has to have a "project," one thing with which to be identified. Pat was dedicated to promoting the concept of volunteerism, the idea of people helping each other and not waiting for the government to do things they can do for themselves. But she bridled at the idea that volunteerism was her "project," or that her interests had to be compartmentalized. She once said, "People are my real project," and she proved it time and time again.

She traveled around the country talking with people in every kind of program—programs for young people, for old people, for the handicapped, programs to help children get a head start on reading, programs for city and community beautification. She made over 150 trips out into the country, some with me and many on her own. And not once did she lose sight of the fact that she was not meeting groups, but individuals, not constituencies, but people. I remember being told once about an afternoon when she had been on a tour of a medical facility and stopped to embrace a little girl blinded by rubella. For a few minutes, while the tour waited, she talked to the child and held her close. When someone came over and told her that the child was deaf as well as blind, Pat answered she had known that. "But she knows what love is," Pat said. "She can feel love."

Life in the White House is active and intense. For one thing, it is a city home and there is always the sense and sound of traffic outside. Sometimes there would be the sound of demonstrations. Inside, it often seemed as if there were never any real privacy as the household staff went about their work, and in the basement the kitchens were constantly bustling with preparations for the steady stream of breakfasts, luncheons, teas, receptions, and official dinners.

We tried at the beginning to cut back on some of the trappings. Pat and I agreed that we should reduce the number of stewards and aides who surround a President wherever he goes. I told Haldeman to have the two Navy medics who had served full time as the President's masseurs reassigned to some more productive duty. I immediately stopped what was to me the almost incredible practice of having the President's bed from the White House flown ahead whenever he traveled outside Washington so that he would never have to sleep in a strange bed. I said that I would need only Manolo and possibly one steward to take care of my clothes and meals when I went on weekend working trips to Camp David or Key Biscayne. We ordered the decommissioning of the two large Navy yachts that had been maintained exclusively for the President's use. We also tried to cut down on the numbers and security requirements of the Secret Service who were always with us.

But even so, life in the White House was confining, and this made the home we bought in summer 1969 for our retirement in San Clemente even more special for us. It is an old Spanish house situated on a beautiful high point directly above the beach. The constant sound of the waves gives it serenity, and the palm and eucalyptus trees surrounding it provide natural protection that made it possible for us to take at least semiprivate walks. We named the house La Casa Pacifica—the Peaceful House. A small complex of offices was built on the Coast Guard station next door, and these became the Western White House.

Because of the distance we were able to visit San Clemente only a few times a year. More often we would go for a weekend to Key Biscayne or to Camp David. In some respects, Pat ran three households—in Washington, California, and Florida—and she made each of them a home for us even if we were there for only a few days.

Over the years of our life in politics, Pat's strength of character continued to grow, and her gentle sensitivity to people became even more acute. She was often criticized by feminist radicals of the women's liberation movement, but she held to her guiding principle: the right of a woman to choose her role in life. And by her actions she proved that it was possible to be both an independent woman and a supportive wife. She was not at all dismayed when she was sometimes accused of being inhibited. In personal encounters she is lively, informal, and witty, but she felt that it was important for a First Lady to be dignified. She recognized that the role is in many ways a representative one. She was traditional, but in a warm way that transcended time and place. And, most important, she was comfortable with herself, sure of herself in a world of rapidly changing values.

During the vice presidential years, Pat and I had traveled together to fifty-three countries. Eisenhower used to think of us as a team—and so did I. While I spent the days in meetings, she went to meet the local people in schools, hospitals, factories, orphanages. I remember the awe and respect on the faces of our hosts in Panama when she insisted on visiting and shaking hands with the tragic inhabitants of a leper colony there.

At night, she would come back to our rooms in time to change into a gown for glittering state dinners.

Pat became for thousands of people abroad the personification of American good will: it was there in her voice, her smile, her eyes. That spoke to the people in the countries we visited in a way that speeches, toasts, and communiqués never could.

Pat was the first First Lady to serve as the President's official diplomatic representative abroad. In this capacity she went to Peru to take supplies gathered by volunteer workers in America to the victims of a devastating earthquake. Braving danger and enduring fatigue, she climbed amid the rubble to embrace homeless children and bring a message of American love and concern. In gratitude for this trip, the President of Peru invested her with the Grand Cross of the Order of the Sun, the oldest decoration in the Americas. She was the first North American woman ever to receive this signal honor.

During our trips to China and the summits in the Soviet Union, Pat showed her mastery of the art of personal diplomacy. She shook hands with dancing bears at the circus, drew children to her in schools and hospitals, visited communes, factories, department stores, and danced a step with the Bolshoi Ballet school.

In 1974, she led the U.S. delegation to the inaugural ceremonies for the President of Venezuela and the President of Brazil. In 1972 she represented me in Africa at the inauguration of the President of Liberia and then traveled on for meetings with the heads of state in Ghana and the Ivory Coast. She returned home from Africa on January 9.

Diary

Pat was obviously elated by her trip. She was particularly impressed by the President of the Ivory Coast. She pointed out that he did not believe in using force against South Africa, and I realized that this is the reason that many in the State Department don't like him because he does not take the usual line which is totally anti-South Africa without regard to the consequences, even if it means a war which no one would win.

I have concluded, after having grave doubts about the independence movements in Africa, that perhaps it is best to allow these countries to start with their first faltering steps and learn to walk alone. They are going to mess a lot of things up but it allows them to have dignity and develop capability which comes only from having responsibility. They would never acquire it in a colonial status or in a dependent status.

The amazing thing is that Pat came back looking just as fresh as a daisy despite an enormously difficult, taxing schedule. She had press conferences in each country, had had conversations with the Presidents, and then carried it all off with unbelievable skill.

As Julie put it, what came through was love of the people of the countries she visited for her, and, on her part, love for them.

Sometimes our family was called square and as far as we were concerned, that was just fine. In the environment of Washington, "square" often means rooted in principles that ignore chic, transitory fashions.

On our first Sunday in the White House we held the first White House worship service in the East Room. It was our idea to have these short inspirational services, each conducted by a distinguished preacher of a different faith and with choirs from different parts of the country.

Each time we would invite between two and three hundred people—from congressional leaders to White House policemen and telephone operators. The worship services meant Pat and I could avoid the exploitation of religion that too often took place when we attended regular church services outside and were accompanied by television crews and pursued by large numbers of tourists and curiosity-seekers who had no interest whatever in the service. This bothered me personally, and I thought that it must be an irritating nuisance and distraction to the others who had come to worship.

There was a flurry of criticism about the worship services. Traditionalists said that they were too watered down to be meaningful; nonbelievers said religion had no place in the White House; and editorialists complained that we were breaking down the separation between church and state. But Pat and I consider the worship services to have been among the high points of our years in the White House. They gave many thousands of people an opportunity to join us. More important, they set a national example of reverence.

Our whole family has always loved theatre, movies, and music. Our favorite relaxation after dinner at Camp David or in Florida or California was to watch a movie. Sometimes we would experiment with films we had never heard of; sometimes we would choose current hits; and sometimes old family favorites.

Pat and I looked forward to the evenings of entertainment at the White House as much as any of our guests. We felt that performers invited to entertain after state dinners should reflect the whole spectrum of American tastes—and, incidentally, our own eclectic preferences. Among the hundreds of memorable evenings, I particularly remember Golda Meir rushing impulsively to embrace Isaac Stern and Leonard Bernstein when they performed after a state dinner in her honor. Beverly Sills, Roberta Peters, Merle Haggard, and the Carpenters covered the range from classical to country and rock. Pearl Bailey was her warmly humorous and inimitable self; and Frank Sinatra, in his first appearance at the White House, had tears in his eyes when he thanked me afterward. Tony Bennett, Johnny Cash, Glen Campbell, Art Linkletter, and Bob Hope were among the others who came to perform.

In addition to the after-dinner entertainment, Pat initiated a series of special Evenings at the White House to which guests were invited to enjoy the artistry of a great performer, whether it was Nicol Williamson reading from *Hamlet*, Red Skelton cracking jokes, or Sammy Davis, Jr., singing and dancing. Sammy and his wife spent the night with us after his performance and—in fulfillment of a lifelong dream—he slept in the Lincoln Bedroom.

More than once, in performances that would have dismayed my Aunt

Jane, I sat down at the piano for some rollicking sing-alongs of old favorites like "When Irish Eyes Are Smiling" and "God Bless America."

In addition to honoring the performing arts, Pat also took a special interest in handicrafts and the fine arts. She welcomed many craft groups to the White House and their work was often displayed in the East Wing corridor. Pat was also the first First Lady ever to arrange a one-man art exhibition at the White House, inviting Andrew Wyeth to show some of his paintings in the East Room.

Except for the POW dinner in 1973, which was a unique historical event, I think that the most memorable of all our White House social occasions was Duke Ellington's seventieth birthday on April 29, 1969, when I presented him with the country's highest civilian honor, the Medal of Freedom. We invited more than 200 guests, including Cab Calloway, Earl Hines, Billy Eckstine, Mahalia Jackson, Harold Arlen, and Richard Rodgers. In making the presentation, I said, "In the royalty of American music, no man swings more or stands higher than the Duke."

I braved the piano accompaniment to "Happy Birthday" and when the formal program was over, and some of the greatest jazz musicians had performed some of his greatest songs, I said, "I think we all ought to hear from one more pianist." I went over to Duke's chair and led him to the piano.

The room was hushed as he sat quietly for a moment. Then he said he would improvise a melody. "I shall pick a name—gentle, graceful—something like Patricia," he said.

And when he started to play it was lyrical, delicate, and beautiful—like Pat.

1972

My attitude and outlook as this climactic year began were reflected in a note I dictated on January 9, 1972—my fifty-ninth birthday.

Diary

The 59th year, now complete, has been perhaps the most successful from the standpoint of accomplishment to date. The 60th offers immense opportunities and, of course, equally great dangers. The main thing is to maintain a cool and objective attitude throughout and if possible to stay above the battle and not be buffeted by ups and downs in the polls and by the inevitable political attacks.

On the third anniversary of my inauguration as President, I held a dinner for the Cabinet and the White House senior staff. In my after-dinner remarks I talked about the year ahead: "This is January 20, 1972, and tonight the fourth quarter begins. The football analogy tells us that the fourth quarter really determines the game," I began. "We are only here for about four quarters—maybe longer, but you can only assume the fourth quarter. But in those four quarters, let us be sure that nothing was left undone that could have been done to make this a more decent country, in terms of our relations between ourselves and in terms of all the infinite problems we have."

PRESIDENTIAL POLITICS: 1972

On January 5, 1972, I sent a letter to the chairman of my New Hampshire campaign committee announcing my candidacy for re-election. Eleven Democrats and two other Republicans sought the presidential nomination in 1972. The other Republicans were antiwar California Congressman Paul McCloskey and right-wing Ohio Congressman John Ashbrook.

Some of the Democratic candidates—Edmund Muskie, George McGovern, Wilbur Mills, and Vance Hartke—were already campaigning in New Hampshire, each hoping to make a national impact by a decisive showing in this first primary contest on March 7. Others—including Hubert Humphrey, George Wallace, Henry Jackson, and John Lindsay—calculated that it was better not to risk an initial battering but to emerge as fresh faces in the second primary a week later in Florida.

Because the Republican National Committee would have to preserve an official neutrality until the convention and because after our 1970 experience I wanted to keep politics out of the White House, I decided to set up a separate campaign organization. It was called the Committee to Re-elect the President, a name we abbreviated with the initials CRP.

The front-runner on the Democratic side was Edmund Muskie. At the end of 1971 he was running even with me in the public opinion polls. Muskie's liabilities were an explosive temper and a reputation in political circles for indecisiveness. His principal problem was the ambition of his former running mate, Hubert Humphrey, whose entry into the race would draw away from him the support and votes of many traditional rank-and-file Democrats.

Of the other Democratic candidates, George Wallace was the one we had to take most seriously. If he ran again as a third-party candidate, he would undoubtedly draw a large number of conservative votes from me.

George McGovern, the extreme liberal dark horse, attracted only mild interest because his chances of getting the nomination seemed so remote. If by some miracle he could be nominated, I had no doubt that he would be the easiest Democrat to beat. The hardest would be the one who resolutely avowed his noncandidacy: Teddy Kennedy.

Noncandidacy would have been the best strategy for Kennedy in any event, but he probably had no choice in the aftermath of the party at Chappaquiddick, Massachusetts, in July 1969, when his car went off a bridge and a young woman in the car was drowned. Kennedy was given nationwide television time to explain his version of the events. His speech was finely crafted, but many felt that his story was full of gaps and contradictions. I could not help thinking that if anyone other than a Kennedy had been involved and had given such a patently unacceptable explanation, the media and the public would not have permitted him to survive in public life.

Personally, however, I felt deeply sorry for Ted Kennedy. When I saw him at a meeting in the Cabinet Room a few days later, I was shocked by how pale and shaken he looked. I spoke to him in the Oval Office for a few minutes afterward and tried to reassure him that he must resolve to overcome this tragedy and go on with his life.

In politics it is possible to feel genuine personal concern for an opponent and still be coldly objective about his position as a competitor. Even as I felt real sympathy for Teddy Kennedy, I recognized, as he must have done, the far-reaching political implications of this personal tragedy. In the short term, I knew that Chappaquiddick would undermine Kennedy's role as a leader of the opposition to the administration's policies. In the longer term, it would be one of his greatest liabilities if he decided to run for President in 1972.

It was clear that the full story of what had happened that night on Chappaquiddick had not come out, and I suspected that the press would not try very hard to uncover it. Therefore I told Ehrlichman to have someone investigate the case for us and get the real facts out. "Don't let up on this for a minute," I said. "Just put yourself in *their* place if something like this had happened to *us*." In fact, our private investigator was unable to turn up anything besides rumors.

After a grand jury heard the case, the presiding judge, James Boyle, issued a report stating that Kennedy could not have been telling the truth in his testimony. Kennedy immediately issued a statement saying that Judge Boyle's report was "not justified." Public opinion polls showed that most people did not think that Kennedy was telling the truth about Chappaquiddick; but they also showed that Massachusetts voters did not think he should have to resign from the Senate because of it. The following year they gave him an overwhelming vote of confidence by returning him to the Senate with 63 percent of the vote. Even with Chappaquiddick to overcome, Teddy Kennedy would still have been the most formidable Democratic nominee in 1972.

I thought that Muskie had a fair chance of beating me and that Humphrey, backed by labor, could come very close. Any Democrat would have the advantage of the sheer size of the Democratic party, which in 1972 outregistered the Republican party by millions of voters. It also seemed possible that they would have the added assistance of George Wallace running against me at the head of a third party.

Finally, it seemed increasingly likely that all of the candidates would be able to campaign against a war that I was not going to be able to win and that I would not yet be able to end.

George McGovern was the most extreme of the antiwar candidates. His solution to an immensely complex problem was appealingly easy to his supporters. "If I were President," he said, "it would take me twenty-four hours and the stroke of a pen to terminate all military operations in Southeast Asia." He said he would withdraw all troops within ninety days, whether or not our POWs were released. He said that President Thieu should plan to flee to whatever country would take him. Even if the POWs were not released, McGovern would not resume fighting because, as he put it during the campaign, "begging is better than bombing."

The difference between McGovern and the other Democrats on Vietnam was fundamental: for the others, the war was an issue; for McGovern, it was a cause.

Muskie beat McGovern in New Hampshire, 46 percent to 37 percent. Considering Muskie's commanding lead at the beginning of the campaign, the commentators described the 9 percent margin as a serious setback for him. Virtually overnight this media attention transformed McGovern from a fringe candidate to a serious contender.

In the second primary, in Florida, George Wallace aroused the voters with his call to "send a message to Washington." The message was: no busing. Wallace won the Florida primary with 41.5 percent of the votes. Hubert Humphrey was second. Senator Henry Jackson was third. Muskie, who had denounced Wallace as a racist, came in fourth with only 8.8 percent.

McGovern won the important Wisconsin primary on April 4 and also won in Massachusetts and Nebraska. To me his steady climb was as welcome to watch as it was almost unbelievable to behold. By the end of the spring, only Humphrey and Kennedy were left to stop him.

On our side, the primary results were no less gratifying because they were expected; despite the fact that I did no campaigning, I received overwhelming majorities in all the Republican primaries.

CHINA

At 7:30 on the evening of July 15, 1971, I spoke to the nation from a television studio in Burbank, California. I talked for only three and a half minutes, but my words produced one of the greatest diplomatic surprises of the century.

I began, "I have requested this television time tonight to announce a major development in our efforts to build a lasting peace in the world." Then I read an announcement that was being made at that very moment in Peking:

> Premier Chou En-lai and Dr. Henry Kissinger, President Nixon's Assistant for National Security Affairs, held talks in Peking from July 9 to 11, 1971. Knowing of President Nixon's expressed desire to visit the People's Republic of China, Premier Chou En-lai, on behalf of the Government of the People's Republic of China, has extended an invitation to President Nixon to visit China at an appropriate date before May 1972. President Nixon has accepted the invitation with pleasure.
>
> The meeting between the leaders of China and the United States is to seek the normalization of relations between the two countries and also to exchange views on questions of concern to the two sides.

Behind this brief announcement lay more than two years of complex, subtle, and determined diplomatic signals and negotiations. Despite the almost miraculous secrecy we had been able to maintain, the China initiative was actually one of the most publicly prepared surprises in history.

The first time I raised the idea of the importance of relations between the United States and Communist China was in my article in *Foreign Affairs* in 1967. In my inaugural address I had referred indirectly to it when I said, "We seek an open world . . . a world in which no people, great or small, will live in angry isolation." Less than two weeks later, on February 1, I wrote a memorandum to Kissinger urging that we give every encouragement to the attitude that the administration was exploring possibilities of rapprochement with the Chinese. "This, of course, should be done privately and should under no circumstances get into the public prints from this direction," I added. During 1969 the Chinese ignored the few low-level signals of interest we sent them, and it was not until 1970 that we began a serious approach to opening a dialogue to see where, if anywhere, it might lead.

The first serious public step in the China initiative had been taken in February 1970 when I sent the first Foreign Policy Report to Congress. The section on China began:

> The Chinese are a great and vital people who should not remain isolated from the international community. . . .
>
> The principles underlying our relations with Communist China are similar to those governing our policies toward the U.S.S.R. United States policy is not likely soon to have much impact on China's behavior, let alone its ideological outlook. But it is certainly in our interest, and in the interest of peace and stability in Asia and the world, that we take what steps we can toward improved practical relations with Peking.

The leaders in Peking clearly understood the significance of the language in this report. Two days later, during a meeting in Warsaw with U.S. Ambassador Walter Stoessel, the Chinese ambassador dramatically suggested moving their hitherto sporadic and unproductive meetings to Peking. He also hinted that they would welcome a high-ranking American official as head of the delegation.

In March 1970 the State Department announced a relaxation of most of the official restrictions against travel to Communist China; in April we announced a further easing of trade controls.

Plans for moving the Warsaw talks to Peking received a setback in May when the Chinese canceled a scheduled meeting in protest of the Cambodian operation. For a few weeks it seemed as if the China initiative had collapsed. But the underlying logic of the initiative was based on clear-cut assessments of mutually advantageous interests, and I was not surprised when, after a few months, the Chinese signaled that they were willing to resume our diplomatic minuet. In July, they released American Roman Catholic Bishop James Edward Walsh, who had been arrested in 1958 and held as a prisoner for twelve years.

Early in October I gave an interview to *Time* magazine. I said that: "If there is anything I want to do before I die, it is to go to China. If I don't, I want my children to."

On October 25 President Yahya Khan of Pakistan came to see me, and I used the occasion to establish the "Yahya channel." We had discussed the idea in general terms when I saw him on my visit to Pakistan in July 1969. Now I told him that we had decided to try to normalize our relations with China, and I asked for his help as an intermediary.

"Of course we will do anything we can to help," Yahya said, "but you must know how difficult this will be. Old enemies do not easily become new friends. It will be slow, and you must be prepared for setbacks."

The next day President Ceaușescu of Romania arrived on a state visit. I had also discussed the need for a new Chinese-American relationship with him in Bucharest in 1969. My toast at the dinner in his honor was the first occasion on which an American President had intentionally referred to Communist China by its official name, the People's Republic of China; even my Foreign Policy Report had called it "Communist China." This was a significant diplomatic signal.

In my meeting with Ceaușescu the next day, I said that, even short of the ultimate ideal of re-establishing full diplomatic relations with China, there could be an exchange of high-level personal representatives. He agreed to pass this word along to Peking, and this was the beginning of the "Romanian channel."

A month later, on November 22, I dictated a memorandum for Kissinger:

> On a very confidential basis, I would like for you to have prepared in your staff—without any notice to people who might leak—a study of where we are to go with regard to the admission of Red China to the UN. It seems to me that the time is approaching sooner than we might think when we will not have the votes to block admission.
>
> The question we really need an answer to is how we can develop a position in which we can keep our commitments to Taiwan and yet will not be rolled by those who favor admission of Red China.
>
> There is no hurry on this study but within two or three months I would like to see what you come up with.

In fact, things were to move much faster than I had anticipated.

On December 9 Chou En-lai sent word through President Yahya that my representative would be welcome in Peking for a discussion of the question of Taiwan. Chou stressed that the message did not come from him alone but had been approved by Chairman Mao and by Lin Piao, still a powerful figure at that time. With characteristic subtlety, Chou concluded with a play on words. "We have had messages from the United States from different sources in the past," he said, "but this is the first time that the proposal has come from a Head, through a Head, to a Head." Through Pakistani Ambassador Agha Hilaly we replied that any meeting should not be limited to a discussion of Taiwan, and we proposed that Chinese and American representatives meet in Pakistan to discuss the possibility of a high-level meeting in Peking in the future.

On December 18, American writer Edgar Snow had an interview with his old friend Mao Tse-tung. Mao told him that the Foreign Ministry was considering the question of allowing Americans of all political colorations—left, right, and center—to visit China. Snow asked whether a rightist like Nixon, who represented the "monopoly capitalists," would be permitted to come. Mao replied that I would be welcomed, because as President I was, after all, the one with whom the problems between China and the United States would have to be solved. Mao said that he would be happy to talk to the President, whether he came as a tourist or as President. We learned of Mao's statement within a few days after he made it.

Early in 1971 the Romanian channel became active. Ambassador Corneliu Bogdan called on Kissinger with the news that after our conversation in October, Ceauşescu had sent his Vice Premier to Peking, and Chou En-lai had given him a message for me. It read:

> The communication from the U.S. President is not new. There is only one outstanding issue between us—the U.S. occupation of Taiwan. The P.R.C. has attempted to negotiate on this issue in good faith for fifteen years. If the U.S. has a desire to settle the issue and a proposal for its solution, the P.R.C. will be prepared to receive a U.S. special envoy in Peking. This message has been reviewed by Chairman Mao and by Lin Piao.

Chou En-lai had also commented that in view of the fact that I had visited Bucharest in 1969 and Belgrade in 1970, I would be welcome in Peking.

We were encouraged by this message. As Kissinger noted, the tone was reassuringly free of invective, and the absence of any references to Vietnam indicated that Peking would not consider the war an insurmountable obstacle to U.S.–Chinese rapprochement.

I did my best to make sure that the Lam Son operation at the beginning of 1971 did not cut off this budding relationship as the Cambodian operation had threatened to do the year before. In a press conference on

February 17 I stressed that our intervention in Laos should not be interpreted as any threat to China. In Peking the *People's Daily,* the official government newspaper, vehemently rejected my statement: "By spreading the flames of war to the door of China, U.S. imperialism is on a course posing a grave menace to China. . . . Nixon has indeed fully laid bare his ferocious features, and reached the zenith in arrogance."

On February 25, 1971, five days after this tirade was published, I submitted to Congress my second Foreign Policy Report. This time a section dealing with the People's Republic of China canvassed the possibilities for an expanded relationship between our nations and reflected the eventuality of Peking's admission to the UN. It concluded:

> In the coming year, I will carefully examine what further steps we might take to create broader opportunities for contacts between the Chinese and American peoples, and how we might remove needless obstacles to the realization of these opportunities. We hope for, but will not be deterred by a lack of, reciprocity.
>
> We should, however, be totally realistic about the prospects. The People's Republic of China continues to convey to its own people and to the world its determination to cast us in the devil's role. Our modest efforts to prove otherwise have not reduced Peking's doctrinaire enmity toward us. . . . So long as Peking continues to be adamant for hostility, there is little we can do by ourselves to improve the relationship. What we can do, we will.

On March 15 the State Department announced the termination of all restrictions on the use of American passports for travel to mainland China. On April 6 a breakthrough occurred in a totally unexpected way: we received word from the American Embassy in Tokyo that an American table tennis team competing in the world championships in Japan had been invited to visit the P.R.C. in order to play several exhibition matches.

I was as surprised as I was pleased by this news. I had never expected that the China initiative would come to fruition in the form of a Ping-Pong team. We immediately approved the acceptance of the invitation, and the Chinese responded by granting visas to several Western newsmen to cover the team's tour.

On April 14 I announced the termination of the twenty-year-old embargo on trade between us. I also ordered a series of new steps taken for easing currency and shipping controls applying to the P.R.C. The same day Chou En-lai personally welcomed our table tennis players in Peking.

When I spoke to the convention of the American Society of Newspaper Editors in Washington, a few days later, I was asked about the meaning of the recent events involving the P.R.C. I replied that we were seeing an ordered policy process beginning to bear fruit. I said that I would have to disappoint the editors if they were looking for hot headline news, but the very nature of the new relationship made that impossible. I concluded with an observation that I am sure many of my listeners dismissed as simply a personal digression; in fact, it was a direct clue.

"The other day was Easter Sunday," I began. "Both of my daughters, Tricia and Julie, were there—and Tricia with Eddie Cox—I understand they are getting married this June—and Julie and David Eisenhower.

"And the conversation got around to travel and also, of course, with regard to honeymoon travel and the rest. They were asking me where would you like to go? Where do you think we ought to go?

"So, I sat back and thought a bit and said, 'Well, the place to go is to Asia.' I said, 'I hope that sometime in your life, sooner rather than later, you will be able to go to China to see the great cities, and the people, and all of that, there.'

"I hope they do. As a matter of fact, I hope sometime I do. I am not sure that it is going to happen while I am in office. I will not speculate with regard to either of the diplomatic points. It is premature to talk about recognition. It is premature also to talk about a change of our policy with regard to the United Nations."

At this point a bull in the form of Ted Agnew inadvertently careened into this diplomatic China shop. During a long postmidnight session with a group of reporters in his hotel room after he arrived for the Republican Governors Conference in Williamsburg, Virginia, Agnew told them that the favorable media coverage of the table tennis team's visit to Peking had helped the Communist Chinese government score a propaganda triumph. He noted that some reporters had sent back almost lyrical descriptions of the contented and productive lives led by the residents of Peking.

Agnew had expressed his reservations about our trade and visa overtures to the Chinese Communists at a recent NSC meeting, but I had never imagined that he would discuss his doubts with reporters. I told Haldeman to get word to Agnew to stay off this topic.

The tempo began to speed up considerably. On April 27 Ambassador Hilaly came to the White House with another message from Chou En-lai via President Yahya. After the ritual insistence that Taiwan was the principal and prerequisite problem, which had to be resolved before any relations could be restored, the message added that the Chinese were now interested in direct discussions as means of reaching that settlement, and therefore "the Chinese government reaffirms its willingness to receive publicly in Peking a special envoy of the President of the U.S. (for instance, Mr. Kissinger) or the U.S. Secretary of State or even the President of the U.S. himself for a direct meeting and discussion."

In some important respects this message raised as many problems as it solved. Taiwan was still mentioned as the central issue. Further, the Chinese spoke of publicly receiving an envoy in Peking. I felt that in order for the initiative to have any chance of succeeding, it would have to be kept totally secret until the final arrangements for the presidential visit had been agreed upon. With advance warning conservative opposition might mobilize in Congress and scuttle the entire effort.

Kissinger and I spent the next few days trying to decide who to send to Peking for these initial talks.

The best man, we agreed, would be David Bruce, but we ruled him out because he was our negotiator in Paris and the Chinese would undoubtedly resent our sending someone so closely identified with Vietnam. We also considered Cabot Lodge, but he was even more identified with Vietnam than was Bruce.

"Well, what about Bill then?" I asked. "If we send the Secretary of State, they'll sure as hell know we're serious." Kissinger rolled his eyes upward. I knew that he would have opposed Rogers on personal grounds regardless, but in this case he had good policy reasons. The Secretary of State had too high a profile for these first talks. Besides, there was almost no way he could go to China secretly.

Finally I said, "Henry, I think you will have to do it."

He objected that, like Rogers, he had too much visibility.

I said, "I am confident that a man who can come and go undetected in Paris can get in and out of Peking before anyone finds out."

At my news conference on April 29 I gave another major clue to what was afoot. But once again even the most rigorous monitors and analysts of Nixon rhetoric failed to pick up the point I was making.

Since none of the reporters had asked me anything about the specific possibility of a visit to China, I asked it of myself. At the end of my reply to a general question about our China policy, I said, "I would finally suggest—I know this question may come up if I don't answer it now—I hope, and, as a matter of fact, I expect to visit mainland China sometime in some capacity—I don't know what capacity. But that indicates what I hope for the long term. And I hope to contribute to a policy in which we can have a new relationship with mainland China."

About the same time the issue of *Life* containing Edgar Snow's December interview with Mao appeared on the newsstands. Now it was public that Mao would welcome me to Peking.

Messages and signals had been going back and forth for more than two years. We had proceeded carefully and cautiously through the Yahya and Romanian channels. Now Kissinger and I agreed that we had reached a point at which we had to take the chance of making a major proposal, or risk slipping back into another long round of tentative probing. I decided that the time had come to take the big step and propose a presidential visit.

On May 10, therefore, Kissinger called in Ambassador Hilaly and gave him a message for Chou En-lai via President Yahya. It stated that because of the importance I attached to the normalizing of relations between the two countries, I was prepared to accept Chou's invitation to visit Peking. I proposed that Kissinger undertake a secret visit in advance of my trip in order to arrange an agenda and begin a preliminary exchange of views.

The die was cast. There was nothing left to do but wait for Chou's reply. If we had acted too soon, if we had not established a sufficiently strong foundation, or if we had overestimated the ability of Mao and Chou to deal with their internal opposition to such a visit, then all our long careful efforts would be wasted. I might even have to be prepared for serious international embarrassment if the Chinese decided to reject my proposal and then publicize it.

For almost two weeks we waited, wondering what kind of decision-making process was under way in Peking.

Then on May 31 we received a message from President Yahya Khan through Ambassador Hilaly. It read:

1. There is a very encouraging and positive response to the last message.
2. Please convey to Mr. Kissinger that the meeting will take place on Chinese soil for which travel arrangements will be made by us.
3. Level of meeting will be as proposed by you.
4. Full message will be transmitted by safe means.

Two nights later, we gave a state dinner for President Somoza of Nicaragua. After Pat and I had finished having coffee with our guests in the Blue Room, I went to the Lincoln Sitting Room to do some paperwork and reading. In less than five minutes Kissinger walked in. He must have run most of the way from the West Wing, because he was out of breath.

He handed me two sheets of typewritten paper. "This just arrived in the Pakistani Embassy pouch," he said. "Hilaly rushed it over, and he was so excited when he gave it to me that his hands were shaking."

Kissinger stood beaming as I read the message:

> Premier Chou En-lai has seriously studied President Nixon's messages of April 29, May 17, and May 22, 1971, and has reported with much pleasure to Chairman Mao Tse-tung that President Nixon is prepared to accept his suggestion to visit Peking for direct conversations with the leaders of the

> People's Republic of China. Chairman Mao Tse-tung has indicated that he welcomes President Nixon's visit and looks forward to that occasion when he may have direct conversations with His Excellency the President, in which each side would be free to raise the principal issue of concern to it. . . .
>
> Premier Chou En-lai welcomes Dr. Kissinger to China as the U.S. representative who will come in advance for a preliminary secret meeting with high level Chinese officials to prepare and make necessary arrangements for President Nixon's visit to Peking.

"This is the most important communication that has come to an American President since the end of World War II," Kissinger said when I had finished reading.

For nearly an hour we talked about the China initiative—what it might mean to America and how delicately it must be handled lest we lose it. It was close to midnight before we noticed the time, and Kissinger rose to go.

"Henry, I know that, like me, you never have anything to drink after dinner, and it is very late," I said, "but I think this is one of those occasions when we should make an exception. Wait here just a minute."

I got up and walked down the corridor to the small family kitchen at the other end of the second floor. In one of the cabinets I found an unopened bottle of very old Courvoisier brandy that someone had given us for Christmas. I tucked it under my arm and took two large snifters from the glass cupboard. As we raised our glasses, I said, "Henry, we are drinking a toast not to ourselves personally or to our success, or to our administration's policies which have made this message and made tonight possible. Let us drink to generations to come who may have a better chance to live in peace because of what we have done."

As I write them now, my words sound rather formal, but the moment was one not just of high personal elation, but of a profound mutual understanding that this truly was a moment of historical significance.

On July 6 I flew to Kansas City to address a large group of Midwestern news media executives attending one of the periodic briefings on administration policies that we held in different parts of the country.

Kissinger was in the middle of a ten-day mission to the Far East and just days away from his secret trip to Peking. Before he got there I wanted to place on the record an outline of the reasons for approaching China.

I told the gathering that the potential of China, though obscured to most American observers by its isolation, was such that no sensible foreign policy could ignore or exclude it. "That is the reason why I felt that it was essential that this administration take the first steps toward ending the isolation of mainland China from the world community," I said. Despite the recent flurry of activity I said that I did not hold out any great hopes of rapid advances in our relations. "What we have done is simply opened the door—opened the door for travel, opened the door for trade," I said. "Now the question is whether there will be other doors opened on their part. . . . Mainland China, outside the world community, completely isolated, with its leaders not in communication with world leaders, would be a danger to the whole world that would be unacceptable, unacceptable to us and unacceptable to others as well. So consequently, this step must be taken now. Others must be taken, very precisely, very deliberately, as there is reciprocation on the other side."

My speech received relatively little attention in Kansas City. As we were to learn later, however, it received a great deal of attention in Peking.

We arranged that Kissinger would fly to Vietnam for consultations early in July and then stop in Pakistan on the way back. There he would develop a stomachache that would require him to stay in bed and not be seen by the press. Then, with President Yahya's cooperation, he would be taken to an airport where a Pakistani jet would fly him over the mountains into China. The stomachache was scheduled for July 9–11. Kissinger would then fly to San Clemente to report to me.

Kissinger's trip was given the codename Polo after Marco Polo, another Western traveler who made history by journeying to China. Everything went without a hitch. His indisposition in Islamabad received only minor attention from reporters covering him. They accepted the story that he would be confined to bed for at least a couple of days and began making arrangements for their own entertainment.

Because of the need for complete secrecy and the lack of any direct communications facilities between Peking and Washington, I knew that we would have no word from Kissinger while he was in China. Even after he had returned to Pakistan it would still be important to maintain secrecy, so before Kissinger left, we agreed on a single codeword—Eureka—which he would use if his mission were successful and the presidential trip had been arranged.

Although I was confident that the Chinese were as ready for my trip as we were, I did not underestimate the tremendous problems that Taiwan and Vietnam posed for both sides, and I tried to discipline myself not to expect anything lest I begin to expect too much.

On July 11 Al Haig, who knew our codeword, phoned me to say that a cable from Kissinger had arrived.

"What's the message?" I asked.

"Eureka," he replied.

Kissinger's description of his time in China was fascinating. The Chinese had agreed to virtually everything we proposed regarding the arrangements and schedule for my trip. The preliminary talks had covered the whole range of issues and problems that lay between our two countries. He found the Chinese tough, idealistic, fanatical, single-minded, remarkable, and uncomfortably aware of the philosophical contradictions involved in their arranging a visit by their capitalist archenemy. "These were men in some anguish," Kissinger said.

Most of all, Kissinger was impressed by Chou En-lai. The two men spent seventeen hours together in meetings and informal conversation, and Kissinger found that "he was equally at home in philosophic sweeps, historical analysis, tactical probing, light repartee. His command of facts, and in particular his knowledge of American events, was remarkable." At one point Chou asked about my Kansas City speech, and Kissinger had to admit that he had read only the press reports. The next morning at breakfast Kissinger found a copy of my speech, with Chou's underlinings and marginal notations in Chinese, lying on the table with a note requesting that he return it because it was Chou's only copy.

In a brilliant summing up of his long report after the trip, Kissinger wrote:

> We have laid the groundwork for you and Mao to turn a page in history. But we should have no illusions about the future. Profound differences and years of isolation yawn between us and the Chinese. They will be tough before and during the summit on the question of Taiwan and other major issues. And they will prove implacable foes if our relations turn sour. My assessment of these people is that they are deeply ideological, close to fanatic in the intensity of their beliefs. At the same time they display an inward security that allows them, within the framework of their principles, to be meticulous and reliable in dealing with others. . . .
>
> Our dealings, both with the Chinese and others, will require reliability, precision, finesse. If we can master this process, we will have made a revolution.

On July 15 I made the televised announcement that I would be going to Peking. Most of the initial reactions were overwhelmingly positive. Max Lerner wrote, "The politics of surprise leads through the Gates of Astonishment into the Kingdom of Hope."

Some commentators joined the more partisan Democrats in tempering their praise with speculation that my motives had been political. Most of the serious criticism, however, came, as I had expected, from the conservatives. Congressman John Schmitz of California charged me with "surrendering to international communism" by accepting the invitation. George Wallace did not actually condemn the trip, but he warned me against "begging, pleading, and groveling" before the Chinese Communists. He told reporters that he suspected the trip was actually a diversionary tactic to get people's minds off "inflation and the high cost of pork chops."

The reaction abroad to our China initiative was generally favorable, but there were some understandable reservations. Our friends in Taiwan were terribly distressed. However, they were reassured that we did not withdraw our recognition of their government and did not renounce our mutual defense commitment. The Japanese presented a particularly difficult problem. They resented the fact that they had not been informed in advance, but we had no other choice. We could not have informed them without informing others, thus risking a leak that might have aborted the entire initiative.

As soon as I returned to Washington from San Clemente, I held a briefing for the bipartisan leadership in the Cabinet Room. I stressed the need for secrecy, because the more we had to put things into words, the less freedom of movement we would have in our dealings with the Chinese. I understood how difficult it would be for many of them, but I had to ask that they trust me. To a man, they came through splendidly. John Stennis said, "The President has made a good move; now it's up to him to follow through, and I'm going to back him up."

Mike Mansfield said, that the China initiative was like the Manhattan Project: secrecy was absolutely essential to the success of each.

Kissinger returned to China on October 20 for Polo II. This time his six-day trip was publicly announced. Its purpose was to prepare the agenda for the meetings I would have with the Chinese leaders and to work out the basic language of the communiqué that would be issued at the end of my trip.

The draft communiqué that I had approved for submission to the Chinese had followed the standard diplomatic formula of using vague and conciliatory language to patch over the most heated and insoluble problems.

Kissinger was somewhat taken aback when Chou stated that our approach to the communiqué was unacceptable. He said that unless it expressed our fundamental differences, the wording would have an "untruthful appearance." He dismissed our proposed draft as the sort of banal document the Soviets would sign without meaning it and without planning to observe it.

The Chinese then handed Kissinger a counterdraft that took his breath away. If ours had smoothed over differences, theirs underscored them. With great self-control, Kissinger read it and calmly said, "We cannot have an American President sign a document which says that revolution has become the irresistible trend of history, or that 'the people's revolutionary struggles are just'!"

The Chinese seemed disconcerted, but Kissinger continued. We could not allow any references to racial discrimination; we opposed it as much as did the Chinese, but mention in this communiqué would be interpreted as criticism of American domestic problems. Similarly, their proposed references to China as "the reliable rear area" of North Vietnam, and to Chinese support for the Indochinese peoples' "fighting to the end for the attainment of their goal" were unacceptable phrasing while Americans were fighting or being held prisoner in Indochina.

After this initial session, Kissinger found that the Chinese were willing to compromise on a communiqué that would state the underlying goals of the summit while retaining each side's basic position expressed in noninflammatory language.

Kissinger summed up these long and sometimes difficult sessions by saying that the Chinese were willing to pursue their objectives by banking on the thrust of history rather than on the specific wording of a communiqué. "They will continue to be tough," he wrote, "but they essentially accept our arguments that we can often do more than we say, that the process must be gradual, and that some issues must be left to evolutionary pressures. This involves great risks for them, at home and abroad, given their past public demands and dissidents in their own camp."

Kissinger reported that toward the end of the talks Chou had specifically pointed out that they could be in real trouble if my administration was not in power. "He shares what he described as your wish that you preside over the 200th anniversary of America's birth."

While Kissinger was in China on Polo II, the United Nations General Assembly moved to vote on the question of admitting the People's Republic of China as a member nation. I instructed Kissinger to stay away an extra day so that he would not have just arrived home when this controversial vote was taken.

As early as August we had publicly withdrawn our opposition to consideration of this question and indicated our support of the concept of the "two Chinas," Chiang Kai-shek's Republic of China on Taiwan and the Communist People's Republic of China, each to have membership in the world organization.

It had not been easy for me to take a position that would be so disappointing to our old friend and loyal ally, Chiang. I had learned as early as the spring, however, that the traditional vote bloc opposed to Peking's admission had irreparably broken up, and several of our erstwhile supporters had decided to support Peking at the next vote. Personally, I have never believed in bowing to the inevitable just because it is inevitable. In this case, however, I felt that the national security interests of the United States lay in developing our relations with the P.R.C. Besides, regardless of what happened in the UN, I was determined to honor our treaty obligations by continuing our military and economic support for an independent Taiwan.

On October 25 the UN voted 76 to 35, with 17 abstentions, to expel Taiwan and to admit the P.R.C. as the sole government representing China. This went much further than we had expected: we had thought that our greatest problem would be in convincing Taiwan to stay after the P.R.C. had been admitted to equal status.

A few days before leaving for China, I invited the great French writer and philosopher André Malraux to the White House.

Malraux had known Mao Tse-tung and Chou En-lai in China during the 1930s and had kept up intermittent contact with them through the years. His description of the Chinese leaders in his *Anti-Memoirs* was among the most valuable and fascinating reading I had done in preparation for my trip.

Malraux was then seventy years old. Time had not dimmed the brilliance of his thought or the quickness of his wit. Even after his elegant French had been filtered through a State Department interpreter, his language was original and striking.

During the talk I had with him in the Oval Office, I asked whether just a few years ago he would have thought that the Chinese leaders would agree to meet with an American President.

"This meeting was inevitable," he replied.

"Even with the Vietnam war?" I asked.

"Ah yes, even so. China's action over Vietnam is an imposture. There was a period when the friendship between China and Russia was cloudless, when they allowed Russian arms to pass over their territory on the way to Vietnam. But China has never helped anyone! Not Pakistan. Not Vietnam. China's foreign policy is a brilliant lie! The Chinese themselves do not believe in it; they believe only in China. Only China!

"For Mao, China is a continent—it is an Australia by itself. Only China is important. If China has to receive the Sultan of Zanzibar, then China will. Or the President of the United States. The Chinese don't care."

I asked Malraux for his impressions of Mao. "Five years ago," he said, "Mao had one fear: that the Americans or the Russians, with ten atom bombs, would destroy China's industrial centers and set China back fifty years at a time when Mao himself would be dead. He told me, 'When I have six atomic bombs, no one can bomb my cities.' " Malraux said that he had not understood what Mao meant by that. He continued, "Then Mao said, 'The Americans will never use an atom bomb against me.' I did not understand that either, but I am repeating it for you because often it is what one does not understand that is most important. I did not ask Mao any more questions about it, because one does not ask Mao questions."

Malraux rushed on with a torrent of words and ideas.

"You will be dealing with a colossus," he said, "but a colossus facing death. The last time I saw him he told me, 'We do not have a successor.' Do you know what Mao will think when he sees you for the first time?" he asked. "He will think, 'He is so much younger than I!' "

That evening at a dinner in his honor in the Residence, Malraux advised me on how to approach my conversation with Mao.

"Mr. President, you will meet a man who has had a fantastic destiny and who believes that he is acting out the last act of his lifetime. You may think he is talking to you, but he will in truth be addressing Death. . . . It's worth the trip!"

I asked him again what came after Mao. Malraux replied, "It is exactly as Mao said, he has no successor. What did he mean by it? He meant that in his view the great leaders—Churchill, Gandhi, de Gaulle—were created by the kind of traumatic historical events that will not occur in the world anymore. In that sense he feels that he has no successors. I once asked him if he did not think of himself as the heir of the last great Chinese emperors of the sixteenth century. Mao said, 'But of course I am their heir.' Mr. President, you operate within a rational framework, but Mao does not. There is something of the sorcerer in him. He is a man inhabited by a vision, possessed by it."

I remarked that this kind of mystique was present in many great men. People who knew Lincoln said that they always felt he was looking beyond the horizon—as if there were a space between the earth and the sky where his gaze was focused. On the day of his assassination he had told his Cabinet about a dream he had the night before: he had seemed to be in some "singular indescribable vessel" moving with great rapidity toward an indefinite shore. "We don't know where or what the shore is but we must avoid the shoals in trying to reach it," I said.

Malraux said, "You have spoken of avoiding the shoals to reach the shore. I feel that Mao has the same view. And even though both you and he are aware of the shoals, neither of you knows what lies on the shore beyond. Mao knows, however, that his harbor is Death."

Later, over coffee, Malraux told me, "You are about to attempt one of the most important things of our century. I think of the sixteenth-century explorers, who set out for a specific objective but often arrived at an entirely different discovery. What you are going to do, Mr. President, might well have a totally different outcome from whatever is anticipated."

At the end of the evening I escorted Malraux to his car. As we stood on the steps of the North Portico, he turned to me and said, "I am not de Gaulle, but I know what de Gaulle would say if he were here. He would say: 'All men who understand what you are embarking upon salute you!' "

On February 17, 1972, at 10:35 A.M. we left Andrews Air Force Base for Peking. As the plane gathered speed and then took to the air, I thought of Malraux's words. We were embarking upon a voyage of philosophical discovery as uncertain, and in some respects as perilous, as the voyages of geographical discovery of a much earlier time.

Diary

As Henry and Bob both pointed out on the plane, there was almost a religious feeling to the messages we received from all over the country, wishing us well. I told Henry that I thought it was really a question of the American people being hopelessly and almost naïvely for peace, even at any price. He felt that perhaps there was also some ingredient of excitement about the boldness of the move, and visiting a land that was unknown to so many Americans.

We stopped briefly in Shanghai to take aboard Chinese Foreign Ministry officials and a Chinese navigator; an hour and a half later we prepared to land in Peking. I looked out the window. It was winter, and the countryside was drab and gray. The small towns and villages looked like pictures I had seen of towns in the Middle Ages.

Our plane landed smoothly, and a few minutes later we came to a stop in front of the terminal. The door was opened, and Pat and I stepped out.

Chou En-lai stood at the foot of the ramp, hatless in the cold. Even a heavy overcoat did not hide the thinness of his frail body. When we were about halfway down the steps, he began to clap. I paused for a moment and then returned the gesture, according to the Chinese custom.

I knew that Chou had been deeply insulted by Foster Dulles's refusal to shake hands with him at the Geneva Conference in 1954. When I reached the bottom step, therefore, I made a point of extending my hand as I walked toward him. When our hands met, one era ended and another began.

After being introduced to all the Chinese officials, I stood on Chou's left while the band played the anthems. "The Star-Spangled Banner" had never sounded so stirring to me as on that windswept runway in the heart of Communist China.

The honor guard was one of the finest I have ever seen. They were big men, strong-looking, and immaculately turned out. As I walked down the long line, each man turned his head slowly as I passed, creating an almost hypnotic sense of movement in the massed ranks.

Chou and I rode into the city in a curtained car. As we left the airport, he said, "Your handshake came over the vastest ocean in the world —twenty-five years of no communication." When we came into Tienamen Square at the center of Peking, he pointed out some of the buildings; I noticed that the streets were empty.

Madame Chou was waiting for us when we arrived at the two large government guesthouses where our official party was to stay. We had tea in the sitting room, and then Chou said that he was sure everyone would like to rest before the state banquet.

About an hour later I was getting ready to take a shower when Kissinger burst in with the news that Chairman Mao wanted to meet me. Late that night I described the atmosphere of the meeting.

Diary

Coming in on the plane Rogers had expressed concern that we ought to have a meeting with Mao very soon, and that we couldn't be in a position of my seeing him in a way that put him above me, like walking up the stairs or him standing at the top of the stairs.

Our concerns in this respect were completely dissipated at about two o'clock when Henry came into the room breathlessly, and told me that Chou was downstairs and said that the Chairman wanted to see me now at his residence. I waited about five minutes while Henry went downstairs, and then we drove to the residence.

We were escorted into a room that was not elaborate, filled with books and papers. Several of the books were open to various pages on the coffee table next to where he was sitting. His girl secretary helped him to his feet. When I shook his hand, he said, "I can't talk very well." Chou later told me that he had been sick for about a month with what was described as bronchitis. This, however, was not known to the Chinese public.

Everybody, including Chou, showed him the deference that was due him. Two or three of the military and the civilian people were standing in the room, and about ten minutes through the conversation Chou waved them out. I noted, however, that they remained standing in the hall watching.

The transcript of the conversation may not have caught probably the most moving moment, when he reached out his hand, and I reached out mine, and he held it for about a minute.

> It is obvious that he has a remarkable sense of humor. He kept bringing Henry into the conversation, and while it was supposed to be ten or fifteen minutes it extended to almost an hour. I saw Chou look at his watch two or three times and realized that I probably should break it up in order not to tax him too much.
>
> It was interesting to note that later at the plenary session, Chou constantly referred back to the meeting with Mao and what Mao had said.

Several Chinese photographers had rushed in ahead of us in order to record our first meeting. We all sat in overstuffed armchairs set in a semicircle at the end of the long room. While the photographers continued to bustle around, we exchanged bantering small talk. Kissinger remarked that he had assigned Mao's writings to his classes at Harvard. Indulging in characteristic self-deprecation, Mao said, "These writings of mine aren't anything. There is nothing instructive in what I wrote." I said, "The Chairman's writings moved a nation and have changed the world." Mao, however, replied, "I haven't been able to change it. I've only been able to change a few places in the vicinity of Peking."

Although Mao spoke with some difficulty, it was clear that his mind was moving like lightning. "Our common old friend Generalissimo Chiang Kai-shek doesn't approve of this," he said, with a sweeping gesture that might have meant our meeting or that might have taken in all China. "He calls us Communist bandits. He recently made a speech. Have you seen it?"

"Chiang Kai-shek calls the Chairman a bandit," I replied. "What does the Chairman call Chiang Kai-shek?"

Mao chuckled when my question was translated, but it was Chou who answered. "Generally speaking, we call them 'Chiang Kai-shek's clique,'" he said. "In the newspapers sometimes we call him a bandit; he calls us bandits in turn. Anyway, we abuse each other."

"Actually," Mao said, "the history of our friendship with him is much longer than the history of your friendship with him."

Mao remarked on Kissinger's cleverness in keeping his first trip to Peking secret. "He doesn't look like a secret agent," I said. "He is the only man in captivity who could go to Paris twelve times and Peking once, and no one knew it—except possibly a couple of pretty girls."

"They didn't know it," Kissinger interjected, "I used it as a cover."

"In Paris?" Mao asked with mock disbelief.

"Anyone who uses pretty girls as a cover must be the greatest diplomat of all time," I said.

"So you often make use of your girls?" Mao asked.

"*His* girls, not mine," I replied. "It would get me into great trouble if I used girls as a cover."

"Especially during an election," Chou remarked as Mao joined in the laughter.

Referring to our presidential election, Mao said that in honesty he had to tell me that if the Democrats won the Chinese would deal with them.

"We understand," I said. "We will hope that we don't give you that problem."

"I voted for you during your last election," Mao said with a broad smile.

"When the Chairman says he voted for me," I replied, "he voted for the lesser of two evils."

"I like rightists," Mao responded, obviously enjoying himself. "People say that you are rightists—that the Republican Party is on the right—that Prime Minister Heath is also to the right."

"And General de Gaulle," I added.

Without dropping a beat, Mao said, "De Gaulle is a different question." Then he continued, "They also say the Christian Democratic Party of West Germany is to the right. I am comparatively happy when these people on the right come into power."

"I think the most important thing to note is that in America, at least at this time, those on the right can do what those on the left can only talk about," I said.

When the conversation moved to the history of our meeting, Mao remarked, "The former President of Pakistan introduced President Nixon to us. At that time, our ambassador in Pakistan refused to agree to our having any contact with you. He said that President Nixon was no better than President Johnson. But President Yahya said, 'The two men cannot be compared.' He said that one was like a gangster—he meant President Johnson. I don't know how he got that impression, although we on our side were not very happy with your former Presidents, beginning with Truman through Johnson. In between there were eight years of a Republican President. During that period probably you hadn't thought things out either."

"Mr. Chairman," I said, "I am aware of the fact that over a period of years my position with regard to the People's Republic was one that the Chairman and the Prime Minister totally disagreed with. What brings us together is a recognition of a new situation in the world and a recognition on our part that what is important is not a nation's internal political philosophy. What is important is its policy toward the rest of the world and toward us."

Although the meeting with Mao dealt mainly with what he called the "philosophy" of our new and potential relationship, I raised in general terms the major substantive questions we would be discussing. I said that we should examine our policies and determine how they should develop in order to deal with the entire world as well as the immediate problems of Korea, Vietnam, and Taiwan.

I went on, "We, for example, must ask ourselves—again in the confines of this room—why the Soviets have more forces on the border facing you than they do on the border facing Western Europe? We must ask ourselves, What is the future of Japan? Is it better—and here I know we have disagreements—from China's standpoint for Japan to be neutral and totally defenseless, or is it better for Japan to have some mutual defense relations with the United States? One thing is sure—we can leave no vacuums, because they can be filled. The Prime Minister, for example, has pointed out that the United States 'reaches out its hands' and that the Soviet Union 'reaches out its hands.' The question is, which danger does the People's Republic of China face? Is it the danger of American aggression—or of Soviet aggression? These are hard questions, but we have to discuss them."

Mao was animated and following every nuance of the conversation, but I could see that he was also becoming very tired. Chou had been discreetly glancing at his watch with increasing frequency, so I decided that I should try to bring the session to a close.

"I would like to say, as we finish, Mr. Chairman, that we know you and the Prime Minister have taken great risks in inviting us here. For us also it was a difficult decision. But having read some of your statements, I know that you are one who sees when an opportunity comes, and then knows that you must seize the hour and seize the day."

Mao's face beamed when the translator came to these words from his own poem.

I continued, "I would also like to say in a personal sense—and I also say this to you, Mr. Prime Minister—you do not know me. Since you do not know me, you shouldn't trust me. You will find I never say something I cannot do. And I always will do more than I can say. On this basis, I want to have frank talks with the Chairman and, of course, with the Prime Minister."

Mao pointed toward Kissinger and said, " 'Seize the hour and seize the day.' I think that, generally speaking, people like me sound like a lot of big cannons!" Chou laughed, and it was clear that we were in for another bit of self-deprecation. "For example, things like, 'The whole world should unite and defeat imperialism, revisionism, and all reactionaries, and establish socialism.' "

"Like me," I said. "And bandits."

Mao leaned forward and smiled. "But perhaps you as an individual may not be among those to be overthrown," he said. Motioning toward

Kissinger, he continued, "They say that he is also among those not to be overthrown personally. If all of you are overthrown, we wouldn't have any more friends left."

"Mr. Chairman," I said, "your life is well known to all of us. You came from a very poor family to the top of the most populous nation in the world, a great nation.

"My background is not so well known. I also came from a very poor family, and to the top of a very great nation. History has brought us together. The question is whether we, with different philosophies, but both with feet on the ground, and having come from the people, can make a breakthrough that will serve not just China and America, but the whole world in the years ahead. And that is why we are here."

As we were leaving, Mao said, "Your book, *Six Crises,* is not a bad book."

Looking at Chou, I smiled and shook my head and said, "He reads too much."

Mao walked us to the door. His walk was a slow shuffle, and he said that he had not been feeling well.

"But you look very good," I replied.

"Appearances are deceiving," he said with a slight shrug.

The first plenary session with Chou at the Great Hall of the People was cut short because of the unscheduled meeting with Mao, and we talked only in general terms about the way our meetings would proceed. Chou preferred a format in which one side presented its views on a subject at one session and the other side responded at the next.

The most difficult and touchiest part of the trip would be the joint communiqué, and I reaffirmed our pragmatic approach to it. "The conventional way to handle a meeting at the summit like this, while the whole world is watching," I said, "is to have meetings for several days, which we will have, to have discussions and discover differences, which we will do, and then put out a weasel-worded communiqué covering up the problems."

"If we were to act like that we would be not only deceiving the people, but we would be deceiving ourselves," Chou replied.

"That is adequate when meetings are between states that do not affect the future of the world," I said, "but we would not be meeting our responsibility for meetings which the whole world is watching, and which will affect our friends in the Pacific and all over the world for years to come. As we begin these meetings we have no illusions that we will solve everything. But we can set in motion a process which will enable us to solve many of these problems in the future. The men in this room and the women in this room have fought a long hard struggle for a revolution which has succeeded. We know you believe deeply in your principles, and we believe deeply in our principles. We do not ask you to compromise your principles, just as you would not ask us to compromise ours."

Perhaps the mention of opposing principles triggered the thought, because Chou remarked, "As you said to Chairman Mao this afternoon, today we shook hands," he said. "But John Foster Dulles didn't want to do that."

"But you said you didn't want to shake hands with him," I countered.

"Not necessarily," Chou replied. "I would have."

"Well, *we* will shake hands," I said, and once again we shook hands across the table.

Chou seemed to warm to the subject, and he continued. "Dulles's assistant, Mr. Walter Bedell Smith, wanted to do differently, but he did not break the discipline of John Foster Dulles, so he had to hold a cup of coffee in his right hand. Since one doesn't shake hands with the left hand, he used it to shake my arm." Everyone laughed, including Chou. "But at that time, we couldn't blame you," he said, "because the international viewpoint was that the socialist countries were a monolithic bloc, and the Western countries were also a monolithic bloc. Now we understand that that is not the case."

"We have broken out of the old pattern," I agreed. "We look at each country in terms of its own conduct rather than lumping them all together and saying that because they have this kind of philosophy they are all in utter darkness. I would say in honesty to the Prime Minister that my views, because I was in the Eisenhower administration, were similar to those of Mr. Dulles at that time. But the world has changed since then, and the relationship between the People's Republic and the United States must change too. As the Prime Minister has said in a meeting with Dr. Kissinger, the helmsman must ride with the waves or he will be submerged with the tide."

By the time we met for the banquet at the Great Hall of the People an hour later, the Chinese group seemed to be much more at ease. Perhaps it was because Mao had now given his official blessing to the visit—or perhaps it was simply that we had already begun to get along well with each other.

In my toast I tried to give idealistic expression to the pragmatic underpinnings of the China initiative:

> We have at times in the past been enemies. We have great differences today. What brings us together is that we have common interests which transcend those differences. As we discuss our differences, neither of us will compromise our principles. But while we cannot close the gulf between us, we can try to bridge it so that we may be able to talk across it.

> So, let us, in these next five days, start a long march together, not in lockstep, but on different roads leading to the same goal, the goal of building a world structure of peace and justice. . . . The world watches. The world listens. The world waits to see what we will do. . . .
>
> There is no reason for us to be enemies. Neither of us seeks the territory of the other; neither of us seeks domination over the other; neither of us seeks to stretch out our hands and rule the world.
>
> Chairman Mao has written, 'So many deeds cry out to be done, and always urgently. The world rolls on. Time passes. Ten thousand years are too long. Seize the day, seize the hour.'
>
> This is the hour, this is the day for our two peoples to rise to the heights of greatness which can build a new and a better world.

After the toasts, the orchestra played "America the Beautiful," and I remarked that this was one of the songs I had chosen for my inauguration in 1969. Chou raised his glass and said, "Here's to your next inauguration!"

When we met at the Great Hall of the People the next afternoon I reminded Chou that despite what he might be reading in some American press reports of the trip, I had no sentimental illusions about what was going on: "Now we say, and most of our rather naïve American press buys this line, that the new relationship between China and America is due to the fact we have a basic friendship between our peoples. But the Prime Minister knows and I know that friendship—which I feel we do have on a personal basis—cannot be the basis on which an established relationship must rest; not friendship alone. I recall that a professor of law when I was a first-year student said that a contract was only as good as the will of the parties concerned to keep it."

Chou sat motionless, his face intent but impassive.

"I believe the interests of China as well as the interests of the United States urgently require that we maintain our military establishment at approximately its present levels," I said. "And, with certain exceptions which we can discuss later, I believe that we should maintain a military presence in Europe, in Japan, and also maintain our naval forces in the Pacific. I believe that the interests of China are just as great as those of the United States on that point."

As I had intended, this statement created a slight stir on the Chinese side of the table.

"Let me now make what I trust will not be taken as an invidious comparison," I continued. "By religion I am a Quaker, although not a very good one, and I believe in peace. All of my instincts are against a big military establishment and also against military adventures. As I indicated a moment ago, the Prime Minister is one of the world's leading spokesmen for his philosophy, and so he has to be opposed to powers such as the United States maintaining huge military establishments. But each of us has to put the survival of his nation first, and if the United States were to reduce its military strength, and if we were to withdraw from the areas of the world which I have mentioned, the dangers to the United States would be great—and the dangers to China would be even greater.

"I do not impute any motives to the present leaders of the Soviet Union," I said. "I have to respect what they say. But I must make policy on the basis of what they do. And in terms of the nuclear power balance, the Soviet Union has been moving ahead at a very alarming rate over the past four years. I have determined that the United States must not fall behind. If we did, our shield of protection for Europe, and for the nations of the Pacific with which we have treaties, would be worthless."

Applying this approach to the question of America's relationship with Japan, I said that the Chinese had framed their position on the subject in terms of their ideology and philosophy: they called for the withdrawal of American troops from Japan and the abrogation of our treaty of mutual defense, thus leaving Japan neutral and unarmed.

"I think that the Prime Minister, in terms of his philosophy, has taken exactly the correct position with respect to Japan," I said, "and I think that he has to continue to take it. But I want him to understand why I think strongly that *our* policy with respect to Japan is in the security interests of his country even though it is opposed to the philosophic doctrine which he espouses.

"The United States can get out of Japanese waters, but others will still fish there. If we were to leave Japan naked and defenseless, they would have to turn to others for help or build the capability to defend themselves. If we had no defense arrangement with Japan, we would have no influence where they were concerned.

"If the United States is gone from Asia, gone from Japan," I said, "our protests, no matter how loud, would be like firing an empty cannon. We would have no effect, because thousands of miles away is just too far to be heard.

"Now I realize that I have painted here a picture which makes me sound like an old cold warrior," I continued, and Chou laughed softly. "But it is the world as I see it, and when I analyze it, it is what brings us, China and America, together, not in terms of philosophy and not in terms of friendship—although I believe that is important—but because of national security I believe our interests are in common in the respects I have mentioned."

The Chinese regarded the Soviet Union with a mixture of utter contempt and healthy fear. Chou was completely aware of the symbolism and impact of my coming to Peking before going to Moscow, and he thoroughly enjoyed the fulminations of the Soviet press against my visit. "You have come here first," he said, "and Moscow is carrying on like anything! They are mobilizing a whole mass of their people, their followers, to curse us. But let them go on. We don't care."

Later on, when he had loosened up considerably, he told an amusing story that he said took place during a Sino-Soviet border flare-up in 1969. "We had a hot line between the Soviet Union and ourselves then," he said, "but it had already become cold because the Kremlin never used it. At the time of the Chen Pao border incident, however, Kosygin picked it up and called us. When our operator answered, he said, 'This is Premier Kosygin. I would like to speak to Chairman Mao.' The operator, completely on his own, said, 'You are a revisionist, and therefore I will not connect you.' So Kosygin said, 'Well, if you will not try to reach the Chairman, will you please connect me with Prime Minister Chou.' But the operator gave the same unauthorized reply and broke the connection."

About halfway through the meeting Chou took some small white pills. I guessed that they were for his high blood pressure. I was impressed by his mental acuity and his stamina; I noticed that some of the younger men on both sides became drowsy as the afternoon lengthened and the translators droned on and on, but despite his seventy-three years Chou remained alert and attentive throughout the four-hour session.

"The most pressing question now is Indochina, where the whole world is watching," he said. "The Democratic Party tried to put you on the spot by alleging that you came to China to settle Vietnam. Of course this is not possible. We are not in a position to settle it in talks."

I said that I fully understood the limitations of our talks and that I had no illusions about being able to settle the Indochina war in Peking. "This is simply an issue in which the only gainer in having the war continue is the Soviet Union," I said. "They want us tied down, because they want to get more and more influence in North Vietnam as a result. From all the intelligence we get, they may even be egging on the North Vietnamese to hold out and not settle."

Chou made clear that, in his opinion, the later we withdrew from Vietnam, the more difficult and unsatisfactory the withdrawal would be for us. He knew the tenacity of the North Vietnamese. "Ho Chi Minh was a very old friend of mine," he said. "I knew him in France in 1922." Chou pointed out that I had admitted that de Gaulle acted wisely in withdrawing from Algeria; despite the domestic political difficulties that a similar decision would cause me, he felt that it was nonetheless the right thing to do regarding Vietnam. He said, "Our position is that so long as you are continuing your Vietnamization, Laosization, and Cambodianization policy, and as long as they continue fighting, we can do nothing but to continue to support them."

When I summarized the American position, I said: "Let me cut away the eight points, the five points, and the thirteen points and all the other points and come right down to what our offer really is. If I were sitting across the table from whoever is the leader of North Vietnam and we could negotiate a cease-fire and the return of our prisoners, then all Americans would be withdrawn from Vietnam six months from that day. And let me also point out that when this was suggested to the North Vietnamese as far back as the middle of last year, they rejected it and insisted there had to be a settlement in which we had to impose a political settlement as well as to resolve the military side."

I said, "I realize that there are views to the contrary, but when a nation is in a position like we are in, where around the world there are nations that depend on us for their defense, if we did not behave honorably we would cease to be a nation worth having as a friend, and which the people of the world could depend upon as an ally."

While I was in these meetings with Chou, Pat carried out a full schedule that included visits to the Peking Zoo and the Summer Palace. When we met at the guesthouse that evening, she remarked that although the Chinese she had met were gracious and eager to cooperate, she felt that our reception was somehow restrained. She had been kept from meeting people, and the only contact she had had with anyone other than her official guides was on a visit to the kitchen of the Peking Hotel. We discussed the tremendous problems our visit presented to the Chinese leadership, not just in terms of their relations with the Soviet Union, North Vietnam, and the entire Communist world, but also in terms of their own internal politics. Two decades of virulent anti-American propaganda could not be undone overnight, and the Chinese masses would take time to assimilate the new line emanating from Peking.

That night we were taken to the Peking Opera by Chou and by Chiang Ching, Mao Tse-tung's wife. They had arranged a special performance of the theatrical extravaganza *The Red Detachment of Women,* which she had devised and staged.

From briefing material I was aware that Chiang Ching was an ideological fanatic who had strongly opposed my trip. She had led a checkered and contradictory life, from her younger days as an aspiring actress to her leadership of the radical forces in the Cultural Revolution of 1966. For many years she had been Mao's wife in name only, but there was no better name in China, and she had used it for all it was worth to build up her personal faction of supporters.

As we settled into our chairs, Chou mentioned that in 1965 Khrushchev had come to a performance of this show and had sat in the very place I was now sitting. He suddenly became flustered and corrected himself: "I mean Kosygin, not Khrushchev."

While we waited for the overture to begin, Chiang Ching told me about some American authors she had read. She had enjoyed *Gone with the Wind* and had seen the motion picture. She mentioned John Steinbeck, and she asked me why another of her favorite authors, Jack London, had committed suicide. I couldn't remember, but I told her that I thought it was alcoholism. She asked about Walter Lippmann and said that she had read some of his articles.

Chiang Ching had none of the easy humor or warmth of Mao, Chou, and the other men I met. I had observed the same characteristic in the young women who acted as interpreters and in several others we met during our week in China. The women of the movement, it struck me, were more humorless and more single-minded in their total dedication to the ideology than were the men. In fact, Chiang Ching was unpleasantly abrasive and aggressive. At one point that evening she turned to me and in a challenging voice asked, "Why did you not come to China before now?" Since the ballet was in progress at the time, I did not respond.

I had not been particularly looking forward to this ballet, but after a few minutes I was impressed by its dazzling technical and theatrical virtuosity. Chiang Ching had been undeniably successful in her attempt to create a consciously propagandistic theatre piece that would both entertain and inspire its audience. The result was a hybrid combining elements of opera, operetta, musical comedy, classical ballet, modern dance, and gymnastics.

The story deals with a young Chinese woman in prerevolutionary times who leads her townspeople in a revolt against an oppressive landlord. Emotionally and dramatically the production was superficial and artificial. In many respects, as I noted in my diary, it reminded me of the ballet *Spartacus* that we had seen in Leningrad in 1959—in which the ending was changed so that the slaves won.

After each evening's social event Kissinger would meet with the Vice Foreign Minister and go over each new draft of the official communiqué word by word. Sometimes Chou would join them; sometimes Kissinger would walk across the small bridge connecting the two guesthouses and report to me on the progress they were making or the problems they had run up against. As a result of these nocturnal negotiations, few of us got very much sleep, and Kissinger got hardly any.

Taiwan was the touchstone for both sides. We felt that we should not and could not abandon the Taiwanese; we were committed to Taiwan's right to exist as an independent nation. The Chinese were equally determined to use the communiqué to assert their unequivocal claim to the island. This was the kind of disagreement that our formula for drafting the communiqué was supposed to take into account: we could state our position and they could state theirs. In this case, domestic political considerations led Kissinger and me to try to convince the Chinese of the necessity of exercising moderation.

We knew that if the Chinese made a strongly belligerent claim to Taiwan in the communiqué, I would come under murderous cross fire from any or all the various pro-Taiwan, anti-Nixon, and anti-P.R.C. lobbies and interest groups at home. If these groups found common ground on the eve of the presidential elections, the entire China initiative might be turned into a partisan issue. Then, if I lost the election, whether because of this particular factor or not, my successor might not be able to continue developing the relationship between Washington and Peking. In the official plenary sessions with Chou, therefore, I spoke very frankly about the practical political problems a strongly worded communiqué on Taiwan would cause me.

We knew that no agreement concerning Taiwan could be reached at this time. While both sides could agree that Taiwan was a part of China —a position supported by both the Peking and Taiwan governments— we would have to oppose the use of military force by Peking to bring Taiwan under Communist rule.

Our lengthy discussions resulted as we expected: we could only agree to disagree and to reflect our differences in the communiqué. Thanks largely to Kissinger's negotiating skill and Chou's common sense, the Chinese finally agreed to sufficiently modified language.

One reason we found the Chinese appeared to be so agreeable to deal with was their total lack of conceit or arrogance. Unlike the Soviets, who ritually insisted that everything they had was the biggest and the best, the Chinese were almost obsessed with self-criticism and with seeking advice on how to improve themselves. Even Chiang Ching, when I told her how impressed I was with her ballet, said, "It is good to know that you find it acceptable, but tell me how you would go about improving it." As Chou continually referred to their need to understand and overcome their imperfections, I could not help thinking of Khrushchev's boastful bombast and how much healthier the Chinese approach was. Of course, I knew that it was only an approach, a conscious decision to view themselves in this way, and that in fact they were absolutely convinced of the ultimate superiority of their culture and philosophy, and that in time it would triumph over ours and everyone else's.

However, I found myself liking these austere and dedicated men. When Pat and I toured the Forbidden City, our host was the seventy-two-year-old Minister of Defense, Marshal Yeh Chien-ying.

Diary

He was a totally delightful man with great inner strength. He made the interesting comment that the American music and the Chinese music seemed to fit in together, and that American and Chinese journalists hit it off well. I think he is totally correct in this respect, particularly where Americans have a little depth and subtlety and are not the abrasive, loud types that would grate upon the Chinese. One of the benefits of our relationship is that Americans today, as distinguished from the late nineteenth-century Americans, are very different from the Europeans, the British, French, Dutch, et al. We have no sense of arrogance—we honestly, almost naïvely, like people and want to get along with them. We lack often a sense of subtlety but that will come after we've had a few hundred more years of civilization. It is the subtlety of the Chinese which is most impressive to me. I had read about it and heard about it, and seen it in quotations. Chou En-lai, of course, adds to Chinese subtlety the far-ranging experience of a world diplomat.

On our third night in Peking, Pat and I were taken to a gymnastics and table tennis exhibition.

Diary

The gymnastic event was a colorful spectacle and, as was the case with the ballet the night before, had the feeling of enormous dedication and singleness of purpose in the whole production.

The way that they brought out their equipment, and the opening march with the red flag, was strikingly strong. The appearance of both the girls and men, as well as, of course, up to the superb Ping-Pong event left an impression that was not only lasting, but also foreboding.

Henry could not be more right in his warning that as the years went on, not only we but all the people of the world will have to make our very best effort if we are to match the enormous ability, drive, and discipline of the Chinese people.

When I went to bed that night I found that I could not get to sleep. At five o'clock I got up and took a hot bath. I climbed back into bed and lighted one of the Chinese-made "Great Wall" cigars my hosts had thoughtfully provided, and sat puffing on the cigar and making notes about the events of the momentous week.

On Saturday, February 26, we flew with Chou in his plane to Hangchow, in eastern China. By this time he and I were talking quite freely to each other.

Diary

Chou En-lai and I had a very interesting conversation on the way to the airport in Peking. He spoke of Mao's poem which he

> wrote on returning to his hometown after thirty-two years. He returned to the point he has made quite often, that adversity is a great teacher. I related it to adversity generally, and pointed out that an election loss was really more painful than a physical wound in war. The latter wounds the body—the other wounds the spirit. On the other hand, the election loss helps to develop the strength and character which are essential for future battles. I said to Chou that I found that I had learned more from defeats than from victories, and that all I wanted was a life in which I had just one more victory than defeat.
>
> I used also the example of de Gaulle in the wilderness for a period of years as a factor which helped to build his character. He came back with a thought that men who travel on a smooth road all their life do not develop strength.
>
> Chou said that I had a poetic turn of mind like Mao, when I had in my last toast said that it was not possible to build a bridge across 16,000 miles and twenty-two years in one week. Much of the Mao poetry, of course, is simply a colorful and vivid example.
>
> He referred again to his admiration for *Six Crises*, and I jokingly said that he shouldn't believe all the bad that the press said of me, and that I would follow the same practice with regard to him.

Hangchow is built around large lakes and gardens. In the days when the emperors used it as a summer resort, it was known as the most beautiful city in China. I knew that Mao enjoyed taking vacations there and staying in an exquisite old palace that had been turned into a government guesthouse.

Even though we were in Hangchow in the cloudy off-season, it was easy to see why Mao was drawn to the city. Mountains rise mistily in the background, and the lakes are full of lotus flowers. The pagoda-like guesthouse, with its sloping green tile roofs, was set in the middle of a lake on an island called "Island of Three Towers Reflecting the Moon." It was rather musty, but it was immaculately clean, and Pat and I later agreed that our stay there was the most delightful interlude of the trip.

During the more than fifteen hours of formal talks I had with Chou we covered a wide range of issues and ideas. Since all our discussions during this trip were so frank, it was understandable that the Chinese were nervous about the possibility of leaks. I am sure that Chou had no trouble imagining the propaganda use the Kremlin would have for the transcripts of our talks. During a discussion of the internal opposition to some of my decisions during the Indo-Pakistan war, Chou referred to the Jack Anderson leak. "The records of three of your meetings were made public because all sorts of people were invited," he remarked with a sardonic smile. I felt a real concern beneath his bantering tone. In fact, in our first conversation on the way in to Peking from the airport, Chou had mentioned how important the Chinese considered confidentiality in our relationship, and Chairman Mao had made the same point very emphatically during our meeting.

To assuage Chou's fears, I outlined the strict procedures we planned to follow to keep our future contacts secret. "The Prime Minister may think we're being too careful," I said, "but as you know, we had the Pentagon Papers from the previous administration, and we've had the Anderson papers from this administration. Dr. Kissinger and I have determined that this will never happen in the new relationship that we have established with your government."

I said I was determined that when the fate of our two countries—and possibly the fate of the world—was involved, we would be able to talk in confidence.

When we began to talk about the situation in the Middle East, Chou jokingly said, "Even Dr. Kissinger doesn't want to discuss this problem, because being Jewish he is afraid that they suspect him."

I said, "My concern in the Middle East—and, incidentally it is Dr. Kissinger's too, because while he is Jewish he is an American first—our concern is much bigger than Israel. We believe the Soviet Union is moving to reach its hands out in that area. It must be resisted. That is why we took a position in the Jordanian crisis, for example, warning the Soviets that if they move aggressively in that area, we will consider our own interests involved."

I emphasized that my visit had bipartisan support and that other visits by Democrats as well as Republicans would now be perfectly in order. "As I have indicated to the Prime Minister, it is important to have policy carried forward whoever sits in this chair next year," I said. "Under our system, I may be here next year, and I may not. I want to be sure that whether a Democrat or Republican occupies the presidency, this beginning we have made is carried forward. It is bigger than any one party or any one man. It involves the future for years to come."

As we became more at ease and more familiar with each other, our conversations occasionally became light, even humorous.

During one of our airport drives, Chou told me about a meeting between Chairman Mao and Emperor Haile Selassie a few months before my trip to China was announced. Mao had asked the old Emperor whether he thought that the "socialist devil," as he humorously called himself, should sit down and talk with the "capitalist devil." I said, "I expect that many of your colleagues must have thought the reason I didn't bring a hat with me was because I couldn't find one to fit over my horns."

A recurring theme in our conversations was age. As Malraux had said, the Chinese leaders were obsessed by the amount that remained to be done and by the little time that was left them in which to do it.

> *Diary*
> Chou came to the age factor two or three times. I said that I was enormously impressed by his vitality and that age really was a question of not how many years a person lived but how much he lived in those years. I seemed to sense that he felt that being involved in great affairs kept a person alive and young, but there was a haunting refrain throughout that he felt that the current leadership was near the end of the road with still very much to be done.

All the Chinese leaders we met seemed particularly struck by the youth of our entire party. In our first meeting Chou singled out Dwight Chapin, who was only thirty-one and looked even younger. "We have too many elderly people in our leadership. So on this point we should learn from you," he said. "I have found that you have many young men; Mr. Chapin is very young indeed, and Mr. Green is not very old either." Marshall Green, the Assistant Secretary of State for East Asia and Pacific Affairs, was fifty-six.

Despite the fact that I was almost a quarter of a century younger than Mao, I approached this trip as if it were the last chance I would have to do something about the Sino-American relationship. As I put it in a diary dictation shortly after returning home, "I am really probably older than they are—I have only ten months to live (politically)—or at most four years and ten months, and I must get results now. That is why now is the hour for me, even more than for them, despite the fact that they are older in conventional terms."

One afternoon as we were discussing the need for patience in the solution of problems, Chou said, "I can't wait ten years. You have ten years. Mr. President may be re-elected to a third term."

"That's against the Constitution," Kissinger interjected.

"After four years then you can run again, because your age permits you to do that. But in view of the age of the present leaders of China, it is not possible. They're too old," Chou said.

"Mr. Prime Minister," I replied, "former Presidents of the United States are like British kings; they have great responsibility but no power. I mean one who is out of office."

"But your career is quite rare in history. You have been Vice President for two terms, then lost and then won an election again. It's quite rare in history."

Our joint statement, issued from Shanghai at the end of the trip, has become known as the Shanghai Communiqué.

Following the formula Kissinger had worked out during Polo II, the communiqué broke diplomatic ground by stating frankly the significant differences between the two sides on major issues rather than smoothing them over. Thus the text is surprisingly lively for a diplomatic document.

The first substantive section begins: "The U.S. side stated" and then details our positions on each of the major issues discussed. This is followed by a section that begins: "The Chinese side stated" and then covers the same ground in counterpoint.

Thus the U.S. side proclaimed its support for the eight-point peace plan proposed by us and the South Vietnamese in Paris on January 27; the Chinese side stated its support for the seven-point proposal put forward by the Vietcong in February.

We stated our intention to maintain close ties with and support for South Korea; the Chinese endorsed North Korea's plan for unification of the Korean peninsula, and called for the abolition of the UN presence in South Korea.

We affirmed that we placed the highest value on our friendly relations with Japan and said that we would continue to develop the existing close bonds; the Chinese side stated that it "firmly opposes the revival and outward expansion of Japanese militarism and firmly supports the Japanese people's desire to build an independent, democratic, peaceful and neutral Japan."

The Chinese stated their claim to be the sole legal government of China and their conviction that Taiwan is a province of China. They affirmed that the liberation of Taiwan was China's internal affair in which no country had a right to interfere, and demanded that all American forces and military installations be withdrawn from Taiwan. They concluded by stating that "the Chinese government firmly opposes any activities which aim at the creation of 'one China, one Taiwan,' 'one China, two governments,' 'two Chinas,' and 'independent Taiwan' or advocate that 'the status of Taiwan remains to be determined.' "

The wording of the American section on Taiwan avoided a clash by stating simply: "The United States acknowledges that all Chinese on either side of the Taiwan Strait maintain there is but one China and that Taiwan is a part of China. The United States government does not challenge that position. It reaffirms its interest in a peaceful settlement of the Taiwan question by the Chinese themselves." We stated our ultimate objective of withdrawing American troops from Taiwan but did not put any final date on it, and we agreed in the meantime to reduce our forces and installations on Taiwan progressively "as the tension in the area diminishes."

Perhaps the most vitally important section of the Shanghai Communiqué was the provision that neither nation "should seek hegemony in the Asia Pacific region and each is opposed to efforts by any other country or group of countries to establish such hegemony." By agreeing to this provision both the P.R.C. and the United States were imposing restraints on themselves. But far more important, particularly as far as the Chinese were concerned, was that the provision subtly but unmistakably made it clear that we both would oppose efforts by the U.S.S.R. or any other major power to dominate Asia.

As I look back on that week in China two impressions stand out most vividly. One is the awesome sight of the disciplined but wildly—almost fanatically—enthusiastic audience at the gymnastic exhibition in Peking, confirming my belief that we must cultivate China during the next few decades while it is still learning to develop its national strength and potential. Otherwise we will one day be confronted with the most formidable enemy that has ever existed in the history of the world.

My other most vivid memory of the trip is the unique personality of Chou En-lai. My meeting with Mao Tse-tung was too brief and too formal to have given me much more than a superficial personal impression. But many hours of formal talks and social conversation with Chou made me appreciate his brilliance and dynamism.

Unlike many world leaders and statesmen who are completely absorbed in one particular cause or issue, Chou En-lai was able to talk in broad terms about men and history. Even though his perspective was badly distorted by his rigid ideological frame of reference the extent of his knowledge was impressive.

After one of the banquets in Peking, I made notes of our conversation.

Diary

It was interesting to note the remarkable knowledge of history that Chou En-lai displays, and, also, how his historical perspective is shaped by his ideology. For example, he sees the French intervention in the Revolutionary War as being by volunteers [led by Lafayette] and not by the French government.

Chou also sees Lincoln [as one] who "after many defeats," as he put it, finally prevailed because he had the people on his side. While it is true that Lincoln is one of the few great figures in history, he was a total pragmatist. He did not fight the war for the purpose of freeing the slaves, although he was unalterably op-

> posed to slavery; and when he freed the slaves, he did not free them as an end in itself—he did so as a purely tactical, military maneuver, freeing only the slaves in the South but not in the Northern border states.

I regret that Chou did not live long enough for me to meet him again when I visited China for the second time in February 1976. I feel that although our acquaintance was brief and necessarily somewhat restrained and even wary, we had formed bonds of mutual respect and personal esteem.

During our last long session together in the guesthouse in Peking, Chou said, "In your dining room upstairs we have a poem by Chairman Mao in his calligraphy about Lushan mountain. The last sentence reads, 'The beauty lies at the top of the mountain.' You have risked something to come to China. But there is another Chinese poem which reads, 'On perilous peaks dwells beauty in its infinite variety.' "

"We are at the top of the mountain now," I said.

"That's one poem," he continued. "Another one which I would have liked to have put up, but I couldn't find an appropriate place, is 'Ode to a Plum Blossom.' In that poem the Chairman meant that one who makes an initiative may not always be one who stretches out his or her hand. By the time the blossoms are full-blown, that is the time they are about to disappear." He took a small book from his pocket and read the poem.

> "Spring disappears with rain and winds
>   and comes with flying snow.
> Ice hangs on a thousand feet of cliff
>   yet at the tip of the topmost branch the plum blooms.
> The plum is not a delicious girl showing off
>   yet she heralds spring.
> When mountain flowers are in wild bloom
>   she giggles in all the color."

"Therefore," Chou continued, "we believe we are in accord with the idea you have expressed: you are the one who made the initiative. You may not be there to see its success, but of course we would welcome your return," he said.

Kissinger diplomatically pointed out that even if I won re-election, a return visit would not be very likely.

"I was only trying to illustrate the Chinese way of thinking," Chou said. "It does not matter anyhow."

Chou referred to the fact that I had changed the name of *Air Force*

One to *The Spirit of '76* shortly before this trip. "Regardless of who is the next President," he said, "the spirit of seventy-six still exists and will prevail. From the standpoint of policies, I hope that our counterpart will be the same so that we can continue our efforts. We also hope not only that the President continues in office but that your National Security Adviser and your assistants continue in office. Various changes may be bound to come. For example, if I should suddenly die of a heart attack, you would also have to deal with a different counterpart. Therefore, we have tried to bring more people to meet you. I hope you won't complain that I am too lengthy in my words."

I assured him that, on the contrary, I was very interested in what he was saying.

"This belongs to the philosophic field, but also to the political point of view. For example," he said, pointing to the book of poems open in his lap, "this poem was written after a military victory over the enemy. In the whole poem there is not one word about the enemy; it was very difficult to write the poem."

"Of course, I believe it is very useful to think in philosophic terms," I said. "Too often we look at problems of the world from the point of view of tactics. We take the short view. If the one who wrote that poem took the short view, you would not be here today. It is essential to look at the world not just in terms of immediate diplomatic battles and decisions but the great forces that move the world. Maybe we have some disagreements, but we know there will be changes, and we know that there can be a better, and I trust safer, world for our two peoples regardless of differences if we can find common ground."

I described the real nature of my thinking behind the China initiative in notes I made at 2:30 A.M. on Friday, February 24, of points I planned to make in my meeting with Chou that afternoon. Perhaps if I could have publicized these notes the conservative critics of the China initiative would at least have felt reassured that I had not approached the Chinese naïvely.

> The first was to emphasize the immense potential of the Chinese living overseas, and the need for the P.R.C. to use that potential and learn to live with it, rather than to blunt it by trying to drive them into the system.
>
> The second was to emphasize that RN would turn like a cobra on the Russians, or for that matter on anyone else, if they break their word with him. My record in Vietnam helped in getting this point across.
>
> The third was to emphasize, in a very personal and direct way, my intense belief in our system and my belief that in peaceful competition it would prevail. I think we have gotten that across. I believe that it is essential not to let the assumption exist at all on their part that their system will eventually prevail because of its superiority.

> Related to this point is that we are not going to become weak—that our system is not coming apart at the seams—and that all of the public criticism, etc., of our system should not be taken as a sign of weakness.

In my toast at the banquet on our last night in China I said, "The joint communiqué which we have issued today summarizes the results of our talks. That communiqué will make headlines around the world tomorrow. But what we have said in that communiqué is not nearly as important as what we will do in the years ahead to build a bridge across 16,000 miles and twenty-two years of hostility which have divided us in the past."

I raised my glass and said, "We have been here a week. This was the week that changed the world."

ITT

The day after we returned from China, Jack Anderson began a series of newspaper columns in which he claimed to have unearthed a major administration scandal. His charges were based on a memorandum allegedly from Dita Beard, a lobbyist for International Telephone and Telegraph Corporation, to one of her ITT superiors. Anderson said that the memo implied that a government anti-trust settlement with ITT had been influenced by an ITT contribution toward the upcoming Republican convention and that John Mitchell and I had pushed for favorable treatment for ITT because of this contribution. Mrs. Beard supposedly managed this whole deal almost single-handedly.

In fact, the anti-trust settlement in question had been a favorable one for the government and not for ITT, which was required to divest itself of holdings representing $1 billion in sales. On the first trading day after this settlement ITT's stock fell 11 percent. Furthermore, the money that allegedly influenced the settlement was not a contribution to the Committee to Re-elect the President or to the Republican Party, but to the city of San Diego so that the city could bid to be the site of the 1972 Republican National Convention. It is standard practice for local businesses to help underwrite a city's convention bid, and the Sheraton division of ITT, which was in the process of opening a new hotel in San Diego, saw the contribution as a promotional investment: the nationwide publicity and prestige that would come with being the presidential staff headquarters during convention week would be worth the payment to San Diego.

My own role in the ITT anti-trust matter consisted of one angry phone call to Dick Kleindienst almost a year earlier at the time of three Justice Department anti-trust suits against ITT. Kleindienst, Mitchell's deputy, was in charge of the case due to the fact that Mitchell had excused himself because an ITT subsidiary had been a client of our former law firm.

As I saw it, the Justice Department suits were a clear violation of my anti-trust policy. I was convinced that American companies would be able to compete in the international market only if they were as big and strong as the government-sheltered monopolies in so many foreign countries, and therefore I had instructed that big businesses were to be broken up only when they violated the laws of fair competition and not simply because they were big. I had made this position clear at staff and Cabinet meetings—and now some subordinate officials in the Justice Department were pursuing a course that deliberately contradicted it. ITT officials felt they were being unfairly sued and descended upon Washington in an effort to get the suits dropped. They had seen members of Congress from both parties and also everyone they could reach in the administration who would give them a hearing. When one case came to trial at the end of 1970, the court agreed that the suit was groundless and ruled against the Justice Department.

Several weeks later I learned that the Justice Department was going to appeal this decision to a higher court. I called Kleindienst and ordered him not to do it. The original suit had been contrary to my specifically stated policy, and I was was not going to countenance further defiance by any subordinate or by any department. Two days later, when my anger had cooled, I was approached by John Mitchell. He was sensitive to the tempers and the egos at the Justice Department. He urged me to retract my order to Kleindienst, advising that if I did not, there would be resignations within the department and that would mean noisy congressional hearings and a general political mess. He explained the policy conflict as the result of unintentional confusion. I agreed to refrain from interfering in the Anti-Trust Division's decision to appeal the case.

As it turned out—for reasons wholly unrelated to my call to Kleindienst or to any contributions toward the selection of the Republican convention site—the Justice officials prosecuting the case decided to settle it and not proceed with the appeal. Months later both Watergate Special Prosecutors, Archibald Cox and Leon Jaworski, investigated the ITT case and concluded that there had been no quid pro quo involved in the settlement. When the tapes of my conversations with Mitchell and Kleindienst were turned over, they proved that my motive in ordering that no appeal be filed was policy and not politics. But this vindication was more than a year away. In that pre-election spring of 1972, the Democrats played the ITT issue to the hilt. And by the way we reacted we played right into their hands.

Dick Kleindienst, who at the time of the Anderson columns had been nominated to succeed John Mitchell as Attorney General, immediately called for new Senate hearings at which he could defend his honor. This turned out to be a tactical disaster. The committee holding the hearings included Teddy Kennedy—a front-running noncandidate—and his friends Birch Bayh and John Tunney. They quickly turned the hearings into a forum in which to berate the administration. Larry O'Brien at the Democratic National Committee joined in and the networks gave prominence to the easy accusations while the sometimes complicated explanations got lost in the clamor. I thought that the committee's Democrats had traded in hearsay and indulged in melodramatics.

Diary

If I ever get time to write a book, at some time in the future, there is going to be a hard-hitting chapter on this point. Where a committee is investigating subversives, inevitably the press attacks the procedures which the committee is following. When a committee is investigating business or government officials, including even the President, the press is totally silent with regard to outlandish procedures that it would immediately condemn if the investigation were being aimed at subversives.

Of course, what is needed is a single standard. Fair procedures should be followed in both cases—something I have always insisted upon. It bugs the press that I have done so, because they know that their objection is not to *how* a committee investigation is conducted, but to *what* is being investigated.

They just don't like to admit they had a double standard.

A year later I was to find out how hypocritical Kennedy in particular had been. Testifying before Congress, former Chairman of the Securities and Exchange Commission William Casey reported that for all Kennedy's sanctimonious grandstanding during the ITT hearings, three months later he had phoned Casey to urge that an investment banking firm headed by one of his friends not be named as a defendant in a civil suit the SEC had filed against ITT. Casey ignored Kennedy's intervention.

Day after day the White House staff raced around trying to minimize the political damage and keep any embarrassing material from the committee's partisan clutches. There were rumors that the memo itself was a forgery, so Colson sent someone out to see Mrs. Beard and to encourage her to deny publicly its authenticity. I later learned the man's name: E. Howard Hunt. In fact, Mrs. Beard did subsequently testify that the memo Anderson had published was a forgery; her secretary filed an affidavit that she had not typed the Anderson version; the man to whom it was addressed testified that he had never received it.

The whole ITT episode left us, and particularly Mitchell and Kleindienst, worn out. We had lost a massive partisan public relations battle; ITT left a sour taste in the mouths of the public even though they did not know exactly what had been involved.

Since I had no other choice, I tried to be philosophical about this situation.

Diary

Colson gave me a report on the ITT case, and said that he had really tried to shake up the staff a bit in terms of their pessimism with regard to the attacks. I told him this is only the beginning of a much greater assault at a later point—for us to stand firm.

I think we have got to find tougher language to throw at some of our Democratic friends. Instead of doing the nation's business, they are spending all their time in smears.

Haldeman had pointed out that Joe Kraft in his column, and Connally later in the day, in recounting a conversation he had with [NBC news anchorman John] Chancellor, made the same point to the effect that the administration was reacting too much to the disclosures. It is likely that this is the case, but I think that at the beginning the problem was that we didn't know what really was involved, and the mistake was that we should have, as Haldeman suggested, simply laid the whole record on the table, and not have been concerned about it.

NORTH VIETNAM INVADES THE SOUTH

The optimistic days when I had envisioned ending the Vietnam war within a year were now long past. For more than a year the North Vietnamese had played a cynical game with the peace talks in Paris. Whenever Kissinger would make a substantial new proposal in one of the private sessions, they would either ignore or reject it. Then in the public sessions they would vehemently attack us for not showing any flexibility or interest in reaching an agreement. They would haggle about details, but on the bottom line they never wavered: they would not agree to a settlement unless we agreed to overthrow Thieu.

On August 16, 1971, we offered the complete withdrawal of American and allied forces within nine months after an agreement; on September 13 they rejected this proposal and continued to insist on the overthrow of Thieu as the sine qua non for reaching any agreement. In the meantime they used the public meetings in Paris to berate us for not wanting to negotiate seriously.

It was a very skillful propaganda maneuver, and it took in many American critics of the war. For example, in September 1971 McGovern visited Paris and spent six hours talking with Xuan Thuy. Afterward he told reporters that he had been assured that the North Vietnamese would return all our POWs as soon as we agreed to set a date for our withdrawal. *These were exactly the terms that we had offered on May 31, 1971, and they had rejected, on June 26, 1971.* When Kissinger confronted Xuan Thuy with this duplicity at their next meeting, Thuy coldly replied, "What Senator McGovern says is his problem."

More to make sure that we had overlooked no opportunity for a settlement than out of any belief that we would succeed in obtaining one, I decided to make another attempt at breaking the deadlock. Therefore in October we got Thieu's approval on a major new plan that provided for all U.S. and allied forces to be withdrawn from South Vietnam within six months of an agreement, for all POWs to be exchanged on both sides, and for a cease-fire throughout Indochina. Thieu also accepted an internationally supervised presidential election in South Vietnam within six months after an agreement was reached and went to the extraordinary length of agreeing that he and Vice President Ky would resign from office one month before the election so that all candidates would run on an equal footing.

Armed with this dramatic new plan, we proposed another secret session for November 1, 1971. The North Vietnamese countered by suggesting November 20, and we accepted. On November 17 they canceled, saying that Le Duc Tho was ill. We offered to meet as soon as he was recovered or to meet with any other qualified representative.

No further word came from Hanoi, but there were ominous reports of a big military buildup north of the DMZ as well as a continued stepping up of enemy activity in the South. When Saigon was shelled—in clear violation of the terms of the 1968 bombing halt agreement—I ordered that our bombing raids be resumed over North Vietnam. The domestic outcry was immediate and intense.

On January 13, 1972, I approved the withdrawal of 70,000 more American troops from Vietnam over the next three months. Coming on the eve of a new session of Congress and just before the beginning of the presidential primaries, I felt that the number had to be significant in order to underscore the downward direction of my withdrawal policy. By May 1, less than four months away, there would be only 69,000 Americans remaining in Vietnam, and they too would be getting ready to leave. Even as I made this announcement, however, I was facing the unsettling prospect that a successful Communist invasion of South Vietnam might seriously jeopardize the safety of those decreasing numbers of Americans still there.

The leak to columnist Jack Anderson during the Indo-Pakistan war had added a disturbing new element to our situation. The Navy yeoman we suspected of being the source of the leak had had access to papers dealing with Kissinger's secret negotiations in Paris, and we had no way of knowing whether any information about them had been passed on to Anderson or others. If the American people learned about the secret negotiations through a newspaper leak, there would be political and diplomatic hell to pay. I was also concerned because one of Kissinger's aides who had resigned because of Cambodia was now working as Muskie's foreign policy adviser in his presidential campaign. Since this man had been privy to the secret negotiations in Paris, we could not be certain that he would not tell Muskie.

Therefore I decided to make a speech revealing publicly the peace plan that the North Vietnamese had not been interested in hearing from us privately and, at the same time, to reveal the existence of the secret channel. The time had come to show the sincerity of our approach and expose the cynical tactics of the Communists.

In the speech, which I made from the Oval Office on January 25, 1972, I said that Kissinger had been holding secret meetings with the North Vietnamese since August 1969. I explained that over the past thirty months Kissinger, Rogers, and I had carefully tailored our public statements to protect the secrecy of the meetings because we were determined to do nothing to jeopardize any chance they had for success. But there had been no success, and it was time to try another way.

Referring to the cynical game the North Vietnamese had played with McGovern regarding the POWs in September 1971, I said, "Nothing is served by silence when it misleads some Americans into accusing their own government of failing to do what it has already done. Nothing is served by silence when it enables the other side to imply possible solutions publicly that it has already flatly rejected privately."

I said that just as secret negotiations can sometimes break a public deadlock, I now felt that public disclosure might help to break a secret deadlock. I described the major points of our dramatic new proposal that Hanoi had not even deigned to receive.

I said that we were still interested in almost any potential peace agreement, but I repeated that the only kind of plan we would not consider was one that required us to accomplish the enemy's goals by overthrowing our South Vietnamese ally. I also warned, "If the enemy's answer to our peace offer is to step up their military attacks, I shall fully meet my responsibility as Commander in Chief of our armed forces to protect our remaining troops."

I concluded, "Honest and patriotic Americans have disagreed as to whether we should have become involved at all nine years ago; and there has been disagreement on the conduct of the war. The proposal I have made tonight is one on which we all can agree."

While the path to the Chinese Summit had unfolded relatively smoothly, the way to the Soviet Summit was strewn with pitfalls. During the first few months of 1972, our intelligence indicated that vast quantities of Soviet arms were pouring into North Vietnam. "I think that what offends me most about the Soviets is their utter lack of subtlety," Kissinger said when we learned this. "They're just trying to blacken China's eyes because of your trip. They want to increase their influence in Hanoi, but they don't see the danger of giving new toys to the North Vietnamese fanatics."

On January 25, I wrote a letter to Brezhnev informing him of my speech that night and stating, "The Soviet Union should understand that the United States would have no choice but to react strongly to actions by the North Vietnamese which are designed to humiliate us. Such developments would be to no one's benefit and would serve to complicate the international situation." Dobrynin pretended to be surprised that we were thinking so negatively, and Brezhnev's reply a few days later was terse and testy.

On March 30 I was sitting in the Oval Office talking to Kissinger when one of his staff members sent a note into him. He read it and said, "The North Vietnamese have attacked across the DMZ. This is probably the beginning of the offensive we have been expecting."

It was more than just an offensive. It was a full-scale invasion, and over the next few weeks the main force of the North Vietnamese Army—an estimated 120,000 troops—trampled across the internationally recognized neutral territory of the DMZ and pushed deep into South Vietnam.

Tragically, the Communist spring offensive also once again unleashed that barbaric strain of North Vietnamese brutality that so marked their conduct of the Vietnam war. I was shocked by the reports that came in. At both An Loc and Quangtri, as terrified civilians rushed to flee the scene of combat, North Vietnamese troops indiscriminately slaughtered thousands of them.

During the spring offensive, the Communists took over Binh Dinh province on the central coast of Vietnam, and intelligence reports came in telling of public executions by the Communists of hundreds of individuals suspected of having connections with the Saigon government. In one hamlet forty-seven local officials were reported to have been buried alive. A few months later we learned of still another barbaric mass murder near Quang Ngai province, where Communist forces gathered together more than a hundred civilians and selected forty of them for execution. They added a grisly twist by stringing land mines around the chosen victims and then, as their wives and children watched, detonated the mines, blowing the helpless captives to bits.

I viewed the North Vietnamese invasion as a sign of desperation. They clearly felt that Vietnamization was working. If it were not, they would have waited and let it fail. I felt that if we could mount a devastating attack on their home territory while pinning down their Army in the South, we would be in a very good position for the next round of negotiations. We decided to go all out in applying military pressure to North Vietnam and diplomatic pressure to its Soviet suppliers. I issued orders for the Pentagon planners to begin assembling a massive attack force of aircraft carriers, cruisers, and destroyers for sea bombardment and B-52s for aerial raids on North Vietnam. On April 4 the State Department publicly announced that Soviet arms were supporting the North Vietnamese invasion. At their next meeting, Kissinger confronted Dobrynin with the alternatives that either the Soviets had actually planned the invasion or their negligence had made it possible.

Despite this, Brezhnev gave a noticeably warm reception to Secretary of Agriculture Earl Butz when he arrived in Moscow to discuss trade agreements, and during this period we signed several joint agreements dealing with education and cultural exchanges. We also began talks aimed at settling the lend-lease debts the Soviets had owed since World War II. It seemed clear that Moscow was moving ahead on the summit regardless of the flare-up in the war.

Without making any specific promises, Dobrynin told Kissinger that the North Vietnamese would adopt a very responsive approach when the private talks resumed in Paris on April 24. He also repeated an earlier suggestion that Kissinger make a secret visit to Moscow so that Vietnam and other agenda items could be discussed with Brezhnev before the summit. I agreed with Kissinger that he should accept this invitation.

We were also completely agreed on our overall strategy and goals as he prepared for his trip to Moscow. However, his opinion on the tactics he should follow in his talks was somewhat different from mine. In my conversation with Kissinger and in the instructions I sent him in Moscow, I stressed that I wanted him to make Vietnam the first order of business and to refuse to discuss anything that the Soviets wanted—particularly the trade agreements for which they were so eager—until they specifically committed themselves to help end the war. Kissinger, however, continued to feel that flexibility must be the cornerstone of any successful negotiation, and he urged me to let him feel out the situation rather than risk everything by imposing any rigid preconditions.

We were in complete agreement on the importance of keeping up the military pressure on North Vietnam, including the bombing. Any sign of weakness on our part might encourage the Soviets to provide more arms in hopes of giving the North Vietnamese a military advantage. I also wanted the South Vietnamese to be confident that we still stood resolutely behind them. The morale of the South Vietnamese government and armed forces would be crucial to their ability to resist this attack.

I felt that the North Vietnamese invasion had moved the war into a final stage. Now one of two things must happen: if the South Vietnamese, with American air support, could repel the invasion or even halt it, then we would effectively have won the war and a negotiated settlement on favorable terms would result. If, however, the North Vietnamese armies were able to sweep down and join with the Vietcong in routing the South Vietnamese forces and taking Saigon, then the war would be lost and the remaining 69,000 American troops in serious danger.

Kissinger agreed, and, perhaps to cheer me up, said that even if the worst happened and we had to pull out in the face of an enemy victory, I would still be able to claim credit for having conducted an honorable winding down of the war by the dignified and secure withdrawal of 500,000 troops. Most people would give me credit for that, and everyone would be so glad the war was over that the domestic situation would not be impossible to handle.

I considered this prospect too bleak even to contemplate. "I don't give a damn about the domestic reaction if that happens," I said, "because if it does, sitting in this office wouldn't be worth it. The foreign policy of the United States will have been destroyed, and the Soviets will have established that they can accomplish what they are after by using the force of arms in third countries." Defeat, I said, was simply not an option.

I recorded my reflections on the situation that had now developed in Vietnam.

Diary

It is ironic that having come this far, our fate is really in the hands of the South Vietnamese.

If we fail it will be because the American way simply isn't as effective as the Communist way in supporting countries abroad. I have an uneasy feeling that this may be the case. We give them the most modern arms, we emphasize the material to the exclusion of the spiritual and the Spartan life, and it may be that we soften them up rather than harden them up for the battle.

> On the other hand, the enemy emphasizes the Spartan life, not the material, emphasizes sacrifice and, of course, with the enormous Soviet technical help on missiles, guns, etc., they have a pretty good advantage.
>
> I think perhaps I was too insistent and rough on Henry today, but I am so disgusted with the military's failing to come up with any idea, and failing to follow through that I simply had to take it out on somebody. Also, Henry, with all of his many virtues, does seem too often to be concerned about preparing the way for negotiations with the Soviets. However, when he faces the facts, he realizes that no negotiation in Moscow is possible unless we come out all right in Vietnam.
>
> What really matters now is how it all comes out. Both Haldeman and Henry seem to have an idea—which I think is mistaken—that even if we fail in Vietnam we can still survive politically. I have no illusions whatever on that score, however. The U.S. will not have a credible foreign policy if we fail, and I will have to assume the responsibility for that development.

A subtle occasion to apply pressure on the Soviets arose when I attended a ceremony at the State Department for the signing of an international convention banning biological warfare. With Dobrynin seated among the ranks of diplomats listening to my remarks, I said that we must recognize that a great responsibility rests upon the great powers to follow the principle that they should not directly or indirectly encourage any other nation to use force or armed aggression against one of its neighbors. There was no doubt that I was talking about the Soviet Union and North Vietnam.

Just before I left the State Department Auditorium, I went over to shake hands with Dobrynin. I told him that Pat had greatly appreciated Mrs. Dobrynin's recent invitation to get together for a talk about our trip to Moscow. Later that afternoon Dobrynin called Kissinger and suggested that the ladies' meeting be arranged for the next day.

Pat had asked Kissinger to brief her on the situation. He told her, "You could say how much you're both looking forward to the trip, and that you hope nothing will poison it, such as the current developments in Vietnam."

The meeting was very successful. Pat showed great skill and subtlety. When she raised the point that we did not want anything like Vietnam to interfere with the summit, Mrs. Dobrynin had squeezed her hand and vigorously nodded in agreement.

During the next weeks we pursued a combined policy of applying military pressure on the North Vietnamese and diplomatic pressure on the

Soviets. Even while the summit plans were going forward, I was determined not to indulge the Soviet fiction that they could not be held responsible for what North Vietnam did, despite the fact that the invasion had been made possible by the massive infusion of new Soviet weapons and ammunition.

In order to have the necessary military impact, I was convinced that the bombing, which had begun in the southern part of North Vietnam, would have to be brought to the enemy's heartland around the Hanoi-Haiphong area. The risks of aircraft loss and additional casualties and prisoners of war in these more heavily defended regions were very great, and Laird expressed grave concern about the congressional furor that would follow further escalation of the bombing while Rogers feared that it might endanger the Soviet Summit. Still, I felt that it had to be done, and I approved the plans for operation "Freedom Porch Bravo"—a weekend of heavy B-52 raids aimed at destroying the oil depots around Hanoi and Haiphong, which were being used to fuel the invasion.

The operation was a complete success, and on Sunday morning April 16 I told Haldeman, "Well, we really left them our calling card this weekend."

Meanwhile, on April 15 the situation took a very serious turn: the North Vietnamese canceled the Paris meeting scheduled for April 24. This was the meeting that the Soviets had hinted might be the decisive one for reaching a settlement. I told Kissinger that I did not think he should take his secret trip to Moscow until we found out what kind of game they were playing.

Kissinger complained to Dobrynin that we had trusted his assurances about this meeting, and warned that its cancellation created serious obstacles to his presummit trip. "The President questions what progress can be made in Moscow if the Soviet Union cannot assure even a meeting with the North Vietnamese on an agreed date," Kissinger told him.

That night I assessed some of the possible political ramifications of these events.

Diary

Henry obviously considered this a crisis of the first magnitude. I laid down the law hard to him that under these circumstances he could not go to Moscow. I told him that what the Russians wanted to do was to get him to Moscow to discuss the summit. What we wanted to do was to get him to Moscow to discuss Vietnam. I can see that this shook him because he desperately wants to get to Moscow one way or the other. He took it in good grace. Then I told him that we had to consider our option with regard to imposing a blockade.

He walked over with me to the EOB. We stayed down deep on

the lawn because there were several groups of tourists, and I was in no mood to talk to anybody at this point.

Later on in the afternoon I had a pretty candid talk with Henry about what we had to look forward to in the future. I said that what we were really looking at was a cancellation of the summit and going hard right on Vietnam, even up to a blockade.

I said under these circumstances, I had an obligation to look for a successor.

I ran down the list, including Rockefeller, Burger, Reagan, and Connally—if we could get him to change his party. Somebody like Burger, or Connally, without the scars on him that I had and with my support, might make it against a fractured Democratic Party.

Henry threw up his hands and said that none of them would do, and that any of the Democrats would be out of the question. I said that if we could get Henry to stay on that we could get continuity in foreign policy. Henry then became very emotional about the point that I shouldn't be thinking this way or talking this way to anybody—which, of course, he would have realized I wouldn't. He made his pitch that the North Vietnamese should not be allowed to destroy two Presidents.

After the dinner for the OAS, the military aide came and said I had a call from Kissinger. I went up and took it, and he told me that Dobrynin was still desperate to have him come to Moscow. Vietnam would be the first subject on the agenda. There was some talk even of having the North Vietnamese Foreign Minister there.

After the dinner I told Henry that I had reconsidered the situation and felt that we had to have an open option on the summit. We had to play out the string completely on the negotiating front, and he should go to Moscow.

The next day our bombers accidentally hit four Soviet merchant ships at anchor in Haiphong Harbor. The Soviets immediately protested what they called our "gangster activities." One of Dobrynin's staff handed a note to one of Kissinger's staff warning that the Soviets would be taking "all appropriate steps" to protect their ships "wherever they would be." An oral protest was made and then a similar note was delivered to the American Ambassador in Moscow. Diplomatically it was interesting—and important—that these protests were kept relatively low-keyed.

I issued orders that we hold absolutely firm in our position. Soviet weapons had made the North Vietnamese offensive possible, and I was not going to let them get off the defensive on this point.

Before Kissinger left for Moscow, he sent me a memorandum describing the strategy he intended to use at the meetings. As I read it I felt the memo did not adequately reflect my instructions about insisting upon a Vietnam settlement as a prerequisite for discussions on any other subject. In our last meeting I had even told Kissinger that if the Soviets proved recalcitrant on this point, he should just pack up and come home.

In their first meeting, Brezhnev protested that the Soviet government did not have as much influence in Hanoi as we seemed to think. He said that the Soviets had refused to answer any new requests for military equipment from the North Vietnamese. When he claimed that they had not supplied all that much equipment in the first place, Kissinger reminded him of the massive tonnage they had sent. In the end Brezhnev refused to promise to put any pressure on Hanoi to achieve either a de-escalation or a final settlement. The most he would agree to do was to forward our latest proposal to Hanoi even though he expected it would receive a negative reaction there. This was a far cry from the Soviets' earlier assurances that the April 24 meeting in Paris, now canceled, would probably see the fruition of the negotiations.

Having reached this impasse, Kissinger proceeded to move on to further discussions of summit agenda items. He was able to arrange the entire agenda except for the most sensitive elements of SALT, which would require direct negotiation between Brezhnev and me. But I was disappointed as I read his daily cable reports, because I felt that we might have missed the last opportunity to see how far the Soviets were willing to go to get the summit. I also feared that they would interpret Kissinger's willingness to negotiate without first getting a firm Soviet commitment to restrain the North Vietnamese as a sign of weakness rather than a sign of pragmatism.

In the other areas of discussion, however, there was remarkable progress. Brezhnev produced a SALT proposal that was considerably more favorable than we had expected, and as Kissinger reported, "If the summit meeting takes place, you will be able to sign the most important arms control agreement ever concluded."

Given Kissinger's achievements on the summit issues, I felt that there was no point in gainsaying his performance after the fact. If he had followed my instructions and insisted on a Vietnam settlement as the first order of business, perhaps Brezhnev would have dug in, called his bluff, and told him to go home—and that might have meant the end of the summit, with everything that it could accomplish, while still producing no progress on Vietnam. That was a risk I had thought worth taking. In any event the summit was held, and undoubtedly it owed a large measure of its success to Kissinger's negotiations during this secret visit to Moscow.

Two days after Kissinger's return I decided to make a short televised speech announcing a troop withdrawal from Vietnam. I felt that a further reduction of our forces while the enemy's invasion was under way would dramatize our desire for peace. Therefore I announced that an additional 20,000 troops would be withdrawn from Vietnam over the next two months, bringing our total force there on July 1, 1972, to only 49,000 men.

I described the military situation in Vietnam in the plainest possible words: "What we are witnessing here—what is being brutally inflicted upon the people of South Vietnam—is a clear case of naked and unprovoked aggression across an international border. There is only one word for it—invasion." I said that the bombing of North Vietnam would continue until the military offensive had stopped. "I have flatly rejected the proposal that we stop the bombing of North Vietnam as a condition for returning to the negotiating table," I said. "They sold that package to the United States once before, in 1968, and we are not going to buy it again in 1972."

It was a tough speech, and afterward I wished that I had made it even tougher.

The North Vietnamese rescheduled the April 24 meeting for May 2. On April 30 Pat and I attended a barbecue party at John Connally's ranch in Texas. I made a few remarks and then answered questions. One guest wanted to know whether I had thought about bombing the dikes in North Vietnam. I replied that naturally I had thought about it, but that it would involve an enormous number of civilian casualties. I continued, "We are prepared to use our military and naval strength against military targets throughout North Vietnam, and we believe that the North Vietnamese are taking a very great risk if they continue their offensive in the South. I will just leave it there, and they can make their own choice."

I knew that the news of this reply would reach Hanoi before the May 2 meeting, and I thought that it might help to strengthen our hand.

That evening I dictated a memorandum for Kissinger outlining my instructions for dealing with the North Vietnamese:

> What you must have in mind is that if they get a delay as a result of their talk with you, we shall lose the best chance we will ever have to give them a very damaging blow where it hurts, not just now, but particularly for the future.
>
> Forget the domestic reaction. Now is the best time to hit them. Every day we delay reduces support for such strong action.
>
> Our desire to have the Soviet Summit, of course, enters into this, but you have prepared the way very well on that score, and, in any event, we cannot let the Soviet Summit be the primary consideration in making this decision. As I told you on the phone this morning, I intend to cancel the Summit unless the situation militarily and diplomatically substantially improves by

May 15 at the latest or unless we get a firm commitment from the Russians to announce a joint agreement at the summit to use our influence to end the war.

In effect we have crossed the Rubicon and now we must win—not just a temporary respite from this battle, but if possible, tip the balance in favor of the South Vietnamese for battles to come when we no longer will be able to help them with major air strikes.

We know from experience, based on their record in 1968, that they will break every understanding. We know from their twelve secret talks with you that they talk in order to gain time. Another factor is that as we get closer to the Democratic Convention, the Democratic candidates and the supporters of Hanoi in the Congress will increasingly give them an incentive to press on and not make a deal with us with the hope that they can make a deal with the Democrats after the election.

I will be talking with you about the statement you will make when you see them, but my present intuition is that you should be brutally frank from the beginning—particularly in tone. . . . In a nutshell you should tell them that they have violated all understandings, they stepped up the war, they have refused to negotiate seriously. As a result, the President has had enough and now you have only one message to give them—Settle or else!

MAY 1972

On May 1, the day Kissinger was to leave for Paris, I received a letter from Brezhnev that increased my fear that we had failed to impress upon the Soviet leadership my unshakable determination to stand up in Vietnam. Brezhnev bluntly asked me to refrain from further actions there because they hurt the chances of a successful summit.

Kissinger was completely absorbed in mapping out his strategy for his May 2 meeting with Le Duc Tho. I spent several hours trying to make sure that we agreed on the strategy he should follow at the meeting.

Late in the afternoon after an hour and a half session on SALT Kissinger came back into the Oval Office, where I was meeting with Haldeman. He had just received a message. "It's from Abrams," he said, "Quangtri has fallen to the Communists. The battle for Hué is beginning."

We were silent for a moment while he looked over the document. "Abrams says that Quangtri isn't that important except for the effect it will have on South Vietnamese morale, but the loss of Hué would be a very serious blow."

"What else does he say?" I asked.

Kissinger cleared his throat uncomfortably, and said, "He feels that he has to report that it is quite possible that the South Vietnamese have lost their will to fight, or to hang together, and that the whole thing may well be lost."

I could hardly believe what I heard. I took the cable and read it for myself.

"How can this have happened?" I asked.

"The South Vietnamese seem to go in cycles," Kissinger suggested. "They're very good for about a month and then they seem to fold up. This crisis has been building up for about a month, and now they're caving in on schedule."

"Whatever happens, this doesn't change my thinking about the negotiations," I said. "I don't want you to give the North Vietnamese a thing. They'll be riding high because of all this, so you'll have to bring them down to the ground by your manner. No nonsense. No niceness. No accommodations. And we'll just have to let our Soviet friends know that I'm willing to give up the summit if this is the price they have in mind to make us pay for it. Under no circumstances will I go to the summit if we're still in trouble in Vietnam."

And then I thought of the bleak possibility—it was conceivable that all South Vietnam would fall. We would be left with no alternative but to impose a naval blockade and demand back our POWs.

"And then we're defeated," I told Haldeman and Kissinger.

"Then we will just have to tighten our belts," Kissinger replied glumly.

Shortly after I arrived in the office on the morning of May 2, 1972, Bob Haldeman came in with the news that J. Edgar Hoover had died in his sleep during the night.

I was deeply saddened by the news. I was also taken by surprise. Even though he was seventy-seven years old, Hoover had a vigor and drive that made him seem much younger. He had become the Director of the Bureau of Investigation in 1924. Over the next forty-eight years his strong patriotism and his political astuteness enabled him to be the loyal servant of seven Presidents. He had been a part of our national life for as long as I could remember; he was already a national hero when I first met him in 1947.

Information was one of the primary sources of Edgar Hoover's power. He usually knew something about everything that was going on, and that knowledge made him as valuable to his friends as it made him dangerous to his enemies. He reached a pinnacle of power and prestige during the Eisenhower years. When Kennedy became President, Hoover was already sixty-six years old, and many of Kennedy's advisers urged him to replace Hoover. Robert Kennedy found some of his activist plans as Attorney General hampered by Hoover's influence in the Justice Department, and the result was a period of very strained relations.

I remember sitting with Hoover in his house during a visit to Washington in 1961, listening to him go on about "that sneaky little son of a bitch," who happened to be the President's brother and Hoover's boss. Never in all the years I knew him, however, did I hear him speak disrespectfully of John Kennedy or any other President he had served.

It was under Lyndon Johnson that Hoover became a presidential confidant. Lyndon Johnson's admiration for Hoover was almost unbounded. I remembered his telling me in 1968 that if it hadn't been for Edgar Hoover, he could not have been President. Johnson's fascination with information and gossip was as insatiable as Hoover's own. In many ways the relationship was probably not a healthy one because, as subsequent Senate investigations have shown, it was under Johnson that Hoover allowed the FBI to reach its peak of political involvement.

When I became President, I asked Hoover to stay on as Director, but I was aware that because of his advancing age and the internal problems his long tenure was causing within the Bureau, I would have to begin thinking about a replacement.

In 1971, John Ehrlichman and others on the staff felt strongly that in the interests of the FBI, the administration, and of Hoover himself, we should take the initiative and get him to resign voluntarily before we reached the point where he might be forced to resign under pressure. We heard the reports that the Bureau's morale was sagging and that the characteristics that had once been Hoover's source of strength—his discipline and his pride—were now seen as temperament and ego.

That year Robert Mardian, an Assistant Attorney General under Mitchell, was told about still other problems. He reported a message of concern from William Sullivan, who had been one of Hoover's closest aides in the FBI. Sullivan apparently felt that Hoover was trapped in outdated notions of the communist threat and was not moving with flexibility against the new violence-prone radicals. Sullivan also worried that Hoover was becoming personally erratic and had recently turned on Sullivan himself and planned to fire him.

Mardian reported that Hoover might try to use the seventeen wiretaps we placed on administration aides and reporters in 1969 as blackmail leverage in order to retain his position in the Bureau. I did not believe that he would ever do such a thing. There had long been rumors that Hoover kept his position because of threats and subtle blackmail of various Presidents, but I had always regarded them with skepticism. I was also convinced that however much he might be tempted to disclose political shenanigans, Hoover would never deliberately expose national security wiretaps, the disclosure of which might have an adverse effect on our efforts to end the war and on our other foreign policy initiatives. But the FBI was in a period of great upheaval, and even though the taps had been discontinued, I could not permit the reports of them to fall into the hands of someone who, like Ellsberg, would see the chance to publicize them and become a media hero.

Sullivan had the FBI's copies of the wiretap reports, so I told Mardian to get them from him so that all copies would be kept at the White House. Later Ehrlichman said he was going to keep them himself, and I approved. That was the last I heard of any supposed threat from Hoover. I never said anything to him about it.

In October 1971 Ehrlichman sent me a brilliantly argued memorandum written for him by G. Gordon Liddy, a member of the White House staff and a former FBI agent. The memorandum analyzed in detail the complex situation presented by Hoover's long tenure as Director and concluded with a strong recommendation that he should resign.

While Ehrlichman favored immediate action, John Mitchell had a more restrained view. He knew Hoover's weaknesses, but he felt that an attempt to replace him—especially if it involved a public confrontation—could be very difficult for me and could make the administration very unpopular. He pointed out that despite all the criticism, Hoover still had very substantial support in the country and in Congress. To millions of Americans J. Edgar Hoover was still a folk hero.

I told both Ehrlichman and Mitchell that I thought most of the new wave of anti-Hoover criticism involved predictable charges from predictable sources. His most prominent public critics opposed him not because of his policies but because he was a symbol of beliefs and values that they opposed, particularly his crusade against domestic communism and subversion, his strong stand for tougher anticrime legislation, and his opposition to legal and judicial permissiveness. I would never desert a great man, and an old and loyal friend, just because he was coming under attack.

I did, however, have two other concerns: one pragmatic and one political. What bothered me most deeply was the fact that Hoover's increasingly erratic conduct was showing signs of impairing the morale of the FBI. I told Mitchell, "The real problem, as so often happens in cases like this, is that the man himself has become the issue. That great ego which for so many years was directed almost totally to serving the Bureau and the nation is now being put into the service of the man himself. I'm sure Edgar isn't even aware that it is happening. But we have to face the fact that he is thinking too much of himself and not enough about the cause he wants to serve."

My second concern was based on my own political realism: I could not be sure that I would be re-elected for a second term. I was aware of what could happen to the FBI in the hands of a politically motivated opposition party, and the last thing I wanted to do was give the Democrats a chance to appoint a new Director who would unquestioningly carry out their bidding against Republicans for the next four or eight years.

Mitchell finally suggested that the ideal compromise would be to persuade Hoover that he should voluntarily announce his decision to retire on his seventy-seventh birthday in 1972. Such an announcement would both undercut the mounting criticism and avoid charges that he had been forced out.

Since the Director of the FBI is under the administrative control of the Attorney General, Mitchell would ordinarily have been the one to raise the question of Hoover's voluntary resignation with him. But as Mitchell put it, "Mr. President, both you and I know that Edgar Hoover isn't about to listen to anyone other than the President of the United States when it comes to this question." I knew that he was right. Although it would be painful for both of us, I decided to invite Hoover to have breakfast with me at the White House and to raise the subject with him then.

At our breakfast Hoover was as alert, articulate, and decisive as I had ever seen him. It was obvious that he was trying to demonstrate that despite his age he was still physically, mentally, and emotionally equipped to carry on.

I told him that I knew he was sensitive about some of the recent attacks on him in Congress, and about a very negative conference on the FBI at Princeton University.

"You shouldn't let things like that get you down, Edgar," I said. "Lyndon told me that he couldn't have been President without your advice and assistance, and as you know, I have the same respect for you as well as a deep personal affection that goes back nearly twenty-five years." Having said this, I tried to point out as gently and subtly as I could that as an astute politician he must recognize that the attacks were going to mount in number and intensity in the years ahead. It would be a tragedy if he ended his career while under a sustained attack from his long-time critics instead of in the glow of national respect that he so rightly deserved.

He responded very directly. He said, "More than anything else, I want to see *you* re-elected in 1972. If you feel that my staying on as head of the Bureau hurts your chances for re-election, just let me know. As far as these present attacks are concerned, and the ones that are planned for the future, they don't make any difference to me. I think you know that the tougher the attacks get, the tougher I get."

It was obvious that he was not going to take the initiative in offering his resignation. I had been through this kind of situation in 1952 when I told Eisenhower that he should make the decision whether or not I was a liability to his campaign. Now Hoover was taking exactly the same position with me: he would submit his resignation only if I specifically requested it. I decided not to do so. My personal feelings played a part in my decision, but equally important was my conclusion that Hoover's resignation before the election would raise more political problems than it would solve.

It has now become fashionable to think of our years of concern over organized crime and subversive communism as a national neurosis. Because Hoover was at the forefront of the anticrime and anticommunist movements of the postwar period, he has been painted, since the revision, as the chief neurotic. But Hoover had done the job that the public demanded for forty-eight years.

During his long and controversial life he made many enemies. He received much criticism, some of it deserved. But he took a bad rap from the critics who charged him with being "anti" one group or another. He was strongly pro-American and only against any group or individual he concluded might be engaging in activities that threatened the security of his country.

Diary

He died at the right time; fortunately, he died in office. It would have killed him had he been forced out of office or had he resigned even voluntarily. I remember the last conversation I had with him about two weeks ago when I called him and mentioned the fine job the Bureau had done on the hijacking cases. He expressed his appreciation for that call and also expressed his total support for what we are doing in Vietnam. I am particularly glad that I did not force him out at the end of last year.

I tried Buchanan on the statement [on Hoover's death] and I think improved upon it in one respect when I said that while I had ordered the flags to be flown at half-mast the flag at the FBI would always fly high due to the courage of J. Edgar Hoover in resisting the vicious attacks on his organization.

While we were trying to decide on Hoover's successor, I received Kissinger's report of his May 2 meeting with the North Vietnamese in Paris. The Communists had been icy and snide, and after putting up with three hours of insult and invective, Kissinger broke off the talks.

Diary

I found with no surprise that the North Vietnamese had given nothing whatever, and that it was the most unproductive of all of Henry's trips. This is the one weakness in his approach to some of these problems. He is so understandably obsessed with the idea that there *should* be a negotiated settlement and that we ought to be able to obtain it with everything that we have set in motion, that he cannot get himself to see clearly why there really isn't enough in it for the enemy to negotiate at this time. I had a long talk with Haig, in which we concluded that we had to have a two-day strike rather than the one-day-separated-by-another-day as Henry had recommended earlier in the week. We have very few cards to play at this point.

I have sent Henry a message indicating that I thought he should think seriously on the plane on the way back about our breaking off the summit before the Russians make that move.

Haig emphasized that even more important than how Vietnam comes out is for us to handle these matters in a way that I can survive in office. I am not sure that this will be possible and in any event I am totally committed to the idea that rather than going out like Johnson did, that I must make whatever hard choices have to be made, and take whatever risks need to be taken, to preserve the position of the U.S. in Vietnam.

Of course, the weak link in our whole chain is the question as to whether the South Vietnamese have the will to fight. Certainly Abrams has been very strongly shaken in this respect as we compare his memorandum of May 1, with his memorandum of just a week before. I wired Thieu today personally to keep his spirits up, because I think it is vitally important that we not be responsible for his losing his courage at this very difficult time when bad news is coming in from the war front. The real problem is that the enemy is willing to sacrifice in order to win, while the South Vietnamese simply aren't willing to pay that much of a price in order to avoid losing. And, as Haig points out, all the air power in the world and strikes on Hanoi-Haiphong aren't going to save South Vietnam if the South Vietnamese aren't able to hold on the ground.

When Kissinger returned from Paris that night he was still discouraged by Le Duc Tho's arrogant conduct. He felt that there was now almost no chance that the Soviet Summit could take place, and he agreed with my initial inclination that we should cancel it immediately in order to prevent the Soviets from doing so first.

We discussed the overriding questions: Would cancellation of the summit be the key to winning the war? Would it shock the Soviets into finally putting some pressure on the North Vietnamese? Would it free us to lift all restrictions and bomb them until they gave in? We agreed that it was unlikely to do any of these things.

Then, I said, I would have to consider the problems it would cause. It would dash a lot of domestic hopes for peace, and that would give the Democrats a real issue. It would unleash a worldwide propaganda offensive in which the Soviets could claim that they had crumbled our foreign policy. "It's hard to see how cancellation is a really rational choice when you look at it this way," I concluded.

The problem, as Kissinger saw it, was that we could not bomb and have the summit too. And now we would have to bomb because we had said we would unless we got some meaningful action in Paris. The Soviets knew this, and unless they thought we were going to back down on our threat, it was highly likely that they would cancel the summit themselves and blame the cancellation on our bombing. That would be the worst possible outcome: a domestic outcry over the bombing and cancellation of the summit as well.

The arguments on both sides seemed persuasive. It was hard to see how I could go to the summit and be clinking glasses with Brezhnev while Soviet tanks were rumbling through Hué or Quangtri. That would show callousness, or weakness, or both. For us to cancel the summit, however, would inevitably be criticized as an impulsive action that dashed the hopes for progress toward a more peaceful world.

I decided to take the risk of postponing a decision for at least a few days. In the meantime I was determined to keep up a strong front despite all the recent setbacks. I began by sending a blunt reply to Brezhnev's letter of May 1 in which he had warned me against taking any actions in Vietnam that might hurt the chance of a successful summit. I said that the North Vietnamese had tricked us and apparently hoped that their offensive would force concessions from us:

> But this, Mr. General Secretary, will not happen, and I must now decide on the next steps in the situation that has been created. In the light of recent events, there does not seem much promise in communicating to you additional substantive considerations; there is now no basis for believing that this will have a positive effect on the situation. As Mr. Le Duc Tho made clear, Hanoi is contemptuous of communications transmitted by a third party. The fact remains that Soviet military supplies provide the means for the D.R.V.'s [Democratic Republic of (North) Vietnam] actions and promised Soviet influence if it has been exercised at all has proved unavailing.

I told Haldeman that he and Kissinger should brief John Connally on the situation and get his opinion. Haldeman reported that Connally emphatically said, "Most important—the President must not lose the war!

And he should not cancel the summit. He's got to show his guts and leadership on this one. Caution be damned—if they cancel, and I don't think they will, we'll ram it right down their throats."

I discussed the issue with Kissinger, Haldeman, Connally, and Haig: "As far as I'm concerned, the only real mistakes I've made were the times when I didn't follow my own instincts," I told them. "After the EC-121 was shot down I knew that we should have moved in and bombed North Korea. When we didn't, everybody figured we were pushovers, and we've been paying for that ever since. When we went into Cambodia, I knew that we should have bombed North Vietnam at the same time. If we'd done that then, the damned war would be over now. Now in this case, my instinct is that one thing is clear: whatever else happens we cannot lose this war. The summit isn't worth a damn if the price for it is losing in Vietnam. My instinct tells me that the country can take losing the summit, but it can't take losing the war."

I believed that it was essential that we take decisive action to cripple the North Vietnamese invasion by interdicting the supplies of fuel and military equipment the enemy needed for its push into South Vietnam. I consequently directed that plans be prepared immediately for mining Haiphong Harbor and for bombing prime military targets in Hanoi, particularly the railroad lines used for transporting military supplies.

I went to Camp David to prepare the speech announcing my decision. On Sunday night I recorded the events of that tense weekend.

Diary

Julie went up with me Friday at four o'clock, and Tricia and Eddie joined us around six o'clock. We saw a good comedy with Bob Hope that night.

I told Julie about the decision on Friday and Tricia on Saturday.

Julie seemed concerned about it in terms of whether it would work. She obviously has done a lot of reading about past failures on the military side in Vietnam. She also was aware of the fact that many had become so disillusioned with the war that we might not have enough public support for it. I mentioned the fact that if we did not do this the United States would cease to be a respected great power. She rejoined with the observation that there were many who felt that the United States shouldn't be a great power. This, of course, is the kind of poison that is fed into so many of the younger generation by their professors. She was sure, however, that David would totally agree with the decision, and she seemed sensitive to what the needs were.

Tricia's reaction was immediately positive because she felt we had to do something, and frankly didn't know what else we could do to avoid a continued deterioration in the battle areas.

Pat came up very late Friday night. I had just come back from Birch where I had been working on the speech. I saw the light on in Pat's room, and when I went in, she got up and came over, and put her arms around me, and said, "Don't worry about anything."

Over the weekend I talked to John Mitchell and he said he thoroughly approved of the decision.

Henry seemed pleased by the fact that all but one of his staff were for the blockade, including his Vietnam expert, who is somewhat of a dove. All of his staff say that it will kill the summit. Mitchell disagrees with that as did Connally.

I discussed with Kissinger the necessity to prepare a contingency plan for summit cancellation. As of this morning, he had raised his 20 percent possibility of a noncancellation to 25 percent, although he still cannot see how the Russians can react otherwise. I constantly bring him back to the point that Connally had made when we reached the decision: we can lose the summit and a number of other battles but we cannot lose in Vietnam. Not only the election, but even more important, the country, requires that the United States not lose in Vietnam. Everything is to be concentrated toward the goal now of seeing that we do not lose now that we have crossed the Rubicon.

The drafts we went through on the speech will tell the story of how it developed. Perhaps the most important section was that on the Soviet Union, and Henry was very impressed with what I finally came up with on my own. It had to be done with great subtlety and I think we have stated the case as well as we possibly can to give them a way out if they want to find one.

This whole period has been terribly hard on the family. Tricia and Eddie have decided to stay up there at Camp David. I am so glad that both girls are making great use of it, because no one knows, as I told Rose, whether we will have it to use after this year, and I want them to have the most pleasant memories of these years.

On Monday morning I informed the NSC that I had decided to go ahead with the bombing and mining, and that I would announce the decision in a televised speech that night.

Diary

Monday was a pretty tough day because the NSC meeting ran over three hours, with Laird opposing the decision and Rogers

> saying he would be for it if it worked. Connally and Agnew predictably took a very strong position for it. The record will speak for itself. Of course, in fairness to Laird and Rogers, both of their reputations are on the line, and I think they have very serious doubts about whether the action will succeed. The real test, of course, will be whether they support once the decision is made and on that I have no doubt.

The biggest question mark remained the Soviet reaction. On Monday morning I sent a four-page letter to Brezhnev explaining what I had decided to do and why. I reiterated my dedication to developing our new relationship into a foundation for world peace and said that I did not intend to let the situation forced upon us by the actions of the North Vietnamese divert us from the path upon which our two countries had embarked:

> In conclusion, Mr. General Secretary, let me say to you that this is a moment for statesmanship. It is a moment when, by joint efforts, we can end the malignant effects on our relations and on the peace of the world which the conflict in Vietnam has so long produced. I am ready to join with you at once to bring about a peace that humiliates neither side and serves the interests of all the people involved. I know that together we have the capacity to do this.

The final copy of my speech was not ready until after five o'clock, and I marked it up for reading and then went to get a haircut at 5:30. I had my usual light prespeech dinner of a small bowl of wheat germ for energy around six, and then went over the text until half past seven.

I jogged in place for about ten minutes and took a long cold shower before going over to the West Wing for a meeting with the joint congressional leadership in the Roosevelt Room.

The room was comfortable and warm, with a fine fire burning in the fireplace. I looked around at the familiar faces, some tense, some wary, all alert: Carl Albert, Hugh Scott, Bill Fulbright, Mike Mansfield, John Stennis, George Aiken, Jerry Ford, Hale Boggs, and half a dozen others. Some would oppose me, others would only reluctantly support me while wishing that I had not made this decision. As I described the situation and the actions I had decided to take no one interrupted or asked any questions.

I acknowledged that this was very strong medicine. It had been a very difficult decision for me to make and I knew that it would be a very difficult decision for them to support.

"If you can give me your support, I would appreciate it," I said. "If you cannot, I will understand."

There was complete silence as I rose and left the room.

Kissinger had invited Dobrynin to come to the White House shortly before I was to deliver the speech. When he described what I was about to say, Dobrynin became terribly agitated. "Why are you turning against *us* when it is Hanoi that has challenged you?" he asked.

Kissinger remained cool. Dobrynin said that he did not see how matters could do anything except take a very bad turn.

I delivered the speech at 9 P.M. After describing the military situation and the deadlock in the negotiations, I said, "There is only one way to stop the killing. That is to keep the weapons of war out of the hands of the international outlaws of North Vietnam." I continued, "I have ordered the following measures which are being implemented as I am speaking to you. All entrances to North Vietnamese ports will be mined to prevent access to these ports and North Vietnamese naval operations from these ports. United States forces have been directed to take appropriate measures within the internal and claimed territorial waters of North Vietnam to interdict the delivery of any supplies. Rail and all other communications will be cut off to the maximum extent possible. Air and naval strikes against military targets in North Vietnam will continue."

I then presented a new peace proposal, which became the reference point for the terms of the final settlement the following January:

> First, all American prisoners of war must be returned.
>
> Second, there must be an internationally supervised cease-fire throughout Indochina.
>
> Once prisoners of war are released, once the internationally supervised cease-fire has begun, we will stop all acts of force throughout Indochina, and at that time we will proceed with a complete withdrawal of all American forces from Vietnam within four months.
>
> Now, these terms are generous terms. They are terms which would not require surrender and humiliation on the part of anybody. . . . They deserve immediate acceptance by North Vietnam.

I concluded with the carefully phrased message to the Soviet Union that I had personally drafted: "We expect you to help your allies, and you cannot expect us to do other than to continue to help our allies, but let us, and let all great powers, help our allies only for the purpose of their defense, not for the purpose of launching invasions against their neighbors. . . . Our two nations have made significant progress in our negotiations in recent months. We are near major agreements on nuclear arms limitation, on trade, on a host of other issues. Let us not slide back toward the dark shadows of a previous age. We do not ask you to sacrifice your principles, or your friends, but neither should you permit

Hanoi's intransigence to blot out the prospects we together have so patiently prepared."

Criticism in Congress and the media was immediate and shrill. Teddy Kennedy said that the mining was a "futile military gesture taken in desperation. I think his decision is ominous, and I think it is folly." The St. Louis *Post-Dispatch* stated that the nation would not support me because "in this case, the cause of war isn't one of honor but of dishonor." The *Wall Street Journal* reported that informed diplomatic observers were now guessing that the summit would be postponed indefinitely. Most of the television reports were focused on this question, and the network commentators unanimously concluded that my speech had seriously jeopardized the summit. NBC's Moscow correspondent said that it would be hard for the Kremlin to swallow my decision, and that it would "practically kill prospects of a summit."

The reticence of the military planners continued to be a problem.

The bombing proposals sent to me by the Pentagon could at best be described as timid. As I wrote in a long memorandum to Kissinger, "I am concerned by the military's plan of allocating 200 sorties for North Vietnam for the dreary 'milk runs' which characterized the Johnson administration's bombing in the 1965–68 period."

Having gone through the agony of making the decision and having accepted the political risks it would involve, I was determined to have it carried out the way I intended. I continued the memo:

> I cannot emphasize too strongly that I have determined that we should go for broke. What we have got to get across to the enemy is the impression that we are doing exactly that. Our words will help some. But our actions in the next few days will speak infinitely louder than our words.
>
> I am totally unsatisfied at this time at the plans the military have suggested as far as air activities are concerned. . . .
>
> Our greatest failure now would be to do too little too late. It is far more important to do too much at a time that we will have maximum public support for what we do.
>
> What all of us must have in mind is that we must *punish* the enemy in ways that he will really hurt at this time. . . .
>
> Now that I have made this very tough watershed decision I intend to stop at nothing to bring the enemy to his knees. I want you to get this spirit inculcated in all hands and particularly I want the military to get off its backside and give me some recommendations as to how we can accomplish that goal. . . .
>
> I think we have had too much of a tendency to talk big and act little. This was certainly the weakness of the Johnson administration. To an extent it may have been our weakness where we have warned the enemy time and

> time again and then have acted in a rather mild way when the enemy has tested us. He has now gone over the brink *and so have we.* We have the power to destroy his war-making capacity. The only question is whether we have the *will* to use that power. What distinguishes me from Johnson is that I have the *will* in spades. If we now fail it will be because the bureaucrats and the bureaucracy and particularly those in the Defense Department, who will of course be vigorously assisted by their allies in State, will find ways to erode the strong, decisive action that I have indicated we are going to take. For once, I want the military and I want the NSC staff to come up with some ideas on their own which will recommend *action* which is very *strong, threatening,* and *effective.*

The Soviet news agency TASS issued a stinging denunciation of the mining as "fraught with serious consequences for international peace and security" and an emergency meeting of the Politburo was held in the Kremlin on the morning after the speech. I was fully prepared for an official statement condemning my actions and canceling the summit.

The next day Dobrynin met with Kissinger in the Map Room. Ignoring the usual pleasantries, Dobrynin coldly announced that his government had instructed him to read an official note. To Kissinger's immense relief, it turned out to be a relatively mild and private protest about the blockade and about a Soviet seaman who had been killed when a bomb accidentally hit a Soviet ship in Haiphong Harbor. When they met again the next afternoon, Kissinger casually asked why the Soviets had made no mention of the summit.

"We have not been asked any questions about the summit," Dobrynin replied, "and therefore my government sees no need to make a new decision."

Kissinger said, "*Should* we have asked any questions about the summit?"

"No," Dobrynin replied, "you have handled a difficult situation uncommonly well."

During their meeting I had been visting Manolo at the hospital where he was recuperating from surgery. The moment I returned Kissinger rushed into my office to tell me the news. "I think we have passed the crisis," he said exuberantly. "I think we are going to be able to have our mining and bombing and have our summit too."

The next day, Dobrynin called Kissinger saying he had a message from Moscow. It turned out to be about procedural details for the summit. He even brought up the question of the state gifts to be exchanged. The Soviets were planning to give me a hydrofoil for use at Key Biscayne, and he said that Brezhnev would not look unkindly on receiving a new car for his collection of luxury automobiles.

It now seemed certain that the summit had survived the speech. The media pundits and congressional critics who had been predicting disaster dropped the cancellation line and began to concentrate on allegations that our bombers were hitting civilian targets.

Early Monday morning, May 15, I was back at my desk ready for a heavy day of meetings and appointments. I was talking with Don Kendall late in the afternoon when Bob Haldeman came in and asked if he could see me for a moment in the private office. When the door was closed behind us, he said, "We just got word over the Secret Service wire that George Wallace was shot at a rally in Maryland."

I asked if he was alive. Haldeman said he was. He said that the gunman was white, but we didn't know anything more about him yet.

The shock of the Wallace shooting forced memories back to the horror of the assassinations of John Kennedy, Martin Luther King, and Robert Kennedy. However terrible and stunning this new blow, I was determined not to let the country be talked into a climate of fear.

An editorial in the New York *Times* the next morning suggested that because of the mood of violence in the country, candidates should stay away from outdoor rallies and campaign only on television or in closed halls where security could be assured. I told Haldeman that under no circumstances would I let my Secret Service detail be increased.

Around noon John Connally came to my office after having announced his resignation and George Shultz's nomination as Secretary of Treasury. I told him and others in the room I was going for a walk.

"When?" Ron Ziegler asked.

"Right now," I said. "Come on."

I decided to walk with Connally back to the Treasury Building. When we emerged from the East Wing just across the street from the Treasury Building a small crowd gathered, and I stopped to talk with some young people with cameras and several foreign visitors. A rather distinguished-looking man said that he was a lawyer who had gone to the University of Virginia Law School. As I started to cross the street, he said, "Thank you for coming out today."

At the end of the week I went to see Wallace at the hospital.

Diary

I stopped in to see Wallace on my way to Washington Friday morning. I was again impressed about the attractiveness of Mrs. Wallace. She has great verve, and I can see must be an enormous asset to him in his campaigning.

He seemed very up for the meeting although I sensed that he did not hear or understand too well at times. He was very proud of the showing he had made in the primaries. I told him that I would send somebody out to brief him after the Russian trip, which pleased him. He said that he would like to consider going to Walter Reed at another time, and I told him it would be available at any time when he was in the Washington area—that it provided perfect security and was a particularly nice room.

He is, though a demagogue, somewhat sentimental in terms of his strong patriotism, like most Southerners, and it came through loud and clear in the meeting. He pointed out that he had taken on both Humphrey and Muskie on the ground that they had voted for all the actions that got the United States into the war in Southeast Asia and now were criticizing what I was doing to get us out. There was a floral flag by his bed, and as I left I told him to keep the flag flying high. He saluted and said, I certainly will to my Commander in Chief. I saluted back and left the room.

SUMMIT I

On Saturday, May 20, *Air Force One* left Washington for Salzburg, Austria, en route to Moscow. After we were airborne, Kissinger came into my cabin and exuberantly said, "This has to be one of the great diplomatic coups of all times! Three weeks ago everyone predicted it would be called off, and today we're on our way."

At 4 P.M. on Monday, May 22, after staying overnight in Salzburg, we landed at Moscow's Vnukovo Airport.

A light rain had begun to fall just before we arrived. President Nikolai Podgorny officially greeted me; Kosygin and Gromyko were also there. Aside from a small crowd standing behind the fence and waving little paper flags, it was a very cool reception. As our motorcade raced along the broad and completely empty streets toward the Kremlin, I noticed that fairly sizable crowds were being kept behind police barriers a block away down the side streets.

Pat and I had been given an entire floor of rooms in one of the large wings of the Grand Palace inside the Kremlin. As we were looking around our ornately opulent quarters, Kissinger arrived with the news that Brezhnev was waiting to welcome me in his office.

Brezhnev's office was the same room in which I had first met Khrushchev, thirteen years before. Like Khrushchev, Brezhnev looked exactly like his photographs: the bushy eyebrows dominated his face, and his mouth was set in a fixed, rather wary smile. I was sure that neither of us, standing shoulder to shoulder in the kitchen at the American Exhibition thirteen years before, had imagined that we would one day be meeting at the summit as the leaders of our countries.

We shook hands and stood talking while tea was brought in for us. He gestured to a long table at one side of the room, and he and I sat down on opposite sides of it with the Soviet translator Viktor Sukhodrev at the end. There had been concern expressed that I should have a State Department translator present also. But I knew that Sukhodrev was a superb linguist who spoke English as well as he did Russian, and I felt that Brezhnev would speak more freely if only one other person was present.

Brezhnev's tone was cordial, but his words were blunt. He said that at the outset he had to tell me that it had not been easy for him to carry off this summit after our recent actions in Vietnam. Only the overriding importance of improving Soviet-American relations and reaching agreements on some of the serious issues between us had made it possible.

After he had made this almost obligatory statement, he warmed perceptibly as he began to talk about the necessity and advantages of developing a personal relationship between us. He said that the name of Franklin D. Roosevelt was warmly cherished in the memory of the Soviet people, who remembered him as the first President to extend diplomatic recognition to the Soviet Union in 1934 and as the leader of the alliance against Hitler during World War II.

I said that I had studied the history of the relationships between Stalin and Roosevelt and between Stalin and Churchill. I had found that during the war differences between subordinates were usually overcome by agreement at the top level. "That is the kind of relationship that I should like to establish with the General Secretary," I said.

"I would be only too happy, and I am perfectly ready on my side," he replied expansively.

"If we leave all the decisions to the bureaucrats, we will never achieve any progress," I said.

"They would simply bury us in paper!" He laughed heartily and slapped his palm on the table. It seemed to be a good beginning.

About a half hour later we met again for the state dinner in the beautiful fifteenth-century Granovit Hall in the heart of the oldest part of the Kremlin. The parquet floor had been polished to a high gloss, and the vaulted walls were covered with huge icon-like paintings in rich gold and brown tones. Sitting next to each other at the head table, Brezhnev and I looked directly across the room at a several-times life-size mural of Christ and the Apostles at the Last Supper. Brezhnev said, "That was the Politburo of those days." I responded, "That must mean that the General Secretary and the Pope have much in common." Brezhnev laughed and reached over and shook my hand.

As usual, the time change made it impossible for me to fall asleep that first night. I finally got up around 4:30 and pulled on slacks and a jacket and decided to go out for a walk around the Kremlin grounds. In Moscow's northern latitude it was already almost clear daylight. I could hear the boats on the river and the sounds of truck traffic from the streets outside the red brick walls. I paused for a minute to look up at the American flag flying atop our residence amid the gold onion-top domes and red stars of the Kremlin churches and towers.

In the first plenary session at 11 A.M. with Brezhnev, Kosygin, Podgorny, Gromyko, and Dobrynin, I decided to establish the straightforward tone I planned to adopt during the entire summit.

"I would like to say something that my Soviet friends may be too polite to say," I began. "I know that my reputation is one of being a very hard-line, cold-war-oriented, anticommunist."

Kosygin said dryly, "I had heard this sometime back."

"It is true that I have a strong belief in our system," I continued, "but at the same time I respect those who believe just as strongly in their own systems. There must be room in this world for two great nations with different systems to live together and work together. We cannot do this, however, by mushy sentimentality or by glossing over differences which exist."

All the heads nodded on the other side of the table, but I guessed that in fact they would have much preferred a continuation of the mushy sentimentality that had characterized so much of our approach to the Soviets in the past.

That afternoon Kissinger and I had a two-hour meeting on SALT with Brezhnev and Andrei Aleksandrov, his adviser on U.S.–Soviet affairs. Despite the impatience he affected with the details and numbers, Brezhnev was obviously very well briefed on the subject. He used a red pencil to sketch missiles on the notepad in front of him as we discussed the timing and techniques of control and limitation.

When I said we felt that specific provisions for verifying that each side was fulfilling its obligations would give necessary reassurance to both sides, he turned to me and in an injured tone of voice said, "If we are trying to trick one another, why do we need a piece of paper? We are playing clean on our side. The approach of 'catching each other out' is quite inadmissible."

We held another long meeting that evening to discuss the important and controversial question of how far the new Soviet ABM systems would be situated from Moscow. When we began our discussion, Brezhnev casually cut three hundred kilometers from the figure that had been agreed upon just a few hours earlier. "Regarding the ABM question," he said, "this now appears to be cleared up. Twelve hundred kilometers is OK with us."

"Fifteen hundred," I said.

"You mean we should put it in China?" he said with mock exasperation.

"Well, as the General Secretary will find out, I never nit-pick," I replied.

"Fifteen hundred kilometers is all right," he said without missing a beat. "You wanted us to move eastward and so now we agree. It would be easier for us to accept twelve hundred, but fifteen hundred is all right, too, and we won't speak of it anymore."

It is a technique of Communist negotiators to introduce some ideal but impractical change in an area where the details have already been agreed upon. When we were wrangling over specific provisions of the SALT proposal, which both sides had agreed would last for five years, Brezhnev suddenly asked, "Why not make it for ten years? Why only five?" Kissinger calmly pointed out that the Soviets themselves had originally wanted the agreement to last for only eighteen months.

"I would consider this interim agreement a great achievement for us and all the world," I said. "I want to reach a permanent agreement, but my time is limited—less than five years. After then, I am out—swimming in the Pacific. Maybe even before."

"Don't go out before that, Mr. President," Brezhnev said.

Surprise is another favorite technique of Communist negotiators. After the ceremony on Wednesday afternoon when we signed an agreement on cooperation in space exploration, Brezhnev and I walked out of the room together. He began talking about the dinner planned for us at one of the government dachas outside Moscow that evening. As we neared the end of the corridor, he took my arm and said, "Why don't we go to the country right now so you can see it in the daylight?" He propelled me into an elevator that took us down to the ground floor where one of his limousines was parked.

We climbed into the limousine and were on our way while the Secret Service and the others rushed around trying to find cars and drivers to follow us. The middle lane of all the main streets in Moscow is reserved solely for party officials, and we drove along at a very fast clip.

As soon as we arrived at the dacha, Brezhnev suggested that we go for a boat ride on the Moskva River. This was exactly what Khrushchev had done thirteen years before. But times had changed: he led us not to a motorboat but to a small hydrofoil bobbing gently in the water. The pilot was skilled, and we had a smooth ride. Brezhnev kept pointing to the speedometer, which showed us traveling at ninety kilometers an hour.

We discussed work habits, and he told me he did not use a Dictaphone. I recalled that Churchill had told me that he much preferred to dictate to a pretty young woman. Brezhnev and the others agreed, and

Brezhnev jokingly added, "Besides, a secretary is particularly useful when you wake up at night and want to write down a note." They all laughed uproariously.

Everyone was in a good humor when we got back to the dacha, and Brezhnev suggested that we have a meeting before the dinner, which was scheduled for eight o'clock.

Kissinger and I sat with Winston Lord and John Negroponte of the NSC on one side of the table, facing Brezhnev, Kosygin, Podgorny, and Sukhodrev on the other side. For the next three hours the Soviet leaders pounded me bitterly and emotionally about Vietnam.

I momentarily thought of Dr. Jekyll and Mr. Hyde when Brezhnev, who had just been laughing and slapping me on the back, started shouting angrily that instead of honestly working to end the war, I was trying to use the Chinese as a means of bringing pressure on the Soviets to intervene with the North Vietnamese. He said that they wondered whether on May 8 I had acted out of thoughtless irritation, because they had no doubt that if I really wanted peace I could get a settlement without any outside assistance. "It's surely doubtful that all of the American people are unanimously supporting the war in Vietnam," he continued. "Certainly I doubt that families of those who were killed or maimed or who remain crippled support the war."

When Brezhnev finally seemed to run out of steam, Kosygin took up the cudgel. He said, "Mr. President, I believe you overestimate the possibility in the present circumstances of resolving problems in Vietnam from a position of strength. There may come a critical moment for the North Vietnamese when they will not refuse to let in forces of other countries to act on their side."

This was going too far. For the first time I spoke. "That threat doesn't frighten us a bit," I said, "but go ahead and make it."

"Don't think you are right in thinking what we say is a threat and what you say is not a threat," Kosygin replied coldly. He said, "This is an *analysis* of what may happen, and that is much more serious than a threat."

Kosygin seemed to gather force as he concentrated his scorn on President Thieu, to whom he referred as "a mercenary President so-called." When I continued to show no reaction to this tirade Kosygin's composure began to break. "You still need to retain the so-called President in South Vietnam, someone *you* call the President, who had not been chosen by anyone?" he asked.

"Who chose the President of *North* Vietnam?" I asked him.

"The entire people," he replied.

"Go ahead," I said.

When Kosygin concluded, Podgorny came to bat. His tone was more cordial, but his words were just as tough. While Podgorny and Kosygin were taking their turns at trying to hammer me down, Brezhnev got up and paced the floor.

After about twenty minutes, Podgorny suddenly stopped and Brezhnev said a few more words. Then there was silence in the room. By this time it was almost eleven o'clock. I felt that before I could let this conversation end, I had to let them know exactly where I stood.

I pointed out that I had withdrawn over 500,000 men from Vietnam. I had shown the greatest restraint when the North Vietnamese began their massive buildup in March, because I did not want anything to affect the summit. But when the North Vietnamese actually invaded South Vietnam, I had no choice but to react strongly.

"The General Secretary remarked earlier that some people may have wondered whether the action I took last month was because of irritation," I said. "If that were the case, I would be a very dangerous man in the position I am in. But that is not the case. On the contrary, my decision was taken in cold objectivity. That is the way I always act, having in mind the consequences and the risks.

"Our people want peace. I want it too. But I want the Soviet leaders to know how seriously I view this threat of new North Vietnamese escalation. One of our great Civil War generals, General Sherman, said, 'War is hell.' No people knows this better than the Soviet people. And since this new offensive began, 30,000 South Vietnamese civilians, men, women, and children, have been killed by the North Vietnamese using Soviet equipment.

"I would not for one moment suggest that the leaders of the Soviet Union wanted that to happen. What I am simply suggesting is that our goal is the same as yours. We are not trying to impose a settlement or a government on anybody."

They listened intently to what I said, but none of them made an attempt to respond.

With that we went upstairs, where a lavish dinner was waiting for us. I made my usual joke about not giving Kissinger too many drinks because he had to go back and negotiate with Gromyko. They seemed vastly amused by this and they proceeded in a comic charade to pretend to ply him with vodka and Cognac. There was much laughing and joking and storytelling —as if the acrimonious session downstairs had never happened.

While we were eating, Kosygin remarked that it was a good omen for our future relations that after three hours of the kind of hard-hitting discussions we had just completed, we could still have a relaxed and personally friendly conversation over dinner. I responded that we must recognize our differences and discuss them honestly. He nodded his head vigorously and raised his glass in another toast.

It was after midnight by the time we got back to the Kremlin. Kissinger and Gromyko immediately began a meeting on the critical questions still standing in the way of a SALT agreement.

I was in my room getting a back treatment from Dr. Riland around 1:00 A.M. when Kissinger came in with the news that the Soviets were continuing to hold out for their position, which was unacceptable to us. It was possible that they were hoping that the domestic pressures on me to return home with a SALT agreement would force me to settle for their terms. I had anticipated this possibility before we left Washington, and I was ready to call their bluff.

Kissinger had further news, however, for which I was not prepared. He reported that the Pentagon was in almost open rebellion and the Joint Chiefs were backing away from the SALT position to which they had previously agreed. Kissinger did not have to remind me—although he did so in the most urgent terms—that if word of this split reached the press, or if the Pentagon refused to support a SALT agreement I brought back from the summit, the domestic political consequences would be devastating.

"The hell with the political consequences," I said. "We are going to make an agreement on *our* terms regardless of the political consequences if the Pentagon won't go along." I determined not to allow either the Pentagon on the right or the Soviets on the left to drive me away from the position I believed was in the best interests of the country.

"Just do the best you can," I said, "and remember that as far as I'm concerned, we don't have to settle this week."

Kissinger spent several more hours that night trying to hammer out an acceptable agreement. The meeting finally broke up in the early morning with the issue still deadlocked.

The next night we went to a gala performance of *Swan Lake* at the Bolshoi Theatre. I sat between Kosygin and Podgorny, with Pat on Kosygin's right. Protocol did not require Brezhnev to attend, and I welcomed the opportunity to see how his colleagues acted away from his forceful presence.

Between the second and third acts a woman in the audience stood up and, turning toward our box, yelled, "Viva Vietnam!" She was quickly removed. We later learned that she was the wife of an Italian journalist who worked for a pro-Communist newspaper. At the next intermission Kosygin remarked that if we left Vietnam our prestige would grow, rather than suffer the way French prestige did after the defeats at Dien Bien Phu and in Algeria. That was the only mention of substantive issues all evening, and Podgorny immediately moved on to say that his favorite part of the ballet was the dance of the four swans in the second act.

Kissinger resumed his meetings with Gromyko after the ballet. The next morning he reported that they had gone as far as they could with the actual negotiations. Their meeting had broken up without any agreement having been reached.

Later, Kissinger and I were meeting in my apartment when Dobrynin arrived with the news that the Politburo had held a special session and agreed to accept our final position.

Everyone's spirits were high at the dinner we gave at Spaso House, the ambassador's residence, that night. Brezhnev was at his most expansive. The pièce de résistance of the meal was a flaming Baked Alaska. When it was brought in, Brezhnev said, "Look! The Americans really are miracle workers! They have found a way to set ice cream on fire!"

Just after eleven that night in the Kremlin, Brezhnev and I signed the ABM treaty and the Interim Offensive Agreement, thereby establishing a temporary freeze on the numbers of ICBMs and submarine-launched missiles that each side could possess until a permanent agreement was negotiated. Pat had asked me if she could attend the historic ceremony. Since none of the other wives would be there, I suggested that she wait until the official party had entered and then slip in and stand behind one of the large columns. She did, and watched the signing.

The next day we flew to Leningrad. We visited the Piskaryev Cemetery, where many of the hundreds of thousands who died during the Nazi siege of the city are buried. We were running late, so the advance man recommended that I cut the scheduled stop at the small museum there. The young girl who was acting as our guide was obviously upset when she heard that I might not complete the itinerary. I said that of course I would visit the museum. I was deeply moved when she showed me the diary of Tanya, a twelve-year-old girl buried in the cemetery. She translated from the entries describing how one after another the members of Tanya's family died; the final sad entry read: "All are dead. Only Tanya is left." The girl's voice choked with emotion as she read these words. "Tanya died too," she said as she brushed tears from her eyes.

I was asked to sign the visitor's book before we left. I wrote: "To Tanya and all the heroes of Leningrad." As I walked away, I said, "I hope it will never be repeated in all the world."

We flew back to Moscow, and on the next day, Sunday, we went to services at Moscow's only Baptist church, the All-Union Council of Evangelical Christian Baptists. The unaffected singing of the congregation made me think of the early Christians. I was surprised to see such a large number of young people in the congregation. I was told later that many of the older men and women had either been frightened away or displaced by KGB agents.

I spent the rest of the day preparing my television broadcast to the people of the Soviet Union. As in 1959, I felt that this would be a very important opportunity for me to present the American viewpoint on international issues to the Russian people without any editing or control by the Soviet government.

In the speech I discussed the dangers of an unchecked arms race, and I underlined America's sincere desire for peace. At the end I described my experience the day before at the cemetery in Leningrad and said:

> As we work toward a more peaceful world, let us think of Tanya and of the other Tanyas and their brothers and sisters everywhere. Let us do all that we can to ensure that no other children will have to endure what Tanya did and that your children and ours, all the children of the world, can live their full lives together in friendship and in peace.

Brezhnev told me after the broadcast that my conclusion had brought tears to his eyes.

The greatest surprise of the summit came during my next to last meeting with Brezhnev. I went to his office for what was supposed to be a half-hour courtesy call, and we ended up spending two hours talking about Vietnam. Unlike at our meeting at the dacha, however, he was calm and serious.

After some initial skirmishing, he said, "Would you like to have one of our highest Soviet officials go to the Democratic Republic of Vietnam in the interest of peace?"

I replied that such a visit might make a major contribution to ending the war, and I said that I would suspend bombing during the period the Soviet official was in Hanoi.

As I was leaving, we paused by the door, and I said, "You have my commitment that privately or publicly I will take no steps directed against the interests of the Soviet Union. But you should rely on what I say in the private channel, not on what anyone else tells you. There are not only certain forces in the world, but also representatives of the press, who are not interested in better relations between us."

The major achievement of Summit I was the agreement covering the limitation of strategic arms. The ABM treaty stopped what inevitably would have become a defensive arms race, with untold billions of dollars being spent on each side for more and more ABM coverage. The other major effect of the ABM treaty was to make permanent the concept of deterrence through "mutual terror": by giving up missile defenses, each side was leaving its population and territory hostage to a strategic missile attack. Each side therefore had an ultimate interest in preventing a war that could only be mutually destructive.

Together with the ABM treaty, the Interim Agreement on strategic missiles marked the first step toward arms control in the thermonuclear age. The Interim Agreement froze the levels of strategic missiles to those then actually existing or under construction. Under this agreement, the United States gave up nothing, because we had no programs that were affected by the freeze. The Soviets, however, had a substantial missile deployment program under way. It is not possible to state how extensive that deployment might have been in the absence of the agreement. But had it continued, it would have put us increasingly at a disadvantage in numbers of missiles and would almost certainly have forced us into a costly building program just to maintain the then-current ratios. By maintaining those ratios the agreement would allow the two sides to begin negotiations for a permanent agreement on offensive weapons free from the pressures of an arms race.

In addition to these major achievements in the area of arms control, there were a number of other agreements signed at Summit I, including the establishment of a joint commercial commission to encourage more trade, and agreements on pollution control and on medicine and public health, especially research on cancer and heart disease. In addition to the establishment of a joint commission to expand cooperation in several areas of science and technology, there was an agreement on a joint orbital mission in space, which came to fruition in 1975 with the Apollo-Soyuz space docking.

Finally, we signed a document containing twelve "basic principles of mutual relations between the United States and the U.S.S.R.," which set forth a code of behavior both sides agreed to follow. This code dealt not only with bilateral relations and measures to reduce the risk of nuclear war but also with the reduction of tension and conflict, especially the kind that could involve the major powers, in their relations with other areas of the world.

These summit agreements began the establishment of a pattern of interrelationships and cooperation in a number of different areas. This was the first stage of détente: to involve Soviet interests in ways that would increase their stake in international stability and the status quo. There was no thought that such commercial, technical, and scientific relationships could by themselves prevent confrontations or wars, but at least they would have to be counted in a balance sheet of gains and losses whenever the Soviets were tempted to indulge in international adventurism.

Because of the pervasive bugging I did not dictate any diary entries while we were in the Soviet Union. The Soviets were curiously unsubtle in this regard. A member of my staff reported having casually told his secretary that he would like an apple, and ten minutes later a maid came in and put a bowl of apples on the table.

I did, however, keep extensive notes during the trip, and I made several long dictations from them the weekend after we returned.

Diary

I emphasized to Henry my evaluation of the Soviet leaders in which I said that Robert Conquest's comment to the effect that they were intellectually third-rate was simply off the mark. I said that we constantly misjudge the Russians because we judge them by their manners, etc., and we do not look beyond to see what kind of character and strength they really have.

Anybody who gets to the top in the Communist hierarchy and stays at the top has to have a great deal of political ability and a great deal of toughness. All three of the Soviet leaders have this in spades, and Brezhnev in particular. His Russian may not be as elegant, and his manners not as fine, as that of some of his sophisticated European and Asian colleagues, but like an American labor leader, he has what it takes, and we can make no greater mistake than to rate him either as a fool or simply an unintelligent brute. Chou En-lai had the combination of elegance and toughness, a very unusual one in the world today.

There is no question that the Russian leaders do not have as much of an inferiority complex as was the case in Khrushchev's period. They do not have to brag about everything in Russia being better than anything anywhere else in the world. But they still crave to be respected as equals, and on this point I think we made a good impression.

It was interesting to note that all the Soviet leaders like good clothes. Brezhnev was even somewhat of a fashion plate in his own way. He had an obviously very expensive gold cigarette holder and lighter.

I noted that all three of the Soviet leaders wore cuff links. I recalled how subtle the change had been from the days of Khrushchev, when he insisted on dressing more plainly than the rest of us.

Kosygin is really all business, a very cool customer with very little outward warmth. He is by Communist terms an aristocrat; while Podgorny is more like a Midwestern senator; and Brezhnev like a big Irish labor boss, or perhaps an analogy to Mayor Daley would be more in order with no affront intended to either.

They seemed to get along well and to have a good personal relationship with each other. I pointed out to Kissinger in a note when Kosygin, Brezhnev, and Podgorny were having one of their colloquies, that it sounded like the scrambler we had in our room which we turned on whenever we wanted to knock out the listening device.

Brezhnev was very warm and friendly. As we were riding in the car out to the dacha, he put his hand on my knee and said he hoped we had developed a good personal relationship.

[Austrian Chancellor Bruno Kreisky had] analyzed Brezhnev as being a "bear-hug" type of man who was likely to have physical contact with whoever came to see him. I couldn't help thinking that Brezhnev and Johnson would have been quite a pair if they had met at Glassboro, instead of Kosygin.

At one point, he said to me, "God be with you." At another point he referred to me as "the present President and the future President."

He told me how an older party man, when he had just begun party work, emphasized the importance of personal relationships in politics and government and party work. I rather wondered who it might have been because this sounded somewhat like Stalin.

There is no question about Brezhnev's overall strength. First, he is five years younger than the other two. Second, he has a strong, deep voice—a great deal of animal magnetism and drive which comes through whenever you meet him. Third, while he sometimes talks too much and is not too precise, he always comes through forcefully, and he has a very great shrewdness. He also has the ability to move off of a point in the event that he is not winning it.

His gestures were extremely expressive. He stands up and walks around, a device he often used during the course of our meetings. Henry recalled one instance in which Brezhnev said, 'Every time I stand up I make another concession.' He must, of course, have been affected by the fact that my own conduct was, by comparison, totally controlled. Some would say this was a mistake but, on the other hand, I am inclined to think it may have impressed him more than if I had been more outwardly emotional in responding to his various charges.

Brezhnev at one point said to me, "I am an emotional man, particularly about death in war." I told him that while my reputation was for being unemotional, I was just as emotional as he was about this issue.

He asked about Mao. I responded that despite poor health, he was sharp from an intellectual standpoint. Brezhnev responded that Mao is a philosopher, not practical, a God-like figure. He said the Chinese were terribly difficult to understand, and then went on to say, "We Europeans are totally different from them."

He said it was really shocking that in the Cultural Revolution they cut off people's heads in the public square. Of course, it's only been twenty years or so since the Communist leaders liquidated their opponents rather than letting them become non-persons, as had been the case with Khrushchev.

He made a great point of the fact that "some people" do not want this meeting to succeed—obviously referring to the Chinese.

An interesting sidelight: unlike the Chinese, who were totally obsessed with the smaller countries of Africa, Asia, and Latin America, the Soviet leaders hardly talked at all about any of the smaller countries except for North Vietnam and a brief mention of North Korea. It was also interesting to note that the Soviet leaders did not raise the subject of Cuba at all, and they were very mild on North Korea.

I noted the great changes since 1959. There were far more cars in the streets, and the people were better dressed.

In a totalitarian state they have to put on a fetish of having some contact with people, but they really don't do much better than the Chinese in setting these things up in a way that appears to be spontaneous. I am constantly amazed by the total gulf that exists between the Communist ruling classes and the people. I always spoke to the waiters or nodded to them as we left the various dinners, but the Communist leaders acted as if they were non-persons. They treated them as a totally different class.

I pointed out on one of the occasions that our meeting was not a fortuitous affair. The situation in the world required that the meeting be held. The world expected much from the meeting, and we justified the world's hopes. The meeting was well prepared, and now we must go forward to do away with the hotbeds of war that exist in the world. What we must not do is to repeat history. Yalta led to an improvement of relations, but then to a sharp deterioration thereafter. Reading about Yalta gives one great pause because it was not what was agreed to at Yalta, but the failure of the Soviets to keep the agreement, which led to all the troubles after that time.

We are now faced with the major task of giving implementation to the documents we have signed.

JUNE 1972

The morning after our return from the Soviet Summit, I had a heavy schedule of meetings and a congressional briefing on the SALT treaty in an effort to line up support behind it. That afternoon I went with my family to Florida. I carried with me a briefcase full of the domestic reports and decision memoranda that had piled up while we were away.

John Connally came down on Monday. He was leaving the administration and was preparing for his return to Texas.

"Well, I saw Tommy Corcoran a couple of days ago," he said as he settled into a chair in my study, "and he told me Teddy Kennedy now says he wants the nomination. But I think it's too late. McGovern and his people have the bit in their mouths, and they're running with it."

I said that we should not underestimate Kennedy's residual appeal. Even McGovern's supporters, no matter how emotionally committed to their man, would rally around Kennedy. "I understand Hubert isn't going to make it," I said, and Connally nodded.

"Whatever you do," Connally said, "keep the door open for Democrats and independents. If McGovern is nominated, you will see an unprecedented defection."

"Don't worry," I said. "I learned something in 1960. The door will not only be open—I've been weaving a welcome mat."

On June 6 George McGovern won the California primary. The early polls had projected a 20-point landslide, but Hubert Humphrey narrowed the difference to only 5.4 percent; with one more week of campaigning, Humphrey might have won. But California settled it: McGovern would win the nomination.

The Democrats were about to nominate a man who had called for immediate unilateral withdrawal from South Vietnam without any assurances concerning the return of our POWs; who favored unconditional amnesty for draft dodgers; who proposed a reduction in the defense budget that would cut the Air Force in half, reduce the number of Navy warships, and slash the personnel assigned to NATO posts without requiring any reciprocal reductions from the Soviets; and who pledged to cut off aid to our NATO ally Greece while increasing overall foreign aid totals by some 400 percent, with most of the money earmarked for African countries.

McGovern's approach to welfare was for the federal government to give $1,000 to every man, woman, and child in America, funded largely by the tax-strapped middle-income group. HEW calculated that this program alone would cost some $50 billion a year.

His tax reform proposals, ostensibly aimed at closing loopholes and redistributing the tax burden more fairly, were too much even for the New York *Times*, which described them as "drastic" with "often woolly estimates of potential gains and losses." Hubert Humphrey, during the California primary, had called them "confiscatory," and "a lot of bunk." By the end of the campaign, we estimated the domestic proposals put forth by McGovern would add $126 billion to the federal deficit.

McGovern told the Washington *Post* that busing was "essential" for integration. He called J. Edgar Hoover "a menace to justice." He said that when he was elected President, the demonstrators who had threatened chaos and spat obscenities at the police would be "having dinner at the White House."

All these extreme stands and statements were on the record, but as late as July only one panelist in ten on a *Time* magazine citizens' panel considered George McGovern a radical, while the rest were equally divided over whether he was really a liberal or a moderate conservative! This confusion existed largely because early in the campaign the media had played down the radical or inconsistent elements of McGovern's programs. Many reporters sympathized with McGovern's positions; many just liked his enthusiastic and engaging collection of amateur staff members and volunteer workers.

Fortunately, not all reporters abdicated their critical faculties or their obligation to be objective. "Reader beware," wrote Godfrey Sperling, columnist for the *Christian Science Monitor*, on June 8. "A love affair between a number of newsmen and George McGovern is bursting into full bloom and even though we are talking—by and large—about tough-minded, professional observers, this congenial relationship is bound to affect their copy." He continued:

> In fact, in this reporter's judgment, it already has. For months now Senator McGovern has been talking about a program that would pretty much revolutionize our society . . . Yet, at least until the last week or so Senator McGovern has pretty much been given a "free ride" from the press. . . . As of now, I would say that many of those newsmen who accompany McGovern along the campaign trail have already let their bias show through—not so much by what they have written about McGovern but by what they have not written about him and his programs. Their omissions tell a great deal.

The biggest political danger McGovern could pose, as I saw it, would be if he decided to change his positions in order to pick up the support of moderate Democrats. I noted in a memo to Mitchell dictated on June 6, the day of the California primary:

> The McGovern strategy is becoming very clear now that he believes that he has the nomination wrapped up. His going to the Governors Conference

> for the purpose of "clarifying" his stand on amnesty, marijuana, abortion, and welfare is a case in point. I know there are those who will say that he can't get away with it any more than Goldwater was able to get away with it. . . . There are two very significant differences. McGovern is more clever and less principled than Goldwater and will say anything in order to win. And second, McGovern will have about 100 percent support from the media in his effort to clean himself up so that he can beat us in the final. This points up the necessity at this time to get *Democrats* and *independents*, not Republicans, to nail McGovern on the left side of the road which his record so clearly identifies him with.

By summer, when my campaign organization began moving into high gear, I almost immediately began hearing about problems connected with it. There were rumors about slack field organizations, about unnecessary discourtesies to local people, and, repeatedly, about the dislike local campaign workers were developing toward the size and slickness of the CRP's Washington headquarters. When I asked what was wrong, I was usually told, "Mitchell's too tired to focus on it," or "ITT nearly wore Mitchell out," or, more simply, "It's Martha."

Haldeman and I decided to send Fred Malek, then a member of the White House staff, over to the CRP to bring things under control. Malek was a tough young businessman whose specialty was organization and management. We decided to hold off for a few more weeks, however, primarily out of concern that Mitchell would view the move as an implicit criticism of his performance rather than as a recognition that he did not have the help he needed.

On June 12 we celebrated Tricia and Ed's first wedding anniversary with a trip on the *Sequoia*. Pat arranged for us to have the same hors d'oeuvres we had liked so much at the wedding reception. After the sail we watched a videotape of the wedding and reminisced about that day and about the year that had gone by so quickly.

President Luis Echeverría of Mexico arrived in Washington for a state visit on June 15. We had a long talk about water salinity problems and ended up with a lively but friendly discussion about the treatment of American private enterprise in Latin America. At the end, he said that he thought my re-election was vitally important to the world.

Later in the day the Saudi Arabian Defense Minister, Sultan ibn 'Abd al-Aziz, came in to bring me greetings from his brother, King Faisal.

In the afternoon I met with Ehrlichman about what appeared at first glance to be a panicky position taken by Bill Ruckelshaus of the Environmental Protection Agency on banning the pesticide DDT. The long day ended with a state dinner in honor of President Echeverría.

Friday, June 16, began with a Cabinet meeting on the Republican platform proposals. Then I had an hour-long session with James Hodgson, Elliott Richardson, and members of my staff on welfare reform. My official schedule ended at 12:45 P.M. with a posthumous presentation ceremony of the Medal of Freedom for John Paul Vann, the courageous head of the Second Regional Assistance group in South Vietnam, who was killed in a helicopter crash.

In the afternoon, I left for a weekend in Florida. I was on my own; Pat was making appearances on the West Coast, and the girls were with their husbands. In my briefcase I had a Buchanan campaign memorandum, the briefing materials on welfare reform, and my well-thumbed copy of Irving Kristol's *On the Democratic Idea in America.* I also brought a copy of *Triumph and Tragedy*, the last volume of Churchill's World War II series, because after the recent Soviet Summit I wanted to reread his analysis of the Yalta conference.

THE WATERGATE BREAK-IN

I spent Friday afternoon and all day Saturday on Grand Cay, a small island in the Bahamas owned by my old friend Bob Abplanalp. The weather was spotty, but I went for a swim and took a walk around the island. The caretaker's wife gave me two brightly colored shirts she had made for me, and I talked with her twelve-year-old daughter, who showed me some of the turtles she had been raising.

On Saturday, June 17, I called the mainland only once, to check in with Haldeman. We talked for four minutes. I asked him to find out where I could reach John Connally, who was on a thirty-five-day trip around the world. I also told him to be sure that we had a plank in the Republican platform supporting federal aid to parochial schools. In the afternoon I went boating with Rebozo and Abplanalp.

On Sunday morning, June 18, Rebozo and I left for Key Biscayne. When I got to my house I could smell coffee brewing in the kitchen, and I went in to get a cup. There was a Miami *Herald* on the counter, and I glanced over the front page. The main headline was about the Vietnam withdrawals: *Ground Combat Role Nears End for U.S.*

There was a small story in the middle of the page on the left-hand side, under the headline: *Miamians Held in D.C. Try to Bug Demo Headquarters.*

I scanned the opening paragraphs. Five men, four of them from Miami, had been arrested in the Democratic National Committee headquarters at the Watergate, a fashionable hotel, office, and apartment complex in Washington. The story said that one of the five men had identified himself as a former employee of the CIA; three of the others were Cuban natives. They had all been wearing rubber surgical gloves. It sounded preposterous: Cubans in surgical gloves bugging the DNC! I dismissed it as some sort of prank. I looked at the feature story at the bottom of the page dealing with the campaign: *How McGovern Camp Figures to Win.* I left the paper on the counter and went to make some phone calls.

I reached Haldeman at the Key Biscayne Hotel, where he was staying with the rest of the traveling staff. We briefly discussed whether to have a signing ceremony for the higher education bill. Then we turned to some intriguing news about George Meany—news that had the potential of becoming one of the most important developments of the 1972 campaign. Meany had told George Shultz that if Humphrey failed to get the Democratic nomination, he would not support McGovern. Meany's—and that meant a large part of organized labor's—benevolent neutrality would breach the traditional Democratic coalition and be a tremendous boost to my campaign.

I called Tricia and Julie, who wished me a happy Father's Day, and I talked to Pat, who was in Los Angeles on a three-day series of appearances that had begun in Texas and was scheduled to end in South Dakota. I talked with Al Haig and then with Kissinger, who had stopped over in Hawaii en route to Peking. In the afternoon I called Chuck Colson to discuss the Meany development with him. Then I went for a long swim in the ocean.

Shortly after 6 P.M. I reached John Connally in Australia and received a glowing report on his trip. I called Colson again for a short talk about my concern that most of the media would be sympathetic to McGovern. Rebozo came over for dinner, and we watched a movie. Afterward I called Jack Nicklaus, who had just won the U.S. Open in Pebble Beach. I congratulated him on his victory and commiserated about the putts that had seemed to go in the hole and out.

I decided to make an early night of it. Before I went to bed, I sat in my study reading the last chapters of *Triumph and Tragedy.*

A steady sun and a light breeze made Monday a beautiful day. I did not bother to look at the morning paper but went straight to my study to make calls. The Watergate break-in was still the furthest thing from my mind as I talked with Julie, Tricia, Rose Woods, Al Haig, and Billy Graham. I also talked with Chuck Colson; the only note that I dictated in my diary about our conversation recounted our detailed analysis of a new set of poll figures covering everything from confidence in presidential leadership to the economy. I made two short calls to Haldeman concerning the day's schedule, and then he came over and we met for an hour. We discussed the possibility that George Wallace would become a third-party candidate, the increase in food prices, the appointment of a new Chief of Protocol, and the schedule for the coming week. In the afternoon I went boating and took a long walk before dinner. At 7:48 P.M. I boarded *Air Force One* for the flight to Washington.

Late that night, back at the White House, I brought my diary up to date. Buried amid observations on the weekend's weather and reflections on the general benefits of relaxation was my first entry dealing with Watergate.

Diary

I almost decided to go back Sunday night, but a hurricane passed nearby, and the winds were so strong that we thought it would be a rather miserable ride although we probably could have gotten out without too much difficulty.

The following day the winds had passed on, and it was the best of all the days. In fact, the best of the six days, including the three immediately after returning from Moscow two weeks ago, and these three. The extra day, with good long swims in the morning and the afternoon, gave me, it seemed to me, a much bigger lift than I had realized was possible. I must make it a point to try to get three full days in the future, and, of course, always try to get the situation developed where I can have peace of mind and good weather if possible.

I am convinced that it is essential to get more exercise. I think one of the reasons that I feel tonight not only more rested but frankly more sharp and more eager to get work done is because I have had rest, and also have had the fresh air and the exercise. I am going to try a routine of bowling for a half hour at the end of each day before coming over to the Residence. This may have a good effect.

On the way back, I got the disturbing news from Bob Haldeman that the break-in of the Democratic National Committee involved someone who is on the payroll of the Committee to Re-elect the President. Mitchell had told Bob on the phone enigmatically not to get involved in it, and I told Bob that I simply hoped that none of our people were involved for two reasons—one, because it was stupid in the way it was handled; and two, because I could see no reason whatever for trying to bug the national committee.

Bob pointed [out] one of Chotiner's operatives had said that a McGovern aide had told him that they had our committee rooms bugged. The problem here, of course, is to get somebody on the PR side who will get out some of the negatives on the other side like this, so that this story just doesn't appear to be a clumsy attempt on our part to get information illegally from the Democrats.

I also urged Bob to keep Colson and Ehrlichman from getting obsessed with the thing so that they were unable to spend their time on other jobs. Looking back, the fact that Colson got so deeply involved in the ITT was a mistake because it kept him from doing other things that in retrospect were more important to do. The best thing probably to have done with ITT was just to let it run its course without having our whole staff in constant uproar about it. I hope we can handle this one in that way.

Pat was in a very good mood tonight, and had felt that her visit to South Dakota was a success. She said the governor had expressed concern that I had always done so well in South Dakota, that he had to run this year as a Democrat and was worried about it. Of course, with McGovern on the ticket he may have a much better chance.

The CRP employee who had been arrested at the Watergate was James McCord. A former CIA security officer, McCord was employed by both the Committee to Re-elect the President and the Republican National Committee as a consultant on security for buildings, documents, and personnel. One of his responsibilities was to protect the Republicans from exactly the kind of thing he had been caught doing to the Democrats. Haldeman had also heard that the money found on the arrested men—over $1,000 in $100 bills—had apparently come from the CRP.

Because of McCord's connection to the CRP, his arrest had turned the Watergate break-in into a hot news story. Larry O'Brien in hyperbolic terms claimed that "the bugging incident . . . raised the ugliest questions about the integrity of the political process that I have encountered in a quarter century of political activity." John Mitchell, as chairman of the Committee to Re-elect, had issued a statement that the arrested men were not acting on behalf of or with the consent of the CRP, and that he himself was surprised and dismayed at the reports of McCord's involvement.

My reaction to the Watergate break-in was completely pragmatic. If it was also cynical, it was a cynicism born of experience. I had been in politics too long, and seen everything from dirty tricks to vote fraud. I could not muster much moral outrage over a political bugging.

Larry O'Brien might affect astonishment and horror, but he knew as well as I did that political bugging had been around nearly since the invention of the wiretap. As recently as 1970 a former member of Adlai Stevenson's campaign staff had publicly stated that he had tapped the Kennedy organization's phone lines at the 1960 Democratic convention. Lyndon Johnson felt that the Kennedys had had him tapped; Barry

Goldwater said that his 1964 campaign had been bugged; and Edgar Hoover told me that in 1968 Johnson had ordered my campaign plane bugged. Nor was the practice confined to politicians. In 1969 an NBC producer was fined and given a suspended sentence for planting a concealed microphone at a closed meeting of the 1968 Democratic platform committee. Bugging experts told the Washington *Post* right after the Watergate break-in that the practice "has not been uncommon in elections past . . . it is particularly common for candidates of the same party to bug one another."

In fact, my confidence in the CRP was undermined more by the stupidity of the DNC bugging attempt than by its illegality. The whole thing made so little sense. *Why?* I wondered. Why then? Why in such a blundering way? And why, of all places, the Democratic National Committee? Anyone who knew anything about politics would know that a national committee headquarters was a useless place to go for inside information on a presidential campaign. The whole thing was so senseless and bungled that it almost looked like some kind of a setup. And yet the trail undeniably led back to the CRP. On Sunday morning the idea of Cubans in surgical gloves bugging the DNC had seemed totally ridiculous. By Monday night it had become a potential issue in the presidential campaign.

On Tuesday morning, June 20, my first day back in Washington, there was a new twist.

A front-page headline in the Washington *Post* proclaimed: *White House Consultant Tied to Bugging Figure.* The story, attributed to "federal sources close to the investigation," said that the name Howard Hunt had been found in the address books of two of the men caught inside the DNC headquarters. It stated that until March 29, 1972, Hunt, a former CIA agent, had worked at the White House as a consultant to Chuck Colson. The mention of Colson's name gave me a start. It was one thing if the CRP was involved, or even a former lower-level White House staff member like Hunt. But Colson was a member of my inner circle of aides and advisers, and if he was drawn in it was a whole new situation. I had always valued his hardball instincts. Now I wondered if he might have gone too far.

The Democrats were already mounting an attack. The DNC filed a $1 million suit against the CRP for invasion of privacy and violation of civil rights. This suit would enable their lawyers to call as witnesses and depose under oath almost the entire CRP and White House staff. In this way, while ostensibly probing the DNC bugging, they could ask questions about any and every aspect of our campaign. As *Time* put it, the true aim of the Democrats' suit was "to preoccupy Republicans in court during the fall, to keep the case in public view to subvert the seemingly unstoppable GOP campaign." Publicly the Democrats were full of righteous indignation at the Watergate break-in. Privately they were rejoicing at this unexpected election-year dividend.

Ken Clawson, our Deputy Director of Communications, received an insight into what we were going to be up against when he had lunch with Dick Harwood, an editor at the Washington *Post*. Before coming to the White House, Clawson had been a *Post* reporter, and after the lunch he visited with some of his former colleagues. He was told that Katharine Graham, the paper's publisher, was personally going to direct an army of reporters assigned to delve into the Watergate story. "We're in for a hell of a barrage," Clawson warned members of the staff.

At 2:20 Tuesday afternoon Colson came in to see me. We spent several minutes discussing the way the newspapers were stretching his connection with Hunt in order to draw him into the scandal and the question of who might be the source of the news leaks.

Colson said that Haldeman was "pulling it all together," and that, in Colson's own opinion, so far we had handled it the right way.

I thought that one problem we would have to deal with soon was what the arrested men were going to say. I thought we would be vulnerable to any charges or accusations—true or false—they might make. I said that I had been told they were all "pretty hard-line guys." I told Colson that, as I understood it, we were going to have "this funny guy" take credit for the whole thing. I meant McCord, but Colson evidently thought I meant his friend Howard Hunt.

Colson was quick to defend Hunt. He insisted that Hunt was just too smart and too sophisticated to have been involved in something as amateurish as the Watergate break-in. I agreed that if we didn't know better we would have thought that the whole thing had been deliberately botched up.

Colson said that after he heard about the break-in he figured it might have been something the Cubans had organized on their own. Everyone knew that the Cuban émigré community feared that McGovern would decide to resume diplomatic relations with Castro. Feelings ran sufficiently high that it was by no means impossible that anti-Castro Cubans would want to bug the Democrats to obtain information about such intentions.

I thought for a moment about the double standard that was sure to be adopted by McGovern and by the New York *Times* and the Washington *Post*: they had tacitly sanctioned Ellsberg's illegal release of top-secret government documents, but they were sure to register high moral dudgeon about something as comparatively minor as an unsuccessful break-in at a political party headquarters. I sardonically suggested that someone give a speech urging that the Watergate break-in crew be given a

Pulitzer Prize like the one the New York *Times* had been given for publishing the Pentagon Papers.

I told Colson that my understanding was that we were just going to leave the Watergate matter where it was, with the Cubans.

Colson came back to Hunt. He said the fact that Hunt's name was in the address books of the arrested men was the most logical thing in the world. The morning paper had pointed out that Hunt had been a CIA agent for more than twenty years, and that all the arrested men had CIA ties. But Colson told me that the connection was even stronger: Hunt had trained Cuban exiles for the Bay of Pigs operation. This information seemed to reinforce the whole Cuban connection.

Colson said that the biggest hazard Watergate represented for us was the risk of our becoming preoccupied with it simply because the media and the Democrats were sure to be. He said that the whole thing was "something which normally wouldn't amount to that much. They're just going to blow their cool out because they haven't got any other place they can lay a glove on us."

He then told me that the New York *Times* had a problem of its own. During my Soviet Summit trip the paper had run an ad calling for my impeachment because of my policy on the Vietnam war. A formal complaint had been filed against the paper, charging that it had failed to require the necessary identifications from the people who paid for the ad and therefore violated the campaign fund disclosure law. I was pessimistic about our ability to get any political mileage out of that. The *Times*, I knew, would just stonewall it.

Before Colson left my office, I tried to cheer him up. "Dumbest thing," I said. "Nothing loses an election. Nothing changes it that much. . . . You look at this damn thing now and it's gonna be forgotten after a while."

The main problem was that the Democrats would be able to keep the Watergate issue alive with their depositions. We were going to try to delay them until after the election, but there was no guarantee we could do so. Colson, however, was not at all worried about this. He said that he would love to have depositions taken from the White House staff, because "everybody's completely out of it. . . . This is once when you'd like for people to testify." He said it with complete conviction. I hoped that it was true.

I met with Bob Haldeman twice on Tuesday, June 20: from 11:26 A.M. until 12:45 P.M., and again from 4:35 until 5:25 in the afternoon. What was said during the morning meeting will never be known completely because the tape of that conversation is the one with the 18½-minute gap. Some of what we talked about during those 18½ minutes can be reconstructed from the notes Haldeman took. According to them, one of my first reactions to the Watergate break-in was to instruct that my EOB office be checked regularly to make sure that *I* was not being bugged by anyone. They also indicate a concern about the political ramifications of the Watergate incident and a desire to divert its impact by mounting our own counterattack.

The best indication of anything else that may have been said about the Watergate break-in in that morning conversation is our discussion of the same subject just a few hours later that afternoon. It has always been my habit to discuss problems a number of times, often in almost the same terms and usually with the same people. This is the way I try to elicit every possible piece of information and advice and examine every possible angle of a situation before making a decision. I am confident that our discussion about the break-in covered much the same points at 11:26 in the morning as it did just five hours later at 4:35 in the afternoon: that any of our own people, at any level, had embroiled us in such an embarrassing situation; and that the investigations and depositions, if they went too far in pursuing all the angles available, would hand the Democrats a major campaign issue.

In the afternoon meeting Haldeman said he thought that John Mitchell had not known about the break-in plan beforehand. I agreed. For one thing, Mitchell was just too smart to be involved in any such thing. I said that I thought Mitchell had been surprised by it. Haldeman observed that it was true, however, that the men who were caught were supposed to be a pretty competent bunch of people and had been doing other campaign-related things.

Haldeman told me what he had heard about the possible reasons for the break-in. Apparently the arrested men had gone in to repair some electronic equipment that had already been installed but was not working properly, and to take pictures of whatever they found inside. Later he mentioned they had expected to find some financial information about the Democrats.

In subsequent weeks and months I heard many other theories about the reason for the break-in and bugging of the DNC. One was that the men were trying to verify a tip that the Democrats were planning to disrupt our convention by printing counterfeit tickets for distribution to demonstrators; another was that they had been planning to photograph classified documents that were illegally held by the DNC. I heard so many different stories because I asked the same question so many times: *Why bug the DNC?*

In our conversation that afternoon Haldeman ran through some of the other information he had picked up during the day. Haldeman said that, as he understood it, McCord was going to say that he was working with the Cubans, who had been putting in the bug for their own political reasons. Haldeman told me that Howard Hunt had either disappeared or was in the process of doing so, but he would come back if wanted. Haldeman indicated that the appearance of Hunt's name in the address books would be explained on the basis of his ties to the Cubans; he told me, as Colson had, that Hunt had been involved in the Bay of Pigs operation while he was in the CIA; in fact Haldeman had learned that one of the Cubans had been Hunt's deputy for the operation. Haldeman said that our people were making an effort to keep the incident tied to the motive of Cuban nationalism. The problem, of course, was that now, through Hunt, ties to Colson and to the White House were being uncovered. The newspapers had reported that Hunt worked at the White House on projects involving international narcotics intelligence and the declassification of documents. Haldeman said that he was not sure exactly what else Hunt had done; he knew only that it had been based on his prior experience in intelligence. Later in the conversation, he mentioned that Hunt had been involved in the "Diem thing"—our effort to unearth the facts on President Kennedy's involvement in the coup against President Diem in 1963, a coup that resulted in Diem's death. I recalled that Colson had alluded to Hunt's intelligence background.

Haldeman said that as far as the intelligence activities for the CRP were concerned, all of us—including Colson—had known that some were going on. But despite the Hunt connection, Haldeman said that he did not think that Colson had known specifically that the Watergate bugging project was under way. I said I thought he had, but then I said that that was just second-guessing him. Later in the conversation Haldeman, however, reassured me even more strongly about Colson: he said that a check had been made and that he was sure Colson was not involved.

Haldeman reported that my offices in the White House and the EOB had been swept for bugs, and none had been found. Of course, he reminded me, there was our own taping system.

Haldeman said he felt like the whole thing was a nightmare; something like this just doesn't happen, he said. I agreed. Fortunately, he said, Mitchell had been several steps removed—or perhaps it was unfortunate, because if he hadn't been so far removed it probably would never have happened. There was always the problem of circumstantial evidence, however, and there was clearly still going to be an effort to try to tie Mitchell in. Haldeman said half jokingly that maybe it would be better if we just said that yes, we were spying on the Democrats and that we had hired McCord to do it because we were scared to death that a crazy man was going to become President and sell the country out to the Communists!

I asked Haldeman how Howard Hunt was involved in the Watergate incident. He said that on the night of the break-in Hunt had been waiting across the street from the Watergate in the motel room from which the bugs were going to be monitored. Haldeman was not sure, however, about Hunt's relationship to McCord or McCord's to the Cubans.

I was still confused about just how Hunt's name had come up, and Haldeman again ran through the story of the address books. He also told me that one of the Cubans had a check from Hunt for about $6.90, payable to Hunt's country club.

I said that in a sense the involvement of the Cubans, McCord, and Hunt made it appear that it was in fact some kind of Cuban operation. Whatever the case, I saw that a Cuban explanation for the break-in would have two advantages for us: it would protect us from the political impact of the disclosure of the CRP's involvement, and it would undercut the Democrats by calling attention to the fact that the Cuban community in the United States feared McGovern's naïve policy toward Castro.

Haldeman mentioned in passing something about the wiretapping and concern about "Liddy's budget." He then returned to the problem of the Democrats' depositions, which, he said, were clearly the toughest thing for us. I expressed my continuing bafflement over the origins of the whole thing. "The Democratic committee isn't worth bugging," I said to Haldeman as our conversation on the subject drew to a close.

June 20 had been a full day. I had had an hour session with Ehrlichman on busing and other domestic issues; made several phone calls to members of Congress and the staff; and held a long meeting with Al Haig. As far as Watergate was concerned, as I walked back to the Residence that night I felt confident. My primary concern had been whether anyone at the White House was involved, and Haldeman and Colson had reassured me on that score. Haldeman had been equally reassuring that Mitchell had had nothing to do with it. With these reassurances, I was ready to go on the offensive.

That evening I called John Mitchell. We talked for about four minutes and I recorded what he told me in a brief diary note I made later that night: "He is terribly chagrined that the activities of anybody attached to his committee should have been handled in such a manner, and he said that he only regretted that he had not policed all the people more effectively . . . in his own organization."

On the phone Mitchell sounded so embarrassed by the whole thing that I was convinced more than ever that it had come as a complete surprise to him. He also sounded completely tired and worn out.

After talking with Mitchell, I called Haldeman. When both he and Colson had mentioned the Bay of Pigs that afternoon, they had stimulated my thinking, and I told him about my new idea for handling the public relations aspect of the Watergate incident. I suggested that if the

Cuban explanation for the break-in actually caught on, I would call Rebozo and have him get the anti-McGovern Cubans in Miami to start a public bail fund for their arrested countrymen and make a big media issue out of it. If they used it to revive the Democrats' inept handling of the Bay of Pigs and to attack McGovern's foreign policy ideas, we might even make Watergate work in our favor.

I worked in the EOB office that night until nearly 11:30. I took some of the time to bring my diary up to date. After recounting the day's events, I closed with this note: "I felt better today than I have really for months—relaxed and yet able to do more work than even we usually do with far more enthusiasm."

Watergate was an annoying problem, but it was still just a minor one among many.

In our conversation on Wednesday morning, June 21, Haldeman told me that Gordon Liddy was "the guy who did this." I asked who Liddy was, and Haldeman said he was the counsel for the finance committee at CRP. When I said I thought McCord was the man responsible for the break-in, Haldeman said no, it was Liddy; we didn't know what McCord's position was, but everyone seemed to think he would hang tight.

Ehrlichman had come up with the idea of having Liddy confess; he would say he did it because he wanted to be a hero at the CRP. This would have several advantages: it would cut off the Democrats' civil suit and minimize their ability to go on fishing expeditions in the depositions connected with it; it would divert some of the press and political attacks by establishing guilt at a low level instead of letting it be imputed to a high one; and finally, since all the arrested men felt that Liddy had been in charge, once Liddy admitted guilt it wouldn't matter what else they thought because everything would tie back to Liddy. Then, Haldeman said, our people would make an appeal for compassion on the basis that Liddy was a poor misguided kid who read too many spy stories.

I said that after all this was not a hell of a lot of crime and in fact if someone asked me about Ziegler's statement that it was a "third-rate burglary," I was going to say no, it was only a "third-rate *attempt* at burglary." Haldeman said the lawyers all felt that if Liddy and the arrested men entered a guilty plea they would get only fines and suspended sentences since apparently they were all first offenders.

I said I was for Ehrlichman's plan. We had to assume the truth would come out sooner or later, so if Liddy was the man responsible, he should step up and shoulder the blame. My only reservation, I said, would be if this would involve John Mitchell—in that case I didn't think we could do it. A day earlier Haldeman seemed certain Mitchell was not involved. Now he was not so reassuring. He had already told me that Mitchell was concerned about how far the FBI's investigation was going and thought that someone should go directly to the FBI and get it turned off. Haldeman said, too, that Ehrlichman was afraid that Mitchell might be involved. When Haldeman had all but put the question directly to Mitchell when they had talked earlier that morning, he had received no answer; so he could not be sure whether Mitchell was involved or not. He indicated that Mitchell had seemed a little apprehensive about Ehrlichman's plan because of Liddy's instability and what might happen when Liddy was really put under pressure. In any case, he said, Ehrlichman had just developed the plan that morning, and everyone was going to think about it before anything was done.

I still believed that Mitchell was innocent; I was sure he would never have ordered anything like this. He was just too smart and, besides, he had always disdained campaign intelligence-gathering. But there were two nagging possibilities: I might be wrong and Mitchell might have had some involvement; and even if he had not actually been involved, if we weren't careful he might become so circumstantially entangled that neither he nor we would ever be able to explain the truth. Either way, I hoped that Liddy would not draw him in. I said that taking a rap was done quite often. Haldeman said that we could take care of Liddy and I agreed that we could help him; I was willing to help with money for someone who had thought he was helping me win the election.

I never personally confronted Mitchell with the direct question of whether he had been involved in or had known about the planning of the Watergate break-in. He was one of my closest friends, and he had issued a public denial. I would never challenge what he had said; I felt that if there were something he thought I should know, he would have told me. And I suppose there was something else, too, something I expressed rhetorically months later: "Suppose you call Mitchell . . . and Mitchell says, 'Yes, I did it,' " I said to Haldeman. "Then what do we say?"

We also talked about the White House side of the problem that morning. I said that I was concerned about what I thought was a bad rap the White House was getting because of the fact that Hunt had worked for Colson. I asked again about whether Haldeman thought Colson was involved, and Haldeman said that as nearly as anyone could be convinced of anything, he was convinced Colson was not.

Haldeman said that what he considered to be the real problem for the White House had nothing to do with the Watergate break-in itself, but concerned what he called "other involvements"—things that an investigative fishing expedition into the break-in could uncover and exploit politically. That was what made the Democrats' civil suit the biggest problem for the White House. Hunt had done a lot of unrelated things for Colson that could be uncovered in the kind of freewheeling legal depositions the Democrats clearly had in mind. I knew that Colson's major project in the last several months had been ITT; I asked Haldeman what he meant—the declassification of papers, or ITT? Haldeman identified Hunt as the man who had gone to Denver and talked to Dita Beard during the ITT investigation. He said there were apparently other "fringe bits and pieces" that would come out if Hunt was called. At one point he said that this was why it was important for us not to overdefend Colson and for Colson not to overreact: he was clean on the bugging, but vulnerable on his other connections with Hunt. Haldeman said that Hunt's political connection was the reason it was felt he should disappear. He also said that this was another reason for getting to the FBI: as of now there was nothing that put Hunt into the case except his name in the address books.

At the end of our discussion I came back to the frustrating situation concerning the break-in. I told Haldeman that it seemed that the Democrats had been doing this kind of thing to us for years and *they* never got caught. Haldeman agreed that the Democrats always seemed to get off easier. He said the press just never went after them the way they went after us. Later in the day, I said that every time the Democrats accused us of bugging we should charge that we were being bugged and maybe even plant a bug and find it ourselves!

When I saw Colson that afternoon, we talked about the morning's press coverage of the break-in, and about the McGovern campaign. Thinking ahead to my press conference scheduled for the next day, I came back to the break-in and observed that taking it at its worst we could at least knock down strongly the idea that the White House was involved. "We didn't know a goddamn thing about it," I said. The conversation ranged over several other topics and then came back to Watergate. I asked Colson what he thought about the plan to have Liddy take the rap and then just cut our losses. He said that he would be for anything that would cut our losses and get us out of it. But, he added, he was deliberately staying out of the whole thing so that he could make an honest affidavit that he knew nothing about it.

Colson again defended his friend Howard Hunt, calling him "a dedicated patriot." He just could not believe that Hunt had engineered the Watergate break-in.

On the morning of Thursday, June 22, I reviewed the briefing material for my press conference that afternoon. Ziegler and Buchanan had written me a memo warning that the reporters were pushing to escalate the break-in story and would try to force me to make a comment that would keep the story alive: *Nixon Concerned* or *Nixon Calls for Investigation* was the kind of headline they were after. It would be important for me to strike the right balance in what I said about the break-in; showing too little concern would cause as bad a news story as showing too much. There was not much more for me to say. Mitchell had already said that such activities could not be condoned and that he was surprised by them; and Ziegler had already issued a statement on Colson's behalf denying Colson's involvement.

When I saw Haldeman, I predicted that the main Watergate question at the press conference would be whether there was any White House involvement. I knew that the reporters would pounce on any modifiers or qualifiers in my answer, so I thought I should just state unequivocally that there was no involvement whatever. Haldeman said he thought that on the direct basis of White House involvement, we were absolutely clean.

He said that the day's Watergate news was all good. For one thing, the Democrats had made a legal mistake by filing a class action suit against the CRP. The Democratic judge who would have heard the case had been replaced by a Republican judge. When the lawyer for the Democrats, Edward Bennett Williams, had insistently demanded immediate depositions, the judge had said that he would meet with him after the weekend to make decisions about the timing.

Further good news was the fact that the FBI still had no case on Howard Hunt. We knew that he had been at the scene, but they did not. Haldeman said that the FBI had no warrant out for him and therefore did not care whether he had disappeared. The final good news was that the FBI could not trace the hundred-dollar bills that the break-in crew had been carrying the night they were arrested. This was good news, because the money was another route by which the break-in could be tied to the CRP. The FBI had got only as far as a Miami bank, and Haldeman said that they would evidently have to go through a South American country in order to trace it finally.

As of June 22, then, the situation provided at least some grounds for hope. The Cuban explanation for the break-in was still holding, and the issue was thoroughly confused. Haldeman said there would continue to be an effort to crank up the Cuban story. He observed that because of what we knew we tended to read too much into what we saw—things that others could not see.

I said that the main thing was what the networks would be doing if they thought they had something on the White House or the CRP. The Cubans were not much of a story, but the networks, I said, would "play it to beat hell" if they thought they had something on us.

Haldeman said that it was being arranged that some members of the Cuban community would start to say how scared they were of McGovern. They were also getting out the fact that two of the arrested men were registered Democrats. He said that there was even some thought of having Liddy leave the country. The FBI was not after him now, and he could come back if something on him surfaced—for instance, if some of the men in jail decided to talk. In the meantime, Haldeman said,

McCord would stay in jail and keep an eye on the others. Later that afternoon I called Ron Ziegler into my office and asked him what he thought I should say about the bugging incident. Then I looked up over my glasses and asked, "Were you there?"

For a moment his round eyes in his boyish face grew wide. "At the bugging incident?" he asked, slightly choked.

"No, you were in Florida weren't you?" I said, and laughed out loud.

"Did you mean was I at the Watergate, Mr. President?" he repeated as he, too, started to laugh.

"Oh, I'll tell you," I said, adding that somebody should say the arrested men were just trying to win a Pulitzer Prize.

When I went into the press conference on the afternoon of June 22, there were two things about Watergate I was prepared to say: that no one in the White House had been involved in the break-in, and that I absolutely believed John Mitchell's statement denying that he had known anything about it. Of the seventeen questions asked that afternoon, only one involved the break-in, and my prediction about it turned out to be completely accurate:

> Q: Mr. O'Brien has said that the people who bugged his headquarters had a direct link to the White House. Have you had any sort of investigation made to determine whether this is true?
>
> A: Mr. Ziegler and also Mr. Mitchell, speaking for the campaign committee, have responded to questions on this in great detail. They have stated my position and have also stated the facts accurately.
>
> This kind of activity, as Mr. Ziegler has indicated, has no place whatever in our electoral process or in our governmental process. And, as Mr. Ziegler has stated, the White House has had no involvement whatever in this particular incident.
>
> As far as the matter now is concerned, it is under investigation, as it should be, by the proper legal authorities, by the District of Columbia police, and by the FBI. I will not comment on those matters, particularly since possible criminal charges are involved.

On Friday, June 23, 1972, I had breakfast with Jerry Ford and Hale Boggs, who were leaving on a trip to the People's Republic of China. After breakfast I went to the Oval Office and Alex Butterfield, one of Haldeman's assistants, brought in several routine papers and documents. Then Haldeman came in as he did every morning, unhurried, ready to begin the day.

We talked about the schedule for Kissinger's return from China that afternoon and about plans for a meeting with Rogers. Then we turned to what Haldeman referred to as the "Democratic break-in thing."

All the good news of the previous day had gone bad, and we were back in what Haldeman called "the problem area." The FBI, he said, was not under control because Acting Director Pat Gray did not know how to control it, and the investigation was leading into some productive areas. In particular, the FBI was apparently going to be able to trace the money after all. "And it goes in some directions we don't want it to go," Haldeman said. As I understood it, unless we could find some way to limit the investigation the trail would lead directly to the CRP, and our political containment would go by the boards.

Haldeman said that Mitchell and John Dean had come up with an idea on how to deal with this problem. Dean was a bright young man who had worked at the Justice Department until 1970, when he succeeded Ehrlichman as White House Counsel. In this capacity Dean had the responsibility for keeping track of and attending to any legal problems affecting the President or the White House.

As Haldeman explained it, General Vernon Walters, the Deputy Director of the CIA, was to call Pat Gray and tell him to "stay the hell out of this . . . business here. We don't want you to go any further on it." The FBI and the CIA had a longstanding agreement not to interfere in each other's secret operations. Haldeman said that this call would not be unusual. He said that Pat Gray wanted to limit the investigation but simply didn't have a basis on which to do so; this would give him his basis. Haldeman said that this would work well because the FBI agents on the case had already come to the conclusion that the CIA was involved in some way.

Haldeman explained that unless something was done, the money would be traced to the contributors who had given it and from there to the CRP. I asked what the contributors would say if they did not cooperate with the investigation—they would have to say that they had been approached by the Cubans. I asked if that was the idea. Haldeman said it was if they would go along; but that would mean relying on more and more people all the time, and the plan to call in Walters would prevent having to do that, and all it would take to set the plan in motion would be an instruction from the White House.

I asked how Haldeman planned to handle it and then observed that we had protected CIA Director Richard Helms from a lot of things. Helms had rarely approached me personally for any kind of assistance or intervention, but I remembered the visible concern on his face less than a year earlier over the possible publication of a book by two disaffected CIA agents. Helms had asked if I would back up legal action by the CIA, despite the fact that there would be cries of "suppression." I had told him that I would.

I mentioned Hunt; he had been involved in a lot of earlier CIA operations, including the Bay of Pigs. I postulated an approach by which we would say to Helms and Walters, "You open that scab and there's a hell of a lot of things." I told Haldeman to say that we felt it would be very detrimental to have the investigation go any further, alluding to the Cubans, to Hunt, and to "a lot of hanky-panky that we have nothing to do with ourselves."

I asked again what had become an almost ritual question: "Did Mitchell know about this thing to any much of a degree?"

"I think so," Haldeman answered. "I don't think he knew the details, but I think he knew."

I said I was sure that he could not have known how it was going to be handled—that had to have been Liddy. Haldeman speculated that the pressure on Liddy to get intelligence might have come from Mitchell.

"All right, fine, I understand it all," I said abruptly. "We won't second-guess Mitchell and the rest. Thank God it wasn't Colson."

Haldeman reassured me that the FBI, after interviewing Colson, had concluded that the White House had had no role in Watergate; they were convinced it was a CIA operation. I said that I was not sure of their analysis, but I was not going to get involved.

"You call them in. Good. Good deal," I said as we brought our discussion of the subject to a close. I told Haldeman to "play it tough," because that was the way the Democrats always played it "and that's the way we are going to play it."

We moved on and talked about the resignation of our Chief of Protocol, a congressional effort to attach a Social Security benefits increase to the bill extending the temporary national debt ceiling, the devaluation of the British pound, the media coverage of my press conference, and busing. Then I came back to the idea to call in Helms and Walters. Howard Hunt clearly provided the best justification for approaching Helms. Hunt's CIA background would give Helms and Walters a plausible reason for going to the FBI; and Hunt's involvement in the planning of the Bay of Pigs would give Helms added incentive.

I thought back again to the time I had instructed Ehrlichman to ask Helms for the CIA's files on the Bay of Pigs, and the Diem assassination. I remembered how he had been unwilling to give them up. Even after I had personally requested that he do so, the Bay of Pigs report he turned over to us was not complete. I saw that Howard Hunt would give us a chance to turn Helms's extreme sensitivity about the Bay of Pigs to good advantage. I was not sure whether the CIA actually had any bona fide reasons to intervene with the FBI. There was enough circumstantial evidence to suggest that they might. But, in any case, Howard Hunt would provide a good way of suggesting that they do so. If the CIA would deflect the FBI from Hunt, they would thereby protect us from the only White House vulnerability involving Watergate that I was worried about exposing—not the break-in, but the political activities Hunt had undertaken for Colson.

I was concerned that Haldeman handle the matter deftly. I did not want him to strong-arm Helms and Walters, nor did I want him to lie and say there was no involvement. I wanted him to set out the situation in such a way that Helms and Walters would take the initiative and go to the FBI on their own. I told Haldeman to say that I believed this thing would open up the whole Bay of Pigs matter—to say that the whole thing was a sort of comedy of errors and that they should call the FBI in and say that for the sake of the country they should go no further into this case.

After this half-hour meeting with Haldeman I held a ninety-minute session on the economy and then conducted several brief ceremonial meetings. When I had finished, I buzzed for Haldeman to come in again. I wanted him to understand that I was not interested in concealing Hunt's involvement in Watergate from Helms and Walters or even from the FBI; in fact, I said that he should level with Helms and Walters and tell them that we knew Hunt had been involved in Watergate. But then he should point out that the whole Cuban involvement in Watergate would make the CIA and Hunt look bad; and the whole thing might possibly reopen the Bay of Pigs controversy, and that would be bad for the CIA, for the country, and for American foreign policy. I also did not want Helms and Walters to get the idea that our concern was political—which, of course, it was. However, I also did not want Haldeman actually to misrepresent to them that our concern was *not* political. He should simply say that our concern was because of "the Hunt involvement."

When Haldeman came back from his meeting with Helms and Walters that afternoon, he said that he had not mentioned Hunt at the outset. He had simply raised the possibility that the FBI was exploring leads that would be harmful to the CIA and to the government. Helms had volunteered the information that he had in fact already received a call from Pat Gray expressing fear that the FBI investigation had run into a CIA operation. Helms said he had told Gray that there was nothing that the CIA knew of at that point, but Gray had asserted that that was what it looked like to him.

Haldeman said he had gone on to point out that the problem was that this matter would track back to the Bay of Pigs and to people who had no involvement in the Watergate matter except by contacts or connections. That was when he mentioned Hunt. At this point, Haldeman said that Helms got the picture and said he would be happy to be helpful but would like to know the reason. Haldeman said he made it clear to Helms that he was not going to get specifics but rather generalities. It had been left that Walters would go to see Gray and take care of the matter. It seemed that our intervention had worked easily. As far as I was concerned, this was the end of our worries about Watergate.

During the remaining few days in June when I discussed the Watergate break-in it was mainly to express my irritation that nothing seemed to be happening to settle the case and remove it from the public eye. Until that was done the media and the Democrats would continue to batter us with it. On June 26 I asked Haldeman if there was any way to get the people involved to plead guilty so that the White House could forget about the case and not have it hanging over us. I asked who was keeping track of the situation for us. He told me that it was being watched by John Dean, John Mitchell, and others.

Haldeman said that guilty pleas would have to await the indictments, and the indictments were being delayed because the FBI kept investigating and uncovering new things. But, he said, we could hope we had turned that off. Later in the day Haldeman said that one of the problems was that the CRP had used the men involved in the Watergate bugging on other standard intelligence and political projects as well. Otherwise, he said, we could cut them loose and sink them without a trace. Haldeman said that he did not know what the other projects were.

For all my concern about Mitchell's vulnerability and despite occasional doubts by me and others about the extent to which he might have been involved, I was still basically convinced of his innocence. I assumed that he had known about the campaign intelligence operations in general, but not about the bugging in particular.

On June 28 I said to Haldeman that, as I understood it, Mitchell had not known specifically about the bugging. Haldeman answered that, as he understood it, that was correct. The next day I said my hunch was that one of the lower-level people at the CRP had said to Mitchell that they were trying to get information. That was standard political practice by both sides. Mitchell would have assumed that they were talking about planting an informant and said, "Don't tell me anything about it." Instead, they had gone and bugged the DNC.

On Friday morning, June 30, a newspaper story attributed to unidentified sources said that Howard Hunt's safe at the White House had been opened and among the contents turned over to the FBI were the architectural plans of the DNC offices, wiretapping equipment, and a gun. Ziegler immediately checked the story and found that there had been an unloaded gun. But there were no such plans, and the so-called wiretap equipment was a walkie-talkie. Haldeman said that some other things in the safe had been handled at a high, discreet level in the Bureau. I asked why Hunt had a safe at the White House if, as I had been told, he had not actually worked as a consultant for several months. Haldeman said that he had simply left these things behind. At one point Haldeman said that the whole thing was so ludicrous that Dean had not discounted the possibility that we were dealing with a double agent who purposely blew the operation. Otherwise it was just too hard to figure out.

I was surprised because this story indicated that the FBI was still going after Hunt. I had thought that they were going to keep away from him as a result of Haldeman's meeting with Helms and Walters. Haldeman said that apparently Pat Gray did not know how to follow through. The U.S. Attorney's office at the Justice Department was pushing hard, making it difficult for them to limit the investigation. I said that Walters should go see the Justice Department officials, too.

The story about Hunt's safe raised my concern that Colson might have had something to do with Hunt on the bugging project. But once again Haldeman said that Colson had told the FBI "the straight truth"—that he had worked with Hunt only on matters totally unrelated to the bugging.

Haldeman had informed me the day before that Liddy had been fired from the CRP after he refused to talk to the FBI investigators; Liddy had understood that this would happen and agreed to it. I asked again whether Haldeman thought Mitchell knew in advance of Liddy's bugging plans. Haldeman said he did not think Mitchell had known specifically but that Liddy had worked on general intelligence and counter-intelligence activity for Mitchell. I observed that such practices were standard in campaigns.

Then Haldeman told me that Gordon Liddy had once worked at the White House on narcotics problems for Bud Krogh on Ehrlichman's Domestic Council. Haldeman was not sure whether it was just Hunt or Liddy too who had worked on the Pentagon Papers investigations. I said that these were perfectly legitimate projects, and we went on to other things.

Later in the day Haldeman told me about the latest ideas for dealing with the Watergate matter. Liddy was going to write a "scenario" that would tie together all the loose ends: he would take responsibility for planning the entire Watergate operation and say that no one higher up had authorized it. As for the money used to finance his activities, he would explain that he had obtained it by cashing a check that he was supposed to have returned to the campaign contributor who wrote it. When I asked why Liddy had in fact been given this campaign check, Haldeman said that apparently Liddy was supposed to have converted it into cash in Mexico, exactly as he had done, but then had gone the further step of using it for his own covert operation. Haldeman said that they had not yet worked out how to handle the issue of Hunt's role.

I told Haldeman that I really believed that Mitchell was telling the truth—that he had not known. Haldeman agreed that he had probably ordered an information-gathering operation, not knowing that bugs were going to be planted.

I expressed my hope that some Cuban motive could be retained in our explanations of the origins of the break-in. I said that the story had to be true to some extent—why else would the Cubans have risked so much? Most of all, I urged Haldeman to move quickly on the whole matter. We should cut our losses and "get the damn thing done."

I was particularly concerned that Colson not get dragged in, which was almost bound to happen if the investigation continued as an endless fishing expedition. Haldeman, however, said that the problem went beyond Colson, because Hunt and Liddy were tied to Krogh, and all of them were tied to Ehrlichman and his aide David Young.

I replied that if this connection was because of our Pentagon Papers investigations, there was nothing the matter with that. Haldeman said that it was the investigation itself—"the process," he called it—that was the problem. I asked what he meant. He said again that it was just "the process" that they had used. I did not pursue the question, but I repeated emphatically that in my view, it was perfectly all right.

My thoughts turned back to Liddy. Earlier I had asked Haldeman about his family, and Haldeman said that whatever needs they had, we would take care of them. Haldeman ventured that if Liddy were saddled with a very long sentence—which would clearly be unfair when measured against all precedents—we could wait a discreet interval and then parole or pardon him after the election. I agreed.

As the meeting was ending, I came back to the matter of Liddy's confession and urged that we get it over with. It would involve the CRP, and I didn't like it. But it wouldn't cripple us in the campaign; the Bobby Baker scandal had not hurt Johnson's margin. "You can't cover this," I said to Haldeman, adding that the best thing was just to get the guy in charge to go ahead and accept the blame. "It's just such a ridiculous goddamn thing," I said.

Shortly before I left Washington to spend the week of July 4 in California, Colson and I talked again about the exaggerated news coverage that was being given to the break-in. In sheer exasperation, I said it would help if someone broke into our headquarters and did a lot of damage—then we could launch a counterattack. Colson agreed and pointed out that several of our campaign files actually had been missing. I reemphasized my desire to get the break-in off our backs because of the impression it would leave, if it lingered, that the White House had ordered bugging and snooping. I observed that Bobby Kennedy had actually *done* it; but we could not afford even the *impression* of having done it.

My extensive diary notes from June 21 to June 30 are predominantly about foreign policy, domestic issues, campaign planning, and personal and family observations. On June 30, the night before I left for California, I dictated a brief reflection about where we stood on Watergate:

> *Diary*
> The major problem on the Watergate is simply to clean the thing up by having whoever was responsible admit what happened. Certainly I am satisfied that nobody in the White House had any knowledge or approved any such activity, and that Mitchell was not aware of it as well.

It was in these days at the end of June and the beginning of July 1972 that I took the first steps down the road that eventually led to the end of my presidency. I did nothing to discourage the various stories that were being considered to explain the break-in, and I approved efforts to encourage the CIA to intervene and limit the FBI investigation. Later my actions and inactions during this period would appear to many as part of a widespread and conscious cover-up. I did not see them as such. I was handling in a pragmatic way what I perceived as an annoying and strictly political problem. I was looking for a way to deal with Watergate that would minimize the damage to me, my friends, and my campaign, while giving the least advantage to my political opposition. I saw Watergate as politics pure and simple. We were going to play it tough. I never doubted that that was exactly how the other side would have played it.

I would have preferred to tell the story of these days as they really happened, with Watergate discussions of thirty and forty minutes interspersed among hours of conversations, deliberations, and decision-making on the whole range of interesting, boring, important, and insignificant matters that fill the days of a President. Instead perspective has been sacrificed to clarity, and several complex dimensions have been reduced to a single comprehensible one. Yet all the discussions about Watergate that took place during the week after the break-in totaled no more than a small fraction of the more than seventy-five hours I spent in the office and working at home. I have sometimes wondered whether, if we had only spent more time on the problem at the outset, we might have handled it less stupidly.

Martha Mitchell was vivacious and pretty in a flamboyant, self-amused way. She was flirtatious, determined to be outrageous, and bound to dominate any room she entered. When I first met her I thought that she might indeed be "the only fun that poor man has," as she later described herself. The man was her husband, who kept a watchful eye to protect her, smiled at her antics, and never seemed to let anything ruffle his calm exterior.

After the election, when Mitchell resisted my request that he come to Washington as Attorney General, I was sure that concern about Martha was behind his reticence. Finally I broached the matter directly with him. I said that I thought Washington might be just what Martha needed. The limelight and attention surrounding his position would give her confidence and do her good. He was skeptical, but in the end he agreed.

I was both right and wrong in my judgment. Martha blossomed like a sweep of azaleas in Washington. She was excellent news copy, and she cultivated a reputation for saying exactly what she thought by saying exactly what she thought. Before long she was a national celebrity. Her lively originality made her much sought after for television shows and party fund-raisers. At one point she had a phenomenally high 76 percent national recognition factor in the Gallup poll. Her constituency consisted of those who actually liked her opinions, those who liked the fact that she spoke out, and those who enjoyed the fact that she must be causing embarrassment to Mitchell and me. I knew she was not always in complete control of herself, and sometimes that worried me. But I kept such worries to myself because I did not ever want Mitchell to feel uncomfortable with me because of her.

Although Martha enjoyed great popularity and success in Washington, her troubles remained, and she was frustrated and tormented by emotional problems she could neither understand nor control. As early as March 1971 Bebe Rebozo had confidentially raised with me the fact that Mitchell was having increasing difficulty with Martha. One day at Key Biscayne, I asked Rebozo why Mitchell put up with her. He said that he had once asked Mitchell the same question, and he had replied simply, "Because I love her."

In the past there had been long bouts of crying and hysterics. Now, with Watergate, there was talk of suicide.

John Mitchell had been exhausted and drained by the ITT attack. Now he was trying to run a presidential campaign amidst the worries and distractions of the Watergate publicity. In the two weeks after the break-in, Martha began a new series of phone calls to the press, saying that she had given her husband ultimatums to get out of politics and insisting that she was a "political prisoner." She drew added suspicion to Mitchell when she said, "I love my husband very much but I'm not going to stand for all those dirty things that go on."

"He can't cope with this," Haldeman told me. Billy Graham called Rose Woods to see if there was anything he could do to help. But we did nothing because we knew that Mitchell would have resented it. He would say that it was his problem, and he must deal with it himself. Only once in a low moment did he break down and confide to Haldeman, "You and the President don't realize how much time I have to spend keeping her on an even keel—or how much it's affected my ability to run the campaign."

I felt that some members of the press deliberately exploited Martha Mitchell during this period. Months later it would become clear to all that her wild claims that she had a manual containing procedures for the Watergate break-in and that she herself knew all the details were simply ploys to get attention. But even at the time it was obvious to those who came into contact with her that she had very serious emotional problems. Nonetheless, many reporters encouraged her to further excesses, primarily, I felt, because they thought that by doing so they were tightening the screws on Mitchell. By the end of June I was reluctantly beginning to think that Mitchell would have to leave the campaign.

I considered John Mitchell to be one of my few close personal friends. I believed that I owed my election as President in 1968 largely to his strength as a counselor and his skill as a manager. I had referred to him as one of the few indispensable men, and that was how I felt about him. The thought of losing his help was bad enough. The thought of his having to resign under pressure amid a barrage of controversy and negative publicity was very hard for me to accept. But the combination of having to fend off Watergate publicity and having to take care of Martha would inevitably distract him too much from important campaign tasks.

I had no illusions that Mitchell's departure would put an end to our Watergate problems. It would take much more than that. On June 26, when Haldeman and I were discussing this, he ventured that the only way to put an end to Watergate would be to hang the blame directly on Mitchell. "I won't do that to him. To hell with it," I said, "I'd rather lose the election."

Even as I had begun to think that Mitchell would have to resign, Mitchell was coming to the same conclusion himself. In personal terms, he saw that there was no other choice, and in typical Mitchell style, instead of bringing us a problem to solve, he came to us with a solution. On June 29 he met with Haldeman and told him that Martha's condition was very serious. She could not cope with the criticism he was getting on Watergate, and he was afraid she would harm herself. Later, when I asked Haldeman if Martha was aware of the real Watergate problem, he said no. Mitchell had commented, however, that Martha was smart, and she recognized that her public complaints would give him a reason to ease out of the front line of the controversy by resigning.

I had lunch with Mitchell in my EOB office on June 30. It was a painful session. He looked worn out and his hand shook so much that he had to put his soup spoon down after the first taste. Later in the afternoon I asked former Minnesota Congressman Clark MacGregor if he would take over the campaign, and he agreed. I felt that MacGregor would infuse new life and spirit into the CRP. He had a rare ability to charge people up, and he would do an effective job of reorganization. We also decided to follow up on our earlier plan to send Fred Malek over to shake things up. "We'll clean that son of a bitch up," I told Haldeman, "and we'll run this campaign."

We made the announcement of Mitchell's resignation and MacGregor's appointment on July 1.

Several weeks later on two different occasions I dictated about John Mitchell and the Watergate break-in.

Diary

Here I think we have had a slip-up due to the fact that Mitchell was so obsessed with the problems he had with Martha. Whether it was getting the organization at 1701 [Pennsylvania Avenue, the CRP headquarters] honed down, or whether it was watching over things like this we just didn't have the discipline we should have had and that we would have had had he been able to pay attention to business.

I am continually amazed whenever I am with John Mitchell about his vast knowledge of people over the country and also in all kinds of fields.

Mitchell has particular knowledge about all kinds of fishing, how the tides operate in various parts of the East Coast, as well as, of course, a wide knowledge of every kind of food and how it is prepared—in addition to having already the deserved reputation for knowing more about more political figures in both parties than perhaps any man in the United States.

Without Martha, I am sure that the Watergate thing would never have happened.

THE GRAY PHONE CALL

When I arrived in California on July 1 for an eighteen-day stay, I faced an unusually busy period. Al Haig and Sir Robert Thompson returned from Vietnam with a firsthand assessment of the situation there, and Kissinger and I were working on the strategy for his upcoming meeting with the North Vietnamese, the first since the May 8 bombing and mining. There was also a great deal of campaign planning to be done following Mitchell's departure. On July 6 I had a long meeting with MacGregor and Malek to discuss campaign organization and management. This day was to turn out to be memorable for a completely unexpected reason, and that night I recounted the events that would later assume such importance:

Diary

Today we got some of the disturbing news with regard to the developments in the Watergate case, almost by accident.

When I saw the account in the *Times* of the FBI's action on the hijacking case in which they killed two hijackers, and unfortunately a passenger as well, on Pacific Southwest Airlines, I called the new Director [Pat Gray] and told him to congratulate the men for me and also to give my congratulations to the Pan Am captain and the police sergeant or retired policeman who had been responsible for the spectacular killing of the hijacker in Vietnam at Saigon Airport.

When I had passed on the message, he proceeded to tell me that he was greatly concerned about the Watergate case and that Walters had come in to see him today indicating that the CIA had no interest in the matter and that pursuing the investigation would not be an embarrassment to the CIA.

He said that he and Walters both felt that some people either at the White House or at the committee were trying to cover up things which would be a mortal blow to me—rather than assisting in the investigation.

When Ehrlichman came in he was astounded to find out that I had had this conversation. He then told me that the problem was that the unraveling of the case would not be particularly embarrassing as far as this instant matter was concerned, but that it would involve the activities which were perfectly legitimate but which would be hard to explain in investigating the Ellsberg case, the Bay of Pigs, and the other matters where we had an imperative need to get the facts.

From my conversation with Haldeman on June 23 I had understood that Gray had *wanted* help from Walters in controlling an investigation that he agreed was getting out of hand. On June 30 Haldeman had told me that Gray wanted to limit the investigation but was under pressure from the U.S. Attorney's office. But now Gray was telling me, and in the most vivid language, that he was upset about what he saw as attempts on the part of the White House to frustrate the FBI's inquiry. I was suddenly confronted with the one thing that I had most wanted to avoid: White House involvement in Watergate. I told Gray emphatically to go ahead with his full investigation.

> *Diary*
> Certainly the best thing to do is to have the investigation pursued to its normal conclusion. In any event, we have to live with this one and hope to bring it to a conclusion without too much rubbing off on the presidency before the election. It is one of those cases where subordinates in a campaign, with the very best of motives, go off on some kick which inevitably embarrasses the top man. In this instance, however, how we handle it may make the difference as to how we come out.
> In any event, as I emphasized to Ehrlichman and Haldeman, we must do nothing to indicate to Pat Gray or to the CIA that the White House is trying to suppress the investigation. On the other hand, we must cooperate with the investigation all the way along the line.

I told Ehrlichman to be sure that both Helms at the CIA and Gray at the FBI knew that I wanted a full investigation and that we were not attempting to suppress anything. I said we should also be sure to level with Clark MacGregor so he did not make statements he would have to retract later.

"Let's take the heat," I told Ehrlichman. "It won't be that bad."

The first mention I recall of Jeb Magruder's possible involvement in the Watergate break-in came while I was in California, when Ehrlichman told me that Magruder was going to be questioned in the investigation. Magruder had been brought into the White House by Haldeman in 1969 and was considered one of Haldeman's protégés, and it would be a personal blow to Haldeman if Magruder were drawn into the Watergate web. I dictated in my diary that night, "Haldeman is naturally very 'tender,' as Ehrlichman pointed out, with regard to Magruder. I feel just as deeply about it as he does." Magruder had left the White House staff in May 1971 to help set up the CRP, where he was assigned to handle the managerial details for Mitchell. Magruder had been Liddy's immediate superior and had been responsible for authorizing money for him.

Ehrlichman thought that Magruder might have to take the Fifth Amendment because even if the prosecutors could not establish any direct involvement in the planning and execution of the bugging, his relationship to Liddy was such that they might be able to draw him in as part of a conspiracy.

On Saturday afternoon, July 8, Ehrlichman and I went for a walk on the beach. It was a beautiful California day, and we could see the surfers bobbing on their boards in the water far down the coast. As we walked along the conversation turned to Magruder.

Diary

I told John Ehrlichman in a long walk on the beach that under the circumstances the question is whether Magruder is going to be better off in the event that he anticipates what will happen and voluntarily indicates what his role was and takes responsibility for the action, or whether he will face the fact that he will be questioned on such matters and then be forced at a later time to resign. I strongly urged the first course in his own interests.

Ehrlichman reflected on Gray's phone call and suggested that Gray and Walters might have failed to cooperate in limiting the FBI investigation because they felt that someone on the White House staff—perhaps Colson—was responsible for Watergate and was trying to put me on the spot in order to protect himself. Not knowing that in fact there was no White House involvement, Ehrlichman said, Gray and Walters probably thought that they were serving my interests by insisting on a wide-ranging investigation.

We discussed the subject of clemency. Watergate was a political shenanigan, and Magruder, Hunt, Liddy, and the five defendants were apparently first offenders. Three years earlier the NBC television producer caught illegally bugging the Democrats had been let off with a light fine and a suspended sentence. The political climate that was being built up around Watergate made it unlikely that there would be such even-handed treatment for anyone involved in the DNC bugging.

Ehrlichman and I agreed that there should be no commitments of any kind on clemency at this time.

In a later conversation with Ehrlichman I suggested that if felonies were committed by demonstrators in this campaign, as they had been in the past, and the participants were booked and charged, I might grant a general political pardon after the election that would encompass both the Watergate bugging and the felonies committed by the opposition. This would not, however, include felonies that involved the use of violence, bombing, or physical injury. I did not consider those to be in the same minor league with the Watergate bugging.

There was certainly a precedent for pardons of political offenses. When Harry Truman became President, dozens of his fellow Democratic workers in the Kansas City Pendergast machine had been convicted of vote fraud in the 1936 elections. Truman began pardoning them before he had been in office a month. By the end of his first year in the White House, he had pardoned fifteen people and restored them to full participation in future political activity.

My discussions with Ehrlichman were in no sense an authorization or a promise of clemency or pardons. Any decision would have to be made later. I summarized it at one point in my diary: if there were equivalent offenses on both sides, "that will provide the necessary basis we will need for pardoning the individuals involved in this caper in the event they are convicted."

> *Diary*
> Everyone agrees that this incident was so clumsily handled that it probably doesn't deserve the criminal penalty that such incidents would ordinarily bring, but in any event, with the political implications involved, we have to be prepared to deal with it firmly before the election. After the election, of course, it will be very difficult to handle it in any other way than an even-handed way, and I hope that such an opportunity presents itself.

THE DEMOCRATS' NOMINEE

The 1972 Democratic convention in Miami was a political shambles. After Humphrey's defeat in 1968, the party machinery had been taken over by radical reformers who sought to cleanse it of the "old politics" of the traditional organizations and power blocs by replacing them with the "new politics" of minority groups and radical activists. As a result the 1972 convention was unlike anything that had been seen before. Television audiences looked on hour after hour as representatives of the "new politics" used the convention to air and argue their currently fashionable frustrations: women, blacks, homosexuals, welfare mothers, migrant farm workers. Speakers were indulged and self-indulgent. There was no semblance of orderly procedure.

George McGovern had been one of the principal sponsors of the delegate reforms, and his nomination for President on July 12 was an indication of how well they had succeeded. He chose Senator Thomas Eagleton of Missouri as his running mate. Eagleton was young, attractive, Catholic, and a favorite with organized labor.

I invited John Connally to join me in San Clemente on the last night of the Democratic convention. After dinner we settled down in the living room to watch the acceptance speeches.

Hours passed as we waited for McGovern and Eagleton to appear. A new party charter was debated. Then thirty-nine other vice presidential candidates were nominated, including Mao Tse-tung and Martha Mitchell. The scene had the air of a college skit that had gotten carried away with itself and didn't know how to stop. Finally Connally gave up and went home. Pat and I continued to watch as first Teddy Kennedy took the microphone, then Hubert Humphrey, and then, at 2:48 A.M. in Miami—prime time on Guam, as some wit observed—McGovern himself at last appeared.

Diary

They panned to Humphrey on several occasions. He really looked like a very sad figure. I was glad that Henry called him today. He said that he wanted to be of assistance to us in foreign policy and seemed to be disappointed at what happened at the convention, not just from a personal standpoint, but generally.

I called Haldeman immediately after the acceptance speech and he said, "Well, they nominated the wrong man." Kennedy looked very good, although some thought he looked fat. He has a magnetic smile, a lot of style, and a brilliantly written speech.

As they had done on every other convention night in every other campaign, my family gave me their assessments of the opposition. Pat thought McGovern's best assets were a rather dignified bearing and an apparent sincerity. Julie had pneumonia and had not been able to stay up, but she thought Eagleton was too glib. Tricia said succinctly of McGovern, "He's a boring evangelist, and there's nothing more boring than an evangelist who's boring."

My thoughts returned to the look on Hubert Humphrey's face as he had watched McGovern's acceptance speech. Humphrey was an honorable and resourceful opponent. He did not fear showing his patriotism, his feelings, or his flaws. However close he might come to getting the nomination if he tried again in 1976, I knew that he would never make it. Time had now passed him by—just as it would have passed me by if I had lost to him in 1968.

The next day I sat in my study near the windows facing the ocean and wrote a letter to him.

I had very little by which to measure McGovern personally. I knew only what he said on the issues—but that was enough. I thought it was critically important to the future of the country that his radical ideas not prevail in November. I feared he would now ease off his radical positions—something, I observed, a far-right candidate would never do.

Diary

The extremists on the right of the Goldwater type would rather lose fighting for principle than to win by compromising principle. The extremists on the left, on the other hand, have usually shown that when the chips are down they will compromise principle in order to get power. This is why the communists usually beat the right-wingers, because the right-wingers are always fighting for principle, and the communists are willing to

THE WHITE HOUSE
WASHINGTON,

July 15, 1972

Dear Hubert,

As your party's convention comes to an end, I know how deep your disappointment must be.

You can take comfort in the fact that through the years you have earned the respect of your opponents as well as your supporters for being a gallant warrior.

As I am sure you will recall after Churchill's defeat in 1945 his wife tried to console him by saying that maybe it was a "blessing in disguise

Churchill answered - "If this is a blessing it is certainly very well disguised."

You must feel as he did. But like him - you have many years of service ahead.

As friendly opponents in the political arena I hope we can both serve our parties in a way that will best serve the nation

Sincerely

Dick

Pat joins me in sending our best to Muriel & to you.

compromise principle until they get into power and then they, of course, crush out their opposition.

Putting it in a nutshell—the radicals of the left want power. They will compromise on issues in order to get power, recognizing that when they get power they can do what they want on the issues. They don't believe as deeply in principle as they pretend, and not nearly as deeply as do the radicals on the right.

In the first three days following his nomination George McGovern irretrievably lost the support of his own party.

Indications of his unreliability had appeared during the convention, when he had ignored or reneged on embarrassing or inconvenient commitments. For example, he had said that he would support a feminist challenge to the South Carolina delegation, but backed out when the challenge was made. Both before and after the nomination he asked Larry O'Brien to remain as Democratic National Chairman, and then backed down when his own staff raised objections. He introduced Pierre Salinger to a public meeting as his personal candidate for vice-chairman of the DNC, and then abandoned him when opposition arose. John Connally shook his head in disbelief. "Lack of character," he said. "It will do him in before the campaign is over." In March 1973 the new DNC Chairman, Robert Strauss, told Haldeman after the Gridiron Dinner, "You fellows just don't know McGovern—you think he's an evil man. He is just the stupidest man there ever was."

In San Clemente the reaction to McGovern's nomination and conduct was little short of exuberant. He had consciously abandoned conservative and moderate Democrats; and the ethnic groups, traditionally a Democratic blue chip, could find in him nothing of the hearty patriotism and pride that they had looked for in their party in the past. With these defections we had a chance not just to win the election but to create the New Majority we had only dreamed of in 1970. Only organized labor and George Wallace remained in doubt.

There were rumors that George Wallace was disgusted with the turn of events in Miami and was once again considering making a bid for the presidency as the nominee of a third party. Harry Dent, a former Republican State Chairman of South Carolina who served as a political aide on the White House staff, and several other White House political contacts were on the phone to Montgomery daily, keeping abreast of the situation there. Finally I asked Connally to take over the "Wallace watch." "Go down there and see him, and let me know what he wants," I said.

On Tuesday, July 25, Connally saw Wallace and told him frankly what he himself believed: that Wallace would not help himself by becoming involved with a third party, and that the only way to get the Democratic Party back on its feet for the future was to "beat the hell" out of McGovern in November.

Connally called me the next day to report that Wallace would announce that he was definitely not going to run for President on a third-party ticket. "And all he really wants from you is to be sure that his message on the issues was heard. He said the Democrats hadn't listened to a word he and his constituents were saying." Connally later told Colson, "We might well say that this was the day the election was won."

I called Wallace and told him I knew it had been a terribly hard decision for him to make. "But you can't let yourself get discouraged by this," I said. "You have so many good years left." I told him that Connally was my closest political adviser, and if there was anything he wanted to discuss with regard to political matters, Connally would be available to him at any time. I also told him that Haig would give him foreign policy briefings, because I knew Wallace supported me on national defense issues.

Diary

I spoke to Haldeman and he was going to have *Sunrise at Campobello* taken to Wallace so he can see it.

I am also going to look into the possibility of a salt-water swimming pool for him, since I told him this would enable him to swim with his feet afloat and would greatly reduce the effort he would have to make swimming only with his arms.

On July 17 I received word that after a three-hour meeting, the executive board of the teamsters' union had voted 16 to 1 to endorse me for reelection. I invited their president, Frank Fitzsimmons, and his board to come to San Clemente.

Diary

This could have been one of the most important watershed meetings in American politics in this century.

I told them that when I had a tough decision to make sometimes members of the Cabinet, members of the administration, most of the media, and even most businessmen were reluctant to stand up and stand with me; but that I found that representatives of labor were really tough and strong in the crunch when the interests of the country were involved. This, of course, is the gospel truth, and they all knew that I meant it very sincerely when I said it.

I also pointed out that as far as they were concerned that most of them were registered Democrats—however, I did not consider

> that Democrats this year would be deserting their party, because the issues, particularly of national defense and foreign policy, transcended party lines, and that the Democratic candidate, who was undoubtedly sincere and against whom I had no personal animosity and hoped he had none against me, simply took a line which was out of tune and out of step with that of great numbers of his party.

I had walked out to the driveway with Fitzsimmons. I asked him what he thought George Meany's reaction would be to the teamsters' decision to endorse me. "Well," he said, "the old son of a bitch really has a problem now. I happen to know that 90 of the 130 members of the AFL-CIO board won't take McGovern. Hah," he chuckled, "after Meany hears what we did today, he'll be in such a stew he's gonna piss down his leg."

On July 19, my first full day back in Washington, I spent most of the morning going over domestic and legislative items. Then I asked Ehrlichman for an update on Watergate. He said that Dean was meeting with Mitchell that very morning to discuss it. He said that he did not think that the defense that had been worked up for Magruder was going to work. In Ehrlichman's judgment, Magruder would probably have to "take a slide."

I asked what that would mean. Ehrlichman said that Magruder would just have to take the lumps whatever they were; he would have to take the responsibility. Ehrlichman said he did not think a story could be contrived that indicated that Magruder had not known what was going on. But, he said, Dean was working on the problem that morning.

I asked if Magruder had in fact known. Ehrlichman's opinion was typically emphatic. Lord yes, he said, he was in it with both feet.

In that case, I said, there must not be any "contrived" story. I said I would like to see the thing worked out, but I knew that the two worst actions in this kind of situation were to lie and to cover up. If you covered up you would inevitably get caught, and if you lied you would be guilty of perjury. That was the story of the Hiss case and the 5 percenters under Truman. It was a tragic thing for Magruder, I said, and I hated to see it happen, but that was the way it was. I reiterated what I had said in San Clemente in early July: it would be easy to pardon Magruder later along with others in both parties who were charged with political offenses during the campaign.

That would do it, Ehrlichman agreed—as he put it, lay the foundation—but we would have a better feel for everything after Dean had talked with Mitchell. He told me that Hunt and Liddy were about to be drawn into the grand jury proceedings through the testimony of a lawyer Hunt had contacted on the night of the break-in and asked to represent the arrested men.

Still thinking about Magruder, I asked if he could invoke the Fifth Amendment. Ehrlichman did not think so and speculated that if he did he would still be convicted by someone else's testimony. He felt that Magruder should simply go in and say that it was a bad thing, but that he had got carried away and now he felt terrible about it.

Magruder's whole life would be ruined for this one mistake. I wondered if he could not accept only the ultimate responsibility by saying that he had simply given an instruction to get all the information possible but had not expected it to be carried out this way. I said I thought it would be unfortunate if he should say that he had actually ordered wiretapping. Ehrlichman agreed that it should be kept at the Liddy level if possible, but repeated that he had too little information at that point to say anything more.

I said that the problem was a tough one, but the important thing was just to get it over and done with. Ehrlichman said he had told Dean that things must move as quickly as possible.

I asked whom Dean was working with on this, Ehrlichman or Haldeman. He said that both of them had been talking with Dean more or less together right along. I asked what Magruder was saying. Ehrlichman said that Magruder was saying that he had wanted to get a lot of information for a lot of different reasons, and that he had given Liddy the responsibility for getting it.

As Ehrlichman saw it, the problem was that once Magruder started talking, no one could tell what the scope of the examination might be and where it might end up.

I said that I supposed the main question was whether it would stop with Magruder or whether it would go on to Mitchell or Haldeman. Ehrlichman agreed and said that he and Haldeman had raised that question with Dean. Dean was unsure whether Magruder was tough and stable enough to be able to hold the line if pressed by interrogators.

I asked Ehrlichman if he thought Mitchell had known about the bugging. He replied that he assumed so but that he did not really know. I said I could not believe that Mitchell knew. Ehrlichman said that transcripts had been made of the tapped DNC calls, and he had a feeling—which, he acknowledged, might be unfair—that Mitchell might have seen them. I asked if Haldeman had seen them. Ehrlichman said no—in fact, he could not find anyone in the White House who ever saw them or who ever knew about the Watergate bugging operation. He said that Haldeman and Dean had had a meeting with Mitchell, Magruder, and some others on an earlier and different intelligence plan that had been proposed but had been disapproved. As a result of their decision in that earlier meeting Haldeman and Dean had a right to feel that nothing like the Watergate operation was going on. After this earlier plan had been disapproved, however, others in the CRP went ahead with the Watergate bugging operation without there ever having been another meeting involving White House people, Ehrlichman said.

Ehrlichman said it was still a tough question whether Magruder would assume responsibility and say that Mitchell had not known anything. He observed that sometimes tough questioning can lead a man into saying things he does not intend to say. I thought surely Magruder would be able to hold up when so much stood or fell on whether Mitchell became implicated. But Ehrlichman said that a good lawyer could keep at him until he broke him down. This was a particular danger in the Democrats' suit against the CRP: their lawyer was Edward Bennett Williams, who was well known for his dazzling courtroom technique.

I asked Ehrlichman what the best tactic would be on the criminal case. He said that if we had our way, it would be to let Liddy and Hunt go and to hold it there. But if Magruder was going to be involved through third-party testimony, he said, the next best tactic would be to rationalize a story that would not lead to his conviction.

I tried to estimate the public relations effect on the charges of a "cover-up" if the five men arrested at the Watergate and Hunt and Liddy were actually convicted. I said that even though Hunt had worked at the White House, I was not really bothered by the negative publicity that would ensue from his conviction. Ehrlichman observed that Liddy had also worked in the White House, and there would be some of that in the news stories as well.

Ehrlichman said that he was still hopeful that Dean and Mitchell would conclude that what Ehrlichman called the "Magruder scenario" would work. But, he said, there was no sense in starting it if it was going to be disproved; that would only be doubly damaging. I agreed. Then we would have both a cover-up and a conviction, which is what had happened to Truman in the Hiss case.

Ehrlichman said that Dean had been admonished not to contrive a story that might not succeed. He repeated his feeling that if any risk remained, Magruder might as well just go "whole hog."

I was still worried about Magruder when I saw Colson later that afternoon. I told him, as I had Ehrlichman, that we simply had to get the thing done and cut our losses. Since Howard Hunt was about to go before a grand jury, I asked Colson how he assessed the situation. He replied that in the first place he did not think that Hunt would feel he had done anything wrong. Hunt, he said, was such an ideologue and so committed to the country that, if he had a good lawyer and were properly coached, he would take the heat rather than talk. He said that the only place that he would worry about Hunt was that he might say that he had tried to "psychoanalyze" Ellsberg because the SOB was an enemy. I said I didn't see any way Ellsberg could be relevant to this case. "I wouldn't worry about that," I said.

We discussed Magruder's situation and my concern whether he would hold up under questioning. Colson said that if it weren't for the political notoriety the whole bugging episode would mean nothing more than a suspended sentence for those involved, as happened in cases of industrial espionage. We agreed that it would be a terrible thing for Magruder to go through and have on his record. I mentioned to Colson the idea I had discussed with Ehrlichman of granting a general pardon after the election covering both Democrats and Republicans who were guilty of political offenses.

When Haldeman came in that afternoon, he was pessimistic about Magruder's chances of not being indicted. He said that there would be testimony implicating Magruder and that the only thing to do now was to try to cut it off before it hit Mitchell. I asked if Magruder could do that. Haldeman said that Magruder said he would, but there was some question whether he could.

Haldeman reported that Ehrlichman felt that we should just get it over with quickly. Haldeman agreed that it was probably better to take whatever losses there were. I said it was just a damn shame about Magruder and repeated my feeling about the possibility of an eventual pardon. We talked about other things, but then I came back to Magruder and asked what we could do to help the "poor son of a gun." Haldeman said he would be assisted in getting legal help. I told Haldeman that I hoped Magruder would leave the campaign before he was indicted. It would be better for him, and for us.

Haldeman and I agreed that the main thing now was that Mitchell come out clean. Whatever the actual case, I told Haldeman, Magruder simply had to draw the line on anything that might involve Mitchell.

I asked Haldeman if Colson had been called before the grand jury. He said no, but he might be called for a deposition in the civil suit. He then told me that the grand jury was apparently talking about calling Ehrlichman. I was surprised and asked why. Haldeman said it had to do with Hunt's having worked for Bud Krogh. I again asked what could be the interest in Ehrlichman, and Haldeman said that Dean had tried to find out from the Justice Department but apparently they were not saying.

The next afternoon Haldeman told me that it looked as if Magruder was not going to be indicted for the Watergate break-in. Evidently there was a distinction that could be drawn about whether the decision was *knowledgeable*—and therefore indictable. Haldeman said that Magruder's line would be that he had not known of this specific action—

"which apparently is true," Haldeman added. Magruder would say that he had authorized sums of money for Liddy without knowing the uses to which they would be put. He would admit to being guilty of stupidity but not of criminal conduct.

So Magruder was now at least technically safe. He had been part of the campaign's intelligence-gathering operation, but he had not been specifically aware of the Watergate break-in. At least that was what he was apparently saying. I was skeptical, as I think we all were, but I nonetheless thought that it was now up to the Justice Department to make its case against him if they could.

Haldeman said that Mitchell did not think we should make Magruder leave the CRP. There would be advance warning if he was going to be indicted; if he was, he could leave then. Haldeman observed that Ehrlichman and Mitchell represented two different approaches to handling the entire matter: Mitchell was of the "stonewall-it-to-hell-with-everybody" school, while Ehrlichman was of the "complete-panic-cut-everything-off-and-sink-it-immediately" school. Haldeman felt both were wrong.

In the late afternoon of July 25 Haldeman brought me a wire service bulletin from McGovern's post-convention vacation headquarters in South Dakota. McGovern and Eagleton had just held a press conference at which the vice presidential candidate disclosed that on three separate occasions between 1960 and 1966 he had admitted himself to hospitals for treatment of mental depression; on two of them his treatment had included electroshock therapy. He said that he still occasionally took tranquilizers.

After Eagleton's statement McGovern had said, "Tom Eagleton is fully qualified in mind, body, and spirit to be the Vice President of the United States and, if necessary, to take over the presidency on a moment's notice. I wouldn't have hesitated one minute if I had known everything that Senator Eagleton said here today." A reporter asked him if the decision to keep Eagleton on the ticket was irrevocable, and McGovern replied, "Absolutely."

My diary records the prediction I made that day to John Connally on how McGovern would handle the situation: "I suggested that McGovern would give him four or five days and then have his major newspapers call for him to resign and then have him replaced by the national committee."

I was therefore surprised the next day when McGovern made an even stronger statement, telling reporters that he was "1000 percent" behind Eagleton and that he had no intention of dropping him from the ticket. But when Haldeman came in with that afternoon's New York *Post* calling for Eagleton's resignation, I felt sure that despite McGovern's public statements, this was the beginning of the process I had predicted to Connally.

> *Diary*
>
> It is my view that if Eagleton is not dropped from the ticket this weekend that they have a very serious problem in letting the thing ride along. It will appear that they have a finger in the air, waiting for public opinion and the polls to tell them what to do. As I pointed out, this tells us a hell of a lot about McGovern.
>
> The main test of a man is whether he has the character to make tough decisions and then to lead his associates to follow him on those decisions.

On July 27 Jack Anderson reported a shockingly false story: he charged that Eagleton had been arrested several times on charges of drunken and reckless driving. In short order the Washington *Post,* the Los Angeles *Times,* and the New York *Post* were calling for Eagleton to get off the ticket. McGovern repeated that he was 1000 percent behind his running mate, and Eagleton denied the charges and gamely defended himself. He insisted that he would stay on the ticket. His gutsy and unshakable belief in himself won sympathy, if not real political support.

On Sunday, July 30, Eagleton appeared on *Face the Nation.* Jack Anderson was one of the panel of questioners. He apologized for the drunk-driving charges but refused to retract them, claiming he was still checking them. I thought back to the fund crisis in 1952 and about how Anderson's mentor, Drew Pearson, had done a similar thing to me. I could empathize with Eagleton's frustration, and I admired his aplomb. He was as courageous as Anderson was contemptible.

At one point the program took a turn that bordered, I thought, on the incredible. One of the reporters remarked how much Eagleton was sweating. Eagleton pointed out that the lights were very hot. The reporter persisted and pointed out that others on the show were not sweating that much and then commented on Eagleton's nervous fidgeting with his hands. I dictated that night, "I perspire even though I may not be under any tension whatever!" I thought it was a predatory performance.

In the meantime McGovern had started to seed the ground for a reversal of his support for Eagleton.

> *Diary*
>
> The way the McGovern-Eagleton thing adds up now, it seems to me, is that McGovern probably will be forced to put him off the ticket because of the opposition of the McGovern media and the professionals in the party. In the event he is able to replace

> him with Kennedy, this will make it a whole new ball game. If he is unable to get Kennedy, it's difficult to see how he could improve the ticket.

The next night McGovern dropped Eagleton. I thought immediately of Eagleton's family. I knew that their agony must have been like that we had suffered during the fund crisis—except that our suffering had been redeemed by a happy ending. I remembered that Eagleton had brought his young son to the Oval Office the year before, and I wrote a letter to the boy. A few weeks later I received his reply.

THE 1972 CAMPAIGN

The 1972 presidential election, with its landslide result, should have been the most gratifying and fulfilling of all my campaigns. Instead it was one of the most frustrating and, in many ways, the least satisfying of all.

During most of my first term I had assumed that my opponent in 1972 would be Kennedy, Muskie, or Humphrey. I thought that I could probably beat Muskie or Humphrey; a campaign against Teddy Kennedy would be much more difficult to predict because it would involve so many emotional elements. Any one of these men would have been a formidable opponent, and for three and a half years I fully expected to have to fight hard for re-election.

Even after McGovern emerged from the primaries as the front-runner, I still could not believe that he would actually be nominated. I thought, as did many political observers, that at the last minute the convention would turn to Kennedy. Only after McGovern was nominated did I accept the fact that I was virtually assured of re-election without having to wage much of a campaign.

Against Kennedy or Muskie or Humphrey I would have had to fight a close-in, one-on-one battle. Against McGovern, however, it was clear that the less I did, the better I would do. This was a totally unaccustomed situation for me, and it was not one in which I felt particularly comfortable or even knew instinctively what was best to do.

There were five basic components of my 1972 election strategy. First, I planned to spend the month and a half following the Republican convention in the White House doing my job. The choice between the candidates was so sharp and the issues spoke so clearly for themselves that there was no need for me to hammer them home.

Second, Senator Bob Dole of Kansas, the highly articulate Chairman of the Republican National Committee, and various members of the Cabinet and the administration would travel throughout the country as presidential "surrogates," talking about our general record and achieve-

Personal

THE WHITE HOUSE

WASHINGTON August 2, 1972 -

Dear Terry -

When I saw the picture in *Life* a week ago I was reminded of our meeting at the White House when your father introduced you to me after I signed the Construction Safety Bill. I thought you might like to have a copy of the White House Photographer's picture of that meeting.

I realize these past few days have been very difficult ones for you and the members of your family. Speaking as one who understands + respects your father's decision to continue to fight for his party's nominees and against my administration's policies, I would like to pass on to you some strictly personal thoughts with regard to the ordeal your father has undergone.

Politics is a very hard game. Winston Churchill once pointed out that politics is even more difficult than war. Because in politics you die many times; in war you die only once".

But in those words of Churchill we can all take some comfort. The political man can always come back to fight again.

What matters is not that your father fought a terribly difficult battle and lost. What matters is that in fighting the battle he won the admiration of foes and friends alike because of the courage, poise and just plain guts he showed against overwhelming odds.

Few men in public life in our whole history have been through what he has been through. I hope you do not allow this incident to discourage or depress you.

Years later you will look back and say "I am proud of the way my dad handled himself in the greatest trial of his life".

Sincerely Richard Nixon

PS I hope your arms are completely healed.

Friday, September 1, 1972

Honorable Richard Nixon
The White House
Washington D.C.

Dear Mr. President,

I just came home from summer camp. That explains why I did not answer your letter sooner.

I guess very few thirteen-year-olds get handwritten letters from the President. Although I am a Democrat, I think you must be a wonderful man to take the time to write to some unimportant person like me.

Do you know what my Dad said when he read your letter? He said, "It's going to make it all the tougher to talk against Nixon."

I think both Dad and you are excellent politicians. Even though you and Dad don't always agree, I think the country is lucky to have both of you.

My favorite subject in school is history. I now feel I am a part of history since you wrote a letter to me.

Thank you, Mr. President very, very much.

With appreciation,
Terry
Eagleton

ments as well as about their own specialized issues. Ideally, one surrogate would precede McGovern's appearance in each major city and another would follow him as soon as he left.

Third, I wanted to develop the most efficient and effective campaign committee organization humanly possible. We succeeded in this so well that Theodore H. White called the Committee to Re-elect the President "one of the most spectacularly efficient exercises in political technology of the entire postwar era."

Fourth, I planned to use the last weeks of the campaign to broadcast thirteen radio speeches covering my philosophy of government as well as my positions on the major campaign issues.

Finally, at the very end, I planned to emerge from the White House and campaign personally during the last two weeks before the election in states where the presidential vote might be close, or where my presence might pull in a Republican candidate in a tight local race. This was a dramatic reversal of roles for one who had been the party wheelhorse in so many other national campaigns. I knew there would be resentment on the part of some of the party workers and particularly by some Republican candidates who were hoping that my landslide could pull them in. But I thought then—and I still believe—that what we did was the only way to run the campaign of 1972 and the best way to pull in enough new blood from the Democrats to give the Republican Party the New Majority momentum that could give it a whole new lease on political life.

In view of my plans for highly limited personal campaigning, I decided that we should try to help Republican candidates with money. Nearly a million dollars went from our campaign funds into various Senate and House races. I posed for pictures and sent tape-recorded endorsements to every Republican candidate except the two running for the Senate in Mississippi and Arkansas. The Republicans in those races had no chance against Democratic incumbents James Eastland and John McClellan, who had stood with me in every international crisis in the first term and whose support I would need in the next four years.

After McGovern had been nominated I knew that the most difficult thing for us about the 1972 campaign would be the tendency to relax. Even if complacency did not cost us the election, it might cost us the renewed energy that comes with the completion of a campaign.

"We have to develop a sense of mission," I told Haldeman, "and not back into victory by default."

The most exciting aspect of the 1972 election for me was that McGovern's perverse treatment of the traditional Democratic power blocs that had been the basis of every Democratic presidential victory for the last forty years had made possible the creation of a New Republican Majority as an electoral force in American politics. I was confident that if we could only make a first inroad, we could follow through with these New

Majority groups. I believed that I had a much greater affinity with most of them than had their erstwhile Democratic allies, and I made this point in two separate diary entries, one as a general observation and the other after a meeting with a group of labor union supporters in New York at the end of September.

Diary

The American leader class has really had it in terms of their ability to lead. It's really sickening to have to receive them at the White House as I often do and to hear them whine and whimper and that's one of the reasons why I enjoy very much more receiving labor leaders and people from middle America who still have character and guts and a bit of patriotism.

The meeting with the labor leaders was the best of all. They were friendly, all out, and I hope we can find a way to see that this alliance is not broken immediately after the election—and that they not revert to their usual partisan, Democratic position. Frankly, I have more in common with them from a personal standpoint than does McGovern or the intellectuals generally. They like labor as a mass. I like them individually. The same thing can be said of all other groups or classes, including young, black, Mexicans, etc.

I do not believe that any administration in history has gone into a re-election campaign with a more impressive record than ours in August 1972. There was no major area of American life in which we had not made progress or proposed dramatic new alternatives.

Inflation averaged 6.1 percent in 1969; after only one year our New Economic Policy had cut it to 2.7 percent. The GNP had increased at an annual rate of only 3.4 percent in the first quarter of 1969; by the third quarter of 1972 it was rising at 6.3 percent, the fastest gain since 1965. All during the campaign the stock market was moving toward the 1000-point record that it achieved in November 1972.

The real earnings of Americans had not increased at all from 1965 to 1970; now they were moving up at an annual rate of 4 percent. Each year of the Nixon administration had set a new record in gross farm income. Average income per farm was 40 percent higher than the average from 1961 to 1968.

We had reduced federal income taxes by 66 percent for a family of four making $5,000, and by 20 percent for a family of four making $15,000. Overall federal taxes on individuals had decreased by $22 billion.

We had proposed the first major welfare reform since the program's inception. It was our proposal for a new national health insurance program—one that shared the cost between those who could afford to pay for health insurance, employers, and government—that survived the several socialized medicine schemes proposed by others. We had nearly doubled the funding for the fight against cancer and increased by ten times the funding for the attack against drug abuse. Seizures of narcotics and dangerous drugs had increased by 400 percent. The rise in crime had been 122 percent from 1960 to 1968; in 1971 it was only 6 percent; in the first half of 1972 it was only 1 percent.

We had proposed and won congressional approval for the nation's first formal research institute for learning and education. We passed a landmark mass transit bill which meant that funding which had been no more than $175 million per year rose to $400 million in 1971 and to $1 billion in 1973. We presented a revolutionary proposal for federal revenue-sharing with the states and hard-pressed cities. We also proposed a complete reorganization of the federal government. We offered the first comprehensive program for the environment in history, aimed at striking a balance between the dreams of the environmentalists and the realities of job-producing industry. Our Legacy of Parks program launched what would eventually become 642 parks in fifty states, parks designed not for elitists but the average citizen.

Our administration had completely changed America's spending priorities: in fiscal 1968, 45 percent of the budget was being spent for defense and 32 percent for "human resources," such as education, social services, health. By fiscal 1973 those figures had been reversed. We increased spending for the arts by almost 500 percent. We increased Social Security benefits by 51 percent.

Draft calls were 299,000 in 1968; they were 50,000 in 1972, and we were on our way to the elimination of the draft and the creation of an all-volunteer Army.

We had a superb record, but we had to make it known to the voters—or at least to remind them of our achievements. At the beginning of the summer I wrote a memorandum to John Ehrlichman asking him to move from his role of overseeing the conception of domestic policies to the role of overseeing their execution:

> You have handled the development of the programs with superb organizational ability and substantively have seen to it that they have come out along the lines of my own thinking. . . .
>
> As I look back over the past three years, our great failing, particularly in the domestic area, has been that once the President shoots the big gun, the infantry doesn't follow in adequately to clean up and to hold the territory. . . . As I see it now the gut issues are cost of living, busing, drug abuse, and possibly tax reform as it relates to the property tax. There are of course

> other subsidiary issues like the environment, revenue-sharing, etc. . . . And then of course there are always the issues where the opposition is on the attack. . . .
>
> The way that I look at most of our domestic programs is that we have done an excellent job of conceiving them and a poor job of selling them. . . . Great ideas that are conceived and not sold are like babies that are stillborn. We need some deliveries within the next few months even if they have to be Caesarean. I will approve any programs you have to bring about those deliveries, provided of course you recognize my total opposition to any abortions.

My relationship with George Meany during the first three and a half years of my first term as President could be described as tempestuous. I had known him for twenty-five years, from the days I served on the House Labor Committee. He was tough, smart, and combative. Philosophically, he was liberal on economic issues and conservative on social issues; politically, he was a partisan Democrat. But when it came to foreign policy and national defense, he was a patriot first and partisan second.

We knew that in June Meany had told George Shultz that he would not support McGovern if he won the nomination. After the Democratic convention he called Shultz again. He was outraged that McGovern had dumped Pierre Salinger—not because of any particular affection for Salinger, but because Salinger was McGovern's man, so McGovern should have stood by him. "He don't stick to his people," Meany said bitterly.

On July 19 a bulletin came over the wires announcing that, for the first time in its history, the AFL-CIO executive council had adjourned without voting any presidential endorsement. It was a moment to ponder and savor: for the first time in seventeen years the AFL-CIO was not going to endorse the Democratic candidate for President.

On July 28 I played golf with Meany, Bill Rogers, and George Shultz at Burning Tree, just outside Washington. As we went down the first fairway, Meany said brusquely, "Eagleton should have told McGovern, but now McGovern has handled it like a fool, vacillating from one side to the other."

It was about 6:30 when we got back to the clubhouse and sat on the porch to have a drink. Rogers and Shultz joined me in ordering cigars so that we could keep Meany company. We sat for almost an hour in the twilight, all of us smoking our cigars and three of us listening to Meany talk. He said that McGovern was going to lose by a virtual landslide. In the circumstances, he said, though labor disagreed with some of my policies, it was in labor's interest to remain neutral in the presidential race and concentrate on saving its favorite Senate and House members. Pouring money into McGovern's campaign would be tantamount to throwing it away.

As we left the porch and walked toward our cars, Meany cleared his throat and said to me gruffly, "I want you to know now that I am not going to vote for you, and I am not going to vote for McGovern. But you'll be doing all right with the Meany family." He said Mrs. Meany and two of his three daughters would vote for me. The other daughter, he said, "will just follow her old man and not vote for anybody."

Then, just as we were about to separate, he put his hand on my shoulder and said, "Just so you don't get a swelled head about my wife voting for you, I want to tell you why—she don't like McGovern."

During the first days of August McGovern sought a new vice presidential running mate. He tried Teddy Kennedy, Edmund Muskie, Abraham Ribicoff, Larry O'Brien, Hubert Humphrey, and Governor Reubin Askew of Florida—all without success.

I spent the weekend of August 4 at the vacation home of Tom McCabe, a good friend from the Eisenhower days, on Assateague Island off Maryland's Eastern Shore. Mitchell, Rebozo, and Abplanalp came with me. The television set at the house did not work so we listened to the radio to hear McGovern announce that Teddy Kennedy's brother-in-law Sargent Shriver would be his new running mate.

As early as June I had heard from visitors to the LBJ Ranch that Johnson was not going to support McGovern if he was nominated. After the Democratic convention I called Johnson and put the question to him directly.

"I don't want to embarrass you," I began, "but you know that John Connally is organizing Democrats who want to support me. A number of people have been contacted who are close to you, and they have indicated a desire to join the group, but only if it wouldn't embarrass you. I appreciate your position in your party, but I would like to ask if you would remain neutral with respect to supporters who want to join John's group."

"Let me just read you a letter, Mr. President," Johnson said, and I could hear a rustling of papers. "This is the standard reply I'm sending out to Democrats who write me about what they should do because they're so disenchanted with McGovern. It says that because of the honor I have been given by my party over forty years, I am going to support the Democratic ticket at all levels. However, I go on to say—and no one will fail to catch this—that I have always taken the position that what an individual does in a presidential campaign is a matter of conscience, and I'm not going to interfere with that decision. Now what do you think of that?"

"I can only say that I'm very grateful, Mr. President," I replied.

A few weeks later Johnson sent me some campaign advice through

Billy Graham: "Ignore McGovern, and get out with the people. But stay above the campaign, like I did with Goldwater. Go to ball games and factories. And don't worry. The McGovern people are going to defeat themselves."

Billy said that when he had raised the question of the Watergate bugging business, Johnson had just laughed and said, "Hell, that's not going to hurt him a bit."

One of the first things I had to decide about the 1972 campaign was whether to change the ticket by choosing a new running mate. By the middle of 1971 Ted Agnew had become increasingly disenchanted with his role as Vice President. He felt, as does almost every Vice President to some degree, that the White House staff did not treat him with proper respect, and that I had not given him major substantive responsibilities. It was then that word came to us from Bryce Harlow that there was a very good chance that Agnew, on his own, would withdraw from the ticket early in 1972 to take advantage of attractive offers outside government.

During the first term Agnew had become an articulate and effective spokesman for conservative positions and issues. In this role he was wrongly underrated by the press as well as by his partisan critics. But as I began preparing for the 1972 election, I also had to look ahead to 1976. I believed that John Connally was the only man in either party who clearly had the potential to be a great President. He had the necessary political "fire in the belly," the energy to win, and the vision to lead. I even talked with Haldeman about the possibility of Agnew's resigning before the convention and my nominating Connally to replace him, although I knew that such a move was a remote possibility at best. The only serious option would be to replace Agnew with Connally as the nominee for Vice President at the convention.

Early in 1972 I discussed the vice presidency with Connally. His reactions ran from mixed to negative. I sensed that he did not think the second spot would be the best route to the White House for him. He said that none of us could calculate the depth of Republican opposition to him as a Johnny-come-lately.

I had a meeting with John Mitchell a few days later. I told him bluntly that I thought Connally should be President in 1976 and that I was weighing the possibility of giving him a head start, if he wanted it, by making him my running mate. Mitchell agreed that Connally was the man to run in 1976, but he argued strongly against making any changes in the ticket in 1972. Connally was still a Democrat, and Mitchell thought that putting him on the ticket might backfire with the conservative New Majority Republicans and Democrats, particularly in the South, among whom Agnew had become almost a folk hero. "Party workers have to believe that loyalty is rewarded, or there won't be any party workers," Mitchell warned.

He felt that Connally would be more helpful in the campaign as the Chairman of Democrats for Nixon than he would by becoming a Republican before the election. Moreover, Connally had told Mitchell that in no circumstances did he want to be Vice President.

In fact, Mitchell urged me to give Agnew a definite commitment. If we waited too long, he warned, Agnew might want to get a deal in exchange—possibly even a pledge to support him for the nomination in 1976. "Besides," Mitchell said, "I feel sorry for him. He's having some financial problems, and he needs to be able to plan his future."

On June 12 I asked Mitchell to tell Agnew that I had made the decision definitely to have him on the ticket again as my running mate. I said that we would not announce it until after the Democratic convention. This would generate interest by creating suspense; it might also lead the Democrats to soft-pedal their attacks on him at their convention just in case I decided to choose someone else.

At the beginning of August I tried to block off time to work exclusively on my acceptance speech, but there were inevitably distractions that made concentration difficult. I mentioned a particularly nettling one in my diary on August 16: "McGovern is striking out more wildly now, trying to say that I was indirectly responsible for the bugging of the Democratic headquarters." McGovern indeed was pulling out all the stops on Watergate. In one of his speeches at this time he had said that the break-in was "the kind of thing you expect under a person like Hitler." Other Democratic leaders were equally vehement in their denunciations, having seized upon Watergate as the best way to distract public attention from their own candidate.

The Democrats had mounted a particularly strident attack based on the fact that a large number of the contributors to my campaign preferred that their contributions remain anonymous. Many of them were Democrats of long standing and considerable prominence who thought it important to defeat McGovern but who would find it awkward to be named publicly. Anonymity for contributors was legal if the contribution was made before April 7, 1972, but the Democrats framed the issue and the media presented it as a case of secrecy versus openness in the political process and thus put us on the defensive in the battle for public opinion. By September the Washington *Post* would be printing leaks from anonymous sources on partisan congressional staffs. For example, there was one that charged Finance Chairman Maury Stans with being tied to $700,000 in illegal campaign funds that had been laundered through Mexico. Stans categorically denied the story. In the months ahead the CRP finance committee would be accused of monitoring the private bank accounts of potential contributors, of having laundered contributions in Luxembourg, and of having raised money from high-ranking Arabs and other illegal foreign sources. The charges were all false.

From the very beginning, I wanted to fight back. I saw no reason why McGovern and his supporters and contributors should be immune. If there was any campaign advantage to incumbency, it had to be access to government information on one's opponents. I remembered the IRS leaks of my tax returns to Drew Pearson in the 1952 campaign and the politically motivated tax audits done on me in 1963. The Democrats, while in office, had made little effort to camouflage their political pressure on the key government agencies. It seemed that even when they were out of power their supporters—particularly among the bureaucrats in the IRS—continued to do the job for them. I heard numerous reports—clearly too frequent to be coincidental—of close personal and political friends who had been subjected to constant and, in my view, vindictive, investigation by the IRS since the time I lost to Kennedy in 1960.

So far our own efforts to use this power had been halfhearted and ineffective. I dictated a diary note about this in the spring of 1972: "This has really been a shameful failure on our part, and it is hard for me to understand it, in view of the fact that I had so often pointed out that after what they did to us when we were out of office we at least owed it to ourselves in self-defense to initiate some investigations of them." Even now it frustrates me to think that our efforts to gain whatever political advantage we could from being in power were so tentative and feeble and amateurish in comparison to the Democrats'. I prodded my staff to change this; on August 3 I reflected on the situation we faced and the problem I saw behind it.

Diary

I emphasized to Haldeman and Ehrlichman the necessity of our getting information on some of our Democratic opponents that they constantly were getting out against us. It is ironic that when we were out of office they really used to crucify us—now that we are in office they still do, due to the fact that the bureaucrats at the lower level are all with them.

The problem we have here is that all of our people are gun-shy as a result of the Watergate incident and don't want to look into files that involve Democrats. Haldeman said after the election we really could then take the steps to get loyalists in various positions that were sensitive. Of course, we should have long ago. Certainly we have been above reproach in this respect and have not used the enormous powers of the office—the Internal Revenue files, the Justice Department files—to go after some of the hanky-panky operations of our Democratic opponents.

I repeatedly urged Haldeman and Ehrlichman—though without apparent success—to have IRS checks made on McGovern's key staff and contributors. In one memo on the subject I said that anything that came up that might indicate "shady dealings" should be got out early. "Of course, if nothing turns up, drop the whole matter," I wrote. "But let's be sure that we've gone the extra mile and developed material before we drop the matter."

Larry O'Brien was one Democrat who was a grand master in the art of political gamesmanship. O'Brien had been tutored in the Kennedy political machine and further shaped by his years with Lyndon Johnson. He was a partisan in the most extreme and effective sense. After the Kent State tragedy, he virtually accused me of killing the four students. Whether the issue was Vietnam or Watergate, he could be counted on to hit hard, and not always above the belt.

An IRS investigation of Howard Hughes's financial empire had revealed that Hughes was paying O'Brien's Washington lobbying firm a large yearly retainer, reportedly almost $200,000. There were rumors about whether O'Brien had reported all the money and paid taxes on it. I was as doubtful as I was hopeful that we would nail him on this issue; as I noted in my diary, "I would be very surprised if he would have allowed himself to get in such a box." The IRS had planned to interview O'Brien at some point regarding the Hughes retainer; I ordered Haldeman and Ehrlichman to have the audit expedited and completed before the election.

Whatever the findings of the audit, I thought, it would be a pleasant —and newsworthy—irony that after all the years in which Howard Hughes had been portrayed as my financial angel, the Chairman of the Democratic National Committee was in fact the one profiting from a lucrative position on Hughes's payroll.

In the end the IRS cleared O'Brien after a routine audit, and my desire to check up on him and on McGovern's supporters was soon deflected by the heightening demands of the campaign schedule and the major new developments at the Vietnam peace talks.

On August 20, the day before the Republican National Convention opened, Pat and the girls went to Miami while I stayed at Camp David to put the finishing touches on my acceptance speech.

I watched television the next night to see the documentary about Pat that was shown on a huge screen in the convention hall. Jimmy Stewart had already given her an unforgettably eloquent introduction, and when the lights came up after the film, Pat suddenly appeared in person at the podium, standing with her arms out wide. It was a gesture uniquely hers, graceful and gracious. The program was running late, and, with infallible instinct, she spoke just a minute to say thank you. The cameras cut to Julie and Tricia, and I could see the loving pride in their smiles. I noted, "That was characteristic of the whole convention as far as the appearance of Pat, the girls, David and Ed are concerned. No First Family ever looked better than they did. No family looked more the all-American type than they did."

I flew to Miami on Tuesday afternoon, August 22. That night I made an unscheduled appearance at the open-air youth rally, and the reception I received overwhelmed me. Pam Powell, the daughter of Dick Powell and June Allyson, escorted me onto the stage. Hands above their heads, four fingers outstretched, the thousands of young people took up a chant that I was hearing for the first time: *"Four more years! Four more years!"* It was deafening. It was music. This was a new kind of Republican youth: they weren't square, but they weren't ashamed of being positive and proud.

The picture that is probably most remembered from the 1972 convention is of Sammy Davis, Jr., impulsively hugging me on the stage at the youth rally. When the crowd finally quieted down, I described my first meeting with him at a White House reception a few weeks earlier. We had both talked about our backgrounds and about how we both came from rather poor families. "I know Sammy is a member of the other party," I said. "I didn't know when I talked to him what he would be doing in this election campaign. But I do know this. I want to make this pledge to Sammy. I want to make it to everybody here, whether you happen to be black or white, or young or old, and all of those who are listening. I believe in the American dream. Sammy Davis believes in it. We believe in it because we have seen it come true in our own lives." For me—and, I think, for many others—the youth rally was the highlight of the convention. That night at the convention hall I was renominated for a second term by a vote of 1,347 to 1.

The next night outside the hall the frustrated demonstrators attempted to set fire to buses filled with delegates. They slashed tires, pelted delegates with rocks and eggs, and marched on the hall wearing their own gas masks and brandishing night sticks. My eyes burned from the lingering sting of tear gas as I entered the hall to accept my fifth and last nomination by a Republican convention.

Inside the hall neither the predictability of a well-organized program nor the absence of a hard-fought nomination battle could mute the enthusiasm of the crowd. The delegates had picked up the slogan I had heard at the youth rally. Over and over they shouted: *"Four more years! Four more years!"*

The day after the convention I addressed the American Legion in Chicago and then spoke at the dedication of Dwight D. Eisenhower High School in Utica, Michigan. Then we flew across the country to San Diego, where another big crowd was waiting, and then took the short helicopter flight up the coast to San Clemente. The enthusiasm of all these crowds was exciting and contagious and deeply satisfying. There was an emotional quality to their receptions and reactions that neither the staff nor I had been able to sense in Washington, where many of the columns and news stories attributed my support more to the widespread disappointment with McGovern than to any intrinsic quality in my own candidacy.

> *Diary*
> Certainly, no one could say that we didn't have the jumpers and the squealers in Michigan and San Diego and San Clemente, although it will, as usual, be difficult to get the press to write it. I am inclined to think that our people are going to be far more the jumpers and squealers than the McGovern people unless he begins to catch on and begins to inspire and lift up, rather than simply talk in the dour, Calvinistic way which characterizes his approach up to this time.
>
> The crowd in San Diego was really fantastic. It must have been about 15,000. My talk was not really up to what it should have been. By this time I was having some fatigue and I just wasn't able to put that much into it.
>
> We then went on to San Clemente. It was a beautiful flight over the coast, and when we got here the staff, of course, had prepared me for a surprise. They had said that it was simply going to be the four mayors and a few friends from the area. It turned out to be one of the great crowds of the day. It was a very emotional crowd.
>
> By the time we got back to the residence we were really bushed. Pat had dinner with me in the study—she had a second helping of chicken but I was not really in a condition to eat much and was glad that King came in to finish off my steak. Pat has been a really tremendous trouper in this past week.
>
> I finished the day sitting out at the pool and smoking a cigar from Iran.

On Wednesday, August 30, Haldeman came in with a morose look.

"Bad news," he said glumly, "I really mean it—it's really bad." Then he handed me the latest Gallup poll:

Nixon	64%
McGovern	30%
Undecided	6%

When I looked up he was smiling. So was I. It was the largest post-convention point spread in favor of a Republican candidate in Gallup's history.

My first press conference of the campaign was scheduled for August 29. Watergate was obviously going to be one of the subjects raised. Ehrlichman assured me that there was still one thing of which we were certain: John Dean, the Justice Department, and the FBI all confirmed that there had been no White House involvement.

In the press conference I was asked whether I thought that there should be a Special Prosecutor appointed for Watergate. I answered that a Special Prosecutor was hardly necessary, since the FBI, the Justice Department, the Senate Banking and Currency Committee, and the General Accounting Office were all conducting investigations. I said that I had ordered total cooperation by the White House. "In addition to that," I continued, "within our own staff, under my direction, Counsel to the President Mr. Dean has conducted a complete investigation of all leads which might involve any present members of the White House staff or anybody in the government. I can say categorically that his investigation indicates that no one in the White House staff, no one in this administration, presently employed, was involved in this very bizarre incident. . . . What really hurts in matters of this sort is not the fact that they occur, because overzealous people in campaigns do things that are wrong. What really hurts is if you try to cover it up."

At a Cabinet meeting on September 12, Attorney General Kleindienst reported that the indictments on the Watergate break-in and bugging would be handed down in three days and that no one at a high level in the CRP or anyone in the White House would be named. He had anticipated the predictable Democratic charges of a whitewash and had therefore totted up some impressive statistics. The FBI had made this the biggest investigation since the Kennedy assassination: 333 agents in fifty-one field offices had followed 1,897 leads through 1,551 interviews for a total of 14,098 man-hours.

The indictments handed down on September 15 named only Hunt, Liddy, and the five men arrested in the Democratic headquarters. My lengthy diary entry for that day indicates the relative unimportance I continued to attribute to Watergate at that time. In it I described a meeting with Nelson Rockefeller and a two-hour session on taxes with Connally, Burns, Shultz, Stein, and Ehrlichman; I reflected on several passages from Robert Blake's *Disraeli,* which I was currently rereading; I noted a conversation with Julie in which she was concerned about the way she had handled a reporter's question on Vietnam; I mentioned my concern because Pat was suffering from a prolonged earache but would not slow down her schedule; I commented on a recent radio speech by Connally; and I recounted a meeting in the Oval Office with singer Ray Charles. My only reference to Watergate was one short sentence near the end: "This was the day of the Watergate indictment, and we hope to be able to ride the issue through in a successful way from now on."

At Haldeman's suggestion, I saw John Dean later that day and thanked him for his work. I had known ever since the week after the break-in that Dean, as White House Counsel, was keeping track of all the different Watergate problems for us, including the FBI investigation, the grand jury, the Democratic civil suit, the libel suit Maury Stans had filed against Larry O'Brien and the CRP's countersuit against the DNC, and Texas Representative Wright Patman's attempt to hold pre-election hearings on the CRP's finances. Summing up his status report on these matters, Dean said, "Three months ago I would have had trouble predicting where we'd be today. I think that I can say that fifty-four days from now [Election Day] that not a thing will come crashing down to our—our surprise."

I said that the whole thing was a can of worms, and a lot of what had happened had been "awfully embarrassing." But I told Dean that the way he had handled it had been "very skillful, because you—putting your fingers in the dikes every time that leaks have sprung here and sprung there."

Dean covered the whole range of the different cases he was handling. The GAO report charging that the CRP had violated campaign finance rules had been referred to the Justice Department, Dean said, where there were reports of hundreds of other alleged violations—including charges against McGovern, Humphrey, and Jackson as well. The GAO was also planning to audit the use of funds by the White House staff. "I think we can be proud of the White House staff," Dean said, adding that the GAO would find nothing if they did investigate. Patman's unabashed partisan attempt to hold hearings on CRP finances was the next pre-election assault we faced. I told Dean that the whole thing was simply "public relations," and he agreed.

"We just take one at a time," Dean said.

"And you really can't just sit and worry yourself about it all the time, thinking 'the worst may happen' but it may not," I replied. "So you just try to button it up as well as you can and hope for the best . . . and remember that basically the damn thing is just one of those unfortunate things and, we're trying to cut our losses."

Then we turned to my long-time determination to restructure the bureaucracy in Washington—so that even if it were not favorable to us, at least it would no longer be serving the Democrats.

Two days later I recalled my impressions of this meeting.

> *Diary*
>
> I had a good talk with John Dean and was enormously impressed with him. I later told Haldeman, who said that he brought him into the White House, that he had the kind of steel and really mean instinct that we needed to clean house after the election in various departments and to put the IRS and the Justice Department on the kind of basis that it should be on. There simply has to be a line drawn at times with those who are against us; and then we have to take the action to deal with them effectively. Otherwise, they will be around to deal with us when their opportunity comes to them.

As the polls continued to indicate a Nixon landslide, McGovern and Shriver became desperate. They launched a strident campaign of personal attacks. McGovern said that my policy on Vietnam sought a "new level of barbarism" in order to save my own face. Three times he compared me to Hitler and the Republican Party to the Ku Klux Klan. He said that any working man who supported me "should have his head examined."

Shriver called me "Tricky Dicky," a "psychiatric case," "power-mad," the "greatest con artist" who spent most of the time "figuring out ways to keep America number one in the power to kill and destroy people abroad," and "the number-one bomber of all time." I told George Christian, President Johnson's former Press Secretary who was working with Connally in Democrats for Nixon, that Johnson should be pleased that Shriver had called *me* the number-one bomber. Christian laughed and said, "I don't believe so, Mr. President. LBJ never likes to be number two in anything."

While these increasingly shrill and acrimonious charges were being hurled against me I continued to stay on the job in the White House, aloof from the rising emotional tides of the campaign. Some diary notes I made after a weekend at Camp David in early September convey the striking contrast between the campaign as I experienced it and as McGovern and Shriver waged it.

> *Diary*
>
> Around noon, since it was such a beautiful day—clear blue—I

went into the pool for a while. It was one of those days when I was able to lie on my back and look up at the leaves. I was reminded of the fact that in the spring the leaves turned over in the wind and the leaves in the spring and the fall were really so very much alike. One portrays the beginning of summer, the other the beginning of winter—one the beginning of life, the other the beginning of death.

I expect the situation to get rougher in the next week and throughout. It is very clear that McGovern had finally learned that what he has to do is simply to attack and he is doing so in a very vicious and irresponsible way. Our people, of course, as I pointed out to Colson, are reacting in their usual honest and stupid way, by defending rather than attacking.

McGovern's going to all the big cities at this time for street rallies is an indication of their desperation because eight weeks before the election is much too soon to hit the big cities.

My campaign was running like clockwork. Ted Agnew, Clark MacGregor, Bob Dole, and their teams were doing a magnificent job. They were not only effective spokesmen for the administration but kept McGovern on the defensive with sharp thrusts against his far-left views. In September I began adding some political appearances to my schedule, but it was still the most restrained campaign of my career; consequently, I remember it primarily as a series of episodes.

One of the most memorable was a campaign trip I made to Texas on September 22 that ended with an enthusiastic Democrats for Nixon barbecue at the Connally ranch.

Diary

I told Connally as we were sitting around about 11:30 or 12 it is vitally important that Teddy Kennedy not pick up the pieces after this election. It is important that people like John Connally pick them up because the country simply can't afford to have the likes of Kennedy and McGovern as even possible Presidents in the years ahead.

Pat pointed out a New York *Times* article on Mrs. McGovern said that the Nixons were from the fifties and the McGoverns from the seventies. I just hope the press continues to think this way because in the end they're going to take a hell of a beating.

I woke up twice in the night, once at 2, and once at 4—even though I was terribly tired when I went to bed. Finally at 7 o'clock I woke up again. When I got up, opened the blinds, looked out on beautiful green countryside, at the cows in the pasture, rang for breakfast, to my great pleasure instead of my wheat germ they insisted on sending in some of their country sausage, which was totally and perfectly delicious. I am going to have to mix up the breakfasts and lunches just a bit in order to get away from such a drab and uninteresting diet.

At the end of September George McGovern received the official editorial endorsement of the New York *Times*. The Washington *Post* withheld a formal endorsement but made clear its preference for McGovern. In my diary I noted my reaction when I heard about the *Times*'s endorsement: "I said that I learned the news with relief because I didn't want anybody on the staff to urge me to meet with their editorial board and thank God we had not done so. Nobody had had the temerity to suggest that I do so. And as I pointed out to Haldeman there should be a letter to the *Times* or a statement that the *Times* basically *should* endorse McGovern because he stood for everything they stood for—permissiveness, a bug-out from Vietnam, new isolationism, etc."

The *Post*'s decision came as no surprise either. On June 26 I had dictated this note on a report Kissinger gave me from columnist Stewart Alsop, who had been to dinner with the paper's publisher: "Henry told me of an interesting conversation he had had with Stewart Alsop. Stewart, apparently, is still critically ill and had been out to dinner with Kay Graham. He had been arguing emphatically with regard to the necessity to support RN because of what he had accomplished in foreign policy, and also the danger of having McGovern in the presidency. He said that Kay Graham finally blew up and said, " 'I hate him and I'm going to do everything I can to beat him.' "

On September 26 we held a dinner in New York for campaign contributors. One encounter during that evening particularly stayed in my mind.

Diary

One thing that made a very great impression upon me was when a relatively young man—at least he seemed young to me; I would imagine he was forty, he could have been forty-five—said to me that he'd lost his son in Vietnam in 1970 and he was still for me and for my foreign policy.

When I think of such men as this and the mothers of the boys as well as their wives, I realize how very important it is to see not only that we end the war, but that we end it in a way that will make their sacrifices not be in vain, which is what I told him as we were being hauled away.

The crowd that turned out to greet Pat and me in Atlanta on October

12 was estimated at between 500,000 and 700,000. To the dismay of the Secret Service, a man in the crowd outside the hotel grabbed me and shouted above the noise, "Thanks for making the South a part of America again." I later told Ehrlichman, "The South is teaching the Democratic Party a lesson about patriotism."

During a long motorcade in Ohio I was warned that there were some unfriendly demonstrators waiting for us a short way ahead. Since there had also been a bomb threat, the Secret Service wanted to close the top of my car and increase the speed during this particular part of the route.

Diary

One thing I did do was when the Secret Service wanted to speed up, I told them to slow down. I said we must not run from these people, so we slowed down to a snail's pace and I waved out the window, as did Pat on the other side, at all the nutheads in the nasty crowd.

When I saw some of the antiwar people and the rest, I'd simply hold up the "V" or the one thumb up; this really knocks them for a loop, because they think this is their sign. Some of them break out into a smile. Others, of course, just become more hateful. I think as the war recedes as an issue, some of these people are going to be lost souls. They basically are haters, they are frustrated, they are alienated—they don't know what to do with their lives.

I think perhaps the saddest group will be those who are the professors and particularly the younger professors and the associate professors on the college campuses and even in the high schools. They wanted to blame somebody else for their own failures to inspire the students.

I can think of those Ivy League presidents who came to see me after Kent State, and who were saying, please don't leave the problem to us—I mean, let the government do something. None of them would take any of the responsibility themselves.

Now the responsibility is theirs, although I imagine they will find another issue. The black power thing is gone—the environment has fizzled out—the war will be gone—the question is, what next? I suppose it will be big business or corruption or what have you, but it will be difficult to find one that emotionally will turn the kids on like the war issue.

It will be good that the college administrators and professors will have to look within themselves—look in the mirror—and realize that it is they who have the responsibility—that they are at fault if the young people are not inspired. They can't blame it on government or anybody else.

Although my direct involvement in the campaign was limited, it was intense. By the end of the campaign I had made dozens of speeches and informal remarks.

> *Diary*
> I had a rather curious dream of speaking at some sort of a rally and going a bit too long and Rockefeller standing up in the middle and taking over the microphone on an applause line. Of course, this is always something that worries a person when he is making speeches, as to whether he is going too long. It is a subconscious reaction. It is interesting.

Since my strategy was to minimize my own campaigning, my family took over the burden of crisscrossing the country making appearances. All together, Pat, Julie, and Tricia covered seventy-seven cities in thirty-seven states in the nine weeks from the end of August to Election Day. David was in the Navy and had to stay on the sidelines, but Ed Cox plunged right in and went onto college campuses to face some of the toughest audiences of all. His easy manner and quick, organized mind enabled him to hold his own and make a strong impression everywhere he went.

In all their speeches and in all their press conferences, there was never a misspoken word. They were heckled, shoved, hissed, and subjected to obscene shouts from demonstrators, but they pressed on like professionals, with poise and grace. Even when Pat was being cursed by angry young men and women in Boston, she was serene and natural—which infuriated them even more; I am sure they had no idea how much they hurt her. Tricia passed on to us her strategy when confronted by a crowd of burly demonstrators: "Please," she would say quietly, "don't push the children."

Julie, who was steely enough to mean it when she said that she would give her life for South Vietnam's freedom, was soft enough to leave the dinner table in tears when she thought about how David, who loved politics so much, would miss the election because his ship would be in the Mediterranean.

> *Diary*
> Julie called me after the Gromyko dinner, very thoughtfully waiting until then, to ask me about whether she could go to see David since he could not return for the election. I, of course, approved it all the way.
> To hell with the election if it interferes with a few days that

> they may have together at this time when it means so much to them.
>
> I recall that in 1960, after the defeat, Julie was the one who at least as far as her open feelings were concerned really never gave up. I remember going in to her bedroom at the Forest Lane house just to kiss her good night, and she would say, "Daddy, can't we still win?" This was two weeks or so after the election.
>
> In 1960 during the first debate she had been worried about whether Daddy had won or not. Tricia had very loyally stepped up and said, "Of course he did."
>
> I remember in 1962 the reaction was somewhat different. Julie had said congratulations on taking on the press after the election, whereas Tricia seemed more reserved and more worried about it.
>
> Looking back that ten years I certainly made it hard for the family with my own reactions and I shall never forget how when I told them we were going to New York, Tricia went in and tore up all her notebooks. They had really hated the school in California because of the number of Birchers that were always giving them hell.

I knew that the road had been hardest of all for Pat. For almost twenty years of public life she had been wife, mother, and full-time campaigner. She had done it all not because she loved the attention or reveled in the publicity—she didn't. She had done it because she believed in me. And she had done it magnificently. Now she was loved by millions, and no woman ever deserved it more. My deepest hope was that she felt that it had all been worth it.

VIETNAM BREAKTHROUGH

As we anticipated, the summer of 1972 produced another series of propaganda maneuvers by Hanoi in an attempt to exploit American domestic opinion. This time they used the ploy of claiming—falsely—that American bombers were deliberately hitting the crucial system of dikes and dams in North Vietnam in order to kill large civilian populations in the resulting floods. Antiwar leaders accepted these claims uncritically. Teddy Kennedy charged that we had a "policy of deliberately bombing dikes." In one of my press conferences I tried to introduce at least an element of logic regarding this charge: if in fact we had decided on a policy of deliberately bombing the dikes and dams, we could have destroyed the entire system in a week. But despite all the propaganda claims, no major junctures were hit and there were no massive floods.

On July 27 former Attorney General Ramsey Clark, the man described by George McGovern as "perfect for head of the FBI if you could get him," left for Hanoi under the auspices of a Swedish group inquiring into "U.S. crimes in Indochina." He made a broadcast over Radio Hanoi stating that our bombing should be stopped immediately. On August 12 he told reporters that he had visited a POW camp and found the health of the American POWs "better than mine, and I am a healthy man." On Clark's return, Teddy Kennedy had him come to Capitol Hill to testify on the good treatment the POWs were receiving.

While Clark was in Hanoi, Shriver waded in, "revealing" that the Nixon administration, as he put it, "blew" a historic opportunity for peace in 1969 when I failed to follow up on progress that had been made in the Paris peace talks during the last months of the Johnson administration. Shriver also claimed that he had resigned as ambassador to France in protest of my war policy. Bill Rogers was furious when he heard about this. He publicly denounced Shriver's claims as "bunk" and political fantasy. Rogers's statement was particularly effective; it was characteristic of the forceful and articulate way he defended my foreign policy in public forums during the campaign. The next day the State Department released Shriver's letter of resignation as ambassador. It was hardly a protest. On the contrary, he wrote that he had "accomplished the objectives I went to Paris to achieve—the beginnings at least of peace in Vietnam and the reawakening of friendship between the U.S.A. and France."

Connally called me to say that President Johnson was "mad as hell" about Shriver's charge. Johnson had indicated that his already minimal support for McGovern would be even less because of this incident. Johnson called Haldeman to tell him that he had never informed Shriver of what was going on in the Paris negotiations. "I never trusted him, the SOB, not even then," Johnson said.

A few days after Ramsey Clark returned from Hanoi, a UPI report revealed that Pierre Salinger, on George McGovern's instructions, had directly approached the North Vietnamese delegation in Paris. His purpose was to see if the Communists would release some American POWs. The goal was laudable, but the contact had all the earmarks of a political ploy. Moreover, the Logan Act prohibits a private citizen from unauthorized contacts with foreign governments with the intent to influence disputes between our government and theirs. McGovern, therefore, had some serious questions to answer about the Salinger mission.

When confronted with this story, McGovern told reporters, "Pierre Salinger had no instructions whatsoever from me." Salinger evidently was stupefied by this statement, because McGovern had not only sent him on the mission but had made the arrangements through a prominent antiwar leader. McGovern had been caught in a serious and discreditable falsehood.

All McGovern's efforts to attack me on the war were to no avail. At the end of August we received word that public support of my conduct of the war had actually risen. A Harris poll found in early September that 55 percent supported continued heavy bombing of North Vietnam, 64 percent supported the mining of Haiphong Harbor, and 74 percent thought it was important that South Vietnam not fall into the hands of the Communists. McGovern and his followers were out of touch with the majority of the American people. But the North Vietnamese, who were avid observers of American public opinion, apparently got the message.

After three years of disappointing and unproductive stalemate the U.S.–North Vietnamese private channel suddenly became active in August 1972. For the first time the Communists actually seemed to be interested in reaching a settlement. Kissinger and I assumed that they had come to the conclusion that McGovern did not stand a chance of becoming President and had therefore decided to explore the possibility that they could get better terms from me before the election than after it. In addition they were undoubtedly concerned by our contacts with Moscow and Peking and with the success of Vietnamization; we knew also that the May 8 mining and bombing had taken a heavy military toll.

At a two-day session on September 26 and 27 the North Vietnamese presented a new ten-point program. Although it was more forthcoming than anything in the past, on the key political and military issues it was still unacceptable. The next meeting, scheduled for October 8, would clearly be the decisive one for determining whether the new momentum could carry through to a settlement before the November 7 election. I was not optimistic in this regard, but I decided to orchestrate as much pressure on the meeting as possible.

When Soviet Foreign Minister Andrei Gromyko arrived in Washington for the signing of the SALT agreement on October 3, I invited him to come to Camp David. When he repeated the familiar refrain that U.S.–Soviet relations could improve if the problem of Vietnam were removed, I told him that when Kissinger returned to Paris the next week, he would lay on the table the last offer we were going to make. If the North Vietnamese said no, then the negotiating track would be closed and we would have to turn to some other methods after the elections.

It seemed unlikely that, even if the North Vietnamese wanted to, we would be able to negotiate an acceptable agreement in just five weeks. Nonetheless I felt that we should prepare Thieu for the outside possibility that the Communists really were determined to conclude a settlement before our election. Haig flew to Saigon and assured Thieu that we would not rush headlong into an agreement. But he also described the difficult domestic situation we would face if the Communists made a reasonable offer and we refused to act upon it. Then they would be able to put the blame on Thieu for blocking peace.

Thieu was visibly shaken. He was suspicious of the motives behind the North Vietnamese proposals and unsettled by our willingness to accept them as even a basis for negotiations. He railed against Kissinger, who, he said, did not "deign" to consider Saigon's views in his negotiations. Haig tried to reassure him. Finally Thieu broke into tears.

I sympathized with Thieu's position. Almost the entire North Vietnamese Army—an estimated 120,000 troops that had poured across the DMZ during the spring invasion—were still in South Vietnam, and he was naturally skeptical of any plan that would lead to an American withdrawal without requiring a corresponding North Vietnamese withdrawal. I shared his view that the Communists' motives were entirely cynical. I knew, as he did, that they would observe the agreement only so long and so far as South Vietnam's strength and America's readiness to retaliate forced them to do so. But I felt that if we could negotiate an agreement on our terms, those conditions could be met. I sent Thieu a personal message: "I give you my firm assurance that there will be no settlement arrived at, the provisions of which have not been discussed personally with you well beforehand." Knowing his penchant for headstrong action, however, I reminded him of the dangers inherent in stirring up his domestic situation as well as our own.

On October 5 we received word of a recent conversation between Premier Pham Van Dong of North Vietnam and the French Delegate General in Hanoi. For the first time Dong had sounded optimistic regarding the likelihood of peace. He had admitted that his experts had paid too much attention to American antiwar leaders and added that I would probably have a freer hand after the election.

In my press conference that same day the questions focused on the prospects for a peace settlement before the election. I replied that in no circumstances would the election determine the character of our negotiations: "If we can make the right kind of a settlement before the election, we will make it. If we cannot, we are not going to make the wrong kind of a settlement before the election."

As the October 8 meeting approached, I felt that we had done everything possible to encourage Hanoi toward a settlement: their troops were being pounded by our renewed bombing, and now presumably the Soviet leaders would be urging the North Vietnamese to take the best terms they could get and end the war before the election. In the meantime, the prospects of my re-election by a landslide were increasing every day.

Kissinger and Haig arrived in Paris on Sunday, October 8, for the crucial meeting with the North Vietnamese. That evening they sent a brief reporting cable: "Tell the President that there has been some definite progress at today's first session and that he can harbor some confidence the outcome will be positive."

On Monday Kissinger reported that the meetings were tense and volatile but that "we are at a crucial point." On Tuesday we received only a one-paragraph message that was more tantalizing than enlightening: "The negotiations during this round have been so complex and sensitive that we have been unable to report their content in detail due to the danger of compromise. We know exactly what we are doing, and just as we have not let you down in the past, we will not do so now."

That night George McGovern made a much-heralded nationally televised campaign speech on Vietnam. He said that on the day he was inaugurated President, he would stop all bombing and begin the immediate withdrawal of all American troops and military equipment from South Vietnam. He also committed himself to stop all military and economic aid to Saigon. He had no plan for ensuring the return of the POWs but said that he expected Hanoi to respond favorably to his policies. James Reston wrote that McGovern "went so far in meeting Hanoi's war aims that he may actually have lost more support by his TV speech than he gained." Joseph Kraft said of McGovern's speech that "apparently without knowing it, he is prepared to accept worse terms than the other side is offering."

On October 11 Kissinger reported only that both sides had decided to stay another day in the anticipation that they were sufficiently close to a major breakthrough. On that day we established a ten-mile bombing-free circle around Hanoi.

Kissinger and Haig arrived back at the White House on the evening of October 12 and came immediately to the EOB office to report to me.

Since the first days of the administration Kissinger and I had talked about the "Big Three" in foreign policy—China, the Soviet Union, and Vietnam—and our goals involving each of them. So far we had succeeded with two of them: we had achieved an opening to China and we had embarked upon a new relationship with the U.S.S.R. Only the third goal—a settlement of the war in Vietnam—had continued to elude us. As Kissinger began his report of the Paris negotiations, he was smiling the broadest smile I had ever seen. "Well, Mr. President," he said, "it looks like we've got three out of three!"

He described the negotiating sessions in great detail. After some rhetoric and bluster, Le Duc Tho had presented a new proposal that met almost all our major requirements: there would be a cease-fire, followed in sixty days by the withdrawal of American forces and the return of POWs on both sides. The North Vietnamese would not specifically agree to withdraw their troops from the South because they maintained the fiction that they had no troops in South Vietnam at all. This charade was particularly galling to Thieu. Now Kissinger had brought back terms that would achieve our and Thieu's objective while allowing the North Vietnamese to save face: no troop withdrawals would be required of them, but the provisions of the agreement regulating the replacement of forces and closing the border sanctuaries in Laos and Cambodia would effectively cut them off from their source of supplies and force them either to return to the North or gradually to wither away in the South. The Communists had finally dropped their demands for a coalition government and had agreed to the face-saving substitute of a National Council of Reconciliation and Concord to be composed of representatives of the government, the Vietcong, and neutral members. Unanimity would be required in its votes; thus Thieu would be protected from being outvoted by the Communists and their supporters. Equally significant, they dropped their demand that Thieu resign. These provisions alone amounted to a complete capitulation by the enemy: they were accepting a settlement on our terms.

There was also a provision embodying the principle of American economic aid to North Vietnam, which I considered to be potentially the most significant part of the entire agreement. The Communists tried to claim that this money would be reparations for the war they charged we had unleashed upon them; but however they tried to justify it, taking money from the United States represented a collapse of communist principle. More important, our aid would inevitably give us increasing leverage with Hanoi as the North Vietnamese people began to taste the fruits of peace for the first time in twenty-five years.

Several unresolved issues remained to be negotiated at a final session in Paris on October 17. Only two of them were major. The first involved the release of Vietnamese civilian prisoners. The North Vietnamese would be accused of betraying their Vietcong allies unless they tried to secure their release as part of the agreement. The second involved the provision for replacement of war matériel by both sides. The Communists wanted it done on the "principle of equality." Neither we nor the South Vietnamese could ever accept this, however, because it would immediately reduce the arms advantage that South Vietnam held over the Vietcong, which we saw as essential for maintaining the peace. Our position was that worn-out existing armaments should be replaced on a one-to-one basis.

Cautioning Le Duc Tho that I would have to review the agreement and approve it, Kissinger had agreed that after the final session in Paris on October 17, he would go to Saigon for three days in order to present the agreement to Thieu and to obtain his approval of it. Kissinger would then go to Hanoi on October 22, where he would initial the agreement with the North Vietnamese leaders. He would return to Washington, and a joint announcement would be made on October 26. The cease-fire would begin on October 30, when the agreement would be signed in Paris by the Foreign Minister of each party.

I asked that some steaks be brought over on trays from the White House mess, and I asked Manolo to bring a bottle of Château Lafite-Rothschild so that we could toast Kissinger's success. I noticed that Haig seemed rather subdued, but I assumed that he was just tired after the exertions of the last few days. Finally I asked him directly how he felt about these terms from Thieu's point of view. He replied that he honestly felt this was a good deal for Thieu. He was worried, however, about how Thieu himself would react to it.

Kissinger had promised to let the North Vietnamese know my reaction within forty-eight hours after his return to Washington. The next day, I instructed the Pentagon to reduce our bombing of North Vietnam to 200 sorties and ordered restrictions on B-52 raids. That night we sent a message to Paris: "The President accepts the basic draft for an 'agreement on ending the war and restoring peace in Vietnam' except for some technical issues to be discussed between Minister Xuan Thuy and Dr. Kissinger on October 17, and subject to the following substantive changes without which the U.S. side cannot accept the document." One of the changes I asked for was the deletion of a paragraph that tied various military obligations of the two South Vietnamese parties—the Saigon government and the Vietcong—to political sections of the agreement. We wanted political matters to be covered solely in the political chapter. Two other changes clarified ambiguities in the text.

The North Vietnamese replied with an official note saying that they felt we were demanding changes in points that had already been agreed upon. They said that only minor technical changes could now be considered and demanded that we not make changes like the ones I had listed. The election deadline was clearly a two-way street: just as we would use it to pressure them to accept our terms, they would try to use it to stampede us into a hasty and ill-considered settlement.

Therefore when I read this message I told Kissinger that in no circumstances should we consider any terms that we felt were less than acceptable.

Diary

I said that as far as the election was concerned, a settlement

> would not particularly help us, that there were risks insofar if Thieu blew it or the North Vietnamese blew it which could hurt us. But nothing that happened could be fatal—it could probably just narrow the gap. Under the circumstances, we had to do what was right. As I pointed out to him, if it was the right time to settle the war and if this was the right plan we should not delay it until after the election, when the pressures upon the enemy might be less than now.
>
> My study of previous settlements indicates that there come pressure points when a settlement can be made, and if the opportunity is missed then the war will drag on for months, and even years, before it comes again. This probably is one of those pressure points. It is an opportunity we must play out to the hilt, because we would never forgive ourselves if we miss this opportunity and then had the election go by and found that the thing would drag on and on. In any event, we have it in the right posture now. We will do what is right without any regard for what effect it will have on the election, and that will probably turn out best for the election as well.

Kissinger raised the possibility of a bombing halt as a demonstration of good will on our part. I ordered another reduction of our daily attack sorties from 200 to 150, but there was no question that a total bombing halt would be a far more dramatic action. I told him, however, that I was absolutely opposed to one before the election. If everything worked out satisfactorily in Paris and Saigon and he was able to go on to Hanoi, then I would consider a bombing *pause* for the few days he was there. But there would be no bombing *halt* until the agreement was signed. I was not going to be taken in by the mere prospect of an agreement as Johnson had been in 1968. Just before Kissinger left for Paris, I gave him a letter I had written the night before. In it I told him to do what is right for an honorable peace, without regard to the election.

Kissinger's meeting with Xuan Thuy on October 17 was tense and pressured. On the prisoner issue, Kissinger rejected as unacceptable the Communist position that we free all Vietcong civilians held by Saigon; some of these prisoners were terrorist murderers. Kissinger told Xuan Thuy that the South Vietnamese would never accept this and there was no point in his writing down something that could not be implemented. The Communists also opposed our strict interpretation of the provisions for the replacement of war matériel and failed to give us satisfactory language regarding American POWs being held in Laos and Cambodia. It was obvious that there would have to be some slippage in the schedule for completion. They pushed for Kissinger to settle the remaining issues in Hanoi. Knowing my adamant views on this point, Kissinger replied that he could not go to Hanoi until we had a completed agreement. Although some of the points were left unresolved, Kissinger departed for Saigon. He had already cautioned the Communists that Thieu had to be consulted before we would sign any agreement. Kissinger had only been able to schedule three days in Saigon to go over the agreement, even though he knew Thieu would be skeptical about its terms and unhappy that it had been suddenly and unexpectedly concluded without his participation. There was no question that the North Vietnamese were trying to use the pressure of the election deadline to strain our relations with Thieu and to create domestic political problems for him by making it appear that the agreement was being imposed on him from Washington without allowing him time to prepare his public opinion for some of its superficially less than advantageous terms. But Kissinger had gambled that Thieu would overlook such problems and seize the tremendous advantages the agreement would give him if he approached it positively and treated it like the victory it was.

The next day I sent a note to the North Vietnamese informing them that, in my opinion, another meeting would be needed before Kissinger could go to Hanoi and before we could stop the bombing. I reiterated that the questions relating to civilian prisoners and replacement of matériel still had to be settled, as well as understandings relating to the withdrawal of North Vietnamese forces from Laos and Cambodia. I offered a new schedule that would extend the original one for three or four days to allow another meeting between Kissinger and Le Duc Tho. I added that as a sign of good will we would maintain the current restrictions on bombing sorties and B-52 raids while the negotiations were in progress, and I reaffirmed my intention to complete the agreement within the proposed new schedule.

The North Vietnamese were now clearly determined to get a pre-election agreement. They sent a reply completely accepting our position on the questions of arms replacement and unconditional release of our POWs in North Vietnam. I sent a cable to Pham Van Dong saying that the agreement could now be considered complete. Only the matter of the unilateral declarations, which included the arrangements for a cease-fire and the return of American POWs in Laos and Cambodia, still had to be clarified, and I therefore suggested a further twenty-four-hour delay so that these questions could be considered and settled. I said that once these problems had been taken care of, we could be counted on to proceed with the schedule as amended, leading to the signing on October 31. On October 21 the North Vietnamese replied by accepting our position on the unilateral declarations.

When Kissinger arrived in Saigon on October 18, he carried with him a letter I had written to Thieu. In it I said, "I believe we have no reasonable alternative but to accept this agreement." I assured Thieu that I would view any breach of faith by the Communists with the utmost gravity.

Kissinger found Thieu polite but noncommittal. During one tense and emotional session with the entire South Vietnamese National Security Council and the ambassadors to the Paris talks, he was bombarded with skeptical questions. Reporting afterward, Kissinger said that the South Vietnamese leaders had exhibited a surprising awe of Communist cunning and a disquieting lack of confidence in themselves. It was clear that they were having great psychological difficulty with the prospect of cutting the American umbilical cord. As Kissinger saw the situation, we were up against a paradoxical situation in which North Vietnam, which had in effect lost the war, was acting as if it had won; while South Vietnam, which had effectively won the war, was acting as if it had lost.

There were undoubtedly psychological reasons for this attitude, but there were also practical personal, political, diplomatic, and military factors behind Thieu's conduct. Because of the way the U.S. media portrayed Thieu, many Americans thought of him as a petty tyrant who suppressed his political opponents. Political dissent was substantially curtailed in South Vietnam, but Thieu still had to deal with an elected National Assembly and face a formidable range of open domestic political opposition. It was by no means certain that he could survive in power unless he could convince his people that the peace agreement was one that would benefit South Vietnam. They had fought and sacrificed too much and they knew the enemy too well to be seduced by the Communists' professed sincerity or willingness to abide by the terms of any agreement. They were the ones who would have to remain in their country after the last Americans had left, and they were naturally reluctant to accept any agreement that might put them at a disadvantage. Since the provisions of any agreement were bound to be controversial, Thieu would have to make it clear that he was neither surrendering any of South Vietnam's vital interests nor accepting terms dictated to him by Washington. The problem was that this would take time, and time was the one thing we did not have if we were to keep to the agreed signing schedule.

Thieu would also be concerned about the military consequences of an immediate agreement. Many military analysts believed that the North Vietnamese were so insistent on keeping October 31 as the deadline for a cease-fire agreement because they had geared up to capture and control as much territory in South Vietnam as possible by that date. As early as the beginning of October a captured COSVN directive had revealed plans to draw South Vietnamese forces into the northern regions so that the provinces in the Mekong Delta and around Saigon would be vulnerable to a last-minute offensive; the document also set out plans for terrorist activities after the cease-fire. Haig was seriously concerned about this.

Diary

Haig believes the real problem is the fact that the North Vietnamese are moving very, very strongly around Saigon at this time to get as much territory as they can. Some of the intelligence indicates that they instructed their cadres the moment a cease-fire is announced to kill all of the opponents in the areas that they control.

This would be a murderous bloodbath, and it's something that we have to consider as we press Thieu to accept what is without question a reasonable political settlement but which must also be justified on security grounds.

On October 20 we began Operation Enhance Plus, a massive airlift of military equipment and supplies to South Vietnam. If the agreement was signed on schedule on October 31, we would have to adhere immediately to its provisions for limited matériel replacement. Therefore it was important to complete as much of the envisaged Vietnamization as possible before the cutoff deadline.

I wanted to make sure once again that Kissinger understood my feelings about not rushing to reach a settlement before the election and about not forcing a break with Thieu by pushing him too fast, so that night I sent him another cable:

> As you continue discussions with Thieu, I wish to re-emphasize again that nothing that is done should be influenced by the U.S. election deadline. I have concluded that a settlement which takes place before the election which is, at best, a washout, has a high risk of severely damaging the U.S. domestic scene, if the settlement were to open us up to the charge that we made a poorer settlement now than what we might have achieved had we waited until after the election . . . .
>
> As I outlined yesterday, we must have Thieu as a willing partner in making any agreement. It cannot be a shotgun marriage.

On October 21 Dobrynin delivered what he described as an urgent message from Brezhnev. The North Vietnamese had complained to him that we were reneging on our agreement and he wanted to let us know that the Soviet government expected us to adhere to the proposed schedule.

Also that day word reached Washington that Pham Van Dong had given an exclusive two-hour interview to Arnaud de Borchgrave of *Newsweek*. When asked whether Thieu could be part of a tripartite coalition government after the cease-fire, Dong had given the opposite impression of what the North Vietnamese had agreed to in Paris. He replied that the National Council of Reconciliation and Concord might actually be or become a coalition government. This was bound to infuriate Thieu and make it even more difficult for him to accept the agreement.

The North Vietnamese were pursuing a cleverly calculated strategy. By agreeing to every point we raised they were building a perfect record in the event they decided to publicize the story of the negotiations. By positioning the agreement as a Communist victory—as Dong had done with de Borchgrave—they were not only saving face domestically and internationally but initiating a psychological battle against Thieu. And by such heavy-handed ploys as deliberately changing words in their translation of the text of the agreement into Vietnamese, they were trying to create friction and suspicion between Saigon and Washington. Thus, even as they were reeling from the effects of our bombing and mining and were troubled by our relationship with their allies in Moscow and Peking, the North Vietnamese were trying to achieve the stunning irony of accomplishing from a position of weakness what they had not been able to attain from a position of strength. They were trying to drive a wedge between us and Thieu; if they succeeded, they might yet use our public opinion to force us to withdraw and give them the chance they wanted to destroy Thieu's government and conquer South Vietnam. I was determined not to let them succeed.

I had Haig send Kissinger another cable on October 21, urging him to push Thieu as far as possible, short of actually making him break with us. I added that if there appeared to be no chance of obtaining Thieu's agreement, Kissinger should inform him that we would have to consider making a separate agreement with the enemy. At this point this was not something I considered doing or that I thought would be necessary, but I wanted to impress Thieu with the seriousness of my determination to complete a settlement as soon as the terms were right.

In Kissinger's judgment the problem was not so much that Thieu would reject the agreement outright and provoke us into breaking with him as that he would stall without giving any answer and thus force us past the signing deadline. He therefore proposed that, in the absence of any indication of Thieu's reaction to the agreement, or even in the event that he refused to go along with it, he should go on to Hanoi as scheduled. With urgent eloquence he pointed out that cancellation of "the final leg," as he called it, would cause many difficult problems, of which the most serious was his continuing conviction that once our election was over the Communists would feel far less pressure to settle and might decide to resume fighting:

> In recent weeks we have played a tough, ruthless game of using our election deadline as blackmail against the other side. In this process we have obtained concessions that nobody thought were possible last month, or for that matter last week. . . .
>
> Washington must understand that this is not a Sunday school picnic. We are dealing with fanatics who have been fighting for twenty-five years and have recently lost the cream of their manhood in the war. They have taken very painful decisions to make the major concessions they have. We cannot be sure how long they will be willing to settle on the terms that are now within our grasp. To wash out the final leg could cost us dearly.

I felt strongly, however, that the North Vietnamese would exploit Kissinger's presence in Hanoi as a propaganda victory and use it to turn American public opinion against Thieu, and I refused to consider the final leg as an option unless and until the settlement had been agreed to by all parties.

On the morning of October 21 Kissinger met with a South Vietnamese working group headed by the Foreign Minister, who opened the session with a prayer and then presented twenty-three proposed changes in the draft agreement. Kissinger immediately accepted sixteen of them as minor and probably manageable. The remaining seven, however, raised impossible demands, including the specified withdrawal of North Vietnamese troops from South Vietnam and the virtual elimination of the National Council of Reconciliation and Concord. He explained that the Communist forces, already weakened by battle and deprived of reinforcements, would eventually wither away; he also pointed out that with the unanimity required for any vote, the Council would end up being a protection rather than a handicap for Saigon. The meeting was cordial, and Kissinger felt that he had been able to present his arguments persuasively. But there was still no word from Thieu, and time was passing. In his cable after the meeting with the South Vietnamese working group Kissinger said:

> I have requested an appointment with Thieu this evening to determine his intentions. Clearly we cannot wait much longer to make our choice since we are rapidly becoming prisoner of events. In retrospect, it is now clear that I made a mistake in agreeing to a fixed date for the final leg. Doing so got us more concessions than any of us thought possible, but it is clearly making us pay at this end. That is water over the dam. I think when you read the records of our talks here you will find that we have been extremely patient with Thieu.

In the meantime the North Vietnamese accepted our formulation of the unilateral declarations regarding Laos and Cambodia. I immediately sent a letter to Kissinger for him to give to Thieu when they met. In it I said that I had now studied the entire agreement, including Hanoi's recent concessions, with the utmost care, and I urged him to accept it for the most practical and compelling reasons:

> Were you to find the agreement to be unacceptable at this point and the other side were to reveal the extraordinary limits to which it has gone in meeting demands put upon them, it is my judgment that your decision would have the most serious effects upon my ability to continue to provide support for you and for the government of South Vietnam.

As the presidential campaign moved through the summer and fall of 1972, the conventional political wisdom was that I might try to turn the war to my political advantage by producing a settlement right before the election. It was ironic that, primarily because of McGovern's extremism, but also because of his inept campaign, the political pressure turned out to be exactly the opposite. The opinion polls confirmed my own intuition that, in terms of voter support, my handling of the war was generally viewed as a positive issue for me and a negative one for McGovern, who was perceived as weak and favoring surrender. Therefore any settlement that was hastily completed in time for the election would look cynical and suspicious. The hawks would charge, however unfairly, that I had given away too much in order to meet a self-serving deadline, and the doves would claim, however erroneously, that I could have obtained the same terms in 1969.

As Kissinger pointed out, the risk in waiting until after the election was that the Communists might decide to keep fighting. I was prepared to step up the bombing after the election, but there was no way of knowing whether that would make them adopt a more reasonable position before the American public's patience ran out, before the bombing began to create serious problems with the Chinese and Soviets or before Congress just voted us out of the war.

> *Diary*
>
> The problem, of course, is that we just don't know whether the enemy has a breaking point or, if it has, when it will come. We don't know, too, whether that situation may become too difficult for us from a political standpoint in the United States after the election, despite the fact that we may win a very significant mandate.
>
> I am inclined to think that the better bargaining time for us would be immediately after the election rather than before. Be-

> fore the election the enemy can still figure there is an outside chance their man can win or at least that he could come closer and that we, therefore, would be under pressure to have a settlement.
>
> Immediately after the election we will have an enormous mandate, we hope, for bringing the war to a successful conclusion, and the enemy then either has to settle or face the consequences of what we could do to them.

My advisers differed about whether it would be easier to get a peace settlement before the election or after it. Kissinger felt strongly that the North Vietnamese would be under much more pressure to negotiate before the election because they would expect to get better terms from me while the war was still an issue in the campaign. He was concerned that once the election had passed, they might revert to their earlier intransigence and let the war drag on at a reduced level in the hope that American public opinion would eventually force us to withdraw.

Others, Haig among them, felt that the North Vietnamese would be more likely to make concessions after the election when I would be armed with a landslide mandate and when I would at any rate be less constrained than I had been during my first term. Personally, I leaned toward this opinion, but I was completely prepared to conclude an agreement before the election if the North Vietnamese would agree to the terms we required and if Thieu could be persuaded to come along. Thieu's apparent determination to postpone an agreement as long as possible presented us with a difficult problem. The knowledge that the North Vietnamese were playing out a cleverly calculated strategy aimed at separating us from Thieu and getting us over a barrel in terms of public opinion did not make that problem any easier to handle.

So far, in fact, it looked as if the North Vietnamese strategy had succeeded. If the negotiating record were made public, it would show that they had virtually capitulated and agreed to everything we required. If we now decided to delay signing the agreement because of Thieu's objections to it, or if we demanded changes in it because of him, then the North Vietnamese were likely to go public with their case and demand that we sign. Thus Thieu would be isolated as the sole obstacle to peace. American public opinion would be stirred up against him by the antiwar leaders and the media, and there would be tremendous pressure brought to bear to jettison him and sign the agreement on our own.

I did not feel that I could let this happen. Even in November, when Thieu's conduct became infuriating, I still felt that if we abandoned him South Vietnam would fall to the Communists within a matter of months, and our entire effort there would have been for naught. I was confident that Thieu would eventually join us in signing an agreement at some point before Congress returned in January and took matters out of our hands by voting to cut off all appropriations for the war and for aid to South Vietnam. So while I hoped that Thieu would accept the agreement before the November election, I was prepared to give him until the end of December to make whatever domestic preparations he felt were necessary before agreeing to sign. In the meantime, I felt that the most important thing was to keep the negotiations going.

On Sunday, October 22, at 8 A.M. in Saigon, Kissinger was finally summoned to Thieu's office. If Thieu had decided to go along, there would still be time for Kissinger to go to Hanoi as we had agreed and for the agreement to be signed in Paris according to the schedule on October 31. Immediately after this meeting Kissinger sent a cable that was phoned to me at Camp David as I was getting ready for bed just after midnight: "We have just finished two-hour meeting with Thieu that was tense and highly emotional. However, I think we finally made a breakthrough and can keep to the original schedule with his support."

I felt an enormous sense of relief and satisfaction when I received this news. By the time I awoke the next morning, another cable had arrived from Kissinger:

> Thieu has just rejected the entire plan or any modification of it and refuses to discuss any further negotiations on the basis of it. He insists that any settlement must contain absolute guarantees of the DMZ, total withdrawal of North Vietnamese forces, and total self-determination of South Vietnam without any reference as to how this is to be exercised.
>
> I need not tell you the crisis with which this confronts us.

Later in the day Kissinger sent a cable explaining how Thieu had called him back in the late afternoon and completely reversed the position he had taken in the morning. "It is hard to exaggerate the toughness of Thieu's position," Kissinger stated. "His demands verge on insanity."

I immediately sent a message to Pham Van Dong through the North Vietnamese delegation in Paris, reminding Hanoi that we had always taken the position that we could not proceed unilaterally: "Unfortunately the difficulties in Saigon have proved somewhat more complex than originally anticipated. Some of them concern matters which the U.S. side is honor-bound to put before the D.R.V. [Democratic Republic of Vietnam] side." Citing the breach of confidence of the de Borchgrave interview as a major reason for the problems with Saigon, I informed them that I was calling Kissinger back to Washington for consultations, and asked that they take no public action until we could send a longer message within twenty-four hours. I reaffirmed our commitment to the substance and basic principles of the draft agreement and our commitment to achieving a negotiated settlement at the earliest opportunity.

Haig called Dobrynin in and explained that difficulties in Saigon required us to postpone the arrangements for signing a settlement. He said that it was important that the Soviets enjoin restraint on their partners, and that Hanoi not indulge in public polemics over the delay.

In the meantime we received a sternly worded reply from the North Vietnamese, stating that they could not accept the reasons I had given for requesting a delay and warning that unless we strictly carried out our commitments regarding the agreement and the schedule for signing it, we would bear the "consequences" for continuing the war.

On October 23 Kissinger and Thieu had a final meeting. Thieu repeated his three main objections to the agreement: its failure to establish the DMZ as a secure border; the potential of the National Council of Reconciliation and Concord to become a coalition government; and the continued presence of North Vietnamese forces in South Vietnam. Kissinger repeated his belief that, while Thieu's concerns were not unjustified, the terms of the agreement were, in fact, a major victory over the Communists. He nonetheless agreed to invite the North Vietnamese to Paris and present Thieu's demands to them there, but he stressed that it was unlikely we would be able to achieve all of them. "What is important is that all the sacrifices that have been made should not have been made in vain," Kissinger told Thieu. "If we continue our confrontation you will win victories, but we will both lose in the end. It is a fact that in the United States all the press, the media, and intellectuals have a vested interest in our defeat. If I have seemed impatient in the last days it is because I saw opportunity slipping away. This is why I leave with such a sense of tragedy."

The next day I sent another message to Premier Dong requesting one final meeting. I declared that the text developed at this meeting would be considered final, and as a token of good will I offered to suspend all bombing of North Vietnam north of the 20th parallel. This message crossed wires with a curt statement from the North Vietnamese insisting that the agreement was complete and no further meeting was necessary. They were ready to receive Kissinger in Hanoi as scheduled; if we delayed, the war would continue. They requested an answer by the next day.

Our answer, which we sent on October 25, was tempered but firm. We stated that we shared their regret that a brief delay in signing was necessary, but we pointed out that we could not sign a document that asserted the concurrence of one of the parties when that concurrence did not exist. We repeated our request for one more meeting between Kissinger and Le Duc Tho and repeated that the text they agreed upon would be considered final. We went even further than I had the day before and undertook that as soon as the text had been completed and while we were consulting with our allies, we would completely stop the bombing of North Vietnam. The message concluded:

> It is up to the D.R.V. to decide whether to sacrifice all that has been achieved by a policy of public vilification and private intransigence. For the D.R.V. to insist on demands beyond the power of the U.S. to fulfill will permit no other conclusion than that it seeks a pretext for prolonging the conflict.

At this point Thieu made a speech to the National Assembly in Saigon. Although he railed against the major provisions of the agreement, he did so in a way that did not rule out his coming along at some later time.

Diary

Thieu's speech was sort of a mixed bag. The most important thing that came out of it, however, was that of the two theories that Henry had laid out—either Thieu was crazy or that he was crazy like a fox—the second proved to be true.

What happens here is that really he is preparing himself for a cease-fire but also proving that he is participating in it in insisting that he is not going to have a coalition government, etc.

On the day of Thieu's speech I signed two veterans' benefits bills at a ceremony in the East Room.

Diary

As I spoke to the veterans I was again terribly moved when I saw the blind veterans and those in wheelchairs.

It makes me realize what a debt we owe to these people, and how important it is to have the kind of peace that will really contribute to no more wars, rather than one that is simply a hiatus between two wars.

How they can still be for us is difficult to understand, but there must be a lot of character in our people, that they will suffer so much and still stand up for what is right for the country.

On Thursday, October 26, what we had been fearing happened: the North Vietnamese went public with the peace agreement. They broadcast the general provisions of the agreement over Radio Hanoi, including the October 31 signing timetable. They revealed two of my cables to Pham Van Dong and insisted that we were dragging out the talks in order to cover up our "scheme of maintaining the Saigon puppet regime for the purpose of continued war of aggression."

Kissinger had already planned to hold a press conference on October 26 in order to reassure the North Vietnamese that we were serious about reaching an agreement as well as to distract attention from Thieu's obstructionism. Now his press conference took on an additional purpose and importance: we had to use it to undercut the North Vietnamese propaganda maneuver and to make sure that our version of the agreement was the one that had greater public impact.

In his opening remarks Kissinger said, "We believe that peace is at hand. We believe that an agreement is within sight, based on the May 8 proposals of the President and some adaptations of our January 25 proposal, which is just to all parties."

Public attention focused on this turn of phrase, "Peace is at hand." Another statement later in the briefing would also come back to haunt us. Kissinger said, "We believe, incidentally, what remains to be done can be settled in one more negotiating session with the North Vietnamese negotiators, lasting, I would think, no more than three or four days, so we are not talking of a delay of a very long period of time." When Ziegler told me that the news lead from Kissinger's briefing was "Peace is at hand," I knew immediately that our bargaining position with the North Vietnamese would be seriously eroded and our problem of bringing Thieu and the South Vietnamese along would be made even more difficult. No less disturbing was the prospect of the premature hopes for an early settlement that would be raised at home, while the McGovern supporters would naturally claim that we were trying to manipulate the election. Kissinger himself soon realized that it was a mistake to have gone so far in order to convince the North Vietnamese of our bona fides by making a public commitment to a settlement.

On the positive side, there was no doubt that Kissinger's briefing had succeeded in completely undercutting the enemy's ploy and superseding their false interpretation of the proposed peace agreement.

Diary

The North Vietnamese thought they were going to surprise us by going public through the NLF with a somewhat distorted and garbled version of the peace plan. Consequently, Henry went public and indicated that "peace was at hand." This was really going considerably further than I would have gone, and I know Henry was worried about it. However, when I talked to him

> about what I should say when we went to [campaign in] Kentucky, he very much did not want me to back off from what he had said.

The North Vietnamese ignored Kissinger's briefing and delivered a message that they were still expecting him in Hanoi to initial the agreement. We sent them a note repeating that we understood their disappointment at our inability to meet the October 31 signing schedule and proposing a final meeting on November 1 with November 20 as the new target date for initialing the agreement.

We agreed not to request any further changes after the agreement had been reached at this final session, and we repeated the offer to suspend all bombing of North Vietnam as soon as the agreement had been completed and while we were consulting our allies about it. We said: "The U.S. side wishes to reaffirm its belief that with a cooperative attitude and good will on both sides, all remaining obstacles can be overcome. The major problem now is to focus on the future and to end recriminations about the past." In a reference to their having publicized the negotiations we added: "Public pressure tactics can only retard progress."

At the same time, we sent a note to Peking saying that it would be greatly appreciated if the Chinese would use their considerable influence in Hanoi to help bring about the peace that was now so near; and I wrote to Brezhnev asking him to use his influence to urge North Vietnam to work with us to complete the agreement on a realistic schedule.

I also sent a strong message to Thieu: "If the evident drift towards disagreement between the two of us continues, however, the essential base for U.S. support for you and your government will be destroyed."

> *Diary*
>
> We are now in a position where if he doesn't come along after the election we are going to have to put him through the wringer. I think then he will come along.
>
> What really concerns him, Henry believes, and I am inclined to think he is right, is that he is terrified of the idea of the Americans being gone from South Vietnam. Abrams, on the other hand, who is certainly no opponent of Thieu's, feels strongly that the time has come for us to get out and that we simply have to cut the umbilical cord and have this baby walk by itself. If they can't do it now, with all we have fed it in the way of arms and ammunition and training, etc., they will never be able to do it.

The avalanche of speculation created by Kissinger's "peace is at hand" statement put us in a very delicate position. Although I did not want to dampen optimism needlessly, I could not allow the impression to remain that a settlement would be the guaranteed outcome of the next Paris meeting. Even if the North Vietnamese gave in to every requirement, there was no assurance that Thieu would go along. In fact, he had made a public speech condemning the proposed settlement as an "agreement to surrender." Therefore, on November 2, in a televised campaign speech, I stated: "We are not going to allow an election deadline or any other kind of deadline to force us into an agreement which would be only a temporary truce and not a lasting peace. We are going to sign the agreement when the agreement is right, not one day before. And when the agreement is right, we are going to sign, without one day's delay." McGovern responded with a charge that I had purposely misled the people about the prospects of peace.

On the same day that I made this speech I authorized some relaxation of the restriction on B-52 raids over North Vietnam that had been in effect since October 13. The plan now was to exert increasing pressure on Hanoi by beginning the bombing near the DMZ and then moving it slightly farther north each day. It seemed to work almost immediately: two days after it began the North Vietnamese agreed to meet with us in Paris on November 14. The election would be over by then; the American people would have chosen their President for the next four years and their decision would have a determining impact on the outcome of the war. Although the differences between McGovern and me were fundamental in almost every area, we were most diametrically opposite in the matter of the Vietnam war. He had pledged to end the war immediately by beginning a unilateral withdrawal without insisting on any arrangements for the return of our POWs. I had pledged to continue fighting until I was convinced that we had achieved a peace that was worthy of our sacrifices, that preserved the independence of South Vietnam, that had a chance of lasting after we had withdrawn our forces, and that assured the return of our POWs and an accounting of our MIAs.

THE CORRUPTION ISSUE

Ignored or rebuked by the majority of voters on the Vietnam war and nearly every other issue, McGovern and the Democrats began to focus on "corruption in government." It may have been completely coincidental that at the same time the Washington *Post* ran a series of news reports—attributed largely to anonymous "sources"—about alleged corruption in the Nixon campaign. As McGovern was quick to recognize, the *Post*'s articles had far more influence in Washington and on the rest of the national media than his or Shriver's campaign rhetoric, and he began to incorporate the charges made by the *Post* into his speeches. These stories reached their peak two weeks before the election, on October 25, and then ended as soon as the election was over. This too may have been coincidental, but that is not the way we saw it in the White House at that time.

For example, on October 3 the *Post* reported an allegation by "sources" that Bill Timmons had been named as one of the people who had received reports from the Watergate wiretaps. The allegation was false, and Timmons denied it. It was still false when the *Post* repeated it three days later, this time on the front page under a big headline.

On October 8 I commented in my diary on the effect this kind of story had.

> *Diary*
>
> Julie was worried about the story in the paper to the effect that Timmons, [Robert] Odle, and one other White House aide had had access to the reports on Watergate. She said that if any of them are really guilty that we really ought to get rid of them. I told her not to be concerned about it, that the reports were false. It does show how sensitive she, and probably others like her in the campaign, are about this issue.
>
> She mentioned the fact that she had seen Sherman Adams. It is a tragedy really what happened to Adams and I must remember to have him to the White House for some occasion. After all of his service to Eisenhower, he should not have been forced to leave under a cloud for an offense that was, at best, a question of judgment and not one of illegality or morality. I tend to agree with Jerry Persons when he says that Adams is an impeccably honest man and left his job a relatively poor man.

On October 10 the *Post* had a new front-page allegation. Under the headline *FBI Finds Nixon Aides Sabotaged Democrats,* the story began: "FBI agents have established that the Watergate bugging incident stemmed from a massive campaign of political spying and sabotage conducted on behalf of President Nixon's re-election and directed by officials of the White House and the Committee for the Re-election of the President."

The story charged that a young man named Donald Segretti had recruited fifty operatives for an undercover campaign that involved "following members of Democratic candidates' families; forging letters and distributing them under candidates' letterheads; leaking false and manufactured items to the press; throwing campaign schedules into disarray; seizing confidential campaign files and investigating the lives of dozens of Democratic campaign workers."

Donald Segretti had been a college friend of my Appointments Secretary Dwight Chapin and of Gordon Strachan, an aide to Haldeman.

Chapin and Strachan had hired Segretti to become what they called "a Republican Dick Tuck." Tuck was a Democrat whose name had become synonymous with ingenious gags aimed at Republican candidates; he was the master of what were then called "dirty tricks": planting embarrassing signs in campaign crowds, changing schedules in order to create confusion, and generally spreading disruption. Segretti, like Tuck, was supposed to use his imagination and his sense of humor to cause minor disarray among the opposition.

Chapin read the *Post*'s story with incredulity. He had not kept tabs on Segretti's activity, but the sinister implications of the *Post*'s account were nothing like what he had authorized. Segretti expressed outrage.

As I saw it then, by printing this story less than a month before the election, the *Post* was accusing Segretti of spying and sabotage for the same kind of thing that had been dubbed creative mischief when Tuck had done it. Furthermore, it was grossly untrue and unfair to link Segretti to the Watergate break-in.

A few days later reporters from the *Post* phoned the White House to warn that they were about to run a new story that would charge that Chapin and Hunt were Segretti's contacts and directed his activities. This would tie Chapin by implication into the Watergate break-in stories. The reporters also said that they were going to charge that Chapin and Hunt had briefed Segretti on what the grand jury would ask about his activities. Both these charges were untrue, and Chapin issued a statement denying them.

The story that was actually published on the front page of the *Post* on October 15 had been subtly changed from the one the reporters had described to us over the phone. They did not, however, inform Chapin that any changes were going to be made or give him an opportunity to modify the wording of his denial accordingly. The story as run did not accuse Chapin of briefing Segretti on the grand jury, and weakened the alleged connection with Hunt. The story now began: "President Nixon's Appointments Secretary and an ex-White House aide indicted in the Watergate bugging case both served as 'contacts' in a spying and sabotage operation against the Democrats."

Of course the problem was that there was no way of separating facts from fiction in this kind of story three weeks before a presidential election. The most damaging parts were completely false; but it was true that Chapin had hired Segretti to cause disarray in the Democrats' campaigns. And there were other political hazards involved in trying to set the story straight. Haldeman had given Chapin approval to have Segretti paid by my lawyer and campaign aide, Herb Kalmbach. Thus there was the danger of focusing the story more strongly on the White House. Ziegler denied that Chapin directed any campaign of spying and sabotage, denounced the "hearsay, innuendo, and guilt by association," and then doggedly refused to comment on the specifics. The White House press corps was furious.

The diary note I dictated that night conveys the way I felt about these charges against Chapin stemming from his Segretti contacts.

Diary

The big story on Chapin broke today and it was certainly guilt by association, hearsay, etc. McCarthyism at its very worst. In any event, as I told Haldeman, we could not be knocked off balance by these stories because they were going to be stepped up in tempo this week.

Haldeman indicated that Chapin felt he was expendable. I said under no circumstances would we move in that direction because it was not fair since the press were simply using a double standard on all of this. It is rather ironical that they excused the Dick Tuck and other operations as being just good clean fun, but where we are doing it, it is grim and vicious espionage and sabotage of the worst type.

A few days later I added a further observation.

Diary

I passed on to Haldeman my midnight thought to the effect that the latest attack on Chapin et al. was the "last burp of the Eastern establishment."

As the news reports about Segretti and the Watergate affair continued, McGovern announced that he knew *he* was being sabotaged, and on October 19 he called my administration a "cutthroat crew . . . a corrupt regime." On October 24 he charged—falsely—that the Republicans wiretapped the phones of Democratic presidential candidates in the primaries and "had us followed and members of our families followed all the time." In the meantime Teddy Kennedy decided that this was the sort of thing he should investigate personally. He announced that his Senate Subcommittee on Administrative Practices would begin a probe of Segretti and questionable campaign tactics.

On the morning of October 25, the Washington *Post* ran a large front-page picture of Bob Haldeman under the headline: *Testimony Ties Top Nixon Aide to Secret Fund.* The story said that Haldeman was one of five men authorized to approve payments from a secret cash fund at the CRP. It claimed that the fund had been "uncovered during the

FBI Watergate bugging investigation. It financed an apparently unprecedented spying and sabotage campaign." The story stated that Haldeman had been one of those who had approved expenditures of hundreds of thousands of dollars for these activities. The reporters said that Hugh Sloan, the CRP's treasurer, had given testimony to this effect before the grand jury and that Haldeman had been questioned about it by the FBI.

It was true that there was a cash fund at the CRP set aside for intelligence-gathering and other campaign projects that had to be handled discreetly. And Haldeman, acting in my name, theoretically could presumably approve money from any fund connected with my campaign. But he had not directed the payments from the CRP fund, nor had he been interviewed by the FBI. Nor had Hugh Sloan given the testimony described in the story.

Diary

We got the news with regard to the *Post* story on Haldeman. It obviously disturbs him but he is a strong man and took it very, very well. He says that the story was inaccurate insofar as the Hugh Sloan testimony was concerned, but in any event the *Post* is going to continue to nibble away. Haldeman spoke rather darkly of the fact that there was a clique in the White House that were out to get him. I trust he is not getting a persecution complex.

I called Haldeman after I got back to the Residence and tried to reassure him by saying that I was relaxed about it, that I knew we were going to have to take some heat in the next two weeks, but that we would sail through and not be knocked off balance.

It is interesting to note that Ben Bradlee of the *Post* says that this administration is committed to the destruction of the press. This of course is total nonsense and he knows it. I think what he fears is what's going to happen to the Washington *Post* news sources after the election—and we have every right, in fact every responsibility, to see to it that people who would give us a fair shake get a break over others who are going to give us the knife.

Considering that McGovern was supposed to be the peace candidate, his supporters resorted to surprisingly violent and destructive attacks against my campaign and even against my supporters. At one of my appearances in San Francisco there occurred what one observer called a "state of siege": the hotel was ringed by helmeted police in riot gear while groups of demonstrators stopped traffic and threw rocks. This demonstration was promoted by leaflets distributed from the McGovern headquarters in nearby Berkeley. In Los Angeles, McGovern's Southern California campaign coordinator admitted to approving the use of telephone banks at their headquarters to promote a massive demonstration against me there; leaflets advertising this effort were handed out at approximately fifty McGovern headquarters. The Ervin Committee was later told that a McGovern spokesman had falsely represented to the press that this effort had not been authorized. In Morgantown, West Virginia, demonstrators tried to shout down a speech by Tricia. In Columbus, Ohio, guests attending a Republican fund raiser at which Ted Agnew spoke were spat upon and subjected to shouts and obscenities. In Washington, D.C., the Democrats for Nixon headquarters was stormed by nearly a hundred people who tore down posters, destroyed campaign material, damaged office equipment, and stole office supplies. When the violators departed, they left McGovern campaign leaflets behind.

Far more serious was the use of outright violence aimed at my campaign. CRP headquarters in Phoenix and Austin were completely destroyed by arsonists. Our headquarters in Dayton, Ohio, was broken into twice and equipment and records damaged; the second time, McGovern slogans were painted on the walls and windows. In Minnesota one of our headquarters buildings was broken into, and materials and literature were destroyed and motor oil dumped over boxes containing mailing literature. At the Alameda County headquarters in California, a bomb exploded, causing extensive damage.

It became routine to find scurrilous literature handed out in advance of appearances. One pamphlet passed out by McGovern campaign workers in Los Angeles neighborhoods with heavy Jewish populations included the line: "Nixon brings the ovens to the people rather than the people to the ovens."

After the campaign it was revealed that, for all its sanctimony, the McGovern high command was not above considering organized spying of its own. At the highest levels of their campaign it was proposed that a paid operative be planted aboard Ted Agnew's campaign airplane to spy on Agnew and report his activities to the McGovern camp. According to Senate Watergate Committee records, one of those responsible for this plan claimed that the same thing had been done successfully against my campaign in 1968.

There was also a break-in at the office of Dr. John Lungren, my personal physician in Long Beach, California. No money or drugs were taken, but my medical files were removed from a locked closet and left strewn about the floor of the office.

Diary

Haldeman and Ehrlichman talked about it during the day.

> Colson was ecstatic and wanted to get it out right away. Ehrlichman, however, probably had the better judgment and said that it might lead to the conclusion either that we had set it up, or it really didn't amount to anything at all. The most important thing, as I told Haldeman, was to conduct an investigation—to report the situation so that there would be no indication of cover-up in the event that the people that broke in had something.

The demonstrators and arsonists detracted heavily from the spirit of this last campaign. More frustrating to me, however, was the double standard that permitted massive and frequently distorted coverage of Watergate while virtually ignoring the many serious violations of law and ethics committed against us. In light of what I saw being done against us in this campaign, the righteous moralizing about Segretti's activities rang hollow.

The last political rally of my career as a candidate took place at Ontario, California, a few miles and twenty-six years from where the first one had taken place in Pomona. We arrived at night, after a two-day final campaign swing through Illinois, Oklahoma, Rhode Island, North Carolina, and New Mexico. The night before we left Washington, Tricia had come into the Lincoln Sitting Room and said, "I want this week to be a real last hurrah."

The overflow crowd at the Ontario airport seemed to sense the emotional and symbolic meaning of the moment for me. I told them how I had been all across the nation during the past few weeks. I said, "I want to tell you something about this country. . . . There was a time, and it was not too long ago, when if you traveled through the country, you would see it deeply divided—the West against the East, the North against the South, the cities against the farms, and so forth. But let me tell you, wherever you go across America, this nation is getting together."

I talked about our goals and then turned back to California and talked about how good the people of California had been to us, sharing our victories and standing by us in our defeats.

"This, of course, not only is the last rally of this campaign that I will speak to," I said in conclusion, "it is the last time I will speak to a rally as a candidate in my whole life, and I want to say to all of you here who worked on this, to all of you who took the time to come, thank you very much for making it probably the best rally that we have ever had."

On election eve, November 6, 1972, I dictated various recollections of my day in San Clemente.

Diary

Today I went down to the Red Beach, walked two miles, went in the water for about twenty minutes. The tide was out further than I have ever seen it—a real ebb tide. Whether this is a good sign or a bad sign only time will tell.

When I went further down the beach—I decided to first go just to the half-mile mark and then went on to the peace sign [which someone had carved in the red sandstone cliff], which is about three-quarters of a mile. Interestingly enough, the peace sign had been worn down by the weather. It was very dim. It looked like a man with a frown on his face. This may be an indication that those who have held up this sign finally have had their comeuppance and they are really in for some heavy depression.

Rose joined Pat and me for dinner that evening. On the East Coast millions had already watched a brief election eve address that I had recorded on videotape earlier in the day. I said that I would not insult anyone's intelligence by rehashing the issues and making a last-minute plea for votes. I said that this election was probably the clearest choice between the candidates for President ever presented to the American people in the twentieth century.

My diary for election eve concluded on a rather subdued and analytical note.

Diary

Well, this wraps it up for the first four years, because as I have often thought over this past year I really only had until November 7 to be President because if I lost the election on November 7—tomorrow—then the presidency would be in someone else's hands.

We are not going to lose it, of course, lacking a miracle beyond which nothing has been seen up to this point. When I think of the ups and downs through the years, and particularly in this last year, I must say that someone must have been walking with us. The Peking trip, the Moscow trip, the May 8 decision, and then the way we have handled the campaign—must deserve some grudging respect from even our critics. The only sour note of the whole thing, of course, is Watergate and Segretti. This was really stupidity on the part of a number of people.

We flew back to Washington on Election Day. When we arrived at the White House at 6 P.M., we were greeted by a cheering staff. In my room I found an envelope propped up on my pillow. It contained a handwritten letter from Henry Kissinger:

> Election Day 1972
>
> Dear Mr. President—
>
> It seems appropriate before the votes are counted to tell you what a privilege the last four years have been. I am confident of the outcome today. But it cannot affect the historic achievement—to take a divided nation, mired in war, losing its confidence, wracked by intellectuals without conviction, and give it a new purpose and overcome its hesitations—will loom ever larger in history books. It has been an inspiration to see your fortitude in adversity and your willingness to walk alone. For this—as well as for the unfailing human kindness and consideration—I shall always be grateful.
>
> With warm and respectful regards,
> Henry

Our family had dinner together while waiting for the polls to close and for the first returns to come in. About an hour later the cap on one of my top front teeth snapped off. It had held firmly in place for twenty-five years, since the time it had been fitted in 1947.

I was to appear on television in a few hours, so we called my dentist, Dr. William Chase. He came to the White House, and after a half hour's work he was able to give me a hastily crafted temporary cap. I was in considerable discomfort, and I knew that if I smiled too broadly the cap might fall off.

I returned to the Lincoln Sitting Room and continued putting down notes for the remarks I would be making later. After a while I got up and put on a tape of *Victory at Sea.*

Ed and David brought me the first reports at 7:30. They were elated because it was already apparent that I was going to win by a landslide. Even if it was not really a surprise, the moment was still exciting for all of us.

Shortly after eight o'clock Haldeman began phoning over more detailed reports from the election-monitoring teams that had been set up in the West Wing offices. In state after state we were winning big. Texas, for example, was going to be ours by more than a million votes. But there was also bad news: we were not picking up enough congressional seats to provide the legislative support my own New Majority mandate would need. When all the results were in, Republicans gained 12 seats in the House, but lost two seats in the Senate. The new lineup of governors —31 Democrats to 19 Republicans—meant a loss of one state house for the Republican Party. I was concerned about our failure to do better in Congress, but I was at least certain that no Republican candidate had lost for lack of money. On examination I found that in many cases our candidates had been defeated by younger liberals who had labor support and labor money. I thought that this would be our challenge as a party before the 1974 off-year elections: to revamp and renew ourselves so as to get candidates who could successfully appeal to voters and wage winning campaigns.

At about 11:40 P.M. George McGovern conceded and sent me a telegram:

> CONGRATULATIONS ON YOUR VICTORY. I HOPE THAT IN THE NEXT FOUR YEARS YOU WILL LEAD US TO A TIME OF PEACE ABROAD AND JUSTICE AT HOME. YOU HAVE MY FULL SUPPORT IN SUCH EFFORTS. WITH BEST WISHES TO YOU AND YOUR GRACIOUS WIFE PAT. SINCERELY, GEORGE MCGOVERN.

Ed thought the message was gracious, but Tricia and Julie thought it cold and arch. I thought it was merely carefully worded. I expressed my reaction in my diary: "It was a tough experience for him and I am not as hard-nosed about it as some might be because with all the mistakes he made, he feels that he has done the best he can and he is being put upon."

Thousands of calls and cables began pouring in to celebrate the great victory. One was from Johnson City:

> THE WAY IN WHICH YOUR FELLOW MEN EXPRESSED THEIR APPROVAL OF YOUR RECORD THESE LAST FOUR YEARS MUST BE A GREAT COMFORT TO YOU AND I KNOW IT WILL GIVE YOU THE STRENGTH SO NECESSARY IN THE TIMES AHEAD. YOU AND YOUR FAMILY HAVE ENDURED MUCH BUT I KNOW TODAY THAT IT IS WORTH IT ALL. LADY BIRD AND I WILL DO ANYTHING WE CAN TO EASE YOUR BURDEN AND HELP YOU MAKE A GOOD PRESIDENT IN THE DAYS AHEAD. LYNDON B. JOHNSON.

The dimensions of the victory were gratifying. I received 47,169,841 votes, and McGovern received 29,172,767: 60.7 percent to 37.5 percent. This was the second largest percentage of the popular vote in our history of two-party politics, and the greatest ever given a Republican candidate. Only Lyndon Johnson, running against Goldwater in the unique circumstances of 1964, had received fractionally more: 61.1 percent. I received the largest number of popular votes ever cast for a presidential candidate and the second largest number of electoral votes. No presidential candidate had ever won so many states.

The support was both wide and deep—it was truly a New Majority landslide of the kind I had called for in my acceptance speech in August. I won a majority of every key population group identified by Gallup except the blacks and the Democrats. Four of these groups—manual workers, Catholics, members of labor union families, and people with only grade school educations—had never before been in the Republican camp in all the years since Gallup had begun keeping these records.

A few days later I described in my diary a curious feeling, perhaps a foreboding, that muted my enjoyment of this triumphal moment.

Diary

It makes one feel very humble at a time like this.

I had determined before this election evening to make it as memorable a one as possible for everybody concerned. The tooth episode probably interfered to a considerable extent. Certainly by the time that I had to prepare for the office telecast I was not as upbeat as I should have been.

The rest of the family seemed to think that they got enough of a thrill out of it. I think the very fact that the victory was so overwhelming made up for any failure on my part to react more enthusiastically than I did.

I am at a loss to explain the melancholy that settled over me on that victorious night. Perhaps it was caused by the painful tooth. To some extent the marring effects of Watergate may have played a part, to some extent our failure to win Congress, and to a greater extent the fact that we had not yet been able to end the war in Vietnam. Or perhaps it was because this would be my last campaign. Whatever the reasons, I allowed myself only a few minutes to reflect on the past. I was confident that a new era was about to begin, and I was eager to begin it.

THE END OF THE WAR

My first priority after the election was to end the war. Now that the pressure was removed, I hoped that both parties would enter the negotiations with the idea that after some hard bargaining each would accept an agreement embodying less than their most extreme position. I knew that it was not going to be easy. None of the objective factors had changed, but now that there was no election deadline, it remained to be seen what the Communists' negotiating tactics would be. Both Saigon and Hanoi were already playing a frustrating game with us. Thieu, while urging that we put forward his demands—some of which were bound to be unacceptable to the North Vietnamese—was still pretending that he was prepared to go it alone. And Le Duc Tho was pretending that the Communists were completely sincere in their desire to conclude an agreement on its merits and then to observe its terms. From our intelligence sources we knew that Thieu was secretly telling his military leaders to be ready for a cease-fire before Christmas; and we knew that the North Vietnamese were still planning to capture as much territory as possible just before the cease-fire in order to be able to turn it to their advantage.

The next meeting with the North Vietnamese was scheduled for mid-November. If anything was to come from it, Thieu's cooperation was now essential. I decided that Haig, whom Thieu trusted and liked, would once again be the best emissary. He left for Saigon on November 9, carrying another letter I had written to Thieu. In it I dealt point by point with the objections Thieu had raised to the terms of the October agreement and clarified the positions that we would present to the North Vietnamese at the next Paris meeting. "We will use our maximum efforts to effect these changes in the agreement," I wrote. "I wish to leave you under no illusion, however, that we can or will go beyond these changes in seeking to improve an agreement that we already consider to be excellent."

I also urged Haig to remind Thieu that although I had won the White House by a landslide, he must remember that the Senate was now even more dovish than it had been before the election. There was no question that if we did not have a settlement completed before Congress returned in January, and if it appeared that Thieu was the obstacle to achieving one, the Senate would cut off the funds that South Vietnam needed to survive. The situation was as simple, and as certain, as that.

Thieu handed Haig a reply that repeated his objections, particularly regarding the presence of North Vietnamese troops in South Vietnam. I responded by reiterating that we would not be able to obtain all the adjustments he had requested. I pointed out that far more important than what was *said* in any agreement was what we would *do* in the event the enemy renewed its aggression. "You have my absolute assurance that if Hanoi fails to abide by the terms of this agreement it is my intention to take swift and severe retaliatory action," I wrote.

Haig left Saigon convinced that Thieu would come along in the end. There was no doubt in his mind that Thieu knew that total intransigence would be fatal. In the meantime, however, he had been careful not to push Thieu too far. He reported on November 12:

> We are now dealing with a razor's edge situation. Thieu has firmly laid his prestige on the line with his entire government and I believe if we take a totally unreasonable stance with him, we may force him to commit political suicide. I am not sure that this would serve our best interests and therefore

recommend the scarier approach of trying to work this problem with Thieu right up to the wire.

Haig correctly pointed out that if we broke with Thieu and then found that the North Vietnamese were still intransigent, we would have burned both our bridges. He concluded, "The price of keeping Thieu aboard is of course risky but I do not believe unacceptable at this juncture."

I agreed with Haig's assessment, and in my diary I noted, "Of course, we may come to the hard place where we have to simply tell Thieu it's this or else, but this does not need to come at this moment." I told both Kissinger and Haig that I felt December 8 was the final date by which we must have signed an agreement in order to make sure that everything was completely settled by the time Congress reconvened. If Thieu could not be convinced to come along by then, I could be reluctantly prepared to reach a separate agreement.

Whether we could meet the December 8 deadline would depend upon the outcome of the November 20 meeting in Paris.

Diary

Assuming that we get any kind of movement from the North Vietnamese on the agreement this week, and assuming we get what we consider to be a good agreement—well, as a matter of fact, we consider the present one to be good, but this will make it better—then we have to put it to Thieu hard: he either accepts the agreement and goes along with it, or we will have to go our separate ways.

As I told Henry when he began to rumble around to the effect that we have a very good record in this instance, I said, Henry, we're not concerned about being right on the record. What we are concerned about is to save South Vietnam and that's why we had to temporize with Thieu as much as we did, because our interest is in getting South Vietnam to survive and Thieu at present seems to be the only leader who could lead them in that direction.

It would, of course, be a disappointment in the event that Thieu does not go along, but under those circumstances we shall simply have to make our own deal, get our prisoners, have our withdrawal, try to save Cambodia and Laos, and then say that Vietnamization has been completed and Thieu then can do what he likes.

On November 20 Kissinger met with Le Duc Tho for more than five hours. Tho opened by reading a lengthy speech complaining that we had reneged on the October agreement. While its tone was no different from the standard rhetoric we had come to expect, the charges that we had unilaterally prevented an agreement were unacceptable. Kissinger immediately cited chapter and verse from earlier sessions in which he had informed the Communists that the South Vietnamese would have to be consulted before any agreement could be signed. Kissinger finished his opening remarks by reiterating our desire to negotiate seriously to end the war and our intention to maintain the essence of the agreement that had been achieved in October.

He then presented the proposed changes. By the time the ones requested by the South Vietnamese had been applied to the text of the agreement and added to the changes and clarifications we wanted, there were more than sixty of them. Le Duc Tho seemed somewhat taken aback by their number. Most of the changes were relatively minor and uncontroversial. But a few were substantive, the most significant of them involving Thieu's insistence on a pull-back of some of the North Vietnamese forces out of South Vietnam. There was also a proposal that the DMZ be respected by each party; the presence of North Vietnamese troops in the South would be a violation of this provision. Le Duc Tho simply took note of the list and indicated that he might have some changes of his own to propose. Kissinger had made no distinction between the changes we wanted and those we were presenting on behalf of the South Vietnamese. His approach, however, made it clear that we were prepared to negotiate on all of them. At the close of the meeting he was asked whether this was actually our final proposal. Kissinger replied, "I would put it this way. It is our final proposal, but it is not an ultimatum." Kissinger suggested that the technical experts meet that night to study the proposed changes. As the session adjourned on a friendly note, it seemed possible that the Communists would treat the proposals as a basis for negotiation and that an agreement might be reached during this round. That morning I dictated in my diary, "The next two days will tell the tale as to whether we get an agreement."

At the meeting the next day, however, the North Vietnamese countered our proposed changes and hardened their position on the remaining unresolved issues; in some areas they even pulled back to their position *before* October 8. It seemed that Kissinger's fears had been realized and that the North Vietnamese, relieved of the pressure of our election deadline, were prepared to stall the negotiations in an attempt to exploit our differences with Thieu. When Kissinger reported that there had been another tense and totally unproductive meeting on November 22, I sent him a message, which I said he could use if and when he saw fit—or not at all—in an effort to get the negotiations moving. The message was in the form of a directive stating that unless the other side showed the same willingness to be reasonable that we were showing, he should discontinue the talks and we would have to resume military activity until they were ready to negotiate. It continued:

> They must be disabused of the idea they seem to have that we have no other choice but to settle on their terms. You should inform them directly without equivocation that we do have another choice and if they were surprised that the President would take the strong action he did prior to the Moscow Summit and prior to the election, they will find now, with the election behind us, he will take whatever action he considers necessary to protect the United States' interest.

After the next session in Paris on November 23 Kissinger reported that although he had made limited progress in specific areas, we were still far apart on some of the provisions that Thieu considered most important. Therefore we had to face the fact that barring a sudden change by the North Vietnamese, we were not going to have an acceptable deal. He felt that as long as Saigon held out for so many substantial alterations, not only would no agreement be reached but the North Vietnamese would continue to retract concessions they had already granted.

Kissinger considered that we now had two options open to us. Option One would be to break off the talks at the next meeting and dramatically step up our bombing while we reviewed our negotiating strategy in order to decide what kind of agreement we would be prepared to accept with and without the South Vietnamese. This was the option Kissinger favored. Option Two would be to decide upon fall-back positions on each of Thieu's major objections and present them as our final offer. If the North Vietnamese agreed to them, we could still claim to have improved on the October terms. This proposal, as Kissinger put it, "would be substantially better optically, and marginally better substantively, than the agreement we concluded in October. It gives Thieu the minimum that he has asked for if he wanted to be reasonable, which he shows absolutely no inclination of being at this time."

The corollary of Option Two would be a complete break with Thieu if he refused to accept the agreement it produced. I knew that this would be a serious step to take, but I strongly opposed breaking off the talks and resuming the bombing unless it was absolutely necessary to compel the enemy to negotiate. I was also becoming irritated by some of Thieu's tactics, and I felt that we could no longer be in the position of forestalling an agreement solely to buy him time. Therefore, if Kissinger could reach a satisfactory agreement, I wanted him to do so. Then Thieu could make his own decision about joining us or going it alone.

In my message replying to Kissinger's cable I made it clear that I did not consider that Option One was open to us any longer:

> In my view the October 8 agreement was one which certainly would have been in our interest. You should try to improve it to take account of Saigon's conditions as much as possible. But most important we must recognize the fundamental reality that we have no choice but to reach agreement along the lines of the October 8 principles.

Almost immediately I became concerned that, in my attempt to encourage Kissinger to pursue Option Two, I might have overstated my reluctance to resume the bombing if there was no other choice left to us to make the enemy negotiate seriously. I felt it was essential that he not be denied this bargaining chip, and consequently I sent him a cable the next morning, November 24, saying that if the Communists remained intransigent, he could suspend the talks for a week so that both sides could consult with their principals. I said that I would be prepared to authorize a massive bombing strike on North Vietnam in that interval:

> I recognize that this is a high-risk option, but it is one I am prepared to take if the only alternative is an agreement which is worse than that of the October 8, and which does not clear up any of the ambiguities which we and Saigon are concerned about in the October 8 draft.
>
> Our aim will continue to be to end the war with honor. And if because of the pursuit of our strategy and the accident of the timing of the election we are now in a public relations corner, we must take our lumps and see it through.
>
> In giving this direction, we all must realize that there is no way whatever that we can mobilize public opinion behind us as in the case of November 3, Cambodia, and May 8. But at least with the election behind us, we owe it to the sacrifice that has been made to date by so many to do what is right even though the cost in our public support will be massive.

When Kissinger informed Le Duc Tho that I was prepared to take actions as strong as the ones of May 8, the North Vietnamese immediately became more conciliatory. This seemed to confirm our suspicions that their intransigence was in fact a negotiating tactic. They did not want the talks to end any more than we did and were therefore prepared once again to engage in serious negotiations.

The problem, as Kissinger presented it in his reporting cable that afternoon, was that while we had now considerably improved the agreement over the October 8 terms, there was no possibility that we could come near anything that would satisfy all of Thieu's requirements. We knew from cable intercepts that Thieu was in a deliberate stalling pattern; this meant that no improvements in the agreement would have any effect on him until he decided that he had sufficiently prepared his people to accept it. So despite our intensive efforts and the improvements we had been able to make in the agreement, a major break with Thieu seemed inevitable if we were going to complete the agreement right away. Kissinger therefore once again recommended a week's recess during which we could force a reckoning with Thieu and then, on the basis of his decision, formulate our own final position.

I still believed, however, that it was important to keep the negotiating channels open and working. I considered Thieu's position to be ill-advised, and I felt more strongly than ever that if we could get a good agreement, we should do so and let Thieu make his choice accordingly. I immediately replied to Kissinger that I thought it preferable for him to stay in Paris and continue talking as long as there was even a remote chance of reaching an agreement. I said that I would even "take risks in that direction."

The North Vietnamese were still stonewalling the negotiations, however, so after another inconclusive session on November 25, Kissinger and Le Duc Tho agreed on the desirability of recessing the talks for several days.

I met with Kissinger as soon as he returned from Paris.

Diary

He arrived back around 10:30 and we spent an hour on it at that time. I had to back him off the position that we really had a viable option to break off the talks with the North and resume the bombing for a period of time. It simply isn't going to work. While we must play the card out with the North Vietnamese as if it would work that way, we must have no illusions that we now have no option except to settle.

We sent a message to the North Vietnamese that we would return to the talks with the idea of making one last effort. In order to demonstrate our good faith and desire to reach a settlement, I ordered a reduction of the bombing of North Vietnam.

On November 29 Kissinger ushered Nguyen Phu Duc, President Thieu's personal representative at the Paris talks, into the Oval Office. We thought that if I made a brutally tough presentation to Duc, that would succeed in bringing home to Thieu the precariousness of his position and the danger of being left on his own. I said that it was not a question of lacking sympathy for Saigon's predicament; but we had to face the reality of the situation. If we did not end the war by concluding a settlement at the next Paris session, then when Congress returned in January it would end the war by cutting off the appropriations. I had already informed Thieu that I had canvassed the staunchest congressional supporters of my Vietnam policy regarding the October terms, and they had unanimously avowed that if Thieu alone were standing in the way of accepting such terms, they would personally lead the fight against him when Congress reconvened.

On November 30 I met with Kissinger, Haig, Laird, and the Joint Chiefs of Staff to discuss our military plans in the event that the talks were broken off or that the agreement reached was subsequently violated by the Communists. In the former case there were contingency plans for three-day and six-day bombing strikes against North Vietnam. In the latter case I was adamant that our response be swift and strong. "If Hanoi violates an agreement, our response must be all out," I said. "We must maintain enough force in the area to do the job, and it can't be a weak response. Above all, B-52s are to be targeted on Hanoi. We must have our own unilateral capability to prevent violations."

Kissinger's next meeting with the North Vietnamese was scheduled for Monday, December 4. If no settlement emerged from this meeting, it would be very difficult to predict how or when the war would end. Kissinger would need all his formidable skills not only to convince the North Vietnamese that we would stay in and continue fighting unless they agreed to a settlement, but to convince the South Vietnamese that we would stop fighting and get out unless they agreed to one. Kissinger himself was optimistic that it would take only a few days to conclude an agreement; in fact, he said, there was a 70–30 chance that he could have the whole thing "wrapped up" by Tuesday night. He blamed his "peace is at hand" statement for having caused many of our present troubles, and he talked about resigning if he was unable to conclude an agreement. I told him that he should not even be thinking in such terms.

On Sunday night I noted: "We enter a very tough week and a very crucial one, but some way I think it's got to come out because the great forces of history—what is really right—are moving us in those directions. Only insanity and irrationality of some leaders may move us in other directions."

All our hopes were dashed on Monday. Le Duc Tho not only categorically rejected every change we had requested, but also withdrew some that had already been agreed upon during the last round and introduced several new and unacceptable demands of his own. Now, even if we decided to conclude an agreement without Thieu, the terms were no longer acceptable to us. Kissinger cabled: "We are at a point where a break-off of the talks looks almost certain." In a long report analyzing the meeting he stated:

> It is not impossible that Tho is playing chicken and is waiting for us to cave tomorrow. But I do not think so. There is almost no doubt that Hanoi is prepared now to break off the negotiations and go another military round. Their own needs for a settlement are now outweighed by the attractive vision they see of our having to choose between a complete split with Saigon or an unmanageable domestic situation. . . .
>
> The central issue is that Hanoi has apparently decided to mount a frontal challenge to us such as we faced last May. If so, they are gambling on our unwillingness to do what is necessary; they are playing for a clear-cut victory through our split with Saigon or our domestic collapse rather than run the risk of a negotiated settlement.
>
> This is the basic question; the rest is tactics. If they were willing to settle now, I could come up with acceptable formulas and would not need to bother you. Assuming they are going the other route, we are faced with the same kind of hard decisions as last spring.

Kissinger felt that Le Duc Tho's conduct once again left us with only two options: either we must agree to go back and accept the terms of the October agreement without any changes, or we must run the risk that the talks would break off. He pointed out that the first option was unacceptable. It would be tantamount to overthrowing Thieu; as Kissinger put it, "He could not survive such a demonstration of his and our impotence." It would leave us with no way of explaining our actions since October, and it would provide Hanoi with an enormous propaganda victory. Most important, agreeing to return to the October terms would deprive us of any credibility in policing the agreement, because the Communists would know that if we were willing to swallow this backdown, we would also lack the capability to react to any violations. Kissinger concluded that while the October agreement had been a good one, intervening events had made it impossible to accept now.

Kissinger continued: "Therefore I believe we must be prepared to break off the negotiations. The question is how we do it." He felt that we now had two tactical choices in this regard. The first was to propose settling on the basis of where we had stood in the previous week's round;

that would at least enable us to keep the changes and improvements Le Duc Tho had agreed to. The problem with this option was that neither Hanoi nor Saigon was likely to accept it.

The second tactical choice, and the one Kissinger recommended, was to insist on retaining those changes to which the North Vietnamese had already agreed while boiling down our remaining requirements to only the most basic ones involving the clear delineation of the non-governmental nature and functions of the National Council of Reconciliation and Concord and the necessity of having in the agreement some formulation of the principle that North Vietnamese troops did not have the right to remain indefinitely in the South. The Communists were unlikely to accept these requirements, but if for some reason they did, we could use the improvements they represented over the October terms as a lever to bring Thieu along. None of these points was sufficiently critical that the North Vietnamese, if they had genuinely wanted an agreement, could not have accepted them.

If the Communists refused and the talks broke off, we would have no choice but to step up our bombing as a means of making them agree to a redefined negotiating position. Kissinger recommended that I go on television to enlist the support of the American people for the stern measures that would be required. "I believe that you can make a stirring and convincing case to rally them as you have so often in the past with your direct appeals," he wrote.

I disagreed with Kissinger in this regard. Instead of a frantic and probably foredoomed attempt on my part to rally American public opinion behind a major escalation of the war, I preferred an unannounced stepping up of the bombing. This would be coupled with a press conference by Kissinger to explain where we stood in terms of the new attempts at reaching a settlement, and why the negotiations had broken down. In my opinion, however, this was still only the option of last resort.

Diary

What Henry does not understand is what I tried to get across to him yesterday before he left, and that is that rallying the people as we did November 3 on Cambodia, and then May 8 has now reached the point of no return.

Expectations were raised so high prior to the election and since the election that to go before the American people on television and say that we have been tricked again by the Communists, that we were misled by them, and that now we have to order resumption of the war with no end in sight and no hope, is simply going to be a loser.

In his cable Kissinger raised the idea of his resigning. "I have no illusions about what a break-off in the talks will do to us domestically," he wrote. "If this happens, I will talk to you upon my return about my own responsibility and role."

Diary

I told Col. [Richard] Kennedy [of the NSC staff] that Henry simply has to get out of his head this idea of resigning and all that sort of thing. This is not personal. This is just one of those things where we are in a box and we have to do the very best we can to do what is right and work our way out of it. It will be tough but in the end we are going to win.

On Tuesday morning, December 5, I received a cable from Kissinger. In the event the negotiations broke off, he saw no alternative to stepping up the bombing drastically, and seizing the public relations initiative by using a presidential speech to rally the American people. He suggested in another cable that he insist upon Thieu's demand for the withdrawal of all North Vietnamese troops from South Vietnam as a way of causing Tho to break off the talks. Then he would return to Washington, and I would deliver the television address, in which I would set forward clear and achievable objectives that would essentially add up to a complete American withdrawal in exchange for the return of our POWs. We would then continue bombing until the North Vietnamese agreed to return all our prisoners; he estimated that this would take between six and eight months. "These are issues that the American people can understand. . . . And I am confident that you can rally them once again," he concluded.

I remained unconvinced of the wisdom and the feasibility of this course of action. It was my firm conviction that we must not be responsible—or be portrayed as being responsible—for the breakdown of the talks.

Diary

We must cast this if we possibly can in the light that the North Vietnamese rather than we were responsible for the breakdown in negotiations; and then we should talk in as low-key a manner as possible, and act as strongly as possible without making a big to-do about the fact that we were stepping up the bombing, etc., and in effect resuming the war with no end in sight after raising the expectations of the people primarily as a result of Henry's now-famous "peace is at hand" statement.

As far as the people are concerned, they assume that we have

> been bombing all along which, of course, is a fact, although the level of bombing has been lower than the high level immediately after May 8. Time will tell us tomorrow as to whether or not we have a way out, but I must say that four weeks after the election the situation is certainly not a very happy prospect.

There was clearly a difference of opinion between Kissinger and me regarding the best strategy to pursue. Once again he felt that we had reached a point where the only thing we could do was break off the talks and step up the bombing to make the North Vietnamese agree to a settlement. And once again I believed it was important to keep the talks going for as long as there was even a remote chance that they might yield a settlement.

Lest there be any misunderstanding about the way I wanted to proceed at what was likely to be the most critical and delicate stage of the entire negotiations, I gave Haldeman detailed instructions for a message to be sent to Kissinger outlining the course he should follow in his next meeting with Le Duc Tho:

> We should avoid any appearance of a dramatic break-off by our side. Instead we should treat the situation as a case where the talks have reached an impasse at this time and each side is returning home for consultation. If there is any such dramatic break-off, it should come from their side, not ours. In any event, our side should not appear to be taking the initiative in ending the talks. We should ask for a recess for the purpose of further consultation.
>
> Then when you return to U.S. you should conduct a low-key, non-dramatic briefing to explain the current situation very briefly and to indicate our continuing plan to maintain military operations until a satisfactory settlement is reached. You would indicate that we are ready to resume negotiations at any time when it will be productive to do so.
>
> I have talked to a very few of the hard-liners here in total confidence, and it is their strongly unanimous view that it would be totally wrong for the President to go on TV and explain the details of why the talks have failed.

Kissinger sent his reply through Haldeman. "We had better face the facts of life," he said. "If there is no agreement in the next forty-eight hours, we may be able to pretend that the talks are in recess long enough to permit me to give a briefing after my return. But soon after there will be no way to keep either of the Vietnamese parties from making the stalemate evident. Furthermore, if we resume all-out bombing this will be even more true. Thus in the event of a stalemate we have only two choices: to yield, or to rally American support for one more effort which

I do not believe the North Vietnamese can withstand. If we are to attempt to rally the American people only the President can adequately do that eventually."

On Wednesday, December 6, Kissinger and Le Duc Tho met for six hours. The North Vietnamese position remained essentially unchanged. After the meeting Kissinger sent a cable stating that we had reached a crossroads and must decide what we wanted to do. Again, he refined the choices to two options. Option One involved making one last attempt at reaching a settlement: we would scale down our requirements to the absolute minimum and then present them as our rock-bottom position. There was no reason to think that the North Vietnamese would respond to this approach, and there was a risk involved even if they did, because Thieu was almost certain to reject it and break with us. As Kissinger pointed out, "You must therefore realize that if you authorize me to proceed along the above lines and we succeed, you will face a major confrontation with the G.V.N. Unless you are prepared to undertake such a confrontation you should not instruct me to follow this course."

Option Two involved provoking a break-off of the talks by making some unacceptable demand and resuming massive bombing until the North Vietnamese agreed to return our POWs in exchange for our military withdrawal from Vietnam. Kissinger still felt that if we could keep up the bombing for six months—through the summer of 1973—the North Vietnamese would be forced to accept this straight prisoners-for-withdrawal trade as the basis of a settlement. It was to be presumed that Congress would not cut off funds if it could be shown that the North Vietnamese were not willing to return our POWs. Kissinger said: "If we are willing to pay the domestic and international price, rally the American people, and stay on our course, this option has fewer risks than the other one, given the G.V.N. attitude."

After giving Kissinger's cable the most serious consideration, I responded with a long message containing my step-by-step instructions for the next morning's session:

> After reading all your messages, I am again enormously impressed by the skillful and dedicated way that you're handling a terribly difficult situation.
>
> Before a decision of this importance is made, it is imperative that I talk with you personally. To accomplish this goal, I suggest that you start tomorrow's session by saying that the President has read all of your messages and a full transcript of the conversations to date. He is, frankly, shocked by the total intransigence of the North Vietnamese and particularly by the fact that they have backed off of the commitments they made in October. Then, I want you to go down a list of specific questions on all of the proposals that

are contained in your minimum position contained in your last message, adding to it the specific question about whether they will agree to any language covering the withdrawal of North Vietnamese forces from South Vietnam. I assume that their answers to virtually all of these questions will be negative, but the purpose is to make the record clear once and for all. I then want you to ask them what is their final offer. You will then tell them that you will report the answers they have given to the President directly and then you will contact them as to the time and the conditions for further meetings.

If the negotiations are to be broken off, it must be absolutely clear that they were responsible for breaking off the negotiations rather than me.

I also am firmly convinced that we should not paint ourselves into a corner by saying like "This is our last offer" or "This is our final meeting." Leave a crack of the door open for further discussion.

I realize that you think that if I go on television that I can rally the American people to support an indefinite continuation of the war simply for the purpose of getting our prisoners back. I would agree that this is a possibility at this time. But, that can wear very thin within a matter of weeks, particularly as the propaganda organs—not only from North Vietnam but in this country—begin to hammer away at the fact that we had a much better deal in hand, and then because of Saigon's intransigence, we were unable to complete it.

However your meeting comes out today, if it does not end in a settlement, and of course I know and agree with you that there is a very remote possibility that you will make a breakthrough on the settlement side, we will embark on a very heavy bombing in the North. But we are going to do it without a dramatic television announcement of it. The thing to do here is to take the heat from the Washington establishment, who know the difference, for stepping up the bombing which will occur for a few days, and simply act strongly without escalating publicity about our actions by what we say about them.

On December 6 we gave Dobrynin an urgent message that we would be presenting our rock-bottom position at the next meeting and that failure to make progress would result in termination of the talks. He seemed to be very disturbed, and reiterated that the Soviets had been working continuously on North Vietnam to get them to accept an agreement. A few days later I stepped up the pressure by calling him and telling him that it was definitely in Moscow's interest that the negotiations wind up now because both Moscow and Washington had bigger fish to fry and it was in our mutual interest to eliminate this irritant in order to enable our mutual relations to continue to improve. We also informed the Chinese ambassador in Paris that the situation had become critical, and that before taking "grave steps" we wanted to bring the issues before Chou En-lai, because such action would obviously affect our ability to develop Sino-American relations in the ways that both our governments wanted.

When Kissinger and Le Duc Tho met on December 7, very little was accomplished. There was some progress the next day, however, and by the morning of December 9 there remained only one major unresolved issue, the DMZ. In fact, the North Vietnamese had already agreed to it during the November negotiations. But now Le Duc Tho was insisting on a new and vague clause about both sides "assessing regulations" for movement across the DMZ, which had the effect of calling its integrity into question. I sent a cable to the North Vietnamese, saying that I felt the inclusion of their new clause would make rapid conclusion of the agreement difficult and suggesting that the language they had agreed to at the November 23 session be restored.

On December 9, with only this one remaining item to negotiate, I allowed myself to begin feeling optimistic about the possibility of having an agreement before Christmas. It would be painful if Thieu refused to go along, but there was no question that we had done everything possible to help him and that now we had to look to our own interests and conclude an agreement if the terms were acceptable. I thought back over the roller-coaster events of the past week, which had begun with Kissinger's recommending breaking off the talks and bombing, and which seemed to be ending with a settlement in sight.

Diary

In essence, as Haldeman and I add things up we think what happened here is that Henry went back to Paris firmly convinced that he would quickly, within a matter of two days, reach agreement with the North Vietnamese. As a matter of fact, he told me that the meetings would only last two days—Monday and Tuesday.

The North Vietnamese surprised him by slapping him in the face with a wet fish.

The North wants to humiliate the South and us as well if possible. The South wants to drive the North out of South Vietnam and get us to stick with them until this goal is accomplished. As far as we are concerned, we must bring the war to an end on an honorable basis as quickly as possible.

Expectations have been built so high now that our failing to bring the war to an end would have a terribly depressing effect on this country, and no television speech is ever going to rally the people, despite Henry's feelings based on past performances that this could be the case. As I have pointed out in previous memos, and as I see it now very clearly, the country can be rallied when it's on its back and when you ask it to get up and fight. On the

> other hand, when the country is already very optimistic, to go in and tell them that things are in a hell of a shape doesn't rally them—it simply rallies our opponents and depresses our friends.
>
> For better or for worse, we are on a course now where we have no choice but to make the very best settlement that we can and then to do the best that we can to see that it is enforced.

On December 10 the North Vietnamese replied to my cable, saying that they considered their position on the DMZ to be very reasonable. It seemed clear that they had made a decision to stall the negotiations.

That afternoon I decided to stir things up and remove any doubts about our resolution. I telephoned Dobrynin and told him that I personally did not favor any of the compromise language that Kissinger was suggesting regarding the DMZ. I said that Hanoi should abide by the language it had already agreed to, and I told him bluntly that it was definitely in Moscow's interest to aid the negotiations and get them over with since we both had bigger fish to fry. As it stood, I said, Hanoi's preoccupation with changing the DMZ arrangement could risk concluding an agreement that had now been largely achieved. Dobrynin asked for some time to communicate with Moscow.

At the meeting on Monday, December 11, the North Vietnamese were totally inflexible on the DMZ issue. Kissinger's report characterized their conduct as composed of equal parts of insolence, guile, and stalling.

They were somewhat more forthcoming the next day, but there was still no real progress. That night Kissinger reported that he had come to the conclusion that Hanoi had decided to play for time: Le Duc Tho was purposely trying to prevent either a settlement of the war or a break-off of the talks. It was possible that they simply planned to exploit the increasingly obvious split between us and Saigon, and I could not help thinking it was ironic that the North Vietnamese intransigence at the negotiating table may have been at least in part a result of our unsuccessful attempts to pressure Thieu into accepting an agreement. There was no doubt that the Communists had infiltrated the Saigon government, and that Hanoi was therefore aware of our warnings of congressional fund cutoffs in January. I noted in a diary entry a week later on December 18: "We are right on a tightrope here and I fear that as a result of the infiltration of the South Vietnamese that the North Vietnamese figure that they have us where the hair is short and are going to continue to squeeze us. That is why we had to take our strong action."

Of course it was also possible that the leaders in Hanoi were divided and were still making up their minds about whether to conclude the agreement. In any case, the result was the same: stalemate. Kissinger described the situation in his cable:

> Their consistent pattern is to give us just enough each day to keep us going but nothing decisive which could conclude an agreement. . . .
>
> On the other hand, they wish to ensure that we have no solid pretext for taking tough actions. They keep matters low key to prevent a resumption of bombing.
>
> They could have settled in three hours anytime these past few days if they wanted to, but they have deliberately avoided this. For every one of their semi-concessions they introduce a counterdemand. . . .
>
> The North Vietnamese strategy seems to me to be as follows: they have reduced the issues to a point where settlement can be reached with one exchange of telegrams. I do not think they will send this telegram, however, in the absence of strong pressures.

At the next meeting, on December 13, Le Duc Tho made it clear that he had no intention of reaching an agreement. He was scheduled to return to Hanoi for consultations the next day, so Kissinger suggested that the talks be recessed and no more meetings be held until after Christmas. That night I noted, "As I had somewhat anticipated, this day, December 13, is really one of the toughest days we have had during the administration."

Kissinger and I completely agreed on the cynicism and perfidy of the North Vietnamese. He even thought that Le Duc Tho's occasional fainting spells during the talks had been contrivances aimed at gaining a negotiating advantage by eliciting sympathy for him. Gritting his teeth and clenching his fists, Kissinger said, "They're just a bunch of shits. Tawdry, filthy shits. They make the Russians look good, compared to the way the Russians make the Chinese look good when it comes to negotiating in a responsible and decent way!"

I had reluctantly decided that we had now reached the point where only the strongest action would have any effect in convincing Hanoi that negotiating a fair settlement with us was a better option for them than continuing the war. Kissinger and I agreed that this meant stepping up the bombing. The only question was how much bombing would be needed to force Hanoi to settle. Kissinger recommended reseeding the mines of Haiphong Harbor, resuming full-scale bombing south of the 20th parallel, and intensifying bombing in southern Laos. My intuition was that something far more extensive was required. When I checked and found that the area south of the 20th parallel was largely rice paddies and jungle, I told Kissinger, "We'll take the same heat for big blows as for little blows. If we renew the bombing, it will have to be something new, and that means we will have to make the big decision to hit Hanoi and Haiphong with B-52s. Anything less will only make the enemy contemptuous."

Kissinger pointed out that Hanoi and Haiphong were heavily defended with Soviet surface-to-air (SAM) missiles. If we attacked them, we would have to be prepared for new losses and casualties and POWs. "I know," I said, "but if we're convinced that this is the right thing to do, then we will have to do it right."

On December 14 I issued an order, to become effective three days hence, for the reseeding of the mines in Haiphong Harbor, for resumed aerial reconnaissance, and for B-52 strikes against military targets in the Hanoi-Haiphong complex. The bombing plan included sixteen major transportation, power, and Radio Hanoi transmitter targets in Hanoi, as well as six communications command and control targets in the outlying area. There were thirteen targets in the Haiphong area, including shipyards and docks. When the first plans came in for the bombing, I was appalled to find that the planes had to be borrowed from different commands, involving complicated logistics and large amounts of red tape. The day after the bombing began, I think I shook Admiral Moorer when I called him and said, "I don't want any more of this crap about the fact that we couldn't hit this target or that one. This is your chance to use military power effectively to win this war, and if you don't, I'll consider you responsible." I stressed that we must hit and hit hard or there was no point in doing it at all. If the enemy detected any reticence in our actions, they would discount the whole exercise.

The order to renew bombing the week before Christmas was the most difficult decision I made during the entire war; at the same time, however, it was also one of the most clear-cut and necessary ones.

Diary

Henry talked rather emotionally about the fact that this was a very courageous decision, but I pointed out to him that there was no other choice—that we were going to be here for four years and that even though we made a good, cheap peace now, to have it break within a matter of a year or two would leave us with nothing to be proud of and beyond that would leave us with terrible choices—much worse choices—later than we would have at the present time. We are going to face up to the music at this time with the hope that this will gain their attention and keep them from reacting to us later.

We decided that Kissinger would conduct a public briefing on the state of the negotiations. It was vitally important that we lay responsibility for the current impasse where it belonged—squarely on the North Vietnamese. I met with him several times to review what he would say; I also dictated two long memoranda covering the points I considered it important for him to make. I felt that we had to get across that the North Vietnamese had agreed to a settlement, then reneged on a number of points, and now were refusing to negotiate seriously. I also said that Kissinger should criticize Thieu for insisting on total victory when what we wanted was a just peace that both sides would be able to keep and live with.

In the early morning hours of Sunday, December 17, our planes reseeded the mines in Haiphong Harbor. Within twenty-four hours 129 B-52s took part in bombing raids over North Vietnam.

Diary

The tough decision has now been made and is under way with regard to the bombing around Haiphong. I have just learned about one B-52 shot down. Henry said they expected as many as three. Of course, there are two more waves to go, but they expect on the second and third waves the amount of SAM opposition to be down or at least suppressed. At least, we can only pray that that will be the case and hope that it is the case.

Two more B-52s were shot down during the day.

Diary

I suppose all the decisions are hard—the May 8 one in retrospect may have been the most difficult one, although Cambodia was just as difficult in its way, and November 3 was difficult. But this one was heartrending due to the fact that everything was moving along in the right direction. And, also, because there is such great uncertainty as to what reaction there will be as a result of what we have done.

In any event, the decision is made and we cannot turn back. Henry has been up and down, understandably. For example, this morning he seems to be down more than up. I have called Moorer to be sure to stiffen his back with regard to the need to follow through on these attacks. I suppose that we may be pressing him too hard, but I fear that the Air Force and the Navy

> may in carrying out orders have been too cautious at times in the past, and that our political objectives have not been achieved because of too much caution on the military side. We simply have to take losses if we are going to accomplish our objectives.
>
> I remember Churchill's admonition in his book on World War I, that one can have a policy of audacity or one can follow a policy of caution, but it is disastrous to try to follow a policy of audacity and caution at the same time. It must be one or the other. We have now gone down the audacious line and we must continue until we get some sort of a break.

Many people could not understand why I did not "go public" with the reasons for the December bombing. As I have already indicated, I did not feel that the American people were ready to be rallied at this time as they had been on November 3 and on May 8. But more important, I was convinced that any public statements on my part would have been directly counterproductive to the possibility of resumed negotiations. If I had announced that we were resuming bombing for the purpose of forcing the North Vietnamese to negotiate, their national pride and their ideological fanaticism would never have allowed them to accept the international loss of face involved in caving to such an ultimatum. So I did it with the minimum amount of rhetoric and publicity, and it succeeded exactly as I had intended. Our brief but massive use of force got the message through to Hanoi while still allowing them to back off their intransigent position without having to acknowledge that they were doing so because of military pressure from us.

On the morning of December 18, in a message to the North Vietnamese in Paris, we said that after having carefully reviewed the record of the recent negotiations, we had decided that they were deliberately and frivolously delaying the talks. We proposed returning to the text of the agreement as it had stood after the November 23 session, with the addition of one or two subsequently negotiated changes. On this basis we would be prepared to meet again at any time after December 26 to conclude an agreement.

I decided that we would also make every possible effort to convince Thieu that in the event the North Vietnamese agreed to resume negotiations, it was imperative that he join us in offering reasonable terms Hanoi would be willing to accept. We considered Agnew, Laird, and Connally for this unenviable job, but finally I said, "Haig is still the man to carry the message to Garcia."

Haig arrived in Saigon on December 19, carrying the strongest letter I had yet written to Thieu. In it I stated: "General Haig's mission now represents my final effort to point out to you the necessity for joint action and to convey my irrevocable intention to proceed, preferably with your cooperation but, if necessary, alone. . . . I have asked General Haig to obtain your answer to this absolutely final offer on my part for us to work together in seeking a settlement along the lines I have approved or to go our separate ways." Haig told Thieu that I had dictated the letter personally and that no one else in our government had seen it. After Thieu had read the letter through twice, he looked up and said that it was obvious that he was not being asked to sign an agreement for peace but rather an agreement for continued American support. Haig replied that as a soldier and as someone completely familiar with Communist treachery, he agreed with Thieu's assessment.

Thieu seemed almost desperate. He argued that the cease-fire would not last more than three months: then, when the last American had gone, the Communists would resume their guerrilla warfare. But this time they would fight with knives and bayonets, being careful not to do anything sufficient to justify American retaliation. In this way my guarantees to enforce the agreement would never be put to the test, and the Communists would have a free hand against him and his government.

After this meeting Thieu leaked word to reporters that we had tried to force him to accept an ultimatum and that he had refused. I was shocked when I learned this, and I felt we would now be justified in breaking with him and making a separate peace with Hanoi. But I was still reluctant to allow our annoyance with him to lead us to do anything that might bring about Communist domination of South Vietnam.

December 20 was the third day of heavy air strikes over North Vietnam. Ninety B-52s flew three waves of attacks against eleven targets. Six planes were lost. On December 21 there were thirty B-52 sorties flown against three new targets. Two planes were lost.

My major concern during the first week of bombing was not the sharp wave of domestic and international criticism, which I had expected, but the high losses of B-52s. I noted on December 23, "I raised holy hell about the fact that they kept going over the same targets at the same time. I was, therefore, not surprised, although deeply disappointed, when we lost five planes on the second or third day. Finally, we got the military to change their minds." The Pentagon began scheduling the strikes at different times and on different routes, thus denying the enemy the knowledge of when and where the strikes would take place and thereby reducing their ability to shoot down our planes.

On December 22 we sent a message to the North Vietnamese requesting a meeting for January 3. If they accepted, we offered to stop the bombing north of the 20th parallel on December 31 and suspend it for the duration of the meeting.

The media reaction to the December bombing was predictable. The Washington *Post* editorialized that it caused millions of Americans "to cringe in shame and to wonder at their President's very sanity." Joseph Kraft called it an action "of senseless terror which stains the good name of America." James Reston called it "war by tantrum," and Anthony Lewis charged that I was acting "like a maddened tyrant." In Congress there were similarly critical outbursts from members of both parties. Republican Senator William Saxbe of Ohio said that "President Nixon . . . appears to have left his senses on this issue." And Mike Mansfield said that it was a "stone-age tactic."

> *Diary*
>
> On the negative side, the columnists and the media broke down about the way they had during the election and on all the Vietnam decisions previously.
>
> The record of the liberal left media on Vietnam is perhaps one of the most disgraceful in the whole history of communications in this country. I am not referring to the honest pacifists who have been against the war from the beginning, but to those in the media who simply cannot bear the thought of this administration under my leadership bringing off the peace on an honorable basis which they have so long predicted would be impossible.
>
> The election was a terrible blow to them and this is their first opportunity to recover from the election and to strike back.

It was especially gratifying to receive calls of support from Nelson Rockefeller and Ronald Reagan. Senator James Buckley also stood behind me, as did Howard Baker, Bob Taft, and Chuck Percy. One of my strongest supporters was John Connally, who called daily to report some new and positive sampling of public opinion.

As the criticism outside mounted, the pressure inside the White House became intense. I could feel the tension in the people I passed and greeted as I walked back and forth to the EOB. I knew how sincerely troubled many of them were because of the bombing; I understood how difficult the bombing made it for many of them to face their friends and even their families during what should have been a happy holiday season.

Pat and I spent Christmas at Key Biscayne. It was the first Christmas we had been alone without the girls. Tricia and Ed were in Europe traveling, and Julie was also there to be with David. Pat and I naturally urged them to go, but I think we were both depressed to find how empty the house seemed without them. Casting a dark shadow over everything was the knowledge that if the bombing did not succeed in forcing the North Vietnamese back to the negotiating table, there was no way of knowing how—or whether—the Vietnam war would end. I made several diary entries during this holiday period.

Diary

This is December 24, 1972—Key Biscayne—4 A.M.

The main thought that occurred to me at this early hour of the morning the day before Christmas, in addition to the overriding concern with regard to bringing the war to an end, is that I must get away from the thought of considering the office at any time a burden. I actually do not consider it a burden, an agony, etc., as did Eisenhower and also to a certain extent Johnson. As a matter of fact, I think the term glorious burden is the best description.

On this day before Christmas it is God's great gift to me to have the opportunity to exert leadership, not only for America but on the world scene, because of the size of the mandate and also the strength of the country.

In a sense, of course, this is not true because immediately after World War II our power was greater because of the monopoly of the bomb and the weakness of Europe and Japan as well as the weakness of China and Russia. But then, there were other world leaders on the scene. Today, except for Chiang Kai-shek most of the World War II greats are gone. This, on the one hand, imposes an enormous responsibility but, of course, at the same time the greatest opportunity an individual could have.

From this day forward I am going to look upon it that way and rise to the challenge with as much excitement, energy, enthusiasm, and, wherever possible, real joy that I can muster.

God's help will be required as will the help of loyal people on the staff and the family.

A new group of Nixon loyalists, of course, is an urgent necessity, but this really begins a new period and this tape concludes with that thought—a period of always reminding myself of the glorious burden of the presidency.

At 6 P.M. Saigon time on December 24 a twenty-four-hour Christmas truce I had approved began in Vietnam. No planes flew. No bombs were dropped. For a day we were at peace.

On Christmas Day I made phone calls to many of our long-time friends and supporters across the country.

Diary

All in all, the Christmas calls didn't produce anything important or different, except not too much talk about the bombing. My guess is that they were all concerned about the media handling of it. Reagan mentioned that and said CBS under World War II circumstances would have been perhaps charged with treason.

Martha Mitchell sounded very up when I called her, which is encouraging because John Mitchell has gone through hell with her and I am glad that she is finally recovering. Perhaps the two weeks or so down here will make a great difference in getting all of them back on the track in a way that John can continue to be effective politically because he is one of the wisest men, one of the strongest men, we have on our whole team.

Henry called to wish us a Merry Christmas but obviously needed a little cheering up, which I was totally able to do because I am confident we are doing the right thing.

It is inevitable that not only the President but the First Lady become more and more lonely individuals in a sense who have to depend on fewer and fewer people who can give them a lift when they need it, even though ironically there are millions more who know them and who would help if they could just be given the chance to do so. It is a question not of too many friends but really too few—one of the inevitable consequences of this position.

As this Christmas Day ends I am thankful for Manolo and Fina, for the wonderful Filipinos and the staff, for Bebe, for Julie and Tricia, Pat, for all of those who basically are our family at a time that the girls are so far away.

Harry Truman died on the day after Christmas. According to his wishes, he lay in state at the Truman Library in Independence, Missouri. On December 27 Pat and I flew there to pay our respects to him and to call on Mrs. Truman.

There was considerable pressure from some of the staff to continue the Christmas truce for a few more days. But I disagreed completely. In fact, I personally ordered one of the biggest bombing raids for

December 26: 116 B-52 sorties were flown against targets in the Hanoi-Haiphong area.

That afternoon the North Vietnamese sent the first signal that they had had enough. We received a message from them condemning what they called "extermination bombing," but they did not require that the bombing be stopped as a precondition to their agreeing to another meeting, which they proposed for January 8 in Paris. We replied that we would like the technical talks to begin on January 2 if the Kissinger meeting was to be delayed until January 8. We offered to stop the bombing above the 20th parallel once the arrangements for the meeting had been completed and had been publicly announced. On December 28 the North Vietnamese gave in and confirmed the January 2 and January 8 dates.

At 7 P.M. Washington time on December 29 bombing above the 20th parallel was suspended. The next morning we announced that the Paris negotiations would be resumed and that Kissinger would meet with Le Duc Tho on January 8.

Diary

The real question is whether the announcement today will be interpreted in the public mind as having been the result of a policy that worked. Of course, it will not be so interpreted by our opponents in the media and the Congress.

I have gone over this with Chuck Colson and he in turn with John Scali [Special Consultant to the President]. They both recognize that much of the media will try to say, "Why was the bombing necessary?" or might even try to say we were forced back to the table because of the world outcry and all that sort of thing.

Henry always looks at it in terms of the merits, and on the merits we know that what this is is a very stunning capitulation by the enemy to our terms.

Most of the TV reporters and the next morning's newspapers put the emphasis on the bombing halt rather than the resumption of talks, and most of them indicated that it was not clear whether the return to negotiations was the result of the bombing, or whether the bombing halt was the result of the enemy's agreement to return to negotiations. It was frustrating not to be able to set them straight. As I said to Colson, "We'll just have to trust to the good judgment of the people to see it. Certainly the press isn't going to make the point for us."

Pat and I spent New Year's Eve at Camp David. I watched the Redskins beat the Cowboys on television, 26 to 3. Just before midnight I looked back over the day and then ahead to the coming year.

> *Diary*
>
> I let all the staff off today and had Manolo cook some eggs and bacon [for dinner]. I had about half a martini and then some white wine, bacon and eggs.
>
> As the year 1972 ends I have much to be grateful for—China, Russia, May 8, the election victory, and, of course, while the end of the year was somewhat marred by the need to bomb Hanoi-Haiphong, that decision, I think, can make the next four years much more successful than they otherwise might have been.
>
> 1973 will be a better year.

On January 2 I called Lyndon Johnson at his ranch in Texas. We shared a few reminiscences of Harry Truman, and he said that he did not know whether he would be able to attend the memorial service in Washington because he had experienced severe heart pains after attending the recent Texas-Alabama football game and his doctor had told him not to travel.

The conversation turned to Vietnam, and Johnson said, "I know what torture you're going through over the war, and I want you to know that I'm praying for you every day."

I told him, "I know that you tried to do the right thing when you were here, and that is what I am trying to do as well."

We continued to play the Soviet and Chinese strategies for whatever they might turn out to be worth. Kissinger went to see Dobrynin and told him that the things the Soviets wanted—a Mideast settlement, a European security conference, nuclear weapons agreements—would have to stay on the back burner until Vietnam was settled. And I wrote a letter to Chou En-lai, saying that the Vietnam war impeded the kind of further progress that would benefit both our countries.

On January 2, 1973, the day before Congress officially reconvened, the House Democratic Caucus voted 154 to 75 to cut off all funds for Indochina military operations as soon as arrangements were made for the safe withdrawal of U.S. troops and the return of our POWs. Two days later Teddy Kennedy proposed a similar resolution to the Senate Democratic Caucus, where it passed 36 to 12. The atmosphere of the congressional leadership breakfast at the White House the next morning was tense. At the end I made a short speech about my reasons for the bombing and why I was sure it was the only way to get a settlement. I concluded, "Gentlemen, I will take the responsibility if these negotiations fail. If they succeed, then we will all succeed."

I was not surprised at the conduct of the Democratic liberals. Ever since the election I had virtually written off any hope of receiving support or cooperation from them. I could see that they were going to try to use the Vietnam issue to pull themselves together after the McGovern debacle. Their strategy seemed obvious: if we got an agreement, they would say that it was because they had pressured me to stop the bombing and return to the negotiating table; if we failed to get an agreement, they would insist on the military withdrawal that most of them had favored all along.

On January 6, before he left for Paris, Kissinger and I met at Camp David to discuss the negotiating strategy he should follow. During the last round of negotiations in December he had described the two options from which we had to choose. Under Option One we would agree to an immediate settlement on the best terms we could negotiate. Under Option Two we would break with Thieu and continue the bombing until the North Vietnamese agreed to return our POWs in exchange for our complete withdrawal.

I was determined that this round of negotiations would produce an agreement, and I strongly conveyed my sentiments to Kissinger.

Diary

Adding it all up I put it to Henry quite directly that even if we could go back to the October 8 agreement that we should take it, having in mind the fact that there will be a lot of details that will have been ironed out so that we can claim some improvement over that agreement. I told him that a poor settlement on Option One was better for us than Option Two at its best would be.

He has finally come around to that point of view, although he believes that both from the standpoint of South Vietnam and perhaps our own standpoint in the long term, we might be better off with Option Two. I think he overlooks the fact that as far as our situation here is concerned, the war-weariness has reached the point that Option Two is just too much for us to carry on.

The war continues to take too much of our attention from other international issues, such as the Mideast, and it also has a detrimental effect on our international relations, not only with the Soviet and the Chinese but even with our allies.

As I told him goodbye at the door of Birch Lodge, I said, "Well, one way or another, this is it!" That night I tried to list all the pluses and minuses to see if I could find some clue to the way things would turn out.

Diary

The first day may tell us a great deal. Certainly as of the end of last week there was a good chance that the enemy was coming back to negotiate a settlement. The international support they have had and the support from the Democrats in Congress may cool them off and convince them that they can hang on longer.

Henry, of course, is going to continue to play the hard line, indicating that I might resort to resumption of the bombing in the Hanoi area, even though I have told him that as far as our internal planning is concerned we cannot consider this to be a viable option.

He feels that another card we have is the threat to withdraw the agreement altogether. He believes that Hanoi wants an agreement now for the reason that this gives them some standing in the South, whereas an American bug-out ironically would still leave them with the necessity of winning militarily in the South.

Some minor straws in the wind are that the technical talks have made some progress this week on the four easier issues, with the four tougher ones left for next week. Also, the fact that the North Vietnamese have launched offensives in the South may indicate that they are trying to grab territory and villages, etc., prior to the time that a cease-fire takes place.

Another plus item is that the South Vietnamese seem to be coming more into line. Our intelligence indicates that Thieu is telling visitors that it is not a peace agreement that he is going to get, but a commitment from the United States to continue to protect South Vietnam in the event such an agreement is broken. This, of course, is exactly the line I gave him in my letter which Haig delivered to him.

In the midst of the tense days of the December bombing and the furore it provoked, new Watergate problems began to surface. On December 8 Howard Hunt's wife was killed in a plane crash; since then Hunt had apparently been disconsolate and on the verge of a breakdown. Now that Hunt was about to face a jail term, Colson began to worry about him.

On the White House staff there were the first signs of finger-pointing, tentative and without evidence. I could sense that people were getting unsettled and worried. I dictated in my diary on January 3.

Diary

One disturbing note was Haldeman's comment to the effect that Colson may have been aware of the Watergate business. I am not sure actually that he was. Haldeman's point was that Colson was insisting on getting information with regard to attempts of the Democrats to disrupt our convention, etc. Of course, Colson may have been insisting on such information but he may not have been aware of what means were being used to obtain this information. I simply can't believe, based on my conversations with Colson, that he would have been so stupid as to think we could get such information through attempting to bug the other side.

I made another note about this problem three days later, on Saturday, January 6.

Diary

Colson told me on Friday that he had tried to do everything he could to keep Hunt in line from turning state's evidence. After what happened to Hunt's wife, etc., I think we have a very good case for showing some clemency.

It was Colson's view apparently that either Haldeman or Ehrlichman or both might have been more deeply involved than has been indicated. Of course, it is all hearsay. Colson's point is that Magruder is a name-dropper and that Magruder may have mentioned the names of Haldeman and Ehrlichman in telling the Watergate people to get information. Apparently, according to Colson, too, some of the meetings took place in Mitchell's office at the Justice Department. This would seem hard for me to believe but then again during the campaign people are not as rational or responsible as they normally would be. This, I know, must be a great burden for Haldeman and Ehrlichman during this past tough week and I could see that something was eating them without knowing what.

I was concerned about these speculations, but I saw them at least in part as manifestations of the routine staff animosities that had long existed between Colson and Mitchell and Colson and Ehrlichman.

It now seems clear that I knew Colson was sending messages of reassurance to Hunt through his lawyer—messages that Hunt took to be signals of eventual clemency. I did not believe that any commitments had been made. I cannot even rule out the possibility that I knew similar reassurance was being given the other defendants. I certainly do not remember it, but where Watergate is concerned I have learned not to be categorical. In any event, I was relieved when, in early January, Hunt and the others pleaded guilty. I thought this would spare us the difficulties of a noisy public trial and all the distraction that would produce at such a critical time.

On Monday, January 8, Kissinger met with Le Duc Tho for four and a half hours. Nothing was accomplished, but in Kissinger's report to me that night he pointed out that it would probably not be realistic to expect the Communists to give in or give up on the first day back after the bombing. I was naturally disappointed, but there was nothing to do but wait and hope. That night I recorded some reflections on the eve of my sixtieth birthday.

> *Diary*
>
> All in all, as the day is finished I look back over the past ten years and realize how life can seem to be at an end as it appeared to be on January 9, 1963, and then has turned completely around by January 9, 1973. It all has to do with spirit, as I emphasized to Colson, who is only forty-one years of age. He was obviously depressed tonight, probably because of the Hunt matter, etc., but I think I lifted him a bit by what we said.
>
> We will get a report from Kissinger today which should tell us one way or another whether there is going to be any breakthrough in the talks.
>
> I noted in the paper this morning that they made a great point out of the fact that the protocol was icy when Henry arrived. This does not bother me because so far when they have had a warm reaction to Henry's arrival, they make no progress. Perhaps having it exactly the opposite may bring a different result.

About noon on January 9 Haldeman came into the Oval Office with a cable from Kissinger.

"What happened?" I asked.

"I think you should read this for yourself, Mr. President," he said solemnly.

I took the paper, put on my glasses, and began to read: "We celebrated the President's birthday today by making a major breakthrough in the negotiations. In sum, we settled all the outstanding questions in the text of the agreement."

Kissinger warned against undue optimism: "The Vietnamese have broken our heart several times before, and we just cannot assume success until everything is pinned down, but the mood and the businesslike approach was as close to October as we have seen since October." He concluded, "What has brought us to this point is the President's firmness and the North Vietnamese belief that he will not be affected by either congressional or public pressures. Le Duc Tho has repeatedly made these points to me. So it is essential that we keep our fierce posture during the coming days. The slightest hint of eagerness could prove suicidal."

I immediately dictated my reply:

> I greatly appreciated your birthday greetings and your report. I totally agree with the need to maintain absolutely "eyes only" secrecy on developments until we have everything completely nailed down. . . .
>
> You should continue a tough posture and, above all, not let the other side filibuster. If the other side stays on this track and doesn't go downhill tomorrow, what you have done today is the best birthday present I have had in sixty years.

The momentum continued through the next session, and Kissinger reported that at the current rate of progress the agreement should be concluded within three or four days.

On January 11 Kissinger cabled, "We finished the complete text of the agreement, including the provisions for signature." It was nine days short of four years since I had entered the White House and inherited the task of ending the Vietnam war.

When the announcement was made that Kissinger was going to fly directly to Key Biscayne from Paris in order to report to me on the progress of his meetings with the North Vietnamese, there was widespread speculation that an agreement had been concluded. In a brief statement at the airport before leaving Paris, Kissinger flashed one of his enigmatic, owlish smiles and said the talks had been "useful."

He arrived in Key Biscayne several hours later, and we talked until after 2 A.M. He described all the tension and drama of the intricate negotiations. Even though he was tired from the talks and the long flight, he still displayed his characteristic thoroughness and enthusiasm. In the early hours of the following morning I recorded some notes about the conclusion of our meeting.

> *Diary*
>
> After we met, I walked out to the car with him and I told him that the country was indebted to him for what he had done. It is not really a comfortable feeling for me to praise people so openly. I prefer to do it a little bit more discreetly. I recall this was one of Eisenhower's characteristics as well. On the other hand, Henry expects it, and it was good that I did so. He, in turn, re-

sponded that without my having the, as he put it, courage to make the difficult decision of December 18, we would not be where we are today.

On January 15 at ten o'clock in the morning all bombing and mining of North Vietnam were stopped for an indefinite period, and we made a public announcement of our actions. The bombing had done its job; it had been successful, and now it could be ended. It was good news for all of us.

Diary

I had Henry call Pat and give her a rundown on affairs shortly after the announcement. Henry said that the four years he had known Mrs. Nixon he had never heard her sound so elated—that she was enormously pleased.

Julie just wanted to call. She was bubbly and upbeat and she and her mother, who was apparently in the room with her, were very proud of what had happened. I began to answer by indicating that the stopping of the bombing I suppose was pretty popular and all that sort of thing. She says, no, that isn't what she meant. She and her mother were proud of the fact that I had gone ahead and done what was right.

I had heard that Mike Mansfield was telling people how restrained and responsible the Senate had been during the past week of negotiations, and I noted in my diary, "It is interesting to note that Mansfield had reacted as he had. Of course, they cut Henry's legs off before he ever went."

There was also a discordant note to record that same day.

Diary

It is ironic that the day the news came out stopping the bombing of North Vietnam, the Watergate Four plead guilty. When I saw the headlines in the *Times*—spies plead guilty in Watergate—I realized what the press would have done if they had not had another story that would override it.

There is a new wrinkle to this which is rather curious. Colson told me that the problem in Hunt's case and with the case generally was that a confession might lead to Haldeman and even Ehrlichman. On the other hand, Haldeman told me that what the *Time* magazine and New York *Times*'s exposés were going to say was that the line ran from Liddy to Colson to Mitchell. Only an ultimatum served on the *Times* that if they used this they would be subject to a libel suit with malice being proved kept them from using that particular item.

I frankly am at a loss to know how it happened and it is probably just as well, but my guess is that Colson was not as aware of it as Haldeman et al. thought he was.

Whether Haldeman was aware of it, I simply don't know, although I think he would be intelligent enough to have stayed a mile away from such stupid activity.

Obviously the judge is going to throw the book at them and this will present quite a problem when it comes to a pardon. It is interesting to note that funds for providing income for them are coming from a Cuban committee here in Florida and it is also interesting to note that just this week Teddy Kennedy comes out with an article indicating that we should renew relations with Castro. Certainly these men would not have taken such enormous risks unless they felt deeply that the McGovernites et al. and the Democrats generally represented a threat to institutions and ideas they deeply believed in.

We had reached agreement on terms with the North Vietnamese but we still had to persuade Thieu to join us in signing the agreement. Thieu had made good use of the time since October and was in a considerably stronger position vis-à-vis the Communists than he had been then. I had always believed that his common sense and patriotism—if not his instinct for survival—would make him come along when we reached the absolute deadline for concluding an agreement before Congress intervened and took the conduct of the war out of my hands. Now we were at that point, and my estimation of Thieu would be put to the test. Soon after Kissinger had returned to Washington on January 14, Haig left for Saigon.

On the morning of January 16 he met with Thieu and handed him a letter from me. In it I said that I had irrevocably decided to initial the agreement on January 23 and sign it on January 27. "I will do so," I wrote, "if necessary, alone." I continued:

> In that case I shall have to explain publicly that your government obstructs peace. The result will be an inevitable and immediate termination of U.S. economic and military assistance which cannot be forestalled by a change of personnel in your government. I hope, however, that after all our two countries have shared and suffered together in conflict, we will stay together to preserve peace and reap its benefits.
>
> To this end I want to repeat to you the assurances that I have already conveyed. At the time of signing the agreement I will make emphatically clear that the United States recognizes your government as the only legal govern-

> ment of South Vietnam; that we do not recognize the right of any foreign troops to be present on South Vietnamese territory; and that we will react strongly in the event the agreement is violated. Finally, I want to emphasize my continued commitment to the freedom and progress of the Republic of Vietnam. It is my firm intention to continue full economic and military aid.

With this letter and this guarantee I did not feel that I could do any more. Up to this point I had not felt that I could do any less. The decision now lay with Thieu.

> *Diary*
>
> Thieu's choice is simply whether he wants to commit suicide or go along with a settlement that could save his country as well as himself. The question, as he put it to his National Security Council, was whether he should be a hero now by turning down the settlement, or a statesman that would save his country later. This is exactly the case. I just told Henry, however, that I doubted if he would be a hero if he turned down the settlement, because the South Vietnamese are losing upward of 250 to 300 killed in action every week, and I imagine they are pretty tired of the war too and would like to have a cease-fire.

It appeared that, true to form to the end, Thieu was going to play it right down to the wire.

In their second meeting on January 17 Haig and Thieu had a brief and emotional encounter during which Thieu gave him a sealed letter addressed to me. Haig returned to the embassy and read the letter. It was, as Haig described it, brittle and uncompromising. I immediately sent a letter in return challenging Thieu's points one by one and confronting him with an inescapable conclusion: "We have only one decision before us: whether or not to continue in peacetime the close partnership that has served us so well in war."

On January 18 it was jointly announced in Washingon and Hanoi that the Paris negotiations would resume on January 23 "for the purpose of completing the text of an agreement." Peace fever broke out everywhere, and reporters flatly stated, with an assurance they could not know was justified, that a settlement was in the bag.

As we anxiously awaited further word from Saigon, Bunker cabled that he had not been able to get an appointment with Thieu because he was engaged in all-day religious ceremonies connected with his daughter's marriage. Bunker and Haig both felt that Thieu was stalling simply in order to be able to say that he had done all he could. They felt he saw my inauguration on January 20 as his last deadline.

In the meantime Haig had traveled to Bangkok and Seoul. The Thai leaders and President Park had no confidence that the North Vietnamese intended to abide by the agreement. But they understood the political realities of the American scene, and they agreed to support the settlement publicly and privately to urge Thieu to sign it.

After one last stab at resistance and another series of letters between us, Thieu finally decided to accept the agreement. Looking across his desk at Bunker, he said, "I have done my best. I have done all that I can do for my country." Even though his conduct had been almost unbearably frustrating, I had to admire his spirit.

Now we had to wait while the final arrangements were made and until the North Vietnamese locked themselves into signing the agreement by announcing it publicly in Hanoi.

On January 20 I was sworn in for my second term as the thirty-seventh President of the United States. I had hoped that my second inauguration would take place in peacetime. But the inevitable delays, added to the dangers of becoming committed publicly to any specific date, pushed the peace agreement into the post-inaugural period. Instead of being able to describe in my inaugural address the blessings of a peace achieved, I could only describe a peace that was near achievement and talk about the ways we could try to make it more than just an interlude between wars.

I am sure that many who heard my words on that cold January afternoon thought I was engaging in conventional inaugural rhetoric when I said, "We have the chance today to do more than ever before in our history to make life better in America—to ensure better education, better health, better housing, better transportation, a cleaner environment—to restore respect for law, to make our communities more livable—and to ensure the God-given right of every American to full and equal opportunity." But I fully believed that, backed by my November mandate and based on my determination to proceed despite the opposition or the political cost, we could actually succeed during my second term in bringing America closer than ever before in history to the attainment of these goals.

This would be my last inaugural address, and I had decided to use it in order to impart a sense of the inspirational tone that I wanted to give to my second term.

I concluded, "We shall answer to God, to history, and to our conscience for the way in which we use these years. As I stand in this place, so hallowed by history, I think of others who have stood here before me. I think of the dreams they had for America and I think of how each recognized that he needed help far beyond himself in order to make those dreams come true. Today I ask your prayers that in the years ahead I may have God's help in making decisions that are right for America, and I pray for your help so that together we may be worthy of our challenge. . . . Let us go forward from here confident in hope, strong in our faith in one another, sustained by our faith in God who created us, and striving always to serve His purpose."

That night, before leaving for the inaugural balls, I went to the Lincoln Sitting Room and recorded some memories and impressions, beginning with inaugural concerts at the Kennedy Center the night before.

Diary

When Mike Curb stepped up at the end of the performance and said that the President had done more to bring peace in the world than anybody else, I thought we would get a few boos. Interestingly enough, he got a pretty good cheer for it, which allayed one of the fears I had as we went to these inaugurals, having read earlier that eleven of Eugene Ormandy's orchestra members requested the right not to come, and he had put his foot down and told them to come. When Steve Bull informed him that I would not be coming down to the platform because it simply couldn't be worked out from a logistic standpoint, Ormandy said that he would have liked to have me come to the stage and stand there beside him "just to show those left-wing sons of bitches." What a man he is.

Inaugural morning, after getting up, I ran 500 steps in place. It left me a little breathless, but I thought it was a good idea to be in as good shape as I could for the ceremonies to take place later in the day.

Before going downstairs, I stepped into the Lincoln Bedroom in the spot where the Emancipation Proclamation was and where I understood Lincoln's desk was located and bowed my head for a moment, and prayed that I might be able to give the country some lift, some inspiration, and some leadership in the rather brief inaugural that I had prepared.

The ride down to the Capitol gave us some indication of what we could expect later in the way of demonstrators. Little clusters of them had gotten into strategic places along the route. Pat and the others didn't hear them, but they were yelling "f–u–c–k," etc., and were a pretty vicious lot.

The inauguration went on schedule—perhaps the best of any that I have seen. The public address system was superb, no hecklers could be heard, although way in the background I think there were a few who let out a few obscenities as I began to speak and then subsided or probably somebody subsided them.

Mrs. Agnew kissed Agnew—Pat did not kiss me. I am rather glad she didn't. I sometimes think these displays of affection are very much in place, as was the case election night. Other times, I don't think they quite fit and on this occasion I didn't really think it quite fit.

[At the inaugural luncheon in the Capitol] I could feel somewhat of a chill. I was thinking how much worse it would have been if we hadn't had the recent developments this week with regard to the possible settlement in Paris. It came not far ahead of the sheriff, and not far enough, I am sure, to avoid some jolt in the polls.

I don't give one damn what the polls say insofar as affecting my decisions. I only care about them because they may affect my ability to lead, since politicians do pay attention to them.

I stood up all of the way through the inaugural parade. Pat got up about a third of the way down and when the demonstrators began to throw eggs and debris, the Secret Service asked her to sit down, and she refused. She was absolutely right. There was one incident where a demonstrator broke out and started to charge the car. The Secret Service agents were on top of him like lightning and brought him down with a tackle.

My feeling is that this may well be the last of the inaugural balls. I just can't imagine that people pay all that money to stand in that huge mob. One girl from Massachusetts was practically hysterical crying, "I love and respect you so much!" Even though we were leaving, I danced with her for a few minutes. Pat, who notices those things a little more than I do, said that the girl was dressed in a rather plain gown, one that perhaps she had made herself, and it had probably cost her a great deal to come. In any event, the dancing was the great hit of the evening. People who came in afterward said the girls and even some of the boys were crying because we had mixed with them so much.

It is obvious that we have to get across more of what Rossiter has called "affability." The staff just hasn't been able to get it across and so I am going to have to do all of these things publicly which demonstrates that. On the other hand, you can't overplay it.

Time passed slowly waiting for January 23 and the announcement of the Vietnam settlement. In the early evening of January 22, while our waiting had yet to be rewarded, Lyndon Johnson died.

Diary

With his death there will be, I trust, the same reappraisal of his place in history as was the case of Truman on his death, although, of course, it will not be nearly as fulsome because not enough years have passed and because there are too many current hatreds which divide the country.

The sadness in Johnson's case is that he did not live to see his position in history really established by reason of our winning a peace with honor in Vietnam. On the other hand, his family will see it and that is, of course, extremely important, and he will know it I am sure.

I also had an interesting reaction as I was thinking about the reason LBJ went down in the polls and so forth in early 1968. What happened was that he did isolate himself—he quit fighting for his policies in public—he did not generate the public support for them. As a matter of fact, he seemed to be running away from them. It was when my November 3 speech came along that we really ginned up some public support for winning a peace with honor. LBJ gave away this ground, and that was why he really failed in the end and was driven out of public office.

I think that Lyndon Johnson died of a broken heart, physically and emotionally. He was an enormously able and proud man. He desperately wanted, and expected, to be a great President. He drove himself to outdo his predecessor.

After I won the election in 1968, and through the remaining years of Johnson's life, I saw what some have described as the "better side" of his character. He was courteous, generally soft-spoken, and thoughtful in every way. He was not the pushing, prodding politician or the consummate partisan of his earlier career.

Above all Johnson wanted to be loved—to earn not only the approval but also the affection of every American. Much of his overblown rhetoric and many of his domestic policies were rooted in this compulsive quest for approbation. Johnson should have allowed himself to be guided by his moderately conservative instincts, which would have led him to avoid huge spending programs at a time when America was deeply involved in a costly war. Seeking both guns and butter is a policy that works only in the very short term. I think that Johnson belatedly came to understand this, because through the four years of my first term I cannot recall an instance when he urged me to go forward with any of his Great Society programs.

Johnson's slogan in the 1964 campaign was "All the way with LBJ." But he found that where the liberals in the media and the left wing of his own party were concerned, it was either all the way with them or none of the way. They applauded his liberal domestic programs, and they praised the Great Society. But the consensus he worked so hard to develop disintegrated when he would not follow their demands for a U.S. bug-out in Vietnam, and they turned on him with a bitterness and ferocity that depressed him and hurt him deeply. He had catered and almost pandered to them, but he could no longer win them.

The hatefulness of the attacks on Johnson's Vietnam policy was symbolized by that awful, mindless chant shouted by antiwar demonstrators: "Hey, hey, LBJ, how many kids did you kill today?" First it frustrated him, then it disillusioned him, and finally it destroyed him. Like Herbert Hoover, he had the misfortune of being President at the wrong time. He might have been a great peacetime President, but the combination of war abroad and at home proved too much for him.

I kept in frequent touch with Johnson while I was President, either directly or through mutual friends. When he returned to Texas he was busy with the preparation of his memoirs—a project from which he derived no enjoyment—and the plans for his presidential library—a project from which he drew much satisfaction. He had his wife and family, including his grandchildren, and his beloved Texas land. But he still longed for the popular approval and affection that continued to elude him. He was uniquely able to understand some of the things I was experiencing, particularly with Congress and the media over Vietnam, and we became quite close. Although I was glad that he did not support McGovern, I thought it was sad that his party treated him so badly. I made a diary note at the beginning of October 1972 that captured something of my feelings and something of our relationship.

Diary

LBJ had told Bobby Baker that he felt he only had a couple of months to live. He ought to have an operation but he was afraid that the operation for removing some of his lower intestines—he has suffered from diverticulosis for years—might be fatal as far as his heart was concerned. He apparently finally got a haircut after getting some criticism about the length of his hair. He is terribly sensitive to how people criticize him on a personal basis. He said, according to Bobby Baker, that President Nixon was probably the best President in history. Whether this is a real view held by him or not is irrelevant. He is in one of those rather emotional states which often come over him. He must be terribly depressed because he is such a proud man and is now being left alone by his party. He doesn't want McGovern under any circumstances but, of course, feels that he can't leave his party. As he puts it, he has been sucking at the tit of the Democratic Party for years and can't let go now, even though the milk may have turned a bit sour because of what the poor cow is eating.

A few weeks earlier I had made a note of a message from Johnson that Rogers Morton passed on to me.

Diary

Morton had talked to Johnson by phone. He said that Johnson seemed to be in one of those moods when he was concerned about going into the hospital again for a rather serious operation, and was looking down toward the end of the road. He said that he closed his conversation in a very sentimental vein, and said, "Tell the President I love him." This, of course, is typical of Johnson who has his violent ups and downs, but is a man strongly motivated by the heart rather than the head.

A week after Johnson's funeral I learned the answer to a question that had bothered me ever since his death.

Diary

I had an interesting little historical note. I asked Kissinger about whether LBJ really knew that we had an agreement. In addition to the call I had made on the 2nd, Haldeman called him on the 15th and told him that we had stopped the bombing. Johnson had answered, "Well, I know what that means." Haldeman said there had been a breakthrough in the talks. And Kissinger had sent him some papers with regard to the peace settlement the same day. So actually before he died he did know what had happened.

At 10 P.M. on January 23, I made a brief statement announcing that a settlement had been reached in Paris and that a Vietnam cease-fire would begin on January 27.

After I finished the broadcast in the Oval Office, I went back to the Residence. As I entered the Solarium, Pat came over and put her arms around me. Julie and Tricia and Ed were also there, and we sat talking about how my announcement had made it official that America was finally at peace for the first time in twelve years. I went to the Lincoln Sitting Room and had a light dinner there by myself. I played several records and sat watching the fire. I had specifically asked that all telephone calls be shut off. Just before I went to bed, I wrote a short note:

Dear Lady Bird,

I only wish Lyndon could have lived to hear my announcement of the Vietnam peace settlement tonight.

I know what abuse he took—particularly from members of his own party—in standing firm for peace with honor.

Now that we have such a settlement, we shall do everything we can to make it last so that he and other brave men who sacrificed their lives for this cause will not have died in vain.

On January 25 I met with Kissinger.

Diary

I had a good talk with Kissinger, sitting over by the fireplace in the Oval Room. I told him what a superb job he had done.

He told me about his daughter, who had been approached in Cambridge to sign a resolution against the bombing. He said that to try to involve a thirteen-year-old was a terribly vicious thing.

He seems at the moment convinced that he should talk to our friends and not try to pander to our enemies. I told him that I didn't want us to have any hatred or anything of that sort toward our enemies. On the other hand, we had to recognize—and that's one of the things that our terribly difficult decision in December meant—we had to recognize that our enemies had now been exposed for what they really are. They are disturbed, distressed, and really discouraged because we succeeded, and now we have to start to play to those who are willing to give us somewhat of a break in writing the history of these times.

At midnight on January 27 the cease-fire went into effect and the killing stopped—at least for a time. I had always expected that I would feel an immense sense of relief and satisfaction when the war was finally ended. But I also felt a surprising sense of sadness, apprehension, and impatience. Sadness, because Lyndon Johnson had not lived a few extra days to share the moment with me and receive the tribute I would have paid him. Apprehension, because I had no illusions about the fragile nature of the agreement or about the Communists' true motives in signing it. And impatience, because I was acutely aware of all the things we had postponed or put off because of the war.

On January 28 I convened a special Cabinet meeting. Commenting on Johnson's death, I remarked that this was the first time in years that we did not have a living former President, and I talked a little about the ages of various Presidents when they died. "TR was sixty-one," I said, and FDR was only sixty-two or -three. Coolidge was sixty-one. In fact it looks like the sixties are the dangerous age! I don't have any fears for myself in that regard. Whatever happens will happen. The important thing is that each of us has to approach each day as if it might be our last day here. That's why each of us has to make every day count and do something with it."

Then I passed around the table leather binders that I had asked Haldeman to have made. Inside each was a large desk calendar covering the four years from January 20, 1973, to January 20, 1977. Next to each of the dates was printed the number of days left in my administration.

I had written a special message for the front of each calendar.

Every moment of history is a fleeting time, precious and unique. The Presidential term which begins today consists of 1461 days--no more and no less. Each can be a day of strengthening and renewal for America; each can add depth and dimension to the American experience.

The 1461 days which lie ahead are but a short interval in the flowing stream of history. Let us live them to the hilt, working every day to achieve these goals.

If we strive together, if we make the most of the challenge and the opportunity that these days offer us, they can stand out as great days for America and great moments in the history of mankind.

Richard Nixon

Washington, D.C.
January 20, 1973

The Presidency
1973–1974

1973

In an interview just before the 1972 election I said that over the next four years my administration would become known as having advocated the most significant reforms of any administration since that of Franklin Roosevelt in 1932. But the reforms I had in mind would be very different from those of the New Deal. I told my interviewer, Garnett Horner of the Washington *Star*, "Roosevelt's reforms led to bigger and bigger power in Washington. It was perhaps needed then. . . . The reforms that we are instituting are ones which will . . . diffuse the power throughout the country and which will make government leaner but in a sense will make it stronger. After all, fat government is weak, weak in handling the problems." In a brief talk to the White House staff on the day after the election I put it more simply: "There are no sacred cows," I said. "We will tear up the pea patch."

At the beginning of my second term, Congress, the bureaucracy, and the media were still working in concert to maintain the ideas and ideology of the traditional Eastern liberal establishment that had come down to 1973 through the New Deal, the New Frontier, and the Great Society. Now I planned to give expression to the more conservative values and beliefs of the New Majority throughout the country and use my power to put some teeth into my New American Revolution. As I noted in my diary, "This is going to be quite a shock to the establishment, but it is the only way, and probably the last time, that we can get government under control before it gets so big that it submerges the individual completely and destroys the dynamism which makes the American system what it is."

During my first term, all my attempts at reorganizing or reforming the federal government along more efficient and effective lines had been resisted by the combined and determined inertia of Congress and the bureaucracy. This was partly for partisan reasons: Democratic institutions naturally resist a Republican President. But it was also because the plans and programs I submitted threatened the entrenched powers and prerogatives that they had built up over many decades through several administrations. For various reasons I had had to acquiesce in this situation and accept the fact that no major reorganization reform or voluntary fiscal restraint would come from Congress during my first term. Now, however, armed with my landslide mandate and knowing that I had only four years in which to make my mark, I planned to force Congress and the federal bureaucracy to defend their obstructionism and their irresponsible spending in the open arena of public opinion.

In my first press conference of the second term, on January 31, 1973, I minced no words. I said, "The problem we have here is basically that the Congress wants responsibility. . . . But if you are going to have responsibility, you have to be responsible, and this Congress . . . has not been responsible on money. The difficulty, of course, and I have been a member of Congress, is that Congress represents special interests."

During the first term I had also had to contend with the increasing hostility of the media. Agnew had told some home truths about their power and their bias, but I had had to observe the official fiction that the President and the media do not have a fundamentally adversary relationship. Now in the second term, however, I planned to let them know that I would no longer uncomplainingly accept their barbs or allow their unaccountable power to go unchallenged.

I took off the gloves in the January 31 press conference when I announced the peace settlement in Vietnam. I said that we had done the best we could against great obstacles and had finally achieved a peace with honor. "I know it gags some of you to write that phrase," I said, "but it is true, and most Americans realize it is true."

By the time a new President was elected in the bicentennial year of 1976, I hoped to have given America the beginning of a new leadership class whose values and aspirations were more truly reflective of the rest of the country. This was not a uniquely conservative perspective. Pat Moynihan had written gloomily in 1969, "Since about 1840 the cultural elite in America have pretty generally rejected the values and activities of the larger society."

My fears about the American leadership classes had been confirmed and deepened by what I had seen and experienced during my first four years as President. In politics, academics, and the arts, and even in the business community and the churches, there was a successful and fashionable negativism which, in my judgment, reflected an underlying loss of will, an estrangement from traditional American outlooks and attitudes. The Vietnam war had completed the alienation for this group by undermining the traditional concept of patriotism.

I had watched this malaise continue to grow and spread during my first term. I saw it in the way the media made heroes out of student rebels while either ignoring those who held to traditional values or presenting them as uninformed or unenlightened. In 1970 Pat Moynihan had added another observant note: "Someone should be pointing out that when an upper-middle-class Ivy Leaguer says something particularly outrageous, official America is supposed to respond that 'he is trying to tell us something.' But when a young construction worker says something in response, we are to conclude that he is a dangerous neo-fascist who must be silenced."

I also saw it in the more subtle attitudes that permeated the liberal-dominated cultural milieu. The fact that they seemed to be less significant did not, in my opinion, make them any less disturbing. During the campaign, for example, I had been annoyed by something I saw in a film we watched one night at Camp David.

Diary

We saw an interesting movie last night called *The Man*, and what really struck me about it was the way that they had an American flag in the lapel of the Secretary of State—who was, of course, depicted as a very bad character. Haldeman told me that he had seen the picture *The Candidate* and that in that case too they put an American flag on the Republican candidate. I told Haldeman that I was going to wear the flag, come hell or high water, from now on, and he said that MacGregor was now letting people know that since the President wore a flag many of them might want to do so also to show their support of the President and their support of the country. Of course, this must be carefully done so that there is no indication of throwing doubts on the patriotism of people who are on the other side. It's really curious how people have come to run down the country the way they do.

This was not a politically motivated prejudice on my part. I felt that we were at a historical turning point. My reading of history taught me that when all the leadership institutions of a nation become paralyzed by self-doubt and second thoughts, that nation cannot long survive unless those institutions are either reformed, replaced, or circumvented. In my second term I was prepared to adopt whichever of these three methods—or whichever combination of them—was necessary.

I thought that America needed a new sense and spirit of positive pride, and now that the Vietnam war was over I felt that I could be instrumental in creating it. I felt that the Silent Majority of Americans, with its roots mainly in the Midwest, the West, and the South, had simply never been encouraged to give the Eastern liberal elite a run for its money for control of the nation's key institutions.

It may seem ironic in view of the scandal that was about to overtake me and my administration and bring my presidency to an untimely end, but in the first weeks and months of 1973 I was planning to provide America with a positive and, I hoped, inspirational example of leadership that would be both a background and an impetus for a new rebirth of optimism and decisiveness and national pride.

I had three main areas of reform in mind for my second term. I wanted to reform the budget and terminate wasteful and ineffective programs, and I planned a massive reorganization and reduction of the federal bureaucracy and White House staff. As columnist Nicholas von Hoffman later wrote, "What Richard Nixon contemplated doing was actually running the government, something no President in seven decades had attempted." Finally, I intended to revitalize the Republican Party along New Majority lines. I had no illusions about the reaction such reforms would provoke from the bureaucracy and Congress or the kind of coverage they would receive from the media. But I was ready, willing, and, I felt, able to do battle for them because I believed in them and because I thought they were the right thing for America.

I summarized all my hopes and plans in some notes I made on January 11 on my large desk blotter in my study at Key Biscayne. This was to have been the blueprint for my second term as President.

Before the election I had asked Caspar Weinberger, Director of the Office of Management and Budget, and John Ehrlichman to make a review of the federal grant programs. They found that of the more than a thousand programs they studied, at least 115 were riddled with waste. For example, the federal farm subsidy program was making 42 percent of its payments to the richest 7 percent of the farmers. Another federal program was still promoting student enrollment in teaching programs, even though we now had a national surplus of 70,000 teachers that was causing serious unemployment problems. Despite a surplus of hospital beds, we were still subsidizing hospital construction. All told, the budget cutbacks I proposed in the first federal budget of my second term, which I sent to Congress on January 29, would have saved $6.5 billion in 1973 and $16.3 billion in 1974. It was a bold suggestion to cut programs that were receiving millions of dollars a year and represented thousands of jobs and government contracts, but I was prepared to take that heat. "Cynics," wrote Eileen Shanahan in the New York *Times*, "who never believe that anyone is committed to anything, have had a hard time grasping the seriousness that Mr. Nixon accords these goals."

1-11-73

Goals for 2d term:

Substance:

Russia - SALT
China - Exchanges
Mideast - Settlement
Europe - Community - Trade -
Latin America -

Defense & Intelligence -
Cut duplication
Improve Hardware
Restore respect

3 Reform goals
3 Foreign goals -
3 Domestic Goals

Intl Monetary & Trade

Domestic:

Crime - Drugs -
Education -
Health -
Land Use -
Race -
Labor - Management -
Prices & wages - (Cut size of govt - make efficient)
Reform -
Growth -
SST?

Spirit? -
Excitement? -

Political:

Strengthen Party -
Better Candidates for '74
New Majority -
New Establishment -
Press -
Intellectual
Business -
Social -
Arts -

RN Campaign in '74?

Personal

Restore Respect for Office -
New idealism, respect for flag - country
Compassion - understanding -

We finally moved to reorganize, reduce, or abolish the remaining behemoths of the Great Society that had done little to aid the poor, and which were now primarily serving the interests of the federal bureaucrats who administered them. Of the $2.5 billion it took to run the Office of Economic Opportunity, 85 percent was filtered out in salaries and overhead before it ever reached the poor. It disserved the poor to keep funding programs that didn't work, but I was prepared for the inevitable accusations from the poverty lobby and the liberals in Congress and the media that we were callous and heartless in proposing these cuts—and I did not have to wait long. "President Nixon's new budget takes the breath away," Joseph Kraft wrote in words of intended criticism that came as music to my ears. "It moves to impose on our whole society his belief in the work ethic."

A year earlier, on January 24, 1972, I had sent Congress a request for placing a ceiling on federal spending. Since Congress had never established a method for staying within an overall budget as it voted on individual appropriations, congressmen and senators had never before been forced to accept responsibility for the fact that passage of some worthwhile project might have the ultimate effect of forcing the government into deficit spending. The legislators had thus been enjoying the best of both worlds: they could vote for whatever spending measures their consciences, their constituents, or their party leaderships urged upon them, while not having to accept the blame for the inflation and tax increases that result from federal deficit spending. Needless to say, there was not much congressional enthusiasm for blowing this comfortable cover, but they did establish a committee to recommend new procedures for budgetary control.

I came back again in January 1973 with a challenge to Congress not only to hold spending to $250 billion that year but to agree to establishing projected spending limits through 1975. Many congressmen had sincere and serious questions concerning who would establish the spending priorities and what criteria would be used. But others were simply frightened by the prospect that budgetary restraints might inhibit their ability to campaign for re-election on a platform of how much federal money they had obtained for their districts. I had made a choice on which programs deserved priority. It was up to Congress to do the same. A reporter wrote in the New York *Times*, "The new budget proposed so sweeping a challenge both to programs and to Congress that it provoked not just surprise but shock, awe and anger. . . . Congress showed signs that it would rally to the defense one by one of the sacred cows the President had so badly defiled."

While my budget with its proposed spending ceiling was sending shock waves through Congress, my plan for government reorganization was sending seismic tremors through the federal bureaucracy. Congress had smothered my attempt in 1971 to streamline the government, so I had asked Ehrlichman and Roy Ash, the incoming Budget Director, to set up task forces and consult with constitutional lawyers to determine how much reorganizing I could legally do on my own. They advised that I could in fact create by executive authority a system closely resembling the one I had requested in the 1971 reform proposal.

We decided to organize six of the eleven Cabinet departments and some of the hundreds of federal agencies under four general management groups: Human Resources, Natural Resources, Community Development, and Economic Affairs. George Shultz would head Economic Affairs and one of the current Cabinet secretaries would be named Counsellor to the President for each of the remaining three areas. These men would then be directly responsible to me for all the programs under their supervision. For example, in 1972 it took seventy-one different signatures to buy one piece of construction equipment for certain federally funded urban renewal projects; five agencies and fifty-six signatures could be required in order to hire one person. Nine federal departments and twenty agencies all had responsibilities for educational programs. Local water and sewer projects alone involved seven different agencies. Under my reorganization plan, the Counsellor in charge would be responsible for eliminating duplication and inefficiency.

I also announced my renewed determination to break the hammerlock the federal government had on the nation's taxes and return some of the revenue to local levels. From 1960 to 1970 the number of categorical grant programs—programs that gave local and state governments federal money for projects which were then controlled and monitored by federal officials—had multiplied from 44 to more than 500. In 1969 a poll found that a majority said big government was a bigger threat to the country than either big business or big labor. I did not consider this an unreasonable fear.

In 1969, 1970, and 1971 I had introduced proposals embodying the principle of revenue-sharing, by which money would be returned from the federal government to state and local governments to spend according to their own needs and priorities. General Revenue-Sharing was passed by Congress in 1972; it provided for a simple return of money without program or project restrictions. During its first year of operation, over $5 billion was designated for return to state and local governments. There were also several Special Revenue-Sharing programs, which would return money with only the provision that it be spent for programs within broadly defined areas: urban development, law enforcement, education, job training, transportation, and rural development.

Special Revenue-Sharing would have replaced 125 categorical grant programs that were bound up in red tape, but so far Congress had not passed any of its component parts. I reintroduced four of them in 1973.

On a practical level, revenue-sharing was a way of revitalizing local government and local responsibility. On a philosophical level, it was the first change in the direction of federal growth in forty years—no less than the New American Revolution we called it.

On a political level, revenue-sharing exacerbated the hostilities in Washington, where it threatened sections of the bureaucracy with obsolescence, and where no one was eager to relinquish any amount of power or control.

I moved immediately after the election to pare down radically the size of the executive branch. When I took office in 1969, the executive office of the President numbered more than 4,700 employees. We announced that by the end of 1973 we intended to cut that figure by 60 percent. I regretted that during the first term we had done a very poor job in the most basic business of every new administration of either party: we had failed to fill all the key posts in the departments and agencies with people who were loyal to the President and his programs. Without this kind of leadership in the appointive positions, there is no way for a President to make any major impact on the bureaucracy. That this was especially true of a Republican President was confirmed a few years later by a study reported in the *American Political Science Review*. Researchers Joel Aberbach and Bert Rockman found that in 1970 only 17 percent of the top career bureaucrats in the executive branch were Republican; 47 percent were Democrats and 36 percent were independents, who "more frequently resemble Democrats than Republicans." The authors of this study confirmed that the frustration we felt with the bureaucracy was based on solid reasons: "Our findings document a career bureaucracy with very little Republican representation but even more pointedly portray a social service bureaucracy dominated by administrators ideologically hostile to many of the directions pursued by the Nixon administration in the realm of social policy." A different study, by Bernard Mennis, concentrated on the foreign service bureaucracy and found that only 5 percent of foreign service officers considered themselves Republicans.

I was determined that we would not fail in this area again, and on the morning after my re-election I called for the resignation of every noncareer employee in the executive branch. Most of the resignations would not be accepted: my action was meant to be symbolic of a completely new beginning. In the weeks before the election, while rereading Blake's *Disraeli,* I had been struck by Disraeli's description of Gladstone and his cabinet as "exhausted volcanoes." I announced that my second term would not suffer the same malady; I was determined that we would not settle into the lethargy that had characterized Eisenhower's second term after an overwhelming re-election victory in 1956. I also wanted the Cabinet members, especially the new ones, to feel that they had complete freedom to choose their staffs for the second term. In some cases I planned to transfer White House staff members into the Cabinet departments to see to it that our policies would be followed.

As much as it was within my power, I was determined during the second term to break the Eastern stranglehold on the executive branch and the federal government. I urged that we reach out into the West and Midwest for fresh talent. I told Haldeman and Ehrlichman that I wanted an administration infused with the spirit of the 1972 New Majority. I gave them four explicit criteria for selection: loyalty, breadth, creativity—and moxie. I wanted to appoint labor leaders, women, and members of ethnic groups, such as Poles, Italians, and Mexican Americans, that had not been adequately represented in the government in the past.

The call for resignations included the entire White House staff and all Cabinet members. I see this now as a mistake. I did not take into account the chilling effect this action would have on the morale of people who had worked so hard during the election and who were naturally expecting a chance to savor the tremendous victory instead of suddenly having to worry about keeping their jobs. The situation was compounded by my own isolation at Camp David, where I spent eighteen days in the four weeks after the election, holding more than forty meetings with old and new appointees and making plans for the second term.

It was one thing for the Democrats to hold all four aces in Washington—the Congress, the bureaucracy, the majority of the media, and the formidable group of lawyers and power-brokers who operate behind the scenes in the city. It was another thing to give them the fifth ace of a timid opposition party.

As I began the new term I had a sense of urgency about the need to revitalize the Republican Party lest the New Majority slip away from us. We even deliberated for several days about starting a new party. There was no question that the party had ability—it had some of the most able and principled men and women in public life. It seemed to me that what we most lacked was the ability to *think* like a majority party, to take risks, to exhibit the kind of confidence the Democrats had because of their sheer numbers. During the campaign I made a note about this after I had addressed the Democrats for Nixon rally at John Connally's ranch.

> *Diary*
>
> We simply need more people on our side who have the love of politics that many of our Democratic friends seem to have in such great abundance. As I have told Connally, the Republicans are more inhibited, more restrained, more proper. The Democrats let it all out and love to shout and laugh and have fun. The Republicans have fun but they don't want people to see it. The Democrats, even when they are not having fun, like to appear to be having fun.

We made plans to revamp the party's organizational structure. I talked with Bob Dole, George Bush, Clark MacGregor, Barry Goldwater, and Jerry Ford about ways we could get the best candidates in every nationwide race in 1974 and 1976. I felt there was a sense of excitement growing about our opportunities and prospects; if we worked hard and were lucky, by 1974 we might have laid the foundations for the first Republican Congress in twenty years.

It was clear that Congress was determined to do battle. Connally reported to me that the mood on Capitol Hill was "the most vicious thing I have ever seen. They are mean and testy." No sooner had the Vietnam peace agreement been announced than the complaints began over the reorganization plans, the proposed budget cuts, the December bombing, and what was soon labeled as the attitude and style of the "Imperial Presidency." In the past there had been similar instances of attempts by Congress to reassert its power and re-establish its prerogatives after the ending of a war. With this precedent in mind I prepared myself for a long and hard fight to get my programs passed and working.

Congressional frustration was exacerbated by the Gallup poll in January, which showed me with an approval rating at 68 percent. Respect for Congress, as measured at the end of 1971, had fallen to an all-time low of 26 percent. Walter Lippmann said that he did not believe that Congress had the wisdom to decide what programs should be proposed or how the country should be led.

I was a man of the Congress and I was proud of the fact. But by 1973 I had concluded that Congress had become cumbersome, undisciplined, isolationist, fiscally irresponsible, overly vulnerable to pressures from organized minorities, and too dominated by the media.

I knew that part of my disenchantment was the simple result of seeing things from the perspective of the White House end of Pennsylvania Avenue rather than from Capitol Hill. Nevertheless, I thought that dramatic changes had taken place in Congress in the twenty-six years since I first came to Washington.

In 1947 it was still possible for a congressman to run his office, do his homework, keep in touch with his constituents, and have his eye on his political fortunes. But the federal government had become so big and the business of government so extensive that even the most conscientious congressman had to delegate a large part of his responsibilities to the personal and committee staffs that had correspondingly swelled in size and influence.

Then radio and television had demonstrated their power to make a politician a national figure overnight, putting a premium on color and controversiality rather then steady industriousness. This situation had a fundamental impact not only on the relationship between Congress and the White House but on the traditional relationships within Congress itself. More and more members refused to accept party discipline and, in effect, went into business for themselves.

Vietnam had precipitated perhaps the most serious and significant change of all: the passing of the tradition of bipartisan support for a President's foreign policy. The long years of war and the national confusion over Vietnam had eroded this concept and further divided Congress against the President, and the two houses against themselves.

In early 1973 it seemed to me that Congress was looking everywhere except to itself for solutions to its problems of inefficiency and ineffectiveness. I thought it was absurd for members of Congress to complain that the executive branch had stolen their power from them. On the contrary, modern Presidents had merely moved into the vacuum created when Congress failed to discipline itself sufficiently to play a strong policy-making role.

The "Imperial President" was a straw man created by defensive congressmen and by disillusioned liberals who in the days of FDR and John Kennedy had idolized the ideal of a strong presidency. Now that they had a strong President who was a Republican—and Richard Nixon at that—they were having second thoughts and prescribing re-establishment of congressional power as the tonic that was needed to revitalize the Republic.

Congress was naturally anxious to find a scapegoat for its problems. The Democratic leadership decided that the best way both to assert their party's majority power and to recover Congress's former prestige would be to take a piece out of the executive branch's hide. After I proposed my budget ceiling and my government reorganization programs, Washington columnists Evans and Novak consulted their inside sources and reported that a "venomous" congressional counterattack was being planned. Hubert Humphrey announced that a "constitutional crisis" was fast approaching.

The first battle lines were drawn in the ostensibly peripheral areas of procedural prerogatives. In early January the Senate Democratic Caucus voted 35 to 1 to narrow the President's traditional authority to invoke executive privilege. The same day a bipartisan bloc of fifty-eight senators introduced legislation that would for the first time in our history limit the President's war powers. On February 5 the Senate voted to require confirmation of the Budget Director, a position that had been filled by presidential appointment without confirmation for the fifty-two years since it had been created.

The major public battles in the executive-legislative conflict were also being fought on the issue of the impoundment of funds. Presidents since Thomas Jefferson had considered it their prerogative, and indeed their responsibility, to withhold the expenditure of congressionally appropriated funds for projects that were not yet ready to begin or if inflation was especially severe and putting more money into the economy would make it worse. This is known as impoundment. In fact, as of January 29, 1973, I had 3.5 percent of the total budget impounded; Kennedy impounded 7.8 percent in 1961, 6.1 percent in 1962, and 3 percent in 1963; Johnson impounded 3.5 percent in 1964 but increased steadily to a high of 6.7 percent in 1967. The Democratic Congress had not challenged my Democratic predecessors for their heavier use of the practice, so I saw the 1973 impoundment battle as a clear-cut partisan attack on me.

Despite my plea for fiscal restraint and my requests for a budget spending ceiling, by March Congress had already prepared fifteen major spending bills that alone would have exceeded the 1974 budget by $9 billion. As a Washington *Post* article on March 28 pointed out, despite "pious statements" about the need for economy, I continued to get resistance on spending cuts. Nor was it a strictly partisan phenomenon. For example, very few Senate Republicans regularly stood with me on opposing the major budget-busting spending bills. I told Hugh Scott that I was going to give up on the Senate unless we got some solidarity in our ranks.

In the midst of this developing confrontation between Congress and the presidency, the Senate Democratic Caucus called for a full-scale investigation of 1972 campaign practices. What they meant, of course, was an investigation of *Republican* campaign practices and of Watergate in particular. Mike Mansfield chose Senator Sam Ervin of North Carolina to head the probe.

Some of my staff and advisers felt that Ervin was a lucky choice for us. They thought that the media would be hard pressed to make much of a hero out of someone whose voting record many liberals viewed as downright segregationist. But I knew that Ervin, for all his affected distraction and homely manner, was a sharp, resourceful, and intensely partisan political animal. As I noted in my diary, I saw Mansfield's move as a purposeful ploy in the congressional campaign to put the presidency on the defensive: "An indication of the fact that we are going to have a very hard four years is Mansfield's announcement that he wants Ervin's committee to investigate Watergate. Mansfield is going to be deeply and bitterly partisan without question. The Democrats actually are starting four years early for their run for the White House."

WATERGATE RECURS

At the time of my re-election I had known that for almost five months we had done everything we could to minimize the impact of the Watergate break-in. John Dean, who had ended up with the day-to-day responsibility in this area, had parried the problems of the Democrats' civil suit depositions, the Patman hearings, the GAO investigations, and the various exposés by the press. He had followed the grand jury and the progress of the FBI investigations in order to keep us from being surprised by anything that emerged from them; he had counseled people who were called to testify; and he had urged officials of the Justice Department to be sensitive to the political ramifications of the case and not to veer off into unrelated areas. I thought that he had acted like a smart political lawyer handling a volatile political case.

As certain as I was that we had done everything we could to contain the scandal, I was equally as confident that we had not tried to cover it up. For one thing, there was no question that the FBI's investigation had been extensive. Mitchell and Colson had both been questioned; even Magruder, about whom we all had suspicions, had testified before the grand jury three times and, however narrowly, had pulled through. Despite the tremendous political sensitivity of the whole case, I had not put personal pressure on the Justice Department, as I was sure other administrations would have done. After all this, there was no evidence that anyone in the White House had been involved in the Watergate break-in.

I could sense that a cloud of suspicion still hung over the White House, but I attributed that to all the election-eve publicity about Segretti and to McGovern's charges of corruption. I felt sure that it was just a public relations problem that only needed a public relations solution.

I decided after the election that both Chuck Colson and Dwight Chapin should leave the White House. Colson was a lightning rod for criticism for political reasons quite apart from Watergate and Ehrlichman in particular urged that he leave as soon as possible. I thought that his departure would help reduce our political vulnerability and give us a fresh start. Colson was naturally concerned that if he left the White House it would look as if he were guilty of something, and our solution was to announce that he would be leaving but to postpone his actual departure until March. I analyzed the decision on November 13, and again on November 18.

Diary

There are risks involved as we know because of the attacks to which Colson will be exposed. However, I do not want to leave the impression that he is leaving under fire because it is an unfair rap for him and also would be an inaccurate way to interpret my actions for getting in a new team as we start the new administration.

Colson is probably right on the issue—I think he is actually clean on Watergate and Segretti—but in the minds of most people he has become the issue. It is a very sad commentary that an individual can be bruised and battered and maligned and libeled and then becomes expendable. But in politics I fear that is the case.

Of course John Ehrlichman would go further than most. We would have lost half the staff by this time had he had his way because of course he is a stickler for getting rid of anybody who has even the appearance of wrongdoing. I would never take this approach because of the human equation.

I believe that where it is the appearance of evil, that an individual should be given a chance to clean the record, to defend himself. The consequences of backing off of people when they come under attack could simply encourage the piranha fish to go to work with a vengeance and leave nothing but the skeleton.

Dwight Chapin's case was even more painful for me. He had been with me since the beginning of my bid for the presidency in 1967. He was young and bright, and he had his whole career ahead of him. But his association with Segretti had made it impossible for him to stay in the White House. My feelings were complicated even more by the knowledge that it was I who had insisted to Haldeman and others on the staff that in this campaign we were finally in a position to have someone doing to the opposition what they had done to us. They knew that this time I wanted the leading Democrats annoyed, harassed, and embarrassed—as I had been in the past. Segretti just turned out to have been the wrong choice for that role.

When John Dean had made his initial report concerning Segretti in early November, he had described Segretti's activities as standard political mischief, and I had observed in my diary that "I was glad to note from talking with Haldeman today, after his talk with Dean, that the Segretti group were not involved in anything other than the Dick Tuck kind of games even though they were perhaps better organized than some of the Dick Tuck operations, although if anything less effective."

But in mid-November, after we had Dean interview Segretti so that we would know exactly what he had done and what Chapin's vulnerability might be, we had learned then that all his activities had not been so innocent as we had originally thought.

Segretti had hired a plane to fly over Miami during the Democratic convention trailing a sign that read: "PEACE POT PROMISCUITY VOTE McGOVERN." Pretending to be one of the organizers, he ordered 200 pizzas and flowers and entertainment for a big Muskie dinner in Washington. On April Fool's Day he printed flyers inviting people to an open house with free lunch and drinks at Humphrey's headquarters in Milwaukee. He paid people to carry "Kennedy for President" signs outside Muskie meetings. All of this was in the realm of standard political fare. But he crossed the boundaries of pranks when he sent out phony letters on stationery from different Democratic campaign offices claiming that two of the Democratic candidates had records of sexual impropriety and that another had a history of mental instability.

I felt that an element of double standard was at work in the media's treatment of Chapin and Segretti. I remembered, for example, that little was written about the vicious anti-Catholic mailers that were sent to heavily Catholic precincts in Wisconsin during the 1960 primary between Humphrey and Kennedy. The letters, postmarked from Minnesota, were designed to look as if they came from Humphrey supporters. A magazine investigation later traced the letters to a friend of Bobby Kennedy's.

I felt too that the *Post*'s stories about Segretti were exaggerated and unfair. As it turned out, the reporters who uncovered the story had not been above dirty tricks of their own in using private sources to obtain access to Segretti's telephone bills and confidential credit information. As John Dean would say to me a few months later, "The intent when Segretti was hired was nothing evil, nothing vicious, nothing bad, nothing. Not espionage, not sabotage. It was pranksterism that got out of hand." Even so, Chapin was irreparably damaged. I believed that it was in his own interest that he leave rather than endure the press assault that was sure to come if he remained in the White House. He was able to get a good job in private industry, but the experience was still sad and painful. As I indicated in my diary, "Chapin took it like a man, and is going to be well placed and will do a superb job. On the Segretti thing, the decision to let it all hang out is, of course, right. I think also the decision to have Chapin leave is the right thing to do. As I have pointed out to Haldeman, time is a great healer."

In mid-November I was still looking for some kind of positive action that would put us out in front and leave Watergate, at last, behind us. On November 22 I read Haldeman and Ehrlichman a letter from one of our supporters who had written to the White House urging me to clean things up. "This theory that it's just going to go away won't work," I said. "It looks like I'm trying to hide something." At the same time a number of conservative columnists had begun to criticize us because of our failure to dispel the residue of suspicion. "Our friends," I dictated one night, "are even harder on us than the other side: conservatives are held up to a higher standard."

I said that we should get out some kind of public statement highlighting the findings of the FBI and grand jury investigations: that there was no White House involvement in Watergate, and no involvement by high-ups at the CRP. I was also ready to go with a detailed accounting of the Segretti episode, regardless of the embarrassment that would cause us.

Not everyone agreed with such a course of action. I heard that Dean in particular thought we should just leave well enough alone. The news stories had died down, so there was no immediate need to respond to new charges. There was, in fact, the danger that anything we did would only create new publicity that would focus new pressure on Magruder or even Mitchell. Finally, there was the legal argument that the Watergate trial was about to begin and anything said by the White House would prejudice the jury about the evidence.

These were all good arguments, but I still wasn't satisfied with inaction. On December 8 I suggested to Haldeman that Dean talk to the press. On December 10 and again on December 11 I pushed for a public statement of some kind that we could issue. But nothing happened. Haldeman and Ehrlichman and I were all working long hours on reorganization, a far more gratifying and, in our view at the time, more important task than the knotty Watergate problem. And then, in the weeks before Christmas, my own time was almost completely absorbed by the unfolding events concerning Vietnam.

While our main attention was focused elsewhere, the Watergate situation became considerably more complicated. In the last weeks of December and the beginning of January, the ground began to shift, however subtly. The Watergate trial was about to begin and the pressure was mounting on the defendants. The vibrations were felt in the White House, particularly in the case of Howard Hunt, whose despair following the death of his wife had been communicated to Colson.

Colson cared deeply about Hunt personally; they had been friends for many years. It is also true that implicit in Hunt's growing despair was a threat to start talking, although I was never sure exactly about what.

In this period, just as had been the case in the days immediately following the Watergate break-in, we began to act on unspoken assumptions, presumptions, and unverified fears. Each person began expressing concern that the others were vulnerable: Haldeman and Ehrlichman said that they thought Colson might be more involved than he was acknowledging; Colson said the same about both of them. This was the period when Colson went to see Hunt's lawyer to reassure Hunt. We were on the verge of a Vietnam settlement, engaged in a wrestling match with Congress over the budget, and about to face some highly publicized Watergate hearings. No one wanted to take any chances.

On January 8, I made a diary note about a conversation with Colson.

Diary

Colson made the interesting point that those that engaged in this activity did so with the thought that in the event they were apprehended that we would move on whoever was the prosecutor and see that nothing happened. Of course, this is very hard for me to believe that they could have had such ideas but I suppose they were thinking back to the Johnson era when he used all the powers of his office to protect himself and others at the time of the Bobby Baker investigation.

By February I was still concerned about the widespread impression of a cover-up that had set in, yet there was little we could do. Whatever our suspicions, we did not actually know who was responsible, and I was not going to force someone to change his testimony just to solve a public relations problem for me. Still, as I said to Colson, "The President's losses got to be cut on the cover-up deal," because "we're not covering up a damn thing." Colson emphatically agreed.

A diary note I dictated on February 14 summed up the situation as I saw it during those first weeks of the new year.

Diary

The real concern here on Colson's part seems to be the possibility that Hunt may blow. He seems to have the obsession that he killed his wife by sending her to Chicago with the money or whatever it was that she was doing at that particular time. He doesn't want to take the $250,000 insurance because of the fact that he takes the blame for killing his wife. Under these circumstances I can see how if the judge calls him in, threatens him with thirty-five years in jail, that he is very likely to be tempted to take immunity and talk about everything he knows.

I really don't know what he knows. Ehrlichman and Haldeman claim they don't know, and of course the same is true of

Colson. I think all of them may know a little more than they indicate but how much I simply can't say. The real problem in the whole thing I think is Mitchell and of course the second man there [Magruder].

I don't know what the situation is, but in any event we are going to have to take our lumps and get the thing over as quickly as we can. I say as quickly as we can although the strategy may be to delay as long as we can and let it drag on and on. I am inclined to think that perhaps the latter is the better thing although it seems to draw blood little by little all the way along.

After Edgar Hoover's death in May 1972 I had named Pat Gray, then an Assistant Attorney General, as Acting Director of the FBI. Gray had earned a reputation in Washington as one of the most efficient, sound, and genial administrators in the city. As Acting Director during the summer and fall of 1972 Gray had overseen the Bureau's Watergate investigation. He was proud of the extent and intensity of that investigation, and he was eager to defend it in any forum.

I decided to nominate Gray to be the FBI's permanent Director, and I met with him on February 14 to discuss the post. I assured him that I was not worried about anything that might come out at his nomination hearings involving Watergate: "I'm not concerned about the substance, about the facts coming out," I said. My only concern was the condition he would be in after the partisan battering he could expect to receive in the hearings.

He responded that he was ready. "I'm not ashamed for it to hang out because I think the administration has done a hell of a fine job in going after this thing," he said. He told me that at the end of the first week he had called in the agents working on the investigation and "just gave them unshirted hell and told them to go and go with all the vim and vigor possible." He said that the week after the break-in even Larry O'Brien had said that he was very happy with the job the FBI was doing.

Gray was sure that he could convince even nonbelievers that the FBI had proceeded without showing favor in the Watergate investigation. He certainly believed it himself.

Diary

At least getting Gray before the committee he can tell a pretty good story. It is a true story of a thorough investigation and this of course knocks down the cover-up. As I emphasized to Ehrlichman and Haldeman and Colson, but I am not sure that they all buy it, it is the cover-up, not the deed, that is really bad here. Of course, the deed may prove to be pretty bad if it involves Mitchell and to a lesser extent if it involves Magruder.

Suddenly it was the end of February and the Ervin hearings were breathing down our necks, and we had still not decided the critical issue of whether we would invoke executive privilege and refuse to let any White House aides testify. Haldeman's, Ehrlichman's, and Dean's efforts to come up with a strategy always seemed to get sidetracked by other things. At the same time, the Republicans in Congress were beginning to grow anxious; some were even insisting publicly that I do something about Watergate. I reflected in my diary: "It is hard to understand how those we have supported so strongly have to make asses of themselves by taking up the cry of the opposition on a matter of this sort when they know very well that there could not possibly be any involvement at the White House level." Ehrlichman and I decided that instead of working through him and Haldeman, I would work directly with John Dean. I thought that perhaps this way I could break the roadblock. For months I had deliberately left the Watergate strategy and planning to others. But not only had the problem not been solved or contained; now it was starting to snowball. I decided to give it my personal attention.

When I met with Dean on February 27, it was the first time I had talked with him since he had reported to me on September 15, the day the Watergate indictments were handed down.

Diary

The talk with John Dean was very worthwhile. He is an enormously capable man. Dean went through quite an amazing recitation as to how Johnson had used the FBI. Apparently he had the FBI do bugging or at least intelligence work on even the New Jersey Democratic convention [in 1964].

I made another note after I had met with him again the next day, February 28.

Diary

I had another very good talk with John Dean. I am very impressed by him. He has shown enormous strength, great intelligence, and great subtlety. He went back and read not only *Six Crises* but particularly the speech I made in the Congress and it made the very points that I am trying to get across here—that the Truman administration had put up a stone wall when we

> tried to conduct an investigation. They wouldn't allow the FBI or the Justice Department or any agency of government to cooperate with us and they were supported totally by the press at that time.
>
> I am glad that I am talking to Dean now rather than going through Haldeman or Ehrlichman. I think I have made a mistake in going through others, when there is a man with the capability of Dean I can talk to directly.

As Dean and I walked to the door at the end of that conversation, we speculated on all the people the Ervin Committee would hope to get up before them in hearings—they would like nothing better than to interrogate Haldeman, Colson or Ehrlichman.

"Or possibly Dean," Dean added.

I was quick to reassure him, "In your case I think they realize you are the lawyer and they know you didn't have a goddamned thing to do with . . . the campaign," I said emphatically.

"That's right," Dean stated.

"That's what I think," I said.

Dean and I continued to meet during the first weeks of March. We discussed Ervin Committee strategy and the statement that we issued on March 12, asserting our right to claim executive privilege on all present and former White House aides. We talked about Pat Gray's confirmation hearings. We also discussed the information he was gathering on Democratic political abuses. And on March 13 we went over the questions he thought I was likely to be asked about Watergate in my press conference in two days.

This press conference on March 15 was bound to be an even more heated one than usual. With equal measures of naïveté and stubbornness, Gray had allowed his hearings before the Senate Judiciary Committee to become a disaster. He turned over raw FBI files to the committee for public release, thereby managing to outrage everyone from the American Civil Liberties Union to his subordinates in the FBI. In each successive appearance he had brought John Dean's name further and further into the controversy; at one point he even implied that Dean might have illegally shown FBI reports to Donald Segretti. Dean had the White House press office deny that he had mishandled FBI reports, but the Democratic members of the Judiciary Committee saw that they were on to a live issue and they began to insist that Dean had to testify before Gray could be confirmed.

I was fully prepared to defend Dean, and in our meeting on March 13 we agreed that if I were asked about the demands that he appear as a witness that I would say that he would respond to questions under oath in a letter. I said I would finesse other Watergate questions by reasserting our intention to cooperate with the Ervin Committee's investigation. Dean added that I could say we had cooperated with the FBI in the past and would cooperate with a proper investigation by the Senate committee.

"We will make statements," I said.

"And, indeed, we have nothing to hide," Dean affirmed.

"We have furnished information; we have nothing to hide," I repeated.

Then Dean and I began a review of the facts, first from the standpoint of my press conference and then from the standpoint of our potential vulnerabilities before the Ervin Committee. I thought that I knew them all. On Watergate I thought that our principal worries were Magruder and Mitchell, although I was sure the Ervin Committee would try to draw in Haldeman as well. I was still prepared to assert unequivocally and to defend unreservedly that there was no White House involvement in the Watergate break-in.

Dean cautioned me that there would be new revelations during the Senate Watergate hearings, but he added that he did not think that it would "get out of hand." I thought I knew what he meant: the Democrats on the committee, spurred on by the media, were going to try to increase the drama by drawing in a "higher-up."

"Let's face it," I said. "I think they are really after Haldeman."

"Haldeman and Mitchell," Dean agreed.

I said that Haldeman's problem was Chapin. Haldeman had given Chapin and Gordon Strachan, another Haldeman aide, the approval to start the Segretti operation, and the press was continually trying to link Segretti to Watergate. But Dean reassured me that Chapin had not known anything about Watergate.

"Did Strachan?" I asked, almost perfunctorily.

"Yes," Dean answered.

I was startled. "He knew?"

"Yes."

"About the Watergate?"

"Yes," he repeated.

I was stunned. Until two months ago, Gordon Strachan had worked in the White House. If he had known about the break-in, that would be bad enough in itself, but I immediately saw the even deeper problem it would pose. It was well known that Haldeman's staff acted as an extension of Haldeman; it would not seem likely that Strachan would have known about anything as important as the Watergate break-in plan without having informed Haldeman of it.

"Well, then, Bob knew," I said. "He probably told Bob then." But in the same breath I added, "He may not have."

Dean was reassuring on this point. He said that Strachan was "judicious" in what he relayed to Haldeman. He described Strachan as "tough as nails." He told me that Strachan had been questioned on two separate occasions and had said, "I don't know anything about what you are talking about." Dean seemed to be implying that Strachan had lied.

"I suppose we can't call that justice, can we?" I remarked. "The point is, how do you justify that?"

"He didn't have to be asked," Dean said. "It just is something that he found is the way he wanted to handle the situation."

Strachan had been such a peripheral and minor figure in all our thinking about Watergate during the past few months that it was difficult to believe that he was suddenly a major problem.

"But he knew? He knew about Watergate? Strachan did?" I asked again.

"Uh huh," Dean answered.

"I'll be damned. Well, that's the problem in Bob's case, isn't it? It's not Chapin, then, but Strachan, 'cause Strachan worked for him."

I still had difficulty accepting the fact that, according to Dean, Strachan had known about the Watergate bugging. If this was true, then nine months of denials of White House involvement were undermined. Later in the meeting Dean seemed to modify the problem presented by Strachan. He said that we could still truthfully say that there had been no White House involvement in that no one had known about the DNC break-in. Strachan had evidently known about the existence of the bug after the fact, but he had not been part of any criminal conspiracy. It was a lawyer's distinction, but by that technicality at least, the White House was still not "involved." In any case, my first instinct was not to accuse or even criticize, but to consolidate.

Running down the list of other potential vulnerabilities, Dean gave me his conclusions about each of them. He said that Magruder had known even more than Strachan; that Colson had not known specifically about Watergate; and that Mitchell had known about the overall intelligence-gathering but not about the actual details of the break-in. Dean observed that his own name had come up—he had been dragged in as the man who sent Liddy to the CRP. It was true, he said, but he had done so only because they had asked for a lawyer, and he had been told that Liddy was a good one. He had passed on that information to Magruder and Liddy had been hired.

We were on the eve of a partisan Senate inquisition, suddenly facing serious new and undefined vulnerabilities. "Well, what about the hang-out thing? . . . Is it too late to, frankly, go the hang-out road?" I asked and then answered my own question, "Yes, it is."

"I think it is," Dean replied.

"I know Ehrlichman always felt that it should be hang-out," I said.

Dean said that he thought he had convinced Ehrlichman that he would not really want to "hang out" either. "There is a certain domino situation here," Dean said. "There are going to be a lot of problems if everything starts falling. So there are dangers, Mr. President. I'd be less than candid if I didn't tell you . . . there are. There's a reason for us not —not everyone going up and testifying."

I raised again the possibility of issuing some kind of White House statement. But Dean argued that regardless of the truth of our assertion that there had been no White House involvement in the Watergate break-in, the partisan Democrats and the media would never believe any statement we issued. He also warned that people would not believe or understand the true story of the Segretti case. "They would have to paint it into something more sinister," he said, "something more involved, a part of a general plan."

At my press conference on March 15 the first question was on Watergate and on John Dean's role in the investigation.

I defended Dean and said that it was unprecedented and unthinkable that the Counsel to the President would accept a summons to appear before a congressional committee. Dean was covered not only by executive privilege but also by the time-honored confidentiality of the lawyer-client relationship. I said that I was prepared to allow him to furnish information; this in itself was more cooperation than was required by the Constitution or by precedent. I reminded the reporters that other administrations had been less cooperative than we; I reminded them that I was cooperating in a way that Truman had refused to during the Hiss case.

The questioning kept returning to Watergate with a relentlessness, almost a passion, that I had seen before only in the most emotional days of the Vietnam war. It was during this conference that for the first time I began to realize the dimensions of the problem we were facing with the media and with Congress regarding Watergate: *Vietnam had found its successor.*

I also knew immediately—even while I was answering the questions in the way that Dean and I had discussed and agreed upon—that our current approach to Watergate was not going to work. We were already on the defensive. We were already behind. We already looked as if we had something to hide.

With the doggedness of one who suddenly finds himself surrounded by a raging storm, I clung to my one landmark—even though it was now apparently anchored upon a technicality: that no one in the White House had been involved in the Watergate break-in. I had been told that Strachan had known about the bugging after the fact—but he had not been part of the decision to do it. Even if that was all we could say, I felt that we should at least be finding persuasive new ways in which to say it. Then we could start defending ourselves from there.

After my press conference I decided to press more firmly than ever for a written statement from Dean that would repeat what he had been saying to us all these months: that there was no evidence against Colson, Chapin, or Haldeman on Watergate.

When I saw Dean again on March 16, I suggested that he go to Camp David and concentrate exclusively on preparing this statement. I was pushing Dean for a statement again the next day, when he told me that he, Dean himself, had been present at meetings in John Mitchell's office at the Justice Department at which Gordon Liddy's intelligence-gathering plans had been discussed. Dean hastened to add that he had said that such things should not be talked about in front of the Attorney General. He said that he had reported to Haldeman and had told him that if something like that was going on, the White House had to stay "ten miles away from it—because it just is not right and we can't have any part of it." He said that Haldeman had agreed with him. "That was where I thought it was turned off," he said.

"But you didn't hear any discussion of bugging, did you?" I asked. "Or did you?"

"Yeah, I did," he answered. "That's what distressed me quite a bit." He explained that Liddy had said at the meeting that they ought to do some bugging. Mitchell had not agreed to it but had simply sat puffing on his pipe, saying nothing. I could visualize the scene and Mitchell's inscrutability—the manner he always adopted when having to tolerate amateurs.

I told Dean that he would not have to mention the talk about bugging when he described this meeting in the statement he was going to prepare. I rationalized that, after all, he had tried to stop it, and Mitchell had not approved it. Dean said that it would be an embarrassment that the White House knew about the existence of an intelligence operation, even though we thought it was to be a legal one. I was not bothered by that and said that if we had to justify it we could, on the basis of all the violence and demonstrations against us. At least, unlike previous administrations, we hadn't used the FBI.

Later I came back to the problem of our vulnerabilities. I said that, as I understood it, in Dean's view they were Mitchell, Colson, Haldeman indirectly and possibly directly; and, on the second level, Chapin. Dean said that he would add his own name. I asked why. He said it was because he had been "all over this thing like a blanket." I said I knew that, but his activities had taken place after the bugging and I did not see the problem. I said that, unlike the others, he had no criminal liability. "That's right," Dean agreed.

When we came back to Strachan, Dean appeared to be altering what he had told me four days earlier when he said that Strachan had not known about the break-in. He said that Liddy had told him that he was not really sure how much Strachan knew.

Dean told me that Liddy had named Magruder as the man who had pressured him to go ahead with the break-in. I asked who had pressured Magruder, and Dean theorized that Strachan had probably urged in general terms that people get moving on gathering intelligence. Once again I asked what kind of intelligence they were after. But now, nine months after the break-in, even Dean still had no answer to why, of all places, they had gone into the DNC. "That absolutely mystifies me," he said.

Things seemed to grow more complicated every day. There was a rumor that Magruder was saying in private that Colson and Haldeman had known about the break-in. I did not believe the accusation, but I thought that, as Dean observed, if Magruder ever saw himself sinking he would reach out to grab anyone he could get hold of. Now there were all these other circumstantial associations and involvements. I told Dean I could see no alternative to trying to "cut her off at the pass" by saying simply that Liddy and his bunch had done the break-in as a part of their job. Then we would put everything out on Segretti. "It isn't nearly as bad as people think it was," I said.

Then Dean said that there was one other potential difficulty: Ehrlichman had a problem with both Hunt and Liddy. "They worked for him?" I ventured, thinking that some kind of circumstantial mud might be slung because of that. Dean then told me that Hunt and Liddy, laden with CIA equipment, had broken into the office of Daniel Ellsberg's psychiatrist.

"What in the world—" I said.

Dean told me that they had done it in an effort to get Ellsberg's psychiatric records in connection with the Pentagon Papers. But he didn't know why. "This is the first I ever heard of this," I responded.

Dean added that it was possible that Ehrlichman had not known beforehand that this break-in was going to take place. As I noted in my diary, "I had my talk with Dean. He mentioned the vulnerability that would be involved with Ehrlichman apparently with something that had to do with an investigation in the Ellsberg case which seemed to me to be somewhat ridiculous. Apparently they were trying to get some information on him from Ellsberg's doctor about his psychiatric conditions."

The ground had shifted once again. Just four days earlier Dean told me that Strachan had had knowledge of the Watergate bug. And now this.

Still, I was convinced that nothing to do with Ellsberg would ever come up during the Ervin hearings, and that meant that we had more important problems than Ellsberg now.

The old pattern of delay and inactivity continued to plague our handling of Watergate. At one point Dean proposed sending a letter to the Gray hearings saying that he had recommended Liddy to the Re-election Committee solely as a legal counsel and that the White House had fully cooperated with the FBI. I urged that he sign it under oath, and the idea lapsed and died.

I needed desperately to get my mind on other things. We were faced with the possibility of having to resume bombing in Laos as retaliation for the failure of the North Vietnamese to abide by the cease-fire provision of the Paris peace agreement. The domestic economy was disturbingly volatile, and George Shultz was about to concede that the relaxation of controls in Phase III of the economic policy had been premature.

I was also thinking about the need to set new foreign policy goals for the second term. Now that the Vietnam war had ended, we could turn our attention to the other area of the world where war was always imminent and where the danger of a great-power nuclear confrontation was far greater than in Southeast Asia. On February 3 I had made the first of several similar notes.

Diary

I hit Henry hard on the Mideast thing. He now wants to push it past the Israeli elections in October, but I told him unless we did it this year we wouldn't get it done at all in the four-year term.

The Egyptian [Hafez Ismail, adviser to President Sadat] is coming over. What he works out I don't know, but I feel that some way we have got to get the Israelis moved off of their intransigent position. Needless to say, we can't move to the all-out Egyptian or Arab position either, but there is some place in between there where we can move. The interim settlement is, of course, the only thing we can talk about—that's the only thing the Israelis will ever go for—and the Egyptians are just simply going to have to take a settlement of that sort—or the Arabs are—with the assurance that we will do the best we can to get a total settlement later.

I spoke to Henry about the need to get going on the Mideast. I am pressing him hard here because I don't want him to get off the hook with regard to the need to make a settlement this year because we won't be able to make it next year and, of course, not thereafter with '76 coming up. He brought that up himself so apparently the message is getting through. What he's afraid is that Rogers, et al. will get ahold of the issue and will try to make a big public play on it and that it will break down. This is the point that I had made to Heath—that we couldn't go to the summit here and fail and, of course, the British understand this totally.

> On the other hand, Henry has constantly put off moving on it each time, suggesting that the political problems were too difficult. This is a matter which I, of course, will have to judge. He agreed that the problem with the Israelis in Israel was not nearly as difficult as the Jewish community here, but I am determined to bite this bullet and do it now because we just can't let the thing ride and have a hundred million Arabs hating us and providing a fishing ground not only for radicals but, of course, for the Soviets. I think actually the radicals are our greater danger because the Soviets will have their people be somewhat responsible whereas the radicals are likely to act in totally unmanageable ways.
>
> As I told Bob, I thought that Henry was having a letdown now because he realized that he had participated in the three great events perhaps of the postwar era—the Soviet, the China, the Vietnam—and that everything else would pale by significance. The Mideast he just doesn't want to bite, I am sure because of the enormous pressures he's going to get from the Jewish groups in this country.
>
> Henry needs to have another great goal. Haig feels strongly that it should be Europe. Henry I noticed had picked up this theme in my last talk with him. I kept hammering, however, with Haig the necessity of doing something about the Mideast.

I also needed some personal time to work on my own schedule. So far I had been keeping up a frenetic pace. In the two months since the second term had begun, I made ten major speeches, held three press conferences, submitted the 1974 budget with the proposed spending ceiling, and sent up new legislative proposals on the environment, health, education, manpower training, law enforcement, and transportation. Golda Meir, King Hussein of Jordan, and British Prime Minister Edward Heath had visited Washington. So far there had been little opportunity to make the public appearances that would be necessary to build support for my policies, and I needed to begin getting out into the country. In fact, I had planned to make a national tour after the end of the war to express my gratitude to the people for their steadfastness during that long ordeal. I was also thinking about making a trip to Latin America after Easter.

Haldeman shared my frustration that the White House was doing and saying nothing on Watergate. He was especially eager to go public on Segretti, tell exactly what had happened, and clear up the mystery.

When we met on Tuesday evening, March 20, he complained that others kept insisting that anything he might say on Segretti would hurt people involved "on the Watergate side."

"I still think I'm being had in a sense . . . being tarred in order to protect some other people," Haldeman said; he added that Chapin, who was also ready to go public with a full explanation on Segretti, was being "far worse tarred in order to protect other people." I said the problem was that the people who seemed to have Watergate vulnerabilities were our friends. Haldeman agreed. He observed that whereas Segretti might represent bad judgment, Watergate was a serious problem, and Dean kept insisting that the whole situation was linked: to break loose and tell everything on Segretti might jeopardize others.

But this brought us back full circle to an unacceptable conclusion, because to follow Dean's advice and to accept his cautious admonitions, was to stay stuck right where we were: making no public statements, fighting with Congress over executive privilege, and giving the impression of a White House cover-up—the worst possible situation for us to be in.

"It isn't really worse—it isn't worse than John Mitchell going to jail for either perjury or complicity," Haldeman countered. I had to agree. I said that I had also considered that. I had questioned, too, whether Magruder would have done such a thing on his own.

Haldeman pointed out that whatever our own conjectures about Mitchell's involvement might be, Dean seemed to think it was possible that Mitchell had not approved the break-in. And Magruder had claimed under oath that he himself had not, which was possible if you accepted the premise that Liddy was acting under a broad authority. But there was always the question of whether Liddy would take the heat or start throwing off onto others. In any event, Dean's approach continued to be containment at Liddy. If no new factors—such as White House statements—were introduced, Dean seemed to think that there was a chance Mitchell would not be drawn in, Haldeman said.

So it was now March 20 and we were back exactly where we had been four days after the break-in nine months earlier: no one was sure about Mitchell or—on a firsthand basis—even about Magruder, but the circumstantial involvements and vulnerabilities surrounding Watergate were so great that even false allegations made by a Liddy or a Magruder could be fatal.

At the end of the meeting Haldeman and I again discussed the idea of putting out a public statement of a general kind. When I mentioned Dean's argument that it would open too many doors, Haldeman said we should just make the statement and see. The doors were evidently going to open anyway, he said. That was exactly how I felt. If the facts were going to come out, I said, "I would rather have us get them out to the

Nixon plans a public Stmt.

extent we can in a forthcoming way." We agreed that the statement should not purport to be complete lest something come up later and undermine it. Rather it should indicate a willingness to answer further questions as they arose.

Before our meeting ended, almost as an afterthought, Haldeman brought up one other problem that Dean had raised with him. He explained that $350,000 in cash had been transferred out of campaign funds in 1972 and brought to the White House to help pay for such political projects as private polling. The money had not been used, and after the election it had been transferred back to CRP. I asked what the problem was with that and he said that it would establish the existence of a "secret fund" which the papers would exploit. "Not that it worries me, not that it's ever worried me," he said. But he added, "Maybe there's more to it than . . . I've found."

I phoned Dean shortly after Haldeman left my office. He seemed slightly agitated. He told me that he would like to meet with me to review the "broadest implications of this whole thing." He said, "You know, maybe about thirty minutes of just my recitation to you of facts so that you operate from the same facts that everybody else has. . . . We have never really done that. It has been sort of bits and pieces."

I said that we should meet at ten o'clock the next morning, March 21. Then I turned to my continuing request that he draw up some kind of general statement that we could release from the White House. I suggested that he might give an oral report to the Cabinet, just to reassure them of what he had told me: that no one in the White House was involved in the break-in. As usual when the idea of a statement arose, Dean's reaction was cool. He repeated his suggestion that before issuing any kind of a statement he should meet personally with me. "No, I want to know. I want to know where all the bodies are first," I replied. Thinking of my discussion with Haldeman about the need to avoid any statement that purported to be definitive, I said that I was thinking about a "complete statement but make it very incomplete"—by that I meant no chapter and verse, just general conclusions such as "Haldeman is not involved in this, that and the other thing; Mr. Colson did not do this. . . . Taking the most glaring things. If there are any further questions, please let me know."

Diary

It was a rather hard day here because we began to get more and more involved in what was really at the bottom of the Watergate-Segretti business, and we seemed always to come up with answers that were basically dead ends as far as getting facts were concerned.

I don't mean to leave it that way actually. It isn't getting at the facts but it's really getting out our side of the story.

I got Dean late in the day, about seven o'clock. He apparently, according to Ehrlichman, had been a little bit discouraged today, although I have been spending a lot of time with him and apparently it bucked him up considerably. He had been trying to keep all of these loose ends from coming apart and he said he would like to have a half hour with me at some point where he could just lay it all out so that I would know everything that he knew and would know all the hazards of whatever might be involved in having members of the White House staff either testify and make statements or what have you. I set it for tomorrow at ten o'clock in the morning.

All in all, though, from what Dean said tonight, he and Moore have come down on the side of not putting out any statement at this point, simply stonewalling the thing.

The point that I raised with both Haldeman and Ehrlichman was that if these questions are going to come out anyway, perhaps it is best just to let them come out on our own initiative rather than having them forced out.

I had also learned that the district court judge was about to hand down sentences on Hunt, Liddy, McCord, and the other men arrested at the Watergate.

Diary

One of the major concerns is what will happen when the judge moves on Friday. He is apparently going to be extremely tough, which does not surprise me.

They think that McCord in this instance might crack because he doesn't want to go to jail and that he might say to the judge after a few days that he is willing to tell all. The question is how much he knows. Certainly he knows a hell of a lot about Mitchell. Mitchell is the one I am most concerned about.

All in all, recalling the fact that a few years ago this would have been inauguration day—March 20—we have many problems that are residues of the campaign. Haldeman said ironically that it was just one of those breaks where if it hadn't been for a night watchman who saw the tape on the door or something like that the Watergate thing would never have come out and none of the other things would have been involved. But that's one of the costs of trying to run a campaign and of having some well-intentioned but rather stupid or at least people with very poor judgment working for you.

> Mitchell just didn't keep his hand on the tiller at a time when he was having all the problems with Martha although I do not blame him for it. I know why it happened. No one could have a better friend or supporter than Mitchell and no man who is stronger in the crunch, but at the present time we are really caught here without really knowing how to handle it.

THE MARCH 21 CONVERSATION

It was just after ten o'clock on Wednesday morning, March 21, when John Dean came into the Oval Office.

After some desultory remarks about the Gray hearings, he said he had thought that we should talk because in our earlier conversations about Watergate he had had the impression that I did not know everything he knew. And that, he said, made it difficult for me to make judgments that only I could make.

"In other words, I've got to know why you feel that . . . we shouldn't unravel something," I said.

"I think . . . there's no doubt about the seriousness of the problem . . . we've got," he began. "We have a cancer—within—close to the presidency, that's growing. It's growing daily. It's compounding—it grows geometrically now, because it compounds itself. That'll be clear as I explain, you know, some of the details of why it is, and it basically is because, one, we're being blackmailed; two, people are going to start perjuring themselves very quickly that have not had to perjure themselves to protect other people and the like. And that is just—and there is no assurance—"

"That it won't bust," I supplied.

"That won't bust," he repeated.

He began reciting details. Some of them I had heard before. Some were variations of things I had heard before. And some were new.

Haldeman, he began, had asked him to set up a "perfectly legitimate" intelligence operation at the CRP. Dean had asked one of his aides to draw up a plan for "normal infiltration . . . buying information from secretaries and all that sort of thing." Dean said that Ehrlichman, Mitchell, and others reached a consensus that the aide he had selected was not the right person to handle the matter; they wanted a lawyer. It was at that point, he said, that he recommended Liddy to handle the intelligence functions. This was the first time Dean told me this: earlier he had said only that he had recommended Liddy to the CRP to act as a legal counsel.

Dean repeated the story of his own indignation when Liddy had presented his incredibly outlandish intelligence plan to Mitchell in the Attorney General's office, and of how he had told Liddy and Magruder, "You just can't talk this way in this office and . . . you should re-examine your whole thinking." He repeated his account of Haldeman's subsequent agreement that Dean and the White House should stay away from such activities. "I thought, at that point, the thing was turned off," he said.

That, as I understood it, was the extent of his firsthand knowledge. He then turned to details he had learned only after the break-in, while he was trying to put together what had happened; these were his extrapolations and conjectures.

It appeared that after the meeting in Mitchell's office, Hunt and Liddy had appealed to Colson for help in getting the authorization for their plans. Colson had thereupon called Magruder, urging him to "fish or cut bait" on Hunt and Liddy. I asked if Colson had known just what Hunt and Liddy's plan was. Dean said he assumed that Colson had had "a damn good idea what they were talking about."

Colson! My earliest fears returned. Up to now I had been told by everyone, including Dean, that Colson was not involved. "Colson then, do you think, was the person who pushed?" I asked. Dean said he thought Colson had *helped* to push. He also thought that Haldeman had pushed through Strachan, but Haldeman's push for some intelligence-gathering had been based on the innocent assumption that nothing illegal was being planned. "I think that Bob was assuming that they had something proper over there," Dean affirmed.

Dean conjectured that Magruder had reported the Colson and Strachan "pushes" to Mitchell, and in the face of all this pressure Mitchell had puffed on his pipe and said, "Go ahead," without really reflecting on what it was all about. That was Dean's theory of how the DNC bugging got under way. I was finding it hard to keep my bearings: just twenty-four hours earlier Haldeman had implied that Dean thought Mitchell had *not* approved the break-in.

Dean said that after the bug was installed, Strachan had received some of the information from it and passed the report on to Haldeman. Haldeman might not have known where the information came from, Dean said, but Strachan did.

Magruder, Dean said, was "totally knowledgeable" and had perjured himself. Dean said that Magruder had set up a "scenario" that he ran by Dean, asking, "How about this?" Dean said that he had responded, " 'Well, I don't know . . . if this is what you're going to hang on, fine.' " Dean said that, despite Magruder's testimony, Magruder had specifically instructed Liddy to go back into the DNC. Dean said, however, that he honestly believed that no one in the White House had known that; but he added, in apparent contradiction, that he thought Strachan had known.

Turning to the post-break-in activities, Dean said that he himself was "under pretty clear instructions not to really investigate this," that he had acted "on a theory of containment." "Sure," I said, remembering Haldeman's comment the night before, that Dean hoped to contain the blame for the break-in at Liddy and not let it be pushed higher to Mitchell.

Dean said that he had followed the FBI and the grand jury's investigations at all times. He said that soon after the arrests at the Watergate the defendants had warned, "We've got to have attorneys' fees . . . if you are asking us to take this through the election." Dean said that arrangements were made for the payments at meetings where he and Mitchell were both present. "Kalmbach was brought in. Kalmbach raised some cash," he added.

I asked if this had been put under the cover of a Cuban committee. Dean said yes, and that Hunt's lawyer had also been used. I added that "I would certainly keep that cover for whatever it's worth. Keep the committee."

Then Dean delivered his punch line: "Bob is involved in that; John is involved in that; I'm involved in that; Mitchell is involved in that. And that's an obstruction of justice."

I didn't understand. I thought Dean had to be overdramatizing.

"How was Bob involved?" I asked.

Dean said that Haldeman had let him use a $350,000 cash fund, which had been held at the White House, to make payments to the defendants. Dean said that he, Haldeman, and Ehrlichman had decided that there was "no price too high to pay to let this thing blow up in front of the election." This was a new twist. The night before, Haldeman had said that the money had been returned unused to the CRP and that the only problem it presented was that the media would call it a "secret fund." "I think you should handle that one pretty fast," I said. Dean agreed.

Dean said that McCord had talked to someone in the White House about commutation of his sentence. "And as you know, Colson has talked to, indirectly to, Hunt about commutation," he said. "All these things are bad . . . in that they are problems, they are promises, they are commitments. They are the very sort of thing that the Senate is going to be looking most for."

Now Dean arrived at the heart of what had precipitated his current state of concern. Five days earlier a lawyer for the CRP had received a message from Howard Hunt and had passed it directly to Dean: Hunt was demanding $122,000 for attorneys' fees and personal expenses. Dean said that when he had received this message, he told the CRP lawyer, "I'm not involved in the money. I don't know a thing about it, can't help you."

Hunt's message had been accompanied by a threat: " 'I will bring

John Ehrlichman down to his knees and put him in jail. I have done enough seamy things for he and Krogh that they'll never survive it.' " Hunt's deadline, according to Dean, was "close of business yesterday."

"What's that, on Ellsberg?" I asked. Dean replied, "Ellsberg, and apparently some other things. I don't know the full extent of it."

"I don't know about anything else," I said, thinking back to January and Colson's speculation that Hunt could draw in Haldeman or Ehrlichman and their simultaneous speculation about what Hunt would do to Colson. Dean said that he didn't either, and then he told me about all the other people who knew about the Ellsberg break-in, among them the Cubans who had been arrested at the Watergate and their lawyers.

Hunt's threat was just the most urgent and dramatic example of the larger problem of the continuing blackmail possibilities for all the defendants. If we continued to pay it, that would compound the obstruction of justice. Beyond that, there was the question of how to raise the money, and even how to deliver it, without involving the White House. I asked how much money he would need. Dean estimated that payments for all the defendants would require a million dollars over the next two years.

I said that it would not be easy, but that I knew where we could get the money. In fact, I had no specific way in mind, but I assumed that, if it were sufficiently urgent, we could raise it from some of the people who had been large contributors in the past.

Dean went back to his account of the "growing cancer" on the presidency. He said that Bud Krogh was forced to perjure himself on the Ellsberg matter. This news about Krogh came as another blow to me. He was one of my favorites among the younger staff members; I knew he was a principled man. But apparently he had testified that he did not know the Cubans, when, in fact, he did—not from Watergate, of course, but from Ellsberg.

"Perjury is an awful hard rap to prove," I said without much conviction.

We returned to the threat from Hunt. Out of all the new details and confusion one thing was clear: Howard Hunt was a time bomb, and his deadline was yesterday. In two days he would be sentenced, and he would be sure to make good on his threat.

"Just looking at the immediate problem, don't you have to handle Hunt's financial situation damn soon?" I asked. "You've got to keep the cap on the bottle that much in order to have any options—either that or let it all blow right now."

"That's right," Dean said. I told him to go ahead with his discourse on the facts. After he had finished, he returned to what he called the growing situation. The problem would be if the Watergate case started breaking and there was a criminal case against Haldeman, Mitchell, Ehrlichman, and himself. He said he thought that he, Haldeman, Ehrlichman, and Mitchell should talk about the whole thing and about how to carve it away from the presidency.

"You're not involved in it," he said to me.

"That is true," I replied.

"I know, sir, it is. Well, I can just tell from our conversations that these are things that you have no knowledge of."

We had arrived at the real question and the real problem: what were the alternatives? I posed the hypothesis that when he met with Haldeman, Ehrlichman, and Mitchell, they might conclude that there was nothing that could be done to keep the whole matter from breaking open. I asked Dean what would be done then: "Are you going to put out a complete disclosure? Isn't that the best plan? That'd be my view on it," I said.

Dean hedged. He introduced the alternative of calling another grand jury with immunity for some witnesses. I thought he had Magruder in mind, but it became clear he was thinking of himself. He told me he thought he faced the possibility of a jail term.

"Oh, hell no," I said, "I can't see how you can." By his own account, he had denounced Liddy's bugging plan; he was not involved in the handling of the money; and he had not offered clemency or given any perjurious testimony. But he was obviously worried, so I asked him to explain to me again his own problems on obstruction of justice. I told him that I couldn't see how a legal case could be made against him. He explained that he had been a "conduit for information" about the blackmail.

As he had talked I had been worrying about the blackmail and the risks of not paying it. I told him, "Let me put it frankly: I wonder if that doesn't have to be continued," and I started to work my way through that maze. At least if we had the million dollars and a way of delivering it, that would hold off everything for a while. Or would it? There was the problem of Hunt and his expectation of clemency: money would not satisfy him if he had been led to expect his freedom. Dean said that the others would be after clemency, too, and added, "I am not sure that you will ever be able to deliver on the clemency. It may be just too hot."

"You can't do it till after the '74 elections, that's for sure," I said. "But even then your point is that even then you couldn't do it."

"That's right," he replied. "It may further involve you in a way you shouldn't be involved in this."

"No, it's wrong; that's for sure," I said.

That was no answer; we were back at the starting point.

Dean was clearly depressed. He said almost apologetically that there had been some bad—as well as some necessary—judgments made before the election, but now it had become a burden in the second term that would not go away. I tried to reassure him; this was no time for recriminations. "We're all in on it," I said, and I told him again that I thought he was overplaying the possibility that he himself might have criminal liability.

Dean said that he did not have a solution to all these problems, but he thought we should think about cutting losses rather than compounding the matter with further payments. I agreed with him—with the exception of Hunt. We were already out of time on him, and if he started hurling charges at the White House there was no way of knowing what damage he could do to my closest aides—Colson, Ehrlichman, Haldeman, Mitchell—and therefore to me.

"But at the moment, don't you agree that you'd better get the Hunt thing?" I asked. "I mean, that's worth it, at the moment."

"That's worth buying time on, right," Dean replied.

We then agreed that Dean would meet right away with Mitchell, Ehrlichman, and Haldeman. "We've never had a real down-and-out with everybody that has the most to lose," he said.

I buzzed for Haldeman to join us. In our conversation Dean had told me that he and Haldeman had talked that morning about the same things he and I were discussing, and at the time I assumed that Haldeman understood all the problems Dean had described to me. But when Haldeman joined us, he seemed to be learning for the first time about Hunt's blackmail demand; about Colson's phone call to Magruder, which may have triggered approval of the Watergate plan; and about Colson's apparently flat promise of a Christmas pardon for Hunt.

When Haldeman was seated I told him that we were at the point of decision. As I saw it, in terms of our overall strategy, we had two options. If we decided that the potential criminal liabilities for everyone were too great, we could yield nothing, fight back, and refuse to testify before the Ervin Committee. "Hunker down," Dean had called it earlier; "cover it up, is what we're really talking about." This was undeniably attractive—if it would work. "I don't want any criminal liability," I told Haldeman. "That's the thing that I am concerned about for members of the White House staff, and I would trust for members of the committee."

At the same time, this option only locked us into a vicious circle, which I described for Haldeman: the only way to stall off disclosures from the defendants would be to pay blackmail; it was possible to do that; but even if we decided that such a desperate measure was justifiable and worth the risk for now, we still had the problem of having to deal with eventual demands for clemency—and clemency was something we simply could not offer; so we ended up back where we began.

On the other hand, if we decided, as I said to them, that "in the end we are going to be bled to death and it's all going to come out anyway, and then you get the worst of both worlds. . . . And we're going to look like we covered up. So that we can't do"—then we had to go with the second option: to get ourselves in the best possible position, whether by offering to go before the grand jury or the Ervin Committee, or by putting out a public statement, and then to let it all blow, take our chances, and just try to survive.

Haldeman was unequivocal about the course we should take. "I don't see how there's any way you can have the White House or anybody presently in the White House involved in trying to gin out this money," he said. I asked Dean if our consensus then was not to say to the defendants, "I'm sorry, it is all off," and let them talk. "That's the way to do it, isn't it? . . . If you want to do it clean?" I asked. Dean did not seem sure; but Haldeman was and said, "See, then when you do it, it's a way you can live with." He stated the problem with blackmail: paying the initial sum was one thing; "but what do you need tomorrow and next year and five years from now?" He pointed out that he had told Dean this during previous months when Dean had said there was a money problem.

As for the payments up to this time, I said that our cover story was going to be that the Cuban committee had taken care of the defendants through the election.

"Well, yeah. We can put that together," Dean said. "That isn't of course quite the way it happened, but—"

"I know, but it's the way it's going to have to happen," I said.

I again asked Dean if his recommendation was to go "the clean way," just letting it all go now.

This time he did not hedge. His answer was no. He again urged the desirability of having our people go before a grand jury, where, unlike the Senate Watergate Committee, there would be rules of evidence.

"You can say you forgot, too, can't you?" Haldeman asked.

A lawyer always advises his client that it is better to say he doesn't recall and err on the side of forgetfulness than hazard a guess or try to reconstruct a memory. Yet this would not help much in committee hearings where taking the Fifth Amendment, or claiming inability to recall, would mean automatic conviction in the eyes of the public. Dean reminded Haldeman that a grand jury also has its hazards—it was a high-risk perjury situation. The Hiss case demonstrated the dangers of a perjury charge. "That's right," I said, "just be damned sure you say I don't remember; I can't recall, I can't give any honest answer to that that I can recall."

I favored the grand jury idea. Ehrlichman had recommended as a solution that we request the Watergate grand jury be reconvened to hear testimony from the White House staff. That would provide an orderly way for us to present the facts. "It should be done through a grand jury, not up there in the klieg lights of the committee," I said at a later point.

I came back one last time to the problem of Hunt. We agreed that no more payments should be made to all the defendants, but Hunt was still the time bomb. I told Haldeman that the reason the Hunt problem worried me was that "it had nothing to do with the campaign . . . it has to do with the Ellsberg thing." Even the grand jury approach would be too late if, in two days' time when the sentencing of the defendants took place, Hunt lashed out. It was Hunt who threatened to leave us with no options, not even the option to do in any orderly way what was responsible and right.

I turned to Dean. "That's why for your immediate thing you've got no choice with Hunt but the 120 or whatever it is. Right? Would you agree that that's a buy-time thing, you better damn well get that done, but fast?"

"I think he ought to be given some signal, anyway to—" Dean said.

"Well, for Christ's sakes get it in a way that. . . . Who's going to talk to him?" I interjected.

Dean reiterated that the problem was having no way to get the money, and we talked about the problems with delivering it. Once again we discussed the idea of recalling the grand jury. Then I came back to Hunt.

"Try to look around the track. We have no choice on Hunt but to try to keep him—" I began.

"Right now we have no choice," Dean said.

"But my point is, do you ever have any choice on Hunt? That's the point," I said. We had arrived once again back at the beginning, the inescapable circle now complete. Even the extreme measure of paying blackmail was not a solution; it would only buy us a little time.

Then Dean came up with an alternative, another way of buying time for ourselves: we might get Judge Sirica to postpone his sentencing for two weeks. That would take the pressure off as far as Hunt was concerned and give us the time we needed to get everyone before the grand jury. I liked this idea immediately and told Dean to go ahead with it.

"I think it is good, frankly, to consider these various options," I said as the meeting closed, "and then once you . . . decide on the plan—John —and you had the right plan . . . before the election. And you handled it just right. You contained it. Now after the election we've got to have another plan because we can't have, for four years, we can't have this thing —you're going to be eaten away. We can't do it."

Haldeman agreed. We had to turn off any further involvement at the lowest possible cost but at whatever cost it took; because, as he pointed out, it was now beginning to get near me.

"Well, the erosion is inevitably going to come here apart from anything, you know, people saying that the Watergate isn't a major concern. It isn't," I said, "but it will be. It's bound to be."

"We cannot let you be tarnished by that situation," Dean said earnestly. I was grateful for his concern—and fully in agreement with it.

"I say that the White House can't do it. Right?" I said, and the meeting ended.

Only two decisions had emerged: Haldeman was to have Mitchell come down from New York immediately for a talk with Dean and Ehrlichman; and Dean was to try to get the sentencing postponed.

I went directly from this meeting to greet the young Russian Olympic gymnast Olga Korbut and some of her teammates, who were visiting the United States. After that there was a session on our efforts to hold down federal spending. But all the time Howard Hunt and his threats and demands for money were weighing on my mind.

As soon as these meetings were over I called in Rose Woods and asked her if we had any unused campaign funds. She told me that we did—she would have to see how much. It turned out to be $100,000, and when Haldeman came in a little later I mentioned it to him. Once again he flatly rejected the idea of our involvement in paying more money. "You should stay out of this," he said.

Later that afternoon Haldeman, Ehrlichman, and Dean came over to the EOB office for a long talk about Watergate. Looking back on it now, I can see that we were all operating from different bases of knowledge and with different perceptions of our own personal vulnerabilities. Haldeman seemed primarily concerned about the danger that Magruder might falsely accuse him of having known about the break-in beforehand, rather than about his knowledge of the payments to the defendants, which Dean had indicated was the real danger. In fact, as late as the following morning Haldeman would still seem unaware of the severity of Dean's conclusion: I mentioned the fact that Dean was concerned about his own knowledge of payments to defendants, and Haldeman mused that he and Ehrlichman had worked on that with Dean. "Perhaps he thinks I'm tied into that, too," Haldeman commented.

On the afternoon of March 21 Ehrlichman seemed even less briefed than Haldeman on the details of the situation: he indicated that he still thought that Gordon Strachan's problem involved his failure to report disbursements of campaign funds. Ehrlichman appeared unaware that Strachan may have had knowledge of the bugging. These differing perceptions, and the chasms they created in our overall understanding, are apparent now. At the time, however, the problem only seemed very complicated, and our strategy sessions were just frustrating and inefficient minuets around the problem.

That night I dictated a long diary note about a day that was later to be seen as a disastrous turning point in my presidency. In it I noted:

Diary

As far as the day was concerned it was relatively uneventful ex-

> cept for the talk with Dean. Dean really in effect let it all hang out when he said there was a cancerous growth around the President that simply was going to continue to grow and that we had probably to cut it out rather than let it grow and destroy us later. He obviously is very depressed and doesn't really see anything—other course of action open, but to move to let the facts out.
>
> As I examined him it seems that he feels even he would be guilty of some criminal liability, due to the fact that he participated in the actions which resulted in taking care of the defendants while they were under trial. As he pointed out, what is causing him concern is that every one of the various participants is now getting his own counsel and that this is going to cause considerable problems, because it will be each man for himself, and one will not be afraid to rat on the other.

The next day, March 22, Haldeman and I again reviewed the increasingly volatile situation regarding Watergate. When our conversation turned to Liddy and the widespread rumors that he and the other defendants were going to be slapped with thirty-five-year sentences, I said that I thought it had been only right to raise money for them. "I don't mean to be blackmailed by Hunt, that goes too far," I told Haldeman, "but we're taking care of these that are in jail . . . we're sorry for them. We do it out of compassion." Haldeman agreed, saying that was why it seemed to him that there was no need for Dean to be concerned about an obstruction of justice. After all, the defendants had pleaded guilty, Haldeman said: "When a guy goes and pleads guilty, are you obstructing justice?"

I said I couldn't understand Dean's concern about his own involvement in an obstruction of justice—after all, by his own account he hadn't delivered the money to the defendants. I said that I thought that was why Hunt's direct demand to him for money had set him off in such a way. "You understand, that that would have constituted goddamn blackmail if Dean had gotten the money," I said. But since Dean had not done it, I could not see that he had any problem.

In retrospect it is clear that on March 21 John Dean was trying to alert me to the fact that what I had assumed for nine months was the major Watergate problem—the question of who had authorized the break-in—had been overtaken by the new and far more serious problem of the cover-up. I left the meeting only troubled by the new dimensions of what he had described rather than galvanized into action by the urgency and peril of our situation. Dean did not tell me the extent of his own active and conscious role in the cover-up, and so I treated much of what he said as conjecture and deduction, instead of as a firsthand report on an explosive situation that was already out of hand. I responded accordingly, by openly running through every available option. Even Dean's insistence that the authorization of payments to the defendants was an obstruction of justice seemed to me more a reflection of his personal depression than a statement of a considered legal conclusion. Only three weeks later, when I finally saw the whole cover-up mosaic in perspective and realized the position the payments to the defendants played in it, would I understand what Dean had really been trying to tell me.

I left the March 21 meeting more disturbed than shocked; more anxious than alarmed. The practical effect of my failure to grasp the full import of what I had been told was that I doggedly persisted in the same course I was on before the conversation: I continued to concentrate on the question of who was vulnerable because of prior knowledge of the break-in, and to look for some way to change our public relations posture so that the White House did not look so defensive where Watergate was concerned.

On the afternoon of March 22, in a meeting in the EOB with Haldeman, Ehrlichman, Dean, and me, John Mitchell urged that we waive executive privilege and allow all White House aides to testify before an executive session of the Ervin Committee. He said it was the only way to move the White House into a new public posture. When someone jokingly called this decision a "modified limited hang-out," I said, "Well, it's only the question of the thing hanging out publicly or privately."

"If we're in the posture of everything short of giving them a public session," Dean himself said at one point, "you're not hiding anything."

We also decided that it was time to get some kind of report or statement from Dean. "I think it's certainly something that should be done," he concurred.

Everyone agreed a statement or report was needed, but everyone seemed to have a different idea about what it was needed for. I wanted it as proof of the truth of my public statements that there was no one in the White House involved in Watergate. I wanted a document that would show that I had said it because I had been told it and believed it. I did not want it to include all of Dean's theories and conjectures—just answers to the broad charges. There was also talk of Dean's report as a document that could be given to the Ervin Committee to define the degree of the involvement of different individuals and therefore help limit the number of witnesses subpoenaed. And there was talk about publicizing the document in order to preempt some of Ervin's thunder by setting out some of the new facts about Watergate in a way that would make them old news before the hearings began. Ultimately, though, the use of the document would have to be defined by what was in it. "The proof is in the pudding," Dean said at one point. Whatever it was, I thought we had to have it. "If it opens up doors, it opens up doors," I said.

When the meeting ended I was relieved. The day before, I had posed two alternative courses: to yield nothing and fight back, or to try to position ourselves so the story would come out as much as possible on our own terms. Now, as of March 22, we had made the first move on the second course.

We had always thought that one important reason for avoiding public statements on Watergate or for volunteering any testimony would be to avoid putting increased pressure on John Mitchell. Therefore I worried about his reaction to this new strategy. I saw him alone after the others had gone. I did not want him to think that I was pushing him out on his own.

I said that I did not think Sherman Adams should have been sacked, even though he had made a mistake. That had been a cruel decision, and I was not going to react cruelly in this case. I was not going to turn against my friends. Then I thought of the beating everyone was going to take before the Ervin Committee. "I don't give a shit what happens," I said to Mitchell. As far as I was concerned they could "plead the Fifth Amendment, cover up or anything else, if it'll save it—save it for them. That's the whole point. On the other hand . . . I would prefer, as I said to you, that you do it the other way. And I would particularly prefer to do it that other way if it's going to come out that way anyway. . . . The story they get out by leaks, charges and so forth, and innuendos, will be a hell of a lot worse than the story they're going to get out by just letting it out there."

I knew that Mitchell would understand that this was my oblique way of confronting the need to make a painful shift in our Watergate strategy, a strategy that so far had been a dismal and damaging failure. Now we had to take a chance and go the other way. It was a relief to know that Mitchell had already come to this conclusion.

The next morning, March 23, Judge John Sirica called an open court session for the purpose of announcing the Watergate sentences. Shortly before the session began, he was handed a letter from James McCord. In it McCord said that political pressure had been exerted to keep him silent; that perjury had been committed at the trial; and that offers of clemency had been made in return for silence. Sirica read the letter in open court.

I had gone to Florida for the weekend, and I was in my study in Key

Biscayne when a call came from Ehrlichman. I dictated a diary note soon after: "I have just received a telephone call from John Ehrlichman with regard to McCord's bombshell on the Watergate thing. I suppose this is something that had to be expected at some point and in my view it is just as well to get it over with now. Let's find out where the bodies are buried and what he has to say."

Sirica freed McCord on bond. He gave a provisional sentence of thirty-five years in jail to Hunt and forty years to each of the other four. Liddy, who had already been cited for contempt because of his refusal to talk, was given a final sentence: six years and eight months to twenty years in jail and a $40,000 fine. These sentences were an outrage. Murderers had received more lenient sentences in the District of Columbia. Sirica admitted severity and justified it as a tactic aimed at getting the defendants to talk. Later Gordon Liddy would wryly remark that he and Sirica were men of like minds because they both believed that the end justifies the means.

Diary

I rather gather that it may go more the Mitchell–Magruder route than the White House route. Whatever the case may be we are now forced to some sort of a position on Watergate. The main thing we have to get off our backs, of course, is the whole problem of political pressure.

As I told Ehrlichman, since the thing is going to come out, let's prick the boil early and get it over with. I asked him whether or not he didn't think we ought to have the President take the lead in calling for a grand jury and offer that everybody in the White House should be called upon to testify.

He said he would talk to Mitchell about that and also talk to Dean about it, but he is off to California for some church affair and will not be back until Sunday, so I will get ahold of Haldeman and Ziegler but I am going to have to make up my mind on this too. I am going to give Dean a call and get his judgment on it. Perhaps Kleindienst as well.

Of course, right at the moment, I guess we're all a bit depressed. I have to be with the Watergate thing going, and not knowing what's going to come out of it. But I think the most important thing now is to get the White House cleaned and cleaned fast on this matter. Now that the judge has moved, I think the more I lean to the idea that we should be calling for a grand jury.

The CPI figures came out—the worst in twenty years—the market continues to go down. So it's just one of the those bad Marches which seem to be congenital as far as our administration is concerned. March is usually a very bad month and then April is a month for action. We shall see.

I told Haldeman to get in touch with Colson and find out exactly what he had said to Hunt about clemency, including whether or not he had mentioned my name. Colson said that when he had met with William Bittman, Hunt's lawyer, Bittman had made references to the fact that Hunt hoped to be out of prison before the end of the year. In response Colson had told Bittman that he was Hunt's friend and would try to do what he could. He said that he had not been specific and had not mentioned me. Colson conceded that what Bittman inferred from his comments might be different from what was actually said.

Haldeman asked Colson about Dean's new disclosure that it had been Colson's call to Magruder urging action on Hunt's and Liddy's intelligence-gathering plans that may have precipitated the Watergate break-in. Haldeman reported that Colson had seemed startled by this question. He said he had not realized that the fact of the call was generally known. He swore that he had not known what it was that Hunt and Liddy were actually proposing.

Haldeman contacted Mitchell about my plan to request another grand jury to look into Watergate. He was against it. He said that at this point it would just give credibility to everything McCord had said and damage the rights of others. Dean agreed with Mitchell and said that we should not overreact. But at this point overreaction on our part was hardly the problem. McCord's letter was explosive news, and I kept pushing for something I could say or do that would enable us to get control of the rush of events: if not another grand jury, then perhaps I should appoint a Special Prosecutor of some kind. But there was always resistance from someone. On March 25 I made a note about the preceding day.

Diary

Yesterday continued our soul-searching with regard to the Watergate matter. I had a long talk with Haldeman, and he told me about Dean's plan of possibly going up to the grand jury, asking for immunity, and then telling all. I am not sure that this is in our interests because we would be giving in on our strongest case where executive privilege is concerned. I mentioned to Haldeman that everybody named by the grand jury, or particularly named in the letter on Thursday by McCord, would have to volunteer to go immediately before the grand jury and present everything that he knew.

Haldeman finally came down, and not reluctantly as a matter

of fact, on my side that what we had to do was to have appearances before the grand jury.

Colson is the one that is dragging his feet the most here and I can understand why, but he is the one perhaps who is the most clever in terms of being able to handle himself before the grand jury.

My concern is that the Cubans may have talked freely to McCord about their hopes and promises for immunity and that this is going to look like an administration cover-up in massive proportions or an obstruction of justice.

Colson swears that anything he said to Bittman he had made a thorough memorandum on later, and that he had limited it to Hunt only on the basis of old friendship. He said that he would intercede for him and he had reason to think that his intercession would be listened to. This, of course, is itself bad enough, and Colson overstated it somewhat.

I talked to Haldeman about the difficulty of any kind of clemency. He agreed nothing could happen before the 1974 elections and whether it could happen then or right at the end remains to be seen. Hunt might be an exceptional case because of his longtime service, the fact that he was not involved as the others were, the fact, too, that he has this very serious personal problem with his wife dead and his children having no one really to care for them.

I talked to Haldeman about the necessity of getting this whole thing cleaned up. I said that we simply wouldn't be able to govern, we couldn't do the job we could do for the country if we allowed it to go on. I said that each man had to go up there and I said when a man was charged he probably had to take a leave of absence. I was thinking then of Magruder.

I said the problem is that, if we go that far, what happens if someone in the White House is charged? Haldeman immediately reacted and said, "Well, that's exactly of course what they want. To drive somebody in the top command out of office and indicate that the whole White House is shot through with corruption." And he's right. We have to find a way to cut this thing off at the pass before it reaches that point, because there's no question in my mind that neither Haldeman or Ehrlichman are guilty.

The Colson matter is something else again. What happens there troubles me a great deal and only time will tell whether he can dig himself out of what appears to be a pretty complex and difficult situation.

I made a note on the 24th, yesterday, that it was exactly sixty days after the Vietnam speech, March 23, our high point in the polls, that the whole Watergate thing came apart, or at least blew up into its rather massive proportions. I recall, too, Theodore Roosevelt coming back after his fantastically successful trip abroad and being received virtually with a ticker tape parade in New York City, and then a few months later being turned down by his own party for leadership and not even being made a delegate to the convention.

It was also on Friday, March 23, that James McCord had a private interview with Samuel Dash, the chief counsel of the Ervin Committee. On March 25 Dash held a press conference and proclaimed McCord's account "full and honest." Even some of the reporters present were perplexed at such a blatantly prejudicial move; some of them speculated that Dash deliberately intended to heighten pressure on them to find leaks. As they soon found out, the search for leaks was not to be that difficult. As would become typical of the Committee's "fairness," the substance of McCord's secret session with Dash immediately leaked.

It turned out that one of McCord's particular targets was John Dean. On the night of March 25 we learned that the next morning's Los Angeles *Times* was going to report that McCord had "told Senate investigators" that Magruder and Dean had had prior knowledge of the Watergate break-in. Dean told Ziegler that the story was libelous and that his attorney was going to inform the paper to that effect. The story appeared regardless, under the headline: *McCord Says Dean, Magruder Knew in Advance of Bugging*. Haldeman called Dean again and received another flat denial. At first I thought about simply announcing that Dean would volunteer to go before the grand jury, but I decided to wait. When Ziegler came to see me before his regular morning press briefing, I told him to express confidence in Dean but to avoid statements on Magruder.

This story in the Los Angeles *Times* marked a major new stage in my perception of the seriousness of the Watergate issue.

Diary

We have tended to sort of live in the idea that while the Watergate wasn't all that big an issue in the country, that it was primarily a Washington–New York story, but now it is far more than that and with the media giving it an enormous assist, it will become worse, particularly as the defendants, if they do, begin to crack and put out various episodes of recollections which may or may not be true but which leave a terrible stigma of possible guilt on the part of the White House staff. Rogers told us that Roger Mudd had positively gloated while reporting the McCord letter.

The other side of the coin is that most of our friends in the press, including Dick Wilson, Bill White, Roscoe Drummond, Vermont Royster, are now pointing out that what was a caper in June now appears to be like a massive cover-up and one that could leave a serious mark on the President and the administration for the balance of the four years unless we take action frontally to clear the thing up.

I think this is correct.

The day has been a hard one, but all in all the day must be a terribly hard one for others. I think of the men who are in prison, I think of course of Haldeman and Ehrlichman, naturally, Mitchell who must be concerned. Needless to say, Magruder who knows he must have committed perjury before the court and Dean who is really the one who deserves the most consideration because he was acting always as a counsel, giving his best advice and always avoiding anything which would smack of illegal or improper activities.

Haldeman had talked with Dean during the day. Dean had said, "The more I look at it, the more I am convinced that if we try to fight it we're going to lose eventually, and the longer we take to lose, the worse we are going to look." Dean told Haldeman that we should revive the idea of going before a grand jury to talk about everything, without invoking executive privilege. I still wasn't sure this was the right course. Dean also told Haldeman that earlier Mitchell had suggested someone be sent to "take McCord's pulse." Dean said that out of this somehow there seemed to be a view floating around that a one-year clemency commitment had been made. Dean also indicated concern because he himself had called Liddy at one point and reassured him not to worry. My diary continued:

Diary

There's also the question as to how much promises were made on the clemency side. Of course Dean puts it on the basis that they were blackmailing us, but on the other hand, as I told Haldeman, that while there might not be any legal basis for prosecution for people paying blackmail, on the other hand, in terms of the President keeping such people on his staff, there just wouldn't be any way to do so. I didn't put it quite so bluntly as that to him, but that is my considered judgment.

According to Haldeman, Dean's concern in testifying before the grand jury was that he told Haldeman he really didn't know how to answer insofar as Mitchell's involvement was concerned because he did not have what he considered to be totally substantiated evidence with regard to Mitchell's role.

Dean also told Haldeman that he didn't have any knowledge beyond a certain point on Magruder because Magruder had not confided in him. He told Haldeman that the only involvement he had with Magruder was that before Magruder went to the grand jury he came to see Dean and asked Dean to question him on the basis that Dean thought the grand jury would raise so that we could get a dry run, and that he, Dean, did that. He said that Magruder had acquitted himself well on the answers, but he said, "I have not gone on an off-the-record type thing in any way with Jeb to get the truth out of him, so I don't know what the truth is from Jeb."

Dean has also raised with Haldeman the point that he did not know the full extent of Gordon Strachan's knowledge.

Haldeman said he asked Dean if Strachan had perjured himself, and Dean said, "No, he hasn't." I pointed out to Haldeman that if Dean went before the grand jury that the grand jury would then call Haldeman, Mitchell, Colson, Ehrlichman, and possibly others that would come out in Dean's questioning and that under those circumstances they would have to go before the grand jury too. Haldeman said again that Colson is very reluctant to expose himself to a grand jury. Dean told Haldeman that he purposely had not questioned Colson on activities other than Watergate which Colson seemed to be worried about because Dean really didn't want to know about those things. I told Haldeman that I didn't know of anything that Colson had done that was illegal unless he had the Cubans doing some damn thing in some other area. Haldeman answered, "He may have." I said, "Do you think he did?" Haldeman answered, "I don't know—I really don't know."

It was in this period that Dean called from Camp David and told Haldeman's assistant, Larry Higby, that while Dean's report might not be a good defense as far as the rest of the White House staff were concerned, it was a very good defense of John Dean.

Everything was growing more and more fluid on Watergate. I still sought some actions that would put the White House out in front of the controversy—some symbols to demonstrate that *we*, and not just the Ervin Committee, were on the side of right.

For a while I considered an idea Dean had suggested of appointing a special presidential commission somewhat like the Warren Commission that had investigated President Kennedy's assassination. Dean had said that he liked the idea because it would stretch things out beyond the 1974 elections. I could then consider granting clemency. But Bill Rogers, whom I had asked to give us advice about Watergate, was strongly opposed to the idea of such a commission. He warned that its members would all try to make names for themselves, and in the end it would be the main thing remembered about the Nixon administration. I finally came around to this view, and I told Haldeman and Ehrlichman, "The idea that a commission might get through the 1974 election. . . . I think the damn thing is going to come out anyway, and I just think you better cut the losses now and just better get it over with much sooner and, frankly, sharper."

I suggested another possibility: I would go to Judge Sirica and tell him to do whatever he thought was best—either call a new grand jury or appoint a Special Prosecutor. Rogers liked this idea. But Colson was against having a Special Prosecutor in any circumstances; he said bluntly that he thought nearly everybody in the White House except himself was involved in the post-June 17 activities, and therefore we should not deliberately increase our vulnerability. Dean also opposed the Sirica idea. He reminded Haldeman of the solution that he had proposed earlier whereby we would obtain immunity for him—that is, for Dean—and then send him to the grand jury. That way, he said, he would head off the possibility that Magruder would unfairly implicate everyone else.

On March 27 Dean phoned Haldeman. He said that he and Paul O'Brien, one of the attorneys retained by the CRP to deal with its Watergate litigation, had concluded that Mitchell had in fact approved the Watergate bugging plan. Dean believed that Mitchell was now using the White House to protect himself; he said Mitchell and Magruder were mixing "apples and oranges" for their own protection. Magruder, for example, was apparently saying that the whole intelligence plan had first been cooked up by Dean on Haldeman's instructions. Magruder even alleged that Strachan had once called him and told him that "the President wanted it done."

From a combination of hypersensitivity and a desire not to know the truth in case it turned out to be unpleasant, I had spent the last ten months putting off a confrontation with John Mitchell. Now it seemed impossible to avoid. I talked with Haldeman and Ehrlichman about having Mitchell come in to give us his personal account of what had actually happened regarding the bugging plan and the break-in.

Before we were able even to reach any decision on this, we had to deal with another problem that had recently emerged. Dean was now saying that if he went before the grand jury, he would contradict Magruder's—

and possibly Mitchell's—earlier testimony. For one thing, there had in fact been *two* meetings in Mitchell's office at which the Liddy plan was discussed. Magruder had testified that there had been only one and that it had dealt with the new campaign spending laws. Dean was not sure how Mitchell had testified on this point. Dean and Magruder had both indicated that Mitchell was putting pressure on them to hold to the original version that there had been only one innocuous meeting. Haldeman said that he was going to advise Magruder to go to the court and say, "I lied," and correct the record. I asked if Magruder could not still stick to his original story, but Ehrlichman said that he could not because there were too many crosscurrents. I agreed and wondered if we could help him get immunity.

On March 28 Haldeman arranged for Mitchell, Magruder, and Dean to meet and see if they could settle the conflict over the number and subject of their meetings with Liddy.

First, Mitchell came in alone to see Haldeman. He said that his first mistake had been not turning the thing off when Liddy first proposed it. But, he said, he just had not paid much attention to it at the time.

Magruder told Haldeman that Liddy had been ordered to prepare a plan for campaign intelligence-gathering before he ever got to the CRP; he was not sure who had ordered it. Magruder was sure, however, that it had been John Dean's idea to lie about the number of meetings with Liddy. Although Magruder's version had to be regarded skeptically, we got a glimpse of how far Dean had gone to keep the Watergate situation under control. Magruder reported that Dean had not only suggested that Magruder say that there had only been one meeting but had urged Magruder to destroy his desk diary, in which there was a note of the two meetings. Magruder also said that it was Dean who had suggested that he lie about the purpose of the meetings and say that they were on the new campaign laws. In fact, Magruder said that he had testified the way he had only to protect Dean. He pointed out that he would not have hurt his own case by admitting that the meetings were on intelligence; but such an admission would have hurt Dean, by drawing him into the intelligence-planning network.

So Jeb Magruder had perjured himself to protect John Dean—and now Dean was going to do Magruder in by exposing him as a perjurer.

Haldeman said that Magruder had been pathetic and had asked about the possibility of clemency. Haldeman had tried to reassure him but made it clear he could make no commitments.

After these meetings with Mitchell and Magruder, Haldeman met with Dean, who said that he could not do what Mitchell and Magruder wanted him to do—to corroborate their accounts of no prior knowledge.

He said the only way to avoid this problem would be for him not to testify at all. When Haldeman told me this, I debated whether we should use executive privilege to keep Dean from having to testify.

Dean told Haldeman that he had decided that we all needed the advice of a criminal lawyer. He said that he was going to get one himself whom we could all use to advise us.

The Ervin Committee continued to leak prejudicial stories, and big headlines now proclaimed that McCord had linked Mitchell to prior approval of the plan. At the same time a publicity-seeking Republican member of the committee, Lowell Weicker of Connecticut, began attacking Haldeman, accusing him of having been "fully aware" of the political espionage schemes. The senior Republican on the committee, Howard Baker of Tennessee, privately expressed dismay over Weicker's "histrionics," but there was nothing he or we could do as Weicker found in abundance the publicity he sought.

Conservative Republican Senators James Buckley, John Tower, and Norris Cotton publicly called on me to allow White House aides and former aides to testify before the Ervin Committee. George Bush, Chairman of the Republican National Committee, privately pleaded for some action that would get us off the defensive.

On the afternoon of March 29 I made the decision to waive executive privilege for Watergate testimony and send Dean to the grand jury. Ehrlichman wrote out a page of notes for the announcement, and we asked Ziegler to call a special press briefing.

Ziegler, however, raised practical objections: most of the reporters had already left the White House for the day, and we were only a few hours away from the major television speech I was to make that night. I agreed to Ziegler's suggestion that we wait until the next day to make the announcement. I have sometimes wondered what would have happened if the announcement had been made immediately, as I had intended. Since Dean himself had recently favored this idea, it had not occurred to me that he would have changed his mind in the matter of a few days. But when we talked with him about it, he strenuously objected and said that his lawyers now told him that he should not offer to go to the grand jury.

So we had to cancel this announcement and scrap this plan, and another day went by and nothing was done.

In my speech that night I announced a temporary price freeze on meat and warned Hanoi about its breaches of the Indochina cease-fire. I also heralded the homecoming of the last group of POWs. "For the first time in twelve years," I said, "no American military forces are in Vietnam." In Washington, however, attention was already focused on Watergate. Scarcely anyone in the media seemed to care about Vietnam anymore—not now that the Vietnam news was good and the Watergate news was bad.

At the end of the month there was a new volley of leaked Watergate stories. The Associated Press, in a story picked up by the networks, quoted sources who said McCord indicated Haldeman had to have known about the break-in scheme. In the New York *Times* "reliable sources" said that McCord had linked Haldeman only by hearsay but had flatly said that Colson knew. Other sources told the Washington *Post* that McCord had not implicated Haldeman at all.

In my diary I noted, "I marvel on the strength of Haldeman. He is a really remarkable man and I only hope to God that we can find a way to keep him immunized from all this, although it's going to be terribly difficult to do so with all the effort being made to get him."

Before we left for San Clemente on March 30, Ziegler announced that members of the White House staff would cooperate fully if they were called before the grand jury. He also revealed that negotiations were under way with the Ervin Committee for a relaxation of our stand on executive privilege.

I asked Ehrlichman to take over Dean's responsibility for handling the Watergate problem. Dean was under too much attack and was obviously going to be coming under still more. In order to establish a lawyer-client privilege, Ehrlichman drew up a letter for me to sign, officially charging him with these responsibilities.

The night after our arrival in California I presented the Medal of Freedom to film director John Ford at a dinner in his honor in Los Angeles. He was seventy-eight years old and terminally ill, but he insisted on being helped to the microphone to acknowledge the award. He told the large audience of celebrities that he had cried when he watched the POWs returning home. "Then," he said, "I reached for my rosary and said a few decades of the beads, and I uttered a short fervent prayer, not an original prayer, but one spoken in millions of American homes today. It is a simple prayer, simply 'God bless Richard Nixon.' "

On April 2 President Thieu arrived in San Clemente for a state visit. He was concerned about the blatant lack of good faith demonstrated by the Communists in their violations of the Paris peace accords. I fully shared his concern, and I reassured him that we would not tolerate any actions that actually threatened South Vietnam. He was grateful for my reassurances, but I knew that he must be concerned about the effect the domestic drain of Watergate would have on my ability to act forcefully abroad.

Ehrlichman moved decisively into his new role as the White House's Watergate man. He devised a negotiating strategy for dealing with the Ervin Committee and began a general fact-gathering inquiry.

On April 5 the CRP's lawyer, Paul O'Brien, came to San Clemente to give his assessment of the case. Ehrlichman found that O'Brien had still another version of the current facts and situation. According to O'Brien's information, Magruder was now saying that Colson had phoned him not once but twice to urge action on the Hunt-Liddy plan. And while only the week before Dean had told us that O'Brien felt that Mitchell had approved the plan, now O'Brien told Ehrlichman that Mitchell had not known of the break-in in advance, but that there was no question that Magruder had.

On April 5, the same day O'Brien met with Ehrlichman, we turned back to the problem of Pat Gray's confirmation hearings as FBI Director. The Senate Judiciary Committee had been holding the nomination hostage until Dean appeared to testify before them. The chances of getting Gray confirmed were slim, and even if we managed to get enough votes, he was now so damaged that I did not think he could be an effective Director. I therefore asked Haldeman to call him and ask that he request to have his nomination withdrawn. Gray called me back immediately and in a manly way did as I had asked.

Later that afternoon Ehrlichman met briefly with Judge Matthew Byrne, the man Attorney General Kleindienst and Henry Petersen had been enthusiastically recommending for weeks as a prospective FBI Director. Byrne was a Democrat and a respected member of the bench. The only drawback was that once Gray's nomination was withdrawn, it would be important to propose someone else right away. If we decided to name Judge Byrne, we would have to wait until he finished presiding over Daniel Ellsberg's trial for unauthorized possession of classified documents.

Diary

The call to Pat Gray was a difficult one. He has been really a great fellow. He said that he was always loyal to the President, and that the people on his staff he had already told were crushed. I said that nobody could feel worse about it than I do.

I met Judge Byrne, briefly, walked out the office door and talked to him for a moment. I was impressed by his real steel-like handshake. He has good tough, cold eyes and is the right age, forty-two years. Unfortunately his case isn't over for a month.

I had a call from Connally. As I expected, Connally was greatly disturbed about Watergate and thought that somebody had to walk the plank. Connally had raised the point with George Bush that there are too many people around the President and that they isolate the President from what is really going on. Of course what we have to realize here is that some of these people overlook the fact that we have some major successes and that we must be doing something right.

I received a rather astonishing message through Harlow from Agnew to the effect that he would speak up on Watergate, but only at a price and that was that he would have to see the President. I told Ehrlichman to pass the message to Harlow that I didn't want under any circumstances to ask Agnew to do something that he was not convinced he ought to do on his own, that under the circumstances he should just chart his own course and of course I would chart my own course. I only hope that Bryce delivered this message in the rather meaningful way that I tried to convey it.

I told Haldeman it was so fortunate that neither he nor I had been told about the Watergate thing before it broke. I am not sure what we would have said, although I think we would have turned it off because of its utter stupidity.

Kissinger came in. Told me that he thought I should stick by Haldeman. I said, "Suppose there is appearance of guilt?" He said, "Even if he is guilty in part they are after him because they know he is the strong man in the administration. He is the most selfless, able person you've got, and you have got to have him."

We have had in four months more problems than most second term Presidents have in four years. In December we had the charge of isolation and the bombing. In January, after it seemed that the war was going to be over, the charge of heartlessness, congressional relations, impoundment, and so forth in the budget. In February, they began to go on the economy, and in March it's Watergate. So every month there's something and each of them has an eroding effect.

One very perceptive point was made that Watergate would not hurt us in the event the other things held up reasonably well. But if, for example, the economy also goes to pot then Watergate accentuates other failures. That is why it is so important to get back to do the domestic things well and the economic things and so forth not just for the purpose of diverting attention, but so the people will not be thinking that the administration is coming apart at the seams, which is exactly what happened in the Truman years. It wasn't just the 5 percenters, it was the fact that added to the 5 percenters, they thought the Truman administration was just no damn good. We must not allow that thing to set in with us.

In early April Dean had advised us that his lawyers were going to meet with the U.S. Attorneys to feel them out on what would be involved if Dean went to the grand jury. Then on April 7 he told Haldeman, with whom he had been in frequent contact during the time we were in California, that he was going to have an off-the-record meeting with the U.S. Attorneys the next day. He said there was no interest in post-break-in activities. In anticipation of being called before the grand jury, he asked to meet with Haldeman and Ehrlichman as soon as they got back to Washington. On April 8, the morning of our return to Washington, I made a note about the unfortunate way the whole situation seemed to be developing, but which still expressed optimism about our ability to survive it.

Diary

Colson has been calling to say he has evidence that Mitchell may be trying to set up Haldeman as a scapegoat. I am not going to allow any of this division business to hurt any of our people. Everyone is going into business for himself for understandable reasons, but we're not going to let it go to the point that one destroys another.

In retrospect as I look back over the past months since the Congress came back into session, I think I've tended to become too depressed, and actually obsessed would be a better word, with the problems of the moment. We have three problems now, the question of prices, the question of Watergate, and the question of the increased disturbances in Vietnam. But compared with the massive problem we had with regard to the war and what we have gone through over the past four years, these problems do not appear all that difficult. They are solvable and they will pass. With the war we simply didn't know whether we were going to be able to see it through.

Haldeman and Ehrlichman met with Dean as soon as we returned to Washington. He told them that he was going to appear before the grand jury.

When I heard this I said that Mitchell would have to decide whether he was going to tell Dean to lie about the meetings with Liddy. I said of Dean, "John is not going to lie." Ehrlichman said that the smartest thing Dean could do would be to go down to the prosecutors and appear to be cooperative.

"Right," I replied.

Ehrlichman said that Dean's strong feeling was that this was the time when "you just have to let it flow." I agreed with this totally.

On April 10 Ted Agnew asked Haldeman if he could come over to his office; he wanted help on a problem. He told Haldeman that someone who had once worked for him in Baltimore was being questioned in a probe of kickbacks and campaign contributions. Agnew assured Haldeman that he himself was innocent of any wrongdoing, but the man apparently had records of efforts to solicit campaign contributions from those who had benefited from his administration, and Agnew thought that there was a potential for embarrassment. He wondered if someone from the White House would see Maryland Senator J. Glenn Beall, Jr., the brother of the Baltimore prosecutor, and alert him that we didn't want Agnew's name to come up in an unnecessary or embarrassing way.

Haldeman gave me a report on the meeting. I was very concerned at the prospect of Agnew's being dragged through the mud unfairly, but in view of all the other problems and our strained relations with Capitol Hill, I did not see how we could do anything to help him. In fact, the climate was such that anything we did to try to help might boomerang and be made to appear that we were trying to cover up for him.

On April 13 Dean told Haldeman and Ehrlichman that the White House was still not a target in the grand jury's Watergate investigation, even though the prosecutors were beginning to develop material on the post-June period.

Magruder, however, seemed to sense that his days were numbered. Earlier he had sent word to Haldeman that if he went to the prosecutors his testimony would bring down John Mitchell. This could mean only one thing: Magruder was going to claim that Mitchell had authorized the bugging. He had asked for Haldeman's advice, and Haldeman had responded that he should do what his lawyers told him to do—in other words, that he should come forward.

When Ehrlichman met with Colson and David Shapiro, Colson's lawyer, Colson said that after Howard Hunt testified before the grand jury on the following Monday, both Mitchell and Magruder would be indicted.

It seemed as if our return to Washington had somehow been a catalyst, and charges and countercharges were now flying in every direction. I did my best to gather everyone in and control the finger-pointing, but a panic was setting in that was beyond anyone's control. Colson said that Magruder was putting out the story that Haldeman, Mitchell, Colson,

Dean, and I had all known about the Watergate break-in plans. Magruder, however, called one of Haldeman's aides and said that his testimony would hurt Mitchell, Strachan, and Dean, but not Haldeman.

Haldeman reported that Colson was claiming that Ehrlichman and Dean had told him to promise clemency to Hunt in January, but that he was smarter than that and had not done so. Ehrlichman had a different version. By his account he had instructed Colson not to tell Hunt anything about a pardon and not to raise the matter with me.

Things were obviously about to happen very quickly. We could no longer avoid facing the unpleasant fact that the whole thing was completely out of hand, and that something had to be done to get the White House out in front. Now it was not just a question of knowledge of the Watergate break-in or a subsequent cover-up, but the possibility of having to respond to accusations that I had not acted promptly on the knowledge obtained during the past few weeks. Regarding this last point, Ehrlichman observed that the information Dean had been giving us over the past weeks and months had not been direct. Dean had only presented different theories of what might have happened and who might have known about it, based on secondhand knowledge—so we had had no clear-cut legal responsibility to act on it. But Magruder's phone call to Haldeman's aide the day before, when he had said explicitly that he would bring down John Mitchell, was firsthand "action knowledge," and we could no longer afford to stand idly by.

About three weeks had now passed since John Dean had first told me that there was a cancer close to the presidency. Since then Watergate had been an almost constant preoccupation. I had tried to grapple with the facts only to find that they were not like the pieces of a puzzle that could be assembled into one true picture. They were more like the parts of a kaleidoscope: at one moment, arranged one way, they seemed to form a perfect design, complete in every detail. But the simple shift of one conjecture could unlock them all and they would move into a completely different pattern.

For example, on March 13 Dean told me that Gordon Strachan knew about the bugging and implied that Strachan had committed perjury. On March 17 he indicated it was possible Strachan had known about the break-in. On March 20, however, Haldeman said Strachan had not known about the break-in and had not lied—rather, "forgot" and had not been well questioned. On March 21 Dean said he thought Strachan knew about the break-in. On March 26 Dean told Haldeman that he did not know the full extent of Strachan's knowledge but that Strachan had not perjured himself. On April 14 Strachan would deny to Ehrlichman any advance knowledge of the break-in. At the end of April, however, I was told that Magruder had passed a lie detector test concerning

Strachan's advance knowledge, and Strachan had taken the same test and failed. Years later Strachan told me that in fact he had passed that test. Strachan was never charged with knowledge of the Watergate wiretap.

There was also kaleidoscopic confusion surrounding the question of Colson's involvement. From the very beginning Haldeman and Ehrlichman had told me that Colson was not involved in any way. Then on March 13 Dean said that Colson did not know the specifics of Watergate but, like others, "knew something was going on over there." On March 21 Dean told me that a call from Colson may have triggered the bugging plan and that he "assumed" Colson had had "a damn good idea" what he was urging. On March 23 Colson completely denied any such knowledge. Five days later, however, both Magruder and Mitchell were speculating that Colson *had* known. An April 8 news report revealed Colson took a lie detector test on the question of prior knowledge and passed it. He was never charged with prior knowledge of the break-in.

A similarly confused and crucial question involved Haldeman. Both Dean and Magruder said that Haldeman and Strachan had received copies of the Watergate bugging reports and that Haldeman may have known what the information in them represented and where it had come from. Haldeman told me that while he may in fact have received these reports, he had not known anything about their source. As it later turned out, he and Strachan had *not* received any of them and had, when these charges were made against them, assumed that innocent intelligence reports they had received might have been the Watergate bugging transcripts.

The most basic and the most sensitive question of all involved John Mitchell's role. For ten months everyone had speculated about whether Mitchell knew in advance. On March 21 Dean told me that he did not know the answer. But on March 27 he told Haldeman that both he and Paul O'Brien had decided that Mitchell *had* approved the break-in. On April 5, however, O'Brien told Ehrlichman he had concluded that Mitchell *had not* approved it. On April 14 Mitchell would tell Ehrlichman he had not. No such charge has ever been brought against him.

We kept thinking that if we could only establish all the facts, then we could construct a way out of the situation that would minimize if not foreclose any possible criminal liability for the people involved. But we never felt confident of the facts, and every alternative course of action, from wholesale appearances before the grand jury to Special Prosecutors to presidential commissions, met with objections from one or the other of my aides and friends who suddenly found himself in a vulnerable position.

As a result, in the three weeks after March 21, when Dean had officially put me on notice about the implications of the cover-up, we did nothing more than stew and worry about the shifting facts and continue to look for any way to prevent damage. By April 14, when everything began to fall apart, all that was left to me was to try to get myself into a position to be able to claim that I had cracked the case, trying to garner some credit for leadership that I had failed to exert.

I decided that the step needed to show some action would be to ask John Mitchell to come down to Washington. That would also alert him to the fact that we were in a position where we had to act. Rather than simply turn over the information to the prosecutors, I wanted Mitchell to have the chance to go in on his own.

Ehrlichman said that he would tell Mitchell that "the President strongly feels that the only way this thing can end up being even a little net plus for the administration . . . is for you to . . . make a statement that basically says, 'I am both morally and legally responsible.' " Ehrlichman said that if both Mitchell and Magruder stonewalled, we would have no choice but to tell them that I was in possession of a body of knowledge that forced me to act.

For the first time I was in the position of having to face and force a confrontation about Watergate with John Mitchell.

Haldeman still did not believe Mitchell was guilty. "I don't think Mitchell did order the Watergate bugging, and I don't think he was specifically aware of the Watergate bugging at the time it was instituted. I honestly don't," he insisted. I agreed that the evidence was not enough to convince me that Mitchell was guilty. But it was almost certainly going to be enough to ensure that he would have to go before a grand jury. Haldeman suggested that perhaps if Mitchell went in and took the blame, the investigators and the press might not care about the cover-up anymore. I said pessimistically that they shouldn't, but they would.

"The Mitchell thing is goddamn painful," I said, and I told Ehrlichman to tell Mitchell that this was the toughest decision I had ever made—tougher than Cambodia, May 8, and December 18 put together. I said he should tell Mitchell that I simply could not bring myself to talk to him personally about it. I said to Ehrlichman, "Frankly, what I'm doing, John, is putting you in the same position as President Eisenhower put me in with Adams. But John Mitchell, let me say, will never go to prison. I agree with that assumption. I think what will happen is that he will put on the goddamnedest defense."

When we turned to the subject of John Dean, who was about to be called before the grand jury, Ehrlichman argued against making Dean leave. He felt that Dean's role in the post-June activities had not been at such a serious level that his departure was necessary. He also thought that Dean would get better and more respectful treatment from the grand jury if he still worked at the White House. Furthermore, as we all recognized, putting Dean outside the White House walls might make him turn against us.

"Dean only tried to do what he could to pick up the goddamn pieces, and everybody else around here knew it had to be done," I said.

"What Dean did was all proper," Haldeman added, "in terms of the higher good."

I picked up a theme that had first been introduced by Ehrlichman: if Dean was guilty, he was no more so than was half the staff—"and, frankly, than I have been since a week ago, two weeks ago," I added.

As far as Magruder was concerned, I asked Ehrlichman to talk to him and tell him that he was wrong if he thought that by keeping silent he was serving my interests. I told Ehrlichman to put in the personal "grace notes" that could help to ease the pain of the situation. I suggested that he tell Magruder of my affection for him and for his family. In fact, I had been thinking the night before about Magruder's young children in school, and about his wife. "It breaks your heart," I said. I thought back to Haldeman's comment two weeks before on how pathetic Magruder had been with his plea for clemency. I told Ehrlichman to tell Magruder that this was a painful message for me. "I'd just put that in so that he knows that I have personal affection," I said. "That's the way the so-called clemency's got to be handled."

Ehrlichman met with Mitchell at 1:40 P.M. on April 14. After their meeting he reported to me that Mitchell was an innocent man in heart and mind, but that he had not missed an opportunity to lob "mudballs" at the White House. He had refused to admit any responsibility for the break-in.

Mitchell confirmed Magruder's story that it was Dean who had talked Magruder into lying to the grand jury about the number and content of the meetings with Liddy. I was shocked, first by the report that Mitchell had been present at such meetings, and second by this apparent confirmation that Dean had talked Magruder into lying.

"What does Dean say about it?" I asked.

"Dean says it was Mitchell and Magruder," Ehrlichman replied. With a wry smile he added, "It must have been the quietest meeting in history, because everybody's version is that the other two guys talked."

Ehrlichman also had a disturbing report of his most recent talk with Dean, who was now saying that "everyone in the place" was going to be indicted. Dean had pointedly hinted to Ehrlichman that the prosecutors were after bigger targets than John Dean—they were aiming at targets like John Ehrlichman.

The problem was apparently the money—the fact that Dean had asked Haldeman and Ehrlichman for money for the Watergate defendants. Dean's "hypothesis," as Ehrlichman called it, was that Haldeman's and Ehrlichman's approval of the use of Kalmbach to obtain funds had been as damaging as action. I said that I still could not believe that the prosecutors could charge Haldeman and Ehrlichman with conspiracy simply because they had been asked whether it was all right to raise the money in the first place. "Technically, I'm sure they could. Practically, it just seems awfully remote," Haldeman said, "but maybe that's wishful thinking."

In the early evening of April 14 I dictated a long diary entry about the day.

Diary

I have just had bacon and eggs and waiting to go over to the White House Correspondents' Dinner. It's rather ironic that the winners of the awards are from the Washington *Post.* While their stories for the most part were libelous, on the other hand it is significant that yesterday and today for the first time the Watergate case really broke apart and I learned the facts on it.

In meeting on Friday, I mentioned to Ehrlichman for the first time the idea of Haldeman and Dean taking a leave of absence. He came back and said it wouldn't work with Haldeman and I don't think he thinks it would work with Dean, because as it turns out Dean has ways that he could implicate both Haldeman and Ehrlichman, not in a way that they couldn't defend, but in a way that might be embarrassing. In any event, there is a solid reason for Dean not having a leave of absence because it would be in effect admitting his guilt before the ax fell on him.

Interestingly enough, Haldeman said that when Magruder came in to see him and say, "Goodbye, I'm going to jail," he said he was like a man with a terrible load lifted off him, a totally different man. He has resigned himself to what is going to happen and is going to live with his fate.

It seems that Colson is going to be a major target, according to Magruder, of the U.S. Attorney. If Dean cracks, Colson will have had it apparently. Colson is probably telling the literal truth when he says that he did not know that the Watergate was going to be bugged. On the other hand he seems to be deeply implicated in urging action on the Liddy project and so forth, and to get the material on O'Brien, whatever he meant by that I don't know, but Mitchell also had talked about getting material on O'Brien.

It is also quite clear that Dean was more of an actor in this whole thing than he led us to believe—or it may be that Magruder is shading it a bit this way too. Dean tells the story a very different way, particularly with regard to the question as to whether or not he advised Magruder how to testify. In this respect, Mitchell knocks Dean, because he indicates that Dean told Magruder how to testify in the meeting that Mitchell sat in with them. Dean seems to have been quite active in that.

I have a note here saying, "the loose cannon has finally gone off," that's probably what could be said because that's what Magruder did when he went in and talked to the U.S. Attorney. I am glad that he did so, however; it is time to get the whole damn thing out and cleaned up.

It's really a terrible thing what is happening to all these men. They all did it with the best of intentions, with great devotion and dedication, but they just went one step too far and then compounded the whole thing through this program of trying to cover it up. It's too bad we were unable to do something about it. I suppose during the election campaign there was a feeling we couldn't do anything for fear of risking the election. Yet that was a mistake, as it turned out, because we were just postponing the day that we would have to face up to it. Immediately after the election, of course, would have been the time to move on it frontally, and yet we did not move then for reasons that I probably will understand later. I just wasn't watching it that closely then and nobody was really minding the store. We were leaving too much to Dean, Mitchell, et al.

At the end of our conversation today, Haldeman brought up the subject himself of resignation. He said quite bluntly he didn't want to do it and didn't feel he should but that he might have to come to that. I didn't commit on it because I think we might have to consider it sometime, although my present inclination, as I indicated to Ehrlichman yesterday and to Kissinger this morning, is that we really had to draw the wagons up around Haldeman and protect him due to the fact, first, that he was really innocent, despite some tangential relationships with the whole affair, and also since it would be such a massive admission of guilt upon the part of the administration that it would really be hard to indicate that we had any character at all in the future.

It will be difficult enough to have Mitchell and most of the campaign people implicated, with Dean possibly a candidate, but to have Haldeman go I think would be the extra blow.

Here what we have to do of course is to enlist some of the Republicans to stand with us. And yet the very thing I predicted is beginning to happen when you see people like John Anderson, Johnny Rhodes, George Aiken, Mathias, of course, as would be expected, and Saxbe popping off, this is the kind of thing that could escalate and get into a general situation as happened in the case of Sherman Adams when Bridges stirred it all up.

Agnew denied the story to the effect that he was appalled by the way Watergate was being handled by the President. Agnew was apparently concerned about some grand jury investigation in Maryland which could involve one of his people and some very damaging memoranda apparently of conversation with Agnew with regard to contributors prior to the time they got state contracts. Of course this is a common practice in states. I said facetiously to Haldeman when he told me about it, "Thank God I was never elected governor of California."

Kleindienst seems to be a strange actor here. Ehrlichman called him at my direction and he had just finished playing golf. He seemed to be amazed the way the ball was bouncing, but still came out for a Special Prosecutor, which Mitchell is totally opposed to and which I think would be a great mistake. Particularly now that the U.S. Attorney is moving so effectively in the case to substitute a Special Prosecutor, it would be a slap in the face for him and also a vote of lack of confidence in our system of justice.

An ironical note was the [Harold] Lipset revelation this morning, where he had been engaged in bugging in 1966, received only a misdemeanor after being charged with a felony, and got a suspended sentence. And yet he was chief investigator for the Ervin Committee. The double standard is really shocking here with the *Post* trying to put the very best face on it all and Dash saying that you have to have somebody as an investigator who has had some experience in doing some things that were wrong.

I told Haldeman today that Rogers must not leave. It's going to be a hell of a blow to Henry but it's the only thing to do, we cannot have anybody leave if we can possibly avoid it while we are under heat on this thing.

The only bright thing that happened over these past three days, one of the few bright things, was that the Gallup poll advance which is going to come out Monday indicated 60–33 [approval–disapproval]. This is probably the last time we will see one that high for some time unless we get a couple of breaks toward the end of the next year. But on the other hand, it does show that as of this time the Watergate has not seriously affected the public—only 5 percent apparently were affected, although Gallup is taking another poll which will probably indicate that more were affected as a result of the stories that have broken in the past few days.

I had a good meeting with Haig and Henry with regard to

> Vietnam. Everything seems to pile up here with Vietnam now a problem and the economic stuff.
>
> I am going to get at that tomorrow if I can possibly get loose from some of this stuff to do so, and I will do so.
>
> I had just made a note to suggest possibly that Ehrlichman talk to Ervin about the disclosures of the day. It's sort of a way-out one, but we might take a crack at that.
>
> In any event, that's all for this day.

This was to be my last full diary dictation until June 1974. Events became so cheerless that I no longer had the time or the desire to dictate daily reflections.

As my diary for January indicates, I knew by then that money was going to the defendants through a Cuban committee, at a time we were hoping Hunt and the others would plead guilty and avoid the publicity of a trial. I do not believe I was ever asked to approve Kalmbach's involvement in raising funds prior to that time, nor that I was aware of the transfer of the $350,000 from the White House to the Re-election Committee and then, at least in part, to the defendants. In early April Ehrlichman told me that O'Brien, the CRP lawyer, had said that in legal terms motive would be the key to guilt or innocence in the authorization of these payments: if the purpose had been to provide attorneys' fees and family support, then they were legal; if the purpose had been to buy silence from the defendants, that would be an obstruction of justice.

> *Diary*
>
> The purpose of course was to see that the defendants would get adequate counsel and that their families would be taken care of during the period when they were in jail, which I suppose would be a perfectly legitimate thing to do. But I suppose it could be said that they were being paid to shut up and not talk. Now whether or not this is a crime—not for the purpose of getting them to shut up about evidence they had about other people, but even about themselves, particularly in view of the fact that they were guilty—remains to be seen.

By mid-April it had become clear that these payments were going to be the biggest problem of all. When Haldeman and Ehrlichman began trying to reconstruct their motives they began to see how the shadow of the Watergate cover-up had fallen across everything and made it impossible to present earlier actions or decisions in their true earlier light. Were the payments intended to silence the defendants about the guilty involvements of others? Or were they simply intended—as I think they were—to pay attorneys' fees and provide family support lest the defendants grow bitter and begin hurling charges. They were a guard against human nature and a hedge against the political problem, not an effort to suppress information based on firsthand knowledge of guilt.

When it came to questions of motive the real answer lay in each man's mind and each man's conscience. I didn't know that answer, nor did I know what each participant was claiming. I did know, however, that the best chance to survive intact would be if everyone who had been involved in the whole unfortunate episode stayed together and maintained the position that the payments had not been intended to buy silence. Since the payments were open to different interpretations, it would take only one person's admission that they were hush money to taint everyone else's actions—including unthinking and innocent actions. That was what Dean would do if he said that the money had been raised for the protection of the guilty and that all the participants in the money-raising had known it. "I wish we could keep Dean away from that," I said, and I told Haldeman and Ehrlichman that I thought everyone involved should get together and stick to the line that they did not raise the money to obstruct justice. When we discussed it again a few days later, I said, "I don't mean a lie, but a line."

After I returned from speaking at the Correspondents' Dinner, I called first Haldeman and then Ehrlichman. I reiterated to both my concern that the participants in the money-raising have the same explanation of the motive for it. I also said that I wanted Colson alerted to what was happening so that if he were called before the grand jury he would not walk into a perjury charge. I also told both men that I had come to the view that the best way of handling the Ervin Committee was just to go ahead and send everyone up for public testimony. Haldeman had come to the same view himself and even thought we should agree to televised public sessions.

I told them both what I had been thinking that evening as I prepared my remarks for the Correspondents' Dinner. However melodramatic it might seem, it was true that what the American President did over the next four years would probably determine whether there was a chance for some kind of uneasy peace in the world for the next twenty-five years. It was in foreign affairs that presidential leadership could really make a difference. "Whatever legacy we have, hell, it isn't going to be in getting a cesspool for Winnetka," I told Ehrlichman, "it is going to be there." Then I added, "And I just feel that I have to be in a position to be clean—forthcoming."

I told Ehrlichman of my special concern for Haldeman—Haldeman was clearly the most vulnerable. "You have had a hell of a week—two weeks. And of course poor Bob is going through the tortures of the damned," I said, adding, "He is a guy that has just given his life, hours and hours and hours, you know, totally selfless and honest and decent." I said some people would argue that anyone against whom charges had been made should be fired. "I mean you can't do that," I said to Ehrlichman. "Or am I wrong? . . . Is that our system?"

"That isn't a system," Ehrlichman answered, "that is a machine."

"Whatever we say about Harry Truman," I said, "while it hurt him, a lot of people admired the old bastard for standing by people who were guilty as hell, and, damn it, I am that kind of person. I am not one who is going to say, look, while this guy is under attack, I drop him."

On Sunday afternoon, April 15, after the White House worship service, Dick Kleindienst came to my EOB office and told me that Haldeman and Ehrlichman were being drawn into the criminal case on Watergate. He did not think the information he had to date was sufficient to bring an indictment; but he felt that, circumstantially at least, very serious questions were being raised. He said that the main accuser was John Dean. Dean had in effect acknowledged his own role in obstructing justice and was now drawing others in. I asked him if there was enough evidence to ask Haldeman to take a leave of absence from the staff. He said that there was not now, but that there might be any day. He said that he thought I should consider whether Haldeman and Ehrlichman should take leaves of absence now, in anticipation of what might come.

Kleindienst was highly emotional and his voice choked periodically. He had been up nearly the whole night, and his eyes were red with fatigue and tears. He described the charges: Dean had alleged that shortly after the break-in Ehrlichman had told him to "deep-six" materials from Hunt's safe and to get Hunt out of the country; Haldeman was accused of knowing that the $350,000 he sent back to the CRP was used to pay the defendants; and there was a question whether Haldeman had actually seen budget proposals from Magruder that outlined the bugging plans.

These charges, based on Dean's accusations, did not seem to me to be sufficient evidence to indict either of them. And if I were to let them go now, I argued, it would label them as guilty before they had a chance to establish their innocence. I told Kleindienst that I wanted more details concerning the evidence and a concrete recommendation about what I should do.

He returned later that afternoon with Henry Petersen. I liked Petersen immediately. He was a Democrat who had served in the Justice Department for twenty-five years, first in the FBI and then in the Criminal Division. His allegiance was to the law and not to any administration. Kleindienst had found Petersen cleaning his boat and brought him straight to the White House, dressed in a smudged T-shirt, tennis shoes, and jeans.

Petersen told me that he thought Haldeman and Ehrlichman should resign. He acknowledged that the evidence against them was not solid. But he added, "The question isn't whether or not there is a criminal case that can be made against them that will stand up in court, Mr. President. What you have to realize is that these two men have not served you well. They already have, and in the future will, cause you embarrassment, and embarrassment to the presidency."

I defended them. Haldeman had denied any prior knowledge of the bugging and break-in; and both men claimed innocence of motive on the payments to the defendants. In effect, I was being asked to sentence them on charges that the prosecutors were not able to prove. I was being asked to prejudice their cases, perhaps irreparably, in the public eye, in order to avoid embarrassment.

"I can't fire men simply because of the appearance of guilt. I have to have proof of their guilt," I said.

Petersen straightened and said, "What you have just said, Mr. President, speaks very well of you as a man. It does not speak well of you as a President."

I urged him to talk to Haldeman and Ehrlichman and get their side of the story, but he said that first he wanted to build his case against them. I asked him if he would come back the next day and bring me the charges in writing.

It was after five o'clock. Bebe Rebozo had come up from Florida that morning, and he was waiting for me outside my office when I emerged. We decided to go for a sail on the *Sequoia*. It was a warm spring evening, and as we sat out on the deck I gave him an outline of the Justice Department's case against Haldeman and Ehrlichman.

I asked him how much money I had in my account in his bank. I said that whatever happened, they had served me loyally and selflessly and I wanted to help with their legal expenses. Rebozo absolutely rejected the idea that I use my own savings. He said that he and Bob Abplanalp could raise two or three hundred thousand dollars. He added that he would have to give it to Haldeman and Ehrlichman in cash and privately, because he wouldn't be able to do the same thing for the others who also needed and deserved help.

As the *Sequoia* prepared to dock, I dreaded having to go back to the White House and face the bleak choices I knew were waiting there.

I forced a cheerful voice as I greeted Haldeman and Ehrlichman when they entered the EOB office at 7:50 that evening.

While Rebozo and I had been on the *Sequoia,* they had been meeting with Bill Rogers. Rogers, they said, felt that no one should be suspended from the staff before formal charges had been brought against him. If an individual was indicted, Rogers thought he should then go on leave of absence. Rogers said that Dean, who had already confessed to the prosecutor his own criminal involvement, should submit his resignation now to become effective at some future date; in the meantime, he thought, Dean should take a leave of absence.

I gave Haldeman and Ehrlichman a report on my meetings with Kleindienst and Petersen and told them that Petersen had indicated that Dean was going to be offered the "good offices" of the U.S. Attorney in return for his cooperation. They were stunned, as I had been, that both Kleindienst and Petersen felt that they should leave the White House.

John Dean sent me a message that said that he hoped I would understand that the motivation for his action was loyalty, and that he was ready to meet with me at any time. I first checked with Petersen and then arranged to meet with Dean.

At 9:15 that night Dean entered the EOB office. I sat in my easy chair, and he sat in a straight-backed chair facing me. It was nearly three weeks since we had last talked.

His voice, as before, was uninflected. He said, "You ought to know that I briefed Bob and John every inch of the way on this." He said that regardless of what their motives may have been, Haldeman and Ehrlichman were involved in an obstruction of justice. "Obstruction of justice is as broad as the imagination of man," he commented dryly. He said that all of them were involved in a "conspiracy by circumstance." I was struck by the fact that whenever Dean talked about Ehrlichman, his voice would take on a vindictive edge.

As we went over some of the charges, Dean seemed almost cocky about his own position. It seemed clear from his comments that he was confident that his lawyers were going to succeed in plea-bargaining with the prosecutors, and I took this to mean that he expected to get immunity.

At one point I said that I could now see that I should not have discussed the question of clemency for Hunt with Colson. He made no response. When the meeting was over, we shook hands and said good night.

I met with Haldeman and Ehrlichman again at 10:15 P.M. I told them about Dean's verdict of "conspiracy by circumstance" and ran through some of the other things he had told me. They both still felt that I should follow Rogers's advice and get Dean's resignation in hand so that when it became known that he was plea-bargaining, it would not appear that I had condoned his crimes, but Petersen was insistent that I not fire Dean or even force him to leave the White House lest such a move adversely affect his decision to cooperate with the prosecutors.

I told Ehrlichman that Petersen had asked me about the fact that non-Watergate materials from Hunt's safe had been turned over to Pat Gray right after the break-in. Dean was claiming that Gray had been given these materials, but Petersen said that Gray had denied even receiving them. Ehrlichman had been present when Dean had turned them over to Gray; they had been given to him instead of to the FBI agents in charge of the investigation in order to reduce the risk of leaks. He could not understand why Gray would have denied receiving them. Ehrlichman picked up the phone and asked the operator to call Gray at home. Haldeman and I listened as he asked Gray about the documents from Hunt's safe. We watched the blood drain from his face as he listened to Gray's reply. After he replaced the receiver he turned to us, his lower lip thrust forward bitterly. "Well, there goes my license to practice law," he said. Pat Gray had destroyed Howard Hunt's files.

When I met again with Dean on Monday morning, April 16, I gave him two draft letters: one tendered his resignation, the other requested a leave of absence. In accordance with Rogers's recommendation, I told him that I wanted him to sign both letters, although neither would be released until his departure from the staff.

The night before, Dean had been self-assured and even cocky. Now he was tense. He challenged every mention of himself with a question about Haldeman and Ehrlichman. I told him they were willing to take leaves if I asked them. He said he would take the draft letters I gave him and do drafts of his own. Dean looked at me at one point late in the conversation and said, "I think there is a mythical belief . . . that [Bob and John] don't have a problem, I'm really not sure you're convinced they do. But I'm telling you, they do."

We talked again about the meeting in which he had told me of the "cancer on the presidency." He said it had taken place on the Wednesday before the sentencing of the Watergate defendants; that would have been March 21.

I asked him about what had happened after that meeting. He said that when Mitchell came down to Washington, Ehrlichman had asked if the Hunt matter had been "straightened out," and Mitchell had replied that he thought the problem was solved. Haldeman and Ehrlichman would have a different version of what had happened on March 22: they said that Mitchell had asked *Dean* if the problem had been handled, and then rhetorically answered himself by saying that he guessed it had been taken care of. I said that I was ready to assume some culpability for knowledge of the demands at that point, but he said that he did not think I had to.

I made a point of telling Dean that I thought all national security matters such as the 1969 wiretaps were privileged. He assured me that he agreed, and that he had no intention of raising them.

Dean reminded me that once he had said that he was incapable of lying. "I want you to tell the truth," I said emphatically. "That's the thing that . . . I have told everybody around here, said, 'Goddamn it, tell the truth.' 'Cause all they do, John, is compound it." I added, "That son of a bitch Hiss would be free today if he hadn't lied about his espionage."

Petersen came to see me again that afternoon, April 16. I told him that I had asked Dean for his resignation—not to announce it, but just to have it in hand. Petersen said he had no problem with that. I asked if he still felt that Haldeman and Ehrlichman should leave. "Mindful of the need for confidence in your office—yes," he said. "That has nothing to do with guilt or innocence." I wondered how he could expect me to live with myself if I deserted my friends simply for the sake of appearances. He gave me his written note of the allegations against them. In summary, the charges were:

Ehrlichman—the "deep-six" instruction and informing Liddy through Dean that Hunt should leave the country.

Haldeman—Magruder said that budget information on the Liddy plan had been given to Strachan, opening the possibility that it had gone to Haldeman. Dean had told Haldeman of the Liddy proposals after they were made and apparently no one had issued any instructions that the program be discontinued. Magruder said he had summaries of the bugging transcripts delivered to Strachan—again raising a possibility that they had been shown to Haldeman.

All our decisions and all our discussions in those days were taking place against a rising flood tide of pressure from the media and Congress. Watergate had acquired dominant status on the television news. Almost daily, every major newspaper had a story based on a leak about some aspect of the case.

I felt that some kind of statement had to be made from the White House, and on April 17 I walked into the press room and announced that we had reached an agreement with Senator Ervin by which all members of my staff would appear voluntarily to testify under oath when requested to do so by his committee. They would answer all relevant questions, unless executive privilege was warranted. Then I added:

> On March 21, as a result of serious charges which came to my attention, some of which were publicly reported, I began intensive new inquiries into this whole matter. . . . There have been major developments in the case con-

> cerning which it would be improper to be more specific now, except to say that real progress has been made in finding the truth.
>
> If any person in the executive branch or in the government is indicted by the grand jury, my policy will be to immediately suspend him. If he is convicted he will, of course, be automatically discharged.

At Ehrlichman's request I also expressed my personal opposition to the granting of immunity in this case:

> I have expressed to the appropriate authorities my view that no individual holding, in the past or at the present, a position of major importance in the administration should be given immunity from prosecution. The judicial process is moving ahead as it should. . . . I condemn any attempts to cover-up in this case, no matter who is involved.

I had formulated the language of this "no immunity" passage with Petersen. I indicated to him only that my concern was to avoid the appearance that would be created if high White House staff members, after acknowledging participation in crimes, were to get off without any penalty. But that was only part of the reason. Another part was Ehrlichman's and Colson's argument that if immunity were dangled before Dean it would be an incentive for him to lie about others, secure in the knowledge that he was protected from the consequences of his own testimony; the final part was my calculation that without immunity Dean might be less likely to turn against me in hope that I would grant him an eventual pardon.

Dean obviously understood what I had done. Len Garment sent word to me that the immunity passage of my statement had Dean "charging around the White House like a wild animal."

Two days later the Washington *Post* reported that Jeb Magruder was telling everything to the prosecutors and that his story would bring down John Dean. The story said that he had accused Mitchell and Dean of helping plan the break-in. This report, coupled with my April 17 statement, triggered Dean. He called Ziegler and said threateningly that he was going to have to "start calling in some friendly reporters." That afternoon he issued a statement: "Some may hope or think that I will become a scapegoat in the Watergate case. Anyone who believes this does not know me, know the true facts, nor understand our system of justice."

I told Ziegler to respond by saying that we were not after scapegoats, but the truth.

It was already clear that there was not one truth about Watergate. There was the factual truth, which involved the literal description of what had occurred. But the factual truth could probably never be completely reconstructed, because each of us had become involved in different ways and no one's knowledge at any given time exactly duplicated anyone else's.

There was the legal truth, which, as we now understood, would involve judgments about motive. There was the moral truth, which would involve opinions about whether what had been done represented an indictment of the ethics of the White House. And there was the political truth, which would be the sum of the impact that all the other truths would have on the American people and on their opinion of me and of my administration.

I can see that long before I was willing to admit it to myself consciously, I knew instinctively that Haldeman and Ehrlichman were going to have to leave the White House. Even while I believed that they had a good chance of being vindicated on the charges of criminal conduct, I knew that the circumstantial facts were so damning that they would not be able to survive the political test. I recognized that if they stayed, they would damage the White House and damage me.

I told myself that I had not been involved in the things that gave them potential criminal vulnerability. I was sure that I had heard nothing about the break-in in advance; I had seen none of the reports based on the phone bug; I had known nothing about Ehrlichman's alleged instruction to Dean to "deep-six" the material from Hunt's safe; and I was sure that no one had asked me about bringing in Kalmbach to raise funds, or about using the $350,000 cash fund for the payments to the defendants.

But there were things that I had known. I had talked with Colson about clemency; I too had suspected Magruder was not telling the truth, but I had done nothing about my suspicions; I had been aware that support funds were going to the defendants; and on March 21 I had even contemplated paying blackmail. The difference was that Haldeman and Ehrlichman had become trapped by their circumstantial involvement; so far, I had not.

I was faced with having to fire my friends for things that I myself was a part of, things that I could not accept as morally or legally wrong, no matter how much that opened me to charges of cynicism and amorality. There had been no thievery or venality. We had all simply wandered into a situation unthinkingly, trying to protect ourselves from what we saw as a political problem. Now, suddenly, it was like a Rorschach ink blot: others, looking at our actions, pointed out a pattern that we ourselves had not seen.

I was selfish enough about my own survival to want them to leave; but I was not so ruthless as to be able to confront easily the idea of hurting people I cared about so deeply. I worried about the impact on them if they were forced to leave; and I worried about the impact on me if they didn't. So the next two weeks were governed by contradictory impulses: I tried to persuade them to go—while I insisted that I could not offer up my friends as sacrifices. I said that we had to do the right thing no matter how painful it was—while I cast about for any possible way to avert the damage, even if it took us to the edge of the law.

This put me in an increasingly difficult situation with respect to John Dean. Since Haldeman's and Ehrlichman's defense lay in discrediting Dean, as long as I kept him on the staff I would appear to be lending credence to his charges against them. I felt that I could not ignore Henry Petersen's private request not to fire Dean, but I knew the detrimental impact that would have on the public perception of Haldeman's and Ehrlichman's guilt.

There was also a personal consideration I could not ignore. I had already alienated Dean by going along with the idea of preventing his obtaining immunity. Now I knew that if I seemed to turn on him, he would almost certainly turn on me. I wanted to handle John Dean very gingerly.

I also had to recognize and admit a confusion and ambivalence about Dean's role. He had been given the brief to contain the Watergate damage. If no one had known at the time all the lengths to which he was having to go to do so, was that his fault or ours? There was a legal difference, but how much of a real difference could we claim between the fact that he had coached Magruder's grand jury testimony while knowing firsthand that Magruder was lying, and the fact that we had wanted him to help Magruder get through the grand jury while only *suspecting* Magruder was lying—but doing nothing to confirm or dispel our suspicions?

It had come down in the end to a question of Dean's judgment: we had wanted Dean to do what had to be done to keep the matter under control—but with the unspoken assumption that he would stop short of getting us in trouble. Dean, however, had simply done what he thought had to be done while failing to project all the consequences.

It was too late to wonder whether someone else in that role—someone without Dean's vulnerabilities from having been present at the Liddy meetings—would have recognized earlier the trap being set for himself and us. By the spring of 1973 it mattered little anymore whether Dean had in fact acted from a genuine belief that what he was doing was necessary to protect the White House, or primarily because he had wanted to protect himself, or whether, under the great pressures he faced, he was even able to make the distinction.

Whatever Dean's motives before or after, I also believed that he was earnestly concerned about the presidency when he came to see me on March 21. Ulterior concern had partly been responsible for bringing him there—the press attention that resulted from Pat Gray's confirmation hearings; my pressure on him to prepare a written statement on Watergate and to answer the charges against him by a letter signed under oath, an idea born of my ignorance about what such action would do to him; and Hunt's direct demand for $122,000. When he walked into my office, however, I believe that he had genuinely hoped to save the presidency from an encroaching cancer. I am sure he hoped that I would react strongly and take charge of the situation. Instead I contemplated buying time with one more payment to Hunt and calmly analyzed the political problems involved in granting clemency to the defendants after the 1974 election.

As early as April 15 I had broached the idea that Haldeman and Ehrlichman possibly take leaves of absence by suggesting that they might find themselves being worn down by press leaks and press charges. On April 17 I did so again. They both disagreed. Ehrlichman said that Dean was the one who should leave. He asked if I felt that Dean's charges were valid. I assured him that I did not, and that I saw that Dean's involvement was on a much more serious level than his own. "Then that's the way it ought to be put," Ehrlichman said. "He brought in a lot of silly garbage about me which doesn't add up to a nickel's worth of a lawsuit."

Ehrlichman said that, furthermore, there were indications that during the original Watergate investigation, Henry Petersen had passed grand jury information to Dean, who was then acting as White House Counsel. That night I called Petersen and told him not to give me any information from the grand jury unless he specifically thought I should have it.

Despite their initially tough front, it was not easy for Haldeman and Ehrlichman to sustain their optimism. That night they reported to me that while their lawyers did not think that the evidence against them was legally sufficient, they had advised them that there was a real chance that it would be a difficult case when so many fine points of motive and intention were involved. The law on obstruction of justice was very loose and broad. As Ehrlichman summed it up, it was possible for them to "beat the rap, but we're damaged goods."

I wanted to be reassuring, but I could think of nothing encouraging to say that any of us would believe. "I think we've just about had it," Ehrlichman continued, "I think the odds are against it."

The two of them joked mordantly about Ehrlichman's making a living handling traffic cases. I made an offer to help pay their legal fees. They thanked me but declined the offer.

After we had discussed the charges at great length, Ehrlichman said, "I'm just not willing to believe the process will result in an indictment . . . I just can't accept that."

"You've gotta have faith that the system works," Haldeman agreed.

I said that we would celebrate their acquittal together. "We'll have the goddamnedest party at Camp David," I promised. But it was just bravado. Deep inside I knew that none of us was confident of the outcome.

At Haldeman's and Ehrlichman's request I met with their lawyers.

They told me that they did not think the cases against their clients were indictable, but they realistically admitted that the prosecutors were zealots and therefore anything could happen. They urged me not to force Haldeman and Ehrlichman to leave, because to do so would be taken as an admission of their guilt. They requested instead that I make a public statement of faith and support for both of them. They said that Henry Petersen was a man I should not trust, and they urged me to stay away from his advice. Later, when Haldeman reminded me of this, I could only say, "He's all I've got, Bob."

It was 7:40 on the night of April 19 that we received word of the first press leaks that Dean and his lawyers had designed as a way of bolstering his case for immunity. Each leak would go a little further: "upping the ante," I called it. In what soon became a grim pattern, we would receive a call, usually from the Washington *Post* or the New York *Times,* just a few minutes before the first-edition deadlines, asking for immediate comment on a complicated Watergate story. If we could not meet the deadlines, the stories would be printed without our response.

On this first night the Washington *Post* called to alert us that they were planning to publish a report that an associate of Dean's said he was "not going to go down in flames," and that he would implicate people "above and below himself." They said that Dean would charge Haldeman with having engineered the cover-up in order to hide the involvement of presidential aides in the DNC bugging, and that the so-called "Dean report" attesting to "no White House involvement" in Watergate had been more or less made up out of whole cloth.

The next morning the *Post* ran the story on the front page.

That same day, April 20, the New York *Times* reported without attribution John Mitchell's first alleged public acknowledgment that he had ever heard of the buggings in advance. According to the *Times,* Mitchell had told "friends" that he had heard of the bugging plot but rejected it and did not know who had ordered that it go ahead.

Throughout this whole period I had tried to keep up a fully active schedule. On Wednesday, April 18, for example, I spent nearly two hours in a congressional leadership meeting on energy policy and then proceeded into another meeting with congressmen on Soviet emigration policy. Prime Minister Giulio Andreotti of Italy was in Washington for a state visit and Rainer Barzel, the chairman of West Germany's Christian Democratic Union, came in for an informal talk. I met with John Volpe, our ambassador to Italy, and then attended a two-hour session on the economy. On April 19 I met with American Jewish leaders on the issue of the emigration of Soviet Jews. On April 20 I held a Cabinet meeting for two hours on energy and the economy and then flew to Florida for the Easter weekend.

Originally, Haldeman and Ehrlichman had planned to come with me to Key Biscayne so that there would be no interruption of their normal duties. But as the weekend neared I felt that I needed time to think, and they felt the same way. They decided, therefore, to go to Camp David instead.

On the evening of April 20 Ron Ziegler came to my house. "Bob will accept the fact that they should leave if the inevitable happens," I told him as we watched the sun setting into Biscayne Bay, "but he won't accept that it is inevitable."

"I know the kind of thing we're going to be up against," Ziegler answered. "I saw Mitchell on television tonight. They were juxtaposing the public statements he made earlier with what he is saying now, trying to humiliate him. You can't have your Chief of Staff and your major domestic adviser going through that kind of thing every day." Ziegler said that in three days alone he had been asked over 300 questions on Watergate in his daily briefings. I asked him to call Haldeman and tell him this, as his own personal feeling about the situation. Before I had left for Florida for the weekend, Haldeman had urged that I not get just one-sided "panicky" advice about what I should do. He had asked me to check with Pat Buchanan and find out how he felt. I had done so, and I wanted Ziegler to read to Haldeman what Buchanan had written to me:

> Anyone who is not guilty should not be put overboard . . . however, presidential aides who cannot maintain their viability should step forward voluntarily . . . if done sooner it will be a selfless act . . . if it is dragged out, the result will be that they were forced . . .
>
> Howard K. Smith questioned on television: Will Nixon be the Eisenhower who cleans his house himself, or the Harding who covered up for his people? This in ruthless candor is the question.
>
> If Haldeman leaves without Ehrlichman, it is still a cover-up: they can't be separated. If there is any chance Ehrlichman's name is going to come up in the grand jury, he should go.
>
> There is a *Titanic* mentality around the White House staff these days. We've got to put out the life rafts and hope to pull the presidency through.

Later I phoned Ziegler to find out what had been said when he had delivered his message. He told me that Haldeman had been "thoughtful."

The next morning, April 21, the Miami *Herald* quoted "associates" of Mitchell who claimed that Magruder had gone over Mitchell's head to the White House to obtain approval of the bugging plan. The Washington *Post* said that Dean had documentary evidence to support his charges about the bugging and the cover-up. And the New York *Times* reported that Dean had supervised payoffs of more than $175,000 to defendants, a charge Dean denied.

On Easter morning there were four different Watergate stories on the front page of the Washington *Post*. According to the major one, the grand jury was investigating whether Haldeman had a fund of $350,000 from which he ordered payments to defendants to keep quiet. The story was attributed to a "high-placed source in the executive branch." Sources said that Dean had tried to stop the payments but was ordered to go ahead with them by higher-ups. A source also said that Dean was prepared to implicate Ehrlichman in Watergate.

The Washington *Star* said that Haldeman and Ehrlichman both were targets. The *Star* also quoted "sources" as saying that Mitchell had personally approved the bugging plans, although "sources" close to Mitchell were quoted as saying that Mitchell believed it was the White House that had done so. Colson, in an alleged attempt to take care of himself, was reported to have given the prosecutors documentary evidence establishing a cover-up.

Although not a single charge of any kind had been made against me directly, a Gallup poll reported that over 40 percent of the people thought I had known about the Watergate bugging in advance. In the same poll 53 percent thought that the bugging was nothing more than "just politics—the kind of thing both parties engage in."

It had been my habit for years to place phone calls to my staff on Easter Sunday. This troubled Easter morning I started with Chuck Colson. He heatedly denied "distorted stories" about him in the newspapers. He said that he wanted to tell me again that the phone call he had made to Magruder that was now being alleged to have precipitated the whole Watergate episode had been innocent. I said that I believed him completely. We wished each other well on Easter.

Next I called Dean. "On Easter morning, I want you to know someone is thinking of you," I began. "I want to wish you well—we'll make it through. You said that this is a cancer that must be cut out, I want you to know I am following that advice."

Dean said that he was grateful for the call. His appreciation seemed real. He said that at some point he would like to discuss with me how he should plead. He said he didn't know if he should take the Fifth Amendment. I told him that he should feel free to come see me.

At one point Dean said rather coolly, "I know how that line got in the statement, the one about no immunity." We talked about Gray's destruction of documents and the sequence of events surrounding Hunt's demand—the events that had led to our meeting of March 21.

I told him I still considered it proper for us to meet about his plea because he had not yet been dismissed from the White House. "You're still my counsel," I said.

At 9:45 I called Haldeman. "I don't want this Easter to go by without reminding you how much tougher it was last Easter," I said. He agreed that this was true.

I called Ehrlichman next. He wished me a good Easter, but he warned, "Don't move too fast and start picking up Carl Rowan's and Joe Kraft's lines that this entire government is corrupt because of all of this. Stay steady."

I went in to gather the family for the Easter church service. There is a kind of unspoken consensus that works in our family. During some crises they will be with me hourly, advising me on every change in mood they perceive and canvassing all the possible options. In this case, however, they had decided that my problem was that I had too many pressures coming in from every direction, and they tried to make it easier for me by talking about other things. Julie had sent me a note when we arrived in Florida. It said simply, "We love you. We stand with you."

When we had finally got the Vietnam peace agreement on January 23, I had told the family that one welcome personal benefit would be that we would no longer be harassed by sign-carrying hecklers as we had been during our first four years. The war was over, but now signs had reappeared. Now they were Watergate signs. Eventually they became even uglier and more personal than the antiwar signs had ever been.

When Pat and I left the church that morning, several people in the crowd held up signs. One of them read: "Is the President honest?" A woman rushed over in front of it, holding up a crudely done sign of her own: "Yes, the President is honest."

Later in the day Ziegler told me that Dean had called him to say how much he had appreciated my call. Ziegler had asked him about the newspaper reports that "sources close to Dean" were saying that his "Dean Report" to which I had alluded in my press conference of August 29, had never actually been written. "If I had a chance to discuss that statement with the President before he made it, it certainly would have been phrased differently," Dean told Ziegler. He added, "I wish someone had told me I was conducting an investigation, Ron—I just reported daily to John and Bob."

This exchange angered and depressed Ziegler. His office had kept the detailed notes from phone calls between Dean and Jerry Warren, the Deputy Press Secretary, when Warren had called Dean almost daily to ask him for guidance on responses to Watergate questions in the briefings. "No one in the White House involved" had been a staple of Dean's response. He had also talked frequently about his "investigation," which, he said, had begun on the day after the break-in. Dean had also given very clear instructions about how Ziegler should defend him when he was under attack: he should say that Dean had had no contact with Liddy on intelligence-gathering matters; that he had not shown FBI materials to anyone; and that he had not delayed turning over items from Hunt's safe to the FBI. Now Dean was completely undercutting Ziegler, who wondered if he would be able to go before the press and brief again.

On Monday morning, April 23, I had a three-hour session with Ziegler, Pat Buchanan, and Chappie Rose. I had asked Rose, a fine lawyer and personal friend from the Eisenhower days, to fly down to Florida to give me some outside counsel.

As Buchanan summarized the options, there were four: we could do nothing, but the evidence was too strong for that; we could fire everyone, but the evidence was too weak for that; we could ask them to take leaves, but that would just postpone the injury. "The answer is their resignation," he said. But Chappie Rose was less certain. He thought that it might be prejudicial to their rights to force them to resign. Ziegler played an effective devil's advocate against both views.

At the heart of the problem, as I had increasingly come to see it, was the White House itself. Haldeman and Ehrlichman had lost the confidence of the staff; no work was being done; everyone was tired, drained, and distracted.

For hours we debated the question, and the longer we went over the charges, the more inevitable the outcome seemed. At one point Rose sadly quoted Gladstone: "The first essential for a Prime Minister is to be a good butcher."

"Ten years from now," I said, as much for myself as the others, "this will be a few paragraphs. In fifty years it will be a footnote. But in the meantime I have got to run the office of President, and I can't when they are under constant attack. The country can't feel that the President is burdened and obsessed. The Mideast is boiling, and the international economic situation is in a crisis. There are too many things that need attention."

As the session drew to an emotional end, we all agreed that Haldeman and Ehrlichman had to resign.

I asked Buchanan if he would call Haldeman and tell him that I had come to this conclusion. I said that he should let them know that I was not forcing it. I still wanted it to be their decision. But this was my opinion. The next step would be theirs.

Buchanan said that he thought Ziegler should do it. The personal ties were closer there, and maybe that would make it less painful. Ziegler stared out the window. Haldeman had been responsible for bringing him on my staff; now he was being asked to pass on the word that Haldeman must resign. He said nothing.

"There are no good choices," I said for all of us.

After making the call, Ziegler told me that Haldeman had been predictably stoic and fair. He had said that while he disagreed with the decision, he would accept it.

Within a few hours, Haldeman called Ziegler back. Evidently he had talked to his lawyers, and also to Ehrlichman, who had resisted strongly and had persuaded Haldeman to change his mind. Ehrlichman maintained that he was in a different situation and that even if Haldeman resigned, he should not. Ehrlichman thought the charges against him were much weaker and that therefore he was detachable. And there was no question that he wanted to be detached.

Haldeman argued to Ziegler that I was overreacting. "In all the other important decisions the President has operated from strength," he said, "and just because this is painful doesn't mean it is strong." He urged that I see his lawyers again. "This would be the first real victory of the establishment against Nixon," he insisted. "This is what the media wants, and sooner or later they will see it as phony. It won't help."

Even though I knew that the decision would have to be mine, I sought the advice of several men I particularly trusted and respected. I asked Ziegler to call Bill Rogers, who said that it appeared to him that Haldeman could not survive in his job and that that should be the determining consideration. He felt that Ehrlichman was a closer case. John Connally's view was that if the allegations against them were untrue, then they should not have to go; but if they could not refute the allegations in a way that would demonstrate their untruth there was no alternative. "Someone has to walk the plank," he said, repeating what he had told me when the whole thing first broke open in March.

Bryce Harlow said, "If Haldeman, Dean, and Ehrlichman have undertaken actions which will not float in the public domain, they must leave quickly—they are like a big barnacle on the ship of state, and there is too much at stake to hang on for personal reasons." Leaves of absence would be wrong, he said, because they would only postpone the inevitable and in the end would be less fair to the men themselves. Kissinger, too, had come to the view that something had to be done to break what he called the "miasma of uncertainty" that had come to surround the working of the entire administration.

On Tuesday night, heading back to Washington from Key Biscayne, I thought about Haldeman's argument that this decision should be made with the same toughness and disregard for the popular and easy course that had characterized the decisions on Cambodia, May 8, and December 18. But there was a difference. In those other decisions involving policy I always knew that if I were given a chance to present the whole case to the people they would be behind me. In those instances I had been acting on strong and recognizable principles. With Watergate there was no way to gain public support even on the principle of loyalty to one's staff or friends because the circumstantial case against them was too strong to be ignored or easily explained away.

Eisenhower had not saved me in the fund crisis; I was saved because I had been able to save myself. I did not believe Haldeman and Ehrlichman were guilty of criminal motives; but I did not know if they could ever prove their innocence. I told Ziegler, "What I am saying is that this, too, will *not* pass."

When Haldeman and Ehrlichman came in later that morning, they told me that they were not getting the same recommendations from Rogers and Connally as I seemed to think that Rogers and Connally were giving. I knew, however, that they were mistaking kindness for ambivalence. "Everyone," I said, "agrees we must do something."

Ehrlichman seemed uneasy and restless during this conversation, and suddenly he said that he had been thinking and had decided that there ought to be a candid assessment of the threat in all this to the President. "Now let me . . . just spin something out for you," he said, "probably a far out point." He said that if Dean were "totally out of control," it was "entirely conceivable" that I might be faced with a resolution of impeachment on the ground that I had committed a crime and no other legal process was available except impeachment. He knew in general of my conversation with Dean on March 21 about the break-in and the cover-up. He said that as far as he knew, what Dean had fell far short of any commission of a crime by me.

"I think really the only way that I know to make a judgment on this," Ehrlichman said, "is for you to listen to your tapes and see what actually was said then, or maybe for Bob to do it." He suggested that before I took "any precipitous steps" I'd better know what my "hole card" was.

I knew that what he was saying, both explicitly and implicitly, was true. Explicitly, he was saying that I should recognize how exposed I would be if he and Haldeman were forced to leave, and that before forcing them to, I should assess the worst possible consequences of that exposure. Implicitly, I believe, he was saying that if I decided I were equally as involved as they, I should consult my own conscience before forcing them to leave.

In the last two weeks of April I began seriously facing the possibility that I would be Dean's next target and that I had personally supplied him with the ammunition during our March 21 conversation. I became preoccupied with it and began bringing it up repeatedly. After reading the transcripts of these discussions, it is clear that I gave a number of different versions of it. In talks with Ehrlichman, Dick Moore, and Henry Petersen, I tried to make it sound more ambiguous than it really was, or even to pass it off as having been facetious.

When I was honest with myself, however, I had to admit that I had genuinely contemplated paying blackmail to Hunt—not because of Watergate, but because of his threat against Ehrlichman on the break-in at Ellsberg's psychiatrist's office and against the administration in general. I had also talked with Dean about the possibility of continuing payments to the other defendants. Furthermore, in that conversation Dean had made me aware of payments to defendants that he said constituted an obstruction of justice.

I told Haldeman and Ehrlichman at one point that we could not risk having Dean turn on me with this conversation, even if it meant having to give him immunity. Haldeman countered that I could not let Dean have the permanent handle of blackmail over me, either. I decided that Haldeman should listen to our tape so that we would know exactly what had actually been said and decided on that fateful afternoon.

Before long a disturbing thought occurred to me; I couldn't get it out of my mind: what if Dean had carried a tape recorder at our March 21 meeting, a small tape recorder, concealed in his jacket but capable of catching every word. He would be able to use parts of the conversation in a very damaging way.

In the afternoon of April 25 Kleindienst called me with an urgent request for a meeting. He had a new problem: he felt that the Justice Department would have to turn over material on the break-in at Ellsberg's psychiatrist's office to the court that was hearing the government's case against Ellsberg for having taken the Pentagon Papers. That had been the ruling within the department; besides, if they did not make their possession of the material known, Dean would undoubtedly hold it over their heads.

On April 18, a week earlier, at Ehrlichman's urging, I had talked on the phone with Henry Petersen about the break-in. I had told him to stay out of it. "Your charge is Watergate. This is national security," I had said. Dean had told me that Krogh had felt that he was acting on a national security mandate, and there was no question in my mind that the Ellsberg investigation as a whole was part of a national security crisis of the highest order.

When Petersen asked me if any evidence had been obtained during the break-in, anything that would have to be turned over to the court hearing Ellsberg's trial, I said no. "It was a dry hole," I told him.

Now Kleindienst was saying that the Justice Department felt that the material had to be revealed. Without hesitation I said that he should go ahead. As I did so, I thought how everything was about to become even bleaker for John Ehrlichman.

At 4:40 P.M. on April 25, Haldeman came back in to report on his first couple of hours of listening to the tape of my March 21 conversation with

Dean. He said that it was interesting to learn that Dean had given me a different version of events from the one he had been telling Haldeman.

Haldeman confirmed that I had said to Dean, "We could get the money." But, he said, "You were drawing Dean out."

Haldeman was familiar with my habit of getting other people's ideas by indirection, by purposely not stating my own opinion until the end of a conversation lest it inhibit others, or alternatively, by stating an extreme position or proposition to see how others reacted. He also knew that in conversations I tend to think a problem through out loud, even considering totally unacceptable alternatives in the process of ruling them out—a lawyer's typical mental exercise. In this case all these factors were partial—but only partial—explanations for some of the things I had said.

I had only one other defense in the matter of the March 21 tape: no action had been taken as a result of that conversation. I had not finally ordered any payments be made to defendants, and I had ruled out clemency.

I thought about Haldeman's report during the afternoon and called him at home twice that night. I said that I had always wondered about the taping equipment, "but I'm damn glad we have it, aren't you?"

"Yes, sir," he answered, adding that even the one section he had been through that day was "very helpful."

I said that despite the passages I would have preferred not to have said, there were also some good things on the tape that helped balance it out.

By April 26 the prosecutors' talks with Dean had broken down. Dean immediately began sending threatening new signals to the White House. He talked with Len Garment and told him that Watergate was just the tip of the iceberg. He said that there were things that had been done in 1970 that he could expose. And he kept saying that he had documentary evidence of the cover-up.

That same day the New York *Daily News* had the story that Pat Gray had burned evidence from Hunt's safe. The source who leaked the story placed the blame squarely on Dean and Ehrlichman, saying that they had ordered Gray to do it. When I learned about the story, I called Kleindienst and told him that I thought Gray should resign. First, however, I wanted Henry Petersen's view of the situation.

Petersen said that Gray was going to accuse Ehrlichman and Dean of instructing him to destroy the papers, vowing that he had done it only because he had confidence in them. I was outraged. I knew from the genuine panic I had watched spread across Ehrlichman's face when he talked to Gray on the phone that he had never ordered such a thing. I said that Petersen must tell Gray that he could not solve this problem with another lie. I asked that he and Kleindienst meet and give me a recommendation about what I should do in this situation.

Ehrlichman wanted the White House to put out a statement saying that the story was not true. When I called Ziegler in and told him this, he said that he thought Ehrlichman should put the statement out in his own name. He was right: eventually these would all be testimonial areas, and we could not be in the position of vouching for one side over the other.

"You must take a leave," I told Haldeman and Ehrlichman. I said that they should prepare letters requesting leaves of absence by Saturday. I said that Haldeman and Ehrlichman should go first, so that it would be clear that they were not being forced to go as Dean would be.

At 7:28 that night the *Post* called with another story: "sources" said that Haldeman and Ehrlichman had been told by Dean on March 20 that "the jig is up" and that they should be prepared to go to jail. The story was not true, but there was no way to fight Dean's guerrilla tactics. The stories revealing that Gray had destroyed documents also indicated that among these materials was a forged cable implicating President Kennedy in the Diem assassination. This had evidently come from Dean, who apparently had seen the material before giving it to Gray.

By the next morning, April 27, two new stories had surfaced about Ehrlichman on subjects unrelated to Watergate. The items were scurrilously false, and Ehrlichman tried valiantly to combat their effect on public opinion.

I flew to Mississippi that morning for a ceremony dedicating a naval training center being named in honor of John Stennis. I invited Stennis to come with me on *Air Force One*. On the way down, as we sat alone in my cabin, this old friend said that he wanted to give me some advice. "The time is now," he said. "We say down in our country that the rain falls on the just and the unjust. Time is running out."

When Stennis introduced me to the enthusiastic crowd at the dedication, he addressed me directly: "You do not panic when the going gets tough. I believe you have what it takes to tough it through. We admire that."

Pat Gray called while we were in Mississippi to say that he had decided to resign. William Ruckelshaus, head of the Environmental Protection Agency, agreed to take over Gray's post temporarily.

I asked Ehrlichman to make up a list for me of all the national-security-related activities that he thought Dean might be able to expose. On the plane on the way back to Washington he went over three of them with me: Ellsberg, the 1969 wiretaps, and the yeoman episode during the Indo-Pakistan war. Ehrlichman was not sure what else there might be, because Dean's access to the files had been almost unlimited.

Ziegler came into my cabin to report that the Washington *Post* had a new story from "reliable sources" to the effect that "someone" had talked to the prosecutors and had implicated me directly in the cover-up. When we got to Washington, the New York *Times* had called with information that Dean was implicating me. Later the Los Angeles *Times* would call to get a comment on the same report.

I called Henry Petersen and asked him to come over. It was an emotional session. I demanded to know if the stories were true: had Dean implicated me? Petersen went out to check with his office, and a few minutes later he came back and said that the stories were not true. He said that earlier in the week Dean's lawyer had said, "We'll bring the President in—not on this case but in other areas." At the time the prosecutors had thought that this was just bombast and posturing as a part of the effort to gain immunity for Dean. And indeed, they had not yet produced any evidence implicating me. I called Ziegler in and told him that the story had to be killed immediately.

Before Petersen left, he said that he would like to recommend that I move on Dean now. He thought that the added pressure from me would be better for the government's position against him. And he urged once more that Haldeman and Ehrlichman also leave.

When Haldeman came in later, he told me that his lawyers felt that he and Ehrlichman were being taken advantage of because they were loyal and Dean was not. "They think Petersen and Dean are playing you."

I said that our plan should be that he and Ehrlichman would take leaves of absence beginning Sunday, or even Saturday. On Monday I would inform Dean that he was being fired. I asked that Ray Price begin preparing a speech for me, leaving open whether I would be announcing leaves of absence or actual resignations.

HALDEMAN AND EHRLICHMAN RESIGN

On Friday night, April 27, I flew to Camp David. On Saturday morning an early fog settled over the valley. I had breakfast on the porch and then went to the small library to work. About ten o'clock I walked into the living room looking for Manolo and a cup of coffee. I was startled to see the fire blazing and Tricia sitting on the couch in front of it.

She said that she had been awake all night talking with Julie and David about Watergate and the decisions that had to be made. They had talked with Pat for a long time early in the morning, and they wanted me to know that they all agreed that there was no choice but to have Haldeman and Ehrlichman resign. The attacks on them had destroyed their ability to serve in their high positions. "I want you to know that I would never allow any personal feeling about either of them to interfere with my judgment," she said. "You know I never felt that the way they handled people served you well—but I promise you that I made my decision carefully and objectively."

Tears brimmed in her eyes; but, unlike Julie, Tricia would seldom allow them to overflow. "I am speaking for Julie, David, and Mama as well," she said. "That is our opinion. But we also want you to know that we have complete confidence in you. If you decide not to take our advice, we will understand. Whatever you do, just remember we will support you, and we love you very much."

I asked her if she would like to stay with me through the day, but she said she knew it would be better if she went back. I hugged her, and she was gone.

Bill Rogers arrived at 11:30 and argued strongly that leaves of absence were no longer a viable answer—resignation was now the only choice. I valued his opinion because I had learned over the years that he had excellent political as well as legal judgment and that as a loyal friend he would tell me what I needed to hear and not just what I might want to hear. I told him I had come to the same conclusion. Otherwise we were just setting ourselves up for an even messier and more painful separation later on.

I asked him if he would convey this to Haldeman and Ehrlichman for me. He said that he did not think his relationship with them was good enough to do that—nor even objective enough, as mine had been with Adams. There had been some bitterness between them after the election during the reorganization, and he was concerned that they might feel that he was bringing personal feelings to the task.

That evening Ehrlichman called me. He was cordial but bluntly direct. He told me that he thought I should recognize the reality of my own responsibility. He said that all the illegal acts ultimately derived from me, whether directly or indirectly. He implied that I was the inspiration behind them and mentioned such things as the forged Diem cable. He also implied, I thought, that I should resign.

I was sitting in the living room after his call when Ziegler came in. He had just learned that the next morning's Washington *Post* had a story from "reliable sources" that Dean had evidence to prove that he was under the direction of Haldeman and Ehrlichman when he engaged in a cover-up and that he also had knowledge of "illegal activities" going back to 1969.

I asked Ziegler if he would call Colson for me and find out what had happened on the Diem cable. He came back a few minutes later and said that Colson had sworn that he himself had not known about the forgery. "The President," Colson had added, "knew zero."

Early on Sunday morning I called Haldeman and asked if he would come up to Camp David. He said that he would, and so would Ehrlichman—but that they would like to have separate meetings with me. I knew then that he realized what I was going to say. I knew that he realized we had reached the end.

Haldeman arrived in the early afternoon. We walked to the windows and haltingly attempted small talk. The fog and clouds had lifted by then, revealing the layers of green spring trees covering the mountainside.

Then I said that I believed resignation was the right course for him. I said this was the hardest decision I had ever made. I meant it. He knew that I rarely spoke about religion, and I thought he looked somewhat surprised when I told him that from my first day as President on January 20, 1969, I followed my mother's custom of getting down on my knees every night and praying silently for those in my administration who were going through difficult times, but most of all for guidance that I would do what was right the next day in meeting my responsibilities. I told him that when I went to bed last night I had hoped, and almost prayed, that I wouldn't wake up this morning.

I said that I knew this wasn't fair, but I saw no other way. I told him I felt enormous guilt. I knew that the responsibility, and much of the blame for what had happened, rested with me. I had put Mitchell in his position, and Colson's activities were in many cases prompted by my prodding.

Even at this moment Haldeman's effort was to reassure me. He was proud and secure. He said that he accepted this decision even though he did not agree with it, and that I must always feel I could call on him. "What you have to remember," he said, "is that nothing that has happened in the Watergate mess has changed your mandate in the non-Watergate areas. That is what matters. That is what you do best." He said that he would go to another cabin and write his letter of resignation.

After he left I walked out onto the porch and was standing there looking down into the valley when Ehrlichman arrived. I shook hands with him and said, "I know what a terribly difficult day this is for you. I am sure you realize what a difficult day it is for me." When I told him about my feelings the night before, he put his arm around my shoulders and said, "Don't talk that way. Don't *think* that way."

Back in the sitting room I told him that I wanted to be as helpful in any way that I could, including assistance with the great financial burden I knew he would now be carrying, not only because of the need to support his family but because of the mounting attorneys' fees.

His mouth tightened and he said quickly, "There is only one thing I would like for you to do. I would like for you to explain this to my children."

With controlled bitterness he said that the decision I had made was wrong and that I would live to regret it. "I have no choice but to accept it, and I will," he said. "But I still feel I have done nothing that was without your implied or direct approval."

"You have always been the conscience of the administration," I said. "You were always for the cleanest way through things."

"If I was the conscience, then I haven't been very effective," he said.

Later that afternoon I had Kleindienst come up to see me. We both knew that his situation at the Justice Department had become intolerable. His close association with Mitchell now made it impossible for him to stay on. He had been the publicist of what he sincerely believed to have been the "greatest investigation since the Kennedy assassination," and it had blown up in his face. We agreed that he should resign and be replaced by Elliot Richardson, who was then Secretary of Defense. I deeply regret now that Kleindienst's departure was timed to coincide with the others; it falsely conveyed the impression that he was somehow involved in Watergate.

After Kleindienst left I stood for a few minutes waiting for Haldeman and Ehrlichman to return with their letters, looking out the picture window and watching the day darken into evening. Ziegler was standing silently near the couch behind me.

"It's all over, Ron, do you know that?"

"No, sir," he said. He thought that I was referring only to the terrible events of the past few days and hours.

"Well, it is. It's all over," I repeated.

When Haldeman and Ehrlichman returned, they showed their letters to me and to Bill Rogers, who had now joined us. Ehrlichman asked me to use the specific sentence, "John Dean has been fired," in my television speech. I knew how he felt. Ehrlichman had been loyal and would defend me and our administration. Dean was disloyal and would look out only for himself. By allowing Dean to "resign" I would be forcing Haldeman and Ehrlichman to share the same public disrepute as their accuser.

We walked out to their car. They said bolstering things like, "Get up for your speech tomorrow night."

"I wish I were as strong as you," I said. "God bless you both." The car drove away.

They had been my closest aides. They were my friends. I tried to make it up to them the next night by saying in my speech what I deeply believed: "Today, in one of the most difficult decisions of my presidency, I accepted the resignations of two of my closest associates in the White House—Bob Haldeman, John Ehrlichman—two of the finest public servants it has been my privilege to know."

They deserved the best possible chance to save themselves, and in asking them to leave I had ensured that they would never be able to prove that their motives had been innocent. I had done what I felt was necessary, but not what I believed was right. I had always prided myself on the fact that I stood by people who were down. Now I had sacrificed, for myself, two people to whom I owed so much.

I stayed at Camp David to work with Ray Price on the final draft of the speech I was to deliver the next night, Monday, April 30. As I handed him the draft, I said, "Ray, you are the most honest, cool, objective man I know. If you feel that I should resign, I am ready to do so. You won't have to tell me. You should just put it in the next draft."

He said that I should not resign, that I had a duty to complete the job I had been elected to do. He said he knew how heartbreaking my decision on Haldeman and Ehrlichman had been, but he tried to ease it for me by saying that I had done what I had to do.

I felt as if I had cut off one arm and then the other. The amputation may have been necessary for even a chance at survival, but what I had had to do left me so anguished and saddened that from that day on the presidency lost all joy for me.

My speech on April 30, 1973, was the first time I formally addressed the American people specifically on Watergate. All that most people understood of the complex situation that had precipitated the speech was that my two closest aides were being accused of participation in the Watergate cover-up, while one of my best friends, my former Attorney General, was being accused of having ordered the break-in and bugging.

No matter how much we protested to the contrary, as soon as Haldeman and Ehrlichman resigned, people assumed it was because they were, at least to some extent, guilty of the charges against them. The spotlight automatically turned next to me: people were waiting for a yes or no answer to the question of whether I was also involved in Watergate. That was what they looked for from my April 30 speech. I made the decision of how I would answer this question less on the basis of logical calculation than on political instinct. I made it without stopping to realize that this speech would be a major turning point and that my answer, once given, would have to see me through whatever lay ahead.

I believe that a totally honest answer would have been neither a simple yes or no.

If I had given the true answer, I would have had to say that without fully realizing the implications of my actions I had become deeply entangled in the complicated mesh of decisions, inactions, misunderstandings, and conflicting motivations that comprised the Watergate cover-up; I would have had to admit that I still did not know the whole story and therefore did not know the full extent of my involvement in it; and I would have had to give the damaging specifics of what I did know while leaving open the possibility that much more might come out later.

I sensed that the inept way we had handled Watergate so far had put us so much on the defensive that there would have been no tolerance for such a complicated explanation from me at this late date. And the instincts of twenty-five years in politics told me that I was up against no ordinary opposition. In this second term I had thrown down a gauntlet to Congress, the bureaucracy, the media, and the Washington establishment and challenged them to engage in epic battle. We had already skirmished over the limitations of prerogative and power represented in confirmation of appointments, the impoundment of funds, and the battle of the budget. Now, suddenly, Watergate had exposed a cavernous weakness in my ranks, and I felt that if in this speech I admitted any vulnerabilities, my opponents would savage me with them. I feared that any admissions I made would be used to keep the Watergate issue—and the issue of my behavior in office—festering during the rest of my term, thereby making it impossible for me to exert presidential leadership.

Given this situation and given this choice—given my belief that these were the stakes—I decided to answer no to the question whether I was also involved in Watergate.

I hoped that, after the agony of the past weeks, a firm statement of my innocence, accompanied by the symbolic cleansing of the administration with the departure of Haldeman, Ehrlichman, and Dean and followed by an active rebuilding with new people along open lines, would convince people that the various Watergate probes could and should be brought to a quick conclusion. I was counting on the polls, which showed that the majority of people, even some of the 40 percent who already thought I knew of the break-in in advance, still agreed with me that the whole thing was "just politics." I knew I was good at being President, at the really important things, and I was counting on people to become impatient with Watergate and exert pressure on Congress and the media to move on to something else and to get back to the things that mattered. I actually hoped that this speech would at last and once and for all put Watergate behind me as a nagging national issue. I could not have made a more disastrous miscalculation.

In the April 30 speech I gave the impression that I had known nothing at all about the cover-up until my March 21 meeting with Dean. I indicated that once I had learned about it I had acted with dispatch and dispassion to end it. In fact, I had known some of the details of the cover-up before March 21, and when I did become aware of their implications, instead of exerting presidential leadership aimed at uncovering the cover-up, I embarked upon an increasingly desperate search for ways to limit the damage to my friends, to my administration, and to myself.

I talked in terms of responsibility and the fact that "the man at the top must bear the responsibility. . . . I accept it." But that was only an abstraction and people saw through it. Finally, I clung to excuses. The fact that they happened to be excuses that I really believed made little difference. In a sense Watergate *had* grown out of the end-justifies-the-means mentality of the causes of the 1960s. It was also true that if we often made the mistake of acting like an administration under siege, it was because we *were* an administration under siege. And I believed it was true that if I had not been preoccupied with Vietnam and other policy issues, I might have probed until I sensed the full dimensions of the cover-up and perhaps precipitated action sooner—if not on ethical grounds, at least because I would have recognized that we were marching headlong into a trap with no exits.

But these were still only excuses. They were not an accounting of my role. They were not explanations of how a President of the United States could so incompetently allow himself to get in such a situation. That was what people really wanted to know, and that was what my April 30 speech and all the other public statements I made about Watergate while I was President failed to tell them.

It was as if a convulsion had seized Washington. Restraints that had governed professional and political conduct for decades were suddenly abandoned. The FBI and the Justice Department hemorrhaged with leaks of confidential testimony, grand jury materials, and prosecutorial speculation. And on Capitol Hill it seemed as if anything could be leaked and anything would be indulged, under the guise of righteous indignation over Watergate.

In reporting the story the members of the Washington press corps were fired by personal passion. They felt that they had embarrassed themselves by uncritically reporting the months of White House denials, and so they frantically sought to reassert their independence by demonstrating their skepticism of all official explanations. In their determination to prove they were not the tools of the White House they went to the other extreme and became the shills for faceless and nameless leakers.

In December 1971 the Washington *Post* had proudly announced a new policy: it would always insist on public accountability for public business—government officials would not be allowed to talk on a "source" basis. In the spring of 1973, however, the *Post* guaranteed anonymity to anyone who proffered an exciting and exclusive Watergate leak or story. Other papers followed this lead, reacting to the combination of commercial pressure and professional competitiveness. They called it "investigative journalism," but it was not that at all. There is nothing "investigative" about publicizing leaks from sources in the FBI, the Justice Department, or congressional committees who have easy access to confidential material. This was rumor journalism, some true, some false, some a mixture of truth and fiction, all prejudicial. That it was a dangerous form of journalism should have been understood by the *Post*, whose editor, Ben Bradlee, has since observed: "We don't print the truth. We print what we know, what people tell us. So we print lies."

A symbiotic relationship developed between the leakers on the Ervin Committee and its staff and the leakers in the prosecutor's office on the one hand, and their media publicists on the other. The reporters gathered daily outside the committee rooms or buttonholed bureaucrats in hallways to try to get a Watergate headline. The subject had already prompted a new ferocity in reporting: grand jurors were hounded by newsmen, itself a potential offense; in some cases other political dirt was ferreted out and traded for Watergate information. The emphasis was on having a story—any story—before someone else got it. The competition for Watergate stories debauched ordinary journalistic standards. No longer did reporters feel required to substantiate the truth of a charge before printing it. They shifted this traditional professional responsibility by saying that the person accused had the obligation to prove that the report was *not* true—and to do so before a stated deadline in order to get them to drop the story.

Many of the reporters argued that because there had been a cover-up of Watergate, the system of justice could no longer be trusted to work on its own. Before very long this argument became the self-justifying rationale for a vigilante squad of anonymous "sources" and competing reporters who, in effect, took the law into their own hands. Louis Nizer said during this period: "I fear McCarthyism in reverse. People are being perhaps destroyed by headlines where there are as yet no proven facts before a jury in a trial. . . . It's one thing to dig up information and even to give it to a prosecutor to pursue, and it is another to become so drunk with the triumph as to begin taking rumor and putting it as a headline. . . . This is the time to be cautious. You see, it is easy to agree with a violation of civil rights when the fellow who is getting it is a man that we are tickled to death is getting it."

But neither the pleas of conscience-stricken colleagues nor the criticism of dismayed outsiders could stop the stampede.

The New York *Times* carried at least one Watergate story on its front page every day but one during each of the months of May, June, and July 1973. A later study showed that an average of 52 percent of the front pages of the major American newspapers was occupied by Watergate stories on days when the Ervin Committee was in session; the average was 35 percent on days when the committee did not meet. The network news shows were devoting a third to half of their time to Watergate.

In many cases the sheer quantity of Watergate stories derived from the nature of the subject itself: each new disclosure seemed to ignite another, like a string of firecrackers. In other cases, however, the quantity of Watergate stories derived from the process of reporting: the competition for stories created a self-perpetuating momentum, and a day without a Watergate headline became a day you had been scooped. Often the same stories were repeated from day to day with only minor changes, and sometimes without any changes at all, and then rehashed again on the weekends in Watergate "updates" or "analyses."

In some cases the press created the monsters it denounced. For example, it was the Washington press corps that created the idea of the Plumbers as a repressive White House "police force." Many people are still astounded to learn that the Plumbers unit consisted of only four men who worked together for just a little over two months in 1971.

In early April 1973 allegations that Senators Muskie, Percy, Proxmire, and Javits had been under surveillance by the White House were being widely reported. *Newsweek* printed reports that the offices of Senators Mansfield and Fulbright had been bugged. Both stories were untrue. On May 3 the Washington *Post* claimed that the Nixon administration had tapped the telephones of at least two newspaper reporters as part of the Pentagon Papers investigation and that the taps were supervised by Hunt and Liddy. Hunt and Liddy were said to have overseen a "so-called 'vigilante squad' " of wiretappers, and, according to the *Post*'s story, it was decided at a campaign strategy meeting that some members of this squad would be used to wiretap the telephones of Democratic presidential candidates. This story was not true. On May 17 the *Post* claimed that a "vast GOP undercover operation" had originated in 1969, and asserted that both the Watergate and Ellsberg break-ins were part of an "elaborate, continuous campaign of illegal and quasi-legal undercover operations conducted by the Nixon administration since 1969." The authority cited for this staggering accusation was "highly placed sources in the executive branch." In the story we were accused, among other things, of having had copies of Senator Eagleton's health records before they were leaked (which was not true); of having used paid provocateurs to encourage violence at antiwar demonstrations early in the first term and during the 1972 campaign (also untrue); and of having undertaken undercover political activities conducted by FBI "suicide squads" against people we regarded as opponents of the administration (also untrue). The reporters said that there were more instances of political burglaries and bugging than had yet been revealed (untrue). They said that groups of radicals, reporters, White House aides, and Democrats all got the same treatment of bugging, spying, infiltration, and burglary (untrue).

In early June the *Post* reported the accusation of "one Senate source" who claimed to have evidence of several other White House burglaries and to know who had participated in them and who had directed them. The charge was untrue; the alleged evidence was never produced. *Newsweek* said that the administration had a secret police force that undertook unauthorized wiretaps and burglaries against radicals (untrue). NBC's legal correspondent Carl Stern reported charges that "massive" wiretapping had been done on McGovern's phones by the Justice Department, ostensibly to monitor incoming radical calls, but in fact to provide information to the CRP (untrue). The Baltimore *Sun* said that testimony before the Ervin Committee would reveal a national network of wiretaps used to supply political information on the Democrats to the CRP (untrue). The Washington *Post* reported that taps had been placed on the phones of Ellsberg and of New York *Times* reporters Neil Sheehan and Tad Szulc, and reports from them fed to the Plumbers (untrue). The New York *Times* reported that we had placed a bug on the phone of friends of Mary Jo Kopechne, who died in Teddy Kennedy's car at Chappaquiddick. None of these stories was true.

There was also a flagrant double standard. In 1973, thirteen years after the alleged event, John Kennedy's doctor claimed that his offices had been broken into during the 1960 campaign and described it as a break-in in a style similar to the burglary of the offices of Ellsberg's doctor. All three networks carried the story. John Lungren, my personal physician, thereupon told of the break-in at his office during the 1972 campaign and even offered reporters copies of the police photographs that had been made at the time. Only one network, CBS, bothered to carry this story.

When Bob Haldeman and John Ehrlichman left the White House, we knew their ability to make a defense before grand juries and in the courtrooms would depend on their ability to demonstrate that their motives had never been criminal or corrupt. Judgments about motives inevitably depend upon delicate and often intangible impressions of personal credibility. After the treatment they received from Congress and the media in the first few days of May, they had no hope of ever receiving a fair hearing.

On the first night after they had left the White House, John Chancellor of NBC proclaimed them "by far" the most unpopular of the 2½ million federal employees, and he quoted congressional "sources" who said that there was "dancing in the halls" over their downfall. ABC said that the reaction on Capitol Hill "couldn't have been happier" because they were both "thoroughly disliked." Hugh Sidey had already reviled them in his *Time* column.

By the end of April the news was full of leaks of John Dean's accusations against them and charges of "cover-up" by nameless congressional sources. But these were not their only malicious accusers. On April 25 a headline in the New York *Times* charged: *Data from Taps Reportedly Sent to White House.* The accusation came from anonymous "federal investigators" who said they had determined that officials of the White House were regularly apprised of the information obtained through the Watergate tap. They mentioned Haldeman as a possible recipient. The accusation was untrue.

On May 27 the *Times* said there was evidence that Haldeman was directly linked to the Ellsberg break-in. This was also untrue. On June 17 the Washington *Post* ran a large front-page story asserting that Gordon Strachan was going to say that Haldeman had been sent the plans for the bugging operation. The next day the New York *Times* ran the same charge. Strachan never made such a claim. Ehrlichman was similarly savaged. For example, on June 13 the Washington *Post* reported that "Watergate prosecutors" had a memo that had been sent to Ehrlichman that "described in detail" plans to burglarize the office of Ellsberg's psychiatrist. The story directly contradicted Ehrlichman's insistence that he had had no prior knowledge of the plans. There was no such memo.

Daniel Schorr of CBS described the situation succinctly when in the fall of 1973 he commented:

> This past year, a new kind of journalism developed, and I found myself doing on a daily routine some things I would never have done before. There was a vacuum in investigation, and the press began to try men in the most effective court in the country. The men involved in the Watergate were convicted by the media, perhaps in a more meaningful way than any jail sentence they will eventually get.

As the months went by and the leaks continued, some voices were raised in concern and protest. Democratic Senator William Proxmire likened the press coverage to McCarthyism. Elliot Richardson urged that reporters develop a code of fairness relating to the use of leaked information. And Special Prosecutor Archibald Cox accused the press of considering itself a fourth branch of government and said that he had misgivings about its role in Watergate. ABC's Harry Reasoner denounced *Time* and *Newsweek*: in a broadcast commentary about the way those news magazines had treated Watergate, he said that "Week after week their lead stories on the subject [of Watergate] have been more in the style of pejorative pamphleteering than objective journalism, and since they are highly visible and normally highly respected organs of our craft, they embarrass and discredit us all."

At the time of the Agnew investigation in September 1973 James Reston wrote:

> It is easy to understand why the Agnews and the Ehrlichmans resent all this, for they are condemned even before they can state their own cases, and obviously they have a justifiable grievance. The newspapers have not resolved or even grappled with the problem effectively. They know that they ought to try to do something to protect the grand jury process, but they have not. . . . The press is ducking this problem, but it cannot do so much longer. It cannot insist on policing the power of the government without policing itself.

The media's performance during this period was irresponsible. Yet to this day exhibiting the same arrogance they are quick to denounce in other institutions, most reporters prefer self-congratulation to self-examination where Watergate is concerned.

On May 2 Bob Haldeman came to see me. Just two days earlier he had been entrusted with some of the most important responsibilities in government. Now he slipped in privately to avoid causing me any embarrassment.

He said he had been thinking about the decision I had made not to replace him but to function as my own Chief of Staff. He wanted to urge that I change my mind. In fact, I had already reached a similar conclusion. Details drain away energy even in good times; now, with Watergate, there was no way that I could handle everything myself.

We had the same man in mind to succeed him: Al Haig. Haig had left Kissinger's staff in January to become Vice Chief of Staff of the Army. He was steady, intelligent, and tough, and what he might have lacked in political experience and organizational finesse he made up for in sheer force of personality. He also had the enormous stamina that the job required. He knew how to drive people, and he knew how to inspire them. Equally important to me, he understood Kissinger.

I asked Haldeman if he would make the initial approach. Haig said he would accept; he asked only that I think further about the public reaction to having a military man as the White House Chief of Staff. After talking with me about this, Haldeman called Haig back and said that he was still the man I wanted.

When I met with Haig at noon the next day I told him that I knew what a great sacrifice I was asking him to make. With his abilities he would certainly have been in a position to become Chief of Staff of the Army and possibly Chairman of the Joint Chiefs of Staff.

I explained that I did not want him to become involved in the handling of Watergate. I wanted him to stick exclusively to running the White House staff and organizing the information I needed for making policy decisions. Still, I knew that taking this job would mean far more for him than just forfeiting military advancement and perquisites. We were in for a long and bloody struggle, and for Haig it would be like volunteering to return to combat with no guarantee of the outcome and with no medals at the end.

A day earlier John Connally had courageously announced that he was switching his affiliation and allegiance to the Republican Party; it was, he said, his ideological home. On May 7 he agreed to come back on the White House staff as an adviser without pay. We decided that rather than define his duties specifically, we would tailor them to his abilities as he went along.

Over the next weeks we began to regain momentum rebuilding the administration as I appointed William Colby Director of the CIA and moved James Schlesinger from the CIA to the Pentagon as Secretary of Defense. I also appointed a strong new head of the FBI, Clarence Kelley, the Chief of the Kansas City Police. Mel Laird and Bryce Harlow agreed to return to the White House as Counsellors to the President, and Haig brought in Fred Buzhardt, the General Counsel of the Defense Department, to assist Len Garment in handling Watergate.

Much of the Watergate criticism had centered on the White House press office. Connally, Laird, and Haig all believed that Ron Ziegler should leave. They had nothing against him personally, but they felt he was a symbol of the old Haldeman order, and that his credibility with the press corps was irreparably damaged. I knew that this was true, but I thought it was unfair to Ziegler. So did Kissinger, who said that we would always regret it if we hurt innocent people in an effort to palliate the press.

Haig looked for someone who might restore the credibility of the press office. Not surprisingly, there were few volunteers for the bloodletting that now accompanied the daily briefings in the White House press room. Ziegler's deputy, Jerry Warren, began to take over the podium much of the time, and Ziegler became more of an adviser to me. Despite his youth and occasional brashness, Ziegler was tough-minded and could analyze problems with honesty and incisiveness.

We had taken some hard blows, but slowly we were gathering strength and beginning to climb back on our feet again. Many friends and supporters at home and abroad offered their reflections and their assistance.

I received a note from Harold Macmillan:

> Although I now live remote from current affairs, thinking more of the past than of the present, I feel impelled, in view of our long friendship, to send you a message of sympathy and good will.
>
> I trust that these clouds may soon roll away, and that you may be able to

take up with enthusiasm the task of promoting the Peace and Prosperity of the world, to which you have already made such a notable contribution.

Our ambassador to Italy, John Volpe, wrote to me after an audience with Pope Paul VI at the Vatican:

> His Holiness said that history will record that you have done more than anyone else to capture world respect as an effective peacemaker during the last four years . . . He told me that he simply cannot understand how Americans writing in the American press can so brutally tear down their own country and its institutions. He is confident, however, that you will be able to pass through this difficult period and continue your fine work for world peace. The Holy Father said he will offer his prayers and a mass for your intentions.

I received a message from former Japanese Prime Minister Sato:

> With profound personal sympathy, today I heard you speak to the American people on the television. You are right when you said, "America is the hope of the world." As an old personal friend of yours, I have firm and quiet confidence in you that you, as the great leader of this hope, will succeed in re-establishing the greater authority and integrity of your own office. Would you please accept my own prayer.

And one afternoon a note arrived from my old friend Clare Boothe Luce:

> From "The Ballad of Sir Andrew Barton": "Sir Andrew Barton said, 'I am hurt, but I am not slain! I'll lay me doun and bleed awhile, and I'll rise and fight again!' "

Through the months of May, June, and July I held meetings with eleven different foreign leaders, presided over fourteen congressional meetings covering major legislation, conducted four Cabinet meetings, chaired thirteen major sessions on the economy and energy, delivered four major public speeches, and prepared for the upcoming summit meeting with Brezhnev.

During this period we also devised a new plan for election reform, moved to increase food production, and, in mid-June, reimposed a limited price freeze in order to steady the economy while we considered our post-Phase III moves. We set up a new Office of Energy Policy, and with Agnew standing by to cast the tie-breaking vote we pushed the vitally important Alaska pipeline bill through the Senate. We continued our efforts at budget reform and government reorganization; by June we had actually accomplished what our critics had said was impossible: we had kept federal spending for 1973 under $250 billion. And although the cost in terms of political abrasion was extremely high, every one of my vetoes of budget-busting legislation was sustained.

Despite this visible and productive activity, we were haunted by the specter of "paralysis." The threat was invoked constantly as the media monitored our pulse and judged that Watergate had sapped my ability to lead. For me, it was a no-win situation. If I had no officially announced schedule for a particular day, it was reported that I was secluded, brooding, paralyzed; if I had an active schedule, it was reported that I was contriving activity in order not to appear paralyzed.

If I talked about Watergate, I was described as struggling to free myself from the morass. If I did not talk about Watergate, I was accused of being out of touch with reality. If I tried to summon the nation to consider economic or foreign policy problems, I was accused of trying to distract attention from Watergate. Watergate had become the center of the media's universe, and during the remaining year of my presidency the media tried to force everything else to revolve around it.

THE POWs RETURN

The fighting in Vietnam took place far from Washington, but scarcely a day passed when the sacrifice and suffering of those who served there were not brought home to me in a very personal and agonizing way. In the letters sent to the next of kin of the men who had been killed in action, I could never find words adequate to express the grief I shared with them. The posthumous presentations of Medals of Honor, at which the families accepted the decoration, were always emotionally wrenching experiences for me. From time to time I made telephone calls to the wives or mothers of men who had been killed in action. It tore me up inside to do it.

During the Christmas season of 1969 Pat and I met with twenty-six wives and mothers of POWs and MIAs. The women spoke respectfully but passionately of the urgent need to get their loved ones released as soon as possible. Tears filled Pat's eyes, and mine as well, as we listened to them tell of the effect of the years of waiting on them and their children, and the terrible uncertainty of not knowing whether their men were alive or dead. From that time on, each POW was an individual to me, and obtaining their release became a burning cause. My long-time friend and chief military aide General Don Hughes did a superb job of handling White House liaison with the families of our POWs and MIAs.

The most dramatic, and heartbreaking, attempt at their release came in November 1970. Late in the summer Mel Laird and the Pentagon presented me with a proposal that we make a daring swoop-and-seize rescue raid on a POW camp inside North Vietnam. They decided to make the raid on the large POW installation at Sontay, the same town outside Hanoi that Pat and I had visited in 1953, when it had served as a refugee camp. Complete secrecy and clockwork precision might allow us to surprise and overpower the camp's guards and remove as many as ninety Americans before a counterattack could be mounted. When I received the plan, I immediately approved it. Early in the month I had received reports that as many as twenty-eight American POWs had recently died because of torture and ill-treatment. I said that I wanted the POWs to have Thanksgiving dinner at the White House.

After two and half months of rigorous training and rehearsal, the raid took place on November 20. By midafternoon in Washington, we knew that it had failed. The raiding party had found the cells empty; the prisoners had been moved. Apparently all the intelligence reports used for planning the operation had been several weeks old. Even if I had known when the operation was being planned that the reports were out of date, I believe I would still have given my approval.

Although the raid did not achieve its purpose, it was a significant psychological success. From intelligence sources we learned that it caused serious concern among the North Vietnamese military and political leaders, because it revealed their vulnerability to a kind of attack they had not experienced before. Later, when the POWs were home, I learned that the raid had also had a positive effect on their treatment as well as on their morale. Shortly after the raid the North Vietnamese moved most of the men from scattered camps throughout the country to a single prison in Hanoi, which became known as the Hanoi Hilton. The men were then able to organize themselves, and obtained more consistent—if not substantially better—treatment from their captors.

Our POWs had been courageous in action; they were even more courageous in captivity. That was one of the reasons that as the war ended, I continued to oppose amnesty for draft dodgers and deserters. I said in one press conference, "I can think of no greater insult to the memories of those who have fought and died, to the memories of those who have served, and also to our POWs, to say to them that we are now going to provide amnesty for those who deserted the country or refused to serve."

The first of the 591 POWs were released in Hanoi on February 12 and flown directly from Hanoi to Clark Air Force Base in the Philippines. I wanted the flag to be flying proud and high on the day the first prisoners returned to American soil. I called Lady Bird Johnson and asked her if we might cut short the official thirty-day period of national mourning during which all flags were flying at half-staff for President Johnson. She said she would like to think about it and call me back in a few minutes. When she called to give her approval, she said she was sure that this was what Lyndon would have wanted.

The scene at Clark Air Force Base was tremendously moving as one by one the men came down the ramp, walking or hobbling on crutches, saluting the flag. Some made eloquent statements. Some fell to their knees to kiss the ground. I had been concerned that they might have been so scarred by what they had been through that they would be bitter and disillusioned, or broken and unable to adjust to the conditions they would find at home. But these were no ordinary men. These were true heroes.

The first man off the first plane, Navy Captain Jeremiah P. Denton, stepped before the microphones and said, "We are honored to have had the opportunity to serve our country under difficult circumstances. We are profoundly grateful to our Commander in Chief, and to our nation for this day. God bless America."

As a token of the joy I felt at the return of the men, I personally bought more than 600 orchid corsages and had one sent to each of the wives or mothers. I was delighted when I heard that some of them had worn the flowers to greet their husbands and sons as they arrived home.

Over the next few days the returning men talked to reporters. Air Force Colonel James Kasler said, "We went to Vietnam to do a job that had to be done. And we were willing to stay until that job was complete. We wanted to come home, but we wanted to come home with honor. President Nixon has brought us home with honor. God bless those Americans who supported our President during this long ordeal."

And Air Force Captain David Gray, Jr., spoke with warm simplicity. "A loving God made me an American, and to America I return. A loving President preserved my honor, and with honor I return. A loving wife waited with strong heart, and to her I return. Thank you, Heavenly Father. Thank you, President Nixon. Thank you, Lynda. Thank you, America."

On the morning of February 12, I received a call from Air Force Colonel Robinson Risner, the senior officer of the first POW group to return home. For seven and a half years he had been held captive in North Vietnam; for much of that time he had been kept in solitary confinement.

When I picked up the phone, he said, "This is Colonel Risner, sir, reporting for duty."

We talked for just a few minutes, and I told him that I looked forward to seeing him and all the other men at the White House. At the end of our brief conversation he said that talking to me had been the greatest moment of his life.

Diary

Risner's comment to the effect that this was the greatest moment in his life, of course, had a very sobering effect as far as I was concerned. It made me feel extremely humble, to hear this man who had suffered so long and had taken such great risks as far as his life was concerned, to speak in this way. He spoke at the very last by saying that he and the men with him would be supporting me as long as they lived.

On March 6 Captain Jerry Singleton and Major Robert Jeffrey, both Air Force officers, came to meet me at the White House.

Diary

At ten o'clock I met the first POWs I have seen. It was a very moving experience to see their wives and the two of them—gaunt, lean, quiet, confident, with enormous faith in the country, in God, and in themselves.

Apparently they had been exposed to enemy propaganda throughout and had never given in to it. For example, they were shown still photos of the big crowds demonstrating against the President. They, of course, heard tapes of messages from Ramsey Clark, Jane Fonda, and the other peacenik groups, but they had nothing but contempt for them.

I only hope that these men do not have a terrible letdown now that they are back. I don't think they will. I think after what they have been through they have become stronger as a result of being put through the fire of adversity. They are like fine steel rather than soft iron.

It was not long before the returning men had confirmed the widespread use of torture in the prison camps. Some were tortured for refusing to pose in propaganda photos with touring antiwar groups. Miss Fonda said that the POWs were "liars" for making such claims; one POW had his arm and leg broken because he refused to meet with Miss Fonda. It was during her trip to North Vietnam in 1972 that she broadcast appeals over Radio Hanoi asking American pilots to quit flying bombing runs over North Vietnam. I met with other POWs whenever I could arrange time in my schedule. Among them was the ranking officer of the group, Air Force Brigadier General John P. Flynn, who had been a POW for five and a half years. When I escorted him to the door after our talk, I told him how deeply sad I was that he had been away from his home and family for so many years and had had to endure such terrible conditions.

He said, "Mr. President, don't give that a second thought; how else could John Peter Flynn be standing here in the office of the President of the United States?" He smartly snapped to attention, saluted, and left the room before I could respond. It was fortunate that he did. I was so choked up with emotion that I don't believe I could have thought of anything to say worthy of the moment.

On March 12 I had long meetings with Colonel Risner and Captain Denton.

Diary

I asked Risner about how he was able to take what he had been through. I had not realized that he had been four years in solitary confinement. At this point he said, "It isn't easy for me to say this." His voice broke, and he said, "It was faith in God and faith in my country."

He obviously was a man who had been through the tortures of the damned. He explained in detail some of the torture he had gone through but did not make a big thing out of it.

He told me how he had gotten to the point that he was ready to break because his nerves had been shattered. He didn't know what was happening to him. He had a hot flash on the back of his neck—he felt that he was coming apart but he would exercise and then finally fall asleep for a few hours.

I asked about the effect of the bombing. They pointed out that as far as the other fighter planes were concerned, their captors would get out and make as if they were shooting at them and all that sort of thing. But when the B-52s came, they came out of the blue despite the bad weather and all the rest, with shattering effect.

He said that they all cheered and hollered and hugged each other when the bombing was going on. He said their captors thought they were all crazy. Apparently some of the plaster fell down off of the walls as a result of the reverberations—one of their captors came in and said, "Aren't you aware of the fact that they are trying to kill you or kill the civilians?" They answered that this was in no way what was involved, and that they knew the bombing was aimed at only military targets.

Denton spoke movingly about his deep concern about the country. He is a deeply religious man. He, whenever I mentioned his suffering and the rest, came back to what I had been through. He was most generous in his respect—said that he could see the same suffering in my eyes that he could see in the eyes of his fellow POWs. I told him that after knowing what they had been through, what I had been through was nothing. But he realized, as he said, that I had been pretty much alone in the decisions that I had made.

He pointed out that the North Vietnamese said that the trouble with Nixon is that he flip-flops. Of course, this was a compliment, not a condemnation. He said that the North Vietnamese knew that Nixon was a very tough fellow, and he was convinced that the recognition of that fact was what eventually brought them around to a settlement.

He made an interesting analogy on the point that the North Vietnamese really thought that the President was off his rocker —was totally irrational. He said that it was absolutely essential for them to think that. He said, as a matter of fact, that that is what saved the POWs because the North Vietnamese thought that they were so irrational that they could not break them and they could not take risks with them.

In fact, Risner or Denton said (I think it was Denton) that he would be willing to stay eight, twelve, or sixteen years if necessary to see that the United States came out of Vietnam in the right way. They did not want to come back with their heads down.

He said that the settlement that Harriman would agree to in '68 would have been a shameful thing and that they could not possibly have felt proud if it had ended on that basis.

Denton kept coming back to the fact that he didn't know what was going to happen to the country after I left the office. He feels very strongly we must use this precious time—he said three years or so—for the purpose of seeing that America's foreign policy role is played as well as it possibly can be.

I said that the history of civilization showed that the leader class rather than the common people were those that first disintegrated. That here in our country the problem was not the common people who stood by us—they were the silent majority.

It is now ten minutes until one on the 13th of March. As I sleep in this comfortable room with the blackout curtains, the air conditioning, a very comfortable bed, I think of how really easy we have it—I think of what they went through—and I realize how we could probably do far more than we do—take more physical punishment actually than we do—live certainly a much more austere life than we do.

On March 3 we had one of our evenings at the White House, at which Sammy Davis, Jr., performed. Afterward he suggested that we organize a gala entertainment honoring the POWs. I discussed this with Pat, and she said that we should go all out and also give a formal dinner in honor of the men and their families.

There were monumental problems involved. In the past the largest number ever served dinner at one time at the White House had been the 231 senior citizens we invited for Thanksgiving in 1969. Now we were considering having more than 1,300 people. Some of the staff members urged that we move the affair into one of the local hotel ballrooms that were properly equipped to deal with such a large number of people, but Pat and I felt that the whole point of the evening was to honor these men at the White House.

Since there was no way that we could possibly accommodate, much less seat, more than a few hundred people inside, Pat arranged for the construction on the South Lawn of a canopy that was itself larger than the whole White House. Then she found and rented enough china and crystal that were sufficiently elegant for an occasion of this importance. Hundreds of bottles of champagne were chilled in ice-filled aluminum canoes, and crates of strawberries for the dessert mousse were run through the blenders at the Pentagon kitchens because the White House simply could not handle such large quantities. Pat was busy for weeks making the preparations and supervising the arrangements for everything from individual place cards to the flower centerpieces on each of the 126 tables.

We wanted to arrange excellent entertainment for after dinner, and Pat and her staff worked with Sammy Davis and Bob Hope and our long-time California friend, television producer Paul Keyes. Her only condition was that she did not want a "girlie" show; she felt that would be inappropriate for the men and their families. The result was a beautifully produced, tasteful, and deeply moving program that everyone who saw it will always remember.

On May 24, the day the POW dinner was held, the flag flying over the White House was the same one that had flown at Clark Air Force Base on February 12 when the first group of POWs returned from Hanoi.

In the afternoon Pat and the girls attended a tea for the wives. Tricia recorded the scene in her diary:

> Mama, Julie, and I attended a reception honoring the wives of the POWs prior to the dinner at the White House.
>
> The press attended the reception too, and while we were scattered through the reception room surrounded by the wives, the reporters surrounded us. Instead of asking us questions about the occasion or even showing a humane concern about the POW families, the press immediately and gleefully bombarded us with Watergate questions.
>
> Finally the POW wives could support this attack no longer and they, un-

asked, began telling the reporters how fine Richard Nixon was. They said things like, "He is the greatest President our country has *ever* had" and "If it were not for him our husbands would still be prisoners."

While the women were having tea, I addressed the men in the State Department Auditorium. My speech was interrupted many times by applause, but I was surprised at the reaction to one particular sentence. Only two weeks earlier Daniel Ellsberg's trial had been dismissed, and he had gone free. When I said, "And let me say, I think it is time in this country to quit making national heroes out of those who steal secrets and publish them in the newspapers," the men leaped to their feet and shouted their agreement.

It had rained all day and much of the evening, and the South Lawn was soggy when the first guests began arriving for the dinner. Many of the women's long dresses got splattered with mud, but nothing could dampen the high spirits of that night. Pat had decided to open the entire White House, so the men and their families wandered through all the rooms, examining the decorations and taking photographs.

Before the dinner an invocation was offered by Navy Captain Charles Gillespie, the POW who had acted as their chaplain in Hanoi. Then the POW chorus of thirty-five men sang a hymn that one of them had written in prison.

Everyone stood at attention as a fanfare announced an all-service honor guard for the presentation of the colors. In place of the full-size American flag, there came a tiny flag held aloft on a short staff. It was the flag that had been secretly made by Air Force Lieutenant Colonel John Dramesi in a North Vietnamese prison, fashioned from a white handkerchief, patches of red underwear, gold trim from a blanket, blue cloth from an old jacket, and string from a Red Cross package. As the honor guard entered, all eyes turned toward the tiny patchwork flag, and beginning with the front tables, a cheer grew and grew until it filled the canvas tent.

During most of the dinner Pat and I walked around from table to table, posing for photographs and signing autographs. When I came to the table at which John Stennis was seated, he turned to the men and said, "You fellows wouldn't be here if it weren't for the guts of this man."

When the dinner was over, I rose to begin the toasts. "The most difficult decision that I have made since being President was on December 18 of last year," I said, and before I could continue there was a thunderous burst of cheering and applause. "And there were many occasions in that ten-day period after the decision was made when I wondered whether anyone in this country really supported it. But I can tell you this: after having met each one of our honored guests this evening, after having talked to them, I think that all of us would like to join in a round of applause for the brave men that took those B-52s in and did the job, because as all of you know, if they hadn't done it, you wouldn't be here tonight."

I said that I wanted to propose a toast not just to Pat as First Lady but to all the brave wives and mothers of the prisoners. Tricia noted in her diary, "When all the men rose to toast their wives and families, all the sacrifice, poignance, sadness, past and future, was caught in that moment."

General Flynn responded to the toast: "I would like to state . . . that we do not consider ourselves a unique group of men. Rather we are a random selection of fate. . . . Mr. President, concerning your decision on December 18, I would like to assure you, sir, that we knew you were in a very lonely position. The decision was contested, but I would like to also report to you that when we heard heavy bombs impacting in Hanoi, we started to go and pack our bags, because we knew we were going home, and we were going home with honor."

The men presented me with a plaque inscribed to "Our leader—our comrade, Richard the Lion-Hearted."

Bob Hope opened the entertainment. All the stars of the show had entertained the men in South Vietnam, many of them as part of Hope's annual Christmas shows. John Wayne got the biggest hand when he said to the POWs, "I'll ride into the sunset with you anytime." Just before he left the stage, he looked down at me sitting in the front row of tables and said, "I want to thank you, Mr. President, not for any one thing, just for everything."

There were famous pop and country singers, comedians and motion picture personalities on the program, and the place of honor at the end was for Sammy Davis, Jr. He sang and danced and, with tears in his eyes, had special praise for the women whose prayers had "brought you cats home."

Then I introduced Irving Berlin. His age and failing health had made it impossible for him to participate in any other part of the evening, but as he began the first notes of his most famous song, his voice came out loud and strong. Many now wept openly as we repeated the stirring and simple verse over and over until, at the end, some of the men almost seemed to be shouting so that the words could be heard all the way to Hanoi: "God bless America, my home sweet home."

The show did not end until after midnight and the dancing went on until after two o'clock, but Pat and I went upstairs around 12:30. I kissed her goodnight and then went to the Lincoln Sitting Room. As I sat before the fire, listening to the sounds of the music and laughter coming up from downstairs, I felt that this was one of the greatest nights in my life. There were no words then, and there are really none now, that could describe the joy and satisfaction that I felt at the thought that I had played a role in bringing these men back home, and that they, who were so completely courageous and admirable, genuinely seemed to consider the decisions I had made about the war to have been courageous and admirable ones.

I reached in my pocket and pulled out a small piece of paper that the wife of one of the POWs had handed to me. It was a short handwritten note on Statler-Hilton stationery:

> Dear Mr. President:
>
> When I was living in solitary confinement and conditions were especially bad, men would often send notes of encouragement to others who were under great pressure. The notes were hidden in the bath areas and were a great comfort to the recipient. The standard message was "Don't let the bastards get you down."
>
> Don't let the bastards get you down, Mr. President.
>
> Joy and Bob Jeffrey

The contrast between the splendid lift of this night and the dreary daily drain of Watergate suddenly struck me with an almost physical force. When Tricia and Julie came upstairs from the party a little later, I invited them to join me in the Lincoln Sitting Room. Tricia made a diary note of that meeting:

> We went down expecting that he wanted to talk over the splendid event and what had led up to it and made it possible.
>
> When we saw his face, we realized that his spirit was troubled. It was obvious that his low spirit was more than the natural letdown that frequently follows the conclusion of a speech or an event where much energy has been expended. He began to talk quietly, without undue passion, about the press's rather negative reception of all the POW ceremonies in Washington. He correctly stated the reason for this apathy: in giving a good play to the ceremonies they feared they would build him up.
>
> He called Paul Keyes and thanked him for arranging the entertainment. They joked for a few minutes, but it was almost painful for us to see how sad Daddy's face looked despite the laughter in his voice.
>
> After he hung up we were all silent for a moment and then, very simply, he said to Julie and me, "Do you think I should resign?"
>
> It was not what he said but the way he said it that produced an internal earthquake in us. Instead of saying it with levity, he said it with a seriousness that produced a wave of exclamations such as "Don't you dare!" and "Don't even think of it!" from us.
>
> He really wanted us to give him reasons for not resigning. This was not difficult for us to do: we said he should stay in office because he had done

nothing wrong. There was no reason to resign. The country would not thrive as well with anyone else in office. He smiled at us and tried to say something to cheer us up, but it was almost more than I could bear to stay there and see his sadness on what should have been a night of jubilant triumph for him as it was for everyone else.

And so the evening concluded—an evening representing a great historical and personal achievement for Daddy, marred by a great personal tragedy. I could not help but think how man lives in the hope of perfection, but lives in the reality of imperfection in himself and in those around him.

THE MAY 22 STATEMENT

John Dean's news-making accusations against Haldeman and Ehrlichman failed to gain him immunity from prosecution.

He later claimed that he had been very careful not to try his case in the press, and he testified before the Ervin Committee that he had not done so. But the New York *Times* reported flatly that Dean's attorney was behind the leaking.

On May 4 Dean had informed Judge Sirica that he had a safe-deposit box full of classified documents taken from the White House, which he planned to use to buttress his Watergate case. We had no idea what the documents might be. The only clues were the press reports noting that one of these documents was forty-three pages long and carried one of the highest security classifications in the government. Fred Buzhardt took the security classification and the number of pages mentioned in the press leaks and started searching until he found what he was sure was the document: the June 1970 Interagency Intelligence Report—the Huston Plan.

In April Dean had promised me categorically that he would not reveal anything involving national security matters, but now he seemed to be willing to breach that promise if it would help him gain immunity from prosecution.

Justice Department officials who had seen the document said that it involved a national security matter and did not relate to Watergate. But Senator Ervin pounced on the chance to make news. He told reporters that it was an "operation to spy on the American people in general," and he cited it as evidence of the administration's "Gestapo mentality."

Even so, I was almost relieved that this was Dean's bombshell document, because I was certain that we could completely defend and explain it in a way that people would understand.

A few days later General Vernon Walters, Deputy Director of the CIA, notified us that several of his "memcons"—memoranda of conversations—dating from June 1972 were about to be subpoenaed by the Senate Armed Services Committee, which was investigating the question of CIA involvement in the Watergate break-in and its aftermath. One of Walters's memcons covered the conversation held among Helms, Haldeman, Ehrlichman, and himself on June 23, 1972. Other Walters memcons covered subsequent conversations with John Dean and with Pat Gray. The subject of all the memcons was Watergate. Walters brought the memcons to the White House to get a ruling on whether they were covered by executive privilege. The minute we saw them we knew we had a problem.

Walters's memcon of the June 23 meeting with Haldeman and Ehrlichman noted that Haldeman had commented on the embarrassment being caused by Watergate and then said that it was my desire that Walters go to see Pat Gray and suggest that he not push the inquiry further, particularly into the Mexican money that appeared to have financed the break-in.

One of the things that made the memcons so troublesome was the fact that Walters was one of my old friends; he would not have contrived them to hurt me. In addition, his photographic memory was renowned, and he was universally respected as a scrupulous and honest man.

Buzhardt, however, noticed that the June 23 memcon had not actually been written on June 23, but five days later, on June 28. During those five days John Dean had approached Walters and asked if the CIA could help put up the bail for the Watergate defendants to get them out of jail and pay their salaries if they were convicted. He had also asked obliquely if the CIA might assume some of the responsibility for the break-in. Walters had reacted to Dean's overtures with dismay and alarm; he had refused, insisting that he would do nothing unless he received a direct order from me. In fact, Dean had undertaken this approach to Walters without my knowledge, and he dropped his request.

Buzhardt postulated that on June 28, when Walters wrote the memcon of the June 23 meeting, he had unconsciously reconstructed the conversation from the perspective of what he felt Dean was trying to do, rather than from what Haldeman and Ehrlichman had actually said.

It had been almost a year since that conversation; so much had happened in the meantime. But I was certain that the motive could not have been as transparently political as it looked. What could we have been thinking? It must have been concern over the perennial competition between the FBI and CIA. I saw Haldeman on May 10 and 11 and again on May 18. He was positive beyond a doubt that that had been our motive. He told me again, as he had when we met on April 25, that I had told Dean on March 21 that we could raise a million dollars but it would be wrong and it would not work.

Back in April I had talked to Haldeman and Ehrlichman about the difficulty of recalling events that were many months past. "How do you remember back that far? . . . You remember the things you want to remember." Now we ourselves rationalized the implications of Walter's memcons; we confusedly reconstructed events around our recollection of our motive—we remembered what we wanted to remember.

I was relieved by Haldeman's certainty. I asked whether he could recall even the slightest hint of political concern in calling in the CIA. He said he was positive that there had been no political concern whatever.

By mid-May we were inundated with new charges. In addition to all the Watergate allegations and accusations, the 1969–70 wiretaps were now public; so was the Plumbers unit, and we knew that Dean had a copy of the Interagency Intelligence Report. No distinction was being made between legitimate national security concerns and exclusively Watergate problems. In the April 30 speech I had dealt in a very general way with the broad concepts of responsibility and blame. Now I could see that we were going to have to provide a detailed response to the many specific Watergate allegations.

In a statement issued from the White House on May 22 I described the 1969 wiretaps and the events that had created the need for them. I also described the 1970 Interagency Intelligence Report and the establishment of the Plumbers. Then I turned to Watergate. I denied prior knowledge of the break-in, and I made a blanket denial of any awareness of or participation in the cover-up. I said that we had called in the CIA to make sure that no secret CIA operations were uncovered by the Watergate investigation and that the investigation did not lead to any inquiry into the Special Investigations Unit. I stated, "It was certainly not my intent, nor my wish, that the investigation of the Watergate break-in or of related acts be impeded in any way." I said flatly that it was not until "my own investigation" that I had known of any fund-raising for the men convicted of the break-in at the DNC. And I said that I had not authorized any offer of executive clemency for any of these defendants. Thus I set more traps that would be sprung by the tapes months later.

The May 22 statement came as a shock to the American public. It was the first time that a President of the United States had publicly admitted that there had been such things as government-approved break-ins. At that time the activities that were later revealed by the 1975 Senate study of intelligence activity were not yet widely known outside some political and journalistic circles in Washington. Thus there was no cushion of preparation, no context of public awareness and acceptance, for my contention that what I had approved in the Huston Plan and the wiretaps was not only objectively justifiable but based on the precedent of presidential decisions and practices as far back as FDR. In 1973 *Newsweek* said that the Huston Plan was "the most wide-ranging secret police operation ever authorized." Later William V. Shannon wrote in the New York *Times*, "There was nothing really new or unprecedented in the methods proposed in the 1970 plan."

There were even denials that any precedents existed. For example, the Washington *Post* reported that Kennedy and Johnson had generally felt that wiretapping was too damaging to employ. After a press conference in which I responded to questions about the history of government-authorized break-ins, Johnson's Attorneys General Nicholas Katzenbach and Ramsey Clark said that they did not know about such things. And Sam Ervin used the nationally televised forum of the Watergate hearings to pontificate erroneously that J. Edgar Hoover would not have authorized any break-ins. Thus were the conventional pieties kept intact and my explanation of my actions undermined.

In the face of the sanctimony that greeted my May 22 statement, I decided that I wanted all the wiretaps of previous administrations revealed. It was Robert Kennedy who had authorized the first wiretaps on Martin Luther King. Ultimately King was subjected to five different phone taps and fifteen microphone bugs in his hotel rooms. The Kennedys had tapped newsmen. They had tapped a number of people instrumental in the passage of a sugar import bill they considered important. I wanted to get out the particulars of Lyndon Johnson's political use of the FBI. He had had thirty FBI employees at the 1964 Democratic convention monitoring events and overseeing wiretaps on Martin Luther King. The Mississippi Freedom Democratic Party—a group that threatened to pose a political problem for him—was tapped, and the reports were relayed directly to the White House. His Press Secretary asked for name checks on Goldwater supporters. His Attorney General had authorized a tap on an author who had written a book about Marilyn Monroe and Bobby Kennedy. Hoover's aide, William Sullivan, wrote, "To my memory the two administrations which used the FBI most for political purposes were Mr. Roosevelt's and Mr. Johnson's. Complete and willing cooperation was given to both." I wanted everything out on the Democrats. My staff resisted me, and for several weeks we debated back and forth about it. I felt like a fighter with one hand tied behind his back: most of my advisers argued that if I revealed the activities of previous administrations, it would look as if I were trying to divert attention from myself by smearing others. If I did not, however, I was afraid that I would remain portrayed as a willful deviant from past practice and be condemned for my legal and legitimate uses of the same tactics my predecessors had used not only more extensively but for blatantly political purposes. In the end, I was persuaded against it, and we did nothing.

If the public reaction to the May 22 statement was negative, the reaction in the White House briefing room was almost violent. Len Garment helped Ziegler with the briefing, and the reporters interrupted them constantly, shouting and jeering.

By the summer the White House and my campaign organization were under investigation by the FBI, the Ervin Committee and four other congressional committees, the General Accounting Office, one House committee, grand juries in Los Angeles, New York, Florida, and Texas, and the Miami District Attorney's office. More than a dozen civil suits had been filed. Now we also had a Special Prosecutor, Archibald Cox, whose sole responsibility was the investigation of Watergate.

The Ervin Committee had a staff of 92; the Special Prosecutor's office had a staff of 80. We had fewer than 10 people: Fred Buzhardt and Len Garment, who bore the full-time burden; Charles Alan Wright, a distinguished constitutional scholar from the University of Texas Law School who helped on a part-time basis; and young lawyers to assist them. Compared with the forces ranged against us, we were like a high school team heading into the Super Bowl.

At the end of May it was clear that Dean's effort to gain immunity from the federal prosecutors had failed. All that was left for him was to push harder for Senate immunity in the hopes that his testimony before the Ervin Committee would renew pressure in his favor that might make the Justice Department reconsider its decision.

On Sunday morning, June 3, there were front-page headlines in the New York *Times* and the Washington *Post*: *Dean Said to Tell of 40 Meetings with Nixon in 1973* and *Dean Alleges Nixon Knew of Cover-up Plan.* I quickly scanned the *Post*'s story. It began: "Former presidential counsel John W. Dean III has told Senate investigators and federal prosecutors that he discussed aspects of the Watergate cover-up with President Nixon or in Mr. Nixon's presence on at least thirty-five occasions between January and April of this year, according to reliable sources." The story in the *Times* similarly reported that Dean had said that I had met with him alone and in small groups more than forty times between January and April, and that in these meetings I had shown "great interest" in making sure things were "taken care of."

I read on in the *Post* and felt a sudden sense of dread as I came to another part of the story. "One of the strongest charges," according to the *Post*, was Dean's assertion that in March 1973, shortly before the Watergate burglars had been sentenced, I had met with him and asked him how much the defendants would have to be paid to ensure their continued silence. Dean was said to have told me that the additional cost would be about $1 million, and I was said to have replied that there would be no problem in paying that much money. Dean claimed that after January I had begun calling him personally to "find out the status of the cover-up," and on March 21 he had told me that "to save the presidency" it would be necessary for Haldeman, Ehrlichman, and Dean himself to disclose fully their involvement in the Watergate affair. He charged that after that meeting I had met with Haldeman and Ehrlichman and then told Dean that I would not tolerate any division in the White House ranks and warned him that he would stand alone if he went to the prosecutors.

I felt discouraged, drained, and pressured. I asked Haig whether I shouldn't resign. His answer was a robust no, and he urged me to steel myself to taking whatever time and effort would be required to listen to the tapes of the Dean meetings and to construct an unassailable defense based on them. I agreed to see what we could do in this regard, and Haig said that he would make the necessary arrangements.

A check of my daily logs showed that I had met with Dean twenty-one times and made or received thirteen phone calls from him between February 27 and April 1973. Except for the March 21 conversation I had little or no recollection of any of the rest of them. As I sat looking at this list, an uneasy feeling came over me as I wondered what we might have talked about in all those conversations.

Monday, June 4, was the first time I listened to a tape. Steve Bull brought a tape machine to my EOB office and cued the first one for me. I put on the earphones and pressed the "play" button. The reel began unwinding. Sounds drifted in and out; voices overrode each other. Gradually, as my ears became accustomed, I could pick up more and more. I listened to conversation after conversation with Dean in February and March, all before March 21. At the end of the day I was both exhausted and relieved.

I knew that there would be problems, but I was sure that they could all be explained. I had said that I first learned about the cover-up on March 21, and the tapes showed that in the conversations prior to March 21, Dean and I had talked about Watergate, the Ervin Committee, executive privilege, and political retaliation against the Democrats strictly as political problems. Dean had told me that no one in the White House was involved in the Watergate break-in.

He had reassured me that from the White House point of view, Watergate and Segretti were not nearly so bad as they had been made to appear in the press. He had agreed with me that he himself had had nothing to do with campaign activities. And he had certainly not disclosed his own role in the cover-up to me before our meeting on March 21.

I called in Haig and Ziegler to tell them the good news: I felt the tapes proved Dean was lying. For just a moment after I had read all the newspaper stories, I was worried that maybe Dean and I *had* talked about a cover-up. But now that I had reviewed the tapes, I told Ziegler I felt enormously relieved. "Really, the goddamn record is not bad, is it?" I remarked almost cheerily.

The day that John Dean was scheduled to begin his testimony before the Watergate Committee, June 18, was also the day that Leonid Brezhnev was to arrive in Washington to begin the second U.S.–Soviet Summit. At the last minute Ervin—"with some degree of reluctance," as he himself said— postponed Dean's appearance for a week, until after the summit.

SUMMIT II

By early spring of 1973, the Soviets appeared to be moving full speed in pursuit of détente. Brezhnev, according to press and intelligence reports, had conducted a quiet purge of the Politburo, apparently in order to remove anti-détente recalcitrants. In February he wrote me a letter outlining his expectations for the summit, saying that he looked forward to the signing of a treaty on the nonuse of nuclear weapons; to useful discussions of the Middle East; to the completion of a further SALT agreement; to the signing of trade and economic agreements and agreements to cooperate in the areas of science, technology, health, and peaceful uses of nuclear energy; to discussion of relations between the two Germanys; and to talks concerning European security and mutual and balanced force reductions in Europe. Considerable progress had already been made in building on the agreements for cooperation in economic and other non-military areas we had reached in Moscow in 1972. The prospects for a successful summit appeared good.

But problems were beginning to develop at home, even apart from Watergate. In the year between the first and second Soviet Summits, a fusion of forces from opposite ends of the political spectrum had resulted in a curious coalition. Kissinger later described it as a rare convergence, like an eclipse of the sun. On the one side the liberals and the American Zionists had decided that now was the time to challenge the Soviet Union's highly restrictive emigration policies, particularly with respect to Soviet Jews. On the other side were the conservatives, who had traditionally opposed détente because it challenged their ideological opposition to contacts with Communist countries. My request in April 1973 for congressional authority to grant most-favored-nation trade status to the Soviet Union became the rallying point for both groups: the liberals wanted MFN legislation to be conditioned on eased emigration policies; the conservatives wanted MFN defeated on the principle that détente was bad by definition.

I have never had any illusions about the brutally repressive nature of Soviet society. But I knew that the more public pressure we placed on the Soviet leaders, the more intransigent they would become. I also knew that it was utterly unrealistic to think that a fundamental change in the Soviet system could be brought about because we refused to extend MFN status.

I felt that we could accomplish a great deal more on the Jewish emigration issue when we were talking with the Soviets than when we were not. As I said to one group of American Jewish leaders, "The walls of the Kremlin are very thick. If you are inside, there is a chance that they will listen to you; if you are outside you are not even going to be heard." That was the approach we adopted. Although we did not publicly challenge the Soviet contention that these questions involved Soviet internal affairs, both Kissinger and I raised them privately with Brezhnev, Gromyko, and Dobrynin. This approach brought results. In March 1973 Dobrynin informed Kissinger that the high exit tax, which the Soviets described as the repayment of state educational expenses by those who wanted to move abroad, had been removed and only a nominal fee was now being required of émigrés from the Soviet Union to Israel. He said that a similar approach would be maintained in the future. Brezhnev sent me a personal note claiming that 95.5 percent of the requests for emigration visas to Israel during 1972 had been granted. Whether or not this claim was exaggerated, the statistics are proof of undeniable success: from 1968 to 1971 only 15,000 Soviet Jews were allowed to emigrate. In 1972 alone, however, the number jumped to 31,400. In 1973, the last full year of my presidency, nearly 35,000 were permitted to leave; this figure is still the record high.

On December 11, 1973, the House of Representatives passed a trade bill that in effect prohibited MFN for the Soviet Union because of its restrictive emigration policies. I met with Dobrynin on December 26 and expressed my profound contempt for the alliance that had combined to defeat MFN, but I said that we must not let temporary setbacks, no matter how discouraging, interfere with or poison the relations between the two superpowers that still held the future of the world in their hands. In the end, the congressional action unfortunately but predictably had an effect that was exactly the opposite of what was intended: the number of Jews allowed to emigrate declined from 35,000 in 1973 to 13,200 in 1975.

Brezhnev's plane landed at Andrews Air Force Base on the afternoon of June 16. Because we had decided not to begin the summit officially until Monday, I had gone to Florida for the weekend. I called him from Key Biscayne shortly after he arrived at Camp David, where he would spend two days resting and adjusting to the time difference between Washington and Moscow. I had never heard him sound so friendly and completely uninhibited as he did on the phone that afternoon. I said that I wanted to welcome him to the United States. Even before Dobrynin, who was on an extension line to act as our interpreter, could begin the translations, Brezhnev said "thank you" three or four times in English.

I told him to get as much rest as he could because I knew from experience that it would take some time to recover from jet lag. He said that he appreciated my thoughtfulness in providing a place as private and comfortable as Camp David, and that he regretted that his wife had not been able to take the trip with him. I said that Pat and I would look forward to having her come with him during the Fourth Soviet Summit, which would take place in America in two years. At least as far as atmosphere was concerned, Summit II was off to the best possible start.

The Soviets were fully aware of Watergate, but they made little effort to conceal the fact that they could not completely understand it. Dobrynin told Kissinger that he was utterly dismayed by the way Americans were acting over the whole affair. He called it a "mess" and said that no other country would permit itself the luxury of tearing itself to pieces in public.

Dean's testimony before the Ervin Committee had been postponed until after Brezhnev's departure, but the drumbeat of Watergate leaks and accusations from him and his nameless associates, and from various anonymous Ervin Committee sources, continued. On the morning Brezhnev arrived, the Washington *Post* published a front-page report revealing that "sources" said I was going to abandon Ehrlichman and Haldeman in a last-ditch effort to save myself. The story was absolute fiction, but perhaps more than many others, it contributed to the impression that the Nixon White House was a viciously cynical place where I would turn on my closest aides to save myself. Our denial of this front-page fabrication was relegated to page five of the next day's edition. Archibald Cox also chose the day of Brezhnev's arrival to hold a press conference, at which, in reply to reporters' questions, he stated that he was studying whether or not he could indict me before an impeachment had taken place. Having said this, he hastened to add that, of course, such a study was only academic.

Just before eleven o'clock on Monday morning Brezhnev's car came up the curving driveway to the South Portico of the White House. In my welcoming speech I said, "The hopes of the world rest with us at this time in the meetings that we will have." His response was warm: "I and my comrades, who have come with me, are prepared to work hard to ensure that the talks we will have with you . . . justify the hopes of our peoples and serve the interests of a peaceful future for all mankind."

After the brief speeches we walked out onto the rain-soaked lawn to review the honor guard. As we came to the end of the front line of troops and were about to walk by the rear ranks, Brezhnev could no longer suppress his animation and joviality. He waved enthusiastically at the spectators, who were applauding and waving American and Soviet flags, and then strode over to them just like an American politician working the crowd at a county fair. He shook hands with several people and grinned broadly as they reached out to him until I reminded him that we had to complete the ceremony. As we walked back to the South Portico, he threw his arm around my shoulders and said, "See, we're already making progress!"

Our first meeting in the Oval Office was private, except for Viktor Sukhodrev, who, as in 1972, acted as translator. Brezhnev began by assuring me that he spoke for the entire Politburo. I replied that, despite domestic differences, I spoke for the majority of Americans. He nodded his head vigorously.

We reviewed our general schedule and agenda for the next few days. As we talked he became more animated. Several times he grabbed my arm and squeezed it to emphasize the point he was making. I couldn't help thinking that the last time such tactile diplomacy had been used in that room was when Lyndon Johnson wanted to make a point.

Brezhnev became very serious when explaining his views about the relationship between our two countries. He said, "We know that as far as power and influence are concerned, the only two nations in the world that really matter are the Soviet Union and the United States. Anything that we decide between us, other nations in the world will have to follow our lead, even though they may disagree with it." It was clear, although he did not mention China, that he wanted this summit to demonstrate that the U.S.–Soviet relationship was more important than the U.S.–Chinese relationship, and that if we had to choose between the two our ties to the Soviet Union would prevail.

I replied that, while I recognized the reality of our pre-eminence as the two nuclear superpowers, we both had allies. "They are all proud people," I said, "and we must never act in such a way that appears to ignore their interests."

At 12:30 our private session ended, and the other participants for both sides came in. Brezhnev quoted the Russian proverb that he would invoke several times during the visit. "We say," he remarked to me, " 'Life is always the best teacher.' Life has led us to the conclusion that we must build a new relationship between our countries." Then he turned to the others in the room and announced that he had already invited me to return to Russia in 1974 and that I had accepted the invitation.

I thought back to 1959, when I had sat in this same office for the first meeting between Eisenhower and Khrushchev. Khrushchev had known that he was speaking from a position of weakness and had felt that it was therefore necessary to take a very aggressive and boastful line. Since then the power balance had evened out, particularly as the gap in the decisive area of nuclear development and capability had been closed. Brezhnev could afford to speak more quietly. In 1973 the United States overall still held the stronger hand, but Brezhnev could laugh and clown and vary his stern moods with warmth, based on the confidence that comes from holding very good cards.

That night there was a state dinner in his honor at the White House. As Brezhnev and I greeted the guests in a receiving line in the Blue Room, he was clearly impressed and somewhat surprised by the broad cross section of political, business, and labor leaders, many of whom opposed each other politically but who had gathered socially under the President's roof to meet the Soviet leader. I was reminded again of how isolated the Russians still are by history and geography, as well as by their communist ideology. Several times Brezhnev asked me, "Do they all support the new Soviet-American initiatives?" In my toast I said, "Not only in this room but across this country, regardless of whatever the organization may be, the overwhelming number of Americans support the objective of Soviet-American friendship."

The first talks with Brezhnev held few surprises. He expressed his disappointment that we had not been able to grant MFN status, but he understood that the fault lay beyond my control in Congress. The Soviets were not yet ready to have limitations imposed on their own multiple-warhead missile development, so he remained adamant against expanding the SALT agreements at this summit. He did, however, reluctantly acquiesce in my insistence that we set the end of 1974 instead of 1975 as the deadline for reaching a permanent SALT accord.

At public functions Brezhnev's demeanor remained ebullient. He obviously enjoyed the attention he was receiving, and, like a skilled actor or a born politician, he knew how to hold center stage. At one signing ceremony, he toasted the event so vigorously that he spilled champagne on his suit and hid his face behind a handkerchief in an exaggerated display of embarrassment. At another signing ceremony he initiated an elaborate pantomime of pretending to race me to see who could finish signing the various copies first.

On Tuesday night we went for a sail aboard the *Sequoia* and then boarded helicopters and flew to Camp David to continue our discussions there. I presented him with a windbreaker bearing the Seal of the President with "Camp David" beneath it on one side and "Leonid I. Brezhnev" on the other. He was delighted and wore it most of the time we were there, including during our photo session with the press. I also presented him with an official gift commemorating his American visit: a dark blue Lincoln Continental donated by the manufacturer. It had black velour upholstery and "Special Good Wishes—Greetings" engraved on the dashboard. Brezhnev, a collector of luxury cars, did not attempt to conceal his delight. He insisted upon trying it out immediately. He got behind the wheel and enthusiastically motioned me into the passenger's seat. The head of my Secret Service detail went pale as I climbed in and we took off down one of the narrow roads that run around the perimeter of Camp David. Brezhnev was used to unobstructed driving in the center lane in Moscow, and I could only imagine what would happen if a Secret Service or Navy jeep had suddenly turned a corner onto that one-lane road.

At one point there is a very steep slope with a sign at the top reading, "Slow, dangerous curve." Even driving a golf cart down it, I had to use the brakes in order to avoid going off the road at the sharp turn at the bottom. Brezhnev was driving more than fifty miles an hour as we approached the slope. I reached over and said, "Slow down, slow down," but he paid no attention. When we reached the bottom, there was a squeal of rubber as he slammed on the brakes and made the turn. After our drive he said to me, "This is a very fine automobile. It holds the road very well."

"You are an excellent driver," I replied. "I would never have been able to make that turn at the speed at which we were traveling."

Diplomacy is not always an easy art.

Our meetings at Camp David included long sessions on SALT, European security, and the mutual and balanced force reduction talks concerning the comparative military strengths of the NATO and Warsaw Pact countries.

The most difficult and significant subject we negotiated at Summit II related to the proposed Agreement for the Prevention of Nuclear War. In our contacts before the summit, Brezhnev had strongly urged that we agree to a treaty on the nonuse of nuclear weapons. But Kissinger and I recognized that the practical effect of such a treaty would be to prevent, or at least to inhibit, us from using nuclear weapons in defense of our allies or of our own vital interests. In fact, we felt that a major reason for Brezhnev's interest in a nonuse treaty might be his suspicion that we were about to conclude a military agreement with Peking. The Soviets felt that a renunciation of the use of nuclear weapons would greatly undercut our usefulness to the Chinese in the event of a Sino-Soviet war. The Soviet fears were unfounded as far as our relations with Peking were concerned. But a treaty of the kind they wanted would have wreaked havoc among our NATO allies in Europe and with countries like Israel and Japan that depended on our nuclear protection against the threat of Soviet attack.

In May Kissinger had worked out a formula that went part way in meeting the Soviet proposals without undercutting our allies and other nations that would look to us for assistance if they were subjected to a Soviet attack. Rather than a treaty renouncing nuclear weapons in the event of war, Kissinger proposed that we should both renounce the use of force not only between us but between each of us and third countries, and agree to consult with each other when the danger of the use of nuclear weapons seemed imminent. I knew that Brezhnev would not be completely satisfied with this formula because it did not preclude the further development of our relations with Peking. But it was better than nothing for his purposes, and he agreed to accept it. We signed the agreement on Friday, June 22, in a formal ceremony in the East Room of the White House.

Later that afternoon we flew to California. As we passed over the Grand Canyon en route, *Air Force One* made a low sweep so that Brezhnev could see the spectacular play of light and shadow on the canyon walls. "I've seen many pictures of this in newsreels and in cowboy movies," Brezhnev said.

"Yes," I replied, "John Wayne."

Suddenly he jumped back from the window, hunched his shoulders, put his hands to his hips, and drew imaginary six-shooters from imaginary holsters.

On the short helicopter ride from El Toro to San Clemente, I had Brezhnev sit by the window so that he could get a good view of the freeway network and the suburban landscape beneath us. I could sense that he was impressed, particularly by the number of cars on the roads and by the large number of private houses. I told him that some of the beachfront houses were owned by wealthy people, but most of the others belonged to people who worked in factories and offices and were typical of what he would see if he had the time to travel over other parts of the country.

It was a beautiful summer evening in San Clemente, so I took Brezhnev for a ride in my golf cart. We had suggested that he stay at the commandant's large house at nearby Camp Pendleton Marine Base, but he insisted on staying with us. I think that he wanted to do so in order to emphasize our personal relationship. Although our house in San Clemente is very beautiful, it is very small by the standards of Soviet leaders, who are used to the dachas and villas of Czarist nobles, and it is not at all equipped to accommodate state visitors. The only extra bedrooms were Julie's and

Tricia's. Because Tricia had recently redecorated hers, we put Brezhnev there. The room is only about ten by fifteen feet, and Tricia had chosen wallpaper with a large floral design in soft lavender and blue. It was amusing to picture a bear of a man like Brezhnev ensconced amid such feminine decor.

During our talks in Washington and at Camp David, Brezhnev had been very restrained on the subject of China. In a meeting in my San Clemente office on Saturday afternoon, however, he spoke about China for several minutes with only thinly veiled concern. He was apparently still worried that we were contemplating some secret military arrangement, possibly a mutual defense treaty, with the Chinese.

I assured him that, while we would continue our policy of communication with China, we would never make any arrangement with either China or Japan that was inconsistent with the spirit of the Agreement for the Prevention of Nuclear War that we had just signed in Washington. I knew that this was not what he had been getting at, but I could not be in the position of agreeing to establish a reporting relationship with him on our dealings with the Chinese.

I told him that I really did not believe that his concern about the Chinese was justified. He asked me why, and I said that it was not a judgment based on any of the conversations I had had with the Chinese leaders but on the realities of military power. I expressed my opinion that it would be at least twenty years before the Chinese would acquire a sufficient nuclear capability to risk an aggressive action against the Soviet Union or any other major nuclear power.

Brezhnev said that he disagreed with me on this question.

"How long do you think it will be until China becomes a major nuclear country?" I asked him.

He held up his two hands with fingers outspread, and at first it struck me he was making some kind of gesture of surrender, but then he stiffened his fingers and said, "Ten, in ten years, they will have weapons equal to what we have now. We will be further advanced by then, but we must bring home to them that this cannot go on. In 1963, during our Party Congress, I remember how Mao said: 'Let 400 million Chinese die; 300 million will be left.' Such is the psychology of this man." Brezhnev gave the impression that he did not think that the Chinese policies would change, even after Mao's death; he was certain that the entire Chinese leadership was instinctively aggressive.

I turned the conversation to Cambodia, a subject I had already raised several times during our meetings. I pointed out that the renewed North Vietnamese activity there was a major threat to world peace. "If that continues," I said, "the reaction of many people in this country will be that Soviet arms made it possible." Brezhnev became highly agitated and strongly denied that any new Soviet military equipment had been sent to Indochina. He said that the Soviet Union was 100 percent for a speedy termination of the war in Cambodia and Laos, and he promised to speak in strong terms to the North Vietnamese. As far as the appearance of new weapons in the area was concerned, Brezhnev said he thought the Chinese might be responsible, not only for the weapons themselves, but for spreading stories that they were being sent by the Soviets.

At the end of the meeting Brezhnev urged as diplomatically as his obviously strong feelings allowed that we not enter into any military agreements with China. He said that he had refrained from raising the question in 1972, but now he was worried about the future. He asserted that the Soviets had no intention of attacking China. But if China had a military agreement with the United States, he said, "that would confuse the issue."

We adjourned from the ideological rigors of the Sino-Soviet split to a poolside cocktail party. The guest list read like a Hollywood *Who's Who*, and we had a receiving line so that Brezhnev would have a chance to meet everyone. While a strolling mariachi band filled the twilight with gay music, Brezhnev greeted each guest warmly and in several cases showed a familiarity with old movies that indicated either that he had been very well briefed or that he had been spending time in the private screening rooms in the Kremlin.

In my remarks I noted that there were many cowboy and movie stars among the guests, but I reassured Brezhnev that they had checked their pistols and holsters at the door. In response he made a very gracious speech: "I am here in the home of President and Mrs. Nixon, and I feel happy."

After the reception we had a small dinner for him. Our dining room seats only ten people, and we made the dinner deliberately informal so that he could feel at home. In my toast I remarked that he had told me how he usually ate very lightly at the big state dinners, and went home afterward to have a late dinner with his wife, an excellent cook. I said that I considered this private dinner in our home to be even more meaningful than the formal and official dinners we were both so accustomed to attending. I pointed out that he was the first foreign visitor who had ever stayed in our house with us, that he was sleeping in Tricia's room, and that Dobrynin and Gromyko were sharing the small guest cottage that David and Julie stayed in when they visited us together.

"As you can see, Mr. Chairman," I said, "this is not a large house, but it is our home. On such an occasion our thoughts turn away from the affairs of state to our families and loved ones wherever they may be. I want our children to grow up in a world of peace, just as I am sure you want your children and grandchildren to grow up in a world of peace.

What the meetings that you and I have had last year and this year have done is contribute to that goal. I only hope that Russians and Americans in future generations may meet as we are meeting in our homes as friends because of our personal affection for each other, and not just as officials meeting because of the necessity of settling differences that may exist between our two countries. Therefore I propose this toast of course to your health, and that of our other guests, but even more to Mrs. Brezhnev, to your children and our children and all the children of the world who, we trust, will have a happier and more peaceful future because of what we have done."

As my toast was translated, Brezhnev's eyes filled with tears. He impulsively got out of his chair and walked toward me. I rose and walked toward him. He threw his arms around me with a real bear hug and then proposed an eloquent toast to Pat and our children and all the children in the world.

After dinner he asked the other guests to excuse us for a moment. Then he took Pat and me aside and said, "We have already exchanged official gifts, but I have brought something with me which is for you and Mrs. Nixon alone." He gave Pat a scarf that had been handwoven by artisans in his home village. "It is a modest gift," he said, "but every stitch in this piece of fabric represents the affection and friendship which all the people of the Soviet Union have for the people of the United States and which Mrs. Brezhnev and I have for you and President Nixon." Tears again came to his eyes as he spoke.

After this rather emotional dinner, Brezhnev said that he was tired because of the three-hour time change from Washington, and he planned to go to bed early. I walked with him to the door of Tricia's room and we said good night there. I decided to have an early night myself, and I was reading in bed in my pajamas around 10:30 when there was a knock at my door. It was a Secret Service agent with a message from Kissinger: the Russians wanted to talk.

I asked Manolo to light a fire in my upstairs study, and I had just finished dressing when Kissinger came in.

"What is this all about?" I asked.

"He says he wants to talk," he replied.

"Is he restless or is this a ploy of some kind?" I asked.

"Who ever knows with them?" Kissinger answered with a shrug.

We went to the study, where Brezhnev, Dobrynin, and Gromyko soon joined us.

"I could not sleep, Mr. President," Brezhnev said with a broad smile.

"It will give us a good opportunity to talk without any distractions," I replied as I settled into my easy chair.

For the next three hours we had a session that in emotional intensity almost rivaled the one on Vietnam at the dacha during Summit I. This time the subject was the Middle East, with Brezhnev trying to browbeat me into imposing on Israel a settlement based on Arab terms. He kept hammering at what he described as the need for the two of us to agree, even if only privately, on a set of "principles" to govern a Middle East settlement. As examples of such principles, he cited the withdrawal of Israeli troops from all the occupied territories, the recognition of national boundaries, the free passage of ships through the Suez Canal, and international guarantees of the settlement.

I pointed out that there was no way that I could agree to any such "principles" without prejudicing Israel's rights. I insisted that the important thing was to get talks started between the Arabs and the Israelis, and I argued that if we laid down controversial principles beforehand, both parties would refuse to talk—in which case the principles would have defeated their purpose.

Brezhnev was blunt and adamant. He said that without at least an informal agreement on such principles he would be leaving this summit empty-handed. He even hinted that without such an agreement on principles he could not guarantee that war would not resume.

At one point he made a show of looking at his watch and furrowing his brow. "Perhaps I am tiring you out," he said. "But we must reach an understanding."

As firmly as he kept demanding that we agree on such principles—in effect, that we jointly impose a settlement that would heavily favor the Arabs—I refused, reiterating that the important thing was to get talks started between the parties themselves.

This testy midnight session was a reminder of the unchanging and unrelenting Communist motivations beneath the diplomatic veneer of détente. Brezhnev was aware of the slow but steady progress we had been making in reopening the lines of communication between Washington and the Arab capitals; and he was also aware that if America was able to contribute toward a peaceful settlement of Arab-Israeli differences, we would be striking a serious blow to the Soviet presence and prestige in the Middle East. From his point of view, therefore, his use of shock tactics at the ostensibly impromptu meeting in my study in San Clemente was a calculated risk. Brezhnev could not seriously have expected me to rise to the meager bait he held out in return for what would amount to our abandoning Israel. Whether he already had a commitment to the Arabs to support an attack against Israel is not clear, but I am confident that the firmness I showed that night reinforced the seriousness of the message I conveyed to the Soviets when I ordered a military alert four months later during the Yom Kippur War.

In the joint communiqué Brezhnev and I signed the next morning there was no effort to use diplomatic language to conceal that we had not been able to reach any common ground for our differing views on this difficult subject. The short section on the Middle East stated, "Each of the parties set forth its position on this problem."

Brezhnev and I made our parting remarks in front of microphones in the flower garden next to the house. He said that he would see me next time in Moscow. At the end he said "goodbye" in English.

After Brezhnev left, I tried to put Summit II in perspective. It was too soon after the 1972 SALT agreements for another major breakthrough in that area, but I did make it clear at every opportunity that 1974 would be the year of decision, when we would have to make progress in ironing out our differences, particularly on offensive weapons. I knew that the Soviets were moving much faster than we were in this area. Unless we got some agreement soon, we might face a situation in which we would be weaker than the Soviets in the eyes of our allies, our friends, and the neutral countries. Therefore, in addition to pinning Brezhnev down to a new agreement by the end of 1974, I specified that we would be talking about reductions and not just limitations of nuclear weapons.

There were several important agreements signed at Summit II covering specific areas: transportation, agriculture, oceanic studies, taxation, commercial aviation, the peaceful uses of atomic energy, and trade. These continued the process that we had begun in 1972 of building an interlocking web of relationships to increase the Soviets' stake in stability and cooperation.

This summit also gave me an opportunity to get to know Brezhnev better and to try to take his measure as a leader and as a man. I had spent forty-two hours with him in 1972, and now thirty-five hours with him in 1973. However superficial this kind of personal contact may be, it can still provide important insights.

I found Brezhnev more interesting and impressive than I had during our first meeting. Away from the constraints of the Kremlin he was able to indulge the more human and political sides of his personality. At one of the signing ceremonies, when his antics made him the center of attention, I jokingly said, "He's the best politician in this room!" He seemed to accept my statement as the highest possible praise.

His conduct and humor were almost impish at many of his public appearances. Whenever possible, I acted as his straight man on these occasions, but it was sometimes difficult for me to balance politeness against dignity.

Brezhnev showed the typically Russian combination of great discipline at times with total lack of it at others. An amusing symbol of this inconsistency was his fancy new cigarette case with a built-in timer that automatically rationed out one cigarette per hour. This was the way he was going to cut down on his chain-smoking. As each hour began, he would ceremoniously remove the allotted cigarette and close the box. Then, a few minutes later, he would reach into his jacket and take another cigarette from the ordinary pack that he also carried. Thus he was able to continue his habit of chain-smoking until the timer went off and he could take another virtuous cigarette from the box.

At Summit I, I could not help making mental comparisons between Brezhnev and Khrushchev. During Summit II, however, I had a chance to observe and analyze the differences between them in more depth and detail. They were alike in the sense that they were both tough, hard, and realistic leaders. Both interlarded their conversation with anecdotes. Khrushchev was often quite vulgar; Brezhnev, however, was just earthy. Whereas Khrushchev had been crass and blustering, Brezhnev was expansive and more courteous. Both had a good sense of humor, but Khrushchev more often seemed to be using his at the expense of others around him. Khrushchev seemed to be quicker in his mental reflexes. In discussions, Brezhnev was hard-hitting, incisive, and always very deliberate, whereas Khrushchev had tended to be more explosive and more impulsive. Both men had tempers, and both were emotional. I was struck by the simple look of pride on Brezhnev's face as he told me that he was about to become a great-grandfather, and that we now had still another generation for which to guarantee peace.

Despite the shortness of Brezhnev's visit, I felt that he had seen a diversity of American life for which no briefing books and studies could possibly have prepared him. I know that he returned home with a far better understanding of America and Americans than he had before he came.

On June 25, the day Brezhnev left Washington, the House of Representatives agreed to a Senate bill immediately cutting off funds for U.S. bombing actions in Cambodia. The effect of this bill was to deny me the means to enforce the Vietnam peace agreement. We were faced with having to abandon our support of the Cambodians who were trying to hold back the Communist Khmer Rouge, who were being supplied and supported by the North Vietnamese in violation of the peace agreement. The Cambodians were completely and justifiably bewildered; they could not understand why we were suddenly deserting them—especially when the military tide seemed to be turning in their favor.

Congress, however, was not prepared to hear any arguments and was determined to go forward despite the consequences. This congressional insensitivity had been dramatically symbolized a few weeks earlier as Kissinger was preparing to leave for a meeting with Le Duc Tho over violations of the cease-fire agreement. We had pleaded with Congress not to send Kissinger to Paris with no negotiating leverage, but Mike Mansfield's response was typical: he offered his "sympathies" but nothing more. In short order, two separate Senate committees voted to cut off funds for combat activities.

The cutoff bill passed on June 25. I vetoed it, and in my veto statement I said, "After more than ten arduous years of suffering and sacrifice . . . it would be nothing short of tragic if this great accomplishment, bought with the blood of so many Asians and Americans, were to be undone now by congressional action." The House of Representatives sustained my veto the same day, June 27, but it seemed clear that another cutoff bill would be proposed and that I could not win these battles forever. Therefore, we agreed to a compromise that set August 15, 1973, as the date for the termination of U.S. bombing in Cambodia and required congressional approval for the funding of U.S. military action in any part of Indochina. At least this gave us more time, but the invitation to aggression represented in any cutoff date remained unchanged.

I was determined that the historical record would mark Congress's responsibility for this reckless act, and on August 3, shortly before the scheduled mandatory cutoff, I wrote to House Speaker Carl Albert and Senate Majority Leader Mike Mansfield:

> This abandonment of a friend will have a profound impact in other countries, such as Thailand, which have relied on the constancy and determination of the United States, and I want the Congress to be fully aware of the consequences of its action. . . . In particular, I want the brave and beleaguered Cambodian people to know that the end to the bombing in Cambodia does not signal an abdication of America's determination to work for a lasting peace in Indochina. . . .
>
> I can only hope that the North Vietnamese will not draw the erroneous conclusion from this congressional action that they are free to launch a military offensive in other areas in Indochina. North Vietnam would be making a very dangerous error if it mistook the cessation of bombing in Cambodia for an invitation to fresh aggression or further violations of the Paris agreements. The American people would respond to such aggression with appropriate action.

I knew that since Congress had removed the possibility of military action I had only words with which to threaten. The Communists knew it too. During this period Kissinger held one of his regular luncheon meetings with Dobrynin. When Kissinger raised the question of the Communist violations of the cease-fire in Cambodia, the Soviet ambassador scornfully asked what we had expected, now that we had no negotiating leverage because of the bombing cutoff imposed by Congress. Kissinger tried to be as menacing as he could, even though he knew that Dobrynin was right.

"There should be no illusion that we will forget who put us in this uncomfortable position," he said.

"In that case," Dobrynin replied, "you should go after Senator Fulbright, not us."

For more than two years after the peace agreement the South Vietnamese had held their own against the Communists. This proved the will and mettle of the South Vietnamese people and their desire to live in freedom. It also proved that Vietnamization had succeeded. When Congress reneged on our obligations under the agreements, the Communists predictably rushed in to fill the gap. The congressional bombing cutoff, coupled with the limitation placed on the President by the War Powers Resolution in November 1973, set off a string of events that led to the Communist takeover in Cambodia and, on April 30, 1975, the North Vietnamese conquest of South Vietnam.

Congress denied first to me, and then to President Ford, the means to enforce the Paris agreement at a time when the North Vietnamese were openly violating it. Even more devastating and inexcusable, in 1974 Congress began cutting back on military aid for South Vietnam at a time when the Soviets were increasing their aid to North Vietnam. As a result, when the North Vietnamese launched their all-out invasion of the South in the spring of 1975, they had an advantage in arms, and the threat of American action to enforce the agreement was totally removed. A year after the collapse of South Vietnam, the field commander in charge of Hanoi's final offensive cited the cutback in American aid as a major factor in North Vietnam's victory. He remarked that Thieu "was then forced to fight a poor man's war," with his firepower reduced by 60 percent and his mobility reduced by half because of lack of aircraft, vehicles, and fuel.

The war and the peace in Indochina that America had won at such cost over twelve years of sacrifice and fighting were lost within a matter of months once Congress refused to fulfill our obligations. And it is Congress that must bear the responsibility for the tragic results. Hundreds of thousands of anti-Communist South Vietnamese and Cambodians have been murdered or starved to death by their conquerors, and the bloodbath continues.

Congress's tragic and irresponsible action, which fatally undermined the peace we had won in Indochina, was buried amid the media's preoccupation with John Dean's testimony before the Ervin Committee. On Monday, June 25, when Dean took the stand, all over the country—even in the compound in San Clemente—the hypnotic monotone of his voice drew people to their television sets. The three television networks gave these sessions all-day gavel-to-gavel coverage.

JOHN DEAN TESTIFIES

Dean testified for five days. It took him one full day to read his 245-page opening statement, which contained most of his charges against me. The cornerstone of his testimony was his accusation that for at least six months, since my meeting with him on September 15, 1972, I had been an active complicitor in the Watergate cover-up. *Dean Tells Panel President Discussed Cover-up in September, March, April* was the Washington *Post* headline after his first day of testimony; *Dean Tells Inquiry That Nixon Took Part in Watergate Cover-up for Eight Months* was the headline in the New York *Times.*

I did not watch the hearings, but the reports I read filled me with frustration and anger. Dean, I felt, was re-creating history in the image of his own defense.

Dean testified that on September 15, 1972, he had expressly discussed the Watergate cover-up with me. He stated that he had specifically told me that he could make no assurance the whole thing would not "unravel" someday, and that he had expressed his concern that "the cover-up" could not be "maintained indefinitely." He said that he had told me that all he had done was "assist in keeping it out of the White House" and that I had expressed appreciation for the difficult job he had performed. Dean said that he, thinking of Magruder's perjury, had told me that others had done more difficult things than he.

As the tape of that conversation shows, Dean had not said anything about others having done more "difficult things" or about his "keeping it out of the White House." Nor had he said anything about things starting to "unravel." On the tape, in fact, he said exactly the opposite: "Three months ago," he said, "I would have had trouble predicting where we'd be today. I think that I can say that fifty-four days from now that not a thing will come crashing down to our surprise."

There were ambiguous statements on the tape, to be sure. For example, I had talked about "putting your fingers in the dikes every time that leaks have sprung." But I was thinking of the fact that he was monitoring so many congressional, civil, and criminal investigations that had potential political impact. It was clear from the tape that however much Dean was concentrating on the criminal vulnerabilities, I was concentrating solely on the potential for political embarrassment.

Dean testified that in our meeting on February 28, 1973, he had described for me his own legal problems concerning "obstruction of justice." He said that he had given me a "general picture" of his "conduit activities" and left me clearly aware of his role in the "cover-up." Here too the tape shows that exactly the opposite occurred. In that meeting I had said to Dean that he, at least, had no vulnerability to the Watergate committee: "I think they realize you are the lawyer and they know you didn't have a goddamn thing to do with the campaign," I said.

"That's right," Dean had replied.

The tape shows that I said that the important thing about the whole Watergate mess was my own isolation from it. "That, fortunately, is totally true," I said.

"I know that, sir," he had affirmed.

Now, four months later, he was testifying that this conversation was one of the reasons he was convinced of my involvement in the cover-up.

Dean testified that on March 13 he had told me about the money being paid to the Watergate defendants. If that were true, it would have undercut my public assertion that I had first learned about the cover-up on March 21. But Dean was wrong, and it seemed to me that he must have deliberately changed the correct date, because as recently as our conversation of April 16, 1973, he had remembered that our "cancer on the presidency" discussion had taken place "on the Wednesday before they were sentenced"—and that was March 21.

In his testimony concerning the meeting of March 17 Dean made another omission that seemed too significant to be accidental. This was the meeting in which he had told me about the break-in at Ellsberg's psychiatrist's office. As the tape shows, I had reacted with utter shock. But Dean apparently wanted to leave an impression that knowledge of the Ellsberg break-in was a motive for my role in the Watergate cover-up. He testified that the meeting consisted of a "rambling conversation" with only brief reference to Pat Gray's confirmation hearings and the general problems confronting the White House. That same day I observed that, unlike others, he had not participated in the break-in and had no criminal liability. "That's right," Dean agreed.

Dean testified that on March 21, 1973, he had finally told me everything. He said flatly under questioning: "On March 21 I certainly told the President everything I knew at that point in time." As the tape proves, however, he did not tell me the extent of his active involvement in suborning perjury, in promising clemency, or in revealing confidential FBI information to the lawyers for the CRP. He did not tell me, nor did he tell the Watergate Committee, that he had also destroyed evidence from Howard Hunt's safe. He minimized his role in the fund-raising and said his primary problem was the fact that he had been a "conduit of information" on paying blackmail to defendants. Because of all these things I thought he was being inadvertently, unfairly, and tangentially drawn in; as late as March 26 I had dictated in my diary that Dean had always acted as counsel, giving his best advice and "avoiding anything that would smack of illegal or improper activities."

Dean implied that since the first days after the break-in everyone in the White House shared the understanding that there was White House "involvement" in the Watergate bugging, even if there was no direct participation in ordering the June 17 break-in. But in March I was stunned by his assertion that Gordon Strachan knew about the existence of the bug, and the information that a Colson phone call may have triggered it—and this was nine months after the break-in.

In his testimony Dean said that I had "never at any time" asked him to write a report concerning Watergate. In fact, I had pointedly suggested on March 22 that he go to Camp David, away from the phone, and prepare a written report.

Dean now implied that from the beginning he had had actual knowledge of Magruder's involvement and perjury and that everyone else did too. Yet on a tape from March 22 Haldeman says of Magruder: "On the other hand, we don't, we can't, prove he perjured himself, that's Dean's opinion." On March 26 Dean was still saying that he did not have any firsthand "off-the-record" knowledge of whether Magruder was involved in the break-in and therefore he could not be sure whether Magruder had committed perjury.

In the spring both Haldeman and I had repeatedly urged Dean to put out the full story regarding Segretti, and he had consistently resisted; now he charged that the White House effort to "cover-up" the Segretti episode was "consistent with other parts of the general White House cover-up" which followed Watergate. Similarly, he now insisted that our efforts to thwart a partisan pre-election move to hold congressional hearings on Watergate were in part an effort to avoid "unraveling the cover-up"; at the time, however, I had analyzed the problem of the hearings this way: "That's what this is, public relations." "That's all it is," John Dean had agreed.

Dean claimed that during March and April Haldeman and Ehrlichman had tried to protect themselves at his expense and that he had only been concerned that the truth be told. Ironically, it had been Dean who had done the manipulating. In March he minimized the problem his testimony would pose to others, apparently hoping to gain White House sponsorship for immunity. "Let's say the President sent me to the grand jury to make a report," he said on the afternoon of March 21, "who could I actually do anything to or cause any problems for? As a practical matter, firsthand knowledge, almost no one." After his first contacts with the prosecutors he kept up his phone calls to Haldeman, his appearance of mutual concern, and his references to "potential" problems on the cover-up, problems he thought possibly could be handled. Only in mid-April, when his bargaining with the prosecutors was under way, did he let it be known that Haldeman and Ehrlichman were in fact his bargaining chips and that he had been positioning himself to get the most from their destruction.

I saw John Dean's testimony on Watergate as an artful blend of truth and untruth, of possible sincere misunderstandings and clearly conscious distortions. In an effort to mitigate his own role, he transplanted his own total knowledge of the cover-up and his own anxiety onto the words and actions of others. In an effort to seem just a subordinate actor, he took the many different levels of understanding, awareness, and concern of those around him and fused them into one.

But as soon as Dean's testimony was over, I once again made the mistake I had been making since the Watergate break-in: I worried about the wrong problem. I went off on a tangent, concentrating all our attention and resources on trying to refute Dean by pointing out his exaggerations, distortions, discrepancies. But even as we geared up to do this, the real issue had already changed. It no longer made any difference that not all of Dean's testimony was accurate. It only mattered if *any* of his testimony was accurate. And Dean's account of the crucial March 21 meeting was more accurate than my own had been. I did not see it then, but in the end it would make less difference that I was not as involved as Dean had alleged than that I was not as uninvolved as I had claimed.

There was another respect in which Dean's testimony caught us unprepared. According to news reports, the Ervin Committee's Democratic members and staff had urged Dean to be sure to build up his opening statement with plenty of "atmospherics" about the White House. He readily obliged, and even more than what he had to say about Watergate, it was from this that we would never recover. This was what gave the political opposition the one thing that they could only have dreamed of: a way of metastasizing Watergate into the other areas of my administration. John Dean dredged up every political machination he could find and offered them as representative of everything we did. He forced the Nixon White House through the prism of his own defense—which was that he was largely the victim of the environment—and produced a portrait devoid of dreams, ideals, serious work, or important goals. He talked about my attempt to have the IRS do checks on our political opponents with no attempt to show how widespread the practice had been among the Democrats in previous years. The fact that we had hired a political investigator was treated as a sinister innovation, when in fact checking up on the political opposition has been part of politics since time out of mind. We paid our investigator with political funds; other administrations had even used the FBI. Dean produced an "enemies list," which even he has since admitted was vastly overplayed by the media. Into all this he folded controversial national security activities—the seventeen wiretaps designed to find the source of foreign policy leaks, the Huston Plan, and the Plumbers—ascribed them to paranoia, and made no effort or attempt to re-create the valid concerns that had produced them.

If the May 22 statement was the American public's first introduction to covert activities undertaken by the government for national security, Dean's testimony was a primer in the dark underside of White House politics. Thanks to the way he did it, everything was perfectly arranged for the Democrats to distance themselves from their own political past and proclaim that my administration had invented original sin.

The Ervin Committee, formally the Senate Select Committee on Presidential Campaign Activities, was a fascinating study in the weaknesses of human nature in general, and in particular of the partisanship and weaknesses of congressional human nature when exposed to massive publicity. The senators and their staffs soon made the heady discovery that whatever they said—or leaked—made news. The result was a steady hemorrhage of leaks usually aimed at undermining the defense of potential witnesses such as Haldeman, Ehrlichman, and Mitchell.

Mike Mansfield publicly chastised the committee. Archibald Cox later compared their tactics to McCarthy's. Senator James Buckley suggested that Ervin interrogate the staff under oath to see who was doing it. Ervin's reply was that that would injure morale. An occasion when a leaker was tracked down and punished exemplified the committee's standard of fairness: Majority Counsel Samuel Dash suspended a staff member who leaked unfavorable comments about Samuel Dash.

The Justice Department prosecutors complained that the committee's leaks and hearings were shattering their cases, and Special Prosecutor Archibald Cox appealed to Ervin not to proceed with open hearings because the publicity would undermine the chance that a prospective defendant could receive a fair trial. Earl Warren had once called it "frontier justice" to haul prospective defendants up before public hearings. But Ervin said that everything had to be done to air the truth. It didn't take long to discover that they had a very special truth in mind.

For example, among the documents the Ervin Committee received from John Dean were two memoranda from Hoover's assistant, William Sullivan. They outlined sensational political abuses of the FBI by earlier Democratic administrations. Ervin's executive assistant announced that the committee would not go into these matters because the allegations were "far, far too personal" and unsubstantiated. "Personal cheap shots," he called them, "rather distasteful."

The original draft of the committee's final report was going to call an aspect of George McGovern's postcampaign fund distribution an "apparent violation of the spirit of the law." When McGovern objected, Ervin had the section removed.

In 1964 Lyndon Johnson's protégé and Senate aide Bobby Baker had been charged with having run a high-finance influence-peddling operation. Many felt that the scandal touched and possibly implicated several Senators and even Johnson, who by then was President. The Democratic majority in Congress voted to keep the Baker case out of public hearings and refused to call any White House aides to testify. Three members of the Ervin Committee—Ervin himself and Senators Daniel Inouye of Hawaii and Herman Talmadge of Georgia—had gone on record seven times to restrict any congressional investigation of the Bobby Baker case. They evidently felt that Watergate deserved a special exception.

Maury Stans was lectured by Ervin for having used dummy committees for campaign funds. Senator Joseph Montoya of New Mexico later claimed that he was "shocked" by the discovery of forgeries on his own campaign finance report, and had no comment when it was reported that $100,000 had been put into dummy committees in Washington after the money had been laundered to prevent disclosure.

The Democrats' chief committee investigator was Carmine Bellino, whose prior political activity for the Kennedys had included tailing a former Republican Congressman during the 1960 campaign. Ervin praised him as a "faithful public servant of exemplary character."

As the first group of witnesses came before the committee, their treatment was in direct response to their willingness to grovel and to implicate others. If they stood up and defended themselves, they were badgered and humiliated. If they exhibited at least a modicum of self-abnegation, they were given first lectures and then commendations. Bernard Levin, the London *Times*'s political commentator, wrote:

> The conduct of the Chairman, Senator Sam Ervin, is so deplorable that the lack of any serious protest against his behavior is in itself a measure of the loss of nerve on the part of so many distinguished Americans, in the press, the academic world and politics itself, who would once, in similar circumstances, have been campaigning vigorously to bring him to heel. . . .
>
> Worse, however, than Senator Ervin's yokum-hokum is the way in which he has clearly decided that some of those appearing before him under suspicion of various malpractices are heroes, and some villains. . . . The technique, of course, was exactly the one used by Senator Joseph McCarthy. . . .
>
> What is really wrong with this inquisition is that it appears to be a judicial process but is in fact a political one. . . . Men are having their reputations destroyed in full view of millions; worse, men who may shortly have to face a criminal trial are having their cases literally prejudged, without any of the safeguards of true legal proceedings.

The Democrats on the committee were able to get away with such tactics because they were the majority and because the Republicans were understandably nervous about Watergate. The Republicans on the committee, with the exception of Weicker, worked diligently and seriously to follow up on leads they thought would provide balance. But they had neither the money, the manpower, nor an objective press to help promote and publicize their work.

A fitting epitaph to the fairness and standards employed by the Ervin Committee was provided by Senator Ervin himself when, on March 10, 1974, UPI reported a conversation with him in which he said that an impeachable offense had to be a federal crime and that "no evidence was produced in the Senate Watergate hearings to support impeachment." Another reporter present at the same interview at the same time had written the identical story, so clearly that was what he had said. Before long, Ervin was confronted with the political import of his statement and the adverse effect it might have on the Democratic impeachment move then under way. Finding himself trapped between political necessity and the dictates of principle, he made a quick and ironic choice: despite the documentation refuting him, he apparently chose to contain the damage by denying that he had ever made the statement.

Most Americans are resigned to a modicum of hypocrisy in politics. I am convinced, however, the historians will eventually conclude that even the serious issues raised and abuses revealed by Watergate did not justify such abuses of power as were committed by members of the Ervin Committee. With their prejudicial leaks, their double standards, and their grandstanding behavior, they only confirmed my feeling that this was a partisan attack, a determined effort to turn something minor into something major, and we had to fight back.

There was ample historical precedent for refusing to permit testimony by any White House aides before the Ervin Committee. But I recognized that with the emotional climate now surrounding Watergate, there would be little public tolerance or understanding if I did so. Therefore I waived all executive privilege and permitted members of the White House staff to submit to the Ervin panel's questions. The result was an unprecedented degree of cooperation by the executive branch with a congressional inquiry: 118 hours of public testimony from present and former White House aides and hundreds of hours in informal or private sessions. Even so, the committee members were not satisfied. They still wanted open access to White House files.

Under the Constitution the three branches of government operate like a three-part free-standing scale: each compensates, supplements, and checks the others. But no one branch has the right to dominate, by demanding and receiving the internal working documents of another. The precedent for this point of view goes back to George Washington, who as President refused to surrender executive branch documents to the House of Representatives.

Sam Ervin himself had defended congressional immunity to subpoenas from another branch in 1972, after Democratic Senator Mike Gravel of Alaska read portions of the classified text of the Pentagon Papers into the *Congressional Record.* The question that reached the Supreme Court was whether one of Gravel's aides could legally be compelled to testify about the senator's unauthorized reading of the papers, and Ervin was one of those who argued in a friend-of-the-court brief that one branch should not be allowed to compel testimony about the internal affairs of another branch. The brief insisted: "If an aide must feel that the advice he offers, the knowledge he has, and the assistance he gives to his senator may be called into question by the executive, then he is likely to refrain from acting on those very occasions when the issues are the most controversial and when the senator is most in need of assistance."

Ervin had demonstrated the same approach to the separation of powers in an earlier case involving another of his Democratic friends. During the hearings after Johnson nominated Abe Fortas as Chief Justice, Ervin asked Fortas about a discussion he had had with the President but immediately and genially added, "I will not insist upon your answer because it is a prerogative of communications in the executive branch of the government." He was not to be so genial when given a partisan advantage against a Republican President during Watergate.

On July 7 I sent a letter to Ervin anticipating a formal request for presidential papers. I noted that when historical precedent was examined, our cooperation with the investigation was already extraordinary. There were rumors that they were going to subpoena me personally, so I reminded them that when Harry Truman had been subpoenaed to appear before a committee of Congress in 1953, he had refused.

I told the members of the committee that, like Truman, I would not appear, nor would I provide documents:

> No President could function if the private papers of his office, prepared by his personal staff, were open to public scrutiny. Formulation of sound public policy requires that the President and his personal staff be able to communicate among themselves in complete candor, and that their tentative judgments, their exploration of alternatives, and their frank comments on issues and personalities at home and abroad remain confidential.

Ervin, despite his erstwhile defense of the virtues of separation of powers and the concept of privileged communications, now denounced my "abstruse arguments about separation of powers and executive privilege." On July 12 he sent a letter to the White House saying that he feared our two positions "presented the very grave possibility of a fundamental constitutional confrontation." He requested a meeting to try to avoid such a conflict. It was typical that Ervin's letter to me was leaked to reporters even before it had been delivered to the White House, and that we first learned about it from the reports on the news wires.

THE WHITE HOUSE TAPES REVEALED

I awakened at 5:30 A.M. on July 12 with a stabbing pain in my chest. It had begun before I went to bed; now it was nearly unbearable. It reminded me of the pain I experienced when I had cracked a rib playing football at Whittier. I switched on the light and tried to read, but I was too uncomfortable to be able to concentrate, so I turned the light out again and lay awake until morning.

The White House physicians gave me a brief examination and arrived at different diagnoses: Dr. Tkach thought it was pneumonia; Dr. William Lukash thought it might be simply a digestive disorder. They agreed that I should have a complete battery of tests.

I was lying restlessly in bed about midday when Haig came in and told me that Senator Ervin was on the phone and wanted to speak with me. He was calling about his letter. We talked for sixteen minutes. My voice was subdued because every breath I took caused a sharp pain.

Ervin began by saying that his committee had sent me "a little note."

"I read about your letter," I answered. "Your committee leaks, you know."

He said he did not know how his letter had gotten into the papers and that while they did not want to have a confrontation, they took the view that executive privilege did not cover criminal or political acts. "You want your staff to go through presidential files," I said. "The answer is no. We disagree on that. But I'll think over your letter."

Even this short exchange had fatigued me, but I went on. "What is it you specifically want? I am not going to have anyone going through all my files. We should start, if we have this meeting, by your telling me the areas you think you want."

He said he thought that staff members could work out specifics, but he repeated the totally unacceptable formulation in his letter that had requested presidential papers "relevant to any matters the committee is authorized to investigate." Taken literally, this would mean that his staff would have to go through *all* the papers just to be able to know which ones they wanted to request.

Despite the pain I raised my voice slightly. "Your attitude in the hearings was clear. There's no question who you're out to get," I said.

"We are not out to get anything, Mr. President," he said, "except the truth."

I settled back onto the bed and told him that no one from his staff was going to go through any White House files. I said I was willing to consider a meeting—but just between him and me. "A man-to-man talk might be useful," I said. "I'm cooperating in every way possible, but I have the responsibility to defend the office of the President—just as you thought you had to defend the concept of separation of powers before the Supreme Court. If you have the same objective you had in Gravel's case, we'll get along just fine."

He seemed a bit nonplussed and indicated that he was not optimistic about our being able to work things out. He said he would report to the committee and insisted again that it was not out to get anybody.

I looked up at Haig and Ziegler, who had been in the room during the call. I told them it must have been the fever that had kept me from giving Ervin the cool answers that undoubtedly would have been more effective for our cause. "But," I added, "I said what I believe."

I got up and dressed, and despite the fact that I had a 102-degree temperature, I decided to keep my scheduled appointments for that day. There is a national commotion every time a President is even the slightest bit ill, so I wanted to postpone any indication that I was not feeling well until the last possible moment. I had a half-hour meeting with West German Foreign Minister Walter Scheel, and then Bill Timmons came in to discuss legislative problems. After that I received a report from the members of a commission I had appointed to study the question of fire prevention.

When the schedule was completed, chest X-rays were taken, which confirmed Tkach's diagnosis: I had viral pneumonia. That evening I was driven to Bethesda Naval Hospital.

I was determined to show that even in the hospital I was able to carry out my duties as President. As I received inhalation therapy and underwent tests and X-rays, I continued to take calls and to see Ziegler and Haig. I phoned Kissinger and reviewed the plans for Phase IV of our economic policy with Shultz. The worst thing about the pneumonia was the inability to sleep because the discomfort was so great. During the nights I lay awake counting the minutes. I ended up staying on the phone until late at night, checking on the day's events.

By Sunday, July 15, my temperature had dropped below 100 degrees. For the first time since I entered the hospital I was able to eat a full meal. I had even slept two full hours on Saturday night.

Early Monday morning Haig called to tell me that Haldeman's former aide Alex Butterfield had revealed the existence of the White House taping system to the Ervin Committee staff and that it would become public knowledge later that day.

I was shocked by this news. As impossible as it must seem now, I had believed that the existence of the White House taping system would never be revealed. I thought that at least executive privilege would have been raised by any staff member before verifying its existence.

The impact of the revelation of our taping system was stunning. The headline in the New York *Daily News* was *Nixon Bugged Own Offices*.

Fred Buzhardt sent a letter to Ervin confirming that the system described by Butterfield did exist and pointing out that it was similar to the one that had been employed by the previous administration. Buzhardt's letter provoked swift reactions laced with righteous indignation. *LBJ Aides Disavow System* was the Washington *Post*'s headline. Johnson's former domestic aide, Joseph Califano, said, "I think this is an outrageous smear on a dead President." Arthur Schlesinger, Jr., said that it was "inconceivable" that John Kennedy would have approved such a taping system. Kennedy's former aide, Dave Powers, then curator of the Kennedy Library, denied that there were tapes. But Army Signal Corps technicians who had installed the Johnson taping system gave Fred Buzhardt sworn affidavits about the placement of the machines and microphones, and within a few days the archivist at the Johnson Library in Austin confirmed the existence of the LBJ tapes. Then, the next day, the Kennedy Library admitted that in fact there were 125 tapes and 68 Dictabelt recordings of different meetings and phone conversations.

Haig and I spent several hours in my hospital room talking about what the revelation of the existence of the tapes would mean. I reflected ironically that just a few months before, on April 10, after I had met with two of the POWs, I had told Haldeman to get rid of all the tapes except those dealing with important national security events. I had made a diary note about it afterward.

Diary

I had meetings with Stockdale and Flynn today. They were just as moving as the meetings I had had earlier with Risner and with Denton. I hope that we have tapes of these conversations.

As a matter of fact, I had a good talk with Haldeman about the tapes—decided that we would go back over the period of time that they have been taken and destroy them except for the national security periods in Cambodia, May 8, and probably December 18, having in mind the fact that otherwise either he or I would be the only ones that could listen to the tapes and decide what could be used—and that would take us just months and months of time.

But this discussion had taken place in the midst of our concerns about Watergate, and three weeks later he was no longer there to do it.

In the hospital I raised the idea of whether we should not destroy the tapes now. Haig said he would have a talk with the lawyers about it. In the meantime we agreed that the taping system itself must be removed.

Over the next three days, while the doctors anxiously tried to keep my meetings to a minimum, I discussed the situation with Haig, Ziegler, Buzhardt, and Garment. Legally the tapes would not actually be evidence until they were subpoenaed. But since we knew that the Ervin Committee or the Special Prosecutor would subpoena them momentarily, it would be a highly controversial move to destroy them. Nonetheless, Buzhardt felt that the tapes were my personal property and he favored destroying them. Garment considered the tapes to be evidence, and while he did not favor releasing them, he made it clear that he would strongly oppose any move to destroy them. Haig made the telling point that, apart from the legal problems it might create, destruction of the tapes would forever seal an impression of guilt in the public mind. When Ted Agnew came to the hospital to visit, he told me I should destroy them.

We contacted Haldeman to find out what he thought I should do. His advice was to claim executive privilege and not surrender an inch of principle to the witch-hunting of Ervin and his committee staff. Haldeman said that the tapes were still our best defense, and he recommended that they not be destroyed.

When I had entered the hospital on July 12, I had been looking forward to fighting our way out of the slump into which Dean's testimony had sent us. But by the time I prepared to leave the hospital on July 20, the revelation of the tapes had changed everything. In the early morning hours of July 19 I had made a note on my bedside pad:

> We must go forward on the business of government for three years. It's the only way we can get by this ordeal. We mustn't let this continuing investigation get to us as the revelation of the existence of the tapes did to Garment and some of the members of the staff. We must be strong and competent. We must go ahead.
>
> Should have destroyed the tapes after April 30, 1973.

It was a beautiful summer day when I returned to the White House from the hospital. Most of the staff had come out to the Rose Garden to greet me, and as I walked up the steps to the Oval Office I turned around and spoke to them. That brief speech remains my favorite of all the statements I made during this difficult period:

> I feel that we have so little time in the positions that all of us hold and so much to do. With all that we have to do and so little time to do it, at the end of the next three and a half years to look back and think that, but for that day, something went undone that might have been done that would have made a difference in whether we have peace in the world or a better life here at home, that would be the greatest frustration of all.

I turned to the predictable comments the staff would be hearing that, because of my illness and the rough assaults being directed toward me, I should consider either slowing down or resigning. I gave my answer to that idea in one of my father's favorite words: "poppycock." I talked about all the things we could accomplish—prosperity without war, controlling crime, drugs, providing opportunity. Then I said:

> There are these and other great causes that we were elected overwhelmingly to carry forward in November. And what we were elected to do we are going to do, and let others wallow in Watergate, we are going to do our job.

If I had indeed been the knowing Watergate conspirator that I was charged as being, I would have recognized in 1973 that the tapes contained conversations that would be fatally damaging. I would have seen that if I were to survive, they would have to be destroyed.

Many factors bore on my decision not to destroy the tapes. When I listened to them for the first time on June 4, 1973, I recognized that they were a mixed bag as far as I was concerned. There was politically embarrassing talk on them, and they contained many ambiguities, but I recognized that they indisputably disproved Dean's basic charge that I had conspired with him in an obstruction of justice over an eight-month period. I had not listened to the March 21 tape, but Haldeman had, and while I knew it would be difficult to explain in the critical and hostile atmosphere that now existed, he had told me that it could be explained, and I wanted to believe that he was right.

I was also persuaded by Haig's reasoning that destruction of the tapes would create an indelible impression of guilt, and I simply did not believe that the revelation of anything I had actually done would be as bad as that impression. On Saturday, July 21, I made a note outlining this rationale: "If I had discussed illegal action, I would not have taped. If I had discussed illegal action and had taped I would have destroyed the tapes once the investigation began."

Finally I decided that the tapes were my best insurance against the unforeseeable future. I was prepared to believe that others, even people close to me, would turn against me just as Dean had done, and in that case the tapes would give me at least some protection.

Once I had decided not to destroy the tapes, I had to decide whether to release them to the Ervin Committee and the Special Prosecutor or to invoke executive privilege. When President Andrew Jackson had been presented with a congressional request for a White House staff document that had been read at a Cabinet meeting, he had said, "As well might I be required to detail to the Senate the free and private conversations I have held with those officers on any subject relating to their duties and my own." Jackson had thought that this example was a ludicrous extreme but that extreme turned out to be the most moderate position espoused by the Special Prosecutor and the Ervin Committee.

I know that most people think that executive privilege was just a cloak that I drew around me to protect myself from the disclosure of my wrongdoing. But the fact that I wanted to protect myself did not alter the fact that I believed deeply and strongly in the principle and was convinced then—as I am now—that it stands at the very heart of a strong presidency. Even though the application of the principle to this case was flawed by the nature and extent of my personal interest and involvement, I did not want to be the first President in history who acquiesced in a diminution of the principle.

There were other, less abstract reasons for not turning over the tapes. I sensed what Agnew and Buzhardt were sure of: the very existence of the tapes was a tantalizing lure for the political opposition. As far as the Democrats were concerned, fighting the battle to get the tapes could be as politically rewarding as winning it. But if even one tape was yielded, it would only heighten the desire for two more. In his eloquent argument before the court of appeals, our constitutional specialist Charles Alan Wright likened the pressure for the tapes to a "hydraulic force":

> Once there is a hole below the waterline of a ship, no matter how small, the tremendous hydraulic pressure of the sea quickly broadens the gash in the ship and the ship is in danger.
>
> And it will be that way, too, if the hydraulic pressures of Watergate are thought to permit to tolerate even a very limited infraction of the confidentiality that every President since George Washington has enjoyed.

Shortly after I had heard about Butterfield's disclosure I had written on my bedside notepad: "Tapes—once start, no stopping."

And, finally, I simply was not sure what was on the tapes. If I had been confident that they were without ambiguity and would show me speaking like the romantic ideal of a President pursuing justice undeterred, I suppose that I might have found some way to overcome my inhibitions about releasing them. But they did not—at least the few that I had heard did not—and I could only fear what might be on the others that I had not heard and could not remember. Therefore, I decided to invoke executive privilege to prevent disclosure of the tapes. On Monday, July 23, I sent Senator Ervin a letter informing him that I would not supply any tapes for his committee's investigation.

As soon as Ervin received my letter he convened his committee, which voted unanimously to subpoena five of the taped conversations and a mass of documents relating directly or indirectly to the "activities, participation, responsibilities, or involvement" of some twenty-five individuals in "any alleged criminal acts related to the presidential election of 1972." Cox moved to subpoena nine conversations.

I now believe that from the time of the disclosure of the existence of the tapes and my decision not to destroy them, my presidency had little chance of surviving to the end of its term. Unfortunately my instinct was not so clear or sure at the time, and I did not see that while destroying the tapes might have looked like an admission of guilt, invoking executive privilege to keep them from being made public appeared hardly less so. In the end my refusal damaged the very principle I thought I was protecting. I was the first President to test the principle of executive privilege in the Supreme Court, and by testing it on such weak ground—where my own personal vulnerability would inevitably be perceived as having affected my judgment—I probably ensured the defeat of my cause. Once the public got the impression that I was trying to hide something, the attempts by Ervin and Cox to get the tapes gained increasing public support.

And quite apart from what was on the tapes, the very fact of their existence and the struggle being fought over their possession were about to do what I had been fearing most from the start: they were about to paralyze the presidency.

After hearing Dean's testimony, the Ervin Committee had recessed for a week. When its hearings resumed in July, the media coverage had tapered off considerably, so the witnesses who appeared in rebuttal to Dean did not have nearly so much impact. Only Dean had received complete live television coverage from all three networks on all five days of his testimony. An unnamed television news executive summed up the situation in an article in the Los Angeles *Times* when he said that the networks looked on these hearings as theatre, and as long as they were lively and controversial they would be broadcast. No one was particularly concerned about fairness. As the executive put it, "A man on defense can never match a man on the attack in terms of audience response."

The committee finally began to lose steam. It continued to hear witnesses, but it no longer provided the entertainment television viewers had come to expect; it had simply become overexposed.

Its public death blow was dealt by Pat Buchanan. Appearing as a witness, he responded to the senators with sharp, combative, commonsense answers and documented illustrations of the fact that it was the Democrats who had set the precedents for dirty tricks in American politics. Ervin was visibly shaken and reportedly angry that his staff had exposed him to such embarrassment.

Before long, most of the committee members were looking for a way to close down the hearings. Finally they came up with a face-saving justification: they sanctimoniously announced that they were concerned about prejudicing the rights of defendants.

On August 7, after 37 days of hearings totaling more than 325 hours of network time, the Watergate part of the Ervin Committee's hearings ended. More than 20 percent of that television time had gone to John Dean. When Ervin's gavel banged this section of the investigation to a close, there had been an average of 22 hours of television news shows, specials, and daytime programming on Watergate for every week since the hearings began.

On August 15 I made my second speech to the nation about Watergate. I talked about what I called "the overriding question of what we as a nation can learn from this experience and what we should now do." I said: "The time has come to turn Watergate over to the courts, where the questions of guilt or innocence belong. The time has come for the rest of us to get on with the urgent business of our nation."

I repeated what I called "the simple truth": that I had had no prior knowledge of the Watergate break-in; that I neither took part in nor knew about the subsequent cover-up activities; and that I had neither authorized nor encouraged subordinates to engage in illegal or improper campaign tactics. I said that far from trying to hide the facts, "my effort throughout has been to discover the facts—and to lay those facts before the appropriate law enforcement authorities so that justice could be done and the guilty dealt with."

This speech, with its call to turn Watergate over to the courts, hit a responsive chord. The numbers of telegrams and phone calls to the White House immediately after it was over were the biggest since the days of my Vietnam speeches. People were tired of Watergate.

It was my belief then, and it is still my belief today, that the Democratic majority in Congress used the Watergate scandal as an excuse for indulging in a purposeful policy of ignoring and actually overriding the landslide mandate that my programs and philosophy had received in the 1972 election. Unfortunately, by the way I handled Watergate, I helped them do it.

TRYING TO REGROUP

Three months of Watergate torpor had slowed Congress's work on domestic and foreign affairs to a near halt. My anger at this situation came through in my toast at the state dinner for Prime Minister Tanaka of Japan in July:

> It is so easy these days to think in other terms, to think in the minuscule political terms that I think tempt us all from time to time and tempt those who represent the people in both countries—make a small point here, work in the murky field of political partisanship—but what really matters is this: after our short time on this great world stage is completed and we leave, what do we leave?
>
> Do we leave the memory only of the battles we fought, of the opponents we did in, of the viciousness that we created, or do we leave possibly not only the dream but the reality of a new world, a world in which millions of the wonderful young children . . . may grow up in peace and in friendship. . . .
>
> And so, let others spend their time dealing with the murky, small, unimportant, vicious little things. We have spent our time and will spend our time in building a better world.

I was determined not to give up on my election mandate, and in the fall of 1973 I decided to send a second State of the Union message to remind Congress and the American people of the important and unfinished domestic agenda that had gone unattended during the Watergate spring and summer. The September 10 message was launched at a press conference on September 5, during which I reviewed the major categories of national concern: inflation, national defense, and energy.

We had succeeded in holding down spending in 1973 and, despite Watergate, had managed to sustain all my vetoes of budget-busting spending bills. But Congress was now threatening to pass increases that would exceed the budget by at least $6 billion. I therefore called for an effort to keep spending within the budget in order to cut inflation and keep prices down.

In terms of constant dollars, defense spending in 1973 was actually $10 billion less than it had been in 1964 before the Vietnam war began.

The draft had been ended and our defense forces were numerically lower than at any time since before the Korean war. Yet the Senate was moving to cut overseas troop strength by nearly 25 percent—without demanding any corresponding cuts by the Soviets. We were winning only narrowly in the congressional appropriations battle for the Trident nuclear submarine and the other important weaponry we needed to give us leverage in SALT.

During the past three years I had sent Congress seven proposals dealing with energy policy and legislation. Congress had not yet acted on any of them. This inaction, I warned, was keeping us at the mercy of the producers of oil in the Mideast, and I asked that immediate attention be paid to this vitally important area of national and international concern. The message described many of the more than fifty bills and programs that I had sent to Congress in 1973 alone and that had been ignored or brushed aside. These included a new federal housing program; proposals for trade reform; proposals for tax reform, particularly in the form of property tax relief for the elderly; environmental bills; education, health, and human affairs bills; and bills relating to crime prevention and control.

On August 22 I announced that I would nominate Henry Kissinger to succeed Bill Rogers as Secretary of State. On September 22 we held the swearing-in ceremony in the East Room, and after Chief Justice Burger had administered the oath, Kissinger talked about our discussion five years earlier during the transition—my insistence that we should not be hampered by preconceptions, or avoid any new departure in the effort to bring peace. He said our objective—achieving a structure of peace—was the same today as then:

> We mean a world which had not just eased tensions but overcome them; a world not based on strength but on justice; a relationship among nations based on cooperation and not equilibrium alone.

Then he added movingly:

> There is no country in the world where it is conceivable that a man of my origin could be standing here next to the President of the United States.

During this period I took stock of the situation within the White House staff. What I saw disturbed me, but I had no solution. Despite my determination that it should not happen, Haig had become bogged down in Watergate; it was like quicksand pulling him back each time he tried to get free to work on foreign and domestic policy problems.

Al Haig, I am sure, would be the first to acknowledge that he ran a very protective White House. It probably would have surprised the press corps to hear the assessments from Cabinet and staff that beneath Haig's far more affable and accessible exterior he was in many ways a more rigid administrator than Bob Haldeman. In fact, Haig purposely set out to structure this kind of White House operation because he felt that during the first term we had made our big mistakes over little things. Watergate was the most obvious case in point: if it had been handled effectively at the outset, it would never have reached this point. Haig was determined not to let this kind of mistake happen again. To prevent it, he drew more and more authority and responsibility to himself.

One problem that Haig had to deal with immediately was that the morale of the White House staff had begun to sink seriously. For many it was a case of sheer physical exhaustion: people who had been used to working ten-hour days were now working twelve and fourteen and seventeen hours a day, trying to handle their own work as well as pitching in on Watergate. But there was also a growing sense that no matter how hard we worked or what we did, we did not gain any ground. Each answer to each charge simply led to another charge requiring another answer—Watergate had become a bottomless pit. We now had a Watergate staff of twelve pitted against the opposition's two hundred. We had no comparable task forces of researchers and investigators to challenge theirs. We needed a well-planned overall strategy, but our lawyers were pulled from case to case with little time to think much beyond the next day's tactics. And I knew that among my lawyers and staff as well there was already a haunting uncertainty about the truth: they recognized that some of my defenses did not hold up to good logic or common sense, and they were naturally reluctant to go out on a limb to expound them.

John Connally soon became disenchanted with his role at the White House. We had planned to match his duties to his talents, but because of Watergate there was never time, and his actual duties as Counsellor to the President remained undefined. While we were in San Clemente in June, Connally told me that he would be leaving before long. He said that he was still supportive but he felt that he had to move on. I tried to talk him into staying, but my heart was not in it; I could not ask a man I liked and respected—and who I hoped would succeed me in the White House in 1976—to tie himself to my troubles.

In a parting press conference Connally told reporters how he felt about their attitudes toward me. "I frankly feel like at this moment if he flew to the moon that you all wouldn't give him credit for courage," he said. "You would say he was fleeing out of fear."

I was also concerned about signs of dissatisfaction in Shultz, Laird, and Harlow. Shultz was discouraged by the downturn in the economy and disillusioned by my handling of Watergate. I considered him one of the ablest members of the Cabinet and asked him to stay on. He did for six months, but finally he said, "I can't, Mr. President. I'm just pooped." I understood. I could not bring myself to urge him to continue to go through the fire that was raging around us. Laird and Harlow felt I was not consulting with them enough on Watergate. There were two reasons that I did not like to discuss the subject with them. First, I felt that it was important for as many people on the staff as possible to stay away from Watergate; second, it was simply a painful subject for me to discuss with anyone. After a while it became easier and easier for me to rely solely on Haig, Ziegler, and the lawyers in dealing with Watergate, even though I knew that this further contributed to the frustration and isolation felt by Laird, Harlow, and others.

On August 29 District Judge John Sirica ruled against us in the Special Prosecutor's suit for nine tapes. No court had ever before in our history compelled a President to produce documents that he had determined not to surrender. Because of the principle of separation of powers, a court can issue an order, but a President has a right—and some scholars would argue, a responsibility—not to obey that order if it infringes on the prerogatives of his independent branch of government. I felt then, and I feel now, that it was fully within my power to refuse to obey Sirica's ruling. In any other case, that is what I would have done. But I recognized the political reality of the Watergate situation, and instead of defying Sirica's order on constitutional principles, I decided to observe the regular procedures of the judicial system and appeal his decision to a higher court.

From the first time that the idea was suggested to me, I had objected to the creation of an independent Watergate Special Prosecutor. For one thing, I thought it was a slap at the ability of the Justice Department to do the job; for another, it was all but inevitable that under the warm glow of press attention and adulation by the Washington establishment, prosecutorial zeal would assume a life of its own.

Unfortunately, in my April 30 speech I had said that I was giving Elliot Richardson "absolute authority to make all decisions bearing upon the prosecution of the Watergate case and related matters." I had, in essence, and as events turned out, put the survival of my administration in his hands. From the time Richardson's confirmation hearings as Attorney General began it was clear that the Senate would hold his nomination hostage until an independent Watergate Special Prosecutor was appointed. Richardson felt compelled to yield to the pressure and began conducting a search for a candidate to fill the position. It took him two weeks and several refusals before he finally selected Professor Archibald Cox of the Harvard Law School.

If Richardson had searched specifically for the man whom I would have least trusted to conduct so politically sensitive an investigation in an unbiased way, he could hardly have done better than choose Archibald Cox. The Washington *Post* described Cox as having "longstanding ties to the Kennedy family." The Boston *Globe* reported that he had actually been recommended to Richardson by Teddy Kennedy. During the 1960 campaign Cox had been in charge of preparing John Kennedy's position papers; he had been a Muskie alternate delegate at the Democratic National Convention in 1972; and he publicly acknowledged that he had voted for McGovern. In a newspaper interview only two weeks before his appointment Cox had caustically criticized John Mitchell as "insensitive" to the importance of civil liberties and mentioned that he had sharp "philosophical and ideological" differences with my administration. When Kissinger learned of the Cox appointment he was shocked. He told me, "Cox will be a disaster. He has been fanatically anti-Nixon all the years I've known him."

Cox was sworn in as Special Prosecutor on May 24. Teddy Kennedy and Mrs. Robert Kennedy were among his guests at the ceremony.

The Special Prosecutor was supposed to supervise the investigation into Watergate and initiate prosecutions if they were justified or required. But shortly after his appointment in May, Cox may have subconsciously revealed his ultimate intention when he told reporters that his great-grandfather had taken part in Andrew Johnson's defense against impeachment. The news reports noted that he smiled as he observed that this family history was "a funny little quirk—or I should say, could become a funny little quirk."

Appointing Archibald Cox was bad enough. But Richardson then compounded the mistake by approving a charter for the Special Prosecution Force that, instead of limiting its responsibility to the area of Watergate, gave it virtual carte blanche to investigate the executive branch. Because of the arm's-length position that we had to observe if the Special Prosecutor was to have any credibility as an independent investigator, we had no role in formulating this charter, which began quite properly by granting him full powers in "investigating and prosecuting offenses against the United States arising out of unauthorized entry into the Democratic National Committee Headquarters at the Watergate." But then it went on to include "all offenses arising out of the 1972 Presidential Election for which the Special Prosecutor deems it necessary and appropriate to assume responsibility, allegations involving the President, members of the White House staff, or Presidential appointees, and any other matters which he consents to have assigned to him by the Attorney General." In addition the charter extended full authority for conducting grand jury proceedings, determining whether to grant immunity, initiating prosecutions, and framing indictments. The Special Prosecution Force was granted virtually unlimited funds, and there was no time limit placed on its activities. It was specifically stated that the Special Prosecutor could be removed only if he were to commit "extraordinary improprieties."

I was shocked and angry when I learned the extent of this charter. Haig talked to Richardson, who insisted that the phrases "allegations involving the President" and "members of the White House staff or Presidential appointees" should be read only in connection with the earlier reference to the 1972 presidential campaign. Of course, it did not work out that way, and Richardson later conceded that he had not foreseen the problems that would arise from giving the Special Prosecutor such unrestricted power.

It did not take long for my worst fears about the Special Prosecution Force to be realized. Of the eleven senior staff members Cox chose, seven had been associated with John, Bobby, or Teddy Kennedy. They included a former Special Assistant to Ramsey Clark, who also served as the head of George McGovern's task force on crime, a former Democratic congressional candidate, and a researcher and speechwriter for Sargent Shriver. The Chicago *Tribune* reported that only one of the top ten staff men was a Republican.

The partisan attitude that permeated the top ranks of the Watergate Special Prosecution Force was exceeded by the fervor of the junior members of its staff, most of whom were brash young lawyers intoxicated with their first real taste of power and with the attention being paid to them by a flattering and fawning press. Reports came back to me of arrogant young men using unsubstantiated charges to threaten and intimidate my personal friends and members of my staff.

Immediately after Cox was appointed, he began his inquiries about White House files. On May 30 he asked about the status of eight files; on June 5 he added six more; on June 11 he wrote asking for the tape of the April 15 conversation with John Dean that I had mentioned to Henry Petersen; the same day he asked for an inventory of twelve files. Then he requested my daily appointment logs covering all my meetings with fifteen different people; then he asked for ITT materials; and then narrative testimony from me. In July there was a leak caused by his staff that he was starting to look into the purchase of my house in San Clemente to see if any union, corporate, or campaign money had been used. His staff asked for information on government wiretapping and tried to call Secret Service agents to find out the details of their operations. Cox himself acknowledged that this went overboard.

Even though Cox's charter presumably restricted him to the 1972 campaign, he launched an investigation into 1970 campaign funds. He began investigating Secret Service personnel for their handling of demonstrators at rallies even as Richardson pointed out that the Justice Department was already defending some of the men involved in civil actions arising from these incidents. Ranging still further afield, Cox investigated the Plumbers and then launched an investigation of Bebe Rebozo.

By October 12, four months after the Special Prosecutor took over the case that the Justice Department had said was already 90 percent completed, they had brought only one indictment, and that one did not even relate to Watergate. It did not take long to see that they interpreted their power to investigate "all offenses arising out of the 1972 Presidential Election" to mean primarily those alleged to have been committed by the Nixon camp. For example, in 1974 the Special Prosecution Force let the statute of limitations lapse on a campaign fund-raising violation committed by Democratic Finance Chairman Robert Strauss. When a similar situation arose with our Finance Chairman Maury Stans, they asked the court for a waiver of the statute to prevent it from running while proceedings were pending.

No White House in history could have survived the kind of operation Cox was planning. If he were determined to get me, as I was certain that he and his staff were, then given the terms of their charter it would be only a matter of time until they had bored like termites through the whole executive branch. The frustrating thing was that while I saw them as partisan zealots abusing the power I had given them in order to destroy me unfairly, the media presented them and the public largely perceived them as the keepers of the sacred flame of American justice against a wicked President and his corrupt administration. Whenever I tried to state my point of view, I was inevitably discounted as being self-interested and self-serving. I could not imagine any other President allowing a man who derived his authority from the White House to use that power independently to conduct a partisan inquisition at the administration's expense. I certainly did not intend to be the first. Thus, by fall a clash was inevitable, and, thanks to the charter Richardson had given him, Cox was so powerful that the outcome was far from predictable.

AGNEW ACCUSED

Ted Agnew's problems with the U.S. Attorney in Baltimore had remained a peripheral concern of mine ever since April 1973, when Haldeman had first mentioned to me that Agnew was afraid of being embarrassed by the investigations under way there.

In June Elliot Richardson had informed Haig that serious allegations were being made about Agnew; by the middle of July the vague allegations had become a series of specific charges that Agnew while governor of Maryland had taken money in return for granting state contracts. There were also charges that he continued to receive money in return for these past favors while he was Vice President. Agnew was convinced that the young Baltimore prosecutors were out to make a name for themselves at his expense; he pointed out that one of them had worked in Muskie's 1972 campaign—a credential that hardly bespoke detachment.

By the end of July Haig had another report from Richardson. This time it was unequivocal. Haig quoted Richardson as having said that he had never seen such a cut-and-dried case. He said that Agnew was potentially indictable on more than forty counts.

On August 1 Richardson sent Agnew a letter informing him that he was being investigated on allegations of conspiracy, extortion, bribery, and tax fraud. When Haig told me this, I felt that it was time for me to become involved. I arranged to meet with Richardson on Monday, August 6; I asked Buzhardt and Garment to see him before this meeting because I wanted their independent analyses of the case against Agnew. I knew that we were dealing with political dynamite and that I had to be scrupulously careful about the information I was receiving and how it was assessed. After their meeting with Richardson, Buzhardt and Garment sent back gloomy evaluations: they agreed with Richardson that this was one of the most solid cases they had ever seen.

John Mitchell had already sent word to me that Agnew felt that Richardson was out to get him. Agnew remembered that Richardson had opposed his nomination in 1968, and he pointed out that they had disagreed repeatedly on policy matters during meetings of the Domestic Council. Agnew also was convinced that Richardson saw himself as a potential presidential candidate.

Half an hour before my meeting with Richardson on Monday morning, August 6, the White House press office received the first inquiry about rumors that the Vice President was under investigation. We knew that it would be only a matter of time before the story broke.

After a general review of the allegations against Agnew, Richardson told me that the witnesses were believable and in some cases had irrefutable documents. He said there were accusations that the payments had continued through the vice presidential years. Objectively I recognized the weight of Richardson's evidence, but emotionally I was still on Agnew's side. I wanted to believe him. I told Richardson that I expected him to assume full responsibility for seeing to it that Agnew was not railroaded by biased U.S. Attorneys and a predatory press corps.

The next morning, August 7, the *Wall Street Journal* had the scoop: a story attributed to "knowledgeable attorneys" stated that Agnew was under investigation. Haig had told me that Agnew was wavering between fighting and resigning.

That afternoon I met for an hour and a half with Agnew. He walked into my office with the same easy, confident stride he always had and began our conversation by declaring that he was totally innocent of the charges. He said they would not hold up in court, and that if it should ever go that far he would be proved innocent. He repeated to me his feeling that someday the prosecution team in Baltimore would be shown up for what it was.

I told him that I had confidence in his integrity, that I believed him and would stand by him unless clear and final evidence was presented to me that forced me to think otherwise. When he said that he was planning a press conference for the next day, I urged him to consider carefully before he said anything that might haunt him later.

I told him that one man whose fairness I could completely vouch for was Henry Petersen. I said I would arrange with Richardson for Petersen to undertake his own independent investigation of the case and to prepare his own independent recommendation.

By August 8 the newspapers and the networks had begun reporting a series of leaks and attacks on Agnew that became so irresponsible that the New York *Times* and the Washington *Post* ended up criticizing on their editorial pages what was being done on their own news pages.

On August 8 Agnew marched indignantly into the EOB briefing room and denounced the leaks. "I have no intention to be skewered in this fashion," he said. "I have nothing to hide." He denied charges that he received $1,000 a week in kickbacks, calling them "damned lies." He was asked if he had ever had a political slush fund financed by Baltimore County contractors. "Never," he replied. He was asked if he had ever received money for his personal use from any person or company doing business with the state of Maryland or the federal government. "Absolutely not," he said.

Haig and Buzhardt came in to tell me that Agnew's press conference looked like a short-term political triumph. In view of the evidence that was bound to come out, however, they did not see how it could be anything but a long-term disaster. Buzhardt shook his head and said that he could not see how Agnew could have made such blanket denials—"never," "absolutely not"—that simply would not hold up.

I faced an impossible dilemma. I knew the charges against Agnew were serious and completely persuasive to responsible people. But this knowledge was private. The press leaks, and Agnew's impassioned denials, had convinced many people that the charges were a vendetta against him. If I actively defended him, and the charges were later substantiated, I would have succeeded only in further eroding my own already dwindling credibility. If I took a neutral position, Agnew's supporters would think I had let him down. In the end I chose the second course as the sounder approach and decided I would simply have to bear the brunt of the criticism that was to come.

Agnew continued to fight back. On August 21 he had issued a statement charging that some Justice Department officials had decided to indict him in the press regardless of whether the evidence supported their position. Elliot Richardson went on television to deny that the leaks were coming from the Justice Department; later he had to acknowledge that his department was in fact probably responsible for some of the stories.

The concerted press attack against Agnew caused me to reconsider my belief in the dependability of the investigation going on in Baltimore. In a press conference on August 22 I warned that any Justice Department or United States government employee who had leaked information would be dismissed immediately upon discovery.

On September 1 Agnew came in, at his request, in order to bring me up to date on the situation. The strains were beginning to show. He told me bitterly how the prosecutors were pressing him for a wide range of personal financial data going back to 1962. He said that he was considering whether it would not be better for him to seek impeachment by the House than to have a trial in the federal court.

From talking with Agnew I understood the manner in which he had come to think about his actions as governor. State government salaries were meager. He was sure that three-quarters of the governors in other states had done the same kind of thing, namely, accepted campaign contributions from contractors doing business with the state. As he saw it, the whole trumped-up case simply involved campaign contributions that had been used to help meet expenses legitimately incurred by him and his family in their public roles. He argued that the contractors were all well qualified and that there had been no quid pro quo involved. He heatedly denied having received money while Vice President. Once again he complained about the Baltimore prosecutors. He said they were trying to track down everything he had ever bought, and every detail of his personal life.

I was genuinely sympathetic to Agnew, and I shared with him his painful concern about the effect this controversy would have on his family and friends. I said that I could not and would not ever judge his case; but I urged that he, as a lawyer, try to analyze it as objectively as he could. Only then would he be able to make decisions in his own best interests.

I could see that he was no longer as sure as he had been in our first meeting that the charges against him were not provable in court; now he reflected on the fact that no court anywhere near Washington or Maryland could possibly treat him fairly.

On the morning of September 10 Fred Buzhardt and Al Haig brought Agnew a new assessment. Buzhardt, who at my request and with Agnew's consent was keeping me informed of developments in the case, told Agnew that Justice Department officials were convinced that he would be indicted, convicted, and sentenced to a jail term. The gravity of Haig and Buzhardt's report must have had some effect. Within days, Agnew's lawyer, Judah Best, had made the first tentative overtures toward negotiations with the Justice Department.

In the midst of these negotiations I met with Agnew again. He had come a long way since that first session six weeks earlier at which he had protested his complete innocence. Now he asked what I thought he should do and talked poignantly about the problems of going away and starting a new life.

Once again I said that this was a decision only he could make, because only he knew the facts and only he knew those who would be testifying against him. He said that he simply was not going to leave under the terms Richardson was proposing: Richardson wanted to drive him into the ground, he said, and he would fight in court before he would allow that. He would risk jail rather than grovel. After this meeting I had Haig and Buzhardt tell Richardson that he must not force the country into the nightmare of a trial by insisting on unreasonably tough terms.

On Friday, September 21, Buzhardt reported to me that he thought there had been a breakthrough. Richardson and Best had reached agreement on language that would not commit Agnew to a "knowing" acceptance of money for preferential treatment, while still acknowledging that others would allege it. Agnew was going to think about it over the weekend, so Monday would be the day of decision. "I think it is just about over," Buzhardt said.

But Saturday morning brought a new set of leaks. The Washington *Post* carried a front-page story "from two sources" revealing that Agnew's lawyers were bargaining on a plea. Then CBS reported that Henry Petersen had told his associates, "We've got the evidence. We've got it cold."

Buzhardt reported that Agnew was outraged; he was convinced that the leaks had come from the Justice Department and were part of a deliberate strategy to weaken his position in the negotiations. By Sunday he had once again decided to fight.

On Monday morning, September 25, I met with Richardson and Pe-

UNITED PRESS INTERNATIONAL

The historic handshake with Premier Chou En-lai in Peking on February 21, 1972.

PEOPLE'S REPUBLIC OF CHINA

The meeting in Chairman Mao Tse-tung's house in Peking.

One of RN's most vivid memories of the 1972 China trip was this audience—made up of both men and women—at the gymnastic exhibition they visited in Peking.

WHITE HOUSE PHOTO

WHITE HOUSE PHOTO

At the Great Wall of China in 1972.

WHITE HOUSE PHOTO

Shaking hands with Leonid Brezhnev after signing the SALT agreement in the Kremlin, May 26, 1972.

Campaigning for re-election in October 1972, in Atlanta, Georgia.

WHITE HOUSE PHOT

UNITED PRESS INTERNATIONAL

With Prime Minister Golda Meir of Israel following a White House dinner on March 1, 1973.

At the POW dinner, May 24, 1973, Irving Berlin leads the singing of "God Bless America." Sammy Davis, Jr., joins in. The flag made in captivity by a POW is displayed in the background.

WHITE HOUSE PHOTO

Summit II: with Brezhnev on the South Portico of the White House after his arrival ceremony in June 1973.

WHITE HOUSE PHOTO

Summit II: with Brezhnev in RN's second-floor study at La Casa Pacifica in San Clemente in June 1973.

With Pat and Bebe Rebozo in San Clemente, August 20, 1973.

WHITE HOUSE PHOTO

WHITE HOUSE PHOTO

The tense press conference of October 26, 1973, following the controversial firing of Archibald Cox as Watergate Special Prosecutor and after the military alert during the Yom Kippur War.

WHITE HOUSE PHOTO

With President Anwar Sadat of Egypt in Alexandria during the Middle East trip in June 1974.

Summit III: sailing on the Black Sea in the Crimea in June 1974. Brezhnev (right) and translator Viktor Sukhodrev point out Yalta.

WHITE HOUSE PHOTO

WHITE HOUSE PHOTO

With Tricia in the Rose Garden, August 7, 1974.

WHITE HOUSE PHOTO

RN with Julie after informing the family of his decision to resign, August 7, 1974.

WHITE HOUSE PHOTO

Meeting with Vice President Ford on August 8, 1974, RN's last full day as President.

WHITE HOUSE PHOTO

RN's farewell to the Cabinet and White House staff in the East Room on the morning of August 9, 1974.

WHITE HOUSE PHOTO

WIDE WORLD PHOTOS

tersen. Petersen went over the principal allegations and gave me his conclusion that it was an "open-and-shut case." He said that Agnew would be found guilty and would have to serve a prison term. Richardson said that he was now ready to send the evidence to the grand jury. I asked Richardson to have the Justice Department prepare an opinion on the question of whether it would be constitutional to indict a Vice President while he was still in office. The Constitution specifically provides that a President can be removed from office only by being impeached and convicted; only then can he be indicted in criminal proceedings and brought to trial for his offenses. Although the Vice President is not specifically mentioned in this clause of the Constitution, I argued that a case could be made that he would be in the same position.

Agnew came in at 10:30 A.M. He told me that he had decided to go to Speaker Carl Albert and request that the House of Representatives undertake a full impeachment inquiry. He still adamantly denied having received any money while Vice President and said that the charges were just part of the effort to sink him. He told me that he would reconsider resigning only if he were granted complete immunity from prosecution. Then, for a moment, his manner changed, and in a sad and gentle voice he asked for my assurance that I would not turn my back on him if he were out of office.

That afternoon Agnew went to Carl Albert's office and presented his formal request for an impeachment proceeding. Though I seriously doubted that it would be granted, I had the congressional relations staff talk with leading House Republicans, urging them to support the request. The next day Albert let it be known that he was rejecting it. The same day, the Justice Department alerted me that its study had concluded that a President could not be indicted while in office, but a Vice President could. I asked that Agnew be informed of this development. That evening Agnew and his family left for California. Haig's impression was that he was going away to think things over, talk with his family, and perhaps prepare them for his resignation.

Agnew's troubles had taken a serious toll. The news stories continued to deluge us and made the Watergate stories seem even worse than they already were. In addition, Agnew's staff had become embittered about our cautious position because they didn't understand the weight of the case against him. Confidence in government—and confidence in me—was already reeling from Watergate and was now being eroded even further. While I still felt enormous personal sympathy for Agnew, over the past days I had grown increasingly disturbed by his prolongation of what seemed an inevitable end and felt he had to resign.

I was at Camp David on Saturday afternoon when Haig called with the latest development. Agnew had just spoken to a group of Republican women in Los Angeles and told them that during the past several months he had been living in purgatory, finding himself confronted by undefined, unclear, and unattributed accusations. As the audience cheered and waved signs reading "Spiro is my hero," Agnew had proclaimed his innocence, attacked Justice Department officials, and shouted: "I will not resign if indicted! I will not resign if indicted!"

When I received Haig's call, I had just finished talking with Rose Woods, who had come up earlier in the day to start typing the conversation from the tapes subpoenaed by the Special Prosecutor.

I had already begun to anticipate that the court of appeals would rule against us. I wanted to break the paralysis caused by the court battles. Rather than take the case to the Supreme Court I had begun to consider a compromise: submitting written summaries of the tapes subpoenaed by the Special Prosecutor and by the Watergate Committee after national security discussions and other matters irrelevant to Watergate had been deleted.

I had asked Rose to do a quick run-through of the subpoenaed tapes to give us the gist of the conversations without taking the time to prepare complete transcripts. She is such a fast typist that I thought it would take her only a couple of days to finish the whole lot. But she found that the quality of the tapes was so bad and the voices so hard to distinguish that she had to go phrase by phrase, listening to each section several times in order to make out the words. After several hours she had finished only one short passage of the first tape.

I took the earphones and listened myself. At first all I could hear was a complete jumble. I ran the machine back and listened again. Gradually I could make out a few words, but at times the rattling of a cup or the thump of a hand on the desk would obliterate whole passages. The tapes of conversations with John Dean that I had listened to in June had almost all been Oval Office conversations and John Dean's flat, uninflected voice had been picked up reasonably well. It had not occurred to me that the other recordings would not be of the same quality. But in the EOB office the different microphone placements and seating arrangements, the shape of the room, and the height of the arched ceilings apparently created entirely different acoustics. Nor had I considered the problem of understanding a highly modulated voice like Ehrlichman's.

Steve Bull, a White House staff aide, had come to Camp David with Rose to help her locate the subpoenaed conversations on the tapes and cue them on the machine for her. At one point Bull hit upon the ambiguity in the Special Prosecutor's subpoena. The subpoena requested a "Meeting of June 20, 1972, in the President's Executive Office Building ('EOB') Office involving Richard Nixon, John Ehrlichman and H. R. Haldeman from 10:30 A.M. to noon (time approximate)." Bull could not find such a meeting in the logs, which showed only a conversation with

Ehrlichman alone, beginning at 10:25 and lasting until 11:20, followed by a separate conversation with Haldeman alone. Bull and Haig talked by phone, and Bull asked about the confusion. Haig talked to Buzhardt and called back to say that, according to Buzhardt, only the Ehrlichman conversation was subpoenaed, not the Haldeman conversation that followed it.

By Sunday night, when we returned to Washington, Rose had worked twenty-nine hours with a Sony tape recorder and a typewriter, and she still had not finished even the first conversation with Ehrlichman.

On Monday morning, October 1, I met with Ziegler, Haig, Laird, and Kissinger and then spent an hour with the President of the commission of the European communities before going to a military promotion ceremony and a bill-signing ceremony. I was in the EOB office when Rose came in visibly agitated.

She said she thought she might have caused a small gap in the Haldeman part of the June 20 tape. For a moment I thought she must have meant the Ehrlichman conversation, because I knew that that was the one she had been working on. When I realized it was the Haldeman conversation I reassured her and told her that since the Haldeman conversation had not been subpoenaed, there was nothing to worry about.

She explained what had happened. At Steve Bull's request the Secret Service had given her a new tape recorder that morning. It was a Uher 5000 machine, a kind that she had never worked with before. Unlike the manually operated Sony she had used at Camp David, the Uher had a foot-pedal control that would help speed up the work considerably by allowing her to type without having continually to shift position back and forth from typewriter to tape recorder. She had been using this new machine only about half an hour when she finally came to what seemed to be the end of the Ehrlichman conversation. She ran the tape ahead to be sure that Ehrlichman had in fact left the room. She had reached a part where she heard Haldeman talking about schedule matters—she heard him say something about Ely, Nevada—when her phone rang and she turned to reach for the phone. When she finished the call, she turned back and started to listen to the tape again. All she could hear was a shrill buzzing sound. She did not know how it had happened. She said she had not heard any words after the reference to Ely. She guessed that she had been on the phone for about four or five minutes.

I called Haig in and told him what had happened, and we checked with Buzhardt to make sure that I was right, that the Haldeman conversation had not been subpoenaed. Buzhardt confirmed this, so the peculiar incident did not seem to present any problem. It had been a busy morning, so Haig and I went for a long drive around Washington in order to talk about the problem that was foremost in my mind: what to do about Agnew. Compared to this, a few minutes missing from a non-subpoenaed tape hardly seemed worth a second thought.

During a press conference on October 3 I again had to walk a verbal tightrope on the Agnew issue. I first came to his defense, urging that he not be tried and convicted in the press. But when the question was asked if there was any truth to Agnew's charge that this had been just a political investigation, I answered that while I had been briefed only on what the witnesses might say, the charges were serious.

After the press conference I left for a weekend in Florida. I asked Buzhardt to come with me. That afternoon he received a call from Judah Best, who said that Agnew was ready to resume discussions about a plea. Best flew to Florida and met with Buzhardt until late into the night. Earlier Best had pointed out to Buzhardt that Agnew was just a few months short of being eligible for retirement with a federal pension. He had wondered if there were not some way to give him a consultancy that would keep him on the government payroll and carry him over the pension deadline. I told Buzhardt that we could not do it at this time. Agnew had also asked if he could keep his Secret Service protection for a while, and he was concerned about what would happen to his staff. I promised that I would see to it that his Secret Service protection was extended, and that we would do our best to find jobs for his staff members.

It was agreed that on Saturday, October 6, Buzhardt would call Richardson to arrange for the talks to begin again.

OCTOBER 1973

On that same Saturday morning we received a cable from Ken Keating, our ambassador in Tel Aviv, reporting that Golda Meir had just told him that Syria and Egypt were in a final countdown for war. Israel was about to be attacked on two fronts: by the Syrians from the north in the Golan Heights, and by the Egyptians from the south in the Sinai Peninsula.

The news of the imminent attack on Israel took us completely by surprise. As recently as the day before, the CIA had reported that war in the Middle East was unlikely, dismissing as annual maneuvers the massive and unusual troop movement that had recently been taking place in Egypt. They had similarly interpreted the dramatic step-up in Syrian military activity as a precautionary move because the Israelis had recently shot down three Syrian jets.

I was disappointed by our own intelligence shortcomings, and I was stunned by the failure of Israeli intelligence. They were among the best in the world, and they, too, had been caught off guard. For the first time since 1948 the Israelis were about to go into a war without having positioned their equipment or having their reserve troops on standby. It was also Yom Kippur—the Day of Atonement—the holiest day in the Jewish calendar, when most Israelis, including many in the armed forces, would be spending the day at home with their families or in synagogue at prayer. It was the one day of the year when Israel was least prepared to defend itself.

It was tragic enough that war was once again going to plague this troubled area. But there was an even more disturbing question mark in the background concerning the role of the Soviet Union. It was hard for me to believe that the Egyptians and Syrians would have moved without the knowledge of the Soviets, if not without their direct encouragement.

In the last few hours before the fighting actually began, Kissinger contacted the Israelis, the Egyptians, and the Soviets to see if war could be prevented. But it was too late. At eight o'clock that morning the Syrians attacked Israel from the north and the Egyptians attacked from the south.

By the end of the first day of fighting, the Egyptians had crossed the Suez Canal and begun a thrust into the Sinai. In the north the Israelis were pushing the Syrians back in the Golan Heights, but they were unable to rout them as they had in earlier conflicts. Israeli losses were heavy. Mrs. Meir, however, was confident that if the Israelis had three or four days in which to mount a counteroffensive, they could turn the military tide on both fronts. We had convened a special meeting of the UN Security Council right after the fighting began, but there was little interest on either side in holding cease-fire discussions. The Soviets objected to our having called the Security Council into session; they clearly thought that the Arabs would win the war on the battlefield if they had enough time to secure their early victories. The French and the British —also Security Council members—were trying to stay at arm's length; they did not share our uniquely close ties with Israel and they knew that Arab oil was at stake in this confrontation.

As far as the American position was concerned, I saw no point in trying to impose a diplomatic cease-fire that neither side wanted or could be expected to observe. It would be better to wait until the war had reached the point at which neither side had a decisive military advantage. Despite the great skepticism of the Israeli hawks, I believed that only a battlefield stalemate would provide the foundation on which fruitful negotiations might begin. Any equilibrium—even if only an equilibrium of mutual exhaustion—would make it easier to reach an enforceable settlement. Therefore, I was convinced that we must not use our influence to bring about a cease-fire that would leave the parties in such imbalance that negotiations for a permanent settlement would never begin. I was also concerned that if the Arabs were actually to start losing this war, the Soviet leaders would feel that they could not stand by and watch their allies suffer another humiliating defeat as they had in 1967.

We had a particularly delicate situation insofar as the Egyptians were concerned. Beginning in February 1973, with a view toward building better relations, we had had a series of private contacts with them. While we had to keep the interests of the Israelis uppermost during this conflict in which they were the victims of aggression, I hoped that we could support them in such a way that we would not force an irreparable break with the Egyptians, the Syrians, and the other Arab nations. We also had to restrain the Soviets from intervening in any way that would require us to confront them. Underlying all the military complications was the danger that the Arabs would try to bring economic pressure to bear on us by declaring an oil embargo.

The immensely volatile situation created by the unexpected outbreak of this war could not have come at a more complicated domestic juncture. Agnew was beginning the final plea-bargaining negotiations that would lead to his resignation, and I was faced with the need to select his successor. The media were slamming us with daily Watergate charges, and we had just begun reviewing the subpoenaed tapes in preparation for reaching a compromise with the Special Prosecutor in the unfortunate but likely event that the court of appeals ruled against us. And Congress was pushing to assert its authority by passing a far-reaching bill to restrict the President's war powers. All these concerns would be interwoven through the next two weeks. Just as a crisis in one area seemed to be settling down, it would be overtaken by a crisis in another area, until all the crises reached a concerted crescendo as we neared the brink of nuclear war.

By the end of the third day of the Yom Kippur War it was clear that the Israelis had been overconfident about their ability to win a quick victory. The initial battles had gone against them. They had already lost a thousand men—compared with the fewer than 700 lost in the entire 1967 war—and were on the way to losing a third of their tank force. By Tuesday, October 9, the fourth day of the war, we could see that if the Israelis were to continue fighting, we would have to provide them with planes and ammunition to replace their early losses. I had absolutely no doubt or hesitation about what we must do. I met with Kissinger and told him to let the Israelis know that we would replace all their losses, and asked him to work out the logistics for doing so.

At 6 P.M. Steve Bull stepped in and announced my next appointment. "Mr. President," he said, "the Vice President." Ted Agnew walked in behind him. He had come to inform me officially of what I already knew: he had decided to resign.

We shook hands and sat down in the chairs in front of the fireplace. I spoke first, saying that I knew his decision had been very difficult for him. I knew that he was by nature a man who would almost rather have lost everything fighting, even from his disadvantaged position, than have won the assurance that he would not go to prison at the price of having to compromise with his opponents. I told him how much I had appreciated his hard campaigning in 1968, 1970, and 1972 and the dedicated way he handled all his assignments from me. I asked about his wife and family; I knew how painful it had been for them.

He was particularly embittered by what he considered the hypocrisy of the members of Congress who had formerly served as governors. He repeated his belief that most of the governors in other states had followed practices such as those common in Maryland. He emphasized that he had always awarded contracts on the basis of merit, and he felt that the amounts he had received had been so small that no reasonable critic could claim that they could have influenced him to make a decision that contravened the public interest. He said that he could not see that what he had done was unethical.

He mentioned that after a few months he would like to have some kind of foreign assignment; he thought that he could be particularly effective in a Far Eastern country, perhaps Japan. He said he would appreciate anything that I could do to get some corporation to put him on a retainer as a consultant. I said that if an opportunity arose in which I could help, I would do so. At one point he said that he supposed the IRS would be harassing him the rest of his life. "You know, they were even charting up how much I paid for my neckties," he said bitterly.

Our meeting was over. I shook his hand and told him that I wished him well. I said that he could always count on me as a friend.

The next day Agnew walked into the federal courtroom in Baltimore and announced that he was pleading nolo contendere to one count of having knowingly failed to report income for tax purposes, and that he was resigning as Vice President.

The judge sentenced him to three years' probation and a $10,000 fine.

Ted Agnew's resignation was a personal tragedy for him and for his family, and a national tragedy as well. I wrote to him on October 10, the day he resigned:

> As Vice President, you have addressed the great issues of our times with courage and candor. Your strong patriotism, and your profound dedication to the welfare of the nation, have been an inspiration to all who have served with you as well as to millions of others throughout the country.
>
> I have been deeply saddened by this whole course of events, and I hope that you and your family will be sustained in the days ahead by a well-justified pride in all that you have contributed to the nation by your years of service as Vice President.

On the morning of October 10 I met with the Republican and Democratic congressional leaders. I said that our objective was to achieve peace without losing the support we had been able to build up in both the Arab and Israeli camps. So far we had succeeded, and neither side felt that we had turned against it. It was clear that none of these men, not even the most ardently pro-Israel among them, was enthusiastic about the prospect of a Mideast war that might involve American participation. Mike Mansfield said, "Mr. President, we want no more Vietnams."

"Is Israel going to lose?" one of the leaders asked apprehensively.

"No," I replied. "We will not let Israel go down the tubes."

Later that morning, as Agnew was entering his plea in a courtroom in Baltimore, the Israeli ambassador came to the White House to deliver a letter from Golda Meir. She wrote:

> Early this morning I was told of the decision you made to assure us the immediate flow of U.S. matériel. Your decision will have a great and beneficial influence on our fighting capability. I know that in this hour of dire need to Israel, I could turn to you and count on your deep sympathy and understanding.
>
> We are fighting against heavy odds, but we are fully confident that we shall come out victorious. When we do we will have you in mind.

I had been checking almost hourly with Kissinger to see how our resupply effort was coming. The reports were not good.

"Defense is putting up all kinds of obstacles," he said. Defense Secretary James Schlesinger was apparently concerned about offending the Arabs and therefore did not want to let any Israeli El Al transport planes land at American military bases. Kissinger had finally persuaded him to relent if the planes first stopped in New York and had their tail markings painted over. I agreed that it was important not to offend the Arabs gratuitously, but we now had reports that a massive Soviet airlift of weapons and supplies was under way to Syria and Egypt, and that three Soviet airborne divisions had been put on alert. The Arabs were obviously trying to consolidate their initial military victories. It was unthinkable that Israel should lose the war for lack of weapons while we were spraying paint over Stars of David. "Tell Schlesinger to speed it up," I told Kissinger.

The situation was further complicated when we received intelligence information that our strong ally King Hussein had decided to send a small contingent of Jordanian soldiers to fight with the Syrians. General Brent Scowcroft, who had replaced Haig as Kissinger's deputy, called the Israeli ambassador and expressed our hope that Israel would not widen the war by attacking Jordan.

In the midst of the developing Mideast crisis I had to turn my attention to the selection of the new Vice President.

Several members of Congress came to the White House to talk to me about it. Many of the Democrats were understandably apprehensive at the prospect of the sudden elevation of a strong Republican to a position of such national prominence. Since I would not be able to run again in 1976, my Vice President would enjoy many of the advantages of incumbency if he became the Republican nominee. There was already a drumbeat of demands from the more partisan Democrats that I not appoint anyone who was going to run for President in 1976; they wanted a caretaker Vice President who would simply fill out Agnew's unexpired term.

Mike Mansfield in particular urged that I go the caretaker route. His own choices were Senator John Sherman Cooper of Kentucky and Bill Rogers. He said that Connally, Rockefeller, or Reagan would meet with very strong opposition in Congress. This was, and I am sure was meant to be, a signal that if I nominated one of these dynamic Republican presidential contenders, the Democrats would turn very partisan. I said that the primary criterion had to be the man's qualification for the job, and I deliberately mentioned Jerry Ford as an example of a qualified man. Mansfield lighted his pipe, took some deep puffs, and made no comment.

I asked Republican Party leaders to list their recommendations for Vice President in order of preference and send the lists to Rose Woods. On the afternoon of October 11 I left for Camp David with Rose's compilation of the recommendations and the text of an announcement speech that at my direction had been prepared with four optional endings—for John Connally, for Nelson Rockefeller, for Ronald Reagan, and for Jerry Ford.

Among the approximately 400 top party leaders from all sections of the country and from Congress, the Cabinet, and the White House staff whose recommendations I had solicited, Rockefeller and Reagan were in a virtual tie for first choice; Connally was third; Ford was fourth. Ford, however, was first choice among members of Congress, and they were the ones who would have to approve the man I nominated.

John Connally had been my own first choice. As early as October 6 I had asked Haig to call him and see whether he would take the position if it were offered to him. I had also wanted to know Connally's own assessment of his chances of confirmation. Over the next few days we did some quiet checking, and the reports were all the same: Connally simply could not make it. He would be opposed by an overwhelming number of Democrats who would fear him as the strongest possible Republican candidate in 1976. With all the problems I was having with Watergate, I could not become embroiled in a massive partisan slugging match over the selection of the new Vice President.

I had Haig call Connally again and tell him that, while he still remained my first choice, I was very seriously concerned whether he could survive a confirmation battle. Connally replied that he had been checking through his own sources and had reached the same conclusion.

Looking at the other choices, I concluded that nominating either Rockefeller or Reagan would split the Republican Party down the middle and result in a bitter partisan fight that, while it might not be fatal in terms of confirmation, might leave scars that would not be healed by 1976. This left Jerry Ford.

From the outset of the search for a new Vice President I had established four criteria for the man I would select: qualification to be President; ideological affinity; loyalty; and confirmability. I felt that Jerry Ford was qualified to be President if for any reason I did not complete my term; I knew that his views on both domestic and foreign policy were very close to mine and that he would be a dedicated team player; and there was no question that he would be the easiest to get confirmed.

I returned to the White House early on Friday morning, October 12, and told Haig of my decision. The only other person we informed was Connally. He agreed immediately that Ford was the right choice in the circumstances. I wondered if Connally remembered, as I did, that I had once told him about a conversation I had had with Jerry Ford in 1972, when Ford had told me that in his view Connally was the man for 1976.

Later that morning a somber-faced Haig brought me the news: the court of appeals, in a 5–2 decision, had ruled against us in the tapes case. We now had one week to decide if we wished to appeal the decision to the Supreme Court.

Hugh Scott and Jerry Ford arrived to talk about the congressional schedule for the next few days. I revealed nothing of my decision about the vice presidency. According to some reporters, Ford had been hoping that during this visit he would learn that he was going to be named Vice President, and I was amused by news accounts that he had appeared downcast when he left the White House.

During the afternoon I learned that the plans for resupplying Israel with military equipment had become seriously bottlenecked. Because Israel was a war zone, no insurance company was willing to risk issuing policies for chartered private planes flying there. In order to get around the insurance problem, we raised with the Pentagon the idea of mobilizing a part of the Civil Reserve Air Fleet. The option of flying supplies to the Azores for transshipment to Israel was also considered, and after much discussion we were able to persuade the reluctant Portuguese government to agree to this plan. In the meantime, however, the Soviet airlift was assuming such massive proportions and the Israeli shortages, particularly ammunition, were becoming so serious, that I concluded that any further delay was unacceptable and decided we must use U.S. military aircraft if that was what was necessary to get our supplies through to Israel. I asked Kissinger to convey my decision to the Pentagon and have them prepare a plan. I was shocked when he told me that the Pentagon's proposal was that we send only three C-5A military transport planes to Israel. Their rationale was that sending a small number of planes would cause fewer difficulties with the Egyptians, the Syrians, and also the Soviets. My reaction was that we would take just as much heat for sending three planes as for sending thirty.

I called Schlesinger and told him that I understood his concern and appreciated his caution. I assured him that I was fully aware of the gravity of my decision and that I would accept complete personal responsibility if, as a result, we alienated the Arabs and had our oil supplies cut off. I said if we could not get the private planes, we should use our own military transports. "Whichever way we have to do it, get them in the air, *now,*" I told him.

When I was informed that there was disagreement in the Pentagon about which kind of plane should be used for the airlift, I became totally exasperated. I said to Kissinger, "Goddamn it, use every one we have. Tell them to send everything that can fly."

Shortly after seven o'clock on Friday evening, October 12, I had Haig place the call to Jerry Ford at home to tell him that he was my choice for Vice President and to ask if he was prepared to accept. Ford asked if we could call back on another number so that his wife, Betty, could share the call on an extension phone.

After talking with both Jerry and Betty, I went to the Residence to tell Pat the news. "Good," she said. "I guessed it."

At nine that night the announcement was made at a televised ceremony in the East Room. Afterward the family joined me while I ate dinner. I had just finished a small steak when Haig came in to discuss the latest Soviet message, which had been delivered to the White House earlier in the evening.

The message stated that they had heard we were supplying Israel with bombs, air-to-air missiles, planes, and tanks. They said that they had also heard rumors that 150 American Air Force pilots were going to Israel disguised as tourists. No threats were made, but the menacing tone and intention of the message were clear. Of course, there was no mention of the massive Soviet airlift, which was by then supplying an estimated 700 tons of weapons and matériel daily to Syria and Egypt.

This message was premature. Our airlift to Israel had not yet begun at the time he wrote, but the next day, Saturday, October 13, at 3:30 P.M., thirty C-130 transports were on their way to Israel.

By Tuesday we were sending in a thousand tons a day. Over the next few weeks there would be more than 550 American missions, an operation bigger than the Berlin airlift of 1948–49. I also ordered that an additional ten Phantom Jets be delivered to Israel.

In fact, the Israelis had already begun to turn the tide of battle on their own, and with our infusion of new supplies they were able to push all the way to the outskirts of Damascus and were close to encircling the Egyptian forces in the Sinai.

It was not until Saturday morning that I finally had time to go over the decision of the court of appeals, which had ruled against us in the Special Prosecutor's suit for the nine tapes.

In one sense the ruling was a victory, because the court accepted our argument that wholesale access to executive deliberations would cripple the government. The majority opinion said that the ruling should be considered an "unusual and limited" requirement for a President to produce material evidence. But such a victory was relative at best because the majority on the court rejected our contention that only a President could decide whether such material was or was not privileged. Instead they arrogated that power to themselves.

The ruling was a serious blow to me personally, even though I had tried to prepare myself for it, as indicated by notes I had made for discussion with Haig and Ziegler:

> We must not kid ourselves; we must face these facts.
>
> After our August 15 statement, Gallup showed us with 38 percent support; since then we've had the August 22 press conference, the September 5 press conference, and a backbreaking schedule of foreign and domestic newsworthy events. We hear from some of our friends in Congress that Congress is in a better mood; that Ervin is going down in public esteem; that the news is not as biased as it was.
>
> Yet both Gallup and Harris show our support going down from 38 in Gallup to 32, and in Harris the number of resignation rising to 31, with 56 opposed.
>
> The question is: are we facing the facts? Aren't we in a losing battle with the media despite the personal efforts I have made over the past month particularly? Are we facing the fact that the public attitudes may have hardened to the point that we can't change them?

The situation was intolerable. Week by week, month by month, we were being worn down, trapped, paralyzed. The Ervin Committee continued its leaks and accusations. It had been four and a half months since Haldeman and Ehrlichman resigned; four months since Cox was named. Nothing had been resolved. The investigations dragged on. Despite the fact that a President can only be impeached, rumors that he wanted to indict me continued. Strong conservatives in Congress and on my staff had long felt that he had to go, both because of the liberal enclave he had established and also because of the parasite he had become, dangerously draining the executive month after month. Firing him seemed the only way to rid the administration of the partisan viper we had planted in our bosom. Whether or not we decided to appeal to the Supreme Court in this particular tapes case, I knew that it would be only a matter of days before Cox would be back for more, and then more after that.

This ruling had come at the worst possible time: we were in the midst of a major world crisis in the Middle East, and in the aftermath of the shattering domestic trauma of the resignation of a Vice President. But any such considerations were extraneous to the timetable imposed on us by the ruling. We had until midnight on Friday either to comply or to file a further appeal.

Appointing a Special Prosecutor had been a major mistake, one that I knew would be difficult and costly to remedy. If I could develop an acceptable compromise on the battle for the tapes, I decided to fire Cox and return the Watergate investigation to the Justice Department, where it had been considered 90 percent complete months earlier and where the investigators would not have the interest Cox and his staff had in self-perpetuation.

When the idea of supplying summaries instead of transcripts of the subpoenaed tapes had first been explored at the end of September, we had begun thinking of finding some outside person who could verify their accuracy. Fred Buzhardt suggested Senator John Stennis of Mississippi. Stennis was a Democrat, the Chairman of the Senate Select Committee on Standards and Conduct, a former judge, and one of the few men in Congress respected by members of both parties for his fairness and integrity. Summaries, we felt, would not compromise the critical question of precedent.

On Sunday, October 14, I saw Stennis for a few minutes after the White House worship service and mentioned the possibility of his verifying the accuracy of some tape summaries. He felt he could handle the job.

The next day, Monday, October 15, Haig called in Elliot Richardson. Cox was officially Richardson's subordinate, and therefore Richardson would be the one who would have to fire him. Richardson, however, was an unpredictable element. He had publicly acknowledged the constitutional foundations of my refusal to hand over tapes when they were first subpoenaed; but he had also promised at his confirmation hearings that he would not fire Cox except for "extraordinary improprieties," and Richardson might feel that if he fired Cox he too would have to resign for breaking his promise to the Senate. After their meeting Haig confirmed that this was indeed how Richardson felt. Besides, I thought, no one could ignore the reality of the situation: Cox had become a Watergate hero.

Richardson's resignation was something we wanted to avoid at all costs. Haig and I decided to approach him with a compromise: we would not insist on firing Cox, but we would go ahead with the Stennis plan. I was still determined that this would be the end of our compromises with Cox. Haig told Richardson this and reported back that Richardson felt that the plan was good and reasonable and that Stennis was perfect for the job. He also said that he had received Richardson's assurance that if Cox refused to accept the Stennis compromise, Richardson would support me in the controversy that was bound to ensue. Haig said that Richardson was confident there would be no problem and that Cox, who had been his mentor at Harvard Law School and with whom he had been friendly ever since, would agree to the compromise.

On Monday Haig and Buzhardt went to see Stennis and confirmed the arrangements. Stennis would verify the line-by-line third-person summaries of the tapes that we produced and attest to the propriety of whatever omissions we made of material that dealt with irrelevant or national security matters. We had also decided to provide the verified summaries to Ervin and Baker for the Watergate Committee.

On October 17 I met in the Oval Office with four Arab Foreign Ministers. Afterward the Saudi Foreign Minister told reporters, "We think the man who could solve the Vietnam war, the man who could have settled the peace all over the world, can easily play a good role in settling and having peace in our area of the Middle East."

At 8:45 P.M. on Thursday, October 18, we received word of a proposal the Soviets intended to submit to the UN Security Council for a joint Mideast cease-fire resolution. The combination of Israeli successes and our military airlift had proved too much for the Arabs and their Soviet sponsors, who proposed a resolution based on the three principles of a cease-fire in place, immediate withdrawal by the Israelis to the borders described in UN Resolution 242—in other words, to the pre-1967 borders—and the beginning of consultations on a peace agreement.

These terms reflected the familiar Soviet insistence that before any discussions of peace could begin, the Israelis would have to give up the territory they had gained in the 1967 war. This demand was utterly unrealistic, since the Israelis saw this territory not just as their leverage in any negotiations but as essential to their national security in the present environment. Besides, the recent Israeli battlefield successes had given them a decided military advantage, and there was no chance whatever that they would accept willingly the same terms the Arabs would have tried to impose if they had been the victors.

I sent a response that did not commit us to accepting the Soviet proposal but stressed the importance of keeping communications open. I said that our détente would remain incomplete unless peace was achieved in the Middle East and both of us had played a part in it.

In the meantime Haig reported that Richardson had talked with Cox but could not persuade him to compromise. Cox was unwilling to accept Stennis's verification. Richardson told Haig that Cox didn't have the sense of who Stennis was—his integrity—that Washington insiders had. Not only that, Cox wanted specific assurances of total access to all White House documents and tapes in the future. Haig reported that even Richardson thought this was unreasonable. More than ever I wanted Cox fired.

On Thursday and Friday, October 18 and 19, Richardson met twice with Haig, Wright, Garment, and Buzhardt. Haig told me that Richardson had suggested as an alternative to firing Cox, putting what he called "parameters" around him. The Special Prosecutor, as a part of the executive branch, was required to obey the orders of his superiors. The parameters could include an instruction that he was forbidden to sue for any further presidential documents. In the meantime we would bypass Cox with the Stennis compromise by offering the transcripts to the court and to the Ervin Committee.

Haig told me that our lawyers had analyzed Cox's possible reactions to Richardson's proposal and decided that he had three possible choices: he could accept the Stennis compromise; he could reject it and do nothing; or he could reject it and resign. According to Haig, everyone was certain that Cox, if he did not accept the Stennis compromise, would resign in protest against it; this would pose no problem for Richardson.

On October 19, while we were still trying to determine the best way to deal with Cox, a letter arrived from Brezhnev. He said that the situation in the Middle East was becoming more and more dangerous. Since neither the United States nor the Soviet Union wanted to see our relations harmed, he stated that we both should do our utmost to keep events in the Middle East from taking an even more dangerous turn. He suggested that Kissinger come to Moscow for direct talks.

We had reached a critical juncture in the war. The Israelis were now defeating the Arabs on the battlefield, and over the next few days the Soviets would have to decide what they were going to do about it. In the afternoon I sent Congress a request for $2.2 billion in emergency aid for Israel. On October 17 the Organization of Arab Petroleum Exporting Countries had voted to reduce crude oil production. Within a few days after my request for aid to Israel, Abu Dhabi, Libya, Saudi Arabia, Algeria, and Kuwait had imposed total oil embargoes on the United States.

Even so, I felt that we could do no less for Israel at such a critical time.

Later that same afternoon, October 19, Haig brought me word of what he called a "tepid" complaint from Richardson about some of the terms of our plan for dealing with Cox. "It's no big problem," Haig said.

At 5:25 P.M., Sam Ervin and Howard Baker arrived at my office. They had been reached in New Orleans and Chicago respectively and brought to Washington aboard Air Force jets. When I told them about the Stennis compromise, they both seemed pleased and relieved.

Ervin was very respectful during the meeting. Toward the end I told him that I regretted that I had talked to him so bluntly on the telephone in July. He said that he had not realized at the time that I was ill and that no apologies were necessary. After Baker and Ervin had agreed to the Stennis compromise, Haig notified the members of the White House staff, the Cabinet, and Jerry Ford. Everyone was elated by the news.

It was reported to me later that Bryce Harlow, who was helping Haig make the calls to the Cabinet, mistakenly called Elliot Richardson. He quickly apologized, but Richardson gave a petulant reply: "I have never been treated so shabbily." Harlow reported this incident to Haig, who immediately called Richardson and said that he was astonished to hear what he had said to Harlow. Richardson apologized. He told Haig that he was very tired and had had a drink and that things were looking much better to him now.

I announced the Stennis compromise in a statement released at 8:15 that night. I began with a reference to the extremely delicate world situation at that very moment:

> What matters most, in this critical hour, is our ability to act—and to act in a way that enables us to control events, not to be paralyzed and overwhelmed by them. At home, the Watergate issue has taken on overtones of a partisan political contest. Concurrently, there are those in the international community who may be tempted by our Watergate-related difficulties at home to misread America's unity and resolve in meeting the challenges we confront abroad.

Then I described the Stennis compromise and stated that the verified summaries would be sent to Judge Sirica and to the Ervin Committee. Having done this, I announced the instruction to Cox to cease and desist from his Watergate fishing expedition:

> Though I have not wished to intrude upon the independence of the Special Prosecutor, I have felt it necessary to direct him, as an employee of the executive branch, to make no further attempts by judicial process to obtain tapes, notes, or memoranda of presidential conversations. I believe that with the

statement that will be provided to the court, any legitimate need of the Special Prosecutor is fully satisfied and that he can proceed to obtain indictments against those who may have committed any crimes. And I believe that by these actions I have taken today, America will be spared the anguish of further indecision and litigation about tapes.

The initial congressional and public reaction to the Stennis compromise was favorable. Congressional colleagues of both parties expressed confidence in Stennis. David Broder wrote a column describing him as the logical man for the job.

I had immediately agreed to Brezhnev's suggestion that Kissinger go to Moscow for direct talks about the Middle East. At midnight on October 19, just before Kissinger was to leave for Moscow, I phoned him to discuss his trip.

The next morning, Saturday, October 20, I sent a stern letter to Brezhnev. I purposely mitigated the hard language in the text with a handwritten note extending best personal regards from Pat and me to him and Mrs. Brezhnev. Brezhnev, I knew, would understand what this mixture conveyed: if he was willing to get behind a serious peace effort, I would not consider that the Soviet airlift had affected our personal relationship or deflected the course of détente.

Shortly after Kissinger arrived in Moscow, he sent me a letter from Brezhnev, echoing the sentiments of my letter and containing a similar handwritten postscript: "Mrs. Brezhnev is grateful for the regards and in turn joins me in sending our best personal regards to Mrs. Nixon and to you."

Early Saturday afternoon Cox called a press conference. Adopting the air of a modest and even befuddled professor, he said, "I am certainly not out to get the President of the United States. I am even worried, to put it in colloquial terms, that I am getting too big for my britches, that what I see as principle could be vanity. . . . It is sort of embarrassing to be put in the position to say, well, I don't want the President of the United States to tell me what to do." He said that he was going ahead with his request for the tapes despite the compromise I had offered. He said he questioned whether anyone but Elliot Richardson could give him instructions that he was legally obligated to obey.

I strongly felt that I could not allow Cox to defy openly a presidential directive. I thought of Brezhnev and how it would look to the Soviets if in the midst of our diplomatic showdown with them I were in the position of having to defer to the demands of one of my own employees. Furthermore, I thought that Cox had deliberately exceeded his authority; I felt that he was trying to get me personally, and I wanted him out.

Shortly after two o'clock Haig called Richardson and asked him to fire Cox. Richardson said that he would not, and that he wanted to see me in order to resign. There were rumors that Richardson in conversations with others was now trying to back off from his own role in the formulation of the Stennis compromise and the cease-and-desist directive to Cox.

When Richardson arrived at the White House, Haig appealed to him to withhold his resignation at least until the Mideast crisis had been resolved. The impact of his resignation during this crisis, while Kissinger was meeting with Brezhnev, might have incalculable effects, not just on the Soviets' assessment of our intentions and our strength, but on the morale within our own government. I later asked Len Garment, "If I can't get an order carried out by my Attorney General, how can I get arms to Israel?" But Richardson refused to wait even a few days.

Shortly after 4:30 he was ushered into the Oval Office to tender his resignation. It was an emotional meeting. I talked to him about the gravity of the decision he was making and the ramifications of the things it might precipitate. I told him how serious I thought the next days were going to be with respect to the situation in the Mideast, and I repeated Haig's arguments in a personal appeal to him to delay his resignation in order not to trigger a domestic crisis at such a critical time for us abroad. Again he refused. He thanked me for being such a good friend and for having honored him with so many high appointments.

Richardson's Deputy, William Ruckelshaus, was the next in line to succeed as Attorney General, but he let us know that he too would resign rather than fire Cox. I feared that we were in for a whole chain of such resignations, and I was not sure where it would end. I was, however, prepared to see it through.

The third-ranking official in the Justice Department was the Solicitor General, Robert Bork. The resignations of his two superiors placed Bork in a painfully difficult position. He was no "yes man." But however much he might personally have opposed my decision to fire Cox, he was a constitutional scholar and he felt that I had the constitutional right to do so and that he therefore had the duty to carry out my orders. He said that he would fire Archibald Cox.

At 8:22 P.M. on Saturday, October 20, Ziegler went to the White House briefing room and announced that Cox was being fired, that Richardson and Ruckelshaus had resigned, and that the office of the Watergate Special Prosecutor was being abolished and its functions transferred back to the Justice Department.

The television networks broke into their regular programming with breathless, almost hysterical, bulletins. Later that evening there were special reports on all networks. Commentators and correspondents talked in apocalyptic terms and painted the night's events in terms of an administration coup aimed at suppressing opposition. John Chancellor of NBC began a broadcast thus: "The country tonight is in the midst of what may be the most serious constitutional crisis in its history. . . . That is a stunning development and nothing even remotely like it has happened in all of our history. . . . In my career as a correspondent, I never thought I would be announcing these things." Some called it the "Night of the Long Knives" in a tasteless and inflammatory comparison with Hitler's murderous purge of his opposition in 1934. Within twenty-four hours the television and press had labeled the events with the prejudicial shorthand of "Saturday Night Massacre."

On Monday evening the network news shows ran nineteen different attacks on me by various congressmen; these were balanced by only five defenses, three of them by Bork.

"Has President Nixon gone crazy?" asked columnist Carl Rowan; Ralph Nader said I was "acting like a madman, a tyrant, or both"; "smacks of dictatorship" was Edmund Muskie's judgment. "A reckless act of desperation by a President . . . who has no respect for law and no regard for men of conscience," was Teddy Kennedy's comment. Senator Robert Byrd said that the Cox firing was a "Brownshirt operation" using "Gestapo tactics." "The wolves are in full cry," countered the New York *Daily News*. The *Star* stated, "The jackboots that some observers seem to hear . . . are largely in their own minds."

By Tuesday, October 23, there were twenty-one resolutions for my impeachment in varying stages of discussion on Capitol Hill. Six newspapers that had formerly been staunch supporters of the administration now called for my resignation. By October 30, in a straight party-line vote, the House Judiciary Committee had voted itself subpoena power; on November 15 the House voted to allocate $1 million to begin the process of impeachment.

Although I had been prepared for a major and adverse reaction to Cox's firing, I was taken by surprise by the ferocious intensity of the reaction that actually occurred. For the first time I recognized the depth of the impact Watergate had been having on America; I suddenly realized how deeply its acid had eaten into the nation's grain. As I learned of the almost hysterical reactions of otherwise sensible and responsible people to this Saturday night's events, I realized how few people were able to see things from my perspective, how badly frayed the nerves of the American public had become. To the extent that I had not been aware of this situation, my actions were the result of serious miscalculation. But to the extent that it was simply intolerable to continue with Cox as Special Prosecutor, I felt I had no other option than to act as I did.

In Moscow on Sunday, October 21, Kissinger and Brezhnev produced the draft of a proposed cease-fire agreement. Brezhnev was to inform Sadat and Asad of its terms, and Kissinger left for Tel Aviv to present it to the Israelis. While he was en route, I sent Mrs. Meir a letter expressing my regret that there had not been more time for consultation and describing the provisions of the proposed agreement:

1. A cease-fire in place.
2. A general call for the implementation of UN Resolution 242 after the cease-fire.
3. Negotiation between the concerned parties aimed at establishing a just and durable peace in the Mideast.

These terms were especially notable because they were the first in which the Soviets had agreed to a resolution that called for direct negotiations between the parties without any conditions or qualifications. It was also the first time that they had accepted a "general call" for adherence to Resolution 242 and not insisted on Israeli withdrawal from the occupied territories as a prerequisite for any further negotiations.

Both the Arabs and the Israelis accepted the terms—without much enthusiasm, to be sure—and on Monday, October 22, the cease-fire went into effect. Within hours, however, the Israelis charged that the Egyptians were violating it and resumed an active offensive and completed their encirclement of the 20,000-man Egyptian Third Army on the east bank of the Suez Canal.

Kissinger, now back in Washington, received a message from the Soviets blaming the Israelis for the breakdown of the cease-fire and informing him that Sadat had suggested that the United States and the Soviet Union agree on measures to ensure the physical disengagement of Egyptian and Israeli forces. Twenty minutes later, at 11 A.M. on October 23, I received an urgent message from Brezhnev over the Washington-Moscow hot line. Although it began, "Esteemed Mr. President," the words were hard and cold. Brezhnev ignored the Egyptian provocations and charged the Israelis with rupturing the cease-fire. He urged that the United States move decisively to stop the violations. He curtly implied that we might even have colluded in Israel's action.

I sent a reply that, according to our information, Egypt was the first party to violate the cease-fire. I added that this was not the time to debate the issue. I said that we had insisted that Israel take immediate steps to cease hostilities, and I urged Brezhnev to do the same on the Egyptian side. I closed by saying that he and I had achieved a historic settlement over the past weekend and should not permit it to be destroyed.

By the time I reached Camp David that afternoon, Brezhnev had sent a message that the Egyptian side was ready for another cease-fire if the Israelis would agree. We sent back a reply urging him to press Syria as well as Egypt to accept the cease-fire. I concluded, "I continue to believe that you and we have done a distinct service to the cause of peace."

That same day, Tuesday, October 23, Charles Alan Wright was scheduled to appear before Judge Sirica and announce my decision on the subpoenaed tapes. The Stennis compromise had fallen apart in the wake of the Cox firing, and shortly before Wright was to leave for the court I met with him, Haig, Garment, and Buzhardt to make the final decision.

I could see that we were going to have to act swiftly or risk an impeachment resolution being raced through the House. This threat argued for yielding the tapes. At the same time, I knew the implications of such compliance, both for the principle of executive privilege and for my personal situation. As a third option I could appeal the decision to the Supreme Court. But that would force an even more binding decision, possibly a negative one, and even greater damage would be done to the presidency and the doctrine of separation of powers.

There were other considerations as well: some congressmen were hinting that Ford's confirmation would be dependent on my surrendering the tapes. Finally, I felt that there was a need to relieve the domestic crisis in order to reduce the temptation the Soviets would feel to take advantage of our internal turmoil by exploiting the international crisis in the Middle East. Everyone at the meeting agreed that I should yield the tapes. It was a wrenching decision for me. I consoled myself that at least these tapes might finally prove that Dean had lied in his testimony against me. That afternoon Wright appeared before the bench and announced, "This President does not defy the law."

On October 24 the second Mideast cease-fire went into effect. But there were alarming new intelligence reports: we received information that seven Soviet airborne divisions, numbering 50,000 men, had been put on alert; and eighty-five Soviet ships, including landing craft and ships carrying troop helicopters, were now in the Mediterranean.

That afternoon Sadat publicly requested that Brezhnev and I send a joint peacekeeping force to the Middle East. The Soviets would obviously back this idea, viewing it as an opportunity to re-establish their military presence in Egypt. Through John Scali, now our ambassador to the UN, we also picked up rumors that the Soviets were plotting for the nonaligned nations to sponsor and support a joint U.S.–U.S.S.R. force whether we liked it or not.

I decided to use our newly opened lines of communication with Egypt to send Sadat a straightforward message:

> I have just learned that a resolution may be introduced into the Security Council this evening urging that outside military forces—including those of the U.S. and U.S.S.R.—be sent to the Middle East to enforce the cease-fire. I must tell you that if such a resolution is introduced into the Security Council, it will be vetoed by the United States for the following reasons:
>
> It would be impossible to assemble sufficient outside military power to represent an effective counterweight to the indigenous forces now engaged in combat in the Middle East.
>
> Should the two great nuclear powers be called upon to provide forces, it would introduce an extremely dangerous potential for direct great-power rivalry in the area.

At nine o'clock that night a new message arrived from Brezhnev. He claimed to have hard information that Israeli armed forces were fighting Egyptian forces on the east bank of the Suez Canal. We knew that this was not true; it had been a relatively quiet day on the battlefront. There was clearly some ulterior motive behind Brezhnev's message, and we would have to wait and see what it was.

An hour later another message from Brezhnev arrived. Kissinger called Dobrynin and read it to him just to be sure there was no mistake, because this message represented perhaps the most serious threat to U.S.–Soviet relations since the Cuban missile crisis eleven years before. Brezhnev repeated his assertion that Israel was fighting despite the Security Council cease-fire. Therefore he urged that the United States and the Soviet Union each immediately dispatch military contingents to the region. He called for an immediate reply and stated that if we did not agree to the joint action he proposed, the Soviets would consider acting unilaterally.

When Haig informed me about this message, I said that he and Kissinger should have a meeting at the White House to formulate plans for a firm reaction to what amounted to a scarcely veiled threat of unilateral Soviet intervention. Words were not making our point—we needed action, even the shock of a military alert.

Late that night I sent Sadat another message, outlining the Soviet proposal and explaining, as I had in my earlier message, why I found intervention unacceptable:

> I asked you to consider the consequences for your country if the two great nuclear countries were thus to confront each other on your soil. I ask you further to consider the impossibility for us for undertaking the diplomatic ini-

tiative which was to start with Dr. Kissinger's visit to Cairo on November 7 if the forces of one of the great nuclear powers were to be involved militarily on Egyptian soil.

We are at the beginning of a new period in the Middle East. Let us not destroy it at this moment.

In the meantime Kissinger, Haig, Schlesinger, Scowcroft, Moorer, and Director Colby of the CIA met at eleven o'clock in the White House Situation Room. Their unanimous recommendation was that we should put all American conventional and nuclear forces on military alert. In the early morning hours we flashed the word to American bases, installations, and naval units at home and around the world.

When we were sure the Soviets had picked up the first signs of the alert, I sent a letter to the Soviet Embassy for immediate transmission to Moscow. It was directly to Brezhnev from me, and beneath the diplomatic phraseology it minced no words:

Mr. General Secretary:

I have carefully studied your important message of this evening. I agree with you that our understanding to act jointly for peace is of the highest value and that we should implement that understanding in this complex situation.

I must tell you, however, that your proposal for a particular kind of joint action, that of sending Soviet and American military contingents to Egypt, is not appropriate in the present circumstances.

We have no information which would indicate that the cease-fire is now being violated on any significant scale. . . .

In these circumstances, we must view your suggestion of unilateral action as a matter of the gravest concern involving incalculable consequences.

It is clear that the forces necessary to impose the cease-fire terms on the two sides would be massive and would require closest coordination so as to avoid bloodshed. This is not only clearly infeasible but it is not appropriate to the situation.

I said that I would be prepared to agree that some American and Soviet personnel go to the area, but not as combat forces. Instead, they might be included in an augmented UN force. But even this kind of arrangement would have to follow carefully prescribed lines:

It would be understood that this is an extraordinary and temporary step, solely for the purpose of providing adequate information concerning compliance by both sides with the terms of the cease-fire. If this is what you mean by contingents, we will consider it.

Mr. General Secretary, in the spirit of our agreements this is the time for acting not unilaterally but in harmony and with cool heads. I believe my proposal is consonant with the letter and spirit of our understandings and would ensure a prompt implementation of the cease-fire. . . .

> You must know, however, that we could in no event accept unilateral action. . . . As I stated above, such action would produce incalculable consequences which would be in the interest of neither of our countries and which would end all we have striven so hard to achieve.

At 7:15 A.M. on October 25 a message arrived from President Sadat that he understood our position and that he would ask the UN to provide an international peacekeeping force.

I met with Haig and Kissinger at eight, and less than an hour later I briefed the bipartisan leadership on these latest events. The room was hushed as I described the exchanges of the last few hours. When the leaders left, they said that they were fully in support of my actions and my policy, including the military alert.

While we were still waiting for word from Brezhnev that would indicate the Soviet reaction, Kissinger held a press conference. It had been a severe shock to the American people to wake up and find that during the night our armed forces had been placed on worldwide alert, and four of the questions at Kissinger's press conference specifically related to whether the decision to call the alert had been based entirely on the military aspects of the situation. Some even obliquely wondered whether the decision had been totally rational. One reporter commented, "As you know, there has been some line of speculation this morning that the American alert might have been prompted as much perhaps by American domestic requirements as by the real requirements of diplomacy in the Middle East."

Kissinger was taken aback by the hostile and skeptical atmosphere in the room, and he replied icily: "It is a symptom of what is happening to our country that it could even be suggested that the United States would alert its forces for domestic reasons. We do not think it is wise at this moment to go into details of the diplomatic exchanges. . . . Upon the conclusion . . . we will make the record available. . . . And I am absolutely confident that it will be seen that the President had no other choice as a responsible national leader." Later in the press conference he acknowledged that we were undergoing a major domestic crisis, and he added: "It is up to you ladies and gentlemen to determine whether this is the moment to try to create a crisis of confidence in the field of foreign policy as well. . . . But there has to be a minimum of confidence that the senior officials of the American government are not playing with the lives of the American people."

As Kissinger was parrying these questions, a message arrived from Brezhnev. In a few short sentences he announced that the Soviet Union was going to send seventy individual "observers" to the Middle East. This was completely different from the military contingent he had described in his earlier letter. I responded to his message in a similarly low-keyed tone, but strongly expressed my opposition to sending even independent observers:

> I propose that at this time we leave the composition of the UN Observer Force to the discretion of the Secretary-General. . . . We do not believe it necessary to have separate observer forces from individual countries operating in the area.

I evaluated the Soviet behavior during the Mideast crisis not as an example of the failure of détente but as an illustration of its limitations—limitations of which I had always been keenly aware. I told the bipartisan leadership meeting on October 25, "I have never said that the Soviets are 'good guys.' What I have always said is that we should not enter into unnecessary confrontations with them."

The Soviet Union will always act in its own self-interest; and so will the United States. Détente cannot change that. All we can hope from détente is that it will minimize confrontation in marginal areas and provide, at least, alternative possibilities in the major ones.

In 1973 the Soviets, with their presence in the Middle East already reduced, feared that they would lose what little foothold they had left. As our direct approaches to Egypt and the Arab countries had met with increasing success, the Soviets had undoubtedly compensated with increased anti-Israeli bravado. Perhaps this indirectly encouraged the Arab countries, which were fanatically determined to regain the occupied territories from Israel if the Soviets would supply the means. Although Brezhnev heatedly denied it when I talked to him at Summit III in Moscow in June 1974, the Soviets may have gone even further and directly urged the Arabs to attack, lured by the tantalizing prospect that they might actually win a quick victory over the Israelis if they could combine surprise with their vastly superior numbers. The Soviets might also have assumed that the domestic crisis in the United States would deflect or deter us from aiding Israel as much or as fast as we had in the past.

Any such high hopes were dashed by the Israeli counteroffensive made possible by the American airlift. For the second time in six years the Arabs lost most of the Soviet equipment that had been sent them. Moreover, for the first time in an Arab-Israeli conflict the United States conducted itself in a manner that not only preserved but greatly enhanced our relations with the Arabs—even while we were massively resupplying the Israelis. Once they realized that military victory was now beyond their reach for at least the next several years, the Egyptian and Syrian leaders were ready to try the path of negotiation. Thanks to our new policy of carefully cultivated direct relations with the Arab capitals, the Arab leaders had a place other than Moscow to turn.

So obsessive had Watergate become for some reporters and publications that suggestions continued to be made that I had purposely provoked or encouraged the Mideast crisis to distract attention from Watergate and to demonstrate that I was still capable of leadership and action. With this in mind, and thinking about the reporting on the Cox firing, I faced this problem head on at a press conference on October 26. "I have never heard or seen such outrageous, vicious, distorted reporting in twenty-seven years of public life," I said. "And yet I should point out that even in this week, when many thought that the President was shell-shocked, unable to act, the President acted decisively in the interests of peace, in the interests of the country, and I can assure you that whatever shocks gentlemen of the press may have, or others, political people, these shocks will not affect me in my doing my job."

At the end of October there was another hot-line exchange. Brezhnev made a formal complaint about what he called Israeli hostilities; in particular he referred to their handling of food and medical supplies intended for the trapped Egyptian Third Army. He also stated that the recent U.S. alert had surprised him, and he complained that it had not promoted a relaxation of tension.

In my reply I said we would do our part to assist the transport of supplies to the wounded Egyptians in the Third Army. In response to his criticism of the alert I quoted the words he had written threatening to take unilateral action unless we joined his plan to send U.S. and Soviet forces to the Middle East. I stated, "Mr. General Secretary, these are serious words and were taken seriously here in Washington."

I followed up on November 3 with a letter to Brezhnev stating the importance of respecting the principle stated in our agreement on the prevention of nuclear war: that efforts at gaining unilateral advantage at the expense of the other party were inconsistent with the objectives of peaceful relations and the avoidance of confrontations. I repeated the fact that the peace of the world depended on the policies and actions of our two countries—in both a positive and a negative sense.

After almost three weeks Brezhnev replied to this letter. He indicated a willingness to pick up the dialogue of détente where it had left off before the Mideast crisis, and he closed with an unusually personal reference: "We would like, so to say, to wish you in a personal, human way energy and success in overcoming all sorts of complexities, the causes of which are not too easy to understand at a distance."

At the beginning of November Golda Meir came to Washington. We met for an hour in the Oval Office, and she expressed her gratitude for the airlift. "There were days and hours when we needed a friend, and you came right in," she said. "You don't know what your airlift means to us."

"I never believe in little plays when big issues are at stake," I said.

I urged a policy of sensible restraint for Israel. "Sometimes, when you have a situation of attrition, even winners can lose," I reminded her. "The problem that Israel must now consider is whether the policy you are following can succeed. Lacking a settlement, the only policy is constantly being prepared for war. But that really is no policy at all." I said that she could be remembered as the leader who created an Israel that was not burdened with a huge arms budget or with having to fight a war every five years.

Mrs. Meir seemed to understand the essential common sense of what I was saying. She also seemed to appreciate my lack of illusions about the limitations of détente or the nature of the Soviet threat. "When the Europeans talked about détente," she said, "they were bleary-eyed and naïve. But you know exactly what you are doing and who your partners are."

On November 5 Kissinger began the first of many journeys to the Middle East in which he personally guided first Israel and Egypt, and then Israel and Syria, along the unfamiliar and often painful road toward a peaceful settlement of their differences. On November 7, 1973, after six years of tense estrangement, the United States and Egypt resumed diplomatic relations.

After Cox had been fired, I had intended that Henry Petersen and his Justice Department staff would be allowed to complete the Watergate investigation, which they had begun and which was properly their responsibility. But it was evident that Congress was determined to have another Special Prosecutor. It was equally evident that I was in no political position to prevent it.

Robert Bork, as Acting Attorney General, began searching for a new Special Prosecutor. A few days later Haig reported to me that he and Bork had concluded that Leon Jaworski, a successful Houston lawyer, a former president of the American Bar Association, and a prominent Texas Democrat, was the right man for the job. Haig had already tentatively approached Jaworski, who had said he would accept if he could have our agreement that in the event we came to an impasse he could sue me in the courts for evidence. I agreed to this condition, and, as a further guarantee, we announced that there would have to be a supportive consensus of the Majority and Minority Leaders of the House and Senate and the ranking majority and minority members of the House and Senate Judiciary Committees before he could be fired.

Within ten days of the Cox firing and after the high political price I had had to pay for ridding myself of him, I was back in the same trap of having to accept a Watergate Special Prosecutor. But there was one major difference: I had been told that, unlike Cox, Jaworski would be fair and objective. Although as a Democrat he would be under pressure from other Democrats to score partisan points, I was led to believe that he respected the office of the presidency and that therefore he would not mount court challenges just for the plaudits and publicity he would thereby receive. Haig said that Jaworski recognized that the staff assembled by Cox was excessively anti-Nixon and that he was determined not to become their captive. He told Haig that he planned to bring in his own people and would see to it that the staff limited its activity to relevant and proper areas. Haig liked Jaworski and was impressed by him; he told me that Jaworski would be a tough prosecutor but not a partisan who was simply out to get me. On November 1, we announced that Leon Jaworski would be the Special Prosecutor.

I also needed a new Attorney General. The political situation created by Richardson's resignation dictated that in order to get my nominee confirmed, I would have to select someone who would not have to contend with charges of excessive personal loyalty to me. Senator William Saxbe of Ohio had long since established that he was a man without that problem. As my father would have put it, he was as "independent as a hog on ice." His appointment was announced the same day as Jaworski's.

SETBACK AND RALLY

In late September, when we were first preparing for the Stennis compromise, Steve Bull had had some difficulty locating several of the nine subpoenaed conversations. The Secret Service had catalogued the tapes, but their system was informal at best and haphazard at worst. In one case, Bull finally found an apparently missing conversation on a reel that had been erroneously labeled. In the case of a June 20, 1972, phone conversation with John Mitchell, I remembered that I had talked to him from a phone that was in the Family Quarters and therefore not connected to any recording equipment. In another case, that of an April 15, 1973, conversation with John Dean, the tape simply could not be found.

Near the end of October, about a month after Bull's initial search, Fred Buzhardt conducted one of his own. He confirmed that the phone call to Mitchell was from the Residence and had never been recorded. He also confirmed why Bull had not been able to find a tape of the April 15 meeting with Dean.

I usually did not go to the EOB office on Sundays. The Secret Service, who monitored the taping system, had not anticipated that I would have several unusually long conversations there on Saturday and Sunday, April 14 and 15. Thus by the time I sat down with Dick Kleindienst at 1:15 on Sunday afternoon, the reel of tape was near the end. It ran out in midsentence during our conversation, and the afternoon and evening meetings of April 15 with Haldeman, Ehrlichman, Petersen, Kleindienst, and Dean were never recorded.

On October 30 Buzhardt informed Sirica that two of the subpoenaed conversations had never been recorded. We readily agreed to have a panel of experts investigate our explanation for each case. We also offered my written notes of the April 15 meeting with John Dean and the tape of my meeting with him the next day, because a comparison of the April 15 notes and the April 16 tape indicated that we had covered much the same ground in the two sessions.

I was sure that a full explanation of how and why the phone call to Mitchell and the meeting with Dean had failed to be recorded would clear things up completely. I simply did not understand the degree of public anticipation that had developed around these nine subpoenaed tapes; now I can see that it was largely the result of the degree to which my personal credibility had sunk.

The news was met with an outburst of anger and indignation. The next day the media began reporting about two "missing tapes." This was both unfair and misleading: the use of the word *missing* implied that the two tapes had existed in the first place. People felt that I was toying with their patience and insulting their intelligence.

For the first time since the Watergate affair began, the New York *Times* urged editorially that I resign the presidency. *Time,* in its first editorial in fifty years, also said that I should step down. Even old friends, among them the Detroit *News* and ABC's Howard K. Smith, began to express doubts. It was in the wake of the two so-called missing tapes that Senator Edward Brooke of Massachusetts became the first Republican in Congress to urge that I resign.

When Barry Goldwater saw the frenzied turn events were taking, he went on the air to ask people to "curb their wild stampede, to pause a moment in their tumult and trumpeting" and give thought to the consequences of the hysteria if it continued uncurbed. "In God's name, cool it," he said.

On November 1 I wrote a frustrated note on the top of a briefing paper:

> There were no missing tapes.
> There never were any.
> The conversations in question were not taped.
> Why couldn't we get that across to people?

That same day I left for a weekend in Florida. I looked forward to the chance to get some rest and to try to assess the damage. I had no idea that our problems with the tapes were just beginning.

In April 1973, in a phone conversation with Henry Petersen, I had unthinkingly said that I believed that my April 15 conversation with John Dean had been recorded on tape. Petersen reported my remark to Cox, who later wrote to us requesting this tape for his investigation. In order to avoid revealing the existence of the taping system, I told Buzhardt to write to Cox and tell him that the "tape" I had had in mind was actually the Dictabelt I had made after the meeting. Now it turned out that the April 15 conversation had never been recorded because the tape had run out. But there was worse news still to come. We were about to learn that no Dictabelt could be found either.

I had not actually checked when I told Buzhardt to tell Cox there was a Dictabelt. I had simply assumed that I had made one, since I had been doing so almost daily in that period; my notes of the meeting were clearly marked for dictation. But we could not find a Dictabelt for that conversation.

I had put Buzhardt in an untenable position: first I had had him send a letter to Cox in order to divert him from a tape recording to a Dictabelt; now there was no Dictabelt. Len Garment felt that the public revelation of this latest blunder would throw us into a fatal spin. Beyond that, both he and Buzhardt felt that they were not making any progress or doing any good. We were always in a completely reactive situation, and there seemed to be no prospect for changing that pattern no matter what we did.

On Saturday, November 3, Garment and Buzhardt had come to Florida. Haig brought me a diluted report of his meeting with them, but I sensed what he was saying between the lines: even before we finally confirmed that there was no Dictabelt, they felt they had had it. I could not blame them. They had been hopelessly undermanned, chronically overworked, and regularly undermined by events and now by me. They had both urged, and Haig concurred, that we look for another lawyer, perhaps someone from outside the White House, who would deal with nothing but Watergate.

That weekend in Florida was a new low point for me personally and a turning point for our approach to dealing with Watergate. Even as I realized the depth to which we had plunged, I recognized that there was only one way out. We were under relentless attack by the opposition, and now we were faced with defections by our supporters as well. More than anything else, we had to stop that erosion. "We will take some desperate, strong measure," I told Ziegler, "and this time there is no margin for error."

First, I had to address the increasing number of demands for my resignation. On November 7, at the end of a televised speech on the energy crisis, I turned over the last typed page of the text to the handwritten notes I had made only a few hours earlier. I said:

> Tonight I would like to give my answer to those who have suggested that I resign.
>
> I have no intention whatever of walking away from the job I was elected to do. As long as I am physically able, I am going to continue to work sixteen to eighteen hours a day for the cause of a real peace abroad, and for the cause of prosperity without inflation and without war at home. And in the months ahead I shall do everything that I can to see that any doubts as to the integrity of the man who occupies the highest office in this land—to remove those doubts where they exist.
>
> And I am confident that in those months ahead, the American people will come to realize that I have not violated the trust that they placed in me when they elected me as President of the United States in the past, and I pledge to you tonight that I shall always do everything that I can to be worthy of that trust in the future.

I decided to begin meeting with different congressional groups until I had personally talked to every Republican in Congress and to all my supporters on the Democratic side. This would not be just a way of presenting my side of the Watergate case and answering whatever questions they had about it; it would also provide an opportunity for beginning to rebuild the badly damaged bridges of communication and shared purposes that had been among the casualties of Watergate. All told, in nine separate two-hour sessions over the next week, I met with 241 Republican and 46 Democratic senators and congressmen. In each meeting I ran over the charges and answered questions, repeating the defense spelled out in my public statements. I explained to Ed Brooke that I would not consider resigning because it would change the American system of government. I remember sitting with Eastland, McClellan, Stennis, and Long, the deans of the Senate, and starting to review the Watergate charges with them. Jim Eastland leaned forward and said, "Mr. President, we don't need to hear any explanations. We don't even want to talk about Watergate. Just tell us what to do to help." Seventy-year-old John Stennis leaned over to Eastland and said, "Quiet, Jim. Let the boy speak."

I told these congressional groups that we would issue white papers on the major charges. I also said that we were contemplating releasing transcripts or summaries of the tapes that had been turned over to the court—something that they had all urged.

Some of the congressmen suggested that I try to put Watergate to rest by making one grandstand play or one dramatic gesture that would answer all the questions and exorcise all the demons. Some suggested that

I voluntarily appear before a joint session of Congress and stay until I had answered every question that every member wanted to ask. The suggestion was well intentioned, but I had no confidence whatever that any single gesture would be successful at this late date. Watergate had gone too far for me to be able to dispel it in one speech. As I told one Republican group that urged this as a solution, if I gave a speech and said, "I didn't do it," the Democrats would say, "The son of a bitch is lying"; and the Republicans would say, "Ho hum, he is probably lying but he is our son of a bitch."

I also said that if the charges against me continued in the same partisan way, "I will go down—and I will go down gracefully—but I will not resign." And I tried to tell them I understood what a burden Watergate had been on them: "You have all worked hard, your careers are involved, you are worried about the polls and about whether the money is going to come in for your campaigns. You are wondering why in hell the President can't clear it up and so forth. I'm worried about it too, because these last few months have not been easy."

And I urged some sense of perspective. "I know people say I shouldn't talk about meetings with Brezhnev and Mao, that people aren't interested in that," I said. "But I know that in the history books twenty-five years from now what will really matter is the fact that the President of the United States in the period from 1969 to 1976 changed the world."

In one meeting Jacob Javits leaned over to me reassuringly and said, "Lincoln was called a lot worse things than you, remember that." "I'm catching up," was all I could reply.

The media, ever in search of a simple label for complex events, latched on to one coined by *Newsweek*. An article in the magazine had referred to my stepped-up activities and my televised remarks against impeachment as "Operation Candor." The intent of the label, of course, was to trivialize my effort and to imply that candor was something I thought could be turned on and off like a faucet. A sloppy press corps soon forgot that this label had been its own invention and started using it regularly without putting it in quotation marks or explaining its origin. On December 2 an editorial in the New York *Times* stated authoritatively that: "President Nixon's counteroffensive on Watergate, billed by the White House as 'Operation Candor,' is visibly collapsing."

THE 18½-MINUTE GAP

It was during one of the congressional briefing sessions on November 15 that someone asked, "Is there another shoe to drop?"

As far as I'm concerned," I replied, "as to the guilt of the President, no." But I added, "If the shoes fall, I will be there ready to catch them."

Late that afternoon Haig came into the Oval Office looking strained and worried. He said that the lawyers had been preparing an index of the tapes that were to be turned over to Sirica. After checking the original subpoena against a supplementary document that had been sent by Cox during the summer, they had now decided that Buzhardt's earlier interpretation, based on the subpoena alone, was wrong. The supplementary document made it clear that the subpoena *did* cover the June 20, 1972, conversation with Haldeman—the tape with the gap.

It was a nightmare. How in hell, I asked, could we have made a mistake about something as fundamental as whether or not a particular conversation was covered by a subpoena? I asked if we could still argue that it wasn't covered by the subpoena. Haig said that he would get Haldeman's notes from June 20, 1972, and try to reconstruct what had been said during the missing segment of our conversation. When the notes finally arrived, they turned out to be a mixed blessing. While they made it clear that we had been talking about Watergate, they indicated that the conversation had been in general terms about the political impact of the incident:

> be sure EOB office is *thoroly* ckd re bugs at all times—etc.
> what is our counter-attack
> PR offensive to top this—
> hit the opposition w/ their activities
> pt. out libertarians have created public callousness
> do they justify this less than stealing Pentagon papers, Anderson file etc.?
> we shld be on the attack—for diversion—

There was still more bad news about the gap that day: I learned that it did not run for just the four or five minutes that Rose had estimated as the length of time she had spent on the telephone. Buzhardt informed me that, after playing the tape through, they found that the gap ran 18½ minutes. No one could explain how or why it had happened or account for the shrill buzzing sounds that punctuated the otherwise blank portion.

When we left for a few days in Florida on November 17, Buzhardt stayed in Washington to see if the 18½ minutes of conversation could be electronically recovered. He was also going to see if he could re-create the circumstances that had caused the gap and the peculiar sounds that now appeared on the tape.

On the way back to Washington on Tuesday, November 20, I stopped off in Memphis, Tennessee, to attend a meeting of the Republican Governors Conference. In a private and freewheeling session we covered every major foreign and domestic issue, including Watergate. At one point in the meeting I was asked if there were going to be any more Watergate bombshells. I immediately thought of the tape with the 18½-minute gap—that was certainly in the bombshell category. But we still had not heard from Buzhardt whether the conversation could be recovered, or, failing that, whether we could find some logical explanation of how it had happened. I knew that if I indicated even the remotest possibility of a new bombshell, I would have to say what it was—and I still was not sure of the answer to that myself.

For all these reasons I answered, "If there are, I'm not aware of them."

On the plane on the way back to Washington Haig told me that Buzhardt confirmed that the missing portion of the June 20 conversation was not recoverable. Furthermore, Buzhardt had had no success in his efforts to reproduce the buzzing sound.

The headline in papers all across the country the next morning was my assertion that there would be no more Watergate bombshells. That same morning Buzhardt told Jaworski and Sirica about the 18½-minute gap, and Sirica announced it to the press.

I know that most people think that my inability to explain the 18½-minute gap is the most unbelievable and insulting part of the whole of Watergate. Because of this, I am aware that my treatment of the gap will be looked upon as a touchstone for the candor and credibility of whatever else I write about Watergate. I also know that the only explanations that would readily be accepted are that I erased the tape myself, or that Rose Mary Woods deliberately did so, either on her own initiative or at my direct or indirect request.

But I know I did not do it. And I completely believe Rose when she says that she did not do it. I can only tell the story of the 18½-minute gap—as incomplete and unsatisfactory a story as I know it is—from the vantage point of having watched it bring my reputation and my presidency to new lows of public confidence and esteem.

Haig told me that Garment and Buzhardt were completely panicked by the discovery of the 18½-minute gap. They suspected everyone, including Rose, Steve Bull, and me. Suspicion had now invaded the White House. I even wondered if Buzhardt himself could have accidentally erased the portion beyond the five-minute gap Rose thought she might have caused. Using the simple criterion of access to the tapes, there were many possible suspects. Haig and others joked darkly about "sinister forces" being responsible for the gap, but I think that we all wondered about the various Secret Service agents and technicians who had had free daily access to the tapes, and even about the Secret Service agents who had provided Rose with the new but apparently faulty Uher tape recorder just half an hour before she discovered the gap. We even wondered about Alex Butterfield, who had revealed the existence of the tape system. He had had access to all the tapes; in fact, he had regularly listened to random passages to make sure that the system was working properly. But it would have taken a very dedicated believer in conspiracies to accept that someone would have purposely erased 18½ minutes of this particular tape in order to embarrass me.

After an inconclusive public hearing the matter of the gap was turned over to the grand jury and a panel of court-appointed experts. I believe that the story of these experts represents one of the biggest, and least known, scandals connected with Watergate. The White House is not without blame, because we approved the six "experts" appointed by the court. If we had checked, we would have found that they were experts in the theory of acoustics but not the practicalities of tape recorders.

In a January report the experts concluded that the buzzing sounds had been put on the tape "in the process of erasing and rerecording at least five, and perhaps as many as nine, separate and contiguous segments. Hand operation of the keyboard controls on the recorder was involved in starting and again in stopping the recording of each segment." This conclusion was widely reported; not so widely reported was the fact that it came under immediate attack from other scientists and tape specialists, one of whom called it more a "news release than a solid investigation."

One electronics firm pointed out that the apparently incriminating sounds and magnetic marks attributed by the panel to specific manual erasures could have been made accidentally by a malfunction in the machine that caused the internal power supply to sputter on and off. *Science* magazine reported that other experts agreed with the feasibility of this alternate hypothesis. The only test that the court's experts made of this hypothesis prior to the release of their preliminary report in January was made on a *Sony,* not a Uher 5000. They apparently failed to see this as a lapse in standard scientific testing procedure.

One of the court's experts testified that in testing the machine Rose had used, they "of necessity had to open up the interior . . . and tighten down several screws and quite conceivably, for example, may have tightened a ground connection to a point where it was making more firm contact than previously." When they found a defective part they replaced it —and threw the defective one away! He acknowledged that after they had worked on the machine it no longer produced the buzzing sound they had noticed beforehand.

After this extraordinary admission, Rose's attorney, Charles Rhyne, said, "So in effect you obliterated the evidence which anyone else would need to test your conclusions, did you not?"

"Yes, in large part," was the answer.

Richard Salmon, national manager of Uher of America, Inc., in Inglewood, California, the manufacturer of the machine Rose had used, scathingly criticized the court experts' report. He said that on some of their specially modified machines pressing the "rewind" button in a certain way would cause the machine to erase automatically. Salmon said that by using a display "of great experience and electrical intelligence" —in other words, technical jargon—"they covered up a weak report."

The court paid these six experts $100,000 for their work. It was worthless as a legal document, but it produced more than its money's worth of incriminating headlines.

Rose Woods testified under oath concerning the 18½-minute gap before a court hearing and the grand jury. In the hearing she was subjected to hours of merciless cross-examination on this issue. On July 17, 1974, Leon Jaworski informed Rose's attorney that no case had been developed of any illegal action of any kind by Rose and that no charges would be made against her. He said that his assistant, Richard Ben-Veniste, agreed. Jaworski, however, did not make a public announcement of this fact, and to this day many people are not aware that Rose was exonerated by the Special Prosecutor in regard to the 18½-minute gap.

In late 1973, after the 18½-minute gap had been revealed and it seemed as if nothing worse could happen to us, something worse did.

PROPERTY AND TAXES

From the start of my political career, I had tried to be scrupulously careful in the handling of public money. I grew up in a home where politics was frequently discussed, and where the greatest contempt was reserved for politicians on the take. If anything, I have always gone far beyond most people in government to document and account for public money, whether campaign or government funds. This was why the accusations of financial impropriety made during the fund crisis of 1952 had been particularly searing and embittering.

After the 1968 election I decided to sell all of my stocks and outside holdings. This divestiture was not required by law, but I thought it would be worth going the extra measure to avoid even the appearance of a conflict of interest. I took most of the money from the sale of the stocks and the sale of our New York apartment and put it into the purchase of two houses in Florida and a house in California.

The San Clemente property was a 26-acre tract of land. Personally I could afford to buy only the house itself and the surrounding grounds, about 5.9 acres. In order to keep the adjacent property under my control, I bought the entire tract with the help of a loan from my friend Bob Abplanalp. In December 1970 I sold the 20.1 acres, plus an additional 2.9 acres I had acquired from a neighboring tract, to Rebozo and Abplanalp and retained only the house and the 5.9 acres I had wanted in the first place. In 1973 Rebozo sold his portion to Abplanalp.

In what now seems a bitter irony we decided to keep these transactions private, not because there was anything improper about them, but because I knew how the Washington press corps would play up my acquisition of such a large and expensive property, and the fact that I was doing it with loans from my friends. Once Watergate snowballed and reporters began to tear the skin off every aspect of my life, this innocent secrecy led to suspicions that I could not dispel.

On May 13 Ervin Committee "sources" leaked a story to a California newspaper alleging that up to "$1 million in campaign funds" might have been used to buy my California property. Even when Ervin claimed that he had never heard of such a thing, the newspaper would not retract its story, which was quickly picked up by the national wire services. Early in July a leak caused by the Cox office produced a story indicating that they too were investigating whether union, corporate, or campaign money had been used to buy any of my houses. The stories mushroomed. Other newspapers spread leaked reports that my San Clemente property was underassessed for tax purposes, and papers all across the country carried the story. Subsequently the Orange County Assessment Appeals Board determined that the charge was not true, but it had already left its impression. I sensed that unless we stopped this kind of story immediately, my personal integrity would come under as much of a cloud as my political integrity was now under.

I had nothing to hide concerning my finances and believed that the only defense against these kinds of charges was to put out everything. Therefore we ordered the General Services Administration to begin assembling every document that related to government expenditures at my homes. On May 25 we released a statement recounting the details of the purchase of my property in San Clemente and Key Biscayne. I also paid over $25,000 to have an audit of these transactions prepared, and I released the report to the press on August 27.

Despite these efforts the stories continued to be fabricated and to be printed. For example, the Washington *Star* falsely alleged that C. Arnholt Smith, a wealthy Californian then facing indictment for tax evasion, possibly helped in the purchase of my property. UPI reported that the "Senate Watergate Committee is investigating the possibility that $100,000 given by billionaire Howard Hughes was used to help pay for President Nixon's San Clemente home, a committee source said." ABC reported the equally outrageous charge that I had "a secret private investment portfolio" of $1 million in corporate campaign funds. Jack Anderson later charged I had Swiss bank accounts filled with cash. *Newsweek* even charged that I manipulated family property in such a way that my daughter Tricia may have filed false income tax returns. All these stories and charges were totally false. For at least the third time that I was aware of in my political career, someone in the IRS bureaucracy violated the law and leaked my tax returns to the press. The reporter who wrote the story based on this illegal act won the 1974 Pulitzer Prize for journalism.

At the end of November I announced that I was planning to release my tax returns in their entirety. The IRS, which had twice earlier reviewed and approved my 1971 and 1972 tax returns, informed us that because of all the publicity they were going to reopen their examination. In the meantime, Texas Democratic Congressman Jack Brooks, one of the most partisan men in Congress, used his subcommittee of the House Committee on Government Operations to hold hearings on government expenditures on my houses.

Every modern President has maintained property outside Washington for a change of pace and for the kind of privacy that is impossible in the capital. Johnson regularly visited three locations; Kennedy visited five. I had two of my own—in San Clemente and Key Biscayne—and I also sometimes used Bob Abplanalp's island in the Bahamas. For me as for other Presidents, the government made expenditures on the places I regularly visited in order to ensure my safety when I was working or relaxing there. When I took office, four of my thirty-five predecessors as President had been assassinated and serious attempts had been made on the lives of several others. On the day Robert Kennedy died, Congress passed a new law that established extraordinary security measures to protect all future presidential and vice presidential candidates and incumbents. The legislation called for the full cooperation of government agencies in meeting requests by the Secret Service for protective devices. I was the first President in office after the legislation was passed to receive all the increased protection it provided. At the request of the Secret Service, the General Services Administration, which handles government buildings and supplies, installed intricate warning devices and electronic alarms on the grounds all around my houses; bulletproof glass was put into the windows; special outside lighting was installed. Secret Service command posts and outposts were constructed; landscaping was arranged and rearranged according to Secret Service requirements.

In the end GSA spent $68,000 on my house at San Clemente. The bulk of this amount went for electrical security systems, fire protection, and the replacement of a gas heater with an electric heating system after the Secret Service decided that the less expensive gas system I would have installed was not sufficiently safe. I spent $217,000 of my own money on furnishings and improvements to the San Clemente house.

GSA spent $137,000—all but $7,000 of it on bulletproof glass—on the two adjacent houses I owned in Key Biscayne. We used one as a family residence and the other as an office and work area. At the same time I personally spent $76,000 for remodeling the houses and for improvements on the grounds.

In addition to the money spent on the houses themselves, GSA spent $950,000 on the grounds. This amount covered the installation of security lighting and alarm systems, walls, guard stations, and relandscaping to restore the areas torn up when the protective equipment was installed.

I was no more eager than anyone else would be to pay for anything that could be legitimately construed as a proper government expense, but a General Accounting Office study concluded that with scattered exceptions, almost all of the $1.1 million spent on my personal properties in California and Florida was spent for protective purposes. In fact, all but $13,400 was specifically requested by the Secret Service. Other items, such as flagpoles and office furniture for my study, were procured under the auspices of the GSA. Flagpoles had routinely been placed at the homes of Presidents and Vice Presidents before me; and the office furniture would all revert to GSA after I left office.

Whenever a President travels there are scores of security and support personnel who have to travel with him to make sure that he is safe and to make sure that his communications facilities are as extensive and secure as they are at the White House or at Camp David. I felt that we also had to take these expenditures into account lest we be accused of trying to hide them. Therefore at my instructions GSA audited every penny the government had spent in San Clemente, Key Biscayne, and Grand Bahama, and on security for my daughters at their homes. More than 20,000 man-hours were devoted to combing 10,000 accounting records and 1,600 files. In the end it cost the government $313,582—50 percent more government money than had been spent on the houses—to answer the congressional and press inquiries. On August 6 we released the totals arrived at by GSA: $1.1 million had been spent on the houses and grounds; $2.5 million had been spent on the office complexes and security measures on government property near the houses; the Defense Department spent $6.1 million for routine presidential communications equipment and support, 60 percent of which would be completely recovered when the equipment was taken away after my presidential term ended; $211,000 more had been spent directly by the Secret Service on equipment connected with their security needs, 90 percent of which would be recovered after I left office.

The next morning, the Washington *Post* and the New York *Times* ran almost identical headlines: *$10 Million Spent on Nixon Homes* wrote the *Post*; *$10 Million Spent at Nixon Houses* wrote the New York *Times*. Other newspapers and the television news shows adopted the same line. Not surprisingly, many people felt that this money had been spent on the homes themselves.

Over the next months we tried to correct those stories by pointing out that almost all the money had been spent on security measures. Only 2 percent of that amount had been spent at the houses themselves; almost 90 percent, or $8.9 million, had been spent on administrative and protective support totally divorced from my personal property. But it was a hopeless public relations battle.

Representative Brooks was determined that his house subcommittee hearings would make the most of the story and his plans were only temporarily foiled when two of the subcommittee members, one of them an anti-Nixon Democrat, toured the San Clemente house and pronounced the government expenditures justifiable. The *Wall Street Journal* editorialized, "In short, despite all those headlines, the spending at San Clemente seems to have been a non-story. . . . It might be wise, too, to think about how the press might undo non-stories when they arise."

Before my administration most of the requests for government expenditures at a President's private property had been made orally and informally. The Defense Department had handled the majority of such requests and expenditures for Lyndon Johnson. I was told that Brooks, who had been one of Johnson's most intimate political allies, carefully confirmed the inaccessibility of the full Johnson record before proceeding against me. Even from what little could be reconstructed, however, it was apparent that at least $5 million had been spent on various Texas sites for Johnson, including the LBJ Ranch; the Haywood Ranch and boathouse in Llano County; his suite at Brooke Army Medical Center, San Antonio; and his office at KTBC, the television station Mrs. Johnson owned in Austin. Over $99,000 was spent remodeling and redecorating Johnson's office in Austin; a million dollars was spent carrying out his request for a major redesign of the federal office building there and for construction of a helipad on the roof of the building so that he could fly directly there from the LBJ Ranch. A small house Johnson owned near his ranch was remodeled by GSA according to his detailed instructions, and he then leased it to the Secret Service. Spiro Agnew, incidentally, had provided the Secret Service with two rooms in his house in Maryland without any charge.

Probably the most astonishing testimony to come before Brooks's subcommittee related to expenditures for President Kennedy at Hyannisport; Middleburg, Virginia; Palm Beach; Squaw Island, Massachusetts; and Atoka, Virginia. The records of these expenditures had been kept by a naval aide to Kennedy, and the subcommittee was told that the aide had accidentally dropped them overboard while his ship was either in the Philippines or somewhere near Europe.

In preparing his tally of government expenditures on my houses and properties, Brooks added up every penny paid to every person working, however remotely, in any connection with the presidential office during every trip. Thus he included the salaries of people like cleaners and custodial staff who would have been on the government payroll regardless of my trips. In this way he came up with a total of $17 million. He put it in a report labeled "Confidential," which was promptly leaked. The headline in the New York *Times* was: *U.S. Aid to Nixon Estates Put at $17 Million.* Brooks's subcommittee began its work in the fall of 1973; the final report, however, was not issued until May 1974—just in time for the opening gavel of the House Judiciary Committee's hearings on impeachment. One of the worst distortions to come out of Brooks's investigation was the idea that Bob Abplanalp had benefited from government expenditures at his Grand Bahama home. In fact, when the Secret Service requested the installation of intrusion alarms, fire detection systems, and special generators, Abplanalp paid for them out of his own pocket. He also built a bunkhouse for the Secret Service agents and allowed the government free use of other buildings on the property. All these would have been completely legitimate government expenditures, but Abplanalp paid for them himself, thereby personally saving the government more than $1 million.

I still held the naïve belief that all suspicion and press speculation about my taxes could be dispelled by the facts. Therefore we began to prepare my tax returns for release to the public. I thought that in this way we would firmly and conclusively put to rest the malicious accusations about how I had bought my homes and whether I had paid the taxes I owed.

In a press conference on November 18 I described my finances over the years. I reminded the reporters of the fact that after fourteen years as congressman, senator, and Vice President, I had a net worth of $47,000 and a 1958 Oldsmobile that needed an overhaul. Such money as I had been able to accumulate was the result of earnings when I was in private life, mainly when I was with the law firm in New York. I concluded:

> I made my mistakes, but in all of my years of public life, I have never profited, never profited from public service—I have earned every cent. And in all of my years of public life, I have never obstructed justice. And I think, too, that I could say that in my years of public life, that I welcome this kind of examination, because people have got to know whether or not their President is a crook. Well, I am not a crook. I have earned everything I have got.

This was not a spur-of-the-moment statement. The attacks on my personal integrity were more disturbing for me and my family than all the other attacks put together. I thought it was essential to put my defense in down-to-earth, understandable language. But it was a mistake. From then on, variations of the line "I am not a crook" were used as an almost constant source of criticism and ridicule.

The first articles on my December 8 release described the extent of the disclosure I had undertaken: "With the release of his income taxes and assorted deeds, mortgages, canceled checks and legal agreements, President Nixon has probably made the fullest disclosure of personal finances in the history of the country." But within only a matter of hours other news reports complained that "most of the issues" were still unresolved. Before long I concluded that the release of the income tax returns had been a mistake. It was the same old story: those who had been demanding that I put out my returns did not really want conclusive proof that the stories about the allegedly illegal purchases of my houses and the supposedly vast secret investment portfolios were false. They seized on the fact that I had large deductions as if it were immoral not to pay more taxes to the government than the law required be paid. They were only looking for ways to keep the stories alive and for any new vulnerability that might turn up.

There were two particular issues raised about my tax returns that were highly complex and on which tax lawyers disagreed. One involved a question about whether I had made a taxable capital gain when I sold some of the San Clemente property to Rebozo and Abplanalp. The accountant who had prepared my taxes insisted that I had not. He found support from some tax professionals and arguments from others. The other controversial question concerned the deduction I had taken for the donation to the National Archives of my prepresidential papers. The idea had come from Lyndon Johnson in 1968 when he told me about the statute providing for the deduction, which, he said, he had been taking for years. He urged that I take advantage of it and recommended that I employ the same expert appraiser he had used to assess the value of his papers. It turned out that a number of public figures had been taking advantage of such deductions long before I found out about them; they included Governor Pat Brown, John Kenneth Galbraith, George Wallace, Hubert Humphrey, Theodore Sorensen, and Arthur Schlesinger, Jr.

Ralph Newman, the appraiser recommended by Johnson, found that in my prepresidential files there were more than a million papers, worth approximately $2 million. In December 1968 I gave a specific portion of these papers to the government and took the allowable tax deduction. Early in 1969 I instructed John Ehrlichman to do what was necessary to make another and larger gift of papers that would spread out the maximum legitimate deductions over the next several years. The papers were delivered to the National Archives on March 27, 1969. A donation of 600,000 documents was appraised at $576,000.

In December 1969 Congress added an amendment to my tax reform act that repealed the provision allowing for any deductions for donations of papers. This amendment was made retroactive to July 25, 1969.

I was confident that the members of my staff and my lawyers, to whom I had delegated the responsibility for preparing my tax returns and executing the documents for the donation of my papers, had taken this change of the law into account and had had everything in order. I was shocked and totally frustrated when, in 1973, I found that this was not the case. A question was raised first by the press and then by the IRS itself about whether the paperwork for my papers donation had actually met the retroactive July deadline.

In the first week of December Bryce Harlow urged that I let the Joint Congressional Committee on Internal Revenue Taxation review the controversial papers gift deduction and the question about the capital gain. He had worked with this committee in the past and found them thorough and objective. Kenneth Gemmill, a prominent tax attorney who helped advise us, shared his views.

On December 8, therefore, I wrote a letter to Wilbur Mills, the chairman of the joint committee, and asked that these two questions be examined. I said that in the event the committee determined that the items had been incorrectly reported, I would pay whatever tax might be due.

On December 13 Mills replied that the joint committee had agreed to consider the case. But he added a new twist. "The committee believes," he wrote, "that the examination should be of all tax items for 1969 through 1972 for the examination to be meaningful." That same day the New York *Times* quoted Mills as saying that he was critical of the deductions I had taken, even if they were legal. "A public official who files a tax return has to be holier-than-thou," Wilbur Mills had said.

I began to fear that I had walked into another trap. My fears were soon borne out. In ordinary times the joint committee may have been, as Harlow had said, objective. But these were not ordinary times. Some of the committee members turned out to be weak and irresponsible; their large staff turned out to be even worse. Philadelphia *Bulletin* columnist Adrian Lee examined the political affiliations of the twenty-five members of the committee's staff and could not find one Republican.

On March 8, 1974, before the committee had reached any findings, Chairman Mills said publicly that he thought I would quit office after their report on my taxes came out. On March 18 he predicted that I would be out of office by November because of "dismay" over my taxes.

Harlow's reports from the joint committee grew increasingly bleak. The staff had broken a promise by sending its draft report directly to the committee without even giving my lawyers a chance to review its findings or to file their own briefs in support of my case.

In the meantime things on our side were falling disastrously apart. I learned that, without my knowledge, the deed for the gift of the papers had in fact been backdated by one of the lawyers handling it for me. My tax attorneys argued that the deed was not crucial to the gift, and that the important thing was that I had expressed my intent to make the donation and had delivered the papers to the archives three months before the July 25 deadline. Previous court cases supported that view, but the unnerving disclosure of the backdated deed considerably undermined my position with my few supporters on the committee.

The members of the joint committee actually met only twice to consider the question of my taxes: once to accept the assignment in December 1973 and once to receive the thousand-page staff report in April 1974. A majority of the members were not even sufficiently concerned to go over the report or to hear my side of any of the major controversial issues. Senator Carl Curtis of Nebraska decried the staff's work. "No other taxpayer in our country has been treated with the harshness that was given the President of the United States in that report," he said.

In addition to finding against me on the papers donation and the capital gains question, the committee staff report found that I should reimburse the government for the air fare when Pat and the family flew on *Air Force One* with me if they were not performing official functions. No other President had ever been charged for his family in this way; in fact, I was the first President to have reimbursed the government for unofficial flights by members of my family when I was not on board the plane.

The committee staff also disallowed the kind of deduction I had taken for the use of my Florida house as an office, on the ground that I did not have to use my house for this purpose because the government could have built me an office there!

The Republicans on the joint committee expressed shock that the staff had arrogated such power to itself and had then wielded it so arrogantly. Harlow was promised that my supporters would insist that the whole matter be turned over to the IRS, but in the end all of them, with the exception of Carl Curtis, bowed to pressure and did nothing. The political heat was too great.

By this time I had also received a new ruling from the IRS. Although my tax return had been approved in two earlier audits, the IRS now reversed itself and said that I should pay back the deduction I had taken for the gift of the papers, and also pay tax on the San Clemente transaction as a capital gain.

There was an ironic twist involving the gift of the papers. As far as the joint committee and the IRS were concerned, I had not made a legally proper gift. But as far as GSA was concerned I had, and they therefore refused to return my papers to me. In other words, I lost both the deduction and the papers.

My lawyers urged that I go to tax court and fight the ruling. They said that the joint committee and the IRS had clearly bowed to political pressures and that I would win the case in court. But I had already lost the case as far as public opinion was concerned, and at that point that was what mattered to me most. Besides, I had agreed to abide by the joint committee's ruling, and I could hardly go back on that now.

On April 3 I issued a brief statement that I had heard of the joint committee's decision to release a staff analysis of my taxes even before the committee members had had an opportunity to meet and evaluate the staff's findings. I said that I would pay the taxes due because of the disallowance of the deduction for the papers donation and also the taxes on the capital gain.

Over the next several days we received $47,000 from citizens who wanted to help me pay the taxes. Pat and I were deeply touched. Of course, we returned the money. On April 17 Tricia walked into the Lincoln Sitting Room. She said that she and Ed had decided to sell their wedding gifts and give Pat and me the money for the taxes. I assured her we could get a loan to cover the amount. "We don't want to loan the money to you," she said, "we want to give it to you."

In the end, 36 people on the staffs of GSA, GAO, two House committees, the White House staff, and the Secret Service had worked 67 days on the inquiries about Key Biscayne; 33 people had worked for 137 days on San Clemente; the joint committee staff of 23 had put 6 people full-time on my finances, and they worked with 5 full-time IRS people. There had been no fraud on my part, and no impropriety, but the effect of the tax issue was a devastating blow, coming as it did in the crucial months when the Judiciary Committee was beginning to weigh impeachment.

THE ASSAULT BECOMES PERSONAL

Eugene McCarthy once compared the press corps to a flock of blackbirds: one flies off the wire and the others fly off, one flies back and the others return. Something that starts as an idle discussion within the Washington press corps will soon be repeated in wider circles among the Washington establishment, and before long it is being reported, interpreted, and analyzed without a thought to where it originally came from.

As an example of this phenomenon, at some point in the hot, muggy summer of 1973, some of the more influential members of the Washington press corps concluded that I was starting to go off my rocker. They decided that my decision not to answer the Watergate charges until after the Ervin hearings had ended, and my isolation from the press on Watergate, showed that I was peculiarly out of touch with reality. Later that summer, my desire to take private drives without being followed by the press and photographed every moment—something done by President Johnson before me and by President Carter after me—was treated as a sign of mental pathology.

Since they were already thinking along these lines, the press corps had a ready-made explanation when I displayed an outburst of anger at Ron

Ziegler in New Orleans. This trip was one of my first public appearances after the Watergate hearings, and we were counting on the large and enthusiastic crowds that had been predicted to help dispel the idea that I was isolated and unpopular because of Watergate. While we were on *Air Force One* we received a Secret Service report that there was a serious threat of an assassination attempt. Personally I would have been willing to take the risk; but I could not endanger the safety of the crowds. Therefore I had to enter the city by an unannounced route.

My temper was already frayed by the time we arrived at the hall where I was scheduled to speak. When I saw Ziegler at the head of a pack of reporters, following right behind me into the VIP waiting room, I took out my frustration by giving him a solid shove and an unmistakable instruction to put the press in the special room that had been provided for them. I apologized immediately afterward to Ziegler, but the incident sent hot flashes through the press corps, and it was portrayed as the desperate flailing of a man at the end of his tether. CBS network news showed the pushing episode *twice* in slow motion.

It was in his influential "Nixon Watch" column in the next issue of *The New Republic* that John Osborne first put into print the talk among reporters that they had detected "something indefinably but unmistakably odd" in my gait and gestures in New Orleans. Some speculated that I was drunk. Osborne, however, said that he believed the assurance of my aides that I did not drink in the daytime, especially not before a speech. His verdict was that it "may just have been the tension taking its toll."

Several weeks later this idea was presumably what accounted for the contention by some reporters and commentators that I had maniacally manufactured the military alert at the time of the Yom Kippur War as a result of the desperate personal and political straits I was in because of Watergate. Considering the combined pressures of the Agnew resignation, the troubled economy, the oil embargo and the fuel shortage, and the Cox firing and its aftermath, many reporters apparently decided that I could only be in a state of mental overload. By early December, the New York *Times* ran a story with the headline *State of Nixon's Health Is a Dimension of Watergate Affair Constantly Being Gauged.* At the daily press briefings reporters began asking questions about whether I was under psychiatric care, if I were using drugs, and if I still prayed or believed in the efficacy of prayer. Theodore White once called reporters' conduct "macabre sadism." There was even a rumor in the press room that I was wearing makeup to disguise a fatal illness. This was a forerunner of the theory that I *planned* to get a serious illness and use that as my excuse for resignation. The final evolution of this bizarre amateur psychiatry was a deduction at the time of my resignation and in the period immediately following it that my problem was a death wish and that I yearned for dramatic extinction.

All these things were conceived, perpetuated, promulgated, and then analyzed by a comparatively small but immensely influential press corps living in the rarefied environment of Watergate-obsessed Washington, feeding on its own inbred ideas.

During this summer and fall of 1973 Pat and I seldom discussed the daily news stories and television broadcasts. She was magnificent in this period of exceptional adversity, just as she had always been before. She felt that in the end we would come out all right and that, above all, we must not allow the attacks to depress us to the point that we would be unable to carry out our duties effectively.

I think of one time in particular when, after an especially difficult day of unrelenting attacks about Watergate, we had to attend the state dinner for Prime Minister Norman Kirk of New Zealand. When the entertainment was over, we saw the Kirks to their car. Just as Pat and I started back through the Grand Foyer on our way upstairs, the Marine Band began playing "The Sound of Music." Following Pat's impulse, we took each other's hands and danced a short fox trot over to the stairs. The press was astonished and the guests delighted. It is a moment I shall always remember.

I believe that the attacks on my financial probity and integrity were the ones that hurt Pat most of all. When she had to join me in signing the statement relating to the preparation of the audit of our taxes, I could sense her tightly controlled anger. She said that she could understand the political attacks that were being made because of Watergate, but she thought that the attacks on our personal and financial integrity were totally unfair. She pointed out how careful she had been in the White House and through all the years we were in government. With a visible shudder she said that this reminded her of the agony and humiliation we had had to endure during the fund crisis in 1952.

At one point a Washington gossip columnist went to extraordinary lengths of innuendo to accuse Pat of unethically keeping jewels given to her as state gifts. In fact, Pat had the jewels listed in a gift register so that there would be no question when they went to the Nixon Library after our administration. Publicly she was charitable about the insults. "It's for the birds," she said laughingly. But privately, she came to me in despair. "What more can they possibly want us to do?" she asked.

Tricia did not make many public appearances during this period, but whenever she was staying with us for a few days she would come to the Lincoln Sitting Room late at night just to be with me while I worked. I knew that deep inside she ached with concern, but she never let Pat or me see it. On a few occasions when we talked about Watergate, she said,

"We always have to look down to the end of the road. In the end it will come out all right and that is all that really matters." Ed was a source of steadiness and support for the whole family.

Julie decided that she wanted to go out and fight, and she threw herself into the battle with characteristic verve and intensity. She made as many as six appearances in different parts of the country in one week. David was just starting a new job as a sportswriter with the Philadelphia *Bulletin*, but he joined her when he could. They lived in the front lines of Watergate, and they suffered its brutal assaults every bit as much as I did.

The annual Radio and Television Correspondents' Dinner in Washington is an event at which the political humor of the after-dinner skits and speakers is usually sharp and irreverent. Julie specifically asked to attend the 1973 dinner to prove that we were not ashamed or afraid to appear in public at such events. David decided to go with her and lend his moral support. On the night of the dinner, however, his car ran out of gas as he was driving to meet her. He hitchhiked the rest of the way, but he did not make it in time and Julie had to attend the dinner alone.

Most of the after-dinner humor had to do with Watergate, and the jokes were cutting and brutal. Julie sat with courage through every derisive laugh. After the program she was approached by Ambassador Guillermo Sevilla-Sacasa of Nicaragua, the dean of the Washington diplomatic corps. He whispered to her, "Your father still has one friend." She had steeled herself to the vicious jibes, but this kindness broke her heart. She could no longer hold back the tears, and with all the eyes fixed on her she rushed out of the room.

I did not want Julie to take the brunt of the Watergate questioning, but she could not bear the fact that there did not seem to be anyone else who would speak out for me. Whenever I suggested that she not become so involved, she always replied, "But Daddy, we have to fight."

My immediate family were not the only ones close to me who found themselves under merciless attack from the press. My brothers Don and Ed were called in for questioning. Reporters and investigators also turned on my friends Bob Abplanalp and Bebe Rebozo.

For Bebe Rebozo, 1973 was the beginning of an eighteen-month nightmare of harassment. He was investigated by the IRS, the GAO, and the Miami District Attorney, in addition to being scandalously hounded by the Ervin Committee staff.

Bebe Rebozo is one of the kindest and most generous men I have ever known. He is a man of great character and integrity. Yet anyone who read only the press stories about him, his business dealings, or his friendship with me would have had to conclude that he combined the worst traits of Rasputin and Al Capone.

The main vehicle for the attack was a $100,000 campaign contribution from Howard Hughes. Rebozo had accepted the money on his understanding that it was intended for the 1972 presidential campaign. He kept it in a safe-deposit box in his bank. In 1970, a serious power struggle erupted within the Hughes empire, marked by vicious infighting among several factions. Rebozo remembered the 1962 California gubernatorial campaign and the issue that had been made then of the loan from the Hughes organization to my brother Don. He wanted to make sure that I was not embarrassed again by any connection with Howard Hughes, so he decided not to mention the money to me and simply to hold on to it until after the election, when he thought it could either be used to help pay any deficit the campaign had incurred or for the 1974 congressional election.

In 1973 the IRS was in the midst of conducting an investigation of Hughes's holdings, and Rebozo knew that he would be asked about the $100,000 contribution. He had told me about the money by now, and I said that unless we could obtain the approval of the Hughes organization to put it into the 1974 campaign, we should return it. The money was accordingly returned to Hughes's representative in June 1973. A check of the serial numbers on the bills confirmed that they had all been issued before Rebozo had received the money, thus supporting his claim that he had left the money untouched in the safe-deposit box until he returned it, exactly as he had said.

When the Ervin Committee found out about the Hughes contribution they had a field day with leaks and innuendos, ironically confirming Rebozo's worst fears about the damaging publicity this innocent transaction could create.

There were reports that the Ervin investigation was going to charge that the Hughes money had been put to my personal use and that the money had been a quid pro quo for a Civil Aeronautics Board ruling favorable to Hughes's airline. Other stories reported charges that it was in exchange for an anti-trust favor. UPI said that the Ervin Committee was investigating whether the money had helped to pay for the purchase of my San Clemente home. Some stories referred to the contribution as a "payoff." All these widely reported stories were false.

On October 8 Rebozo was interviewed by the Ervin Committee. UPI ran a report alleging that he had been "hazy" on what happened to the money while it was in his possession. This was outrageously false. The New York *Times* reported charges that the contribution may have been part of an effort to stop a scheduled atomic test, since Hughes feared the effects of nuclear testing in Nevada on his Las Vegas properties. Another article reported that the contribution might have been in exchange for favors on Hughes's tax-exempt medical institute. That story, like the others, was untrue.

The Hughes contribution was not the only weapon used to harass Rebozo. On August 1 ABC had reported that investigators were checking reports that huge sums of illegal campaign contributions had been laundered through gambling casinos in the Bahamas with the aid of his bank, the Key Biscayne Bank; on August 20 ABC reported a story from "committee sources" that the Ervin Committee had subpoenaed the bank's records in connection with contributions run through the Bahamas of possibly $2 million or more. There were no such contributions, and there had been no such "laundering" of them.

On October 22 ABC reported the alleged existence of an illegal "private investment fund" administered on my behalf through the Rebozo bank: "Described by sources close to the investigation as the 'Nixon Checkers Fund of 1973,' the alleged investment portfolio is being probed to determine whether large unreported political contributions may have been diverted to Nixon's personal use." The story said that two corporations might have contributed more than $1 million. The charges were totally false.

In the meantime the Ervin Committee's pursuit of Rebozo was ruthless. It is described in detail in *At That Point in Time,* by the committee's Minority Counsel Fred Thompson. He tells how, in sets of twos and threes, staff investigators went to Miami four separate times to interview Rebozo, each group repeating the questions of the previous group. The committee interviewed his family and his business friends and subpoenaed financial records of everyone with whom he had engaged in business transactions over a period of six years. They also interviewed everyone to whom he had written a check over the last six years.

Rebozo was subjected to fourteen weeks of IRS audits, an investigation by the GAO, an investigation by the Ervin Committee, and an investigation by the Miami District Attorney, and finally the Watergate Special Prosecutor. When in January 1975 Leon Jaworski finally confirmed that there was no evidence for a case against Rebozo, the New York *Times* did not carry the story at all and the Washington *Post* carried only a short report. Not one of the television networks, which had been reporting the false allegations nightly, even mentioned Jaworski's statement.

By the time the Rebozo investigation was finally concluded in October 1975, the Special Prosecutor's office had issued more than 200 subpoenas, questioned 123 people ranging from me to the gardener at my Key Biscayne home, and hauled 28 people before a grand jury. In 1978 internal staff documents from the Special Prosecution Force were made public that showed the lengths to which the investigators were willing to go. A memo by the head of the Rebozo investigation acknowledged that the informant who had prompted their investigation of the secret multimillion-dollar Bahamian bank account supposedly maintained for me by Rebozo turned out to be a "con man with a criminal record" who had made an identical allegation years earlier against Earl Warren. The documents he had shown to back up his story were "determined to be fraudulent." The memo concluded, "Like so many of the Rebozo allegations, it seemed at first to have great potential. Like so many, it lacked critical details. And like so many, it proved utterly baseless."

But this was years later, and in the meantime the Special Prosecutor's office had investigated Rebozo for sixteen months, evidently caring little that they made his life hell.

An estimated $2 million had been spent investigating Bebe Rebozo. In the end all the allegations and innuendos proved false, and he was officially vindicated. In the meantime, of course, he had been unmercifully harassed and defamed. But those who had made the charges, and those who had printed and broadcast them, despite his complete exoneration by the Special Prosecutor's office, did not have the decency to retract them or to apologize for the damage they had done. Bebe Rebozo endured a modern-day Star Chamber of political persecution. His crime was that he was Richard Nixon's friend.

Earlier in 1973 polls had shown that despite a widespread assumption that I was involved in the Watergate cover-up, a majority of the public still believed I was a man of high integrity. The effect of the year's relentless assault was that it began to succeed in doing what the charges of a political cover-up alone could not do: it began to undermine that confidence in my integrity. In the spring of 1974 columnist Nicholas von Hoffman would write:

> But the formal process of legal impeachment has to wait upon a kind of informal social impeachment whereby the man is stripped of the reverence, protections, and deference with which we treat our presidents. He has to be tried, convicted, disgraced and expelled before he is formally accused. . . .
>
> Until a few months ago any American president could have sent the IRS American Express slips and doodles . . . and gotten a pass. . . . Small unflattering tidbits about Nixon and his family are now broadcast and repeated with the special satisfaction of the self-righteous.

Von Hoffman predicted that an inevitable train of events had been set in motion based more on the imperatives of good drama than on questions of impeachable guilt or innocence. He stated that I was going to be impeached "although nobody quite knows why. . . . Nixon's policies such as they were would never get another man impeached. Nevertheless one senses the decision has been made. . . . None of this has to do with whether there are enough votes . . . to do him in now. Before too long there will be."

During my meetings with congressmen in November I had said that I might make the subpoenaed tapes public, in summary form if not in full transcripts. The congressional leadership, particularly Hugh Scott, had strongly urged that I do so. Pat Buchanan was assigned to go over these transcripts and compare them with John Dean's testimony. When I read Buchanan's report of his findings, I was reassured by the thought that anyone reviewing the tapes would agree with my view that Dean had lied when he charged that I had conspired with him for eight months on a Watergate cover-up. I knew that the March 21 tape would cause an uproar. But I was sure that in the end people would recognize that it was what I had done that mattered, not what I said, much less what I had temporarily contemplated.

Haig brought Garment, Harlow, Ziegler, and communications aides Ken Clawson and Dick Moore in on the decision. Each of them first read the tapes, then Buchanan's summaries. Haig tried to soften his report of their opinion for me, but I could tell that they did not share my optimism that if we could weather the many admittedly rough passages, the tapes in their entirety would prove that Dean had lied and I had told the truth. Harlow in particular thought that the tapes would be deadly because the conversations on them were just too realistically political for public consumption.

Buchanan, however, was strongly in favor of releasing the transcripts. I shared his belief that if we could survive the first shock waves, the tapes would end up proving Dean a liar. But I also appreciated Harlow's insight into possible public and congressional reactions, and I felt that in our present parlous situation these considerations would have to be treated as paramount. Therefore, despite the expectations that had been raised by announcing our intention to release the transcripts, I decided not to do so.

On December 2, 1973, William Greider wrote in the Washington *Post*: "What the public has to understand is that if it asks Congress to impeach and try Mr. Nixon, it is really asking for much more than that. Impeachment on these offenses implicitly requires Democrats and Republicans alike . . . to render judgment not just on Mr. Nixon, but on the political past."

"1973 will be a better year," I had dictated in my diary in December 1972. Now, at Camp David on December 23, 1973, I wrote across the top of a page of notes I was making: "Last Christmas here?"

1974

It was difficult to believe that only eight months had passed since Haldeman and Ehrlichman had left, and since the full fury of Watergate had descended on me. It had been a brutal eight months, an endless cycle of blows and rallies followed by further blows. In May I had felt that there was a chance to renew, rebuild, and recover. Now I was reduced to analyzing my situation in the stark terms of the possibilities of simple survival.

It was after the weekend of Cox's dismissal that I first considered what my actions had precipitated. I made notes to myself that I labeled "Analysis":

1. Cox had to go. Richardson would inevitably go with him. Otherwise, if we had waited for Cox making a major mistake which in the public mind would give us what appeared to be good cause for him to go would mean that we had waited until Cox had moved against us.

2. We must learn from the Richardson incident what people we can depend on. Establishment types like Richardson simply won't stand with us when chips are down and they have to choose between their political ambitions and standing by the President who made it possible for them to hold the high positions from which they were now resigning.

3. As far as the tapes were concerned we need to put the final documents in the best possible PR perspective. We must get out the word with regard to no "doctoring" of the tapes.

4. We must compare our situation now with what it was on April 30. Then the action with regard to Haldeman and Ehrlichman, Gray, Dean, and Kleindienst did not remove the cloud on the President as far as an impression of guilt on his part was concerned. In fact it increased that doubt and rather than satisfying our critics once they had tasted a little blood they liked it so much they wanted far more. Since April 30 we have slipped a great deal. We had 60 percent approval rating in the polls on that date and now we stand at 30 percent at best.

5. Now the question is whether our action on turning over the tapes or the transcripts thereof helps remove the cloud of doubt. Also on the plus side, the

Mideast crisis, probably if the polls are anywhere near correct, helped somewhat because it shows the need for RN's leadership in foreign policy.

6. Our opponents will now make an all-out push. The critical question is whether or not the case for impeachment or resignation is strong enough in view of the plus factors I noted in previous paragraph.

At 1:15 A.M. on January 1, 1974, I made this note: "The basic question is: Do I fight all out or do I now begin the long process to prepare for a change, meaning, in effect, resignation?"

Over the past months I had talked about resignation with my family, with a few close friends, and with Haig and Ziegler. But the idea was anathema to me. I believed that my resignation under pressure would change our whole form of government. The change might not be apparent for many years; but once the first President had resigned under fire and thereby established a precedent, the opponents of future Presidents would have a formidable new leverage. It was not hard to visualize a situation in which Congress, confronted with a President it did not like, could paralyze him by blocking him on legislation, foreign affairs, and appointments. Then, when the country was fed up with the resulting stalemate, Congress could claim that it would be better for the country if the President resigned. And Nixon would be cited as the precedent! By forcing Presidents out through resignation, Congress would no longer have to take the responsibility and bear the verdict of history for voting impeachment.

My notes continued:

The *answer—fight*. Fight because if I am forced to resign the press will become a much too dominant force in the nation, not only in this administration but for years to come. Fight because resignation would set a precedent and result in a permanent and very destructive change in our whole constitutional system. Fight because resignation could lead to a collapse of our foreign policy initiatives.

I made another list of notes for myself later that morning, New Year's Day, 1974:

Decision to fight:

1. Resign sets precedent—admits guilt.
2. Lets down friends.
3. Fight now makes possible fight for future as a man of principle.
4. Only substance, not politics, must affect this decision.

Priorities:

1. Press conference and media meetings.
2. Organize our hard core in the House, Senate, among top governors and our friends like Kendall, etc., who were working under Flanigan's direction.

3. Mobilize the Cabinet.
4. Buck up the staff.

Substantive areas:

1. Rodino, Jaworski, et al.
2. Foreign policy initiatives.
3. Run the shop well on the domestic front (energy, et al.).

Style:

1. Confidence.
2. Compassion.
3. Color—the necessity for the interesting.

Be *strong* against unprecedented adversity but avoid intemperate remarks or conduct.

I made still another note on January 5, at 5 A.M.:

Above all else: Dignity, command, faith, head high, no fear, build a new spirit, drive, act like a President, act like a winner. Opponents are savage destroyers, haters. Time to use full power of the President to fight overwhelming forces arrayed against us.

As I assessed the situation, impeachment was not going to be decided on the basis of the law or historical precedent. Impeachment would be an exercise in public persuasion: while I was trying to restore public confidence in my ability to lead, my opposition would be trying to condition the public to the idea that I had to be removed from office.

THE LAST CAMPAIGN

I had thought that 1972 was going to be my last political campaign. But at the beginning of 1974 I recognized that I was about to embark on the campaign of my life.

I was sure that, regardless of the substantive issues involved in the impeachment effort, it was the politics of the situation that would determine the outcome. At each stage the Democrats would be taking the political temperature, trying to determine whether the Republicans would be worse off in the 1974 congressional elections and in the 1976 presidential campaign with a discredited President still in office, or with a new President bearing the political burden of his predecessor's impeachment or resignation. Pressure on the Democratic Congress was intensified by polls that showed that opinion of Congress was at its lowest percentage in the polls' history—even lower than mine!

Many congressional Republicans were now also considering impeachment as a strictly political question in terms of the upcoming off-year elections—in which many of them had an obvious and immediate interest. For them, however, impeachment would clearly be a double-edged sword, because as much as they might want to be rid of me now that it appeared I would be a drag on the party's fortunes in 1974 and 1976, they recognized that many Republicans, particularly the party workers, were outraged by the idea, and that the general public might consider their willingness to see me impeached self-interested and disloyal.

As I increasingly saw it, therefore, the main danger of being impeached would come precisely from the public's being conditioned to the idea that I was going to be impeached. In the end, therefore, it would come down to a race for public support: in other words, a campaign. But this time, instead of campaigning for a political office, I would be campaigning for my political life.

As of December, the opinion polls showed that the people were still undecided. Fifty-four percent were against requiring me to leave office. At the same time, 45 percent would respect me more if I resigned so that the nation could concentrate on other problems than Watergate. The very thing I had been counting on to work in my favor had begun to work against me. In April 1973 I had hoped that the public would get tired of Watergate and apply pressure to Congress and the media to move on to other things. But the congressional and media assault and the controversy over the White House tapes had so embroiled me in Watergate that the public was increasingly seeing me as the roadblock and their desire to move on to other things was affecting their willingness to have me removed. Unless I could do something to stem this tide, it would sweep me out of office.

As I had in every other campaign, I tried to weigh my strengths and weaknesses. As usual, the Democrats had the political edge because they had the numerical majority. Therefore impeachment was *possible* no matter what I did to try to stop it. It was *probable* if the Republicans decided not to help me or not to help me enough.

In fact, my Republican support in Washington had been steadily eroding. By the end of 1973, as the impeachment hearings drew near and as the prospect of the off-year elections threatened to become a personal barometer of public sentiment about me, even the solid middle-ground Republicans, including the party leadership in Congress, had begun to send out signals that unless I could dramatically turn the tide for myself, they would have to begin moving to arm's length. I complained that it was typical Republican minority-party jitters, but in fact it was largely my own fault. Too many who had tried to defend me in the past had been burned, and many no longer felt sufficiently confident or motivated to take further risks for me.

My problems were compounded by the fact that all my activities with my congressional supporters had become uncomfortably self-conscious. No congressman could afford to seem to be too firmly committed to my camp lest he be accused of not considering the case against me on its merits—despite the fact that many on the other side were openly campaigning for impeachment. Normal phone calls and invitations to White House briefings were called into question by the press, and word started to come back that these activities might be made to look like attempts to influence votes and that congressmen would be grateful if I would leave them alone until after the impeachment question had been settled. This effectively barred any real strategy; my primary campaign weapon would have to be doing my job well and continuing to push for recognition of the fact that Watergate mattered so much less than the things I did well. At the same time, increasing irritation and factionalism began to build between the party's liberal and conservative elements. With nerves rubbed raw from all the months of Watergate, and the usual uncertainties of an off-year election campaign, each group tended to view any policy action I took as a concession to the other side in an effort to win votes on impeachment.

Across the country several small but dedicated support groups began to appear. Don Kendall did a superb job trying to rally the business community; Rabbi Baruch Korff of Massachusetts spent his personal savings for an ad that launched a nationwide movement of people who felt that the current assault was not just against me personally but against the presidency as well. Peter Flanigan coordinated the liaison with many of the groups.

The Cabinet had held firm during the rocky passages of the last eight months. Some of them, such as Commerce Secretary Fred Dent and Agriculture Secretary Earl Butz, went out into the country to speak in my behalf. Others stayed in Washington and showed their loyalty simply by doing their jobs despite all the pressures they had to endure. The White House staff was equally superb. I cannot ever adequately thank all those who stood by me. But despite the valor of the staff, everyone was completely exhausted. I do not for a moment concede that we were outclassed, but from the beginning we had been hopelessly outmanned. We reached out for new people. One was James St. Clair, a prominent Boston lawyer who came in to head the legal team. Dean Burch, former Chairman of the Federal Communications Commission, took over the political operation of the White House staff. Ken Cole, the Executive Director of the Domestic Council, became Assistant to the President for Domestic Affairs. These appointments were well received, and they created a certain welcome momentum around the White House. But it would not last long.

Mel Laird soon announced that he was leaving the White House to begin a new career in the private sector. Jerry Ford had been sworn in as Vice President on December 6, and Laird indicated publicly that he expected Ford would take over many of the domestic policy and congressional liaison functions he had handled. However, Evans and Novak, the Washington *Post* columnists who so regularly reflected Laird's point of view that they were jokingly referred to around Washington as his publicists, wrote that his departure was a signal to Republicans that they were no longer duty-bound to protect the President.

By the end of 1973 my longstanding political opponents began consolidating their efforts to make sure that I would be impeached. The ACLU distributed a fifty-six-page handbook that described ways to hasten and ensure impeachment. The principal ACLU spokesman was candid about their motivation: "There's no civil rights movement. There's no war. There's no social-action movement. I hate to use the word, but it's liberal chic. Impeachment is there." Stewart Mott, McGovern's principal contributor, under the guise of a "public interest" group, published a broadside accusing me of twenty-eight indictable crimes ranging from the war in Vietnam to the Watergate break-in. After Cox was dismissed, Ralph Nader's organization began phoning around the country to promote impeachment. The AFL-CIO announced that impeachment could no longer be avoided and began a nationwide campaign, sending out four million leaflets on "Nineteen Points for Impeachment." An AFL-CIO lobbyist observed in January 1974 that "when the timing is good" they were going to make an "all-out lobbying effort on the Hill" to have me impeached. The serious impact of organized labor's decision to go all out for impeachment was underscored by the fact that nineteen of the twenty-one Democratic members of the House Judiciary Committee had received a total of $189,196 in campaign money from organized labor in the 1972 election. Two of the Republican members had received $2,100. Committee Chairman Peter Rodino had received $30,923.

The question of impeachment would first be debated, and the evidence to justify it would first be investigated, by the House Judiciary Committee—and one had only to be able to count to know that the House Judiciary Committee was a stacked deck. Twenty-one of its thirty-eight members were Democrats; seventeen were Republicans. Of the twenty-one Democrats, eighteen either came from the party's liberal wing or had reputations as hard-core partisans. Realistic observers of Washington politics conceded at the outset that these eighteen Democrats, despite their pieties about objectivity, were all going to vote for impeachment.

The three remaining Democrats were Southern conservatives: Walter Flowers of Alabama, Ray Thornton of Arkansas, and James Mann of South Carolina. They were the only unpredictable element on the Democratic side, because they had supported me in the past, often going against their party, on matters pertaining to national defense and budget restraint.

The consensus in Washington was that of the seventeen Republicans on the committee, eleven would stand by me. Among the remaining six, some were liberals who had rarely supported me on policy matters, some were facing difficult re-election campaigns, and some had already shown signs of personal disaffection because of Watergate. My only hope of averting a recommendation for impeachment from the committee would be either to hold every Republican and pick up two of the Southern Democrats, or to hold sixteen Republicans and win all three of the Southerners. Either of these outcomes was possible, but extremely remote.

Whatever the opposition from without, there was also an enemy within: the tapes. The biggest danger I saw in the year ahead was that both the Special Prosecutor and the House Judiciary Committee would begin requesting more and more tapes—always with the disclaimer that each request would be the last. But there would never be an end to these requests until all 5,000 hours of tapes had been requested and surrendered. These investigations had taken on a life of their own—I did not understand why more people could not see that. The various investigators were no longer trying to determine the truth of any particular charges against me. They wanted to go through everything, to pursue every lead, no matter how remote, until they found something that would in their view finally justify my removal from office. And for me the continuing nightmare of the tapes was the possibility that, given enough time and enough tapes, they might find what they were looking for.

I wanted to stop it. In the past I had made the grievous mistake of saying I was going to stop it but failing to do so. Then, after paying the political price for refusing, we would cave when the pressure started to build. I regretted not having followed my instincts about this in the past and wanted to begin following them right away. I even talked about destroying the tapes. I argued that the best strategy would be to go to Congress and fling down the gauntlet and declare that enough is enough. I said that I wanted to do it in the State of the Union message on January 30: I would announce that I would provide nothing more to the House Judiciary Committee or the Special Prosecutor.

I was persuaded against it by the argument that using the State of the Union to draw lines and force confrontations would not only heighten the impeachment issue but completely overshadow the important national policy issues in the speech.

So the tapes sat there in the EOB. The ones I had already reviewed were bad enough; now what might be on the others haunted us all. I thought of the peculiar reality for me of Churchill's observation: "The longer one lives, the more one realizes that everything depends upon chance. If anyone will look back over the course of even ten years experience, he will see that tiny incidents, utterly unimportant in themselves, have in fact governed the whole of his fortune and career."

I had no way of remembering everything that was on the tapes, but I was sure that there were many more of the rough political patches that had already brought us to this point. I might survive any number of them, but eventually the accumulated weight would bring me down. Tricia later showed me a note from her diary that reminded me that sometimes people around you understand things better than you understand them yourself:

> Something Daddy said makes me feel absolutely hopeless about the outcome. He has since the Butterfield revelation repeatedly stated that the tapes can be taken either way. He has cautioned us that there is nothing damaging on the tapes; he has cautioned us that he might be impeached because of their content. Because he has said the latter, knowing Daddy, the latter is the way he really feels.

So many people had gone out on so many limbs for me already—and I knew better than most of them just how shaky some of those limbs had really been. Now others would have to take that risk if we continued to fight: Haig, Ziegler, the lawyers, the congressmen and senators who would support me during the impeachment hearings, the White House staff. I would have to inspire these people for the battle, even though I knew that in many respects the case was not very inspiring. What enabled me to justify fighting on and asking these people to fight with me and for me was that although the *case* was badly flawed, I convinced myself that the *cause* was noble and important.

As I came to see it, the cause now involved the nature of leadership in American politics. I felt that if I could be hounded from office because of a political scandal like Watergate, the whole American system of government would be undermined and changed. I never for a moment believed that any of the charges against me were legally impeachable—none of them involved "Treason, Bribery, or other high Crimes and Misdemeanors" as enumerated in the Constitution. If I had felt that I was actually guilty of a legally impeachable offense I would not have allowed anyone to extend himself in my defense. I would have resigned immediately. But this impeachment was going to be a political phenomenon; this was confirmed when the House Judiciary Committee could not reach agreement on the constitutional definition of impeachment. In December the New York *Times* reported that two-thirds of the committee's members believed that an impeachable offense did not even have to be a violation of the law. Later, instead of deliberating until a consensus on a definition was reached, it was decided that each member would be allowed to make up his own mind along the way. If there had ever been any doubts before, this decision made it clear that a political rather than a legal standard would govern the impeachment proceedings.

I felt that in terms of the important elements of presidential leadership, I still had much to contribute to America and the world. As crippled as I was and was bound to remain throughout the rest of my term because of Watergate, I was still more experienced than Jerry Ford, who had only just been confirmed as Vice President. And experienced leadership was needed. The North Vietnamese were clearly preparing for a new offensive in Cambodia and South Vietnam, aimed at testing our willingness and ability to enforce the Paris agreement. The Soviets were holding back from concluding a comprehensive SALT agreement and would need a firm U.S. position to encourage them in the right direction. At home, the economy was extremely shaky in the aftermath of its experience with controls, and the impact of the Arab oil embargo was going to make it a long hard winter for whoever was in the White House. The temptation to lash out against the Arabs would have to be kept in check in order to capitalize on the tremendous success of our policy during the Yom Kippur War.

I was aware that the way I had handled Watergate so far and the inherent flaws in my case might endanger the very things I believed required my staying in office. I realized that for many people I had made a mockery of national security and executive privilege by using them, as they saw it, to cover my own guilt. I also realized that many people felt I was irreparably damaging the strength of the presidency by persisting in my determination to be a strong President despite the weakness created by Watergate.

But I did not agree. Rightly or wrongly, I convinced myself that I was being attacked by old opponents for old reasons. I was instinctively geared to fight for my survival. After living and fighting in the political arena for so long, I was not going to give up now and leave the presidency because of something like Watergate. I would fight and do and say whatever I thought was necessary to rally my forces and maintain their confidence for this last campaign.

On January 9, 1974, while I was spending a few days at Sunnylands, the magnificent Palm Springs home of my friend Walter Annenberg, I received a call from John Connally. He is not a man who becomes easily or unnecessarily alarmed, but he sounded agitated as he talked to me. He said that he had just been in Washington and talked to one of his close friends, who was the best source of political intelligence he had ever known. His friend had told him that a group of Republicans, primarily in the House but including one or two senators, some top party leaders among them, had been meeting privately and had concluded that my staying in office would be highly detrimental to all Republicans running in 1974. Some of these people, Connally said, were men who had been my friends in the past. He referred to the group as the "Arizona Mafia." I asked if Goldwater was a part of it, and Connally replied that while Goldwater might be aware of the group's existence and intentions, he was not one of its prime movers. He made it clear that the group was not limited to Arizonans; there were men from the East and the Midwest participating in the discussions. "Some of them are men you think are your very good friends," he said.

The supposed strategy of this alleged group was to delay the vote in the House Judiciary Committee until after the Soviet Summit in June. Then they would have some selected Republican leaders come to the White House and request that I resign in the best interests of the party, particularly because so many of my supporters in the House would lose their seats if I were still in office in November. Connally said that his source had emphasized that Jerry Ford had no knowledge of the group's existence.

Connally repeated that his source for this disturbing intelligence was extremely reliable, and he insisted that I should not brush it off as just another rumor. He urged me to have it checked very carefully. I told him that I would.

When I mentioned this information to Haig he was skeptical, and I agreed that it was the kind of thing that could be expected to turn up in the Washington rumor mills in times like these. Haig checked with Goldwater and reported that Goldwater claimed, and appeared, to be standing firm.

At that time I did not believe there could be an organized Republican conspiracy to force me out of office. However, survival matters most in politics. Washington is ruled by Darwinian forces, and if you are in serious political trouble, you cannot expect generosity or magnanimity for long. Often a consensus develops, sometimes no more than a shared instinct, that the burden of the wounded must be removed in order for the rest to survive.

The State of the Union address was scheduled for January 30 at 9 P.M. Pat and I sat silently in the car on the way from the White House to the Capitol. She knew as well as I did how tense the situation had become. The whole family had discussed whether the members of the House and Senate would receive the speech courteously or whether there might even be an open demonstration of hostility.

As soon as I entered the Chamber door, however, there was a loud, almost raucous burst of applause and cheers. Our small but vocal group of Republican and Democratic loyalists cheered so lustily that their colleagues felt obliged at least to stand, if not to follow suit.

This 1974 State of the Union address was to be the final summing up of my domestic stewardship. I was able to say at the outset: "Tonight, for the first time in twelve years, a President of the United States can report to the Congress on the state of a Union at peace with every nation of the world."

I believe that, had it not been for Watergate, the actual state of the American Union in 1973 would have been acknowledged as proof of the validity of the political philosophy on which I had run in 1972. The events of 1973 almost seemed designed to demonstrate just how inadequate the politics of the left would have been in dealing with the problems we had confronted and in solving them successfully. For example, the Mideast war ironically turned many of the prominent Vietnam doves back into hawks when Israel's safety and survival were at stake. The recurrent inflation showed how recklessly the traditional liberal Democratic dollar politics would have affected the economy. Even Teddy Kennedy and Wilbur Mills tacitly acknowledged this by revising their highly publicized compulsory national health insurance proposal to make it resemble mine. And the realities of the energy crisis forced pragmatic reevaluations of the fashionable but one-sided environmentalist bias.

The country I had been elected to lead five years earlier had been on the ropes from domestic discord. The cities had been burning and besieged; the college campuses had become battlegrounds; crime was increasing at an alarming rate; drug abuse and drug addiction were increasing; the military draft cast a disruptive shadow over the lives of young Americans; there was no program to deal with the protection of our natural environment; and there were vital areas of social reform and governmental operation that needed attention and consideration.

In the five years of the Nixon administration we could point to some signal successes. The cities were now quiet; the college campuses had once again become seats of learning; the rise in crime had been checked; the drug problem had been massively attacked, abroad as well as at home; the draft had been eliminated; and we had submitted to Congress the nation's first environmental program, as well as major plans for national health care, education reform, revenue-sharing, and government reorganization. In this State of the Union I outlined ten landmark accomplishments that I felt would be possible in 1974: we could break the back of the energy crisis and lay the foundation for meeting our energy needs from our own resources; we could achieve a just and lasting settlement in the Mideast; we could check the rise in prices without causing a recession; we could enact my health care proposals and thereby begin to provide high-quality insurance for every American in a dignified way at an affordable price; we could make states and localities more responsive to local needs; we could make a crucial breakthrough in mass transportation; we could reform federal aid to education in ways that would make it do the most for those who needed it the most; we could begin the task of defining and protecting the right of personal privacy for every American; we could finally and belatedly reform the welfare system; and we could begin establishing an international economic framework in which Americans would share more fully.

As the speech progressed I was surprised and moved by the warm reception it was accorded. By the end I had been interrupted by applause more than thirty times. At one point I came to a line I had not thought particularly exceptional: in discussing the overriding aim of establishing a new structure of peace in the world, I said, "This has been and this will remain my first priority and the chief legacy I hope to leave from the eight years of my presidency." Suddenly the rafters seemed to ring. Almost all the Republicans and even a number of Democrats were on their feet, applauding and cheering. I looked up to my family. They were beaming.

When I had finished the address, I turned over the last page of my text and concluded with an extemporaneous and personal note. The Chamber was completely hushed as I said:

> I would like to add a personal word with regard to an issue that has been of great concern to all Americans over the past year. I refer, of course, to the investigations of the so-called Watergate affair.
>
> As you know, I have provided to the Special Prosecutor voluntarily a great deal of material. I believe that I have provided all the material that he needs to conclude his investigations and to proceed to prosecute the guilty and to clear the innocent.
>
> I believe the time has come to bring that investigation and the other investigations of this matter to an end. One year of Watergate is enough.
>
> And the time has come, my colleagues, for not only the executive, the President, but the members of Congress, for all of us to join together in devoting our full energies to these great issues that I have discussed tonight which involve the welfare of all of the American people in so many different ways as well as the peace of the world.
>
> I recognize that the House Judiciary Committee has a special responsibility in this area, and I want to indicate on this occasion that I will cooperate with the Judiciary Committee in its investigation. I will cooperate so that it can conclude its investigation, make its decision, and I will cooperate in any way that I consider consistent with my responsibilities to the office of the presidency of the United States.
>
> There is only one limitation. I will follow the precedent that has been followed by and defended by every President from George Washington to Lyndon B. Johnson of never doing anything that weakens the office of the President of the United States or impairs the ability of the Presidents of the future to make the great decisions that are so essential to this nation and the world.

Another point I should like to make very briefly. Like every member of the House and Senate assembled here tonight, I was elected to the office that I hold. And like every member of the House and Senate, when I was elected to that office, I knew that I was elected for the purpose of doing a job and doing it as well as I possibly can. And I want you to know that I have no intention whatever of ever walking away from the job that the people elected me to do for the people of the United States.

Now, needless to say, it would be understatement if I were not to admit that the year 1973 was not a very easy year for me personally or for my family. And as I have already indicated, the year 1974 presents very great and serious problems, as very great and serious opportunities are also presented.

But my colleagues, this I believe: with the help of God, who has blessed this land so richly, with the cooperation of the Congress, and with the support of the American people, we can and we will make the year 1974 a year of unprecedented progress toward our goal of building a structure of lasting peace in the world and a new prosperity without war in the United States of America.

Back at the White House I found the whole family elated by the reaction to the speech, particularly the ovation that had followed my statement about the eight years of my presidency. Everyone felt that this was a positive sign that there was still a great deal of solid support for me in Congress.

The State of the Union speech seemed to have a generally positive reception. For a while it even seemed to supply the momentum that I had been seeking to break out of the Watergate morass. *New Confident Nixon* was the headline in the New York *Times*.

I decided to take advantage of this situation while it lasted, and I made several trips out into the country. On February 18 I went to Huntsville, Alabama, where more than 20,000 people gathered for an Honor America Day rally. George Wallace was my host, and he could not have been friendlier. On March 15 I went to Chicago for a televised question-and-answer session. The next day I flew to Nashville for the opening of the new Grand Ole Opry House. Three days after that I held a press conference at the convention of the National Association of Broadcasters in Houston. Inspired by the success of these appearances, and buoyed by the obviously sincere enthusiasm of the people I met, I made a note to myself that I would take my case directly to the country right after the Soviet Summit in June.

In the meantime Congress, distracted by impeachment, passed only about half the number of bills it had passed in a similar period the year before.

On December 21, 1973, UN Secretary-General Kurt Waldheim had opened the Geneva Peace Conference on the Middle East. Syria did not attend, but Egypt, Israel, Jordan, the United States, and the U.S.S.R. sent representatives. On December 22 the initial round of talks ended, with instructions to Egypt and Israel to begin immediate discussions on the disengagement of their forces along the Suez Canal.

From January 10 through January 17, 1974, Kissinger began what came to be known as his "shuttle diplomacy." President Sadat had requested that Kissinger help work out the disagreements between Egypt and Israel relating to the disengagement of their troops. Thanks to the success of our earlier policies, Kissinger had become a common denominator for the two countries: a man both sides felt they could trust, representing an administration both sides thought could and would be evenhanded. The opening of these negotiations with Kissinger as the go-between called for great faith on the part of Golda Meir and for exceptional courage on the part of Anwar Sadat. Kissinger repaid Mrs. Meir's trust and President Sadat's courage with a tireless effort to adjust each side's position until an agreement had been produced that would make a substantial beginning in resolving the differences between Israel and Egypt.

On January 17 the Egyptian-Israeli troop disengagement was finally achieved. It was a tribute to Kissinger's enormous stamina, his incisive intellect, and, not least, his great personal charm. It was an even greater tribute because he had to cope with the burden of a President weakened by political attack at home.

After I announced the disengagement, I called Mrs. Meir. She sounded as if a weight had been lifted from her. "Your statesmanship has played a key role," I said to her. "It would not have happened except for what you did in October," she replied. "You and Dr. Kissinger deserve great credit for bringing this about," I responded. Before I hung up, she added warmly, "Take care of yourself and get plenty of rest."

I also called President Sadat. "Congratulations on your statesmanship. I'm looking forward to meeting and working together with you for a permanent peace in the Middle East," I said. "Thanks to you and your wise guidance, and the efforts of Dr. Kissinger," he replied.

ENERGY

During the winter of 1973–74 America had an encounter with the future. We passed a milestone of national awareness when we recognized for the first time that the bounty of energy resources we had taken for granted for so long was not as limitless as we had once thought.

This was not something that had happened overnight. The predicament of the 1970s was the result of shortsighted government policies compounded by decades of wasteful habits.

The United States, with only 6 percent of the world's population, was consuming one-third of the energy used on earth, and the supply of fuel was getting tight.

As early as 1971 I had turned my personal attention to giving an impetus to the production of nuclear energy. I ordered the first American breeder reactor project to begin in the spring of 1971.

By June 4, 1971, our study of the imminent energy problem had evolved into the first Presidential message on energy in our history. In it I urged the continuation of the development of the breeder reactor and committed the administration to the creation of a program for converting coal into clean gaseous fuels and to the acceleration of oil and gas lease sales on the outer continental shelf. I also proposed that all the federal government's energy resource development programs—some fifteen of them—be brought together under one agency. I said, "This message points the way for America—at considerable cost in money, but an investment that is urgent and, therefore, justified—points the way for finding new sources of energy and, at the same time, clean energy that will not pollute the air, will not pollute the environment."

On April 18, 1973, I sent Congress five major new requests involving the energy program. In the twenty-two months since my first message the worsening energy situation had been almost ignored. On our own, the administration had increased funding for experimental research and development by nearly 50 percent, but legislation was needed to forestall the crunch that we saw coming.

I asked Congress to deregulate natural gas and let the price rise with the market so that there would be more money and more incentive in the private sector for additional development. I also requested tax credits for oil exploration, approved extending the deadline on unreasonable environmental regulations, and ended the mandatory quotas on imports. By executive action I tripled the offshore acreage for oil and gas leases. I made requests for further research and development on nuclear and geothermal energy and on shale oil energy resources. I also announced the creation of an Office of Energy Conservation and proposed a new Cabinet-level department dealing exclusively with energy, the Department of Energy and Natural Resources.

In mid-May we began to insist on the voluntary sharing of gasoline resources between the major retailers and independent dealers. On June 29 I named John Love, governor of Colorado, to head the new energy office. I renewed my appeal to Congress, calling for a $10 billion program for energy research over the next five years, to match the anticipated $200 billion that would be spent in the private sector.

I asked that people voluntarily reduce road speeds to fifty miles an hour; this alone would have saved 25 percent of the fuel consumed traveling at seventy miles an hour. I said that the government was going to reduce its energy consumption by 7 percent over the next year and urged that personal consumption voluntarily be cut by 5 percent.

I again appealed to Congress on September 10, when I urged passage of seven bills, including one approving construction of the Alaska pipeline, and others covering deepwater port construction to make bigger fuel imports possible, the deregulation of natural gas, and new legislation on strip mining.

The first distant rumble of a possible Arab oil embargo began in the spring of 1973. By mid-summer King Faisal of Saudi Arabia was warning that unless our policy toward Israel changed, there would be a reduction of the oil sent to us. We stood our ground, and I said in a press conference on September 5: "Both sides need to start negotiating. That is our position. We are not pro-Israel and we are not pro-Arab, and we are not any more pro-Arab because they have oil and Israel hasn't. We are pro-peace and it is the interest of the whole area for us to get those negotiations off dead center."

After the outbreak of the Mideast war on October 6, the Arab position hardened, and by the end of October we were confronted with a full-scale embargo. By November it was clear that we were going to fall as much as 10 percent behind our energy needs, a figure that could rise as high as 17 percent by winter, depending upon weather conditions.

On November 7 I went on television to announce to the American people what I called the "stark fact": we were heading toward the acutest shortage of energy since World War II.

I called for a three-stage conservation effort, involving executive action, state and local action, and congressional action. Heating in federal buildings would be lowered to between 65 and 68 degrees, and I urged the same for private houses. I called for car pooling and asked state and local governments to set speed limits at fifty miles an hour. I asked Congress to pass an emergency energy act that would give me the authority to relax environmental restrictions on a case-by-case basis as I deemed necessary, and would impose special restrictions on the use of energy resources. I asked that the country be returned to daylight-saving time and called for the imposition of a nationwide speed limit of fifty miles an hour on federal highways.

I recalled the dedication that had characterized the Manhattan Project and the unity of spirit that had made the Apollo program a success. It was clear that when the American people decided a particular goal was worth reaching, they could surmount every obstacle to achieve it. Then I announced the beginning of Project Independence, with the goal of attaining energy independence for America by 1980.

Unfortunately only two of the proposals I requested—daylight-saving and a lowered speed limit—made it out of Congress before the Christmas recess. With the important exception of the Alaska pipeline bill, which I signed on November 16, Congress had failed to pass one major energy bill that I had requested.

Although the congressional response was disappointing, the American people rallied through the long winter months of 1973 and 1974. Conservation was working; but the crisis still existed. On November 25 I had to tighten controls still further, banning the sale of gasoline on Sunday, requesting cutbacks in outdoor lighting, and announcing that we were going to have a cutback on gasoline allocations by 15 percent in order to have enough heating oil.

The White House Christmas tree had 80 percent fewer lights that year. And instead of flying to California on *Air Force One* for the holiday season, Pat and I flew on a commercial airliner. We returned on a small Air Force Jetstar that had to make one refueling stop and got us back to the White House at 3 A.M.

Despite the truly valiant nationwide conservation effort, it was a long winter of energy discontent. Lines at gas stations lengthened. People had to get up in the early hours of cold mornings to get in line for fuel. Even then, a station might not open because its allotted shipment did not arrive. If it did open, it was often only a short time until the supply ran out.

Before long the energy crisis had generated a serious new economic crisis. As early as the spring of 1973 gasoline prices had taken the biggest leap in twenty-two years. The oil-producing countries had the leverage, and they were using it. The National Petroleum Council said that it feared the energy crisis might lead to a recession. The uncertainty began to snowball. A Harris poll showed that 54 percent thought we were heading into a recession. The stock market, which had topped a record high of 1000 at the start of my second term, was now down in the 800s. Every wild rumor gained some nervous credence: gasoline was going to rise to a dollar a gallon; bread would rise to a dollar a loaf. The Wholesale Price Index climbed 18.2 percent in 1973 and the Cost of Living Index registered the biggest rise since 1947. Most of these increases resulted directly from food and fuel prices.

There was no easy place to lay the blame. There was even a lingering disbelief on the part of many Americans that the crisis was real. But every report I received assured me that the crisis had not been contrived by the oil companies. The cause seemed clear: foreign oil imports had risen from $4 a barrel before the crisis to $12 a barrel afterward, and the domestic oil companies were passing on this increase to consumers.

Nor was there a particular school of economics to be made the scapegoat. Walter Heller, economic adviser to several Democratic administrations, said, "The energy crisis caught us with our parameters down.

The food crisis caught us too. . . . This was a year of infamy in inflation forecasting. There are many things we just don't know."

As the situation worsened the pressure for radical action—and specifically, for gas rationing—increased. Soon Senators Mansfield, Proxmire, and Jackson were spearheading a campaign to impose rationing. A number of governors also called for it, and before the winter was over they had been joined by several of my energy experts within the administration.

I strongly opposed this idea. My personal experience at the OPA had convinced me that rationing does not work well even in wartime when patriotism inspires sacrifice. I knew that in peacetime an enormous black market would develop and the entire program would become a fiasco. The huge bureaucracy required to implement rationing would cost millions of dollars, and, like any bureaucracy, it would be determined to perpetuate itself long after it was needed. I was sure that rationing would end up being a cure worse than the illness.

By January 19 I could report real progress: in the month of December national gas consumption was 9 percent below what had been predicted; use of electricity was down 10 percent; the federal government had actually cut back on its energy usage by more than 20 percent; and by executive action I had established a Federal Energy Office in the executive branch and placed Deputy Secretary of the Treasury Bill Simon in charge. Simon moved swiftly to impose a strong hand and was soon dubbed the nation's "energy Czar."

Congress had adjourned for the Christmas holidays without passing any of the legislation I requested, so I met its return in January 1974 with a new appeal for four short-term actions and eleven other priority requests. In my State of the Union address I warned that the energy crisis was now our foremost legislative concern.

From the moment the Arab oil embargo began we had worked unceasingly to end it. Kissinger discussed the problem with both King Faisal and President Sadat. After one of his meetings with Sadat in December, Kissinger sent me a memo describing how he had reminded Sadat of our unique role in bringing peace to the Middle East:

> I told Sadat that without your personal willingness to confront the domestic issue nothing would have been possible.
>
> Sadat promised me he would get the oil embargo lifted during the first half of January and said that he would call for its lifting in a statement which praised your personal role in bringing the parties to the negotiating table and making progress thereafter.

I followed up with a letter to Sadat on December 28:

> For my part, I pledge myself to do everything in my power to ensure that

> my second term as President will be remembered as the period in which the United States developed a new and productive relationship with Egypt and the Arab world. . . .
>
> However, the clearly discriminatory action of the oil producers can totally vitiate the effective contribution the United States is determined to make in the days ahead. Therefore, Mr. President, I must tell you in complete candor that it is essential that the oil embargo and oil production restrictions against the United States be ended at once. It cannot await the outcome of the current talks on disengagement.

A few weeks later, after the Egyptian-Israeli troop disengagement in January, we began urging Sadat even more insistently to help lift the embargo. At the end of the month he wrote to tell me that he had dispatched a special envoy to King Faisal and the other Arab leaders and that they had now agreed to lift the embargo, and a meeting to affirm this decision would be held in February. Unfortunately the meeting turned out to be a stalemate and the embargo continued.

Sadat soon sent me another message through our UN Delegate Shirley Temple Black, who had seen him privately. "I will lift the embargo," he told her. "I will lift it for President Nixon."

By mid-March there were reports that the embargo would be lifted conditionally, depending on the foreign policy behavior of the United States. I addressed these reports in a question-and-answer session in Chicago on March 15:

> The United States, as far as the embargo is concerned, is not going to be pressured by our friends in the Mideast or others who might be our opponents to doing something before we are able to do it. And I would only suggest that insofar as any action on the embargo is taken, that if it has any implications of pressure on the United States it would have a countereffect on our efforts to go forward on the peace front, the negotiation front, because it would simply slow down, in my opinion, our very real and earnest efforts to get the disengagement on the Syrian front and also to move towards a permanent settlement.

Finally on March 18, after almost six months, seven of the nine Arab states finally agreed to lift the oil embargo. The decision was not supposed to be conditional on American policy, but it was to be subject to review in June.

The Arab oil embargo caused America's economic output to decline by as much as $15 billion during the first quarter of 1974. But it can be said that the energy crisis of 1974 had at least one positive effect: it made energy consciousness a part of American life.

As the oil embargo was ending, Kissinger resumed his shuttle diplomacy. Now his goal was a Syrian-Israeli troop disengagement. By this time both he and I recognized that we were in a race against time before another incident, inadvertent or otherwise, further froze the Syrian and Israeli positions and perhaps even drew the Egyptians back into the conflict. We were also racing against growing uncertainty in the thinking of some of the Mideastern leaders as the impeachment turmoil steadily threatened to undermine my position. On March 21 I received a report from Henry J. Taylor, a columnist and former ambassador to Switzerland, who had recently seen Sadat. "I am very worried about the President," Sadat had told Taylor. "I need time," he added with concern. "I wonder if I am going to have it. I need six months. You know what I would like to do? I would like to come to Washington and fight for President Nixon."

A WAR OF ATTRITION

On Friday, March 1, John Mitchell, Bob Haldeman, John Ehrlichman, Chuck Colson, Robert Mardian, Gordon Strachan, and Kenneth Parkinson, who had been one of the CRP's lawyers, were indicted on charges of conspiracy and, except for Mardian, on charges of obstruction of justice. All but Parkinson, Colson, and Mardian were also charged with having given false testimony. On March 7 Colson, Ehrlichman, Liddy, and three others were indicted for the break-in at the office of Ellsberg's psychiatrist.

The indictments were not a surprise, but they were still a blow. These men were about to face trials in a city where it would be almost impossible for them to have an impartial jury; a poll taken in Washington showed that 84 percent of the people there already thought they were guilty.

Earlier in the year Haig told me that Jaworski had reassured him that no one currently in the White House was going to be named by the grand jury—including me. Instead, we thought, he was sending grand jury material relating to me to Judge Sirica in a sealed report. On March 18 Sirica directed that this material be sent to the House Judiciary Committee. He also stated that, contrary to recent leaks, the grand jury's report was only a straightforward compilation of evidence and drew no accusatory conclusions.

The political prospects for Republican members of the House and Senate who faced re-election in November 1974 continued to worsen. I believed that the two issues of prosperity in the domestic economy and peace in the world, the same two issues that had swayed off-year elections for as long as I had been in public life, would ultimately tip the balance in this one, too. But many prospective candidates apparently felt that Watergate was going to overshadow everything else and that they would have a better chance to win with Jerry Ford as President.

There were to be five special elections held in the first few months of 1974. Ordinarily these would have attracted only minor interest, but in the superheated climate of the time the media treated them as highly important and significant votes of confidence for me. Of the five, Republican candidates won only one.

On March 19, 1974, Republican Senator James Buckley of New York became the first of my major conservative supporters to call for my resignation. He told reporters that he feared the effects of the "melodrama" of a Senate trial, in which "the Chamber would become a twentieth-century Roman Colosseum, as the performers are thrown to the electronic lions."

I addressed myself to Buckley's point in a press conference that same day:

> While it might be an act of courage to run away from a job that you were elected to do, it also takes courage to stand and fight for what you believe is right, and that is what I intend to do. . . . From the stand-point of statesmanship, for a President of the United States, any President, to resign because of charges made against him which he knew were false and because he had fallen in the polls, I think would not be statesmanship. It might be good politics, but it would be bad statesmanship. And it would mean that our system of government would be changed for all Presidents and all generations in the future.

Four days earlier at a question-and-answer session in Chicago I addressed a similar question by recalling that Senator Fulbright had once demanded Truman's resignation when he was at a low point of his popularity. "Some of the best decisions ever made by Presidents," I said, "were made when they were not too popular."

In March and April I knew that what had been at best only a remote chance to block impeachment in the House Judiciary Committee had now become almost nonexistent. When Chairman Peter Rodino addressed the House of Representatives on February 6—the day of a resolution ratifying the impeachment inquiry—he had said: "We are going to work expeditiously and fairly. . . . Whatever the result, whatever we learn or conclude, let us now proceed with such care and decency and thoroughness and honor that the vast majority of the American people and their children after them will say, 'That was the right course. There was no other way.' "

Among the members of the committee who sat solemnly by when Rodino said this was John Conyers of Michigan, who had already told the Washington *Star* on March 17, that talk of conscience, evidence, and constitutional factors was "all crap." In the New York *Times Magazine* on April 28 he had described his role on the committee as "making sure Rodino doesn't get *too* damn fair." Another member was Father Robert Drinan of Massachusetts, who had urged impeachment for nearly a year and was frequently seen wearing an "Impeach Nixon" button on his clerical lapel. Robert Kastenmeier of Wisconsin had decorated his office with "Impeach Nixon" bumper strips. Charles Rangel of New York had been quoted by the Associated Press as saying, "There is no doubt in my mind that the President of the United States is a criminal." And Jerome Waldie of California had opened a letter to his constituents by thanking them "for supporting my efforts to impeach President Nixon." These were some of the committee members who, in Rodino's view, were going to proceed with "care and decency and thoroughness and honor" in their investigations into whether the evidence would justify the framing of articles of impeachment against me.

The Democratic majority chose John Doar as their counsel. Renata Adler, who served as one of Doar's aides, has since written in *Atlantic Monthly* that he had advocated my impeachment "months before he became special counsel, long before the inquiry began."

In March, James St. Clair wrote to Doar asking to participate in the hearings and to cross-examine witnesses. The committee finally and reluctantly agreed to allow St. Clair to participate in the closed sessions and to question witnesses, although it would not allow him to cross-examine them. When St. Clair wrote asking if he could see the grand jury material that Sirica had sent to the committee, he was refused.

On March 7 I dictated a memo to Haig in which I said that as far as the impeachment inquiry was concerned, "the law case will be decided by the PR case." That was what I felt we had to get across to St. Clair, Buzhardt, and our supporters in Congress. On March 15 I wrote another note: "St. Clair sees it too much as a trial, not a public relations exercise. We must work on him to get him to understand what we are up against."

My failure to use the State of the Union speech to draw the line firmly once and for all as far as providing more tapes was concerned proved to be the error I had feared it would be. Jaworski on one side, and now the House Judiciary Committee on the other, kept pressuring us for more and more. The Ervin Committee, whose initial request for five taped conversations had been rejected by the court, issued a new series of subpoenas for some 500 tapes and thousands of documents.

We had voluntarily turned over tapes in a civil case brought by Ralph Nader. Nader's lawyer, William Dobrovir, took a copy of one of these tapes and played it, as he was later quoted, "just for fun," at a cocktail party in Georgetown. The Special Prosecutor's office was outraged, but Dobrovir excused himself by saying that it had been an impulsive mistake. He was contradicted by his hostess, who said that he had told her in advance of his plan to bring the tape and play it and that she had told at least one of the guests about it beforehand. Dobrovir had also played the tape for a CBS television news reporter.

In December Jaworski came to us with a plea for access to another group of tapes. Haig told me that Jaworski had assured him that this would be his last request for tapes relating to the break-in and cover-up, and, on this assurance, we yielded. Thus, as of January 8, 1974, every request for tapes or documents that Jaworski had made had been met.

On January 8 and 9 St. Clair received letters asking for more than forty additional tapes—twenty-five of them relating to the break-in and cover-up. Haig was surprised, shocked, and disillusioned by Jaworski's action.

St. Clair wrote Jaworski and reminded him of the specific narrowness of the court ruling requiring us to surrender the nine subpoenaed tapes. Nor could Jaworski maintain that he needed these new tapes in order to obtain Watergate convictions: the year-end report of the Special Prosecution Force stated that enough evidence had been received to consider major indictments, and a prosecutor is not supposed to recommend an indictment unless he feels he already has the evidence needed to get a conviction. Two weeks later Jaworski trapped himself with his own words. In an interview he thought was off the record he revealed that as far as he was concerned, his office already "had the full story of Watergate." St. Clair told Jaworski that I would not give up any more tapes. Jaworski met with St. Clair and seemed to give him yet another assurance that this one additional request would be the last. Haig also met with Jaworski and reported that he was being very expansive and cooperative in evaluating the situation. My notes on Haig's report show these as the major points made by Jaworski:

1. Jaworski had told Haig that the staff he had inherited from Cox had a number of "fanatics" on it and that he was having great difficulty in keeping them under control.
2. Jaworski told Haig that Haldeman was worse off than Ehrlichman. He told him that he was prepared to let Ehrlichman off easy, but that Ehrlichman's attorney had taken too tough a line and, consequently, he had no choice but to proceed against Ehrlichman in the same way that he was proceeding on the charges against Haldeman.
3. Jaworski made what Haig and I considered to be a very interesting comment that "Sirica was really a friend of the President." Sirica, he felt, would not like the attitude of the members of his, Jaworski's, staff who were, in his

view, more interested in "getting the President" than in getting the facts.
4. Jaworski disliked Rodino and considered him "publicity mad."
5. Jaworski liked St. Clair.
6. With regard to the additional tapes and documents that Jaworski had just requested, he urged Haig to give him "the softest possible turn-down," and Haig said that we ought to "use Vaseline" in responding to these requests and in handling Jaworski.

On February 13 St. Clair wrote to Jaworski again, saying that he hoped he would have reconsidered the broad scope of his request, and, for the second time, respectfully declining the request for more than forty additional tapes.

Jaworski immediately wrote to Senator Eastland, the Chairman of the Senate Judiciary Committee, acknowledging that he could bring indictments on the evidence he had, but arguing that new tapes "may contain" evidence necessary for future trials. This kind of reasoning could be applied to any and all documents in the presidential files. It was hard to see where, if anywhere, Jaworski would ever draw a line.

The escalating pattern seemed never ending. Because of the original Special Prosecutor's request we had turned over eight conversations; we had also given the prosecutors more than 700 documents. We had voluntarily provided access to seventeen additional tapes since the first court ruling. Now they were back asking for more than forty more.

The House Judiciary Committee would prove no different from the Special Prosecutor in its insatiable demands for tapes and other materials. On March 6 I announced that we would turn over to the committee all the materials we had given to the Special Prosecutor; these comprised some nineteen tapes and more than 700 documents. I also agreed to provide literally boxloads of documents requested by the committee from departments and agencies, ranging from meetings of the Cost of Living Council to high-level sessions on import quotas. I agreed to answer in writing and under oath any question from the committee. I also indicated that I was willing to be interviewed under oath, if that was deemed necessary.

At this time the committee's range of investigations covered scores of policy and political areas—from the secret Cambodian bombing in 1969 to the Cost of Living Council's decisions about the price of hamburger. And the list was still growing.

Before the committee had narrowed down any of its areas of investigation into anything like specific charges against me, and before it had even looked at the 700 documents or listened to the nineteen tapes, a letter was sent demanding over forty more tapes.

I met with House Republican Leader John Rhodes, and he agreed that the committee's request was extremely broad. He confided that some of the committee members had not even known all Doar was doing. But Rhodes was emphatic when he said that, as unjust as it undoubtedly was, no Republican congressman could afford to defend a refusal by the White House to produce any additional evidence the committee requested.

I had to face the fact that we were over a barrel and that my weakened political situation gave the Judiciary Committee license for an unrestrained fishing expedition. I had no practical choice but to comply with their demands. If I refused, they would vote me in contempt of Congress. I made a note on March 22, 1974, at 2 A.M.: "Lowest day. Contempt equals impeachment."

Since the first of the year impeachment had been like a shifting sea. One day it would be calm, and there would seem to be a chance we could survive. The next day it would turn stormy and survival seemed unlikely. By the end of March almost every day was stormy. In New York, John Mitchell and Maury Stans were on trial in the Vesco case. Some news reports from the trial implied that John Dean had been unrattled in his testimony, whereas Stans and Mitchell had seemed shaken and had not been very effective. Ultimately, both Stans and Mitchell were found innocent, and the jurors told the press that it was Dean they had not believed. But we did not know that in March when the impeachment hearings were gearing up.

The bombshell of my having to pay $400,000 in new taxes because of the disallowance of the deduction for my donation of my papers was still reverberating, and we had just been hit with the leaks that Brooks's subcommittee was charging that $17 million of government funds had been spent on my personal property. The court-appointed tape "experts" had also recently issued one of their series of reports on the 18½-minute gap. In California, John Ehrlichman, on trial for the break-in at Ellsberg's psychiatrist's office, asked and obtained a court subpoena for me to appear at the trial.

We had also received word that John Connally was about to be drawn into a grand jury investigation over illegal contributions alleged to have been made to him from milk producers' organizations. In normal times the Justice Department would not have considered moving against a former Secretary of the Treasury, three-term Governor, and Secretary of the Navy solely on the basis of a highly unreliable informant who succeeded in having the Special Prosecutor's office drop serious charges being brought against him in a totally unrelated matter. But these were not ordinary times. Whenever I met with Connally, he would brush off his own troubles. He was innocent, he said, and there was no way that he could ever be found otherwise. He turned out to be right: in 1975 he was ultimately acquitted on all charges. But in the meantime this was another numbing blow. "Just one time," I said to Ziegler, "will we ever just one time get a break in this long, tortuous year?"

On April 13, for the first time, the Harris poll reported a bare majority, 43 percent to 41 percent, was now in favor of my impeachment.

Haig, Buzhardt, St. Clair, and I decided that because of the political realities of the situation, we had to compromise on the House Judiciary Committee's request for more tapes. We decided to supply the committee with written verbatim transcripts from which only material unrelated to Watergate had been excised. This ultimately became the "Blue Book," a massive, 1,300-page document officially titled *Submission of Recorded Presidential Conversations to the Committee on the Judiciary of the House of Representatives by President Richard Nixon.* Our hope was that this response might, through its sheer bulk, bring home to the public what was being asked of me.

It soon became clear that there were many gray areas in the conversations—material not entirely unrelated to "Watergate," as that term had constantly expanded in meaning—but unrelated to my knowledge and action on the cover-up, which were the issues actually before the committee.

Buzhardt suggested the phrase "Material Unrelated to Presidential Action Deleted," which was typed in the Blue Book transcripts wherever such a deletion was made. In order to verify our decisions in this regard, we offered to invite Rodino and the ranking Republican on the committee, Edward Hutchinson of Michigan, to come to the White House and hear any of the uncut original tapes they chose.

Before we could even complete the Blue Book in response to the House Judiciary Committee's request for 42 tapes, we received a letter requesting 142 more tapes and documents relating to Watergate, the Huston Plan, Daniel Ellsberg, wiretaps, and the visit of Judge Byrne to San Clemente. Not long after this, Peter Rodino warned that the committee might soon be asking for still more tapes and documents dealing with my income taxes, the San Clemente property, campaign dirty tricks, and other matters.

Just before midnight on April 20 I made a note:

D Day
1. Any more tapes will destroy the office.
2. Leaving the question open will only invite more unreasonable demands.
3. Better to fight and lose defending the office than surrender and win a personal victory at disastrous long-range cost to the office of the presidency.

At nine o'clock on the night of April 29 I made a televised address in which I announced that I was yielding the transcripts of the tapes requested by the House Judiciary Committee so that the committee could reach an informed judgment and because the American people were entitled to the facts and the evidence that demonstrated those facts. I said that I hoped that by violating the principle of confidentiality this once I could restore it for the future.

I said that the transcripts I was releasing included all the relevant portions of the subpoenaed conversations, "the rough as well as the smooth, the strategy sessions, the exploration of alternatives, the weighing of human and political costs. . . . These materials—together with those already made available—will tell it all."

Then I continued:

> I realize that these transcripts will provide grist for many sensational stories in the press. Parts will seem to be contradictory with one another and parts will be in conflict with some of the testimony given in the Senate Watergate Committee hearings.
>
> I have been reluctant to release these tapes not just because they will embarrass me and those with whom I have talked—which they will—and not just because they will become the subject of speculation and even ridicule—which they will—and not just because certain parts of them will be seized upon by political and journalistic opponents—which they will.
>
> I have been reluctant because, in these and in all the other conversations in this office, people have spoken their minds freely, never dreaming that specific sentences or even parts of sentences would be picked out as the subjects of national attention and controversy. . . .
>
> I am confident that the American people will see these transcripts for what they are, fragmentary records from a time more than a year ago that now seems very distant, the records of a President and of a man suddenly being confronted and having to cope with information which, if true, would have the most far-reaching consequences not only for his personal reputation but, more important, for his hopes, his plans, his goals for the people who had elected him as their leader.
>
> In giving you these records—blemishes and all—I am placing my trust in the basic fairness of the American people.
>
> I know in my own heart that through the long, painful, and difficult process revealed in these transcripts I was trying in that period to discover what was right and to do what was right.

It is not possible to describe what it is like to see long-forgotten conversations suddenly reappear as lengthy transcripts. We are conditioned to think of the written word as a form of planned communication, and when the words of an ordinary conversation are put on paper they acquire a rigidity that, despite a literal accuracy in terms of what was said, may completely fail to capture or reflect the nature of the meeting or conversation as it actually took place. An observation can seem like an intention; an offhand comment appears deliberate and premeditated; a passing thought can strike the reader as a prescription for action. Seeing the words there in lifeless type on a page, you realize that there is no way to explain how at one moment in a discussion one person is a devil's advocate and the next moment the roles all shift. Outsiders reading only the words of those conversations about Watergate could know nothing of the torment, the spectrum of concern that lay behind them. More than for the substance, the transcripts would be criticized for the tone of the discussions.

Much of the impact of Watergate throughout the past year had come from the fact that it was breaking new ground in the political awareness of the American people by introducing them to things like government-authorized wiretaps and break-ins, White House taping systems, and the political use of the IRS. As much as many may have suspected beforehand that such things took place, I had to bear the brunt of having revealed the particulars that confirmed those suspicions.

And so it was with the Blue Book transcripts. The American myth that Presidents are always presidential, that they sit in the Oval Office talking in lofty and quotable phrases, will probably never die—and probably never should, because it reflects an important aspect of the American character.

But the reality of politics and power in the White House is very different. It is a rough game, and the men I have known who have made it there reflect the ability to play rough when necessary and come out on top. There is noble talk in the Oval Office to be sure, high-minded and disinterested. But there are also frustration, worry, anxiety, profanity and, above all, raw pragmatism when it comes to politics and political survival.

With the Blue Book transcripts, as with so many other Watergate revelations, I was in the position of telling the American people things that they did not want to know.

The reaction to the Blue Book was oddly delayed. On May 3, four days after it had been released, I went to a rally in Phoenix. A crowd of 15,000 had gathered inside the auditorium, and when a group of about 150 demonstrators started yelling "Out now," they were shouted into silence. Afterward, at a reception at Barry Goldwater's mountaintop house, both he and John Rhodes came up individually to say how pleased they were with the reception and to assure me that I could continue to count on their support.

By the time I had returned to Camp David from this cross-country swing, however, a surge of negative reaction to the Blue Book had begun to register. Hugh Scott denounced its contents as a "deplorable, shabby, disgusting, and immoral performance by all." The *Wall Street Journal* said editorially that while it could see no good grounds in the transcripts for recommending impeachment, "Still, there is such a thing as moral leadership . . . the 'bully pulpit.' This is what Mr. Nixon has sacrificed for once and all." The Chicago *Tribune* called for my resignation, while other old friends, including the Omaha *World-Herald*, the Kansas City *Times*, the Cleveland *Plain Dealer*, and the Charlotte *Observer*, echoed their sentiments or even endorsed impeachment. They were joined by the Los Angeles *Times*, the Miami *Herald*, and the Providence *Journal*. Jerry Ford felt that he had to make a comment on the transcripts, so he said, "They don't exactly confer sainthood on anyone," and he admitted that he was disappointed by them.

More and more Republicans began to talk about resignation. John Rhodes, his mind apparently changed from just a few days earlier, now said he would accept my decision to resign if I were to make it. He said that my chances of winning in the House had been steadily reduced; at the moment he put the percentage at 51 to 49 against impeachment. John Anderson, the Chairman of the House Republican Conference, suggested that I consider resigning. In the Senate, Marlow Cook of Kentucky and Richard Schweiker of Pennsylvania called for outright resignation, and Milton Young of North Dakota said I should use the Twenty-fifth Amendment to step aside until I had been proved innocent. Barry Goldwater drew attention when he said he was sure I would resign if I were impeached by the House.

I was determined not to panic. I would respect everyone's views and understand the necessity they felt to express them. But I would not quit.

Haig was stunned by the swell of criticism. He said that the combination of the Chicago *Tribune* editorial and Scott's and Rhodes's statements suggested to him a calculated effort to force me out of office. He worried further about news reports of an "informal" conversation Jerry Ford had had with reporters in which he was quoted as having described his concern that my authority had been "crippled" and that Russia might try to take advantage of this situation. Ford was reported to have said that my failing influence could be seen in Teddy Kennedy's successful efforts to secure a congressional cutback on aid to Vietnam, and that he had talked to Kissinger about these concerns but not to me. After this report was published, Ford issued a "clarification," but the damage was done.

Soon the resignation rumors started taking wild turns: there was a report that Ford had asked his staff to go on "red alert," and another that I was going to step down within forty-eight hours and that Kissinger was about to fly back from the Middle East to receive the letter of resignation. There was even a rumor that I had had a stroke.

In an effort to scotch these rumors Haig told reporters that I would consider resignation only if I thought it was in the best interests of the country, and Ziegler released a statement that I had personally approved:

> The city of Washington is full of rumors. All that have been presented to

> me today are false, and the one that heads the list is the one that says President Nixon intends to resign. His attitude is one of determination that he will not be driven out of office by rumor, speculation, excessive charges, or hypocrisy. He is up for the battle, he intends to fight it and he feels he has a personal and constitutional duty to do so.

The Blue Book proved conclusively that I had not known about the break-in in advance, and that Dean was wrong when he said that he and I had discussed the cover-up over a period of months. On the other hand, it undercut the impression I had left in my public statements that I had reacted like a prosecutor when Dean informed me of the cover-up. But however damaging any or all of it may have been, nothing on the tapes amounted to an impeachable offense.

Unfortunately the main Watergate issue had already shifted, and, as had been the case throughout the past thirteen months, I was in the position of settling a point after everyone had already moved on to another one. The release of the transcripts was good strategy to the extent that it proved conclusively that Dean had not told the truth about everything; and to the extent that it showed that in the areas where he had told the truth, my actions and omissions, while regrettable and possibly indefensible, were not impeachable.

But public opinion is not a court of law, and there would be no trial on this evidence. This was politics, and the effect of the Blue Book was to force Republicans even further into a political corner with me. The transcripts raised the distinctions that responsible congressmen would have to make between what was constitutionally impeachable and what was politically insupportable.

The Blue Book itself would be undermined in early July when the House Judiciary Committee, after suggesting that we had deliberately dropped the most damaging sections from some of the tapes, released its own book of transcripts.

In fact, most of the discrepancies between the committee's version and ours were minor ones that arose because the committee arranged to have its copies of the tapes electronically enhanced, and consequently picked up many words that we had described as "unintelligible." Some of these additional words or sentences helped our case more than hurt it.

But there was one admittedly serious discrepancy that dominated all the others. It was the section of the March 22 tape covering my final discussion with John Mitchell, in which I told him that unlike Eisenhower who cared only that he was "clean," I cared about the men. I told Mitchell that they could go before the Ervin Committee and "stonewall it, let them plead the Fifth Amendment, cover up, or anything else" if they thought they had to. Then I added, "On the other hand, I would prefer . . . that you do it the other way." This section was not in our version of the transcripts.

Transcripts Link Nixon to Cover-up was the Washington *Post* headline when the Judiciary Committee revealed the discrepancy. It was utterly ridiculous to assume that we would have deliberately omitted a damaging section of a tape that we knew the Judiciary Committee already had in its possession. But we took terrible heat for it at the time because we simply did not know what had happened. Only months later, when it no longer mattered, did Fred Buzhardt figure out the answer. Apparently, according to Buzhardt, the committee's copies of the tapes must have been copied from the originals at a higher volume, with the result that the final section of the March 22 tape, which was inaudible on our copy—and evidently also on the Special Prosecutor's copy, which had been made at the same volume level—could be heard on the committee's copy. The bitter irony was that this innocent discrepancy had made us look both sinister and foolish.

On May 5, in the middle of the uproar over the Blue Book, Al Haig met with Leon Jaworski in the Map Room at the White House. Jaworski told Haig that I had been named an unindicted coconspirator by the Watergate grand jury. If this was true, then Jaworski had not been honest with Haig earlier in the year when he had told him that no one in the White House had been named.

We knew Jaworski had doubted whether I could constitutionally be indicted while I was President. But he knew that by naming me an unindicted coconspirator he would have a wild card to produce in the courts when he needed it to get more tapes and to guarantee that he could use the tapes in the Watergate trials. Later Archibald Cox, of all people, would denounce Jaworski's action, calling the technique he used "just a back-handed way of sticking the knife in." By having me charged by the grand jury, a forum that could not judge me, he could prejudice me before the House Judiciary Committee, the forum that could.

Jaworski had a deal to propose: he told Haig that if we would give him eighteen of the sixty-four tapes he had subpoenaed, leaving open the possibility that defendants would request additional ones in the trials, he would drop his suit for the rest and not reveal at this time that the grand jury had named me an unindicted coconspirator. If I would not agree to what he called his "compromise," he was going to announce the grand jury's action in open court in order to strengthen the case against me.

Even after taking so many low blows from so many sources over so many months, I was still surprised that Jaworski would resort to what I felt was a form of blackmail. But the thought of actually ending the courtroom battle over the tapes was like a siren song. Haig felt it too. He said, "We're at the point that we can see the barbed wire at the end of the street. What we have to do is mobilize everything to cut through it." St. Clair, however, was opposed to the so-called compromise; he felt that to cave now would forfeit our position that we would give no more.

Haig urged me at least to listen to the eighteen tapes and not reject the offer out of hand. I returned from Camp David in the evening of May 5, 1974, and went to the EOB office shortly after eight o'clock to begin this task.

I worked until late that night and for several hours the next morning listening to more tapes. I broke just before midday for some appointments and a talk with Scowcroft about the situation in the Middle East. In the afternoon I listened to the tape of my June 23, 1972, conversation with Haldeman—the tape that would emerge publicly three months later as the "smoking gun." I heard Haldeman tell me that Dean and Mitchell had come up with a plan to handle the problem of the investigation's going into areas we didn't want it to go. The plan was to call in Helms and Walters of the CIA and have them restrain the FBI.

I listened further and heard myself asking if Mitchell had known about "this thing to any much of a degree." "I think so. I don't think he knew the details, but I think he knew," Haldeman had answered. His voice did not have a great deal of conviction when he said it, but there he was, a week after the break-in, telling me that he thought Mitchell knew.

I had indicated in all my public statements that the sole motive for calling in the CIA had been national security. But there was no doubt now that we had been talking about political implications that morning. I thought back to my discussion with Haldeman about this very problem in May 1973, when he had insisted that our only motive had been the national security concern that the FBI's investigation might expose CIA operations. I knew he believed it completely then, and so had I. I also knew that no one would ever believe it now. I consoled myself with the thought that there must be other things that were not apparent on these tapes, things that would explain our later belief that we had been thinking about national security. The city was now full of new reports—and provocative new questions—about the CIA's apparent awareness of the break-in before it happened and about its activities during the cover-up. Surely we could not have been so wrong as to have completely rationalized a national security concern where none existed. I thought that perhaps there would be something else, something helpful on another tape.

In the afternoon I talked to Scowcroft, who sent in a report from Kissinger. My letter to Mrs. Meir had apparently had some effect and the Israelis had presented a peace proposal that Kissinger thought had a chance of actually being accepted by the moderate Arab governments.

I wrote across the bottom of the page: "Personal message to K from RN: You are doing a superb job against great odds—regardless of the outcome. But let us hope and work for the best."

The contents of the June 23, 1972, tape were not my primary reason for deciding against Jaworski's "compromise." In another example of miscalculation I did not recognize the tape then as the "smoking gun" it turned out to be. I knew that it would hurt—but so had so many other things, and we had survived them. And perhaps the Court would rule in our favor; in the meantime I did not feel others should listen and have to be answerable for what they heard.

Now I can see that I should have asked Buzhardt to listen to all three June conversations with Haldeman, give me his independent judgment on them, and then have put them out—even though they were in several respects inconsistent with Haldeman's and my public statements of our recollection of the purpose of the meetings. That would have been damaging, but far less so than being forced to make the tapes public after the Supreme Court's decision compelled me to do so.

By this time, however, I had come around to St. Clair's and Buzhardt's view that we should draw the line on producing any further tapes. My instinct was still that we had to put a stop to it.

On Wednesday I notified them both that I had decided not to give up any more tapes. "Perhaps this is Armageddon," I told Ziegler, "but I would rather leave fighting for a principle." That afternoon St. Clair called Jaworski and told him my decision. On May 22 I sent a letter to the House Judiciary Committee informing them that I would not supply any more tapes in response to the constantly escalating requests for them. Now the lines were drawn. April 26 had been a symbolic milestone: if I succeeded in completing my full term as President I would be in the White House for one thousand more days. May 22 was another milestone: with this letter to the House Judiciary Committee, whatever happened, I was about to begin the last leg of the Watergate road.

In January 1973 Washington observers had predicted that I could count on having a margin of between 74 and 125 votes on an impeachment resolution in the House. By March 1974, this margin had been badly worn down by House Judiciary Committee accusations and the attacks on my finances. After the Blue Book was released, Timmons reported a defection of at least twenty-five House members. In mid-May Jerry Ford said that the odds that the committee would vote impeachment were 50–50. The atmosphere spawned more rumors. Now that few people seemed to care about the question of who had ordered the break-in, there was new information that the Democrats themselves had prior knowledge and that the Hughes organization might be involved. And there were stories of strange alliances. In mid-May I received a call from Connally. He had known Jaworski in Texas, and he said he was calling to pass along something Jaworski had told him. The message was: "The President has no friends in the White House."

But then the tide seemed to change, and by June it looked as if things were actually beginning to brighten. Whatever other reasons there might have been, a major one was that the Judiciary Committee's patently unfair tactics had started to backfire.

Rodino had opened the committee's investigation of the evidence with the announcement that the proceedings would be governed by rules of confidentiality. After this announcement the committee had voted itself into closed sessions and then promptly started to leak everything that came into its hands. Every tape was labeled "highly damaging" by the partisans on the committee; my finances were described as even "more explosive." When St. Clair requested that the committee go into open sessions rather than continue its prejudicial game, he was rebuffed.

One of the clearest examples of the committee's conduct was a leak about my diary dictation for the night of March 21, 1973, the day that Dean had described the "cancer" growing close to the presidency. Committee leakers told UPI that I had dictated: "Today is March 21. It wasn't a very eventful day." This leak, which indicated that I was totally blasé about the information Dean had given me—presumably because I was already part of the cover-up—went out over the networks and wires. In fact, what I had dictated was: "As far as the day was concerned it was uneventful, except for the talk with Dean."

The leaks, the posturing, the publicity-mad behavior of the House Judiciary Committee members and staff undermined all their talk about "fairness." At the same time the highly emotional first reaction to the contents and language of the Blue Book transcripts had run its course. On June 5 Timmons reported that Tom Railsback of Illinois, one of the swing Republicans on the committee, was saying that the evidence was simply not overwhelming in the way it would have to be in order to justify impeachment. Robert McClory of Illinois, another Republican, said optimistically that the committee was now evenly divided: eleven votes for impeachment, eleven against, and sixteen on the fence. John Rhodes called me to say that he had found that the attitude in the House and on the Judiciary Committee had grown more positive over the past week. St. Clair said that his experience always told him when things were going bad because there was what he called a "smell of guilt in the courtroom." He said, "There just isn't a smell of guilt in that committee."

There were also reports of new grass roots organizations cropping up across the country to help me. And Haig had finally started to organize the staff into task forces to fight impeachment.

On June 7, 1974, I resumed making detailed diary dictations at the end of each day. I began the first one by summing up the situation as it had appeared at the start of the summer.

Diary

I am not going to try to recap the events of this very difficult time, but will try to put some of the immediate developments in perspective and include some observations with regard to various collateral issues that have arisen.

I have kept in almost daily touch with Timmons in the past couple of weeks, and he believes that we have been gaining slowly but surely among both the Southerners and the Republicans.

Teddy White, interestingly enough, had talked to Rose and then had talked to Ziegler today. He said that two weeks ago he thought that the House would have voted an impeachment and that we would have won in the Senate by a margin of five or six votes. Now he believes that, as he puts it, we have bottomed out and that the House will not vote impeachment if a vote were to occur today.

John Connally strongly held the same opinion. Connally believes, for example, that those who vote for impeachment will find that the next time they come up for election they will be wiped out. Of course, we have been thinking for over a year now that the tide was turning, and then events occur which seem to put us behind the eight ball again.

What will motivate the House members at the present time I think may be their concern that if they impeach, they run the risk of taking the responsibility for whatever goes wrong in foreign and domestic policy after that. They also may be concerned from the Democratic standpoint that if they impeach, they put in office as an incumbent Ford, who would have a united party and an administration behind him against whoever they ran for President. This the Democratic pros must not look to with any relish.

On the plus side, the 18½-minute-gap matter I think is being resolved fairly satisfactorily, although we never know what Jaworski may do.

Bebe is going through another intensive going over with, he said, about a hundred subpoenas to his restaurants, the yacht club, etc. What this poor man has gone through is really unbelievable and it is amazing that he has been able to stand up as well as he has.

I saw Don and Eddie after the luncheon for [Prince] Fahd [of Saudi Arabia]. Both brothers have stood up splendidly under torturous conditions. Don has about forty thousand dollars in legal bills. Eddie has one of twenty thousand for legal fees.

Al Haig told me that the Senate Watergate Committee had a pretty devastating report on Humphrey and also one on Mills.

The Republicans have it, but no one of the Republicans, of course, will leak it. The trouble is that the Republicans, like conservatives generally, are responsible and play with Marquis of Queensberry rules, whereas the liberals go just the other way.

The irony of this whole situation is that we are being accused of playing a foul game during the election and so forth, whereas what we have done as compared with previous administrations is hardly worth mentioning, but with the double standard that exists in the media, anything that comes out that hurts the conservatives, and particularly the President, gets enormous play—anything that comes out against one of the Democrats gets a one-day play and then is dropped.

I think one thing that seems to disturb our opponents in the media, in the Congress, and in partisan circles the most is that I have hung on. As I look back over the year, I don't know quite how I have done it. I have had times of considerable discouragement although I have pretty generally been able to cover it so people are unable to see it.

I remember, looking clear back, in May 1973 I think it was, while we were in the swimming pool in Florida, and David was sitting in the Jacuzzi, and he said that he had been thinking about all these things and he felt that all that was necessary was for me to "persevere," as he put it. And that is, of course, about all we've been doing—persevering.

Looking back over the year and just highlighting the events, the mistakes are quite apparent. First, the April 30 speech. Possibly the decision on Haldeman–Ehrlichman was right, although I am not absolutely sure that it was under the circumstances now.

But going on from there, certainly the first major mistake was the appointment of Richardson as Attorney General. Richardson's weakness, which came to light during the Cox firing, should have been apparent.

Then, of course, came the bombshell of the tapes. This occurred, unfortunately, while I was out at the hospital, and I remember when Haig came in and told me about it and we discussed it. Later Agnew came in and said, maybe you ought to destroy them. Frankly, we thought about it. We should have done it, because none had been subpoenaed at that time. But here Garment, I think primarily, stepped in with the idea that it would be a destruction of evidence or what have you. But all the sorrow and difficulties we have had about the eighteen minutes and the so-called two missing tapes, and, of course, then the tapes themselves and the Supreme Court case would have been avoided had we just bitten the bullet then. But having failed to do so we went on down the line.

The Agnew resignation was necessary although a very serious blow, because while some thought that his stepping aside would take some of the pressure off the effort to get the President, all it did was to open the way to put pressure on the President to resign as well. This is something we have to realize: that any accommodation with opponents in this kind of a fight does not satisfy—it only brings on demands for more.

Of course, the Cox firing probably was the right thing to do even with all the pain and suffering that it caused because, according to Buzhardt and others, Cox was ready to indict the President at that time and that could have been at a time that it could have had a fatal effect with the House, even though our public standing then was probably somewhat higher than it is now.

I think what has irritated me the most has been the handling of my personal finances. We have an excellent case, but we simply couldn't get a proper hearing on it.

On May 20, 1974, the district court hearing Jaworski's suit for the sixty-four new tapes ruled in his favor. I decided to appeal the decision. Jaworski immediately moved to bypass the court of appeals, requesting that the Supreme Court take the case directly. On May 31 the Supreme Court agreed to Jaworski's unusual request. This meant that a final decision could come in as little as a month.

By the end of May Kissinger had spent thirty-two days traveling back and forth between Jerusalem and Damascus in the long and often frustrating attempt to achieve a disengagement between Syrian and Israeli troops. The Egyptian-Israeli disengagement had been easier because Sadat had adopted the attitude that if the major issues could be resolved, the minor ones could be settled at the ongoing Geneva Conference. But the hatred between the Syrians and the Israelis went too deep for them to be able to think this way.

Kissinger was at his finest in these sessions, probing like a surgeon the concerns that separated the two parties, indefatigably seeking the areas of mutual interest that would make an accord possible.

But on May 16 Scowcroft brought Haig a message from Kissinger that he was coming back; he had done the superhuman and it still was not enough. I sent back a firm message of encouragement directing that he give it one more try. I knew he was exhausted, but he was too close to a settlement to let the momentum slacken.

On May 22 I wrote Mrs. Meir to "urge that you and your Cabinet make a supreme effort to seek a compromise which would permit an agreement on the disengagement of forces on the Golan Heights and enable us to move another step away from strife and bloodshed."

On May 29 the prize was won. The impossible had been achieved. Both Israel and Syria accepted the terms, and the disengagement agreement was signed on May 31.

The next step in the American effort had to be an attempt to consolidate the new trust and extend the new dialogue. It was important to move fast while the momentum was still fresh. Plans were therefore activated for a series of major summits in the Mideast. I decided to make personal visits to Egypt, Syria, Saudi Arabia, Jordan, and Israel to help firm up the gains we had made and to lay the groundwork for more progress in the future.

While Kissinger was forging the Syrian-Israeli disengagement, the House Judiciary Committee turned to the topics of wiretaps and the Plumbers. Kissinger had already testified before the Senate Foreign Relations Committee about both subjects, but now the House Judiciary Committee had been given the materials on the case and was treating them with characteristic irresponsibility. The committee began a systematic series of leaks implying that there were discrepancies in Kissinger's statements. Several Foreign Relations Committee members reaffirmed their belief in Kissinger's veracity, but the press would not let up. Early in his first press conference after his shuttle tour de force the questions took an ugly and accusatory turn. He was asked about reports that he had given false testimony to the Foreign Relations Committee and whether he had obtained a lawyer because of the prospect of perjury. His jaw angrily set, Kissinger fired back, "I do not conduct my office as a conspiracy."

This sudden attack on his character and truthfulness, added to the strains of a month of tense shuttling between Israel and Syria, set Kissinger's nerves on edge. He kept his composure during the press conference, but afterward he was shaken and disillusioned. As he analyzed the situation, he was the major symbol of the positive foreign policy accomplishments of the Nixon administration; even while the full-scale attempt to impeach me was under way, he had had the effrontery to show the nation and the world that the United States under my leadership was still able to command respect in the world and achieve significant results despite the drag of Watergate. I agreed with this analysis completely: the voracious forces of the opposition could not allow that to continue.

THE MIDEAST TRIP

Shortly before leaving for the Mideast on June 10, 1974, I dictated two notes about the way the domestic situation had developed.

Diary

As the week ends and as the trip begins, there seems to be a feeling that the momentum is changing somewhat, although we have felt this before and have been disappointed.

One thought that has occurred to me, which I developed at Camp David as I took a walk down the nature trail on a very muddy path, is that from now until approximately the first of August when the Supreme Court will rule, the thing to do is to just treat every day as basically the last one and not to be constantly concerned about what may happen in the future. I have tried to do this over the past year and a half, but it has been very difficult at times because we seem always to be fighting the battle or trying to deal with some new development.

But all in all, looking back over this last fifteen or sixteen months, to me the great tragedy is that it seems to be a year and a half almost that is lost. We have accomplished some good things but I have had to spend an inordinate amount of my time thinking about this problem, and, of course, emotionally it has taken a great deal out of me. We certainly have made our mistakes but perhaps the year has taught us all somewhat more compassion and understanding, although I must say that it has also brought clearly to light the unbelievable battle in which we are engaged and how high the stakes are and how bitter and fanatical the opposition is. We simply have to stick it out.

On June 5 I held a meeting for some of the leaders of the American Jewish community. I was disturbed by what I considered to be their shortsighted outlook.

Diary

I pointed out that hardware alone to Israel was a policy that made sense maybe five years ago but did not make sense today, and that they had to have in mind that each new war would be more and more costly because their neighbors would learn to fight, and there were more of them. And that second, looking into the future, someone would have to hold the ring against the Russians, as we did with the alert in 1973.

I made it very clear there is going to be no blank check in our conversations with the Israelis although, of course, I expressed sympathy for their military needs and, of course, enormous respect for their bravery, etc.

As a matter of fact, whether Israel can survive over a long period of time with a hundred million Arabs around them I think is really questionable. The only long-term hope lies in reaching some kind of settlement now while they can operate from a position of strength, and while we are having such apparent success in weaning the Arabs away from the Soviets and into more responsible paths.

On June 9 we had a lively family dinner. Afterward, while the girls and their husbands went downstairs to watch a movie and Pat went upstairs to finish her packing, I went to the Lincoln Sitting Room and dictated a note describing the problems and opportunities I saw in the historic trip we were to begin the next morning.

Diary

I don't know whether I got across adequately the point that not just this trip when it is concluded, or the two and a half years remaining when it is concluded, will mean that we have secured our goal of a lasting peace. It is going to require tending thereafter by strong Presidents for the balance of this century. And who knows what can happen thereafter.

All I must do is to do everything possible to see that we leave a structure on which future Presidents can build—a structure based on military strength, diplomatic sophistication, intelligence, and, of course, a strong strain of idealism which will lead to progress despite some rough waters through which we will have to pass toward our goal of a permanent peace in that area.

As I complete this day, June 9, I begin this trip recognizing the profound importance it will have for the future as far as the Mideast is concerned, and as far as the American position in the world.

I was fully aware that the success or failure of this trip might make the decisive difference in my being able to continue to exercise presidential leadership abroad and at home despite the merciless onslaught of the Watergate attacks.

Diary

The irony of it all is that, as I told Ziegler, the press—or at least most of the press—will be more obsessed with what happens with the minuscule problems involved in Watergate than they are with the momentous stakes that are involved in what I will be doing and saying in the Mideast.

This is probably a turning point in terms of the whole so-

> called Watergate issue, but also a turning point insofar as the presidency itself is concerned. I am going to devote myself over this next ten days to doing everything possible to restore some respect for the office as well as for the man.

During the flight to our first stopover, Salzburg, Austria, Haig told me that Kissinger was upset about an editorial in that morning's New York *Times* that accused him of having dissembled in his Senate testimony about the 1969 wiretaps. He said that Kissinger was talking about holding a press conference in Salzburg in order to answer this charge.

"A *Times* editorial isn't a charge, Al," I said. "It's nothing more than a *Times* editorial, and that doesn't mean a goddamn thing. If he holds a press conference, he'll only play into their hands by giving them a Watergate lead for their first story from this trip." I said that if Kissinger felt he had to have a press conference, he should at least not be defensive but approach the question positively on the ground that the wiretaps were legitimate and necessary.

But Kissinger was in no mood to take this advice. He called a press conference and opened it with a long and emotional statement. After going through the details of his testimony on the wiretaps, he introduced an aggrieved personal note. "I have been generally identified, or, it has been alleged that I am supposed to be interested primarily in the balance of power," he said. "I would rather like to think that when the record is written, one may remember that perhaps some lives were saved and that perhaps some mothers can rest more at ease, but I leave that to history. What I will not leave to history is a discussion of my public honor."

The real bombshell came during the question period that followed when, in reply to a question, he said, "I do not believe that it is possible to conduct the foreign policy of the United States under these circumstances when the character and credibility of the Secretary of State is at issue. And if it is not cleared up, I will resign."

I issued a public statement expressing my understanding of Kissinger's desire to defend himself against malicious leaks, adding that all Americans would recognize, as I did, that his honor needed no defense.

> *Diary*
>
> All in all, what really concerns me about this attack on Kissinger is the total irresponsibility of the *Times* and Washington *Post* and all of our opponents at a time we are traveling abroad to take him on on this flimsy issue. The mistake that he made, of course, was to hypo his case with the threat to resign, which, among other things, is an empty cannon.

The first reaction to Kissinger's threat to resign was a resounding chorus of support for him. Within a few days, however, even a few of his supporters were calling his Salzburg performance a tantrum, while a small band of critics was claiming that it had been a calculated maneuver to distract attention from the charges against him. But in the end his threat to resign had the effect he desired and put his critics on the defensive. Later, the Senate Foreign Relations Committee reconsidered his testimony and announced that he was still in good standing with them. This, at last, seemed to put the matter to rest.

We stayed overnight in Salzburg in order to get used to the time change.

Diary

I felt good this morning except for the fact that my left leg is having exactly the same symptoms it had when I was in Hawaii and had what was diagnosed as a blood clot. I am having Lukash come over and take a look at it since he was the one who measured it before.

It is much larger than the right leg and it really makes me quite lame. I, of course, will not allow them to do anything which will disrupt the trip at this point.

I was suffering from phlebitis, an inflammation of a vein. After Lukash examined the leg he told me that the danger of phlebitis is that a blood clot might form and break loose into the bloodstream; if it reached the lungs, it could cause a fatal embolism. Fortunately, he seemed to think that the swelling in my leg was in fact the aftermath of the inflammation and that the greatest danger had already passed. He told me to wrap the leg in hot towels at least four times a day and to stay off it as much as possible.

Later I called Haig in and showed him my swollen leg. I told him that I wanted the few people who knew about it to keep it absolutely secret.

We landed in Cairo on June 12 in the hot afternoon sun. President Sadat and his wife were waiting at the airport, and I was immediately impressed by both of them. Sadat is a handsome man, somewhat taller than I had expected from his pictures. In the car he turned to me and said with intense feeling, "This is a great day for Egypt."

As soon as we started on the road to Cairo, I got the first taste of what was perhaps the most tumultuous welcome any American president has ever received anywhere in the world. For mile after mile along both sides of the road people were packed a hundred deep. In Cairo itself the streets and large squares were overflowing. Conservative estimates put the crowd at over a million.

But even more impressive than the sheer number was the obvious sincerity of the crowd's emotion. Sadat seemed to sense what I was thinking, because he leaned over and shouted in my ear so that I could hear him. "This is a real welcome from the heart," he said. "These people are here because they want to be here. You can bring people out, but you can't make them smile." We passed under large arches that had been built across the streets, decorated with huge pictures of Sadat and me, proclaiming us "Great Men Dedicated to Peace and Progress." The noise was overwhelming as a million people yelled "Nik-son, Nik-son, Nik-son!" at the top of their lungs.

When the motorcade finally reached the palace where we would be staying, Sadat suggested that we delay our first meeting for an hour or two. I thought he was simply being polite because of the exertion of standing up and waving for almost an hour under the blazing sun. Only later during the visit did Mrs. Sadat tell me that he took a nap every afternoon. He had suffered two mild heart attacks as recently as 1970 and as a result took extremely cautious care of himself. I later made a diary note: "The thing that I am really concerned about is what would happen if he were to pass from the scene."

In our conversations Sadat showed great subtlety and sophistication. He did not press me privately about U.S.–Israeli ties, although publicly he made a strong appeal for the return of the occupied territories, the rights of the Palestinians, and the status of Jerusalem. Describing his dealings with the Soviets, he said that he had asked them for military help before the October war, and they had not come through. With surprising candor he said, "We just gave up on them."

The crowds got bigger each day we were in Egypt. They jammed the entire route on our three-hour train ride from Cairo to Alexandria as Sadat and I stood waving from an open coach. It was hot and dusty, and the swelling in my leg grew painful from standing so long. But I realized that Sadat felt it was important for as many people as possible to see us together. It was a way of confirming the new Egyptian-American relationship.

One of the pool of reporters aboard the train asked Sadat about the principal contribution the United States could make for continuing peace in the Middle East. In his reply he referred to some of the handmade signs we had seen along the route: "It is to keep the momentum of the whole thing going on, and I must say you have read what my people wrote. They wrote, 'We Trust Nixon.' . . . President Nixon never gave a word and didn't fulfill it. He has fulfilled every word he gave. So if this momentum continues, I think we can achieve peace."

I made a diary note about these phenomenal crowds: "I think the estimates that approximately six and a half to seven million people that we saw in Egypt is an honest one. It is in that kind of ball park at any rate. One wonders whether they came out simply because they think we are bringing a bag full of money to deal with their problems. Certainly something of that enters into it. I think more than that was what Sadat told me: that they really feel very strongly a feeling of affection for the Americans. Part of that, of course, is their irritation with the Russians."

Egypt is the key to the Arab world, and thanks to Sadat and the Egyptian people, the trip got off to an excellent start. Our objectives were to provide support to Egypt in pursuing its moderate course and to encourage and strengthen Sadat in his roles as leader of his country and as a constructive and essential influence for any future Middle East negotiations. At the conclusion of the visit, we issued a statement of principles of relations and cooperation between Egypt and the United States that set forth the basis for working together for peace in the Middle East and new plans for economic cooperation. We also agreed to negotiate an agreement under which we would sell non-military nuclear reactors and fuel to Egypt for the production of electrical power.

When we landed in Jidda, Saudi Arabia, the temperature was above 100 degrees. Even so, King Faisal was at the airport waiting to greet us. He looked much older than his admitted sixty-seven—according to our intelligence reports, seventy-two—years.

Faisal saw Zionist and Communist conspiracies everywhere around him. He even put forward what must be the ultimate conspiratorialist notion: that the Zionists were behind the Palestinian terrorists. Despite this obsession, however, and thanks to his intelligence and the experience of many years in power, Faisal was one of the wisest leaders in the entire region.

Saudi Arabia was not directly involved in the Middle East peace negotiations, but Faisal's stature in the Arab world and the substantial financial support he provided to Syria and Egypt gave him a vital role in maintaining the momentum toward peace. I was also able to discuss with him the serious global impact of the high oil prices caused by the recent Arab oil embargo and to encourage his moves to moderate oil prices.

I was as surprised as the reporters who clustered around us when Faisal said at the departure ceremonies, "Anybody who stands against you, Mr. President, in the United States of America or outside the United States of America, or stands against us, your friends in this part of the world, obviously has one aim in mind, namely, that of causing the splintering of the world, the wrong polarization of the world, the bringing about of mischief, which would not be conducive to tranquillity and peace in the world. Therefore, we beseech Almighty God to lend His help to us and to you so that we both can go hand in hand, shoulder to shoulder in pursuance of the noble aims that we both share, namely, those of peace, justice, and prosperity in the world."

My visit to Syria required the most delicate diplomacy of the entire Mideast trip. Syria had been one of the most radically pro-Soviet, anti-Israeli, and anti-American of the Arab nations.

The problems that my visit presented to President Asad were summed up in the story he told me about his eight-year-old son. The boy had watched our airport arrival ceremonies on television, and when Asad returned home that night, he went up to his father and asked, "Wasn't that Nixon the same one you have been telling us for years is an evil man who is completely in control of the Zionists and our enemies? How could you welcome him and shake his hand?" Asad smiled at me and said, "That is the question all my people will ask, and that is why we have to move at a very measured pace as we develop our relations in the future. After all, for years my people have been taught to hate the Americans; and in recent years they have been taught particularly to hate the Nixon who represents the capitalists who have always supported the Israelis. The same Nixon who saved Israel in 1973!"

The agreement to disengage forces in the Golan Heights had been an achievement of substantial proportions, and my visit was an opportunity to encourage, support, and nurture the new Syrian-American relationship that Kissinger had begun. I was convinced that Asad would continue to play the hardest of hard lines in public, but in private he would follow the Arab proverb that he told me during one of our meetings: "When a blind man can see with one eye it is better than not being able to see at all." I was very impressed with President Asad.

Diary

As far as Asad was concerned he exceeded my expectations on the conversations I had had with Henry. He was, as Henry had said, a tough negotiator, but he has a great deal of mystique, tremendous stamina, and a lot of charm. He laughs easily, and I can see he will be a dynamic leader if he can just maintain his judgment. In our last conversation he came down very very hard against any separate peace. But on the other hand, he seemed to be quite reasonable with regard to the various regional approaches we were making. All in all he is a man of real substance, and at his age—forty-four—if he can avoid somebody shooting him or overthrowing him, he will be a leader to be reckoned with in this part of the world.

Pat noted that he had a flat head in the back which she said

> was probably because he hadn't been turned when he was a baby. What he reminded me of, curiously enough, was that he had a forehead like Pat Buchanan's, and my guess is he has the same kind of brain and drive and single-mindedness that Pat has. The man really has elements of genius, without any question.

In the Syrian capital of Damascus, the oldest continuously inhabited city in the world, American flags were flying for the first time in seven years. Everywhere we went large and friendly crowds turned out to welcome us, despite the fact that our movements and itineraries were given no publicity by the Syrian authorities. I viewed this as a measure of the people's strong desire for friendship with America, for an alternative to the Soviets, and for peace. I noted in my diary, "These people want to be friendly with the U.S. and it runs right down to the rank and file and it goes to the fact that they know the Russians. The Americans, of course, may be in that category soon if we are unable to produce on the peace initiatives that we have begun."

In his toast at the state dinner in my honor President Asad said, "Let us open a new page and begin a new phase in the relations between our two countries." For a President of Syria, this was a dramatic statement. At the conclusion of my visit we announced the resumption of diplomatic relations between our two countries, and I stated our willingness to resume educational and cultural exchanges and to cooperate in Syrian economic growth.

When I said goodbye to Asad at the airport, he kissed me on both cheeks—the highest compliment that can be paid a visitor and an extraordinarily important gesture for the man who, until a few months earlier, had been the leading anti-American firebrand of the Arab world.

I later reflected on this breakthrough in our relations with Syria.

> *Diary*
>
> All in all, Syria is by far the most difficult country we have in terms of working out some kind of positive continuing relationship. On the other hand, they desperately want to have another string in their bow. They want us in there, probably to play us against the Russians, and that's why on the way back I said that we must explore every possible way to make some moves toward the Syrians in the economic area.

My receptions in Egypt and Syria and my conversations with Sadat and Asad confirmed the tremendous potential of the new role of the United States as a force for peace in the Arab world. If we could provide the lead, these two pragmatic and patriotic men were willing to seek a compromise settlement with Israel as a prerequisite for turning their attention to the development of their own countries. I was also encouraged to see the extent to which the Soviets had alienated their former Arab clients; it was particularly interesting to discover that this was not just the case at the leadership level. As was frequently the case, Manolo, who was traveling with me, was an excellent source of information and insights.

Diary

Manolo gave some interesting sidelights about the trip when we asked him about which country he liked the best. He said that he liked Egypt the best because the Egyptians were so friendly. He said that they all said they were glad to see the Americans come in and the Russians leave. It reminded me of my first conversation with Sadat, where he said that in six months America had gained more in Egyptian popular support than the Russians had been able to gain in twenty years.

Manolo said that the Egyptians told him over and over again that the Russians were grim and mean; they lived apart and did not treat the people kindly. He ran into the same thing in Syria, where one of the people working in the kitchen told him that the Americans were smiling and the Russians were always grim. I think one thing we have going for us in this part of the world, and I trust in other parts of the world, is the fact that, with all of our faults, and with the exception of some arrogant Americans, particularly in the foreign service and some business types, most Americans basically like other people. Putting it another way, they want to be liked, and so they go overboard in trying to win other people. The Russians, with their inferiority complex and their single-minded communist determination, are a very different breed. They don't let their good qualities show through except when they are dealing with what they consider to be absolute equals.

I recalled a conversation I had had with Sadat in which I had told him that I thought that the real problem between China and Russia was that, deep down, the Chinese consider themselves superior and more civilized than the Russians. Sadat had smiled and said, "You know, that's exactly the same way we feel: we Egyptians are more civilized than the Russians."

Our reception in Israel, although warm by ordinary standards, was the most restrained of the trip. This was partly because of Israeli domestic problems. Golda Meir had resigned just two months earlier and Yitzhak Rabin had taken over as Prime Minister, heading up a fragile coalition. Given the unpopularity of my Mideast policy in many quarters in Israel, Rabin was understandably unwilling to be more than correct in the treatment he accorded me but he was also bluntly anxious to know how much more aid he could depend on from us.

The primary purpose of my meetings with Rabin and his top Cabinet officials was to make it clear to them that while we would not waver in our total support for Israel's security, we would insist on their playing a sincere and serious part in maintaining the momentum of the peace negotiations that we had begun with Kissinger's shuttle diplomacy and had now confirmed with my trip. In addition to a thorough discussion of the economic and military needs of Israel and a review of further steps that might be taken toward peace, we proposed in a joint statement issued at the conclusion of the visit that we negotiate an agreement on nonmilitary nuclear reactors and fuel supply similar to the one we had concluded with President Sadat.

At the state dinner at the Knesset, the Israeli parliament building, I said that I would exercise the presidential prerogative of breaking precedent: although Golda Meir was no longer Prime Minister, I wanted to propose a special toast to her before the traditional toast to the head of state. I said that of all the world leaders I had met none had greater courage, intelligence, stamina, determination, or dedication to their country than Golda Meir. She was sitting nearby at the head table, and I could see how flustered and flattered she was. I continued, "I thought that I, having worked with her, having become her friend, and she has been my friend, that I might have the honor and the privilege to ask you to join me in a toast to the former Prime Minister. Prime Minister Golda Meir. To Golda."

Typically eloquent even when taken by surprise, she made a brief reply. "As President Nixon says, Presidents can do almost anything, and President Nixon has done many things that nobody would have thought of doing. All I can say, Mr. President, as friends and as an Israeli citizen to a great American President, thank you."

In my formal toast I talked frankly about the task confronting the new Prime Minister and the Knesset:

> There are two courses that are open to them. The one is an easy one, an easy one particularly politically, I suppose, and that is the status quo. Don't move, because any movement has risks in it, and therefore resist those initiatives that may be undertaken, that might lead to a negotiation which would perhaps contribute to a permanent, just, and durable peace.
>
> But there is another way. The other, I believe, is the right way. It is the way of statesmanship, not the way of the politician alone. It is a way that does not risk your country's security. That must never be done. But it is a way that recognizes that continuous war in this area is not a solution for Is-

> rael's survival and, above all, it is not right that every possible avenue [not] be explored to avoid it in the interest of the future of those children we saw by the hundreds and thousands on the streets of Jerusalem today.

Our last stop in the Middle East was in Jordan, where I was once again impressed by the charm and intelligence of King Hussein. He and I spent over two hours in a private discussion of his unique role in assisting the settlement of conflicts. He had long been a staunch and loyal friend of the United States, sometimes to his considerable peril, and he affirmed that he would continue to do his part on behalf of restraint and moderation on the long road that lay ahead.

In his toast at the state dinner he gave for us, Hussein generously summed up the meaning of my trip as he saw it: "Mr. President, we join with you in all the hopes and expectations you must have for this memorable 'Journey for Peace' that you are undertaking, and we in the Arab world are grateful that you have made it," he said. "Although you know better than anyone else perhaps that a journey for peace seems to have no ending, your coming to us at this time has been perfectly timed to preserve the momentum that American initiative had begun under your inspired and inspiring leadership."

I concluded my toast that night by saying: "I do not tell you where this journey will end. I cannot tell you when it will end. The important thing is that it has begun."

There was a large crowd waiting on the South Lawn of the White House to welcome Pat and me. Jerry Ford led the official delegation of Cabinet members. He said, "Mr. President, about ten days ago, I was here with many others to wish you Godspeed. Our prayers were with you at that time, and I think it might be appropriate now to quote from that biblical injunction: 'Blessed is the peacemaker.' "

During the next few days, even while preparing for Soviet Summit III, I briefed congressional leaders on the opportunity we had to exert leadership for peace in the Middle East, and I reflected on the Mideast trip in the practical perspective of the domestic reaction to it.

> *Diary*
>
> We must have gotten some lift from the trip, although it seems almost impossible to break through in the polls. Of course, this is not surprising after the terrible banging we are taking. As I pointed out to Ziegler, when he was telling me about the five or six minutes that we were getting on each network while we were away, I said, 'Compare that with the eight or ten minutes that they have been hearing on Watergate for over a year!' We can't

complain too much about the coverage in the Mideast. It was good. It was very hard to knock the trip. And I think it had an impact. How great and how lasting only time will tell.

The most important thing, of course, is to keep working to make sure the trip bears the fruits of peace—or at least of progress. Sadat constantly emphasized the point that it was unnatural for the Egyptians and the Americans to be enemies, and natural for us to be friends. It was this theme that we heard in Saudi Arabia and also in Syria and Jordan: natural and unnatural, normal and abnormal, etc. This to me is the most significant benefit from the presidential trip as distinguished from all the negotiations. The Arabs really want to be friends of the Americans, and now it's up to us to be their friends and also to prove that friendship with America is worthwhile.

With the congressional leaders I stepped out a little bit ahead of Henry in indicating that we would make Israel strong enough that they would not fear to negotiate, but not so strong that they felt they had no need to negotiate. I would add to that, Israel should also be strong enough so that their neighbors would not be tempted to attack them, and would have an incentive to negotiate.

One thing the Mideast trip did was to put the whole Watergate business into perspective—to make us realize that all the terrible battering we have taken is really pygmy-sized when compared to what we have done and what we can do in the future not only for peace in the world but, indirectly, to effect the well-being of people everywhere. This, I suppose, is what we must always keep front and center regardless of what happens in the future.

On June 13, while I was in Egypt, Fred Buzhardt had suffered a heart attack. Once I was assured that he was going to pull through, I tried to assess the impact his illness would have on our legal situation. This was a particularly busy and important period because we had briefs to file and oral arguments to prepare for the tapes case before the Supreme Court. We also had to prepare for the pretrial hearings in the Watergate cover-up case on defense motions for documents, and to respond to demands for documents from the district court that was hearing the Ellsberg break-in case. There were several other lesser legal battles also being waged. We were trying to assert a claim of executive privilege in a suit brought by Common Cause; and we were getting ready to file an appeal on Sirica's decision to release a section of the September 15, 1972, tape that he himself had earlier judged did not relate to Watergate—one in which I had talked about IRS information on our opponents. And as if these were not enough, the Ervin Committee was still demanding more information, Kissinger was returning to testify on the wiretaps before the Senate Foreign Relations Committee, and the House Judiciary Committee was continuing its rapacious demands for more tapes. Buzhardt's enforced absence would be a serious blow.

There was at least one relatively bright spot: there were reports of behind-the-scenes problems at the House Judiciary Committee. The leaks from both members and staff had become so frequent that Democrats as well as Republicans were expressing their disapproval. An anonymous committee member was quoted in the Washington *Post*, "I think we are a little embarrassed by what we have done."

On June 21, two days after my return from the Mideast, the House Judiciary Committee finished hearing all the evidence on all the charges against me; it ran over 7,000 pages and ultimately filled thirty-eight large printed volumes. The quantity of the evidence was overwhelming, but its quality was weak; most of it had little or no direct bearing on my own actions.

There were also other optimistic signs. Washington columnists noted that John Rhodes, for the first time in weeks, was beginning to emerge as a leader in my behalf. The House pro-impeachment Democrats were now reported to be pushing hard for an early House floor vote because they felt the committee's slow pace had let the momentum slip. The Washington *Post* ran a front-page story that the committee had begun to polarize.

On June 22 I telephoned Louisiana Democrat Joe Waggonner. A veteran of seven terms in the House, Waggonner headed an informal group that sometimes numbered as many as a hundred House Democrats, mainly Southerners, who had often given me support on key issues. He had been a great source of strength to me throughout the whole Watergate period; hardly a week went by that he did not call to reassure me of his continued support. But he was always totally realistic, and he never tried to encourage me falsely. Now he was saying that he had seventy anti-impeachment votes in his group that he thought were pretty solid. The only thing that might change them, he said, would be if for any reason I were held in contempt of the Supreme Court. Other than that he did not think there was any chance for an impeachment. He ended this conversation, as he did every one I ever remember having with him, by saying, "God bless you."

I calculated that if Waggonner had 70 Democratic votes, we would need only 150 Republicans to make a majority against impeachment. That was not an unrealistic goal. On June 22 and 23 I reflected on the tentative new sources of support showing up in Congress, and even in the House Judiciary Committee itself.

Diary

Thank God some of our Republicans on the committee led by [Charles] Wiggins [of California], are standing up. This may be the new factor that could change this situation—change it, that is, with the one caveat—that what happens in the Supreme Court is going to put us to a real test.

I still hope and feel, however, that there would be a fairly good chance this time that the Court, as it looks down to the future of this country and the future of the presidency and for that matter the future of the Court itself, will not want to set such a devastating precedent. But the Court all lives in Washington, are affected by the Washington stories, and the poison they see in the Washington *Post* must really seep in. It's very difficult for people to read it every day and not be affected by it.

In thinking today, after my call with Joe Waggonner, when he said that unless there was contempt of the Supreme Court we would win the impeachment, I realized that we really are looking at about thirty days in which the climactic decision with regard to whether we are able to stay in office or whether we will have to, in effect, refuse to comply with what might be an order of the Court which would violate the constitutional precepts which I have laid forward, will have to be made. What I have to do in these next thirty days is to live every one of them up to the hilt and not be concerned about what happens in between. We just have to be sure that we do everything we can to be worthy of whatever responsibilities we have.

The more I think about this whole impeachment process the more I remember what Ayub Khan said: "Trust is like a thin thread. Once you break it, it is almost impossible to put it together again." This is why as time has gone on, when we add up the Dean week which was just a year ago—and the tape issue—and then Agnew—and then following that up with the two-tapes business—the tax business—and all of the other assaults—the Rebozo thing—the eighteen minutes—it's just miraculous that we are still in the game at all.

We can only thank God for the strength of the family, as I have often said—of some of our close friends, and the iron will of Haig, who I think is the strongest man in the whole group—supported, of course, by Ziegler, Buchanan, and others.

I had a very good talk with Bob Haldeman. He is really a tower of strength. I told him that I knew he must be worried about what was going to happen in September and what he must be going through, and that I felt for him very, very deeply, just as I felt for John Ehrlichman and John Mitchell. He said, well, he just lived day by day and didn't think about the outcome in the end.

When I think, incidentally, of my feeling of depression last night I suppose that something might happen in the future with regard to the Court that would end in eventual impeachment, I thought of all of the others who must be going through much worse—sleepless nights and so forth—people who don't have strong physical or emotional faculties as I have. It's really remarkable that we have so many among our own group who have stood up under a terrible battering, and have taken the worst shots that they could get and have still survived.

I talked to Henry. He seemed to think the mood, as he puts it, had changed. Of course, he has said this before. And, Henry, of course, always puts in the caveat, "unless something big develops."

I also talked to Al Haig. He says he really feels better than he has for a year.

As I analyze things on this rather rainy Sunday, June 23, I must say that we are probably, as Al says, stronger than we were a couple of months ago, and we shall now see what happens as we go to the Soviet Union, come back, and as the tension then focuses as it will almost totally on the whole impeachment process. At least the Mideast trip tended to break the momentum and to focus attention on other subjects. Al feels that the press wants to do that—that they are rather tired of the other subject. I trust he's right, although I think that we will find that many of our opponents will not play that game because they desperately want to get us out.

My family and I tried to make the time we spent together as happy and carefree as possible. I worried about the girls constantly. They were young, and they needed freedom to live their own lives; instead they were having to fight my battles day in and day out. Their constant thoughtfulness was a source of great comfort to me. Julie would often leave her copy of the New English edition of the New Testament on my bedstand, opened to some consoling passage. And Tricia would come to the Lincoln Sitting Room at some of my lowest times and just sit with me while I read or worked, in a quiet tribute of love and support.

I was in the Mideast on Father's Day, but there was a telegram for me from the girls: "Dear Daddy, Happy Father's Day. We are so proud of you and love you very much. Julie and Tricia." My sons-in-law joined to send me a telegram: "Mr. President, A triumphant Father's Day. Our admiration and love. Ed and David."

Because of the demands of Ed's job, he and Tricia stayed in New

York and did not make many official appearances. It became a favorite sport of insatiable gossip columnists to fabricate rumors of a "rift" between me and Ed, or even between Tricia and Ed. It finally reached the point that Tricia was forced to issue a statement denying that her marriage was about to break up. In fact, she and Ed seemed to grow stronger and draw closer the more they were forced to endure. In March, without informing me beforehand, they jointly wrote a courageous and eloquent magazine article in my defense.

Julie and David were directly in the blast of the hurricane for the entire final year of my presidency. Living in Washington ensured that they could never escape from the ceaseless media scrutiny or from the stifling atmosphere of the threatened impeachment. Both Julie and David were sturdy young people, but after more than 160 public appearances, many of them searing Watergate sessions, they would have had to be unintelligent and insensitive not to feel the effect. In February 1974 David wrote to me about it:

> Julie has undoubtedly mentioned my low spirits this past week. In a nutshell, nothing in my life prepared me for the thunder clap of criminal charges pressed against people I know and respect and essentially on grounds growing out of dedication to your case. . . .
>
> I never accepted that life could be so unfair and it's unquestionably just the beginning. I spent the better part of this week wrestling with my feelings on the situation. I hope I haven't been misunderstood. Last night I discovered an appropriate thought, "There is no despair so absolute as that which comes with the first moment of our first great sorrow when we have not yet known what it is to have suffered and be healed, to have despaired and recovered hope." The quote was from George Eliot, of course. I wondered when it was you experienced your "despair so absolute"—14 years ago, 1 year ago—ours may have been last week. But the point of the passage and of your experience is hope. Under these circumstances hope means determination. We are happy with any part of redeeming the work you have done for America and we aren't alone either, come what may.

It hurt me to see Julie daily grow quieter and more inward. But the only time I recall that she ever let me know of her despair was when we went to Camp David after the release of the Blue Book transcripts. "Everything is so dreary," she said quietly. By the next day she had bounced back, and within a week she and David decided to hold a press conference in response to the storm of criticism of the transcripts and the calls for my resignation that were now coming from friends and enemies alike.

At one point during their press conference a reporter for CBS began talking about the "sins of the fathers" being visited on their children. His implication was that their spontaneous decision to hold the press conference was part of a calculated move to shield me from reporters. Julie's eyes flashed, but the steel in her character helped her restrain emotion as she said:

> I am going to try to control myself in answering the question, because it really does wound me. . . . I am here because Helen Smith had fifty-five calls from the media. . . . Now if the media has a hang-up, an obsession about resignation and feels they must be reassured by members of the family, I feel as a daughter it is my obligation to come out here.
>
> I have seen what my father has gone through, and I am so proud of him that I would never be afraid to come out here and talk to any members of the press about resignation or anything else, even though it goes against my grain because I know he does not want me out here because he does not want anyone to construe that I am trying to answer questions for him. I am not trying to answer questions for him. I am just trying to pray for enough courage to meet his courage.

Pat was, as always, the strongest of all. She worked to keep our spirits high when we were together as a family, while she showed the world that beneath the woman who was loved universally for her warmth, her easy elegance, and her genius for personal understanding, there was a strength of character unmatched, I believe, in the history of American politics.

She was, as Jerry Ford proclaimed her, "First Lady of the World," and on March 11 she made what was to be the last of her trips as my representative abroad. This time she visited Brazil and Venezuela, where she captivated everyone who saw her. Yet on the plane back reporters immediately started pressing her about Watergate, wanting to know just how much pain she had suffered in the last year, just how bad it had been for her. "I really don't wish to speak of it. It's just a personal thing," she said. "Why bring that into the trip?" She repeated what she had said before: that she loved me and knew that I was an honorable, dedicated person.

She worked hard to be an example of dignity under attack. And still they would not let up.

SUMMIT III

In January 1974, the Soviets had agreed to announce the date of Summit III, scheduled to be held in Moscow in the summer. I evaluated this decision either as an act of faith on their part that I was going to prevail over impeachment, or as an indication of their interest in seeing détente continue regardless of who was President.

What was probably the most crucial and hardest fought battle of Summit III took place not in Moscow but in Washington, where the activities of the anti-détente forces reached almost fever pitch just as I was getting ready to leave for the Soviet Union. The liberals were now in full cry with what had become the currently fashionable outrage over Soviet repression of political dissidents and their restriction of Jewish emigration. The conservatives of both parties were still united in their determination either to limit trade with the Soviets or to ban it altogether. The military establishment and its many friends in Congress and the country were up in arms over the prospect that Summit III might actually succeed in producing a breakthrough on limiting offensive nuclear weapons or a limited nuclear test ban.

This convergence of anti-détente forces would have existed regardless of any domestic political problems. But Watergate had badly damaged my ability to defuse, or at least to circumvent, them as effectively as I otherwise might have been able to do.

When Kissinger went to Moscow on March 24 for four days of talks aimed at setting the agenda for Summit III, he reported that Brezhnev seemed to be confronting some of the same problems as we were of military opposition to a permanent agreement to limit offensive nuclear weapons. Thus we knew from the outset that it would be very difficult to produce a major SALT breakthrough at Summit III.

The U.S. military opposition to a new SALT agreement came to a head at the meeting of the National Security Council on the afternoon of June 20 when Secretary of Defense Schlesinger presented the Pentagon's proposal. It amounted to an unyielding hard line against any SALT agreement that did not ensure an overwhelming American advantage. It was a proposal that the Soviets were sure to reject out of hand.

After the arguments on both sides had been stated, I intervened: "I think we should try to use this time to frame a more practical approach to this problem. We have to accept the fact that Secretary Schlesinger's proposal simply has no chance whatever of being accepted by the Soviets, so we should try to work out something consistent with our interests that will."

There was a moment of silence, and then Schlesinger, who was sitting next to me, said, "But, Mr. President, everyone knows how impressed Khrushchev was with your forensic ability in the kitchen debate. I'm sure that if you applied your skills to it you could get them to accept this proposal."

In my diary that night I recorded: "The NSC meeting was a real shocker insofar as the performance of the Chiefs, and particularly of Schlesinger, was concerned. His statement that he knew that Khrushchev had been very impressed by my 'forensic ability' and that, with my forensic ability, I could sell the idea that he presented, was really an insult to everybody's intelligence and particularly to mine."

Jerry Ford broke the silence that followed Schlesinger's remark and moved the discussion into the broader area of the defense budget. After this had gone on for a few minutes, I made a statement about the way I viewed the development of détente over the two years remaining to me in the White House.

Diary

Ford is on the kick that we ought to have a huge increase in the defense budget, and that that will give us a bargaining position with the Soviets. He's right in one way, of course, and wrong in another, because we aren't going to be able to bluff them in this particular case.

My great concern, as I said at the meeting, is that whoever might succeed me in this office might not fight these bloody battles that I have had to fight over these past five and a half years—for ABM, for big defense budgets, for the Trident submarine, etc. We could have someone who, despite all the white-hot talk that the United States has to be number one and so forth, would cave in to the peacenik views that the establishment press would undoubtedly be expressing once they got one of their own in office.

That is why it is very important, if we possibly can, to get some constraints on the Soviets at this time. Because later on, if we get into a runaway race, it may be that they will be uninhibited and we will be inhibited. As I tried to point out at the NSC meeting, when the President of the United States makes a decision, it's very different from a decision made by the General Secretary of the Soviet Union. We can be very sure that his decision is one that will and can be carried out. He doesn't have to be too concerned about his public opinion, if at all. When the President of the United States makes a decision, however, he can't ever be absolutely sure that his decision will be carried out. It's certainty versus the uncertainty that weakens, not our actual bargaining position so much, but makes it essential that we take this factor into account in negotiating the terms of any deal that we make with the Soviet. Because if we have an agreement which constrains us both, it means that we will be constraining them in something that they will inevitably do. When we constrain ourselves, it may be that we are constraining ourselves in an area where we wouldn't be doing anything anyway. This, of course, was exactly the situation with regard to the '72 agreement.

It is just as well, however, that we don't fight this battle right now, and if we can just find a way to get the proper language so that we can negotiate it in October and November—and also get

> the Soviets to agree to some proper numbers, then I think we will have rendered a great service to our national security as well as to some sort of balance in forces generally.
>
> Many of the Defense people don't want any agreement because they want to go ahead willy-nilly with all the defense programs they possibly can and they do not want constraints. The situation has been compounded by the fact that Henry hasn't been able to work on it. He has been so tied down with the Mideast that he hasn't been able to pull this other one together. Maybe it's just as well, however, because this as I said is not the time to fight this battle.

The battle with the military was not the only major problem affecting Summit III. For the first time since the Watergate break-in, Brezhnev expressed concern about my ability to make decisions domestically. He had gone very far out on a limb for détente, and he was understandably concerned that my sudden or unexpected departure from office would leave him in an embarrassing and exposed position within his own hierarchy.

In April 1974 we received a report from Walter Stoessel, now ambassador to Moscow, describing a meeting at which Brezhnev had seemed particularly concerned that our domestic problems could hinder the course of events. "Brezhnev said he respected the President for fighting back, calling this one characteristic of a statesman, and expressed amazement that the United States had reached a point where the President could be bothered about his taxes. He viewed the President's opponents as 'senseless,' " Stoessel reported.

When Gromyko came to see me on April 11, he opened by reassuring me that despite the anti-Soviet stories and articles that appeared in the American press, the Soviets were firmly in support of détente. Then, in an unusually personal moment, Gromyko said that he simply wanted to say to me that he admired my standing up, "despite certain known difficulties," as he put it. "We admire you for it on the human plane," he said.

The rest of our meeting was spent in a wrangle over SALT numbers, a preview of what was to come in Moscow. Thus far, the Soviets were not yielding. Neither were we. When I walked Gromyko to the door of the West Lobby, he said, "We trust you understand that we want you to come and have the meeting and that nothing should interfere with it."

I indicated that I understood. "We will be cursed by future generations if we fail," I said. "We must succeed."

We left Washington on June 25. Our first stop was Brussels, where I attended ceremonies marking the twenty-fifth anniversary of NATO. I thought that it would be especially useful to dramatize the continuing viability of the Atlantic alliance before sitting down with Brezhnev. In my formal statement to the NATO Council, I said that the period of détente was one of great opportunity but also of great danger. We had to face the fact that European politics had changed completely. We had to accept the fact that fear of communism was no longer a practical motivation for NATO; if NATO were to survive, it would need other binding motives to keep it together.

It was just before I left for Brussels that the story of my phlebitis attack during the Mideast trip broke in the American press. The reporters immediately watched my every movement for signs of a limp or pain. In fact, my leg was still swollen and painful, but I was determined not to betray how much.

> *Diary*
>
> It's amazing that my health is as good as it is, and, as I told Ziegler, the main thing about this leg situation is not to let them build it up in a way that they think the President is crippled mentally as well as physically. I feel that at the present time we have it relatively under control but we must make sure that people never get the idea that the President is like Eisenhower in his last year or so, or like Roosevelt, or, for that matter, even like Johnson when everybody felt that Johnson was probably ready to crack up, and was drinking too much and so forth. I think we can avoid this by proper handling.

With our airport reception in Moscow on June 27, Summit III got off to a very auspicious start. Brezhnev himself was there, bounding across the tarmac, to greet me. A fairly large crowd had been allowed to stand behind barriers and wave paper flags. Unlike 1972, there were also crowds along the streets as we drove to the Kremlin.

Shortly after we arrived, Brezhnev invited me to his office for a private talk. He told me about his recent meeting with Teddy Kennedy and Averell Harriman and said that they both supported détente. I told him it was fine for him to meet with leaders of both parties between now and 1976 because we wanted them all to be in support of détente. "Let's get them all a little pregnant," I said.

He said that he had followed the political situation in the United States, and he was convinced that I would be in until 1976.

After the state dinner that night I suggested to Kissinger and Haig that we have a brief meeting in my car, where we could talk without being bugged. Kissinger had seemed depressed all day. As I had guessed, the domestic harassment over the wiretaps still bothered him, as well as his realization after his talks with Gromyko during the afternoon that our negotiating position had been seriously undercut by the anti-détente agitation within the administration.

On the first day of formal sessions we took up the question of a nuclear test ban. The Soviets, as in the past, would not agree to the necessary on-the-ground verification procedures. I was convinced that without such ironclad verification procedures to make sure that they were abiding by the terms, a total test ban was too dangerous to consider. We also had to take into account that such a ban was no longer as meaningful as it would have been when we were the only two nuclear powers, and in those days the Soviets had refused even to consider it. Now neither France nor the P.R.C.—about which the Soviets were especially sensitive—would halt nuclear testing regardless of what we did; nor would Israel or India stop nuclear research.

During Kissinger's preliminary visit to Moscow in March the Soviets had suggested a "threshold" test ban. Under such an arrangement, nuclear weapons could be tested as long as they did not cross a certain threshold of size and force. Since these infractions could be determined by seismic equipment in each country, on-the-ground verification would not be necessary. But at our afternoon session on the first full day of Summit III Brezhnev suddenly suggested that, instead of wrangling about the threshold levels for a limited test ban, we solve the question by agreeing on a comprehensive test ban.

I recorded in my diary, "During this session, Brezhnev was very tough, just like at the dacha in 1972 on Vietnam. He rewrote the script here, and none of us were prepared because it had been their idea in March, which they had explored with Kissinger, to have a threshold test ban."

Since there was no way to forestall this digression if Brezhnev was determined to have it, I decided that the only way to counter was with a vigorously frank and pragmatic approach. If Kosygin and the others expected me to hedge uncomfortably, they would be disappointed by the tone and substance of my reply. "We discussed this issue in very great depth before I came," I replied. "It is true that some in our Senate favor a comprehensive test ban. At the other end of the spectrum, however, there are equal numbers who favor no ban at all, having in mind the problem of verification. We have tried to restrain both sides by setting a low threshold. This is the only way we will get the support of the majority of our Congress. We cannot go to a total test ban," I said.

After a bit of verbal jousting I came back to the subject: "Speaking quite candidly, we have an ironic situation in the United States, as 1976 approaches, with respect to détente. Those who applaud our efforts toward détente over the past two years now, for reasons that are more partisan than philosophical, would like to see our efforts fail. So, I would not make any enemies if I were intractable here today.

"I do not raise these points to indicate that my position is based simply on these political considerations. I will move in the direction of détente because it is indispensable for the peace of the world, and that is why we want every possible agreement we can make and implement.

"I am in a unique position of being able to bring the American public along in support of détente. I can handle our so-called hawks—but only one step at a time, and I do not want this process to be interrupted. I want it to continue."

I pointed toward the massive gold doors at the entrance to the room. "As we look to those golden doors," I said, "we could say that we all want to reach them. But we will not make it if we try to do it in one step. We will always find, Mr. General Secretary, various factions in the U.S. and in other countries who, for differing reasons, want to see détente fail. And we, on our part, do not want to take a step that we have not prepared the support for. If we did that, we would simply be looking for repudiation."

This bit of plain speaking broke the rhetorical spiral they were building. Brezhnev said he would have to consult with his colleagues and discuss it again later. Then we turned to deciding how early we would have to leave Moscow in order to arrive in the Crimea before nightfall so that I would be able to see the countryside.

I made a diary note of this long and difficult session: "My leg began to swell again after this plenary session. I think I crossed my leg a great deal during it and that seems to start the swelling. It was a pretty tiring exercise, just to hear them go through their usual hard-line statements."

Pat and I flew with Brezhnev from Moscow to the Crimea, where we would continue our discussions at his villa on the outskirts of Yalta on the Black Sea. Since the name Yalta still carried unfavorable connotations, we called this the Oreanda Summit, after the area in which the dacha is situated.

On the way to the Crimea, Brezhnev called his wife from a phone on the plane, and as I noted in my diary, "He is like a child with a new toy when it comes to that sort of thing." I talked to Mrs. Brezhnev and said, "*Ochen priatno,*" a Russian phrase of greeting I had learned, which seemed to please her.

Diary

I told Brezhnev on the plane that the ceremonies at the tomb of the Unknown Soldier in D.C. and in Moscow, where I had laid wreaths, always made me feel the profound importance of the work that we are doing. I said, "That's what our negotiations are all about."

Brezhnev talked about how terrible it was to see thousands of dead people in the war. In winter, he said, it was particularly bad to see them frozen in grotesque shapes. I said, "Like a tragic ballet." Gromyko added, "In the summer when it's hot and the bodies rot it's just as bad."

They have been through some pretty horrible experiences.

The mood lightened during the sixty-four-mile drive from the airport to Oreanda. Brezhnev mentioned my Marine aide, Lieutenant Colonel Jack Brennan. "I like him very much," he said, "he is young and strong and handsome." "The girls all think so, too," I replied, and Brezhnev chuckled for a moment. Then he turned completely serious and looked right at me and said, "Although you and I are older, in history we may do more for our people for peace than any of these younger people."

For most of the hour-and-a-half drive we looked out the windows at the rolling green mountains covered with blue and gold wild flowers. Occasionally we would catch glimpses of the sea in the distance.

Brezhnev clearly loved being in the Crimea, and he enjoyed taking me for walks through the lush greenery surrounding his hillside villa and along the low sea wall. On the first day after we arrived we walked to a small building built partly into the rock, with large picture windows looking out to the sea. He called it a cabana. We went in, took off our coats, and talked privately for over an hour before the others joined us for a plenary session.

Diary

We had a very frank and forthcoming discussion on the subjects he had apparently wanted to talk to me alone about. He looked out to the sea as we sat there and pointed to the hydrofoil. He did some doodling—what it looked like was an arrow with a heart—an arrow through the heart. He first brought up his new idea of a U.S.–Soviet treaty, which others could join, where each country would come to the defense of the other if either country or one of its allies were attacked. This, of course, smacks of condominium in the most blatant sense.

One thing that was particularly interesting about our conversation at the cabana was Brezhnev's complete switch on China. In 1973 he had expressed great concern about it, but now he affected almost complete lack of interest. "Mao is a god," he said, "a very old god. And when he dies there will be a new god." Gromyko, however, took the opposite approach when we talked privately at one of the dinners, warning that the Chinese were a great threat to peace because they had a huge population and would sacrifice anything, including their own cities and their own people, to accomplish their goals.

Diary

Going back to the private session with Brezhnev, I pointed out that if détente unravels in America, the hawks will take over, not the doves, and I urged him to make some sort of a gesture on Jewish emigration if only to pull the rug out from under Jackson and some of the media critics. He proceeded to pull out from his folder the statistics and said he would give them to Dobrynin and Dobrynin would pass them on to Kissinger.

Our conversation ranged freely from the proposed conference on European security to the reduction of nuclear weapons.

Diary

He pointed out, incidentally, that his predictions with regard to the Mideast proved to be true. He said that under no circumstances, however, did he expect that there would be an Arab attack when he warned me about the explosive situation. That they, as a matter of fact, had done everything that they could to stop it. He was expressive with his gestures at this point—grabbed me by the arm and said, trying to hold them back, but, he said, "We were unable to do so."

When the others joined us at the cabana, the conversation returned to the impasse we had reached over multiple-warhead nuclear missiles, or MIRVs.

"Well, let us examine this question," I said, "because if nothing can be agreed upon, we should know it now." I had concluded that he decided to use this ostensibly casual conversation as the final go-round on SALT at Summit III.

Kissinger stated bluntly that the numbers proposed by the Soviets were impossible for us to accept. If we did, we would have to stop MIRV construction within a year, while the Soviets would be able to continue for four more years.

"This will be represented in the U.S. as our accepting a freeze while permitting the Soviet Union to catch up," Kissinger said. Lest the discussion lose sight of the reality of the situation, he introduced a gentle and subtle threat. "This agreement should be seen not only in terms of the numbers that are established but in terms of what each side could do *without* an agreement," he said. "Without an agreement, for example, we could put MIRVs on 500 more Minuteman missiles."

"In this period?" Gromyko asked, somewhat taken aback.

"Yes, in two years," Kissinger replied firmly. He then introduced our counterproposal on MIRVs. It did not go as far as the Pentagon had urged, but it still provided for a substantially greater number for the

U.S. than for the U.S.S.R. "We are restraining our possibilities much more than we are asking for your restraint," Kissinger stated.

The wrangling went on for almost an hour. Suddenly Brezhnev looked across the table at me. In a heavy voice he said, "Mr. President, let me say that if what Dr. Kissinger has outlined is the last word on this subject, there is no basis for an agreement."

He immediately returned to resume the argument with Kissinger, but from that moment I knew that there was no hope for a SALT agreement at Summit III.

Kissinger kept up the fight brilliantly and valiantly. At one point I passed him a note: "Use that 'forensic ability' Schlesinger told us would be sufficient to convince them." But Kissinger could not afford to smile even for a moment. Eventually I sent him another note: "Should be a recess—we appear to be in for endless emphasis on the obvious," and he began steering the discussion to a close. At the first opportunity I broke in and suggested that we keep to the schedule and go on the boat ride that Brezhnev had planned for us.

"I agree. It is time to go out on the water," he said, and immediately led us down to the dock, where we boarded Brezhnev's Soviet Navy yacht for a sail on the Black Sea.

Diary

The boat trip was really done in high style. It was a little rocky and on one occasion some of the plates fell off, but after we all sat down Brezhnev was in good form and the toasts went rather well.

The spirit of Oreanda I described as peace where we reach agreements equally fair to both sides. I also proposed a toast to the diplomats who do the work so that the leaders can rest.

The Brezhnev-Nixon doctrine I described as one that was fair to both nations and one which would leave a legacy of peace for generations to come.

The most interesting session was after lunch, when he joined me in sitting at the back of the boat and we just talked together. He pointed out Yalta and Bear Mountain and all the other points of interest. He became very emotional; he said that he wanted this summit to be one that would be remembered as were the other great events that had taken place, obviously referring, but without saying so, to Yalta.

He put his arm around me and said, "We must do something of vast historical importance. We want every Russian and every American to be friends that talk to each other as you and I are talking to each other here on this boat."

I had many thoughts as the boat went by Yalta and the harbor

—in Crimea the war—one of the most useless wars in history and one where both sides lost terribly. About the only thing good that came out of it was the Red Cross.

I made the point, just to try it out on him, that the danger in advanced nations and, of course, the implication included the Soviet Union among them, is the weakening of character. If he thought it through he could have thought of Mao's Red Guards and the Cultural Revolution. Brezhnev agreed and said sociologists and psychiatrists are now studying this question. The point, of course, was that as people got more material goods they became less "hungry," lost their drive, and become almost totally obsessed with self, selfishness, and every kind of abstract idea.

As we later walked back to the dacha after getting off the boat, Gromyko was on my right and I was glad to have a talk with him. He said that his analysis was that I was doing considerably better politically in the United States. He said, "It's really about nothing."

I said that the Crimea had been the cradle of war in the nineteenth century and that we could make it the birthplace of peace in the twentieth century.

On the boat I had said to Brezhnev that our goal must be the reduction of nukes and Brezhnev responded, "We must destroy the evil that we have created." He again came back to the theme that I was always welcome in the Soviet Union, even after '76.

The long boat ride, after the morning walk and the afternoon session, was very tiring. That night I had dinner with Pat alone on the balcony outside our room.

Diary

As we looked out at the sea, there was a three-quarter moon. Pat said that since she was a very little girl, when she looked at the moon, she didn't see a man in the moon or an old lady in the moon—always the American flag. This, of course, was years before anybody ever thought of a man actually being on the moon or an American flag being there.

She pointed it out to me and, sure enough, I could see an American flag in the moon. Of course, you can see in the moon whatever you want to see.

The next morning Brezhnev and I rode together to the airport. He took advantage of the long ride to importune me again on the Middle East. He said that while Sadat might believe in putting Egypt first,

Nasser had appealed to a stronger sentiment of pan-Arabism. I did not repeat for him my analysis of what I considered to be Sadat's brilliant positioning in the flexible middle ground between those extremes.

> *Diary*
>
> I simply said, "Don't let the Mideast become the Balkans for the U.S. and the Soviet Union. Don't let anyplace else, Southeast Asia, the Mideast, or the Caribbean, become a point of difference between us that draws us into conflict, when there are many more important issues that could draw us together." I had used this argument with him in pointing out how Roosevelt, Churchill, and Stalin had gotten along well, particularly emphasizing the Roosevelt-Stalin relationship in fighting the war, because they did not allow differences on what the peace was going to be like to deter them from their main goal of defeating the Nazis.
>
> Of course, historically, my own view is that this was a mistake —that Churchill was right in insisting that there be more discussion at that point and that we should have made some kind of a deal that would have avoided the division of Europe on the basis that it finally came out.

The subject of religion came up, and Brezhnev said, "What the hell difference does it make what God Americans pray to—we recognize all religions. All we care about is whether they are for peace." He again described his policy on Jewish emigration. He said, "As far as I am concerned, I say let all the Jews go and let God go with them."

He spoke of the destruction of civilization from nuclear war and repeated what Khrushchev had said fifteen years earlier: that we must remember that in such a war, the white race would be destroyed and only the yellows and blacks would remain to rule the world.

During this ride I suggested we have a "mini-summit" before the end of the year. Brezhnev enthusiastically agreed. We felt it should not be held in Washington or Moscow but in some place in between; I used the term *halfway house*, and he mentioned Switzerland. I told him it was essential to reach agreement on offensive weapons before the end of the year. Otherwise, I warned, since no agreement had been reached at this summit, Congress would go forward on a greatly increased defense budget. I suggested that Kissinger return to Moscow in September to arrange the agenda, and then Brezhnev and I could meet again in October, November, or December. I said that we must agree in principle on a reduction of military arms, and he nodded his head vigorously.

When we arrived at the airport, Brezhnev went back to Moscow and

Pat and I flew to Minsk. I noted in my diary: "On the color side, whereas wild flowers predominated in the Crimea, when we were at Minsk there were purple and yellow flowers—so we had the Whittier colors, purple and gold. Great fields of purple flowers."

The crowds that greeted us everywhere during Summit III seemed genuinely and spontaneously warm. Occasionally someone would shout out "Peace is very important." I noted that in nearly every casual conversation, whether with the people in the street or with the leaders in the Kremlin, the subject invariably turned to one of three topics: the desire for friendship and peace with the United States based on equality; the devastation Russia had suffered in World War II; or pride in Russia's cultural heritage, including the Czarist palaces and buildings. In Minsk the people seemed to reach out to us. Some had tears in their eyes. I felt that such things could not go unnoticed by their leaders. "In the end," I noted in my diary with cautious hope, "the Russian leadership must reflect their people's desires."

On our boat ride, Brezhnev and I had agreed that while Pat and I were in Minsk, Kissinger and Gromyko should make one more attempt at reaching an agreement on limiting offensive nuclear weapons. As soon as I was back in my room in the Kremlin, Kissinger came up to report that he had not been able to make any progress whatever. Gromyko had spent the time nit-picking and was apparently unable or unwilling to negotiate seriously.

In order to be able to talk freely, Kissinger and I went outside and walked up and down in the open courtyard. He was concerned because we would be going home empty-handed on SALT. But the Pentagon's last-minute about-face had made it impossible for us to engage in any flexible negotiating. If we had been able to return with even a controversial SALT agreement, Kissinger was convinced that we would have been able to educate public opinion to accept it. "And," he added, "it's a lot better subject to be debating about than Watergate." Despite this disappointment over SALT, he felt that Summit III had been a success even without a SALT agreement, and he said he did not think that I would be impeached now.

"Well, Henry," I said, as we started back upstairs, "we have to do what is right, regardless of the press analysis or the political consequences. You've done a superb job under enormous pressures against overwhelming odds. You can be proud. Now we shall just have to see where events take us. We have done our best."

It was clear by this time that Summit III was not going to produce any big news as far as new agreements were concerned. Some in the press were already trying out a critical line that attributed this failure to my Watergate troubles, implying that the Soviets were holding out either because they thought I might make greater concessions because I needed a foreign triumph to alleviate my domestic problems or because they thought that I was not going to survive and they might get better terms from my successor.

In normal times Summit III would have been hailed as a successful meeting. It produced the threshold test ban, further restrictions on ABMs, agreements to seek controls on environmental warfare and for cooperation in energy, the opening of additional consulates in both countries, and, most important, the oral agreement I made with Brezhnev for a mini-summit before the end of 1974 for the purpose of reaching agreement on limitations of offensive nuclear weapons.

In my judgment my Watergate problems and the impeachment hearings did not play a major part at Summit III. Our intelligence beforehand—and my distinct impression while in the Soviet Union—was that Brezhnev had decided to go all out for détente and place all his chips on my survival and my ultimate ability to deliver on what I promised. It was the American domestic political fluctuations, most of which had preceded Watergate, that cast the greatest doubt on my reliability: the failure to produce MFN status and the agitation over Soviet Jews and emigration had made it difficult for Brezhnev to defend détente to his own conservatives. Similarly, the military establishments of both countries were bridling against the sudden reality of major and meaningful arms limitation and the real prospect of arms reduction if and as détente progressed. These problems would have existed regardless of Watergate.

Diary

There are some, of course, who will want to put blame on Watergate for our failing to get an agreement on offensive nukes but, on the other hand, I think that it came out about right. We went as far as we could go at this point without raising an issue which could have lost us some of our good conservative supporters, and we did just about what the traffic would bear. As it turned out, it's probably just as well that we were unable to reach any agreement with the Russians on the nuclear front, because to have to take this thing on now would mean that we would have to be opposed to some of our best friends prior to the impeachment vote.

The fact was that neither side was prepared to go any further at Summit III. I think that both Brezhnev and I grasped this situation at the outset, and that is what accounted for his highly personal and warm demeanor. We both understood that if the process of détente could be maintained through a holding-pattern summit, we might be able to make a breakthrough at the next meeting.

Overall, I summarized Summit III as a mixed bag; its success or failure would have to be determined in light of the way events developed before the next meeting at the halfway house.

Diary

There is nit-picking to the effect that it was not as successful as the other two. The main thing is that the process went forward, and this is in itself an achievement. Peace is never going to be achieved once and for all—it must be constantly worked on. That's why these continuing summits between major powers must go forward, even though we don't have great announcements to make after each one.

I am inclined to think that in arranging the next summit, it's the informal meetings which provide the greatest opportunity for progress. I think the formal ones—the plenary sessions—produce the least, because everybody's talking for the record and making a record.

Brezhnev has been much more forthcoming when we meet informally in the car or elsewhere than when we are sitting down in a formal group with others present. The larger the group, the less free the conversation is. This is something that is true in all forms of society, but it is particularly true in the Soviet Union and in the Communist states.

On July 2, the last night of Summit III, we gave a reciprocal dinner at Spaso House, the American ambassador's residence. Brezhnev was the most relaxed I had ever seen him. Even Mrs. Brezhnev, who like most Soviet wives seemed uncomfortable in the limelight of Western visits, opened up and talked freely about her family.

Diary

At dinner Brezhnev spoke very warmly, grabbing me by the arm, first, about the meeting that we would have in between—the so-called halfway summit at halfway house—and second, that after 1976 he wants to see me. He said he thought he would be in power after that time and, even though because of our Constitution I would not be in, that I would always be welcome in the U.S.S.R.

Brezhnev's granddaughter was very pretty, and he has a very handsome son-in-law as well. Mrs. Brezhnev commented on Tricia, who had visited Russia, saying when she stepped off the plane she looked like a white winter snowflower. At one point, incidentally, he told me about his great-grandchild—a girl—one and a half. Mrs. Brezhnev said that the child had started walking at ten months and I said that taking the first step was always the hardest. He said, yes, that's true. He said in the case of his great-granddaughter now after that first step the only way they could keep from falling down was to almost run. Brezhnev compared this to U.S. and Soviet relations.

He clowned it up a bit by hitting a couple of keys on the piano, which allowed me to say something about playing a duet the next time he came to the United States. It's very difficult, however, to get the Russian elite to respond to any comments that are humorous, particularly when they are in a large group. Individually they will be warm and friendly, but collectively they immediately freeze—they have to watch to see what the others do before they react.

The last morning in Moscow Brezhnev and I held a final meeting alone in his office. I repeated my strong belief that we should try for a SALT accord by the end of the year so that the United States did not go ahead at an increased pace in the development of arms. I also urged what I called "increased communication" between us for taking care of the kind of problems that had arisen in the Middle East.

At the plenary session before we went to St. Vladimir Hall for the final signing ceremony, I said that we must not be discouraged by the fact that we did not settle every issue every time. It was important simply to keep talking.

Diary

The rest of the plenary meeting was really pro forma. They obviously want to put as good a face as possible on the summit as Brezhnev had in his dinner toast the night before when he interestingly enough took some credit for the Soviet Union and détente for the end of the war in Vietnam and holding off in the Mideast. Obviously, in both of these cases this was an overstatement. I think it would be better stated that in both areas the Soviet Union did not play a positive role, but, on the other hand, while they could not take credit for bringing about either of the peace settlements, they could have intervened more strongly than they did and made it impossible for us to accomplish our goal of having any peace settlement at all.

The Soviets ended Summit III with a flourish of ceremony and spectacle. We signed the protocols on the new limitation of ABMs to one site only, the treaty on the limitation of underground nuclear tests, and a joint statement on negotiations to control environmental warfare.

After the signing ceremony we went to St. George Hall, where a buffet that exceeded even the sumptuousness of the one at the end of Summit I had been laid out on two tables running the length of the vast room. While we were talking and toasting each other, I noticed that the small orchestra on the balcony was playing the music that had been played at Tricia's wedding.

To my surprise Brezhnev, Gromyko, Podgorny, and Kosygin all climbed into the car with me for the ride to the airport. Brezhnev sat on the jump seat in front of me. He was extremely quiet on the way out, letting Kosygin and Podgorny do most of the talking. At the airport we performed the traditional farewell ceremonies. Then Brezhnev and I turned and headed toward *Air Force One*.

Diary

As I was walking to the plane, I said that my only regret was that he was not coming with us back to the United States. And he said that, as a matter of fact, he had been thinking the same thing as we drove out to the airport. I really think he had a feeling of loss, and felt sad that the trip was over. He had looked forward to it—had built it up—had hoped that it would achieve a great deal—and now that it was over he was getting somewhat of a letdown.

I think he realizes that it wasn't a "home run," and yet it did make some progress and we talked on several occasions, including the last time at the dinner, of a meeting, perhaps in November, at a neutral place.

I wondered if it would be the last time that I would see Brezhnev. At times he looked very good but at other times he looked very tired. He started very late in the morning—10:30 or eleven o'clock—for every meeting.

My other feeling was one of disappointment on the fact that we couldn't get some sort of agreement on SALT and that the chance of getting it in the future looked pretty hard.

When I got on the plane, I went back through the cabin and said, "Well, we're home again." I recalled on our '53 trip that every time we got on the plane after some very dreary stops we would eat the rather plain food with great relish because it was safe and clean and we would always say, "Well, we're home again." I am sure everybody felt that way when they got on the plane this time.

IMPEACHMENT SUMMER

All the while we were in the Soviet Union, the impeachment effort at home had continued much as before. A few days after my return the House Judiciary Committee began releasing Doar's compilation of evidence on the Watergate break-in and cover-up, thus ensuring that Watergate would dominate the headlines in the weeks before the crucial vote on impeachment. The Ervin Committee also began to leak and then to release accusations from its supposedly secret report.

Despite its headline impact, however, this so-called evidence was generally admitted to be weak. ABC began its evening news with the announcement that there were "no bombshells." "No startling new disclosures," was NBC's verdict. And CBS reported that there were "no shockers, no startling new revelations." Jack Germond of the Washington *Star* summed up by saying, "The smoking pistol has yet to be found in President Nixon's hand."

That the evidence against me fell flat was satisfying; but the situation was still far from reassuring. On July 5 I summarized the situation as I saw it.

Diary

I remember Harlow saying almost a year ago, this issue has no legs to it. He may be right—may have been right, then—but so much has been added on—the personal taxes and all that sort of thing—so many doubts have been raised that one wonders what the situation is now.

I think of myself worrying as I have from time to time—what was going to happen next—and you get that sinking feeling in the bottom of your stomach and sometimes there are nights that are sleepless. I think of people like Kalmbach and Porter and others who are threatened with being sent to prison for fifteen to twenty years and so forth.

Perhaps as years go on attitudes may change, but they have left some deep scars, as I pointed out to both Ziegler and Haig on the plane coming back from Russia. Scars that will remain in the public mind and will not go away. Our only course of action is to keep fighting right through to the last and not to die a thousand deaths in the meantime.

I talked to Bebe too about this situation. Pat had pointed out that Bebe had been almost—she said that he had been really depressed. The whole purpose of course is to discredit, destroy, harass everybody around the President.

Both Pat and Bebe spoke of Rose and that she was really a

fighter. I am glad that Pat sensed that from her talk with Rose coming home on the plane because Rose has gone through hell on this whole eighteen-minute business and she certainly has stood up with great character and great courage.

Bebe makes the point when I tell him how regretful I am that he and other decent people have to go through all this hell, he says that my own strength has inspired them all. I am inclined to think that I have not been as strong as I could have been or should have been, but I must say when we have such people like this we can't let them down, and I have got to fight every inch of the way.

In any event, if we can get through the Court and by the impeachment vote we will then have a couple of years to do as many good things for the country as we possibly can. What we have to do is to hold ourselves together through this next very difficult two-month period.

On June 27, 1974, Peter Rodino told a group of reporters that all twenty-one Democrats on the House Judiciary Committee were going to vote for impeachment. With this statement he confirmed what no one had dared say publicly before: the votes were in even before the witnesses had been heard or a defense had been made. Rodino was reprimanded by members of both parties. His first reaction was to try to cover up; he even went before his colleagues in the House and insisted that he had not made the statement. But reporters from the Los Angeles *Times* and ABC who had been there and had heard him confirmed the accuracy of the story.

By this time there was no question in my mind that the House Judiciary Committee was going to vote to impeach me. It was the margin of that vote that would assume a vital importance, because it would have a direct effect on the vote of the full House. The critical votes were still the six swing Republicans and the three Southern Democrats. The way these nine men voted would tell me whether I would be impeached by the House. Timmons had reduced it almost to a science: it was a straightforward example of a multiplier effect. He calculated that each vote we lost in the committee would cost us five votes from our supporters on the floor of the House.

In the first week of July, after we returned from the Soviet Union, Timmons felt we would win at least one of the three Southern Democrats and lose at least two of the six Republicans. If we could hold our losses to these numbers in the committee, then we could be optimistic about beating impeachment in the full House. This analysis found reinforcement from several sides. Godfrey Sperling of the *Christian Sci-*

ence Monitor wrote that although Watergate was not worn out as an issue, it appeared to be receding from public conversation. Hugh Sidey, *Time*'s White House correspondent, told Henry Kissinger that his editors had decided that I was going to weather the impeachment storm. John Osborne, *The New Republic*'s White House watcher, told Ron Ziegler that he thought the House would not vote to impeach.

There were other hopeful signs of the sort that political pros might be expected to appreciate: RNC Chairman George Bush called the White House to say that he would like to have me appear on a fund-raising telethon; Don Rumsfeld called from Brussels, offering to resign as Ambassador to NATO and return to help work against impeachment among his former colleagues in Congress; and John Rhodes said he was for me unless he was presented with overwhelming evidence he should not be. Haig told me that his talks with the Cabinet members also indicated that the tide had turned. I was encouraged but not overly optimistic as I heard these reports.

Diary

Whatever the case may be, the big battle now is to try and hold the committee as well as we possibly can during the next couple of weeks. Obviously, the Democrats are going to pull out all the stops.

Dean will come again pretty soon and probably slap me around some more, but we don't think there are any other shoes ready to drop, although from the past track record no one can really be sure.

Getting back to Washington always gets you back into really the depths, although Ziegler says that the press is not nearly as hostile. But there is a depressing atmosphere here, and, of course, when you compound this with the family problem it makes it pretty tough. On the other hand, having survived this long I am convinced that we can see it through to the end—however the end comes out.

On July 12 I signed the Congressional Budget and Impoundment Control Act of 1974, a bill that I considered both a personal and a national triumph. After five years of nagging, urging, and pleading, and despite my weakened position because of Watergate, we had finally pushed through legislation that would make Congress face its responsibility for keeping the federal budget at agreed-upon levels.

After the ceremony Jerry Ford came over to me with his big, confident smile. "Don't worry, Mr. President," he said, "you've got this beat. We have a solid fifty-vote margin in the House, and we can build from there." Bryce Harlow, a man who knew Congress as well as any congressman, was also at the ceremony. He added, "Boss, you've got it won."

I wanted to believe these enthusiastic reports, but I knew Washington too well to think that the forces ranged against me would quit or forfeit the battle so easily. Twenty-five years of political instinct told me that despite the superficial appearances, things were not good; in fact, my instinct was stronger than ever that somehow, on some subsurface level, the political tide was flowing fast, and flowing against me.

I tried to pinpoint the reasons for my apprehension. One was the report of the numbers on my side. According to almost every report, there were approximately a hundred members of the House definitely committed to me, about seventy-five openly against me, and the rest were "undecided." I knew from experience that, more often than not, when a congressman tells someone from the White House that he is undecided on a particular question, he is probably against it and is only trying to be polite in declining to state his opposition before the vote is taken.

Another reason was my knowledge of how forceful, organized, and powerful the Democratic congressional leadership was, and how desperate they would become if it looked as though impeachment was actually going to be voted down. Having brought things this far, they would rightly fear the risk of a backlash if the impeachment drive failed and voters began to feel that the agony of Watergate had been prolonged for partisan motives.

Another major unknown was the Supreme Court, which would soon be handing down its ruling on Jaworski's petition for the sixty-four additional tapes. St. Clair was optimistic, but even he conceded that the Court would probably end up voting along political lines, despite the fact that we had the stronger legal case. In the event that the Court ruled flatly against me in the tapes case, I could decide to defy the ruling. But that would almost certainly bring about impeachment and therefore could not realistically be considered. Another choice was to *abide* by the Court's ruling without actually *complying* with it. This would involve some plan to turn over the tapes only in an excerpted form. In fact, I knew that even this approach would not take care of the real problem. I had not heard all the tapes, but I was concerned that in those thousands of hours of conversations there might be material that would be so damaging that I would not want to turn it over. There was already the June 23 tape, which still worried me. As I had noted in my diary on July 21, "Of course, how we handle the 23rd tape is a very difficult call because I don't know how it could be excerpted properly."

The Supreme Court ruling was going to have a tremendous—and almost certainly a detrimental—influence on the course of my impeachment hearings.

Diary

At this time, I must say, I am not particularly optimistic, al-

> though I would not be surprised about anything. If only [Burger] and his colleagues can look at the terrible impact if they are coming down in a way that totally destroys executive privilege—the impact that it will have in the future on Presidents. If only they can see that we may come up with a reasonable approach.
>
> In any event, if only we could get over this hurdle without tripping and falling and giving the House some ground for impeachment we can then insist on a vote in the House and then move on to other things.
>
> If they leave any air in the balloon at all, if we could find a way to comply or abide, this would be the best of all worlds for us because then they could go on with their vote in the House and then we could in the last two years make up for the time that has been lost over the past year and one-half in doing what we were elected to do, the nation's business.

I also felt that the optimists among my supporters had not taken into account the political realities that would come into play when the full House of Representatives was faced with having to vote on an impeachment resolution. In addition to the partisan Democrats who were sure to vote for impeachment regardless of the evidence, an increasing number of Republicans would become concerned that if I were still in office during the November elections, I would be like an albatross around their necks.

If my support in Congress was halfhearted and disorganized, the White House staff was not in much better shape. Haig's eleventh-hour efforts to organize a group that would lead the fight from within the White House was handicapped by the "arm's length" requirement that our congressional supporters had put on their contacts with us. I knew, too, that they were handicapped psychologically by their own uncertainty about the case, by their fear that there might be still another bombshell—and that they might be out on the front line when it hit.

I was also concerned because the economy, which most voters still named as the issue of number-one concern to them, was standing on wobbly postembargo, postfreeze legs. The Dow Jones average had just hit a new four-year low. To the considerable degree that the economy affected national confidence and that national confidence would affect attitudes toward impeachment, this was a cause for the most serious concern. Unfortunately there did not seem to be much that I could do about the problem. I had convened and attended a number of meetings focusing on it, and there was general agreement that the best course was just to wait and ride it out.

Finally, there were the media. I felt that, consciously or subconsciously, they had a vested interest in my impeachment. After all the months of leaks and accusations and innuendo, the media stood to lose if

I were vindicated. The defenses never caught up with the charges. For example, after all the damaging press and television coverage of alleged abuses of the IRS, when IRS Commissioner Donald Alexander announced the conclusions of a report that found no one had in fact been harassed as a result of White House intervention—a conclusion later supported by the findings of a joint congressional committee investigation—it was run on page thirty-nine of the New York *Times* and received scant coverage elsewhere. Most of the reporters and commentators were still filtering everything through their own Watergate obsessions. For example, Douglas Kiker of NBC reported that the White House was seeking to create the "impression" of a "busy President, back from an important and exhausting peacemaking mission, trying to do his job" despite harassment from the House Judiciary Committee. Months later, House Judiciary Committee impeachment firebrand Jerome Waldie said he doubted that I would have been forced from office "if the press had not desired it."

These were some of the reasons that my own instincts about the outcome of the impeachment effort were more pessimistic than those of most of my advisers. I often thought of something Tricia had observed several months earlier that seemed to me to be a perfect description of our problem. She had said that trying to explain something like Watergate was just like engaging in trench warfare: despite all the effort and all the blood expended, it was simply impossible to advance.

On July 12 we left Washington to spend two weeks in California. We received word aboard *Air Force One* that John Ehrlichman had been convicted of perjury and of conspiring to violate the civil rights of Daniel Ellsberg's psychiatrist. I was deeply depressed by the tragic irony of this development. Ellsberg, who had leaked top-secret documents, had gone free. Ehrlichman, who was trying to prevent such leaks, had been convicted.

When Pat, Ed, Tricia, and I arrived in San Clemente on the afternoon of July 12, everything seemed to be the same as it had been on every other California trip. We all went for a swim in the pool and then had an early dinner. It was a cool, clear night, and Ed and Tricia decided to take a walk before going to bed. They went through the garden and around the pool out to the golf course. When I bought the house in 1969, some local supporters had formed a group called Friends of the President and had raised money to build and maintain a three-hole golf course on Bob Abplanalp's property, adjacent to mine.

In the diary Tricia kept during this period she recorded the shock she and Ed experienced when they saw the golf course that night:

> Wasted, neglected, ugly, dead. The golf course of "Friends" of the Presi-

dent is no more. The sight is sickening, not because it is a sickening sight, but because of what it signifies. Deserted. Killed. The golf course. The man for whom it was created.

Ed and I came upon it on our first stroll around the grounds, and its quality of finality, of hopelessness, smote us with an almost physical intensity. Ed tried to overcome this feeling with nervous levity. He said, "Looks like someone forgot to water the golf course." Of course we both knew someone had remembered not to water it. We made light of it to Daddy by saying we like to see it wild as it was when we first saw San Clemente. He was not fooled, but politely agreed. He trying to spare us. We trying to spare him. No one was spared.

Despite these dark counterpoints, during the first days of our stay the reports from Washington continued optimistic. I tried to be skeptical and detached, but almost irresistibly I found myself charting out in my diary plans for the future.

Diary

I think what we have to do is to remember that once we get past this election then we have just got to call them as we see them and '75 is the year to do it. '73 would have been the year to do it, as we thoroughly expected to do it when we first began '73, but then with the Watergate thing we lost that whole year and now we are in the election year, but '75 will be our last shot at doing the responsible things that need to be done to get our economy back on the right kind of a track and also to deal philosophically with some of these great issues where this may be the last opportunity for a conservative viewpoint to prevail over the radical leftist viewpoint, which McGovern and his colleagues fought for and lost.

We shall always have to keep in mind Tricia's philosophy, that we have got to look down to the end of the road to see that we will come out all right, whatever may be and whatever way it is, and then remember that we will look back and see that we shouldn't have been worried about things all along. This is very hard to do, but it is the only thing that can sustain us through these other critical and difficult times. It is the only thing that has sustained us as a matter of fact through the enormous blows that we have been getting from all sides for such a long time.

As I sit here in my upstairs library, I am looking at a really beautiful portrait, hanging over the fireplace. I don't know whether it is a portrait or probably a photograph touched up of my mother when she was twelve years old. She was born in 1885, which would have meant that she would have been ninety years old now. But her face looked somewhat like Julie, I would say, or a combination of Julie and Tricia (very serious, very thoughtful, and very grown-up for a girl of twelve). She was truly a saint, as Helene Drown used to say. Someday I must write a monograph about her, which I think could be a very moving one.

On July 15 there was a violent coup on the strife-torn island of Cyprus. Fighting between the Greek and Turkish Cypriot factions seemed imminent. I suggested to Kissinger that he send Assistant Secretary of State Joe Sisco over to monitor the situation at the scene. I noted in my diary, "The Cyprus thing brought home the fact that with the world in the situation it is, with the peace as fragile as it is in various parts of the world, a shake-up in the American presidency and a change would have a traumatic effect abroad and a traumatic effect at home."

On July 18, James St. Clair was finally, and very reluctantly, given a chance to present a summary of my defense to the House Judiciary Committee. He did a brilliant job, and the overall impact of his appearance was extremely positive. We heard that this impression heightened even further the panic that had set in among the committee Democrats. Soon thereafter the Democrats voted not to allow St. Clair to present a defense of me on television once the public hearings began.

As these all-important hearings approached, Timmons's reports became troubled. He picked up signs that the Democratic leadership was turning on tremendous pressure in preparation for a fight to the finish. Democratic National Chairman Robert Strauss stated publicly that no responsible man could vote other than for impeachment. And we heard that Tip O'Neill was putting pressure on Rodino which Rodino was passing along to Doar to do something to get impeachment back on the track.

On July 18 I tried to evaluate the situation.

Diary

It is a little bit foggy this morning and in a curious way, I think this is the day that I may probably have been preparing for in terms of really shaking up our own thinking to get prepared for the battle of August and perhaps even, if Timmons's more pessimistic views prevail, the battle for the balance of the year in the Senate.

I began to think really about the whole impeachment process and very objectively and coldly. All in all, it appears very possible although not probable, I would have to say that O'Neill's bunch is going to be able certainly to get a majority vote out of the committee and a very damn close vote in the House. This completely leaves out the thing that has been worrying me earlier in the week—the Supreme Court thing.

The problem we have here is trying to hold the line with the Southerners in the House and that means trying to get at least two of them of the committee, and hopefully, for sure, one. We think we have Flowers.

A climactic struggle: that is what we have entered now and I think I have gotten that through to everybody, although I must say that Haig and St. Clair are thinking along these lines themselves.

Haig has agreed that we have got to get the Cabinet out just as soon as St. Clair gets back. In fact, as he said, we have got to push every button and mobilize every asset that we have got. Haig thinks that at a minimum that we should get fourteen votes in the committee. We would hope we could end up with sixteen; of course if we got eighteen that would be a great victory. Sixteen would be manageable (Haig's term), fourteen would be a bit tough, but he thinks still not beyond the point where we could still win on the floor.

Basically, it is like a campaign. We have got to take some risks when everything is on the line.

On July 19 John Doar stood before the members of the House Judiciary Committee and delivered a passionate and, by all accounts, masterful argument calling for my impeachment. The committee had continued its media blitz, releasing mounds of material on different subjects, designed to crescendo toward the public televised hearings to begin on July 24. Everything was moving quickly now, as we approached the time when the hearings would be ended and the vote would be taken.

Diary

I intend to live the next week without dying the death of a thousand cuts. This has been my philosophy throughout my political life. Cowards die a thousand deaths, brave men die only once.

I suppose it could be said that this is our Seventh Crisis in spades. Because the next month will be as hard a month as we will ever go through, but we can only be sustained by two things: one, in the belief that we are right—we are fighting, as all agree, an assault on our entire system of government.

And second, we will be sustained by the fact that at the end it will be over and even if it is over in the terms of an impeachment, we will just have to live with that.

By this time next week we may have both the Court and the committee vote. We can only hope for the best and plan for the worst.

The weekend of July 20 was the last time there was any real hope. On the night of July 21 we all went to a party for some of our old California friends at Roy Ash's house in Bel Air. Tricia's description of the evening in her diary said it all:

> At times it is like being in the eye of the hurricane. It is quite calm, quite still and if your eyes are closed you don't notice the unnatural darkness which surrounds you. You recall moments isolated in time. Yet they exist in the present. You recall a time without "Watergate" or when Watergate simply meant a rather extravagant place to live. An isolated moment. But then your eyes open and the darkness you see is the darkness of the storm.
>
> The sun last shone at the Ash dinner. Their home in Bel Air was a million light-years away from the turmoil. There was a glow of old about the entire evening. The guests, composed of old friends and others that the Ashes felt could be helpful, were in high spirits.
>
> Ever since the Roy Ash party, dating from the day following it, something was lost. Some support. The straw became so brittle and worn that you could almost hear it breaking asunder.

By the beginning of the week of July 22 there had been no new evidence introduced since late June, when it had been generally acknowledged that the evidence was not sufficient to justify impeachment. Nothing factual had changed, but the political ground began to shift. We heard that John Rhodes was going to help us; and that he was not. We were told that Goldwater had said that he was going to ask me to resign; but when Haig called him, Goldwater laughed and said in absolutely no circumstances had he ever said that, nor would he. Perhaps most disturbing, because it was apparently true, we heard that we were in trouble with the three Southern Democrats on the committee: Wilbur Mills was said to be getting to his fellow Arkansan Thornton, while Rodino was reportedly having private sessions with Flowers and O'Neill was rumored to be putting a strong arm on Mann. Most people don't recall it, but long before the new "evidence" of the June 23 tape was produced, the political consensus had already been reached, and the political consensus was to impeach.

"LOWEST POINT IN THE PRESIDENCY"

On the morning of Tuesday, July 23, the day before the House Judiciary Committee's televised hearings were scheduled to begin, Lawrence Hogan, one of the committee's conservative Republicans, called a press conference. In emotional tones he announced that he had decided to vote for my impeachment. Many of his colleagues, and some news commentators, said that Hogan's effort to jump the gun and thereby gain maximum publicity was an effort to shore up his faltering campaign for governor of Maryland. In San Clemente we tried to minimize the damage Hogan caused by concentrating on the many people who criticized him and his motives. But the fact was that he had dealt us a very bad blow. Later that same day, July 23, Timmons called from Washington. He said it was now certain: we had lost all three Southern Democrats on the committee.

I was stunned. I had been prepared to lose one and had steeled myself for losing two. But losing all three meant certain defeat on the House floor. It meant impeachment.

I told Haig bitterly that if this was the result of our hands-off strategy, we could hardly have done worse by outright lobbying. I said that we had to do something to try to get at least one of the Southerners back.

Haig mentioned that one of George Wallace's aides had sent word that I had only to call on Wallace if there was anything he could do to help me. Here was the opportunity to take up Wallace's offer: perhaps the Alabama governor would be willing to call his fellow Alabamian Walter Flowers and remind him that party loyalty need not include supporting the radical surgery of removing a President from office. I agreed that it was worth a try, and Haig said he would arrange the call.

At 3:52 P.M. in my office in San Clemente I picked up the phone. George Wallace was already on the line.

Diary

When I got Wallace on the phone he played it very cozy. He said he couldn't quite hear me at first, and then said that he hadn't expected the call, that nobody had told him about it.

He said he hadn't examined the evidence. That he prayed for me. That he was sorry that this had to be brought upon me. That he didn't think it was proper for him to call Flowers, that he thought Flowers might resent it and that if he changed his mind he would let me know. I knew when I hung up the phone that he would not change his mind.

The call took only six minutes. When I hung up the phone I turned to Haig and said, "Well, Al, there goes the presidency."

Haig was not ready to give up. He urged that I call Alabama Senator James Allen and ask if he could help with Flowers. I reached Allen in Washington. He was concerned and friendly, but he was too honest to give me any false encouragement. I had to accept the fact that the committee's Southerners were lost.

I called Joe Waggonner, and he said that with the three Southerners gone, he could hope to hold only between thirty and thirty-five of the Waggonner group. This meant that I could not possibly have enough votes on my side when the full House voted. "My guess is," I noted in my diary, "that the Democrats have made a command decision to get me out and Ford in and then tear him up and win in 1976."

That night I sat in my study trying to work on the speech on the economy that I was to give on national television in two days. I tried to organize and outline my thoughts for it, but my mind kept wandering back to the afternoon, and a sense of hopeless loss and despair kept welling up in me.

My options had been reduced to only two: resign or be impeached. I had to decide either to leave the presidency voluntarily, or else confront the hard decision of whether the country could stand six months of having the President on trial in the Senate.

Over the past few weeks I had talked with Haig and Ziegler several times about resigning. Haig argued that resignation would not only look like an admission of guilt, but it would mean a dangerously easy victory for the radicals—not just over me but over the system.

There were also personal factors to consider. My family had already been put through two years of hell, but if I resigned I could expect an onslaught of lawsuits that would cost millions of dollars and take years to fight in the courts. I told Haig that the personal factors must not be the deciding ones. But it was difficult to separate personal considerations from political, party, and national interests.

On the edge of my speech notes I wrote: "12:01 A.M. Lowest point in the presidency, and Supreme Court still to come."

I would not have long to wait.

The next morning I overslept for the first time in several months. I had worked on the speech until 2:30 A.M., and it was after nine o'clock when I picked up the bedside phone. Haig came on the line, and I asked, "How are things going?" In a strained voice he said, "Well, it's pretty rough, Mr. President. I didn't want to wake you until we had the complete text, but the Supreme Court decision came down this morning."

"Unanimous?" I guessed.

"Unanimous. There's no air in it at all," he said.

"None at all?" I asked.

"It's tight as a drum."

This decision in the case of *United States* v. *Nixon* was widely heralded as one of the Court's finest hours. As one television reporter described it, the United States had triumphed. While I understood the reasons for the decision, I thought that the United States had lost. I felt that the presidency itself was a casualty of this ruling.

I asked Haig to come to my study. A few minutes later St. Clair came in, looking very dejected. The problem was not just that we had lost but that we had lost so decisively. We had counted on some air in the Court's ruling, at least some provision for exempting national security materials. We had counted on at least one dissent. For a few minutes we discussed the option of "abiding" by the decision in the Jeffersonian tradition. But after checking with some of our strongest supporters in Washington, we concluded that full compliance was the only option.

I asked St. Clair how long he thought we could take to turn over the sixty-four tapes covered by the decision. He said that with all the problems involved in listening to them and preparing transcripts, we could probably take a month or more.

I thought that we should assess the damage right away. When Haig called Buzhardt to discuss the decision, I took the phone and asked him to listen to the June 23 tape and report back to Haig as soon as possible. This was the tape I had listened to in May on which Haldeman and I discussed having the CIA limit the FBI investigation for political reasons rather than the national security reasons I had given in my public statements. When I first heard it, I knew it would be a problem for us if it ever became public—now I would find out just how much of a problem.

Buzhardt listened to the tape early in the afternoon. When he called back, he told Haig and St. Clair that even though it was legally defensible, politically and practically it was the "smoking gun" we had been fearing. Haig and St. Clair had often remarked that Buzhardt was an alarmist. So Haig called Buzhardt back and asked him to listen to the June 23 tape a second time. After Buzhardt had listened again and made a second report of his impressions, Haig put on a brave front and told me that the tape was apparently "embarrassing" but not completely "unmanageable." "I think we can cope with it," he said.

Diary

The 23rd tape we have talked over time and time again. Fred has listened to it twice, spoken to St. Clair about it. St. Clair wants to talk to Al about it and listen to it on Monday. When St. Clair and Al came up to see me in the Library to discuss what St. Clair should say about complying with the Supreme Court decision, St. Clair rather airily passed off the 23rd tape by saying—"but just two weeks later you told Gray to go forward with his investigation."

On the night that the Court's ruling was handed down, the House Committee began its televised sessions. The Democrats postured shamefully, pretending that they had not made up their minds. My supporters were eloquent—but they were fighting a lost battle. And now, underneath it all, like slow-fused dynamite waiting to explode, was the June 23 tape.

I was swimming in the ocean at Red Beach near San Clemente on July 27 when the House Judiciary Committee voted on the first article of impeachment. It charged that I had engaged in a "course of conduct" designed to obstruct the investigation of the Watergate case. The vote went exactly the way I had feared: all the Democrats, including the three conservative Southerners, were joined by six of the seventeen Republicans. The article was passed, 27 to 11.

I was getting dressed in the beach trailer when the phone rang and Ziegler gave me the news. That was how I learned that I was the first President in 106 years to be recommended for impeachment: standing in the beach trailer, barefoot, wearing old trousers, a Banlon shirt, and a blue windbreaker emblazoned with the Presidential Seal.

Our family dinner that night was not subdued, but it was more quiet than usual. Afterward, in my study, I made some notes about Pat.

Diary

I remember that Tricia said as we came back from the beach that her mother was really a wonderful woman. And I said, yes. She has been through a lot through the twenty-five years we have been in and out of politics. Both at home and abroad she has always conducted herself with masterful poise and dignity. But, God, how she could have gone through what she does, I simply don't know.

That night and the next I sat up very late trying to grasp the new situation I faced and decide on the best course of action to deal with it.

Diary

And so we will be back on Monday. They will listen to the tapes, and my guess is that they might well come in to me and say, "We just don't think this is manageable." I am referring to St. Clair, Haig, et al.

If we do make that decision, then I have a hard call—that call being as to whether I decide to bite the bullet on resignation or whether I continue to fight it through the House and wait until the House vote and then resign on the basis that I can't put the country through the months that would be involved in an impeachment trial.

Al and Ziegler have been splendid in this period. Ziegler

makes the point very strongly that if we ever connote the impression that we have given up, then everybody will run to the hills. Al points out that under no circumstances must we do this for another reason. That if we don't get a third in the House that it would look as if we had run out and so forth.

As a matter of fact, I have had a feeling of calm and strength during this period. This is due in part to the fact that after hearing of the total defection of the Southerners, I realized that we had lost the ball game and faced at least a six-month trial in the Senate.

To a certain extent I think the calmness and strength may have come from somewhere back in my background—perhaps from my father and my mother.

I now recognized in my own mind something that, totally deliberately, I did not convey to my closest associates: the country simply could not afford to have a crippled President for six months.

Diary

We have to try to work out what we can do to live out whatever life I have left as President and thereafter in a decent way.

Looking to the future, I recognize that I would have to face up to the hard fact of how I could take care of our personal expenses in the time ahead. Whether I can sell a book or papers or what have you in order to have the funds that would be needed to maintain an adequate staff in the office and in the house. My present inclination is to sell the property in Florida and take what equity I have there so that I have some cash on hand. As far as the San Clemente house is concerned, I will simply have to make a determination as to whether we want to keep it. It might be that we would be better off to take a reasonably comfortable apartment at some place and live out our lives there.

Needless to say, how we are able to handle our staff like Manolo and Fina—our household staff—and even the minimum staff of Rose and two or three secretaries to work with me on the book, God only knows. But I must not borrow trouble on this at this point. At the present time what I have to do is to recognize that we are in a battle for our lives. It involves the country. The sad thing, as Eddie says, is that the bad guys will have won. He means by that that this would be a very bad thing for the country should I go the resignation route.

Henry came in to see me, very mournful but, bless him, he was thinking only with his heart. A very unusual approach for a

> man who is so enormously endowed with extraordinary intellectual capacity. He said that his wife had told him that history in four years would look back on the President as a hero. And Al, of course, has made the point that history will show me in the end to have been an outstanding President.

We returned to Washington on Sunday, July 28. Tricia recorded the scene:

> In the hall of the second floor of the White House we said goodbye to Daddy and Mama before Ed and I departed for New York. Daddy came as close to outward emotion as he ever does when he said how much it had meant to him for us to be in California with him. Without further expression, I felt as if these words marked an end of an era. That this was a farewell. A chapter ended forever.

Monday, July 29, was our first full day back in Washington. I was shocked to see the difference that just two weeks had made. Impeachment hysteria had taken over the city. The White House staff was cloaked in gloom. It remained to be seen whether anything could be salvaged of the shattered confidence of the tired men and women in the West Wing and the EOB.

On Tuesday St. Clair returned from a long weekend in Cape Cod, where he had gone to get some rest. Even before the California trip Haig told me that St. Clair had become tired and touchy and that we would have to be careful if we wanted to keep him on the staff. St. Clair listened to the June 23 tape and discussed it with Buzhardt. His breezy optimism disappeared. He not only agreed with Buzhardt that this was the smoking gun, but he said that it so contradicted the arguments he had made before the House Judiciary Committee that he would become party to an obstruction of justice unless it was made public.

As we weighed the damage of the June 23 tape, the House Judiciary Committee passed two more articles of impeachment. Article II, passed on July 29, charged that I had committed an impeachable offense by abusing the powers of the presidency. It contained a number of different charges ranging from an alleged attempt to use the IRS for political purposes to the 1969 national security wiretaps. Article III, passed on July 30, charged that I had committed an impeachable offense by defying the committee's subpoenas for tapes and documents. After voting down two more articles of impeachment—one dealing with the Cambodian bombing and the other with my personal finances—the House Judiciary Committee recessed. The next step would be the vote on each of the three articles of impeachment by the House of Representatives. The opening debate was scheduled for August 19.

On the night of July 30 I could not get to sleep. After tossing and turning for a few hours, I finally put on the light and took a pad of notepaper from the bed table. I wrote the time and date at the top—3:50 A.M., July 31—and I began to outline the choices left to me. There were really only three: I could resign right away; I could stay on until the House had voted on the articles of impeachment and then resign if impeached; or I could fight all the way through the Senate.

For almost three hours I listed the pros and cons: what would be the best for me, for my family, for my friends and supporters? What would be the best for the country?

There were strong arguments against resigning. First and foremost, I was not and never had been a quitter. The idea that I would be running away from the job and ending my career as a weak man was repugnant to me. Resignation would be taken by many, and interpreted by the press, as a blanket admission of guilt. Resignation would set a dangerous precedent of short-circuiting the constitutional machinery that provides for impeachment. I also had to consider that my family and many of my supporters would want me to fight and would be hurt and disillusioned if I gave up before the battle was over.

The arguments in favor of resignation were equally compelling. I knew that after two years of being distracted and divided by Watergate, the nation badly needed a unity of spirit and purpose to face the tough domestic and international problems that would not wait through the six months of a Senate trial. Besides, I would be crippled politically as soon as the House voted to impeach, and I did not know whether I could subject the country to the ordeal of a weakened presidency during such troubled and important times. From a practical point of view, I also had to face the fact that if I decided to stay and fight, the outcome of the fight was all but settled: I would be defeated and dishonored, the first President in history to be impeached and convicted on criminal charges.

Another positive effect of resignation, one I knew to be uppermost in the minds of many Republicans, was that it would free the party from having to defend me. The 1974 elections would not become a referendum on Nixon and Watergate, and their campaigns and their congressional seats would not be held hostage to my political fortunes.

It was almost morning by the time I finished making these notes. My natural instincts welled up and I turned the paper over and wrote on the back: "End career as a fighter."

That was what my instincts and my intuition told me was the right thing to do. As bad as Watergate was, it would be far worse to set the precedent of a presidential resignation—even if the alternative was the removal of a President because of a political scandal. *"End career as a fighter"*—the way it had begun. That was the way I really wanted it.

With Buzhardt and St. Clair now on the side of resignation, Haig's position became pivotal. I would need Haig to rally whatever loyal staff was left and to keep the White House running if I chose not to resign but to face a Senate trial.

On Wednesday, July 31, Haig read the transcripts of the June 23 conversations for the first time.

"Well, what do you think?" I asked when he had finished.

"Mr. President," he said, "I am afraid that I have to agree with Fred and Jim St. Clair. I just don't see how we can survive this one. I know what was really happening there, and I know how you feel about it, but I think that we have to face the facts, and the facts are that the staff won't hold and that public opinion won't hold either, once this tape gets out."

That afternoon Ron Ziegler listened to the tape. I could tell that he too now felt the situation was all but hopeless.

THE DECISION TO RESIGN

On Thursday, August 1, I told Haig that I had decided to resign. If the June 23 tape was not explainable, I could not very well expect the staff to try to explain and defend it.

I said that I planned to take the family to Camp David over the weekend to prepare them and then to resign in a televised speech on Monday night. I would stay in Washington for about two weeks putting things in order, and then fly to San Clemente.

Haig said that we could work out the arrangements however I wanted, but he suggested that I resign even sooner, perhaps the next night, Friday, August 2. Since the June 23 tape was in the group to be handed over to Judge Sirica that morning, Haig thought that I should have resigned and been gone from the scene before the tape surfaced publicly. By that time, he said, so much attention would be focused on the new President that the damaging impact of the tape might be muted.

I decided to think about it, and I asked Haig if in the meantime he would take some notes and then have Ray Price begin work on a resignation speech. I told him that I would acknowledge that I had made mistakes; but I did not want Price to write a groveling mea culpa. I wanted him to say that I no longer had the political support in Congress or in the country that I believed I needed to govern effectively.

I also asked Haig to see Jerry Ford and tell him that I was thinking of resigning, without indicating when. I said Haig should ask him to be prepared to take over sometime within the next few days. I told him to impress on Ford the need for absolute secrecy. This was a decision I had to make for and by myself—right up to the end. I told him that I would be put in a humiliating position if it got to the point that the Republican National Chairman or a group of senators or congressmen, or a delegation of Cabinet members, began requesting or demanding that I resign. I knew that if that happened, my lifetime instincts of refusing to cave to political pressure might prevail.

I went over to the EOB office early in the afternoon. Now that the decision to resign had been made, I felt that if I could focus strongly enough on carrying it out in all its details, it would be easier to get through the painful decisions and duties of the next few days. I took off my suit coat and put on my favorite old blue sports jacket.

I asked Ron Ziegler to come over. As soon as he came in, I could see that Haig had already talked to him. I confirmed that I was going to resign.

There was a long moment of silence. Ziegler was by instinct a fighter, like me. He said only, "Mr. President, I know you want me to support your decision, so I will."

I told him that I knew Jerry Ford was not experienced in foreign affairs. "But he's a good and decent man, and the country needs that now," I said.

When I told Ziegler about Haig's advice to move quickly and resign the following night, he argued strongly that such a move would be precipitate. He said that there should be at least enough time to prepare properly. I realized that he was right, if for no other reason than that I owed it to my friends and supporters to give them a chance to react to the June 23 tape and get off the hook while I was still in office, rather than leave them behind holding the bag. The least they deserved was the chance to reverse their position if they wanted. So I tentatively decided to wait until Monday night to resign.

After Ziegler had left, I read some of Timmons's congressional reports and listened to the last group of tapes that had to be turned over to Sirica the following week. Around six o'clock I heard that Bebe Rebozo had just arrived from Miami. I asked Haig if he could arrange a dinner on the *Sequoia,* and an hour later we were sailing up the Potomac under a sultry evening sky.

"You're not going to like this," I said to Rebozo, "but I have decided that I should resign." I will always remember the stricken expression on Rebozo's face when I said this.

"You can't do it," he said. "It's the wrong thing to do. You have got to continue to fight. You just don't know how many people are still for you."

I told him about the June 23 tape and said that once it was released there would certainly be a trial in the Senate, with the likelihood of conviction. He urged that I get Russell Long and other leading senators in to listen to it and not just take the evaluation of a small group of staff.

I said that even if I had a chance in the Senate, the country simply could not afford six months with its President on trial.

As we sailed back toward Washington, I asked Rebozo to help by backing me up with the family. He said he would do everything he could as long as I would promise not to make the decision irrevocable until we made one last try to mount a defense. I agreed. I was touched by his spirit and by his fierce loyalty. But I knew how helpless and hopeless it was.

When we returned to the White House, I went to the Lincoln Sitting Room. It had been a long hard day.

The afternoon of August 2 Haig asked Chuck Wiggins to come in and read the June 23 transcript and give us his preliminary evaluation of its impact.

Haig reported to me that Wiggins said impeachment in the House and conviction in the Senate were now no longer in doubt. He said that when these tapes became known, we would lose all but two or three Republicans on the Judiciary Committee—possibly including himself. He said that unless I planned to withhold the tape from the Court by pleading the Fifth Amendment, I should get ready to resign right away. Like St. Clair, he felt that unless he reported the existence of the tape, he would himself become party to an obstruction of justice. Haig assured him that we would make it public.

That night I began the painful task of telling my family about the June 23 tape and preparing them for the impact it would have on my attempts to remain in office. Tricia's diary recorded the family side of that day:

> Julie called, very down this morning. She informed me that Daddy had had a talk with her that was serious but she hesitated to elaborate over the phone. Immediately I said I was coming right down. She said it was not really necessary. I replied that it was. She agreed.
>
> I pushed the Secret Service button and informed them I would be leaving on the next shuttle for Washington.
>
> Our curious little band departed within ten minutes. While boarding the jet at La Guardia Airport, catcalls, boos, and obscene words were hurled at me by a group of Eastern employees who were lounging around their vehicles. I was caught between two agents, one on the step above me, one on the step below. I attempted to bypass the agent on the step below so that I could verbally take head-on the cowardly group. But the agent was not inclined to cooperate and anyway I thought it more important to make this flight than to protest the treatment.
>
> At the White House, I took the elevator to the second floor, then scurried to the secret stairway at the East Hall and climbed to the third floor. I walked into Julie's room and found her on the telephone. Seeing me, she disengaged herself and I calmly asked her what Daddy had said to her yesterday. "He thinks he must resign." "Why?" "Because he has virtually no support left." "Julie, I can't believe this isn't a nightmare. It cannot be happening."

Julie and I talked some more and I learned that Mama had not been told of Daddy's tentative decision. Mama was in her sitting room at her desk. It is strange how you try to spare those you love from worry. Strange because worry is contagious and is difficult to conceal other than with words. So in the end it is kinder to reveal what the person you are trying to spare already feels. But I was still trying to protect Mama and spare her from grief. Daddy, of course, is always protective of everyone but himself. Mama and I talked briefly and made plans to walk with the dogs later that afternoon.

From her room I entered my own down the hall. I placed a call through the operators to Edward at his office. This is something I refrain from doing, so when he answered he knew the motive had to be serious. Without going into any details, I said it would be "delightful" if he could come down to Washington that evening for dinner. *Delightful* was a codeword we used to connote trouble. We did not have a codeword for disaster.

After the call I met Bebe in the hall. He looked sick and I asked him how Daddy was. Bebe had just been in the Lincoln Sitting Room with Daddy and he surprisingly (for Bebe is closed-mouthed) told me that Daddy had told him about resigning. Bebe suggested that I should go to Daddy and pretend I knew nothing so that Daddy could tell me himself. This I did.

Daddy was seated in his brown armchair with his feet up on the ottoman. He was fussing with a pipe. He greeted me, "Well, honey, when did you arrive?" And then he began a clear description of the June 23 tape and an analysis of his position. I only interrupted when he began to speak of resigning for the good of the country. I told him for the good of the country he must stay in office.

Then as I was leaving I went over to where he was, put my arms around him, kissed his forehead, and without warning I burst into tears and said brokenly, "You are the most decent person I know."

Emotions for me are usually completely controllable externally. But when Daddy said, "I hope I have not let you down," the tragedy of his ghastly position shattered me.

Mama, Julie, Bebe, David, and I had just been called into the Lincoln Sitting Room by Daddy. Daddy had been talking to us for about twenty minutes when Ed arrived and joined our little band. Just prior to Ed's arrival Daddy picked up the receiver of the nearby phone and asked to speak to Al Haig. Once connected he asked Haig to send over the transcripts of the June 23 tape he had just been describing to us. His tone throughout was almost dispassionate but not quite. In about ten minutes Manolo brought us the papers bearing the bothersome words. Ed arrived and the four of us (Julie, David, Ed, and me) removed ourselves from the room to carefully peruse the transcripts. Julie and David read their copy together. Ed and I read our copy. Ed and I agreed the words could be taken one of two ways depending upon who was judging them.

We returned to the Lincoln Sitting Room with its interior deceptively gay-looking from the soft light cast by the fire burning in the fireplace. Each of us in turn expressed his or her opinion. Ed, Julie, and I coming out strongly for not resigning. David was less sure. But all of us were in concert of feeling that we wanted Daddy to do what he felt he should. He spoke of doing the right thing for the country, of how he thought a weak President in the position of being impeached would be a disaster to the country. What would the Soviets not dare to attempt in such a situation? Look what they had already attempted in the last Mideast dispute.

Daddy did not appear overly anguished but rather properly anguished at the events. He was very much in control of his feelings.

Finally there was nothing left to say, and we left Daddy alone in his chair staring into the fire. Undoubtedly more telephone calls would be made and received long after we were gone. We left feeling he still might not resign. In the time we were in that room with Daddy, years had been lived, re-lived.

The future held, he said, either resignation or removal from office by the Senate.

Upstairs Mama, Ed, and I went to the third floor to say good night to Julie and David. We all broke down together, and put our arms around each other in circular, huddle-style fashion. Saying nothing.

I sat alone in the Lincoln Sitting Room that night for several hours, trying to decide the best course of action.

My family's courage moved me deeply. They had been through so much already, and still they wanted to see the struggle through to the end. Pat, who had let the others do most of the talking in our meeting, told me that now, as always before, she was for fighting to the finish.

I decided that instead of resigning on Monday night, I would release the June 23 tape and see the reaction to it. If it was as bad as I expected, then we could resume the countdown toward resignation. If by some miracle the reaction was not so bad and there was any chance that I could actually govern during a six-month trial in the Senate, then we could examine that forlorn option one more time. In a subconscious way I knew that resignation was inevitable. But more than once over the next days I would yield to my desire to fight, and I would bridle as the inexorable end drew near.

I called Haig and told him that Ray Price should stop working on the resignation speech for Monday night and instead begin work on a statement to accompany the release of the June 23 tape.

On Saturday afternoon I decided that we should get out of Washington and go to Camp David. Even up there in the mountains it was hot and humid, so as soon as we could change our clothes we all went for a swim. Then we dressed and sat on the terrace, looking out across the wide valleys. On evenings like this it was easy to see why Franklin Roosevelt had named this place Shangri-la, and I think that each of us had a sense of the mystery and the beauty as well as the history and the tragedy that lay behind our weekend together in this setting.

At every opportunity the young people urged me to fight on. After a swim on Saturday afternoon I was in the sauna when Eddie came in. After sitting for a few minutes in silence, he turned to me in a very controlled but emotional way and said, "You have got to fight 'em, fight 'em, fight 'em."

At dinner on Saturday night we reviewed the situation again, and everyone urged that I at least postpone any decision until after the tape had been released on Monday. I told them I would consider their arguments and delay my decision to resign. For some reason an odd rhyme struck me. I said, "Well, that's settled: we will wait and see. It's fight or flight by Monday night!"

Sunday was a cloudy day, but the clouds did not reach quite to the top of the mountain on which Aspen Lodge is situated. I was awake at dawn, looking out over the great uncharted sea of clouds, pondering the decision yet again.

That afternoon some of the senior staff members and writers came up from Washington. We had decided that a written statement would be better than a speech to discuss the June 23 tape. I wanted the statement to emphasize the fact that as soon as Gray had informed me on July 6, 1972, of his concern about White House intervention, I had told him to press on with the investigation. The lawyers and staff, however, produced a draft that shifted the emphasis of the statement from the contents of the tape to my failure to inform them of its existence.

I handed Haig a page of notes from my yellow pad on which I had formulated the information I wanted the statement to convey. It read: "On July 6 in a telephone conversation FBI Director Gray expressed his concern to me that improper efforts were being made to limit its investigation of the Watergate matter by some White House personnel. I asked him if he had discussed this matter with General Walters. He answered—yes. I asked if Walters agreed with him. He answered—yes. I then told him to press forward with the investigation. This clearly demonstrated that when I was informed that there was no national security objection to a full investigation by the FBI, I did not hesitate to order the investigation to proceed without regard to any political or other considerations. From this time when I was informed that there were no national security interests involved or would be jeopardized by the investigation, the investigation fully proceeded without regard to any political or other considerations."

Haig read the note quickly and said, "It's no use, Mr. President. We've been working all afternoon on this thing, and this is the best we can come up with. I can't make any changes in the statement now. If I do, St. Clair and the other lawyers are going to jump ship, because they claim they weren't told about this beforehand and they based their case before the House Judiciary Committee on a premise that proved to be false."

I did not make an issue of it with Haig. Instead I said, "The hell with it. It really doesn't matter. Let them put out anything they want. My decision has already been made."

THE LAST DAYS

On Monday morning, August 5, the daily press briefing was postponed several times. It was canceled at 1:30, and a statement was promised by three o'clock. Speculation that I was about to resign filled the press lobby. The statement and the lengthy tape transcripts of the June 23 conversations were released at four o'clock. In the rush to produce copies of these transcripts for distribution to the press, some personal references were carelessly and unnecessarily left in.

I had returned to the White House that morning and called the Residence, suggesting that the family have dinner on the *Sequoia.* I did not want them to have to endure the ordeal of watching the evening news broadcasts. I knew what they would be like.

Ed had had to return to New York, so Pat, Julie, David, Tricia, and Rose met me in the Diplomatic Reception Room. As we walked to the cars, about a hundred young staff members, most of them secretaries from the East Wing and West Wing offices, were waiting for us. They stood on the driveway and clapped and cheered. As I shook their hands they said, "Hang in there," "We're still with you," "God bless you, Mr. President."

Out on the river the evening was beautiful. The breeze off the water stirred the sultry air, and we sat on the top deck watching the sunset. When we passed under bridges, reporters and photographers would suddenly surge forward, hanging perilously over the railings, trying to get a closer glimpse or a closer picture.

Everyone valiantly tried to make the evening as happy as possible. They talked about the summer weather and about a movie Julie and David had seen. They talked about the firm way Rose had of fending off impertinent reporters. They talked about everything but what was on everyone's mind.

During dinner I began to reminisce about all sorts of people in so many places who had been good to us over the years. I said that someday, even if it were not for a long time, all the recent experiences we had endured would mean a lot to us because we would see how they had brought us closer together. Everyone agreed that our life in politics had been enriching, the bad as well as the good. There was no talk about resigning that night, but several weeks later I learned that the next morning Pat had begun to organize our clothes, getting them ready for packing.

After dinner the boat turned and began heading back. I had no illusions about what was awaiting us. I knew that while we were sailing on the tranquil river, the city of Washington was being whipped into a frenzy of excitement by the revelation of the June 23 tape. By now everyone would be scrambling for position, and few, if any, would want to be found standing with me.

I asked Rose to call Haig and get a report on the first reactions, and then I went down to my cabin and stretched out on the bed with my left leg elevated as the doctors had ordered.

A few minutes later Rose came down and read me her shorthand notes of her conversation with Haig. "Just tell him that this thing is coming about the way we expected," Haig had told her. Rose continued to read from her notes: "Those in the upper level we expected to be all right are the same—some lower level lost—all ten on first article. The one that Dean Burch talked to regularly"—that would be Goldwater—"is going to keep quiet. Senators Curtis, Cotton, Bennett, Eastland, Stennis, Congressman Waggonner, are very much back of him but concerned about what it will do. He is worried about some others in his group. Rhodes said it was very bad. He didn't say what he was going to do. Talked with three key guys in the Cabinet—no problem with whole Cabinet—all solid."

After Rose left, I turned off the lights and closed my eyes.

I had been planning to hold a Cabinet meeting ever since we returned from San Clemente. Late Monday night I asked Haig to see if he could arrange one for Tuesday morning, August 6.

Although I recognized the inevitability of resignation, no plans had yet been set in motion. Once resignation came, it would be quick and complete; but until then I intended to play the role of President right to the hilt and right to the end. Until my decision had been announced, the government had to remain absolutely stable at home and nations around the world must have no reason to think that America was without a leader. In the meantime I felt that the Cabinet and the White House staff should be reminded that their first responsibility was to their jobs and to the continued functioning of the government.

I knew my Cabinet well, and despite Haig's reports that they were all holding firm I knew that there would be great pressure on them all, and great temptations, to make public demands for my resignation. That was something I had to prevent if I possibly could. I was determined not to appear to have resigned the presidency because of a consensus of staff or Cabinet opinion or because of public pressure from the people around me. For me and no less for the country, I believed that my resignation had to be seen as something that I had decided upon completely on my own.

I was unable to sleep that night, and about two o'clock I walked down to the Lincoln Sitting Room. No fire had been laid, so I stacked some logs together, lighted them with paper, and sat down in my big armchair in front of the blaze. A few minutes later, as I sat lost in thought, the door burst open and two of the night-duty engineers rushed in. When they saw me sitting there, they froze in their tracks. "Mr. President," they said in surprised unison.

Apparently everyone had thought I was in bed, and my amateur fire had set off an alarm. After they recovered from the shock of finding me there, they checked the chimney to make sure that the flue was open.

Just as they left, the younger of the two turned around and said, "Mr. President, I just want you to know that we're praying for you," and quickly closed the door behind him.

I thought about these two men, and about the office workers that afternoon, and about the millions of others like them all across the country who still had faith in me. I knew that by resigning I would let them down.

I went back to bed around three o'clock. We had passed through the first blast of the fire storm, but it was still raging. I knew that it would be following me for the rest of my life.

The Cabinet meeting on Tuesday morning was tense and subdued. During every other crisis of the administration, my entrance had been greeted with applause. Today the Cabinet rose silently as I came into the room and walked around to my chair at the center of the big oblong table.

I opened by saying that we had several major problems to deal with, but I knew that the major subject on their minds was Watergate, and that was what I wanted to talk about first.

I said that I understood how many people were genuinely upset by the June 23 tape. I knew it was a terrible blow to my case because it made clear that there had been discussions about the political advantages of bringing in the CIA. I thanked the Cabinet members for their statements of support in the past. I knew that many times it had not been easy to stand up for me, and I was grateful when they did. The faces were intent, sober, noncommittal.

I said that I had considered resigning. Resignation would certainly lift a great burden from my shoulders. But I also had to think of the presidency itself. I had to consider whether resigning now because of the tremendous pressures on me to do so would establish a precedent that could start America down the road to a parliamentary type of government in which the executive stays in office only as long as he can win a vote of confidence from the legislative branch. I said that I would not expect any member of the Cabinet to do anything that would be personally embarrassing or politically harmful. My problems were my own responsibility, and I only asked that they try to run their departments especially well over the next weeks and months.

I paused, and Jerry Ford, his voice unnaturally low, said that his situation was particularly difficult. It appeared that the vote in the House was going to be unfavorable, and he said that despite his admiration and affection for me, he had decided to remain silent about impeachment from now on. I said that this was the right position, and that no other member of the Cabinet should do anything that might jeopardize his ability to carry on his present responsibilities, or responsibilities he might have in the future, in the event I did leave office.

I repeated that they should not become involved in the impeachment controversy but must instead give their full attention to running their departments. If I became occupied with a Senate trial, I said, I wanted the Cabinet Secretaries to think of themselves as the functioning trustees of the President and the government.

After an uncomfortable pause I said that for the rest of the meeting I wanted to discuss the subjects that the public opinion polls still showed to be the foremost concerns of the American people: inflation and the economy.

There was a brief discussion of the new agricultural appropriations bill, which I said would have to be vetoed because it was an out-and-out giveaway measure, exceeding my budget limitation by $450 million. The discussion then turned to a proposal for an economic summit between Congress and the executive branch sometime in the near future. Saxbe broke in, saying that perhaps we should wait to see if I would have sufficient leadership to implement any of the economic measures we were discussing. As if spurred on by Saxbe, George Bush indicated that he wanted recognition.

Henry Kissinger's deep, thick voice broke in sharply: "We are not here to give the President excuses. We are here to do the nation's business." There was a moment of embarrassed silence around the table, and then the discussion on the economy resumed until the meeting ended.

After the Cabinet meeting I met with Kissinger in the Oval Office. I told him how much I had appreciated his support and his handling of the foreign policy problems over the last months. Then I told him that I felt I had to resign. He said that, as a friend, he had to agree that it was the best thing. He said that if I decided to fight it through to the Senate I would be picked to death and further dishonored in a trial, and the foreign policy of the nation might not be able to survive such a situation. It was one thing for the President to be under political attack as I had been for the last two years; it was quite another thing, he said, for the President to be in the dock for half a year with his chances for survival in office dubious at best.

I told him that I totally agreed with his appraisal and thanked him for his loyal friendship.

After Kissinger had left, I asked Bill Timmons for a report on the latest congressional defections. It was every bit as bad as I expected it would be. Two days earlier we had estimated that I could almost count on having the thirty-four votes I would need to avoid conviction in the Senate. Today, Timmons said, there were only seven men in the Senate I could count on to be with me if I decided to stay and fight. He said that as the party's former standard-bearer, Barry Goldwater had been asked by the Republican congressional leaders to bring me personally their assessment of how hopeless the situation was. I told Haig to make arrangements for Goldwater to see me on Wednesday afternoon. We decided to invite Hugh Scott and John Rhodes to come with him.

Haig said that he had received a phone call from Haldeman, who was strongly opposed to my resigning. If that was my irrevocable decision, however, Haldeman thought that it would be in my interest to grant him and the other Watergate defendants a full presidential pardon as my last act in office. To make this politically palatable he suggested that these Watergate pardons be combined with amnesty for all Vietnam draft dodgers. The next day I learned that John Ehrlichman had called Rose and Julie with a similar recommendation.

Before we could discuss this any further, Steve Bull came in to say that Rabbi Korff was waiting for his appointment. I had asked Ziegler to tell him that I had decided to resign and that he should not try to change my mind. Rabbi Korff summoned his usual eloquence and said that although he would accept whatever I decided, he felt obligated to say what he thought. "You will be sinning against history if you allow the partisan cabal in Congress and the jackals in the media to force you from office," he said. He spoke with the fire of an Old Testament prophet, but he saw that my mind was made up. He said that if I did resign, I owed it to my supporters to do it with my head high, and not just slip away.

When he left, I buzzed for Rose. I told her that I needed her help in telling the family that I did not want them to go through the agony of watching the television news broadcasts reporting more defections over the June 23 tape. There was no need for them to worry over something we could no longer do anything about. "Tell them that the whole bunch is deserting now and we have no way to lobby them or keep them," I said. I also asked her to tell them that my support was so low I could no longer govern, and that I was going to have to resign.

When Rose left, I took a yellow pad from the desk. At the top I wrote, "Resignation Speech." Working quickly, I filled several pages with notes and outlines.

I asked Haig and Ziegler to come over to the EOB. "Things are moving very fast now," I said, "so I think it should be sooner than later. I have decided on Thursday night. I will do it with no rancor and no loss of dignity. I will do it gracefully." Haig said that it would be an exit as worthy as my opponents were unworthy.

We fell silent. Finally I looked up at them and said, "Well, I screwed it up good, real good, didn't I?" It was not really a question.

I gave them additional thoughts I wanted included in the first draft of my speech. They both wrote diligently as I dictated. I wanted to say that this had been a difficult time for all of us, and that the situation had now reached a point where it was clear that I did not retain the necessary support to conduct the business of government in a way that would assure that the best interests of the nation were served. I wanted to include a statement that I understood the motivations and considerations of those who were no longer able to stand with me, and that I would be eternally grateful to those who had.

Then the three of us walked from the EOB back to the White House. As we entered the street between the two buildings, reporters rushed out to watch us.

"One thing, Ron, old boy," I said, "We won't have to have any more press conferences, and we won't even have to tell them that either!"

When we reached the end of the Rose Garden, I looked at Haig's face. I suddenly saw how tired he was, how much all the political stress had taken out of this superb military man. "Buck up," I admonished him, and I put my arm around his shoulders.

We parted at the elevator. As I pressed the button, I turned to them and said, "It's settled then. It will be Thursday night."

Since Julie had prepared dinner for David's parents, who were in Washington for a visit, she and David were at their own apartment as I went up to meet the family in the Solarium. Tricia has described the day in her diary:

> A day for tears. I could not control their flow. I did not even try.
>
> Mama, Daddy, Rose, and I sat in Mama's room for a bit before dinner. The only emotionally sound one was Daddy.
>
> In my room I began clearing our drawers of five years of memories and became shattered at the significance. I threw clippings, writing, mementos into boxes helter-skelter. Boxes which my tears sealed. I shall not open them again for years.
>
> Rose in tears this afternoon told us (Mama, Julie, me) in the Solarium that Daddy had irrevocably decided to resign. Now we must all be as stoical as is humanly possible, and show him that this action has our blessing, praise him for it, and show him we love him more than ever. We must not collapse in the face of this ordeal. We must not let him down.

The evening news reports that night were even worse than on Monday. Goldwater was now being quoted as having said privately, "You can only be lied to so often, and it's time to take a stand that we want out." Del Latta, who had been one of my strongest supporters on the House Judiciary Committee, said that when he heard the June 23 tape, he felt he had been run over by a truck.

I sat in the Lincoln Sitting Room thinking about the resignation speech until 2 A.M. When I walked into my bedroom, I found a note from Julie on my pillow. She must have slipped over from her apartment and put it there.

If anything could have changed my mind at this point, this would have done it. But my mind was made up past changing. Not because I was tired and fatigued, and certainly not because I had given up, but because I felt, deep down in my heart and mind, that I had made the decision that was best for the country. I took Julie's note and put it into my briefcase to make sure that it did not get lost in the massive move that was about to take place.

When I got to the Oval Office at ten o'clock on Wednesday morning, August 7, the countdown toward resignation was already proceeding smoothly. That morning Haig had told Jerry Ford to be ready to assume the presidency on very short notice. The first draft of the resignation speech was waiting on my desk. Ray Price had attached a short memo to it saying that the resignation, although sad, was necessary. He said that he hoped I would leave the White House as proud of my accomplishments there as he was proud to have been associated with me and to be my friend. He ended simply, "God bless you; and He will."

I took the speech and started over to the EOB office. As I walked through the West Wing I heard phones ringing in every office. The switchboard was deluged with calls from people who had stood by me through it all. Many had written to me and my family. Some had collected signatures on petitions. Some had sent in money, hoping to contribute to my defense. They were calling to say that I must fight on. That decision, I had to repeat to myself again, was made. Now I did not want to know about these calls.

Staff members seemed to summon up an extra heartiness for their "Good morning, Mr. President!" as I passed by. I went out the West Basement door into the closed street that separates the White House from the Executive Office Building. The crowds waiting outside the iron fence surrounding the White House surged forward when I came into view. Ed Cox had called it a death watch, but I believed that there was more than simple curiosity involved, I felt that these people were drawn by the sense that history was about to happen, and they wanted to be nearby. I could sense the tension of the Secret Service agents, and I moved as quickly as possible up the broad stone stairs and into the office.

THE WHITE HOUSE
WASHINGTON

August 6

Dear Daddy –

I love you. Whatever you do I will support. I am very proud of you.

Please wait a week or even ten days before you make this decision. Go through the fire just a little bit longer. You are so strong! I love you.

Julie

Millions support you.

I placed a call to Bob Haldeman in California; I felt that I owed it to him to listen to his eleventh-hour plea. A few minutes later he was on the line. The familiar voice sounded energetic and unself-conscious. I told him that I had decided to resign. I said that as much as I was torn by the conflicting principles involved, I thought the country would be better off this way. He urged me to take more time and think it through again, but if I had made up my mind, he would like me to consider issuing a blanket pardon for all the Watergate defendants.

He said the country would be better off if Watergate did not drag on for more months and years with endless subpoenas and lawsuits. With the kind of detachment he used to have when he discussed revenue-sharing, he added that amnesty for Vietnam draft dodgers would deflect criticism of the Watergate pardons.

As he talked, my mind wandered back to the campaign days and the White House days, when his proud and brusque way of dealing with people had aroused fear in some and inspired loyalty in many others. I could not help but feel and share the despair that he must be feeling. I had hoped that after the 1974 election I would be in a position to grant pardons, but I had never foreseen all that would happen. I did not give him an answer.

I called Ziegler for an account of the morning news. He said that Charles Sandman, hitherto one of my strongest defenders on the Judiciary Committee, had said that the June 23 tape was insurmountable and reckoned that I could command fewer than twelve votes in the whole House. He had said that he thought the Senate must vote to convict.

I had promised Julie that I would see Bruce Herschensohn, one of the most ardent loyalists on the staff. He was emotional as he argued against what he suspected was a course already in motion. His voice shook with conviction when he said that seventy-five years from now, when some young person was confronted with a difficult and seemingly hopeless duty, he should be able to look back and say, "President Nixon didn't give up and neither will I." He argued that the example of a President who faced his attackers and went down defending himself would better serve the American people than any immediate relief that the ending of Watergate would bring them.

I thanked Herschensohn for his frankness and said that he was probably right. The decision was not an easy one, but in a case like this perhaps there were no easy decisions, or even any good decisions, but only decisions that had to be made.

Tricia called and asked if she and Ed could come see me. She described our meeting in her diary:

> We lent our support to whatever Daddy decided to do. Because nothing had been announced publicly, we still wanted to caution him to be sure resignation was the only step to take. We were afraid that in a moment of weak-

> ness or discouragement he might make the wrong decision to bring an end to the unbearable harassment. But resignation would not be the end. He would be hounded habitually after leaving office—by trials, lawsuits, etc. We were afraid he would wake up the morning after leaving office feeling he had made a terrible mistake by resigning. Daddy has fought alone many times, almost alone many others. But there comes a point when fighting alone must come to mean fighting against yourself.

A little later Ed and David came in together and argued the case for waiting, even if only for a few days. I told them that I felt that executive authority would be so damaged by a vote of impeachment in the House and a long trial in the Senate that it would be almost impossible to govern.

Ed countered that the most important role for the President was in foreign affairs, and that even crippled by impeachment, I would be a lot stronger and more credible than Ford. He added that from a personal standpoint, my resignation would not accomplish anything. He had worked in the U.S. Attorney's office in New York, and he knew several people on the Special Prosecutor's staff. He said, "I know these people. They are smart and ruthless; they hate you. They will harass you and hound you in civil and criminal actions across this country for the rest of your life if you resign."

After Ed made his point about impeachment not ending my personal troubles, I said to him that this was just like a Greek tragedy: you could not end it in the middle of the second act, or the crowd would throw chairs at the stage. In other words, the tragedy had to be seen through until the end as fate would have it.

David agreed that if I had the personal will to see it through, I should do so. He responded forcefully when I mentioned the argument that I should resign for the good of the party. "You don't owe the party a damn thing," he said. "That was the way Grandad felt, and so should you. Do what you think is best for yourself, and what you think is best for the country." Before they left, they assured me that the family was ready for whatever happened, and would be behind me in whatever I decided to do.

It was after four o'clock. In less than an hour Goldwater, Scott, and Rhodes would arrive. I picked up the draft of the resignation speech again and wrote notes on the bottom of the first page:

> Insert: I have met with leaders of House and Senate, including my strongest supporters in both parties. They have unanimously advised me that because of Watergate matter, I do not and will not have support in Congress for difficult decisions affecting peace abroad and our fight against inflation at home, so essential to lives of every family in America.

Before I realized it, it was five o'clock. I called Steve Bull, who had greeted Goldwater and his colleagues in the West Lobby. "Take the boys into the office," I said, "and make them comfortable until I get over."

They were all seated when I arrived: Barry Goldwater, the former standard-bearer and now the silver-haired patriarch of the party; Hugh Scott, the Senate Republican Leader, and John Rhodes, the House Republican Leader. Over the years I had shared many successes and many failures with these men. Now they were here to inform me of the bleakness of the situation, and to narrow my choices. I pushed back my chair, put my feet up on the desk, and asked them how things looked.

Scott said that they had asked Goldwater to be their spokesman. In a measured voice Goldwater began, "Mr. President, this isn't pleasant, but you want to know the situation, and it isn't good."

I asked how many would vote for me in the Senate. "Half a dozen?" I ventured.

Goldwater's answer was maybe sixteen or perhaps eighteen.

Puffing on his unlighted pipe, Scott guessed fifteen. "It's pretty grim," he said, as one by one he ran through a list of old supporters, many of whom were now against me. Involuntarily I winced at the names of men I had worked to help elect, men who were my friends.

Goldwater said that I might beat Article I and Article III on the House floor, but that even he was leaning toward voting for Article II.

I glanced up at the Presidential Seal set into the ceiling and said, "I don't have many alternatives, do I."

As I looked at their faces, Goldwater and Scott said nothing. Rhodes had not noticed that I had been making a statement rather than asking a question, and he earnestly replied that he did not want to tell the reporters waiting outside that he had discussed any specific alternatives with me.

"Never mind," I said, "there'll be no tears from me. I haven't cried since Eisenhower died. My family has been fine, and I'm going to be all right. I just want to thank you for coming up to tell me."

Scott looked so solemn as they were walking out that I said, "Now that old Harry Truman is gone, I won't have anybody to pal around with." He mustered a bit of a smile.

After the meeting I called Rose and asked her to tell the family that a final check of my dwindling support in Congress had confirmed that I had to resign. I asked her to tell them that Goldwater, Stennis, Scott, and Rhodes were all going to be voting for impeachment. My decision was irrevocable, and I asked her to suggest that we not talk about it anymore when I went over for dinner.

I went back to the Oval Office and asked Kissinger if he could come in. He was contained, quiet, somber. I told him that I had decided to resign the next night. We talked briefly about notifying foreign governments and about sending special messages to the leaders of China, the Soviet Union, and the Middle Eastern countries. Every nation would need reassurance that my departure from the scene would not mean a change in America's foreign policy. They would have little knowledge of Jerry Ford, so I wanted to let them know how strongly he had supported my foreign policy while he was in the House of Representatives and as Vice President, and how they could count on him to continue that policy as President.

For a minute I tried to imagine the different reactions to these cables. What would Chou think in his office in Peking? And how would Chairman Mao take the news, sitting there in the cluttered book-lined study where we had talked just two years ago?

In Moscow it would be the middle of the night when the word arrived. I did not envy the night duty officer who would have to decide whether to wake Brezhnev or wait and give him the news when he got up. Brezhnev had placed so much emphasis on the importance of our personal relationship as the foundation of détente that I suspected his first instinct would be to assess what my resignation would do to his own situation and plan his reaction accordingly.

In Cairo and in Tel Aviv, in Damascus and Amman, the news also would arrive while the cities still slept. Eight weeks ago I had been hailed as a triumphal peacemaker and accorded unprecedented acclaim by their peoples. Now I was resigning the presidency because of a political scandal. How fragile would the peace that we had worked so hard to attain turn out to be?

My mind snapped back to the grim reality of the moment. "Henry," I said, "you know that you must stay here and carry on for Jerry the things that you and I have begun. The whole world will need reassurance that my leaving won't change our policies. You can give them that reassurance, and Jerry will need your help. Just as there is no question but that I must go, there really is no question but that you must stay."

After Kissinger left, I walked alone to the Residence. I had been afraid that this would be the most painful meeting of all. But I had underestimated the character and strength of my family. My wife and daughters remained an indomitable trio. Each one respected the opportunities public life had given her; and when the blows came, each reacted with dignity, courage, and spirit.

Everyone was gathered in the Solarium. Pat was sitting up straight on the edge of the couch. She held her head at the slightly higher angle that is her only visible sign of tension, even to those who know her. As I walked in, she came over and threw her arms around me and kissed me. She said, "We're all very proud of you, Daddy." Tricia was on the couch, with Ed sitting on the arm next to her. Julie sat in one of the bright yellow armchairs, tears standing in her eyes. David stood beside the chair with his hand on her shoulder. Rose, who is as close to us as family, sat on a large ottoman next to my yellow easy chair. I said, "No man who ever lived had a more wonderful family than I have."

I had arranged for Ollie Atkins to take some pictures. Someday, I said, we would be able to talk about this night, and then we would want to remember everything about it. I asked Pat to come down to the Rose Garden for a final photograph, but that was simply expecting too much. Tricia said, "I'll come with you, Daddy."

As we entered the Rose Garden, she took my arm just as she had done three years before when she was married there. Like me, and like my mother, Tricia seldom displays her inner emotions so that people can see them. She smiled at me and looked as young and, if possible, more beautiful than on the day of her wedding.

Finally Ollie said, "I think that's enough, Mr. President." I turned and saw tears in his eyes. I said, "Ollie, keep your chin up!"

We went upstairs, and I asked that the dogs be brought in for the last pictures. No one felt much like posing, so Tricia suggested that we just form a line and link arms as we had done in one of our favorite family photographs taken in front of the Christmas tree in the Blue Room in 1971.

Before Ollie could move into position, Julie broke into tears. I knew that the only way we would get through this night would be to pretend a bravado we did not really feel, so I said that I would have to take over the designing of the photo. I elaborately positioned everyone, and, mercifully, Ollie was quick. After he had snapped some pictures, he turned his head away, but we could all see the tears streaming down his cheeks.

It was too much for Julie. She threw her arms around me sobbing, "I love you, Daddy," she said, and Ollie, through his own tears, captured that moment as well.

I still do not like to look at the pictures from that night. All I can see in them is the tension in the smiles, and the eyes brimming with tears.

No one had much appetite for our last dinner in the White House, so we just asked that trays be brought up to the Solarium. The important thing was that we were together. Because we were there together and so close to each other, it is one of the priceless moments that I will carry with me for the rest of my life. We tried to talk animatedly, even to laugh at the dogs and their comical begging for food. But mostly we ate in silence.

When we had finished, I went to the Lincoln Sitting Room to continue work on the resignation speech. I could even feel a kind of calm starting to settle in now that the family had been told.

Ziegler came over to discuss the arrangements for the speech. As we talked about the tremendous swings of fortune we had known over the past two years and about how tragic it was that everything should end so suddenly and so sadly, he recalled a famous quotation from Teddy Roosevelt I had used often in my campaign speeches. It was the one in which TR had described the "man in the arena,"

> whose face is marred by dust and sweat and blood, who strives valiantly, who errs and comes short again and again because there is not effort without error and shortcoming, but who does actually strive to do the deed, who knows the great enthusiasms, the great devotions, who spends himself in a worthy cause, who at the best knows in the end the triumphs of high achievement and who at worst, if he fails, at least fails while daring greatly.

I decided that I would use this quotation in my resignation speech.

At nine o'clock I picked up the phone to see if Kissinger was still in the office and if he could come over. We talked for an hour about our present relationships with the Chinese and the Soviets, and about our problems in the Middle East, in Europe, and in other parts of the world. We reminisced about the decisions of the past five and a half years. For some reason the agony and the loss of what was about to happen became most acute for me during that conversation. I found myself more emotional than I had been at any time since the decision had been set in motion.

At one point Kissinger blurted out, "If they harass you after you leave office, I am going to resign as Secretary of State, and I am going to tell the world why!"

I told him that the worst thing that could happen to America and to all our initiatives to build a more peaceful world would be for him to resign after I had resigned. There was simply no one else on the horizon who could even shine his shoes, let alone fit into them.

I reminded him how, three years earlier, we had drunk a toast after we received the invitation to go to Peking. I walked down the dark hall to the family kitchen and brought back the same bottle of brandy. Once again we tipped our glasses and solemnly toasted each other. But after a sip we put our glasses down and left them unfinished on the table.

Just as Kissinger was about to leave, I took him from the Lincoln Sitting Room into the Lincoln Bedroom right next to it. In Lincoln's time, long before the West Wing had been built, this had been the President's office. It contains one of the five copies of the Gettysburg Address in Lincoln's own handwriting, as well as the desk he used at his summer

White House—the Old Soldiers' Home in the District of Columbia.

I told Kissinger that I realized that, like me, he was not one to wear his religion on his sleeve. I said that we probably had different religious beliefs if we were to examine them in a strictly technical way, but that deep down I knew he had just as strong a belief in a Supreme Being—just as strong a belief in God—as I did. On an impulse I told him how every night, when I had finished working in the Lincoln Sitting Room, I would stop and kneel briefly and, following my mother's Quaker custom, pray silently for a few moments before going to bed. I asked him to pray with me now, and we knelt.

After Kissinger left, I went back to work on the speech. I wrote: "As a private citizen, I shall continue to fight for the great causes to which I have been dedicated throughout my service as congressman, senator, Vice President, and President—peace not just for Americans, but for all nations, prosperity, justice, and opportunity."

A President's power begins slipping away the moment it is known that he is going to leave: I had seen that in 1952, in 1960, in 1968. On the eve of my resignation I knew that my role was already a symbolic one, and that Gerald Ford's was now the constructive one. My telephone calls and meetings and decisions were now parts of a prescribed ritual aimed at making peace with the past; his calls, his meetings, and his decisions were already the ones that would shape America's future.

Ziegler arrived and described the technical arrangements for the resignation speech and the departure ceremony.

As we walked out of the Lincoln Sitting Room, I asked Manolo to go ahead of us and turn on all the lights. From the outside the second floor of the White House must have looked like the scene of a festive party.

Ziegler and I went into each room: the Queen's Bedroom, the Treaty Room, the Yellow Oval Room that Pat had just redecorated and which we had scarcely had a chance to enjoy.

"It's a beautiful house, Ron," I said, as we walked down the long hallway under the glow of the crystal chandeliers.

I asked Manolo to wake me at nine in the morning, and I started toward my room.

"Mr. President," Ziegler called, "it's the right decision."

I nodded. I knew.

"You've had a great presidency, sir," he said as he turned away.

Thursday, August 8, 1974, was the last full day I served as President of the United States. As on other mornings of my presidency, I walked through the colonnade that had been designed by Thomas Jefferson, through the Rose Garden, and into the Oval Office.

I called Haig in and told him that I wanted to veto the agricultural appropriations bill we had discussed in the Cabinet meeting on Tuesday, because I did not want Ford to have to do it on his first day as President. Haig brought the veto statement in, and I signed it. It was the last piece of legislation I acted on as President.

At eleven o'clock Steve Bull came in and said, "Mr. President, the Vice President is here."

I looked up as Jerry Ford came in, somber in his gray suit. His eyes never left me as he approached. He sat down at the side of the desk, and for a moment the room was filled with silence.

Then I said, "Jerry, I know you'll do a good job."

I have never thought much of the notion that the presidency makes a man presidential. What has given the American presidency its vitality is that each man remains distinctive. His abilities become more obvious, and his faults become more glaring. The presidency is not a finishing school. It is a magnifying glass. I thought that Jerry Ford would measure up well under that magnification.

We talked about the problems he would face as soon as he became President in almost exactly twenty-four hours. I stressed the need to maintain our military strength and to continue the momentum of the peace initiatives in the Middle East. Above all, I said, we must not allow the leaders in Moscow or Peking to seize upon the traumatic events surrounding my resignation as an opportunity to test the United States in Vietnam or anywhere else in the world. We must not let the Communists mistakenly assume that executive authority had been so weakened by Watergate that we would no longer stand up to aggression wherever it occurred.

I said that I was planning to send messages to all the major world leaders that Jerry Ford had been one of the strongest supporters of my policies and that they could count on him to continue those policies with the same firmness and resolve.

Ford asked if I had any particular advice or recommendations for him. I said that as far as I was concerned, the only man who would be absolutely indispensable to him was Henry Kissinger. There was simply no one else who had his wisdom, his tenacity, and his experience in foreign affairs. If he were to leave after I resigned, I said, our foreign policy would soon be in disarray throughout the world. Ford said firmly that he intended to keep Kissinger on for as long as he would be willing to stay.

I also urged him to keep Haig as Chief of Staff, at least during the transition period. Haig, I assured him, was always loyal to the commander he served, and he would be an invaluable source of advice and experience in the days ahead when there would inevitably be a scramble for power within both the Cabinet and the White House staff.

I told Ford that I would always be available to give him advice at any time, but I would never interject myself in any way into his decision-making process. He expressed appreciation for this attitude and said that he would always welcome any of my suggestions, particularly in foreign affairs.

I do not think that Ford knew that he had not been my first choice for Vice President when Agnew resigned, or that he had come in fourth in the informal poll I had taken among Republican leaders. I knew that there were many who did not share my high opinion of Ford's abilities. But I had felt then that Jerry Ford was the right man, and that was why I chose him. I had no reason to regret that decision.

It was noon. It was time for him to go.

"Where will you be sworn in?" I asked as we walked to the door. He said that he had decided not to go to the Capitol because his former colleagues there might turn the occasion into some kind of celebration. I said that I planned to be gone by noon; if he liked, he could be sworn in in the White House, as Truman had been.

I told him about the call I had received from Eisenhower the night before I was inaugurated on January 20, 1969, when he had said that it would be the last time he could call me "Dick." I said, "It's the same with me. From now on, Jerry, you are Mr. President."

Ford's eyes filled with tears—and mine did as well—as we lingered for a moment at the door. I thanked him for his loyal support over the last painful weeks and months. I said that he would have my prayers in the days and years ahead.

After Ford left, I once again walked the familiar route to the EOB office. The West Wing was strangely quiet. Desks that had never been uncluttered were cleared. Only the steady ringing of the phones gave the place a sense of purpose, of life. Everything else seemed frozen.

Fred Buzhardt came in and showed me a letter from Haldeman's attorney, requesting a presidential pardon. Haldeman, ever the efficient Chief of Staff, had included a specially typed page to insert in my resignation speech announcing the pardon and proclaiming a Vietnam amnesty. I told Buzhardt to call the other lawyers after the speech and tell them that I had said no. It was a painful decision not to grant his request, but tying their pardon to the granting of amnesty to Vietnam draft dodgers was unthinkable. And to grant a blanket pardon to all those involved in Watergate would have raised the issue to hysterical political levels. I felt it was vital for the country that my resignation be a healing action, and in the climate then prevailing I was afraid that to couple resignation with a blanket Watergate pardon would vitiate its healing effect.

Haig and Ziegler joined us. Haig had just come from meeting with Jaworski to inform him that I was going to resign. I had told him that I wanted no bargaining with Jaworski. I would not be coaxed out of office by any special deals, or cajoled into resigning in exchange for leniency. I was not leaving from fear, and I would take my chances. "Some of the best writing in history has been done from prison," I said. "Think of Lenin and Gandhi."

Haig said Jaworski believed I had made the right decision, and from their conversation he got the impression that I had nothing further to fear from the Special Prosecutor. I said that, considering the way his office had acted in the past, I had little reason to feel reassured.

Frankly, it galled me that people might think that my decision had been influenced by anything as demeaning as the fear of prosecution, or that the Special Prosecutor and other attackers had forced me out of office. I did not care what else people thought as long as they did not think that I had quit just because things were tough.

I turned to Ziegler and said, "How can you support a quitter? You know, when I was a kid I loved sports. I remember running the mile in track once. By the time we reached the last fifty yards, there were only two of us straggling in for next to last place. Still, I sprinted those last yards just as hard as if I were trying for the first-place ribbon. I have never quit before in my life. Maybe that is what none of you has understood this whole time. You don't quit."

Rose came in to get my final changes for the resignation speech. She was going to type it on the special large-face typewriter we used so that I would not have to wear my glasses on television. She was wearing a pink dress and pink shoes in an attempt, I knew, to defy the darkness of the day.

She said that the family had discussed it, and they wanted to be in the Oval Office when I delivered the speech so that the whole world could see they were with me. I said it was simply out of the question, because I would not be able to get through the speech without breaking up if they were even nearby. She said that they had anticipated my feeling, and so at least wanted to be in the next room when I spoke. I asked her to explain that this was something I would have to do alone, and, as a favor to me, to ask them to stay in the Residence and watch the speech from there.

She said that she also thought I should know that Air Force Colonel Theodore Guy, the head of the POW organization, had called in tears, saying that Rose must not let me resign. I had not given up on them, he had said, and they would not give up on me.

That afternoon I wanted to go from the EOB office back to the White

House without any of the usual groups of staff or press or police watching or taking photographs. Ziegler carried out my wishes completely, and we saw no one as he and I made the short walk.

Packing boxes lined the halls of the Family Quarters. I shaved and showered and then picked out the suit and tie that I had worn in Moscow in 1972 when I delivered my speech on television to the Soviet people. It was slate blue, light in texture, and consequently cool under the hot television lights.

I went back to the EOB for a brief meeting with the congressional leaders to inform them officially that I had decided to resign.

I wanted it to be easy for them, and dignified. These men were veterans, and they knew that the coming and going of Presidents, whatever the individual or personal consequences, is not the only thing that matters to the country.

They were right on time, at 7:30 P.M. Carl Albert, the Speaker of the House, was the first to enter.

Before I said a word he blurted out, "I hope you know, Mr. President, that I have nothing to do with this whole resignation business." I said, "I understand, Carl." We talked about coming to Capitol Hill together in the same freshman class in 1947.

I told them all that I had appreciated their support on many issues through the years, and that I was especially grateful for their support during the last Soviet Summit, when I knew that partisan pressures and temptations had been very great. I said that I had always respected them when they had opposed my policies. I was looking directly at Mike Mansfield when I said this, but he did not react at all. He just sat there in a more dour mood than usual, puffing on his pipe. I said, "Mike, I will miss our breakfasts together," and he nodded, but without much responsiveness. Hugh Scott was cordial and more sympathetic than Mansfield. John Rhodes played his usual pleasant but noncommittal role.

Jim Eastland was the only one who seemed really to share my pain. As a Southerner and a conservative, he was always one of the most underestimated men in the Senate. Throughout my career he had been one of my most trusted counselors. In his face was a look of understanding that spoke more than volumes of words.

Finally I rose and put my arm on Carl Albert's shoulder. "I'll miss our breakfasts, too, Carl," I said.

We said goodbye, and they left.

I took a look around the office. My eyes ran over the familiar elephants, the gavels, the framed cartoons and plaques, the books, and the pictures of Pat and Tricia and Julie. I walked out and closed the door behind me. I knew that I would not be back there again.

I walked quickly into the Cabinet Room. Forty-six men were crowded around the table and in the chairs along the walls. Forty-six friends and colleagues in countless causes over three decades. Some of these men had already been in the House for years before I arrived as a freshman from Whittier; some of them had arrived with me in 1947, full of hope and dreams and plans for America. Together over the past five and a half years we had worked together time and again to form the slim but sturdy coalitions that repeatedly beat back the Goliath of liberal Democrats and liberal Republicans in the Senate and the House.

I started to talk about the great moments we had shared together. Without them, I said, it would have been impossible for me to take the initiatives that led to the new relationships with China and Russia, to progress toward peace in the Middle East, and, above all, to the ending of the war in Vietnam on an honorable basis and the return of our POWs.

I said that I wanted to stay and fight, but that a six-month trial in the Senate was too long for the country. I said that a full-time President would be needed now for the tough calls that would be coming up. The presidency is bigger than any man, I said, bigger than any individual President, and even bigger than their great loyalty. Now it was Jerry Ford they must support with their votes, their affection, and their prayers.

The emotional level in the room was almost unbearable. I could see that many were crying. I looked at my watch. It was approaching 8:30. I had been talking for almost half an hour. When I heard Les Arends, one of my closest and dearest friends, sobbing with grief, I could no longer control my own emotions, and I broke into tears.

"I just hope that I haven't let you down," I said, as I tried to stand up. Everyone was jammed together so tightly that my chair would not move, and Bill Timmons had to pull it back for me. I left the room.

A few minutes later Haig came into the small office next to the Oval Office where I was looking over my speech. He had witnessed the scene in the Cabinet Room, and he was concerned that I might not be able to get through the broadcast. I said, "Al, I'm sorry I cracked up a bit in there, but when I see other people cry, particularly when they are crying for someone else rather than themselves, it just gets to me. I'll be all right now, so there's nothing to worry about."

He said, "Mr. President, the whole group was deeply touched. I know you are going to be able to make a great speech tonight." He left the room, and I sat there by myself.

Two minutes before nine o'clock I went into the Oval Office. I sat in my chair behind the desk while the technicians adjusted the lighting and made their voice check.

At forty-five seconds after nine, the red light on the camera facing my desk went on—it was time to speak to America and the world.

I began by saying how difficult it was for me to leave the battle unfinished, but my lack of congressional support would paralyze the nation's business if I decided to fight on.

> In the past few days . . . it has become evident to me that I no longer have a strong enough political base in the Congress to justify continuing that effort. As long as there was such a base, I felt strongly that it was necessary to see the constitutional process through to its conclusion, that to do otherwise would be unfaithful to the spirit of that deliberately difficult process, and a dangerously destabilizing precedent for the future.
>
> But with the disappearance of that base, I now believe that the constitutional purpose has been served, and there is no longer a need for the process to be prolonged.

Then I came to the most difficult sentence I shall ever have to speak. Looking directly into the camera, I said,

> Therefore, I shall resign the presidency effective at noon tomorrow.

I continued:

> By taking this action, I hope that I will have hastened the start of that process of healing which is so desperately needed in America.
>
> I regret deeply any injuries that may have been done in the course of the events that led to this decision. I would say only that if some of my judgments were wrong—and some were wrong—they were made in what I believed at the time to be in the best interest of the nation.

I talked briefly about America and about the world. I talked about my own attempts in twenty-five years of public life to fight for what I believed in. I recalled that in my first inaugural address I had pledged to consecrate myself and my energies to the cause of peace among nations. I went on:

> I have done my very best in all the days since to be true to that pledge. As a result of these efforts, I am confident that the world is a safer place today, not only for the people of America, but for the people of all nations, and that all of our children have a better chance than before of living in peace rather than dying in war.
>
> This, more than anything, is what I hoped to achieve when I sought the presidency. This, more than anything, is what I hope will be my legacy to you, to our country, as I leave the presidency.

Throughout the speech I looked down at the pages of the text, but I did not really read it. That speech was truly in my heart. At the end, I said: "To have served in this office is to have felt a very personal sense of kinship with each and every American. In leaving it, I do so with this prayer: May God's grace be with you in all the days ahead."

The red light blinked off. One by one the blinding television lights were switched off. I looked up and saw the technicians respectfully standing along the wall, pretending that they were not waiting for me to leave so that they could dismantle their equipment. I thanked them and left the Oval Office.

Kissinger was waiting for me in the corridor. He said, "Mr. President, after most of your major speeches in this office we have walked together back to your house. I would be honored to walk with you again tonight."

As we walked past the dark Rose Garden, Kissinger's voice was low and sad. He said that he thought that historically this would rank as one of the great speeches and that history would judge me one of the great Presidents. I turned to him and said, "That depends, Henry, on who writes the history." At the door of the Residence I thanked him and we parted.

I quickly headed for the elevator that would take me to the Family Quarters. The long hall was dark and the police and Secret Service had mercifully been removed or were keeping out of sight. When the doors opened on the second floor, the family was all waiting there to meet me. I walked over to them. Pat put her arms around me. Tricia. Julie. Ed. David. Slowly, instinctively, we embraced in a tender huddle, drawn together by love and faith.

We sat talking for a few minutes about the day and the speech. Suddenly I began to shake violently, and Tricia reached over to hold me. "Daddy!" she exclaimed, "the perspiration is coming clear through your coat!" I told them not to worry. I had perspired heavily during the speech, and I must have caught a chill walking over from the office. In a minute it had passed.

We talked about the initial reactions to the speech, most of which were favorable. Many of the television commentators and newspaper columnists spoke of it as a speech that was aimed at bringing the country together. But this turned out to be the briefest honeymoon of my entire political life; within a few hours came the second thoughts, negative and critical.

Finally I said that we should try to get some sleep because we had a long day ahead of us tomorrow. As we walked out into the hall, we could hear the sound of a crowd chanting outside. A tragicomic scene followed, described in Tricia's diary:

> On Pennsylvania Avenue voices of a crowd chanting were heard. Mama misinterpreted and thought the group was one of supporters when actually it

consisted of the same people who throughout Daddy's presidency had hounded his every effort. Now they were singing "Jail to the Chief."

Mama tried to propel Daddy towards the window so that he could see the crowd. Ed and I tried desperately to talk loudly so as to drown them out. We hoped Daddy would not hear their sick message. Even so, I am not sure this last injustice did not escape him.

In fact, I had been able to hear the crowds earlier, before the speech. I did not actually know which side they were on. I assumed they were against me, but I did not really care about the shouters, and they did not bother me.

I asked Manolo to bring some bacon and eggs to me in the Lincoln Sitting Room, and I placed phone calls to friends and supporters and staff members until around 1:30. To each I expressed my appreciation for his support, and I told each that I hoped I had not let him down.

There was a knock at the door and Manolo came in to see if there was anything I wanted before he went to bed. I asked him to turn out all the lights in the Residence. Just as last night had been a time for light, tonight was a time for darkness. A few minutes later I stepped out into the darkened corridor. I was not afraid of knocking into anything in the dark. This house had been my home for almost six years, and I knew every inch of it.

I woke with a start. With the blackout curtains closed I didn't know what time it was. I looked at my watch. It said four o'clock. I had been asleep for only two hours, but I was wide awake.

I put on my robe and decided to make myself something to eat.

To my surprise I found Johnny Johnson, one of the White House waiters, in the kitchen. I said, "Johnny, what are you doing here so early?"

"It isn't early, Mr. President," he replied. "It's almost six o'clock!"

I looked at my watch again. It had stopped at four.

I told him that instead of having my usual orange juice, wheat germ, and glass of milk, this morning I would like something a little more substantial. I ordered my favorite breakfast of corned beef hash and poached eggs and asked him to bring it down to the Lincoln Sitting Room.

After finishing breakfast I took a yellow pad from my briefcase and began to think of something to say to the administration officials, Cabinet members, and White House staff, who would be coming to the East Room at 9:30 to say goodbye. After what I had been through during the last twenty-four hours, it was difficult to think of anything new to tell them.

There was a knock on the door, and Haig came in. Almost hesitantly, he said, "This is something that will have to be done, Mr. President, and I thought you would rather do it now."

He took a sheet of paper and put it on my desk. I read the single sentence and signed it:

> I hereby resign the Office of President of the United States.

It would be delivered in a few hours, at 11:35 A.M. on the 2,027th day of my presidency.

After Haig left, I remembered something I had read in a biography of Theodore Roosevelt, and I asked one of the Residence staff to go over to the EOB office and bring me the books from the edge of my desk. I was sure that the TR book was among them. He came back with Herman Wouk's *The Winds of War*, Allen Drury's *The Throne of Saturn*, and *TR* by Noel Busch. I quickly found what I was looking for and put a marker in the place.

When I called Haig to say a final goodbye, he was in the middle of a staff meeting dealing with the problem of making a smooth transition between administrations. Five minutes later, however, he was standing at the door of the Lincoln Sitting Room.

"The hell with the staff meeting," he said. "I would rather spend these last few minutes with you." I said that words could not express my gratitude for everything he had done for me over the years, and I wished him the very best.

Soon it was time to join the family. David and Julie were waiting in the hall. They were not coming with us but would stay to supervise the shipping of our things to San Clemente. Tricia and Ed came out of their room and stood together, waiting for Pat.

She was wearing a pale pink and white dress, and she tried to smile when she saw us waiting. She was wearing dark glasses to hide the signs of two sleepless nights of preparations and the tears that Julie said had finally come that morning. I knew how much courage she had needed to carry her through the days and night of preparations for this abrupt departure. Now she would not receive any of the praise she deserved. There would be no round of farewell parties by congressional wives, no testimonials, no tributes. She had been a dignified, compassionate First Lady. She had given so much to the nation and so much to the world. Now she would have to share my exile. She deserved so much more.

Manolo came over and said that the residence staff had lined up to say goodbye. I gave a little talk to them, saying that I had been in the great palaces of Europe and Asia and had visited with hundreds of princes and prime ministers in houses of great antiquity and splendor. "But this," I said, "is the best house because this house has a great heart, and that heart comes from those who serve in it."

I said that we had not failed to notice the countless ways and times they had made every guest, whether a king or a retarded child, feel welcome in the President's house. Now they must take the same special care of President Ford and Mrs. Ford. "You're the greatest!" I said, as I shook hands with each of them.

It was time to go downstairs. I asked Ed if he would carry the TR book for me. I had decided to read the passage directly from it, and since there was no time to have it copied on the speech typewriter, for the first time I would have to wear my glasses in public.

Just after 9:30 we went to the elevator. As we rode down, Steve Bull described the arrangement of the East Room and told each member of the family where they were supposed to stand behind me on the platform during my speech. He mentioned that there would be three television cameras. At that news, Pat and Tricia became very upset. It was too much, they said, that after all the agony television had caused us, its prying eye should be allowed to intrude on this last and most intimate moment of all. "That's the way it has to be," I said. "We owe it to our supporters. We owe it to the people."

We stood for a moment steeling ourselves for the ordeal beyond the doors. Pat decided not to wear her dark glasses, and Eddie said that it was proper because this was not a moment to be ashamed of tears. I nodded to Bull, and the doors were opened.

Tricia described our entrance in her diary:

> I took three consciously deep breaths to clear the light-headedness that had struck me. One—two—three. I said aloud, "Take three deep breaths." Mama and Julie did so.
>
> As the doors of the hall swung open to the Grand Hall, its beauty was flooded with the startling intensity of the television lights. The warmth they generated surrounded us like a cocoon both pleasant and unpleasant, both comforting and stifling.
>
> The Hall seemed overcrowded with humanity. There seemed to be an electricity in the air produced by the surrounding humanity—an electricity powerful enough to propel our little band forward.
>
> Suddenly I was grabbed from behind. One of the maids (Viola, the laundress, I think) was out of control and sobbing hysterically. I was almost immune from her deep sorrow as I was beyond mere grief itself. I put my arm around her and whispered, "Take care of the new President and his family." Then I extricated myself, conscious of wanting to catch up to the rest of the family who were several steps ahead of me now.
>
> There was a resonance of applause resounding through the House through all who really cared. "Ladies and Gentlemen, the President of the United States of America and Mrs. Nixon. Mr. and Mrs. Edward Cox. Mr. and Mrs. David Eisenhower." Normal. Thunderous applause. Scraping of chairs as people rose to their feet. "Hail to the Chief."
>
> Platform ahead. Step up onto platform. Find name marker. Do not trip

> over wires. Stand on name marker. Reach for Mama's hand. Hold it. Applause. Daddy is speaking. People are letting tears roll down their cheeks. Must not look. Must not think of it now.
>
> The words themselves were unique for Daddy because they were from the heart. Not formal. I was glad that at the end people at last had a glimpse of the fine person he had always been. At last the "real" Nixon was being revealed as only he could reveal himself. By speaking from the heart people could finally know Daddy. It was not too late.

The emotion in the room was overpowering. For several minutes I could not quiet the applause. After I started to talk, I began to look around. Many of the faces were filled with tears. To this day I can remember seeing Herb Stein, a man I had always respected for his cool and analytical intellectual ability and his dry sense of humor, with tears streaming down his face. I knew that if I continued to look around this way, it would be difficult for me to contain my own emotions. So I turned away from the red eyes of the crowd and looked only at the red eye of the camera, talking to all the nation.

By now I was fighting back a flood tide of emotions. Last night had been the formal speech for history, but now I had a chance to talk personally and intimately to these people who had worked so hard for me and whom I had let down so badly.

This was the nightmare end of a long dream. I had come so far from the little house in Yorba Linda to this great house in Washington. I thought about my parents, and I tried to tell these people about them.

> I remember my old man. I think that they would have called him sort of a little man, common man. He didn't consider himself that way. You know what he was? He was a streetcar motorman first, and then he was a farmer, and then he had a lemon ranch. It was the poorest lemon ranch in California, I can assure you. He sold it before they found oil on it.
>
> And then he was a grocer. But he was a great man because he did his job, and every job counts up to the hilt, regardless of what happens.
>
> Nobody will ever write a book, probably, about my mother. Well, I guess all of you would say this about your mother: my mother was a saint. And I think of her, two boys dying of tuberculosis, nursing four others in order that she could take care of my older brother for three years in Arizona, and seeing each of them die, and when they died, it was like one of her own.
>
> Yes, she will have no books written about her. But she was a saint.

I had wanted to find a new way of saying something to the White House staff that would inspire them. I had tried to find a way of urging them, without any platitudes, to look beyond this painful moment. I took the book from Ed, put on my glasses and read the moving tribute Theodore Roosevelt had written when his first wife died:

> She was beautiful in face and form and lovelier still in spirit. . . . When she had just become a mother, when her life seemed to be just begun and when the years seemed so bright before her, then by a strange and terrible fate death came to her. And when my heart's dearest died, the light went from my life forever.

Putting down the book, I said that TR had written these words when he was in his twenties. He thought the light had gone out of his life forever. But he went on, and he not only became President, but after that he served his country for many years, always in the arena, always vital. I said that his experience should be an example for everyone to remember.

> We think sometimes when things happen that don't go the right way; we think that when you don't pass the bar exam the first time—I happened to, but I was just lucky; I mean, my writing was so poor the bar examiner said, "We have just got to let the guy through." We think that when someone dear to us dies, we think that when we lose an election, we think that when we suffer a defeat, that all is ended. We think, as TR said, that the light had left his life forever.
>
> Not true. It is only a beginning, always. The young must know it; the old must know it. It must always sustain us, because the greatness comes not when things go always good for you, but the greatness comes and you are really tested when you take some knocks, some disappointments, when sadness comes, because only if you have been in the deepest valley can you ever know how magnificent it is to be on the highest mountain. . . .
>
> Always give your best, never get discouraged, never be petty; always remember, others may hate you, but those who hate you don't win unless you hate them, and then you destroy yourself.

Finally it was over. We stepped down from the platform. People were clapping and crying as we went by.

Jerry and Betty Ford were in the Diplomatic Reception Room on the ground floor. As I entered the room, Ford stepped forward to meet me. We shook hands.

"Good luck, Mr. President," I said to him. "As I told you when I named you, I know the country is going to be in good hands with you in the Oval Office."

"Thank you, Mr. President," he replied.

Betty said, "Have a nice trip, Dick."

We walked out under the canopy and started down the long red carpet that led to the steps of *Marine One,* the presidential helicopter. Then we were there, quickly shaking hands with Jerry—Pat embracing Betty—kissing Julie—saying goodbye to David. Then I was there alone, Pat,

Ed, and Tricia already inside, standing at the top of the steps in the doorway, turning, looking back one last time.

The memory of that scene for me is like a frame of film forever frozen at that moment: the red carpet, the green lawn, the white house, the leaden sky. The starched uniforms and polished shoes of the honor guard. The new President and his First Lady. Julie. David. Rose. So many friends. The crowd, covering the lawn, spilling out onto the balconies, leaning out of the windows. Silent, waving, crying. The elegant curve of the South Portico: balcony above balcony. Someone waving a white handkerchief from the window of the Lincoln Bedroom. The flag on top of the House, hanging limp in the windless, cheerless morning.

I raised my arms in a final salute. I smiled. I waved goodbye. I turned into the helicopter, the door was closed, the red carpet was rolled up. The engines started. The blades began to turn. The noise grew until it almost blotted out thought.

Suddenly, slowly we began to rise. The people on the ground below were waving. Then we turned. The White House was behind us now. We were flying low next to the Washington Monument. Another swing and the Tidal Basin was beneath us and the Jefferson Memorial.

There was no talk. There were no tears left. I leaned my head back against the seat and closed my eyes. I heard Pat saying to no one in particular, "It's so sad. It's so sad."

Another swing, and we were on course for Andrews, where *Air Force One* was waiting for the flight home to California.

Index